JANE'S
ENCYCLOPEDIA
OF AVIATION

JANE'S ENCYCLOPEDIA OF AVIATION

Compiled and edited by Michael J. H. Taylor

Contributors: Bill Gunston, A. J. Jackson, David Mondey, Malcolm Passingham, John Stroud, Michael J. H. Taylor, Susan H. H. Young

Portland House

New York

PUBLISHER'S NOTE

Jane's Encyclopedia of Aviation was originally published in a five volume set. This new edition is the first time the five volumes have been published as one. The publishers have also taken the opportunity to up-date the encyclopedia with a 40 page appendix written by Michael J. H. Taylor that covers many of the important advances of the last decade.

Jane's Encyclopedia of Aviation
was originally published by Jane's Publishing Company
Limited in 1980

This 1989 edition published by Portland House, a division of dilithium Press, Ltd., distributed by Outlet Book Company, Inc., a Random House Company, 225 Park Avenue South, New York, New York 10003.

Copyright © Studio Editions Ltd., London,
1980, 1989

Printed and bound in the United States of America

Library of Congress Cataloging-in-Publication Data

Jane's encyclopedia of aviation / compiled and edited
by Michael J. H. Taylor.
p.   cm.
ISBN 0-517-69186-8
1. Aeronautics. 2. Airplanes—History. 3. Airplanes-
-Dictionaries. I. Taylor, Michael John Haddrick.
II. Title: Encyclopedia of aviation.
TL509.J29   1989
629.13—dc20   89-8649   CIP

h g f e d c b

Contents

Photograph credits

The location of each photograph credited here is given by a three-element code. The first element is the page number, the second indicates the column, and the third the vertical position in the column. For example, the photograph coded 637/1/M is the middle of three in the first column of page 637. Abbreviations: **T** top, **U** upper, **UM** upper middle, **M** middle, **LM** lower middle, **L** lower, **B** bottom.

Foreword

When historians of the future look back on our twentieth century, they will see it as the first century of powered flight. There were a few flights by lighter-than-air powered airships, and hops of marginal significance by primitive manned and powered aeroplanes, during the second half of the nineteenth century; but the officially recognised first powered, controlled and sustained flights by an aeroplane were accomplished by Orville and Wilbur Wright at Kitty Hawk, North Carolina, on 17 December 1903. Today, before the twentieth century ends, powered flight has progressed to the stage where no two major cities on earth are more than 24 hours apart, and has dropped in on the Moon while doing so.

It has changed to a remarkable degree the whole pattern of life on our planet. After an orgy of airborne destruction in world war, it has made further major wars unthinkable for anyone but a madman. In more peaceful skies, it has brought international travel, even to the other side of the world, within reach of countless millions of ordinary folk. It has speeded mail delivery; transported mountains of freight and food; brought aid to impoverished victims of earthquake, flood and famine; saved the lives of hundreds of thousands of men, women and children injured by accident or conflict; helped to make vast areas of barren land fertile; saved forests and farmland threatened by fire; and much more.

This *Encyclopedia* records in easy-reference form details of many thousands of the aircraft types that have made such activities possible. As in any worthwhile *dramatis personae*, those with only small roles are identified modestly, in a form that reflects their period and importance in the overall story. In the case of more important types, the original edition of the *Encyclopedia* has already demonstrated its ability to meet uniquely the day-to-day requirements of a variety of highly professional readers.

For those with time to browse, it offers a source of never-ending fascination. It explains how the key to the 1903 success of the Wright brothers was the methodical way in which they conducted their experiments. Never doubting that they would fly within a few years, they rejected the flawed theories of earlier pioneers, built a wind tunnel in which to develop more efficient wing sections, made their own engines, and sought out an area with optimum wind and weather conditions to ensure stable flight, away from prying eyes.

Sir George Cayley, in the UK, had earned the title "Father of Aeronautics" half a century earlier as a result of his research, and had flown practical gliders. Subsequent invention of the petrol engine provided, at last, a power plant of sufficiently light weight to thrust into the air a primitive structure of wood, wire and canvas. By the beginning of the twentieth century, everything needed to fulfil the centuries-old dream of flying like the birds was available. In the USA, Doctor Samuel Pierpont Langley might have been first had he not spent more money on a launching gear to fling his "Aerodrome" from a houseboat than the Wrights expended on their entire series of experiments up to December 1903. Instead of flying, the Langley aircraft hit a post on the launch gear and fell into the Potomac river.

Members of the press who had been invited to witness the event commented wryly that if the Aerodrome had been launched upside down it might have gone upward, into the air, rather than downward into the water. Such derision was familiar to the pioneers. The Wrights were still subjected to it after their 1903 flights.

From the start they believed that their Flyer would prove more profitable if they could sell it as a military vehicle, rather than for sport. When they offered it to the US War Department in October 1905, the reply to their letter stated: "It is recommended that the Messrs Wright be informed that the Board (of Ordnance and Fortification) does not care to formulate any requirements for the performance of a flying machine or take any further action on the subject until a machine is produced which by actual operation is shown to be able to produce horizontal flight and to carry an operator".

Before approaching the War Department, the Wrights had achieved a flight of 24.2 miles in 38 minutes 3 seconds, but it was not witnessed by anyone who could inform the Army. On the only occasion when the local press had accepted an invitation to watch a demonstration of the improved Flyer No. 2, the engine had failed to develop its full 15–16 hp. The biplane simply ran off the end of its launch rail and came to a halt.

The Wrights were made of sterner stuff than their predecessors, who had abandoned their experiments in the face of ridicule. By 1908 the US Army could ignore them no longer, and awarded them a $25,000 contract for an improved Wright Model A, with seats for two persons. After an early setback, which cost the life of Orville's passenger, a Model A was accepted into US Army service in 1909 as history's first military aeroplane.

Meanwhile, Wilbur had been busy demonstrating a similar aircraft in France. His flights of up to 2 hours 18 minutes, often with a passenger, convinced the European pioneers that they were far outclassed but also inspired them to greater efforts. In England the three Short brothers, Eustace, Horace and Oswald, founded the world's aviation industry by setting up the first-ever assembly line to build a series of aeroplanes of a single design. The six Wright Flyers that they delivered to members of the Aero Club of the United Kingdom earned them a total of £1,200. Other pioneers, like A.V. Roe in England and Louis Blériot in France, rejected the clumsy front elevator and falling-weight catapult launching gear of the Wright biplanes in favour of what was accepted gradually as the "conventional" aeroplane configuration, with a propeller at the front, tail at the rear and wheels instead of skid landing gear. No longer were aeroplanes able to fly only from places where their launch-gear was situated. On 25 July 1909, Louis Blériot flew across the English Channel, from a point near Calais in France to Dover in England, in 36½ minutes, in his Blériot XI monoplane. It gained him a prize of £1,000 offered by the *Daily Mail* newspaper of London for the first cross-Channel flight. More importantly, it represented the first-ever aeroplane flight between two countries over the sea, pointing the way to international air travel of the future.

Progress was rapid during the following five years. Blériot's flight, more than any other, had captured the imagination of the public. In August 1909 a quarter of a million of them flocked to Rheims, in France, to attend the first international flying meeting. They got their money's worth. Twenty-three aircraft, flown by most of the world's leading pilots, competed for cash prizes in speed, distance and duration competitions, and records were broken every day. The first successful flight in a seaplane was made by Henri Fabre at Martigues, France, in 1910. In the same year Georges Chavez of Peru demonstrated that mountains were no more of a barrier to aeroplanes than were seas, by flying a Blériot monoplane over the Alps, only to die in the crash landing at Domodossola in Italy.

Such events were spectacular, and newsworthy, but the pioneers realised that aeroplanes would be taken seriously only when they were shown to have practical uses. Air freight was carried by air for the first time on 7 November 1910. Two packages of silk were flown from Dayton to Columbus, Ohio, by Philip Parmalee on a Wright biplane. The job was done on behalf of the Morehouse-Martens Company, whose Home Dry Goods Store sold souvenir patches of the silk at a profit of over $1,000. Air mail had its official beginnings three months later, on 18 February 1911, when Frenchman Henri Pequet flew some 6,500 letters five miles from Allahabad to Naini Junction in India, across the Jumna river.

Airline travel by aeroplane – now one of the world's great industries, carrying well over one billion passengers annually – had its modest beginnings on the first day of 1914, when Anthony Jannus launched the first scheduled service by flying a single person between St Petersburg and Tampa, Florida, in a small Benoist flying-boat. His passenger, a former Mayor of St Petersburg, bid $400 in an auction for the privilege; but people airminded and wealthy enough to feel an urge to cross Tampa Bay in half an hour, in a spartan open cockpit, were scarce and the operation closed after four months.

During the following four years, aviation was to have a more deadly purpose, as World War I started in August 1914.

The Wrights had foreseen an unaggressive military future for their aeroplane, suggesting that aerial reconnaissance over a battle area would prove faster, more effective, and less costly in terms of casualties than conventional forays by cavalry. More sinister uses were foreshadowed when their early rival, Glenn Curtiss, dropped dummy bombs from one of his biplanes on to the shape of a battleship marked out on Lake Keuka, New York State, in June 1910. Two months later, Lt Jacob Earl Fickel of the US Army fired his rifle from the passenger seat of a Curtiss biplane at a surface target. A live bomb was dropped from a Wright biplane in January 1911, and a machine-gun was fired from a Wright Model B in June 1912.

By then, such aerial tactics were no longer mere experiments. An Italian Air Flotilla had introduced the aeroplane to full-scale war on 22 October 1911, when Capitano Piazza flew a Blériot monoplane from Tripoli to Azizia, in North Africa, to make a reconnaissance of Turkish enemy forces. On 1 November, his colleague 2nd Lt Giulio Gavotti dropped bombs in anger for the first time on Turkish positions at Taguira Oasis and Ain Zara.

Despite such developments, the military aeroplane was still largely a novelty when war started in Europe in August 1914. Germany had the largest air force, and probably the best, as many of its 258 aircraft were powered by the highly-efficient Mercedes engines that had enabled German pilots to set outstanding altitude and duration records earlier in the year. On the Allied side, France mustered 156 aeroplanes; Britain's Royal Flying Corps entered the field with 63, while the Royal Naval Air Service had 39 landplanes, 52 seaplanes and seven airships. There were no real fighters, as nobody had worked out an entirely satisfactory way of firing a machine-gun from aircraft like the Blériot monoplane and RNAS Tabloid without hitting the propeller.

Pilots of the British aircraft began to cross the Channel on 13 August. With motor car tyre inner tubes wrapped round their waist as makeshift lifebelts, they were ordered to ram any German Zeppelin airships they spotted en route – a far from cheering prospect as they carried no parachutes. Fortunately, none were encountered. Once in France, they lost no time in displaying their prowess. Highly successful reconnaissance flights were started by Captain (later Air Chief Marshal Sir) Philip Joubert de la Ferté in a Blériot XI, and Lt Gilbert Mapplebeck in a B.E.2a, on 19 August. The German air force dropped five bombs on Paris on 30 August. More purposeful was an RNAS raid on Zeppelin sheds at Düsseldorf on 8 October when tiny bombs dropped by Flt Lt R.L.G. Marix from a Tabloid destroyed by fire one of the huge sheds, complete with the new and secret Zeppelin Z.IX that it contained.

The true fighter aircraft was born when employes of Dutchman Anthony Fokker, designing aircraft for the Germans, invented an interrupter gear that "timed" the bullets from a forward firing machine-gun so that they passed between the blades of a spinning propeller. During six months of 1915–16, the Fokker monoplanes almost shot the Allied air forces from the sky, until the British and French learned to shoot back and the years of savage dog-fighting began. This was the era of the first legendary "aces", men like Ball, Mannock, McCudden, Bishop, von Richthofen, Boelcke, Immelmann, Guynemer, Fonck and, when America entered the war, Rickenbacker and Lufbery.

Aviation became a vast industry. In Britain alone, by the summer of 1918, the aircraft industry employed 350,000 men and women, producing aeroplanes at the rate of 30,000 a year. The newly formed Royal Air Force had 22,171 aeroplanes in service and in store; the French had 15,342, the Germans about 20,000. The USA demonstrated its potential by building 15,000 aeroplanes, almost from scratch, in the 21 months after it entered the war, but the only American-designed combat aircraft used operationally were Curtiss flying-boats.

By the end of World War I, most of the basic tactics of aerial warfare had been developed. Fighters shot each other from the sky, and provided escort for the bombers that showered high-explosive and incendiary bombs on battlefield and town alike, and for the reconnaissance aircraft that reported and photographed every move of the unhappy armies on the ground. The first dive-bombers had been built to harass further the infantry in their muddy trenches. Torpedo-planes had scored their first victories against ships at sea; frail seaplanes had, to a large extent, been superseded by carrier-based fighters and bombers; and long-range flying-boats had helped to check the menace of German U-boats in the seas around Britain.

Yet, if the results of aerial warfare in 1914–18 are assessed objectively, it must be admitted that military aircraft had only a limited effect on the outcome of the war, except in the reconnaissance role, which proved of the utmost value. Most aircraft at the time of the Armistice still had structures of wood, wire and canvas, but Junkers of Germany pointed the way to future progress with its J.1 all-metal cantilever monoplane. Of more immediate importance was that the reliability and performance of aero-engines had improved so greatly during the war years that airmen could now contemplate ventures of a kind that would have been adjudged suicidal in 1914.

An independent strategic bombing force formed by the Royal Air Force in June 1918 had little opportunity to prove the war-winning potential claimed by its commander, but four of the Vimy bombers that had been produced for it blazed trails that would one day be followed as major sectors of a worldwide network of commercial air routes. In June 1919, a Vimy flown by John Alcock and Arthur Whitten-Brown made the first non-stop flight across the North Atlantic. Others flew from England to Australia, and contributed to the first flight from London to Cape Town, South Africa. With the war ended, there was no shortage of surplus military aircraft and pilots, and daily scheduled international airline services between London and Paris were started in August 1919, using D.H.16s built from D.H.9A bomber components.

Other bombers and fighters left over from the war pioneered an early form of what would now be called a deterrent policy. Then known as air control, it involved the use of a few squadrons of RAF aircraft to keep the peace in troublesome areas of the Middle East, instead of army garrisons on the ground. Put simply, if local tribesmen in places like Iraq and the North-West Frontier became aggressive, the policy was to drop a note from the air, warning them that their village would be bombed on a specified date if they did not become lawful. Air control never failed, and damage and casualties to both sides were minimal.

By the mid-twenties, the time had come to replace the old D.H.9As, Bristol Fighters and other types used for such tasks. The Royal Air Force took the opportunity to change to metal structures for its combat types, still fabric covered in most cases. Biplane configuration remained standard in air forces; but the airlines had by then begun to switch to monoplanes in some countries, with the Fokker, Ford and Junkers companies setting the pace in design. The process was speeded by the achievements of Macchi and Supermarine monoplane seaplanes in the Schneider Trophy contests. By the late 1930s, all-metal monoplanes were the norm, except for primary training and sport flying. Retractable undercarriages, wing flaps, enclosed cockpits, variable-pitch propellers and other refinements were standard on the faster categories of both military and commercial aircraft.

As airliners grew in size, from the four-seaters of 1919 to four-engined monoplanes able to cross oceans and continents, and link even the farthest outposts of empire with their homeland, some operators like the British Imperial Airways and US Pan American Airways turned from landplanes to flying-boats. Apart from the fact that they were considered safer on long overwater routes, they were able to operate from lakes, rivers, harbours and other sheltered stretches of water in places where there were few large, flat, areas of grass. World War II virtually killed off the big flying-boats. Hard runways were laid down all over the world for use by bombers and troop carrying transports, and were available for landplane airline operations when the fighting was ended.

Much else was changed by World War II. Close support by dive-bombers of the Luftwaffe cleared a path through both East and Western Europe for invading German armies. Hurricanes and Spitfires of the Royal Air Force then won decisively the first battle in history in which armies and navies played only minor roles, in the 1940 Battle of Britain. To what extent the subsequent Anglo-American day and night bombing offensive contributed to victory is still a matter for fierce debate. What cannot be denied is that just two atomic bombs, dropped from US B-29s on Hiroshima and Nagasaki in August 1945, brought the whole war to a rapid end.

Since then, aviation has changed the entire social pattern of the world. The terrifying potential of atomic weapons, available in tens of thousands, has provided a deterrent to a third World War for almost half a century. Most were carried as warheads by land-based and submarine-based missiles, but the financially crippling senselessness of keeping the peace between former Allies of East and West by a policy known as Mutually Assured Destruction (the initial letters of which summed up well its capability!) was recognised by the mid-1980s. Today, the safer and more flexible deterrence of air power is returning to favour.

However, the combat aircraft of today bear little resemblance to those of the

Battle of Britain era. That conflict was won by piston-engined fighters, armed mainly with rifle-calibre machine-guns, and guided to their targets by the new "secret weapon" of ground radar. The Battle was fought at an average speed of about 180 mph, which meant that the slower but more manoeuvrable and more easily repaired Hurricane was at no disadvantage compared with the faster Spitfire and enemy Bf 109. Performance was changed dramatically by the end of the war, when the first jets, such as the RAF's Meteor and Luftwaffe's Me 262, were in action. But they were too late to have any major effect on the course of the conflict.

Today, jet aircraft and their turboprop cousins have replaced piston-engined types for everything but slower, less sophisticated duties. Radar continues to track and control them from the ground, and navigate them in flight in airborne form. Other systems based on radar, infra-red and laser emitters locate military targets, in the air and on the ground, work out the range, and guide the aircraft's air-to-air and air-to-surface weapons. Special electronic systems are designed to detect and jam radar emissions of all kinds. Dispensers carried by aircraft eject flares to decoy infra-red homing missiles away from their target, and metallised strips known as chaff to confuse radar by giving the same radar "echo" as the aircraft itself. All these "black boxes" and defensive/offensive systems can easily cost more than the airframe; but this, too, is changing in the case of aircraft like the US F-117A fighter and B-2A bomber. As first-generation "stealth" aircraft, they have structures made of composite materials such as carbonfire and glassfibre, and special surface finish, to absorb probing radar signals. Their skins are shaped, sometimes bizarrely, to deflect the radar signals in all directions, rather than back to the transmitters. A high price in combat terms also has to be paid for "stealth", as the F-117A and B-2A are both subsonic.

Civil flying has kept pace with all this military development, benefitting from some advances introduced on combat aircraft, such as jet propulsion and navigation radar. Every pound of structure weight that can be saved enables one more pound of revenue-earning payload to be carried. So airliners embody increasing amounts of composite materials, in fins, control surfaces, skin panels and other structures, because they combine great strength with light weight. Some smaller aircraft like the Beech Starship are made almost entirely of composites.

The commercial Boeing Stratoliner of 1938 pioneered cabin pressurisation, enabling its occupants to travel in comfort at high altitude without the need for oxygen masks. Swept wings and delta wings came with jet propulsion, for aerodynamic reasons. That they are not essential was proved by the very first aeroplane to exceed the speed of sound, the straight-wing Bell X-1 of 1947, and by the later X-15 which achieved speeds of up to 4,534 mph.

By vectoring its exhaust nozzles, Britain's Harrier freed combat aircraft from the need for long, vulnerable, runways. Its ability to make vertical or short take-offs and landings rivalled helicopters. Without any rival in the late 1980s is the Anglo-French Concorde supersonic airliner. Most beautiful aeroplane ever built, it made use of the most advanced technology of its time to enable 100 passengers to be carried in luxury and safety at Mach 2, across the North Atlantic, as daily routine. In doing so, the small number of production Concordes spend more time flying at twice the speed of sound than all of the world's military aircraft added together. With the Harrier, Boeing's big Model 747 airliner and specialised freight carriers like America's Hercules and the Soviet Union's Antonov An-225, it represents a peak of achievement beyond the wildest dreams of the pioneers at the dawn of this century of flight.

Glossary

The more important technical terms or acronyms are listed below to help readers understand the technical shorthand used in the Aircraft section of the Encyclopedia.

Afterburning Method of temporarily increasing the thrust of a turbojet or turbofan by burning additional fuel in the jetpipe.

Avionics Aviation electronics, such as communications radio, radars, navigation systems and computers.

Bypass ratio Airflow through fan duct (not passing through core) divided by airflow through core.

CAA Civil Aviation Administration (UK).

Clean Without external weapons or stores.

Derated Engine restricted to power less than potential maximum.

ECCM Electronic counter-countermeasures.

ECM Electronic countermeasures.

ehp Equivalent horsepower, measure of propulsive power of turboprop made up of shp plus addition due to residual thrust from exhaust.

FAA Federal Aviation Administration (USA).

FAI Fédération Aéronautique Internationale.

Ferry range Extreme safe range with zero payload.

Hardpoint Reinforced part of aircraft to which external load (weapon or tank) can be attached.

hp Horsepower.

IFF Identification friend or foe.

IFR Instrument flight rules.

kN Kilonewton (measure of force).

kW Kilowatt (measure of power).

lb st Pounds static thrust.

Mach The ratio of the speed of a body to the speed of sound.

MAD Magnetic anomaly detector.

Monocoque Structure with strength in outer shell, devoid of internal bracing.

NACA US National Advisory Committee for Aeronautics (now NASA).

NASA National Aeronautics and Space Administration.

Pylon Structure linking aircraft to external load.

Radius The distance an aircraft can fly from base and return without intermediate landing.

shp Shaft horsepower, measure of power transmitted via rotating shaft.

STOL Short take-off and landing.

Store Object carried as part of payload on external attachment.

T-O Take-off.

VTOL Vertical take-off and landing.

(For a complete guide to aerospace terminology see *Jane's Aerospace Dictionary*.)

Aircraft A-Z

AAMSA Quail A-9B.

AAMSA Quail A-9B (Mexico) Small single-seat agricultural aircraft powered by one 224 kW (300 hp) Lycoming IO-540-K1A5 flat-six engine. Can be equipped with any type of dispersal equipment. Standard equipment includes 0.64 m³ (22.5 cu ft) glassfibre/polyester hopper, capacity 643 litres (170 US gallons) of liquid or 545 kg (1,200 lb) of dry chemicals. Component sets of the Quail A-9B are sent by AAMSA to its subsidiary Aircraft Parts and Development Corporation of Laredo, Texas, which is responsible for marketing the aircraft. By 1978 43 AAMSA-built Quails had been completed. The Quail was previously known as the Rockwell International Quail Commander.

AAMSA Sparrow (Mexico) The second of Rockwell International's Commander agricultural aircraft to be produced by Aeronautica Agricola Mexicana SA. Powered by one 175 kW (235 hp) Lycoming O-540-B2B5 engine. Max payload 567 kg (1,250 lb). Programme terminated.

Ace Baby Ace Model D (USA) Single-seat light monoplane designed to be home-built by amateur constructors. Suitable engines comprise Continental A65, A85, C65 or C85 (48.5–63.5 kW; 65–85 hp). Wooden parasol wing and welded steel-tube fuselage, fabric-covered.

Ace Baby Ace Model D.

Ace Junior Ace Model E (USA) Basically a side-by-side two-seat version of the Model D usually powered by one C85 engine.

AD flying-boat (UK) Tandem two-seat biplane flying-boat of 1917 powered by one 149 kW (200 hp) Hispano-Suiza engine as standard. Twenty-seven production aircraft built in four batches out of 85 ordered (including a few powered by 97 kW; 130 hp Smith engines).

AD flying-boat

Remaining contracts cancelled in March 1918. Used by RNAS as patrol aircraft armed with one forward-firing Lewis machine-gun and with provision for carrying light bombs.

Ader Avion III (France) Second aeroplane to be completed by Clément Ader; powered by two steam engines. Two attempts to take off in 1897 are believed to have failed, despite claims to the contrary by Ader.

Ader Eole (France) Bat-winged monoplane built by Clément Ader. Became the first piloted and powered (one 15 kW; 20 hp Ader-designed steam engine driving a primitive four-blade tractor propeller) aeroplane to fly from level ground, in an uncontrolled hop at the Château Pereire, Armainvilliers, France, on 9 October 1890. The aircraft covered approximately 50 m (165 ft).

AEG B.I and B.II (Germany) From 1913 Allgemeine Elektrizitäts Gesellschaft (AEG) almost exclusively built military aircraft. The B.I and smaller B.II were two-seat unarmed reconnaissance biplanes of 1914, powered by 74.5 kW (100 hp) Mercedes D.I and 89.5 kW (120 hp) Mercedes D.II engines respectively. These were used in limited numbers during 1914 and 1915,

but their maximum speeds of only 100 km/h (62 mph) and 110 km/h (68 mph) and lack of defensive armament led to their quick replacement.
Data (B.II): *Engine* as above *Wing span* 15.5 m (50 ft 10 in) *Length* 10.5 m (34 ft 5½ in) *Max T-O weight* 650 kg (1,433 lb) *Max level speed* as above

AEG B.III (Germany) Similar to the B.II with the exception of a redesigned tail unit, the B.III of 1915 was intended for reconnaissance and training duties and was one of the last unarmed first-line types to be built.

AEG C.I and C.II (Germany) Built as an armed development of the AEG B.II from the spring of 1915, the C.I reconnaissance biplane was produced in reasonable numbers for the time. After the installation of a 112 kW (150 hp) Benz Bz.III in-line engine maximum speed was raised to 130 km/h (81 mph). Armament comprised a single Parabellum or Bergmann (not widely used) machine-gun mounted in the rear cockpit. The smaller C.II derivative superseded the C.I in production in October of the same year. Refinements included redesigned cockpits and a new gun mounting, plus the provision for carrying four 10 kg (22 lb) bombs in a light attack role.

Data (C.II): *Engine* one 112 kW (150 hp) Benz Bz.III *Wing span* 11.85 m (38 ft 10½ in) *Length* 7.09 m (23 ft 3¼ in) *Max T-O weight* 1,200 kg (2,646 lb) *Max level speed* 138 km/h (85.75 mph)

AEG C.III (Germany) Unsuccessful attempt at producing a reconnaissance biplane with improved vision for the pilot, wider field of fire for the observer and higher maximum speed. Appeared at the close of 1915. Fuselage depth increased to meet upper and lower wings; the pilot in rear cockpit and observer in forward cockpit sitting above upper wing. Same engine as for C.I/C.II. Marginally heavier than C.II but with maximum speed of 158 km/h (98 mph).

AEG C.IV (Germany) Early reconnaissance types had proved the value of aircraft at the battle front and by 1916 all major air forces were carrying out expansion programmes. The C.IV was built by AEG as a follow-on to the unsuccessful C.III, although it reverted to the general configuration of the C.II. Produced by AEG and Fokker, many C.IVs were operated successfully in reconnaissance and observation roles by the German Air Force right up to the Armistice. Others went to the air forces of Bulgaria (which declared war on Romania in September 1916) and Turkey (engaged in war from 1914, but most

Turkish Flying Corps aircraft flown by German pilots). Despite proving to be underpowered, C.IVs were also used as escorts, while a night bomber variant (C.IVN) was produced in prototype form in 1917. It had a wing span of 15.3 m (50 ft 2½ in) and a 112 kW (150 hp) Bz.III engine. Another variant was built as the C.IVa, powered by a 134 kW (180 hp) Argus engine.
Data (C.IV): *Engine* one 119 kW (160 hp) Mercedes D.III *Wing span* 13.46 m (44 ft 2 in) *Length* 7.15 m (23 ft 5¼ in) *Max T-O weight* 1,120 kg (2,469 lb) *Max level speed* 158 km/h (98 mph) *Armament* one forward-firing Spandau and one rear-mounted Parabellum machine-gun. Provision for light bomb load

AEG C.V to C.VIII (Germany) Series of prototype two-seat general-purpose biplanes built in 1916 and 1917; powered by the 119 kW (160 hp) Mercedes D.III engine (C.VII and C.VIII), the 164 kW (220 hp) Mercedes D.IV (C.V) and the 149 kW (200 hp) Benz Bz.IV (C.VI).

AEG C.VIII Dr (Germany) Unsuccessful triplane version of the C.VIII biplane.

AEG D.I and Dr.I (Germany) Unsuccessful biplane and triplane single-seat fighters of 1917.

Artist's impression of Clement Ader's *Eole*.

AEG C.VII.

AEG C.II.

AEG C.IV prototype.

AEG G.IV.

AEG G.II.

AEG DJ.I (Germany) Very streamlined single-seat ground attack biplane of September 1918, featuring I-type interplane struts, armour protection and aluminium fuselage covering. Powered by a 145 kW (195 hp) Benz engine. Armament comprised Spandau machine-guns and bombs.

AEG G.III (foreground) and G.I.

AEG G.V used by DLR.

AEG G.I to G.V (Germany) Series of twin-engined biplane bombers that appeared between 1915 and 1918. The engine power, overall dimensions and bomb-carrying capacity increased with each new version. Initial version was the three-seat K.I (later redesignated G.I) powered by 74.5 kW (100 hp) Mercedes D.I engines. Performance was poor and so led to the development of the G.II, of which a small number were used operationally. Powered by 112 kW (150 hp) Benz Bz.III engines, the G.II was armed with up to three machine-guns and 200 kg (441 lb) of bombs. A number of these aircraft had an extra vertical tail surface on each side of the fin and rudder. The G.III, powered by 164 kW (220 hp) Mercedes D.IV engines, could carry a 50% increase in bomb load but was built only for limited service, mostly away from the major fronts. Therefore the majority of over 540 AEG G bombers built were of G.IV type, powered by 194 kW (260 hp) Mercedes D.IVa engines. G.IVs became operational in late 1916, remaining in service until the Armistice. Even with a warload twice that of the G.II it was not successful in terms of offensive capacity or performance and was often used in a photographic reconnais-

sance role or as a general combat aircraft. The similarly powered G.V of 1918 was designed to overcome earlier shortcomings, carrying three times the bomb load of the G.II. The end of the war prevented it from becoming operational and it was AEG's last bomber.

After the war a number of G.Vs were operated as six-passenger civil transports by Deutsche Luft-Reederei – an airline company financed by and connected with AEG. In fact the G.V in 1919 was the only large German 1914–18 aircraft employed commercially to any great extent. Following early use of the bomber as a make-shift transport (with an open cockpit for passengers) a Limousine version was developed. This had a new cabin fairing attached to enclose the passenger area, a downward-hinging fuselage nose to provide a baggage locker (which could also act as a buffer if the aircraft overturned) and a toilet aft of the cabin.

Data (G.IV): *Engines* as above *Wing span* 18.4 m (60 ft 4¼ in) *Length* 9.7 m (31 ft 10 in) *Max T-O weight* 3,628 kg (8,000 lb) *Max level speed* 166 km/h (103 mph) *Armament* two Parabellum machine-guns and bombs

AEG J.I and J.II (Germany) The J.I was basically an armoured and more powerful version of the AEG C.IV produced in large numbers to equip army co-operation units from 1917. To facilitate its main task of attacking ground forces and positions two Spandau machine-guns were mounted in the floor of the observer's cockpit and were able to fire downward and at forward angles up to the cross-axle of the landing gear. For defence a single Parabellum machine-gun was provided in the usual rear-cockpit position and armour plating was added around the engine and cockpits. The J.Ia version differed in having ailerons fitted to the lower as well as upper wings. The longer J.II of the following year differed further in having horn-balanced tail control surfaces and

upper ailerons. A total of over 600 J.I/J.Ia/J.IIs were built.

After the war J.IIs first passed to Deutsche Luft-Reederei. This airline began what became the first sustained daily passenger aeroplane service in the world with them and DFWs on 5 February 1919 (between Berlin and Weimar). Although early commercial J.IIs retained open cockpits, modified aircraft quickly appeared with an enclosed cabin for two passengers.
Data: *Engine* one 149 kW (200 hp) Benz Bz.IV *Wing span* 13.46 m (44 ft 2 in) *Length* (J.II) 7.9 m (25 ft 11 in) *Max T-O weight* (J.II) 1,765 kg (3,891 lb) *Max level speed* 150 km/h (93 mph)

Aerauto PL.5C (Italy) Unsuccessful high-wing monoplane of early 1950s powered by one 63.5 kW (85 hp) Continental pusher engine. Designed to be towable.

Aerfer Ariete (Italy) Single-seat lightweight fighter development of the Sagittario 2, differing mainly by the addition of a Rolls-Royce Soar RS.2 auxiliary turbojet engine to improve climb etc. Prototype first flew on 27 March 1958.

Aerfer Sagittario 2 (Italy) All-metal single-seat lightweight interceptor and tactical support aircraft developed from the Ambrosini Sagittario. First flown June 1956. Reached Mach 1.1 during a dive from 13,725 m (45,000 ft). Powered by one Rolls-Royce Derwent 9 turbojet engine (16 kN; 3,600 lb st).

Aeritalia AM.3C (Italy) Developed jointly by Aerfer and Aeronautica Macchi for forward air control, observation, liaison, transport of passengers and cargo, casualty evacuation, tactical support of ground forces and similar duties. The first of three prototypes flew on 12 May 1967. Produced to meet orders from the South African Air

Force (40; known in that country as the Bosbok) and the Rwanda Air Force (3). Normal accommodation for two persons in tandem, with dual controls. Provision at rear for two stretchers or a rear seat for one or two persons or freight. Large diversity of armament can be carried on two underwing pylons (standard), each able to carry 170 kg (375 lb) of stores, including machine-guns, rockets, bombs and missiles. Alternatively reconnaissance packs can be fitted under or inside the fuselage.
Data: *Engine* one 253.5 kW (340 hp) Piaggio-built Lycoming GSO-480-B1B6 flat-six *Wing span* 11.73 m (38 ft 6 in) *Length* 8.73 m (28 ft 8 in) *Max T-O weight* 1,700 kg (3,750 lb) *Max level speed* at 2,440 m (8,000 ft) at normal T-O weight 278 km/h (173 mph) *Range* 990 km (615 miles)

Aeritalia G91 (Italy) The original single Bristol Siddeley Orpheus-engined Fiat G91 was designed in accordance with NATO requirements for a standard lightweight tactical strike fighter to equip its forces. The first of three prototypes and 27 pre-production aircraft flew on 9 August 1956. Original production models included the G91R/1 photographic-reconnaissance version (three Vinten 70 mm cameras) and similar R/3 and R/4 with armament changes; G91N modified aircraft to evaluate navigational aids; G91T/1 tandem two-seat version for advanced training at transonic speeds, and similar T/3 and T/4 with equipment changes.

The G91Y is a twin-engined development of the G91 based upon the G91T version. Two prototypes were built (the first flying on 27 December 1966) followed by 20 pre-series G91Ys for the Italian Air Force. Delivery of the initial series of 35 production aircraft to the Italian Air Force began in September 1971, as single-seat light tactical strike-reconnaissance fighters. Armament comprises two 30 mm DEFA cannon and cameras in nose; four underwing attachment points for 1,000 lb bombs, 750 lb napalm tanks, 7 × 2 in rocket packs, 28 × 2 in rocket packs or 4 × 5 in rocket containers. G91s are in service with the air forces of the German Federal Republic (G91R/3 and G91T/3 – including R/3s licence-built in Germany), Italy (G91R/1, R/1A, R/1B, G91T/1 and G91Y) and Portugal (G91R/4).

Aeritalia

Aeritalia AM.3C.

Aeritalia G91Y.

Aeritalia F-104S.

Aeritalia G222.

Data (G91Y): *Engines* two General Electric J85-GE-13A turbojets (each 18.15 kN; 4,080 lb st with afterburning) *Wing span* 9.01 m (29 ft 6½ in) *Length* 11.67 m (38 ft 3½ in) *Max T-O weight* 8,700 kg (19,180 lb) *Max level speed* at s/l Mach 0.95 *Combat radius* 600 km (372 miles)

Aeritalia G222 (Italy) Originally conceived in four separate configurations; all but the military transport version (originally designated G222 TCM) halted at the project stage. Two prototypes built, the first flying on 18 July 1970. The Italian Air Force ordered 44 production G222s and deliveries began in late 1976. These are operated in troop, paratroop or cargo transport roles, or for aeromedical duties. The G222 can operate from semi-prepared airstrips and in all weathers. Others have been ordered by the Argentine Army (3) and the Dubai government (1).

Design of the G222 makes it suitable for adaptation to such roles as maritime patrol and anti-submarine warfare and for several civil applications. Water-bombing tests with the second prototype, designated G222 SAMA, were completed in 1976.

Normal accommodation is for a crew of three and 44 troops or 32 paratroops. Alternative payloads include 36 stretchers and eight atten-

dants or sitting casualties, or 8,500 kg (18,740 lb) of freight, including two light trucks, a truck and a 105 mm howitzer or five freight containers.

Data: *Engines* two 2,535 kW (3,400 shp) Fiat-built General Electric T64-GE-P4D turboprops *Wing span* 28.70 m (94 ft 2 in) *Length* 22.70 m (74 ft 5½ in) *Max T-O weight* 26,500 kg (58,422 lb) *Max level speed* at 4,575 m (15,000 ft) 540 km/h (336 mph) *Range* with 44 troops 2,220 km (1,380 miles)

Aeritalia G222 (projected new versions) An electronic warfare version is under development; designed to carry a pilot, co-pilot and up to ten systems operators. It has a modified cabin fitted with racks and consoles for detection, signal processing and data recording equipment. Externally it has a small thimble radome beneath the nose and a larger radome on top of the tail-fin. Designated G222VS, the prototype first flew 9 March 1978. Other versions of the G222 include the G222RM flight inspection (radio/radar calibration) aircraft, already flown, and the proposed maritime patrol and search and rescue models.

Aeritalia F-104S (Italy) Version of the Lockheed Starfighter single-seat multi-purpose combat aircraft built under licence for the Italian and Turkish air forces (205 and 40 aircraft respectively); the only version in current production. Powered by one General Electric J79-GE-19 turbojet (79.62 kN; 17,900 lb st with afterburning). Nine external weapon attachment points for bombs, rocket pods, auxiliary fuel tanks and air-to-air missiles. Normal primary armament consists of two Raytheon AIM-7 Sparrow III air-to-air missiles under wings and/or two Sidewinders under fuselage and either a Sidewinder or fuel tank on each wingtip. Alternatively an M-61 20 mm multi-barrel rotary cannon can be fitted in the port underside of the fuselage. Max external weapon load 3,402 kg (7,500 lb).

Aeritalia AMX (Italy) Subsonic single-seat combat aircraft under development for the Italian Air Force as a replacement for the G91 in the close air support role, G91Y interdictor and F-104G and F-104S in strike roles, from 1985.

Aermacchi MB 326 (Italy) The first prototype of the original MB 326 flew on 10 December 1957, powered by a Rolls-Royce Viper 8 turbojet engine. The first production version (designated MB 326) was powered by one 11.12 kN (2,500 lb st) Viper 11 engine and 100 were ordered for the Italian Air Force as basic trainers.

Subsequent production versions include the MB 326B/F/M two-seat trainers and light attack aircraft powered by the Viper 11 engine (MB 326B for Tunisia, MB 326F for Ghana, MB 326M

Aeritalia AMX.

licence-built in South Africa as the Atlas Impala Mk 1); MB 326E two-seat trainer with the Viper 11 engine, strengthened wings, six underwing hardpoints, new electronics and equipment (for Italy); MB 326GB two-seat trainer and counter-insurgency aircraft with airframe modifications and the 15.17 kN (3,410 lb st) Viper 20 Mk 540 engine (for Argentine Navy, Zaïre, Zambia); MB 326GC, similar to MB 326GB but assembled in Brazil under licence by EMBRAER as the AT-26 Xavante (for Brazil and Togo); MB 326H two-seat trainer powered by the Viper 11 engine (for Australia); MB 326K single-seat operational trainer and light ground attack aircraft powered by the 17.79 kN (4,000 lb st) Viper 632-43 engine and with standard armament of two 30 mm DEFA cannon (also built as an advanced trainer in South Africa as the Atlas Impala Mk 2; MB 326K for Dubai, Ghana, Tunisia); and MB 326L two-seat advanced trainer version, announced in 1973, which combines the airframe of the MB 326K with the standard two-seat dual control cockpit installation (for Dubai, Tunisia). The MB 326D version is used by Alitalia.

Data (MB 326GB trainer): *Engine* as above *Wing span* over tip-tanks 10.854 m (35 ft 7¼ in) *Length* 10.673 m (35 ft 0¼ in) *Max T-O weight* 4,577 kg (10,090 lb) *Max level speed* 867 km/h (539 mph) *Range* (fuselage, tip, underwing tanks) 2,445 km (1,520 miles)

Aermacchi MB 339 (Italy) Tandem two-seat trainer and ground attack aircraft based upon the airframe and engine of the MB 326K, but with reshaped forward fuselage, an improved cockpit, uprated electronics equipment and other detail changes. First of two flying prototypes flew on 12 August 1976. First of 15 initial production aircraft flew mid-1978. A total of 100 have been ordered to replace MB 326s currently in service with the Italian Air Force.

Up to 1,815 kg (4,000 lb) of external stores can be carried on six underwing hardpoints. Provisions are made on the two inner stations for the installation of two Macchi gun pods, each containing either a 30 mm DEFA cannon or a 7.62 mm GAU-2B/A multi-barrel machine-gun. Other stores can include AS 11 or AS 12 air-to-surface missiles, Matra 550 air-to-air missiles, machine-guns, bombs, napalm containers, rockets, drop-tanks or a photographic pod with four 70 mm Vinten cameras.

Data: *Engine* one Piaggio-built Rolls-Royce Viper 632-43 turbojet (17.79 kN; 4,000 lb st) *Wing span* over tip-tanks 10.858 m (35 ft 7½ in) *Length* 10.972 m (36 ft 0 in) *Max T-O weight* 5,895 kg (13,000 lb) *Max level speed* 898 km/h (558 mph) *Range* (internal fuel) 1,760 km (1,093 miles)

Aermacchi/EMBRAER
AT-26 Xavante.

Aermacchi-Lockheed AL.60, Lockheed-Azcarate LASA 60 and Lockheed 60 (Italy, Mexico and USA) The Lockheed 60 was an all-metal light utility transport aircraft designed and developed by Lockheed-Georgia for production by its overseas associates. The first prototype flew on 15 September 1959. Lockheed-Azcarate SA put it into production as the LASA 60, a six-seater with a tricycle landing gear and powered by the 186.5 kW (250 hp) Continental IO-470-R engine. Demand proved disappointing. Eighteen were built for SAR duties with the Mexican Air Force. The Aermacchi-built Model 60 first flew on 19 April 1961, powered by the 298 kW (400 hp) Lycoming IO-720-A1A flat-eight engine. The AL.60F5 Conestoga was the basic version with a tricycle landing gear. The AL.60C5 was evolved for bush operations in Canada, fitted with a tail-wheel landing gear. Other AL.60C5s went into

Prototype Aermacchi MB
339 I-NINE and the first
five production
examples.

Aermacchi MB 326D used
by Alitalia.

21

**Aermacchi-Lockheed
AL.60C5.**

Aero Ab.11.

Aero 2.

Canadian military service and to the air forces of the Central African Republic and Rhodesia.

Data (AL.60C5): *Engine* as above *Wing span* 11.99 m (39 ft 4 in) *Length* 8.8 m (28 ft 10½ in) *Max T-O weight* 2,040 kg (4,500 lb) *Max level speed* 251 km/h (156 mph) *Range* 1,038 km (645 miles)

Aero 2 (Yugoslavia) First post-war aeroplane of original design to come from the government factories in Yugoslavia. Produced as a two-seat trainer, the first pre-production aircraft flew on 19 October 1946. Built in quantity for the Yugoslav Air Force and for civil use. Powered by either one 108 kW (145 hp) de Havilland Gipsy Major 10 (Models 2B and 2BE) or 119 kW (160 hp) Walter Minor 6-III engine. Aero 2B/C/F had open cockpits; Aero 2BE/D/E and 2H seaplane had enclosed cockpits. Dual controls standard. Max level speed 208 km/h (129 mph).

Aero 3 (Yugoslavia) Development of the earlier Aero 2 powered by a neatly cowled 138 kW (185 hp) Lycoming O-435-A engine. Main external difference was the use of a one-piece transparent sliding canopy over the tandem cockpits of the Aero 3, compared with either open or enclosed cockpits of the Aero 2 – the latter comprising a transparent canopy with sliding sections. Dual controls standard. Aero 3 production started in 1957 and the new aircraft replaced the Aero 2 as the Yugoslav Air Force's standard primary trainer. Currently used by flying clubs.

Data: *Engine* as above *Wing span* 10.5 m (34 ft 5½ in) *Length* 8.58 m (28 ft 1¾ in) *Max T-O weight* 1,198 kg (2,641 lb) *Max level speed* 230 km/h (143 mph)

Aero A.1 (Czechoslovakia) Two-seat biplane trainer, the design of which was developed from a Hansa-Brandenburg type. Powered by one 74.5 kW (100 hp) Mercedes engine. Maximum level speed 100 km/h (62 mph).

Aero A.10 (Czechoslovakia) This five-passenger cabin biplane was the first commercial aircraft built in Czechoslovakia. Construction of the pro-

totype began in 1921 and was completed in the following year. Four production A.10s followed and in 1924 the Czech national airline ČSA (Československé Státní Aerolinie) began using them on the Prague to Bratislava service. Power was provided by one 194 kW (260 hp) Maybach Mb IVa engine, a number of which were left in Czechoslovakia by the Germans.

Aero A.11 (Czechoslovakia) Two-seat general-purpose biplane of mixed construction, developed from the A.12. Normally powered by one 179 kW (240 hp) Walter W-IV engine. Armament comprised one forward-firing Vickers and two rear-mounted Lewis machine-guns. Equipment included photographic and wireless apparatus. About 440 A.11s were built in many different variants from 1923 including: A.11N reconnaissance; Ab.11 light bomber powered by the 179 kW (240 hp) Breitfeld Daněk Perun II engine; and A.11H-S reconnaissance and training aircraft which incorporated structural changes, powered by the 223.5 kW (300 hp) Hispano-Suiza 8Fb engine. A number of the latter were built for Finland. Low-powered trainer variants of the A.11 were also produced with 134 kW (180 hp) Perun I engines.

On 13 September 1925 Captain Vicherek accomplished a Czech duration record in an Aero A.11 by remaining airborne for 13 h 15 min, covering a distance of 1,900 km (1,180 miles). In October 1925, returning a visit made by Polish pilots earlier in the year, four A.11s flew from Prague to Belgrade and Bucharest, and nine flew to Cracow and Warsaw. In 1926 an A.11 was flown on a 15,000 km (9,320 miles) tour of 23 countries in Europe, North Africa and Turkey. On 3 May 1927 one of the Finnish Aero 11H-S did 225 loops in 44 min 52.7 sec.

Data (A.11): *Engine* as above *Wing span* upper 12.78 m (41 ft 11¼ in) *Length* 8.2 m (26 ft 11 in) *Max T-O weight* 1,534 kg (3,381 lb) *Max level speed* 214.5 km/h (133.5 mph) *Range* 750 km (465.5 miles)

Aero A.12 (Czechoslovakia) Two-seat reconnaissance biplane, similar to the Aero 11 but fitted with side radiators instead of the nose type and powered by one 164 kW (220 hp) Walter or 182.5 kW (245 hp) Maybach Mb IVa engine. Ordered in quantity for the Czech Army Air Service.

Data: *Engine* as above *Wing span* 12.78 m (41 ft 11¼ in) *Length* 8.3 m (27 ft 2¾ in) *Max level speed* 200 km/h (124 mph)

Aero A.14 (Czechoslovakia) Version of the Hansa-Brandenburg C.I biplane built in Czechoslovakia by Aero from 1922. Powered by one 171.5 kW (230 hp) Breitfeld Daněk-built

Hiero N engine. Operated by the Czech Army Air Service on wheel and ski landing gears. Others went into commercial service with CSA as two-passenger transports. They were used initially to prove the Prague–Bratislava route in 1923, prior to actual inauguration of the airline on the Prague, Bratislava, Kosice and Uzhorod route on 28 October 1923, using D.II. 50 and Farman aircraft.

Aero A.18 (Czechoslovakia) Single-seat biplane fighter of 1923, 20 of which were built for the Czech Army Air Service. Powered by one 134 kW (180 hp) Walter-built BMW IIIa engine. Specially prepared variants flown successfully in the Czech President's Cup air races of 1923 and 1924.

Aero A.22 (Czechoslovakia) Commercialised version of the Aero A.12. It was identical except for the substitution of two passenger seats in the rear cockpit and removal of military equipment. Used by Aero from 1925 on the highly successful Prague to Marianbad route.

Aero A.23 (Czechoslovakia) Six- or seven-passenger cabin biplane powered by one 335 kW (450 hp) Walter-built Jupiter IV engine. Toilet aft of the cabin. Open cockpit for pilot and co-pilot aft and above the passenger cabin. Seven operated by CSA from 1928 on its proven Prague to Uzhorod and Prague to Marianbad routes. A few remained flying up to the late 1930s.
Data: *Engine* as above *Wing span* 16.6 m (54 ft 11½ in) *Length* 12.22 m (40 ft 1¼ in) *Max T-O weight* over 3,100 kg (6,834 lb) *Max level speed* 185 km/h (115 mph) *Range* 1,100 km (683 miles)

Aero A.24 (Czechoslovakia) Large biplane night bomber powered by two 182.5 kW (245 hp) Maybach engines.

Aero A.25 (Czechoslovakia) Two-seat advanced training aircraft used by the Czech Army Air Service from the late 1920s. Powered by one 138 kW (185 hp) Walter engine. The Aero A.28 was also designed for the same role, but powered by one Hispano-Suiza engine.

Aero A.29 (Czechoslovakia) Twin-float seaplane developed from the Aero A.11. Powered by one 179 kW (240 hp) Breitfeld Daněk Perun II engine. Nine operated as target tugs with the Czech Army Air Service. Max speed 195 km/h (121 mph) at 5,000 m (16,400 ft).

Aero A.30 (Czechoslovakia) Two-seat long-range reconnaissance and light bombing aircraft developed from the Ab.11. Prototype installed with one Avia-built 335 kW (450 hp) Lorraine engine. Production aircraft (built for the Czech

Aero A.30.

Army Air Service from 1927) were powered by 372.5 kW (500 hp) Skoda L engines. Armament consisted of one forward-firing Vickers and two rear-mounted Lewis machine-guns, plus a normal load of 300 kg (661 lb) of bombs. Total of 79 built (including A.230s), remaining in service in the designed role until the mid-1930s.
Data: *Engine* as above *Wing span* 15.3 m (50 ft 2¼ in) *Length* 10.0 m (32 ft 9¾ in) *Max T-O weight* 2,710 kg (5,975 lb) *Max level speed* 235 km/h (146 mph) *Endurance* 6 h

Aero A.32 (Czechoslovakia) Another aircraft developed from the successful Aero A.11, but produced mainly as an army co-operation biplane for the Czech Army Air Service. For this role the A.32 was fitted with two forward-firing Vickers machine-guns – as well as the standard rear-mounted Lewis guns – and could carry twelve 10 kg bombs on racks attached to the inner sections of the lower wings. Power was provided by one Walter-built 335 kW (450 hp) Bristol Jupiter engine.

Aero A.24.

Of the 116 A.32 series aircraft produced from 1928, 16 were built for the Finnish Air Force (all but the first powered by Gnome-Rhône-built Jupiter engines); others were of the refined Ap.32/Apb.32 type for Czech service. The main difference between the two was that the new aircraft had a divided-type landing gear with faired shock-absorbers, whereas the earlier A.32 had a cross-axle Vee undercarriage which was axle sprung on rubber shock-absorber cord. A.32 series aircraft remained in Czech service in the designed role until about 1936. Finnish A.32s served for a shorter time in an attack role, but remained operational as trainers for many years.
Data: *Engine* as above *Wing span* 12.44 m (40 ft 9½ in) *Length* 8.2 m (26 ft 11 in) *Max T-O weight* 1,927 kg (4,248 lb) *Max level speed* 230 km/h (143 mph) *Range* 800 km (497 miles)

Aero A.34 (Czechoslovakia) Two-seat light aircraft powered by one 63.5 kW (85 hp) Walter Vega radial engine.

Aero A.35 (Czechoslovakia) Strut-braced high-wing monoplane, the prototype of which was flown in 1928. Eight production aircraft built: six for the Czech airline CSA (plus the prototype) for its Brno to Uzhorod and other services; and two for a manufacturing company. Each aircraft had a cockpit for the pilot and one passenger under the leading edge of the wing. It had a transparent roof

Aero A.304.

Formation of Aero A.100s.

Aero L-29 Delfins.

section and windscreen. The cabin for four passengers was situated aft of the cockpit and below the wing. Large baggage compartment behind the cabin.

Data: *Engine* one 179 kW (240 hp) Walter Castor radial *Wing span* 14.52 m (47 ft 7¾ in) *Length* 9.75 m (31 ft 11½ in) *Max T-O weight* 1,900 kg (4,189 lb) *Max level speed* 197 km/h (122 mph) *Range* 660 km (410 miles)

Aero A.38 (Czechoslovakia) Biplane airliner of 1929 incorporating the wings, tail unit and Jupiter engine of the A.23 and fuselage and landing gear of the A.35. Only five A.38s were built: three as A.38-1s for CSA and two slightly modified A.38-2s for the French company CIDNA (Compagnie Internationale de Navigation Aérienne), which until 1925 had been known as Compagnie Franco-Roumaine de Navigation Aérienne. The French aircraft differed in being powered by French-built Gnome-Rhône Jupiter 9Ady radial engines. Each aircraft had a cockpit and cabin layout similar to that of the A.35, but had a longer fuselage with eight passengers being accommodated in the cabin, and a toilet installed.

Data (A.35-1): *Engine* one 335 kW (450 hp) Walter-built Bristol Jupiter IV *Wing span* 16.6 m (54 ft 6 in) *Length* 12.8 m (42 ft 0 in) *Max T-O weight* 3,200 kg (7,055 lb) *Max level speed* 190 km/h (118 mph) *Range* 500 km (311 miles)

Aero A.100 (Czechoslovakia) Two-seat general-purpose biplane powered by one 484.5 kW (650 hp) Avia Vr.36 water-cooled geared engine. Built originally as a variant of the A.30 (designated A.430) but developed into a completely new aircraft. Forty-four were built between 1933 and 1935 for the Czech Army Air Service. Armament consisted of two forward-firing Vickers and two rear-mounted Lewis machine-guns (the latter on a flexible mounting that could be stowed to reduce drag), plus bombs.

Data: *Engine* as above *Wing span* 14.7 m (48 ft 3 in) *Length* 10.6 m (34 ft 9 in) *Max T-O weight* 3,220 kg (7,099 lb) *Max level speed* 270 km/h (168 mph) *Range* 950 km (590 miles)

Aero A.101 and Ab.101 (Czechoslovakia) A.101 was a bomber variant of the A.100, 29 being built alongside the general-purpose types. Powered by one 596 kW (800 hp) Praga-built Isotta-

Fraschini Asso-1000 engine. The main differences included a re-shaped vertical tail unit and larger rear cockpit. The Ab.101 was produced from 1936 as a stop-gap bomber, powered by one 641 kW (860 hp) Praga-built Hispano-Suiza 12Ydrs engine. Slightly larger than the previous versions of the A.100; bombs were carried vertically in the forward part of the fuselage on the 'Pantof' system (with pneumatic releases) in addition to those carried horizontally beneath the fuselage. A prone bombing position was provided beneath the pilot's seat. Sixty-four were built, but proved totally inadequate and were quickly replaced.

Aero A.200 (Czechoslovakia) Four-seat light monoplane built for the 1934 Challenge de Tourisme International.

Aero A.204 (Czechoslovakia) Eight-passenger cantilever low-wing monoplane airliner of 1936 powered by two 268 kW (360 hp) Walter Pollux IIR engines. Not adopted by CSA, which instead ordered Walter Castor II-powered Airspeed Envoys, despite the A.204's similar performance.

Aero A.230 (Czechoslovakia) Variant of the A.30 powered by an Avia-built Lorraine engine. Produced from 1930. Main differences included a divided-type landing gear with faired shock-absorbers, two forward-firing guns and reshaped lower wingtips.

Aero A.300 (Czechoslovakia) Medium bomber developed from the A.204/A.304. Powered by two 618.5 kW (830 hp) Bristol Mercury IX engines. Many refinements included strengthened wings and a new tail unit with twin vertical surfaces. No production aircraft completed before the German occupation. Maximum speed was 470 km/h (292 mph). Bomb load 1,000 kg (2,205 lb).

Aero A.304 (Czechoslovakia) Reconnaissance-bomber of 1938 developed from the A.204 airliner. Fifteen built before the outbreak of war; made possible by the minimum of alterations to the basic A.204 airframe. Powered by two 320.5 kW (430 hp) Walter Super Castor 1-MR engines. Bomb load 300 kg (661 lb). One fixed forward-firing machine-gun in nose and another in a dorsal turret.

Following the invasion by Germany in March 1939, making Czechoslovakia a German protectorate, A.304s became transports and trainers with the German and Bulgarian air forces.

Aero MB.200.

Czech Air Force and exported to the air forces of Egypt, Indonesia, Nigeria, Syria and Uganda. The majority of those exported to Africa and the Middle East were of the L-29R light attack version, available with nose cameras and underwing stores.

Provision for a camera gun and gun sight, and either two bombs of up to 100 kg (220 lb), eight air-to-ground rockets or two 7.62 mm machine-gun pods under the wings.

Data (NATO reporting name: Maya): *Engine* as above *Wing span* 10.29 m (33 ft 9 in) *Length* 10.81 m (35 ft 5½ in) *Max T-O weight* with external fuel tanks 3,540 kg (7,804 lb) *Max level speed* 655 km/h (407 mph) *Max range* with external fuel tanks 894 km (555 miles)

Aero L-29 Delfin (Czechoslovakia) Two-seat basic and advanced trainer designed as a modern replacement for the piston-engined trainers formerly in service with the Czech Air Force. First flown on 5 April 1959 while powered by a Bristol Siddeley Viper engine. Production aircraft, powered by one M 701c 500 turbojet engine (8.72 kN; 1,960 lb st) as standard, began coming off the production line in April 1963. More than 3,000 Delfins were built by the close of production; more than 2,000 were supplied to the USSR for use as trainers by the Soviet, Bulgarian, German (Democratic Republic), Hungarian and Romanian air forces. The balance were delivered to the

Aero L-29A Delfin Akrobat (Czechoslovakia) Single-seat version of the Delfin intended specifically for military and sporting aerobatic use. Never put into production.

Aero L-39 Albatros (Czechoslovakia) Two-seat basic and advanced trainer developed to replace the L-29 Delfin. First flown on 4 November 1968. A pre-production batch of ten aircraft joined the flight test programme in 1971. Series production started in late 1972 following official selection of the L-39 to succeed the L-29 as the standard jet trainer of all Warsaw Pact countries, except Poland. By the spring of 1974 the L-39 had begun to enter service with the Czech Air Force.

The L-39 forms part of a comprehensive training system which includes a specially designed pilot training flight simulator, a pilot ejection ground training simulator and vehicle-mounted mobile automatic test equipment. The weapons trainer version is designated L-39Z; a single-seat ground attack version has the provisional designation L-39D (max external stores load 1,100 kg; 2,425 lb, including 500 kg bombs, rockets, air-to-air missiles, gun pods, reconnaissance pod, and an underfuselage pod for a 23 mm cannon).

Aero L-39 Albatros with underwing stores.

Aero L-39 pilot ejection ground training simulator.

Aero Boero 150Ag.

Aero Boero 180.

By May 1977 approximately 1,000 L-39s had been ordered. Of these, about half were already in service with the air forces of Afghanistan, Bulgaria, Czechoslovakia, the German Democratic Republic, Hungary, Iraq and the USSR.

Data: *Engine* one Walter Titan (Motorlet-built Ivchenko AI-25-TL) turbofan (16.87 kN; 3,792 lb st) *Wing span* 9.46 m (31 ft 0½ in) *Length* 12.32 m (40 ft 5 in) *Max T-O weight* 5,270 kg (11,618 lb) *Max level speed* 780 km/h (485 mph) *Max range* with external fuel tanks 1,600 km (994 miles)

Aero MB 200 (Czechoslovakia) Licence-built version of the French Bloch MB 200 bomber, incorporating minor changes and powered by two 633 kW (850 hp) Walter K-14 radial engines. One hundred and twenty-four built in Czechoslovakia between 1936 and 1937. Maximum speed 245 km/h (154 mph).

For other **Aero** aircraft see **LET (Letecké Zavody, Narodni Podnik)**

Aero Boero 95 (Argentina) Three-seat all-metal light monoplane suitable for private or business flying, training and agricultural use. Prototype first flown on 12 March 1959. Versions built included the AB 95 Standard with a 71 kW (95 hp) Continental C-90-8F flat-four engine; AB 95A De Lujo with a 74.5 kW (100 hp) Continental O-200-A engine; AB 95A Fumigador agricultural version with an O-200-A engine and dusting or spraying equipment; AB 95B with a 112 kW (150 hp) engine; and AB 95/115, which was similar to the AB 95B but with an 85.5 kW (115 hp) Lycoming O-235-C2A engine, mainwheel fairings and a more streamlined cowling.

Aero Boero 115BS (Argentina) Final production version of the Aero Boero 95 and 95/115 series. First flown in February 1973. Similar to the AB 95/115 but with a sweptback fin and rudder, increased wing span and greater fuel capacity. Twenty-five built. Production ended in 1976.

Aero Boero 150RV and 150Ag (Argentina) AB 150RV is essentially a lower-powered version of the AB 180RV, certificated in the Normal category. Four built and five ordered by spring 1978. Powered by one 112 kW (150 hp) Lycoming O-320-A2B flat-four engine. AB 150Ag is certificated in the Restricted category for use as an agricultural aircraft and has a similar power plant to that of the AB 150RV. Equipment includes a non-corrosible glassfibre underfuselage tank with a capacity of 270 litres (71.3 US gallons) of liquid chemicals.

Aero Boero 260Ag.

Data (AB 150RV): *Engine* as above *Wing span* and *Length* as for the **AB 180RV** *Max cruising speed* 211 km/h (131 mph)

Aero Boero 180Ag (Argentina) Version of the AB 180 for use as an agricultural aircraft. Ten built and six ordered by spring 1978.

Aero Boero 180, 180RV and 180RVR (Argentina) The AB 180 was the initial version, thought to have first flown in 1967. Built as a four-seater with a wing span of 10.7 m (35 ft 1 in) and as a three-seater with a wing span of 10.42 m (34 ft 2¼ in). This model was followed by the three-seat AB 180RV standard version with a recontoured fuselage, sweptback fin and rudder and increased fuel capacity. First flown in 1972. The AB 180RVR glider-towing version (also first flown in 1972) has a towing hook and a transparent roof panel. A two-seat or pilot and 100 kg (220 lb) underfuselage cargo pack high-altitude version (with optional turbocharger) was also produced as the AB 180 Condor. Total of 45 AB 180RV/RVRs had been built and seven ordered by spring 1978.

Data (180RV/RVR): *Engine* one 134 kW (180 hp) Lycoming O-360-A1A flat-four *Wing span* 10.72 m (35 ft 2 in) *Length* 7.273 m (23 ft 10¼ in) *Max T-O weight* 844 kg (1,860 lb) *Max level speed* (AB 180RV) 245 km/h (152 mph) *Range* 1,180 km (733 miles)

Aero Boero 180SP (Argentina) Biplane version of AB 180 produced by adding short-span lower wings on basic aircraft. Agricultural chemical tankage provided in lower wings.

Aero Boero 210 and 260 (Argentina) Four-seat light aircraft. Prototype of AB 210 powered by one 156.5 kW (210 hp) Continental IO-360 flat-six engine. Proposed development as the AB 260 powered by one 194 kW (260 hp) Lycoming O-540 engine.

Aero Boero 260Ag (Argentina) Single-seat agricultural monoplane, the prototype of which first flew on 23 December 1972. The static test programme and flight certification were due for completion in April 1978. Powered by one 194 kW (260 hp) Lycoming O-540 flat-six engine. Equipment includes a non-corrosible glassfibre tank with a capacity of 500 litres (110 Imp gallons) of liquid or 500 kg (1,102 lb) of dry chemicals.

Aero Commander (USA) See also **Rockwell International**

Aero Commander series (USA) Aero Design and Engineering Corporation was formed in

December 1944 to produce a prototype executive aircraft named the Aero Commander Model L-3805. This first flew on 23 April 1948. The first production version was the Aero Commander 520, a five–seven-seat monoplane powered by two 194 kW (260 hp) Lycoming GO-435-C2B flat-six engines. By the close of production in 1954 150 had been built. Subsequent versions (produced by Aero Commander and North American Rockwell) included the Aero Commander 560, 560A, 560B (70 built) and 560F (1960 model) with 261 kW (350 hp) Lycoming IGO-540 engines; Aero Commander 680 Super (295 built), 680E, 680F and 680FP with 283 kW (380 hp) Lycoming IGSO-540 supercharged engines; Aero Commander 500 (95 built) with 186 kW (250 hp) Lycoming O-540 engines, later superseded by the

Aero Commander Courser Commander.

Aero Commander 500B.

Aero Commander 560F.

Commander 100, subsequently becoming the improved Darter Commander in 1968. A four-seat high-wing light aircraft powered (as the Darter Commander) by one 112 kW (150 hp) Lycoming O-320-A flat-four engine.

Aero Commander 200 (incl Meyers 200B and Interceptor 400) (USA) The Aero Commander 200 was developed from the Meyers 200B and fitted with a 212 kW (285 hp) Continental IO-520-A piston engine. Following a production run the design was taken over by the Interceptor Corporation and is currently produced as the Interceptor 400. A four-seat low-wing monoplane, it is powered by a 496 kW (665 shp) Garrett-AiResearch TPE 331-1-101 turboprop engine, flat rated at 298 kW (400 shp). Max cruising speed is 452 km/h (281 mph).

Aero Commander Jet Commander (USA) See **IAI Westwind**

Aero Design DG-1 (USA) First flown on 25 July 1977, the DG-1 is a custom-built single-seat Unlimited Class racing monoplane of unorthodox design. Power is provided by two Mazda RX-3 rotary engines in pusher and tractor positions. It will also be used in an attempt to break the world speed record for propeller-driven aircraft.

500A with 194 kW (260 hp) Continental IO-470-M engines and the 500B with 216 kW (290 hp) Lycoming IO-540 engines (the 500B was redesignated 500U and called the Shrike Commander); Aero Commander 720 Alti-Cruiser (13 built); Grand Commander with a lengthened cabin for 11 persons and later known as the Courser Commander with 283 kW (380 hp) Lycoming IGSO-540-B1C supercharged engines; Courser-Liner with 283 kW (380 hp) Lycoming IGSO-540-B1A supercharged engines and designed as a convertible passenger/cargo version of the Courser Commander; and Shrike Commander. Details of the Shrike Commander, Shrike Commander Esquire, Commander 685, Hawk Commander and Turbo Commander series can be found under **Rockwell International.**

Aero Commander Darter Commander (USA) In its original form this aircraft was developed by the Volaircraft Corporation and was known as the Volaire Model 1050. When Aero Commander took over Volaircraft it became known as the Aero

Aero Commander Darter Commander.

Aero-Difusión Jodel D.112 and D.119 (Spain) Standard French Jodel aircraft built under licence. Powered by a 48.4 kW (65 hp) Continental A65 engine and a 67 kW (90 hp) Continental C90 engine respectively. Both versions were known as Populanes and the first D.112 was completed in 1954. An improved D.119, known as the D.1190.S Compostela, was subsequently produced with a 67 kW (90 hp) Rolls-Royce/Continental C90-14F flat-four engine.

Aero Spacelines Pregnant
Guppy.

Aero-Flight Streak series (USA) The two-seat low-wing Streak lightplane was produced in three versions from 1946 to 1953: AFA-1 Streak-85 with a 63.3 kW (85 hp) Continental C85-12J engine; AFA-2 Streak-125 with a 93 kW (125 hp) Continental C125 engine; and AFA-3 Streak-165 with a 123 kW (165 hp) Franklin engine. Maximum speed of the latter was 350 km/h (219 mph).

Aero Commander 200.

Aero Design DG-1.

Aero Spacelines Guppy
201.

Aero Spacelines Guppy series (USA) Aero Spacelines initiated the conversion of a Boeing B-377 Stratocruiser into a transport aircraft to carry sections of large American booster rockets. A 5.08 m (16 ft 8 in) section was inserted into the fuselage aft of the wing trailing edge and a huge circular-section bubble structure was built over the top of the fuselage. The new structure had an inside height of 6.02 m (19 ft 9 in) compared with the normal headroom of just under 2.74 m (9 ft 0 in) for the upper deck of the aircraft. The converted aircraft (designated B-377PG Pregnant Guppy) flew for the first time on 19 September 1962. In July 1963 it flew from Los Angeles to Cape Kennedy carrying an inert Saturn S-IV stage. This was the first of many regular flights.

Shortly after the completion of the Pregnant Guppy, the even larger B-377SG Super Guppy was built, capable of accommodating the S-IVB third stage of the Saturn V launch vehicle and the Apollo Lunar Module adapter. It utilised the wing, flight deck and forward fuselage of the Boeing C-97J and incorporated a hinged nose section. Wing span was increased by 4.57 m (15 ft) and the fuselage was lengthened by 9.40 m (30 ft 10 in). The upper fuselage lobe was made large enough to house cylindrical loads with a diameter of 7.62 m (25 ft). Power plant comprised four 5,216 kW (7,000 eshp) Pratt & Whitney T34-P-7WA turboprop engines. The Super Guppy flew for the first time on 31 August 1965.

The Guppy-201 was basically a production

version of the Super Guppy and three were built, each powered by four 3,660 kW (4,912 eshp) Allison 501-D22C turboprop engines. Two are based in Europe and have carried sections of Concorde and Airbus airliners between France and Great Britain, operated by Aéromaritime. A single example of the B-377MG Mini Guppy was built with a 6.86 m (22 ft 6 in) longer fuselage and a wider floor than the Stratocruiser, powered by four Pratt & Whitney R-4360-B6 piston engines. The last of the seven Guppy transports built was the Guppy-101 with a hinged nose and Allison 501-D22Cengines. Apart from their European and NASA use, Guppy transports were flown in America to carry sections of various commercial aircraft between factories.

Data (Guppy-201): *Engines* as above *Wing span* 47.62 m (156 ft 3 in) *Length* 43.84 m (143 ft 10 in) *Max T-O weight* 77,110 kg (170,000 lb) *Max cruising speed* 407 km/h (253 mph) *Range* 813 km (505 miles)

Aerocar Aerocar (USA) In 1948 Aerocar Inc began developing a flying automobile designed by Mr M. B. Taylor. The prototype Aerocar, with a Lycoming O-290 engine, was completed in October 1949. It was followed by a pre-production Aerocar Model I with a Lycoming O-320 engine and four additional Model I Aerocars for demonstration tours. No further production models have been built but a refined Model III Aerocar has been completed and development continues.

Aerocar Imp (USA) Currently under development, the Aerocar Imp is a single-engined homebuilt light aircraft embodying many design features of the Aerocar. Accommodation comprises two seats side-by-side and two rear folding

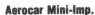

seats. Latest plans are for the installation of two 1,000 cc 74.5 kW (100 hp) motorcycle engines geared to drive a single propeller.

Aerocar Micro-Imp (USA) Similar to the Mini-Imp but built primarily of glassfibre-reinforced paper. Construction of a prototype began in December 1978.

Aerocar Mini-Imp (USA) Single-seat version of the Aerocar Imp. The basic all-metal structure is easily assembled and a folding wing facilitates construction in small areas. Plans and kits of parts for the Mini-Imp are available. By 1979 more than 100 amateur-built examples were under construction and several were flying. Recommended power plant is the turbocharged Revmaster 2100 D.

Aerocar Sooper-Coot Model A (USA) A lightweight homebuilt amphibian first flown in February 1971. Basic structure is of wood but the tailboom and tail unit can be of steel tube and fabric, wood monocoque or all-metal construction. The 'float-wing' configuration permits rough-water operation and all control surfaces are statically balanced. The wings, tailplane and elevators all fold. Over 400 Sooper-Coots are under construction, with 50 already flying.
Data: *Recommended engine* Franklin 134 or 164 kW (180 or 220 hp) *Wing span* 10.97 m (36 ft 0 in) *Length* 6.1 to 6.71 m (20 ft 0 in to 22 ft 0 in) *Max T-O weight* 884 kg (1,950 lb) *Max cruising speed* 209 km/h (130 mph)

Aeromarine 39-A and 39-B (USA) Two-seat biplane trainers produced for the US Navy from 1917. Fifty 74.5 kW (100 hp) Hall-Scott A-7A-powered Model 39-As were completed as landplanes and twin-float seaplanes; followed by 150 74.5 kW (100 hp) Curtiss OXX-6-engined Model 39-B landplanes and single main float seaplanes. Also used for post-war deck landing experiments (see **Chronology** 26 October 1922).

Aeromarine 40F (USA) Two-seat flying-boat trainer of 1918 powered by a 74.5 kW (100 hp) Curtiss OXX-6 engine in pusher configuration. Fifty delivered to the US Navy before the end of World War I. Could also be fitted with skis. The Type 40 was also used for carrying airmail. Max level speed 290 km/h (180 mph).

Aeromarine 75 (USA) Twelve-passenger (plus pilot and mechanic) commercial flying-boat pro-

duced after World War I. Powered by two Liberty engines. Notably used on the Key West to Havana route.

Aeromarine 700 (USA) Two 66.75 kW (90 hp) Aeromarine-engined biplanes (ordered in 1917) fitted with twin floats and used by the US Navy for torpedo-dropping experiments.

Aeromarine AS-1 and AS-2 (USA) Aeromarine built a single AS-1 fighter seaplane with an exposed engine and a uniquely shaped vertical tail positioned below the horizontal tail surfaces and two AS-2 seaplanes. The latter were also powered by a 223.5 kW (300 hp) Wright-Hispano E engine, covered by the slab-sided fuselage, and had a new oval fin and rudder. They were operated by the US Navy during the early 1920s. Max level speed 183 km/h (114 mph).

Aeromere M-100 S (Italy) Single-seat Standard Class sailplane, the prototype of which made its first flight on 19 January 1960. The first production model flew on 12 May 1960. Minimum sinking speed at 67 km/h (41.6 mph) 0.65 m/sec (2.13 ft/sec).

Aeromere Falco F.8.L series (Italy) Designed by Ing. Stelio Frati, the Falco two-seat light monoplane flew in its original form – with a 67 kW (90 hp) Continental engine – on 15 June 1955. Production by Aviamilano Costruzioni Aeronautiche began with the Falco F.8.L Series I, of which ten were delivered to customers from 1956 with 100.6 kW (135 hp) Lycoming engines. Subsequent production version was the F.8.L Series II with a 112 kW (150 hp) Lycoming engine and other improvements. Aeromere Societa Per Azioni then licence-built the Falco as the F.8.L America – modified to conform with US CAR Part 3 requirements and with an ultimate load factor of 8.7 with full load – and the Falco 160 with a 119 kW (160 hp) Lycoming O-320 engine and variable-pitch propeller. The company became Laverda in 1964 and produced the latter

Aeromarine 40.

Aeronca C-3.

aircraft as the Super Falco. It was announced in 1979 that the Super Falco was going to be put back into production by the Sequoia Aircraft Corporation of the USA.

Data (Super Falco): *Engine* as above *Wing span* 8.0 m (26 ft 3 in) *Length* 6.5 m (21 ft 4 in) *Max T-O weight* 821 kg (1,810 lb) *Max cruising speed* 290 km/h (180 mph) *Range* 1,400 km (870 miles)

Aeronautica Umbra Trojani A.U.T.18 (Italy) This company entered aircraft production in 1935 by building bombers for the Italian government. Its one and only aircraft of original design was the A.U.T.18, a single-seat prototype fighter of 1939 powered by a 745 kW (1,000 hp) Fiat A.80Rc.41 engine.

Aeromarine 75 *Mendoza* **after carrying 27 people from Key West.**

Aeromere Falco F.8-L.

Aeronca C series (USA) This company was incorporated as the Aeronautical Corporation of America in November 1928, although it was known as Aeronca. Of its earliest designs the tiny single-seat C-2 did most to establish the company by making many noteworthy flights in America and by setting up several records for its class. Power was provided by a 22.3 kW (30 hp) Aeronca E-107-A two-cylinder engine which gave a maximum level speed of 128 km/h (80 mph). The later C-3 was a two-seat high-wing cabin monoplane powered by a 30 kW (40 hp) Aeronca E-113C two-cylinder engine, with a maximum speed of 149 km/h (93 mph).

The following Aeronca aircraft are listed in numerical then alphabetical order, and care should be taken with different aircraft of similar name that appeared before, during or after World War II.

Aeronca 7 Champion series (USA) In 1941 the name of the company was changed to Aeronca Aircraft Corporation. Between 1946 and 1951 more than 10,000 aircraft of the Champion series were built as two-seat cabin monoplanes with high braced wings and fixed tailwheel-type landing gears. These included the 7AC Champion with 48.4 kW (65 hp) Lycoming engine; 7BC Champion with a fuel injected 63.5 kW (85 hp) Continental O-191-1 or 67 kW (90 hp) Continental O-205-1 engine, a transparent roof and jettisonable doors, supplied to the US Army as the L-16A (509 built) and L-16B (100 built) for liaison and communications duties; 7DC Champion with a 48.4 kW (65 hp) or 63.5 kW (85 hp) Continental engine; and the 7EC Champion with a 67 kW (90 hp) Continental C90-12 engine. (See also **Champion Aircraft**)

Data (7EC Champion): *Engine* as above *Wing span* 10.67 m (35 ft 0 in) *Length* 6.55 m (21 ft 6 in) *Max T-O weight* 658 kg (1,450 lb) *Max level speed* 176 km/h (110 mph) *Range* 560 km (350 miles)

Aeronca 11AC Chief (USA) A variation of the Champion, produced in 1947. Generally similar except for increased fuselage width to accommodate side-by-side seating for two and a lower cowling line to give better visibility.

Aeronca 11CC Super Chief (USA) Generally similar to the Chief, produced in 1948. Fitted with balanced elevator surfaces, it incorporated other modifications to meet the trim requirements of Section 03 of the Civil Air Regulations.

Aeronca 15AC Sedan (USA) The Sedan four-seat cabin monoplane appeared in 1947 and many were subsequently built. Its all-metal structure had fabric covering on the fuselage and metal on the wings. Most were produced with 108 kW (145 hp) Continental C145 engines but a small number had 123 kW (165 hp) Franklin 6A40-165-B3 engines installed. An S15AC twin-float seaplane version was also produced.

Data: *Engine* as above *Wing span* 11.43 m (37 ft 6 in) *Length* 7.7 m (25 ft 3 in) *Max T-O weight* 930 kg (2,050 lb) *Max cruising speed* 183 km/h (114 mph) *Range* 734 km (456 miles)

Aeronca 50 Chief series (USA) Basically similar to the Scout but powered by a 37.25 kW (50 hp) Continental A-50 engine (Model 50-C), Franklin 50 (Model 50-F) or Lycoming engine (Model 50-L). Maximum speed 160 km/h (100 mph).

Aeronca 65 Super Chief series (USA) Version of the Chief with a 48.4 kW (65 hp) engine and other refinements. Produced in several versions with engines including the Continental A-65-8 and Lycoming O-145-B1. A small number impressed into Army service during World War II.

Aeronca K Scout series (USA) The pre-war Scout, with the Chief, established the basic Aeronca layout for two-seat cabin monoplanes which remained virtually unchanged through most of the subsequent series of aircraft marketed under various names. It was of composite construction and seating was for two side-by-side. The Model K was powered by a 30 kW (40 hp) Aeronca engine and the Model KC had a Continental two-cylinder engine of similar power.
Data (Model KC): *Engine* as above *Wing span* 10.9 m (36 ft 0 in) *Length* 6.27 m (20 ft 7 in) *Max T-O weight* 481 kg (1,060 lb) *Max level speed* 149 km/h (93 mph) *Range* 402 km (250 miles)

Aeronca L series (USA) The L series of aircraft, which originated in 1935, differed from all other Aeronca aircraft by being cantilever low-wing monoplanes with a fixed and trousered landing gear, the main units of which were attached to and faired into the wings. Each model had an enclosed cabin for two persons side-by-side with dual controls, covered by a panelled enclosure. The various engines fitted to the aircraft of the series were radials enclosed in Townend cowling rings: the Model LA was fitted with a 52 kW (70 hp) Le Blond; the LB, a 63.5 kW (85 hp) Le Blond; the LC, a 67 kW (90 hp) Warner Junior; and the LD, a 67 kW (90 hp) Lambert.
Data: *Engine* as above *Wing span* 10.9 m (36 ft 0 in) *Length* 6.86 m (22 ft 6 in) *Max T-O weight* (52 kW; 70 hp Le Blond) 763 kg (1,680 lb) *Max level speed* (52 kW; 70 hp Le Blond) 184 km/h (115 mph) *Range* (52 kW; 70 hp Le Blond) 805 km (500 miles)

Aeronca L-3 Grasshopper (USA) In 1941 the US Army purchased four Aeronca Tandem

Trainers (basically a Super Chief with seating for two in tandem and a shorter wing span) for evaluation as light observation and liaison aircraft. These were designated YO-58 Defenders. Production aircraft for the Army began with 50 O-58s, which were subsequently redesignated L-3s. Similarly, improved O-58As became L-3As and O-58Bs became L-3Bs. Nearly 900 of the two versions were built. Production for the Army ended with the delivery of 490 L-3Cs. In addition a small number of Aeronca Model 65s were impressed into the Army as L-3Ds to L-3Js.
Data (L-3): *Engine* one 48.4 kW (65 hp) Continental O-170-3 *Wing span* 10.67 m (35 ft 0 in) *Length* 6.4 m (21 ft 0 in) *Max T-O weight* 590 kg (1,300 lb) *Max level speed* 129 km/h (80 mph) *Range* 313 km (195 miles)

Aeronca Arrow (USA) Two-seat all-metal cantilever low-wing cabin monoplane with a retractable tailwheel-type landing gear. Power was provided by a 67 kW (90 hp) flat-four engine.

Aeronca Chum (USA) Two-seat cantilever low-wing cabin monoplane with a retractable nosewheel-type landing gear. Power was provided by a 63.5 kW (85 hp) Continental C85J engine.

Aeronca TG-5 (USA) Three-seat training glider based on the L-3 Grasshopper. Two hundred and fifty purchased by the USAAF.

Aeroneering Miller Lil' Rascal (USA) Two-seat sporting biplane designed to be constructed by amateurs and schools. Powered by one 63.5 kW (85 hp) Continental C85-8 flat-four engine or a 67 kW (90 hp) Franklin engine.

Aeronca L-16A.

Aeronca 15AC Sedan.

Aero Resources J-2 and Super J-2 (USA) In 1974 Aero Resources took over production of the J-2 two-seat light autogyro from McCulloch Aircraft Corporation. The actual prototype J-2, designed by Mr D. K. Jovanovich, first flew in June 1962. A version known as the Super J-2 was developed from the J-2, powered by a 134 kW (180 hp) Lycoming O-360-A2D flat-four engine.

Aeronca Chum.

Aero Resources Super J-2.

Aerospace General Mini-Copter Configuration 2.

Aerospace Airtrainer CT4, used by No 1 Flying Training School, RAAF.

Aerospace Fletcher FU-24-954.

Aerospace Airtrainer CT4 (New Zealand) In 1974 Aero Engine Services Ltd purchased the Aircruiser lightplane from Victa Ltd of Australia. It was then decided to produce a military trainer version of the aircraft. Consequently it was re-designed and restressed to make it suitable for aerobatic flying with limits of +6 and −3g and renamed the Airtrainer CT4. Other changes from the original Victa Airtourer included a hinged clear perspex cockpit canopy, side-by-side seating for two persons with an optional third seat at rear and stick-type control columns. A prototype CT4 flew for the first time on 23 February 1972. On 1 April 1973 AESL and Air Parts amalgamated to form New Zealand Aerospace Industries Ltd. The Royal Thai Air Force ordered 24 Airtrainers, the Royal Australian Air Force 37 and the RNZAF 13, plus one later (designated CT4B).
Data: *Engine* one 157 kW (210 hp) Rolls-Royce Continental IO-360-H flat-six *Wing span* 7.92 m (26 ft 0 in) *Length* 7.06 m (23 ft 2 in) *Max T-O weight* 1,088 kg (2,400 lb) *Max level speed* 286 km/h (178 mph) *Max range* 1,422 km (884 miles)

Aerospace Fletcher FU-24-950 (New Zealand) The FU-24 was developed by the Sargent-Fletcher Company of the USA initially for agricultural top-dressing work in New Zealand. The prototype flew in July 1954, followed by the first production aircraft five months later. All manufacturing and sales rights were acquired by Air Parts (NZ) in 1964 and production continued in New Zealand (see **Airtrainer CT4** entry above

for amalgamation). The initial production series of 100 was delivered to New Zealand operators for top-dressing work. By June 1978 a total of 256 Fletcher aircraft had been produced, including a number sent to Australia, Bangladesh, Iraq, Pakistan, Thailand, Uruguay and several Pacific island countries.

The current model is the FU-24-950 powered by a 298 kW (400 hp) Lycoming IO-720-A1A or A1B flat-eight engine. The agricultural models have an enclosed cockpit for the pilot and one passenger. Equipment includes a glassfibre hopper for 1,045 litres (230 Imp gallons) of liquid or 1.05 m³ (37 cu ft) of dry chemicals. The utility models have an enclosed cabin for the pilot and up to seven passengers or freight.
Data: *Engine* as above *Wing span* 12.81 m (42 ft 0 in) *Length* 9.7 m (31 ft 10 in) *Max T-O weight* 2,463 kg (5,430 lb) *Max level speed* 233 km/h (145 mph) *Range* 709 km (441 miles)

Aerospace Cresco (New Zealand) A projected new production version of the Fletcher FU-24 powered by a 447 kW (600 hp) Avco Lycoming LTP 101 turboprop or similar Pratt & Whitney or AiResearch engine.

Aerospace General Mini-Copter (USA) The Mini-Copter was intended originally for air-dropping to a pilot who had been forced down behind enemy lines or in terrain unsuited to conventional rescue. It is currently being evaluated by the US Army in an Individual Tactical Air Vehicle (ITAV) role in three configurations: Configuration 1 is the basic version with no landing gear and the fuel tanks and control/rotor unit strapped to the pilot; Configuration 2 consists of a

welded steel tube structure carrying the control/ rotor unit and fuel tanks, and providing a seat for the pilot; Configuration 3 is generally similar to the latter but has the addition of a 67 kW (90 hp) McCulloch flat-four engine. This model takes off as a helicopter using its two 0.187 kN (42 lb) Aerospace General rocket motors (one on the tip of each main rotor blade) but at 48 km/h (30 mph) forward speed the tip units are turned off and the aircraft flies as an autogyro using the McCulloch engine.

Aérospatiale CM 170 Magister and Fouga 90 (France) The first prototype Magister two-seat advanced jet-powered trainer and light attack aircraft flew on 23 July 1952, having been produced by Fouga. This company went on to build production aircraft under its own name for the French Air Force until it became part of Potez in 1958. Production continued under Potez until it became part of Sud-Aviation and later Aérospatiale. Magisters built by all companies (929 constructed between 1953 and 1968) currently serve with the armed forces of 15 countries and the following versions have been built: CM 170 Magister basic version with two 3.91 kN (880 lb st) Turboméca Marboré IIA turbojets; CM 170 Super Magister with two 4.71 kN (1,058 lb st) Marboré VI turbojets; CM 175 Zéphyr, which is similar to the Magister but with equipment for operation from French Navy aircraft carriers (32 delivered); and the new Fouga 90 modernised version with two 6.76 kN (1,520 lb st) Astafan IIG turbofan engines, a new cockpit with a higher rear seat and uprated equipment (prototype flew on 20 August 1978).
Data (CM 170 Super Magister): *Engines* as above *Wing span* over tip-tanks 12.15 m (39 ft 10 in) *Length* 10.06 m (33 ft 0 in) *Max T-O weight* 3,260 kg (7,187 lb) *Max level speed* at 9,000 m (30,000 ft) 725 km/h (451 mph) *Range* at 3,100 kg (6,834 lb) AUW 1,400 km (870 miles) *Armament* two 7.5 or

7.62 mm machine-guns and optional underwing racks for four 25 kg air-to-ground rockets, two Matra 181 launchers with 18 × 37 mm rockets each, two launchers with seven SNEB 68 mm rockets each, two 50 kg bombs or two AS.11 guided missiles.

Aérospatiale N 262 and Frégate (France) A twin-engined light transport aircraft for civil and military applications, first flown on 24 December 1962. Variations in layout and accommodation include the standard airline version with 26 seats (maximum 29 seats); a quick-change passenger/ cargo version with folding seats; a version with a six-person executive suite forward and ten passengers aft; an ambulance version; and an aerial survey version. Military versions can be fitted out to carry 18 paratroops or 29 troops, or as 22-seat utility transports. Naval versions can be equipped for target towing, artillery and missile observation, radar calibration or crew training duties. Standard transport versions have a large cargo door at the front on the port side. The production versions were as follows: the N 262 Series A standard early production version (preceded by Series B) powered by two 805 kW (1,080 ehp) Bastan VIC turboprop engines and delivered from August 1965; the N 262 Series B (designation of the first four production aircraft) built for Air Inter, which became operational in July 1964; and the Frégate (formerly N 262 Series C and D) with uprated Turboméca Bastan VII turboprop engines (each 854 kW; 1,145 ehp), resulting in improved single-engine ceiling, cruising speed and T-O performance at 'hot and high' airfields, which entered production in 1970, alongside the Series A (from the 74th aircraft). Total order of 110 for all versions completed in 1976.
Data: *Engines* as above *Wing span* 22.6 m (74 ft 1¾ in) *Length* 19.28 m (63 ft 3 in) *Max T-O weight* (Frégate) 10,800 kg (23,810 lb) *Max level speed* (Frégate) 418 km/h (260 mph) *Range* 1,020 km (633 miles)

Aérospatiale Mohawk 298 (France/USA) See **Frakes Aviation**

Aérospatiale N 500 (France) Small single-seat VTOL research aircraft intended primarily to evaluate the flight principles of the tilting-duct concept. The prototype was completed in 1967 and made its first tethered flight in July 1968.

Aérospatiale N 3202-B1B (France) Version of the Nord 3202 two-seat basic trainer as modified for use in aerobatic competitions by the *Patrouille de l'Aviation Légère de l'Armée de Terre*. Modifications included an increase in aileron area, installation of a three-blade variable-pitch propeller, a new landing gear and reduction in weight.

Aérospatiale N 500.

Aérospatiale AS 350D Astar.

Aérospatiale SA 315B Lama.

Aérospatiale/HAL SA 315B Cheetah.

Aérospatiale AS 350 Ecureuil/Astar (France/USA) Intended as a successor to the successful Alouette, the six-seat general-purpose AS 350 Ecureuil (Squirrel) helicopter embodies Aérospatiale's new Starflex type main rotor hub (made of glassfibre) with elastomeric spherical stops and oleo-elastic frequency matchers. The first prototype flew on 27 June 1974. The 459 kW (616 shp) Avco Lycoming LTS 101-600A.2 turboshaft-engined version is being marketed only in North America as the AS 350C Astar; the AS 350B Ecureuil, powered by 478 kW (641 shp) Turboméca Arriel, goes to the rest of the world. By March 1978 more than 300 AS 350s had been sold to operators in 14 countries. Deliveries began in the same month.
Data: *Engine* as above *Main rotor diameter* 10.69 m (35 ft 0¾ in) *Length* 13.0 m (42 ft 8 in) *Max T-O weight* 1,900 kg (4,190 lb) *Max cruising speed* (AS 350B) 235 km/h (146 mph) *Max range* (AS 350B) 780 km (484 miles)

Aérospatiale SA 315B Lama/Cheetah (France/India) Design of the SA 315B Lama began in 1968, initially to meet a requirement of the Indian armed forces. The prototype was flown for the first time on 17 March 1969. It combines features of the Alouette II and III. During demonstration flights in the Himalayas in 1969 a Lama, carrying a crew of two and 140 kg (308 lb) of fuel, made the highest landings and take-offs ever recorded, at a height of 7,500 m (24,600 ft). On 21 June 1972 a Lama set a helicopter absolute height record of 12,442 m (40,820 ft).

The production Lama has standard accommodation in the glazed cabin for a pilot and passenger in front and three passengers behind. It can be equipped for rescue, liaison, observation, training, agricultural, photographic, ambulance (two stretchers and an attendant) and other duties. It is capable of transporting an external load of 1,135 kg (2,500 lb) at an altitude of more than 2,500 m (8,200 ft). In an agricultural role it can be fitted with spraybars and an underbelly tank of 1,135 litres (300 US gallons) capacity. An alternative agricultural installation, using two side-mounted glassfibre tanks, was shown for the first time in 1976. Up to 1,000 kg (2,200 lb) of liquid chemicals can be carried in these tanks.

A total of 250 Lamas had been ordered by 84 operators in 26 countries by April 1978, when 215 had been delivered. In addition to manufacture by Aérospatiale, the SA 315B is produced under licence by HAL for the Indian Army as the Cheetah.
Data: *Engine* one 649 kW (870 shp) Turboméca Artouste IIIB turboshaft, derated to 410 kW (550 shp) *Main rotor diameter* 11.02 m (36 ft 1¾ in) *Length of fuselage* 10.26 m (33 ft 8 in) *Max T-O weight* (with externally-slung cargo) 2,300 kg (5,070 lb) *Max cruising speed* (with slung cargo) 120 km/h (75 mph)

Aérospatiale SA 318B Alouette III, SA 319B Alouette III Astazou/Chetak (France/India) The Alouette III seven-seat general-purpose helicopter was evolved from the Alouette II, with

Length of fuselage 9.75 m (31 ft 11¾ in) *Max T-O weight* 1,650 kg (3,630 lb) *Max level speed* 180 km/h (112 mph) *Max range* 720 km (447 miles)

Aérospatiale SA 319B Alouette III Astazou.

Aérospatiale SA 321G Super Frelons.

larger cabin, greater power, improved equipment and higher performance. The prototype flew for the first time on 28 February 1959 and a total of 1,382 Alouette IIIs had been sold to 190 operators in 72 countries by April 1978. All Alouette IIIs delivered up to the end of 1969 were designated SE 3160. Subsequent Alouette IIIs were designated SA 316B, with strengthened main and rear transmission, higher AUW and increased payload. First deliveries of this version were made in 1970. The SA 319B Alouette III Astazou version is a direct development of the SA 316B, from which it differs principally in having an Astazou XIV turboshaft engine (649 kW; 870 shp, derated to 447 kW; 600 shp) with increased thermal efficiency and a 25% reduction in fuel consumption. The sale of Alouette IIIs to India, Romania and Switzerland included a licence agreement to manufacture the aircraft in these countries (200 named Chetaks in India, 130 in Romania and 60 in Switzerland).

Data (SA 316B): *Engine* one 649 kW (870 shp) Turboméca Artouste IIIB turboshaft, derated to 425 kW (570 shp) *Main rotor diameter* 11.02 m (36 ft 1¾ in) *Length* (rotors turning) 12.84 m (42 ft 1½ in) *Max T-O weight* 2,200 kg (4,850 lb) *Max level speed* 210 km/h (130 mph) *Range* 540 km (335 miles) *Armament* 7.62 mm AA52 machine-gun carried internally or 20 mm MG 151/20 cannon carried in an open turret-type mounting, or four AS.11 or two AS.12 missiles, or 68 mm rocket pods. (Armament of SA 319A in naval ASW role includes two Mk 44 homing torpedoes or one torpedo and MAD gear)

Aérospatiale SA 318C Alouette II Astazou (France) This five-seat general-purpose helicopter flew for the first time on 31 January 1961 as a development of the SE 313 Alouette II Artouste. Production ended in 1975 after more than 350 had been completed. Alouette II Astazous remain operational as civil helicopters in many countries and with the French Army in a military role. A twin pneumatic float undercarriage can be fitted as an alternative to the standard skids. A skid gear with longer legs can be substituted to raise the fuselage higher off the ground for flying-crane operations.

Data: *Engine* one 395 kW (530 shp) Turboméca Astazou IIA turboshaft, derated to 268 kW (360 shp) *Main rotor diameter* 10.2 m (33 ft 5⅝ in)

Aérospatiale SA 332 Super Puma.

Aérospatiale SA 321 Super Frelon (France) The Super Frelon is a three-engined multi-purpose helicopter derived from the smaller SA 3200 Frelon. Sikorsky Aircraft of the USA provided assistance in its development. The first prototype, originally designated SA 3210-01, flew on 7 December 1962 powered by 985 kW (1,320 shp) Turmo IIIC₂ engines. The second prototype, flown on 28 May 1963, was representative of the naval version, with stabilising floats on the main landing gear supports. Four pre-production aircraft followed and the French government ordered an initial series of 17 (designated SA 321G) in October 1965.

By May 1978 a total of 97 Super Frelons had been sold to 10 operators in 8 countries, of which 91 had been delivered. Current versions are as follows: SA 321F commercial airliner designed to carry 34–37 passengers or alternative layouts providing for 8, 11, 14, 17, 23 or 26 passengers or freight; SA 321G anti-submarine helicopter, of which 24 were built for service with Flottille 32F of Aéronavale to support the *Redoutable* class of nuclear submarines entering and leaving their base on the Île Longue, operations from the helicopter carrier *Jeanne d'Arc* and minesweeping; SA 321H air force and army version with accommodation for 27–30 troops, 5,000 kg (11,023 lb) of internal or external cargo, or 15 stretchers and two medical attendants, and fitted with Turmo IIIE₆ engines; and SA 321Ja utility and public transport version designed to carry a maximum of 27 passengers or freight.

Data: *Engines* three 1,156 kW (1,550 shp) Turboméca Turmo IIIC⁶ turboshafts *Main rotor diameter* 18.9 m (62 ft 0 in) *Length of fuselage* 19.4 m

Aérospatiale SA 318C Alouette II Astazou.

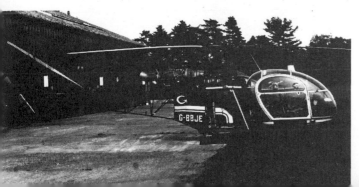

Aérospatiale

(63 ft 7¾ in) *Max T-O weight* 13,000 kg (28,660 lb) *Cruising speed* 250 km/h (155 mph) *Normal range* 820 km (509 miles) *Armament* ASW SA 321G operates normally in tactical formations of three or four aircraft. Four homing torpedoes or two Exocet anti-surface vessel missiles (also available to SA 321H)

Aérospatiale SA 332 Super Puma (France) Derivative of the SA 330 Puma (see entry) with accommodation for 19 passengers. Powered by two Turboméca Makila turboshaft engines, each with a T-O rating of 1,248 kW (1,675 shp). Fitted with Starflex hub. Max cruising speed 289 km/h (179 mph).

Aérospatiale SA 360C Dauphin.

Aérospatiale SA 365C Dauphin 2.

Aérospatiale SA 360C Dauphin (France) The SA 360 was developed as a replacement for the Alouette III. The first of two prototypes flew on 2 June 1972, powered by a 730 kW (980 shp) Turboméca Astazou XVI turboshaft. By early 1978 orders for 70 SA 360s (and the SA 365 variant) had been received from 17 operators in 13 countries. Standard accommodation is for ten persons, although an alternative 14-seat layout is available. An ambulance version carries four stretchers, a medical attendant and two crew. A mixed-traffic version carries six persons at the front of the cabin and has 2.5 m³ (88.3 cu ft) of cargo space to the rear. Executive versions have VIP interiors for four to six passengers. Provision is made for a 1,300 kg (2,865 lb) capacity cargo sling, rescue hoist and a wide range of civil and military equipment, including eight Hot missile launchers.
Data: *Engine* one Turboméca Astazou XVIIIA turboshaft, delivering 783 kW (1,050 shp) for take-off *Main rotor diameter* 11.5 m (37 ft 8¾ in) *Length of fuselage* 10.98 m (36 ft 0 in) *Max T-O weight* 3,000 kg (6,613 lb) *Cruising speed* 275 km/h (171 mph) *Range* 680 km (423 miles)

Aérospatiale SA 361H Dauphin (France) Similar to the SA 360 but powered by a 1,043 kW (1,400 shp) Turboméca Astazou XXB turboshaft engine with a Starflex rotor head. It will be capable of anti-tank operations, armed with eight Hot missiles, area neutralisation using 20 mm cannon/7.62 mm machine-guns and rockets, and assault missions carrying eight to ten troops.

Aérospatiale SA 365C Dauphin 2 (France) This helicopter is a twin-engined version of the SA

360 powered by two 485 kW (650 shp) Turboméca Arriel turboshafts. The prototype flew for the first time on 24 January 1975. Delivery of production aircraft began in early 1978. Variants of the design under development include the SA 365N for shipboard use. This will be offered as a lightweight anti-submarine helicopter carrying torpedoes and MAD and as an anti-ship helicopter armed with AS.15 missiles. The basic helicopter has accommodation for between 10 and 13 persons or can be fitted out as an executive helicopter for four or five passengers, an ambulance with four stretchers and a medical attendant, or for other military and civil roles.
Data: *Engines* as above *Main rotor diameter* 11.68 m (38 ft 4 in) *Length* 13.29 m (43 ft 7¼ in) *Max T-O weight* 3,400 kg (7,495 lb) *Cruising speed* 255 km/h (158 mph) *Range* 465 km (289 miles)

Aérospatiale SE 210 Caravelle (France) The French Secrétariat Général à l'Aviation Civile et Commerciale issued a specification in 1951 for a medium-range aircraft capable of carrying a 6,000–7,000 kg (13,227–15,432 lb) payload at 620 km/h (385.2 mph) over stages of 1,600–2,000 km (994–1,242 miles), mainly for operation between France and North Africa. SNCASE's X210 design was submitted for an aircraft with three rear-mounted SNECMA Atar engines and from this developed the SE 210 Caravelle with two rear-mounted Rolls-Royce Avon turbojets. Four prototypes (two flying) were ordered by the government in July 1953, the first one flying from Toulouse on 27 May 1955. Certification trials were completed by April 1956 and the aircraft then began route proving with Air France.

The Caravelle was a low-wing monoplane with 20° sweepback at quarter-chord and a low-set tailplane. The first production Caravelle Is had two 46.70 kN (10,500 lb st) Avon RA.29 Mk 522 engines and 80 seats. Air France introduced the

type on its Paris-Rome-Istanbul route on 12 May 1959. The similar Caravelle IA entered service with Finnair on 1 April 1960. There was no Caravelle II, but the Caravelle III with 50.71 kN (11,400 lb st) Avon Mk 527s entered service with Alitalia on 23 May 1960. One of the early Caravelle IIIs was fitted with General Electric CJ805-23C turbofans and delivered to General Electric in July 1960. Subsequently Caravelle Is and IAs were brought to Caravelle III standard. The next version was the Caravelle VI of 1961, which was built as the VIN with 54.27 kN (12,200 lb st) Avon Mk 531s, and the VIR with 56 kN (12,600 lb st) Avon Mk 532R or 533R engines and reverse thrust. Sabena introduced the VIN on 18 February 1961 and United Air Lines commissioned VIRs on the New York–Chicago route on 14 July 1961. The VIR had redesigned flight deck windows providing better view, more powerful brakes and six lift-dumping spoilers. Some Caravelle IIIs were modified to VIN standard.

It was planned to follow the Caravelle VIs with the Caravelle Horizon – the 10A with CJ805-23C turbofans and the 10B with Pratt & Whitney turbofans – but only a 10A prototype was produced. It flew on 31 August 1962. Instead of the Caravelle Horizon, Sud-Aviation (as SNCASE had become before the Caravelle appeared) produced the 10R, which was a VIR fitted with 62.3 kN (14,000 lb st) Pratt & Whitney JT8D-1 turbofans; and the Caravelle Super B with the same engines, one metre increase in fuselage length, modified wing root with greater chord and increased sweep, and a bullet fairing at the fin and tailplane junction. Finnair introduced the Super B on its Helsinki–Milan services on 16 August 1964. Alia (The Royal Jordanian Airline) was the first to fly 10Rs, known initially as the 10B1R, in the summer of 1965. All the Caravelles up to the Super B were equipped to carry 80 passengers but

Aérospatiale SE 313B Alouette II.

in 1965–66 some Caravelle IIIs were modified to accommodate 94. The Super B had maximum seating for 109. Maximum weights rose from the original 43,500 kg (95,901 lb) of the Caravelle I to 52,000 kg (114,640 lb) for the Super B. Development from the Caravelle 10R gave a small number of 11R JT8D-7-powered combination passenger/cargo aircraft, first flown in April 1967. Then came the final Caravelle 12 with a fuselage more than four metres longer, JT8D-9 engines, up to 128 tourist-class seats and 56,000 kg (123,459 lb) take-off weight.

A total of 280 Caravelles were built and many are still in service.

Data (Caravelle III): *Engines* as above *Wing span* 34.3 m (112 ft 6¼ in) *Length* 32.01 m (105 ft) *Max T-O weight* 46,000 kg (101,413 lb) *Cruising speed* 779 km/h (484 mph) *Range* 1,740 km (1,081 miles)

Aérospatiale SE 313B Alouette II (France) Two prototypes were built as SE 3120s, the first of which flew on 12 March 1955. Both were powered by Salmson 9 engines and had been developed for agricultural work. The designation SE 3130 Alouette II was originally given to production helicopters, but this was changed to SE 313B Alouette II. Deliveries of the five-seat general-purpose helicopter began in 1957, to the French Army. Twenty-one other countries eventually operated military versions and civil helicopters were also widely used. Production totalled 923 aircraft. Equipment available enabled the helicopter to be used for agricultural, rescue, ambulance (two stretchers and a medical attendant), casualty evacuation, photographic, survey, flying-crane, observation, liaison and close support duties.

Data: *Engine* one 395 kW (530 shp) Turboméca Artouste IIC6 turboshaft, derated to 268.5 kW (360 shp) *Main rotor diameter* 10.2 m (33 ft 6 in) *Length* (blades folded) 9.66 m (31 ft 9 in) *Max T-O weight* 1,600 kg (3,527 lb) *Max level speed* 185 km/h (115 mph) *Range* 300 km (186 miles)

Aérospatiale SE 210 Caravelle VIN.

Aérospatiale SE 210 Caravelle Super B.

Aérospatiale SN 601 Corvette.

Aérospatiale/Westland SA 330E Puma.

Aérospatiale SN 601 Corvette (France) This aircraft was designed to fulfil a number of roles, including commuter and executive transport (6–14 passengers), air taxi, ambulance, freighter and training. It can be equipped for radio aids calibration or aerial photography. The prototype (designated SN 600) flew for the first time on 16 July 1970 and completed more than 270 flying hours before being lost in a crash in 1971. It was powered by two Pratt & Whitney Aircraft of Canada JT15D-1 turbofan engines, each rated at 9.81 kN (2,200 lb st). The first SN 601 production type aircraft was completed in 1972 and deliveries began in September 1974. By mid-1978 a total of 36 Corvettes had been sold or leased. Production was terminated after the fortieth aircraft.
Data: *Engines* two 11.12 kN (2,500 lb st) Pratt & Whitney Aircraft of Canada JT15D-4 turbofans *Wing span* 12.87 m (42 ft 2½ in) *Length* 13.83 m (45 ft 4½ in) *Max T-O weight* 6,600 kg (14,550 lb) *Max cruising speed* at 9,000 m (30,000 ft) 760 km/h (472 mph) *Max range* (12 passengers) 1,555 km (967 miles)

Aérospatiale/Westland SA 341B Gazelles.

Aérospatiale Ludion (France) Displayed for the first time at the 1967 Paris Air Show, the Ludion was an ultra-light jet-lift VTOL aircraft capable of carrying a fully equipped man and a payload of 30 kg (66 lb) to a height of 150–200 m (500–600 ft) above the ground for a distance of more than 700 m (2,300 ft).
Aérospatiale/Socata TB-30 (France) In September 1978 Aérospatiale released details of this tandem two-seat primary trainer. It will cover the full primary flight curriculum of basic training, aerobatics, blind and night flying, close formation and combat manoeuvres, and VFR/IFR navigation for students in both fighter and transport streams. Further uses for the aircraft could include liaison and light tactical close support. Power plant is a 224 kW (300 hp) Lycoming IO-540-K flat-six engine.
Aérospatiale/Westland SA 330 Puma (France/UK) The Puma was developed initially to meet a French Air Force requirement for a medium-sized *hélicoptère de manoeuvre* able to operate by day or night in all weathers and in all climates. In 1967 it was selected for the RAF Tactical Transport Programme and was included in a joint production agreement between Aérospatiale and Westland of the UK. The first prototype flew on 15 April 1965 and the first production aircraft in September 1968. The following versions have been built: SA 330B Puma for the French Army (ALAT) and French Air Force, powered by two 884 kW (1,185 shp) Turboméca Turmo IIIC4 turboshaft engines; SA 330C/H Puma military export versions, powered by two 1,044 kW (1,400 shp) Turmo IVB engines; SA 330E Puma for the RAF (40 helicopters designated HC.1) with Turmo IIIC4 engines; SA 330F/G Puma civil passenger/cargo versions with accommodation for between eight and 20 passengers or cargo and powered by two 1,070 kW (1,435 shp) Turmo IVA engines; and SA 330J/L Puma current civil and 16-troop (or six stretchers and six seated patients or freight) military production versions respectively, powered by two 1,175 kW (1,575 shp) Turmo IVC engines. A total of 573 Pumas had been sold by April 1978.
Data (SA 330J/L): *Engines* as above *Main rotor diameter* 15.0 m (49 ft 2½ in) *Length of fuselage* 14.06 m (46 ft 1½ in) *Max T-O weight* 7,400 kg (16,315 lb) *Max cruising speed* 271 km/h (168 mph) *Max range* 572 km (355 miles) *Armament* (military version) includes a side-firing 20 mm cannon, axial-firing 7.62 mm machine-guns, missiles and rockets

Aérospatiale/Westland SA 341/342 Gazelle (France/UK) The first prototype of this five-seat lightweight helicopter (designated SA 340) flew on 7 April 1967, powered by an Astazou III engine. The first production SA 341 Gazelle flew on 6 August 1971. Ten versions of the Gazelle have been announced: SA 341B British Army version (designated Gazelle AH.1) powered by an Astazou IIIN engine; SA 341C Royal Navy version (designated Gazelle HT.2); SA 341D RAF training version (designated Gazelle HT.3); SA 341E RAF communications version (designated Gazelle HCC.4); SA 341F French Army version with an Astazou IIIC engine (166 procured); SA 341G civil version with an Astazou IIIA engine (a variant, known as the Stretched Gazelle, has additional legroom for rear passengers); SA 341H military export version with an Astazou IIIB engine; SA 342J commercial counterpart of the SA 342L, with a higher max T-O weight and improved 'fenestron' tail rotor; SA 342K military version supplied initially to Kuwait and powered by a 650 kW (870 shp) Astazou XIVH engine;

Aerosport Rail.

and SA 342L military counterpart of the SA 342J. Data (SA 341G): *Engine* one 440 kW (590 shp) Turboméca Astazou IIIA turboshaft *Main rotor diameter* 10.5 m (34 ft 5½ in) *Length of fuselage)* 9.53 m (31 ft 3³⁄₁₆ in) *Max T-O weight* 1,800 kg (3,970 lb) *Max cruising speed* 264 km/h (164 mph) *Range* 670 km (416 miles) *Armament* (military Gazelles only) can include two pods of Matra or Brandt 2.75 in or 68 mm rockets, four AS.11 or two AS.12 missiles, four or six Hot missiles, two forward-firing 7.62 mm machine-guns, reconnaissance flares or smoke markers

Aerosport Quail (USA) Single-seat lightweight cabin monoplane (1,600 cc Volkswagen modified motor car engine), designed to be constructed by amateurs. By 1979 about 375 sets of plans had been sold. Approximately 26 aircraft were under construction and about ten were flying.

Aerosport Rail (USA) Single-seat ultra-light aircraft (Volkswagen motor car engine), plans of which are no longer available to amateur constructors. About 175 sets of plans had been sold by 1977. A new version was expected to be announced in 1980.

Aerosport Scamp A and B (USA) Scamp A is a single-seat light open-cockpit biplane (prototype has 1,834 cc Volkswagen modified motor car engine) designed to be constructed by amateurs. By 1979 more than 640 sets of plans had been sold, 30 Scamps were under construction and 12 were flying. Scamp B is an agricultural cropspraying version of the Scamp, which is assembled in Colombia from Aerosport kits and marketed commercially.

Aerosport Woody Pusher (USA) Two-seat light open-cockpit parasol-wing monoplane (48.5–63.5 kW; 65–85 hp engine) designed to be constructed by amateurs. Plans are no longer available but several hundred sets have been sold and at least 27 aircraft are flying.

Aerotec A-122A Uirapuru (Brazil) The prototype of this two-seat primary trainer made its first flight on 2 June 1965 while powered by an 80.5 kW (108 hp) Lycoming O-235-C1 engine. The second prototype had a 112 kW (150 hp) Lycoming O-320-A engine fitted. In 1967 the Brazilian Air Force ordered 30 production aircraft under the designation T-23, to be powered by 119 kW (160 hp) Lycoming O-320-B2B engines, later increasing the total ordered to 100 for use at the Academia da Força Aérea in Pirassununga, São Paulo State. Others have been sold to Bolivia (18) and Paraguay (8). Twenty-five examples of a civil version of the Uirapuru (designated A-122B) have also been built.

Data: *Engine* as above *Wing span* 8.5 m (27 ft 10¾ in) *Length* 6.6 m (21 ft 8 in) *Max T-O weight* 840 kg (1,852 lb) *Max level speed* 227 km/h (141 mph) *Max range* 800 km (495 miles)

Aerotec A-132 Uirapuru II (Brazil) Generally similar to the A-122A, but span and length are increased. Other changes include a flat-sided fuselage, improved canopy and larger vertical tail surfaces with no ventral fin. Under development.

Aerotécnica AC-12 (Spain) This two-seat light helicopter was developed from the AC-11, the designation given to the Matra-Cantinieau MC-101, for which Aerotécnica held a manufacturing licence. In the AC-12 the 125 kW (168 hp) Lycoming O-360-B2A engine was mounted above the cabin with direct drive through the gearbox to the main rotor. The prototype first flew on 20 July 1956. Twelve delivered to the Spanish Air Force (designated EC-XZ-2s). Max level speed 140 km/h (87 mph).

Aerotécnica AC-14 (Spain) Five-seat helicopter powered by a 298 kW (400 shp) Turboméca Artouste IIB1 turboshaft engine. Also designed to suit agricultural and ambulance roles. A preproduction batch of ten AC-14s (military designation EC-XZ-4) was built, of which the first flew on 16 July 1957. The company ended trading in 1962.

AFU AA-7/AJ-7/AR-7 (Switzerland) Proposed developed versions of the P-16 strike fighter (see **FFA**) powered by SNECMA Atar 9C, General Electric J79 and Rolls-Royce RB.168.25 engines respectively.

Ago C.I and C.II (Germany) Series of twin-boom reconnaissance biplanes, each armed with one machine-gun in the nose. C.I and C.II landplanes had a four-wheel landing gear under the central crew nacelle and a tailskid under each boom. Power was provided by a 119 kW (160 hp) Mercedes D.III and 112 kW (150 hp) Benz III or 164 kW (220 hp) Benz Bz.IV pusher engine respectively. The similarly powered C.I-W (one built) and C.II-W (two built) twin-float seaplane versions were operated by the German

Aerosport Scamp A.

Aerosport Woody Pusher.

Aerotec T-23 Uirapuru.

Agusta A 106 with torpedoes.

Navy in a coastal reconnaissance and defence role. C.Is and C.IIs became operational over the Western Front in the latter half of 1915.

Data (C.II): *Engine* as above *Wing span* 14.5 m (47 ft 6⅞ in) *Length* 9.84 m (32 ft 3½ in) *Max T-O weight* 1,946 kg (4,290 lb) *Max level speed* 138 km/h (86 mph)

Ago C.III (Germany) Experimental development of the C.II powered by a Mercedes D.III engine.

Captured Ago C.IV.

Agusta A 101G.

Ago C.IV (Germany) The C.IV was totally different from Ago's earlier reconnaissance aircraft, being a tractor-engined two-seater with a conventional cross-axle landing gear and distinctively tapered biplane wings. Power was provided by a 164 kW (220 hp) Benz Bz.IV engine driving a two-blade propeller fitted with a spinner. Armament comprised a forward-firing Spandau and a rear-mounted Parabellum machine-gun. Great care had been taken to give the observer the best possible field of fire. Only about 70 production aircraft became operational from early 1917, although large orders had been placed with three manufacturers. In service the C.IV proved fast but unstable and was not popular with crews.

Data: *Engine* as above *Wing span* 11.9 m (39 ft 0½ in) *Max T-O weight* 900 kg (1,984 lb) *Max level speed* 190 km/h (118 mph) *Endurance* 4 h

Ago C.VII (Germany) Improved version of the C.IV. Prototype only.

Agusta A 109 military version.

Ago C.VIII (Germany) Version of C.VII with a Mercedes D.IV. Prototype only.

Ago DV.3 (Germany) Advanced-design single-seat biplane of 1915 powered by a 74.5 kW (100 hp) Oberursel U.I rotary engine. Prototype only.

Ago S.I (Germany) Single-seat ground attack biplane armed with two machine-guns and a cannon. None in service by the Armistice.

Agusta 115 (Italy) Announced in 1961, the 115 was a four-seat general-utility helicopter powered by a 358 kW (480 shp) Turboméca Astazou II turboshaft engine. Alternatively a stretcher could be carried internally and two externally in an ambulance role. No series production was undertaken.

Agusta A 101 (Italy) The first of three prototype A101G multi-purpose helicopters, built for the Italian Air Force, flew for the first time on 19 October 1964. Powered by three 1,043 kW (1,400 shp) Rolls-Royce Bristol Gnome H.1400 turboshaft engines, it had accommodation for 36 passengers or paratroops, 18 stretchers and five attendants or up to 5,000 kg (11,025 lb) of freight. A civil version, designated A 101H, was also projected with three Gnome H.1800 engines. Neither version entered series production.

Agusta A 103 (Italy) Single-seat light helicopter powered by a 63.5 kW (85 hp) Agusta M.V. G.A. 70 engine. No series production was undertaken.

Agusta A 104 Helicar (Italy) Two-seat light helicopter first flown in December 1960. Developed from the A 103 for civil and military use. Powered by one derated 104 kW (140 hp) Agusta M.V.A. 140V engine. No series production was undertaken.

Agusta A 106 (Italy) High-performance single-seat light helicopter. It was designed originally for ASW attack duties carrying two Mk 44 torpedoes and equipment for contact identification. First flight was made in November 1965, powered by a 246 kW (330 hp) Turboméca-Agusta TAA 230 turboshaft engine. The expected production aircraft for the Italian Navy were not built.

Agusta A 109A (Italy) The A 109A is a high-speed, high-performance twin-engined helicopter. The basic version accommodates a pilot and seven passengers. Alternatively, it can be adapted for freight carrying, as an ambulance (for two stretchers and two medical attendants) or for search and rescue. The first of three flying prototypes flew on 4 August 1971. Delivery of production aircraft started in 1976.

Data: *Engines* two Allison 250-C20B turboshafts, rated at 287 kW (385 shp) max continuous power

Main rotor diameter 11.0 m (36 ft 1 in) *Length of fuselage* 10.71 m (35 ft 1¾ in) *Max T-O weight* 2,450 kg (5,400 lb) *Max cruising speed* 266 km/h (165 mph) *Max range* 565 km (351 miles)

Agusta A 109 military version (Italy) Five modified military A 109s were delivered to the Italian Army during 1977. Three are equipped to carry four TOW missiles, the other two for transport and liaison duties. Changes in the military version include dual controls and instrumentation; rotor brake; tail rotor control magnetic brake; sliding doors; environmental control system; emergency flotation gear; non-retractable landing gear; armoured seats; crashworthy fuel tanks; heavy-duty battery; particle separator; external cargo hook; multi-purpose universal supports for external loads; rescue hoist; high-load cargo floor; and infra-red suppression system. Armament is basically two 7.62 mm flexibly mounted machine-guns and two XM-157 rocket launchers, each with seven 2.75 in rockets. Alternative weapons include Hot or TOW missiles; a 7.62 mm Minigun; MG3 7.62 mm machine-gun; an XM-159C launcher for 19 × 2.75 in rockets, Agusta launcher for seven 81 mm rockets, or 200A-1 launcher for 19 × 2.75 in rockets. The military A 109 has also been ordered by the Argentine Army and other foreign operators.

Agusta A 109 naval version (Italy) Under construction for several navies. Intended for anti-surface-vessel, anti-submarine, electronic warfare, armed patrol (stand-off missile guidance, TG-2), coastguard patrol, SAR, aerial ambulance, utility, reconnaissance, liaison and military command post and other duties. Armament can include two torpedoes, AS.12 or AM-10 missiles.

Agusta A 119 (Italy) Projected 11-seat version of the A 109.

Agusta A 129 Mangusta (Italy) Tandem two-seat anti-tank and light attack helicopter for the Italian Army. Powered by two Lycoming LTS 101 or Allison 250-C30 turboshaft engines (derated to 335 kW; 450 shp each for normal operations) and using dynamic components of the A 109. First flight is expected in 1981.

Agusta AZ8-L (Italy) Twenty-two or twenty-six-passenger medium-range transport aircraft powered by four 350 kW (470 hp) Alvis Leonides Mk 22 (503/2) nine-cylinder radial engines. First flight was made on 9 June 1958. Never put into series production.

Agusta CP-110 (Italy) Four-seat cabin monoplane of 1951, powered by a 108 kW (145 hp) Alfa 110*ter* engine. Intended for civil and military use

and evaluated by the Italian Air Force. Maximum level speed 275 km/h (170 mph).

Agusta-Bell Model 47 series (Italy) Agusta began building the Bell Model 47 under licence in 1954. More than 1,100 had been completed by the beginning of 1972 and production continued on a limited basis until 1976. Final versions included standard Models 47G-3B-1, G-3B-2, G-4A, G-5 and J-2A. In addition Agusta developed from the J-2A the AB 47J-3 and high-altitude AB 47J-3B-1 special variants. The former differed from the standard aircraft in having a modified main transmission (an ASW version developed for the Italian Navy carrying one Mk 44 torpedo); and the latter being equipped with exhaust-driven supercharger, high-inertia rotor and servo-control on both cyclic and collective pitch control systems respectively.

Agusta-Bell Model 47G-4A.

Agusta-Bell Model 102 (Italy) Eight- to ten-person general utility helicopter designed for civil and military use. First flown 3 February 1959. Two production aircraft built for passenger services between Milan and Turin. Each was powered by one 447 kW (600 hp) Pratt & Whitney R-1340-S1H4 engine.

Data: *Engine as above Main rotor diameter* 14.5 m (47 ft 7 in) *Length of fuselage* 12.73 m (41 ft 9 in) *Max T-O weight* 3,025 kg (6,670 lb) *Max level speed* 177 km/h (110 mph) *Max range* 400 km (250 miles)

Agusta-Bell 204B and 204AS (Italy) AB 204B is a medium-sized utility helicopter similar to the Bell Iroquois and built under licence. In production from 1961 to 1974 for the armed forces of eight countries and for commercial operation in Italy, Lebanon, Sweden and Switzerland. By the end of 1973 about 250 AB 204-series helicopters had been delivered (incl 204AS). Variants were built with Rolls-Royce Bristol Gnome, Lycoming

Agusta AZ8 in military markings.

Agusta-Bell 204B.

Agusta-Bell 205A-1 used by the Italian Fire Brigade.

T53 and General Electric T58 turboshaft engines. The AB 204AS is a special version for anti-submarine and anti-surface vessel duties with the Italian and Spanish navies. Armament can include two Mk 44 homing torpedoes or AS.12 missiles.

Data (AB 204AS): *Engine* one 962 kW (1,290 shp) General Electric T58-GE-3 turboshaft *Main rotor diameter* 14.63 m (48 ft 0 in) *Length of fuselage* 12.67 m (41 ft 7 in) *T-O weight* 4,310 kg (9,501 lb) *Cruising speed* 167 km/h (104 mph)

Agusta-Bell 205 (Italy) Multi-purpose helicopters built under licence and corresponding to the Bell UH-1D/UH-1H versions operated by the US forces. In service with the armed forces of many countries. Powered by one 1,044 kW (1,400 shp) Lycoming T53-L-13 turboshaft.

Agusta-Bell 206A JetRangers.

Agusta-Bell 205A-1 (Italy) Fifteen-seat commercial utility helicopter. Production started under licence in Italy in 1969.

Agusta-Bell 206 JetRanger and 206B JetRanger II (Italy) Five-seat general-purpose helicopters. AB 206A JetRanger has been manufactured under licence since 1967 for civil and military use (provision for weapons, as for Bell Kiowa). Deliveries of the improved AB 206B JetRanger II began in 1972 and several hundred have been sold for civil and military use. AB 206As built for Sweden (designated HKP 6s) have long-leg ski landing gears for carrying torpedoes, depth-charges, mines or other weapons for anti-submarine and anti-shipping missions.

Agusta-Bell 206L LongRanger (Italy) General-purpose helicopter built under licence.

Agusta-Bell 212.

Agusta-Bell 212 (Italy) Utility helicopter built under licence and corresponding with the Bell Model 212 Twin Two-Twelve. Powered by one 843 kW (1,130 shp) Pratt & Whitney Aircraft of Canada PT6T-3 Turbo Twin Pac. Production deliveries began in 1971 and more than 40 had been delivered by early 1977 to civil and military operators.

Agusta-Bell 212ASW (Italy) Modified version of the standard AB 212 for the Italian Navy, Turkey and other countries. Capable of submarine search, classification and strike; air-to-surface vessel search and strike; SAR; reconnaissance; vertical replenishment of ships; troop transport and fire support; casualty evacuation; and electronic warfare, liaison and utility duties. It can also operate in the stand-off missile guidance role, using its TG-2 system to guide the Otomat missile during the cruise phase of the attack. Powered by one Pratt & Whitney Aircraft of Canada PT6T-3 Turbo Twin Pac, derated to 962 kW (1,290 shp). Armament can include two Mk 44 or Mk 46 homing torpedoes, depth charges or four AS.12 missiles, according to the mission.

Agusta-Bell 214A (Italy) Military version of the Bell Model 214 built under licence. Powered by one 2,215 kW (2,970 shp) Lycoming LTC4B-8D turboshaft engine.

Agusta-Sikorsky HH-3F (Italy) Twenty Sikorsky S-61R multi-purpose rescue helicopters being built initially by Agusta under licence: 12 for the Italian Air Force for SAR duties and others for foreign operators.

Agusta-Sikorsky S-61A-4 (Italy) Derivative of the Agusta-Sikorsky SH-3D. Suitable for a wide range of duties including troop and cargo transport, medical evacuation and search and rescue. Power plant comprises two 1,118.5 kW (1,500 shp) General Electric T58-GE-100 turboshafts. Accommodation for 31 troops or 15 stretchers. VIP transports were ordered by Iran, Libya and Saudi Arabia.

Agusta-Sikorsky SH-3D (Italy) Construction under licence of an initial batch of 24 helicopters for the Italian Navy began in 1967, with deliveries starting in 1969. Additional aircraft are being built for the Italian armed forces.

Ahrens AR 404 (USA) Thirty-passenger or cargo transport aircraft powered by four 314 kW (420 shp) Allison 250-B17B turboprop engines. It is designed to be easy to operate and maintain. A constant-section square fuselage provides maximum volume and simplifies the loading of containers. The prototype made its first flight on 1 December 1976.

Aichi B7A Ryusei (Shooting Star) (Japan) Two-seat cranked-wing torpedo bomber code-named *Grace* by the Allies, of which just over 100 were built from 1944 for Japanese Navy service. Power was provided by a 1,360 kW (1,825 hp) Nakajima Homare 12 radial engine on B7A2 production aircraft.

Data (B7A2): *Engine* as above *Wing span* 14.4 m (47 ft 3 in) *Length* 11.49 m (37 ft 8½ in) *Max T-O weight* 6,500 kg (14,330 lb) *Max level speed* 566 km/h (351 mph) *Max range* 3,040 km (1,889 miles) *Armament* two 20 mm forward-firing can-

non and one rear-mounted 7.92 mm or 12.7 mm machine-gun plus an 800 kg (1,763 lb) torpedo or 1,000 kg (2,205 lb) of bombs

Aichi D1A (Japan) Two-seat dive bomber and reconnaissance aircraft which served with the Japanese Navy from 1934 until 1939. The initial production version was the D1A1 or Type 94 Model 1, powered by a 432 kW (580 hp) Nakajima Kotobuki II-Kai 1 radial engine. One hundred and sixty-two were built and the type first served on the aircraft carrier *Ryujo*. In October 1936 the first strengthened and improved D1A2 (or Type 96) flew, powered by a 455 kW (610 hp) Nakajima Hikari radial engine. A total of 428 aircraft of this version were built, together with a number of D1A2-K trainers. D1A2s sank the American ship *Panay* during the Yangtse Incident and were deployed against the Chinese from July 1937 (see **Chronology**).

Data (D1A2): *Engine* as above *Wing span* 11.4 m (37 ft 5 in) *Length* 9.3 m (30 ft 6 in) *Max T-O weight* 2,610 kg (5,755 lb) *Max level speed* 310 km/h (193 mph) *Range* 925 km (575 miles) *Armament* two forward-firing 7.7 mm machine-guns and one rear-firing 7.7 mm gun plus up to 380 kg (835 lb) of bombs

Aichi D3A (Japan) The two-seat D3A, code-named *Val* by the Allies, was the first all-metal low-wing monoplane dive-bomber to serve with the navy. Developed after studies of the Heinkel He 64 and He 70, the prototype first flew in late 1937 and production of the 801 kW (1,075 hp) Mitsubishi Kinsei 43/44-powered D3A1 or Navy Type 99 Model 11 carrier-based bomber started immediately. The D3A1 was operated against the Chinese. More importantly, however, it was one of the main types of aircraft used in the surprise attack on Pearl Harbor on 7 December 1941. A total of 478 D3A1s were built. Production continued with 816 D3A2s (built as Model 22s), powered by 894 kW (1,200 hp) Kinsei 54 radial engines.

Data (D3A2): *Engine* as above *Wing span* 14.37 m (47 ft 1½ in) *Length* 10.2 m (33 ft 5½ in) *Max T-O weight* 3,800 kg (8,378 lb) *Max level speed*

428 km/h (266 mph) *Range* 1,561 km (970 miles) *Armament* three 7.7 mm machine-guns plus up to 370 kg (816 lb) of bombs

Aichi E11A1 (Japan) Single 462 kW (620 hp) Hiro Type 91-engined night reconnaissance flying-boat, first flown in mid-1937. Seventeen built as Navy Type 98s, each armed with a single 7.7 mm machine-gun. Code-named *Laura* by the Allies.

Aichi E13A (Japan) Three-seat twin-float ship-borne reconnaissance monoplane, powered by one 805 kW (1,080 hp) Mitsubishi Kinsei 43 radial engine. First flown in 1938, the type was selected for production as the E13A1 or Navy Type O Model 1. More than 1,400 were produced, mostly by Kyushu Hikoki. Code-named *Jake* by the Allies, the type opened its operational career by flying over Pearl Harbor before the main attack and subsequently took part in all the major battles involving the navy until the end of the war.

Data: *Engine* as above *Wing span* 14.5 m (47 ft 7 in) *Length* 11.3 m (37 ft 1 in) *Max T-O weight* 4,000 kg (8,818 lb) *Max level speed* 376 km/h (234 mph) *Range* 2,100 km (1,300 miles) *Armament* one rear-mounted 7.7 mm machine-gun (extra 20 mm cannon fitted later to some aircraft) plus optional 370 kg (816 lb) of bombs

Agusta-Bell 212ASW.

Agusta-Sikorsky SH-3D.

Ahrens AR 404.

Aichi E16A Zuiun (Auspicious Cloud) (Japan) Code-named *Paul* by the Allies, the Zuiun was a development of the E13A1, powered by a 969 kW (1,300 hp) Mitsubishi Kinsei 51/54 radial engine. Entering service in 1944 as a twin-float reconnaissance seaplane, it was nevertheless often operated as a dive-bomber in an attempt to help Japan's desperate situation. A total of 252 production aircraft were built.

Aichi H9A (Japan) Anti-submarine and training monoplane flying-boat, powered by two 529 kW

Agusta-Sikorsky HH-3F.

Aichi B7A Ryusei.

Aichi D1A1.

Aichi E13A.

(710 hp) Nakajima Kotobuki 42/43 radial engines. Total of 31 aircraft built, the production H9A1s or Navy Type 2s serving from 1942.

Aichi M6A Seiran (Mountain Haze) (Japan) Submarine-borne light attack seaplane, of which 18 production aircraft were built. Ten Seirans were operational on board submarines when the war ended, never having flown a combat mission.

AIDC/CAF T-CH-1 (Taiwan) Tandem two-seat trainer and light ground attack aircraft, powered by one 1,081 kW (1,450 ehp) Lycoming T53-L-701 turboprop engine. The first prototype flew on 23 November 1973. The second prototype, modified to perform weapon training and counter-insurgency missions, flew on 27 November 1974. Production began in May 1976. Maximum level speed 592 km/h (368 mph).

Aichi D3A.

AIDC/CAF XC-2 (Taiwan) High-wing transport aircraft accommodating 38 passengers or 3,855 kg (8,500 lb) of cargo. The prototype first flew in 1978. Power is provided by two 1,082 kW

(1,451 ehp) Lycoming T53-L-701A engines.
Air Parts Fletcher Fu-24 (New Zealand) See **Aerospace Fletcher Fu-24-950**
Air Tractor Model AT-301 Air Tractor (USA) Single-seat agricultural aircraft, the first example of which made its first flight in September 1973. By 1 January 1978, a total of 175 AT-301s had been ordered. Power is provided by a 447.5 kW (600 hp) Pratt & Whitney R-1340 radial engine.
Air Tractor Model AT-302 Air Tractor (USA) First flown in June 1977, this is a modified version of the AT-301 powered by a 447.5 kW (600 shp) Avco Lycoming LTP 101-600A turboprop engine. Ten had been ordered by early 1978.
Airbus A300B and A310 (International) The 220- to 336-passenger A300 is the first twin-engined wide-body transport. It entered service with Air France on the Paris–London route on 30 May 1974, but its origin can be traced to the mid-1960s when the first discussions for a collaborative project were held. Initial discussions were between France, Britain and Germany, but Britain withdrew from the project – the parties ultimately being Aérospatiale, CASA, Deutsche Airbus and Fokker-VFW, with Hawker Siddeley producing the wings under contract. Britain has now rejoined the programme. The prototype first flew on 28 October 1972. The French and German C of A was granted on 15 March 1974 (for Cat II operation) and US certification was received on 30 May 1974.

This first European wide-bodied aircraft is a large aeroplane with 5.35 m (17 ft 7 in) cabin width. Wing sweep at quarter chord is 28° and the wing itself is claimed to be the most technically advanced design so far employed on a transport aeroplane. Power is normally provided by two wing-mounted General Electric CF6-50C turbofans of 226.9–233.5 kN (51,000–52,500 lb st) but SAS ordered a version with 235.75 kN (53,000 lb st) Pratt & Whitney JT9D-59A engines.

Originally the A300 was produced in two versions, the B2 and the heavier and longer range B4. There was also the B2K for South African Airways with wing root Kruger flaps. The designations have now been changed and are B2-100 (formerly B2), B2-200 (ex-B2K), B4-100 (ex-B4 Stage I), B4-200 (ex-B4 Stage III with increased weight) and A300C4 (ex-B4FC convertible passenger/cargo version). A300F4 is a proposed freighter. The A300 was slow to achieve general airline approval but, as it proved itself in operation to be an outstanding aeroplane and as world traffic recovered from the recession, orders picked up. The major breakthrough was securing an order from Eastern Air Lines for 23, with an option on a further nine. The aircraft has done particularly well in Asia. By March 1979, 21 customers had placed orders for 132 aircraft and taken options on another 57. At that time 61 aircraft had been delivered to 14 airlines.

In service the A300, with its twin-aisle cabins (a typical economy class layout being for 269 seats), has proved popular with passengers and crews, showed a high serviceability rate and low noise characteristics. It could become the most important European transport aeroplane so far produced.

In 1978 the decision was taken to produce the smaller 200-passenger A310 with shortened fuselage and a new and even more advanced wing. The A310 is due to be ready for delivery by the end of 1982 and orders and options exceeded 60 by the first quarter of 1979. There is also a possibility that the Airbus family may be extended by production of the proposed A300B9 'stretched' version for 336 tourist class passengers and the A300B99 long-range version with accommodation for 200–218 passengers.

Data (A300B4-100): *Engines* as above *Wing span* 44.84 m (147 ft 1 in) *Length* 53.62 m (175 ft 11 in) *Max T-O weight* 157,500 kg (347,228 lb) *Max cruising speed* 911 km/h (567 mph) *Max range* 5,930 km (3,685 miles)

Airco (de Havilland) D.H.1 and D.H.1a (UK) Typical of Geoffrey de Havilland's early designs, these aircraft were single pusher-engined biplanes, first flown in 1915 and powered by 52 kW (70 hp) Renault and 89.4 kW (120 hp) Beardmore engines respectively. Both versions had accommodation for a crew of two in tandem, the forward cockpit being stepped down and carrying a single machine-gun. More than 170 served as armed patrol and escort aircraft with the Royal Flying Corps over the Western Front and in the Middle East. They were withdrawn in early 1917, by which time they were totally obsolete. Maximum speed (D.H.1a) 142 km/h (88 mph).

Airco (de Havilland) D.H.2 (UK) Basically a scaled-down version of the D.H.1, the D.H.2 was the RFC's first true single-seat fighter. The prototype first flew in the summer of 1915. While production was getting underway, the new and revolutionary Fokker monoplane (see **Chronology**) was destroying the Allied air forces over the Western Front in what was known as the 'Fokker scourge'. Although in many ways an inferior design, the D.H.2 was highly manoeuvrable and fast, proving a match for the German fighter when it entered operational service in early 1916 – first serving with No 24 Squadron, RFC.

In total 400 D.H.2s were built. Armament remained similar to that of the D.H.1, but the gun had up and down movement only. However, in actual combat the Lewis gun was normally left in a horizontal position to allow the pilot to use all

Aichi M6A Seiran.

his skill in steering his aircraft into a favourable firing position. The type was not withdrawn from first-line service until 1917. By this time German Albatros fighters had regained superiority in the air over the Western Front, although D.H.2s based in the UK or in Macedonia or Palestine did not have to confront such advanced German fighters until late in their career. As noted in the **Chronology**, on 5 August 1916 Maj L. W. B. Rees won the VC when he inadvertently attacked ten German aircraft – he had approached them thinking they were RFC types – and shot down two of them.

Aichi E16A Zuiun.

Data (early production aircraft): *Engine* one 74.5 kW (100 hp) Gnome Monosoupape rotary *Wing span* 8.61 m (28 ft 3 in) *Length* 7.68 m (25 ft 2½ in) *Max T-O weight* 654 kg (1,441 lb) *Max level speed* 150 km/h (93 mph) *Endurance* 2 h 45 min

Airco (de Havilland) D.H.4 and D.H.4A (UK) The D.H.4 was a single-engined day bomber designed by Geoffrey de Havilland and built by The Aircraft Manufacturing Co Ltd (Airco). It first flew in August 1916. It was a biplane of wooden construction, fabric-covered. Its armament normally comprised two forward-firing Vickers and two rear-mounted Lewis guns, plus two 104 kg (230 lb) or four 50 kg (112 lb) bombs carried under the wings. Of the 1,700 ordered (from Airco, F. W. Berwick, Glendower Aircraft, Palladium Autocars, Vulcan Motors, Waring and Gillow and the Westland Aircraft Works, Yeovil) only 1,449 were actually delivered. These were powered by a variety of British and foreign water-cooled engines in the 149–279.5 kW (200–375 hp) range. Although faster than most contemporary fighters, the D.H.4 was vulnerable in battle because of poor communications between the cockpits, and the high fire risk created by the big fuselage fuel tank.

Used by nine RFC and 13 American squadrons in France from the spring of 1917, and by home defence squadrons over the North Sea, it is widely regarded as the finest single-engined bomber of World War I. Naval versions were also built by Westland for RNAS coastal patrols. Among many notable achievements, D.H.4s of No 202 Squadron photographed Zeebrugge before the raid of 22–23 April 1918 in which Wg Cdr Fellowes

AIDC T-CH-1 prototype.

Airbus A300B4-200.

bombed the Mole; Maj Egbert Cadbury shot down Zeppelin L70 on 5–6 August 1918; and a D.H.4 of No 217 Squadron sank a German U-boat in the North Sea on 12 August 1918. D.H.4s were also flown overseas at Basra and in the Aegean Islands, the Adriatic and Russia.

The D.H.4 was mass-produced by Atlantic Aircraft, Boeing, Dayton-Wright and Fisher in the USA, with 298 kW (400 hp) Liberty 12 engines; 3,227, designated DH-4, were completed by the Armistice (1,885 shipped to France, of which about a third became operational) and 4,846 by the end of 1918. Large numbers were subsequently used by the USAAC and Latin American countries in the 1920s. Two American DH-4Bs were used during the first successful flight-refuelling experiments in 1923. Interestingly, more than 60 American post-war variants were produced, including a version with an all-metal fuselage structure and ambulance versions. Two were also built for US air attachés by de Havilland in 1924 and 15 for the Belgian Air Force by SABCA, Brussels, in 1926.

War-surplus D.H.4s were sold to the air forces of Spain, Belgium, Greece, Japan and other countries by the Aircraft Disposal Co Ltd, Croydon. Two were later converted to three-seaters by C. J. de Garis for passenger routes in Australia, one later being sold to QANTAS. An Imperial Gift of 12 was made by Britain to Canada in 1919. These were used for spotting forest fires in the Rockies, flying on skis in winter.

Civil D.H.4s were used by Aircraft Transport & Travel Ltd (AT&T) and the Belgian airline SNETA on cross-Channel services in 1919. G-EAMU *City of Cardiff* was used by S. Instone & Co Ltd for carrying ships' papers. One D.H.4R racer, with a shortened bottom wing and 335.3 kW (450 hp) Napier Lion engine, set up a British closed-circuit record of 207 km/h (129.3 mph) in June 1919. Small numbers were converted by Airco to have glazed cabins, as

Airco (de Havilland) D.H.2.

Airco (de Havilland) D.H.1 (Renault engine).

D.H.4As, for service with No 2 (Communication) Squadron between Kenley and Buc during the 1919 Peace Conference. One was supplied to the River Plate Aviation Co Ltd for charter work in South America and others were used on the Continental services of AT&T, Handley Page Transport Ltd and SNETA.

Data (standard D.H.4): *Engine* one 279.5 kW (375 hp) Rolls-Royce Eagle VIII *Wing span* 14.3 m (42 ft 4½ in) *Length* 9.4 m (30 ft 8 in) *Max T-O weight* 1,575 kg (3,472 lb) *Max level speed* 230 km/h (143 mph) *Range* 700 km (435 miles)

Airco (de Havilland) D.H.5 (UK) The D.H.5 was designed in 1916 as a replacement for the D.H.2 and was the first de Havilland combat plane to be fitted with an interrupter gear for its forward-firing Vickers machine-gun. Particular attention had been given to providing it with the excellent forward vision enjoyed with pusher-engined aircraft, with the result that the upper wing of the biplane had considerable backward stagger. About 550 D.H.5 fighters were built for the Royal Flying Corps, although not all became operational. In service from mid-1917 until January 1918, the aircraft was latterly used for ground attack duties (carrying four 25 lb bombs) as its handling characteristics and high-altitude performance were inferior to those of other British and Allied fighters. Many were thereafter used as advanced trainers.

Data: *Engine* one 82 kW (110 hp) Le Rhône rotary *Wing span* 7.82 m (25 ft 8 in) *Length* 6.71 m (22 ft 0 in) *Max T-O weight* 676 kg (1,490 lb) *Max level speed* 175 km/h (109 mph) *Endurance* 3 h

Airco (de Havilland) D.H.6 (UK) Originally designed as a two-seat biplane trainer for the Royal Flying Corps, the D.H.6 was conventional in every sense and was cheap and easy to build. During its service life it was given many names – mostly detrimental, including 'clutching hand' – mainly because it had very low maximum and stalling speeds but was deliberately made unstable to prepare pilots for the vices of the operational fighter.

More than 2,280 were used by the RFC but were gradually replaced with the arrival of the Avro 504K. After this a number were operated as single-seaters by the RNAS and the US Navy for hunting and attacking German submarines. Nevertheless, the RAF had more than 1,000 D.H.6s in service when the war ended. After the war many D.H.6s were modified for civil flying and were to be seen in the skies of several countries, including Spain, where some were built under licence.

Data: *Engine* one 67 kW (90 hp) R.A.F. Ia, Curtiss OX-5 or 59.6 kW (80 hp) Renault *Wing span* 10.95 m (35 ft 11⅛ in) *Length* 8.32 m (27 ft 3½ in) *Max T-O weight* 920 kg (2,027 lb) *Max level speed* 106 km/h (66 mph) *Endurance* 2¾ h *Armament* 45.4 kg (100 lb) of bombs for anti-submarine duties

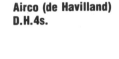
American-built DH-4B.

Airco (de Havilland) D.H.9 (UK) Produced as a replacement for the excellent D.H.4. It used the same wings and tail unit, but the crew positions were brought closer together to improve communications. The D.H.9 was first flown in July 1917. Mass production was undertaken by Airco and 12 sub-contractors. Armament comprised one forward-firing Vickers and one or two rear-mounted Lewis machine-guns, plus up to 209 kg (460 lb) of bombs. However, despite the fact that more than 3,200 were built in Britain for the RFC (plus a few for Belgium, US Navy and Russian forces), performance was inferior to that of the D.H.4, mainly because of the poor 171.4 kW (230 hp) Siddeley Puma engine. With the arrival of the D.H.9A, many D.H.9s were relegated to non-combatant duties although the type continued to serve over the Western Front, in Palestine and Macedonia. D.H.9s were operated by No 99 Squadron, RAF, for mail services to Cologne

and as ambulances in Somaliland. By 1919 all D.H.9s were off RAF charge.

Fitted with a 335.3 kW (450 hp) Napier Lion, one D.H.9 established a world altitude record of 9,296 m (30,500 ft) in 1919. Surplus D.H.9s were included in Britain's Imperial Gifts to Australia, New Zealand, Canada and India; others were sold to Afghanistan, Chile, Estonia, Greece, Ireland, Holland, Latvia and Spain. Commencing in 1925, over 500 were built by Hispano-Suiza in Spain and by SABCA in Belgium. Others were assembled in Holland with Wright Whirlwind radial engines for the Dutch East Indies.

A D.H.9 flown by R. J. P. Parer was the first single-engined aircraft to fly from the UK to Australia (1919–20). The type was also used on the cross-Channel routes of AT&T, KLM and SNETA. Some were converted to D.H.9B standard for two passengers behind and one in front of the pilot. In 1921 the de Havilland Hire Service used eight D.H.9Cs with swept-back wings and a small rear cabin. Local D.H.9B and C conversions operated pioneer scheduled services in Australia, Belgium, Denmark and Spain, on skis in Canada and on floats to survey Burma and Rhodesia. From 1923 D.H.9Js, with 287 kW (385 hp) Jaguar radials, were used for RAF Reserve training.

Data: *Engine* as above *Wing span* 14.3 m (42 ft 4½ in) *Length* 9.4 m (30 ft 5 in) *Max T-O weight* 1,510 kg (3,325 lb) *Max level speed* 176 km/h (109 mph) at 3,050 m (10,000 ft) *Endurance* 4½ h

Airco (de Havilland) D.H.9A (UK) The D.H.9A was a D.H.9 replacement designed for Airco by the Westland Aircraft Works, Yeovil, using the American-built 298 kW (400 hp) Liberty 12 engine in a strengthened fuselage with larger wings. By the end of 1918 885 had been

Airco (de Havilland) D.H.4s.

Airco (de Havilland) D.H.5.

Airco (de Havilland) D.H.4A with glazed cabin for use as an RAF communications aircraft.

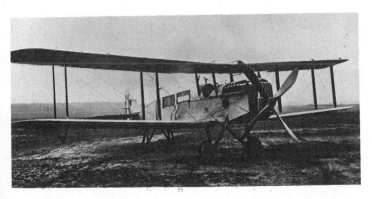

Airco (de Havilland) D.H.6 prototype.

Airco (de Havilland) D.H.9.

Airco (de Havilland) D.H.9A.

built by Westland, with Airco, F. W. Berwick, Mann Egerton, Vulcan Motors and Whitehead Aircraft as sub-contractors. The D.H.9A was the outstanding strategic bombing aeroplane of World War I and carried 272 kg (600 lb) of bombs on external racks. Machine-gun armament comprised one forward-firing Vickers and twin Lewis guns on a Scarff ring over the rear cockpit.

First in service with No 110 (Nizam of Hyderabad) Squadron, RAF, in France in August 1918, this aircraft dropped 10½ tons of bombs on German cities. It was also used by Nos 18, 99 and 205 Squadrons on the Western Front; Nos 47 and 221 Squadrons in Russia (where locally designed copies designated Type R-1 were built); and on coastal patrols by Nos 212 (Dover) and 273 Squadrons.

After the war production continued, several hundred being built by the Westland, Airco, de Havilland, Gloster, Handley Page, Hawker, Parnall and Short companies. These formed the equipment of eight regular UK-based day bombing squadrons and six auxiliary squadrons. From 21 June 1921 the D.H.9As of Nos 30 and 47 Squadrons flew a regular Cairo–Baghdad desert air mail service. An extensive reconditioning programme by the Blackburn, S. E. Saunders and the above manufacturers, as well as the RAF Depot, Ascot, kept the D.H.9A in RAF service until 1931. They were very familiar to the public during demonstrations of wing drill at Hendon RAF Displays and in battle formations during annual war games.

Tropicalised D.H.9As policed Iraq and the North West Frontier of India, where they relieved ground forces of the near-impossible task of keeping resurgent tribesmen under control, carrying spare wheels, goatskins of water, tents and bed-

Observer's cockpit of a D.H.6 specially equipped with Marconi radio.

ding in case of forced descents in hostile territory. Overseas squadrons were also based in Palestine and Egypt. Imperial Gift D.H.9As comprised 29 aircraft for Australia to serve with the RAAF and 11 to Canada for civil forestry patrol and survey work (on skis in winter). In 1919 the RAE, Farnborough, fitted 11 D.H.9As with 335.3 kW (450 hp) Napier Lion engines for use by Aircraft Transport & Travel Ltd on a Forces air mail service between Hendon and Cologne. Two (one with folding wings) were used later for carrier trials on board HMS *Eagle*. The Lion engine also powered the D.H.9R single-seat racer with shortened lower wing in which Capt G. Gathergood raised the British closed circuit record to 241 km/h (149 .43 mph) in November 1919. Surplus stocks of D.H.9A components were used post-war for several prototypes including the A. W. Tadpole; and in the construction of 36 Westland Walrus fleet spotter biplanes. The final derivative, produced in 1926, was the D.H.9AJ Stag with a Bristol Jupiter radial. In 1921 Handley Page converted a D.H.9A fuselage to carry a

thick section monoplane wing, as the H.P. 20, during development of their automatic wing slots. Data: *Engine* 298 kW (400 hp) Packard Liberty 12 *Wing span* 14 m (45 ft 11⅜ in) *Length* 9.2 m (30 ft 3 in) *Max T-O weight* 2,107 kg (4,645 lb) *Max level speed* 185 km/h (114 mph) *Endurance* 5¼ h

de Havilland D.H.10 and subsequent aircraft (UK) See **de Havilland**

Airspeed AS.4 Ferry (UK) Ten-passenger biplane airliner of 1932 with cranked lower wings attached to the upper fuselage. Powered by three 89.4 kW (120 hp) de Havilland Gipsy engines, two on the lower wings and one mounted centrally on the upper wing. Four built: two for Sir Alan Cobham's National Aviation Day tours and two for Midland and Scottish Air Ferries.

Airspeed AS.5 Courier (UK) Five-six-seat cantilever low-wing cabin monoplane with a retractable landing gear. Powered by an Armstrong Lynx IVC engine (AS.5A version) or an Armstrong Siddeley Cheetah V (AS.5B version). First flown on 11 April 1933. Sixteen built; one flown by Sir Alan Cobham in an attempt to fly from England to India non-stop using flight refuelling.

Airspeed AS.6 Envoy (UK) Pilot and eight-passenger enlarged and twin-engined development of the Courier. First flown on 26 June 1934. About 50 built by Airspeed for British, Japanese, Czechoslovakian, Chinese and South African civil operators, plus a small number for the South African Air Force and the RAF (SAAF Envoys carrying bombs and one forward-firing and one dorsal-turreted machine-gun). Mitsubishi also built a number under licence. Engines fitted to Envoys included the Wolseley AR.9, Scorpio I or Aries III, Armstrong Siddeley Lynx IVC or Cheetah IX, Wright Whirlwind R.760 and Walter Castor II.

Airspeed AS.8 Viceroy (UK) One Envoy modified for the 1934 MacRobertson Trophy Race from England to Australia.

Airspeed AS.10 Oxford (UK) The 'Ox-box', as the Oxford became known to members of the RAF, was originally designed as a military development of the Envoy and was built to an Air Ministry specification of 1936. The prototype flew for the first time on 19 June 1937. The first production Oxfords entered service at the Central Flying School in November 1937 as the RAF's first twin-engined cantilever low-wing monoplane trainer. A total of well over 8,500 Oxfords were eventually produced by Airspeed and several sub-contractors and served in training, communications, ambulance and other roles.

Airspeed produced five basic versions of the design for military use, of which three were major types. The Mk I was a weapons trainer, usually fitted with a dorsal gun turret; the Mk II a pilot, radio-operator and navigator trainer; and the Mk V, which was similar to the Mk II but powered by two 335.3 kW (450 hp) Pratt & Whitney Wasp Junior radial engines. Large numbers of Oxfords were delivered to the air forces of Australia, Canada, New Zealand, South Africa, Southern Rhodesia and Portugal, as well as to the Fleet Air Arm, the USAAF and the Free French. A small number of civil Oxfords were also produced (not including military conversions), operated post-war by companies, airlines and flying clubs.

Data (Mk I): *Engines* two 264.5 kW (355 hp) Armstrong Siddeley Cheetah IX or X radials *Wing span* 16.25 m (53 ft 4 in) *Length* 10.52 m (34 ft 6 in) *Max T-O weight* 3,447 kg (7,600 lb) *Max level speed* 293 km/h (182 mph) *Range* 885 km (550 miles)

Airspeed AS.4 Ferry.

Airspeed AS.6 Envoy.

Airspeed AS.8 Viceroy.

Airspeed AS.30 Queen Wasp (UK) Designed as a radio-controlled and unmanned target aircraft, first flown as a piloted aircraft in 1937. A total of seven aircraft were built (incl. prototypes) of 65 production aircraft ordered.

Airspeed AS.39 Fleet Shadower (UK) Prototype carrier-borne high-wing monoplane designed for shadowing enemy naval vessels. Powered by four 97 kW (130 hp) Pobjoy Niagara V engines.

Airspeed AS.45 Cambridge (UK) Prototype tandem two-seat cantilever low-wing monoplane trainer, powered by a 544 kW (730 hp) Bristol Mercury VIII engine.

Airspeed AS.5 Courier.

Airspeed AS.51 and AS.58 Horsa (UK) High-wing military transport gliders with accommodation for 30 equipped troops or freight, including vehicles. The prototype first flew in September 1941 and production AS.51 Horsa Is entered service in the latter part of 1942. The AS.58 Horsa II differed mainly from the Mk I in having a hinged nose section to allow easy loading of freight or vehicles. It is believed that a total of 3,655 Horsas were built. The first operational mission with Horsas was the invasion of Sicily in

Airspeed Oxford I.

Airspeed AS.30 Queen Wasp.

1943, but the greatest triumph was the D-day landings, when huge numbers of Horsa gliders were towed across the Channel by Whitley and C-47 aircraft. The US forces also received several hundred of these gliders.

Airspeed AS.57 Ambassador (UK) The first Brabazon Committee, in its February 1943 report, recommended the Type IIA as a short-haul piston-engined aircraft for British operators and for sale to European airlines. This recommendation resulted in the AS.57 Ambassador, which first flew on 10 July 1947. The Ambassador was a very good-looking high-wing monoplane with triple fins, retractable nosewheel undercarriage and two Bristol Centaurus engines. The trials programme was prolonged, but with 47 seats and 2,012 kW (2,700 hp) Centaurus 661s the Ambassador entered service with British European Airways in March 1952 as the Elizabethan class. BEA operated a fleet of 20 and the total built including prototypes was 23. However, although the Ambassador was a good aircraft, it was too late to attract other orders, the Viscount entering service only a year later.

Data: *Engines* as above *Wing span* 35.05 m (115 ft 0 in) *Length* 24.69 m (81 ft 0 in) *Max T-O weight* 23,587 kg (52,000 lb) *Cruising speed* 386 km/h (240 mph) *Range* 995 km (618 miles) with full payload

Airspeed AS.65 Consul (UK) With the Oxford in mass production and serving well in its designed role as a military trainer, the Airspeed company became aware that there would be a large number of surplus aircraft after the war which could be converted easily and cheaply into civil transports. Modifications to produce the Consul (as the converted aircraft was to be known) from the Oxford included adding two more windows to the cabin, modifying the tail unit, adding a bulkhead between the cockpit and the cabin and recontouring the nose. The first Consul was sold in early 1946 and a further 160 were produced, many being operated by British airlines, companies and private owners but others going abroad, including several to Indo-China.

AISA I-11B (Spain) The prototype I-11 two-seat touring and training monoplane had a tricycle landing gear and flew for the first time in 1950. The I-11B, with a tailwheel landing gear, was developed from it and the prototype first flew on 16 October 1953. The first 70 production aircraft had only basic flying instruments; the second series of 110 were fitted with full blind-flying panels. Some are operated by the Spanish Air Force for liaison and training duties as L.8Cs. Power is provided by a 67 kW (90 hp) Continental C90-12F flat-four engine. Maximum speed is 200 km/h (124 mph).

Airspeed Oxford V prototype.

After service with BEA the Ambassadors passed to several independent airlines including BKS, Dan-Air and Globe Air of Switzerland – some serving as freighters and horse transports. Three were used for a time by Butler Air Transport in Australia, and one was owned by the King of Morocco.

Ambassadors also served as engine test-beds, being fitted with Bristol Proteus, Rolls-Royce Dart and Tyne and Napier Eland turboprops.

AISA Autogyro GN (Spain) Four-seat autogyro with jump take-off capability, expected to make its first flight in 1980.

AJEP (Wittman) Tailwind (UK) AJEP marketed ready-to-fly examples of the Tailwind, a much-modified version of the Wittman Tailwind light aircraft. These are no longer being produced. (See **Wittman Tailwind**)

Akron and Macon (USA) US Navy helium-filled airships designed to be flying aircraft carriers for the Curtiss F9C-2 Sparrowhawk fighter. The USS *Akron* made its first flight on 25 September 1931 and a production Sparrowhawk made its first 'hook-on' using the skyhook on 29 June 1932. Six Sparrowhawks were successfully operated from the airship during several exercises until it crashed into the Atlantic on the night of 3/4 April 1933. On 23 June 1933 the sister ship USS *Macon* was commissioned and the Sparrowhawks, which were not on board *Akron* when it crashed, were detached to this airship. It successfully flew on manoeuvres for 22 months until it too crashed into the Pacific in 12 February 1935.

Data (ZRS4 *Akron* and ZRS5 *Macon*): *Engines* eight and six 417.3 kW (560 hp) Maybach engines respectively *Length* 231 and 239 m (758 ft and 783 ft) respectively *Diameter* 40.5 m (132.9 ft) *Volume* 184,059 m³ (6,500,000 cu ft) *Max level speed* 133.5 km/h (83 mph)

Aktiebolaget Svenska Järnvägsverkstäderna Type 2 (Ö.9) (Sweden) Two-seat reconnaissance or day-bombing biplane trainer.

Aktiebolaget Svenska Järnvägsverkstäderna Jakfalken (Sweden) Single-seat biplane fighter which entered service with the Swedish AF in the first half of the 1930s and remained operational until about 1939. Powered by a supercharged Bristol Jupiter VII radial engine. Maximum speed 300 km/h (186 mph). Armament comprised two forward-firing machine-guns.

Aktiebolaget Svenska Järnvägsverkstäderna Tigerschwalbe (Sweden) Raab-Katzenstein two-seat advanced training biplane built under licence for the Swedish Air Force.

Aktiebolaget Svenska Järnvägsverkstäderna Viking II (Sweden) Four-seat light high-wing cabin monoplane of the mid-1930s, powered by a 149 kW (200 hp) de Havilland Gipsy-Six engine.

Alaparma AP.65 and AP.75 Baldo (Italy) Two-seat twin-boom pusher monoplanes developed from a series of AM designs reaching back to the AM.6 of 1942. Designed by Capt Adriano Mantelli. Power was provided by a 48.4 kW (65 hp) Walter Mikron and 56 kW (75 hp) Praga D engine respectively.

Airspeed AS.39 Fleet Shadower.

Airspeed Horsa Mk II.

Albatros B.I, B.II and B.IIa (Germany) The Albatros B.I and smaller B.II were developed before the outbreak of war in 1914 and were roughly equivalent to the British Royal Aircraft Factory B.E.2, although slower but better looking. Layout was fairly conventional for the time with the pilot occupying the rear cockpit and the observer the front. No armament was provided as aerial combat was a thing of the future. Power was provided by a 74.5 kW (100 hp) Mercedes D.I or an 82 kW (110 hp) Benz Bz.II engine and an ugly exhaust manifold partially obstructed the forward view. However, they were strongly constructed and well liked by their crews and were widely used for reconnaissance duties during the first year of the war on both Western and Eastern Fronts.

Airspeed AS.57 Ambassador.

Airspeed AS.65 Consul.

Manufacture was undertaken by several companies. A seaplane version was also built in small numbers and a few B.IIs were operated by Austro-Hungary. In 1917 the B.II was ordered back into service as the B.IIa dual-control trainer, powered by an 89.4 kW (120 hp) Mercedes D.II or Argus As.II engine.

Data (B.II): *Engine* as above *Wing span* 12.8 m (42 ft 0 in) *Length* 7.62 m (25 ft 0¼ in) *Max T-O weight* 1,070 kg (2,359 lb) *Max level speed* 105 km/h (65 mph) *Duration* 4 h

Interior of an Airspeed Ambassador.

AJEP (Wittman) Tailwind.

Albatros C.I series (Germany) The C.I was a workmanlike and warlike development of the successful B.I. It differed mainly in having the observer in the rear cockpit, armed with a Parabellum machine-gun, and being powered by a 119 kW (160 hp) Mercedes D.III, 112 kW (150 hp) Benz Bz.III or 134 kW (180 hp) Argus As.III. Forward vision was, however, little improved with these engines. C.Is entered service on the Western and Eastern Fronts in 1915 and, in addition to the designed reconnaissance duties, also performed bombing, artillery observation and co-operation and photographic work with great success. The refined C.Ia version had a new radiator mounted over the engine on the upper wing leading edge, while the C.Ib was a Mercedes D.III-powered dual-control trainer. A number may also have been built under licence by Oeffag for the Austro-Hungarian Air Force.

Data (C.I): *Engine* as above *Wing span* 12.9 m (42 ft 3¾ in) *Length* 7.85 m (25 ft 9 in) *Max T-O weight* 1,190 kg (2,623 lb) *Max level speed* 140 km/h (87 mph)

Albatros C.III (Germany) The C.III was the main variant of the Albatros C series of reconnaissance aircraft and became operational during the latter half of 1916 and served into 1917. During the production run the single rear-mounted defensive Parabellum machine-gun was supplemented by a Spandau machine-gun for forward attack. A reasonable bomb load of 91 kg (200 lb) could also be carried in an internal con-

tainer – an advanced concept for the time. Externally, it would have been difficult to tell this version apart from the earlier Cs if it had not been for the introduction of the famous Albatros rounded tailplane and elevators. Standard engine was the Mercedes D.III.

Data: *Engine* as above *Wing span* 11.69 m (38 ft 4¼ in) *Length* 8.0 m (26 ft 3 in) *Max T-O weight* 1,353 kg (2,983 lb) *Max level speed* 140 km/h (87 mph) *Endurance* 4 h

Albatros C.V (Germany) The career of the C.V was short and dogged by trouble. It was aerodynamically a much improved aircraft with a beautifully streamlined fuselage, which tapered into a rounded nose section, and introduced a low-profile rounded fin and rudder. Power was provided by the new 164 kW (220 hp) Mercedes D.IV engine, the cause of its eventual downfall. It was initially produced as the C.V/16, but this model proved heavy to fly and experienced serious problems with its cooling system. To remedy this the C.V/17 was produced, featuring a new lower wing with rounded tips, a new radiator fitted to the upper wing (instead of the two rounded radiators previously fitted to the fuselage sides forward of the wings), balanced ailerons and elevators and other refinements. These made a considerable difference to the handling and cooling, but the problems with the crankshaft of the engine remained and meant that only a small number of C.Vs became operational. Max level speed was 170 km/h (106 mph).

Albatros C.VII (Germany) The success of this aircraft in reconnaissance and other roles somewhat vindicated the C.V. It was generally recognised that the Mercedes engine had been the greatest problem with the C.V and so the new

Albatros C.III.

C.VII was fitted with a 149 kW (200 hp) Benz Bz.IV. A return to the C.V/16's lower wing and radiator layout was made, resulting in an aircraft with fine handling qualities and an excellent performance. C.VIIs served during 1916 and 1917 in all battle areas and were often used as tactical light bombers.

Data: *Engine* as above *Wing span* 12.78 m (41 ft 11¼ in) *Length* 8.7 m (28 ft 6½ in) *Max T-O weight* 1,550 kg (3,417 lb) *Max level speed* 170 km/h (106 mph) *Endurance* 3 h 20 min *Armament* one forward-firing Spandau and one rear-mounted Parabellum machine-gun plus up to 91 kg (200 lb) of bombs carried on racks (optional)

Albatros C.X (Germany) This reconnaissance and artillery observation aircraft entered service in 1917 and was basically a larger and refined version of the C.VII. Powered by the improved and satisfactory 194 kW (260 hp) Mercedes D.IVa engine, it was able to carry wireless and oxygen equipment. In order to maintain the streamlined contours of the fuselage a return was made to the C.V/17 type of radiator. As with earlier Albatros designs production was also sub-contracted to several other manufacturers.

Data: *Engine* as above *Wing span* 14.36 m (47 ft 1½ in) *Length* 9.15 m (30 ft 0½ in) *Max T-O weight* 1,665 kg (3,670 lb) *Max level speed* 175 km(h (109 mph) *Endurance* 3 h 25 min *Armament* as for C.VII

Albatros C.XII (Germany) The C.XII followed the C.X into service on the Western Front, first appearing in the last months of 1917. It was the only production Albatros reconnaissance C-type to make use of the elliptical-section fuselage developed for the D-type fighters. Other refinements included a revised tail unit with a

tailplane of much reduced chord and, therefore, overall area and a new triangular ventral fin on which the tailskid was mounted and inset. C.XIIs remained operational until the end of the war.

Data: *Engine* one 194 kW (260 hp) Mercedes D.IVa *Wing span* 14.37 m (47 ft 1¾ in) *Length* 8.85 m (29 ft 0½ in) *Max T-O weight* 1,640 kg (3,615 lb) *Max level speed* 175 km/h (109 mph) *Endurance* 3 h 15 min *Armament* as for C.X

Albatros C.XV (Germany) Development of the C.XII, via the prototype C.XIV, and put in production in 1918. No C.XVs became operational.

Albatros D.I and D.II (Germany) The D.I and D.II represented Germany's second successful bid within a year to gain total air superiority over the Allies (the first with the Fokker E monoplanes in 1915–16). They were vast improvements over the Fokker and Halberstadt biplane fighters that had filled the gap. Each was an unequal-span biplane with a wooden semi-monocoque fuselage, having the famous Albatros rounded tailplane (see C.III) coupled with the

Albatros B.II.

Albatros D.I.

Albatros

Albatros D.III.

Albatros C.X.

Richthofen's 'Circus' of Albatros D.IIIs.

new rounded fin and rudder of C.V/16 type. The major difference between the versions was that the upper wing of the D.II was lowered to reduce the gap between it and the fuselage so as to improve forward and upper vision. Power was provided by either a 112 kW (150 hp) Benz Bz.II or 119 kW (160 hp) Mercedes D.III engine on the D.I and by the latter only on the D.II. These beautiful fighters each had the shattering firepower of two Spandau machine-guns – the first successful installation of twin guns on a German fighter.

D.Is and D.IIs were first flown on an operational mission in September 1916, led by the legendary ace Oswald Boelcke. He had recently given up flying Albatros Cs and Fokker monoplanes and returned to the Western Front from a tour of other battle areas to take command of the new Jagdstaffel Nr 2 (Jasta 2). Although Boelcke's career on the aircraft was short – he was killed on 28 October when the undercarriage of a colleague's aircraft struck his upper wing – the fighters ravaged Allied D.H.2s, B.E.2s and Nieuports throughout the winter, making up for slightly inferior manoeuvrability with a much higher maximum speed and rate of climb. Twenty D.IIs, powered by 138 kW (185 hp) Austro-Daimler engines, were also licence-built by the Oeffag company for the Austro-Hungarian Air

Force. At the peak of their operational careers with the German Air Force, about 260 D.I and D.II fighters were in service.

Data (D.II): *Engine* as above *Wing span* 8.5 m (27 ft 10½ in) *Length* 7.4 m (24 ft 3¼ in) *Max T-O weight* 888 kg (1,958 lb) *Max level speed* 175 km/h (109 mph) *Endurance* 1 h 30 min

Albatros D.III (Germany) The D.III was a direct development of the D.II. It incorporated a new higher-compression Mercedes D.IIIa engine, rated at 126.7 kW (170 hp), a greater-span upper wing with swept tips, new narrow-chord lower wings and V-type interplane struts. The result was an increase in the service ceiling of nearly 305 m (1,000 ft) and a 33% improvement in the endurance. The type entered service on the Western Front in early 1917 and thereafter joined units in Palestine and Macedonia, where the last of the British D.H.2s had already suffered at the hands of the D.I and D.II. The first two weeks of April 1917 saw the greatest loss of Allied aircraft over the Western Front: nearly 140 RFC aircraft (mostly B.E.2cs) fell to the D.III and other German aircraft in what was known as 'Bloody April'. But time was running out for the Albatros type of fighter as the Allies – fresh from licking their wounds – were already beginning to field a new and war-winning array of fighters which included the S.E.5/5a and others of Spad, Nieuport and Sopwith design. However, by the end of 1917 about 450 D.IIIs were operational – not including those licence-built for the Austro-Hungarian Air Force with 138 kW (185 hp) engines.

Data: *Engine* as above *Wing span* 9.05 m (29 ft 8½ in) *Length* 7.33 m (24 ft 0½ in) *Max T-O weight* 886 kg (1,953 lb) *Max level speed* 175 km/h (109 mph) *Endurance* 2 h *Armament* as for D.II

Albatros D.V and D.Va (Germany) The appearance of the D.V fighter in mid-1917 did not mark the start of a third era of German air supremacy, but instead heralded the beginning of the end. The German authorities, confident in their ability to contain the Allies in the air war, saw little need to develop a radical D.III replacement. Compared with the earlier type, the D.V had a new rounded-section fuselage, a rounded rudder, a faired headrest (usually removed) and a smaller gap between the upper wing and the fuselage. Like the D.III it was powered by a high-compression Mercedes D.IIIa. The D.Va version differed little and entered service a few months later. The resulting fighters had slightly better top

speeds but little else that could be called an improvement. Nevertheless, at the height of their careers in the spring of 1918 more than 1,050 D.Vs and D.Vas were operational on the Western Front, in Italy and Palestine, by which time the Albatros Werke company had already changed over from D.Va to Fokker D.VII production.
Data: *Engine* as above *Wing span* 9.05 m (29 ft 8¼ in) *Length* 7.33 m (24 ft 0½ in) *Max T-O weight* 937 kg (2,066 lb) *Max level speed* 186 km/h (115.5 mph) *Endurance* 2 h *Armament* two forward-firing Spandau machine-guns

Albatros D.XI (Germany) Prototype biplane fighter of 1918 powered by a 119 kW (160 hp) Siemens-Halske Sh.III geared rotary engine.

Albatros G.II and G.III (Germany) Medium bomber powered on the G.III limited production version by two 164 kW (220 hp) Benz Bz.IVa pusher engines mounted on the lower wings. Interesting feature of the design was that the trailing-edges of the inner sections of the lower wings were cut away to allow the engines and large propellers to be fitted further forward on the wings than would otherwise be possible. The G.II prototype first flew in mid-1916 and G.IIIs entered service in Macedonia and elsewhere in the following year. Armament comprised two Parabellum machine-guns – one each in nose and rear cockpits – plus 320 kg (704 lb) of bombs. Maximum level speed 150 km/h (93 mph).

Albatros J.I and J.II (Germany) These were produced by Albatros in 1917 to perform the same duties as the AEG J.I and J.II and were similarly armed. The major production J.I version was also similarly powered to the AEGs and carried armour plating to protect the crew from ground fire. The less successful J.II, powered by a 164 kW (220 hp) Benz Bz.IVa, had extra armour plating to protect the engine and so lost the pointed nose and propeller spinner of the former. Maximum speed of the J.I was 140 km/h (87 mph).

Albatros L.58 (Germany) High-wing monoplane airliner of 1923, originally powered by a single 179 kW (240 hp) Rolls-Royce Falcon engine. Construction was of wood with three-ply covering. The enclosed cabin for six passengers was arranged almost entirely under the wing and the pilot was seated immediately forward of the wing leading edge in an open cockpit. Petrol and baggage were carried in the wings. A small number are known to have entered service in Germany with several companies, while others may have been operated abroad.

Albatros L.59 and L.60 (Germany) Single- and two-seat cantilever low-wing monoplanes of 1923 with trousered landing gear legs. Powered by 41 kW (55 hp) and 60 kW (80 hp) Siemens-Halske radial engines respectively.

Albatros L.68 Alauda (Germany) Two-seat school and touring biplane of 1920 powered normally by a 74.5 kW (100 hp) Siemens engine.

Albatros L.69 (Germany) Racing parasol-wing monoplane designed for the '1925 Deutscher Rundflug'. Powered by an 82 kW (110 hp) Siemens or 74.5 kW (100 hp) Bristol Lucifer engine.

Albatros L.72 (Germany) Slotted-wing biplane transport aircraft of 1926. Two originally built for the publishers Ullstein AG and used to carry newspapers between German cities. Later operated as freight carriers by Luft-Hansa. A single L.72c Albis version was produced in 1927 for another company with enclosed accommodation for four passengers or 400 kg (881 lb) freight.

Albatros L.73 (Germany) Large and impressive eight-passenger biplane airliner of 1926. Powered

Top: Albatros D.V.

Above: Albatros G.III.

Below: Albatros W.4.

Alcock Scout.

Avion-Planeur RF 3, one of a series of lightweight single or two-seat aircraft by Alpavia of France.

originally by two 179 kW (240 hp) BMW Va engines but subsequently fitted with 268 kW (360 hp) BMW Vas. It is believed that four were built for Luft-Hansa, flying night sections of several domestic and international routes until the early 1930s.

Albatros L-75a Ass (Germany) Two-seat advanced training biplane powered by a 268 kW (360 hp) BMW Va engine.

Albatros L.79 Kobold (Goblin) (Germany) Single-seat experimental biplane with symmetrical wing section, specially developed for inverted flight.

Albatros L-82 (Germany) Two-seat folding wing school and touring biplane powered by a 74.5 kW (100 hp) de Havilland Gipsy engine.

Albatros L-100 (Germany) Three-seat cabin monoplane powered by a 82 kW (110 hp) Argus As.8 inverted engine.

Albatros L-101 (Germany) Two-seat school, sport and touring high-wing monoplane.

Albatros W.4 (Germany) The W.4 was a seaplane development of the D.I and 117 were built for the German Navy to defend coastal naval bases from attack. Most were stationed at the important North Sea bases from early 1917, but a small number were deployed around the Aegean Sea area.

Data: *Engine* one 119 kW (160 hp) Mercedes D.III *Wing span* 9.5 m (31 ft 2 in) *Length* 8.5 m (27 ft 10½ in) *Max T-O weight* 1,070 kg (2,359 lb) *Max level speed* 159 km/h (99 mph) *Endurance* 3 h *Armament* as for Albatros D.I

Albatros W.5 (Germany) Designation of five two-seat twin 112 kW (150 hp) Benz Bz.II-engined pusher seaplanes supplied to the German Navy from May 1917 for torpedo attack.

Alcock Scout (UK) One example only of a single-seat fighter produced from components of the Sopwith Pup and Triplane and used operationally by the RNAS in the Aegean from Mudros.

All American Model 10A Ensign (USA) Two-seat all-metal low-wing monoplane with a retractable landing gear. Powered by a 63.5 kW (85 hp) Continental C85-12 engine. Prototype only flew in 1945.

Allied Aviation LRA-1 and LR2A (USA) LRA-1 was an experimental 12-seat flying-boat glider of which four were built for the US Navy in 1943. The LR2A was a projected development of the former type.

Allison Convair 580 (USA) The Allison division of General Motors Corporation was prime contractor for the conversion programme under which operators of Convair 340/440 transports could have their aircraft modified to Convair 580 standard: the existing piston engines were replaced with 2,795 kW (3,750 eshp) Allison 501-D13 turboprops driving Aero-products 606 four-blade propellers. The conversion work was performed by Pacific Airmotive Corporation. By April 1967 100 Convair 580 conversions had been delivered. In May 1969 Pacific Airmotive Corporation became the prime contractor until the company stopped trading in 1972.

Alon Model A-2 Aircoupe (USA) The original two-seat cantilever low-wing Erco 415C was put into production by Engineering and Research Corporation with alternative 48.4 kW (65 hp) and 56 kW (75 hp) Continental engines. Both received Type Approval in 1940. From then about 6,000 Ercoupes were built in various versions and under various names, including Fornaire and Aircoupe. In 1967 the Alon company was taken over by Mooney and the final production versions of this aircraft were built as the A-2 with a new spring-steel landing gear and the M-10 Cadet (one 67 kW; 90 hp C90-16F engine) with a new aft fuselage and a single fin and rudder instead of the usual twin fins and rudders.

Alon Four (A-4) (USA) Four-seat light monoplane first flown in February 1966.

Alpha AVO 68V Samburo (Austria) Two-seat motor-glider powered by a 50.5 kW (68 hp) Limbach SL 1700 E4 engine and first flown in 1977. In production.

Allison Convair 580.

Ambrosini S.7 (Italy) Single- or two-seat cantilever low-wing military trainer of 1953 powered by a 167.7 kW (225 hp) Alfa 115*ter* piston engine. Small number ordered by the Italian Air Force.

Ambrosini Super S.7 (Italy) Slightly larger and more powerful version (onc 283 kW; 380 hp D.H. Gipsy Queen Series 70) of the S.7 designed to provide all training requirements up to the stage where pilots are qualified to join operational jet training units. Armed with one 7.7 mm SAFAT machine-gun and able to carry light bombs or four rockets.

Ambrosini S.1001 Grifo (Italy) The first postwar product of the Ambrosini company, the Grifo light cabin monoplane was built in three versions: as a four-seat tourer with dual wheel control, as a four-seat taxi with single joystick control, and as a two-seat trainer with dual wheel control. During 28–29 April 1948 a production Grifo established a new international distance record for light aeroplanes in Class 1 by flying 4,170 km (2,591 miles) straight line distance from Campoformido, north of Trieste, to Massawa, Eritrea. A two-seat basic trainer was also derived from the Grifo as the S.1002 Trasimenus.

Ambrosini SAI designs (Italy) The Società Aeronautica Italiana was incorporated into the Ambrosini group in 1934. There followed a long series of touring and training aircraft, among which were the SAI.1 two-seat touring biplane, SAI.2 five-seat cabin monoplane, SAI.2S and SAI.3 (produced for the Littorio Rally), SAI.7, SAI.10, SAI.207 lightweight fighter (of which 13 of 2,000 ordered were built during World War II), and SAI.403 fighter (proposed as an SAI.207 replacement).

Ambrosini Sagittario (Italy) Experimental swept-wing aircraft built for aerodynamic research and first flown on 5 January 1953. Constructed of wood and powered by one 3.74 kN (840 lb st) Turboméca Marboré II turbojet engine. Max level speed 560 km/h (348 mph). (See **Aerfer**.)

AmEagle American Eaglet (USA) Single-seat shoulder-wing homebuilt self-launching sailplane, first flown in November 1975. A total of 250 kits to build the aircraft were under construction in early 1978, of which 12 had been completed. Power for take-off and self-recovery is provided by one 9 kW (12 hp) McCulloch 101B two-stroke engine installed aft of the cockpit.

American 1A and 1B airships (USA) 1A was a Wellman-Vaniman-Mallet airship of 1907 with a volume of 7,797 m³ (275,340 cu ft) and powered by a 59.6 kW (80 hp) Lorraine-Dietrich engine. Damaged on first flight. 1B was an enlarged

American Air Racing *Wild Turkey*, a homebuilt single-seat Formula I racing aircraft.

Amiot 143.

All American Ensign.

version of 1910 with two engines and a volume of 9,769 m³ (345,000 cu ft). Abandoned during an attempt to cross the Atlantic.

American Airmotive NA-75 (USA) Single-seat agricultural aircraft comprising a modified Stearman Model 75 (Boeing Kaydet) fuselage, fitted with new high-lift wings of metal construction and dispersal equipment for dusting and spraying. The completed aircraft was made available, as were kits for the conversion. More than 200 Stearmans were fitted with the wings, which permitted loads of more than 908 kg (2,000 lb) to be carried.

Amiot 122-BP3 (France) Large biplane bomber and escort of 1928 powered by a single 484.4 kW (650 hp) Lorraine 18Kd engine and accommodating a crew of three. Eighty production aircraft built from 1929 for the Armée de l'Air and five for Brazil. Offensive load was up to 800 kg (1,764 lb) of bombs and five machine-guns were provided for defence. Maximum level speed was 206 km/h (128 mph).

Amiot 140 (France) Day and night bomber, reconnaissance and attack aircraft, selected for service by the Armée de l'Air in 1933 as the 140M. Forty production aircraft were built.

Amiot 143 (France) Developed from the Amiot 140, the Amiot 143 M5 was preferred by the French Air Ministry to the Amiot 142 (with its liquid-cooled engines) to meet a requirement for a *Multiplace de Combat* (Multi-seat combat aircraft).

The first flight of a 143 was made in August 1934. It was an all-metal cantilever high-wing monoplane with an enclosed pilot's cockpit, manually operated nose and dorsal gun turrets and a large glazed ventral 'balcony' housing the bomb-aimer's position forward and the ventral gunner's position at the rear. The large fixed divided-type undercarriage had wheel spats. The first batch of 50 aircraft was delivered in the winter of 1935–6 to Escadres GB I/22 and GB II/22 at Chartres; from aircraft number 31 the fuselage was slightly lengthened. Total production amounted to 138 aircraft. Normal bomb load was 900 kg (1,984 lb), with 1,600 kg (3,527 lb) as the overload weight, of which the internal capacity was 800 kg (1,764 lb) and the rest carried underwing. Defensive armament comprised a TO 23 nose turret with a single 7.7 mm Lewis gun, a TO 14*bis* dorsal turret with twin 7.7 mm Lewis guns and a further twin Lewis mounting in the ventral location. From 1941 onwards these were replaced by single MAC 7.5 mm machine-guns in each position.

In August 1939 91 Amiot 143s were still in service with first-line Escadres, 29 with training units and six in storage. The 34ᵉ Escadre carried out a number of daylight reconnaissance sorties between the Vosges and the left bank of the Rhine during September 1939. The Amiots also carried out a number of night reconnaissance and leaflet-dropping missions up to the end of the year, reaching into Germany as far as Neustadt. In March 1940 Escadres I/63 and II/63 were withdrawn to North Africa to re-equip with Martin 167F bombers and their Amiot 143s were passed over to the CIB (training unit) at Marrakesh. Interestingly, ten wooden mockups of the Amiot 143 were deployed on French aerodromes at the beginning of the May 'Blitzkrieg' to deceive German bombers, while 30 more were under construction. Up to 10 May French night raiders had been carrying only leaflets, but from then on until the French surrender Amiot 143s dropped a total of 528 tonnes (520 UK tons) of bombs in night raids. However, Amiot 143s are best remembered for their heroic mission of 14 May 1940 when, with fighter escort, they attacked the heavily defended bridges at Sedan during daylight hours. The aircraft of the 34ᵉ and 38ᵉ Escadres bombed from an altitude of 800 m (2,600 ft). Four aircraft were lost in action and all the rest seriously damaged. Amiot 143s were subsequently used for transport and training duties by the Vichy French, except for a few impressed by the Germans.

Data: *Engines* two 596 kW (800 hp) Gnome-

Rhône 14K radials *Wing span* 24.53 m (80 ft 5¾ in) *Length* 18.24 m (59 ft 10½ in) *Max T-O weight* 9,700 kg (21,385 lb) *Max level speed* 310 km/h (192.5 mph) at 4,000 m (13,120 ft) *Range* 1,300 km (807 miles)

Amiot 350 series (France) Eighty-six Amiot 350 series aircraft had been completed before the Germans occupied the Le Bourget factory in June 1940. They stemmed from the famous Amiot 370 record-breaking aircraft which set up five speed-with-load-over-distance records in early 1938 and from the Amiot 340, itself modified from the long-range postal Amiot 341. The Amiot 340 took Gen Vuillemin on his notorious visit to the Luftwaffe in August 1938. Converted to the Amiot 351.01 prototype bomber, it was followed by production Amiot 351s and 354s. Each version had a beautifully streamlined all-metal fuselage, a tapered mid-wing with considerable dihedral and twin Gnome-Rhône 14N radial engines. However, they differed in having twin oval fins and rudders and a large single vertical tailplane respectively. Armament comprised a 20 mm HS 404 cannon on a flexible mounting at the rear of the crew canopy plus single 7.5 mm MAC machine-guns in nose and ventral positions. The bomb load was up to 1,200 kg (2,646 lb). After a limited number of bombing and reconnaissance missions the Amiots were converted by the Vichy French for long-range liaison flights.

Data: *Engines* as above *Wing span* 22.83 m (74 ft 10 in) *Length* 14.5 m (47 ft 6 in) *Max T-O weight* 11,300 kg (24,912 lb) *Max level speed* 480 km/h (298 mph) at 4,550 m (14,928 ft) *Range* 2,495 km (1,550 miles)

Anahuac Tauro 350 (Bull) (Mexico) Single-seat agricultural aircraft powered by one 261 kW (350 hp) Jacobs R-755-SM turbocharged radial engine. The first production Tauro, flown on 5 June 1970, was a 224 kW (300 hp)-engined Tauro 300, of which seven were built. The improved Tauro 350 followed, of which about nine had been completed by spring 1978.

Anatra VI (Russia) Basically a copy of the highly successful French Voisin combat biplane powered by a 112 kW (150 hp) Canton-Unné radial pusher engine. One hundred and thirty-nine were ordered from 1915 for light bombing and reconnaissance duties, but those that actually reached operational units were poorly constructed and disliked by crews.

Anahuac Tauro 300.

Anatra D and DS (Russia) Although both of these reconnaissance aircraft had serious design faults, they were widely operated by the Imperial Russian Air Force and, after the Revolution, by the Red Air Force until replaced in the 1920s. The Anatra D (sometimes known as the Anade) first became operational in mid-1916; all but the first aircraft were powered by 97 kW (130 hp) Clerget rotary engines. In 1917 the 'D' was superseded by the Anatra DS, powered by the 112 kW (150 hp) Salmson-built Canton-Unne radial engine. This version (sometimes known as the Anasal) was armed with a forward-firing machine-gun in addition to the standard rear-mounted Lewis gun. However, it experienced similar cooling problems to those suffered by some versions of the enemy's Albatros Cs. Nevertheless, about 100 were built, bringing the total of Anatra D/DSs to about 380 aircraft.

Anatra VI.

Amiot 354.

Anatra D.

Crosby-built Andreasson BA-4B.

Anderson EA-1 Kingfisher.

Anbo parasol monoplanes (Lithuania) During its 20 years of independence between World Wars I and II the small Baltic republic of Lithuania produced a number of original aircraft designs. Following a series designed in the 1920s by Lieut Dobkevicius, Lieut-Col Gustaitis produced the Anbo I – a two-seat low-wing lightplane – and then a series of parasol-wing military two-seaters. All were built at the Lithuanian Army workshops at Kaunas.

It is believed that batches of up to 24 aircraft of each type were built, the first, the Anbo II, being a low-powered light primary trainer. Anbo III had a 108 kW (145 hp) uncowled Walter Mars radial engine. It differed from the Anbo II in having a robust divided undercarriage instead of a conventional axle type, metal sheet covering over the forward fuselage, redesigned fin and rudder with a curved leading edge, and considerable sweepback on the wings. Although officially designated an advanced trainer, at least one Anbo III had a gun ring over the rear cockpit. The Anbo IV of 1932 was a much heavier design and equipped two Lithuanian Army Air Service squadrons for reconnaissance and general purposes. The undercarriage, fin and rudder and strut-bracing were all of new design and power was provided by a 447 kW (600 hp) Bristol Pegasus L2 radial engine enclosed in a Townend ring. Aircraft of this type participated in a 1934 tour of European capital cities, during which the three Anbo IVs visited the annual RAF Display at Hendon. The formation was led by Col Gustaitis, who by then had been promoted Head of the Army Air Service. Total distance covered was some 9,200 km (5,700 miles).

Later designs included the Anbo V and its development the Anbo 51 – lighter primary trainers powered by the 108 kW (145 hp) Siddeley Genet engine – and the Anbo VI advanced trainer with a 138 kW (185 hp) Curtiss Challenger radial. The final design was the Anbo 41 development of the Anbo IV, again for reconnaissance and general purposes, powered by a 596 kW (800 hp) Bristol Pegasus engine in a long-chord cowling.

Early in 1940, prior to annexation by the Soviet Union, two Lithuanian reconnaissance squadrons were equipped with Anbo IVs and one squadron had Anbo 41s.

Data (Anbo 41): *Engine* as above *Wing span* 13.2 m (43 ft 3 in) *Length* 8.8 m (28 ft 10 in) *Max T-O weight* 2,300 kg (5,071 lb) *Max level speed* 320 km/h (198 mph)

Anderson EA-1 Kingfisher (USA) Two-seat light amphibian designed to be homebuilt by amateurs. Powered normally by one 74.5 kW (100 hp) Continental O-200, Lycoming O-235 or similar engine. By 1978 well over 200 sets of plans had been sold and more than 100 Kingfishers were under construction.

Anderson Greenwood AG-14 (USA) Two-seat light cabin monoplane powered by one 67 kW (90 hp) Continental C90 engine. The prototype first flew in October 1947. Five production aircraft built.

Andreasson BA-4B (Sweden) Single-seat fully aerobatic light biplane, of which plans are available to amateur builders. Also built in small numbers in the UK by Crosby Aviation; three slightly differing models have flown and kits are available.

Andreasson BA-11 (Sweden) Tandem two-seat all-metal biplane intended for single-seat aerobatic, two-seat training or competition flying.

ANF Les Mureaux 113 series (France) André Brunet's Mureaux 110 and 111 were winners of a 1931 French Air Ministry competition to replace

the Breguet 19 in the reconnaissance (R2) category. They were followed by the 110-2, soon redesignated 112. Three Mureaux 112 R2s, two 113 R2s (484.4 kW; 650 hp Hispano-Suiza 12Ybrs engine), one long-range 113G.R and two night-fighting 114 Cn2s appeared in 1933. The Mureaux 117.01 (Hispano-Suiza 12Ycrs) arrived in June 1935, with strengthened wing bracing and a wooden propeller. The later Mureaux 115 R2 01 was a conversion of Mureaux 117 No 76. It had a 641 kW (860 hp) Hispano-Suiza 12Ycrs engine with a frontal radiator in place of the deep under-nose radiator of all the other versions.

The basic design was an all-metal parasol strut-braced monoplane. Two crew members were seated in open tandem cockpits, with the observer/gunner protected by a high windscreen. The divided undercarriage had 'spat'-type wheel fairings, frequently discarded in operational conditions. Production for the Armée de l'Air comprised 49 Mureaux 113s, 119 Mureaux 115s and 115 Mureaux 117s. The Mureaux 113 and 117 were each armed with two synchronised Vickers machine-guns plus twin Lewis guns for the observer and a further machine-gun firing through a ventral trap. The Mureaux 115 had a

20 mm HS-9 cannon or a 7.5 mm MAC machine-gun firing through the propeller shaft, plus four other machine-guns disposed as in the Mureaux 113. Reconnaissance-bomber (R2B2) versions of the Mureaux 115 and 117 also had racks for up to 200 kg (441 lb) of bombs.

Mureaux 113s and 117s started to enter service early in 1935 with the reconnaissance Groupes, then with observation Groupes, and finally replaced Potez 25s with the reserve 'Groupes Aériens Régionaux'. Forty Mureaux 113s were converted to Cn2 configuration in 1934–35 to equip France's two night fighter Groupes and replace their ancient Breguet 19s. The Mureaux 115 began to enter service during 1936.

Nine GARs (redesignated 'Groupes Aériens d'Observation') equipped with Mureaux 115s and nine more with Mureaux 117s were used widely during 1939–40, 11 aircraft being lost in action by the end of April. However, no less than 228 Mureaux aircraft were on hand when the German 'Blitzkrieg' was launched on 10 May 1940, but only 62 were left in Vichy France and North Africa by 25 June. All were subsequently scrapped.

Data (Mureaux 115): *Engine* as above *Wing span* 15.4 m (50 ft 6 in) *Length* 9.95 m (32 ft 7 in) *Max T-O weight* 2,560 kg (5,643 lb) *Max level speed* 340 km/h (211 mph) *Range* 1,000 km (621 miles)

Angkatan Udara Republik Indonesia, Depot Penjelidikan, Pertjobaan dan Pembuatan designs (Indonesia) The Indonesian Air Force's Research, Development and Production Depot began the design of the NU-200 Sikumbang in 1953. In 1961 the new Institute for Aero Industry Establishment came into being, which in turn became known under the name LIPNUR in 1966. Of the aircraft produced since the NU-200, the NU-225 Sikumbang (X-09) ground support monoplane was grounded in 1967, the Kumbang 260 (X-02) four-seater was not completed, the Belalang 85 (X-03) and Belalang 90 entered

Ansaldo A300-4.

production and service (see below), the Kunang 25 (X-04) was grounded, the Super Kunang 35 (X-05) single-seat low-powered light monoplane entered production, and the Kindjeng 150 (X-06) and B-8m Kolentang were flown. Other types were not completed.

The Belalang Model 90 (Grasshopper) prototype first flew in 1958. It was a low-wing modification of the Piper L-4J, which the Air Force used as a primary trainer. After testing the prototype, modification of all the L-4Js into Belalangs began, the original 67 kW (90 hp) Model 90 giving way to the 74.5 kW (100 hp) Continental O-200-A-powered Model 90A.

ANF Les Mureaux 113.

Ansaldo A300 (Italy) The prototype of this general-purpose biplane appeared in 1919, a time when Italy had no independent air force but aviation branches of the Army and Navy. The first production version was the A300-2 two-seat reconnaissance aircraft, powered by a 223.5 kW (300 hp) Fiat A12*bis* engine. It was followed by about 90 production A300-3 three-seaters. However, by far the most important version was the A300-4, which first appeared in 1922. Like the A300-2 it was a two-seater suitable for reconnaissance and light attack duties. Power was provided by a developed A12*bis* engine and armament comprised two forward-firing machine-guns and one rear-mounted gun. When the air force proper was formed in 1923 as the Regia Aeronautica, under the auspices of Mussolini, the number of squadrons was rapidly increased; a total of 60 squadrons in 1924–25 was expanded to 84 by 1926, not including training units. As one of the main types of aircraft available for the expansion, about 700 A300-4s were produced. The later A300-6 was another military version of the basic design.

Ansaldo Balilla Racer.

Two examples of civil airliners were also produced from the basic A300, the A300/C and A300/T, with internal accommodation for four and eight passengers respectively. Both had new cabin structures which extended over the upper wings to give maximum headroom. In 1925 Fiat took over Ansaldo's aircraft division.
Data (A300-4): *Engine* as above *Wing span* 11.24 m (36 ft 10 in) *Length* 8.75 m (28 ft 8½ in) *Max T-O weight* 1,700 kg (3,750 lb) *Max level speed* 200 km/h (124 mph) *Endurance* 3 h 30 min

Ansaldo A-1 Balilla (Italy) The Balilla was the first Italian-designed single-seat fighter to go into service with the air force. The prototype appeared in 1917 and production aircraft began reaching operational units later the same year. Powered by a 164 kW (220 hp) SPA 6A engine the fighter was extremely fast, indeed one of the fastest aircraft to become operational during World War I. But it had several major faults, not least of which were poor manoeuvrability and poor forward vision for the pilot. Nevertheless, 150 were built for service and these supplemented French fighters. Most were operated as bomber escorts or home defence fighters. In the early 1920s Poland received 75 Balillas from Italy and went on to licence-build another 50. These saw action against Russia soon after delivery. Interestingly, one Balilla was fitted with a Curtiss 12 engine in America and took part in the 1921 Pulitzer race.
Data: *Engine* as above *Wing span* 7.67 m (25 ft 2 in) *Length* 6.84 m (22 ft 5 in) *Max T-O weight* 885 kg (1,951 lb) *Max level speed* 220 km/h (137 mph) *Endurance* 1 h 30 min

Ansaldo S.V.A. 5 Primo, 9 and 10 (Italy) The very neat S.V.A.5 single-seat reconnaissance and light bombing biplane was operational in the final year of World War I and remained on strength well into the 1920s, due mainly to its incredibly high speed. It also undertook several impressive post-war long-distance flights, including one from Rome to Tokyo in 1920. Armament comprised two forward-firing Vickers machine-guns. The S.V.A.9 was basically an unarmed training version of the S.V.A.10 two-seater which, unlike the S.V.A.5 and 9, was powered by a 186.3 kW (250 hp) Isotta-Fraschini Semi-Asso engine and carried only one Vickers gun, supplemented by a rear-mounted Lewis gun. A total of 1,300 aircraft

Ansaldo S.V.A.5 Primo.

of the series were produced, including 50 twin-float seaplanes for use by the Italian Navy.
Data (S.V.A.5): *Engine* as above *Wing span* 9.1 m (29 ft 10¼ in) *Length* 8.1 m (26 ft 6¾ in) *Max T-O weight* 1,050 kg (2,315 lb) *Max level speed* 230 km/h (143 mph) *Endurance* 4 h

Antoinette (France) The Antoinette series of large and graceful monoplanes were designed by Léon Levavasseur and named after his daughter. The earliest model proper was the Antoinette III, featuring wing warping lateral control which was stated at the time to be defective. The Model IV retained the 37.2 kW (50 hp) Antoinette engine of the Model III but introduced ailerons to the trailing edges of the outer wing panels. It also had a strange landing gear comprising a pair of narrow-track main wheels under the wings, a tiny forward wheel protecting the propeller during landing and long outrigger units at half-span. The fuselage and wings were aluminium structures, covered with hand-polished fabric. The Models V, VI and VII were basically similar to the IV and proved highly successful. About 80 were built. (See **Chronology** 19 July 1909)

Antoinette Military Monoplane (France) The military Antoinette of 1911 differed from the standard type in having a totally covered airframe, a modified tail unit, long trouser-type fairings over the landing gear legs and wheels, and two seats in tandem.

Antonov A-7 (USSR) Large, 18.97 m (62 ft 3 in) wing span transport glider of which about 400 were built for the Red Air Force from 1940. Usually pulled by Tupolev SB-2 or Ilyushin DB-3 tugs.

Antonov (and WSK-PZL-Mielec) An-2 (USSR/Poland) The An-2 biplane first flew on 31 August 1947 and has been in continuous production from 1948 for military and civil use. More than 5,000 were built in the Soviet Union before production there ended in the mid-1960s with the An-2M specialised agricultural version. A further 8,200 have been built in Poland since 1960, including 3,800 An-2R agricultural aircraft. Most exported Polish aircraft have gone to the Soviet Union, although An-2s from both countries are in widespread service around the world. The An-2 carries the NATO reporting name *Colt*. Soviet-built models include the An-2P basic general-purpose version for ten passengers/14 paratroops, six stretchers or 1,240 kg (2,734 lb) of freight; An-2S agricultural version of An-2P with a hopper for 1,400 litres (308 Imp gallons) of liquid chemicals or 1,200 kg (2,650 lb) of dust; An-2M agricultural version with more efficient dispensing systems and a 1,960 litre (431 Imp gallon) hopper; An-2V floatplane version of An-2P; An-2L water-bomber; and An-2ZA version of An-2P for high-altitude meteorological research.

Polish-built versions include the An-2P 12 adult and two children passenger aircraft; An-2PK five-seat executive transport; An-2P-Photo photogrammetry version; An-2PR television relay version; An-2R agricultural version with a 1,350 kg (2,976 lb) capacity glassfibre-reinforced epoxy-resin hopper or tank; An-2S ambulance for six stretchers and medical attendants; An-2T general-purpose version; An-2TD paratroop transport and training version with six tip-up seats along each side of the cabin; An-2TP cargo/passenger version; An-2M twin-float version of An-2T; and An-2 Geofiz geophysical survey version.
Data (Polish An-2P): *Engine* one 746 kW (1,000 hp) Shvetsov ASz-621R nine-cylinder radial *Wing span* (upper) 18.18 m (59 ft 8½ in) *Length* 12.4 m (40 ft 8¼ in) *Max T-O weight* 5,500 kg (12,125 lb) *Max level speed* 258 km/h (160 mph) *Range* 900 km (560 miles)

Antonov An-10A

Antonov An-3 (USSR) It was reported in 1972 that the Antonov design bureau was engaged on design studies of a turboprop development of the An-2. The new aircraft is intended for agricultural duties and the prototype was said to have been produced by converting an An-2 to have a 716 kW (960 shp) Glushenkov TVD-10A turboprop engine, driving a slow-turning large-diameter propeller optimised for an aircraft operating speed of 140–180 km/h (87–112 mph).

Antoinette.

Antonov An-12.

Antonov An-4 and An-8 (USSR) Military and civil transport aircraft of similar type designed for the Soviet Air Force and Aeroflot respectively. Both aircraft carried the NATO reporting name *Camp*. The prototype of the former was exhibited at Tushino in 1956, powered by two 3,800 kW (5,100 ehp) Kuznetsov turboprop engines and with a cannon in a tail turret.

Antonov An-6 (USSR) Improved version of the An-2 with a supercharged ASh-62 radial engine; reported to have been produced for Aeroflot. Aircraft operated by the Soviet Antarctic expeditions were also referred to as An-6s.

Antonov An-10 and An-10A (USSR) Design of the An-10 airliner began in November 1955 and the prototype (named *Ukraina*) first flew in March 1957. Subsequently more than 500 An-10/10As are believed to have been built. The An-10 was the initial version with accommodation for 84 passengers and a 'play-room' for children at the rear. It entered service in July 1959 on routes from Simferopol to Moscow and Kiev. The An-10A developed version had a 2 m (6 ft 7 in) longer fuselage and accommodated 100 to 130 passengers. It entered service in February 1960. An-10As also operated on skis in the far north of the Soviet Union. No An-10/10As were exported and Aeroflot withdrew the airliners in 1973. Both versions had the NATO reporting name *Cat*. Power was provided by four 2,981 kW (4,000 ehp) Ivchenko AI-20K turboprops.

Antonov An-12 (USSR) This aircraft carries the NATO reporting name *Cub*. Derived from the now-retired An-10 passenger transport (see above), the basic An-12 is a military and civil freight carrier with a redesigned rear fuselage and tail unit which permit air-drop operations. About 850 aircraft were built before production ended in 1973.

The following versions are currently in service with the Soviet Air Forces.

Cub-A, designated An-12BP in the USSR. This type constituted about 85% of the 700 aircraft equipping the VTA (Military Transport Aviation) in 1978, although replacement with Ilyushin Il-76s began in 1974. At peak strength *Cub-A*s

Antonov An-14 Pchelka.

could carry 14,000 men and their equipment (two full army divisions) over a radius of about 1,207 km (750 miles). Military An-12s are also in service with the air forces of India, Algeria, Bangladesh, Egypt, Indonesia, Iraq, Poland, Syria and Yugoslavia. Civil versions are operated by Aeroflot, Polish Air Lines (LOT), Bulair and Cubana.

Cub-B is the version used for electronic intelligence (elint) duties. Examples are known to have four additional blister fairings under the forward and centre fuselage plus other antennae. *Cub-C* is the ECM version in service with the Soviet Air Force and Navy. It has an ogival 'solid' fuselage tailcone, housing electronic equipment instead of a gun position; additional electronic pods are faired into the forward fuselage and ventral surfaces. The gun turret is, of course, deleted in the civil version. All versions carry all-weather equipment.

Data (An-12BP): Engines four 2,983 kW (4,000 ehp) Ivchenko AI-20K turboprops *Wing span* 38.0 m (124 ft 8 in) *Length* 33.1 m (108 ft 7¼ in) *Max T-O weight* 61,000 kg (134,480 lb) *Max level speed* 777 km/h (482 mph) *Armament* two 23 mm NR-23 guns in tail turret

Antonov An-13 (USSR) Single-seat light jet sporting aircraft based on the Antonov A-13 all-metal sailplane.

Antonov An-14 Pchelka (Little Bee) (USSR) Carrying the NATO reporting name *Clod*, the An-14 is a twin-engined light general-purpose aircraft that first flew in March 1958. Production began both for Aeroflot and the Soviet armed forces at the Progress Plant at Arsenyev in 1965 and by the mid-1970s well over 300 aircraft had been delivered. The military version, first seen at the Domodedovo air display in 1967, appeared not to differ from the civilian passenger version externally. An-14s are also in service with the air forces of Bulgaria, the German Democratic Republic and Guinea.

Data: *Engines* two 224 kW (300 hp) Ivchenko AI-14RF radials *Wing span* 21.99 m (72 ft 2 in) *Length* 11.44 m (37 ft 6½ in) *Max T-O weight* 3,600 kg (7,935 lb) *Max level speed* at 1,000 m (3,280 ft) 222 km/h (138 mph) *Range* 800 km (497 miles)

Antonov An-22 Antheus (USSR) Carrying the NATO reporting name *Cock*, the An-22 is a very large, long-range heavy transport. It flew for the first time in February 1965, at which time it was the largest transport aircraft in the world. Deliveries to both the Soviet Air Force and Aeroflot were completed during 1974, with the military air transport force (VTA) receiving between 30 and 50 aircraft. The An-22 is used widely in the underdeveloped areas of the northern USSR, Siberia and the Far East. In 1979 it was still the only Soviet transport capable of airlifting the T-62 tank. Accommodation is for a crew of five or six, 28–29 passengers in the cabin and freight. Maximum payload is 80,000 kg (176,350 lb).

In October 1967 an An-22 established 14 payload-to-height records. With a payload of 100,000 kg of metal blocks it reached a height of

7,848 m (25,748 ft), thereby qualifying also for the intermediate records from 35,000 kg. Max payload lifted to a height of 2,000 m was 104,444.6 kg (221,443 lb). A take-off run of just over one kilometre was reported; the flight duration was 78 minutes.

In 1972 a further series of ten records for speed with payload were set up by Marina Popovich, wife of the Soviet cosmonaut Pavel Popovich. The aircraft averaged a speed of 593.318 km/h (368.671 mph) around a 2,000 km closed circuit with a 50,000 kg payload, qualifying also for the intermediate records from 30,000 kg. In addition the aircraft averaged a speed of 608.449 km/h (378.073 mph) in a flight two days later around a 1,000 km circuit with the same payload. The An-22 also holds three further records for speed with payload over a 5,000 km circuit, established in 1974 and 1975.

Data: *Engines* four 11,186 kW (15,000 shp) Kuznetsov NK-12MA turboprops *Wing span* 64.4 m (211 ft 4 in) *Length* 57.8 m (189 ft 7 in) *Max T-O weight* 250,000 kg (551,160 lb) *Max level speed* 740 km/h (460 mph) *Range* 5,000 km (3,100 miles)

Antonov An-24 (USSR) Carrying the NATO reporting name *Coke*, the An-24 was intended as a replacement for the piston-engined aircraft on Aeroflot's internal feederline routes. The prototype made its maiden flight in April 1960. The production version entered service with Aeroflot in September 1963, flying between Moscow and Voronezh and Saratov. By 1976 Aeroflot had acquired several hundred of the 1,100 or so An-24s built. Other operators, flying a total of 74 An-24s, include Air Guinée, Air Mali, Balkan Bulgarian Airlines, CAAC, Cubana, Interflug, Iraqi Airways, Lebanese Air Transport, Lina

Congo, LOT, Misrair (EgyptAir), Mongolian Airlines, Pan African Air Services and Tarom. Versions have also been supplied to the air forces of the USSR, Bangladesh, the Republic of Congo (Brazzaville), Czechoslovakia, Egypt, East Germany, Hungary, Iraq, North Korea, Mongolia, Poland, Romania, the Somali Republic, Vietnam and South Yemen. The Laotian government acquired six for unspecified duties.

Versions of the An-24 are:

An-24V Srs II Standard version, superseded Srs I in 1968. Powered by two Ivchenko AI-24A turboprop engines. Versions available include mixed passenger/freight, convertible cargo/passenger, all-freight and executive.

An-24P Variant for firefighting duties; provision is made for firefighters to be parachuted from a height of 800–1,200 m (2,625–3,940 ft) to deal with forest fires.

An-24RV Similar to the Srs II version but has a Type RU 19-300 auxiliary turbojet engine in starboard nacelle, instead of starter/generator, to improve take-off and in-flight performance.

An-24T Specially equipped freighter version of the Srs II. Belly freight door replaces normal passenger door at rear of the cabin for cargo loading and airdropping of payload or parachutists. It can also be used for ambulance duties. Single ventral fin is replaced by twin ventral fins, forming a 'Vee', aft of the cargo door.

An-24RT Similar to the 'T' but fitted with a Type RU auxiliary turbojet in a starboard nacelle, as on the An-24RV.

Data: *Engines* as above *Wing span* 29.2 m (95 ft 9½ in) *Length* 23.53 m (77 ft 2½ in) *Max T-O weight* 21,800 kg (48,060 lb) *Normal cruising speed* 450 km/h (280 mph) *Range* 3,000 km (1,864 miles)

Antonov An-26 (USSR) Carrying the NATO reporting name *Curl*, the An-26 was known initially as the 'An-24T with an enlarged freight door'. The An-26, although largely similar to the An-24T, has a completely redesigned rear fuselage of the 'beaver-tail' type and uprated AI-24T

Antonov An-32.

turboprop engines. Essentially a cargo aircraft with airdrop capability, the An-26 can be easily adapted for passenger-carrying, ambulance or paratroop duties. An-26s are in service with the Air Wing of the Bangladesh Defence Force, and the Hungarian, Peruvian, Polish, and Romanian air forces.

Data: *Engines* as above *Wing span* 29.2 m (95 ft 9½ in) *Length* 23.8 m (78 ft 1 in) *Max T-O weight* 24,000 kg (52,911 lb) *Cruising speed* 425–435 km/h (264–270 mph) *Range* 2,250 km (1,398 miles)

Antonov An-28 (USSR/Poland) Carrying the NATO reporting name *Cash*, the An-28 is a development of the piston-engined An-14. It is a short-range twin-turboprop light general-purpose aircraft, expected to enter production with WSK-PZL-Mielec of Poland in 1980. The first prototype flew in September 1969 and had a retractable landing gear and Isotov TVD-850 engines. The An-28 now has a non-retractable tricycle type landing gear and two 723 kW (970 shp) Glushenkov TVD-10B turboprops. A much larger cabin accommodates up to 19 passengers or a variety of alternative payloads, including scientific, medical or agricultural spraying equipment.

Data: *Engines* as above *Wing span* 21.99 m (72 ft 2 in) *Length* 12.98 m (42 ft 7 in) *Max T-O weight* 6,100 kg (13,450 lb) *Max cruising speed* 350 km/h (217 mph) *Range* 1,300 km (805 miles)

Antonov An-30 (USSR) Carrying the NATO reporting name *Clank*, the An-30 was evolved from the An-24RT and An-26 and is the first specialised aerial survey aeroplane produced in the USSR. Principal modifications comprise an extensively glazed nose to allow the navigator a wide field of vision and a raised flight deck to improve the pilot's view and increase the size of the navigator's compartment. The cabin has fewer windows and houses a dark room, film storage cupboard, survey cameras and a control desk.

Two photographers/surveyors normally accompany the flight crew of five, although the photography can be automatic or semi-automatic. Standard equipment includes radio topographic distance measuring equipment and a

radio altimeter, with recording units. Specialised cameras can be fitted for specific missions, as can other survey equipment such as that used for microwave radiometer survey, which gathers data on ocean surface characteristics, sea and lake ice, snow cover, flooding, seasonal vegetation changes and soil types. Capable of conversion into a transport. The prototype first flew in 1974.

Data: *Engines* two 2,103 kW (2,820 ehp) Ivchenko AI-24VT turboprop *Wing span* 29.2 m (95 ft 9½ in) *Length* 24.26 m (79 ft 7 in) *Max T-O weight* 23,000 kg (50,705 lb) *Max level speed* 540 km/h (335 mph) *Range* 2,360 km (1,466 miles)

Antonov An-32 (USSR) Carrying the NATO reporting name *Cline*, the An-32 is a short/medium-range transport intended for operation in high temperatures or at high altitudes. It has an airframe generally similar to that of the An-26 except for much larger ventral fins and a full-span slotted tailplane. Two high-mounted 3,862 kW (5,180 ehp) Ivchenko AI-20M turboprop engines provide greatly increased power, enabling the aircraft to operate from airfields 4,000–4,500 m (13,125–14,750 ft) above sea level in an ambient temperature of 25°C, and permitting 3 tonnes of freight to be transported over a 1,100 km (683 mile) stage length, with fuel reserves. Other modifications include increased hoist capacity and low-pressure tyres for operation from unpaved airstrips.

Alternative payloads include 39 passengers, 30 parachutists or 24 stretchers and a medical attendant.

Data: *Engines* as above *Dimensions* as for An-26 *Max T-O weight* 26,000 kg (57,320 lb) *Normal cruising speed* 510 km/h (317 mph) *Range* 2,200 km (1,367 miles)

Antonov An-40 (USSR) New very large turbofan-powered transport aircraft (in the same class as the Lockheed C-5 Galaxy) reported to be under development as a replacement for the An-22 turboprop freighter.

Antonov An-72 (USSR) Few details regarding this new twin-engined turbofan-powered STOL transport aircraft have been released although it flew for the first time in December 1977. Nominal payload is 5,000 kg (11,023 lb). The news agency Tass reported it as a STOL replacement for the An-26 operated by Aeroflot and other airlines. The military potential of a transport capable of operation from small, unprepared areas in underdeveloped countries, or small fields in Europe, is clear. In this capacity, the An-72 could seemingly fulfil a support role for the new generation of V/STOL combat aircraft expected to replace the Yak-36.

A considerable increase in lift is achieved through the Coanda effect, created by the high-set position of the engines. Other details concerning the An-72's degree of sophistication are still awaited.

Data (provisional): *Engines* two high bypass ratio turbofans, probably related to the Lotarev D-36 engines used in the Yak-42 transport (each 63.2 kN; 14,200 lb st) *Max T-O weight* 29,000 kg (63,935 lb) *Cruising speed* 600–700 km/h (373–435 mph) *Range* 1,000 km (620 miles)

Antonov An-72.

JANE'S

Encyclopedia of Aviation

Volume 2

Aircraft A–Z
Apollo — Cunningham-Hall

Compiled and edited by Michael J. H. Taylor

Contributors: Bill Gunston, A. J. Jackson, David Mondey,

Malcolm Passingham, John Stroud, Susan H. H. Young

Apollo

The expended Saturn IVB stage viewed from Apollo 7 during practice docking manoeuvres.

Apollo spacecraft (USA) North American was selected to develop the Apollo three-man spacecraft in 1961 and contracts covered production of 20 spacecraft, 16 boilerplate versions, 10 full-size mockups, five engineering simulators and evaluators, and two mission simulators. Design of the spacecraft was based on the 'building block' or modular concept. There were three major components: the Command Module housing the three-man crew; a Service Module housing fuel, electrical power supplies and propulsion units; and the Lunar Module (LM).

The Command Module was 3.23 m (10 ft) high with a launch weight of about 5,900 kg (13,000 lb). It consisted of an inner pressurised compartment of aluminium honeycomb and an outer structure of stainless steel honeycomb with a plastic ablative heat shield coating over the entire outer surface. The Service Module was 7.54 m (24 ft 9 in) high with a weight of about 24,040 kg (53,000 lb) and was constructed of aluminium honeycomb.

The Lunar Module (LM) was designed and produced by Grumman. The LM was able to

Apollo 11 with the 'white room' through which the astronauts entered the spacecraft.

detach from the Apollo command/service modules in orbit and carry two astronauts down to the lunar surface. It was, in effect, a two-stage vehicle, each stage being complete with its own liquid-propellant rocket engine. The ascent (upper) stage consisted of a pressurised crew compartment, equipment sections and an ascent rocket engine. The descent (lower) stage, to which the landing gear was attached, contained a gimballed, throttleable descent rocket engine and the ALSEP (Apollo Lunar Surface Experimental Package). After investigating the Moon, the astronauts took off in the upper stage, the lower stage serving as a launch platform and remaining on the Moon. The astronauts rendezvoused again with the command/service modules, jettisoned the LM and returned to Earth. Grumman's contract covered manufacture of 15 flight models and ten test vehicles.

David Scott photographed during an extravehicular activity from the docked Command/Service Modules and Lunar Module of Apollo 9.

Arado Ar.95 landplane.

Aquaflight Aqua I Model W-6 (USA) Aquaflight was formed in 1946 to build the Aqua six-person or pilot and cargo amphibious flying-boat. Power was provided by two 93 kW (125 hp) Lycoming O-290-A engines.

Arado Ar.64 (Germany) Single-seat biplane fighter developed in 1930 from the Arado S.II trainer and powered by a German-built Jupiter radial engine.

Arado Ar.65 (Germany) Development of the Ar.64 powered by a 372 kW (500 hp) BMW VI in-line engine. The first prototype flew in 1931. Delivery of production Ar.65E single-seat fighters began in 1933 and the first Staffel became operational in April 1934. Meanwhile the Ar.65E had been supplanted in production by the slightly heavier Ar.65F, but both versions were transferred to training units from 1935 with the arrival of better aircraft.

Data (Ar.65E): *Engine* as above *Wing span* 11.2 m (36 ft 9 in) *Length* 8.4 m (27 ft 6¾ in) *Max T-O weight* 1,930 kg (4,255 lb) *Max level speed* 300 km/h (186.5 mph)

Arado Ar.66 (Germany) Two-seat biplane trainer powered by a 179 kW (240 hp) Argus As 10 engine.

Arado Ar.68 (Germany) Five prototypes of this new and improved single-seat fighter biplane appeared in 1933, powered by BMW VI or Junkers Jumo 210 engines. The first version to enter production and service (1936) was the Ar.68F, powered by the BMW engine, followed after a small production run by the superior 514 kW (690 hp) Jumo Da- or Ea-engined Ar.68E. Prototype Ar.65G and H versions were subsequently built, of which only the supercharged 533.4 kW (850 hp) BMW 132 Da-engined 'H' was fully developed. But even this failed to enter production despite having four machine-guns and an enclosed cockpit for the pilot. A few Ar.68s remained operational as night fighters during the first months of World War II and were the Luftwaffe's last operational biplane fighters.

Data (Ar.68E): *Engine* as above *Wing span* 11.0 m (36 ft 1 in) *Length* 9.5 m (31 ft 2 in) *Max T-O weight* 2,020 kg (4,453 lb) *Max level speed* 335 km/h (208 mph) *Range* over 483 km (300 miles) *Armament* two forward-firing 7.9 mm MG 17 machine-guns

Arado Ar.76 (Germany) Parasol-wing light-weight fighter and advanced trainer of which a small number were built and operated by the Luftwaffe from 1936. Power was provided by a 179 kW (240 hp) Argus As 10C engine.

Arado Ar.79 (Germany) Side-by-side two-seat training and touring low-wing monoplane of the latter 1930s powered by a 78.2 kW (105 hp) Hirth H.M.504A2 inverted engine.

Arado Ar.95 and Ar.196 (Germany) Developed as a naval torpedo-bomber and reconnaissance biplane for use from a proposed German aircraft carrier. The first prototype (built as a twin-float seaplane) first flew in 1936 and was followed by other seaplane and landplane prototypes, differing in engines fitted. The landplanes featured heavily trousered main landing gear legs. A change of direction led to the delivery of six aircraft to Spain, where they fought during the late stage of the Civil War. Six Ar.95 landplanes and seaplanes were exported to Chile in 1939 and those built for Turkey were retained for use by the Luftwaffe.

Arado Ar.95 seaplane.

The Ar.196 monoplane was a development of the Ar.95 and the first prototype flew in 1938. Following a number of pre-production aircraft, production proper began with twenty Ar.196A-1s, which were delivered from mid-1939. Production continued with A-2 to A-5 versions and a few modified single-float Ar.196Bs, the number of aircraft produced totalling about 435. Ar.196 seaplanes were operational with the German Navy in reconnaissance, patrol and anti-submarine roles throughout World War II and were for many years the standard catapult seaplane of the Navy, up to four being carried on board some battleships.

Data (Ar.196A-3): *Engine* one 671 kW (900 hp) BMW 132K radial (Ar.95A-1: 656 kW; 880 hp

Arado Ar.196.

BMW 132Dc) *Wing span* 12.45 m (40 ft 10 in) *Length* 10.95 m (35 ft 11¼ in) *Max T-O weight* 3,720 kg (8,201 lb) *Max level speed* 312 km/h (193.5 mph) *Range* 1,078 km (669 miles) *Armament* two forward-firing 20 mm MG FF cannon and one 7.9 mm MG 17 machine-gun and one rear-mounted MG 15 machine-gun, plus two 50 kg bombs

Arado Ar.234 Blitz prototype.

Armstrong Whitworth Atalanta, named *Aurora*, in wartime RAF livery.

Arado Ar.96 (Germany) Tandem two-seat monoplane trainer with retractable landing gear. Powered by one 335 kW (450 hp) Argus As.410A engine on Ar.96B production aircraft built from 1940 (prototype had one 179 kW; 240 hp Argus As.10C). The Ar.199 was a development of the design.

Arado Ar.232 (Germany) The Ar.232 was a uniquely styled transport aircraft. The first prototype flew in 1941 powered by two 1,192 kW (1,600 hp) BMW 801MA radial engines. It is believed that only 18 to 20 further aircraft were built as Ar.232As or B-Os and Ar.232Bs, most of which were powered by four 894 kW (1,200 hp) BMW Bramo 323R-2 radials and carried a crew of four and about 4,500 kg (9,920 lb) of cargo (including vehicles).

Ar.232s, including the prototypes, served with the Luftwaffe from 1942 until 1944. A unique feature of the design was its landing gear: a retractable main nosewheel type gear and a secondary gear of ten pairs of smaller wheels on shorter legs situated under the fuselage. The latter were normally off the ground but took the weight of the aircraft during loading and unloading when the main undercarriage legs were reduced in length to facilitate cargo handling.

Data: *Engines* as above *Wing span* 33.48 m (109 ft 11 in) *Length* 23.52 m (77 ft 2 in) *Max T-O weight* 20,000 kg (44,092 lb) *Max level speed* 307 km/h (190.5 mph) *Armament* one 20 mm MG 151 cannon and two or three 13 mm MG 131 machine-guns in nose, dorsal and rear-fuselage positions

Armstrong Whitworth Ensign.

Arado Ar.234 Blitz (Lightning) (Germany) Arado's Ar.234 has the historical distinction of being the world's first turbojet bomber to enter operational service with any air force. That alone is sufficient to make it a very interesting aircraft but, in addition, it was used to explore a number of advanced concepts. With the company number E.370, it was selected to provide the Luftwaffe with a medium-range turbojet-powered reconnaissance aircraft under the designation Ar.234.

An aerodynamically clean shoulder-wing monoplane, its slender fuselage and thin-section wing made difficult the provision of conventional landing gear, leading to a somewhat startling innovation for an aeroplane intended for operational service. This consisted of a jettisonable take-off trolley. Landing was to be accomplished on a centrally mounted main skid, with outrigger skids mounted beneath the engine nacelles.

The first prototype Ar.234 flew on 15 June 1943 powered by two Junkers Jumo 004A turbojets. It was followed by other prototypes introducing such advanced features as a pressurised cockpit for the pilot and RATO units to reduce take-off run. The Ar.234B, which went into production in mid-1944 and then entered service, had narrow-track (but otherwise conventional) retractable tricycle-type landing gear.

Initial operations in the autumn of 1944 were concerned with reconnaissance over Britain, the Ar.234 having ample speed to elude all attempts at interception by the RAF. Ar.234B-2 bombers were involved during the Ardennes offensive (December 1944/January 1945), but their most vital operation was in opposition to the Allied crossing of the Rhine. For attack missions one 1,000 kg bomb could be carried under the fuselage and one 500 kg bomb under each jet nacelle, although a total load of 1,000 kg was normal.

Data (Ar.234B-2): *Engines* two 8.81 kN (1,980 lb st) Junkers Jumo 004B turbojets *Wing span* 14.11 m (46 ft 3½ in) *Length* 12.64 m (41 ft 5½ in) *Max T-O weight* 9,850 kg (21,715 lb) *Max level speed* 690–742 km/h (430–461 mph) *Combat range* 1,630 km (1,015 miles) *Armament* two rear-firing 20 mm cannon and up to 2,000 kg (4,410 lb) of bombs

Arado Ar.240 (Germany) Intended to be produced as a high-speed and high-altitude reconnaissance aircraft, night fighter and bomber, the first prototype flew in May 1940. Further prototypes and pre-production aircraft were completed and tested – most as reconnaissance aircraft but including examples for other roles – until 15 aircraft had been built. With no decision as to

the best role for the aircraft, the programme was terminated in late 1942, just prior to the expected production run. A few completed aircraft were taken into service by the Luftwaffe and used on the Eastern Front. Maximum level speed of the ninth aircraft, powered by two 1,304 kW (1,750 hp) Daimler-Benz 603A-2 engines, was 730 km/h (453 mph).

Arado L. I (Germany) Tandem two-seat light parasol-wing monoplane of 1929 powered by a 30 kW (40 hp) Salmson radial engine.

Arado L.II (Germany) Two-seat cantilever high-wing monoplane of 1930 designed for sport, training or touring.

Arado L.IIa (Germany) Similar to L.II but with braced folding wings and a new landing gear.

Arado S.I (Germany) First product of the Arado company; built in 1925 as a two-seat trainer with sesquiplane wings and powered by a 74.5 kW (100 hp) Bristol Lucifer engine.

Arado S.III (Germany) Two-seat biplane primary trainer powered by a 71 kW (95 hp) Siemens-Halske Sh.12 radial engine.

Arado SC.I (Germany) Developed in 1926 as a two-seat high-performance trainer powered by a 179 kW (240 hp) BMW IV engine.

Arado SC.II (Germany) Two-seat biplane trainer powered by a 238.5 kW (320 hp) BMW Va engine.

Arado SD.I (Germany) Single-seat biplane fighter of 1928.

Arado SD.II and SD.III (Germany) Single-seat biplane fighters of 1929.

Arado SSD.I (Germany) Seaplane version of SD.I.

Arado V.1 (Germany) Single example of a braced high-wing monoplane transport aircraft. Two crew and four passengers sat in fully enclosed cockpit and cabin. Powered by a 372.6 kW (500 hp) BMW Hornet engine. Made several long distance flights and carried mail over the South Atlantic during 1929.

Arado W-2 (Germany) Two-seat cantilever low-wing seaplane trainer of 1928 powered by two Siemens-Halske Sh.12 radial engines.

Archangelskii Ar-2 (USSR) Development of the Tupolev SB-2*bis* powered by two M-105R engines, each rated at 820 kW (1,100 hp) during take-off. Wing area also increased and incorporated other refinements. Operated on the Eastern Front from 1941.

Arctic Aircraft Interstate S1B2 Arctic Tern (USA) Updated and improved version of the Interstate S1A, flown more than 30 years ago. Produced as a two-seat sporting and general utility high-wing monoplane powered by a 112 kW (150 hp) Lycoming O-320 flat-four engine.

Armstrong Whitworth A.W.15 Atalanta (UK) In 1930 Imperial Airways drew up a specification for a new four-engined airliner to serve in Africa between Kisumu, western Kenya, and Cape Town, South Africa. As a complete breakaway from the more traditional biplane airliner and in order to meet the rather exacting performance figures demanded, Armstrong Whitworth designed the A.W.15: a high-wing cantilever monoplane with four engines mounted in the leading edges of the wings, an ingenious short special

Armstrong Whitworth Albemarle prototype configured as a reconnaissance bomber.

Armstrong Whitworth Albemarle II troop carrier.

Armstrong Whitworth A.W.52.

low drag landing gear in which the oleo legs and radius rods and most of the axles were within the fuselage, and fully enclosed accommodation for the crew of three and passengers. Passenger accommodation varied between nine (plus mail and/or freight carried around and beneath the corridor) for the African route and up to 17 for European services. A toilet was provided at the back of the cabin. Named *Atalanta*, the first A.W.15 flew on 6 June 1932.

On 26 September 1932 *Atalanta* flew the route to Brussels and Cologne and thereafter other A.W.15s linked London, Paris and Zürich. In

Armstrong Whitworth
A.W.650 Argosy flown by
Riddle Airlines.

Armstrong Whitworth
Scimitar.

Armstrong Whitworth
Argosy biplane.

1933 four A.W.15s operated the Kisumu–Cape Town route; in the same year Indian Trans-Continental Airways took over the operation of two of the A.W.15s under an agreement with Imperial Airways for a shared service in India. In the following year A.W.15s were used by Imperial Airways on the shared service to Australia, operated with Qantas. In all eight A.W.15s were built. The name *Atalanta* was given to the first aircraft and subsequently the fourth, following an accident to the first, which then took on the name *Arethusa*. The other six were named *Amalthea*, *Andromeda*, *Artemis*, *Athena*, *Astraea* and *Aurora*. In 1940 the remaining five A.W.15s were taken over by BOAC, but were handed over to the Indian Air Force the following year.
Data: *Engines* four 253.3 (340 hp) Armstrong Siddeley Serval III radials *Wing span* 27.43 m (90 ft 0 in) *Length* 21.79 m (71 ft 6 in) *Max T-O weight* 9,526 kg (21,000 lb) *Max level speed* 251 km/h (156 mph) *Range* 1,030 km (640 miles)

Armstrong Whitworth A.W.27 Ensign (UK)
The Ensign class of airliner was designed to an Imperial Airways specification for a new aircraft capable of carrying a large number of passengers and mail over the land sections of the Empire routes to South Africa and Australia. In the event the aircraft was proposed in two forms: the 40-seat 'European' or 'Western' (with 12 passengers in the front cabin, 4 in the card room, 12 in the middle cabin and 12 in the rear cabin, plus 3 toilets) and the 27-seat 'Empire' or 'Eastern'

(with 3 cabins and 2 toilets) which could also be configured as a 20-passenger sleeper. Both versions were externally similar, being shoulder-wing monoplanes with the four 596 kW (800 hp) Armstrong Siddeley Tiger IX radial engines mounted in the leading edges of the wings. The fuselage was long and slim and a retractable undercarriage was fitted, each main leg carrying a single large Dunlop wheel.

The first A.W.27 flew on 23 January 1938 and from October it flew the London–Paris service. Production was slow, mainly because of the company's heavy commitment to the manufacture of bombers for the RAF, but nevertheless three others were completed in time for mail-carrying flights to Australia in late 1938. However, due to engine troubles, all broke down well short of their goal. The sixth production A.W.27 was fitted with 637 kW (855 hp) Tiger IXC engines driving new de Havilland three-blade constant-speed propellers, and had a modified tail unit. This arrangement subsequently became standard on all the A.W.27s.

With the outbreak of World War II the A.W.27s were used to ferry RAF personnel initially to France and then between RAF stations within the UK. During this period several were destroyed or damaged by German fighters. In 1941 the surviving aircraft were re-engined with 671 kW (900 hp) Wright R-1820-G Cyclone radials and were known as A.W.27A Ensign Mk IIs. With the end of the war the airliners were scrapped. Altogether 14 A.W.27s had been built.
Data: *Engines* as above *Wing span* 37.49 m (123 ft 0 in) *Length* 34.8 m (114 ft 0 in) *Max T-O weight* (Mk II) 23,813 kg (52,500 lb) *Max level speed* 338 km/h (210 mph) *Normal range* (in still air) 2,205 km (1,370 miles)

Armstrong Whitworth A.W.35 Scimitar (UK)
Single-seat biplane fighter, the prototype of which was the converted A.W.16 and first flew on 25 June 1934. Four production aircraft were built for Norway, powered by the 540 kW (725 hp) Armstrong Siddeley Panther XI radial engine and armed with two forward-firing Vickers machine-guns and underwing racks for light fragmentation bombs.

Transport of Detroit for US domestic cargo services. Three were delivered to BEA with the 'Rolamat' cargo-handling system, but were handed back with the delivery of Series 220 Argosies. The Argosy 650 Series 200 was basically similar to the Series 100, but had design refinements to reduce structure weight and offer simpler maintenance. The first of the expected production batch of ten flew on 11 March 1964 but was converted to Series 220 standard.

Flight deck of a Whitley bomber.

Armstrong Whitworth A.W.41 Albemarle (UK) Conceived originally by the Bristol company as a medium bomber, the design was taken over by Armstrong Whitworth and reworked into a reconnaissance-bomber. More than 40 were built before it was decided to change the role and produce subsequent aircraft either as special transports or as glider tugs. The first ST.Is and GT.Is entered RAF service in mid-1942 and early 1943 respectively, and subsequent versions brought the total number of Albemarles built to 600. Albemarles took part in the Sicily, Normandy and Arnhem operations. Power was provided by two 1,185 kW (1,590 hp) Bristol Hercules XI radial engines.

Armstrong Whitworth A.W.52 (UK) First flown on 13 November 1947, the A.W.52 was a tail-less research aircraft designed to obtain data to determine the final shape and detailed design of a six-jet tail-less transport aircraft.

Armstrong Whitworth A.W.650 Argosy (UK) The Argosy was designed specifically to meet the requirements for a large-capacity civil and military passenger and freight transport for worldwide service. An initial production run of ten Series 100 aircraft was laid down as a private venture and the first of these flew on 8 January 1959.

The Argosy 650 Series 100 was the basic pressurised version. First deliveries were made in 1960 to Riddle Airlines of the USA, which operated seven until July 1962. Five of these were then taken over by Capital Airways for operation on Logair military charter work inside the USA and the other two were acquired by Zantop Air

The Argosy 650 Series 220 was fitted with four 1,565 kW (2,100 ehp) Rolls-Royce Dart 532/1 turboprop engines and had wider front and rear door apertures and increased weights and performance. Five were purchased by BEA and were operated from autumn 1964 until April 1970. The Argosy 660 was the specialised military transport model. The fuselage was extensively redesigned and upward and downward hinging rear loading doors were fitted; they could be opened in flight for air-drop operations. The Air Ministry ordered 56 for RAF Transport Command as Argosy C.1s, and the first of these flew on 4 March 1961. Deliveries were made between late 1961 and April 1964, and the type entered service officially with 114 Squadron in March 1962. Power was provided by four 1,841 kW (2,470 ehp) Dart RDa.8 Mk 101 turboprops. Military equipment that could be carried included a 105 mm pack howitzer, Ferret scout car and Wombat anti-tank gun, or a Saracen armoured car. Alternatively 54 paratroops, 69 fully equipped soldiers or 48 stretchers could be accommodated. The last military freighters were withdrawn from service in 1971.
Data (C.1): *Engines* as above *Wing span* 35:05 m (115 ft 0 in) *Length* 27.13 m (89 ft 0 in) *Max T-O weight* 47,610 kg (105,000 lb) *Average cruising speed* 433 km/h (269 mph) *Max range* 5,220 km (3,250 miles)

Armstrong Whitworth Argosy (UK) The very impressive three-engined Argosy biplane, which had no type number, left a very firm mark on air transport history although only seven were built. It owed its origin to a 1922 specification for a Middle East transport aircraft and flew for the first time on 16 March 1926, Imperial Airways having ordered two and the Air Ministry one.

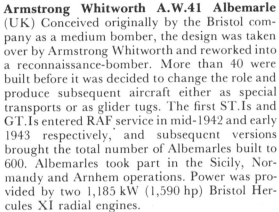

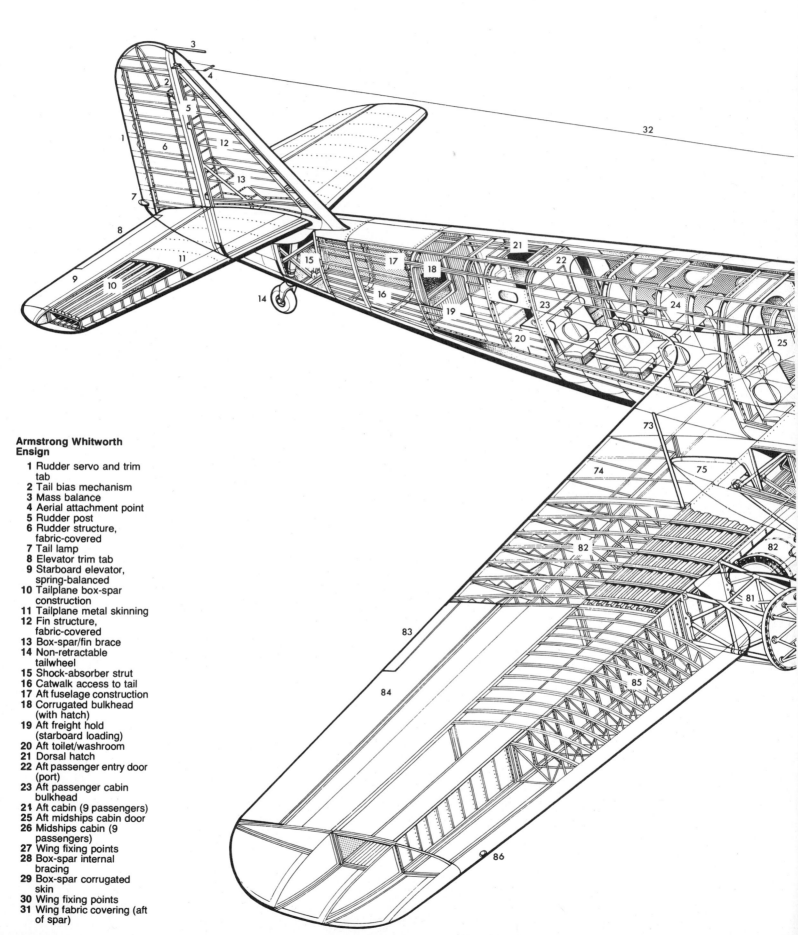

**Armstrong Whitworth
Ensign**

  1 Rudder servo and trim
    tab
  2 Tail bias mechanism
  3 Mass balance
  4 Aerial attachment point
  5 Rudder post
  6 Rudder structure,
    fabric-covered
  7 Tail lamp
  8 Elevator trim tab
  9 Starboard elevator,
    spring-balanced
 10 Tailplane box-spar
    construction
 11 Tailplane metal skinning
 12 Fin structure,
    fabric-covered
 13 Box-spar/fin brace
 14 Non-retractable
    tailwheel
 15 Shock-absorber strut
 16 Catwalk access to tail
 17 Aft fuselage construction
 18 Corrugated bulkhead
    (with hatch)
 19 Aft freight hold
    (starboard loading)
 20 Aft toilet/washroom
 21 Dorsal hatch
 22 Aft passenger entry door
    (port)
 23 Aft passenger cabin
    bulkhead
 24 Aft cabin (9 passengers)
 25 Aft midships cabin door
 26 Midships cabin (9
    passengers)
 27 Wing fixing points
 28 Box-spar internal
    bracing
 29 Box-spar corrugated
    skin
 30 Wing fixing points
 31 Wing fabric covering (aft
    of spar)

32 Aerial
33 Aerial post
34 Port aileron servo and trim tab
35 Port aileron, mass-balanced Frise-type
36 Wing light-alloy skinning, torsion box and leading edges
37 Port navigation light
38 Landing light
39 Port outer oil tank
40 de Havilland variable-pitch propeller
41 Engine exhaust stubs
42 Port 1,590 litre (350 Imp gal) fuel tank
43 Port inner oil tank
44 Armstrong Siddeley Tiger IX engine
45 Aerial mast
46 Cabin ventilation intakes
47 Forward passenger crew entry door (port)
48 Dorsal freight hatch

49 Upper freight compartment
50 Promenade deck (port)
51 Forward cabin (9 passengers)
52 Control cables (above false cabin ceiling)
53 Flight-deck door
54 Flat windscreen
55 Control yoke
56 Nose landing light
57 Pitot head
58 Corrugated bulkheads and flooring
59 Pilot/co-pilot seats
60 Radio operator's position
61 Forward cabin bulkhead
62 Double seats to starboard throughout
63 Single seats to port throughout
64 Forward cabin/freight bulkhead
65 Main freight hold
66 Starboard freight loading hatch

67 Pantry/galley position
68 Forward toilet/washroom
69 Mail compartment beneath wing spar
70 Fuel cocks
71 Box-spar/undercarriage attachment
72 Individual oval windows per seat row
73 Aerial post
74 Split flaps
75 Undercarriage nacelle
76 Retraction jack
77 Main undercarriage legs
78 Mainwheel
79 Radius rods
80 Engine mounting
81 Engine-bearer frame
82 Wing construction
83 Starboard aileron servo tab
84 Starboard aileron
85 Wing ribs
86 Starboard navigation light

Armstrong Whitworth

**Armstrong Whitworth
Awana.**

**Armstrong Whitworth
F.K.3.**

**Armstrong Whitworth
F.K.8.**

In general layout the Argosy was similar to the early Handley Page and Vickers biplane transports, but there were significant differences. Instead of a wooden structure it had a steel-tube fuselage; a wide-track two-wheel main undercarriage replaced the more usual pairs of wheels; and it was powered by three 287 kW (385 hp) Armstrong Siddeley Jaguar air-cooled radial engines instead of the more commonly used water-cooled engines. Accommodation was for 18–20 passengers, sitting in two rows of wicker seats in the fully enclosed cabin. The crew sat in an open cockpit high in the nose.

The Argosies were originally intended for Imperial Airways' trunk routes but initially went into service in Europe – the first service flight being made on 16 July 1926, between Croydon and Le Bourget. The type became well known when used on the *Silver Wing* London–Paris lunchtime services which were inaugurated on 1 May 1927. On 30 March 1929 one of the Argosies received wide publicity when it operated the Croydon–Basle sector of the first United Kingdom to India air mail service (see **Chronology**). During 1929 Imperial Airways took delivery of four Argosy MkII aircraft with 306 kW (410 hp) geared Jaguar IVA engines, automatic slots and increased fuel capacity. The original Argosies were then re-engined to bring them to comparable standard. When Imperial Airways opened the route to Central Africa, with the first departure from Croydon on 28 February 1931, two Argosies were used to operate the Cairo–Khartoum sector (see **Chronology**). One, the *City of Birmingham*,

was lost in a forced landing and had to be replaced in Africa by the last of the original aircraft.

The Argosy remained Imperial Airways' main European aircraft until the much larger Handley Page Heracles class was introduced in 1931, after which they were mainly used as back-up aircraft and for training. They were also used for joyriding. The last survivor was sold to United Airways in 1935 and was used until 1936.

Data (Argosy Mk I): *Engines* as above *Wing span* 27.43 m (90 ft 0 in) *Length* 19.8 m (65 ft 0 in) *Max T-O weight* 8,165 kg (18,000 lb) *Cruising speed* 145 km/h (90 mph) *Range* 668 km (415 miles)

Armstrong Whitworth Atlas (UK) In its original prototype form the Armstrong Whitworth Atlas flew for the first time on 10 May 1925. This was a somewhat larger and heavier sesquiplane than the Siskin, which had preceded it on the production line. It had been designed big (to accommodate essential equipment) and strong (to stand up to punishment) to meet the RAF's requirement for an army co-operation aircraft. The Atlas was, in fact, the first aircraft designed for the RAF for this specific role, which, prior to its entry into service, had been filled by aircraft adapted for the purpose.

It was not until nearly 2½ years after the prototype's first flight that this two-seat aircraft began to enter squadron service. In the interim period the company had used innumerable 'try-it-and-see' ideas to overcome shortcomings in flight characteristics revealed by service testing. Thus came changes in wing dihedral, incidence and sweepback, the provision of new wings, automatic wingtip slots and, in the case of aircraft

for the RCAF, the addition of ailerons on the lower wings. In the long term this effort was worthwhile, for a total of more than 440 were built for the RAF, of which 175 were dual-control advanced trainers. These aircraft were to remain in service until 1934 in the army co-operation role, and as advanced trainers and communications aircraft into 1935. In addition to those built for the RAF, small numbers were exported to Canada, Egypt, Greece and Japan. By no means a great aeroplane, the Atlas was renowned for its rugged reliability and benefited from use of the reliable and developed Jaguar IVC power plant in the Atlas Mk I, and the improved 399 kW (535 hp) Panther IIA in the Mk II version. Equipment included radio, message pick-up hook and cameras.

Data (Atlas Mk I): *Engine* one 298 kW (400 hp) Armstrong Siddeley Jaguar IVC radial *Wing span* 12.06 m (39 ft 6 in) *Length* 8.71 m (28 ft 6 in) *Max T-O weight* 1,823 kg (4,020 lb) *Max level speed* 230 km/h (143 mph) *Range* 772 km (480 miles) *Armament* two 0.303 in machine-guns and four 112 lb bombs

Armstrong Whitworth Siskin prototype.

Armstrong Whitworth A.W.38 Whitley (UK) Most extensively built of all Armstrong Whitworth aircraft was the Whitley heavy bomber, designed to meet the British Air Ministry specification B.3/34. More than 1,800 were produced. Selected for production off the drawing board in 1935 the prototype flew for the first time on 17 March 1936. The second prototype and 34 Mk I production aircraft which followed were all powered by two 592.5 kW (795 hp) Armstrong Siddeley Tiger IX radial engines. Mk IV, V and VII Whitleys, which followed later, had Rolls-Royce Merlin engines – these conferring considerably improved performance.

Whitleys began to enter RAF service in the early months of 1937 and by the outbreak of war in 1939 were wellestablished in the bomber squadrons. Being slower than the contemporary Handley Page Hampden and Vickers Wellington they were classed as night bombers. They were a vital component of Bomber Command operations until their withdrawal from front-line service in 1941. Achieving some of the major milestones of the war, the Whitley was responsible for the first widespread leaflet raids over Germany, in Sep-

tember 1939; the first bombing raid on Germany, in May 1940; the first bombing raid on Italy, in June 1940; and the first paratroop operation over Southern Italy, in February 1941. After its withdrawal from front-line service with Bomber Command the Whitley was converted for use as a general reconnaissance bomber and put into service by Coastal Command. In another converted form it was used to train the first British airborne troops and to take them into action for the first time, in a flight from England to Southern Italy. At the end of the war the type was still in service for training and other miscellaneous duties. (A full description of the type appears in the 1945–46 *Jane's*.)

Armstrong Whitworth F.K.10.

Data (Whitley V): *Engines* two 801.5 kW (1,075 hp) Merlin Xs *Wing span* 25.6 m (84 ft 0 in) *Length* 22.10 m (72 ft 6 in) *Max T-O weight* 12,790 kg (28,200 lb) *Max level speed* 367 km/h (228 mph) *Combat range* 2,414 km (1,500 miles) *Armament* five 0.303 in machine-guns, plus up to 3,175 kg (7,000 lb) of bombs

Armstrong Whitworth Awana (UK) The first product of the post-war Armstrong Whitworth company was the Awana, a 25-seat troop transport biplane. The first prototype flew on 28 June 1923 but failed in competition with the Vickers Victoria to get production orders.

Armstrong Whitworth F.K.3 (UK) During World War I the designer Frederick Koolhoven worked for British companies, among which was Armstrong Whitworth (after the war he designed aircraft in the Netherlands under his own name). The F.K.3 was the result of Koolhoven's attempt to improve upon the B.E.2c, which was being built in the UK by several manufacturers including Armstrong Whitworth. As well as making the aircraft easier to construct he refined the fuselage, increased the wing span and area of the fin and rudder, and put the observer in the rear cockpit.

Armstrong Whitworth Siskin III with experimental low-drag cowling.

Armstrong Whitworth

Armstrong Whitworth Siskin IIIA.

Armstrong Whitworth Wolf.

With the RAF 1a engine installed, maximum speed was increased by 27 km/h (17 mph) to 143 km/h (89 mph). Five hundred production aircraft were built, most serving as trainers but a number as reconnaissance, artillery spotting and light bombing aircraft in Macedonia.

Armstrong Whitworth F.K.8 (UK) Subsequently nicknamed 'Big Ack', the F.K.8 appeared in May 1916 as a large and sturdy armed-reconnaissance biplane, capable also of carrying up to 72.5 kg (160 lb) of bombs for 'hit and run' raids on enemy ground positions. Initial production aircraft, which became operational on the Western Front in early 1917, were powered by 89.4 kW (120 hp) Beardmore engines. Later production aircraft were normally powered by 119 kW (160 hp) Beardmore engines in much neater cowlings with new small radiators on the fuselage sides. An unusual but much appreciated feature of the aircraft was its dual controls, which greatly improved the observer's chances of survival.

In service F.K.8s proved capable of withstanding far more punishment than the Royal Aircraft Factory B.E.2s they at first replaced, and had the speed, manoeuvrability and firepower to give aircrews a reasonable chance of defending themselves. Indeed, the two VCs won by F.K.8 pilots – awarded to A. A. MacLeod and F. M. F. West (see **Chronology**) – were for actions against formations of attacking enemy fighters. It is believed that more than 1,600 F.K.8s were built, serving on the Western Front, as home defence and train-

ing aircraft in the UK, in the Middle East and in India. Of these, nearly 700 were on strength at the end of the war.

Interestingly, after the war, two F.K.8s were among the initial equipment of Queensland and Northern Territory Aerial Services Ltd, which was subsequently known as QANTAS. These aircraft were used by the airline to carry air mail between Charleville and Cloncurry; this represented the Australian government's second air mail contract. The first service took place during 2 and 3 November 1922.

Data: *Engine* as above *Wing span* 13.26 m (43 ft 6 in) *Length* 9.58 m (31 ft 5 in) *Max T-O weight* 1,275 kg (2,811 lb) *Max level speed* 157 km/h (98 mph) *Endurance* 3 h *Armament* one forward-firing Vickers machine-gun and one rear-mounted Lewis gun.

Armstrong Whitworth F.K.10 (UK) Eight two-seat fighting or light bombing F.K.10 quadruplanes were built for the RNAS and delivered in 1917. Powered by 82 kW (110 hp) Le Rhône or 97 kW (130 hp) Clerget radial engines. The pilot sat forward of the wings and the rear-gunner aft.

Armstrong Whitworth Siskin (UK) When the moment arrived after World War I for the RAF to start equipping with new fighter aircraft, the Armstrong Whitworth Siskin – and its contemporary Gloster Grebe – gradually displaced the excellent Sopwith Snipe, which had served so well. The Siskin was to prove an important aircraft for Armstrong Whitworth, helping to establish on a sound basis the new company structure which had resulted from the early post-war acquisition of the Siddeley Deasy company.

In its original form the Siskin was a sesquiplane of wood and fabric construction, with an unusual landing gear which was retained in subsequent aircraft produced by Armstrong Whitworth. The first stage in its evolution to production form for the RAF came with the installation of an early Armstrong Siddeley Jaguar radial engine in the Siskin prototype.

First of the Siskins ordered for the RAF was the single-seat Siskin III prototype. This conformed to Air Ministry requirements for an all-metal frame, both airframe and wings being of a basic metal structure with fabric covering. Power plant of this version was the 242 kW (325 hp) Jaguar III. Sixty-four were built, the first entering service in 1924. Three years later, improved Siskin IIIAs began to enter service with the RAF with a more powerful Jaguar IV engine. For their time, Siskin IIIAs and IIIBs were built in large quantities: almost 400 were supplied to the RAF to equip 11 squadrons.

Siskin IIIAs first entered service in March 1927 and remained active for almost five years. They are remembered as highly manoeuvrable, attractive biplanes, with few vices and plenty of spirit. Siskins were also exported in small numbers, those going to Estonia being used as trainers alongside Avro Avians, 504s and 626s, and remaining active until the outbreak of World War II.

Data (Siskin IIIA): *Engine* one 287 kW (385 hp) Armstrong Siddeley Jaguar IV supercharged radial *Wing span* 10.11 m (33 ft 2 in) *Length* 7.72 m (25 ft 4 in) *Max T-O weight* 1,379 kg (3,040 lb) *Max level speed* 251 km/h (156 mph) at 3,050 m (10,000 ft) *Range* 402 km (250 miles) *Armament* two 0.303 in machine-guns and provision for four 20 lb bombs

Armstrong Whitworth Wolf (UK) Six aircraft built in 1923 for the RAF and the RAF Reserve Flying School as two-seat reconnaissance and training aircraft respectively. Unusual features of the design included the fuselage mounted midway between the biplane wings and a very wide track undercarriage. Power was provided by a 261 kW (350 hp) Armstrong Siddeley Jaguar III radial engine.

Arpin A-1 monoplane (UK) In 1937 M. B. Arpin and Company designed a light two-seat cabin monoplane fitted with a 67 kW (90 hp) Cirus Minor engine driving a pusher propeller, and a tail unit carried on twin booms. It was evaluated by the British Army but failed to win orders.

Arrow Active Mk II.

Arrow Active (UK) High-performance, single-seat all-metal sesquiplane, originally powered by a 74.5 kW (100 hp) Cirus-Hermes IIB engine. An improved version was produced in 1932 as the Arrow Active Mk II, differing mainly by having an additional upper-wing centre-section carried on outwardly splayed struts and an 89.4 kW (120 hp) Gipsy III inverted air-cooled engine.

Arrow Sport and Sport Pursuit (USA) Two-seat light sport and training biplanes of the late 1920s, powered by 44.7 kW (60 hp) Le Blond and 74.5 kW (100 hp) Kinner K-5 engines respectively.

Arrow Model F (USA) Built to a Bureau of Air Commerce contract, the Model F was a light single-seat open-cockpit monoplane designed to investigate the possibilities of using cheap mass-produced motor car engines for aircraft.

Arsenal 0.101 (France) Two-seat light research monoplane of the late 1940s built to serve as an experimental flying test bed for aerofoil sections, ailerons, spoilers, flaps, fairings, etc. The aircraft was made small enough to be tested in a large wind tunnel so that the results could be iompared with those gained from the aircraft's internal equipment during flight tests.

Arsenal VB 10 (France) Before the outbreak of World War II Arsenal de l'Aéronautique was engaged in the development of the Vernisse-Galtier VG 30. It was subsequently redesignated VB 10 and development continued throughout the German occupation. It was a single-seat fighter-bomber of all-metal construction. Power was provided by two Hispano-Suiza HS 12Z engines, each rated at 1,118 kW (1,500 hp) and mounted in tandem in the fuselage with a special coupling to drive two contra-rotating co-axial propellers.

Armament comprised six 12.7 mm machine-guns and four 20 mm cannon, and provision was made for two 500 kg bombs and four rocket projectiles. Maximum speed was estimated at 700 km/h (435 mph). An initial order for 50 production aircraft – to be built by SNCAN (Nord) – was temporarily placed by the French government.

Arsenal VG 70 (France) Designed by M. Galtier, the VG 70 was a research aircraft designed to obtain information for the development of high-speed jet fighters. The aircraft was completed in 1947 and first flew on 23 June 1948. Power was provided by an 8.41 kN (1,890 lb st) Junkers Jumo 004B-2 turbojet engine.

Arsenal VG 90 (France) Designed as a single-seat naval strike aircraft. The first two prototypes were powered by Hispano-Suiza Nene turbojet engines. Both were destroyed in accidents. The third prototype, built in 1952, was powered by a SNECMA Atar 101 turbojet engine.

Arsenal VB 10.

Arsenal VG 90.

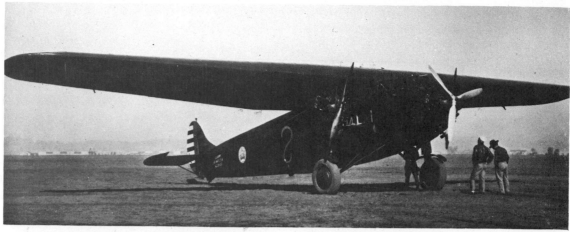

Atlantic C-2A *Question Mark*, which set an endurance record in 1929 using flight refuelling.

Astra C and CM (France) Astra began as a balloon and dirigible manufacturing company. It became French agent for the Wrights in 1909 and for a time built modified Wright biplanes. From 1912 the company built a small series of clean-looking biplanes for civil and military use under the Type C and CM designations respectively. Those built in 1912 were of wooden construction, thereafter of wood and metal. Power was provided by Renault engines of 37.35–74.5 kW (50–100 hp). By 1916, however, the company had reverted to building airships.

Astra-Torres (France) The Société Astra des Constructions Aéronautiques (see above) constructed a series of airships known as the Astra-Torres type – named after the Spaniard Torres Quevedo, who had designed the envelope adopted by Astra. The envelope was of trefoil form instead of the usual circular. Astra XIV, XVII and XIX were purchased by the Royal Navy. Other airships were built for the French Navy between 1916 and 1922.

Ateliers de Constructions Aéronautiques Zeebrugge (Belgium) Otherwise known as ACAZ, this company produced the T.2 two-seat cabin monoplane in 1924; built of duralumin tubes and sheet metal.

Atlantic Aircraft Corporation (USA) This company started business in the USA in 1924 with a contract from the US Army Air Service for remodelling 100 D.H.4 biplanes into D.H.4M2s. It later acquired rights to build Fokker aircraft under licence. In 1926 it became known as the Fokker Aircraft Corporation, but in 1931 was taken over by the General Aviation Manufacturing Corporation. Under the name of Atlantic the company produced the S.III two-seat biplane, which it hoped would be accepted by the Army Air Service as a basic and advanced trainer (fitted with a 149 kW; 200 hp Curtiss OX5 engine). Other aircraft attributed to Atlantic-Fokker and built for the Army included 17 Fokker F.VIIA/3m type aircraft as C-2/2As and C-7/7As, a Fokker F-10A as the C-5, 20 C-14s, one C-15, 14 O-27/B-8s and an XLB-2. All the 'C' category aircraft were transports (the C-15 a specialised ambulance), while the B-8s and XLB-2 were experimental light bombers and the O-27s observation monoplanes. In addition the US Navy purchased seven F.VIIA/3m type aircraft as TA-1s and TA-2s, which subsequently became RA-1s and RA-2s respectively and later still RA-3s. A single F-10A was purchased as the RA-4. (See **Fokker – USA**)

Atlas C4M Kudu (South Africa) The Kudu first flew on 16 February 1974 and is a light transport aircraft accommodating a pilot, co-pilot and four/six passengers. The passenger seats are removable to provide space for 560 kg (1,235 lb) of freight. A trap-door in the cabin floor allows aerial survey and supply dropping. A military prototype first flew on 18 June 1975. The type is in production for the South African Air Force.
Data: *Engine* one 254 kW (340 hp) Piaggio-built Lycoming GSO-480-B1B3 flat-six *Wing span* 13.075 m (42 ft 10¾ in) *Length* 9.31 m (30 ft 6½ in) *Max T-O weight* 2,040 kg (4,497 lb) *Max level speed* 259 km/h (161 mph) *Range* 1,297 km (806 miles)

Atlas C4M Kudu.

Atlas H-10 (USA) Four-seat cabin monoplane of the late 1940s powered by a 149 kW (200 hp) Lycoming O-435 engine.

Atlas Impala (South Africa) Aermacchi M.B.326M licence-built in South Africa as the Impala Mk 1 for the SAAF. The Impala Mk 2 is an improved version – based on the single-seat M.B.326K – which has been developed by Atlas as an advanced trainer for the SAAF and is in production. The Mk 2 is powered by a Rolls-Royce Viper Mk 540 turbojet engine.

Aubert Cigale series (France) The first aircraft designed by M. Paul Aubert for development by Aubert-Aviation was the PA-20 two-seat (side-by-side) trainer, which was exhibited at the 1938 Paris Salon. After World War II the aircraft was revised as the PA-201, winning many competitions. The final version was the PA-204 Super Cigale powered by a 100.5–134 kW (135–180 hp) Lycoming engine. The prototype 100.5 kW (135 hp) version first flew on 27 July 1955 and featured a wider cabin for four persons with improved forward view. A batch of 30 production aircraft was put in hand, including eight for the Aero-Club Air France.

Atlas Impala Mk I.

Auster 5.

Auster Aircraft (UK) Because of the large number of basically similar aircraft produced by this company during the 1940s and 1950s, it is considered expedient to cover the earlier types in the following paragraphs. Many of the later types are covered separately thereafter.

Auster Aircraft Ltd was a successor to Taylorcraft Aeroplanes (England) Ltd which was formed in 1939 to manufacture a cabin monoplane under licence from Taylorcraft Aircraft Corporation of America. The company assumed the name Auster Aircraft Ltd on 7 March 1946.

The British Taylorcraft was produced in a number of different forms for the RAF and the

British Army. The Auster 1 (Cirrus Minor engine), the Auster 3 (Gipsy Major engine) and Auster 4 and 5 (97 kW; 130 hp Lycoming engine) were all used on active service as three-seat artillery spotters or Air Observation Posts. Throughout the war development of the design continued, and although the same basic welded steel-tube structure remained, considerable strengthening was achieved and performance improved. In later models trailing-edge flaps were incorporated. During the war the company built 1,604 Austers for the RAF and the Army Air Corps: 100 Mk 1s, 2 Mk 2s (shortage of Lycoming engines), 467 Mk 3s, 255 Mk 4s and 780 Mk 5s. In addition, six Model H gliders were built.

A civil version of the Mk 5 was produced, known as the Auster Mk 5 J/1 Autocrat. It was basically similar to the military aircraft but had upholstered accommodation and other refinements. This aircraft served also as the basis for all the subsequent civil models produced under different names.

The two-seat Arrow followed the Autocrat into production and subsequently several versions of the basic two- and three-seat airframes appeared. These included the J/3 and J/3A two-seaters with 48.4 kW (65 hp) Continental C65 engines; the J/4 and J/5 with Cirrus and Gipsy Major 1 engines respectively; the J/6, a three-seater similar to the Autocrat but with a 108 kW (145 hp) Gipsy Major 10 engine. A J/7 two-seater with a 74.5 kW (100 hp) Cirrus Minor engine was projected. The four-seat Avis made its appearance in 1947 and was put into production.

In the military field, the basic series of Auster Air Observation Posts continued with the AOP.6.

Auster 1 of 1942.

Auster

Auster AOP series (UK) AOP.6 was developed from the Mk 5 and powered by a 108 kW (145 hp) Gipsy Major 7 engine. Modified fuselage and increased all-up weight. All-metal auxiliary aerofoil flaps below and behind trailing edge, and wings strengthened to take two 52.25 litre (11.5 Imp gallon) fuel tanks. Pilot and observer seated in tandem. Lengthened landing-gear struts allowed larger airscrew. Production completed in 1949. T.7 was a two-seat trainer which could be quickly converted to full AOP standard. Side-by-side seating with dual controls. Third seat could be fitted. AOP.9 had a 134 kW (180 hp) Cirrus Bombardier 203 (military version of 702) engine.

Auster B.8 Agricola (UK) Specialised single-seat agricultural low-wing monoplane powered by a 179 kW (240 hp) Continental O-470-M2 engine.

Auster J/1B Aiglet (UK) Basically a version of the Autocrat with larger tail surfaces and powered by a Gipsy Major 1 engine. Approximately 90 built; many used for crop-spraying.

Auster J/1N Alpha (UK) Conceived as a low-priced light aircraft capable of a variety of duties in varied climatic conditions. Two versions were made available, the J/1 Alpha and the Alpha 5 – differing in having 97 kW (130 hp) Gipsy Major 1 and Lycoming O-290-3/1 engines respectively. Both versions were delivered as new aircraft but many owners of Autocrats brought their aircraft to a similar standard by fitting Gipsy Major engines and a new tail unit with horn-balanced rudder. Accommodation comprised two individual seats at the front and a bench seat at the rear for an adult and two children.

Auster J/1V Workmaster (UK) Agricultural version evolved especially to meet a requirement of Crop Culture Ltd. Fourteen were initially ordered.

Auster J/4 Arrow.

Auster Avis (UK) Four-seat cabin monoplane built as the Mk 1 for civil use and projected as the Mk 2 for military use and as a civil ambulance.

Auster B.4 (UK) Designed and built as a private venture to perform the numerous duties, other than AOP, required of a light military aircraft. It featured a large cabin with a loading door at the rear end. The forward portion of the fuselage was of square section, with a triangular wedge roof to which the tail boom was bolted. The floor provided fittings for seats, stretchers or light freight. Power was provided by a Cirrus Bombardier 702.

Auster J/5B,G,P Autocar (UK) Four-seater designed to be used for passenger-carrying, freight-carrying, crop-spraying, dusting, glider-towing and ambulance duties. The Autocar was Auster's first four-seat aircraft proper to go into production, having first flown in August 1949. Approximately 100 were built, many for export. The three versions were powered by 97 kW (130 hp) Gipsy Major 1, 115.5 kW (155 hp) Cirrus Major 3 and 108 kW (145 hp) Cirrus Major 10 engines respectively. They were known as the Autocar (J/5B), Cirrus Autocar (J/5G) and Autocar 145 (J/5P). A seaplane version was also produced.

Auster J/5F Aiglet Trainer (UK) Two-seat dual-control aerobatic aircraft. Airframe basically similar to the earlier J/5 but with horn-balanced rudder and elevators and wings clipped by 1.22 m (4 ft) to give greater rate of roll. The J/5F was the standard version with a Gipsy Major 1 engine. The J/5FL version was powered by a 108 kW (145 hp) Gipsy Major 10/2 engine and was a two/three-seat trainer of which 15 were built for the Iranian government. Delivery began in July 1958.

Auster AOP.6.

Auster J/5Q and J/5R Alpine (UK) Incorporated features of both the Autocar and Aiglet: basically the wide cabin of the latter and the long-span wings of the former. Variants differed by having Gipsy Major 1 and Gipsy Major 10 engines respectively.

Auster (Beagle) D series (UK) It was announced in 1960 that Pressed Steel Company intended to acquire the whole share capital of Auster Aircraft. This resulted in the formation of the Beagle group, which continued production of the D.5/160 and D.5/180, the latter as the A.113 Husky when fitted with a 134 kW (180 hp) Lycoming O-360-A1A engine. Before the change-over Auster produced three versions of the D series, which had resulted from an extensive development programme of previous types. A major innovation was the use of metal wing spars which, in conjunction with new low-flammability long-weathering plastic-based butyrate dope and paint finishes, made the Ds entirely suitable for use in the tropics. The D.4 was a two-seater with either a 9.75 m (32.0 ft) or 10.98 m (36.0 ft) wing span and an 80.5, 112/119 or 134 kW (108, 150/160 or 180 hp) Lycoming engine; the D.5 was a three-seater offering the two wing spans but only the 119 and 134 kW (160 and 180 hp) engines; and the D.6 was a four-seater with the greater wing span and engines as for the D.5. The first production D.4/108 flew on 12 February 1960; the first D.5/160 on 10 January 1960, and the first D.6/160 on 9 May 1960.

Austin-Ball A.F.B. 1 (UK) Single-seat fighter powered by a 149 kW (200 hp) Hispano-Suiza engine driving a four-blade propeller. Armament comprised a Lewis machine-gun firing through the propeller shaft and a second gun mounted on the upper wing. Designed in accordance with the requirements of a fighter as suggested by Albert Ball, Britain's first great ace of World War I. One prototype only appeared in early 1916.

Avia 14 (Czechoslovakia) Licence-built version of the Soviet Ilyushin Il-14. Three variants produced: the Avia 14-32A with seating for up to 32 passengers, the Avia 14T cargo version of the 14-32A with enlarged loading doors and a reinforced cabin floor, and the Avia 14 Salon (previously known as the 14 Super) with a pressurised fuselage and seating for 42 passengers. The latter differed further in being the only version with circular, instead of square, windows and wingtip fuel tanks.
Data (Avia 14 Salon): *Engines* two 1,416 kW (1,900 hp) Shvetsov ASh-82T piston engines *Wing span* 32.41 m (106 ft 8 in) *Length* 22.3 m (73 ft 2 in) *Max T-O weight* 18,000 kg (39,683 lb) *Normal cruising speed* 300 km/h (186 mph) *Max practical range* 2,500 km (1,550 miles)

Auster B.8 Agricola.

Avia Av-35 (Czechoslovakia) Sometimes referred to as the B-35, this aircraft was a single-seat cantilever low-wing monoplane fighter of 1938 with retractable landing gear and powered by a 633 kW (850 hp) Avia-built Hispano-Suiza 12 Ycrs engine. Armament comprised one 20 mm Oerlikon cannon and two 7.9 mm machine-guns. Prototypes only.

Avia Av-135 (Czechoslovakia) Single-seat cantilever low-wing monoplane fighter with retractable landing gear, derived from the Av-35. Appeared in 1939 and exhibited in prototype form in Brussels that year. Twelve produced during the German occupation for the Bulgarian Air Force; these aircraft were delivered in 1941. They saw limited action against USAAF bombers attacking targets in Romania. Powered by a 633 kW (850 hp) Avia-built Hispano-Suiza 12Ycrs in-line. Max level speed 534 km/h (332 mph).

Avia B 34 (Czechoslovakia) Single-seat biplane fighter of 1931 powered by a 484.4 kW (650 hp) Hispano-Suiza water-cooled engine. Subsequently used to flight test engines for several projected variants.

Avia B 71 (Czechoslovakia) B 71 was the designation given to 54 Tupolev SB-2s acquired by Czechoslovakia from Russia from 1937. Production lines to licence-build the type were also set up in Czechoslovakia by Avia and Aero. The only Czech aircraft completed were finished during the German occupation and were operated by the Luftwaffe and the Bulgarian Air Force for secondary duties.

Avia B-534 (Czechoslovakia) In August 1933 the prototype B-534 biplane fighter made its first

Avia

Auster J/5B Autocar.

Auster Aiglet Trainer.

Auster (Beagle) D.6.

flight. It was a single-seater with unequal-span single-bay wings. The wing structure was of riveted steel with fabric covering, while the fuselage structure was of steel tubes, riveted and bolted together and braced with streamlined wires. The forward portion was covered with detachable panels and the rear portion with fabric. A split-type landing gear was fitted, with the wheels enclosed in streamlined casings. The fighter was, in fact, the result of a line of development which had begun with the B-34, itself built as a possible replacement for the BH-33s then in service. Production B-534s were built with open and enclosed cockpits. A total of 445 were produced. These formed the fighter element of the Czech Air Force right up to the German occupation in 1939. B-534s thereafter found their way into the Luftwaffe, serving as fighters on the Eastern Front and being used for secondary duties elsewhere.
Data: *Engine* one 633 kW (850 hp) Avia-built Hispano-Suiza 12 Ydrs in-line *Wing span* 9.4 m (30 ft 10 in) *Length* 8.2 m (26 ft 10¾ in) *Max T-O weight* 1,980 kg (4,365 lb) *Max level speed* 394 km/h (245 mph) *Range* 600 km (373 miles) *Armament* four 7.7 mm machine-guns, two in each side of the fuselage and firing along troughs in the sides of the engine cowling

Avia BH-1 (Czechoslovakia) Exhibited at the Prague Aero Show in 1920, the BH-1 was a small two-seat low-wing sporting monoplane, somewhat reminiscent of Junkers monoplanes. It was originally powered by a 30 kW (40 hp) Austro-Daimler engine, but overheating caused its replacement with a 1911 37.25 kW (50 hp) Gnome. Maximum speed with the latter engine was 136 km/h (85 mph).

Avia BH-2 (Czechoslovakia) Single-seat light monoplane of 1921 powered by a Bristol Cherub engine.

Avia BH-3 (Czechoslovakia) Cantilever low-wing monoplane fighter of 1921. Ten built for the Czech Air Force powered by either 134 kW (180 hp) BMW IIIa or 179 kW (240 hp) Walter W/IV engine. First wczech production fighter.

Avia BH-4 (Czechoslovakia) Single-seat fighter prototype similar in configuration to the BH-3. Powered by a 164 kW (220 hp) Hispano-Suiza 8Ba engine.

Avia BH-5 (Czechoslovakia) Two-seat light sporting monoplane of 1924 powered subsequently by a 41 kW (55 hp) Walter radial engine.

Avia BH-6 (Czechoslovakia) Single-seat fighter of 1922–23 powered by a Hispano-Suiza 8Ba engine.

Avia BH-7 (Czechoslovakia) Single-seat parasol-wing fighter powered by a 223.5 kW (300 hp) Skoda-built Hispano-Suiza engine.

Avia BH-8 (Czechoslovakia) Single-seat fighter of 1923 powered by a Hispano-Suiza 8Ba engine.

Avia BH-9 (Czechoslovakia) Two-seat low-wing monoplane trainer of 1924 derived from the BH-5. Powered by a 41 kW (55 hp) Walter NZ radial engine. One BH-9 given enlarged fuel tanks set new Czech duration record (designated BH-9A).

Avia BH-10 (Czechoslovakia) Smaller version of the BH-9 and used by the Czech Air Force as a single-seat advanced trainer.

Avia BH-11 (Czechoslovakia) Similar to the BH-9 and delivered to the Czech Air Force as a communications and training aircraft.

Avia BH-12 (Czechoslovakia) Similar to the BH-9 but designed for a competition of touring aircraft in Brussels in 1924, as well as for other competitions and meetings. Structure revised and lightened and wings folded for transport and storage.

Avia BH-16 (Czechoslovakia) Very light single-seat low-wing monoplane powered by a 12 kW (16 hp) Vaslin or similar engine.

Avia BH-17 (Czechoslovakia) Designed at the request of the Czech Air Force in 1923, this single-seat biplane fighter was the result of tests with two experimental aircraft fitted with 223.5 kW (300 hp) Skoda-built Hispano-Suiza 8Fb engines. It was a clean-looking fighter of wooden construction, armed with two forward-firing machine-guns. The cabane structure supporting the upper wing housed the oil and water tanks, the whole being covered over. This resulted in a limited forward view for the pilot and, coupled with weak I-type interplane struts, resulted in only one small batch of aircraft being built in 1924. However, the type was developed into the more successful BH-21.

Avia BH-19 (Czechoslovakia) Single-seat low-wing monoplane fighter of 1924 powered by a 223.5 kW (300 hp) Skoda-built Hispano-Suiza 8Fb engine. Maximum speed approximately 250 km/h (155 mph).

Avia BH-20 (Czechoslovakia) Single-seat advanced training biplane powered by an 82 kW (110 hp) Walter NZ engine.

Avia BH-21 (Czechoslovakia) Improved version of the BII-17 with new N-type interplane struts and a honeycomb radiator fitted under the fuselage (whence it could be withdrawn) instead of the BH-17's radiators mounted between the side Vs of the undercarriage. Approximately 120 BH-21s were built in Czechoslovakia and these operated on wheel and ski undercarriages. In addition 50 were constructed under licence in Belgium.
Data: *Engine* one 223.5 kW (300 hp) Skoda-built Hispano-Suiza 8Fb *Wing span* 8.9 m (29 ft 2½ in) *Length* 6.87 m (22 ft 6½ in) *Max T-O weight* 860 kg (2,392 lb) *Max level speed* 246 km/h (153 mph) *Range* 550 km (342 miles) *Armament* two forward-firing Vickers machine-guns

Avia BH-21R (Czechoslovakia) Racing version of the BH-21 with wings of smaller span and new aerofoil section, reduced gap between the fuselage and upper wing and new Lamblin wing radiators. The boosted Hispano-Suiza engine drove a Reed duralumin propeller. The BH-21R won the President of the Republic's Speed Trophy Contest at Prague in 1925 at a speed of 301 km/h (187 mph).

Avia BH-22 (Czechoslovakia) Lightweight version of the BH-21 for the Czech Air Force, of which 30 were built as advanced and tactics training aircraft to prepare pilots for the transition from standard trainers to fighters. Powered by a 134 kW (180 hp) Hispano-Suiza 8Aa engine. Armament reduced to a camera gun.

Avia BH-23 (Czechoslovakia) Originally known as the BH-22N, this version of the BH-22 was built for training pilots in night-fighter tactics.

Avia BH-25 (Czechoslovakia) Six-passenger (plus pilot and mechanic) commercial airliner. First flown in prototype form in July 1926. Rectangular-section passenger cabin was 2.6 m (8 ft 6½ in) long, 1.3 m (4 ft 3 in) wide and 1.8 m (5 ft 11 in) high. Normally powered by one 313 kW (420 hp) Walter-built Jupiter engine. Five operated by Československá Letecka Společnost on its routes from Prague to Berlin and Vienna (in association with DLH) and to Rotterdam and elsewhere. Four were also operated by Serviciul National de Navigatie Aeriana of Romania.

Avia Av-35.

Avia BH-26 (Czechoslovakia) Two-seat light bombing and reconnaissance biplane powered by a Jupiter engine.

Avia BH-27 (Czechoslovakia) Projected three passenger high-wing cabin monoplane designed to be powered by an 82 kW (110 hp) Walter or similar engine.

Avia BH-28 (Czechoslovakia) Variant of the BH-26 fitted with a 287 kW (385 hp) Armstrong Siddeley Jaguar engine and built to the requirements of the Romanian government.

Avia 14.

Avia BH-29 (Czechoslovakia) Two-seat trainer with a plywood-covered fuselage and staggered wings of orthodox wood and fabric structure. Powered by a Walter NZ engine.

Avia Av-135.

Avia BH-33 (Czechoslovakia) Developed from the successful BH-21, this single-seat biplane fighter first flew in 1927. It won production contracts to equip the Czech Air Force and foreign air forces, despite considerable competition from abroad. The original version was of all-wood construction, except for the ailerons. The improved BH-33E of 1929 introduced a fuselage constructed of steel tubes and equal span wings (the BH-33 had an upper wing of smaller span) with slight dihedral on the lower. As with the first version, the BH-33E was powered by either a Walter-built Jupiter VI or VII engine. The final version was the larger BH-33L powered by a 373 kW (500 hp) Skoda L engine in a much neater cowling, made possible by not having to cowl-in the cylinder heads of the radial engine. Versions of the BH-33 were operated by the Czech Air

Avia

Avia BH-3.

Avia B-71 in Luftwaffe markings

Force for many years and others were exported to Russia and Yugoslavia (BH-33E). Production lines were also set up, under licence, in Yugoslavia (BH-33L) and Poland.

Data (BH-33L): *Engine* as above *Wing span* 9.5 m (31 ft 2 in) *Length* 7.22 m (23 ft 8¼ in) *Max T-O weight* 1,628 kg (3,589 lb) *Max level speed* 297 km/h (185 mph) *Range* 450 km (280 miles) *Armament* two forward-firing Mk 28 machine-guns

Avia B-534s.

Avia BH-33L.

Avia F.IX, F.39/F.IX D (Czechoslovakia) Based on the Fokker F.IX, the Avia F.IX was produced in 1932 as a bomber powered by three 335.5 kW (450 hp) Walter-built Jupiter engines and carrying a warload of up to 1,500 kg (3,307 lb). Twelve were built for the Czech Air Force as heavy bombers and two were exported to Yugoslavia, which also received a licence to manufacture the type. In 1934 Avia produced the F.39 or F.IX D. Unlike the previous aircraft (which was also often known as the F.39) the F.IX D was a 20 passenger commercial airliner powered by three Walter-built Pegasus IIM2 engines, each rated at 410 kW (550 hp). While the bomber had a maximum speed of 210 km/h (130 mph), the airliner could fly at 255 km/h (158 mph). Two F.IX Ds were delivered to ČSA in 1935.

Aviafiber Canard-2 FL (Switzerland) First flown in September 1977, this is a foot-launched sailplane of most unusual configuration. Production was expected to begin in 1978. A powered version was due for completion in 1978.

Aviamilano F8L Falco (Italy) See **Aeromere**.

Aviamilano P.19 Scricciolo (Italy) This side-by-side two-seat light monoplane was designed to meet the requirements of the Aero Club of Italy for a primary trainer. The prototype flew for the

first time on 13 December 1959 and three production versions were produced. The P.19 was the initial production version powered by a 74.5 kW (100 hp) Continental O-200-A flat-four engine. The P.19R was introduced in 1964 for glider-towing and general duties, powered by a 112 kW (150 hp) Lycoming O-320-A1A engine. The P.19 tr was similar to the P.19 but had a retractable landing gear. The first series of 25 production Scricciolos was completed in 1963.

Aviatik B and C series (Germany) The Aviatik B and C series aircraft (often referred to by contemporary British sources as P types because of the B.I.'s P-15A non-military designation) were the German equivalents of the RFC's B.E.2a/bs and B.E.2c/ds respectively. Interestingly, both types originated before the outbreak of World War I and started as unarmed reconnaissance aircraft with the observers in the forward cockpits. Apart from a few Aviatik C. Ias, later C.IIIs and B.E.2ds, this cockpit layout remained standard even when the aircraft were armed with machine-guns for defence against fighters. The first Aviatik version to enter service was the B.I powered by a 74.5 kW (100 hp) Mercedes D.I engine. It was joined soon after the outbreak of war by the 89.4 kW (120 hp) D.II-engined B.II, both versions seeing active service over the Western Front during the first phases of the war. It soon became apparent that aerial warfare was hotting up and the C.I appeared in 1915 with a 119 kW (160 hp) D.III engine and a Parabellum machine-gun for defence. In action the gun had to be manhandled onto rails mounted on each side of the forward cockpit, which greatly restricted the field of fire. The C.II powered by a 149 kW (200 hp) Benz Bz. IV engine was not produced in quantity. The series ended with the refined C.III of 1916, which remained operational until 1917.

Data (C.I): *Engine* as above *Wing span* 12.5 m (41 ft 0¼ in) *Length* 7.92 m (26 ft 0 in) *Max T-O weight* 1,240 kg (2,733 lb) *Max level speed* 142 km/h (88 mph) *Endurance* 3 h *Armament* one Parabellum machine-gun

Aviatik B.II and B.III (Austro-Hungary) Oesterreichische-Ungarische Flugzeugfabrik Aviatik was the Austro-Hungarian branch of the German Aviatik company but produced aircraft of original design. The B.II of 1915 (89.4 kW; 120 hp Austro-Daimler) and the B.III of 1916 (119 kW; 160 hp Austro-Daimler) were basically reconnaissance aircraft, but carried a small number of 10 kg bombs for light offensive missions. Defensive armament of a Schwarzlose machine-gun was standard on the B.III and a developed version of the B.II. The original B.II carried no gun. Following useful but unspectacular service, mostly on the Eastern Front, the Aviatiks Bs began (in 1916) a new career as trainers.

Aviatik B.I.

Aviatik D.I (Austro-Hungary) The D.I has the distinction of being Austria's first single-seat fighter to go into production and the home-designed fighter produced in greatest numbers for her air force during World War I. Basically a single-seat and smaller version of the C.I, the D.I was powered by a range of Austro-Daimler engines of 138–167.7 kW (185–225 hp) and was produced by five companies. Interestingly, it was often referred to as the Berg Scout or Berg D.I after its designer Julius von Berg. As production continued through 1917 and 1918, armament increased from one forward-firing Schwarzlose machine-gun (firing outside the propeller arc) to two guns with interrupter gear. Maximum speed was 186 km/h (116 mph).

Aviamilano P.19 Scricciolo.

Aviation Traders ATL.90 Accountant (UK) Single example of a 28-passenger airliner first flown on 9 July 1957. Power was provided by two 1,297 kW (1,740 ehp) Rolls-Royce Dart 512 turboprop engines.

Aviatik C.I.

Aviation Traders ATL.98 Carvair (UK) The Carvair was a DC-4 conversion to carry heavy freight (incl motor cars) or up to 84 passengers. The prototype flew for the first time on 21 June 1961 and entered service with British United Air Ferries (later British Air Ferries) in March 1962. A total of 23 Carvair conversions were completed. The conversion involved replacing the entire forward fuselage with a new nose section containing a hydraulically operated sideways-opening nose door and an elevated flight deck over the front of the cargo hold.

Aviatik C.I (Austro-Hungary) Following its experience with the B series of reconnaissance aircraft, Aviatik produced the C.I in 1917. Like the B.III, it had a single long cockpit for the pilot (forward) and the observer but was more heavily armed with one forward-firing machine-gun and one rear-mounted gun. Powered by either a 138 kW (185 hp) or 149 kW (200 hp) Austro-Daimler engine, the C.I had a very reasonable performance and was built in considerable numbers by five companies. Only its inherent structural weakness prevented it from receiving the acclamation that might otherwise have come its way. Nevertheless, it remained operational until the end of the war.

Aviatik D.I.

Aviation Traders/Bristol Britannia conversion (UK) Conversion of the Series 300 or 310 Britannia introduced a large hydraulically operated freight door, approx 1.93 m × 3.12 m (6 ft 4 in × 10 ft 3 in) in size, which incorporated a crew entry door. The cargo handling system, which accepted 3.17 m × 2.23 m (10 ft 5 in × 7 ft 4 in) pallets, employed a ball table at the door and roller racking with side guides along the cabin. Total cargo volume was 92.71 m³ (3,274 cu ft). Six conversions were carried out for BUA, Lloyd International and British Eagle.

Aviatik C.VI, modified version of the DFW C.V.

Aviation Traders

Aviation Traders/Vickers Vanguard Merchantman cargo conversion (UK) This cargo conversion of the Vanguard 953 for British European Airways introduced a hydraulically operated freight door 3.48 m long × 2.03 m deep (11 ft 7 in × 6 ft 8 in). Up to 11 pallets measuring 2.74 m × 2.23 m (9 ft 0 in × 7 ft 4 in) or eight of these plus two pallets measuring 3.17 m × 2.23 m (10 ft 5 in × 7 ft 4 in) can be carried. Work on the first Vanguard conversion for BEA began in 1968 and the first flight was made on 10 October 1969.

Avions J.D.M. Roitelet (France) Single-seat homebuilt ultra-light monoplane of 1949 powered by an 18.6 kW (25 hp) Poinsard engine. Built as the first of a proposed production series.

Avions Fairey Belfair (Belgium) Two-seat light cabin monoplane powered by a 46 kW (62 hp) Walter Mikron engine. Its design originated from the single-seat Tipsy S, designed and built in 1935 by Mr E. O. Tips. This aircraft (and the two-seater which followed) met considerable success and manufacturing licences were acquired in England, France, Spain and South Africa. The two-seater became the Belfair after World War II.

Avions Fairey Firefly (Belgium) The Firefly was a very neat single-seat fighter, originally of wooden structure, powered by a 324 kW (435 hp) Felix engine and produced for possible service with the RAF. The Firefly I flew for the first time on 12 November 1925. A second version, produced with an all-metal structure and known as Firefly IIM, followed. Power was provided by a 358 kW (480 hp) Rolls-Royce Kestrel IIS engine. Although the RAF favoured its rival, the Hawker Fury, the aircraft eventually entered production in Belgium for the Aéronautique Militaire, having won a competition against fighters from other countries and survived a terminal velocity dive to prove its strength. The first five Firefly IIMs for Belgium were built in the UK, but the remaining 60 were constructed in Belgium by the Société Anonyme Belge Avions Fairey – a company formed as an offshoot of the British concern to manufacture the fighter. These entered service from 1933. A naval fighter version of the Firefly IIM, known as the Firefly IIIM, failed to gain production contracts.

Data: *Engine* as above *Wing span* 9.6 m (31 ft 6 in) *Length* 7.52 m (24 ft 8 in) *Max T-O weight* 1,492 kg (3,290 lb) *Max level speed* 358 km/h (223 mph) *Armament* two forward-firing Vickers machine-guns

Avions Fairey Fox (Belgium) See **Fairey Fox**.

Avions Fairey Junior (Belgium) The Junior was the first Belgian aircraft of new design to be built after the end of World War II. A single-seat touring and training monoplane, it could be powered by an engine of between 18.6 and 48.4 kW (25 and 65 hp); those fitted included the 46 kW (62 hp) Walter Mikron and 26 kW (35 hp) J.A.P.

Avions Fairey T.66 Tipsy Nipper (Belgium) The Tipsy Nipper is a simple low-cost ultra-light single-seat semi-aerobatic monoplane, which was produced in Belgium as the T.66 Mk 1 and the T.66 Mk 2 until 1961. The former was the initial production version with a 30 kW (40 hp) Pollmann HEPU engine. The prototype first flew on 2 December 1957 and the first production model on 10 March 1959. The Mk 2 was identical except for having a 33.5 kW (45 hp) Stark Stamo 1400A dual-ignition engine. By the end of 1960 Nippers were being flown by aero clubs and private owners in 17 countries. Worldwide rights for the Nipper are currently held by Nipper Components and Kits of the UK.

A.V.Roe biplane (UK) Alliott Verdon Roe's first full-size aeroplane, built with the proceeds (£75) from his award-winning model aeroplane which had flown at Alexandra Palace in April 1907. Originally fitted with a 6.7 kW (9 hp) J.A.P. engine. Failed to become airborne under its own power until re-engined with an 18 kW (24 hp) Antoinette. Achieved its first 'hop' on 8 June 1908.

A.V.Roe triplane (UK) Following earlier unsuccessful work on a triplane, Roe completed the first of two Roe I triplanes in May 1909. An acute shortage of funds had resulted in the use of wood instead of steel tubing for the airframe, the wings being covered in paper, and the installation of the 6.7 kW (9 hp) J.A.P. engine. Crashes during his first attempts to fly at Lea Marshes, Essex, caused damage to the aircraft's wings. But on 13 July 1909 he managed a flight of 30 m (100 ft) to become the first Briton to make a flight in an all-British aeroplane. Ten days later he completed a flight of 275 m (900 ft). A second modified aircraft was later constructed with a 15 kW (20 hp) J.A.P. engine and flew in December 1909.

A.V.Roe II triplane (UK) The Roe II was the first aircraft to be built by A. V. Roe and Company in 1910, and was basically an improved Model I with a 26 kW (35 hp) Green engine. Construction was of spruce, with the wings, fuselage and tail unit fabric-covered. Two were built: the first for the company and for exhibition and the second for sale to W. G. Windham.

A.V.Roe III triplane (UK) This mid-1910 two-seater represented quite an advance over the earlier triplanes, introducing trailing-edge ailerons (on the upper wing of the prototype and the middle wing on subsequent Roe IIIs), tail unit elevator and a rudder of greater area. The 26 kW (35 hp) J.A.P.-engined prototype first flew on 24 June 1910. Three more Roe IIIs were built, all with 26 kW (35 hp) Green engines, one of which was eventually sold to the Harvard Aeronautical Society.

A.V.Roe IV triplane (UK) Roe's last 'pioneering' triplane, the Roe IV was the most elegant of the early aircraft but for some reason reverted to the outmoded wing warping method of lateral control. The bottom wing was of considerably reduced span and chord and the tapering triangular-section fuselage (of which only the forward portion was covered) ended with a new tail unit comprising a tailplane with elevators and a rudder. Power was provided by the standard Green engine. Only one example was built and this was operated at the Avro Flying School from the late summer of 1910.

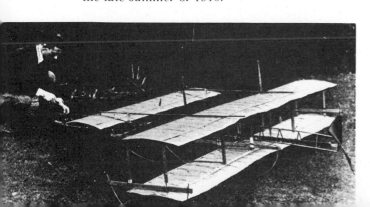

Avions Fairey Fox VIC.

Avro Type D (UK) On 1 April 1911 the first flight took place of the prototype Avro Type D. This aircraft, powered by the familiar Green engine, was A. V. Roe's first biplane since his Roe I and represented the company's first truly successful aeroplane. Easy to fly, it retained wing warping for lateral control. Altogether, about six Type Ds were built, with various engines and as single- and two-seaters.

Avro Type E (UK) Designed and built to a War Office specification, the Type E was a two-seat biplane powered by a 44.7 kW (60 hp) E.N.V. engine. The rectangular-section fuselage was fabric- (rear half) and metal- (forward) covered and great care had been taken to reduce drag to a minimum. The first flight was undertaken on 3 March 1912. Although its maximum speed of 80 km/h (50 mph) and rate of climb were slightly below those required, it handled extremely well and was enthusiastically received by those who piloted it. Its main importance was, however, that it served as a stepping-stone to the Avro 500.

Avions Fairey Firefly IIM.

Avro 500 (UK) In an attempt to improve upon an already fine aircraft, Avro produced a second Type E, which became the prototype Avro 500. It was basically similar to the earlier aircraft but was powered by a 37.25 kW (50 hp) Gnome rotary engine, covered by the angular nose of the fuselage. The large side radiators of the original Type E were not required, and a cut-out in the centre-section of the upper wing improved vision. The first flight was made on 8 May 1912 and, despite reduced power, the 500 could climb to 610 m (2,000 ft) over twice as fast as the Type E. Twenty-one production aircraft were built, including six for the Navy, five single-seaters for No 3 Squadron, RFC (formed in May 1912 from No 2 Aeroplane Company, Air Battalion) and seven two-seat trainers for the Central Flying School (among the first aircraft taken on charge, along with Short biplanes and Maurice Farman S.7 Longhorns).

Avro Type F (UK) Single-seat braced mid-wing monoplane powered by a 26 kW (35 hp) Viale radial engine. Important as the world's first aircraft with a fully enclosed cabin. One aircraft only, first flown on 1 May 1912.

Avro Type G (UK) Two-seat military biplane powered by a 44.7 kW (60 hp) Green engine. Important as the world's first aircraft with two seats in a fully enclosed cabin. One aircraft only, first flown in August 1912.

Alliott Verdon Roe with his 1907 model aeroplane.

A. V. Roe biplane.

Avro 501 and 503 (UK) One 501 and four 503s built as large two-seat military biplanes for the RNAS and for Germany (one 503). Powered by 74.5 kW (100 hp) Gnome engines and operated as land- and seaplanes.

Avro 504 series (UK) Non-specialist readers will know, and perhaps remember, the participation in World War II of such aircraft as the Avro Anson and Lancaster. They may not have heard of the Avro 504, yet this little two-seat trainer must be numbered among the great aircraft of British aviation history.

A. V. Roe triplane I.

Alliott Verdon Roe with the Roe III.

The 504 was designed in 1912 and it was decided to introduce this aircraft to the aviation scene by entering it for the second Aerial Derby, which was scheduled for 20 September 1913, to gain as much interest and free publicity as possible. Thus, it was built behind closed doors and when subsequently flown to Hendon to take part in the race it was seen in public for the first time. It was perhaps something of an anticlimax that it did not win, coming in fourth at an average 107 km/h (66.5 mph). But this was a considerable achievement for an aircraft first flown only three days previously.

Production of 12 504s for the War Office began in the summer of 1913, the first of more than 8,000 for military service to be built during World War I. Successive variants were to remain in production for almost 20 years. The last to be operated by the RAF were seven civil 504Ns impressed for service in 1940 and used for glider-towing.

The 504 was designed for training and private flying, and few could have foreseen that this aircraft would ever be flown in anger. Yet when the RFC's No 5 Squadron flew to France on 13 August 1914, its small force included several 504s.

Although little used in military operations, the type is remembered for an attack on the German Zeppelin sheds at Friedrichshaven, carried out on 21 November 1914 by three 504s of the RNAS, each armed with four 20 lb bombs. One Zeppelin was destroyed in its shed and hits on the associated gasworks resulted in an explosion which caused great damage.

The original 504 (and subsequent 504A) was powered by a 59.6 kW (80 hp) Gnome rotary engine. Successive variants included the 504B with 59.6 kW (80 hp) Gnome or Le Rhône; 504C/D with 59.6 kW (80 hp) Gnome; 504E with 74.5 kW (100 hp) Gnome; 504F with 56 kW (75 hp) Rolls-Royce Hawk; 504G/H with 59.6 kW (80 hp) Gnome; 504J with 74.5 kW (100 hp) Gnome or 59.6 kW (80 hp) Le Rhône; 504K with 97 kW (130 hp) Clerget, 74.5 kW (100 hp) Gnome or 82 kW (110 hp) Le Rhône; 504L seaplane with 112 kW (150 hp) Bentley B.R.1, 97 kW (130 hp) Clerget or 82 kW (110 hp) Le Rhône; and 504N with 112 kW or 134 kW (150 or 180 hp) Armstrong Siddeley Lynx, 112 kW (150 hp) Armstrong Siddeley Mongoose, 74.5 kW or 85.7 kW (100 or 115 hp) Bristol Lucifer, or 149 kW (200 hp) Wright Whirlwind engine. Many other engines were installed experimentally or were specified for aircraft built for foreign civil or military use, or licence-built abroad. Worth mentioning were the 504R Gosports built for the Argentine, Estonian and Peruvian air services, powered by 112 kW (150 hp) Armstrong Siddeley Mongoose engines.

This lightweight but robust biplane proved to be a superb training aircraft. When Maj R. R. Smith-Barry became commander of No 1 Reserve Squadron at Gosport in 1916, he evolved a completely new system of flying instruction based on demonstration and explanation. So good were the results that this squadron was developed into the School of Special Flying – using the Smith-Barry system and Avro 504J – with pupils encouraged to fly these aircraft to the limit of their capabilities. Later 504Ns were equipped especially for use by the RAF's Central Flying School, becoming the first instrument or blind-flying trainer to serve with the RAF.

Extensively built by A. V. Roe for home and

export customers, in both civil and military guises, 504s were also built by manufacturers in Australia, Belgium, Canada, Japan, Netherlands East Indies, and Russia.

In an era when the general public regarded aviation as a form of transportation suited only to the brave or foolhardy, the 504 was used by Sir Alan Cobham's 'Flying Circus' and Capt Percival Phillips' Cornwall Aviation Company, carrying large numbers of civilians on their first flight. It has been reported that Capt Phillips alone carried something like 91,000 passengers into the air, the majority of them in an Avro 504K.

Data (504K): *Engine* 82 kW (110 hp) Le Rhône rotary *Wing span* 10.97 m (36 ft 0 in) *Length* 8.97 m (29 ft 5 in) *Max T-O weight* 830 kg (1,829 lb) *Max level speed* 145 km/h (90 mph) *Range* 402 km (250 miles)

Avro 510 (UK) Large two-seat biplane, the prototype of which was built originally for the Circuit of Britain Race. Powered by a 112 kW (150 hp) Sunbeam Nubian engine. Six seaplanes built for the RNAS in 1914.

Avro 519 (UK) Large biplane of 1916 powered by a 112 kW (150 hp) Sunbeam Nubian engine. Upper wing of much greater span than lower. Four built: two single-seaters for the RNAS and two two-seaters for the RFC.

Avro 531 Spider (UK) Single-seat sesquiplane fighter of 1918 originally powered by an 82 kW (110 hp) Le Rhône engine. Later re-engined with a 97 kW (130 hp) Clerget, with which it achieved 193 km/h (120 mph). Not put in production.

Avro 534 Baby (UK) Light low-powered biplane, the prototype of which appeared in April 1919 as a single-seater, powered by a 26 kW (35 hp) Green engine. Seven other aircraft built as single- and two-seaters. These achieved con-siderable success in handicapped air races and performed notable long-distance flights. Two built as seaplanes, one as the Avro 554 for spotting seals in the Antarctic.

Avro 536 and 546 (UK) Avro 536 built as a modified Avro 504K, featuring a wider fuselage to accommodate a pilot and four passengers (in pairs to the rear of the pilot). Twenty-one produced for joyriding flights. One Avro 536 built as a two-seater for long-distance flying. One Avro 546 produced with enclosed accommodation for the passengers.

Avro 547 (UK) Triplane commercial airliner, the first of only two aircraft built appearing in early 1920. Enclosed accommodation for four passengers. Powered by one 119 kW (160 hp) Beardmore engine. Subsequently purchased by Queensland and Northern Territory Aerial Services (QANTAS). Second more powerful aircraft proved unsuccessful.

Avro 548 (UK) Basically a three-seat and inline engine conversion of the Avro 504K for civil flying. Small numbers produced by Avro and other companies, powered by 60 kW (80 hp) Renault and 89.4 kW (120 hp) Airdisco engines.

Avro 549 Aldershot (UK) Three-seat heavy bomber of 1922 powered by a 484.5 kW (650 hp) Rolls-Royce Condor III engine. Fifteen built for No 99 Squadron, RAF, serving between 1924 and 1926. Maximum bomb load 907 kg (2,000 lb). Maximum level speed 177 km/h (110 mph).

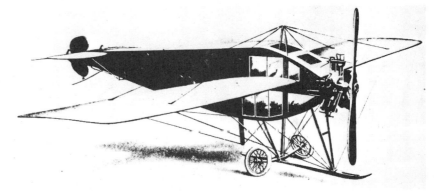

Avro 552 (UK) Basically an Avro 504K fitted with an ex-S.E.5a 134 kW (180 hp) Wolseley Viper engine and an upper wing centre-section fuel tank. Subsequently produced in small numbers as single- and two-seat landplanes and two-seat seaplanes by Avro and Canadian Vickers for RCAF, Argentine Navy and civil use.

Avro 555 Bison (UK) Deck-landing reconnaissance and Fleet gunnery spotting biplane, first flown in 1921. Twelve Bison Is built for the FAA

Avro Type D undergoing trials as a seaplane.

Avro Type D.

Drawing of the Avro Type F.

Avro 500.

Avro

in 1923. One converted to an Avro 555B amphibian with a central float. Main production during 1925–26 comprised 41 Bison IIs, each with the upper wing raised on struts above the fuselage and no dihedral. Operated from the aircraft carrier HMS *Eagle* in the Mediterranean, on board HMS *Furious* and at Hal Far, Malta.
Data: *Engine* one 357.7 kW (480 hp) Napier Lion II *Wing span* 14.02 m (46 ft 0 in) *Length* 10.97 m (36 ft 0 in) *Max T-O weight* 2,630 kg (5,800 lb) *Cruising speed* 145 km/h (90 mph) *Range* 557 km (340 miles)

Avro 558 (UK) Two very light single-seat biplanes built for the 1923 Lympne Trials. Powered by 500 cc Douglas motorcycle and 698 cc Blackburne Tomtit engines.

Avro Type G.

Avro 561 and 563 Andover (UK) Similar in many respects to the Aldershot, the 561 Andover was produced to fly the RAF's Cairo–Baghdad air service. Accommodation was for 12 passengers, or stretchers as an air ambulance. Only three built. A commercial version, produced as the 563, was the first Avro aircraft to be produced specially for airline service on main routes. Only one built. This was subsequently operated by Imperial Airways on its cross-Channel services. Both versions powered by one 484.5 kW (650 hp) Rolls-Royce Condor III engine.

Avro-built Cierva autogiros (UK) See **Cierva**

Avro 504.

Avro 504K.

Avro 581, 594 and 616 Avian (UK) Wooden two-seat Avro 581 Avian powered by a 52 kW (70 hp) Armstrong Siddeley Genet engine; built for the Lympne Trials. As the 581E powered by a 63.3 kW (85 hp) Cirrus II engine, used by H. J. L. Hinkler for the first solo flight to Australia in 1928 (see **Chronology** 7 Feb 1928). In production with various engines as the Avro 594 in the UK and USA between 1927 and 1929. Replaced by the metal fuselage Avro 616 Avian IVM and Sports Avian variant in 1929, produced in small numbers in the UK, Canada and the USA. Two aircraft, named *Southern Cross Junior* and *Minor*, used by Kingsford Smith for the UK–Australia–UK attempts during 1930–31.
Data (Avian IVM): *Engine* 89.4 kW (120 hp) de Havilland Gipsy II *Wing span* 8.53 m (28 ft 0 in) *Length* 7.39 m (24 ft 3 in) *Max T-O weight* 726 kg (1,600 lb) *Cruising speed* 145 km/h (90 mph) *Range* 579 km (360 miles)

Avro 618 Ten series (UK) Following an in-depth look at the Fokker F.VIIB/3m in Holland, Avro acquired a licence to build the aircraft in the UK. The first British-built F.VIIB/3m, known as the Avro 618 Ten (two crew and eight passengers), was exhibited at Olympia in 1929. In all 14 were built, each powered by three 179 kW (240 hp) Armstrong Siddeley Lynx IV radial engines. Among the operators of the Ten could be counted Imperial Airways, Australian National Airways and the Egyptian government. One was supplied for the personal use of the Viceroy of India.

Although Avro went on to produce several variants of the Ten in the light of experience with the aircraft, 1929 also saw the appearance of the Avro-designed 619 Five: a smaller and stouter derivative powered by three 78 kW (105 hp) Genet Major engines. Only four were built. From the 619 Five was developed the 624 Six, of which three were built – two going to China.

The 16-passenger Avro 642/2m originally appeared with two 335 kW (450 hp) Jaguar VID engines and a rounded nose which retained the streamlining of the fuselage. This aircraft was subsequently modified to have a more conventional stepped nose and individual rounded (instead of a continuous glazed section) windows in the fuselage sides. According to the 1934 *Jane's* 'the cabin is large and lofty and can be arranged in a variety of ways to suit various types of air traffic'. Although this was true, only one was ever built. The final variant was the seven-seat 642/4m

powered by four 179 kW (240 hp) Lynx IVC engines. This aircraft was used by the Viceroy of India and replaced the earlier Ten.

Avro 621 Tutor (UK) The original Avro Trainer of 1929 was designed as a replacement for the Avro 504N and featured a welded steel-tube structure and a 115.5 kW (155 hp) Armstrong Siddeley Mongoose IIIA radial engine. Twenty-two were built for the RAF and three for the Irish Army Air Corps. Following evaluation Avro began mass production of the 621 for the RAF under the new name of Tutor. It eventually completed more than 390, including 14 Sea Tutors with long single-step Alclad floats. The structure of the Sea Tutor was specially treated against corrosion by sea water; a metal propeller and hand-turning gear were also standard. Because the latter features were desirable for a seaplane but not a landplane, the Sea Tutor was one of the few types of seaplane that could not be converted into landplane form. Power plant was a 160 kW (215 hp) Lynx engine. In addition, numbers of Tutors were delivered to Denmark, Greece, Poland and South Africa, plus others for civil use. A further 57 were built under licence in South Africa for the air force and a very small number in Denmark for the navy.

Data (Tutor): *Engine* normally one 179 kW (240 hp) Armstrong Siddeley Lynx IVC radial *Wing span* 10.36 m (34 ft 0 in) *Length* 8.08 m (26 ft 6 in) *Max T-O weight* 1,115 kg (2,458 lb) *Max level speed* 196 km/h (122 mph) *Endurance* 2 h 45 min

Avro 626, Prefect and 637 (UK) The 626 was specially designed for the export market for the complete instruction of military flying personnel in all duties, from *ab initio* flying training onwards – including the operation of all normal armament and equipment. It was similar to the Tutor but the fuselage was arranged to accommodate alternatively the armament and equipment for each of the separate branches of training, including offensive and defensive gunnery, bombing, wireless telegraphy, aerial photography, navigation and flying training (including night- and blind-flying). The fuselage differed from that of the Tutor by having in effect three cockpits, while remaining a two-seater. The third and rear cockpit provided the mounting for a turret or gun-ring (as required) or was used for the camera or W/T equipment. Power was provided by either a 179 kW (240 hp) Lynx IVC or 194 kW (260 hp) Cheetah V engine.

The 626 remained in production until 1939; examples were operated by the armed forces of Argentina, Belgium, Brazil, Canada, Chile, China, Egypt, Estonia, Greece, Ireland, Lithuania and Portugal. A special two-cockpit version of the 626, known as the Prefect, was also developed as a navigational trainer. Seven were delivered to the RAF and four to the RNZAF. The 637 was an armed patrol version of the 626, of which eight served with the Kwangsi Air Force.

Avro 631 and 643 Cadet (UK) The Cadet was developed specially for use in civil training schools where a robust aircraft with similar flying characteristics to the Tutor was required, but where it was uneconomic to operate a machine of that size. The Cadet was, therefore, basically a smaller and less powerful version of the Tutor. The original 631 Cadet version of 1931 was powered by a 100.5 kW (135 hp) Armstrong Siddeley Genet Major I radial engine and had wooden wings. Nineteen were built. The 643 of 1934 introduced a raised rear seat for improved forward vision; eight of these were built. The 643 Mk II Cadet of 1934 was powered by a 112 kW (150 hp) Genet Major IA engine with an inverted fuel system and, apart from four aircraft, was produced exclusively for the Royal Australian Air Force (34 aircraft).

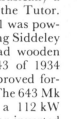

Avro 636 and 667 (UK) The 636 was a two-seat intermediate trainer of 1935, of which not even the prototype was completed. It was designed to be powered by one of several different engines. When fitted with an Armstrong Siddeley Panther and by covering the rear cockpit, it could be transformed into a single-seat fighter. A single-seat version was also envisaged. Four Avro 636s, with the actual Avro designation of 667s, were purchased by the Irish Army Air Corps. These were powered by 343 kW (460 hp) Jaguar VIC engines giving a maximum speed of 282 km/h (175 mph).

Avro 638 Club Cadet and 640 Cadet (UK) Basically a folding-wing version of the Cadet for flying clubs and private owner/pilots. Powered by a 97 kW (130 hp) de Havilland Gipsy Major I, 100.5 kW (135 hp) Genet Major I or 104.3 kW (140 hp) Cirrus Hermes IVA engine. Seventeen were built from 1933. A variant of the design was the Avro 640 Cadet, which accommodated two passengers in front of the pilot. Nine were built, powered by Genet Major I or 104.3 kW (140 hp) Cirrus Hermes IV engines.

Avro

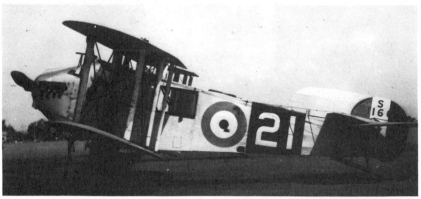

Avro 555 Bison.

Avro 621 Tutor.

Avro 563 Andover.

Avro 641 Commodore (UK) Five-seat cabin biplane of 1934 powered by a 179 kW (240 hp) Armstrong Siddeley Lynx IVC engine. Six built.

Avro 652A Anson (UK) The Anson was derived from the Avro 652 – two of which were built to an Imperial Airways order of 1933 – and was among the first aircraft in Europe to reach high performance by adopting the twin-engined, cantilever low-wing formula with retractable landing gear. Avro designers, having had experience with Fokker aircraft and derivatives, used a similar steel tube fuselage construction and basically moved the wooden wings of the earlier types from a high to a low position.

The production prototype flown in December 1935 was a forerunner of 7,195 Avro-built Anson Is for the RAF, RN, RAAF, SAAF, RCAF, Greece and Egypt. Production Ansons were first issued to No 48 Squadron, which put the RAF's first low-wing, retractable landing gear monoplane into service on 6 March 1936. Armament included two 45 kg (100 lb) and eight 9 kg (20 lb) bombs, a forward-firing Vickers gun and a Lewis gun in a turret amidships. Operational with Coastal Command between 1936 and 1939 and for air-sea rescue until 1942, the majority were delivered as turretless trainers for the Commonwealth Air Training Plan in Canada, Australia and South Africa.

The Anson 10, introduced in 1943, had strengthened floors for continental freight runs by Air Transport Auxiliary. After the war surplus Ansons were sold to civil charter firms and the air forces of Belgium, Holland, Iran, Israel, Norway, Portugal and Saudi Arabia. Increased headroom, introduced in 1944, created the Anson 11 or 12

according to engine. The latter, furnished as a feeder-liner eight-seater, became the Avro 19 Series 1 or Series 2 (tapered metal wing) for the RAF, BEA and civil operators in the UK and abroad. Final variants of 1948–49 were Anson 18 trainers for Afghanistan and India; Anson T.20 (perspex nose) for navigation training in Southern Rhodesia; T.21 (metal nose) for the RAF in the UK; and T.22 radio trainer.

Data (Anson I): *Engines* two 238.6 kW (320 hp) Armstrong Siddeley Cheetah IX *Wing span* 17.22 m (56 ft 6 in) *Length* 12.88 m (42 ft 3 in) *Max T-O weight* 3,476 kg (7,663 lb) *Max level speed* 272 km/h (170 mph) *Range* 1,062 km (660 miles)

Avro 679 Manchester (UK) The Manchester was a twin-engined, medium-range bomber. First flown in prototype form in July 1939 with twin fins and rudders and new 24-cylinder X-type Rolls-Royce Vulture engines. A central fin was added during flight trials. Maximum bomb load was 5,080 kg (11,200 lb). Defensive armament comprised 0.303 in machine-guns in nose, rear and mid-upper rotating turrets. Production aircraft were built by Avro (156 Mk Is) and Metropolitan-Vickers (44).

The bomber first entered service in November 1940 with No 207 Squadron, RAF, and carried out its first operational mission to Brest during the night of 24–25 February 1941. The triple fin arrangement was later deleted and enlarged endplate fins and rudders were fitted to a longer tailplane (Manchester Mk IA). Unfortunately the Vulture engine proved unreliable and the Manchester's operational life ended on 25 June 1942 with a raid on Bremen. A four-engined development of the Manchester became the Lancaster.

Data: *Engines* two 1, 311.5 kW (1,760 hp) Rolls-Royce Vultures *Wing span* 27.46 m (90 ft 1 in) *Length* 20.98 m (68 ft 10 in) *Max T-O weight* 22,680 kg (50,000 lb) *Cruising speed* 473 km/h (294 mph) *Range* 2,623 km (1,630 miles)

Avro 683 Lancaster (UK) Most famous of all Avro military aircraft and without doubt the most successful heavy night bomber to be deployed over Europe during World War II. The Avro 683 evolved almost accidentally as a result of recurrent failure of the insufficiently developed Rolls-Royce Vulture engines installed in the twin-engined Avro Manchester.

Owing to delays in the full development of the

Edwin Aldrin descends from Apollo Lunar Module *Eagle*.

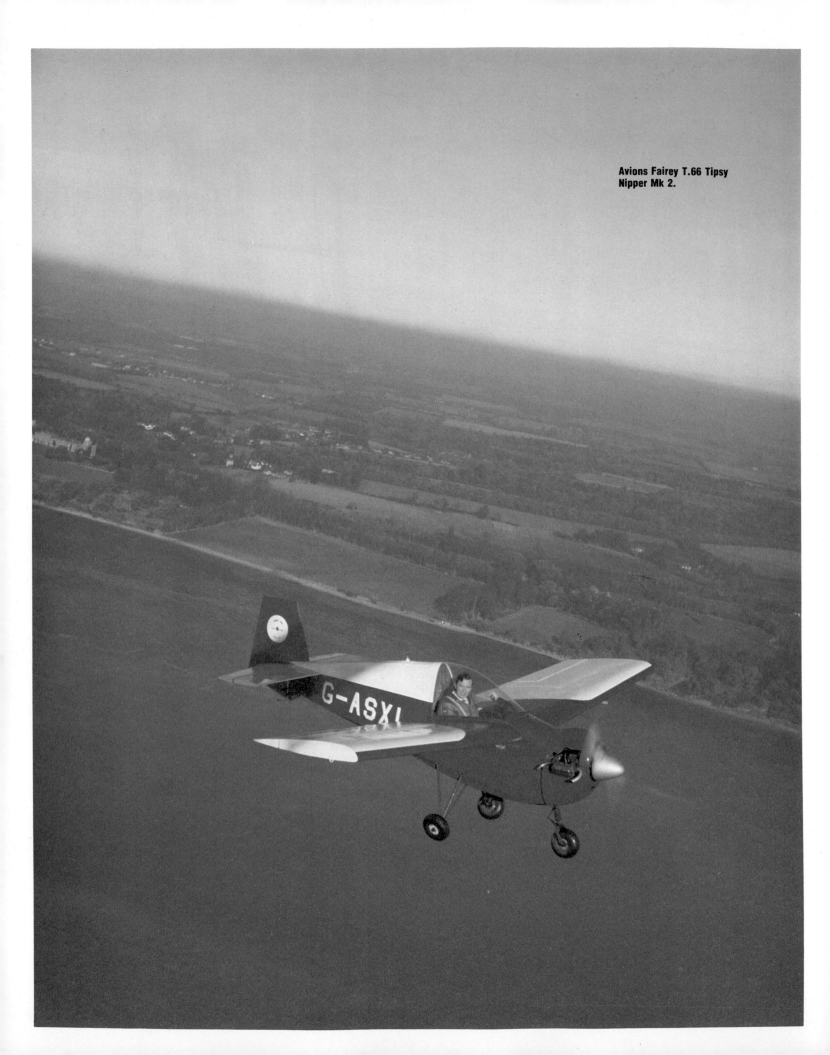

Avions Fairey T.66 Tipsy
Nipper Mk 2.

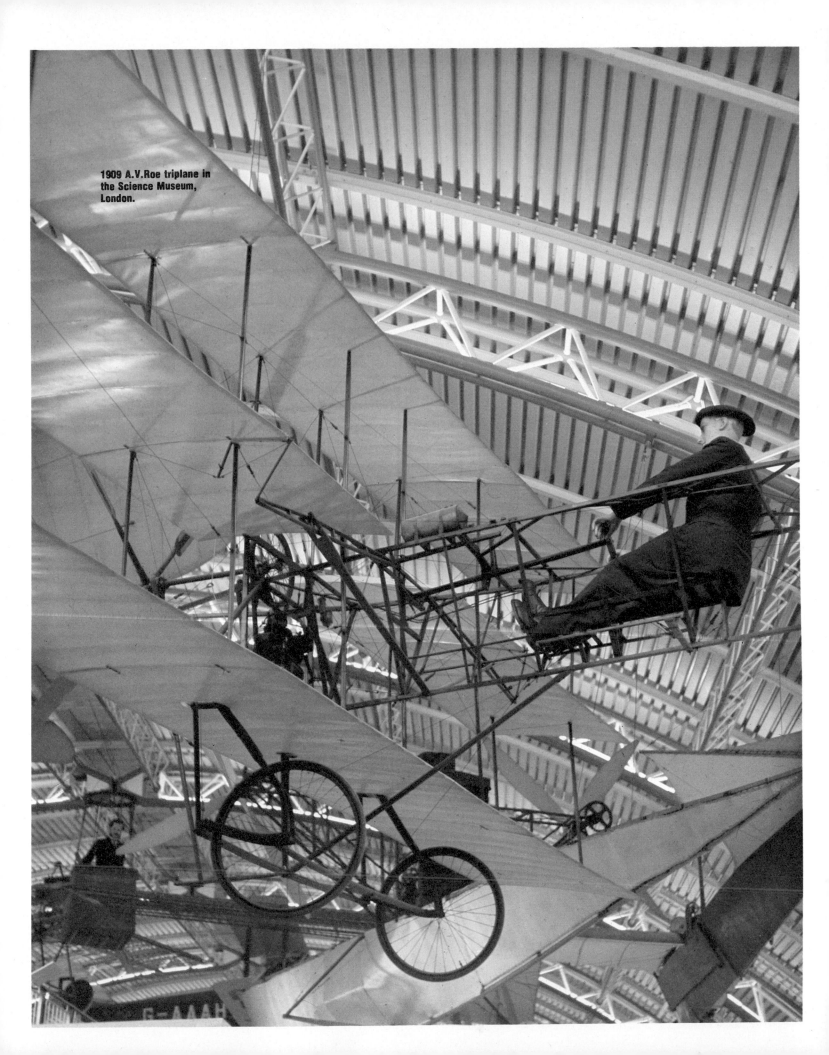

1909 A.V.Roe triplane in
the Science Museum,
London.

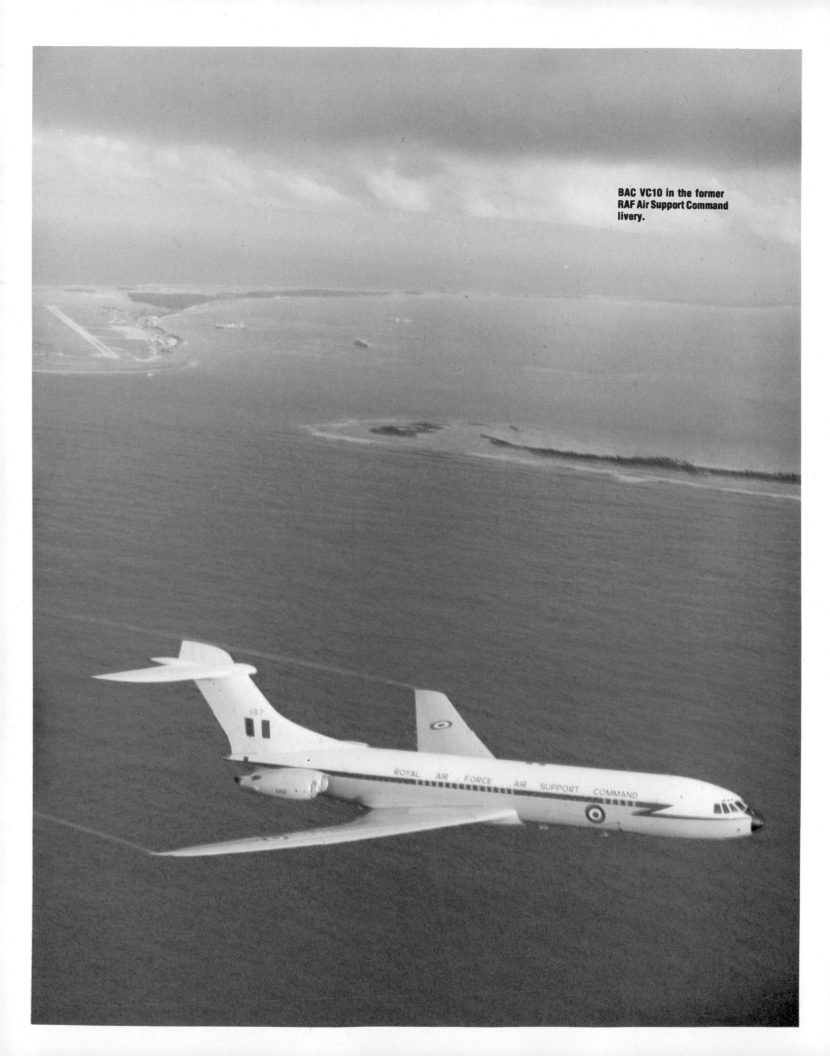

BAC VC10 in the former RAF Air Support Command livery.

BAC Lightning F.6 of No
23 Squadron RAF escorts
a Soviet *Bear*.

Royal Navy BAe Sea
Harrier FRS.1s.

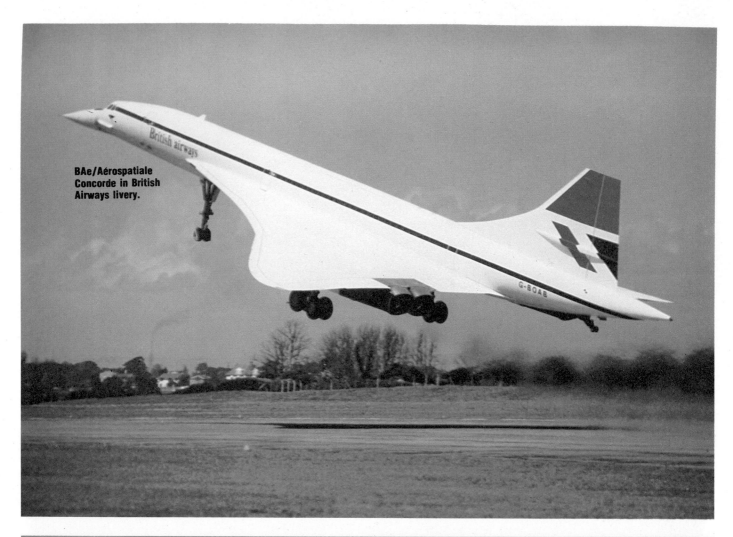

BAe/Aérospatiale
Concorde in British
Airways livery.

Col 18** Bell X-1A.

Bell Model 206L
LongRanger.

Champion (Bellanca)
Super Decathlon.

Vulture engine, the decision was taken in mid-1940 to design a new version of the Manchester with four Rolls-Royce Merlin engines. The first conversion made use of about 75 per cent of the Manchester's parts and assemblies, the principal change being the provision of a new centre-section of the wing with mountings for Merlin engines. This aeroplane became the first prototype of the Lancaster. A second prototype fitted with Merlins and significantly modified in detail was designed, built and flown in just eight months. The first production Lancaster I flew just over five months later, its power plant comprising similar 954 kW (1,280 hp) Rolls-Royce Merlin XX in-line liquid-cooled engines, each driving a three-blade constant-speed and fully feathering propeller. Because of the possibility of some interruption in Merlin production, the Lancaster II was built with 1,229.5 kW (1,650 hp) Bristol Hercules VI radial engines. These fears did not materialise, with the result that only 300 Lancaster IIs were built.

First operational RAF squadron to be equipped with Lancasters was No 44, which used them operationally for the first time on 3 March 1942 – laying mines in the Heligoland Bight. Defended by ten machine-guns and carrying a maximum bomb load of 6,350 kg (14,000 lb), the Lancaster was – and soon proved itself to be – a formidable weapon in the hands of the RAF, which had, by mid-1942, learned a great deal about night bombing operations over Europe. By comparison with contemporary four-engined bombers it was statistically the most effective, dropping 132 tons of bombs for each aircraft lost on operations; the corresponding figure for the Halifax and Stirling were 56 and 41 tons respectively. The Lancaster was so right, from the beginning, that there were very few changes in airframe design during its wartime service. Improved power plants, however, provided steadily improving performance: the Lancaster VII, for example, with 1,207 kW (1,620 hp) Merlin 24 engines, had a maximum take-off weight of 30,844 kg (68,000 lb) by comparison with the 22,680 kg (50,000 lb) of the early Is. Bomb load changed considerably, the cavernous bomb bay being designed originally to carry bombs of up to 4,000 lb, with a total bomb load of 6,350 kg (14,000 lb); it was modified progressively to carry the 22,000 lb *Grand Slam* bomb.

The Lancaster will be remembered for its part in two spectacular operations: the breaching of

the Möhne and Eder dams on the night of 16–17 May 1943 by No 617 Squadron (led by Wing Cdr Guy Gibson); and the sinking of the German battleship *Tirpitz*. Its contribution to victory in World War II is best measured, however, by the total of 608,612 tons of bombs delivered, which represented two-thirds of the total bomb load dropped by the RAF from the time of its entry into service. A total of 7,366 Lancasters were built (including Mk Xs in Canada) and the type remained in front-line service with the RAF until 1954. Canada had some photo-reconnaissance Lancasters in service in 1964.

Data (Lancaster I): *Engines* four 954.5 kW (1,280 hp) Rolls-Royce Merlin 24s *Wing span* 31.09 m (102 ft 0 in) *Length* 21.13 m (69 ft 4 in) *Max T-O weight* 30,844 kg (68,000 lb) *Max level speed* 443 km/h (275 mph) *Combat range* about 2,670 km (1,660 miles) *Armament* ten 0.303 in machine-guns and up to 6,350 kg (14,000 lb) of bombs

Avro 638 Club Cadet.

Avro 641 Commodore.

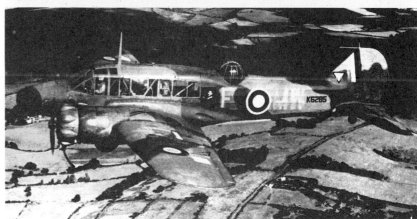

Avro Anson I.

Avro 685 York (UK) The York transport aircraft was developed from the Lancaster bomber. The original prototype first flew in July 1942. The type was intended as an interim transport, pending completion of newer types designed primarily for transport duties. To expedite production the York was designed to incorporate the wings, engines, landing gear and tail unit of the Lancaster. A radically new all-metal square-section large capacity fuselage was introduced. The first prototype was converted to the one-off Mk 2 York, with Bristol Hercules radial engines; and the third prototype *Ascalon* became Churchill's wartime transport. Production by Avro during 1945–48 included 208 for the world trunk routes of RAF

Avro

Avro 685 York.

Transport Command. Civil Yorks were built for BOAC (25), British South American Airways (12), Flota Aerea Mercante Argentina (5) and Skyways (3). One additional York was built by Victory Aircraft, Canada.

Yorks of BOAC, independent operators and the RAF flew 3,000 h during the Berlin Airlift of 1948–49 (see **Chronology**). RAF and BOAC Yorks were withdrawn from service in 1957. Surplus Yorks were used by airlines in the Near East, South Africa and Canada and by the French Navy.

Data: *Engines* four 1,207 kW (1,620 hp) Rolls-Royce Merlin 24s *Wing span* 31.09 m (102 ft 0 in) *Length* 23.93 m (78 ft 6 in) *Max T-O weight* 30,844 kg (68,000 lb) *Cruising speed* 375 km/h (233 mph) *Range* 4,345 km (2,700 miles)

Avro Anson T.20.

Avro 683 Lancaster bombers.

Avro 688 and 689 Tudor (UK) The original Type 688 Tudor was conceived in 1943 to Specification 29/43 as a commercial conversion of the Lancaster for use over the North Atlantic as a quick replacement for the bomber-transports then being used. As then envisaged, the Tudor was to be a modification of the Lancaster IV (later the Lincoln) with a new pressurised fuselage to carry a load of 1,705 kg (3,760 lb) over 6,437 km (4,000 miles). Following the issue of the specification to Avro in March 1944 two prototypes were ordered and production contracts for BOAC (14 aircraft, plus six later) followed later in the same year and in 1945.

Avro 688 Tudor 4B.

While development of the original Tudor con-

tinued – despite many difficulties – a new version with considerably lengthened fuselage was planned. This version was intended for use on the BOAC Empire routes; two prototypes were ordered in 1944, followed by production contracts. By this time the first version of the Tudor was available in its production form, but BOAC requirements had altered. This, and the aircraft's shorter than planned range, meant that the Tudor was no longer required as a passenger-carrying transport. British South American Airways Corporation (BSAAC), however, began using a modified version on their route to South America in 1947, and some of the aircraft laid down for BOAC were turned over to this operator. The Tudor 2 (with the lengthened fuselage) suffered a similar fate, and these were planned for conversion to freighters for BOAC.

Following the unexplained disappearance of two of BSAAC's Tudors in January 1948 and January 1949 while on passenger services, the Minister of Civil Aviation decreed that the type should no longer be used on passenger routes. The ban on passenger carrying lasted until 1954 when a Tudor belonging to Aviation Traders received an unrestricted C of A for passenger flights – following extensive modification to the aircraft which included fitting 1,311 kW (1,760 hp) Rolls-Royce Merlin 623 engines. Virtually all surviving Tudors were similarly modified by Aviation Traders. Five Tudors were later further modified by fitting large freight doors; known thereafter as Super Traders, they remained in service until 1959.

The versions of the Tudor are listed below:

Avro 688 Tudor 1 Powered by four Rolls-Royce Merlin 102, 621 or 623 engines. The original short-fuselage Tudor for the Atlantic route, seating 12–24 passengers. First flown 14 June 1945

Avro 689 Tudor 2 Four Rolls-Royce Merlin 102 or 621 engines. The original long-fuselage version for BOAC South African and Australian routes. Accommodation for up to 60 passengers. Thirty production aircraft ordered in November 1944 and a further 49 in April 1945, plus six to be built in Australia. Order reduced to 50 in 1946 and 18 in 1948. Final 18

were to consist of two Mk 2s for development work, six Mk 5s for BSAAC and ten modified to freighters for BOAC.

Avro 688 Tudor 3 Two additional Mk 1 airframes converted by Armstrong Whitworth for use as VIP transports by ministers.

Avro 688 Tudor 4 Four Rolls-Royce Merlin 621 or 623 engines. A modification of the Tudor 1 to meet BSAAC requirements. Fuselage lengthened by 1.83 m (6 ft) and accommodation for 32 passengers. Four aircraft originally ordered. Subsequently augmented by conversion of BOAC Mk 1s.

Avro 688 Tudor 4B Two Tudor 1s of BOAC contract modified to have lengthened fuselage of the Mk 4 for use by BSAAC, but retaining the flight engineer's station as on Mk 1. Accommodation for 28 passengers.

Type 689 Tudor 5 Four Rolls-Royce Merlin 621 engines. A modification of the Tudor 2, of which six were completed, five for BSAAC. Accommodation for 44 day or 36 night passengers. BSAAC aircraft delivered without passenger seats and used on Berlin Airlift. Sixth airframe converted to have four Bristol Hercules 120 engines.

Avro Super Trader See main text.

Data (Tudor 1): *Engines* as above *Wing span* 36.58 m (120 ft 0 in) *Length* 24.23 m (79 ft 6 in) *Max T-O weight* 32,205 kg (71,000 lb) *Cruising speed* 338 km/h (210 mph) *Range* 5,842 km (3,630 miles)

Avro 691 Lancastrian (UK) The Lancastrian was a high-speed long-range transport conversion of the Lancaster bomber. The first conversions were made in Canada by Victory Aircraft Ltd for Trans-Canada Air Lines and were operated by this company on behalf of the Canadian government on transatlantic mail and passenger services between Montreal and Prestwick. The Canadian Lancastrians were fitted with Packard-built Rolls-Royce Merlin engines and accommodated ten passengers.

Production of the Lancastrian was later undertaken by Avro and deliveries were made to the RAF, BOAC and British South American Airways Corporation. The four main variants of the aircraft were: the Lancastrian C.1, a nine-seat version of which 23 were produced for the RAF but all but two were subsequently operated by BOAC; Lancastrian C.2, which was similar to the C.1 and 38 were produced for the RAF; Lancastrian 3, initially for BSAAC, accommodating 13 passengers (18 eventually delivered, most for

Avro 696 Shackleton MR.3s in SAAF markings.

BOAC); and the C.4 for the RAF, eight of which were delivered.

Avro 694 Lincoln (UK) The last piston-engined bomber to serve with the RAF, the Lincoln conformed to Specification B.14/43 and was virtually a scaled-up version of the Lancaster. Indeed, the first version of the Lincoln was originally known as the Lancaster Mk IV. The first prototype flew on 9 June 1944.

Normally powered by four Rolls-Royce Merlin 85 engines with annular radiators, the Lincoln was armed with twin 0.50 in Browning machine-guns in a Boulton-Paul Type F nose turret; two 20 mm Hispano Mk 4 or Mk 5 cannon in a Bristol B-17 Mk II dorsal turret; twin 0.50 in machine-guns in a Boulton Paul Type D rear turret and up to 6,350 kg (14,000 lb) of bombs.

Avro 694 Lincoln.

Intended for use in the Pacific theatre of war, the Lincoln appeared just too late to go into operational service, but instead became the RAF's standard post-war heavy bomber. Avro built 168 production aircraft, supplemented by 79 from Metropolitan-Vickers and 281 from Armstrong Whitworth. Six were also built in Canada and 54 with nose extensions in Australia by the Government Aircraft Factory at Fishermen's Bend, NSW. Thirty Lincolns were also diverted to the Argentine Air Force. Several versions of the bomber were produced during the production runs: Lincoln B.1 with Merlin 85 engines; B.2 with Merlin 68A engines; Lincoln Mk 3 intended to be the ASR version but became the Shackleton; Lincoln B.4 with Merlin 85s; Lincoln B.15 built in Canada; and Lincoln B.30 Australian version with Merlin 85 or 102 engines.

First issued to the RAF in September 1945, the bomber eventually equipped 20 squadrons. No 97 Squadron and others were detached to Singapore in 1950 for anti-terrorist raids and to Kenya in 1954. One was converted for the bulk uplift of fuel oil and made 45 civil flights during the Berlin Airlift.

Data: *Engines* four 1,304 kW (1,750 hp) Rolls-Royce Merlin 85s *Wing span* 36.58 m (120 ft 0 in) *Length* 23.86 m (78 ft 3½ in) *Max T-O weight* 37,194 kg (82,000 lb) *Cruising speed* 383 km/h (238 mph) *Max range* 5,745 km (3,570 miles)

Avro

Avro Shackleton (UK) The Shackleton was a maritime reconnaissance aircraft with a stressed skin fuselage and Avro Tudor and Lincoln components (see Lincoln Mk 3). Armament comprised four 20 mm cannon, two machine-guns, depth charges and/or bombs, and it carried a nose-mounted ASV scanner. Shackleton MR.1s entered service with No 120 Squadron and other Coastal Command squadrons from 1951; and the production run of 77 aircraft included MR.1As with wider outer nacelles.

The first of 69 MR.2s, each with a streamlined nose and a 360°-scan radar under the rear fuselage, came into use in the UK and Malta in 1952. Thirty-four MR.3s with tricycle undercarriages, auxiliary Viper 203 turbojet engines, improved cockpit canopies, dorsal turrets deleted and wing tip-tanks (giving a 24-hour endurance) were issued in 1957. Eight were delivered to the South African Air Force. In 1971 No 8 Squadron, RAF, re-formed at Kinloss with MR.3s converted to AEW.2s with large ventral radomes for early warning duty; 11 remained operational in 1979 with 7 MR.3s serving in South Africa.
Data (AEW.2): *Engines* 1,829 kW (2,455 hp) Rolls-Royce Griffon 57As *Wing span* 36.52 m (119 ft 10 in) *Length* 26.62 m (87 ft 4 in) *Max level speed* 282 km/h (175 mph) *Range* 4,665 km (2,900 miles)

Avro 698 Vulcan (UK) The first jet bomber to employ the delta-wing configuration. The original Avro 698 Vulcan prototype was developed to Air Ministry Specification B.35/46, issued on 1 January 1947, flying for the first time on 30 August 1952. It was then fitted with four Rolls-Royce Avon turbojets, but was later re-engined with Bristol Siddeley Sapphires and subsequently Rolls-Royce Conways.

A second prototype powered by four Bristol Siddeley Olympus 100s – with a slightly longer fuselage to eliminate the need for shortening the nose-wheel leg during retraction – made its first flight on 3 September 1953. It was later fitted with wings having a redesigned leading edge with compound sweepback and it made its first flight in this form on 5 October 1955. On 31 August 1957 it began flight testing the larger wing of the Vulcan B.2.

All production Vulcans were fitted with wings having the revised leading-edge configuration and two main versions were produced. The first production version was the Vulcan B.1, powered by Olympus Mk 101 or Olympus Mk 102 engines. All of these engines were converted later to Olympus Mk 104 standard. Planned re-equipment of three Bomber Command squadrons of the RAF with this version was completed in 1960. The B.1A version was given electronics in a bulged tail-cone, like the B.2. A total of 45 B.1/1As were built. The B.2 was a developed version with Olympus Mk 201 or 301 engines, wing of increased span (with elevon controls) and the ability to carry the Blue Steel stand-off nuclear bomb. The first production B.2 flew on 30 August 1958. Production was completed in 1964.

Two versions of the Vulcan remain in service. The B.2, with in-flight refuelling capability, currently serves in an overland strike role (not strategic bombing) and carries free-fall nuclear weapons or 21 × 1,000 lb high-explosive bombs. The SR.2 is a conversion of the B.2 for strategic reconnaissance, and one squadron serves with the RAF.
Data (Vulcan B.2): *Engines* four 88.97 kN (20,000 lb st) Rolls-Royce Bristol Olympus Mk 301 turbojets *Wing span* 33.83 m (111 ft 0 in) *Length* 30.45 m (99 ft 11 in) *Max T-O weight* more than 81,645 kg (180,000 lb) *Max cruising speed* 1,005 km/h (625 mph) *Combat radius* 4,630 km (2,875 miles) with flight refuelling

Avro 698 Vulcan B.2.

Avro 701 Athena (UK) Two-seat trainer designed (to Specification T.7/45) for advanced flying training, day and night navigation, gunnery, bombing and photography. It could also be used as a glider tug. Fifteen production aircraft built as T.2 gunnery trainers for the RAF Flying College, Manby, powered by the 954 kW (1,280 hp) Rolls-Royce Merlin 35 engine.

Avro 706 Ashton (UK) Large research aircraft, six of which were built for the Ministry of Supply to act as test-beds for research into jet operations. The first made its maiden flight on 1 September 1950. Powered by four 22.24 kN (5,000 lb st) Rolls-Royce Nene 5 and 6 engines.

Avro 707 (UK) Built primarily to carry out extensive research into the behaviour of delta wings at low speeds and to provide information which would be used in the final design of the Vulcan bomber. The first aircraft made its maiden flight at Boscombe Down on 4 September 1949, but was destroyed subsequently in an accident. It was followed by the 707B for low-speed research, two 707As for high-speed research and a dual-control 707C.

Avro 748 (UK) See **BAe (HS) 748**

Azcarate O-E-1 and E (Mexico) Two-seat light bombing or reconnaissance sesquiplane and two-seat advanced training or sporting sesquiplane respectively (quoted at the time as the Sesquiplane and Biplane). Designed during 1928 by General Brigadier Ingeniero de Aeronautica Juan F. Azcarate, Officer Commanding the Mexico Military Aviation. Four O-E-1s built and ten Es during 1928–29; one of the former flew around Mexico in 58 stages between 30 September and 18 December 1928.

BAC 221 (UK) Redesigned and rebuilt Fairey Delta 2 research aircraft with new delta wings, control surfaces, engine intakes and landing gear. It was instrumented and equipped for use by the Royal Aircraft Establishment, Bedford. Again modified ane returned in 1966, it was used to research subsonic, transonic and supersonic speed ranges up to Mach 1.6 and slim delta wings at low speeds.

BAC (Hunting) H.126 (UK) Jet-flap research aircraft first flown on 26 March 1963. Special features included wings with alternative dihedral angles of 4° and 8°; ailerons and flaps with slots in leading and trailing edges, through which air was passed; narrow slit along trailing edge of wings for ejection of engine efflux; and variable-incidence tailplane hydraulically operated in conjunction with elevator.

BAC TSR.2 (UK) Attack and reconnaissance bomber first flown on 27 September 1964 and designed for service with the RAF. Powered by two 136.2 kN (30,610 lb st) Bristol Siddeley Olympus 22R turbojets. Max level speed Mach 2.05–2.5. Could perform completely automatic sorties without visual reference and had an accuracy of weapon delivery within 'tens of feet'. Cancelled because of defence cut-backs.

BAC VC10 (UK) The prototype of this airliner flew for the first time on 29 June 1962. The VC10 entered service on BOAC's route to West Africa on 29 April 1964. Four production variants and a

Avro 706 Ashton.

Avro 707s flying with Vulcan prototype.

modification of the prototype were produced: the Model 1101, of which 12 went to BOAC accommodated 16 first-class and 93 economy passengers; the Model 1102, of which two went to Ghana Airways, one with a large hydraulically operated cargo door between the standard passenger doors and both with 4% chord leading-edge extension from wing root to fence; the Model 1103, of which three went to British United Airways with cargo door and extended leading edge; Model 1106, of which 14 went to RAF Air Support Command with cargo door, folding hatracks, machined cargo floor, extended leading edge, 97 kN (21,800 lb st) Conway RCo.43 Mk 301 turbofans and fin fuel tank; and the Model 1109, the prototype brought up to airline standard for Laker Airways, with the Model 1106 wing. Standard engines for the VC10 were four 90.6 kN (20,370 lb st) Rolls-Royce Conway RCo.42 turbofans in lateral pairs on each side of the rear fuselage. RAF basic transport

BAC 221.

BAC TSR.2.

BAC Jet Provost T.5s.

BAC (English Electric) Canberra Mk 82 for Venezuela.

BAC VC10.

version designated VC10 C.1. C.2 is the unconfirmed designation of flight refuelling tanker conversions of five VC10s and four Super VC10s.

Data (C.1): *Engines* as above *Wing span* 44.55 m (146 ft 2 in) *Length* 48.36 m (158 ft 8 in) *Max T-O weight* 146,510 kg (323,000 lb) *Max cruising speed* 935 km/h (581 mph) *Range* 6,275 km (3,900 miles) *Accommodation* 150 passengers or 76 stretchers and 6 medical attendants

BAC Jet Provost (UK) The Jet Provost (formerly Hunting P.84) became the standard two-seat basic jet trainer of the RAF, and is only now being replaced by the BAe (HS) Hawk. More than 450 were built. The versions that remain in service comprise: the Jet Provost T.3 unpressurised trainer with a Rolls-Royce Viper Mk 102 turbojet engine (7.78 kN; 1,750 lb st), first delivered to the RAF in June 1959; the Jet Provost T.5 uprated trainer (produced as the BAC 145 Jet Provost) with a pressurised cabin, lengthened nose, redesigned windscreen, canopy and wings (157 RAF T.3/5s retrofitted with VOR and DME and redesignated T.3A/5As); and the Jet Provost T.51/52 unpressurised export models of the T.3 and 4 respectively, with provision for two machine-guns, gun camera and underwing stores including rockets, AS.11 guided missiles, bombs or two reconnaissance packs. The trainer remains in service in the UK, Iraq, Singapore, Sri Lanka, Sudan and Venezuela.

Data (T.5): *Engine* one 11.12 kN (2,500 lb st) Rolls-Royce Viper Mk 202 turbojet *Wing span* 10.77 m (35 ft 4 in) *Length* 10.27 m (33 ft 8½ in) *Max normal T-O weight* 3,866 kg (8,524 lb) *Max level speed* 708 km/h (440 mph) *Range* 1,450 km (900 miles)

BAC Super VC10 (UK) The Super VC10 was designed to carry larger payloads than the standard VC10, for a relatively small increase in take-off distance. The fuselage is 4.27 m (13 ft) longer and accommodates 163–174 economy-class passengers or a mixed payload such as 32 first-class and 99 economy passengers. It has the 4% chord leading-edge extension and Conway RCo.43 engines. Two versions were produced: the Model 1151 for BOAC (17 aircraft equipped to carry 16 first-class and 123 economy passengers) and the Model 1154 for East African Airways with the large freight door (five aircraft, the last delivered in February 1970).

BAC (English Electric) Canberra (UK) Early developments of the turbojet engine, with then very limited power output, restricted somewhat the size and type of aircraft able to take advantage of this new power plant. Thus, it was not until Air Ministry Specification B.3/45 was issued that the English Electric Company was able to design and build Britain's first turbojet-powered bomber – the first such aircraft to serve with the RAF. A prototype flew for the first time on 13 May 1949.

The original intention had been to produce a two-crew aircraft which would rely upon radar for the accurate delivery of its bomb load. But although the four prototypes were built to this configuration, the first production Canberra B.2s carried a crew of three and were configured for visual bombing. Of mid-wing monoplane configuration, these aircraft were powered by two 28.91 kN (6,500 lb st) Rolls-Royce Avon 101 engines and could carry internally 2,722 kg (6,000 lb) of conventional or nuclear weapons. Canberras entered RAF service with No 101 Squadron at RAF Binbrook in May 1951. These aircraft were unarmed, relying (as had the wartime de Havilland Mosquito) on being able to show their opponents a 'clean pair of heels'.

Subsequent variants included: the B.6 bomber with 32.92 kN (7,400 lb st) Avon 109s; the B(I).6 intruder variant; B(I).8 two-seat long-range night interdictor or high-altitude bomber, built also as the B(I).58 for India and B(I).12 for New Zealand and South Africa; a conversion of the B.6 with additional underwing hardpoints for weapons, designated B15; and a generally similar B.16 with more radar equipment. Performance was such that it was logical to develop photo-reconnaissance versions. The PR.3 (based on the B.2) first flew on 19 March 1950 and was followed by the PR.7 (similar to the B.6) and the high-altitude PR.9. Other RAF Canberras included T.4/11/17 and 19 trainers; and the target-towing TT.18.

The Canberra has been supplied to many air forces, has been licence-built in Australia, and has the distinction of being the only modern aircraft of British design to be licence-built in the USA. Under the USAF designation B-57 the Martin Company built 403. At a later date a number of these were converted by General Dynamics to serve as ultra high-altitude strategic reconnaissance aircraft. These were provided with a wing span of 37.19 m (122 ft), two 80 kN (18,000 lb st) Pratt & Whitney TF33-P-11 turbofan engines (replacing the conventional power plant), plus two 14.68 kN (3,300 lb st) Pratt & Whitney J60-P-9 turbojets in underwing pods, and many equipment and avionics changes to fit them for their specialised role.

Data (B(I). 8): *Engines* two 32.92 kN (7,400 lb st) Rolls-Royce Avon 109s *Wing span* 19.49 m (63 ft 11½ in) *Length* 19.96 m (65 ft 6 in) *Max T-O weight* 24,925 kg (54,950 lb) *Max level speed* 871 km/h (541 mph) at 12,190 m (40,000 ft) *Range* 1,296 km (805 miles) *Armament* four 20 mm guns in underfuselage pack, two 1,000 lb bombs or AS.30 missiles underwing, and three internally stowed 1,000 lb bombs

BAC (English Electric) Lightning (UK) W. E. W. Petter, of the English Electric Company, who had been responsible for design of the Canberra bomber, was to achieve another milestone for the RAF in designing its first single-seat

BAC (English Electric) Lightning F.2A.

fighter able to exceed the speed of sound in level flight. So advanced was the design – and so complex the aerodynamic problems which this design posed – that Britain's first transonic wind tunnel was built to facilitate testing. Short Brothers at Belfast were instructed by the Ministry of Supply (MoS) to build a research aircraft able to investigate aspects of Petter's design which the MoS considered more revolutionary than functional. Thus Short's S.B.5 had a wing which could investigate sweepback at 50°, 60° and 69°, landing gear which could be adjusted to cater for the CG changes in these different configurations and, at a later stage, a low-set tailplane. When both wind tunnel testing and S.B.5 confirmed that Petter's design had been right from the outset, the MoS let English Electric get on with construction of two prototypes and a static test airframe.

The first P.1A prototype flew on 4 August 1954, showing very clearly that the company had a significant aeroplane on their hands, but one which needed some further development. The three resulting P.1B prototypes had more powerful engines mounted one above the other in the rear fuselage, with the lower engine well forward of the upper; a changed nose air intake to the engines, with a centrally mounted shock cone; modified airbrakes; plain trailing-edge flaps; and an improved cockpit canopy. The first of these flew on 4 April 1957 and the production F.1 Lightning began to enter service with the Central Fighter Establishment at RAF Coltishall in December 1959.

By the spring of 1966 the fully developed F.6 was beginning to enter RAF service, proving that the RAF had indeed acquired an important aircraft. Speed was in excess of Mach 2 in level flight and the aircraft's operational ceiling was 18,290 m (60,000 ft). As far as the RAF was concerned this represented a quantum jump in performance, but it was not only the performance which was revolutionary. It was also the first RAF fighter designed as an integrated weapons system, which meant that detection of the target and positioning of the Lightning for an interception were carried out by electronic systems. Once the Ferranti fire-control radar had locked on to a target, an airborne computer ensured that steering and interception data were fed to an automatic control system which positioned the Lightning so that its missiles were locked on to the target before instructing the pilot to fire them.

Martin B-57s.

Bachem Ba 349 Natter.

F.3s (which entered RAF service in January 1964) were the major production variant. A total of 338 Lightnings were built by English Electric and the British Aircraft Corporation. These included T.4 and T.5 two-seat trainers, equivalent to the F.1A and F.3 respectively and retaining full operational capability. In addition to those which have seen RAF service, Lightnings have also been supplied to the air forces of Kuwait and Saudi Arabia.

Data (F.6): *Engines* two 72.77 kN (16,360 lb st; reheat) Rolls-Royce Avon 301 turbojets *Wing span* 10.62 m (34 ft 10 in) *Length* 16.23 m (53 ft 3 in) *Max T-O weight* approx 22,680 kg (50,000 lb) *Max level speed* Mach 2 plus *Range* 1,287 km (800 miles) *Armament* Red Top or Firestreak air-to-air missiles, or two rocket packs or two 30 mm guns in ventral packs

Bach Air Transport (USA) Eight-passenger high-wing cabin monoplane of the late 1920s powered by three Wright and/or Pratt & Whitney radial engines. A number built for regular operation on the West Coast of the USA.

Bachem Ba 349 Natter (Viper) (Germany) Vertical take-off interceptor powered by a 19.62 kN (4,410 lb st) Walter HWK 509C-1 rocket motor. First vertical test flight made on 19 December 1944, launched from a steel-girder ramp. Thirty-six completed and a number deployed to intercept bombers but never used in action. Armament comprised 24 73 mm or 33 55 mm rockets carried in nose. Rate of climb was more than 11,280 m (37,000 ft)/min.

BAC (BAC 167) Strikemaster (UK) The Strikemaster was developed from the BAC 145 Jet Provost. It has the same airframe but is powered by a 15.2 kN (3,410 lb st) Rolls-Royce Bristol Viper Mk 535 turbojet engine. It has eight underwing hardpoints, enabling it to carry up to 1,360 kg (3,000 lb) of weapons, including Matra launchers each for 18 × 68 mm SNEB rockets or other rocket packs, four 510 lb ballistic or retarded bombs, 250 kg or 500 kg or smaller bombs, napalm, and other stores (plus the two 7.62 mm FN machine-guns). This makes it suitable for counter-insurgency combat operations, reconnaissance (with the BAe/Vinten five-camera pod), pilot and weapon training.

The first Strikemaster was flown on 26 October 1967 and 155 have been built (including a few for store against possible new orders). The versions so far delivered are listed below:

Mk 55 Designation of five BAC 145s in service with the Sudan Air Force.

Mk 80 Twenty-five ordered for the Royal Saudi Air Force, with deliveries between 1968 and 1969.

Mk 80A Follow-on order for the Royal Saudi Air Force comprising ten aircraft. An additional order for ten aircraft placed in 1977.

Mk 81 Delivery of four aircraft for the People's Democratic Republic of Yemen completed in May 1969.

Mk 82 Twelve aircraft for the Sultan of Oman's Air Force. Delivery completed in December 1969.

Mk 82A Eight ordered for the Sultan of Oman's Air Force. Delivery of a further four was completed in July 1976.

Mk 83 For Kuwait Air Force. Twelve aircraft delivered between 1969 and 1971.

Mk 84 Delivery of 16 aircraft to the Singapore Air Defence Command completed in September 1970.

Mk 87 Six aircraft for the Kenya Air Force. Delivery complcted in 1971.

Mk 88 Total of 16 ordered for the Royal New Zealand Air Force. Operational with No 14 Squadron of RNZAF. Used also for advanced training.

Mk 89 Twelve for the Ecuadorean Air Force. Deliveries completed between 1973 and 1976.

Data: *Engine* as above *Wing span* 11.23 m (36 ft 10 in) *Length* 10.27 m (33 ft 8½ in) *Max T-O weight* 5,215 kg (11,500 lb) *Max level speed* 760 km/h (472 mph) *Range* 2,224 km (1,382 miles)

BAe (BAC) One-Eleven (UK) First announced in 1961, the One-Eleven is a short/medium-range airliner. Five versions have been produced: Series 200 initial production version with 46 kN (10,330 lb st) Spey 25 Mk 506 turbofans and accommodation for up to 89 passengers (56 built, entering service in April 1965 with BUA and Braniff); Series 300 longer range version with 50.7 kN (11,400 lb st) Spey Mk 511 engines and increased standard fuel tankage (nine built);

BAe (BAC) One-Eleven Series 320.

Series 400, a version of the Series 300 modified to US requirements, with lift dumpers and dropout emergency oxygen masks (69 built); Series 475 with fuselage and accommodation of Series 400, wings and power plant of Series 500, and modified landing gear (nine built); and Series 500 stretched version with accommodation for 119 passengers, extended wingtips, strengthened landing gear (80 built, plus about 80 to be built under licence in Romania).

Data (Series 500): *Engines* two 55.8 kN (12,550 lb st) Rolls-Royce Spey Mk 512 DW turbofans *Wing span* 28.5 m (93 ft 6 in) *Length* 32.61 m (107 ft 0 in) *Max T-O weight* 47,400 kg (104,500 lb) *Max level and cruising speed* 871 km/h (541 mph) *Still-air range* 3,484 km (2,165 miles)

BAe (HS) 125 (UK) Developed as a private venture, the BAe (HS) 125 is a twin-turbofan business aircraft which is also suitable for use by armed forces in a variety of roles, including communications, troop carrying, as an ambulance, for airways inspection, and as an economical trainer for pilots, navigators and specialised radio and radar operators. All versions of the HS 125 can operate from unpaved runways without modification.

First flown in August 1962. Over 400 have been sold, with more than 80% for export (including 229 in North America by early 1979).

Production of the Hawker Siddeley 125 Series 1 (8 built), 1A (64 built), 1B (13 built), 2 (RAF Dominie T.1, 20 built), 3 (2 built), 3A (12 built), 3B (15 built), 3A-R and 3A-RA (20 built), 3B-RA (16 built), 400A (69 built), 400B (47 built), 600A (33 built) and 600B (39 built) has ended. The Series 2 navigation trainer version serves as the Dominie T.1 with the RAF, whose No 32 Squadron also operates four Series 400 in the communications role under the designation CC.1 and two Series 600 under the designation CC.2. Other air forces supplied include those of Brazil, Ghana, Malaysia, Mexico and South Africa as well as the Argentinian Navy, Qantas, the Australian Department of Civil Aviation, the Brazilian Government and the South African Department of Civil Aviation.

Current versions are the 125 Series 700A and 700B introduced in 1976. As with earlier versions, the suffix indicates the intended market: the Series 700A being for North America; the Series 700B for the rest of the world. The prototype was a converted Series 600 airframe, re-engined with Garratt-AiResearch TFE 731-3-1H turbofan engines (each 16.46 kN; 3,700 lb st). Similar conversions of existing turbojet-powered 125s are offered but new production Series 700 aircraft embody many other refinements, including improvements to the airframe and interior.

Data (Series 700): *Engines* as above *Wing span* 14.33 m (47 ft 0 in) *Length* 15.46 m (50 ft 8½ in) *Max T-O weight* 10,977 kg (24,200 lb) *Max level speed* 592 km/h (368 mph) *Range* 4,318 km (2,683 miles)

BAe (HS) 146 (UK) Originally announced by Hawker Siddeley in 1973, this short-range airliner was shelved until 1977 when Hawker Siddeley became part of British Aerospace and limited

BAe (HS) 125s under construction.

funding was provided to allow the manufacture of assembly jigs and systems rigs and the resumption of design and tunnel tests. Two versions are projected: the first as the Series 100 with accommodation for 70–90 passengers or a mixed passenger/freight layout, able to operate from short semi-prepared airstrips with minimal ground facilities; the second as the Series 200 80–109 passenger version with greater range, for operation from paved runways. The first flight of a prototype is expected in autumn 1980.

BAe (HS) 748 (UK) The first prototype 748 short/medium-range turboprop airliner (originally designed by Avro) made its maiden flight on 24 June 1960. UK production of the Series 1 (18 built with 1,401 kW; 1,880 ehp Dart Mk 514 engines) and 2 (with 1,569 kW; 2,105 ehp Dart 531 engines, including two Andover CC.2s for the Queen's Flight and four for Air Support Command) has been completed. The Series 2A, which superseded the Series 2 in production, differs only in having two 1,700 kW (2,280 ehp) Rolls-Royce Dart RDa.7 Mk 534-2 or Mk 535-2 turboprops for improved performance. The latter was the standard production aircraft until 1979. Sales (including Andover C.1s for the RAF) totalled 332 by late 1978. (See **Hawker Siddeley Andover**.)

BAe (HS) 748 Coastguarder.

BAe (HS) AV-8A Harrier.

From 1979 the BAe (HS) 748 Series 2A was replaced by a new Series 2B basic model with improved 'hot and high' Dart 536-2 engines, a 1.22 m (4 ft) span increase, modified tail surfaces and other refinements. Modification kits to bring 2As to 2B standard will be made available. The civil transport 748 is available optionally with a large rear freight door, as fitted to military 748s, which also have strengthened floors. Twenty-eight military transports are currently in service with the Belgian Air Force, Brazilian Air Force, Ecuadorean Air Force, Indian Air Force, Nepal Royal Flight and other undisclosed customers.
Data (Series 2A): *Engines* as above *Wing span* 30.02 m (98 ft 6 in) *Length* 20.42 m (67 ft 0 in) *Max T-O weight* 21,092 kg (46,500 lb) *Cruising speed* 452 km/h (281 mph) *Range* 2,483 km (1,543 miles) *Accommodation* 40–58 passengers, or up to 58 troops, 48 paratroops, 24 stretchers and nine attendants or freight in military version
BAe (HS) 748 Coastguarder (UK) Medium-range maritime patrol aircraft based on the 748 Series 2A airliner. Suitable for surface surveillance, fishery protection, pollution/contraband control, search and rescue, tactical surveillance and offshore oilfield patrol. Demonstrator first flew on 18 February 1977. Crew comprises two pilots, two beam observers and a tactical navigator. Fuel tankage increased to 10,047 litres (2,210 Imp gallons).
BAe (HS) Harrier (UK) The Harrier is the

western world's only operational fixed-wing V/STOL strike fighter. When it first entered RAF service with the Harrier OCU (No 233 Squadron) on 1 April 1969, it was the world's first and only operational aircraft of its type. Developed via the P.1127/Kestrel (see **Hawker Siddeley**). Nearly 250 aircraft of the Harrier family had been delivered by 1979. Harriers have also operated from the decks of more than 30 ships, including US, Argentinian, Spanish, Indian, French, Australian and British aircraft carriers; Italian and British cruisers; and US amphibious support ships.
The Harrier GR.1, 1A and 3 are single-seat close-support and tactical reconnaissance versions for the RAF. The former version was fitted initially with the 84.5 kN (19,000 lb st) Rolls-Royce Pegasus 101 vectored-thrust turbofan engine. When retrofitted subsequently with the 89 kN (20,000 lb st) Pegasus 102, it was redesignated GR.1A. Aircraft now in service have the 95.6 kN (21,500 lb st) Pegasus 103 engine as the GR.Mk 3. The designations Harrier T.2, 2A and 4 apply to the two-seat version, retaining full combat capability. The first development two-seater flew on 24 April 1969. The designations apply to the retrofitting of later Pegasus engines as for the single-seat version described above. Harrier Mk 50 (USMC designation AV-8A) is the single-seat version for the United States Marine Corps, with provision for carrying Sidewinder air-to-air missiles. An initial quantity of 12 was ordered in 1969 but subsequent orders brought the total to 102, including eight Mk 54 (TAV-8A) operational trainers. All US Harriers now have Pegasus 103 engines; they equip three USMC combat squadrons. Six Mk 55 AV-8As and two TAV-8As, known as Matadors and designated T/AV-8S, are also operational with the Spanish Navy.
An Advanced Harrier study was completed in 1973 by Hawker Siddeley, Rolls-Royce, McDonnell Douglas and Pratt & Whitney (McDonnell Douglas involvement stemming from a licence to manufacture-'any significant numbers' ordered if the US Government decides to build in the USA). Details of the Advanced Harrier can be found under **McDonnell Douglas**.
Data: *Engine* one Rolls-Royce Pegasus Mk 103

BAe (HS) Sea Harrier FRS.1.

vectored-thrust turbofan, with four exhaust nozzles of the two-vane cascade type, rotatable through 98° from fully-aft position and used to achieve vertical, horizontal or hovering flight, in conjunction with the jet reaction control valves built into the outrigger wheel fairings, nose and extended tailcone, which stabilise the aircraft *Wing span* 7.7 m (25 ft 3 in) *Length* (single-seater with laser nose) 13.91 m (45 ft 7.8 in) *Max T-O weight* over 11,340 kg (25,000 lb) *Max level speed* 1,186 km/h (737 mph) *Range* with one in-flight refuelling 5,560 km (3,455 miles) *Armament* four underwing and one underfuselage pylons for more than 2,270 kg (5,000 lb) of stores including 30 mm guns, bombs, rockets, missiles, reconnaissance pod etc.

BAe (HS) Sea Harrier (UK) First announced in May 1975, the Sea Harrier is a maritime version of the Harrier to equip the Royal Navy's new *Invincible* class of aircraft carriers from 1980. Designated FRS.1s, 34 aircraft have been initially ordered. In addition one standard non-navalised T.4 two-seater has been procured for land-based training. The Sea Harriers will make use of the cruisers' 7° ski-jump ramp at the front of their deck runways. The type is also expected to serve on board the anti-submarine carrier *Hermes*.

The first Sea Harrier to fly made its maiden flight on 20 August 1978 and is a full production type. Major changes compared with the RAF Harriers comprise a raised cockpit, revised operational electronics, and installation of multi-mode Ferranti radar in a redesigned nose that folds to port for carrier stowage. Power is provided by a Pegasus 104 turbofan, which is of similar power to the Pegasus 103 but incorporates anti-corrosion features and generates greater electrical power. *Data: Engines* as above *Wing span* 7.7 m (25 ft 3¼ in) *Length* 14.5 m (47 ft 7 in)

BAe (HS) Hawk (UK) Two-seat basic and advanced jet trainer with capability for close support missions. The pre-production HS 1182 (or Hawk as it became) made its maiden flight on 21 August 1974 and was the first of 176 aircraft ordered for the RAF as Hawk T.1s. About 60 Hawks had been delivered by August 1978.

The Hawk has been designed to be fully aerobatic (stressed to +8 and −4g) and will eventually replace the RAF's Jet Provosts, Gnat Trainers and Hunters for advanced flying training and for radio, navigation and weapons training. Since 1980 the Hawk has also equipped the Red Arrows aerobatic team.

The Finnish Government has ordered 50 Hawk trainers to replace its Fouga Magisters, with initial deliveries in 1980. Component manufacture and final assembly for 46 of these is being undertaken in Finland by Valmet. Eight ground attack/trainer aircraft have been ordered for the Indonesian Air Force and 12 for Kenya. *Data: Engine* one 23.75 kN (5,340 lb st) Rolls-Royce/Turboméca RT.172-06-11 Adour 151 non-afterburning turbofan *Wing span* 9.39 m (30 ft 9¾ in) *Length* excl. nose-probe 11.17 m (36 ft 7¾ in) *Max T-O weight* 7,755 kg (17,097 lb) *Max level speed* 1,000 km/h (621 mph) *Combat radius* 556 km (345 miles) *Armament* trainer version has

BAe (HS) Hawk T.1s.

underfuselage centreline-mounted 30 mm Aden gun and ammunition pack and two inboard underwing pylons each capable of carrying a nominal 454 kg (1,000 lb) of stores, including rockets and bombs. Provision for two outboard underwing pylons and a pylon in place of the ventral gun pack, also each capable of a 454 kg (1,000 lb) load to a total maximum of 2,567 kg (5,660 lb) for close support role. In RAF training roles the normal maximum will probably be about 680 kg (1,500 lb)

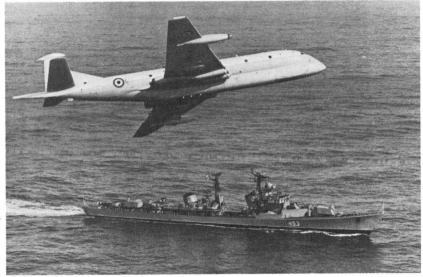

BAe (HS) Nimrod MR.1.

BAe (HS) Nimrod (UK) Although based largely on the airframe of the Hawker Siddeley (de Havilland) Comet 4C, the Nimrod is a new production aircraft with modifications including a shorter, pressurised fuselage; a new unpressurised, underslung pannier for operational equipment, including the search radar, and weapons; enlarged flight deck main windows and 'eyebrow' windows; ESM and MAD equipment in glassfibre fairings on top of the fin and in the tailboom respectively; a searchlight; and Rolls-Royce Spey turbofans. Two of the engines can be shut down to increase endurance and the aircraft can cruise and climb on one engine.

The Nimrod is scheduled to serve well into the 1990s and is designed to combine the advantages of fast transits with low wing loading

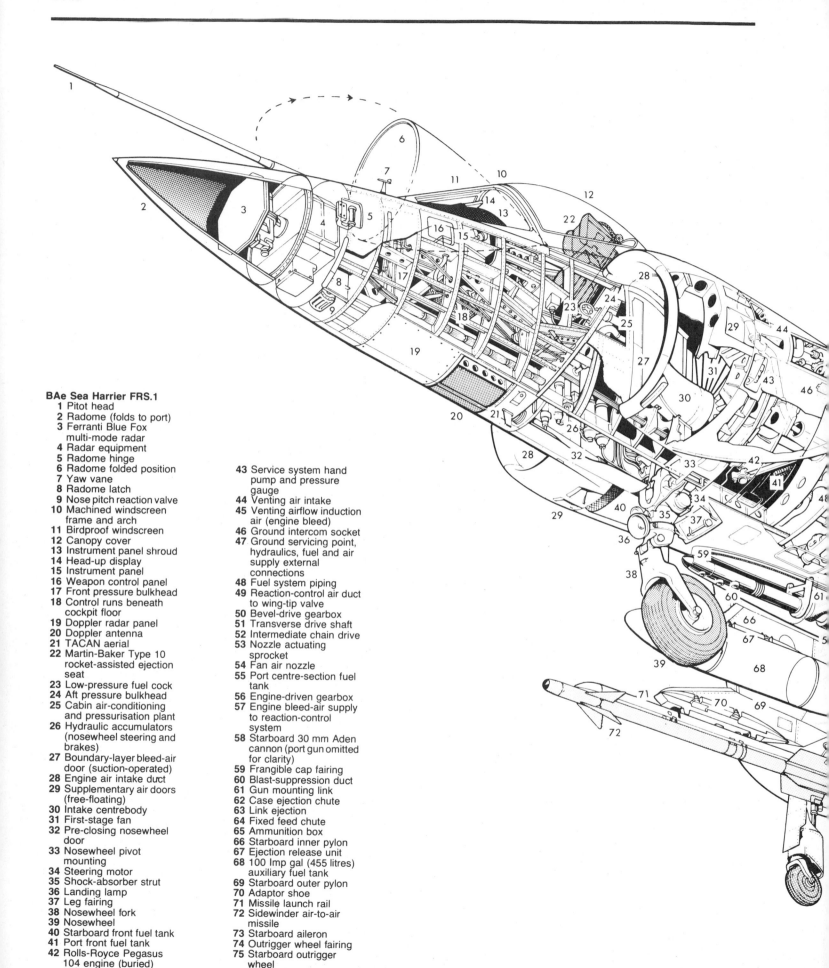

BAe Sea Harrier FRS.1
1 Pitot head
2 Radome (folds to port)
3 Ferranti Blue Fox multi-mode radar
4 Radar equipment
5 Radome hinge
6 Radome folded position
7 Yaw vane
8 Radome latch
9 Nose pitch reaction valve
10 Machined windscreen frame and arch
11 Birdproof windscreen
12 Canopy cover
13 Instrument panel shroud
14 Head-up display
15 Instrument panel
16 Weapon control panel
17 Front pressure bulkhead
18 Control runs beneath cockpit floor
19 Doppler radar panel
20 Doppler antenna
21 TACAN aerial
22 Martin-Baker Type 10 rocket-assisted ejection seat
23 Low-pressure fuel cock
24 Aft pressure bulkhead
25 Cabin air-conditioning and pressurisation plant
26 Hydraulic accumulators (nosewheel steering and brakes)
27 Boundary-layer bleed-air door (suction-operated)
28 Engine air intake duct
29 Supplementary air doors (free-floating)
30 Intake centrebody
31 First-stage fan
32 Pre-closing nosewheel door
33 Nosewheel pivot mounting
34 Steering motor
35 Shock-absorber strut
36 Landing lamp
37 Leg fairing
38 Nosewheel fork
39 Nosewheel
40 Starboard front fuel tank
41 Port front fuel tank
42 Rolls-Royce Pegasus 104 engine (buried)

43 Service system hand pump and pressure gauge
44 Venting air intake
45 Venting airflow induction air (engine bleed)
46 Ground intercom socket
47 Ground servicing point, hydraulics, fuel and air supply external connections
48 Fuel system piping
49 Reaction-control air duct to wing-tip valve
50 Bevel-drive gearbox
51 Transverse drive shaft
52 Intermediate chain drive
53 Nozzle actuating sprocket
54 Fan air nozzle
55 Port centre-section fuel tank
56 Engine-driven gearbox
57 Engine bleed-air supply to reaction-control system
58 Starboard 30 mm Aden cannon (port gun omitted for clarity)
59 Frangible cap fairing
60 Blast-suppression duct
61 Gun mounting link
62 Case ejection chute
63 Link ejection
64 Fixed feed chute
65 Ammunition box
66 Starboard inner pylon
67 Ejection release unit
68 100 Imp gal (455 litres) auxiliary fuel tank
69 Starboard outer pylon
70 Adaptor shoe
71 Missile launch rail
72 Sidewinder air-to-air missile
73 Starboard aileron
74 Outrigger wheel fairing
75 Starboard outrigger wheel

76 Aft-retracting twin mainwheels
77 Torque links
78 Shock-absorber strut
79 Mainwheel leg fairing
80 Pre-closing mainwheel doors
81 Rear exhaust nozzle
82 Nozzle drive chain and sprocket
83 Transverse drive shaft
84 Pressure refuelling point and control panel
85 Hydraulic reservoir
86 Wing front attachment point
87 Centre spar attachment
88 Aft attaching link
89 Machined skin planks
90 Wing front spar

91 Intermediate centre spar
92 Wing fuel tank
93 Rear spar web
94 Tank pressurising air
95 Fuel/air valves
96 Inner pylon fitting
97 Leading-edge dogtooth
98 Leading-edge wing fence
99 Aileron control rod
100 Reaction-control air duct
101 Tandem aileron jack and autostabiliser
102 Aileron hinge
103 Bonded aluminium honeycomb flap structure
104 Port aileron, bonded aluminium honeycomb structure

105 Roll reaction-control valve
106 Outer pylon fitting
107 Navigation light
108 Wing tip
109 Outrigger wheel fairing
110 Hydraulic retraction jack
111 Leg fairing (upper section)
112 Port outrigger wheel
113 Leg fairing (lower section)
114 Torque links
115 VHF aerial
116 ECM fairing
117 Fin structure
118 Bonded aluminium honeycomb rudder structure
119 Fuselage efflux shield

120 Ventral fin
121 Fuselage rear fuel tank
122 Lox container (1.1 Imp gal/5 litres)
123 Avionics equipment bay
124 Airbrake (extended)
125 Avionics bay air-conditioning system
126 Standby UHF aerial
127 Radar altimeter aerials
128 Starboard all-moving tailplane
129 Tandem tailplane jack
130 Port all-moving tailplane
131 Tailplane structure
132 Bonded aluminium honeycomb trailing edge
133 Pitch and yaw reaction-control valves
134 Tail warning radar

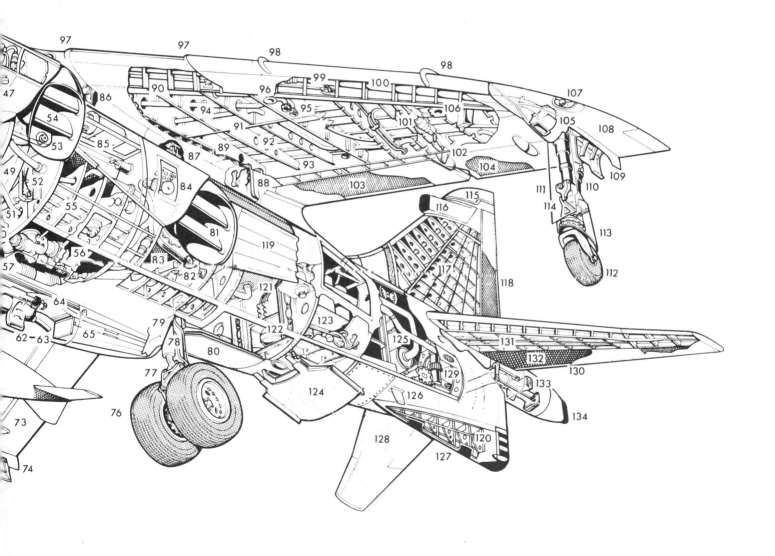

Artist's impression of a
BAe (HS) Nimrod AEW.3.

and good low-speed manoeuvring capabilities when operating in its primary roles of anti-submarine warfare, surveillance and anti-shipping strike. In addition the aircraft can perform day and night photographic missions. The original stand-off surface missile capability (although deleted) could be reactivated if necessary. The first of two prototypes flew in May 1967. Production versions are:

Nimrod MR.1 First flown in June 1968. Delivery of the initial order of 38 began in October 1969 to No 236 OCU, RAF Strike Command at St Mawgan, Cornwall. Current operational squadrons are No 42 (also at St Mawgan) and Nos 120, 201 and 206 at Kinloss, Scotland. Of the eight additional Nimrods ordered in 1972, only the first five are to Mk 1 standard; the three others are for development purposes, one for the MR.2 and two for the Nimrod AEW.3.

Nimrod R.1 Designation of three aircraft delivered to No 51 Squadron at Wyton, Huntingdonshire in 1971. Their mission is reported to include electronic reconnaissance and the monitoring of hostile radio and radar transmissions. This version is distinguishable by the absence of the MAD tailboom.

Nimrod MR.2 Under a programme begun in 1975 all the RAF's Nimrod MR.1s are being refitted with new communications equipment and advanced tactical sensor and navigation systems. The refitted aircraft (to be redesignated MR.2) were scheduled for redelivery by 1980.

Nimrod AEW.3 See next entry.

Ample space and power are available in the

basic Nimrod for additional or alternative sensors such as sideways-looking radar, forward-looking infra-red, infra-red linescan, low light level TV, digital processing of intercepted ESM signals and other new developments. Other possible roles include airborne warning and control (AWACS); long-range search and rescue; sea control and fishery protection.

Data: *Engines* four 54 kN (12,140 lb st) Rolls-Royce RB.168-20 Spey Mk 250 turbofans *Wing span* 35.0 m (114 ft 10 in) *Length* 38.63 m (126 ft 9 in) *Max overload T-O weight* (MR.1) 87,090 kg (192,000 lb) *Max transit speed* ISA + 20°C 880 km/h (547 mph). *Typical endurance* 12 h *Armament* wide range of ASW weapons can be carried in the lower fuselage pannier; sonobuoys and markers can be housed in the pressurised rear fuselage area. A hardpoint is provided under each wing for air-to-surface missiles, rocket or cannon pods, or mines.

BAe (HS) Nimrod AEW.3 (UK) Development of a new radar system by Marconi Avionics – with both essential maritime capability and the ability to satisfy the air defence requirements of central Europe – has made possible the airborne early warning (AEW) version of the Nimrod. The aircraft can provide (at long range and at high or low altitude) detection, classification and tracking of aircraft, missiles and ships; interceptor control; direction of strike aircraft; air defence; air traffic control; and search and rescue facilities. Eleven aircraft have been ordered for the RAF.

Two newly developed and identically shaped scanners (designed specifically for Nimrod) are installed in fore and aft positions, necessitating modification to the aircraft's nose and tail. This arrangement ensures all-round coverage. The pulsed Doppler radar system can be used for ship surveillance as well as aircraft detection. The system also features sophisticated anti-jamming devices to cope with the increasing efficiency of electronic countermeasures.

An airborne computer controls the flow of data from the scanners and correlates track information between the AEW aircraft and the surface control station. Six operator consoles are planned although much of the data control is fully automatic. High standards of communications and navigation are essential to complement the advanced radar and data handling systems. For communications the aircraft carries tactical UHF transceivers, SIMOP HF transceivers, pilot's U/VHF, RATT, secure voice com, LF receiver and data links. Primary navigation electronics consist of dual inertial navigation systems (INS). The secondary navigation system includes a gyro magnetic compass, air data computer, twin VOR/ILS, ADF, Tacan, autopilot and a flight director. ESM (electronic support measures) equipment is housed in the two pods at the wingtips.

The first of four development aircraft (a converted Comet 4C) flew on 28 June 1977, carrying nose-mounted radar only. The first Nimrod to AEW standard was expected to fly in 1980.

Data: *Wing span* 35.08 m (115 ft 1 in) *Length* 10.06 m (33 ft 0 in) *Endurance* more than 10 h

BAe (HS) Trident 2E.

BAe (HS) Trident (UK) Originally the de Havilland D.H.121, the Trident was ordered into production initially to meet BEA's requirements for a short-haul 965 km/h (600 mph) airliner for service from 1963–64 onwards. The first Trident flew on 9 January 1962.

Five versions of the Trident were produced: the Trident 1 (24 built), 1E (15 built), 2E (50 built), 3B (26 built) and Super 3B (2 built). These are described below:

Trident 1 Initial version with three 43.82 kN (9,850 lb st) Rolls-Royce RB.163-1 Mk 505-5 Spey turbofans. Seating for up to 103 passengers.

Trident 1E Basically similar to the Trident 1 but with 50.71 kN (11,400 lb st) RB.163-25 Mk 511-5 Spey turbofans. Increased wing span incorporating full-length leading-edge slats in place of the drooping leading edge of the Trident 1. Seating for up to 115 passengers.

Trident 2E Developed version seating up to 115 passengers. Fuel capacity and max T-O weight increased. Take-off performance improved by use of 53.2 kN (11,960 lb st) RB.163-25 Mk 512-5W turbofans.

Trident 3B High-capacity short-haul development of Trident 1E with fuselage lengthened by 5.0 m (16 ft 5 in) to seat between 128 and 180 passengers. Wing span as Trident 2E, but wing area, wing incidence and flap span increased. Powered by same engines as Trident 2E, but with 23.35 kN (5,250 lb st) RB.162-86 turbojet installed in tail.

Super Trident 3B Announced in 1972 following an order for two by CAAC. Seating for 152 passengers. Increased fuel capacity, max T-O and max zero-fuel weights. Effective range increased by 692 km (430 miles). First example flew 9 July 1975.

Data (Trident 3B): *Engines* as above *Wing span* 29.87 m (98 ft 0 in) *Length* 39.98 m (131 ft 2 in) *Max T-O weight* 68,040 kg (150,000 lb) *Econ cruising speed* 959 km/h (596 mph) *Range* 3,798 km (2,360 miles)

BAe SA-3-120 Bulldog Series 120 (UK) The Bulldog originated in 1968 as a military primary trainer version of the Beagle Pup. It differs substantially, however, from the Pup in having a fully transparent canopy, increased wing span, and strengthened construction to allow full aerobatic operation. First flight was made on 19 May 1969.

The first 98 production Bulldogs were of the Series 100 version and were delivered to Kenya, Malaysia and Sweden. Production continued with the Series 120. The versions so far produced comprise the Model 121 for the RAF as the Bulldog T.1 (130); Model 122 for the Ghanaian Air Force (6), plus seven Mk 122As delivered by 1976; Model 123 for the Nigerian Air Force (32); Model 124 company demonstrator; Model 125 for the Jordanian Royal Academy of Aeronautics but transferred to the Air Force (13); Model 126 for the Lebanese Air Force (6); Model 127 for an undisclosed customer, probably Kenya (9); and Model 128 for the Royal Hong Kong Auxiliary Air Force (2). All are two–three-seaters and have provision for installation of four underwing hardpoints to which can be attached various loads including unguided or wire-guided air-to-surface projectiles; 7.62 mm machine-gun pods; grenade launchers; bombs of up to 50 kg; supply containers up to a maximum of 290 kg (640 lb).

Data (Series 120): *Engine* one 149 kW (200 hp) Lycoming IO-360-A1B6 flat-four *Wing span* 10.06 m (33 ft 0 in) *Length* 7.09 m (23 ft 3 in) *Max T-O weight* 1,066 kg (2,350 lb) *Max level speed* 241 km/h (150 mph) *Range* 1,000 km (621 miles)

BAe SA-3-200 Bulldog Series 200 (UK) Prototype only of a version of the Bulldog (known as the Bullfinch) with retractable landing gear, provision for a fourth seat, and other refinements; suitable for basic, aerobatic and weapon training roles.

BAe Jetstream Mk 1 and Series 200 (UK) Originally the Handley Page HP 137 Jetstream and developed between 1966 and 1970. A number of Handley Page-built Jetstream Mk 1s are in service with operators in Canada, France, the UK, the USA and Zaïre. Some Mk 1s have been converted to Series 200 standard. This later model also originated with Handley Page, was developed subsequently by Jetstream Aviation and is now available from British Aerospace. Approximately 30 civil Jetstreams were in service at the beginning of 1979.

The major production commitment so far has been for 26 military Series 200s (Model 201) for the RAF, the first of which flew on 13 April 1973. The RAF aircraft (designated Jetstream T.1) are generally similar to the civil Series 200 except for having two 743 kW (996 ehp) Turboméca Astazou XVI D engines, 'eyebrow' windows above the flight deck and different instrumentation and electronics installation. They were intended as trainers for pilots of multi-engined aircraft. Sixteen have since been converted to T.2s for observer training with the Royal Navy.
Data (T.1): *Engine* as above; civil Series 200s powered by two 743 kW (996 ehp) Astazou XVI C2 turboprops *Wing span* 15.85 m (52 ft 0 in) *Length* 14.37 m (47 ft 1½ in) *Max T-O weight* 5,700 kg (12,566 lb) *Max level speed* 454 km/h (282 mph) *Range* 2,224 km (1,380 miles) *Accommodation* two pilots and four passengers. Civil Series 200 accommodates 12 passengers in VIP layout or 16 passengers as an airliner

BAe/Aérospatiale Concorde (UK/France) In 1956 both Britain and France began research to determine the feasibility of a supersonic transport and at the end of that year the British Supersonic Transport Aircraft Committee was formed. Discussions followed to investigate the possibility of Anglo-French collaboration and on 29 November 1962 the two governments signed an agreement for the joint design, construction and development of a 100-seat aircraft using established materials and techniques and on a shared basis. Work

on the first prototypes began in April 1965. Final assembly of the first aircraft began in April 1966 and the first Concorde (001) made its initial flight at Toulouse on 2 March 1969, just over two months after the first Tupolev Tu-144.

The Concorde, designed to cruise at above Mach 2, is a slender-fuselage aircraft with ogival delta wing and four 169.3 kN (38,050 lb) thrust Rolls-Royce/SNECMA Olympus 593 Mk 610 turbojets (with reheat), carried in pairs beneath the wing. To improve crew visibility for take-off and landing the nose can be drooped hydraulically. A retractable visor is raised hydraulically to fair in the windscreen in cruising flight.

On 1 October 1969 the Concorde achieved Mach 1 for the first time and in November 1970 the first British and French assembled aircraft each achieved Mach 2.

The two prototypes were followed by two pre-production aircraft, after which 16 production examples were built, eight on the Filton and eight on the Toulouse lines. The first production aircraft flew on 6 December 1973. Concorde services began on 21 January 1976, with Air France opening Paris–Rio de Janeiro services via Dakar and British Airways a Concorde service between London and Bahrain.

Air France initially ordered four Concordes and British Airways five; at one time options were held on more than 70 aircraft.

On 24 May 1976 Concorde North Atlantic service began when Air France and British Airways opened services to Washington, both aircraft arriving together on the inaugural service. Air France began a daily service to John F. Kennedy International Airport, New York, on 22 November 1977; British Airways followed on 12 February 1978.

A joint British Airways/Singapore Airlines Concorde service between London and Singapore started on 9 December 1977. It was suspended after three flights and then reopened in January 1979; in the same month Braniff Airways began leasing Air France and British Airways

BAe/Aérospatiale Concorde.

Concordes to fly interchange services, at subsonic speed, between Washington and Dallas/Fort Worth.

The Concorde has caused more controversy than any other civil aeroplane but has cut the North Atlantic crossing to less than 3½ h and has operated with little disturbance. It is still the only supersonic transport in service, the Tu-144 having been withdrawn after only a short operational life.

Data: *Engines* as above *Wing span* 25.56 m (83 ft 10 in) *Length* 62.1 m (203 ft 9 in) *Max T-O weight* 185,065 kg (408,000 lb) *Cruising speed* Mach 2.2 *Range* 6,580 km (4,090 miles) *Accommodation* up to 128 economy-class passengers normally, but a 144 passenger layout is available

Bakeng Duce and Double Duce (USA) The Duce is a two-seat light sporting parasol-wing monoplane designed for amateur construction. More than 200 sets of plans had been sold by 1979. The Double Duce is a biplane version.

Ball-Bartoe JW-1 Jetwing (USA) Single-seat blown wing research aircraft powered by a 9.79 kN (2,200 lb st) Pratt & Whitney Aircraft of Canada JT15D-1 turbofan engine. First flown 11 July 1977. Jet efflux from the engine is ducted along the wing leading edge and discharged through a slot extending for approximately 70% of the span. A narrow chord augmentor aerofoil surface is mounted above the wing upper surface over the efflux discharge slot.

Barkley-Grow T8P-1 (USA) Eight-passenger all-metal cantilever low-wing commercial monoplane of the latter 1930s powered by two 298 kW (400 hp) Pratt & Whitney Wasp Junior engines. Max level speed 338 km/h (210 mph).

Barling NBL-1 (USA) Triplane heavy bomber of 1923 powered by six 298 kW (400 hp) Liberty engines.

Barnett J-3M and J-4M (USA) Single-seat ultra-light gyroplanes. Plans, materials and kits of parts were made available to homebuilders. J-3M utility version powered by 48.5 kW (65 hp) Continental A65 engine. J-4M higher performance version with 63.5 kW (85 hp) Continental C85 engine and more streamlined nacelle.

Bartel M.1 Maryla (Poland) Single-seat high-wing monoplane fighter powered by a 335.3 kW (450 hp) Lorraine-Dietrich engine. Prototype only.

Bartel M.2/BM.2 (Poland) Two-seat biplane trainer of 1926 with lower wing of greater span than upper. First flown on 7 December 1926. Powered by an 89.4 kW (120 hp) Salmson AC.9 radial engine. Prototype only.

Bartel M.4/BM.4a (Poland) The M.4 or BM.4 two-seat primary trainer was basically a development of the BM.2 and was designed to a Department of Aeronautics specification for a primary trainer for the air force, to be powered by the World War I vintage 59.6 kW (80 hp) Le Rhône rotary engine. The prototype first flew on 20 December 1929 powered by a Walter engine. Eventually 22 were produced as BM.4as. A further 50 were subsequently built by P.W.S. as BM.4hs powered by 78.2 kW (105 hp) Walter Junior or 89.4 kW (120 hp) de Havilland Gipsy III engines.

Beagle Terrier Series 2.

Bartel M.5/BM.5 (Poland) Two-seat intermediate trainer developed from the BM.4. First flown in prototype form on 27 July 1928. Forty production BM.5as and BM.5bs were subsequently built with 164 kW (220 hp) Austro-Daimler and Spa engines respectively, followed by 20 BM.5cs with 223.5 kW (300 hp) Hispano-Suiza engines, all for the air force. A further five BM.5cs were built for the Polish Navy. After some years of service a number of aircraft were re-engined with 164 kW (220 hp) Skoda-built Wright Whirlwind engines as BM.5ds. These remained in service throughout the 1930s.

Beagle Airedale.

Bartlett LC 13-A Zephyr 150 (USA) Developed from the Babcock monoplane of the 1930s, via the Bartlett Blue Zephyr. The post-war Zephyr 150 was a two-seat cabin monoplane with strut-braced mid wings. Power was provided by a 112 kW (150 hp) Franklin 6A4-150-B3 flat-six engine.

B.A.T. F.K.23 Bantam (UK) Single-seat bi-plane fighter of 1918 powered by a 126.7 kW (170 hp) A.B.C. Wasp I radial engine. Only nine built by the British Aerial Transport Company for the RAF, none of which entered squadron service. Used after the war as racing aircraft.

B.A.T. F.K.24 Baboon (UK) Two-seat trainer of 1918 powered by a 126.7 kW (170 hp) A.B.C. Wasp I radial engine. Prototype only; initially on RAF charge but subsequently raced.

B.A.T. F.K.26 (UK) Four-passenger biplane airliner first flown in April 1919. Four built, each powered by a 261 kW (350 hp) Rolls-Royce Eagle VIII engine. One operated by Instone for cross-Channel services.

B.A.T. F.K.28 Crow (UK) Interesting ultra-light single-seater powered by a 30 kW (40 hp) A.B.C. Gnat engine. Pilot sat in open position below wing.

Beagle A.61 Terrier (incl 6A Tugmaster) (UK) Produced by completely rebuilding and furnishing to new high standards ex-army Auster AOP.6 and T.7 monoplanes. The 6A Tugmaster

Beagle B.206.

Beagle Pup.

and Terrier 1 were also rebuilt Auster Mk 6s, but to lower standards. First flight of a Terrier Series 2 was made on 25 April 1962. The type is a three-seat touring and training monoplane.

Beagle A.109 Airedale (UK) The Airedale is a four-seat touring and business aircraft retaining many features of the Auster range. The prototype first flew on 16 April 1961. It was followed by eight pre-production and 42 production aircraft. It has provision for full airline instrumentation and nav/com radio for all-weather operation. Powered by one 134 kW (180 hp) Lycoming O-360-A1A flat-four engine. Maximum level speed 227 km/h (141 mph).

Beagle A.113 Husky (UK) See **Auster D series**

Beagle B.121 Pup (UK) Four versions of the Pup were produced by Beagle: the Pup-100 fully aerobatic light aircraft with accommodation for two adults and powered by a 74.5 kW (100 hp) Rolls-Royce/Continental O-200-A flat-four engine, deliveries beginning in April 1968; the Pup-150 with seating for two adults but with an optional seat for a third adult or two children and powered by a 112 kW (150 hp) Lycoming O-320-A2B engine; the Pup-160 with a 119 kW (160 hp) Lycoming O-320-D2C engine; and the Pup-200 with a 149 kW (200 hp) Continental engine. A total of 128 Pups had been delivered by the close of 1969, when a further 267 aircraft were on order. However the company went into liquidation and the Pup was developed into the Bulldog by Scottish Aviation.

Beagle B.206 (UK) Twin-engined light transport aircraft with accommodation for five to eight persons. The first prototype flew on 15 August 1961, powered by a Continental 194 kW (260 hp) IO-470-A engine, and was smaller than subsequent B.206s. The second prototype had increased dimensions and a 231 kW (310 hp) Rolls-Royce/Continental GIO-470-A engine. The initial commercial version was the B.206 Series I or B.206C. The B.206R was the military production version, ordered for communications and ferrying duties with the RAF under the name Basset CC.1. The B.206-S was a development of the Series I with supercharged engines and other refinements. Deliveries included two ambulance models for the Royal Flying Doctor Service of New South Wales, Australia. By the close of 1969 40 B.206 Series I and II aircraft, 20 Bassets and two B.206Z pre-production types for the Ministry of Technology had been delivered.

Beardmore W.B.III (UK) Development of the Sopwith Pup specifically for shipboard operations. Wings and landing gear could be folded for easy stowage, according to version. Fifty-five delivered as S.B.3Ds and S.B.3Fs. These served on board HMS *Furious*, *Pegasus* and *Nairana*.

Beardmore Inflexible (UK) Monoplane bomber powered by three 484 kW (650 hp) Rolls-Royce Condor II engines. First flown 5 March 1928. Largest British landplane prior to World War II, with wing span of 48.0 m (157 ft 6 in). Maximum speed 175 km/h (109 mph). Prototype only.

Béarn Minicab GY-201 and Super-Minicab (France) The former was a two-seat light cantilever low-wing monoplane powered by a 48.4 kW (65 hp) Continental A65 engine. Ten built for the Service de l'Aviation Légère et Sportive (SALS). The Super-Minicab was a version with a retractable landing gear, slotted flaps and a 67 kW (90 hp) Continental C90 engine. Six built for SALS.

Bede BD-4 (USA) Two–four-seat sporting and utility high-wing cabin monoplane designed to be constructed by amateurs. Well over 2,000 sets of plans sold.

Bede BD-5 Micro (USA) Single-seat lightweight low-wing monoplane, designed to be constructed by amateurs from plans and kits of parts. Seven versions produced: the original BD-5A prototype; BD-5B, first model with conventional tail unit; BD-5D factory-built version of BD-5G; BD-5G improved version of BD-5B; BD-5J jet-powered version, powered by a 0.90 kN (202 lb st) Microturbo TRS 18 turbojet engine instead of the normal piston engine in pusher configuration; BD-5JP factory-built version of BD-5J; and BD-5S sailplane version. Well over 5,000 Micros ordered.

Bede BD-6 (USA) Single-seat lightweight sporting cabin monoplane similar in configuration to BD-4.

Bede BD-7 (USA) Essentially a two–four-seat version of the BD-5; first flown in December 1976.

Bede BD-8 (USA) Easy-to-build single-seat aerobatic aircraft designed in 1973.

Beech Aircraft Company/Corporation (USA) Beech aircraft have been entered (as far as is possible) in order of appearance rather than in numerical Model number.

Beech Model 17 'Staggerwing' (USA) In 1932 Walter H. Beech and his wife Olive Ann Beech founded the Beech Aircraft Company. The first aircraft produced was the Model 17 biplane, which first flew on 4 November 1932. Flight tests at Wichita Municipal Airport indicated a maximum speed of 323 km/h (201 mph) and good all-round performance. This aircraft was sold to the Ethyl Corporation and at the Miami Air Races in January 1933 it won the Texaco Trophy. Beech produced a second aircraft with negative stagger (designated B17L). It entered production in 1934 as the B17L with a 167.7 kW (225 hp) Jacobs engine; 17R with a 335.3 kW (450 hp) Wright engine; and A17F with a 484.4 kW (650 hp) engine. Most of the 18 B17 type aircraft built that year were of the former type. During 1935 36

Beardmore Inflexible.

aircraft were built. In the same year the 212.4 kW (285 hp) Jacobs-engined B17B and improved B17R (with a 313 kW; 420 hp Wright engine) were introduced. A seaplane version of the aircraft also appeared as the SE17B.

During 1936 the basic design was improved with the relocation of the wing flaps and shorter landing gear legs. With these improvements the designations became C17L (167.7 kW 225 hp Jacobs), C17B (212.5 kW; 285 hp Jacobs) and C17R (313 kW; 420 hp Wright). In 1937 the Model 17 was tested with aileron-type full-length flaps mounted on the lower wings and the ailerons on the upper wings. The tail unit of versions of more than 261 kW (350 hp) was also redesigned, giving a much cleaner cantilever type horizontal and vertical structure. The aircraft incorporating these refinements were designated E17B (212.5 kW; 285 hp Jacobs), D17R (313 kW; 420 hp Wright) and D17S (335.3 kW; 450 hp Pratt & Whitney Wasp Junior).

Only three D17W modernised aircraft were

Beech D17S.

Beech

produced: one owned by the famous aviator Miss Jacqueline Cochran set a new US women's speed record on 26 July 1937 of 328.14 km/h (203.895 mph) over a set course. Other records and achievements were gained by this aircraft. In 1938 a fleet of D17Rs were fitted out as ambulances and delivered to the Chinese government, which was fighting an undeclared war with Japan (see **Chronology**). In 1939 Beech delivered its first military aircraft: a number of D17Ss for the US military attachés in London, Rome, Paris and Mexico City.

From 1939 to 1944 Beech produced Model 17s for the USAAF and US Navy, including a total of 164 in 1943 and 192 in 1944. Beech press releases state that 105 and 320 were produced for each service respectively; military records indicate 207 and 342 respectively – the discrepancy probably due to numbers of civil aircraft impressed into military service and those delivered for Lease–Lend to the UK. The USAAF Model 17s were designated UC-43 Travelers and became utility transports and communications aircraft. The naval aircraft became GB-2 Traveler transports.

After the war Beech produced the G17S with a new type of engine mounting, new engine cowling and exhaust system, larger tail control surfaces, a new instrument panel and other refinements. Power was provided by the Wasp Junior engine. However, production of the Staggerwing ended in 1948. In total 781 aircraft of the Model 17 series were built.

Data: *Engine* as above *Wing span* 9.75 m (32 ft 0 in) *Length* 7.96 m (26 ft 1½ in) *Max T-O weight* (UC-43) 2,132 kg (4,700 lb) *Max level speed* 319 km/h (198 mph) *Range* 805 km (500 miles) *Accommodation* four persons

Beech Model 18 'Twin Beech' (USA) On 26 November 1969 the last three Beechcraft Super H18s were delivered to Japan Air Lines. This ended a continuous production run of the Model 18 type that had begun in 1937 – the longest run in aviation history.

Only three years old and with the Model 17 in full production, the Beech Aircraft Company produced the prototype Model 18, a twin-engined cantilever low-wing monoplane of all-metal construction with accommodation for a crew of two and six passengers. This aircraft made its first flight in January 1937. The main feature of the Model 18 design was its truss-type centre section, built of welded high-strength chrome steel tubing, heat treated to a strength of 180,000 pounds per square inch. Power was provided by 238.5 kW (320 hp) Wright R-760-E2 engines.

Although the Model 18 found little initial success among operators in the USA, it was an immediate success with feeder lines in Canada. The first Model 18s went to Prairie Airways of Alberta and Starratt Airways and Transportation of Ontario, the latter company's Model 18A operating on ski and float landing gears.

Throughout the 1930s the Model 18 was improved and five models appeared with Wright, Jacobs and Pratt & Whitney engines. The first military Model 18s were delivered to the Philippine Army Air Corps and were specially equipped for aerial photography. The Model 18 had been selected by the Chief of Staff of the American military mission to the Philippine Commonwealth, Lt Col Dwight Eisenhower. He saw US military interest in an off-the-shelf design that could fulfil specialised needs, and Model 18s par-

ticipated in an Air Corps evaluation competition at Wright Field in 1939. By the outbreak of World War II a total of 39 Model 18s had been sold, including a few for China as pilot trainers and light tactical bombers. The latter were five M18Rs fitted with gun turrets and bomb racks. An order for the USAAF for 150 similar Model 18s followed in 1941. Eventually 5,257 modified Model 18s were supplied to the Allied military forces for training pilots, gunners, bombardiers and navigators, as well as for transporting personnel and cargo. USAAF versions comprised the C-45 transport and communications aircraft, AT-7 navigation trainer, AT-11 Kansan bombing and gunnery trainer, and F2 photographic reconnaissance aircraft. A small number of UC-45Fs were subsequently converted into CQ-3s for directing radio-controlled targets. After the war the ATs and F-2s became T-7/11s and RC-45As. US Navy versions comprised JRB Expeditor transports and SNB Kansan and Navigator weapon and navigation trainers. Some were subsequently used as ambulances and as photo reconnaissance aircraft. Expeditors were also operated by the Royal Canadian Air Force. It has been estimated that 90% of American bombardiers and navigators of World War II were trained in military Model 18s.

In the early 1960s USAF aircraft became known as '60 Dash 2s' and the last 11 C-45s were retired in November 1963. Navy SNB-5s remained operational until July 1972. The US Army operated five Model 18s as utility and liaison transports until 1976. Interestingly, no less than 2,263 Model 18s were refurbished by Beech from 1952 to 1961 under a single US government programme.

Meanwhile, in early 1945 the first post-war commercial version appeared as the new eight-seat Model D18S. This had a 20% increase in all-up weight and increased payload and range. Flush riveting was used in the wing leading edges and other areas, and the engine nacelles were refined. A parallel development was the D18C ten-seat feeder liner powered by two 391 kW (525 hp) Continental R-9A engines. In 1954 the Super 18 (Model E18S) was introduced, featuring a cabin with increased headroom, larger cabin and cockpit windows, new wingtips, increased fuel tankage and other refinements.

Beechcraft T-34C-1s.

Model 18 production continued into 1957 with a total of 6,326 having been delivered. From 1954 until 1969 762 Super 18s were delivered. In 1959 a modification kit was made available to update earlier types to Super 18 configuration and a Volpar modification kit was made available in 1962. The final version of the 'Twin Beech' was the Super H18 powered by 335.3 kW (450 hp) Pratt & Whitney R-985-AN-14B engines, driving three-bladed fully feathering propellers.

Data (C-45): *Engines* two 335.3 kW (450 hp) Pratt & Whitney R-985-AN-1s or AN-3s *Wing span* 14.53 m (47 ft 8 in) *Length* 10.44 m (34 ft 3 in) *Max T-O weight* 3,561 kg (7,850 lb) *Max level speed* 346 km/h (215 mph) *Range* 1,126 km (700 miles)

Beechcraft Bonanza Model 35 (USA) The prototype Model 35 Bonanza flew for the first time on 22 December 1945 and the type went into production as the Model 35 in 1947 (1,500 built). Subsequent versions comprised the A35 of 1949 (701 built), B35 of 1950 (480), C35 of 1951–52 (719), D35 of 1953 (298), E35 of 1954 (301), F35 of 1955 (392), G35 of 1956 (476), H35 of 1957 (464), J35 of 1958 (396), K35 of 1959 (436), M35 of 1960 (400), N35 of 1961 (280), P35 of 1962–63 (467), S35 of 1964–5 (667), V35 of 1966 (622), V35A of 1968–69 (470), and V35B and V35B TC Turbo Bonanza of 1970 – the latter with a turbocharged 212.4 kW (285 hp) TSIO-520-D engine and oxygen system as standard.

In February 1977 the 10,000th V-tail Bonanza Model 35 was completed. This aircraft entered its 32nd year of production in 1978. A total of 10,108 had been delivered by April 1978. The current version is the Model V35B. Beech also offers five 'Super Utility' packages of optional equipment, including a large cargo door on the Models V35B and F33A and 280 litre (74 US gallon) extended-range fuel tanks.

Data (V35B): *Engine* one 212.4 kW (285 hp) Continental IO-520-BA flat-six *Wing span* 10.21 m (33 ft 6 in) *Length* 8.05 m (26 ft 5 in) *Max T-O weight* 1,542 kg (3,400 lb) *Max level speed* 338 km/h (209 mph) *Range* 1,648 km (1,023 miles) at 45% power *Accommodation* enclosed cabin for four or five persons on individual seats, plus space for 122.5 kg (270 lb) of baggage

Beechcraft Bonanza V35B.

Beechcraft

Beechcraft Model 45 Mentor (USA) First appearing in the late 1940s, the Model 45 was inexpensively developed from the Bonanza as a tandem two-seat primary trainer. In March 1953 the USAF selected the Model 45 as its new primary trainer (under the designation T-34A Mentor). A total of 450 were eventually acquired. Power plant consisted of a 168 kW (225 hp) Continental O-470-13 flat-six engine. Just over a year later the US Navy reached a similar decision and eventually acquired 423 T-34B Mentors.

Beechcraft Queen Air B80.

Beechcraft Bonanza A36.

In 1973 Beech received a USN research and development contract to modify two T-34Bs to see whether they could be upgraded for a continuing training role. This involved installation of a 298 kW (400 shp) Pratt & Whitney Aircraft of Canada PT6A-25 turboprop engine and the latest electronics equipment. Designated YT-34C, the first of these flew on 21 September 1973. Beech has received USN contracts for more than 170 new-production T-34Cs out of an anticipated total requirement of nearly 300. The first were delivered in November 1977.

A T-34C-1 armament systems trainer version is also available. In addition to its basic role, it is capable of carrying out forward air control (FAC) and tactical strike missions. Examples have been delivered to the air forces of Morocco (12), Ecuador (20) and Indonesia (16), and the navies of Peru and Argentina.

Data (T-34C): *Engine* as above *Wing span* 10.16 m (33 ft 3⅞ in) *Length* 8.75 m (28 ft 8½ in) *Max T-O weight* 1,938 kg (4,274 lb) *Max level speed* 414 km/h (257 mph) *Range* 1,205 km (749 miles) *Armament* (T-34C-1) four underwing hardpoints for up to 544 kg (1,200 lb) of bombs, Minigun pods or wire-guided anti-tank missiles

Beechcraft Model 50 Twin Bonanza (USA) First of the American light twin-engined aircraft of post-war design. The prototype Twin Bonanza flew for the first time on 15 November 1949. The final civil version was the Model D50E powered by two 220 kW (295 hp) Lycoming GO-480-G2F6 flat-six engines. Accommodation was provided for six or seven persons.

A number of Twin Bonanzas were also acquired by the US Army for communications, liaison and transport duties. Some were later used as navigation trainers. The first aircraft acquired were 55 L-23As powered by 194 kW (260 hp) Lycoming O-435-17 engines. These were followed by 40 L-23Bs and 85 L-23Ds, the latter powered by 253.3 kW (340 hp) Lycoming O-480-1 engines. The L-23As and Bs were subsequently brought up to this standard. The final versions to enter service were six L-23Es (equivalent to the commercial D50E) and 12 specialised RL-23D radar surveillance aircraft. US Army L-23s subsequently became U-8D Seminoles (L-23Ds), RU-8D Seminoles (RL-23Ds), U-8E Seminoles (L-23Es) and U-8F Seminoles (based on the Queen Air 65, see below). The U-8G Seminole was a conversion of earlier models with improved accommodation and GO-480 engines.

Data (U-8D Seminole): *Engines* as above *Wing span* 13.8 m (45 ft 3½ in) *Length* 9.61 m (31 ft 6½ in) *Max T-O weight* 3,175 kg (7,000 lb) *Max level speed* 375 km/h (233 mph) *Range* more than 2,172 km (1,350 miles)

Beechcraft Model 95 Travel Air (USA) The original four-seat Model 95 Travel Air flew for the first time on 6 August 1956 and received CAA Type Certificate on 18 June 1957. Power was provided by two 134 kW (180 hp) Lycoming O-360-A1A engines. Compared with the D95A, the later B95A had a 48 cm (19 in) longer cabin, providing room for an optional fifth seat or couch. The tailplane was also redesigned with an increased span and improved load distribution. Power was provided by IO-360-B1A engines. The D95A was powered by IO-360-B1B engines, as was the final version, the E95A. When production ended in 1967 711 Travel Airs had been built.

Beechcraft Queen Air Model 65, 70 and 80 (USA) First flown in prototype form on 28 August 1958 (four months after its design was started) the Model 65 Queen Air was a six–nine-seat business aeroplane incorporating the features of a modern airliner. It could also be operated as a cargo transport by removing the bulkheads and passenger seating. Production of this version of the Queen Air was terminated at the end of 1971. By then a total of 333 of the original Model 65s and later Model A65s and 71 US Army U-8F Seminoles had been built. Power was provided by two

Beechcraft Baron 58TC.

253.3 kW (340 hp) Lycoming IGSO-480-A1E6 engines in the final version, which had accommodation for a crew of two and four to nine passengers.

In 1968 Beech introduced the Queen Air 70, joining the Queen Air A65 and Queen Air B80 (see below) as the third in a series of 6–11-seat business and utility aircraft. With the same power plant as the A65 and extended wing of the B80, the Queen Air 70 had an operating economy comparable with the A65, while carrying more than a 10% greater load. However, production was terminated at the end of 1971 after 42 had been completed.

The prototype of the original Queen Air 80 (which introduced two 283 kW; 380 hp Lycoming IGSO-540-A1A flat-six engines) flew for the first time on 22 June 1961. It was followed in January 1964 by the Queen Air A80 with increased wing span and AUW, new interior styling, increased fuel capacity and redesigned nose compartment. The A80 was followed in turn by the improved B80 and 11-seat Queen Airliner B80, powered by two 283 kW (380 hp) Lycoming IGSO-540-A1D engines. It is available with the optional Executive or Airline packages, according to the interior layout required. By 1 January 1978 Beech had built a total of 509 Queen Air 80s, A80s, B80s and Queen Airliner B80s.

Data (B80): *Engines* as above *Wing span* 15.32 m (50 ft 3 in) *Length* 10.82 m (35 ft 6 in) *Max T-O weight* 3,992 kg (8,800 lb) *Cruising speed* 362 km/h (225 mph) *Range* 2,441 km (1,517 miles)

Beechcraft Model 33 Debonair (USA) First flown on 4 September 1959, the Debonair was developed as a four-seat executive aircraft. Two versions were produced: the Model C33 with a 167.7 kW (225 hp) Continental IO-470-K engine; and the Model C33A with a 212.3 kW (285 hp) IO-520-B engine. Both were four-seaters. A total of 1,195 Debonairs were built by the end of production in 1966, 21 going for pilot training to Lufthansa. The Debonair was a direct descendant of the Bonanza F33.

Beechcraft Model 55 Baron (incl Baron Model 95-B55) (USA) The original Baron was a four–five-seat cabin monoplane developed from the earlier Travel Air but with more power, better all-weather capability and airframe refinements that included a swept tail-fin. It first flew in pro-

totype form on 29 February 1960 and was licensed in the FAA Normal category in November 1960. The Baron Model 95-B55 was similarly licensed in September 1963.

The current Barons are optional four-, five- or six-seaters with interior features of the Bonanza. In February 1965 the US Army selected the Model 95-B55 as winner of its competition for a twin-engined instrument trainer. Beech identified the military trainer as the Model 95-B55B and the Army ordered 65 as T-42A Cochise. In 1971 Beech delivered five more T-42As to the US Army for service with the army of Turkey, under MAP. Export deliveries of the standard Model 95-B55 have also been made, including 19 for the Spanish Air Ministry and six for the Civil Air Bureau of Japan. These aircraft are used as instrument trainers.

A total of 2,188 civil and military Barons had been delivered by the beginning of 1978.

Data (Model 95-B55): *Engines* two 194 kW (260 hp) Continental IO-470-Ls *Wing span* 11.53 m (37 ft 10 in) *Length* 8.53 m (28 ft 0 in) *Max T-O weight* 2,313 kg (5,100 lb) *Max cruising speed* 348 km/h (216 mph) *Range* 1,036 km (1,141 miles)

Beechcraft Model 23 Musketeer (USA) First flown on 23 October 1961, the Musketeer was designed as a low-cost all-metal two–six-seat light aircraft. Deliveries of the original model were first made in the autumn of 1962 and in October 1965 Beech introduced the new range of Musketeer IIIs (123 kW; 165 hp Continental IO-346-A engine in Custom III). A more powerful engine

Beechcraft Duke B60.

was introduced on the Custom version in March 1967; and an optional aerobatic kit was made available for the Sport and Custom models in 1968. The Musketeer Super R, with retractable landing gear, was introduced in late 1969. The four final models of the Musketeer are listed below:

Custom Standard four-seat Musketeer with a 134 kW (180 hp) Lycoming O-360-A2G engine and non-retractable landing gear.

Sport Two-seat (optional four-seat) sporting and training version with 112 kW (150 hp) Lycoming O-320-E2C engine and non-retractable landing gear.

Super Generally similar to the Custom version but with 149 kW (200 hp) Lycoming IO-360-A2B engine and optional constant-speed propeller.

Super R Generally similar to the Super version but with constant-speed propeller as standard and retractable tricycle-type landing gear.

Production of the Musketeer totalled 2,079 of all models by the end of 1969.

Beechcraft Bonanza Model 36 (USA) This version of the Bonanza, introduced in mid-1968, is a full six-seat utility aircraft developed from the Bonanza Model V35B. It is currently known under the A36 designation and is generally similar to the V35B but has a conventional tail unit with sweptback vertical surfaces. In addition the A36 has large double doors on the starboard side of the fuselage aft of the wing root, to facilitate loading and unloading of bulky cargo when used in a utility role. A total of 1,266 civil versions of the Model 36/A36 had been built by April 1978. A turbocharged version is also available as the A36TC.

Data (A36): *Engine* one 212.4 kW (285 hp) Continental IO-520-BA flat-six *Wing span* 10.21 m (33 ft 6 in) *Length* 8.05 m (26 ft 5 in) *Max T-O weight* 1,542 kg (3,400 lb) *Max level speed* 338 km/h (209 mph) *Range* 1,648 km (1,023 miles) at 45% power

Beechcraft Turbo Baron A56TC (USA) This turbocharged version of the Baron was delivered to customers from September 1967 and a total of 93 were built before production ended at the end of 1971. Power was provided by two 283 kW (380 hp) Lycoming TIO-541-E1B4 engines.

Beechcraft Bonanza Model F33A/C (USA) The F33A version of the Bonanza is a four–five-seat executive aircraft, similar to the V35B but with a conventional tail unit. Its ancestry can be traced to the Model 33 Debonair. The F33C is generally similar to the F33A, but is approved for aerobatic and utility operation. The Model G33 was discontinued in early 1973 after only 49 had been produced.

A total of 2,189 Model 33s had been built by April 1978. Deliveries of F33As and aerobatic F33Cs to foreign air forces comprised 16 F33Cs to Iran, 5 F33Cs to the Mexican Navy, and 74 F33s to the Spanish Air Ministry and Air Force.

Data: *Engine* one 212.4 kW (285 hp) Continental IO-520-BA flat-six *Wing span* 10.21 m (33 ft 6 in) *Length* 8.13 m (26 ft 8 in) *Max T-O weight* 1,542 kg (3,400 lb) *Max level speed and range* as for V35B

Beechcraft Baron Model E55 (USA) The Baron E55 had its origin in the Baron 95-B55 when the Model 95-C55 was added to the Baron series in August 1965. The 95-C55 had 212.4 kW (285 hp) Continental IO-520-C engines, increased tailplane span, swept vertical surfaces, an extended nose baggage compartment and

Beechcraft King Air C90.

other refinements. It was followed by the D55 in October 1967 and subsequently the E55 with an improved interior and systems accessory refinements.

Beech had delivered 1,118 of this Baron series by early 1978.

Data: *Engines* as above *Wing span* as for Model 95-B55 *Length* 8.84 m (29 ft 0 in) *Max T-O weight* 2,405 kg (5,300 lb) *Max level speed* 386 km/h (239 mph) *Range* 2,103 km (1,306 miles)

Beechcraft Baron Model 58 (USA) In late 1969 Beech introduced a new version of the Baron, designated Model 58. Developed from the Baron D55, it differed by having the forward cabin section extended by 0.254 m (10 in), allowing the windscreen, passenger door, instrument panel and front seats to be moved forward and so providing a more spacious cabin. New features included double passenger/cargo doors, extended propeller hubs, redesigned engine nacelles to improve cooling, and a fourth window on each side of the cabin.

Beech had delivered 1,078 of this Baron series (including Baron 58Ps and 58TCs) by early 1978.

Data: *Engines* two 212.4 kW (285 hp) Continental IO-520-Cs *Wing span* as for Model 95-B55 *Length* 9.09 m (29 ft 10 in) *Max T-O weight* 2,449 kg (5,400 lb) *Max level speed* 386 km/h (239 mph)

Range 2,482 km (1,541 miles) *Accommodation* as for E55, except that folding fifth and sixth seats – or club seating comprising folding fifth and sixth seats and aft-facing third and fourth seats – are optional.

Beechcraft Duke Model 60 (USA) Design work on the original version of this four–six-seat pressurised and turbocharged light twin-engined transport started in January 1966. First flight was made on 29 December 1966.

The current version of the latest variant, the B60, has an AiResearch Lexan pressurisation system, with a mini-controller that allows selection of cabin altitude prior to take-off or landing. This system can also change the aircraft cabin altitude at any desired rate from 15 to 610 m/min (50 to 2,000 ft/min). A total of 462 Dukes had been produced by April 1978.

Data: *Engines* two 283 kW (380 hp) Lycoming TIO-541-E1C4 turbocharged flat-six *Wing span* 11.96 m (39 ft 3 in) *Length* 10.31 m (33 ft 10 in)

Max T-O weight 3,073 kg (6,775 lb) *Max level speed* 455 km/h (283 mph) *Range* 2,060 km (1,280 miles) at 68% power

Beechcraft King Air Model 90 (incl 90, A90, B90 and C90) (USA) Introduced in September 1970 the King Air C90 is a pressurised six–ten-seat twin-turboprop business aircraft which superseded the original Models 90, A90 and B90 King Air. It is powered by two 410 kW (550 ehp) P & W Aircraft of Canada PT6A-21 turboprops. Increases in take-off and climb power offer improvements in high altitude and hot weather operation and, since these engines also run cooler, increases in useful life and lower overhaul costs result.

The C90 King Air utilises the more advanced cabin pressurisation and heating system of the King Air 100. A total of 1,227 commercial and military King Air 90s had been delivered by April 1978. One is operated by the USAF as the VC-6B VIP transport and ten C90s went to the Spanish Air Force and Civil Aviation School as instrument trainers and liaison aircraft.

Data (C90): *Engines* as above *Wing span* 15.32 m (50 ft 3 in) *Length* 10.82 m (35 ft 6 in) *Max T-O weight* 4,377 kg (9,650 lb) *Max cruising speed* 412 km/h (256 mph) *Range* 2,374 km (1,474 miles)

Beechcraft Model 99 Airliner.

Beechcraft C-12A.

Beechcraft Sierra 200.

Beechcraft

Beechcraft Skipper.

Beechcraft King Air Model A100 (USA) The Model A100 version of the King Air is a pressurised transport with increased internal capacity and two 507 kW (680 ehp) Pratt & Whitney Aircraft of Canada PT6A-28 turboprop engines, enabling it to carry a useful load of more than two short tons. By comparison with the King Air 90 series, it has a fuselage 1.27 m (4 ft 2 in) longer, reduced wing span, larger rudder and elevator and twin-wheel main landing gear. It is available in a variety of interior configurations, seating six–eight in executive interior configurations, or up to 13 in high-density arrangement, plus crew of two.

A total of 275 commercial and military King Air 100s had been sold by April 1978. First deliveries of the advanced Model A100, comprising five U-21Fs for the Department of the Army, began in October 1971. Two were also supplied to the Spanish Air Force.

Two aircraft equipped with a Beech-developed UNACE package (Universal Aircraft Com/Nav Evaluation) have been delivered to Belgium and Indonesia. UNACE-configured aircraft, which provide an economical means of inspecting and calibrating aviation navigation aids, are operating also in Algeria, Canada, Malaysia, Mexico and the USA. Beech is able to modify King Airs for aerial photography; camera-equipped aircraft have been delivered to Canada, Chile, France, Jamaica, Saudi Arabia and Thailand, as well as to various US organisations.

Data: *Engines* as above *Wing span* 13.98 m (45 ft 10½ in) *Length* 12.18 m (39 ft 11⅜ in) *Max T-O weight* 5,216 kg (11,500 lb) *Max cruising speed* 436 km/h (270 mph) *Range* 2,483 km (1,542 miles)

Beechcraft Model 99 Airliner (USA) The prototype of the original Model 99 flew for the first time in July 1966 and the first delivery of a production aircraft was made on 2 May 1968. The later B99 Airliner, was also an unpressurised high-performance aircraft, with accommodation for 17 persons and designed specifically for the scheduled airline and air taxi market. A total of 164 of these were delivered to 64 operators. The final two versions available were the B99 Airliner, the standard model with a gross weight of 4,944 kg (10,900 lb) powered by two 507 kW (680 ehp) PT6A-28 turboprops; and the B99 Executive offering optional seating arrangements for 8–17 persons and various corporate interiors.

Beechcraft Sierra 200, Sundowner 180 and Sport 150 (USA) In December 1971 Beech introduced a new light aircraft marketing programme centred around three models, renamed from their previous Musketeer designations. In 1974 these designations were changed again to indicate the engine horsepower rating. Current names are Sierra 200 (formerly Model A24R

Bede BD-4.

Bede BD-5J Micro, as evaluated by the USAF.

Partly completed fuselage of a BD-5 Micro.

Musketeer Super R), Sundowner 180 (Model C23, formerly Musketeer Custom) and Sport 150 (Model B19, formerly Musketeer Sport).

The current Sundowner 180 is the basic four-seat version with a 134 kW (180 hp) Lycoming O-360-A4K engine. The Sport 150 is a two–four-seat sporting and training version with a 112 kW (150 hp) Lycoming O-320-E3D engine. The Sierra 200 seats four–six persons and is powered by a 149 kW (200 hp) Lycoming IO-360-A1B6 engine and is the only version with a retractable tricycle landing gear. Factory installed optional equipment packages are available for these aircraft – under the names Weekender, Holiday and Professional.

A total of 3,821 Musketeers, Sundowners, Sports and Sierras had been delivered by April 1978, including examples for military training abroad.

Data (Sundowner): *Engine* as above *Wing span* 9.98 m (32 ft 9 in) *Length* 7.85 m (25 ft 9 in) *Max T-O weight* 1,111 kg (2,450 lb) *Max level speed* 228 km/h (141 mph) *Range* 1,106 km (687 miles)

Beechcraft Baron Model 58P (USA) Pressurised version of the Model 58 Baron, powered by 231 kW (310 hp) Continental TSIO-520-L turbocharged engines. Deliveries began in late 1975 and 128 had been delivered by early 1978.

Beechcraft Baron Model 58TC (USA) Turbocharged version of the Baron Model 58 powered by 231 kW (310 hp) Continental TSIO-520-L turbocharged engines. Unlike the Model 58P, this aircraft is not pressurised. Deliveries began in mid-1976 and 59 had been delivered by early 1978.

Beechcraft King Air E90 (USA) Business aircraft, combining the airframe of the King Air C90 with the 507 kW (680 ehp) PT6A-28 turboprop engines of the King Air A100, each flat rated to 410 kW (550 ehp). Sixty-one delivered to the US Navy as T-44A advanced pilot trainers powered by two 560 kW (750 ehp) P & W AC PT6A-34B engines. Cruising speed of the T-44As is 445 km/h (276 mph).

Beechcraft King Air B100 (USA) Generally similar to the King Air A100 but powered by two 533 kW (715 shp) AiResearch TPE 331-6-252B turboprop engines and first flown on 20 March 1975. Maximum level speed 491 km/h (305 mph).

Beechcraft King Air C100 (USA) Version of the King Air series with 559 kW (750 shp) PT6A-135 turboprop engines, first announced in October 1977.

Beechcraft

Beechcraft Super King Air 200 (USA) Similar to the King Air 100 but with increased wing span, a new T-tail, 634 kW (850 shp) Pratt & Whitney Aircraft of Canada PT6A-41 turboprop engines, additional fuel capacity, increased cabin pressurisation and a higher gross weight. First flown in prototype form on 27 October 1972.

In 1974 Beech received a first contract from the US Army to build and support 34 modified versions designated C-12A. The Army was to receive 20 of these and the USAF 14. Subsequent orders for the US Army, USAF and US Navy brought the total to 133 aircraft. Accommodation is provided for eight passengers, with easy conversion for cargo missions. Standard power plant for the C-12A is two 559 kW (750 shp) PT6A-38s. In addition the US Army ordered three special mission RU-21Js, each having extensive antenna arrays and powered by PT6A-41 engines. A specialised maritime patrol version has also been built as the Maritime Monitor 200T, with an undernose search radome, wingtip fuel tanks to extend endurance to 10.3 h, and a VLF or inertial navigation system. 200Ts are operated by the Irish Air Force and the Japan Maritime Safety Agency.

By early 1978 Beech had delivered 318 Super King Airs to commercial and private operators and 113 military C-12As.
Data: *Engines* as above *Wing span* 16.61 m (54 ft 6 in) *Length* 13.34 m (43 ft 9 in) *Max T-O weight* 5,670 kg (12,500 lb) *Max cruising speed* 515 km/h (320 mph) *Range* 3,495 km (2,172 miles)

Beechcraft Model 77 Skipper (USA) First flown on 6 February 1975 the Skipper is intended primarily as a low-cost trainer for Beech Aero Centres. It utilises new construction techniques to reduce manufacturing costs. Power is provided by an 85.5 kW (115 hp) Lycoming O-235 series flat-four engine. Beech has received orders for more than 600 Skippers, initial deliveries of which began in 1979.
Data: *Engine* as above *Wing span* 9.14 m (30 ft 0 in) *Length* 7.32 m (24 ft 0 in) *Max T-O weight* 748 kg (1,650 lb)

Beechcraft Duchess 76 (USA) Four-seat light aircraft powered by two 134 kW (180 hp) Lycoming O-360-A1G6D opposite-rotating flat-four engines. The first flight was made on 24 May 1977. By May 1978 350 aircraft had been ordered.

The Duchess 76 is planned for use by Beech Aero Centres and is designed for the personal light twin, light charter and multi-engine flight trainer markets. Emphasis has been placed on

Bell P-39 Airacobra.

good low speed flight and single-engine handling characteristics; opposite-rotating propellers are fitted. Weekender, Holiday and Professional optional equipment packages are available.
Data: *Engines* as above *Wing span* 11.58 m (38 ft 0 in) *Length* 8.86 m (29 ft 0½ in) *Max T-O weight* 1,769 kg (3,900 lb) *Max cruising speed* 308 km/h (191 mph) *Range* 1,445 km (898 miles)

Beets G/B Special (USA) Single-seat sporting biplane with open cockpit for the pilot. Designed to be constructed by amateurs; plans available from the Stolp Starduster Corporation.

Bell FM-1 Airacuda (USA) Thirteen aircraft built between 1937 and 1940 for the USAAF as five-seat long-range escort fighters; powered by two 857 kW (1,150 hp) Allison V-1710-13 pusher engines. Armament included two cannon mounted in glazed nose of engine nacelles.

Bell P-39 Airacobra (USA) In 1938 Bell Aircraft produced the Airacobra single-seat fighter featuring a tricycle landing gear, a single Allison engine located behind and below the pilot and driving the propeller by means of an extension shaft, and

Bell P-59 Airacomet.

Bell YFM-1 Airacuda.

Bell X-1A and X-1B.

Bell X-1A being positioned beneath the B-29 motherplane.

a cannon firing through the hollow propeller shaft (in addition to fuselage-mounted machine-guns). Advantages of this layout were said to include superior vision and concentration of firepower in the nose. The first production aircraft (originally ordered by the French government) were delivered to the RAF and became operational in October 1941. In British service the Airacobra I/IA was used for a short time for ground attack duties. It was not well received and production aircraft completed for Britain, but undelivered, were taken on by the USAAF as trainers. New production began with 20 P-39Cs for the USAAF. P-39D (V-1710-35), F (-35), J(-35), K(V-1710-63; E6), L(-63), M(V-1710-83),

N(V-1710-85; E19) and Q versions were eventually built, bringing the total number of Airacobras completed to 9,558. More than half the total production went to Russia to act as interim fighters with the air force pending delivery of large numbers of MiGs and Yaks.

Data (P-39Q): *Engine* one 894 kW (1,200 hp) Allison V-1710-85 *Wing span* 10.36 m (34 ft 0 in) *Length* 9.19 m (30 ft 2 in) *Max T-O weight* 3,765 kg (8,300 lb) *Max level speed* 620 km/h (385 mph) *Range* 1,086 km (675 miles) *Armament* one 37 mm cannon in nose and four 0.50 in machine-guns in wings, plus a 500 lb bomb

Bell P-59 Airacomet (USA) The Airacomet was the first American-designed and built turbojet fighter. It first flew in prototype form on 1 October 1942. One later aircraft was subsequently exchanged for a British Gloster Meteor I fighter so that comparisons could be made between the types. Indeed the Airacomet's engines were developed from the British Whittle.

As noted in detail in the 1945–46 *Jane's*, the Bell Aircraft Corporation was requested in September 1941 to design a fighter to be equipped with thermal jet propulsion units of British Whittle design, and before the end of the month preliminary drawings had been submitted to and approved by the USAAF. To maintain secrecy, this project was given the designation XP-59A – the XP-59 being a totally different fighter project with a pusher radial engine and twin tail-booms. Following trials with the prototype and two other XP-59As (with General Electric Type I-A engines) 13 YP-59As were produced for service trials, deliveries beginning in 1943. Twenty production P-59As with 8.9 kN (2,000 lb st) General

Electric J31-GE-3 engines and 30 P-59Bs with similarly rated J31-GE-5 engines were delivered in 1944 and were used mainly as single-seat trainers.

Data (P-59B): *Engines* as above *Wing span* 13.87 m (45 ft 6 in) *Length* 11.84 m (38 ft 10 in) *Max T-O weight* 6,214 kg (13,700 lb) *Max level speed* 665 km/h (413 mph) *Armament* one 37 mm cannon and three 0.50 in machine-guns in nose; bomb racks provided under the outer wings.

Bell P-63 Kingcobra (USA) The P-63 fighter and fighter-bomber, the prototype of which first flew on 7 December 1942, was a development of the P-39, which it resembled in all its general features. It was never used operationally by the USAAF, the greater proportion of the 3,303 aircraft built being delivered to Russia under Lend–Lease, although numbers served with the Free French. A special modification of the P-63 was, however, evolved to serve as a target in the US Army's live ammunition training programme. This model (designated RP-63) was covered with more than a ton of special duralumin alloy armour plate against which 30-cal lead and plastic frangible machine-gun bullets disintegrated harmlessly. Under the armour were special instruments which, when the bullets struck, transmitted impulses to a spotlight, causing it to flash brightly.

Data (P-63A and RP-63C): *Engine* one 987 kW (1,325 hp) Allison V-1710-93 and one 1,125 kW (1,510 hp) V-1710-117 respectively *Wing span* 11.68 m (38 ft 4 in) *Length* 9.96 m (32 ft 8 in) *Max T-O weight* 4,763 kg (10,500 lb) *Max level speed* 657 km/h (408 mph) *Range* 724 km (450 miles) *Armament* one 37 mm cannon and two 0.50 in machine-guns in nose, plus one or three 500 lb bombs

Bell X-1 series (USA) Three X-1s were built to investigate flight problems at supersonic speed. The type was first air-launched (unpowered) on 19 January 1946; powered flights began in December of that year. On 14 October 1947 the first X-1, piloted by Capt Charles 'Chuck' Yeager, became the first aeroplane to exceed the speed of sound – reaching 1,078 km/h (670 mph) or Mach 1.015 at an altitude of 12,800 m (42,000 ft). The second X-1 was used by NASA for high-speed flight research; the third was des-

Bell X-2.

troyed at Edwards AFB during flight fuelling operations.

The X-1A was similar to the X-1, except for having turbo-driven fuel pumps (instead of a system using nitrogen under pressure), a new cockpit canopy, longer fuselage and increased fuel capacity. In this aircraft a speed of Mach 2.435 was achieved on 12 December 1953; in the following June an altitude of over 27,430 m (90,000 ft) was reached. In 1955 this aircraft was given new wing panels, but was destroyed before its first flight in this configuration.

Following the X-1B (used for thermal research) came the projected X-1C and the X-1D. The latter aircraft was destroyed in August 1951 after being jettisoned from its B-50 carrier-plane, following an explosion.

The last of the series was the X-1E: the second of the original X-1s fitted with wings of 4% thickness/chord ratio (instead of 10%), turbo-driven fuel pumps and a knife-edge windscreen. Ballistic control rockets designed by Bell Aircraft's Rocket Division were included in this aircraft, which was flight tested by NACA. A total of 156 flights were made with the X-1, 21 with the X-1A, 27 with the X-1B, one with the X-1D and 26 with the X-1E.

Data (X-1): *Engine* one 26.7 kN (6,000 lb st) Reaction Motors E6000-C4 (Thiokol XLR-11) bi-propellant rocket motor *Wing span* 8.53 m (28 ft 0 in) *Length* 9.45 m (31 ft 0 in) *Max T-O weight* 6,078 kg (13,400 lb)

Bell XV-3.

Bell X-5.

Bell Model 30s, in original and developed forms.

Bell Model 47G-2A.

Bell Model 47B-3.

Bell X-2 (USA) Two X-2 rocket-powered (Curtiss-Wright XLR25-CW-1) research aircraft built to explore the problems of transonic and supersonic flight. The second aircraft made the first powered flight on 18 November 1955 but was destroyed in a fatal crash on 27 September 1956 after a flight that had achieved an unprecedented Mach 3.2.

Bell X-5 (USA) First flown on 20 June 1951, the X-5 was built to investigate the aerodynamic effects of changing the degree of wing sweepback during flight. Its variable-geometry wings could be swept at angles varying from 20° to 60°. Two X-5s were built powered by Allison J35-A-17 turbojet engines.

Bell X-14 (USA) Experimental VTOL aircraft powered initially by two Bristol Siddeley Viper turbojet engines and later by two General Electric J85s. Used the jet-deflection method of flight, the thrust diverters deflecting the jet efflux towards the ground to raise or lower the aircraft vertically for take-off or landing. At a safe height the efflux was directed slightly rearward to provide some forward thrust in addition to jet lift. When the forward speed was sufficient for the fixed wings to provide adequate lift, the efflux was directed towards the rear. The X-14 made its first hovering flight on 19 February 1957 and first transition from hovering to forward flight on 24 May 1958.

Bell X-22A (Model D2127) (USA) Experimental V/STOL transport aircraft powered by four General Electric YT58-GE-8D shaft-turbine engines mounted in pairs at the root of each wing. These could power the four tilting ducted propellers fitted to the tips of the rear-mounted wings and foreplane for vertical and transitional flight and for control through thrust modulation (by changing the pitch of the propellers). The first flight was made on 17 March 1966 and by May 1969 the aircraft had accumulated 216 short take-offs, 405 vertical and 197 short landings, and 185 transitions from vertical to horizontal flight and vice versa. Flight testing continued into the early 1970s.

Bell XV-3 (USA) Experimental tilting-rotor convertiplane powered by one 335.3 kW (450 hp) Pratt & Whitney R-985 piston engine. Made its first vertical flight on 23 August 1955 and went on to complete more than 250 flights, totalling more than 125 flying hours. It was the world's first tilting-rotor, fixed-wing aircraft to achieve 100% tilting of its rotors, and proved the design practical.

Bell Model 47 (USA) The Bell Aircraft Corporation had an experimental helicopter (Model 30) flying in the middle of 1943 following two years of development work. From it was developed the Model 47, which first flew on 8 December 1945. It went on to receive the first Type Approval Certificate for a commercial helicopter and the first commercial licence awarded by the CAA on 8 March 1946. Among the first orders for the helicopter were a small number of YR-13s for the US Air Force and HTL-1s for the US Navy. Production by Bell continued until 1974, but the type remained in production in Italy as the Agusta-Bell 47 until 1976. For convenience, the major versions are listed below:

Model 47 Pre-production version with 133 kW (178 hp) Franklin engine and car-type cabin for two persons. Delivered to the US Air Force as YR-13s and ten transferred to the US Navy as HTL-1s.

Model 47B First major civil version, similar to the Model 47. Version available as the Model 47B-3 with open bubble-type cockpit. Examples acquired by the US Air Force and Navy.

Model 47D First version with the familiar 'goldfish bowl' canopy; openwork tailboom and ventral tailfin on three-seat Model 47D-1. Examples also delivered to the USAF as H-13Bs and to the US Navy as HTL-2s. Military Model 47D-1s became H-13D/Es (later US Army redesignated OH-13Es) and HTL-4/5s (later TH-13Ls).

Model 47E Powered by one 149 kW (200 hp) Franklin 6V4-200-C32 engine. Number acquired by the US Navy as HTL-3s.

Model 47G Combined three seats of the Model 47D-1 with engine of the Model 47E. Models 47G-2 to 47G-5 similar, but had various Lycoming engines from 149 to 209 kW (200 to 280 hp), and optional metal rotor blades. In production by Bell from 1953 to 1974. Model 47G-3B-2A and Model 47G-5A were final variants. Military examples acquired as the H-13G (later becoming OH-13G and still flown by the US Army for observation duties), HTL-6 for the US Navy (becoming TH-13M and later operated by the US Army as dual-control trainer), H-13H and H-13K (Model 47G-2 and G-3, later becoming OH-13H and K and operated by US Army for observation duties), and TH-13T (Model 47G-3B-1 instrument trainer operated by US Army).

Model 47H Generally similar to the Model 47G series, but with fully-enclosed fuselage and car-type cabin. Powered by one 149 kW (200 hp) Franklin 6V4-200-C32AB engine.

Model 47J Ranger (originally Model 47G-1) Generally similar to Model 47H, but seating four persons; 164 kW (220 hp) Lycoming VO-435 engine. Powered controls and metal rotor blades introduced as standard on Model 47J-2 (194 kW; 260 hp VO-540) in 1960. Military versions acquired as the H-13J by the USAF, HUL-1 by the US Navy (became UH-13P) and HUL-1G by the Coast Guard (became HH-13Q).

Other military versions of the Bell 47 included the Navy HUL-1M (Model 47L, with Allison YT63-A-3 turboshaft engine, became UH-13R) and HTL-7 (Bell 47K with HUL-1 body, dual-controls and power unit, became TH-13N). All USAF Bell Model 47s became UH-13H/J utility helicopters in 1962. In addition, many were built by Westland Helicopters of the UK as Sioux AH.1 (Model 47G-3B-1) for the British Army. Military Model 47s are generally known as Sioux helicopters and remain operational with the forces of about 30 countries. Civil Bell Model 47s also remain in worldwide use.

In Italy Agusta-Bell produced well over 1,100 Model 47s; this number includes two special variants of its own design produced from the J-2A, known as the AB 47J-3 and AB 47J-3B-1. The former has a modified main transmission able to absorb greater power input (a special ASW version was evolved for the Italian Navy carrying a Mk 44 homing torpedo) and the latter is a high-altitude version with a 201 kW (270 hp) Lycoming TVO-435-B1A engine.

Data (Model 47G-3B-2A): *Engine* one 209 kW (280 hp) Lycoming TVO-435-F1A *Rotor diameter*

11.32 m (37 ft 1½ in) *Length of fuselage* 9.63 m (31 ft 7 in) *Max T-O weight* 1,338 kg (2,950 lb) *Recommended cruising speed* 135 km/h (84 mph) *Range* 397 km (247 miles) *Accommodation* three seats in enclosed cabin; can carry 454 kg (1,000 lb) of cargo externally

Bell Model 48 (USA) Virtually a scaled-up version of the Bell Model 47, incorporating the same basic rotor system. Three prototypes were ordered by the USAF in 1946: two as five-seat XR-12s with 410 kW (540 hp) Pratt & Whitney R-1340 Wasp engines; one as the XR-12B with accommodation for ten and powered by a 447 kW (600 hp) R-1340-55 Wasp engine. Later redesignated XH-12/12Bs. Ten pre-production YH-12s followed, each accommodating a crew of two and eight passengers or a pilot, six stretchers and an attendant for emergency rescue and evacuation duties.

Bell Model 61 (USA) The Model 61 or HSL-1 was a large tandem-rotor anti-submarine helicopter which successfully won a design competition organised by the US Navy in June 1950. Power was provided by a 1,788 kW (2 400 hp) Pratt & Whitney R-2800-50 engine. The first of three prototypes flew on 4 March 1953 and 50 production

Bell Model 47J-2A Ranger.

Bell HSL-1.

Bensen B-8M
Gyro-Copter.

Blériot XI monoplane.

Boeing Model 247.

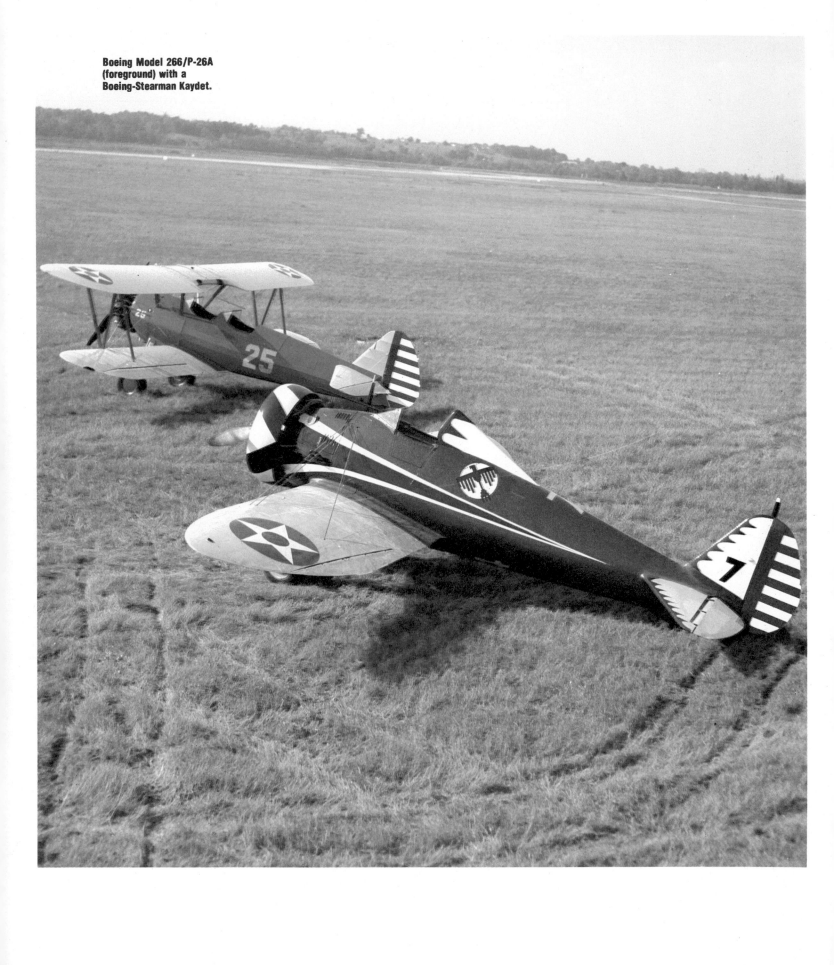

Boeing Model 266/P-26A (foreground) with a Boeing-Stearman Kaydet.

Boeing B-17G Flying
Fortresses.

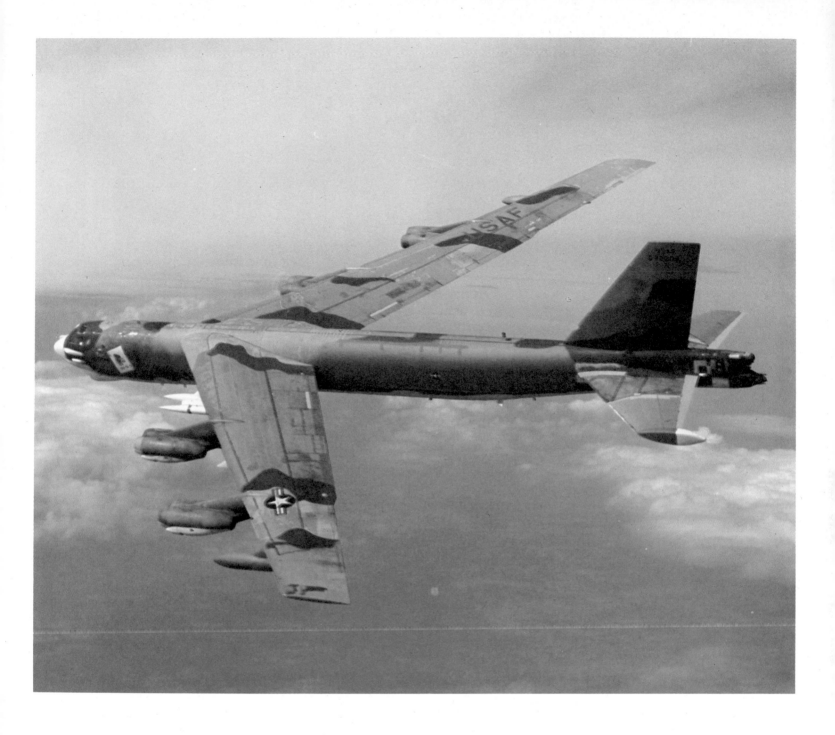

Boeing Model 450/B-47
Stratojet.

Boeing Model 464/B-52G
Stratofortress carrying
SRAM missiles.

Boeing B-29
Superfortress.

helicopters were built. Each carried a crew of four (made up of a pilot, co-pilot and two sonar operators) and was intended to carry lightweight homing weapons, including missiles.

Bell Model 204 (USA) In 1955 the Bell Model 204 won a US Army design competition for a utility helicopter suitable for front-line casualty evacuation, general utility and instrument training duties. The production version was originally designated HU-1, but this was subsequently changed to UH-1. The official US Army name for the helicopter is Iroquois.

UH-1C Iroquois Developed version of the UH-1B. New rotor with blades of increased chord offering higher speed and better manoeuvrability. Superseded UH-1B for the US Army, but was itself superseded by the HueyCobra.

UH-1E Iroquois Similar to UH-1B for US Marine Corps. Pilot and eight troops or 1,815 kg (4,000 lb) of cargo. Could carry rockets and machine-guns.

UH-1F Iroquois Based on UH-1B. Twenty-five ordered by USAF for missile site support

Bell Model 204B.

The first of three XH-40 prototypes flew on 20 October 1956 and was followed by six YH-40 service test models and nine UH-1 preproduction models. The initial production version was the UH-1A Iroquois. The variants are listed below:

UH-1A Iroquois Initial production version powered by one Lycoming T53-L-1A turboshaft engine, derated to 574 kW (770 shp). Deliveries began to the US Army in June 1959. Thirteen modified to carry 16 × 2.75 in rockets and two 0.30 in machine-guns for service in Vietnam with the Utility Tactical Transport Helicopter Company.

UH-1B Iroquois Development of the UH-1A powered initially by one 716 kW (960 shp) T53-L-5 turboshaft engine. Subsequent deliveries with 820 kW (1,100 shp) Lycoming T53-L-11 engine. Crew of two plus seven troops or three stretchers and two sitting casualties. Alternatively 1,360 kg (3,000 lb) of freight. For armed support missions could be equipped with rocket pack and electrically controlled machine-guns. Delivered from March 1961.

duties. Powered by General Electric T58-GE-3 turboshaft engine, derated to 820 kW (1,100 shp) and driving a 14.63 m (48 ft 0 in) rotor. Pilot and ten passengers or 1,815 kg (4,000 lb) of cargo. First delivered in February 1964. Used for classified psychological warfare missions in Vietnam.

TH-1F Iroquois Training version of UH-1F for USAF.

HH-1K Iroquois SAR version for US Navy. Twenty-seven ordered and delivered in 1970. Powered by T53-L-13 engine.

TH-1L Iroquois Training version for US Navy, similar to UH-1E. Powered by T53-L-13 turboshaft, derated to 820 kW (1,100 shp). Improved electronics. Forty-five ordered in 1968.

UH-1L Iroquois Utility version of TH-1L for US Navy. Eight ordered; delivered in 1969.

UH-1M Iroquois US Army version fitted with Hughes Aircraft Iroquois night fighter and night tracker system to detect and acquire ground targets under low ambient lighting conditions. Three deployed with hunter-killer

helicopter groups in Vietnam in 1970 to evaluate system.

RH-2 One UH-1A used as flying laboratory research vehicle.

Model 204B Commercial and military export version of UH-1B with ten seats, 820 kW (1,100 shp) T5311A turboshaft engine and 14.63 m (48 ft 0 in) rotor. Baggage compartment in tailboom. Over 60 commercial 204Bs delivered by end of 1967, in addition to military deliveries.

UH-1P Iroquois Similar to UH-1F but used for special missions.

Agusta-Bell 204B Utility helicopter, similar to Iroquois, produced under licence in Italy from 1961 to 1974 and sold to military and civil customers. By end of 1973 about 250 delivered, including the AB 204AS version for the Italian and Spanish navies, armed with two Mk 44 homing torpedoes or AS.12 air-to-surface missiles depending on anti-submarine search and attack or anti-fast surface vessel role.

Data (UH-1E Iroquois): *Engine* as above *Rotor diameter* 13.41 m (44 ft 0 in) *Length of fuselage* 11.7 m (38 ft 5 in) *Max T-O weight* 4,309 kg (9,500 lb) *Max level speed* 222 km/h (138 mph) *Range* 460 km (286 miles)

Bell Model 205 and 205A-1 (USA) Although basically similar to the earlier Model 204, the Model 205 introduced a longer fuselage, increased cabin space to accommodate a much larger number of passengers, and other changes. The military version of the Model 205 retains the Iroquois name, while the commercial utility version is designated Model 205A-1.

The initial production version for the US Army was the UH-1D powered by an 820 kW (1,100 shp) Lycoming T53-L-11 turboshaft engine, driving a 14.63 m (48 ft) rotor. Accommodation provided for a pilot and 14 troops, or six stretchers and a medical attendant, or 1,815 kg (4,000 lb) of cargo. The first YUH-1D flew on 16 August 1961 and delivery to Army units began two years later. A further 352 UH-1Ds were built subsequently under licence in Germany for the German Army and Air Force. The UH-1D was followed into production by the UH-1H powered by an 1,044 kW (1,400 shp) T53-L-13 engine. By 1976 1,242 had been built, including nine for the RNZAF. Production continues to meet export orders. A further 118 were built under licence in the Republic of China. Originally designated CUH-1Hs, ten similar helicopters were acquired for the Mobile Command, Canadian Armed Forces; subsequently redesignated CH-118s. The designation HH-1H applies to 30 USAF helicopters (similar to UH-1H) for local base rescue.

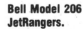

Bell AH-1S HueyCobra.

Bell Model 206
JetRangers.

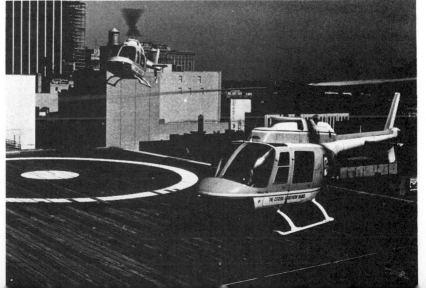

Bell Model 206L-1 LongRanger II.

Bell AH-1Q HueyCobra.

Bell AH-1J SeaCobra.

The commercial Model 205A-1 is a 15-seat utility helicopter developed from the UH-1H, with a T5313B engine derated to 932 kW (1,250 shp). It is designed for rapid conversion for alternative air freight, flying crane, ambulance, rescue and executive roles. External load capacity in the flying crane role is 2,268 kg (5,000 lb). It is also licence-built by Agusta-Bell.
Data (UH-1H Iroquois): *Engine* as above *Rotor diameter* 14.63 m (48 ft 0 in) *Length of fuselage* 12.77 m (41 ft 10¾ in) *Max T-O weight* 4,309 kg (9,500 lb) *Max level and cruising speed* 204 km/h (127 mph) *Range* 511 km (318 miles)

Bell Model 206 (USA) Four-seat lightweight observation helicopter powered by a 186.3 kW (250 hp) Allison T63 turboshaft engine. Produced to a US Army specification and first flown on 8 December 1962. Five delivered; originally designated HO-4s by the Army but subsequently redesignated OH-4As. Evaluated against Hiller and Hughes prototypes. No further production.

Bell Model 206 JetRanger (USA) The Model 206A was the original version of the JetRanger general-purpose light helicopter. The prototype flew for the first time on 8 December 1962, and 660 production aircraft had been delivered by the close of production in 1972, each powered by a 236.4 kW (317 shp) Allison 250-C18A turboshaft engine. This model was followed on the production lines by the Model 206B JetRanger II. Its 298 kW (400 shp) Allison 250-C20 turboshaft engine allows better performance under hot-day/high-altitude conditions. A modification kit to convert Model 206As to JetRanger II standard was offered simultaneously with production JetRanger IIs. By early 1977 Bell and its licensees had manufactured more than 5,000 Model 206 series helicopters (including 1,619 JetRanger IIs), of which 2,200 were for commercial use. The latest version of the Model 206 is the Model 206B JetRanger III powered by a 313 kW (420 shp)

Allison 250-C20B turboshaft engine. This model incorporates the enlarged and improved tail rotor mast, increased capacity oil cooler blower and improved transmission oil temperature gauge of the LongRanger. Modification kits for JetRanger IIs are also offered. By early 1978 the total number of Model 206 helicopters built had risen to 6,000, including 2,279 for commercial use (see also **LongRanger**, **Kiowa** and **SeaRanger**).
Data (Jet Ranger III): *Engine* as above *Rotor diameter* 10.16 m (33 ft 4 in) *Length of fuselage* 9.5 m

(31 ft 2 in) *Max T-O weight* 1,451 kg (3,200 lb) *Max cruising speed* 219 km/h (136 mph) *Range* 608 km (378 miles) *Accommodation* five persons and 113 kg (250 lb) of baggage

Bell Model 206L LongRanger (USA) First announced in September 1973, the LongRanger was developed to meet a requirement for a turbine-powered general-purpose helicopter in a size and performance range between the five-seat JetRanger II and 15-seat Model 205A-1. The original Model 206L LongRanger flew for the first time on 11 September 1974 and production aircraft were delivered from October 1975. It incorporated Bell's Noda-Matic cabin suspension system, which reduces rotor-induced vibration and isolates structure-borne noise from the cabin environment. Accommodation provided for a pilot, co-pilot and five passengers. Alternative layouts allow for two stretchers and two ambulatory patients/attendants, or internal or external freight, or a four-seat executive seating arrangement.

The new Model 206L-1 LongRanger II was certificated in May 1978, introducing a new 373 kW (500 shp) Allison 250-C28B engine. Detail improvements include a redesigned aft cabin to provide 0.05 m (2 in) more headroom for rear seat passengers, new cowlings, firewall, engine mountings and engine deck area structure and other refinements. Deliveries of the Model 206L and L-1 were expected to reach 230 by the beginning of 1979.
Data (LongRanger II): *Engine* as above *Rotor diameter* 11.28 m (37 ft 0 in) *Length overall* 12.46 m (40 ft 10½ in) *Max T-O weight* 1,837 kg (4,050 lb) *Max cruising speed* 215 km/h (134 mph) *Range* 621 km (386 miles)

Bell Model 209 HueyCobra and SeaCobra (USA) First flown on 7 September 1965 (six months after its development was started) the HueyCobra is a development of the UH-1B/C Iroquois intended specifically for armed helicopter missions. A main feature of its design is its extremely slim fuselage, which makes it a difficult

target from the ground. Production versions are listed below:

AH-1G HueyCobra Original version for the US Army powered by a 1,044 kW (1,400 shp) Lycoming T53-L-13 turboshaft engine, derated to 820 kW (1,100 shp). Armed initially with an Emerson Electric TAT-102A six-barrel machine-gun turret, which was superseded by the XM-28 subsystem. Initial contract for 110 production aircraft was placed in April 1966; by October 1968 the total ordered had risen to 838. In January 1970 the US Army ordered 170 more, followed by an order for 70 in 1971. Twenty were also acquired by the Spanish Navy for anti-shipping strike duties and Israel received six. Operational deployment in Vietnam began in 1967. The US Marine Corps acquired 38 during 1969 for transition training and initial deployment, pending delivery of the AH-1J.

AH-1J SeaCobra Modified version of the AH-1G, initially for the US Marine Corps (202 later acquired by Iran, delivered from 1974). A batch of 49 was ordered in May 1969 and deliveries begun in mid-1970. Twenty more were ordered in 1970, the final two becoming prototype AH-1Ts. The SeaCobra has a 1,342 kW (1,800 shp) Pratt & Whitney Aircraft of Canada T400-CP-400 coupled free-turbine turboshaft power plant (a military version of the PT6T-3 Turbo Twin Pac), flat rated for 820 kW (1,100 shp) continuous output. An electrically driven 20 mm turret system (developed by General Electric) is faired into the forward lower fuselage and houses an XM-197 three-barrel weapon (a lightweight M-61 cannon). Four external stores attachment points under the stub wings can accommodate various loads, including XM-18E1 7.62 mm Minigun pods as well as 2.75 in folding-fin rockets. The helicopter also has marine electronics.

AH-1Q HueyCobra Anti-armour version equipped with eight Hughes TOW anti-tank missiles. First of eight pre-production helicopters delivered to the US Army in early 1973, at which time it was expected that nearly half the US Army's AH-1Gs would be converted to AH-1Q standard. Of the 93 aircraft converted from AH-1G to Q standard, 20 have been further modified to AH-1S standard. Sixty-two others in Germany will be brought up to S standard by Dornier.

AH-1R HueyCobra As for AH-1G but with uprated power plant (1,342 kW; 1,800 shp T53-L-703); without TOW missile installation.

AH-1S HueyCobra Advanced version of G/Q equipped to fire TOW missiles; with upgraded power plant (as for AH-1R), gearbox and transmission. US Army planning calls for modification of 690 AH-1Gs to AH-1S, of which 290 (including AH-1Qs) have already been converted and are known as Modernised AH-1S. Also being built are 297 new production helicopters (Production AH-1S) incorporating a flat plate canopy designed to reduce sun glint, an improved cockpit design optim-

Bell AH-1S HueyCobra.

ised for nap-of-the-earth flight and other engineering changes. A follow-on programme will add several survivability features: a turreted cannon, improved fire control and stores management, and other refinements (Upgunned AH-1S). The first new Production AH-1S was accepted by the US Army in March 1977 and 231 had been ordered by the autumn of 1978 – including 100 to initial Production S standard and 98 to Upgunned standard. A third modernisation programme is also planned for all AH-1Ss.

AH-1T Improved SeaCobra Fifty-seven examples ordered by the USMC. First delivered in October 1977. Twenty-three to be modified to TOW missile configuration. The AH-1T incorporates the AH-1J airframe but embodies the dynamic system of the Model 214, technology developed for the Model 309 KingCobra and an upgraded engine (1,469 kW; 1,970 shp Pratt & Whitney Aircraft of Canada T400-WV-402 coupled free-turbine turboshaft).

Data (AH-1S): *Engine* as above *Rotor diameter* 13.41 m (44 ft 0 in) *Length of fuselage* 13.59 m (44 ft 7 in) *Max level speed* 227 km/h (141 mph)

Bell Model 212 Twin Two-Twelve.

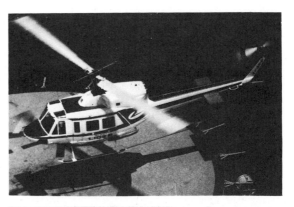

Bell Model 214.

in TOW configuration; AH-1G 277 km/h (172 mph) *Range* 507 km (315 miles) *Armament* one XM-35 six-barrel 20 mm automatic cannon or one XM-28 Minigun/grenade launcher subsystem; up to eight TOW missiles.

Bell Model 212 Twin Two-Twelve (USA) Twin-engined development of the UH-1; developed initially to a Canadian government requirement. Fifty subsequently ordered for the Canadian Armed Forces as CUH-1Ns (later redesignated CH-135s), delivered between 1971 and 1972. Similar UH-1Ns were ordered simultaneously for the USAF (79, delivered from 1970), US Navy (40) and USMC (22). A further 159 were later ordered for the USN and USMC, delivered from 1973 to 1978, and others have been delivered to the air forces of Bangladesh (6) and Argentina (8).

Bell Model 412 advanced-technology, four-blade variant of the Model 212.

A commercial version (known as the Twin Two-Twelve) is also in full production and can carry an external load of 2,268 kg (5,000 lb) – compared with 1,814 kg (4,000 lb) of the UH-1N. Model 212s are also commercially operated with IFR certification.

Bell Model 301 (XV-15).

Data (UH-1N): *Engines* one Pratt & Whitney Aircraft of Canada PT6T-3 Turbo Twin Pac, comprising two PT6 turboshaft engines coupled to a combining gearbox with a single output shaft, producing 1,342 kW (1,800 shp) and rated at 842 kW (1,130 shp) for continuous operation *Rotor diameter* 14.69 m (48 ft 2¼ in) *Length of fuselage* 12.92 m (42 ft 4¾ in) *Max T-O weight* 4,762 kg (10,500 lb) *Max cruising speed* 185 km/h (115 mph) *Range* 400 km (248 miles) *Accommodation* pilot and 14 passengers or cargo

Bell Model 222.

Bell Model 214A and 214C (USA) Developed from the Model 214 Huey Plus, the advanced Model 214A 16-seat utility helicopter is powered by a 2,185 kW (2,930 shp) Lycoming LTC4B-8D turboshaft engine. The initial order for 287 helicopters was placed by the US Army, these being acquired by Iran through the US government. A further six were ordered by the Iranian government in 1977. Deliveries to Iran began in May 1975.

In 1976 the Iranian government ordered 39 Model 214Cs, equipped for search and rescue. Prior to the time of the change of government in Iran, it had been planned that Bell and the Iranian Helicopter Industry (IHI) would co-produce 50 Model 214As and subsequently 350 improved twin-engined Model 214ST (Stretched Twin).

Data: *Engine* as above *Max T-O weight* 6,260 kg (13,800 lb) *Cruising speed* 259 km/h (161 mph) *Range* 456 km (283 miles)

Bell Model 214B BigLifter (USA) Commercial version of the Model 214A powered by a 2,185 kW (2,930 shp) Lycoming T5508D turboshaft engine (1,379.5 kW; 1,850 shp max continuous power). It is able to cruise at 259 km/h (161 mph) with an internal load of 1,814 kg (4,000 lb). A passenger configuration provides seating for 14 persons in addition to the crew of two. An external load of more than 3,175 kg (7,000 lb) can be carried. In an agricultural role this allows nearly four US tons of chemicals to be lifted, or 3,025 litres (800 US gallons) of water or suppressant in a fire-fighting role. The Model 214B-1 differs only in having its max T-O weight for internal load-carrying limited to 5,670 kg (12,500 lb).

Data: *Rotor diameter* 15.24 m (50 ft 0 in) *Max T-O weight* (external loading) 7,257 kg (16,000 lb)

Bell Model 222 (USA) In 1974 Bell announced its intention of developing the Model 222, described as the first commercial light twin-engined helicopter to be built in the USA. The first prototype flew on 13 August 1976. Deliveries of production aircraft were planned to begin in 1979. Standard accommodation is for a pilot and seven passengers, although a high-density ten-seat layout is available. The streamlined configuration of the helicopter is enhanced by the hydraulically retractable tricycle-type landing gear.

Data: *Engines* two Avco Lycoming LTS 101-650C2 turboshafts, each with max continuous rating of 440 kW (590 shp) *Rotor diameter* 12.12 m (39 ft 9 in) *Length of fuselage* 10.98 m

(36 ft 0¼ in) *Max T-O weight* 3,470 kg (7,650 lb) *Max level and cruising speed* 265 km/h (165 mph) *Range* 644 km (400 miles)

Bell Model 301 (USA) Tilt-rotor research aircraft powered by two wingtip-mounted 1,156 kW (1,550 shp) Avco Lycoming LTC1K-4K turboshaft engines, driving 7.62 m (25 ft 0 in) rotors. Engines and rotors turn through 90° for vertical or horizontal flight. The first of two aircraft (designated XV-15 by the US Army) made its first free hovering flight on 3 May 1977.

Bell Kiowa and SeaRanger (USA) On 8 March 1968 the US Army named Bell as winner of its re-opened light observation helicopter competition and awarded the company the first increment of a planned total order for 2,000 OH-58A Kiowa aircraft. The Kiowa is generally similar to the Model 206A but has an increased-diameter main rotor and changes to internal layout and electrics.

The designation CH-136 Kiowa applies to 74 helicopters delivered to the Canadian Armed Forces; 206B-1 Kiowa, to 56 helicopters for Australia and co-produced by Bell and the Commonwealth Aircraft Corporation; OH-58B Kiowa, to 12 helicopters for Austria; OH-58C Kiowa, to three OH-58As converted for higher performance, with an uprated 313 kW (420 shp) Allison T63-A-720 turboshaft engine, an IR reduction package and a flat glass canopy to reduce glint (production pending); and TH-57A SeaRanger, to 40 dual-control trainers for the US Navy.

Data (OH-58A): *Engine* one 236.4 kW (317 shp) Allison T63-A-700 turboshaft *Rotor diameter* 10.77 m (35 ft 4 in) *Length of fuselage* 9.93 m (32 ft 7 in) *Max T-O weight* 1,360 kg (3,000 lb) *Cruising speed* 188 km/h (117 mph) *Range* 490 km (305 miles) *Accommodation* pilot and co-pilot/ observer and two passengers or cargo *Armament* XM-27 armament kit utilising a 7.62 mm Minigun

Bellanca CH.300 (USA) The Bellanca Aircraft Corporation was incorporated in December 1927, taking over the old Bellanca Aircraft Corporation of America. The CH.300 was one of its first products and was a six-seat cabin monoplane powered by a 223.5 kW (300 hp) Wright Whirlwind radial engine. *(Bellanca aircraft are listed in order of appearance and carry the names under which they were reported at the time in Jane's.)*

Bellanca P (USA) Fourteen-seat commercial cabin monoplane powered by a 372.6 kW (500 hp) Pratt & Whitney whornet radial engine.

Bellanca Pacemaker (USA) The Pacemaker of the early 1930s was a six-seat cabin monoplane powered by a Wright Whirlwind or Pratt & Whitney Wasp Junior radial engine of 223.5–298 kW (300–400 hp). Maximum speed with the 298 kW (400 hp) Whirlwind Model E engine was 249 km/h (155 mph). A seaplane version was also produced with twin Edo floats. An example of a version with a 167.7 kW (225 hp) Packard-Diesel engine was flown by Messrs Walter Lees and Frederic Brossy between 25 May and 28 May 1931 to break the world's non-refuelling endurance record, by remaining airborne for 84 hours 33 minutes at Jacksonville, Florida.

Bellanca 14-13 Cruisair.

Bellanca 14-19 Cruisemaster.

Bellanca Skyrocket (USA) The standard Skyrocket was generally similar to the Pacemaker except that power was provided by a 316.7 kW (425 hp) Pratt & Whitney Wasp radial engine. A seaplane version was also produced. Three examples were acquired by the US Navy in 1932 under the RE designation, two being used for radio research and one later going to the Marines as an air ambulance (2 stretchers).

Bellanca de Luxe Skyrocket (USA) Essentially the same as the standard Skyrocket but with a 335.3 kW (450 hp) Wasp SC engine and a number of detail design improvements.

Bellanca Airbus (USA) Eleven–fourteen-passenger commercial sesquiplane of unusual appearance; designed to be powered by a 447 kW (600 hp) geared Curtiss Conqueror, 428.5 kW (575 hp) Wright Cyclone or Pratt & Whitney Hornet direct-drive, or 465.8 kW (625 hp) Wright Cyclone or Pratt & Whitney Hornet geared radial engine. Developed into the Aircruiser.

Bellanca Senior Pacemaker (USA) Six–eight-seat monoplane developed from the Pacemaker. Passenger seats removable for freight carrying. Powered by a 313 kW (420 hp) Wright R-975-E3

Bellanca Model 77-140 Bomber seaplane.

Bellanca

Bellanca Super Viking.

Whirlwind radial engine. Land- and seaplane versions available.

Data (landplane): *Engine* as above *Wing span* 15.39 m (50 ft 6 in) *Length* 8.51 m (27 ft 11 in) *Max T-O weight* 2,540 kg (5,600 lb) *Max level speed* 273 km/h (170 mph)

Bellanca Senior Skyrocket (USA) Generally similar to the Senior Pacemaker, except that power was provided by a 410 kW (550 hp) Pratt & Whitney R-1340 Wasp radial engine. Accommodation for the pilot and five or seven passengers. One acquired by the US Navy in 1938 and designated JE-1.

Data (landplane): *Engine* as above *Wing span* 15.39 m (50 ft 6 in) *Length* 8.69 m (28 ft 6 in) *Max T-O weight* 2,540 kg (5,600 lb) *Max level speed* 298 km/h (185 mph)

Bellanca 260C Model 14-19-3C.

Bellanca de Luxe Senior Skyrocket (USA) Substantially the same as the standard model except that power was provided by a 391.2 kW (525 hp) Pratt & Whitney Wasp radial engine. The aircraft incorporated a number of additional refinements, including complete bonding and shielding of the wireless, Sperry horizon and directional gyro and special internal and external finish.

Bellanca Aircruiser (USA) The Aircruiser first appeared in the early 1930s as a development of the Airbus. As with the Airbus, its sesquiplane wing structure consisted of a conventional top wing and bottom planes of which the inner sections had coarse anhedral and the outer sections sloped up from the extremities of the inner sections to the top plane in the form of aerofoil-sectioned bracing struts. Power was provided by a single Wright Cyclone or Pratt & Whitney Hornet engine. Accommodation was for a pilot and 11–14 passengers. Baggage and mail compartments were positioned forward of the pilot's cockpit. Aft of the cabin was a toilet.

Champion (Bellanca) Citabria.

The Aircruiser met with considerable commercial success as a land- and seaplane. Military examples were delivered to air forces, including those of the USA and Cuba. The USAAC aircraft carried C-27 designations and deliveries began with four Y1C-27s for evaluation. Each accommodated 12 persons and was powered by a 410 kW (550 hp) Hornet engine. The Y1C-27s were followed by ten C-27As with 484.4 kW

(650 hp) R-1860-19 Hornet engines. After tests of one C-27A with a 503 kW (675 hp) Cyclone engine, all 14 aircraft were subsequently re-engined with 559 kW (750 hp) Wright R-1820-25 Cyclone radial engines.

Data (C-27): *Engine* as above *Wing span* 19.81 m (65 ft 0 in) *Length* 13.03 m (42 ft 9 in) *Max T-O weight* 4,377 kg (9,650 lb) *Max level speed* 265 km/h (165 mph) *Range* 1,770 km (1,100 miles)

Bellanca bomber (USA) First appearing in 1933, the Bellanca bomber was basically a twin 535 kW (715 hp) Wright R-1820-F3 Cyclone-engined Aircruiser, with the engines attached to the leading edge of the upper wing. Land- and seaplane versions were offered and the type could also be used as a troop transport, freight carrier or ambulance.

Bellanca 28-90 (USA) Two-seat multi-purpose observation, fighting or bombing braced low-wing monoplane powered by a 671 kW (900 hp) Pratt & Whitney R-1830 Twin Wasp radial engine. The aircraft also had a retractable landing gear; the cockpits were enclosed by a single long canopy.

Bellanca 17-20 (USA) Five-seat low-wing cabin monoplane under construction in 1937.

Bellanca 28-92 (USA) High-performance cantilever low-wing monoplane powered by a 313 kW (420 hp) Ranger engine in the nose and two wing-mounted 186.3 kW (250 hp) Menasco C-65s. Built for the Istres–Damascus–Paris air race.

Bellanca Junior 14-7 and 14-9 (USA) Three-seat cantilever low-wing cabin monoplanes with fixed or retractable landing gears. The 14-7 powered by a 56 kW (75 hp) Le Blond 5E radial engine and the 14-9 by a 67 kW (90 hp) Le Blond 5F. Max level speed of the 14-9 (later called Cruisair) with retractable landing gear 220 km/h (137 mph). A version with an 89.4 kW (120 hp) Franklin engine followed as the Cruisair 14-14.

Bellanca YO-51 (USA) Two-seat short-range army co-operation high-wing monoplane of 1940 powered by a 335.3 kW (450 hp) Ranger SGV-770B-3 inverted V engine.

Bellanca 14-13-3 Cruisair (USA) The post-war Model 14-13 Cruisair is a development of the pre-war Cruisair. The prototype flew for the first time in 13 November 1945. This version was a four-seat low-wing cabin monoplane powered by a 112 kW (150 hp) Franklin 6A4-150-B3 engine and with a retractable landing gear.
Data: *Engine* as above *Wing span* 10.41 m (34 ft 2 in) *Length* 6.48 m (21 ft 3 in) *Max T-O weight* 975 kg (2,150 lb) *Cruising speed* 266 km/h (165 mph)

Bellanca 14-13-3W (USA) This was a general utility version of the 14-13-3 with the inside lined with plywood and the rear seat removable for cargo carrying. The rear floor was also strengthened.

Bellanca 14-19 Cruisemaster (USA) This was basically a higher-performance version of the Cruisair powered by a 141.6 kW (190 hp) Lycoming O-435-A engine. Length was 7.01 m (23 ft 0 in); max T-O weight 1,179 kg (2,600 lb); and cruising speed 290 km/h (180 mph).

Bellanca 260C Model 14-19-3C (USA) Known formerly as International Aircraft Manufacturing Inc (Inter-air), Bellanca Sales Company was a subsidiary of Miller Flying Service. It manufactured new versions of the well-known Bellanca 14-19 four-seat business aircraft in considerably refined form. These can be identified by the single swept-back vertical tail assembly which replaced the original triple-fin tail unit. Power was provided by the 194 kW (260 hp) Continental IO-470-F flat-six engine. Max level speed 315 km/h (196 mph).

Bellanca Viking series (USA) Bellanca Sales Company acquired the assets of Champion Aircraft Corporation in 1970. Following the merger the name Bellanca Aircraft Corporation was adopted, and Bellanca now markets both its own products and those of Champion Aircraft.

From the original Bellanca 260C and Standard Viking 300 series (comprising the 223.5 kW; 300 hp Continental IO-520-D-engined Standard Viking 300, Lycoming IO-540-engined Standard Viking 300, and 231 kW; 310 hp TIO-540-engined Standard Turbo Viking 300) have been developed the current models. These comprise the 223.5 kW (300 hp) Continental IO-520-K-engined Model 17-30A Super Viking 300A; 223.5 kW (300 hp) Lycoming IO-540-K1E5-engined Model 17-31A Super Viking 300A; and the 223.5 kW (300 hp) Lycoming IO-540-K1E5-engined Model 17-31ATC Turbo Viking 300A with two Rajay turbochargers. By the beginning of 1978 a total of 1,528 Vikings of all models had been sold.
Data (Model 17-31ATC): *Engine* as above *Wing span* 10.41 m (34 ft 2 in) *Length* 8.02 m (26 ft 4 in) *Max T-O weight* 1,508 kg (3,325 lb) *Max cruising speed* 357 km/h (222 mph) *Range* 1,512 km (940 miles)

Bellanca Model 19-25 Skyrocket II.

Champion (Bellanca) Citabria (USA) The Citabria ('airbatic' backwards) represents Bellanca's advanced development of the Model 7 Champion airframe. It is a two-seat braced high-wing monoplane of which a total of 4,814 of all models had been sold by 1978. The Citabria Standard (formerly Model 7ECA) is the basic version with an 85.5 kW (115 hp) Lycoming O-235-C1 engine. The Citabria 150 (formerly Model 7GCAA) is similar but has a 112 kW (150 hp) O-320-A2D engine; and the Citabria 150S (formerly Model 7GCBC) has the Model 7GCAA engine and increased wing span.
Data: *Engine* as above *Wing span* 10.19 m (33 ft 5 in) *Wing span* (150S) 10.49 m (34 ft 5 in) *Length* 6.91 m (22 ft 8 in) *Max T-O weight* 748 kg (1,650 lb) *Max level speed* (150) 212 km/h (132 mph) *Range* (150) 977 km (607 miles)

Bellanca Model 8GCBC Scout (USA) This version of the Scout went into production in 1974 with a 134 kW (180 hp) Lycoming O-360-C2E flat-four engine. Accommodation and configura-

Bellanca Aries T-250.

tion are similar to the Citabria. By 1978 a total of 248 had been produced.

Champion (Bellanca) Decathlon (USA) Similar in accommodation and configuration to the Citabria, the Decathlon is an aerobatic competition aircraft designed for loads of +6*g* and −5*g*. It has been arbitrarily cleared for two minutes of inverted flight. By 1978 a total of 292 had been produced. Power plant of the Decathlon is a 112 kW (150 hp) Lycoming AEIO-320-E2B flat-four engine (the former Model 8KCAB version had an -E1B engine). The Decathlon CS has the -E1B engine and a Custom Sport package as standard. The latter comprises wingtip strobe lights, rheostat for cabin lights, competition harness for front seat, quick oil drain and

Champion (Bellanca) Super Decathlon.

Bellanca

three-colour exterior paint scheme. The Super Decathlon has a 134 kW (180 hp) Lycoming AEIO-360-H1A engine.

Bellanca Model 19-25 Skyrocket II (USA) The original Bellanca Aircraft Corporation (see above) merged with companies not engaged in aircraft manufacture and lost its identity in 1959. The present company (Bellanca Aircraft Engineering Inc), formed by Mr August Bellanca and his father, the late G. M. Bellanca, bought all the original Bellanca Aircraft designs with the exception of the 14-19. In 1971 the company was reorganised and construction of the prototype Skyrocket II was started. The first flight was made in March 1975. Orders for about 70 aircraft have been received.

The Skyrocket II is a six-seat light cabin mono-

plane powered by a 324 kW (435 hp) Continental GTSIO-520-F engine.

Data: *Engine* as above *Wing span* 10.67 m (35 ft 0 in) *Length* 8.81 m (28 ft 11 in) *Max T-O weight* 1,860 kg (4,100 lb) *Max cruising speed* 532 km/h (331 mph) *Range* 2,357 km (1,465 miles)

Bellanca Aries T-250 (USA) Designed by Anderson, Greenwood and Company (of which Bellanca is a subsidiary), this is a four-seat cabin monoplane which first flew on 19 July 1973. Production will begin after satisfactory financing has been arranged.

Benes-Mráz lightplanes (Czechoslovakia) Founded in 1935, this company produced several lightplane designs before World War II, including the Be.50 Beta-Minor open two-seat low-wing monoplane (63.3–71 kW; 85–95 hp Walter Minor engine); the similar Be.51 Beta-Minor with an enclosed cabin; the Be. 550 Bibi two-seat cabin monoplane (44.7 kW; 60 hp Walter Mikron II engine); and the open two-seat Be.252 Beta-Scolar (119–134 kW; 160–180 hp Walter Scolar radial engine). These could be used for training and touring and were successful in many interna-

tional flying events before the war (see **LET**).

Bennett P.L.11 Airtruck (New Zealand) This agricultural aircraft was designed by Mr Luigi Pellarini and was the first commercial aeroplane developed in New Zealand. The prototype flew for the first time in August 1960. It subsequently became known as the Waitomo Airtruck and later still the Transavia P.L.12 Airtruk (see **Transavia**).

Benoist flying-boat (USA) Famous as the aircraft used on the first scheduled service of an airline using aeroplanes (see **Chronology** 1 Jan 1914), the Benoist flying-boat made its maiden flight in 1913. It was a two-seat biplane powered by a 56 kW (75 hp) Roberts or 52 kW (70 hp) Sturtevant engine. The wing span was 13.72 m (45 ft 0 in); max T-O weight about 680 kg (1,500 lb); and max level speed 105 km/h (65 mph).

Bensen Model B-8 Gyro-Glider (USA) Simple unpowered rotor-kite which can be towed behind a small car, developed from the earlier B-7. It is available as a single- or two-seater, as a completed aircraft or in kit form.

Bensen Model B-8W Hydro-Glider (USA) Basically a twin-float version of the Gyro-Glider.

Bensen Models B-8M, B-8V and Super Bug Gyro-Copters and B-8MW Hydro-Copter (USA) First flown on 6 December 1955, the Gyro-Copter is a powered autogyro conversion of the Gyro-Glider designed for home construction from kits or plans. The current B-8M has a more powerful engine than the original B-7M and can be equipped with an optional mechanical rotor drive. It is normally powered by a 53.5 kW (72 hp) McCulloch Model 4318AX flat-four two-stroke pusher engine (or 67 kW; 90 hp McCulloch). The similar B-8V can be powered by a 1,600 cc Volkswagen converted motorcar engine or a McCulloch. The Super Bug is an advanced version of the B-8M with a twin-engine installation to spin up the rotor prior to take-off. The Hydro-Copter is a twin-float version of the B-8M.

Bensen Model B-8HD (USA) This 1979 Gyro-Copter is based on the Super Bug design. It uses hydraulic drive to feed about 3 kW (4 hp) from the engine to the rotor, instead of having a separate engine for pre-rotation. This is reported to give the aircraft a take-off run of less than 61 m (200 ft).

Bensen B-8MJ (USA) This is basically a B-8M with a Power Head fitted, enabling the aircraft to take-off vertically without ground roll. It is claimed to provide a 30° angle of climb. Hovering cannot be achieved. Power Heads are available to amateur builders or owners of Gyro-Copters with 50 or more hours of solo flight.

Bensen Model B-8MH Hover-Gyro (USA) Demonstrated in public for the first time in 1976, this is described as a 'Hovering Gyro-Copter'. It is powered by a 52.2–82 kW (70–110 hp) modified water-cooled outboard engine driving the lower of the two rotors; the upper rotor autorotates. One 10.4 kW (14 hp) modified air-cooled go-kart engine drives the pusher propeller mounted at rear.

Bergamaschi C-1 and C-2 (Italy) Single- and

two-seat training biplanes of the 1920s powered by 112 kW (150 hp) Hispano-Suiza engines.

Bergamaschi A.P.1 (Italy) Single-seat close support aircraft; produced as the Caproni A.P.1 (see entry) as this company had become a subsidiary of Caproni in 1931.

Bergamaschi Borea, Ghibli and Libeccio (Italy) See **Caproni Ca 308, 309 and 310**

Berger BX-50A (Switzerland) Single-seat light helicopter flown in prototype form in the 1970s. Powered by a 67 kW (90 hp) Continental C90 flat-four engine.

Berger BX-110 (Switzerland) Two-seat light helicopter powered by a 134 kW (180 hp) Wankel rotating-piston engine. Prototype flew for the first time on 3 June 1974.

Beriev Be-2 (USSR) G. M. Beriev took up seaplane design in 1928 and became subsequently the best-known Soviet designer of water-based aircraft. The Be-2, originally designated KOR-1, was a shipboard reconnaissance seaplane. It entered service in 1938.

Beriev Be-4 (USSR) Originally designated KOR-2, the Be-4 was a single-engined monoplane flying-boat.

Beriev Be-6 (USSR) In 1945 the Beriev bureau at Taganrog became the centre for all Soviet seaplane development. The piston-engined Be-6 (NATO reporting name *Madge*) was a standard military flying-boat during the 1950s. The first flight had been made in 1949. Power was provided by two 1,490 kW (2,000 hp) ASh-73 radial engines mounted on the leading edge of the gull-type wings. Armament comprised 23 mm cannon

Bensen Model B-8HD.

in nose, dorsal and remotely controlled tail gun turrets. Racks were provided for bombs, mines, depth charges and torpedoes.
Data: *Engines* as above *Wing span* 33 m (108 ft 3¼ in) *Length* (approx) 25.6 m (84 ft 0 in) *Max T-O weight* 23,400 kg (51,588 lb) *Max level speed* 415 km/h (258 mph) *Range* 4,900 km (3,045 miles)

Beriev Be-8 (USSR) First flown in 1947, the Be-8 was designed as a lighter and shorter-range counterpart of the Be-6, powered by one 522 kW (700 hp) ASh-21 engine. Only limited production was undertaken. A prototype of a turbojet-powered flying-boat, also designated Be-8, was flown.

Beriev Be-10 (USSR) Based on the Be-R-1 prototype of 1949, the Be-10 was a large swept-wing flying-boat that entered service in about 1960. It was given the NATO reporting name *Mallow*. Four Be-10s took part in the 1961 Aviation Day fly-past over Moscow. Similar aircraft were later demonstrated on Soviet Navy Day. On 7 August

Bensen Model B-8W Hydro-Glider.

Bensen Model B-8MH Hover-Gyro.

Beriev

1961 a Be-10 set up an international speed record for seaplanes, averaging 912 km/h (566.69 mph); and the aircraft went on to set up many other speed, payload-to-height and altitude records.
Data: *Engines* two 63.74 kN (14,330 lb st) Lyulka AL-7PB turbojets *Wing span* (estimated) 24.38 m (80 ft 0 in) *Length* (estimated) 32.92 m (108 ft 0 in)

Beriev Be-6.

Beriev M-12 (Be-12) Tchaika (Seagull) (USSR) This twin-turboprop medium-range maritime reconnaissance amphibian was displayed for the first time in the 1961 Aviation Day fly-past at Tushino Airport, Moscow. Subsequently, during the period 23–27 October 1964, it established six officially recognised international height records in Class C.3 Group II. The aircraft was also able to lift a payload of around ten tons under record conditions. Other speed and speed-with-payloads records have since been set up by the aircraft.

The M-12 (Be-12) has a glazed observation and

Beriev Be-8.

navigation station in the nose (with a long radar 'thimble' built into it) and an astrodome-type observation position above the rear fuselage. A long MAD (magnetic anomaly detection) 'sting' extends from the tail and there appears to be an APU exhaust on the port side of the rear fuselage.

Aircraft of this type have been identified in standard service at Soviet Northern and Black Sea Fleet air bases and were reported to be operational for a period from bases in Egypt. About 100 are believed to have been built.
Data (estimated): *Engines* two 2,980 kW (4,000 hp) Ivchenko AI-20D turboprops *Wing span* 29.7 m (97 ft 6 in) *Length* 32.9 m (107 ft 11¾ in) *Max T-O weight* 29,500 kg (65,035 lb) *Max level speed* 610 km/h (379 mph) *Range* 4,000 km (2,485 miles) *Armament* internal bomb bay; provision for one large and one small external stores pylon under each outer wing panel

Beriev Be-30 and Be-32 (USSR) The Be-30 twin-turboprop light transport did not enter series production. A developed version, the Be-32, set up two time-to-height records from an aerodrome near Moscow. It is said to accommodate 18 passengers or 1,900 kg (4,189 lb) of freight.

Beriev MBR-2 (USSR) This single-engined flying-boat, first flown in 1932, entered production in 1934 as a short-range coastal reconnaissance aircraft. Power was provided by one 507 kW 680 hp) M-17B (BMW VI) engine. Armament comprised 7.62 mm machine-guns in open bow and dorsal positions and underwing racks for up to 300 kg (661 lb) of bombs. The dorsal position was subsequently modified by the fitting of a manually operated gun turret. Of the 1,500 or so aircraft built, a large number were of the improved MBR-2*bis* type with a 641 kW (860 hp) AM-34N engine. Many MBR-2/2*bis* flying-boats were operated during World War II, some with wheel or ski landing gears.
Data (MBR-2*bis*) *Engine* as above *Wing span* 19.0 m (62 ft 4 in) *Length* 13.5 m (44 ft 3½ in) *Max T-O weight* about 4,300 kg (9,500 lb) *Max level speed* 220 km/h (136 mph) *Range* 1,500 km (932 miles)

Berliner-Joyce P-16/PB-1 (USA) Two-seat fighter powered by a 447 kW (600 hp) Curtiss V-1570 engine. Sesquiplane-type wings canted at roots to meet fuselage. Twenty-five evaluation Y1P-16s ordered by the USAAC in 1929, subsequently joining the 1st Fighter Group as PB-1s.

Bernard 18T (France) Eight-passenger commercial monoplane of 1927. May have been the aircraft named *Oiseau Canari* that was flown across the North Atlantic from the USA to Spain in June 1927, while carrying two crew, one passenger and a stowaway.

Bernard 190T (France) Development of the 18T, of which a number were delivered to Compagnie Internationale de Navigation Aérienne for use on its airline routes. Power was provided by one 313 kW (420 hp) Gnome Rhône-built Jupiter radial engine.

BFW U-12 Flamingo (Germany) Bayerische Flugzeugwerke A.G. (later to become Messerschmitt A.G.) was formed from the Udet-Flugzeugbau of 1922. The Flamingo wooden

Kangaroos were also converted into tandem-cockpit dual-control trainers during 1924–26 and were used for refresher flying by RAF pilots and Reservists. They were, however, withdrawn from use in 1928 and broken up.

primary trainer (first flown in 1925) was the last product of the former and was put into production by the new company. It was an equal-span biplane with I-type interplane struts. Power was provided by a 71.5 kW (96 hp) Siemens Sh.11 radial engine. Numbers served in Germany and were exported to Austria and Hungary. Licensed production was also undertaken in Hungary and Latvia.

BFW M-18 (Germany) See **Messerschmitt**

Bird Innovator (USA) Four-engined conversion of the PBY-5A Catalina which received FAA Supplemental Type Certificate on 20 December 1968.

Birdman TL-1A (USA) Single-seat ultra light-weight sporting aircraft powered by an 8.5 kW (11.5 hp) McCulloch MC-101 DT two-stroke engine. Designed to be built by amateur constructors; over 300 kits were under construction by 1979.

Blackburn (UK) Blackburn aircraft are covered in order of appearance, not alphabetically.

Blackburn monoplane No 1 (UK) Single-seat high-wing monoplane completed in 1909. Power was provided by a 26 kW (35 hp) Green engine mounted in front of the pilot.

Blackburn Mercury (UK) Two-seat mid-wing monoplane powered by a 37.25 kW (50 hp) Isaacson, Gnome or Anzani engine. The first of nine aircraft was exhibited at the Olympia Aero Show of 1911.

Blackburn T.B. Twin (UK) Large twin-fuselage twin-engined seaplane of 1915 designed to attack Zeppelin airships with incendiary steel darts. Nine built for the RNAS.

Blackburn R.T.1 Kangaroo (UK) The Kangaroo originated as a twin-engined anti-submarine torpedo-bomber biplane of fabric-covered wooden construction. First flown in January 1918, a total of 20 aircraft were built, ten going to No 246 Squadron, RAF. In June 1918 the operational aircraft attacked 11 U-boats, damaging four; on 28 August 1918 a Kangaroo crewed by Lts Waring and Smith helped sink the UC 70.

After the Armistice the Disposals Board sold all available Kangaroos: the prototype to Lt V. Rendle, a competitor for the Australian government's £10,000 prize; three to the Grahame-White Aviation Company for pleasure flying; and all remaining stocks back to the Blackburn Company. Three of the latter were subsequently modified to carry seven passengers in a glazed cabin and were used from September 1919 on the North Sea Aerial Navigation Company's Leeds to Hounslow service. When the service was extended to Amsterdam in 1920 textiles became the main cargo.

Rendle's attempt to fly to Australia (with co-pilot D. R. Williams and navigator Capt Hubert Wilkins) began at Hounslow on 21 November 1919, but ended in a forced landing in Crete. Five

Data: *Engines* two 201 kW (270 hp) Rolls-Royce Falcon III *Wing span* 22.83 m (74 ft 10¼ in) *Length* 13.46 m (44 ft 2 in) *Max T-O weight* 3,636 kg (8,017 lb) *Max level speed* 158 km/h (98 mph) *Endurance* 8 h

Blackburn T.1 Swift (UK) The Swift was a large single-seat carrier-borne torpedo-bomber biplane with a steel-tube fuselage and wooden wings, fabric-covered. It was the first British aircraft with staggered wings that folded and it appeared to have a curiously upturned nose when on level ground. The prototype was first flown in 1920 and was delivered for trials at Martlesham in January 1921. By May the aircraft had been fitted with deck-arrester claws and delivered to the Development Squadron at Gosport. It thereafter made its first deck landing on HMS *Argus*. The Swift was developed into the Dart (see below) for the Fleet Air Arm.

Seven export Swifts, with radiators below instead of in front of the engine, were built for foreign governments. Two Swift Model Fs were supplied to the US Navy base at Anacostia for evaluation during 1922–23. The remainder were

Blackburn

Blackburn Mercury.

Berliner-Joyce P-16/PB-1.

Berger BX-110.

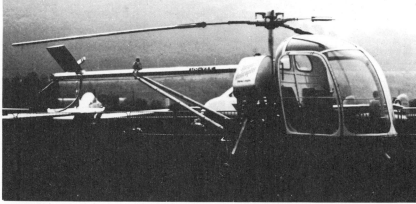

Bird Innovator.

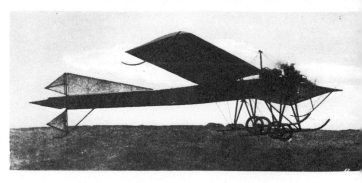

Swift IIs: two of these were taken to Japan by the British Aviation Mission in 1922 for the Japanese Navy; and three were delivered to the Spanish Navy Air Station at Prat de Llobregat, near Barcelona, in 1923.

Data: *Engine* one 335.3 kW (450 hp) Napier Lion IB *Wing span* 14.78 m (48 ft 6 in) *Length* 10.82 m (35 ft 6 in) *Max T-O weight* 2,858 kg (6,300 lb) *Max level speed* 171 km/h (106 mph) *Range* 563 km (350 miles)

Blackburn T.2 Dart (UK) The Dart was the FAA's standard single-seat torpedo bomber from 1923 to 1933. Similar to the Blackburn Swift but with reduced wing span, it could carry a torpedo or underwing bombs. Production ended in 1928 after the 117th Dart had been completed.

The Dart first entered service with No 460 Flight in 1923 on board HMS *Eagle*, stationed in the Mediterranean; and with Nos 461 and 462 on board HMS *Furious*, based in home waters. Shore training was by 'D' Flight at Gosport. The aircraft's low stalling speed of 70.5 km/h (43.5 mph) enabled it to pioneer the technique of deck landing by night on HMS *Furious* in 1926. In 1928 Nos 463 and 464 Flights embarked on HMS *Courageous* for service in the Mediterranean and in the following year a single example was delivered to No 36 Squadron, RAF, for smoke-screen trials. Three Darts were also converted into two-seat advanced-training seaplanes for use on the River Humber by Blackburn's RAF Reserve School, being used between 1925 and 1929.

Data: *Engine* one 335.3 kW (450 hp) Napier Lion IIB or 346.5 kW (465 hp) Lion V *Wing span* 13.86 m (45 ft 5¾ in) *Length* 10.78 m (35 ft 4½ in) *Max T-O weight* 2,895 kg (6,383 lb) *Cruising speed* 161 km/h (100 mph) *Endurance* 1 h

Blackburn R.1 Blackburn (UK) The Blackburn was an ugly carrier-borne Fleet spotter-reconnaissance biplane, accommodating a pilot in an open cockpit in front of the upper wing leading edge, a wireless operator/gunner and a navigator/observer. The latter crew members were provided with a cabin inside the deep fuselage and only needed to venture out into the open for observation or to use the rear-mounted Lewis machine-gun. Thirty production Blackburn 1s, with 335.3 kW (450 hp) Napier Lion IIB engines, were built. The type first entered service on board HMS *Eagle* in 1923. These were followed by 29 346.5 kW (465 hp) Napier Lion-engined Blackburn IIs, entering service in 1926. All were replaced by Fairey IIIFs in 1931.

Data: *Engine* as above *Wing span* 13.87 m (45 ft 6½ in) *Length* 11.02 m (36 ft 2 in) *Max T-O weight* (II) 3,022 kg (6,660 lb) *Max level speed* (II) 157 km/h (98 mph) *Armament* one forward-firing Vickers and one rear-mounted Lewis machine-gun

Blackburn T.3 Velos (UK) The Velos was a two-seat development of the Dart designed for the Greek Navy in 1925. Armament comprised four 230 lb bombs carried under the wings or one torpedo, plus a rear-mounted Lewis machine-gun. Four were built by Blackburn and 12 under licence by the Greek National Aircraft Factory at Athens. They were supplied with wheel or float undercarriages for operation from Tatoi Aerodrome and Phaleron Bay, Athens, and remained in service until 1934.

Two additional Velos were built by Blackburn in 1926: one for seaworthiness trials of Blackburn's new metal floats and the other for a demonstration sales tour of South America in 1927. Both were later converted to tandem-cockpit advanced training seaplanes for use at the

Blackburn Reserve School, joining four others specially built for this role. From 1929 until 1933 these aircraft were flown as landplanes.

Data (seaplane): *Engine* one 335.3 kW (450 hp) Napier Lion IIB or 346.5 kW (465 hp) Lion V *Wing span* 14.78 m (48 ft 6 in) *Length* 10.82 m (35 ft 6 in) *Max T-O weight* 3,175 kg (7,000 lb) *Cruising speed* 121 km/h (75 mph) *Endurance* 3 h 30 min

Blackburn R.B.1 Iris (UK) The five-seat Iris was an elegant biplane flying-boat. The first of only eight built flew on 19 June 1926. The single Iris I, powered by three 484.4 kW (650 hp)

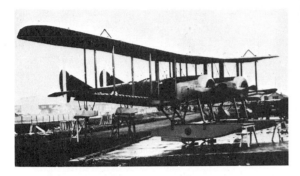

Rolls-Royce Condor III engines, was converted into the II with 503 kW (675 hp) Condor IIIAs. It was followed by four Iris IIIs with 503 kW (675 hp) Condor IIIB engines (entering service with the RAF in 1930); a single Mk IV (the first prototype with 596 kW; 800 hp Armstrong Siddeley Leopard IIIs, mounted as two tractors and one pusher); and three Vs with 615 kW (825 hp) Rolls-Royce Buzzard IIMS engines. A III was also brought up to V standard.

Blackburn T.5 Ripon (UK) The Ripon was a torpedo-bomber with a steel-tube fuselage and wooden wings, first flown as the Ripon I in 1926. The first of 20 aerodynamically cleaner Ripon IIs replaced the Blackburn Darts of Nos 460, 461 and 462 Flights, FAA, on board HMS *Glorious* and *Furious* in 1929.

Forty Ripon IIAs with shorter-span duralumin wing-ribs and smaller rudders were built during 1930–31. Five of these belonging to No 460 Flight went to Buenos Aires on board HMS *Eagle* in 1931 and were used for formation flying over the British Empire Exhibition during March and April. Thirty-one Ripon IICs with additional sweep-back and steel wing-spars were delivered during 1931–32. Earlier marks were thereafter returned

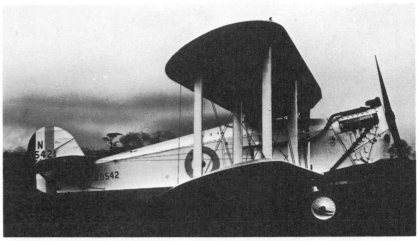

Blackburn Dart.

to Blackburn for modification to this standard. Ripon IICs formed the equipment of Nos 465 and 466 Flights on board *Furious* in 1931, but in 1933 all the Flights were regrouped. The IICs remained in service until 1934.

One Ripon IIF, with a Bristol Jupiter radial engine, was delivered to Finland in September 1929, where 25 others were constructed with plywood-covered fuselages and wheel/float/ski landing gears. These saw service against the Russians during the 1939 'Winter War'.

Data: *Engine* one 424.8 kW (570 hp) Napier Lion XIA *Wing span* 13.67 m (44 ft 10 in) *Length* 11.2 m (36 ft 9 in) *Max T-O weight* 3,568 kg (7,866 lb) *Max level speed* 196 km/h (122 mph) *Range* 1,706 km (1,060 miles)

Blackburn L.1A Bluebird II and L.1B Bluebird III (UK) Following on from the single L.1 Bluebird I of 1924 (designed for use by flying clubs and for touring), Blackburn produced the Bluebird II, a two-seater with side-by-side accommodation and powered by a 59.6 kW (80 hp) Armstrong Siddeley Genet II engine. A total of 13 were eventually built. An improved version of the biplane appeared in 1927 as the Bluebird III, with a wooden-covered rear-fuselage decking and an upper-wing centre-section fuel tank. The prototype, first flown with the Genet engine, was later fitted with a 67 kW (90 hp) A.D.C. Cirrus III. A total of six production Bluebird IIIs followed (see **Bluebird IV**).

Blackburn F.2 Lincock (UK) High-performance single-seat biplane fighter of 1928. Eight built (two Lincock IIIs going to Japan and two to China) powered by 201 kW (270 hp) Armstrong Siddeley Lynx Major radial engines.

Blackburn T.B.Twin.

Blackburn Kangaroo operated by the North Sea Aerial Navigation Company.

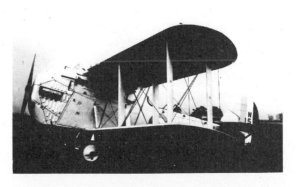

First prototype Blackburn Blackburn.

Blackburn

Blackburn Blackburn on board HMS *Argus*.

Blackburn R.B.2 Sydney and C.B.2 Nile (UK)
Intended as long-range maritime reconnaissance
flying-boats. Only one Sydney built and flown for
the first time on 18 July 1930. Nile not completed.

Blackburn L.1C Bluebird IV (UK) The
Bluebird IV was the most successful version of the
Bluebird two-seater and introduced an all-metal
structure, fabric-covered. Three were built by
Blackburn in 1929, the first being flown to South

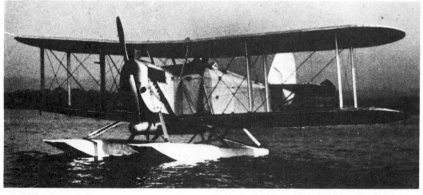

Blackburn Velos.

Africa by Sqn Ldr L. H. Slater between 8 March
and 15 April 1929. Fifty-five were also built by
Saunders-Roe between 1930 and 1931. Thirteen
went to the RAF Reserve School at Brough as
seaplanes; one (flown by E. C. T. Edwards) won
the 1931 King's Cup Race; another was flown by
the Hon Mrs V. Bruce on a solo flight around the
world during 1930–32; and a seaplane version was
flown by Miss Delphine Reynolds on a West
African flight in 1931. The Bluebird IV was also
exported to six countries.
Data: *Engine* one 67 kW (90 hp) A.D.C. Cirrus
III, 89.4 kW (120 hp) de Havilland Gipsy III or
100.6 kW (135 hp) Armstrong Siddeley Genet
Major I *Wing span* 9.14 m (30 ft 0 in) *Length*
7.06 m (23 ft 2 in) *Max T-O weight* 710 kg
(1,566 lb) *Cruising speed* 175 km/h (109 mph)
Range 547 km (340 miles)

Blackburn T.7B (UK) Carrier-borne attack
bomber. The prototype first flew on 28 December
1929 and was sent to Mitsubishi of Japan, which
built 200 production examples for the Imperial
Japanese Navy as Mitsubishi B2M1s and B2M2s.

Blackburn R.B.3A Perth (UK) Five-seat long-
range coastal patrol flying-boat of 1933 powered

Blackburn Iris II.

by three 615 kW (825 hp) Rolls-Royce Buzzard
IIMS engines. Four built, three of which were
operated by No 209 Squadron, RAF, between
1934 and 1936.

Blackburn B-1 Segrave (UK) Four-seat cabin
monoplane powered by two 89.4 kW (120 hp) de
Havilland Gipsy IIIs or similar engine. Six aircraft only: the prototype built by Saunders-Roe
and flown on 28 May 1930 was followed by three
built by Blackburn and two by Piaggio as P.12s.

Blackburn B-2 (UK) Two-seat (side-by-side)
all-metal biplane trainer with a monocoque fuselage and fabric-covered wings. Entire output of 42
aircraft produced for pilot training at civilian
Elementary and Reserve Flying Schools under the
RAF expansion scheme. Blind-flying hood,
camera-gun or vertical camera fitted for advanced
instruction. All transferred to Air Training Corps
squadrons as instructional airframes in 1942. Last
survivor G-AEBJ was still being flown by British
Aerospace in 1979.
Data: *Engine* one 89.4 kW (120 hp) de Havilland
Gipsy III, 97 kW (130 hp) Gipsy Major or Cirrus
Hermes IVA *Wing span* 9.80 m (32 ft 2 in) *Length*
7.39 m (24 ft 3 in) *Max T-O weight* 839 kg
(1,850 lb) *Cruising speed* 153 km/h (95 mph) *Range*
515 km (320 miles)

Blackburn B-5 Baffin (UK) This aircraft was an
improved version of the Ripon with a 421 kW
(565 hp) Bristol Pegasus radial engine in place of
the Napier Lion and its heavy water-cooling system. Two prototypes and 33 production Baffins
served with a single flight at Gosport for dummy
deck-landing and torpedo practice and with Nos
810, 811 and 812 Squadrons on board the aircraft
carriers HMS *Courageous*, *Furious* and *Glorious*
respectively from 1934 until replaced by Sharks in
1936. One batch of 14 Baffins were shipped to
Malta as reserve aircraft when the carriers exercised their squadrons in the Mediterranean.

More than 60 Ripons were re-worked and re-
engined as Baffins during 1934–35. Twenty-nine
surplus Fleet Air Arm aircraft were sold to the
RNZAF during 1937–38 for the Wellington,
Christchurch and Auckland Territorial GR
Squadrons, which combined for wartime coastal
patrols.
Data: *Engine* as above *Wing span* 13.67 m (44 ft
10 in) *Length* 11.68 m (38 ft 3¾ in) *Max T-O
weight* 3,452 kg (7,610 lb) *Cruising speed* 206 km/h
(128 mph) *Endurance* 4 h 30 min

Blackburn B-6 Shark (UK) The Shark was a
carrier-borne torpedo biplane with a buoyant
metal-skinned fuselage and a 521.5 kW (700 hp)
Armstrong Siddeley Tiger IV two-row radial
engine. Production for the Fleet Air Arm was
undertaken between 1934 and 1937, with 238
Shark Is, IIs and IIIs (Pegasus radial engines)
being built, many as seaplanes. Accommodation
was provided for a crew of two and armament

comprised one 1,500 lb torpedo or equivalent bomb load, plus one forward-firing Vickers and one rear-mounted Vickers or Lewis machine-gun. Deck take-offs and landings were aided by the large camber-changing flaps fitted to the aircraft.

Sharks served with Nos 820 and 821 Squadrons on board HMS *Courageous*, No 822 Squadron on board HMS *Furious* and No 705 (Catapult) Flight on the battleships HMS *Repulse* and *Warspite*. The type was also used at Air Gunnery Schools in the UK and Trinidad.

Six Sharks were also delivered to the Portuguese Navy in March 1936 and were based at Bom Succeso on the River Tagus, near Lisbon, where they operated for several years. Four aircraft were built for the Royal Canadian Air Force and 17 IIIs were built under licence by Boeing Aircraft of Canada during 1939–40, mainly for the RCAF.

Data: *Engine* as above *Wing span* 10.74 m (35 ft 3 in) *Length* 14.02 m (46 ft 0 in) *Max T-O weight* 3,651 kg (8,050 lb) *Max level speed* 225 km/h (140 mph) *Range* 1,158–2,027 km (720–1,260 miles)

Blackburn B-24 Skua (UK) The Skua was the Fleet Air Arm's first fighter/dive-bomber and its first operational monoplane. The Skua was also the first radial-engined all-metal cantilever low-wing monoplane with folding wings, flaps, a retractable landing gear and variable-pitch propeller to be produced in Britain. It was first flown in prototype form on 9 February 1937. The crew of two sat in a glazed cabin, the rear-gunner being armed with one Lewis gun and the pilot with four Browning guns mounted in the wings. One 500 lb armour-piercing bomb was carried under the fuselage.

To meet the Royal Navy's urgent requirements 190 Skuas were ordered in July 1936 (six months before the prototype flew) and deliveries were completed in March 1940. Skuas re-equipped Nos

800 and 803 Squadrons on board the aircraft carrier HMS *Ark Royal* and No 801 on board HMS *Furious*. A Dornier Do 18 flying-boat – the first enemy aircraft shot down during World War II by the FAA – fell to the guns of a Skua of No 803 Squadron piloted by Lt B. S. McEwen off Heligoland on 25 September 1939. Although quickly replaced as a fighter, it was a very effective dive-bomber, its greatest success being the sinking of the German cruiser *Königsberg* in Bergen Harbour on 10 April 1940, which was attacked by seven Skuas of No 800 Squadron led by Capt R. T. Partridge RM and nine Skuas of No 803 Squadron led by Lt W. P. Lucy RN. This involved a long-distance night crossing from Hatston, Orkney. The majority were lost 11 days later when both squadrons embarked on *Ark Royal* to cover the Narvik operations.

In June 1940 No 801 Squadron operated over the Dunkirk beaches from a temporary base at Detling, Kent. After brief operations on board *Ark Royal* and *Argus* in the Mediterranean, Skuas were relegated to target-towing in distinctive diagonal black and yellow stripes.

Data: *Engine* one 663 kW (890 hp) Bristol Perseus XII *Wing span* 14.07 m (46 ft 2 in) *Length* 10.84 m (35 ft 7 in) *Max T-O weight* 3,732 kg (8,228 lb) *Max cruising speed* 301 km/h (187 mph) *Range* 700 km (435 miles)

Blackburn Ripon IIA.

Blackburn Lincock III for China.

Blackburn L.1B Bluebird III.

Blackburn B-25 Roc (UK) The Roc was a two-seat Fleet fighter/dive-bomber developed from the Skua but with a wider rear fuselage to accommodate a Boulton Paul power-driven turret with four Browning machine-guns. The entire produc-

Blackburn Perth.

Blackburn

Blackburn B-2.

Blackburn Segrave.

tion of 136 aircraft was subcontracted to Boulton Paul Ltd, Wolverhampton. The first aircraft flew on 23 December 1938. Four Rocs were also flown experimentally with float landing gears.

Rocs served briefly with Nos 801 and 806 Squadrons, FAA, in 1940. When broadsides by the four turret guns proved a failure, Rocs were relegated to second-line duties in the UK, Egypt and Bermuda. Many were painted with diagonal black and yellow stripes in 1940 as target-tugs. Others were used in 1941 for sea searches for survivors of sinking ships and aircraft in the English Channel.

Data: *Engine* one 663 kW (890 hp) Bristol Perseus XII *Wing span* 14.02 m (46 ft 0 in) *Length* 10.85 m (35 ft 7 in) *Max T-O weight* 3,606 kg (7,950 lb) *Cruising speed* 217 km/h (135 mph) *Range* 1,303 km (810 miles)

Blackburn B-26 Botha I (UK) The Botha was designed for Coastal Command RAF as a three-seat twin-engined reconnaissance-bomber, able to carry a torpedo internally or up to 907 kg (2,000 lb) of bombs. Defensive armament comprised a single 0.303 in Vickers machine-gun for-ward and a dorsal turret with two Lewis guns. The first prototype made its maiden flight on 28 December 1938 and the first production Bothas entered service with No 608 Squadron on 28 June 1940, but remained in first-line service only until November of that year. A handful of operational Bothas also went to No 502 Squadron, but were also withdrawn rapidly. Although the Botha was a failure as a torpedo-bomber – mainly due to being under-powered – large numbers served as pilot, navigation, bombing, gunnery and radio trainers until 1944.

Data: *Engines* two 656 kW (880 hp) Bristol Perseus X or 693 kW (930 hp) Perseus XA radials *Wing span* 17.98 m (59 ft 0 in) *Length* 15.54 m (51 ft 0½ in) *Max T-O weight* 8,368 kg (18,450 lb) *Max level speed* 354 km/h (220 mph) *Range* 2,044 km (1,270 miles)

Blackburn B-37 Firebrand (UK) The Firebrand was originally designed and built to Specification N.11/40 as a single-seat Fleet fighter powered by the Napier Sabre liquid-cooled engine. Owing to the unavailability of the latter, a new specification was drawn up as S.8/43 to provide for the use of the Bristol Centaurus air-cooled engine. At the same time the requirements of the specification were broadened to provide for a strike role, carrying a torpedo, bombs and/or rockets. Therefore several versions of the Firebrand appeared, although only small numbers of the early types were built.

Production for the FAA began with nine Firebrand F.Is powered by 1,718 kW (2,305 hp) Napier Sabre III engines. These were followed by 12 TF.IIs powered by similar engines but able to carry an 18 in torpedo; 27 TF.IIIs with 1,878 kW (2,520 hp) Bristol Centaurus IX radial engines; 102 TF.4s with enlarged tail surfaces, wing dive-brakes and other refinements, and powered by the Centaurus IX; and 68 TF.5/5As (plus about 40 TF.4s converted to the later standard) with horn-balanced elevators and other refinements to improve manoeuvrability.

Firebrands entered service with the FAA in September 1945 and so were not used operationally during World War II. However Firebrands remained in first-line service until 1953.

Data (TF.5): *Engine* as above *Wing span* 15.63 m (51 ft 3½ in) *Length* 11.81 m (38 ft 9 in) *Max T-O weight* 7,938 kg (17,500 lb) *Max level speed* 547 km/h (340 mph) *Range* 1,191 km (740 miles) *Armament* four 20 mm Hispano cannon and one 1,850 lb torpedo or bombs/rockets

Blackburn B-101 Beverley (UK) The Beverley C.1 was the production version of the Universal four-engined transport, which was basically a General Aircraft design. The first prototype, powered by four 1,505 kW (2,020 hp) Bristol Hercules 730 engines, was in an unfinished state when Blackburn and General Aircraft merged in 1949. It was transferred to and completed at Brough, flying for the first time on 20 June 1950. A second prototype with four 2,124 kW (2,850 hp) Bristol Centaurus engines and other modifications flew in June 1953 and served as the prototype for the Beverley.

The first production Beverley C.1 made its maiden flight on 29 January 1955 and the type went on to equip several squadrons of RAF Transport Command. Forty-seven C.1s were built and the type remained in service until 1967.

Assisted take-off experiments in 1956 showed that the use of ten Scarab rockets (mounted five on each side of the rear fuselage) enabled a fully loaded Beverley to take off within 365 m (400 yards).
Data: *Engines* four 2,124 kW (2,850 hp) Bristol Centaurus 273s *Wing span* 49.38 m (162 ft 0 in) *Length* 30.30 m (99 ft 5 in) *Max T-O weight* 61,200 kg (135,000 lb) *Max level speed* 383 km/h (238 mph) *Range* 2,092 km (1,300 miles) *Accommodation* 94 troops, 70 paratroops, 48 stretchers and 34 sitting casualties, or freight

Blanchard Brd.1 (France) Three-seat biplane bomber-reconnaissance flying-boat powered by two 194 kW (260 hp) Hispano-Suiza water-cooled engines, driving two-blade pusher propellers. The prototype first flew in 1922 and captured several world seaplane altitude records in 1924. Fourteen aircraft served with naval Escadrille 5R1 between 1923 and 1926. Series-built aircraft carried four machine-guns and up to 400 kg (882 lb) of bombs.

Blériot IV to X (France) The Type IV was a fabric-covered low-wing monoplane, the first Blériot aircraft actually to fly. It was built in 1907 and made a number of short hops in the following year. The Blériot V was described in 1908 as being the first successful Blériot aeroplane. The Type VII (the ancestor of the modern tractor monoplane, with very clean lines) was followed in 1908 by the Type VIII, looking like a crude Blériot XI-type monoplane and featuring a single lever control joystick. This aircraft flew well until it was lost in an accident. The Type IX was similar to the Type VIII but had tandem horizon-

tal tail surfaces which acted as the tailplane and elevators. The Blériot X looked a little like a Wright-type biplane; it was built in 1909 but not developed in any way.

Blériot XI (France) The first flight of a Type XI was made on 23 January 1909 on the power of a 21.5 kW (30 hp) REP engine driving an inefficient four-blade propeller. During April and May the aircraft was refined and fitted with a 16.4–18.6 kW (22–25 hp) Anzani 3 engine and Chauvière two-blade propeller. The central fin that had been fitted was removed and the rudder was enlarged and deepened, and the 'elevons' at the ends of the tailplane were arranged to function solely as elevators.

The most famous exploit of a Type XI was the cross-Channel flight on 25 July 1909 (see **Chronology**). The actual aircraft used is preserved in the Paris Conservatoire des Arts et Métiers. However many Type XIs were built for civil and military use: one became the first aeroplane to be used in a war, when Capitano Piazza of Italy made a reconnaissance sortie over Turkish troops at Azizia on 22 October 1911. Similarly the first bombs to be dropped from an aeroplane were released from a Type XI on 1 November 1911 (see also 12 and 19 Aug 1914 in **Chronology**).
Data: *Engine* as above *Wing span* 7.80 m (25 ft 7⅛ in) *Length* 8.0 m (26 ft 3 in) *Max T-O weight* 300 kg (661 lb) *Max level speed* 75 km/h (47 mph)

Blériot XII (France) The Type XII was similar to the Type XI but powered by a 26 kW (35 hp) engine in original form. It was the first aeroplane to fly with two passengers (Santos-Dumont and Fournier) at Issy-les-Moulineaux on 12 June

Blackburn Skuas.

Blériot

Blackburn Rocs.

Blackburn Botha I.

Blackburn Firebrand TF.4.

Blackburn Beverley.

1909. When later re-engined with a 44.7 kW (60 hp) ENV, it won for Blériot the prize for the fastest lap of the 10 km Reims circuit on 28 June, in 7 minutes 48 seconds. Later pre-World War I Blériot aircraft were similar to the XI/XII types, although many appeared in refined form.

Blériot 110 (France) By the beginning of August 1914 over 800 aeroplanes of 40 different types had been produced by the Blériot works. Shortly after this the factory at Suresnes was built. By the end of the war these were turning out 18 aeroplanes a day. Parallel with the development of the Société Blériot, Louis Blériot helped organise the famous Société Spad and during the war these two companies were amalgamated. After the Armistice aircraft appeared as both Blériot and Blériot-Spad types. The Blériot 110 first flew on 16 May 1930 and was a high-wing monoplane with enclosed accommodation for two. Also known as the 'Blériot Zappata', it was one of a number of special aircraft built for record breaking, ordered by the French government. Between 26 February and 1 March 1931 it flew 8,822.325 km (5,481.928 miles) in a closed circuit. Other records were subsequently achieved.

Blériot 115 (France) Large biplane airliner (three crew and eight passengers) powered by four 134 kW (180 hp) Hispano-Suiza 8Ab or 8Ac engines, two on upper wing and two on lower. First flown 9 May 1923. Prototype and three others built; two under military guise flown from Paris to Goa, Mali.

Blériot 125 (France) Worthy of inclusion because of its unusual design, the Type 125 was a 12-passenger twin-fuselage commercial monoplane of the early 1930s powered by two 372.6 kW (500 hp) Hispano-Suiza engines mounted in tandem between the two huge, bulbous passenger cabins positioned below the wings.

Blériot 127 (France) The prototype Blériot 127M flew for the first time on 7 May 1926 as a four-seat cantilever low-wing multi-purpose monoplane, intended as a day or night escort fighter, day or night bomber, or for long-range reconnaissance missions. A unique feature of the design was the gunners' cockpits mounted in the rear of each engine nacelle, which extended behind the trailing edge of the wings. Each gunner had twin 7.7 mm machine-guns. A third gun cockpit was positioned in the nose of the aircraft. Forty-two production Blériot 127/2s flew with two 'escadrilles de protection' of the 11ème Régiment d'Aviation de Bombardement at Metz between 1929 and 1934.

Data (Type 127/2): *Engines* two 372.6 kW (500 hp) Hispano-Suiza 12Gbs *Wing span* 23.2 m (76 ft 1½ in) *Length* 14.68 m (48 ft 2 in) *Max T-O weight* 4,966 kg (10,948 lb) *Max level speed* 199 km/h (123.6 mph)

Blériot 135 (France). Blériot 115 fitted with 171.4 kW (230 hp) Salmson 9Ab engines. Two operated by Air Union from July 1924 on the Paris–London route.

Blériot 155 (France) Larger development of the Type 135 powered by 171.4 kW (230 hp) Renault 8Fq engines. Two operated by Air Union on the Paris–London route from May to October 1926.

Blériot 165 (France) Developed from the Type 155 as a 16-passenger airliner powered by two 313 kW (420 hp) Gnome Rhône Jupiter 9Ab engines. Two operated by Air Union.

Blériot 5190 *Santos-Dumont* (France) Single example of a large eight-passenger high-wing monoplane flying-boat with a metal two-step hull and stabilising floats. Powered by four 484.4 kW (650 hp) Hispano-Suiza 12Nbr engines (three

tractor and one pusher). During 1934 the aircraft made four experimental crossings of the South Atlantic from Dakar to Natal and back; in 1935 it went into regular service with Air France on the route. An order for three more Type 5190s was withheld as the aircraft thereafter no longer conformed to French official requirements for a transatlantic flying-boat.

Blériot-Spad S.XX (France) Tested by the famous Sadi Lecointe on 7 August 1918, the S.XX two-seat fighter was an instant success and unlimited production at the rate of 300 examples a month was ordered for the Aéronautique Militaire. The Armistice of November 1918 forced an immediate cancellation of the order, but the need for new aircraft led to the delivery of 95 machines from October 1920. They equipped first the 2ème Régiment d'Aviation at Strasbourg, then fighter units at Chateauroux and Dijon. The Japanese Mitsubishi company bought three S.XXs and the Bolivian government one. The prototype S.XX established a world speed record for two-seaters in 1918 at 230 km/h (142.9 mph) and in July 1919 Sadi Lecointe set up an altitude record of 8,900 m (29,200 ft).

The fuselage of the S.XX was a graceful wooden monocoque structure, and the wings were of wooden construction, fabric-covered. Characteristic of André Herbemont's biplane designs, the upper wing had considerable sweepback. Wing bracing was by means of single I-struts either side. Power was provided by a 223.6 kW (300 hp) Hispano-Suiza 8Fb engine with a frontal radiator. The pilot operated two fixed synchronised 7.7 mm Vickers machine-guns and the observer – whose cockpit was immediately behind the pilot's – had a single Lewis gun.

From the S.XX Herbemont developed a series of single-seat racing biplanes (the S.20bis-1 to the S.20bis-6) during 1919–20. They followed the S.XXbis fighter, only two of which were constructed. The racers competed against their arch rivals, the Nieuport biplanes, in a number of competitions. The most radical modifications were made to the S.20bis-5, which had the normal upper wing with cabane struts replaced by a gull-wing attached directly to the upper fuselage. The S.20bis-6 reverted to a more normal wing arrangement, but eliminated its predecessor's large spinner to improve engine cooling. On 3 November 1920 the S.20bis-6 raised the World Absolute Speed Record to 309.012 km/h (192.01 mph).

Data (S.XX): *Engine* as above *Wing span* 9.72 m (31 ft 10 in) *Length* 7.30 m (23 ft 11 in) *Max T-O weight* 1,306 kg (2,879 lb) *Max level speed* 242 km/h (150 mph)

Blériot-Spad 27 (France) Small commercial transport biplane developed from the Spad 18 and first flown in late 1919. Accommodation for a pilot (in an open cockpit) and two passengers in a cabin. Power was provided by a 223.6 kW (300 hp) Hispano-Suiza 8Fa engine. Three were built and were operated between Paris and London by Compagnie des Messageries Aériennes (CMA).

Louis Blériot poses in front of his Type XI monoplane at Dover.

Capitano Piazza and his Blériot XI.

Blériot-Spad 33, 46, 56, 66, 116, and 126 (France) The S.33 was one of the most successful early French commercial aircraft and was developed throughout the 1920s, culminating with the S.126. It was first operated on regular Paris–London services in 1921 by CMA.

The S.33 – originally powered by a 186.3 kW (250 hp) Salmson Z.9 engine but later fitted with a 194 kW (260 hp) CM.9 – accommodated a pilot and four–five passengers (four passenger seats in the cabin). Altogether 40 aircraft were built, serving with several European airlines. From the S.33 was developed the S.46 powered by a 279.5 kW (375 hp) Lorraine-Dietrich 12Da engine, 38 of which were produced. The S.56 was essentially similar to the S.33 but was originally powered by a 279.5 kW (375 hp) Gnome Rhône-built Jupiter engine, had larger-span wings with duralumin spars and wooden ribs, and different cabin windows. The prototype – with a single elongated window on the starboard side of the fuselage and a similar window and two round windows (one on each side) on the port side – set up a height record in 1923 of 8,200 m (26,900 ft) while carrying a 250 kg (551 lb) useful load. About 20 S.56s were built, the major version of which was the Type

Blériot VII.

Blériot-Spad

56/4 with a roomy cabin for six passengers in the centre-section of the fuselage and the open pilot's cockpit in front of the cabin instead of behind. The cabin was well ventilated, heated and amply provided with opening windows. The S.66 designation applied to earlier aircraft incorporating some refinements. The S.116 and S.126 were one-offs with 335.3 kW (450 hp) Renault or Hispano-Suiza engines respectively.

Data (S.56/4): *Engine* one 313 kW (420 hp) Gnome Rhône-built Jupiter radial *Wing span* 13.15 m (44 ft 2 in) *Length* 9 m (29 ft 7 in) *Max T-O weight* 2,712 kg (5,950 lb) *Max level speed* 192 km/h (119 mph)

Blériot 110.

Blériot-Spad 34 (France) This elementary trainer was conceived by André Herbemont, a designer with precise ideas about what was required for an efficient aircraft in that category. As a result pupil and instructor were seated side-by-side for ease of instruction and communication, and the machine had docile handling qualities.

The prototype first flew on 16 July 1920. It was a biplane with a swept-back upper wing and a straight lower wing. Bracing was by single I-struts either side. One hundred and fifty S.34-1 machines were built: 119 went to French military aviation; six to the Navy; and 16 to the Blériot flying school at Buc. Six machines were also exported to Argentina, two to Finland and one to Bolivia. S.34s remained in French service until 1936. The S.34*bis* had a 97 kW (130 hp) Clerget rotary engine in place of the original 59.6 kW (80 hp) Rhône. Six were built, three for the French Navy.

Blériot-Spad S.XX.

Data (S.34-1): *Engine* as above *Wing span* 8.12 m (26 ft 7 in) *Length* 6.45 m (21 ft 1 in) *Max T-O weight* 719 kg (1,585 lb) *Max level speed* 145 km/h (90 mph)

Blériot-Spad 51 (France) Extensive prototype testing of this single-seat fighter biplane began in 1924. Powered by a 313 kW (420 hp) Jupiter engine, it had a wooden rounded monocoque fuselage and fabric-covered metal wings with characteristic sweepback on the upper plane. The S.51-2 development was finally rejected by France, but 50 were exported to Poland and at least one machine went to Turkey.

Blériot-Spad 61 (France) The prototype S.61-1 single-seat fighter biplane flew for the first time on 6 November 1923. In fact it appeared after the S.81 and featured a number of design improvements over its stablemate. The monocoque fuselage of the S.61 was slimmer and more streamlined. Unlike most Herbemont designs, both wings had straight leading edges. The upper wing spanned slightly more than the lower and there was considerable stagger. Bracing was by the familiar I-strut either side. Power was provided by a 335.3 kW (450 hp) Lorraine 12We water-cooled engine with frontal radiator.

The French military showed little interest in the S.61, but Poland ordered no fewer than 250 production S.61-2s and Romania 100. Subsequently Poland initiated licence production and it is believed 30 machines were completed. Polish S.61s formed the bulk of the equipment of the country's fighter regiments by 1928. Two years earlier, on 5 April 1926, a French-built S.61 won a world record for Poland by reaching 6,000 m (19,685 ft) in 14 minutes 38 seconds. Variants of the S.61 included several racers, and Pelletier d'Oisy won the Coupe Michelin in 1926 with an S.61-6d.

Data (S.61-2): *Wing span* 9.53 m (31 ft 3 in) *Length* 6.78 m (22 ft 2 in) *Max T-O weight* 1,531 kg (3,375 lb) *Max level speed* 237 km/h (147 mph) *Range* 600 km (373 miles) *Armament* two forward-firing Vickers machine-guns

Blériot-Spad 81 (France) A large number of fighter prototypes were developed to meet a French Air Ministry requirement of 1922. The only two designs to show promise were André Herbemont's S.81 and Emile Dewoitine's D.1. The latter was too innovative for the Aéronautique Militaire, which ordered 80 S.81s. They went into service from 1924 with the 2eme Régiment d'Aviation at Strasbourg. Armament was two

synchronised 7.7 mm cowling machine-guns. Power was provided by a 223.6 kW (300 hp) Hispano-Suiza 8Fb engine with twin Lamblin radiators. The wings resembled those of the S.61-2 with slight dihedral on the lower only.
Data: *Wing span* 9.61 m (31 ft 6 in) *Length* 6.4 m (21 ft 0 in) *Max T-O weight* 1,266 kg (2,791 lb) *Max level speed* 245 km/h (152 mph) *Range* 500 km (311 miles)

Blériot-Spad 510 (France) The S.510, in being a biplane, was unique among the many contenders to meet a French official requirement of 1930 for a single-seat fighter. It was constructed largely of metal, the fuselage being built up of duralumin and steel; the rear part was a duralumin monocoque. The equal-span wings had a metal structure, fabric-covered, and were braced with I-type interplane struts. Characteristically there was considerable sweepback on the upper wing only. The struts of the fixed landing gear were faired and the wheels had spats. Power was provided by a 715 kW (960 hp) Hispano-Suiza 12Xbrs liquid-cooled engine with a frontal radiator. The open pilot's cockpit was located immediately below the 'cut-out' in the trailing edge of the upper wing.

The prototype was some time in development and did not fly until 6 January 1933. Subsequent modifications included a lengthened fuselage to improve stability and alterations to the ailerons, which were fitted to upper and lower wings. While inferior to the low-wing Dewoitine D.510 monoplane in speed, the S.510 proved itself superior in manoeuvrability and climb-rate. An official order for 60 S.510s was placed in August 1935. Production aircraft were handed over to the Armée de l'Air during 1937. Armament comprised four MAC 1934 7.5 mm machine-guns in the lower wings, replacing the traditional two synchronised guns of the prototype.

The S.510s formed the equipment of the 7ème Escadre de Chasse until shortly before the beginning of World War II. By September 1939, however, they had been handed over to training schools and reserve fighter units. There were unconfirmed reports of S.510s flying on the Republican side during the Spanish Civil War.
Data: *Engine* as above *Wing span* 8.84 m (29 ft 0 in) *Length* 7.46 m (24 ft 5 in) *Max T-O weight* 1,680 kg (3,704 lb) *Max level speed* 372 km/h (231 mph) *Range* 800 km (497 miles)

Bloch 81 (France) Military ambulance monoplane powered by a 130 kW (175 hp) Salmson 9Nd radial engine. Stretcher accommodated in the forward fuselage. The Bloch 80 prototype was followed in 1932 by the first of 20 production Bloch 81s which were used in French overseas territories from 1935, remaining operational during World War II.

Bloch 120 (France) A three-engined all-metal high-wing monoplane for colonial service. Designed in 1933, it was selected to operate the state-owned scheduled air route across the Sahara from Algiers, which extended in 1935 through central Africa to Madagascar. Seven Bloch 120s were eventually operated by the Régie Air Afrique company. Power was provided by three 223.6 kW

Bloch 131.

(300 hp) Lorraine Algol 9Na radial engines. Up to ten passengers could be carried, but the principal task of the civil Bloch 120s was to establish and maintain regular air mail routes throughout French Africa. In addition the Armée de l'Air operated a number of Bloch 120s in the African territories. Several examples were still flying in 1942.
Data: *Engines* as above *Wing span* 20.54 m (67 ft 4¾ in) *Length* 15.3 m (50 ft 2½ in) *Max T-O weight* 6,000 kg (13,228 lb) *Max level speed* 255 km/h (158.5 mph)

Bloch 151 prototype.

Bloch 131 (France) The Bloch 131, developed from Bloch 130.01 *Guynemer* prototype, flew in July 1934. The low-wing Bloch 130 was a smaller version of the Bloch 210, but with a fixed and trousered undercarriage. A total redesign led to the Bloch 131, with a glazed nose and tall single fin and rudder, and powered by two 708 kW (950 hp) Gnome-Rhône 14N radial engines. A retractable undercarriage was fitted. Armament comprised 7.5 mm machine-guns in nose, dorsal turret and ventral positions. One hundred and thirty-nine production Bloch 131s were built for the Armée de l'Air in the RB4 category as four-crew machines intended for bombing and reconnaissance. The first six aircraft were delivered by June 1938, the rest by September 1939. Most went to Reconnaissance Groupes, suffering heavy losses at the beginning of the 'Phoney War' period. From October 1939 the type was used only for occasional night missions and for training. The max bomb load in various combinations was 800 kg (1,764 lb). The single Bloch 133, with a new twin fin and rudder tailplane, was later

Bloch

Bloch 155s and 152s.

Bloch 174.

Bloch 200 prototype without nose turret.

converted to a standard Bloch 131. Following France's capitulation, the Vichy regime used surviving Bloch 131s for target-towing.

Data (Bloch 131): *Engines* as above *Wing span* 20.05 m (65 ft 9 in) *Length* 17.91 m (58 ft 9 in) *Max T-O weight* 8,526 kg (18,797 lb) *Max level speed* 385 km/h (239 mph) *Range* 1,500 km (932 miles)

Bloch 150-157 (France) The Bloch 152 C1 cantilever low-wing monoplane was one of the standard Armée de l'Air fighters during the Battle of France in May–June 1940, but was comparatively unsuccessful. The main problem was that the 745.2 kW (1,000 hp) Gnome-Rhône 14N-25 radial engine powering most Bloch 152s was insufficiently powerful to give good performance; a number had the improved 14N-49 engine and Chauvière 371 variable-pitch propeller, which rendered them more effective. It was clear, however, that the Bloch fighters (while robustly built and stable in flight) lacked manoeuvrability. Nevertheless Bloch-equipped units were credited with 146 confirmed and 34 probable victories by the time of the June 1940 Armistice.

The Bloch 150.01 in its original form had failed to leave the ground in July and August 1935. Redesign, abandoned for a period, was subsequently re-started and a first flight was successfully completed on 29 September 1937. Continual modifications were made to the aircraft and its complete redesign for mass-production led to pre-series MB-151s, the first of which took to the air on 18 August 1938. While testing and further production were taking place, the improved MB-152.01 with a 14N-25 engine, in place of the MB-151's less powerful 14N-35, was tested. The

imminence of war led to additional orders, based on optimistic MB-152 performance figures (reached with inaccurate measuring instruments). The first MB-151 delivered was not accepted by the Armée de l'Air until March 1939, and was regarded as unsuitable for combat. Even after modifications, Armée de l'Air MB-151s were utilised only for training.

The first fighter Groupe to equip with the MB-152 was GC I/1 at Étampes-Mondésir in July 1939. The type was subsequently withdrawn for modification and when war broke out no Bloch fighters were in escadrille service. Re-equipment got under way at the end of 1939 and by the time of the German Blitzkrieg on 10 May 1940, 140 MB-151s and 363 MB-152s had been taken on charge by the French. Some of the former were to see service with navy fighter escadrilles. By the time of the Armistice the number of MB-152s accepted had risen to 482, plus one MB-153 (with Pratt & Whitney Twin Wasp radial) and nine MB-155s. Nineteen more MB-155s were completed by the Vichy French. They differed from the MB-152 in detail and had increased fuel capacity. Externally the main change was in the adoption of a smooth engine cowling. Final aircraft in the series was the sole MB-157 powered by a 1,267 kW (1,700 hp) Gnome-Rhône 14R-4 radial, which achieved a remarkable 710 km/h (441.2 mph) when tested under German supervision in March 1942. The Vichy regime was allowed to retain six (out of nine) MB-152-equipped Groupes after June 1940, but only 215 MB-152s and MB-155s were on charge when the air arm was dissolved by the Germans in November 1942.

Twenty MB-152s were sent to Romania and others (plus some MB-155s) ended their careers as Luftwaffe trainers. Nine MB-151s of a Greek export order were delivered to that country in 1940, but there is no record of their operational use.

Data (MB-152): *Engine* as above *Wing span* 10.54 m (34 ft 7 in) *Length* 9.1 m (29 ft 10 in) *Max T-O weight* 2,800 kg (6,173 lb) *Max level speed* 509 km/h (316.2 mph) *Range* 600 km (373 miles) *Armament* two 20 mm Hispano-Suiza 404 cannon and two 7.5 mm MAC machine-guns.

Bloch 160-162 series (France) The Bloch 160 was a one-off design which flew for the first time in September 1939, and was intended for Air Afrique passenger services. Powered by four 536.5 kW (720 hp) Hispano-Suiza 12X engines, it was a cantilever low-wing monoplane with a retractable landing gear and cabin accommodation for 12.

The design was developed to accommodate 32 passengers, but production as the Sud-Est 161 was delayed during the German occupation. The first SE.161 flew on 17 September 1945. Christened *Languedoc*, 100 of the type were built and used mainly on Air France routes. The SE.161 was a 33-seater (increased to 44), had twin fins and rudders, and was powered by four 857 kW (1,150 hp) Gnome-Rhône 14N radials (later Pratt & Whitney Twin Wasps, redesignated SE.161/P.7). The sole Bloch 162.01 four-engined bomber flew on 1 June 1940 and was subsequently taken over by the Germans and used for clandestine operations. It resembled the SE.161 transport, although of slightly smaller dimensions.

Data (SE.161/P.7): *Engines* as above *Wing span* 29.38 m (96 ft 4 in) *Length* 24.25 m (79 ft 6 in) *Max T-O weight* 22,941 kg (50,576 lb) *Max level speed* 440 km/h (273 mph)

Bloch 174/175 (France) The Bloch 174/175 was the outstanding French reconnaissance-bomber of 1940. The design originated with the MB-170.01 two-seat fighter, which flew for the first time on 15 February 1938. Unfortunately the undercarriage collapsed on landing a month later. On 30 July the three-seat MB-170-02 was air-tested. Further development led to the Bloch 174.01, which flew on 5 January 1939. It was impressive and series production at three SNCASO factories was ordered the following month. About 60 Bloch 174 A3 reconnaissance aircraft had been completed by the time of the June 1940 capitulation.

The MB-174 was a workmanlike low-wing monoplane with two 849.5 kW (1,140 hp) Gnome-Rhône 14N-48/49 radial engines in close-fitting cowlings. It had twin fins and rudders

of oval form. The nose was extensively glazed and pilot and dorsal gunner were accommodated under a raised glazed canopy. Defensive armament comprised two fixed forward-firing wing machine-guns, twin guns on a flexible mounting at the rear of the crew canopy and three further guns ventrally mounted to fire to the rear. All machine-guns were of the 7.5 mm MAC 1934 type. A number of MB-174 A3 aircraft were used for long-range reconnaissance missions over German-held territory during 1940, and displayed excellent performance characteristics. The MB-174 was developed into the MB-175 B3 bomber, with an enlarged bomb bay capable of carrying a maximum of 600 kg (1,323 lb) of bombs. Only 20 had been accepted when the Germans took over deliveries, using 56 MB-175s as trainers. The French Navy took delivery of a post-war MB-175T torpedo-bomber version, some 80 being built.

Data (MB-175 A3): *Engines* as above *Wing span* 17.92 m (58 ft 9 in) *Length* 12.23 m (40 ft 1 in) *Max T-O weight* 7,160 kg (15,784 lb) *Max level speed* 530 km/h (329 mph) *Range* 2,000 km (1,243 miles)

Bloch 200 (France) This angular machine was by far the most important of the early products of the Marcel Bloch (later Dassault) company. It was designed in the spring of 1932 to meet a French Air Ministry BN5 (five-seat night bomber) specification. In fact it was planned as a four-seater, and despite the existence of seven rival designs it was selected as the principal aircraft in its class by the Armée de l'Air. The first of three prototypes built at the Bloch factory at Courbevoie flew on 7 July 1933.

An initial order for 20 was placed in January 1934 and subsequently a further 188 were ordered to a later standard. Bloch built only a small number, the chief output coming from the Potez factory at Méaulte and Hanriot at Bourges. The MB-200 was an all-metal machine, though without stressed skin and with fabric-covered control surfaces. It was powered by two 648 kW (870 hp) Gnome-Rhône GR14 Kirs/Kjrs 14-cylinder radials, in full-length cowlings and driving three-blade fixed-pitch propellers. Landing gear was fixed and large spats (originally fitted) were often left off in operational service. The best feature was the bomb load of 1,200 kg (2,645 lb), which could be increased if necessary to 2,500 kg (5,511 lb). This was carried internally and on overload racks under the wings. Three 7.5 mm

Bloch 200.

Bloch 210s.

Blohm und Voss Bv 138.

Bloch

Blohm und Voss Bv 141.

MAC 1934 or other machine-guns were fitted to three prominent and highly unaerodynamic glazed positions in the nose and above and below the rear fuselage. The main drawbacks of the MB-200 were poor performance (50 km/h slower than the specification) and short range – the fuel capacity being a mere 304 Imp gal.

A combined output from the three factories of 25 per month meant that almost the entire order of 208 was delivered to 12 squadrons of the Armée de l'Air in the course of 1935; a further ten almost identical bombers were supplied to the Aéronavale. The MB-200 faded swiftly from front-line units from 1938 and all had been scrapped or consigned to training by the outbreak of World War II. In 1939 it was the chief French long-endurance crew and navigation trainer.

Blohm und Voss Ha 139 Nordwind.

A further quantity (believed to number 124) were built under licence in Czechoslovakia as the Aero MB-200, Avia assisting as sub-licensee. The licence was signed in 1934 and a pattern aircraft was delivered to Aero in May 1935. Aero made many alterations, the most important being to use NACA-cowled Walter K14 engines of lower power (559 kW; 750 hp) than the GR14s. The MB-200 was a tough and serviceable bomber, but the tendency to spin and crash after failure of an engine made it unpopular, and was probably a by-product of the poor speed.

Blohm und Voss Ha 139 Nordeer on its launching platform.

Data (French MB-200 BN4): *Engines* as above *Wing span* 22.45 m (73 ft 8 in) *Length* 15.8 m (52 ft 6 in) *Max T-O weight* 7,280 kg (16,049 lb) *Max level speed* 230 km/h (143 mph) *Range* 1,000 km (621 miles)

Bloch 210 (France) The Bloch 210.01 prototype flew for the first time in June 1934. It was intended as a twin-float seaplane bomber for the French Navy. A second prototype was designated Bloch 211 N° 1 *Verdun*. Following tests, the production version was ordered as the Bloch 210. A cantilever low-wing monoplane which retained the angular lines of the high-wing Bloch 200, the Bloch 210 was powered by two 678 kW (910 hp) Gnome-Rhône 14N engines and had a retractable landing gear, the main units of which retracted into the engine nacelles. Armament comprised single 7.5 mm MAC machine-guns in a nose turret and semi-retractable dorsal and ventral positions. Maximum bomb load was 1,730 kg (3,814 lb).

The first production machine flew on 10 December 1935. A total of 283 were eventually built for the Armée de l'Air, with which they served in the BN5 (five-crew night bomber) category. Final deliveries to the air force were made in February 1939, by which time the aircraft was obsolete.

By September 1939 238 Bloch 210s served with French bomber Groupes, employed on limited night operations including leaflet raids. However all were withdrawn from first-line service by June 1940. Twenty-four Bloch 210s had also been exported to Romania in 1938 and the Spanish Republicans had received several. Ex-Vichy aircraft were supplied by the Germans to Bulgaria in 1942.

Data: *Engines* as above *Wing span* 22.81 m (74 ft 10 in) *Length* 18.9 m (62 ft 0 in) *Max T-O weight* 10,200 kg (22,487 lb) *Max level speed* 334 km/h (207.5 mph) *Range* 1,100 km (684 miles)

Bloch 220 and 221 (France) The Bloch 220 was an all-metal twin-engined 16-passenger commercial airliner, the prototype of which flew for the first time in December 1935. Power was provided by 682 kW (915 hp) Gnome-Rhône 14N, 16 or 17 radial engines. Sixteen were subsequently operated by Air France. Those still flying after World War II were re-engined with Wright R-1820-97 Cyclones and redesignated Bloch 221s.

Blohm und Voss Bv 138 (Germany) This distinctive and rather pleasant-looking twin-boom reconnaissance flying-boat was nicknamed 'Fly-

ing Shoe' and became operational in Bv 138A-1 form in 1940. Trouble with the three 447 kW (600 hp) Junkers Jumo 205C-4 engines meant that it was little used operationally until the 656 kW (880 hp) Jumo 205D-engined Bv 138B-1s and C-1s entered service. Initially flown mainly over the Baltic and North Atlantic Ocean, Bv 138s later operated successfully over the North Sea and elsewhere (from bases in occupied Norway) in an attempt to search out Allied convoys and then direct U-boats on to them. The Bv 138 finished its career in a mine-sweeping role, carrying a large degaussing 'hoop' around its fuselage to explode magnetic mines. A total of 273 production Bv 138s were completed.

Data (Bv 138C-1): *Engines* as above *Wing span* 26.93 m (88 ft 4¼ in) *Length* 19.85 m (65 ft 1½ in) *Max T-O weight* 17,650 kg (38,911 lb) *Max level speed* 275 km/h (171 mph) *Range* 4,300 km (2,672 miles) *Armament* two 20 mm MG 151 cannon in nose and tail turrets; one 13 mm MG 131 machine-gun in dorsal position; and one side-firing 7.9 mm MG 15 machine-gun. Up to six 50 lb bombs, two mines or depth charges.

Blohm und Voss Ha 139 (Germany) From the foundation of the company in 1933 until World War II, the most important aircraft built by Blohm und Voss was the Ha 139, two of which – the *Nordmeer* and *Nordwind* – were delivered to Deutsche Luft Hansa in 1937. In the summer and autumn of that year they made 14 experimental transatlantic flights between Horta (Azores) and New York, operating from depot ships. In the spring of 1938 *Nordwind* went into service on the regular South Atlantic mail service between Bathurst (Gambia) and Natal (Brazil). Up to the end of June 1939 the seaplanes had successfully completed 100 transatlantic flights: 40 across the North Atlantic and 60 across the South Atlantic. For the 26 transatlantic flights of 1938 between the Azores and New York an improved and larger type of Ha 139, the Ha 139B *Nordstern*, was delivered. The Ha 139 type was also used to a limited extent during World War II as a reconnaissance, mine-laying and ambulance aircraft. Power was provided by four 447 kW (600 hp) Junkers Jumo 205C engines.

Blohm und Voss Bv 141 (Germany) Unique observation aircraft with crew nacelle mounted to one side of the fuselage and tractor engine on the centre-section of the monoplane wing. Small number operated on the Eastern Front from late 1941.

Blohm und Voss Bv 142 (Germany) Designed as an armed reconnaissance aircraft incorporating the wings, fuselage and tail unit of the Ha 139. Powered by four BMW 132H engines. Few built and used as transports by the Luftwaffe.

Blohm und Voss Bv 144 (Germany) Two prototypes built to German order by Breguet as 18-passenger transports with variable-incidence wing.

Blohm und Voss Bv 155 (Germany) Prototype high-altitude interceptor based on the Bf 109. Quantity production contemplated but type never became operational.

Blohm und Voss Bv 222 Wiking (Germany) Six-engined (745.2 kW; 1,000 hp Junkers Jumo 207Cs) flying-boat designed before the war for a proposed transatlantic service by Deutsche Luft Hansa. First prototype flown on 7 September 1940, but crashed. Altogether seven prototypes and seven production Bv 222Cs built and used as military freight and personnel transports. First reported in service in the autumn of 1942 in the Mediterranean area. Max accommodation for 110 troops on two decks.

Blume Bl.502 and Bl.503 (Germany) Designed by Prof Dipl-Ing Walter Blume as a four-seat all-metal touring and sports aircraft to replace his pre-war Arado Ar 79 design. Bl.500 prototype first flew on 14 March 1957 and two production versions were made available: the Bl.502 and Bl.503, with a 112 kW (150 hp) Lycoming O-320-A and a 134 kW (180 hp) Lycoming O-360-A1A engine respectively.

Boeing Model 1 (USA) First Boeing aircraft, designed by William Boeing and Cdr G. C. Westervelt, US Navy, and often referred to as the B and W seaplane. Two built with 93 kW (125 hp) Hall-Scott engines and sold to New Zealand in 1918 for air mail services.

Blohm und Voss Bv 238, developed using experience gained with the Bv 222 to become the largest flying-boat of World War II. Prototype only.

Boeing Model 1, best remembered as the B & W seaplane.

Boeing Model 6, known as the B-1 flying-boat.

Boeing

Prototype Boeing Model 10/GA-1, designated G.A.X.

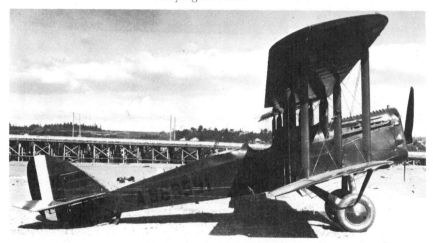

Boeing Model 16/DH-4M-1 of 1923.

Boeing Model 15/FB-1.

Boeing Model 5 (USA) Fifty twin-float seaplane trainers produced for the US Navy during World War I; powered by 74.5 kW (100 hp) Hall-Scott A-7A engines.

Boeing Model 6 (USA) Small two-seat biplane flying-boat of 1919; eventually powered by a 298 kW (400 hp) Liberty pusher engine. Used for carrying air mail.

Boeing Model 10 (USA) Ten experimental ground-attack armoured triplanes, each powered by two 317 kW (425 hp) Liberty 12A pusher engines. Delivered to the US Army Air Service as GA-1s in 1921.

Boeing Model 10 (USA) Two single tractor-engined experimental ground-attack biplanes delivered to the US Army Air Service.

Boeing Model 16 (USA) Basically remodelled de Havilland D.H.4s for extended use as observation, photographic and training biplanes with the USAAS. One hundred and eleven initially converted into DH-4Bs with crew cockpits brought closer together to improve communications. These were followed by 177 DH-4M-1s, which were identical to the DH-4Bs except that the wooden members of the fuselage were replaced by steel tubing. In addition the pilot's seat was modified to accommodate a parachute pack. One hundred and forty-seven DH-4M-1s were re-livered to the USAAS in 1924 and received the Army designation O2B-1, the remainder going to the US Marine Corps.

Boeing Model 63/TB-1 (USA) Three torpedo-bombers built for the US Navy as TB-1s and delivered in 1927.

Boeing Model 15/PW-9 and FB series (USA) The PW-9 was the first Boeing-designed fighter to enter service with the USAAC. The first of three prototypes flew on 29 April 1923 and had wooden sesquiplane-type wings and a fuselage constructed of steel tubes. Power was provided by a 328 kW (440 hp) Curtiss D12 engine. Thirty production PW-9s were built, followed by 25 improved PW-9As (Model 15As) with redesigned wingtips; 40 PW-9Cs (Model 15Cs); and 16 PW-9Ds (Model 15Ds) – the latter aircraft being the first to incorporate a balanced rudder and other refinements.

The US Navy also received examples of the Model 15 from 1924. Deliveries began with ten FB-1s and two FB-2s (Model 53s). The FB-2s were of greater significance because they had deck-landing arrester hooks fitted for experimental operations from America's first aircraft carrier, USS *Langley*. These were followed into service by 27 FB-5s (Model 55s), which differed from the earlier FB-1s by having increased wing stagger, a balanced rudder and a cross-axle landing gear for the attachment of deck landing arrester hooks in place of the split-type landing gear. Power was provided by the 391 kW (525 hp) Packard 2A-1500 engine. FB-5s were operated successfully from USS *Lexington* from 1927.

Data (PW-9C): *Engine* as above *Wing span* 9.75 m (32 ft 0 in) *Length* 7.14 m (23 ft 5 in) *Max T-O weight* 1,438 kg (3,170 lb) *Max level speed* 254 km/h (158 mph) *Range* 628 km (390 miles) *Armament* one 0.30 in and one 0.50 in Browning forward-firing machine-guns.

Boeing Model 21/NB-1 and NB-2 (USA) Two-seat flying and armament trainers of 1924, of which 41 NB-1s and 30 NB-2s were completed for the US Navy/Marine Corps with 164 kW (220 hp) Wright and 134 kW (180 hp) Wright-built Hispano-Suiza E-4 engines respectively.

Boeing Model 40A and 40B-2 (USA) Three-seat mail-carrying biplane of 1927 powered by a 317 kW (425 hp) Pratt & Whitney R-1340 Wasp radial engine (40A). Twenty-four produced for Boeing Air Transport to fly US mail between San Francisco and Chicago. A number were subsequently re-engined with 391 kW (525 hp) Pratt & Whitney Hornet engines and redesignated Model 40B-2s.

Boeing Model 40C (USA) The Model 40C was a further version of the 40A. The cabin was arranged to accommodate four passengers, resulting in the deletion of the rear 0.28 m³ (10 cu ft) mail compartment, leaving only the 0.71 m³ (25 cu ft) forward mail compartment behind the engine.

Boeing Model 40B-4 (USA) The Model 40B-4 was basically a refined four-seat version of the Model 40B-2, the first of which flew in October 1929. Model 40Cs were later brought up to 40B-4 standard. The four passenger seats were arranged in pairs, each being slightly staggered to provide ample shoulder room. All windows were glazed with non-splinterable glass and could be opened. Forced heating and ventilation added to passenger comfort.

Data: *Engine* as above *Wing span* 13.46 m (44 ft 2¼ in) *Length* 10.16 m (33 ft 4½ in) *Max T-O weight* 2,758 kg (6,080 lb) *Max level speed* 206 km/h (128 mph) *Range* 1,046 km (650 miles)

Boeing Model 69/F2B-1 (USA) The designation F2B-1 applied to 32 fighters and fighter-bombers ordered by the US Navy and delivered from early 1928. Like most naval fighters, the F2B-1s were designed to be able to operate as seaplanes or deck-landing fighters, but as far as is known they were only used on wheel landing gears on board USS *Saratoga*. The fuselage and tail unit were of steel and duralumin-tubing construction, while the wings were of wood with duralumin interplane struts. Power was provided by a 317 kW (425 hp) Pratt & Whitney Wasp radial engine. An auxiliary fuel tank could be carried under the fuselage and dropped in an emergency. Max level speed 254 km/h (158 mph).

Boeing Model 77/F3B-1 (USA) In an effort to improve upon the F2B-1 and gain new orders Boeing produced a new prototype fighter which could be fitted with either a central duralumin float and two wingtip floats or a land-type undercarriage. The float landing gear was expected to enable the aircraft to be catapulted from naval vessels. However no orders were placed and the prototype went back to Boeing, where it was fitted with a new swept-back upper wing of increased span. Although it is widely believed that the aircraft then emerged as a landplane, it in fact remained a seaplane until after initial flight tests. From 1928 the US Navy received 73 refined F3B-1s with wheel landing gears, which served on all three of its aircraft carriers.

Data: *Engine* one 317 kW (425 hp) Pratt & Whitney R-1340 Wasp radial *Wing span* 10.06 m (33 ft 0 in) *Length* 7.57 m (24 ft 10 in) *Max T-O weight* 1,515 kg (3,340 lb) *Max level speed* 251 km/h (156 mph) *Range* 547 km (340 miles) *Armament* two forward-firing 0.30 in/0.50 in Browning machine-guns, plus up to 56.7 kg (125 lb) of bombs

Boeing Model 80 and 80A (USA) The Model 80 was a 12-passenger biplane airliner powered by three Pratt & Whitney Wasp radial engines. Four were built for Boeing Air Transport in 1928. A change of power plant to Hornet radials led to the construction of ten 12–18-passenger Model 80As; the passenger seats arranged in four, five or six rows of three. A separate compartment forward of 2.8 m³ (100 cu ft) could accommodate a row of seats or be used for mail, when only 15 passengers were carried. The Model 80As were subsequently redesignated 80A-1s when fitted with auxiliary fins and rudders on each side of the usual large central vertical surfaces.

Boeing Model 95 (USA) First flown in December 1928, the Model 95 was a mail- and cargo-carrying biplane with no passenger accommodation. Power was provided by a 391 kW (525 hp) Pratt & Whitney Hornet radial engine. Twenty-five were built, most going to Boeing Air Transport.

Boeing Model 40As.

Boeing Model 69/F2B-1.

Boeing Model 80.

Boeing P-12 and F4B series (USA) One of the most famous of Boeing's biplane fighters of the inter-war years, the F4B originated as a private venture to develop a replacement for the US Navy's F2B/F3B carrier-based fighters, which had first entered service in 1928. Although they had only been in service for a very short period, Boeing believed it was possible to refine the design to give improved performance without additional power.

Two very similar prototypes were built: Boeing Models 83 and 89. The former had a spreader-bar axle landing gear and an arrester hook; the latter a split-axle landing gear so that a bomb could be carried beneath the fuselage. In other respects they were virtually identical. Following Navy evaluation in the summer of 1928, 27 were ordered as F4B-1s, these combining the split-axle landing gear, bomb carrying provisions and arrester hook. Forty-six F4B-2s, delivered in early 1931, had the spreader-bar axle, a tailwheel, Frise

Boeing P-12s.

Boeing Model 215, designated YB-9 by the Army. From it was developed the Model 246.

Boeing Model 200 Monomail.

ailerons and a neat ring cowling for the engine. They were followed by 21 F4B-3s with a semi-monocoque metal fuselage and 92 F4B-4s which differed by having a larger fin and rudder.

The USAAC ordered ten aircraft similar to the F4B-1 in late 1928, accepting the naval evaluation as being correct. Designated P-12s, these differed only by having the arrester hook and other specifically naval equipment deleted. P-12Bs, of which 90 were built with 317 kW (425 hp) Wasp engines, differed very slightly and were followed by 96 P-12Cs, which were similar to the Navy's F4B-2s. P-12Ds, of which 35 were built, had a more powerful 391 kW (525 hp) Wasp engine. Most extensively built of the Army versions was the P-12E. This had a monocoque fuselage, pilot's headrest faired by a turtleback and the more powerful engine of the P-12D. A total of 135 were ordered in 1931, many remaining in service until replaced by P-26As in 1935. The last few of the order were given 447 kW (600 hp) Pratt & Whitney R-1340-19 engines and the designation P-12F.

Total production for the Army and Navy amounted to 586 aircraft, representing a production record for a basic military design which remained unequalled until the attainment of long production runs during World War II.
Data (F4B-4): *Engine* one 410 kW (550 hp) Pratt & Whitney R-1340-16 radial *Wing span* 9.14 m (30 ft 0 in) *Length* 6.12 m (20 ft 1 in) *Max T-O weight* 1,638 kg (3,610 lb) *Max level speed* 303 km/h (188 mph) *Range* 595 km (370 miles) *Armament* two 0.30 in forward-firing machine-guns.
Boeing Model 200 Monomail (USA) High-performance mailplane powered by a 428 kW (575 hp) Pratt & Whitney Hornet B radial engine. First flown on 6 May 1930, it introduced many advanced features such as a cantilever low wing, retractable landing gear and a specially designed long-chord anti-drag engine cowling. Had three mail compartments with a total capac-

ity of 6.23 m³ (220 cu ft). Max level speed 254 km/h (158 mph); cruising speed at sea level 225 km/h (140 mph). Later converted into the Model 221A eight-passenger transport for Boeing Air Transport.
Boeing Model 246/Y1B-9A (USA) Following single examples of the experimental Model 214 and 215 bombers, Boeing built five Y1B-9As for evaluation by the USAAC. The first flew in July 1932. It was a cantilever low-wing monoplane with a retractable landing gear and accommodation for a crew of five. Power was provided by two 447 kW (600 hp) Pratt & Whitney engines and armament comprised two machine-guns and up to 1,000 kg (2,200 lb) of bombs. However the USAAC ordered Martin B-10 bombers in preference to the Y1B-9As.

Boeing Model 247 (USA) In May 1930 Boeing flew the first example of what must be regarded as a revolutionary design for a civil transport. Prior to the introduction of this machine into service, aircraft of what was then regarded as conventional design were in general use. Conventional meant heavy biplane structures; fixed and often massive landing gear; and engines which, because they were often uncowled, added their proportion of drag to the total.

Learning much from the Monomail exercise and appreciating that a multi-engine design could eliminate its shortcomings, Boeing evolved a new ten-passenger civil transport under the designation of Model 247. Of cantilever low-wing monoplane configuration and powered by two 410 kW (550 hp) Pratt & Whitney Wasp radial piston engines, it flew for the first time on 8 February 1933. Of all-metal structure, with retractable landing gear, controllable-pitch propellers, and wing and tail unit de-icing, the Model 247 was way ahead of all contemporary designs. Able to climb safely on the power of only one engine and with a cruising speed of 249 km/h (155 mph), it virtually made other US airline equipment obsolete overnight. In service it demonstrated that it was capable of reliable and regular transport operations over ranges of up to 1,207 km (750 miles). A specially prepared aircraft with additional fuel tanks in the fuselage took part in the 1934 MacRobertson air race from England to Australia, coming second in the transport category.

A total of 75 Model 247s were built for use by the airlines which comprised the Boeing Air Transport system (soon to become United Air Lines) and for other companies including Luft-Hansa of Germany. Further production was,

however, impeded by the introduction of the much better Douglas DC-1/2/3 family. In 1942 27 Model 247s were impressed for service with the USAAF as heavy cargo and troop transports. After the discovery that the size of the cabin door and cabin interior was totally unsuited to loading cargo, they were used to ferry aircrew and for training purposes. In Army service they were designated C-73 in the cargo and transport category, their original engines replaced by 447 kW (600 hp) R-1340-AN-1s. At the end of the war they were returned to civil airline operations.

Data (247D): *Engines* two 410 kW (550 hp) Pratt & Whitney R-1340-S1H1G Wasp radials *Wing span* 22.56 m (74 ft 0 in) *Length* 15.72 m (51 ft 7 in) *Max T-O weight* 6,193 kg (13,650 lb) *Max cruising speed* 304 km/h (189 mph) *Range* 1,207 km (750 miles)

Boeing Model 266/P-26 (USA) The P-26 'Peashooter' was Boeing's first and last production monoplane fighter. Some 111 P-26As, 2 P-26Bs and 23 P-26Cs were built for the USAAC. The type had monoplane wings, the outer panels of which were externally braced with front and rear wires. The centre-section spars were constructed of steel with ribs and skin covering of aluminium alloy. Split-type trailing-edge flaps were later added to P-26As and were manually operated from the open cockpit. The semi-monocoque fuselage was also of aluminium alloy construction. A fixed, heavily trousered landing gear was fitted and power was provided by a 447 kW (600 hp) Pratt & Whitney R-1340-27 or -33 radial engine. Armament comprised two forward-firing machine-guns of 0.30 in and/or 0.50 in calibre and two 120 lb or five 30 lb bombs could be carried.

Although never used in action by the USAAC, ex-Army P-26s acquired by the Philippine Air Force fought the Japanese during World War II and the 11 Model 281 export fighters for China must also have seen action against Japanese forces. In addition Panama and Guatamala received ex-USAAC P-26s and Spain received an export model.

Data (P-26A): *Engine* as above *Wing span* 8.52 m

(27 ft 11⅝ in) *Length* 7.19 m (23 ft 7¼ in) *Max T-O weight* 1,340 kg (2,955 lb) *Max level speed* 376 km/h (234 mph) *Range* 580 km (360 miles)

Boeing Model 307 Stratoliner (USA) In early 1934 Boeing began design studies for a multi-engine bomber and a basically similar civil transport. When, in June 1934, the USAAC invited proposals for a new bomber, Boeing's Model 299 was revamped to meet the Army specification and duly became built by the thousands as the B-17 Flying Fortress.

The Model 300 was also changed as ideas were developed and in its Model 307 form was basically similar to the B-17, except for a very different fuselage. This was of circular cross-section, a configuration chosen so that the structure would be able to withstand the stresses of pressurisation, thus ensuring a smooth flight for the crew of five and 33 passengers at an altitude above much of the atmospheric turbulence.

The prototype Model 307 (named Stratoliner because of its high cruising ceiling) flew for the first time on 31 December 1938. A total of ten were built: the prototype; five SA-307Bs for Transcon-

tinental & Western Air; three S-307s for Pan American; and a single SB-307B for the late Howard Hughes. TWA's SA-307Bs were impressed for service with the Army's Air Transport Command during World War II, being used as C-75s for VIP transport over the North and South Atlantic.

The Model 307 had the distinction of being the first civil airliner with a pressurised cabin to enter service. It also introduced an extra crew member – known as the flight engineer – to relieve the captain of certain duties such as power plant, fuel and pressurisation management and monitoring.

Data: *Engines* four 820 kW (1,100 hp) Wright R-1820 radials *Wing span* 32.69 m (107 ft 3 in) *Length* 22.66 m (74 ft 4 in) *Max T-O weight* 19,051 kg (42,000 lb) *Max level speed* 396 km/h (246 mph) *Cruising speed* 354 km/h (220 mph) *Range* 3,846 km (2,390 miles)

Boeing

Boeing B-17E Flying Fortresses.

Boeing 314 Clipper (USA) To meet the requirements of Pan American Airways for a long-range flying-boat which would be suitable for operation over the North Atlantic (as well as on other over-water routes), Boeing designed a large high-wing monoplane. It utilised, with little change, the wing which had been developed for the single XBLR-1 (Experimental Bomber Long Range Model 1) which had resulted from a US Army design study awarded in 1934. Before the latter was completed the designation changed to XB-15; during World War II it was redesignated XC-105 when used to carry cargo.

The wing was wedded to a new flying-boat hull of semi-monocoque construction; on either side of the hull, below the wing, a huge hydro-stabiliser was mounted to assist both planing and stability – each contained fuel to supplement the wing tanks. Power plant comprised four 1,118 kW (1,500 hp) Wright Double Cyclone engines, nacelle-mounted at the wing leading edge and driving a Hamilton Standard constant-speed fully feathering propeller. Some measure of the depth of the wing aerofoil section is gained from the fact that each engine was accessible in flight via a companionway built inside the wing structure.

Boeing Model SA-307B Stratoliner in Transcontinental & Western Air livery.

Accommodation was provided for a crew of eight and a maximum of 74 passengers in the Model 314. Day compartments were convertible into sleeping accommodation for up to 40 passengers in upper and lower berths. There were, in addition, a special dining saloon and associated galley, a private drawing room, dressing rooms and toilets. There was also space for some 4,760 kg (10,500 lb) of cargo.

Pan American's initial order was for six Model 314s. The first of these made its maiden flight in June 1938 and all six had been delivered within a

Boeing Model 314 Clipper.

year. Used initially for scheduled services over the North Atlantic, Pan American's 'Boeing Clippers' (so-called because of their individual names, such as *Yankee Clipper*) also gained a wonderful reputation for reliability on the San Francisco–Hong Kong trans-Pacific route. The first six 314s were followed by an order for six 314As with increased engine power and provision for three additional passengers. Subsequently the original six flying-boats were converted to 314A standard.

With the outbreak of war in the Pacific, the US Navy acquired two of these aircraft from Pan Am, plus three from the USAAF, which had used them briefly as cargo transports under the designation C-98. The Navy operated them on special transport duties. Three were sold by Pan Am to BOAC in Britain, also for use on the Atlantic route. These three aircraft, plus those in Navy service, were returned to their original owners at the end of the war, but by then the heyday of the flying-boat had passed into history.

Data (Boeing 314A): *Engines* four 1,192 kW (1,600 hp) Wright R-2600 Twin Cyclone radials *Wing span* 46.33 m (152 ft 0 in) *Length* 32.31 m (106 ft 0 in) *Max T-O weight* 38,102 kg (84,000 lb) *Max level speed* 320 km/h (199 mph) *Cruising speed* 296 km/h (184 mph) *Range* 8,369 km (5,200 miles)

Boeing-Stearman Kaydet (USA) Lloyd Stearman had founded the Stearman Aircraft Company in 1927 at Venice, California, but soon became established at Wichita, Kansas. In 1934 he developed a two-seat biplane trainer of very clean lines as a private venture. Later in the same year the company became a subsidiary of the Boeing Company and this trainer was developed as the Model 70, winning an Army Primary Trainer competition.

For Americans and Canadians, the Boeing-Stearman Kaydet (as it became known) carries the same aura of nostalgia surrounding such aircraft as the Avro 504 and Tutor, de Havilland Tiger Moth, and Bücker Jüngmann and Bestmann. This follows from the fact that well over 8,000 were built for the US Army and Navy, meaning that thousands of men learned to fly on this superb, kindly and forgiving trainer.

Post-war, large quantities of surplus aircraft were acquired by civil operators, many being converted for use as agricultural dusters or sprayers (see **Stearman**).

Boeing B-17 Flying Fortress (USA) Frustrated in their efforts to acquire a fleet of strategic bombers for service with the Army Air Corps, US Army planners – who were devotees of the theories expounded by Brig Gen William 'Billy'

Mitchell – inserted the thin end of an important wedge when they ordered a small number of YB-17 prototypes in January 1936, ostensibly for the nation's defence. Originating as the Boeing Model 299, the prototype was built as a private venture, Boeing gambling heavily on producing a winner that would bring a large military contract. It must have seemed to Boeing that their gamble had failed when, almost at the end of the military trials, the Model 299 crashed on take-off. Fortunately investigation proved that the aircraft had been flown off with the flying controls locked and safety of the basic design was not suspect.

It was not until 1938 that the USAAC was able to place an order for 39 production B-17Bs, the last of this batch entering service in March 1940. These were the first B-17 production aircraft to be equipped with turbocharged engines, providing a higher maximum speed and much increased service ceiling. Of the B-17Cs which followed, a batch of 20 were supplied to the RAF (designated Fortress I) and used operationally in Europe for evaluation, leading to improved B-17D and B-17E aircraft with self-sealing fuel tanks and revised armour and armament.

The B-17E was truly a flying fortress, armed with one 0.30 in and 12 0.50 in machine-guns for defence and able to carry a maximum 7,983 kg (17,600 lb) of bombs. Most extensively built variant was the B-17G (8,680), being built by Douglas and Lockheed Vega as well as at the Boeing plant, Seattle. Pratt & Whitney R-1820-97 radial engines and improved turbochargers enabled the B-17G to operate at an altitude of up to 10,670 m (35,000 ft); and the addition of a chin turret below the nose (containing two 0.50 in machine-guns) provided better defence against the head-on attacks being launched by Luftwaffe fighter pilots in their attempts to reduce the numbers of Fortresses striking daily at strategic targets deep in German territory.

Special variants included the B-40 with up to 30 machine-guns/cannons, which was intended as a B-17 escort, but proved to be an operational failure; BQ-7 pilotless aircraft packed with explosives to be deployed against German targets by radio control, which failed due to unreliable control equipment; CB-17 and C-108 transports; and F-9 long-range B-17 equipped to serve as an air-sea rescue aircraft and able to deploy a lifeboat carried beneath the fuselage.

In Britain, more than anywhere else in the world, the B-17 evokes vivid memories of courageous aircrew who day after day – despite sometimes horrific losses – continued to attack targets in Europe until victory was won. For Boeing, their private-venture gamble paid off: a total of 12,731 Fortresses were built by the Boeing, Douglas and Lockheed team.

Data (B-17G): *Engines* four 894 kW (1,200 hp) Pratt & Whitney R-1820-97 radials *Wing span* 31.62 m (103 ft 9 in) *Length* 22.66 m (74 ft 4 in) *Max T-O weight* 29,710 kg (65,500 lb) *Max level speed* 462 km/h (287 mph) *Range* 3,219 km (2,000 miles) *Armament* 13 × 0.50 in machine-guns, plus bombs

Boeing B-29 Superfortress (USA) Some three years after the first flight of its Model 299 prototype (subsequently designated B-17 Flying Fortress) Boeing approached the USAAC with proposals for an improved version of the B-17. The time was not yet ripe, however, for the Army

The 500th Boeing C-97, delivered to the USAAF/USAF as a KC-97G tanker.

Boeing

special wing aerofoil section and used Fowler-type flaps to provide satisfactory take-off and landing characteristics.

Deliveries of the first production B-29s began in the autumn of 1943; but it was not until 5 June 1944 that they were first used operationally in an attack on Bangkok, followed ten days later by an attack on the Japanese mainland. These initial missions were launched from bases in India; the first B-29 operations from the Mariana Islands began in late November 1944. Maj Gen Curtis LeMay was selected to command the B-29 attacks on Japan in January 1945 and in March initiated low-level incendiary raids by night. These, between 10 and 20 March, destroyed about 83 km² (32 sq miles) of the nation's four most important cities. Finally, on 6 and 9 August, the B-29s *Enola Gay* and *Bock's Car* dropped the world's only two operational atomic bombs on the Japanese cities of Hiroshima and Nagasaki,

had then (in 1938) only recently been permitted to place an initial contract for 39 B-17Bs. However information on changing requirements in relation to operational needs allowed Boeing to keep updating their design, so that at the beginning of 1940, when the USAAF invited proposals for a long-range medium bomber, much of their basic thinking had already been done. The Boeing design (in competition with submissions from Consolidated, Douglas and Lockheed) was sufficiently interesting for three XB-29 prototypes plus a static test airframe to be ordered on 24 August 1940. Consolidated also received an order for three prototypes, their submission being built as the B-32 Dominator.

To provide better conditions for the crew of the B-29 Superfortress (as this aircraft became designated) three pressurised compartments were provided: one for the flight deck which accommodated the pilots, bombardier and flight engineer, connected via a tunnel above the bomb bays to the midships compartment for the observers and gunners; a separate pressurised section was provided for the tail gunner. Armament comprised ten or eleven guns in five turrets, of which four were remotely controlled and sighted from adjacent astrodomes. Because of what was then considered to be a very high wing loading (initially 349 kg/m², 171 lb/sq ft) Boeing developed a

bringing World War II to an end shortly afterwards. Post-war a total of 88 B-29s served with the RAF as Washington B.Is, and the type continued in USAF service as flight-refuelling tankers and for air-sea rescue, photo-reconnaissance and weather reconnaissance.

A developed version of the B-29 with Pratt & Whitney R-4360 Wasp Major engines was built as the XB-44. When ordered into production it was designated B-50 and introduced a number of improvements. The first B-50A flew on 25 June 1947. B-50Bs had increased gross weight; B-50Ds additional fuel capacity; and conversion programmes produced KB-50 tankers, TB-50 trainers and WB-50 weather reconnaissance aircraft. Data (B-29A): *Engines* four 1,639 kW (2,200 hp) Wright R-3350 radials *Wing span* 43.05 m (141 ft 3 in) *Length* 30.18 m (99 ft 0 in) *Max T-O weight* 64,000 kg (141,100 lb) *Max level speed* 576 km/h (358 mph) *Range* 6,598 km (4,100 miles) *Armament* 11 × 0.50 in machine-guns or ten 0.50 in guns and one 20 mm cannon, plus up to 9,072 kg (20,000 lb) of bombs

Boeing Model 377 Stratocruiser (USA) The United States had a significant lead in the design and construction of long-range transport aircraft at the close of World War II, the consequence of an understanding with Britain that the US industry would concentrate on the development of such

Boeing 727 prototype
rollout.

Boeing F4B-4.

Bristol Britannia 301.

Boeing E-4B.

Bristol Sycamore helicopters operated by the Royal Australian Navy.

Bristol/Westland Belvedere HC.1 hauling a Bloodhound missile.

Bristol F.2B Fighter.

Pilatus Britten-Norman
BN-2 Islander.

Bücker Bü 133
Jungmeister.

Cameron Balloons G-OLLI
hot-air balloon, made for
Robertson Foods Ltd.

Cameron Balloons hot-air balloon made for Champion in the shape of a spark plug.

aircraft because of the distances involved in the Pacific war. However, with the end of the war, US manufacturers were soon under considerable pressure from airlines to provide large capacity long-range civil airliners, resulting in some temporary adaptations of military aircraft.

As early as 1942 Boeing had initiated the design of the military transport version of the B-29 Superfortress. This retained the wings, landing gear, power plant, lower fuselage and tail unit of the B-29 with little change. Completely new was the upper fuselage, which formed a double-bubble section when mated to the existing lower fuselage; the new, wider cabin providing increased capacity. A USAAF contract for three prototypes was awarded in early 1943 and the first of these flew on 15 November 1944. Satisfactory testing resulted in an order for ten YC-97 service test aircraft: the first six were almost identical to the prototypes; the next three had the taller fin and Pratt & Whitney R-4360 engines of the B-50, designated YC-97A and furnished as troop carriers; the tenth became a transport aircraft with airline type seats for service with MATS and was designated YC-97B, later C-97B.

The initial contract for production aircraft covered a total of 50 C-97As, the first of which was delivered on 15 October 1949. C-97Cs which followed were ordered for casualty evacuation and all subsequent production (amounting to some 800 aircraft) was for various KC-97 flight refuelling tankers.

Faced with the urgent demand for a long-range civil transport, Boeing proposed an airliner counterpart of the C-97 which entered production in 1947 at Seattle. Built alongside B-50s (using the basic C-97 airframe with B-50 systems), a total of 55 were built and served with major US airlines and BOAC. With accommodation for 55 to 100 passengers, they provided luxurious travel – even boasting a lounge and cocktail bar on the lower deck – and remained in service until 1958.
Data: *Engines* four 2,608 kW (3,500 hp) Pratt & Whitney R-4360 Wasp Major radials *Wing span* 43.05 m (141 ft 3 in) *Length* 33.63 m (110 ft 4 in) *Max T-O weight* 66,134 kg (145,800 lb) *Max level speed* 604 km/h (375 mph) *Cruising speed* 483 km/h (300 mph) *Range* 6,437 km (4,000 miles)
Boeing Model 450/B-47 Stratojet (USA) The Stratojet was a six-engined medium bomber and the first large jet-powered aircraft to be fitted with sweptback wings and tail surfaces. Two prototypes were built, the first making its maiden flight on 17 December 1947. The first production order was placed in September 1948. For convenience the main production versions are listed below:

B-47A Stratojet Initial production version powered by six 23.1 kN (5,200 lb st) General Electric J47-GE-11 turbojets. Eighteen individual JATO solid-fuel rockets fitted to give an emergency take-off thrust of 88.97 kN (20,000 lb st). The first B-47A flew on 25 June 1950. Ten built.
B-47B Stratojet Powered by six 25.8 kN (5,800 lb st) J47-GE-23 engines. Max T-O weight 83,914 kg (185,000 lb). Fitted with drop tanks.

First flown on 26 April 1951. B-47Bs later modified and modernised up to B-47E standard including: the installation of J47-GE-25 engines and water-injection system to give a 17% increase in T-O power; substitution of droppable 33-rocket T-O assist pack for original internal 18-rocket equipment; installation of 4.9 m (16 ft) approach parachutes and ejection seats; re-arrangement of equipment on the flight deck; and substitution of the GE radar-directed tail gun turret with two 20 mm cannon for former 0.50 in guns. Modified aircraft were known as B-47B/IIs. Total of 398 built.
RB-47B Stratojet Conversion of B-47B for high-altitude photographic reconnaissance.
B-47E Stratojet Powered by six 26.69 kN (6,000 lb st) J47-GE-25 turbojets. Remotely controlled tail armament of two 20 mm cannon. Some converted to ETB-47E crew trainers. Total of 1,590 built.
RB-47E Stratojet Day or night long-range photographic reconnaissance version of B-47E with longer nose. First flown 3 July 1953. Length 33.5 m (109 ft 10 in). Total of 240 B-47Es completed as RB-47Es.

Boeing Model 464/B-52H Stratofortress carrying two Hound Dog missiles.

RB-47H Stratojet Special reconnaissance version to locate radar stations. Thirty-two built.
RB-47K Stratojet Similar to RB-47E but equipped for both photographic and weather reconnaissance. Fifteen built.
EB-47L Stratojet Electronic communications version converted from B-47Es. Total of 35 produced.

Boeing 707 prototypes.

**Boeing KC-135
Stratotanker.**

which would have the capability of delivering weapons against any target in the world, it was envisaged that turboprop engines would provide the power plant.

Following initiation of a design competition (involving Boeing and Convair) by the USAAF in 1946, Boeing was awarded a contract for further development of their proposal. This was for a turboprop-powered aircraft of some 158,755 kg (350,000 lb) gross weight. By 1948 this weight had increased by about 37%; but even this did not provide the necessary range, and it was envisaged that flight refuelling would be essential if the 'any world target' requirement was to be met.

Despite these shortcomings, two prototypes were ordered under the designation XB-52 (one became the YB-52); but before these were started the design was changed. The new configuration looked like a scaled-up B-47, with a swept mono-plane wing carrying four pairs of pylon-mounted turbojets. First to fly was the YB-52, on 15 April 1952. Like the B-47 it had four twin-wheel main landing gear units, plus small balancing outrigger wheels which retracted into the wings. The bomb bay could accommodate a thermonuclear weapon plus decoy missiles.

QB-47 Stratojet Fourteen B-47Es modified by Lockheed into pilotless drones for the USAF's R & D Command. First flown in September 1959.

B-47s were subsequently structurally modified to extend their useful life by six to ten years of normal service with the USAF's Strategic Air Command.

Data (B-47E): *Engines* as above *Wing span* 35.35 m (116 ft 0 in) *Length* 32.92 m (108 ft 0 in) *Max T-O weight* 91,625 kg (202,000 lb) *Max level speed* 1,013 km/h (630 mph) *Range* 5,150 km (3,200 miles) *Armament* two 20 mm cannon and up to 9,070 kg (20,000 lb) bombs

Boeing Model 464/B-52 Stratofortress (USA)
In 1945 the USAAF indicated a requirement for a long-range heavy bomber which was to be pow-ered by turbine engines. It must be remembered that at that date the fuel economy of turbojets was far from satisfactory, emphasis having been on developing high output thrust with little concern for fuel consumption. While this approach pro-duced engines which were suitable for new gener-ation fighters and interceptors, they could hardly be considered ideal for any aircraft in which long range was of paramount importance.

Turboprop engines, on the other hand, in which the smooth power of a turbine was used to drive a propeller through the medium of a reduc-tion gear, were proving to be far less thirsty. Thus, when the USAAF approached Boeing to produce a design study for a new strategic heavy bomber

In February 1951 the USAF ordered 13 B-52s, the first B-52A Stratofortress flying on 5 August 1954. This differed from the prototype by having cross-wind landing gear; provision for 3,785 litre (1,000 US gallon) underwing tanks and flight refuelling; and the flight deck changed to provide side-by-side seating for the two pilots. Only three were built before production changed to the B-52B/RB-52B, the first operational version, of which 50 were built. More powerful engines and equipment changes resulted in the B-52C (35 built), B-52D (170), B-52E (100) and B-52F (89).

Most extensively built version was the B-52G, production totalling 193. The increased-capacity integral wing fuel tanks of this version provided greater range; a remotely controlled rear gun-turret enabled the tail gunner to sit more produc-tively alongside the ECM operator; and a Hound Dog stand-off bomb could be carried beneath each wing. Final production version was the B-52H with turbofan engines and a 20 mm multi-barrel gun in the tail; 102 were built to bring total Stratofortress construction to 744.

Major modification programmes have since enabled B-52G/H models to carry 20 Short Range Attack Missiles (SRAM) each and have added an Electro-optical Viewing System (EVS) with forward-looking LLTV and IR capability; this equipment is housed in small under-nose turrets. In the absence of a manned bomber replacement for the B-52, continuing modification and recon-struction programmes are intended to ensure that the USAF's Strategic Air Command will retain a viable strategic bomber for the remainder of the century.

Data (B-52H): *Engines* eight 75.6 kN (17,000 lb st) Pratt & Whitney TF33-P-3 turbo-fans *Wing span* 56.39 m (185 ft 0 in) *Length* 48.03 m (157 ft 7 in) *Max T-O weight* 221,350 kg (488,000 lb) *Max level speed* 1,040 km/h (650 mph) at 6,100 m (20,000 ft) *Range* 20,120 km

Boeing 720 prototype.

(12,500 miles) *Armament* One M-61 20 mm gun in General Electric turret. Up to twenty SRAM attack missiles, plus nuclear free-fall bombs.

Boeing Model 707 (incl KC-135 Stratotanker and VC-137) (USA) The original designation of Boeing's Model 707 prototype was 367-80, which Boeing claims to be partly camouflage to mislead big-eared competitors and partly to show that much of its design derived from earlier studies made for advanced versions of the Model 367 (military C-97). Design and construction of the Stratocruiser and Stratofreighter (together with the company's experience in building large aeroplanes) encouraged Boeing into deciding that the moment had come to utilise the rapidly growing power of the new turbojet engines to carry a new generation of civil transports along the world's airways.

As first flown on 15 July 1954, the 367-80 (known as 'Dash Eighty' to two generations of Boeing's workforce) was a prototype flight-refuelling tanker/transport built as a private venture. For it the company developed a 'flying' rigid flight-refuelling boom which could be lowered to transfer fuel at up to 3,785 litres (1,000 US gallons) a minute. This made it possible for heavily laden aircraft to become airborne without the additional weight penalty of full fuel tanks, or to confer intercontinental range on short-range aircraft.

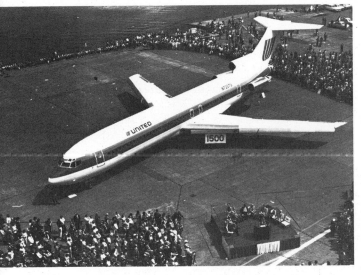

After extensive service testing had confirmed that this tanker could be of vital importance to the USAF (a service which had growing responsibility for world peace-keeping), it was ordered in large numbers under the designation KC-135. With USAF approval to develop a basically similar civil transport, the Dash Eighty was called into use again as a prototype of the civil version, destined to become America's first production turbojet-powered airliner. This led to the introduction of the medium-range Model 707, and the intermediate-range Model 720; but it was the former transport which has been the subject of continuing development and modification. As a result the Model 707-120, which first flew on 20 December 1957, has been displaced by improved versions, but not before Pan American inaugurated the first round-the-world service with the airliner. The Model 707-320C was the version still in production in 1979: a long-range convertible civil transport, capable of operating all-passenger, mixed-passenger/cargo or all-cargo services. Militarised versions of these aircraft have entered service with the USAF as VC-137A and VC-137B VIP transports, plus a single VC-137C presidential transport which is dubbed *Air Force One*.

Model 707-320Cs also serve with the armed forces of other nations: the five used by the Canadian Armed Forces have the designation CC-137. In addition the Model 707-320B was used as the basis of Boeing's submission for an AWACS (Airborne Warning and Control System), which is described separately. The version of the Model

The first Boeing 747.

707 to be offered with 97.9 kN (22,000 lb st) CFM56 turbofans is now designated 707-700 for new production aircraft and 707-320C CFM for existing aircraft refitted with these engines.

Data (707-320C): *Engines* four 84.52 kN (19,000 lb st) Pratt & Whitney JT3D-7 turbofans *Wing span* 44.42 m (145 ft 9 in) *Length* 46.61 m (152 ft 11 in) *Max T-O weight* 151,315 kg (333,600 lb) *Max level speed* 1,010 km/h (627 mph) *Cruising speed* 974 km/h (605 mph) *Range* with max payload 6,920 km (4,300 miles)

Boeing Model 720 (USA) Production of this intermediate-range member of the Boeing four-jet transport family ended at the end of the 1960s. Although a completely different design from the weight and structural strength standpoints, the 720 is almost identical to the 707-120 in external outline and main dimensions, aerodynamic design and control systems. Two versions appeared: the Model 720 with four 55.6 kN (12,500 lb st) Pratt & Whitney JT3C-7 or 57.83 kN (13,000 lb st) JT3C-12 turbojets (entering service with United Air Lines in July 1960); and the Model 720B with four 75.62 kN (17,000 lb st) JT3D-1 or 80 kN (18,000 lb st) JT3D-3 turbofan engines.

Boeing Model 727 (USA) On 5 December 1960 Boeing announced its intention to produce a short/medium-range jet transport designated Boeing 727. A major innovation (compared with this company's earlier designs) was the choice of a rear-engined layout. The upper fuselage section is identical with that of the 707/720 and many parts and systems are interchangeable between the three types.

The 1,500th Boeing 727 (an Advanced 727-200).

The first production version was the Model 727-100 powered by three 62.28 kN (14,000 lb st) Pratt & Whitney JT8D-7 turbofans, with accommodation for up to 131 passengers. It was followed by the 727-100C convertible cargo-passenger; 727-100QC convertible cargo-passenger (using palletised passenger seats and galleys – and advanced cargo loading techniques – to complete conversion from all-passenger to all-cargo configuration in less than half an hour); and 727-100 Business Jet versions. The current production versions are the lengthened 727-200, accommodating 163–189 passengers; Advanced 727-200 with increased fuel capacity, 'Superjet-look' interior and an optional large 'Carry-all' compartment; and 727-200C convertible version for 137 passengers plus cargo in a mixed configuration.

By August 1978 a total of 1,562 Model 727s had been sold, of which 1,366 had been delivered. The 727 is the only commercial transport aircraft to have exceeded 1,000 sales.

Data (727-200): *Engines* three 64.5 kN (14,500 lb st) Pratt & Whitney JT8D-9A turbofans as standard *Wing span* 32.92 m (108 ft 0 in) *Length* 46.69 m (153 ft 2 in) *Max T-O weight* 95,027 kg (209,500 lb) *Max cruising speed* 964 km/h (599 mph) *Range* 2,685–3,966 km (1,670–2,464 miles)

Boeing 737 (incl T-43A) (USA) The decision to build this short-range transport was announced in 1965. Simultaneously a first order for 21 aircraft was placed by Lufthansa. The original Model 737 was designed to utilise many components and assemblies already in production for the Boeing 727. Design began in May 1964 and the first aircraft flew on 9 April 1967. Sales had totalled 605 by August 1978, including 19 737-200s modified as T-43A navigation trainers for the USAF.

The current versions are the Advanced 737-200, accommodating 115–130 passengers and powered by JT8D-9A turbofan engines as standard; Advanced 737-200C/QC standard convertible passenger/cargo model; Advanced 737-200 Executive Jet, similar to the 737-200 but with special business and executive luxury interiors (15 passengers with maximum fuel to enable a range of 5,560 km; 3,455 miles); and Advanced 737-200 Long Range, a higher gross weight model of the Advanced 737-200 for longer-range use, of which two versions have been proposed.

Data (737-200): *Engines* as above *Wing span* 28.35 m (93 ft 0 in) *Length* 29.54 m (96 ft 11 in) *Max T-O weight* 53,070 kg (117,000 lb) *Max cruising speed* (JT8D-15 engines) 927 km/h (576 mph) *Range* (JT8D-15 engines) 4,448 km (2,764 miles)

Boeing Model 747 (incl E-4) (USA) Boeing's success in the design, construction and development of a family of turbine-powered transports (707/720/727 and 737) led in the early 1960s to study and discussion on the next step the company should take as a provider of commercial transports to airlines all over the world. The need to provide large-scale low-cost travel to meet an ever growing demand – allied to the increasing problems of air traffic control – suggested that a solution might be found in building an aircraft with a seating capacity then unheard of.

By August 1965 Boeing had assembled a preliminary design group and only seven months later the decision was made to finalise a design based upon its studies and proposals. Within weeks a firm design proposal (identified as the Model 747) was offered to the airlines and in April 1966 Pan American placed a conditional order for 25.

Not surprisingly the media temporarily choked on the statistics given in the early press release, then found their voices to shout the details to the world at large: 'Wing span of nearly 200 feet; length over 230 feet; a weight at take-off of more than 300 tons; enough fuel in its tanks to carry a

Artist's impression of the Boeing Model 757.

Morris 1000 56 times round the world; and seating for up to 550 passengers!' Every statistic, every dimension was big. Inevitably they called it the 'Jumbo Jet', a name which has remained in common usage with travellers of every nation.

The cabin size came as something of a shock at first view; and it seemed impossible that such an enormous area of seated passengers, galleys, toilets and baggage could leave the ground. Perhaps little attention had been paid to the superb high-lift wing design, with variable-camber and Krueger leading-edge flaps, triple-slotted trailing-edge flaps, spoilers, and high- and low-speed ailerons. To carry the enormous load on the ground, the 747 has a main landing gear comprising four four-wheel bogies. Power plant of the first production 747 – which flew for the first time on 9 February 1969 – consisted of four 208.85 kN (46,950 lb st) Pratt & Whitney JT9D-7A turbofan engines. The inaugural flight on Pan Am's New York–London route was on 22 January 1970, almost five years after the birth of Boeing's great idea.

Since that time many versions have been introduced in passenger, Combi (passenger/cargo) and freighter configurations. A 747-200B powered by 222.8 kN (50,100 lb st) Rolls-Royce RB.211-524B turbofans recorded a take-off at 381,108 kg (840,200 lb) gross weight on 1 November 1976. 747-200F freighters have a nose loading door as standard, this is hinged just below the flight deck so that it can swing forward and upward, giving clear access to the main deck. A side cargo door is available to allow simultaneous nose and side loading. This aircraft can deliver a 90,720 kg (200,000 lb) load of cargo over a range of 7,226 km (4,490 miles). The 747SR is a special short-range version of the 747, carrying up to 550 people.

In February 1973 Boeing received a USAF contract to convert two Model 747Bs for use as Advanced Airborne Command Posts; later in the year this was increased to four. A total of six aircraft are planned and these will replace EC-135 aircraft as they become available with full operational systems. Designated E-4A (first three) and E-4B (remainder, with more advanced equipment), they will be able to operate with an expanded battle staff, allowing improved flexibility and capability by comparison with the older EC-135s.

Data (747-200B): *Engines* four 222.4 kN (50,000 lb st) Pratt & Whitney JT9D-7FW turbofans *Wing span* 59.64 m (195 ft 8 in) *Length* 70.51 m (231 ft 4 in) *Max T-O weight* 365,140 kg (805,000 lb) *Max level speed* 969 km/h (602 mph) *Range* (with 385 passengers and baggage) 10,424 km (6,477 miles)

Boeing Model 747SP (USA) In September 1973 Boeing announced its intention to proceed 'incrementally' with the development of a lower-weight longer-range version of the basic Model 747, for use on lower-density routes. A week later it was announced that Pan American had ordered 10 747SPs (Special Performance) with an option on 15 more.

Retaining a 90% commonality of components

with the standard 747, the SP differs principally in being 14.2 m (46 ft 7 in) shorter. The first flight of a 747SP was made on 4 July 1975. Aircraft belonging to South African Airways and Pan American subsequently set up world records for non-stop distance flown by a commercial airliner and round-the-world speed

Data: *Engines* four 208.8 kN (46,950 lb st) Pratt & Whitney JT9D-7A or similar turbofans *Wing span* as for 747 *Length* 56.31 m (184 ft 9 in) *Max T-O weight* 285,763–315,700 kg (630,000–696,000 lb) *Max level speed* 980 km/h (609 mph) *Range* 9,915–10,841 km (6,161–6,736 miles) *Accommodation* 288–360 passengers

Boeing 747-123 Space Shuttle Orbiter Carrier (NASA 905) (USA) Boeing modified a Model 747-123 as a carrier for the Space Shuttle Orbiter, enabling it to carry the Shuttle 'piggy-back' fashion. The first flight of the NASA 905/*Enterprise* combination was made successfully from the Dryden Flight Research Center, Edwards AFB, California, on 18 February 1977.

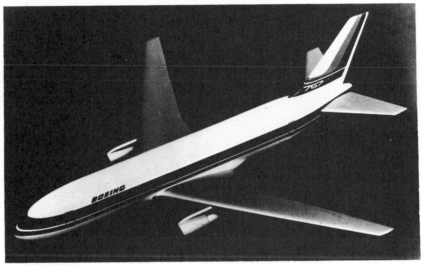

Model of the Boeing 767-200.

Boeing Model 757 (USA) This is a twin-engined (Rolls-Royce RB.211-535, General Electric CF6-32 or Pratt & Whitney JT10D turbofans) short/medium-range transport aircraft with six-abreast passenger seating. On 31 August 1978 Eastern Air Lines and British Airways announced their intention to purchase 21 and 19 respectively, the former taking on option on an additional 24. The 757 retains the same fuselage cross-section as the 707/727/737 family, with an overall length 5.97 m (19 ft 7 in) greater than that of the 727-200 and a wing utilising the same technology used in Boeing's other new, high-efficiency designs. Typical accommodation will be for 177 mixed-class or 195 tourist-class passengers. Max range will be approximately 4,670 km (2,900 miles).

Boeing Model 767 (USA) This aircraft has been proposed in 767-100 and 767-200 versions, accommodating 180 and 197–255 passengers respectively. In July 1978 Boeing announced its intention to launch full-scale development and production of the Model 767, following receipt of an order from United Air Lines for 30 767-200s. Initial deliveries are scheduled for mid-1982.

The aircraft's advanced wing design will include high-lift leading-edge slats and trailing-edge flaps which will provide outstanding take-off and landing performance. The fuselage will be 1.24 m (4 ft 1 in) wider than the Model 727's and power plant for United Air Lines' 767s will comprise two 197 kN (44,300 lb st) Pratt & Whitney JT9D-7R high-bypass-ratio turbofans in pods pylon-mounted on the wing leading edges. Alternative engines will be available for other customers.

Two major work-sharing programmes were

Boeing E-3A Sentry.

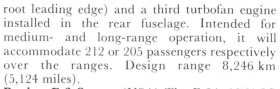

root leading edge) and a third turbofan engine installed in the rear fuselage. Intended for medium- and long-range operation, it will accommodate 212 or 205 passengers respectively over the ranges. Design range 8,246 km (5,124 miles).

Boeing E-3 Sentry (USA) The E-3A AWACS aircraft (see **Boeing Model 707**) being developed and produced for the USAF is equipped with extensive sensing, communications, display and navigational devices. In concept it offers the potential of long-range high- or low-level surveillance of all air vehicles (manned or unmanned) in all weathers and above all kinds of terrain. Its data storage and processing capability would provide real-time assessment of enemy action and of the status and position of friendly resources. By centralising the co-ordination of complex, diverse and simultaneous air operations, such an aircraft would be able to command and control the total air effort: strike, air superiority, support, airlift, reconnaissance and interdiction.

The system has a dual use. Operated by the Tactical Air Command it will be used for airborne surveillance and as a command and control centre for quick-reaction deployment and tactical opera-

Boeing YC-14 (AMST).

announced in 1978. Aeritalia of Italy will produce the wing control surfaces, flaps and leading-edge slats; wingtips; elevators; fin, rudder, and nose radome. CTDC of Japan will produce the wing fairings and main landing gear doors (Fuji); centre-fuselage body panels and exit hatches (Kawasaki); rear-fuselage body panels, stringers, passenger and cargo doors, and dorsal fin (Mitsubishi). Range is expected to be 4,075 km (2,530 miles) with maximum payload.

Boeing Model 777-100 (USA) Generally similar to the Model 767-100 but with an extended fuselage (a plug of 3.94 m; 12 ft 11in in length inserted immediately forward of the wing-

tions. As deployed by Aerospace Defense Command the system will be a survivable early-warning airborne command and control centre for identification, surveillance and tracking of airborne enemy forces, and for the command and control of NORAD (North American Air Defense) forces. The E-3A provides comprehensive surveillance out to a range of more than 370 km (230 miles) for low-flying targets and still further for targets flying at higher altitudes.

The first production E-3A was delivered on 24 March 1977 and by the end of that year five had been delivered. Full production funding for 22 systems had been approved by mid-1978.

The most prominent feature of the E-3A is the elliptical cross-section rotodome carried above the fuselage, housing the surveillance radar and other equipment.

Boeing YC-14 (AMST) (USA) First flown on 9 August 1976, the YC-14 was Boeing's contender for the USAF's advanced military STOL transport requirement for a C-130 Hercules replacement in the 1980s. However funding for the AMST programme has been withheld.

Boeing Vertol Model 76/VZ-2A (USA) Tilt-wing research aircraft powered by a 641 kW (860 hp) Lycoming YT53-L-1 shaft-turbine engine geared to drive a pair of three-blade rotor/propellers mounted on the tilting wing. First flown on 13 August 1957. By May 1961 448 flights had been completed.

Boeing Vertol Model 107/H-46 Sea Knight (USA) The prototype Model 107 twin-turbine transport helicopter flew for the first time on 22 April 1958. Production in the USA ended in the early 1970s. A derivative, built under licence by Kawasaki and known as the KV-107, remains in production in Japan. Several versions were produced for commercial and military use.

The standard commercial version was the 107 Model II powered by two 932 kW (1,250 shp) General Electric CT58 turboshaft engines. Eight of these 25-seat airliners were delivered to New York Airways, which introduced them on scheduled services from July 1962, three having been purchased by Pan American and leased to NYA. Ten were also ordered by Kawasaki prior to licence production in Japan. The designation 107 Model IIA applies to a commercial version with 1,044 kW (1,400 shp) CT58-140-1 turboshaft engines.

Military versions began with the CH-46A Sea Knight (formerly HRB-1) assault transport for the US Marine Corps, powered by two 932 kW (1,250 shp) T58-GE-8B engines. Used in Vietnam from March 1966, it could accommodate 17–25 troops or 1,814 kg (4,000 lb) of cargo over a combat radius of 185 km (115 miles); or 15 stretchers and two attendants. It was followed by the CH-46D Sea Knight; CH-46E (T58-GE-16 engines) with crash attenuating seats, crash and combat-resistant fuel system and other improvements; CH-46F Sea Knight with additional electronics equipment, delivered from July 1968; UH-46A Sea Knight for the US Navy, mainly for use in vertical replenishment (VERTREP) operations between ships at sea; and UH-46D Sea Knight for VERTREP operations (T58-GE-10 engines).

The Canadian Air Force and Army received 60 CH-113 Labrador and 12 CH-113A Voyageur helicopters from 1963 to 1965; the Swedish Navy and Air Force received four and ten respectively, with Bristol Siddeley Gnome H.1200 engines for anti-submarine and mine countermeasures (naval) and search and rescue missions. The total number of Sea Knights ordered was 624.

Data (CH-46D Sea Knight): *Engines* two 1,044 kW (1,400 shp) General Electric T58-GE-10 turboshafts *Rotor diameter* 15.54 m (51 ft 0 in) *Length overall* 25.7 m (84 ft 4 in) *Max T-O weight* 10,433 kg (23,000 lb) *Max cruising speed* 266 km/h (165 mph) *Range* 383 km (238 miles)

Boeing Vertol Model 114 and 234/CH-47 Chinook (USA) In June 1959 the US Army awarded a contract for five YHC-1B prototypes to Boeing Vertol. Evaluated in competition with submissions from four other companies, Boeing Vertol's twin-rotor Model 114 was considered to be nearest to meeting the Army's requirement for a 'battlefield mobility' helicopter. The specification had been a little daunting, for this aircraft was required to carry 40 fully equipped troops or two tons of internal cargo or up to eight tons on an external sling; be suitable for casualty evacuation; and able to airlift any component of the Pershing missile system.

The first prototype made its maiden flight on 21 September 1961 and production aircraft began to enter service in December 1962. Affected by the tri-service designation rationalisation, these were delivered as CH-47As and given the name Chinook. They had straight-in rear loading; non-retractable quadricycle landing gear; and featured sealed and compartmented fairing pods on each side of the fuselage to supplement buoyancy of the sealed lower fuselage, allowing operation from water. Power plant comprised two 1,976 kW (2,650 shp) Lycoming T55-L-7 turboshaft engines.

Versions introduced into service since that time include CH-47Bs, with redesigned rotor blades and 2,125 kW (2,850 shp) T55-L-7C engines; and CH-47Cs (Model 234) with still more powerful turboshafts, strengthened transmission and greater fuel capacity. Nine of this version for the Canadian Armed Forces have the designation CH-147, and introduce an advanced flight control system, improved safety features and a greater

Boeing Vertol

Elicotteri Meridionali-built CH-47C Chinook in Italian Army Aviation markings.

Bölkow BO 102 Heli-Trainer.

Boisavia B.60 Mercurey.

Bölkow BO 46.

maximum take-off weight. Total US Army procurement of the CH-47A/B/C reached 721 by September 1978, while others have been exported.

Chinooks used in Vietnam demonstrated under battlefield conditions their ability to fulfil the task for which they had been designed, carrying in troops and supplies, evacuating casualties and/or refugees and recovering disabled aircraft. The subject of modernisation programmes, these aircraft continue to be regarded as an important component of the US Army's helicopter air logistic forces. Under co-production and marketing rights acquired by Elicotteri Meridionali in 1968, Chinooks are built in Italy for European and Middle East customers.

A new version of the Chinook is the CH-47D, basically a modified CH-147. Powered by Lycoming T55-L-11C engines, it will have provision for glassfibre/carbon fibre rotor blades and three external cargo hooks. Accommodation will be for 44 troops or 24 stretchers. Thirty-three have been ordered by the RAF as Chinook HC.1s, for delivery between August 1980 and the end of 1981. Some 360 US Chinooks may be modernised to this standard. (See also **Model 234LR**)

Data (CH-47C): *Engines* two 2,796 kW (3,750 shp) Lycoming T55-L-11C turboshafts *Rotor diameter* each 18.29 m (60 ft 0 in) *Length overall* 30.18 m (99 ft 0 in) *Max T-O weight* 20,865 kg (46,000 lb) *Max level speed* 304 km/h (189 mph) *Ferry range* 2,142 km (1,331 miles)

Boeing Vertol Model 234LR Commercial Chinook (USA) Announced in 1978 this is a commercial development of the CH-47 Chinook for use as a transport and offshore oilfield support aircraft. Power is provided by Avco Lycoming AL 5512 turboshaft engines.

Boeing Vertol BO 105 Executaire (USA) The BO 105C helicopter has been marketed in the United States, Canada and Mexico since 1972 by Boeing Vertol. The Executaire is an improved version developed by Boeing Vertol and powered by Allison Model 250-C20B engines. Twenty-one had been sold by 1978.

Boisavia B.60 Mercurey (France) Developed from the B.50 Muscadet three-seater, the Mercurey light high-wing monoplane first flew in March 1948 and was produced in small numbers as a four-seat tourer and trainer, glider-tug and agricultural aircraft.

Boisavia B.260 Anjou (France) First flown on 2 June 1956, this was a twin-engined four-seat cabin monoplane produced in prototype form only.

Bölkow BO 46 (Germany) Experimental helicopter first flown on 30 January 1964 and used to flight test the Derschmidt high-speed rotor system.

Bölkow BO 103 (Germany) Single-seat light helicopter which retained most of the features of the BO 102 Heli-Trainer, a non-flying helicopter pilot training simulator.

Bölkow BO 105, BO 208 and BO 209 (Germany) See **MBB**

Bölkow BO 207 (Germany) Four-seat development of the three-seat Klemm Kl 107C, originally known as the Kl 107D, with a 134 kW (180 hp) Lycoming O-360-A1A flat-four engine, modified wings, a full-vision cockpit canopy and other changes. The prototype first flew in October 1960 and 90 had been built by 1964.

Bölkow/Klemm Kl 107 (Germany) The Kl 107 was designed during World War II as a two-seater. The prototype was built by Klemm-Flugzeuge in 1955. It was developed into the Kl

107B and then the three-seat Kl 107C. All rights in this aircraft were acquired by Bölkow and production was undertaken.

Bölkow/Fauvel AV.36 C11 (Germany) Motorised version of the French Survol (Fauvel) AV.36 glider.

Borel hydro-monoplane (France) The twin-float Borel of 1912 was a single-seater and was no more than a seaplane version of the **Morane-Borel** (see below). One was entered in the round-Britain Hydro-Aeroplane trial (see **Chronology**). In 1913 Borel produced a two-seat hydro-monoplane. About eight hydro-monoplanes (with 59.6 kW; 80 hp Gnome rotary engines) were acquired by the Royal Navy. They remained in use as ship spotters at the beginning of World War I. Others were flown in France and Italy.

Borel monoplanes (France) The Morane-Borel of 1911 was powered by a 37.25 kW (50 hp) Gnome engine. In 1912 a pusher-engined monoplane was built, followed in 1913 by a monocoque racer.

Bossi hydro-aeroplane (Italy) The Bossi biplane of 1913 was powered by a pusher engine and was the first Italian seaplane to fly successfully.

Boulton Paul Defiant (UK) At a time when prototypes of the famous eight-gun fighters for the RAF – the Hurricane and Spitfire – were being built, the British Air Ministry thought up a new tactical concept for a two-seat fighter. This was to be crewed by a pilot and air gunner, the latter provided with a power-operated turret, in the belief that both crew members would be able to work more effectively. Boulton Paul and Hawker both submitted design proposals and built pro-

totypes, the Defiant and Hawker Hotspur, but it was the former which was ordered into production. A cantilever low-wing monoplane of all-metal construction, the Defiant had a Boulton Paul power-operated turret containing four 0.303 in Browning machine-guns.

The prototype flew for the first time on 11 August 1937, entered service in December 1939 and was used operationally by No 264 Squadron for the first time on 12 May 1940. Defiants were an immediate success; unsuspecting enemy aircraft making a conventional attack from the rear were subjected to the concentrated fire power of the four Brownings. Within 19 days Defiants were credited with the destruction of 65 aircraft – 38 on one glorious day. Unfortunately for the British, the Luftwaffe pilots were quick to realise there were certain sectors at which the battery of

Bölkow BO 103.

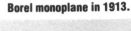

Borel monoplane in 1913.

machine-guns could not be directed. Thereafter they were subjected to attack from below or head-on, against which they had no defence, and they were quickly taken out of front-line daylight service. There was a further brief spell of success in the night fighter role, during the winter of 1940–41, after which Defiants were used largely for target-towing, air/sea rescue, army co-operation and gunnery training.

Data (Defiant I): *Engine* one 767.6 kW (1,030 hp) Rolls-Royce Merlin III *Wing span* 11.99 m (39 ft 4 in) *Length* 10.77 m (35 ft 4 in) *Max T-O weight* 3,787 kg (8,350 lb) *Max level speed* 488 km/h (303 mph) *Armament* four turret-mounted 0.303 in machine-guns

Boulton Paul Defiant I.

Bölkow BO 207.

Boulton Paul

Boulton Paul Overstrand.

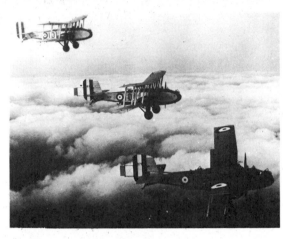

Boulton Paul
Sidestrand IIIs.

Boulton Paul P.71A
Britomart.

Boulton Paul Sea Balliol
T.21.

Boulton Paul Overstrand (UK) The Overstrand was a further stage in the development of the high-performance medium bomber by this company. Essentially a 'super-Sidestrand' and originally known as the Sidestrand V, the production Overstrand that entered service with No 101 Squadron from 1934 became the RAF's first bomber with a power-operated enclosed gun-turret, which overcame the problems associated with firing movable machine-guns at high speed. A total of 24 Overstrands were built, each powered by two 432 kW (580 hp) Bristol Pegasus II M3 radial engines. These remained in service as bombers until 1937, thereafter becoming gunnery trainers.
Data: *Engines* as above *Wing span* 21.95 m (72 ft 0 in) *Length* 14.02 m (46 ft 0 in) *Max T-O weight* 5,443 kg (12,000 lb) *Max level speed* 246 km/h (153 mph) *Range* 877 km (545 miles) *Armament* three Lewis machine-guns in nose, dorsal and ventral positions; plus up to 725 kg (1,600 lb) of bombs

Boulton Paul Sidestrand (UK) Entering service with No 101 Squadron, RAF, in 1928, the Sidestrand was a biplane medium bomber for daylight operations, powered by two 335 kW (450 hp) Bristol Jupiter VI or 343 kW (460 hp) Jupiter VIIIF radial engines (Sidestrand II and III versions respectively). Eighteen were produced, introducing a new high standard of accuracy, performance and manoeuvrability. Armament comprised three Lewis machine-guns and up to 476 kg (1,060 lb) of bombs. Max level speed 225 km/h (140 mph)

Boulton Paul Superstrand (UK) Although only a project, the Superstrand warrants a mention as the third stage in the Sidestrand/Overstrand line of development. Mentioned briefly in the 1935 *Jane's*, it was basically an Overstrand with a retractable landing gear, modified tail unit, a new transparent cupola for the nose gunner and a new enclosed canopy for the pilot which extended aft to terminate in a folding hood for the dorsal/rear gunner.

Boulton Paul P.71A (UK) Twin-engined high-speed commercial biplane, designed for feeder-line service with Imperial Airways. Seating for seven passengers in the main cabin.

Boulton Paul P.108 Balliol and Sea Balliol (UK) Originally designed as an all-purpose advanced trainer to be fitted with an Armstrong Siddeley Mamba or Rolls-Royce Dart turboprop engine. Three versions were produced: Balliol T.1 three-seater with a Mamba engine, first flown in prototype form on 24 March 1948 to become the first aeroplane in the world to fly solely on turbo-prop power; Balliol T.2 two-seater, produced for the RAF (162) with a 928 kW (1,245 hp) Rolls-Royce Merlin 35 piston engine; and Sea Balliol T.21 for the Royal Navy with deck-landing capability (30 built)

Boulton Paul P.111 and P.120 (UK) Research aircraft designed to investigate the delta wing at transonic speeds. First flown on 10 October 1950 and 6 August 1952 respectively.

Bowers Fly Baby 1-A (USA) Single-seat light monoplane designed to be constructed by amateurs; 3,870 sets of plans had been sold by May 1979.

Bowers Fly Baby 1-B (USA) Biplane version of the 1-A using a set of interchangeable wings.

Bowers Namu II (USA) Side-by-side two-seat light monoplane. One only built.

Brantly-Hynes B-2B (USA) Current production version of the B-2 two-seat light helicopter, which was originally produced by the Brantly Helicopter Corporation and later marketed as the

B-2A, B-2B and B-2E by Brantly, ARDC and Brantly Operators Incorporated. By 1970 approximately 400 B-2s had been built. Brantly-Hynes was formed in 1975 and subsequently put the B-2B back into production, powered by a 134 kW (180 hp) Lycoming IVO-360-A1A flat-four engine. Max level speed 161 km/h (100 mph).

Brantly-Hynes Model 305 (USA) Five-seat helicopter of similar configuration to the Model B-2B, but larger in every respect. The prototype first flew in January 1964. It is currently produced by Brantly-Hynes, powered by a 227.5 kW (305 hp) Lycoming IVO-540-A1A flat-six engine. Max level speed 193 km/h (120 mph).

Bratukhin Omega (USSR) Twin-engined twin-rotor research helicopter, first tested in 1941. Max forward speed 180 km/h (112 mph).

Brditschka HB-21 (Austria) Two-seat motor glider first flown in 1973. Basically an enlarged version of the HB-3. Twelve sold by 1978.

Breda A.2 (Italy) Two- or three-seat cantilever low-wing monoplane designed for touring, mail-carrying or training when powered by a 97 kW (130 hp) Colombo 110D engine; and reconnaissance with a 186.3 kW (250 hp) Isotta Fraschini engine.

Breda A.4 (Italy) Two-seat training biplane of 1926 powered by a Colombo 110D as a landplane or 134 kW (180 hp) Hispano-Suiza as a twin-float seaplane. Operated by the Regia Aeronautica.

Breda A.7 (Italy) Two-seat parasol-wing monoplane reconnaissance aircraft of 1926, powered by a 380 kW (510 hp) Isotta-Fraschini Asso engine. Armament comprised one forward-firing Vickers and one rear-mounted Lewis machine-guns. Up to 200 kg (440 lb) of bombs could also be carried. Operated by the Regia Aeronautica.

Breda A.9 (Italy) Two-seat advanced training biplane of 1928 powered by a 149 kW (200 hp) S.P.A. 6A engine. Operated by the Regia Aeronautica.

Breda Ba 15 (Italy) Two-seat cabin monoplane of 1929, usually powered by a 63.3 kW (85 hp) Walter Venus engine, but could be fitted with Cirrus III, de Havilland Gipsy or Isotta-Fraschini engines in the 59.6 kW–89.4 kW (80–120 hp) range. Flown as civil aircraft and operated by the Regia Aeronautica.

Breda Ba 19 (Italy) Single- or two-seat advanced and aerobatic training biplane powered by a 164 kW (220 hp) Alfa-Romeo-built Armstrong Siddeley Lynx or 179 kW (240 hp) Walter Castor engine. Operated by the Regia Aeronautica.

Breda Ba 25 and Ba 28 (Italy) The Ba 25 was a two-seat advanced training biplane powered by a Lynx or Castor engine. It was operated by the Regia Aeronautica as a landplane and twin-float seaplane. The Ba 28 was similar except that power was provided by a 290 kW (390 hp) Piaggio Stella VII (Gnome-Rhône K-7) radial engine.

Breda Ba 27 (Italy) Single-seat braced low-wing monoplane fighter of 1935, of which a small number were produced for China.

Breda Ba 44 (Italy) The Ba 44 of 1934 was a six-passenger cabin biplane powered by two 141.5–153 kW (190–205 hp) Walter Major-Six or 149 kW (200 hp) de Havilland Gipsy engines. Six were produced for Ala Littoria.

Breda Ba 64 (Italy) Single- or two-seat fighter or reconnaissance-bomber powered by a 454.6 kW (610 hp) Piaggio Stella IX or 484.4 kW (650 hp) Alfa-Romeo 125RC radial engine. Armament comprised four forward-firing 7.7 mm machine-

Boulton Paul P.111.

Bowers Fly Baby 1-A.

The original Brantly B-1 of 1946.

Brantly-Hynes B-2B.

Breda

Breda Ba 27 for China.

guns and up to four 100 kg bombs, plus an extra rear-mounted machine-gun as a two-seater.

Breda Ba 65 (Italy) First appearing in 1935, the Ba 65 was a direct development of the Ba 64 and retained the earlier aircraft's general configuration, including the cantilever low wing and retractable landing gear. As with the Ba 64, it was designed as a single- and two-seater for close-support and light bombing duties, as well as reconnaissance. Indeed the first examples to go into service with the Regia Aeronautica were flown in Spain during the Civil War as reconnaissance aircraft and during the invasion of Abyssinia. During World War II, those remaining operational were flown mostly in North Africa. Ba 65s were also exported to Hungary, Iraq, Paraguay and Portugal.

Brantly-Hynes Model 305.

Breda Ba 27 prototype.

Data: *Engine* one 745.2 kW (1,000 hp) Fiat A.80RC.41 or 671 kW (900 hp) Isotta-Fraschini K.14 radial *Wing span* 12.1 m (39 ft 8½ in) *Length* 9.6 m (31 ft 6 in) *Max T-O weight* 2,950 kg (6,505 lb) *Max level speed* 430 km/h (267 mph) as single-seater *Range* 1,100 km (684 miles) as two-seater *Armament* two 12.7 mm and two 7.7 mm machine-guns in wings plus up to 1,000 kg (2,205 lb) of bombs; some Ba 65*bis* had a rear gun turret fitted.

Breda 88 Lince (Lynx) (Italy) Following the realisation that the light bombers in service with the Regia Aeronautica were outdated, the Italian Air Ministry issued a requirement for a modern replacement. Breda produced the Ba 88 in 1937: a mid-wing monoplane with a retractable landing gear and twin Isotta-Fraschini radial engines. With two 745.2 kW (1,000 hp) Piaggio P.XI RC 40 engines and a new tail unit with twin fins, the Ba 88 entered production for the Regia Aeronautica. In December 1937 a Ba 88, piloted

Breda Ba 64s.

by Furio Niclot, set up two international speed records over 100 km and 1,000 km with a 1,000 kg (2,205 lb) payload: 554.35 km/h (344.46 mph) and 524.185 km/h (325.71 mph) respectively. Altogether 105 were produced. However the Ba 88 was not a success and by 1943 only a few remained operational in North Africa.

Data: *Engines* as above *Wing span* 15.6 m (51 ft 2¼ in) *Length* 10.79 m (35 ft 4¾ in) *Max T-O weight* 6,750 kg (14,880 lb) *Max level speed* 490 km/h (304 mph) *Range* 1,640 km (1,020 miles) *Armament* three forward-firing Breda-SAFAT 12.7 mm machine-guns in nose and one 7.7 mm Breda L machine-gun in dorsal turret, plus up to 1,000 kg (2,205 lb) of bombs

Breda-Zappata B.Z.308 (Italy) Twenty-four-seat passenger airliner of 1943 powered by four 1,863 kW (2,500 hp) Bristol Centaurus 568 14-cylinder radial engines. Development continued throughout the 1940s.

Breda-Zappata B.Z. 309 (Italy) Projected twin-engined 11–15-seat short-range airliner.

Breda-Pittoni B.P.471 (Italy) Eighteen-passenger twin-engined transport aircraft flown in prototype form.

BredaNardi helicopters (Italy) Formed in 1971, BredaNardi constructs the Hughes 300C, 500C and 500D helicopters under licence, including the NH-500M-D (TOW) military helicopter which is equipped to carry TOW missiles.

Breguet IV (France) First successful Breguet aircraft, nicknamed 'coffee pot'. In August 1910 it set a record by carrying six people.

Breguet G 3 (France) Completed in 1911, the G 3 biplane was a three-seater, although one photograph that appears in the 1912 *Jane's* shows the aircraft with the pilot and at least nine others on board. Power was provided by a 74.5 kW (100 hp) Gnome engine. A total of 41 Breguet aircraft were sold for military purposes in 1912: France (32), Britain (5), Italy (3) and Sweden (1). This number includes aircraft described below.

Breguet 1911–1912 models (France) The 1911–1912 models included the previously described G 3; the G 2*bis* two–three-seat biplane with a 59.6 kW (80 hp) Gnome engine; C-U1 two-seat biplane with a 59.6 kW (80 hp) Canton

Unné engine; C-U2 two-seat biplane with an 82 kW (110 hp) Canton Unné engine; and the tandem-wing Aerhydroplane with an 82 kW (110 hp) Canton Unné engine. The latter was a peculiar flying-boat with single float-type hull, sponsons and a four-blade propeller driven via a long shaft.

Breguet 1912–13 models (France) The 1912–13 models included the H.I-U3 two-seat hydro-aeroplane with a 149 kW (200 hp) Canton Unné engine; A.G.4 armoured military biplane with a 104 kW (140 hp) engine; and T.O-2 two-seat bi-plane with a 59.6 kW (80 hp) engine. However the most important aircraft from the Breguet stable at this period was a biplane developed from the A.G.4 and powered originally by a 59.6 kW (80 hp) Chenu engine. It cannot be verified whether this aircraft and the T.O-2 are one and the same, especially as it has been referred to as the U.1. Nevertheless aircraft of the developed A.G.4 type were supplied to the military in France, Italy and the UK (RNAS and RFC). The 15 RNAS aircraft (later fitted with 82 kW; 110 hp Canton Unné engines) and the RFC machines were nicknamed 'tin whistle' because of the shape of the fuselage. Some saw service at the start of World War I as reconnaissance aircraft.

Breguet Type V and VI (France) See **Breguet-Michelin**

Breguet 14 (France) This aircraft was the out-standing French day bomber/reconnaissance aircraft of World War I. The Bre 14 A2 reconnais-sance version and the Bre 14 B2 bomber equipped at least 71 French escadrilles on the Western Front by November 1918 and were also used by units in Serbia, Greece, Macedonia and Morocco. The prototype flew for the first time on 21 November 1916. Production was spread over seven manufacturers, in addition to the Louis Breguet factory at Velizy, near Paris, and some 8,000 of the type were built up to 1926.

A robust two-bay unequal-span biplane of mixed construction, it was remarkable for its time in the amount of duralumin used in the fuselage and wing structure. Covering was of fabric. The metal cowling over the 238.5 kW (320 hp) Renault 12Fe engine was extensively louvred and a distinctive frontal radiator was fitted. The Bre 14 A2 was armed with a single fixed 0.303 in Vickers machine-gun on the left side of the fusel-age and twin Lewis guns in the observer's cockpit. The B2 version could be fitted with an additional Lewis gun that fired downwards through the rear

fuselage floor and had a maximum bomb load of 256 kg (564 lb), carried on underwing racks.

The reconnaissance version was followed into production by the bomber in the summer of 1917, the latter differing in having Breguet-designed automatic trailing-edge flaps on the lower wings and transparent panels in the sides of the observer's cockpit. Late production examples of both versions had horn-balanced ailerons, the B2 aircraft thus equipped doing away with the trailing-edge flaps. A single-seat long-range ver-sion, known as the Bre 14 B1, was also built in limited numbers during 1918, and was intended to bomb Berlin. In fact it was little used and never mounted an attack on the German capital. Bre-guet 14s also equipped American and Belgian units during World War I, some powered by Italian Fiat A-12 and A-12*bis* engines.

Breguet 14s remained in service in the colonial/TOE version throughout the 1920s, equipping many overseas units. A number of foreign countries also flew the type. Many ex-French aircraft were handed over to Poland in 1919 and these took part in the fighting with Russia in 1920. The type formed part of the initial equipment of the Czech air arm, and others were operated in Brazil, China (70 with 298 kW; 400 hp Lorraine-Dietrich engines), Denmark, Finland, Greece, Japan, Portugal and Spain. The Spanish equipped four squadrons in Morocco in 1922, using them on missions against Riff tribes-men. A further 40 were obtained in 1923. A small

Two-seat Breda Ba 65 with a 7.7 mm gun in a large dorsal turret.

Single-seat Breda Ba 65s.

Two-seat Breda Ba 65 *bis* with a 12.7 mm gun in a hydraulically operated dorsal turret.

Breda Ba 88 Lince.

Breguet 14 A2.

number of float variants were also built, mostly with a central main float and small wingtip stabilising floats.

During 1919 Breguet 14s made a number of remarkable long-distance flights and Louis Breguet founded the Compagnie des Messageries Aériennes with them, making regular air mail flights linking Paris with Brussels and London. These Bre 14s had special mail containers fitted under the wings. A cabin version with provision for two passengers was built as the Breguet 14T.

Breguet 14T *bis*.

Breguet 17.

Later came the improved Bre 14T*bis* and the three-passenger Breguet 14T2. During the 1920s, the Lignes Aériennes Latécoère company used more than 100 Breguet 14s in various versions on its routes between Toulouse and Dakar (West Africa) and between Natal and Santiago di Chile in South America. The final version worthy of mention was the 14S air ambulance, adapted from the Breguet 14T. This version was widely operated in the 1920s during the campaigns in Morocco and Syria. Each could carry two stretchers in the rear fuselage.

Breguet 16 prototype.

Data (Breguet 14 A2): *Engine* as above *Wing span* 14.86 m (48 ft 9 in) *Length* 8.87 m (29 ft 1¼ in) *Max T-O weight* 1,537 kg (3,388 lb) *Max level speed* 183 km/h (114 mph) *Range* 700 km (435 miles)

Breguet 16 (France) This was a two-seat night bomber development of the Breguet 14, appearing in 1918. The main external differences were wings of greater span, with three pairs of interplane struts either side instead of two, and differently shaped vertical tail surfaces. Maximum bomb load was 550 kg (1,212 lb). Breguet 16s remained in service in Morocco and Syria until March 1927.

Breguet 17 (France) The Breguet 17 was a two-seat (C2) development of the Breguet 14 and was test flown in November 1918. Compared with the 14 it had a reduced wing span, two forward-firing machine-guns, a downward and rearward-firing gun operated through a trap in the fuselage floor and a 335.3 kW (450 hp) Renault Ja engine. Max level speed was 225 km/h (140 mph). Breguet 17s remained in service throughout the 1920s.

Breguet 18T (France) Single example of this larger four-passenger development of the 14T appeared in 1919 powered by a 335.3 kW (450 hp) Renault Ja engine.

Breguet 19 (France) The first prototype Bre 19.01 was displayed at the Salon Aéronautique in 1921 while fitted with a 335.3 kW (450 hp) Breguet-Bugatti engine. However, for the first flight in March 1922, a similarly rated Renault 12Kb was installed. In 1923 the prototype won a Spanish international military aircraft contest and the 11 pre-production machines under construction in France were inspected by a Yugoslav delegation. Sales to both countries followed.

The Bre 19 was mostly of metal construction, with fabric covering only the unequal-span wings, aft fuselage and tailplane. Large-scale production of A2 (observation) and B2 (day bomber) versions, powered by Renault 12K or Lorraine 12 engines, was undertaken; 'Aménagement 1926' machines having increased fuel capacity. More than 1,000 were built for French service, the type equipping many Groupes of the French Aéronautique Militaire from 1925; the last escadrilles did not relinquish their aircraft until 1935. Included in the total were a number of night fighter (Cn2) variants.

Foreign deliveries went to Poland (250), Yugoslavia (160, plus 190 built under licence at Kral-

jevo), Romania (108), China (74), Greece (30), Argentina (25), Turkey (20), Spain (19, plus 177 built under licence by CASA), Venezuela (12), Bolivia (15), Belgium (6, plus 146 built under licence by SABCA) and Brazil (5). One hundred and three Yugoslav Bre 19s were still in service in 1939, many powered by 313 kW (420 hp) Gnome Rhône Jupiter radial engines. Bre 19s were also used extensively during the Spanish Civil War by both sides, but combat losses and lack of spares led to their disappearance from the scene.

Many record flights were made by Breguet 19s including one made by the 'Grand Raid' version named *Nungesser-Coli*, which was flown from Paris to San Francisco and Tokyo to Paris by Costes and Le Brix, covering 57,000 km (35,400 miles) in 350 hours flying time. The pilots are best remembered for making the first non-stop air crossing of the South Atlantic, from Senegal to Natal, Brazil, on 14 October 1927. Also, in September 1929 a Breguet 19 'Super Bidon' named *Point d'Intérrogation* was flown by Costes and Bellonte from Le Bourget to Manchuria to set up a new world distance record of 7,905 km (4,913 miles). A year later it was the first aircraft to fly non-stop from Paris to New York.

In 1928 the Breguet 19*ter* was developed into the improved Breguet 19.7, with a 484.3 kW (650 hp) Hispano-Suiza 12Nb engine, new wings with semi-elliptical tips, redesigned vertical tailplane and increased fuel tankage. Yugoslavia built 75 and a small batch built by Breguet went to Romania. Fifty similar aircraft were exported to Turkey in 1932 and were the last of the breed to be built by Breguet. Forty-eight Yugoslav-built Breguet 19.8s had Wright Cyclone 580 kW (778 hp) radials with long chord cowlings, the last being completed in 1937. Yugoslav Breguets were used later by Croat forces, and two recaptured by Tito's troops were flown during 1945.

Data (Breguet 19 B2): *Engine* as above *Wing span* 14.83 m (48 ft 7¾ in) *Length* 9.51 m (31 ft 2½ in) *Max T-O weight* 2,347 kg (5,174 lb) *Max level speed* 235 km/h (146 mph) *Range* 800 km (497 miles) *Armament* one forward-firing 0.303 in Vickers and two rear-mounted Lewis machine-guns, plus a ventral flexibly mounted gun. Thirty 10 kg or eight 50 kg bombs carried internally and four 100 kg or two 200 kg bombs carried on underwing racks

Breguet 19 'Grand Raid'.

Breguet 26T (France) Six-passenger development of the Breguet 19 with a new fuselage and a 335.3 kW (450 hp) Gnome Rhône-built Jupiter or Lorraine-Dietrich engine. Four built in France, two for commercial use and two for the Armée de l'Air, the latter as ambulances. Two also built in Spain by CASA for commercial operations.

Breguet 27 (France) The Bre 27 was a two-seat sesquiplane of unusual design and appearance. The prototype flew for the first time on 23 February 1929. Intended for observation duties, the Bre 27 offered the observer an extensive field of vision and fire. The nacelle, with the engine at the front and crew cockpits at the rear, tapered away sharply immediately behind the observer's cockpit, and a girder formed a boom to support the tail unit. The lower stub-wing was braced to the upper wing by V-struts either side. The main

Breguet 270 A2.

Breguet

Production Breguet 521 Bizerte with 'glasshouse' cockpit extension.

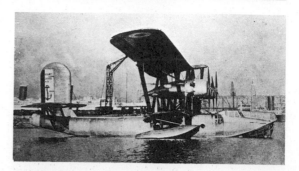

Breguet Saigon.

Breguet 393T.

wheels of the fixed undercarriage were 'spatted'.

A number of experimental versions were built with redesigned tailplanes, landing gears and a variety of power plants. Following three pre-series aircraft, 85 Bre 270s (with 372.6 kW; 500 hp Hispano-Suiza 12Hb engines) and 45 Bre 271s (with 484.4 kW; 650 hp engines) were delivered to the Armée de l'Air between 1931 and 1934. Armament of both versions comprised one fixed forward-firing 7.7 mm Lewis machine-gun and one 7.7 mm Vickers gun operated by the observer. Max bomb load was 120 kg (265 lb). Some aircraft were converted into VIP transports in 1933 by fitting canopies over the cockpits.

Many Bre 270 and Bre 271 aircraft were still in service in September 1939; some were in first-line use but were quickly withdrawn after several had been shot down. Ten Bre 270s were also exported (to Brazil and Venezuela). The 641 kW (860 hp) Hispano-Suiza 12 Ybrs-powered Bre 273 of 1935 was supplied to Venezuela (15) and China (six). Data (Breguet 270 A2): *Engine* as above *Wing span* 17.01 m (55 ft 9 in) *Length* 9.76 m (32 ft 0 in) *Max T-O weight* 2,393 kg (5,276 lb) *Max level speed* 236 km/h (146 mph)

Breguet 521 Bizerte prototype with open nose-gunner's position.

Breguet 280T series (France) Refined version of the Breguet 26T with changes in power plant, wings, tail unit, fuselage and landing gear, and providing an enclosed cabin for the pilot. Production centred around two main models: the 372.6 kW (500 hp) Renault 12Jb-engined Bre 280T, and 432.2 kW (580 hp) Hispano-Suiza 12Lbrx-engined Bre 284T, of which nine and eight were produced respectively. All surviving aircraft were handed over to Air France in May 1933 when the airline was formed from four existing operators of which two, Air Orient and Air Union, had been original users of the type.

Breguet 393T (France) The prototype of this three-engined sesquiplane airliner flew for the first time in January 1931. As the refined Bre 393T ten-passenger airliner powered by three 261 kW (350 hp) Gnome-Rhône Titan Major radial engines, it entered production for Air France. Six were completed.

Breguet 521 Bizerte (France) Developed from the Short Calcutta, the prototype flew for the first time on 11 September 1933. Series aircraft differed mainly in having a long narrow glasshouse extension from the pilots' cabin to the bow of the flying-boat. Thirty were built, powered by three 671 kW (900 hp) Gnome-Rhône 14 Kirs radial engines. These served with 'Exploration' escadrilles of the French Aéronavale from 1935 until the end of World War II, latterly being used as maritime reconnaissance and anti-submarine aircraft. Of these, nine were captured by the Germans and were used during 1943–45 for air-sea rescue.

The Bizerte itself was a sesquiplane with an exceptionally large single fin and rudder. Armament comprised five 7.5 mm Darne machine-guns: one in the cupolas each side at the rear of the cabin, one under each of two sliding hatches (with retractable windscreens) staggered to port and starboard amidships, and one in the extreme tail cockpit aft of the tail unit.

Data: *Engines* as above *Wing span* 35.13 m (115 ft 3 in) *Length* 18.89 m (61 ft 11¾ in) *Max T-O weight* 16,500 kg (35,274 lb) *Max level speed* 255 km/h (158.5 mph) *Range* 2,100 km (1,305 miles)

Breguet 530 Saigon (France) The Saigon was developed in parallel with the Bizerte as a larger and modified 20-passenger commercial version of the Short Calcutta flying-boat. Two were built for Air Union, flying in 1934 with three 585 kW (785 hp) Hispano-Suiza 12Ybr engines.

Breguet 690 series (France) Designed to a 1934 requirement for a new high-performance three-seat fighter, the Breguet 690 was an all-metal cantilever mid-wing monoplane with twin fins and rudders, a retractable landing gear and two 507 kW (680 hp) Hispano-Suiza 14Ab 14-cylinder radial engines. In 1938 the aircraft entered production in the refined Bre 691 form, eventually being produced as the 691C3 three-seat fighter, 691A3 reconnaissance aircraft, 691B2 two-seat light bomber and 691AB2 dive-bomber. The latter version was quickly replaced by the Bre 693 powered by Gnome Rhône 14 M4/M5 engines. The only other version to be series built and to see action during the early stages of World War II was the Bre 695 powered by 596 kW (800 hp) Pratt & Whitney Hornet engines.

Data (Bre 691B2): *Engines* as above *Wing span* 15.35 m (50 ft 4¾ in) *Length* 9.80 m (32 ft 2 in) *Max T-O weight* 5,000 kg (11,023 lb) *Max level speed* 464 km/h (289 mph) *Range* 1,400 km (870 miles) *Armament* one 20 mm Hispano cannon and 7.5 mm machine-guns, plus up to eight 50 kg bombs

Breguet 763 Deux-Ponts and 765 Sahara (France) The 763 and 765 transport aircraft were the production developments of the 761, the design of which began in 1944. The prototype 761 powered by four 1,192 kW (1,600 hp) SNECMA 14R engines flew for the first time on 15 February 1949. A pre-series of three aircraft, designated 761S, was then produced, powered by 1,490 kW (2,000 hp) Pratt & Whitney R-2800 B31 engines.

Breguet 763 Deux-Ponts.

Breguet 765 Sahara.

The 763 was the first production version of the Deux Ponts. Twelve were ordered by Air France in 1951, powered by four 1,788 kW (2,400 hp) R-2800 CA18 engines. The fuselage was generally similar to that of the 761, but the wing span was increased and the wings were reinforced. It was a convertible passenger/cargo airliner with standard accommodation for 59 tourist-class passengers on the upper deck and 48 second-class passengers on the lower. As used by Air France, the 763 was known as the Provence and first entered service in March 1953. All were operated between France and Algiers.

The 765 Sahara was the military transport version with accommodation for 146 fully equipped troops, 85 stretchers and medical attendants or freight (including military vehicles loaded through the large rear-opening ramp). Fifteen were ordered for the French Air Force in 1956 powered by Pratt & Whitney R-2800 CB-16 or CB-17 engines. The first flew on 6 September 1958.

Data (765 Sahara): *Engines* as above *Wing span* 43.0 m (141 ft 0 in) *Length* 28.94 m (94 ft 11½ in) *Max T-O weight* 54,000 kg (119,050 lb) *Max cruising speed* 380 km/h (236 mph) *Range* 4,700 km (2,920 miles)

Breguet 941 (France) This was an unpressurised cargo/passenger transport aircraft utilising the deflected-slipstream STOL technique. The prototype first flew on 1 June 1961 and in 1965 the French government ordered four 941S pre-production aircraft.

Breguet 1001 Taon (France) Although it did not enter production, the Taon is interesting in being a single-seat lightweight ground attack fighter designed to meet a NATO specification. The first prototype made its maiden flight on 26 July 1957.

Breguet 1050 Alizé (France) This three-seat carrier-borne anti-submarine hunter-killer was derived from the 960 Vultur naval strike aircraft. The first prototype flew on 6 October 1956 and was followed by five pre-production aircraft. Orders for 75 production Alizés were placed by the French Navy and the first was officially delivered on 20 May 1959. Sixty-five were in service by May 1961. A further contract for Alizés was received subsequently from the Indian Navy and 12 were delivered, plus two ex-French aircraft. Two French Navy squadrons and one Indian squadron still operate Alizés on board the carriers *Foch* and *Clémenceau* (French) and *Vikrant* (Indian) respectively.

Breguet 693 AB2.

Breguet 695.

Breguet

Breguet 941S.

Breguet 1001 Taon.

Data: *Engine* one 1,565 kW (2,100 hp) Rolls-Royce Dart RDa 7 Mk 21 turboprop *Wing span* 15.60 m (51 ft 2 in) *Length* 13.86 m (45 ft 5¾ in) *Max T-O weight* 8,200 kg (18,078 lb) *Max level speed* 470 km/h (292 mph) *Normal range* 2,500 km (1,550 miles) *Armament* weapons bay accommodates a torpedo or three 160 kg depth charges. Racks for two 160 kg or 175 kg depth charges under inner wings and for six 5 in rockets or two AS.12 missiles under outer wings. Sonobuoys inside front of wheel fairings.

Breguet 960 Vultur (see Alizé).

Breguet 1150 Atlantic (France) The Atlantic is a twin-engined maritime patrol aircraft, of which 40 were delivered to the French Navy (three of which were passed on to the Pakistan Air Force), 20 to the German Navy, 9 to the Royal Netherlands Navy and 18 to the Italian Navy. Production of the standard version ended in 1974. However Dassault-Breguet is devoting considerable design study, research and development effort to a new-generation version to meet a French Navy reuuirement to replace 42 of its present Atlantics in the mid-1980s. The aircraft will have the same airframe and Tyne turboprop engines with entirely new operational equipment, including advanced data processing, radar, electronic warfare, thermal detection, night vision and acoustic submarine detection systems.

Designed under the auspices of the NATO Armaments Committee, the Atlantic first flew in prototype form on 21 October 1961. The current model carries a crew of 12, with a further 12 making up a relief crew when on long-range patrol missions. The aircraft's main weapons are carried in a bay in the unpressurised lower fuselage. Weapons include all NATO standard bombs, 175 kg French or 385 lb US depth charges, HVAR rockets, homing torpedoes (including types such as the Mk 44 Brush or LX4 with acoustic heads) or four underwing air-to-surface missiles with nuclear or high-explosive warheads. Data: *Engines* two 4,550 kW (6,106 ehp) SNECMA-built Rolls-Royce Tyne RTy 20 Mk 21 turboprops *Wing span* 36.30 m (119 ft 1 in) *Length* 31.75 m (104 ft 2 in) *Max T-O weight* 43,500 kg (95,900 lb) *Max level speed* 658 km/h (409 mph) *Max range* 9,000 km (5,590 miles)

Breguet-Michelin BM series (France) In 1915 the Breguet BU3 bomber appeared, powered by a 149 kW (200 hp) Canton-Unné DF9 pusher engine. The pusher-engine layout was one that the French military preferred and 100 production aircraft were ordered, to be built at the Michelin works. Production bombers appeared in 1916 with BM designations on the tail and were powered by the Canton-Unné or 164 kW (220 hp) Renault RE 8Gd engines. The latter engines were subsequently replaced. As a result of an official requirement for a bomber capable of reaching enemy factories, Breguet produced the improved Type V (winner of the October 1915 competition) and Type VI sesquiplanes, capable of carrying 40 7.25 kg bombs on underwing racks. However in service these proved slow and were relegated first to night bombing and then reconnaissance duties, armed with one flexibly mounted 37 mm Hotchkiss cannon for the observer. Meanwhile the RNAS had taken delivery of 25 Type Vs from France and Grahame-White produced another ten for the service with 186.3 kW (250 hp) Rolls-Royce engines. Max level speed of the Type V was 138 km/h (85.5 mph).

Breguet-Richet Gyroplane No 1 (France) On 29 September 1907 this helicopter, powered by a 33.5 kW (45 hp) Antoinette engine driving four huge rotors, lifted a man off the ground. Although the type made the first flight of a helicopter, it is not credited with the 'first free flight' as it had to be steadied by ground crew with poles.

Breguet 1050 Alizé.

Breguet 1150 Atlantic.

mid-wing all-metal monoplane fitted with a 1,267 kW (1,700 hp) Wright Double-Row Cyclone R-2600-8 engine. Production deliveries were made to the RAF in 1942 as SB2A-1s (known as Bermudas and quickly relegated to training and target-towing duties), and to the US Navy from 1943 as SB2A-2s, -3s and -4s; the latter were produced for the Netherlands East Indies but were not delivered and were used instead as trainers. A total of 750 Buccaneers were built.

Breguet 1150 Atlantic.

Breguet-Michelin
Type IV.

Breguet-Short Calcutta (France) In 1931 two Calcutta flying-boats were purchased from Short Brothers, one civil machine and one military. Subsequently Breguet built four more military Calcuttas (similar to the RAF Rangoon) for the French Navy. They served in Escadrille 3E1, together with the imported example, over a long period.

Brewster F2A (USA) The prototype of this single-seat all-metal fighter flew for the first time in December 1937. The first production version was the F2A-1 powered by a 700.4 kW (940 hp) Wright R-1820-34 radial engine. Eleven were operated by the US Navy on board USS *Saratoga* and 44 were exported to Finland. The F2A-1 was the US Navy's first monoplane fighter. These were followed by 43 894 kW (1,200 hp) R-1820-40-engined F2A-2s and 108 F2A-3s for the US Navy. Meanwhile a few fighters had reached Belgium and others were in service in the Netherlands East Indies and with the RAF (called Buffalos). Apart from the Finnish fighters which fought well against the Russians, F2As were used almost exclusively against the Japanese and in all cases met superior aircraft. Heavy British losses in the Far East led to their withdrawal and US Navy action during the Battle of Midway was equally unsuccessful. A total of more than 500 F2As were built.

Data (F2A-3): *Engine* one 894 kW (1,200 hp) Wright R-1820-40 radial *Wing span* 10.67 m (35 ft 0 in) *Length* 8.03 m (26 ft 4 in) *Max T-O weight* 3,247 kg (7,158 lb) *Max level speed* 517 km/h (321 mph) *Range* nearly 1,610 km (1,000 miles) *Armament* four 0.50 in Colt-Browning machine-guns, plus two 100 lb bombs optionally

Brewster SB2A Buccaneer (USA) The Buccaneer was as unsuccessful in its designed role of carrier-borne dive-bomber as the F2A had been as a fighter. First flown on 17 June 1941, this was a

Breguet-Michelin Type V.

Briegleb sailplanes (USA) The BG 12 series of sailplanes were available as kits or plans for amateur construction. By 1978 kits and/or plans had been purchased for 257 BG 12s and 58 BG 12-16s. The company also re-introduced the 1940s-designed BG 6 and BG 7 as plans only.

Bristol Boxkite (UK) First product of the Bristol and Colonial Aeroplane Company and one of the most famous British pioneering aircraft. The first Bristol biplane (similar in many ways to the French Voisin biplane), later known as the Boxkite, flew initially on 31 July 1910 with a 37.25 kW

Brewster F2A Buffalo.

Bristol

Bristol (Prier) monoplane.

(50 hp) Grégoire engine. However the Boxkite was only successful when fitted later with a 37.25 kW (50 hp) Gnome rotary engine. Full production soon got under way and a total of 76 aircraft were constructed, of which the eight exported to Russia constituted the first foreign order for British aeroplanes. One was flown during the British Army manoeuvres, which led to the delivery of the first military aircraft as an army co-operation machine in May 1911. Although very slow and highly susceptible to wind variations, small numbers served with the RFC and RNAS as two-seat trainers during the early part of World War I.

Brewster SB2A-2 Buccaneer.

Bristol Boxkite before a demonstration flight in November 1910.

Bristol Aeroplane Company (UK) Bristol aircraft are described in order of appearance.

Bristol (Prier) monoplane (UK) Second product of the Bristol Company, designed with definite Blériot monoplane features by the Frenchman Pierre Prier. Thirty-four built as single- and two-seat racing and training aircraft for civil and military use.

Bristol (Gordon England) biplane (UK) Five biplanes produced during 1912 from Gordon England designs, the final two (as G.E.3s) being produced for military use in Turkey and looking very similar to the Breguet 'tin whistle'.

Bristol (Henri Coanda) monoplane (UK) Better-known for his remarkable turbine aeroplane of 1910, Romanian Henri Coanda joined the Bristol Company in 1912 and designed a two-seat monoplane of very clean lines. Altogether 36 were built with Gnome rotary engines of 37.25–59.6 kW (50–80 hp), military examples going to the RFC, Italy and Romania.

Bristol (Prier) monoplanes and Bristol Boxkites at the Bristol Flying School at Larkhill on Salisbury Plain in 1911.

Bristol (Henri Coanda) T.B.8 biplane (UK) Henri Coanda's biplane was a development of the monoplane (the latter configuration not being favoured by the British War Office) and appeared in original form in early 1913. Altogether 65 were produced in several versions, the most important of which was the T.B.8, the RNAS receiving 46. Power was provided by a 37.25 kW (50 hp) or 59.6 kW (80 hp) Gnome, 44.7 kW (60 hp) or 59.6 kW (80 hp) Le Rhône, or 74.5 kW (100 hp) Monosoupape engine. RNAS aircraft served until 1916 from stations in the UK and France as trainers and coastal patrol aircraft. Max level speed was 121 km/h (75 mph).

Bristol Scout (UK) As originally designed by Frank Barnwell and first flown in February 1914, the single-seat Scout was a remarkable aircraft for its time, possessing all the design and handling qualities found in later aircraft of World War I but lacking armament. Full-scale production for the RFC and RNAS began with the Scout C, powered by a 59.6 kW (80 hp) Gnome, Clerget or Le Rhône rotary engine. By the end of 1914 it was in service on the Western Front. Altogether 161 were produced. One Scout C, flown by Capt L. G. Hawker on 25 July 1915 and armed only with a hastily fitted cavalry carbine mounted at an angle to fire past the propeller, gained victories over three armed German Albatros two-seaters (see **Chronology** 24 Aug 1915). With the growing menace of Zeppelin airships, some Scouts were fitted with exploding steel-tipped Ranken darts, which could be dropped from high-flying aircraft. Another answer was to operate Scouts from seaplane-carriers to extend their effective range and from the makeshift deck on board HMS *Vindex*.

At the end of 1915 the Scout D appeared, powered by the 59.6 kW (80 hp) engine of the Scout C or alternatively 74.5 kW (100 hp) Gnome Monosoupape or 82 kW (110 hp) Clerget engines. Design improvements included shorter-span ailerons but, more importantly, most carried a machine-gun. A total of 210 were built, serving with the Cs until the latter part of 1916 on the Western Front, in Macedonia, in the Middle East and in the Aegean Sea area.

Data (Scout D): *Engine* as above *Wing span* 7.49 m

Bristol (Henri Coanda)
monoplane.

Bristol (Henri Coanda)
monoplane.

(24 ft 7 in) *Length* 6.3 m (20 ft 8 in) *Max T-O weight* 653 kg (1,440 lb) *Max level speed* 177 km/h (110 mph) *Endurance* 2 h

Bristol F.2 Fighter (UK) The Bristol Fighter is one of the best-remembered military aircraft to be produced by the Bristol Company and remained in first-line service with the RFC/RAF for about 15 years. Designed as a modern replacement for the Royal Aircraft Factory B.E.2, the Fighter originated as the low-powered R.2A. Modification of the design to fit a 141.6 kW (190 hp) Rolls-Royce Falcon I led to the new designation F.2A and the first flight was made in September 1916. Fifty production F.2As were followed by the refined F.2B version, featuring later versions of the Falcon engine (or other engines as production of the airframes outstripped delivery of the engines from Rolls-Royce) and a new centre-section fitted between the lower wings.

Although the service record of the Fighter was destined to be second to none, when it first entered operational service with No 48 Squadron, RFC, in early 1917 it proved a disaster. Instead of being flown in action against attacking enemy fighters as a two-seat fighter, it was flown in the traditional way of a two-seat reconnaissance machine with the pilot trying to line up the aircraft to give the observer/rear-gunner the best field of fire. Consequently, on the first reconnaissance missions over German lines in April, many F.2As failed to return. But the lessons from early mistakes were quickly learned so that when attacked the pilot flew the aircraft as a single-seater using his forward-firing machine-gun. The rear-gunner could then make a secondary attack as the aircraft flew past or could stave off fighters attacking from the rear. Further help was given by the Fighter's excellent maximum speed, equal to that of most contemporary single-seaters.

More than 5,100 Bristol Fighters were built in Britain during and after World War I, but the expected US production lines were abandoned when it was found that the 298 kW (400 hp) Liberty 12 engine made the aircraft nose-heavy. RAF Fighters performed as general-purpose aircraft in India, Iraq and elsewhere until 1932. In all its many years of faithful service with the RAF, the Fighter's greatest achievement was on 7 May 1918, when just two aircraft from No 22 Squadron were attacked by no fewer than seven Fokker single-seat fighters. During the dogfight which followed the Fighters shot down four Fokkers, only to become entangled with another 15 fighters. The ensuing fight resulted in the loss of another four German machines.

Data (F.2B): *Engine* one 141.5–205 kW (190–275 hp) Rolls-Royce Falcon I, II or III; or Hispano-Suiza, R.A.F.4d, Siddeley Puma or Sunbeam Arab of 149–223.5 kW (200–300 hp) *Wing span* 11.96 m (39 ft 3 in) *Length* 7.87 m (25 ft 10 in) *Max T-O weight* 1,292 kg (2,848 lb) *Max level speed* 201 km/h (125 mph) *Endurance* 3 h *Armament* one forward-firing Vickers and one or two rear-mounted Lewis machine-guns, plus up to 109 kg (240 lb) of bombs.

Bristol Scout C.

Bristol F.2A Fighter.

Post-war version of the
Bristol F.2B Fighter.

Bristol

Bristol M.1C monoplane.

Bristol Tourer with
enclosed rear cockpit.

Bristol Taxiplane.

Bristol Racer Type 72,
which made a few flights
in 1922.

Bristol M.1C (UK) Having experienced structural problems with monoplanes before the outbreak of World War I (which had resulted in a temporary ban on aircraft of this configuration), the War Office was not as ecstatic about the new M.1A of 1916 as was its manufacturer, the Bristol Company. Nevertheless, following a number of test aircraft, 125 production M.1C fighters were ordered for the RFC, powered by 82 kW (110 hp) Le Rhône rotary engines. Although these would have proved invaluable on the Western Front, they were sent to less important areas of operations in the Middle East and Macedonia, where small numbers fought air combats and carried out attacks on Turkish ground forces from 1917 until the end of the war.
Data: *Engine* as above *Wing span* 9.37 m (30 ft 9 in) *Length* 6.22 m (20 ft 5½ in) *Max T-O weight* 611 kg (1,348 lb) *Max level speed* 209 km/h (130 mph) *Endurance* 1 h 45 min *Armament* one forward-firing Vickers machine-gun
Bristol Tourer (UK) Developed from the Bristol F.2B Fighter, the Tourer was produced as a two–three-seater with an open or enclosed rear cockpit for the passengers. Power was usually provided by a 171.4 kW (230 hp) Siddeley Puma engine.

Total production amounted to 44 aircraft, of which many were exported.
Bristol Ten-seater and Brandon (UK) The Ten-seater was a large single-engined biplane airliner of 1921, accommodating six passengers facing forwards and two facing aft in the cabin, a pilot and a mechanic (full description appears in the 1926 *Jane's*). Two Ten-seaters were completed: the first with a 335.3 kW (450 hp) Napier Lion engine, serving initially with Instone Air Line on the London–Paris route; the second, powered by a 317 kW (425 hp) Bristol Jupiter IV, served with Imperial Airways between London and Cologne as a freight carrier. The Brandon was a military transport version for the RAF, of which only one was completed and used as an ambulance aircraft.
Bristol Taxiplane and Trainer (UK) The Taxiplane and the Trainer were basically the same aircraft, the former accommodating a pilot forward and two passengers side-by-side aft and the Trainer two in tandem. Power for both was an 89.4 kW (120 hp) Bristol Lucifer engine. Only three Taxiplanes were built, but 24 Trainers were produced for use at the Bristol RAF Reserve Officers' Flying School, and for export to Chile, Bulgaria and Hungary.
Bristol 'Jupiter' Fighter and Type 89 Advanced Trainer (UK) Only three 'Jupiter' Fighters (317 kW; 425 hp Jupiter IV engine) were built, one going to Sweden, where it performed on skis extremely well under Arctic conditions (a detailed account of this aircraft, together with official time-to-height performance figures, appeared in the 1927 *Jane's*). An advanced training version of the Fighter was also produced as the Type 89 (7 built) and Type 89A (14) with 238.5 kW (320 hp) Jupiter IV or VI engines respectively.

Bristol Brownie (UK) Two-seat light aeroplane built for Air Ministry competitions in 1924. Two Brownies competed, one with wooden and one with metal wings, the latter winning second prize of £1,000. Power was provided by a 24 kW (32 hp) Bristol Cherub I engine.
Bristol Boarhound (UK) Two-seat army co-operation biplane, of which two were flown in Mexico.
Bristol Bulldog (UK) Between the World Wars the Bristol Aeroplane Company had very few successful designs. The outstanding one that kept the big factory busy from 1928 until 1935 was the Bulldog, the RAF's standard single-seat intercep-

Bristol Brownie.

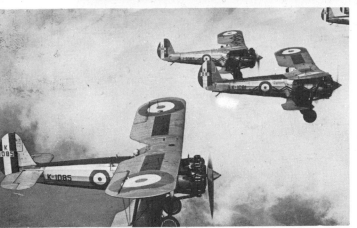

Bristol Bulldog IIs.

tor from the late 1920s until progressively replaced by the Fury and Gauntlet in the mid-1930s.

Capt Barnwell designed the Type 105 Bulldog to meet Air Ministry Specification F.9/26. It was a sturdy unequal-span biplane with a structure chiefly of light alloy, with fabric covering. The Bristol Jupiter engine, which in the initial production Bulldog II was a 328 kW (440 hp) Jupiter VII, was mounted in a streamlined nose with its cylinders projecting uncowled but with streamlined fairings and cooling baffles. The propeller had two wooden blades. From the first flight on 17 May 1927 handling was excellent. Features included Frise ailerons on the large upper wing and an adjustable trimming tailplane. In conformity with standard British practice the armament comprised two 0.303 in Vickers machine-guns with their breeches accessible to the pilot (so that he could clear stoppages with a mallet and recock the offending weapon) and firing along channels in the forward fuselage and between the cylinders of the engine. Four 9 kg (20 lb) bombs could be carried under the small lower wing. Standard equipment included an oxygen bottle and radio.

After final evaluation against the Hawker Hawfinch the Bulldog was selected in 1928, Bristol having quickly produced a Mk II prototype with a longer fuselage and other changes to rectify previous minor faults. The first batch comprised 25 aircraft, of which 23 went to RAF fighter squadrons beginning with No 3 in 1929. Altogether 92 Bulldog IIs were built, one of which was retained for trials with Mercury engines in more advanced forms of cowling. Seventeen went to Latvia, eight to the RAAF, two to the US Navy, two to Siam, 12 to Estonia, three to Sweden and one to Chile.

A civil demonstrator flown in June 1930 was stressed for greater gross weight and led to the main production version, the Bulldog IIA, the usual engine of which was the 365 kW (490 hp) Jupiter VIIF with forged cylinder heads. By November 1933 Bristol had built 262 of this model, of which eight went to Sweden and 253 to the RAF. Four more, called Bristol 105D, were supplied to Denmark with Madsen guns and other changes. Two improved and much faster aircraft with the Mercury engine and Townend ring cowl were designated Bulldog IIIA, leading to the strengthened four-aileron Bulldog IVA, with a 477 kW (640 hp) Mercury VIS2 and full-length cowl. This was beaten by the Gladiator for RAF orders, but 17 were built for Finland in the first two months of 1935. The last Bulldog was an all-stainless-steel Mk IIA for the Air Ministry.

Back in 1931 a Mk IIA had been rebuilt into a dual-control advanced trainer. In December 1932

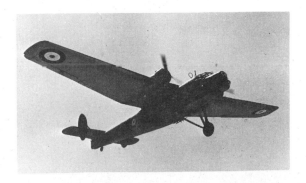

Bristol Bulldog IIAs with experimental ring cowlings around the engines.

a modified trainer, called Bulldog TM (Training Machine), went into production as a standard type for the RAF. By December 1934 no fewer than 60 had been delivered. They were designed so that by fitting different rear fuselages, and adding guns (for which provision was made), they became fighters; but this was never necessary. Bulldogs remained in full RAF service until 1937, and until 1940 with Baltic air forces.

Bristol Bombay.

Bristol

Data (Mk IIA): *Engine* as above *Wing span* 10.3 m (33 ft 10 in) *Length* 7.68 m (25 ft 2 in) *Max T-O weight* 1,660 kg (3,660 lb) *Max level speed* 285 km/h (177 mph)

Bristol Bombay (UK) The Bombay was designed as a transport aircraft for 24 troops or freight, capable also of being operated as a bomber by RAF squadrons based abroad. Power was provided by two 753 kW (1,010 hp) Bristol Pegasus XXII radial engines mounted on the leading edges of the high monoplane wings. Defensive armament comprised Lewis guns in nose and tail positions. The prototype first flew on 23 June 1935 and the first of 50 production aircraft entered service just after the outbreak of World War II. Flown mainly as transports in the Middle East and Mediterranean theatres of war, a number were also employed temporarily as night bombers against Benghasi, Libya, in September 1940. Max level speed was 309 km/h (192 mph).

Bristol Type 138A (UK) Single-seat high-altitude research monoplane powered by a 372.6 kW (500 hp) Bristol Pegasus P.E.6S radial engine. Flown by Sqn Ldr F. R. D. Swain, it achieved a height record of 15,223 m (49,944 ft) on 28 September 1936. On 30 June 1937 it raised the record to 16,440 m (53,937 ft) at the hands of Flt Lt M. J. Adam.

Bristol Type 142 (UK) Single example of a very fast twin 484.4 kW (650 hp) Bristol Mercury VIS 2-powered six-passenger transport aircraft. Built for Lord Rothermere (owner of the *Daily Mail* newspaper), it was later presented to the nation as *Britain First*. From the Type 142 *Britain First* was developed the Bristol Blenheim bomber.

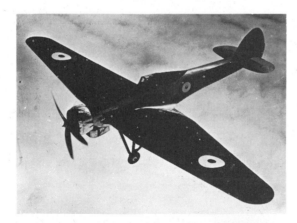

Bristol Blenheim (UK) The often told story of the six-seat executive aircraft built for Lord Rothermere, proprietor of the aviation-supporting *Daily Mail*, usually misses the vital point. Why did he want a fast executive aircraft? Primarily it was to show the world that Britain could build a civil aircraft at least as good as the Douglas DC-1. Bristol's Type 142 first flew on 12 April 1935. When tested at Martlesham Heath in June it proved to be 80 km/h (50 mph) faster than Britain's latest fighter prototype.

The outcome was the Bristol Type 142M, the most important changes being to provide armament, a bomb aimer's position, internal bomb stowage and more powerful 626 kW (840 hp) Mercury VIII radial engines. To make room for a bomb bay in the lower fuselage, the low-wing configuration of the civil Type 142 was changed to mid-wing for the military version, which became named Blenheim. The prototype made its first flight on 25 June 1936, and initial deliveries went to No 114 Bomber Squadron in March 1937.

The requirement for longer range led to evolution of the long-nosed, increased tankage and strengthened landing gear version, named originally Bolingbroke I. These began to enter RAF service in March 1939, by then designated Blenheim IV.

By the outbreak of World War II Blenheim Is had been superseded by Mk IVs in the UK, but remained in first-line service in Greece and the Western Desert. Blenheim IF night-fighters had their armament of two machine-guns supplemented by a four-Browning under-fuselage gun pack. It was these aircraft which pioneered British airborne radar, serving throughout the blitz of 1940–41. Blenheim IVs had their share of early fame – making the first reconnaissance over Germany of World War II on 3 September 1939, the first attack on the German Fleet on 4 September – and were continuously active over Europe on daylight raids until late 1941.

On 24 February 1941 a modified Blenheim, known originally as the Bisley, made its first flight. Powered by two 708 kW (950 hp) Mercury 30 engines, it featured an extensively modified nose and other changes. As the Blenheim V, a total of 940 production aircraft were eventually built in several variants. Although not popular with its crews it remained operational in the Far East until the latter part of 1943.
Data (Blenheim IV): *Engines* two 685.6 kW (920 hp) Bristol Mercury XV radials *Wing span* 17.17 m (56 ft 4 in) *Length* 12.98 m (42 ft 7 in) *Max T-O weight* 6,532 kg (14,400 lb) *Max level speed* 428 km/h (266 mph) *Range* 2,350 km (1,460 miles) *Armament* five 0.303 in Browning machine-guns, plus up to 599 kg (1,320 lb) of bombs

Bristol Beaufort (UK) The Bristol Beaufort torpedo-bomber was designed to meet two Air Ministry specifications (M.15/35 for a torpedo bomber and G.24/35 for a general reconnaissance-bomber); the prototype flew for the first time on 15 October 1938. With a family likeness to the Blenheim IV it was, however, a heavier aircraft powered by two 753 kW (1,010 hp) Bristol Taurus II sleeve-valve radial engines in the original Mk I aircraft, which entered service with the RAF in December 1939. Beaufort Is were followed into service by later versions with 894 kW (1,200 hp) Pratt & Whitney Twin Wasp engines, the total number of Beauforts eventually built amounting to more than 2,100, a third of which were built in Australia.

Coastal Command's first mine-laying operation with Beauforts was mounted on the night of 15–16 April 1940. From then until withdrawn from service in 1944, they were used extensively around Britain's coastline and in the Mediterranean. Beauforts took part in the abortive attempt to prevent escape of the German pocket battleships through the English Channel in 1942.
Data (Beaufort I): *Engines* two 842 kW (1,130 hp) Bristol Taurus VI radials *Wing span* 17.63 m (57 ft 10 in) *Length* 13.59 m (44 ft 7 in) *Max T-O weight* 9,629 kg (21,228 lb) *Max level speed* 426 km/h (265 mph) *Range* 1,666 km (1,035 miles) *Armament* five 0.303 in machine-guns, plus up to 680 kg (1,500 lb) bombs or one 1,605 lb torpedo

Bristol Beaufighter (UK) At the time of the Munich crisis it became alarmingly clear in Britain that the nation had a serious deficiency in modern fighter aircraft and virtually none suit-

able for deployment as long-range escorts or as night fighters. The Bristol Aeroplane Company had flown in 1938 the prototype of a torpedo-bomber, which duly entered service as the Beaufort; to the Bristol design team it seemed that this aircraft had potential for adaptation as a large fighter, one which would have the fuel-carrying capacity for long range or the armament/equipment-carrying capacity for service as a night interceptor.

Bristol Beaufort I.

Bristol Beaufighter TF.X.

Despite some concern from Air Ministry quarters that such a large aircraft might have poor manoeuvrability, four prototypes were ordered, the first making its maiden flight on 17 July 1939. Resembling the Beaufort in its original form – a new fuselage and more powerful engines representing the major changes – the first series aircraft was distinguished mainly by its heavy armament. This comprised four 20 mm cannon mounted in the nose, four 0.303 in Browning machine-guns in the starboard wing and two more in the port wing, making it the most heavily armed fighter in the world.

First deliveries to RAF squadrons began in September 1940. Any disappointment at lack of speed in this early version was more than offset when its capacity as a carrier for the initially bulky AI (airborne interception radar) was appreciated. The first night interception resulting in the destruction of an enemy aircraft, a Junkers Ju 88, was made on the night of 19 November 1940, and Beaufighters equipped with AI Mk IV played a significant part in ending the German night attacks on London in the winter of 1940–41.

Bristol Blenheim V.

Beaufighters operated in the Western Desert as long-range day fighters; with Coastal Command as long-range fighters; as torpedo-carrying aircraft nicknamed 'Torbeaus'; and as anti-shipping strike aircraft armed with eight underwing rockets. On two memorable days, two squadrons of TF.X anti-shipping strike fighters equipped with ASV radar and armed with torpedoes, rockets and bombs sank no fewer than five U-boats.

Bristol Buckingham I.

Bristol Brigand TF.1 armed with rockets and a torpedo.

Beaufighters were built under licence in Australia, where airframe construction was based on 55,000 microfilm negatives sent from Filton to Fisherman's Bend by the Airgraph service. By the time that production ended, the combined total of aircraft constructed in England and Australia amounted to more than 5,560. Many remained in second-line service well into the 1950s.

Data (Beaufighter X): *Engines* two 1,285 kW (1,725 hp) Bristol Hercules XVII radials *Wing span* 17.63 m (57 ft 10 in) *Length* 12.95 m (42 ft 6 in) *Max T-O weight* 11,521 kg (25,400 lb) *Max level speed* 531 km/h (330 mph) *Range* 2,414 km (1,500 miles) *Armament* four 20 mm cannon, one 0.303 in machine-gun, one torpedo, eight rockets and two 250 lb bombs

Bristol Buckmaster I.

Bristol Buckingham (UK) Intended as a day-bomber version of the Beaufighter, the prototype Buckingham flew for the first time on 4 February 1943. Only 119 were completed, all becoming or built as four-passenger (three crew) high-speed transports. Power was provided by two 1,878 kW (2,520 hp) Bristol Centaurus VII or XI radial engines.

Bristol Brigand (UK) The Brigand was designed as a twin-engined three-seat long-range attack aircraft capable of fulfilling the duties of a torpedo-bomber, dive-bomber and fighter to replace the Beaufighter. It used wings, landing gear, engine nacelles and tail unit of a similar type to those of the Buckingham. The prototype first flew on 4 December 1944. Although the first 11 aircraft were delivered as TF.1 torpedo-bombers to Coastal Command, in 1947 the Mk 1 was remodelled as a three-seat general-purpose bomber and most of the remaining 132 production Brigands were delivered as B.1s. However a few saw service as Brigand Mk 2 training aircraft for radar navigators and Met Mk 3 meteorological reconnaissance aircraft.

The Brigand served with the RAF from 1949 until 1958, seeing action in Malaya during the early 1950s. Power was provided by two 1,841 kW (2,470 hp) Bristol Centaurus 57 engines, giving a max speed of 576 km/h (358 mph).

Bristol Buckmaster (UK) Serving with the RAF for a decade from 1945, the Buckmaster was basically a three-seat advanced training version of the Buckingham. One hundred and ten were completed from Buckingham components, with the armament deleted and dual controls installed.

Bristol Brabazon (UK) The Type 167 Brabazon was designed as a fully pressurised passenger airliner specifically for operating the direct London to New York service without having to refuel en route in the west-bound direction. Designated Mk 1, the first aircraft (the second not being completed) began its flight trials on 4 September 1949 powered by eight 1,863 kW (2,500 hp) Bristol Centaurus 20 18-cylinder two-row radial engines. The second aircraft would have been powered by Bristol Proteus turboprops in coupled pairs. It was expected that the Mk 1 would be retained for experimental flight research into the problems associated with very large aircraft, while the Mk 2 would be furnished to carry 100 passengers by day or night, plus a flight crew of seven and eight stewards. However, although the Mk 1 flew well and BEA wanted to use it between London and Nice, France, fatigue cracks in the propeller mounting and other problems ended the project. Normal cruising speed of the Mk 2 at 10,670 m (35,000 ft) was expected to have been about 531 km/h (330 mph).

Bristol Freighter (UK) The Type 170 was designed as an economic passenger, freight/passenger or all-freight transport aircraft to Specification 22/44 to carry a high payload on short-range flights. Because the campaign against the Japanese in Burma was still under way, a second Specification (C.9/45) was issued to provide a military transport capable of carrying into

jungle areas a three-ton payload, including heavy trucks, guns, 28 stretchers and attendants, 36 fully equipped troops, 23 paratroops or other military loads. Large twin nose-doors facilitated loading and unloading of cargo.

The first of the two prototypes flew in December 1945, by which time it was too late to see service during World War II. But surveys had shown that there was a genuine need for a similar aircraft for post-war commercial services and so the Freighter and Wayfarer were put into production, with nose-doors for loading freight or mixed passenger/freight-carrying and without nose-doors but seating for 36 passengers respectively.

Of the 214 Bristol Type 170s built, the best-known of all the versions was the Mk 32 with a lengthened fuselage, ordered by Silver City Airways. This version could accommodate two or three cars and 23 passengers. Apart from the large numbers of commercial versions which were supplied for use in all parts of the world for a variety of duties, the Type 170 was also produced as a military transport and served with the RAAF, RCAF (Mk 31 freighter version), RNZAF and the Pakistan Air Force.
Data (Mk 32): *Engines* two 1,475.5 kW (1,980 hp) Bristol Hercules 734s *Wing span* 32.92 m (108 ft 0 in) *Length* 22.35 m (73 ft 4 in) *Max T-O weight* 19,958 kg (44,000 lb) *Max level speed* 362 km/h (225 mph) *Range* 1,320 km (820 miles)

Bristol Britannia (UK) The Type 175 Britannia, the world's first large turboprop transport aircraft, began as a piston-engined design to meet BOAC's 1947 specification for the MRE (Medium Range Empire) transport to carry

32–36 passengers and be powered by four Bristol Centaurus 662 sleeve-valve engines. The aircraft's size was soon increased and consideration given to the installation of Bristol Proteus turbines or Napier Nomad compound engines.

After some delay, in June 1948 the Ministry of Supply ordered three Centaurus-powered prototypes but stipulated that the second and third should be capable of conversion to Proteus-engined aircraft.

When the first prototype emerged in 1952 it was a much bigger aeroplane with accommodation for more than 80 passengers and powered by Proteus 625 engines. First flight was on 16 August 1952. Development trials were prolonged, partly because of engine icing problems, but on 1 Febru-

ary 1957 BOAC began operating Britannia 102s with 2,906 kW (3,900 hp) Proteus 705s and up to 90 seats on its London–Johannesburg services.

A number of versions were developed from the Series 100 aircraft and on 19 December 1957, BOAC began the first turbine-powered North Atlantic service when it put Britannia 312s on the London–New York route. These were 3.12 m (10 ft 3 in) longer, had accommodation for up to 139 passengers, were powered by 3,070 kW (4,120 hp) Proteus 755s and had a 13,608 kg (30,000 lb) increase in max weight. On the day that BOAC introduced Britannias on the North Atlantic, El Al flew a Britannia 10,328 km (6,100 miles) non-stop from New York to Tel Aviv.

The Britannia was a superb aeroplane but was too late to establish itself before the introduction of turbojet transports; only 85 were built, including 23 Series 250 aircraft for the RAF.

Canadair developed the Britannia design into the military CL-28 Argus and CL-44 Yukon and the CL-44 series of passenger and cargo aircraft.

Bristol Brabazon under construction in January 1948.

Bristol Wayfarer.

Bristol Freighter Mk 21.

Bristol Brabazon.

Bristol

Bristol Britannia 102.

Data (Britannia 312): *Engines* as above *Wing span* 43.35 m (142 ft 3 in) *Length* 37.87 m (124 ft 3 in) *Max T-O weight* 84,345 kg (185,000 lb) *Cruising speed* 574 km/h (357 mph) *Range* 8,545 km (5,310 miles)

Bristol Sycamore.

Bristol Type 173.

The first Bristol/Westland Type 192 Belvedere.

Bristol Sycamore (UK) The Type 171 was the first rotating-wing aircraft to be built by the Bristol Company. Three prototypes were produced, the first (powered by a 335.3 kW; 450 hp Pratt & Whitney R-985 engine) flying for the first time on 24 July 1947. The third prototype (Type 171 Mk 2) was powered by an Alvis 71 engine.

The Type 171 or Sycamore entered service as a civil transport and in a number of military roles, with accommodation varying accordingly. Standard accommodation was for five persons, including one or two pilots and for search and rescue and communications duties it remained similar. As an ambulance a pilot, medical attendant and two stretchers were carried. Standard power plant was a 387.5 kW (520 hp) Alvis Leonides Mk 173 (civil designation) nine-cylinder radial engine mounted vertically in the fuselage centre-section.

The first production model was the Mk 3, designed to be operated as an air taxi or for observation, reconnaissance and air/sea rescue duties. The Mk 4 thereafter became the standard production version, capable of rapid conversion for passenger or freight carrying. Military versions as such began with the Sycamore HC.10, an ambulance version for the British Army. The HC.11

was a communications, observation and transport version for the British Army, capable of carrying externally up to 726 kg (1,600 lb) of slung freight and with a rope ladder for use over unsuitable landing terrain.

Subsequent versions included the HR.12 search and rescue or communications aircraft for RAF Coastal Command; HR.13, as for HR.12 but for Fighter Command; HR.14 search and rescue, ambulance and communications aircraft for the RAF; HR.50 and 51 search and rescue or communications aircraft for the Royal Australian Navy, with a hydraulically-operated side winch, folding 'deck chair' seats and other changes; and Mk 52 for the Federal German forces, basically similar to the HR.14.

Data (HR.14): *Engine* one 387.5 kW (520 hp) Alvis Leonides 73 *Rotor diameter* 14.81 m (48 ft 6¾ in) *Length* (main rotor folded) 14.07 m (46 ft 2 in) *Max T-O weight* 2,540 kg (5,600 lb) *Max level speed* 204 km/h (127 mph) *Range* 430 km (268 miles)

Bristol Type 173 (UK) First flown on 3 January 1952, this was Bristol's second and the first British multi-engined helicopter. Expected to enter service with BEA, it remained a prototype but was used in the development of the Type 192.

Bristol Type 192 and Westland Belvedere (UK) Originally developed by Bristol from the Type 173, this helicopter was later produced by Westland Helicopters following that company's take-over of Bristol in 1960. No prototype was built and the first of 26 production Belvederes for the RAF flew for the first time on 5 July 1958. Three production machines were delivered to the Trials Unit in October 1960 and the Belvedere entered service with No 66 Squadron on 15 September 1961, being operated in the UK and Far East. Belvederes also equipped No 26 Squadron in Aden and No 72 Squadron in the UK.

Data: *Engines* two 1,229.5 kW (1,650 shp) Napier Gazelle NGa.2 (revised) Mk 101 free turbines *Rotor diameter* (each) 14.91 m (48 ft 11 in) *Length*

overall 27.35 m (89 ft 9 in) *Max T-O weight*
9,072 kg (20,000 lb) *Max level speed* 222 km/h
(138 mph) *Econ cruising speed* for max endurance
120 km/h (75 mph) *Range* 715 km (445 miles)
Accommodation crew of two and 19 troops; 12
stretchers, two sitting casualties and a medical
attendant; up to 30 passengers in emergency
rescue role; or 2,721 kg (6,000 lb) of internal/
external freight

Bristol T.188 (UK) Supersonic research aircraft
designed to investigate prolonged flight at speeds
of up to Mach 3. First flown 14 April 1962 powered by two 62.28 kN (14,000 lb st) Bristol Siddeley (D.H.) Gyron Junior DGJ.10R turbojet
engines.

British Army Aeroplane No 1 (UK) Born in
America but later becoming a British citizen,
Samuel Franklin Cody was one of the most colour-
ful and prominent designers working with the
British Army and War Office before and just after
the turn of the century. Having designed and
constructed man-lifting kites and played an
important part in the development of the Dirigible No 1 (see below), Cody began experimenting
in aeroplane design, which finally led to the construction of the British Army Aeroplane No 1.

Piloted by Cody, it first flew on 16 October
1908, achieving a distance of 424 m (1,390 ft) and
therefore making the first officially recognised
powered flight of an aeroplane in Great Britain.
Development of the aircraft continued and on 14
May 1909 he flew over a mile. Cody was killed in
an air accident in 1913.
Data: *Engine* one 37.25 kW (50 hp) Antoinette
Wing span 15.85 m (52 ft 0 in) *Length* (approx)

13.41 m (44 ft 0 in) *Max T-O weight* 1,152 kg
(2,540 lb) *Max level speed* 64 km/h (40 mph)
Accommodation Pilot and passenger

British Army Dirigible No 1 *Nulli Secundus*
(UK) Financed with War Office funds, the British Army Dirigible No 1, known as *Nulli Secundus*,
was completed at the Balloon Factory, Farnborough, under the direction of Col John Capper
and Samuel Cody and first flown on 10 September
1907. It was later modified with stabilising planes
to prevent pitching and flown in revised form on
24 July 1908. Power was provided by a single
37.25 kW (50 hp) Antoinette engine.

British Aircraft Swallow and Eagle (UK)
Originally known as British Klemm and formed
in 1933, the British Aircraft Manufacturing
Company licence-built the Klemm L.25 and L.32
as the Swallow and Eagle respectively. The Swallow was a two-seat light low-wing monoplane
powered by a 56 kW (75 hp) British Salmson or
Pobjoy Cataract radial engine. The Eagle was a
three-seat cabin monoplane powered by a 97 kW
(130 hp) de Havilland Gipsy Major or 138 kW
(185 hp) Gipsy Six engine. Six were built. British
Aircraft also produced 22 examples of an Eagle 2
version.

Britten Sheriff (UK) Designed as a two–four-
seat lightweight training and utility aircraft by the
late John Britten.

Bristol T.188.

Brokaw Bullet.

British Army Aeroplane
No 1.

Britten-Norman BN-2 Islander (UK) The
Islander was designed to be a modern replacement for aircraft in the class of the de Havilland
Dragon Rapide. The prototype first flew on 13
June 1965 powered by two 157 kW (210 hp)
Rolls-Royce Continental IO-360-B engines and
with a wing span of 13.72 m (45 ft). Subsequently
the prototype was re-engined with Lycoming
O-540s and the wing span increased. The production prototype first flew on 20 August 1966 and
deliveries of production aircraft began a year
later. By September 1978 more than 800 aircraft

British Aircraft Swallow.

Britten-Norman

Pilatus Britten-Norman Defender.

Pilatus Britten-Norman Maritime Defender.

Pilatus Britten-Norman Defender.

Pilatus Britten-Norman Maritime Defender.

Pilatus Britten-Norman BN-2 Islander.

of the various models (see below) had been delivered to operators in 118 countries.

The sale of 100 aircraft to the Philippines began in 1974. These were followed by 14 partially completed aircraft, which led to licence production by NAMC of the Philippines.

Initial production aircraft were designated BN-2. Those built from 1 June 1969 until 1978 had the designation BN-2A and the current model is the BN-2B Islander II, which has a higher maximum landing weight and improved interior. Deliveries began in 1979. The basic Islander II is available with a choice of two alternative power plants and either standard 14.94 m (49 ft) span wings or wingtip extensions having raked tips and containing extra fuel. On 25 July 1978 it was announced that Pilatus Aircraft of Switzerland was to acquire all assets of Britten-Norman. The Islander range is now marketed under the name Pilatus Britten-Norman.

Data (BN-2B Islander II with standard wings and nose): *Engines* two 194 kW (260 hp) Lycoming O-540-E4C5 or 224 kW (300 hp) IO-540-K1B5s *Wing span* 14.94 m (49 ft 0 in) *Length* 10.86 m (35 ft 7¾ in) *Max T-O weight* 2,993 kg (6,600 lb) *Max cruising speed* 290 km/h (180 mph) *Range* 1,136 km (706 miles) *Accommodation* up to ten persons, including pilot.

Britten-Norman BN-2 Trislander (UK) In the autumn of 1970 Britten-Norman introduced an enlarged development of the Islander, having a third engine mounted at the rear and a lengthened fuselage seating up to 17 passengers. By mid-1978 orders had been received for more than 80 Trislanders for customers in the UK, Africa, Australasia, USA, Canada, Indonesia and South America.

The current versions are the BN-2A Mk III-2 standard version with an extended nose contain-

Pilatus Britten-Norman BN-2A Mk III-2 Trislander.

ing a baggage compartment; BN-2A Mk III-3, as for Mk III-2 but with autofeather system which feathers the propeller automatically should an engine fail on take-off; BN-2A Mk III-4, as for Mk III-3 plus a standby rocket engine to provide additional thrust should an engine fail on take-off; and Trislander M proposed military version, suitable for carrying troops, paratroops and supplies, as well as for deployment in maritime patrol or search and rescue roles.

Data: *Engines* three 194 kW (260 hp) Lycoming O-540-E4C5s, plus standby rocket engine (Mk III-4) providing 1.56 kN (350 lb) of thrust *Wing span* 16.15 m (53 ft 0 in) *Length overall* 15.01 m (49 ft 3 in) *Max T-O weight* 4,536 kg (10,000 lb) *Max cruising speed* 267 km/h (166 mph) *Range* 1,610 km (1,000 miles)

Britten-Norman Defender (UK) This is a variant of the civil Islander which can be adapted for a wide range of government and military roles such as search and rescue, internal security, long-range patrol, forward air control, troop transport, logistic support and casualty evacuation. Typical underwing loads include twin 7.62 mm machine-guns in pod packs, 250 lb or 500 lb GP bombs, Matra rocket packs, SURA rocket clusters, wire-guided missiles, 5 in reconnaissance flares, anti-personnel grenades, smoke bombs, marker bombs and 227 litre (60 US gallon) drop tanks.

Britten-Norman Firefighter (UK) Firefighting variant of the Islander equipped with four specially designed interconnected liquid tanks with a total capacity of 800 litres (211 US gallons).

Britten-Norman Maritime Defender (UK) Generally similar to the Defender but differs by having a modified nose with a larger search radar. The interior layout provides for the pilot and co-pilot, a radar operator and two observers. Intended for coastal patrol, fishery and oil rig protection duties, as well as search and rescue support, it is suitable for all-weather operation, by day or night, and carries the equipment necessary to fulfil such roles.

Britten-Norman Turbo Islander (UK) Announced in 1975, the Turbo Islander is generally similar to the piston-engined version equipped with the extended baggage nose, except for reinforcement of the wing and fuselage and uprating of the landing gear to cater for a gross weight of 3,311 kg (7,300 lb). There are two versions, the BN-2B-40 with standard wings, and the BN-2B-41 with extended wings. First flight was made on 6 April 1977. Power is provided by two 448 kW (600 shp) Lycoming LTP101 turboprop engines, flat-rated at 298 kW (400 shp). Maximum cruising speed is 354 km/h (220 mph).

Brochet M.B.70 (France) Two-seat light cabin monoplane of the early 1950s, designed to be amateur-built and powered by a 33.5 kW (45 hp) Salmson 9ADB radial engine. Ten were built for the Service de la Formation Aéronautique et des Sports Aériens (SFASA) for distribution among French flying clubs.

Brochet M.B.71 (France) Similar to the M.B.70 except that power was provided by a 56 kW (75 hp) Minié 4.DC.32 engine.

Brochet M.B.80 (France) Development of the M.B.71 with a 10.2 cm (4 in) wider fuselage, balanced control surfaces and a steel spring-type landing gear. Ten built for SFASA.

Brochet M.B.100 (France) Three-seat development of the M.B.70, not intended for amateur construction. Powered by a 67.8 kW (91 hp) Hirth 504 inverted engine. Five built for SFASA.

Brochet M.B.110 (France) Two prototypes were ordered in October 1954 at the instigation of SFASA. The first prototype of this four-seat long-range touring monoplane flew on 12 March 1956. Power was provided by a 126.7 kW (170 hp) SNECMA-Régnier 42O2 inverted engine.

Brochet M.B.120 (France) Two-seat light touring monoplane, the prototype of which first flew on 5 April 1954. It had the airframe of the M.B.100 remodelled as a two-seater, to which lighter wings with landing flaps were fitted. Power was provided by a 67 kW (90 hp) Continental C90 engine.

Brügger MB-3.

Bücker Bü.133 Jungmeister.

Brokaw Bullet (USA) Two-seat high-speed sporting aircraft powered by a 283 kW (380 hp) Avco Lycoming TIO-541-E flat-six engine. Plans are available to amateur builders.

Brügger MB-2 Colibri 2 (Switzerland) Single-seat light low-wing monoplane powered by a 30 kW (40 hp) 1,600 cc modified Volkswagen motorcar engine. Plans are available to amateur constructors and about 140 were under construction or flying in Europe by early 1979.

Brügger MB-3 (Switzerland) Single-seat all-metal light aircraft first flown in 1977. Plans are not available to amateur constructors.

Bryan (Schreder) RS-15 (USA) Single-seat Standard Class sailplane designed for simple, rapid assembly by the homebuilder.

Bücker Bü.131 Jungmann (Germany) Bücker Flugzeugbau was formed in 1933 and the first product was the Jungmann, a light two-seat biplane trainer specially developed for school and other training purposes. The prototype first flew on 27 April 1934. Power was provided by a 59.6 kW (80 hp) Hirth H.M.60R engine in the Bü.131A and a 78.2 kW (105 hp) Hirth H.M.504A inverted engine in the Bü.131B. Before the outbreak of World War II the trainer was being used in 21 countries and licence-built in Holland, Czechoslovakia, Spain and Switzerland. Many remain flying today.

Bücker Bü.133 Jungmeister (Germany) The Jungmann was followed in 1935 by the Jungmeister, a single-seat advanced training biplane, powered in the original version by a 119 kW (160 hp) Siemens Sh.14A engine. It achieved outstanding success as an aerobatic machine before the war and won international competitions in Germany, Holland, France, Switzerland, Romania and the USA. As the Bü.133C it was still in production in 1945. More recently Aero Technik Canary of Germany put the Jungmeister back into production as the Bü.133D-1 with an Sh-14A4 engine,

Brochet M.B.80.

Brügger MB-2 Colibri 2.

Bücker Bü.181 Bestmann.

Buhl Bull Pup.

One of several Burgess seaplanes designed for the US Navy.

and in 1969 as the Bü.133F with a 164 kW (220 hp) Franklin 6A-350-C1 engine.

Bücker Bü.180 Student (Germany) The Student of 1938 was a two-seat light cabin monoplane powered by a 37.25–44.7 kW (50–60 hp) Walter Mikron II or 37.25 kW (50 hp) Zundapp inverted engine.

Bücker Bü.181 Bestmann (Germany) The Bestmann of 1939 was a two-seat cabin monoplane powered by a 78.2 kW (105 hp) Hirth H.M.504 inverted engine.

Bücker Bü.182C Kornett (Germany) Single-seat advanced training monoplane powered by a 59.6 kW (80 hp) Bücker Bü.M 700 inverted engine.

Budd RB Conestoga (USA) Cargo and troop transport aircraft of stainless-steel construction powered by two 894 kW (1,200 hp) Pratt & Whitney R-1830-92 radial engines. First flown in October 1943. The US Navy ordered 200 as RB-1s and the USAAF 600 as C-93s. Owing to manufacturing problems and changes in service requirements, in 1944 the Army cancelled the C-93 and the Navy cut its order to 25. Only 17 were completed as JRB-3s and these were sold to civil operators.

Buhl C.W.3, Airsedans, Airster and Bull Pup (USA) The Buhl-Verville Aircraft Company

(later renamed Buhl Aircraft Company) was formed in 1925 and thereafter produced a series of aircraft up to 1931. The C.W.3 of 1926 was a sturdy two-seat biplane, suitable for freight-carrying, aerial photography, crop dusting and many other roles. The CA-6 Standard Airsedan was a six-seat cabin biplane powered by a 223.5 kW (300 hp) Wright J-6 Whirlwind engine. It was followed into production by the slightly larger CA-8 Senior Airsedan with accommodation for eight and powered by the 391 kW (525 hp) Wright Cyclone engine.

The Sport Airsedan was a three-seater of smaller dimensions than the Standard Airsedan powered by a 149 kW (200 hp) Wright J-5 or 223.5 kW (300 hp) J-6 engine. The single-seat high-performance open-cockpit Airster was a completely different design leaving the sesqui-plane configuration for a braced low wing. Power was provided by a Whirlwind or Pratt & Whitney Wasp Junior engine. The final aircraft was the single-seat Bull Pup light monoplane powered by a 33.5 kW (45 hp) Szekely SR-3 engine.

Burgess Models D to J (USA) The W. Starling Burgess Company and Curtis built several air-craft of original design, but only after it had licence-built established types. Following produc-tion of Farman, Curtiss (Model D) and Grahame-White Baby (Model E) biplanes, it

produced its Models F and J (licence-built Wright Models B and C respectively). One of each was sold to the US Army. Among the civil examples built, one was flown by Harry N. Atwood from St Louis to New York between 14 and 25 August 1911.

The Burgess Model I was of original design and was a twin-float biplane powered by a 44.7 kW (60 hp) Sturtevant engine. Designed for use as a coastal defence aircraft, a single example was sold to the US Army and flown in the Philippines until 1915. The finest aircraft of the series was undoubtedly the Burgess H powered by a 52 kW (70 hp) Renault engine. Six Model H trainers

Burgess Type H.

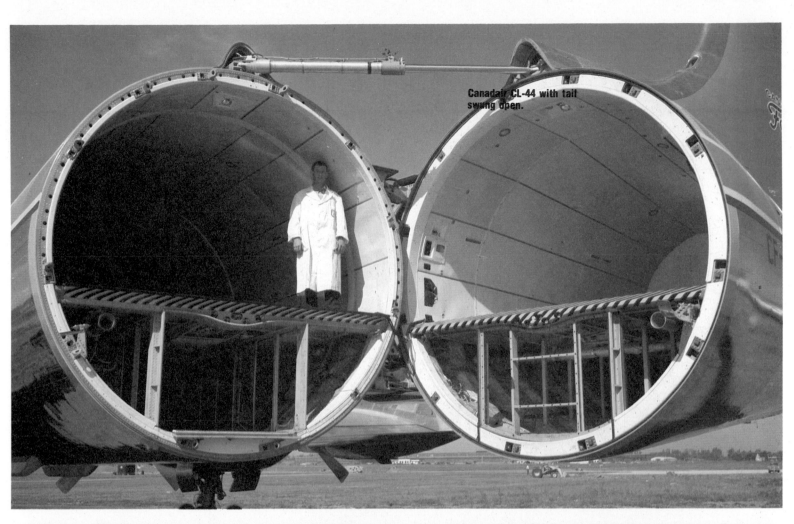

Canadair CL-44 with tail swung open.

Canadair CL-84-1.

Canadair CL-215.

CASA C-101 Aviojet.

Cessna Model 150 assembled in France by Reims Aviation.

**Reims-built Cessna A150
Aerobat.**

**Chance-Vought F7U
Cutlass fighters.**

Christen Eagle II.

Convair 880.

**Convair F-102A Delta
Dagger.**

were purchased by the US Army and these gave excellent service. The company also produced three seaplane variants of the British Dunne tailless biplane and a number of other seaplanes during 1916–18.

Burnelli UB-14B (USA) Vincent Burnelli began experimenting in the design of aircraft in 1920 and produced the Remington-Burnelli Airliner that year. It was followed by the RB-2 of 1924, CU-16 of 1927 and UB-20 of 1929. In 1936 the Burnelli UB-14B transport aircraft was produced with an aerofoil-shaped fuselage for the flight crew and fourteen passengers. Power was provided by two 507 kW (680 hp) Pratt & Whitney radial engines.

Bushby M-II Mustang II (USA) Side-by-side two-seat derivative of the Midget Mustang powered normally by a 119 kW (160 hp) Lycoming O-320 engine. Plans are available to amateur constructors and by 1979 about 800 Mustang IIs were under construction.

Bushby/Long MM-1 Midget Mustang (USA) First flown in 1948, the Midget Mustang is a single-seat fully aerobatic sporting monoplane. Two versions are available for homebuilding: the MM-1-85 with a 63.5 kW (85 hp) Continental C85-8FJ or -12 engine and the MM-1-125 with a 101 kW (135 hp) Lycoming O-290-D2 engine. By 1979 95 Midget Mustangs were flying, with 900 more under construction.

Bushmaster 2000 (USA) Modernised version of the 1920–30s Ford Tri-Motor transport aircraft produced for customers in the early 1970s and powered by 335.3 kW (450 hp) Pratt & Whitney R-985-AN-1 or AN-14B engines.

Butterworth Westland Whirlwind Mk II (USA) Single-seat ⅔-scale replica of the Whirlwind fighter powered by two 48.5 kW (65 hp) 1,600 cc Volkswagen modified motorcar engines. Plans are available to amateur constructors.

CAARP CAP 10 and 20 (France) See **Mudry**

Call-Air A series (USA) From the original Model A of the 1940s, Call-Air developed the A-2 and A-3 two–three-seat cabin monoplanes powered by 93.15 kW (125 hp) Lycoming O-290 and Continental C125 engines respectively. An agricultural version of the A-2 was also produced

with spray booms installed within the wings and carrying a jettisonable tank beneath the fuselage.

The A-4 appeared in 1954 and was built in three versions: the two–three-seat Model 150 cabin monoplane with a 112 kW (150 hp) Lycoming O-320-A2A engine; the similarly powered A-4AG agricultural two-seater with a simplified structure and specialised agricultural equipment; and the A-4 Model 180 with a 134 kW (180 hp) Lycoming O-360-C1A engine. The A-5 was similar to the A-4AG in being a tandem two-seat agricultural aircraft.

The A-6 first flew in December 1957 and was identical to the A-5 but with a 134 kW (180 hp) O-360-A1A engine. During 1959 alone, Call-Air sold 28 A-5s and 17 A-6s. The A-6 was later developed by IMCO and then by Aero Commander and Rockwell into the better known Commander agricultural single-seaters flown today.

Camair Twin Navion (USA) Twin-engined four-seat version of the North American/Ryan Navion light aircraft. The prototype CTN-A was built and flown in 1953. Production began with the CTN-B powered by two 179 kW (240 hp) Continental O-470-B engines and a total of 28 were delivered between 1955 and 1959. The CTN-C was flown in 1960 with 194 kW (260 hp) Continental IO-470-D engines and a number of Bs were brought up to this standard. The CTN-D appeared in prototype form with 224 kW (300 hp) Continental IO-520 engines. Production of new aircraft has been suspended but Camair is able to modify Bs and Cs to D configuration.

Campbell Cricket (UK) Single-seat light autogyro first flown in 1969. Among Crickets delivered were seven for shrimp-spotting duties in Kuwait.

CAMS 30 (France) Exhibited at the Paris Salon de l'Aéronautique in 1922, the CAMS 30 prototype was followed by 22 production aircraft for the French Navy and seven for Yugoslavia. It was a small single-bay biplane flying-boat powered by a 112 kW (150 hp) Hispano-Suiza 8Aa engine

CAMS

Campbell Cricket.

and intended for training. Pupil and instructor sat side-by-side. A single example of the CAMS 30T four-seat tourer was also built.

CAMS 33 (France) Winner of a contest for flying-boats sponsored by the French Navy in 1923, the CAMS 33B was a slim-hulled biplane powered by two 206 kW (275 hp) Hispano-Suiza 8 Fg water-cooled engines mounted in tandem. Pilot and co-pilot sat side-by-side in open cockpits and two gunners had cockpits in the bow and amidships. The two prototypes were followed by a small batch of production machines. Twelve went into French service for coastal reconnaissance duties with Escadrille 1 R 1 based at Cherbourg-Chantereyne, while six were exported to Yugoslavia in 1925.

A single civil variant was known as the CAMS 33C or 33T and had participated in the same competition as the military version. It had a cabin for seven passengers immediately behind the pilots' cockpits.

Data (CAMS 33B): *Engines* as above *Wing span* 17.62 m (57 ft 9¾ in) *Length* 13.23 m (43 ft 5 in) *Max T-O weight* 4,000 kg (8,818 lb) *Max level speed* 175 km/h (108.5 mph) *Range* 820 km (509 miles) *Armament* four machine-guns and light bombs

Bushmaster 2000.

Camair Twin Navion.

CAMS 37 (France) The prototype CAMS 37, a small Hurel-designed flying-boat, appeared in 1926 and featured folding biplane wings to facilitate stowage on board ship. It was followed by two amphibious prototypes. Series-built aircraft retained the mixed construction of the prototypes but had new square-cut fin and rudder assemblies. Accommodation comprised cockpits for a pilot in the forward hull and two gunners in bow and amidship positions. Power was provided by a 335.3 kW (450 hp) Lorraine 12 liquid-cooled engine driving a pusher propeller.

The CAMS 37A amphibian, of which the French Navy ordered 15 examples in 1926 and Portugal bought seven in 1929, was followed in quick succession by the CAMS 37/2 flying-boat; 37A/3 with a reinforced hull; 37A/6 with an enclosed cabin, three of which were used as admirals' barges; 37A/7 or 37LIA liaison amphibian of 1930 with an enclosed cabin; the metal-hulled 37A/9 staff officer transport, four built; and

CAMS 33B.

37/11 unarmed trainer with four open cockpits in the forward hull, delivered from 1937.

The final version to go into production was the CAMS 37/13 or CAMS 37*bis*, which had a metal hull and was strengthened for catapult launching. The CAMS 37/13 flew from a number of French ships and proved successful in a variety of roles, ranging from spotting for the guns of the fleet to casualty evacuation. The CAMS 37 family served at every French naval station as well as aboard the training cruiser *Jeanne d'Arc*. They proved sturdy and reliable both in the air and on water.

Civil versions included the one-off four-seat CAMS 37/12; CAMS 37A, two of which were handed to the local aero club in Martinique by the French Navy in 1936; CAMS 37/10, two utilised for catapult launching trials from the transatlantic liner *Ile de France*; and Guilbaud's famous CAMS 37C or CAMS 37GR, a special long-range version which made a tour around Africa and the Mediterranean between 12 October 1926 and 9 March 1927, covering more than 22,600 km (14,000 miles) in 38 stages without incident or damage to the machine.

Data (CAMS 37/13): *Engine* as above *Wing span* 14.50 m (47 ft 7 in) *Length* 11.37 m (37 ft 3½ in) *Max T-O weight* 3,080 kg (6,790 lb) *Max level speed* 180 km/h (112 mph)

CAMS 46 (France) The CAMS 46E of 1926 was a primary training biplane flying-boat with side-by-side cockpits and dual controls, developed from the CAMS 30 and differing externally in having a modified, more rounded fin and rudder. The CAMS 46ET had a more powerful engine and was intended as an intermediate trainer. One Escadrille of CAMS 46ETs was based at Hourtin for a number of years from 1928 onwards.

CAMS 51 (France) The experimental CAMS 51C biplane flying-boat, powered by two 283 kW (380 hp) Jupiter radial engines, was used by the French Aéropostale company for tests during 1928, prior to the introduction of the CAMS 53 machines. The CAMS 51 R3 was a prototype three-seat bomber-reconnaissance amphibian flying-boat which flew for the first time in January 1927. It was instrumental in the development of the CAMS 55 series.

The similarly designated CAMS 51-3 R or CAMS 51 GR broke the world height-with-load record on 18 August 1927, lifting two tonnes useful load to 4,684 m (15,368 ft). It subsequently made a pioneering flight to South America, opening up French air mail routes to that subcontinent.

CAMS 53, 56 and 58 (France) Built for passenger and air mail services on Mediterranean routes, these flying-boats were designed by Maurice Hurel. Some 30 examples of the CAMS 53 went into service from 1928. They were single-bay unstaggered biplanes with tandem engines. The original CAMS 53 was powered by

two 372.6 kW (500 hp) Hispano-Suiza 12Hbr liquid-cooled engines. Six were built, four for Aéropostale and two others were used by Air Orient. The two-man crew had an enclosed cabin and there was also a cabin for four passengers. Sixteen CAMS 53-1s and five CAMS 53-2s followed, all powered by two 432 kW (580 hp) Hispano-Suiza 12Lbr engines, the latter version having a strengthened airframe. Most CAMS 53s operated up to 1935, giving reliable service. The four CAMS 56 boats differed largely in having two 357.7 kW (480 hp) Gnome-Rhône Jupiter radials. The CAMS 58-0 was considerably strengthened and accommodated a crew of three and six passengers. Power was provided by two 447 kW (600 hp) Lorraine 12Fa engines. The experimental CAMS 58-2 with four 223.5 kW (300 hp) Lor-

raine 9Na radial engines in tandem pairs was followed by two CAMS 58-3 with twin 507 kW (680 hp) Hispano-Suizas, ordered for Air France. Accommodating four passengers, they were found unsatisfactory and soon withdrawn from service. Data (CAMS 53-1): *Engines* as above *Wing span* 20.40 m (66 ft 11¼ in) *Length* 14.82 m (48 ft 7½ in) *Max T-O weight* 6,900 kg (15,212 lb) *Max level speed* 212 km/h (131.5 mph) *Range* 1,125 km (700 miles)

CAMS 55 (France) The prototype of this equal-span single-bay biplane flying-boat flew for the first time in 1928, piloted by its designer Maurice Hurel. Largely of wooden construction, it was followed by two CAMS 55H machines, powered similarly by two tandem 447 kW (600 hp) Hispano-Suiza 12Lbr liquid-cooled engines, and two CAMS 55Js with 372.6 kW (500 hp) Jupiter radials. Standard armament for all CAMS 55 aircraft (of which 112 were built in total) was twin 0.303 in Lewis machine-guns in both bow and midships cockpits, plus two 75 kg G 2 bombs on underwing racks.

A considerable number of variants were completed, but main production versions were the CAMS 55/1 (43 built with Hispano engines); CAMS 55/2 (29 built with Jupiters); and CAMS 55/10 (32 completed from 1934 with Jupiters). The type equipped at one time or another 15 escadrilles of the French Aéronavale, being utilised principally for maritime reconnaissance and coastal patrol. Pilot and co-pilot were seated side-by-side in open cockpits and there was glazing around the bow cockpit affording good downward visibility. Twenty-nine CAMS 55s were still in escadrille service at the outbreak of war in September 1939.

Data (CAMS 55/10): *Engines* as above *Wing span* 20.4 m (66 ft 11¼ in) *Length* 15.03 m (49 ft 3¾ in) *Max T-O weight* 6,900 kg (15,212 lb) *Max level speed* 195 km/h (121.2 mph) *Range* 1,300 km (808 miles)

Canadair CL-44.

Canadair Sabre
production line.

Canadair Four (Canada) The Four or C-4 was designed in its early North Star versions to meet specifications of Trans-Canada Air Lines and the Royal Canadian Air Force. Incorporating the airframe features of the Douglas DC-4 and DC-6, it was powered by four 1,311.5 kW (1,760 hp) Rolls-Royce Merlin 626 engines. Twenty-four were produced for the RCAF in a military version known as the C-54GM; 20 commercial pressurised airliners went to TCA as DC-4M2s; BOAC received 22 in 1949 as Argonauts; and four went to Canadian Pacific Air Lines.

Canadair Five (Canada) A larger and more powerful version of the North Star, the Five was completed during 1950 for the RCAF. Powered by four 1,565 kW (2,100 hp) Pratt & Whitney R-2800-CA15 18-cylinder radial engines, it was used as a long-range crew trainer and VIP transport for government and military officials.

Canadair CL-44.

Canadair 400 and CL-44 (Canada) The CL-44 is still flown today as a long-range freight-carrying aircraft, based on the Bristol Britannia. The first production version had conventional side-loading doors. Twelve were supplied as CC-106 Yukons to the RCAF as personnel and freight transports, the first flying in November 1959.

Commercial Forty-Fours (with four 4,270 kW; 5,730 eshp Rolls-Royce Tyne RTy.12 Mk 515/10 turboprops) were built with swing-tails for straight-in loading as CL-44D4s, and the prototype of this version was the world's first swing-tail long-range transport when it flew for the first time on 16 November 1960. Deliveries began in June 1961 and by 1965 production aircraft had been delivered to Seaboard World Airlines (7), Slick Airways (4), Flying Tiger Line (10), Japan Cargo Airways (3) and Loftleidir Icelandic Airlines (2). One Seaboard aircraft was leased to BOAC.

Canadair Sabre 2s.

228

The last of four CL-44s eventually bought by Loftleidir for transatlantic services was delivered as a CL-44J or Canadair 400 with a 4.57 m (15 ft) longer fuselage and accommodation for up to 214 passengers instead of the normal 178 passengers. It first flew on 8 November 1965. Three CL-44D4s were also converted to this standard for the airline and were operated by Cargolux. Meanwhile, RCAF Yukons had been withdrawn from service by 1972 and these entered commercial service as CL-44-6s.

Data (Canadair 400): *Engines* as above *Wing span* 43.37 m (142 ft 3½ in) *Length* 46.28 m (151 ft 9¾ in) *Max T-O weight* 95,250 kg (210,000 lb) *Max cruising speed* 621 km/h (386 mph) *Range* 5,245 km (3,260 miles)

Canadair Sabre (Canada) During 1949 Canadair began quantity production of the Sabre single-seat jet fighter for the RCAF under licence from North American Aviation Inc. The prototype first flew on 9 August 1950 as an F-86A or Sabre Mk 1. Initial production aircraft were F-86Es or Sabre Mk 2s, powered ey General Electric J47-GE-13 engines. Following the Mk 4, a modified Mk 2, the Mk 6 entered production with an Avro Orenda 14 engine, rated at 32.36 kN (7,275 lb st).

Canadair Silver Star (Canada) Licence-built Lockheed T-33A two-seat jet trainer powered by a 22.67 kN (5,100 lb st) Rolls-Royce Nene 10 turbojet engine.

Canadair CL-28/CP-107 Argus (Canada) The Argus is a long-range maritime patrol aircraft built as a modification of the basic Bristol Britannia design. First flown on 28 March 1957, the first aircraft was accepted by the RCAF in September 1958 and 33 were delivered in total. Two versions were produced: the Argus Mk 1 with a large chin radome housing American APS-20 search radar (13 aircraft); and the Argus Mk 2 with a smaller chin radome housing new equipment including British ASV-21 radar. Production was completed in 1960.

Data (Argus Mk 2): *Engines* four 2,757 kW (3,700 hp) Wright R-3350 (TC18EA1) Turbo

Compounds *Wing span* 43.37 m (142 ft 3½ in) *Length* 39.09 m (128 ft 3 in) *Max T-O weight* 67,130 kg (148,000 lb) *Max level speed* 507 km/h (315 mph) *Range* more than 6,440 km (4,000 miles) *Armament* two bomb bays each able to accommodate 1,815 kg (4,000 lb) of stores, including homing torpedoes; provision for carrying 1,724 kg (3,800 lb) of weapons under each wing

Canadair CL-41/CT-114 (Canada) Two-seat side-by-side jet trainer first flown on 13 January 1960. The CL-41A was the basic trainer version with optional light armament. It became the standard ab initio/basic trainer of the Canadian Armed Forces (190 acquired as CT-114 Tutors). The CL-41G was the tactical combat version, suitable also for training roles; powered by an Orenda-built General Electric J85-J4 turbojet engine of 13.12 kN (2,950 lb st). It was also provided with additional armour plating and can carry up to 1,815 kg (4,000 lb) of weapons on six attachment points under the wings and fuselage. Twenty were delivered to the Royal Malaysian Air Force as Tebuans.

Data (CT-114 Tutor): *Engine* one 11.71 kN (2,633 lb st) Orenda-built General Electric turbojet *Wing span* 11.13 m (36 ft 6 in) *Length* 9.75 m (32 ft 0 in) *Max T-O weight* 3,355 kg (7,397 lb) *Max level speed* 801 km/h (498 mph)

Canadair CL-66/Canadair 540 (Canada) The Canadair CL-66, which was marketed as the Canadair 540, was a development of the Convair 440 Metropolitan with two 2,504 kW (3,360 eshp) Napier Eland NE1.6 Mk 503 turboprops. The first production aircraft flew in January 1960. Two versions were produced as the 540-A 48–64-passenger and 540-B all-cargo airliners. In addition to commercial sales, ten passenger/freight convertible models were delivered to the RCAF as CC-109s.

Canadair CL-84 (Canada) Twin-engined tilt-wing V/STOL experimental aircraft first flown on 19 February 1970.

Canadair CL-90 (Canada) Canadair designation of 200 strike-reconnaissance and 110 fighter versions of the Lockheed F-104G Starfighter built under licence in Canada for the RCAF (CF-104s).

Canadair CL-215 (Canada) The CL-215 is a twin-engined amphibian intended primarily for firefighting but adaptable to a wide range of other duties. First flown on 23 October 1967, production aircraft have been delivered to the Sécurité Civile of France (15), Province of Quebec (15), Spanish government (10 mainly for search and rescue), Greek government (7), Province of Manitoba (1) and the Royal Thai Navy (2 for search and rescue).

Data: *Engines* two 1,566 kW (2,100 hp) Pratt & Whitney R-2800-83AM2AH, -83AM12AD or -CA3 radials *Wing span* 28.6 m (93 ft 10 in) *Length* 19.82 m (65 ft 0½ in) *Max T-O weight* 19,731 kg (43,500 lb) *Cruising speed* 291 km/h (181 mph) *Range* 2,260 km (1,405 miles) *Accommodation* as water bomber a crew of two on flight deck and 2,673 litres (588 Imp gallons) of water in fuselage tanks; as a utility aircraft 8–19 passengers, nine stretchers or other specialised equipment

Canadair CL-600 Challenger (Canada) In 1976 Canadair acquired exclusive rights to design, manufacture, market and support the LearStar 600 from the late William P. Lear Snr. First flown in 1978, it is a 30-passenger or freight-carrying business, cargo and commuter transport aircraft, powered by two 33.36 kN (7,500 lb st) Avco Lycoming ALF 502L turbofan engines. By May 1978 sales of the executive version had reached 102.

Canadian Avro CF-100 and CF-105 Arrow (Canada) First flown in January 1950, the CF-100 was the first and only Canadian-designed and

Canadair Silver Stars.

Canadair CT-114 Tutor (foreground) flies alongside a Canadair-built CF-5B.

Canadair 540.

Canadair Argus 2.

**Canadair CL-215
water-bomber.**

built fighter to enter service. Some 692 were built for the RCAF and 53 for export to Belgium by Avro Aircraft of Canada. The last were retired from training duties in 1980. Power was provided by two 32.36 kN (7,275 lb st) Orenda M11 or 14 turbojet engines.

The CF-105 Arrow was a very advanced interceptor which first flew in 1958. It was cancelled in 1959.

**Canadair CL-84 landing
on board ship.**

Canadair CF-104 (CL-90).

CAP 1–5 (Brazil) Companhia Aeronáutica Paulista was formed to build and repair aircraft. It produced a series of three powered light aeroplanes of original design: the CAP 1 Planalto two-seat advanced trainer; CAP 4 Paulistinha two-seat primary trainer and touring high-wing monoplane (also 4B Ambulancia carrying one stretcher and 4C Paulistinha Radio for military observation and liaison); and CAP 5 Carioca light touring monoplane. The company also built the Saracura primary and Alcatraz secondary training gliders. Production was abandoned in 1948 due to financial problems.

CANSA C.5 and C.6 (Italy) The C.5 was a single-engined (67 kW; 90 hp Fiat A.50 or 97 kW; 130 hp Alfa Romeo 910-8) trainer of the late 1930s produced for civil use. The C.6 was a development of the C.5.

CANSA Lictor 90 and 130 (Italy) Light cantilever low-wing cabin monoplanes of 1935 powered by 67 kW (90 hp) Fiat and 97 kW (130 hp) de Havilland Gipsy Major engines respectively.

Caproni A.P.1 (Italy) Designed by Cesar Pallavicino of the Caproni Aeronautica Bergamasca company, the A.P.1 was intended exclusively for ground-attack work. It was a low-wing cantilever monoplane of mixed construction. The two prototypes built were single-seat machines. Limited production was undertaken and series aircraft

**Canadair CL-600
Challenger.**

had a crew of two seated under a glazed canopy. The trousered undercarriage of the second prototype was replaced by a more simple arrangement and wheel spats could be fitted. Of 66 production aircraft delivered between 1936 and 1938, ten went to Franco's forces in Spain in late 1938, while seven were exported to Paraguay and four to Salvador. The rest were used (largely for propaganda film purposes) by the Regia Aeronautica. There is no record of the A.P.1 ever having seen action. Armament was two wing-mounted 7.7 mm machine-guns plus a further 7.7 mm weapon on a flexible mounting. Up to 400 kg (882 lb) of bombs could be carried.

Data: *Engine* normally one 522 kW (700 hp) Alfa Romeo 125 RC 35 radial *Wing span* 12.0 m (39 ft 4½ in) *Length* 8.69 m (28 ft 6¼ in) *Max T-O weight* 2,230 kg (4,916 lb) *Max level speed* 355 km/h (220.5 mph) *Range* 1,100 km (684 miles)

Caproni biplane (Italy) Large biplane of 1910 powered by an 18.63 kW (25 hp) Miller engine driving two wing-mounted tractor propellers.

Caproni monoplane (Italy) Advanced-looking monoplane of 1913 powered by a 59.6 kW (80 hp) Gnome rotary engine. One of the most successful pre-World War I Italian aircraft.

Caproni Ca 1, Ca 2 and Ca 3 series (Italy) In 1913 pioneer aircraft designer Gianni Caproni designed a bomber of advanced concept powered by three engines, all contained in a central crew nacelle. Two engines drove tractor propellers by means of extension gearing and the third a pusher propeller at the rear of the nacelle. There was little official interest in the design and no construction was undertaken. However a Caproni prototype bomber flew for the first time in October 1914 with a 74.5 kW (100 hp) Gnome rotary engine at the rear of the central nacelle driving a pusher propeller and two 59.6 kW (80 hp) Gnomes conventionally mounted on the lower wings driving tractor propellers. Two booms extended aft of the wing engines to support the triple rudder tailplane. The Italian government was slow to grasp the possibilities of the new design, but eventually a contract was signed for 12 Caproni 300HP

bombers powered by three 74.5 kW (100 hp) Fiat A.10 engines. A further 150 were delivered during the next two years. These aircraft were also known as Ca 1s and were followed by nine Ca 350HP machines (with the third engine replaced by a 112 kW; 150 hp Isotta Fraschini) designated Ca 2.

Ca 3 (or Ca 33) was in fact the alternative designation of the Ca 450HP, 299 of which were built between 1917 and 1919. Powered by three 112 kW (150 hp) Isotta Fraschini V.4B engines, the Ca 3 proved the most successful Allied bomber of World War I, taking part in many outstanding raids. Normal bomb load was 200 kg (485 lb) and defensive 7.7 mm machine-guns were mounted over the nose cockpit and in a precarious open position which comprised a tubular metal structure incorporating a ladder leading from the rear of the central nacelle (just in front of the engine) to a gun ring just behind and slightly higher than the trailing edge of the upper wing centre section.

Caproni A.P.1s.

Caproni Ca 36.

Ca 3s equipped three bomber Gruppi by the end of 1917 and made attacks in numbers on Pola, Kotor naval base, railway junctions and troop concentrations. Licence production was undertaken in France by Robert Esnault-Pelterie, 83 examples being completed. Two French bomber Groupes co-operated with the Italian Ca 3-equipped XVIII Gruppo, which had been sent to the Western Front. They made damaging night raids on targets along the Marne as well as attacking troop concentrations near Amiens. In Italy Ca 3s hindered the Austrian advance from the Piave and gave strong support to the final victorious Italian offensive.

With the revival of Italian air power by Mussolini and the formation of the Regia Aeronautica in 1923, the Ca 3 design was given a new lease of life. A handful of surviving Ca 3s bore witness to the longevity and effectiveness of the design and so orders were given to place it back in production in the Ca 3 mod or Ca 36 versions. A number of minor improvements and production sim-

plifications were incorporated and 153 were built over three years. Eighteen Ca 3 mods took part in the 1925 military manoeuvres. The same year eight machines were sent to Libya in support of the reconquest of that territory. By the end of 1926, however, the last examples had been withdrawn from first-line service.

Immediately post-war 20 Ca 1s and Ca 3s had been briefly utilised as passenger transports. Data (Ca 33): *Engines* as above *Wing span* 22.2 m (72 ft 10 in) *Length* 10.9 m (35 ft 9 in) *Max T-O weight* 3,312 kg (7,301 lb) *Max level speed* 135 km/h (85 mph) *Range* 450 km (280 miles) *Armament* two–four 7.7 mm Revelli machine-guns, plus up to 454 kg (1,000 lb) of bombs

Caproni Ca 4 series (Italy) A number of these sizeable triplane bombers flew operationally over northern Italy during 1918. They were impressive not only in flight – with their three equal-span wings and their multiplicity of struts and wires – but also in the construction techniques employed. Power was supplied by three engines, early aircraft having 223.6 kW (300 hp) Fiat A.12s or Isotta Fraschini V.5s, while later machines had 298 kW (400 hp) American Liberties. One engine was mounted to drive a pusher propeller at the rear of the central crew nacelle; the other two were tractor-mounted in front of the middle wing leading edge in the noses of the twin booms (each with a midships gunner's cockpit) which extended to the rear to support the tailplane.

The prototype and the first three production Ca 4s had angular crew nacelles, but all later examples of the Ca 1000HP (its initial designation arising from the total horsepower provided by the prototype's engines) had carefully contoured rounded nacelles. A third gunner's cockpit was located at the front of the nacelle forward of the side-by-side cockpits for the pilot and co-pilot. Max bomb load was 1,000 kg (2,204 lb). Total production of all versions of the Ca 4 was 42. Six of

Canadian Avro CF-100 Mk 5D.

Caproni monoplane, retrospectively known as the Ca 14.

Caproni

Caproni Ca 42.

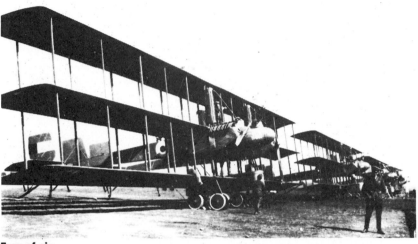

Four of six Liberty-powered Caproni Ca 4s delivered to the RNAS but returned to Italy.

the 23 Liberty-powered Ca 4s built were sold to Britain and used briefly, though not operationally, by the Royal Naval Air Service.

One Ca 4 was converted to a seaplane by the substitution of huge twin floats for the land undercarriage. Post-war, the Ca 48 23-passenger conversion made a notable flight from Milan to London in 1919. Another civil conversion for 30 passengers was tested the following year under the designation Ca 58.

Data (Liberty engines): *Engines* as above *Wing span* 29.9 m (98 ft 1¼ in) *Length* 15.1 m (49 ft 6½ in) *Max T-O weight* 7,500 kg (16,535 lb) *Max level speed* 140 km/h (87 mph)

Caproni Ca 5 series (Italy) Originally known as the Caproni 600HP because of the total horse-power of its three engines, the prototype of the Ca 5 series first flew in 1917. It was intended to

improve upon the performance of the outstanding Ca 3 bomber family and immediate plans were made for a vast production programme involving a number of Italian and American firms. Compared with its predecessor, wing area was increased, the crew nacelle was entirely redesigned and took on a sleeker aerodynamic form, and a new undercarriage was fitted. Various versions with different power plants – including 186.3 kW (250 hp) Fiat A.12s, Isotta Fraschinis of the same power and 261 kW (350 hp) Liberty engines – were developed and production continued from 1918 to 1921.

Unfortunately the Ca 5 was unpopular with its crews. It offered no real advantages over the trusty Ca 3 and the most used engine, the Fiat A.12, had a tendency to catch fire during flight. Nevertheless, 669 aircraft were completed in Italy, including ten examples of the Piaggio-built I.Ca floatplane version; but the end of the war abruptly terminated the American production programme after only five machines had been completed. French construction had also started, but again only a few examples were delivered. Later, the Italians reinstated production of the Ca 3, which easily outlived the Ca 5, on which the Allies had pinned such high hopes. Production orders for the Ca 5 had totalled 3,900 to be built in Italy, 1,500 in the USA and 150 in France.

Ca 5s did operate during 1918 with several Italian units, with the United States Northern Bombing Group and with the French 2ème Groupe de Bombardement. The French and American units co-operated in operations over the Western Front. Defensive armament was two 7.7 mm machine-guns. Max bomb load was 900 kg (1,984 lb).

The Caproni company also developed an eight-passenger civil version in 1919 and the Breda company christened a similar conversion the Italia I, but apart from these little was heard of the Ca 5 post-war.

Data (Fiat engines): *Engines* as above *Wing span* 23.4 m (76 ft 9¼ in) *Length* 12.62 m (41 ft 5 in) *Max T-O weight* 4,920 kg (10,846 lb) *Max level speed* 152 km/h (94.5 mph) *Range* 600 km (373 miles)

Caproni Ca 73 series (Italy) The newly formed Regia Aeronautica, created by Benito Mussolini in 1923, initially relied for its heavy bombing force on the 1916 Ca 3 design. But a modern replacement was needed and development of the new Ca 73 was speeded up. It was intended as Italy's response to the thoughts of its strategic bombing prophet Gen Giulio Douhet, who gained an international reputation for his far-seeing ideas. The prototype flew in 1925. Interestingly the basic design remained unchanged through a large number of versions. It was a two-bay inverted sesquiplane with two engines mounted in tandem between the wings. The undercarriage was of the divided type and the tailplane was of the popular but cumbersome biplane configuration. Armament comprised a single 7.7 mm machine-gun in each of the open nose and midship gunners' cockpits and a ventral tunnel position. Bombs were carried on external racks on the fuselage sides.

Caproni Ca 46, one version of the Ca 5.

Production versions included the Ca 73*bis*, which had Lorraine engines each delivering 335.3kW (450 hp) instead of the original 305.5 kW (410 hp); Ca 82 (originally Ca 73*ter*) with 380 kW (510 hp) Isotta Fraschinis; Ca 80 with 298 kW (400 hp) Jupiter radials; Ca 80S, a paratroop transport/air ambulance; and Ca 82 Co, a colonial bomber/transport. The most radical redesign appeared in the Ca 73*quater* (or Ca 88), which had new control systems and improved constructional features; and the Ca 73*quater*G (or Ca 89), which had 380 kW (510 hp) Isotta Fraschini engines and a manually operated dorsal gun turret, extensively glazed nose for bomb-aiming, as well as a retractable ventral 'dustbin' turret. Underwing racks for the bomb load replaced those originally located on the fuselage sides.

The Ca 73 type remained with the Italian first-line night bomber Squadriglie until 1934. It was operated from Blida aerodrome from 1926 onwards against rebellious desert tribesmen and flown during Italy's North African campaigns of the early 1930s, latterly with the generic designation Ca 74.

Data (Ca 73*quater*G/Ca 89): *Engines* as above *Wing span* 25.0 m (82 ft 0¼ in) *Length* 15.1 m (49 ft 6½ in) *Max T-O weight* 6,200 kg (13,668 lb) *Max level speed* 180 km/h (112 mph) *Range* 650 km (404 miles)

Caproni Ca 97 (Italy) Six-passenger high-wing monoplane transport aircraft of the early 1930s powered normally by a 335.3 kW (450 hp) Jupiter or similar radial engine. Thirteen were operated by the Regia Aeronautica and commercially, some of the civil aircraft being powered by three smaller engines in the 108 kW (145 hp) Walter Mars or 74.5 kW (100 hp) Lorraine-Dietrich class.

Caproni Ca 100 (Italy) The 1928 prototype of this two-seat open-cockpit biplane was followed by 680 production machines for the Regia Aeronautica, built by Caproni and several other firms. Thirty Macchi-constructed Ca 100s were given the suffix 'Idro' and completed as twin-float seaplane trainers.

The 'Caproncino' (as it was affectionately called) was evolved from the de Havilland D.H. 60 Moth, for which Caproni held a manufacturing licence. It had a redesigned tailplane and new wings of typical Caproni format, the lower wing having greater span than the upper one. Various engines were utilised, chiefly the 85.7 kW (115 hp) Isotta Fraschini Asso 80R and 108 kW (145 hp) Colombo S.63 liquid-cooled in-lines and the 63.3 kW (85 hp) Fiat A50 uncowled radial.

The military machines were used as primary trainers and for liaison work. A number of civil tourers were also sold and Ca 100s were exported to Portugal and Peru, the latter country building some under licence. A small batch were also built by Caproni's Bulgarian subsidiary under the designation KB-1.

Data (Colombo S.63 engine): *Engine* as above *Wing span* 10.0 m (32 ft 9¾ in) *Length* 7.3 m (23 ft 10¾ in) *Max T-O weight* 760 kg (1,675 lb) *Max level speed* 180 km/h (112 mph)

An American-built (Standard Aircraft) Caproni Ca 5.

Caproni Ca 73.

Caproni Ca 101 (Italy) The Ca 101 D2 was a high-wing strut-braced cabin monoplane powered by three 179 kW (240 hp) Alfa Romeo D2 uncowled radial engines. It was built in limited numbers as a colonial bomber-transport and achieved notoriety in the Italian campaign in Abyssinia during 1935–6. Strongly constructed and fitted with Handley Page leading-edge slats, the Ca 101s were slow but tough and were effective in providing the advancing Italian columns with bombing support and supplies. Their poor performance was not a problem as there was no air opposition. Armament comprised four 7.7 mm machine-guns firing from a retractable dorsal turret, a ventral bulge and lateral window ports. The bomb load was carried externally under the fuselage.

Although a few civil Ca 101s were flown on colonial passenger routes for several years (with various Walter, Piaggio and Alfa Romeo engines of 149–313 kW; 200–420 hp), the military Ca 101s were withdrawn from first-line service immediately after the Abyssinian campaign. A development of the Ca 101 was also produced for the Regia Aeronautica as the Ca 102, powered by four engines in tandem pairs and with a nose-gunner's position. At least one was flown experimentally.

Data: *Engines* as above *Wing span* 19.68 m (64 ft 6¾ in) *Length* 14.37 m (47 ft 1¾ in) *Max T-O weight* 3,950 kg (8,708 lb) *Max level speed* 208 km/h (129 mph) *Range* 1,000 km (621 miles)

Caproni

Caproni Ca 97.

Caproni Ca 111 (Italy) Intended for long-range reconnaissance duties, the four-seat single-engined Ca 111 was an enlarged and refined development of the earlier Ca 97, 13 of which had been built. It was a high-wing strut-braced cabin monoplane with a fixed undercarriage, the separate main units of which had spatted wheels. Armament comprised three or four 7.7 mm machine-guns and up to 600 kg (1,323 lb) of bombs. Power was provided normally by a 723 kW (970 hp) Isotta Fraschini Asso 750 RC liquid-cooled engine with a nose radiator. One hundred and forty-eight production Ca 111*bis* Ric aircraft followed the prototype and four pre-production machines, and deliveries to the Regia Aeronautica were completed in 1936. Of these, 25 machines were fitted initially with large twin floats and employed by long-range maritime reconnaissance units, but were subsequently converted to landplane configuration. During the Italian conquest of Abyssinia, Ca 111*bis* aircraft were used for reconnaissance, bombing, transport and casualty evacuation. They were later operated against dissident tribesmen in Italy's African empire and after Italy's entry into World War II were utilised in North and East Africa and in the Balkans.
Data: *Engines* as above *Wing span* 19.68 m (64 ft 6¾ in) *Length* 15.3 m (50 ft 2½ in) *Max T-O weight* 5,350 kg (11,795 lb) *Max level speed* 280 km/h (174 mph) *Range* 2,000 km (1,242 miles)

Caproni Ca 113 (Italy) The Ca 113 two-seat aerobatic trainer won fame when a single-seat conversion piloted by Mario di Bernardi won the aerobatic trophy at the 1931 Cleveland Air Races,

USA. It was built in limited numbers for military and civil use. Dual controls were fitted and the type was used as an advanced trainer as well as for aerobatic work. Power was provided either by a 238.5 kW (320 hp) Piaggio Stella VII C 35 or a 179 kW (240 hp) Walter Castor radial engine. The single-seat Ca 113 AQ special conversion, with a supercharged 395 kW (530 hp) Pegasus engine, set a world altitude record of 14,433 m (47,352 ft) on 11 April 1934, piloted by Renato Donati.

The Bulgarian Caproni subsidiary company at Kazanlik built a series of Ca 113 developments between 1937 and 1939, designated KB-2, -3, -4 and -5. Production of all four versions totalled 107.

Caproni Ca 114 (Italy) A single-seat fighter developed from the Ca 113 two-seat biplane. Powered by a 380 kW (510 hp) Bristol Mercury radial engine, it attained 355 km/h (220 mph), but was rejected by the Italian government. A small batch was subsequently built to meet an export order from Peru.

Caproni Ca 123 (Italy) Interesting prototype of a 28-passenger cantilever low-wing monoplane airliner of the mid-1930s, powered by two Gnome-Rhône K-14 radial engines.

Caproni Ca 132 (Italy) Interesting prototype of a 20-passenger three-engined airliner.

Caproni Ca 133 (Italy) Serialled MM 283, the first Ca 133 prototype made its initial flight from Taliedo airfield in December 1934, piloted by Mario di Bernardi. A second prototype was followed by 417 series-built aircraft produced over the next eight years for the Regia Aeronautica. In addition a small batch was exported to Austria.

A high-wing strut-braced monoplane of mixed construction, the Ca 133 was developed from the Ca 101 and Ca 111, but was heavier and aerodynamically more refined. The fixed wide-track undercarriage was provided with wheel spats. Pilot and co-pilot were seated side-by-side in an enclosed cabin, the latter acting as bomb-aimer. Defensive armament comprised four 7.7 mm (0.303 in) Lewis machine-guns, of which two were operated through portholes either side of the fuselage and a third from a rear ventral position. The fourth machine-gun in the Ca 133T version (329 built) was on a flexible mounting operated through the cabin floor, while the remaining 67 bomber-transports each had a retractable dorsal turret.

Caproni Ca 100.

I-BERC

Maximum offensive load which could be carried in the bomb bay was 300 kg (661 lb), while two 250 kg (551 lb) or 500 kg (1,102 lb) bombs could be attached to underfuselage racks. As a transport, 16 fully equipped troops were accommodated. Under-powered with three 343 kW (460 hp) Piaggio P VII C.16 radials in long-chord cowlings, the Ca 133 had a very modest performance. However, known affectionately as the 'Caprona', it was available for the later stages of the conquest of Abyssinia. In 1939 Ca 133s airlifted invasion troops to Albania. By June 1940 it equipped 14 bomber Squadriglie in East Africa, having performed well against minimal air opposition, but suffered heavy losses during the victorious British campaign in 1940 and 1941.

In other theatres of war the Ca 133 was used for transport and liaison work, operating in Italy, in support of the Italian air expeditionary force in Belgium during autumn 1940, in North Africa, the Balkans and on the Russian Front. Ca 133s were also employed as trainers and 21 Ca 133S (Sanitario) specialised air ambulances were augmented by a number of conversions.

A number of Ca 133s were also flown as 16-passenger commercial airliners until the outbreak of war by Ala Littoria on its East African services.
Data: *Engines* as above *Wing span* 21.24 m (69 ft 7½ in) *Length* 15.36 m (50 ft 4¾ in) *Max T-O weight* 6,700 kg (14,771 lb) *Max level speed* 280 km/h (174 mph) *Range* 1,350 km (839 miles)
Caproni Ca 135 (Italy) A twin-engined medium bomber, the Ca 135 was a mid-wing monoplane with twin fins and rudders. It flew for the first time on 1 April 1936. Six were ordered by Peru and deliveries took place in 1938–9. The Tipo Peru had retractable dorsal and ventral gun turrets and 671 kW (900 hp) Isotta Fraschini Asso IX RC 40 in-line engines. Thirty-two Asso-powered bombers were also delivered to the Regia Aeronautica during 1938, but an Italian order for 32 Piaggio P XI RC 11 radial-powered Ca 135*bis* machines was finally diverted to Hungary. Meanwhile eight aircraft with Fiat A 80 RC 41 radials had been flown to assist the Franco Nationalist forces in Spain. Three were lost en route to Majorca (in a storm) and the remaining five were refused by the Spanish, seeing out their days in Italian training units.

Caproni Ca 114.

Caproni Ca 135*bis* in Hungarian service.

Following completion of the original Hungarian order in August 1940, a further 32 machines, designated Ca 135*bis*/U (for Ungaria), were ordered and delivered in early 1942. The Hungarian machines featured extensively glazed noses and glazed ventral panels, and each had a manually operated dorsal turret located just behind the cockpit. Armament comprised two 12.7 mm and one 7.7 mm machine-guns, plus up to 1,600 kg (3,527 lb) of bombs. Although outmoded, these bombers took part in the invasion of the Soviet Union, making some early effective raids in the Ukraine against coastal targets. The last offensive missions were carried out in the summer of 1943.
Data: *Engines* as above *Wing span* 18.8 m (61 ft 8¼ in) *Length* 13.7 m (44 ft 11½ in) *Max T-O weight* 9,600 kg (21,164 lb) *Max level speed* 440 km/h (273 mph) *Range* 2,000 km (1,242 miles)
Caproni Ca 148 (Italy) The Ca 148 was a 1937 development of the Ca 133. Intended for passenger operations in the Italian colonial empire,

Caproni Ca 101.

Caproni

the type was in series production from 1938 to 1943. Over 100 were completed and a number remained in service post-war. The high-wing configuration of the Ca 133 was retained and power was provided by three 343 kW (460 hp) Piaggio Stella VII radial engines.

Caproni Ca 161 (Italy) This was a high-altitude record-breaking biplane, developed from the Ca 113, but radically lightened, being stripped to the barest essentials. Power was provided by a 521.6 kW (700 hp) Piaggio P.XI RC 100 engine, driving a specially designed four-blade airscrew. The wing was a new design of greatly increased span. With the Ca 161 Mario Pezzi took the world altitude record to 15,655 m (51,361 ft) on 8 May 1937. Flying the Ca 161bis he improved on this by reaching 17,083 m (56,046 ft) on 22 October 1938, a record which still stands for piston-engined aircraft. The altitude record for seaplanes was also raised by the Ca 161 Idro NS on 25 September 1939, when 13,542 m (44,429 ft) was attained.

Caproni Ca 309 Ghibli.

Caproni Ca 164 (Italy) Originally intended as a two-seat primary trainer, the Ca 164 was designed by Raffaele Conflenti and retained the inverted sesquiplane layout of the elderly Ca 100. When the prototype accomplished its first flight on 17 November 1938, it displayed worrying qualities and proved unsuitable for its designed task. Therefore most of the 280 machines supplied to the Regia Aeronautica between 1939 and 1941 flew on liaison duties with headquarters and bomber units. The French Armée de l'Air also acquired 100 examples, all being delivered before the June 1940 Armistice. The French machines closely resembled their Italian counterparts, except for slightly modified wheel spats. Power was provided by a 138 kW (185 hp) Alfa Romeo 115 Ibis engine, giving a maximum speed of 217 km/h (135 mph).

Caproni Ca 308 Borea (Italy) Following the appearance of the Ca 306 prototype at the 1935 Milan Exhibition, a series of seven Ca 308 production aircraft was built. Two went to the Italian

Caproni Ca 310.

colonial government in Libya and the rest were utilised by Ala Littoria on passenger routes. Each had accommodation for a three-man crew and seven passengers, plus freight. They were of wooden construction covered with ply and fabric. Power was provided by two 149 kW (200 hp) Alfa Romeo or D.H. Gipsy Six engines. Cruising speed was 210 km/h (130.5 mph).

Caproni Ca 309 Ghibli (Italy) This slim two-crew cantilever low-wing monoplane was intended for general-purpose work with an emphasis on colonial duties. A total of 243 of all versions (including trainers and ambulances) were built between 1936 and 1943 and were used in Libya and in Metropolitan Italy. The Ghibli was a neat aircraft with single strut undercarriage legs and wheel spats and had a large curved single fin and rudder. It could carry up to 336 kg (741 lb) of bombs in an internal bay, the underside of the nose being glazed for bomb-aiming. When armament was installed it comprised two fixed 7.7 mm machine-guns in the wing leading edges and a third gun flexibly mounted in the nose. Power was provided by two 145.3 kW (195 hp) Alfa Romeo 115 engines, giving a maximum speed of 250 km/h (155.3 mph).

Caproni Ca 310 to Ca 316 series (Italy) The Ca 310 to Ca 316 (designed by Ing Cesare Pallaviciono) originated from the Ca 308 Borea and Ca 309 Ghibli. They were all twin-engined general-purpose military monoplanes with retractable undercarriages. The Ca 310 Libeccio prototype took to the air for the first time on 20 February 1937. Two hundred and three Ca 310s went into Regia Aeronautica service, while batches were sold to Peru, Norway and Yugoslavia. The Spanish Nationalists received 16 machines in 1939, but all except three of a 36-aircraft order from Hungary were rejected as unsuitable.

The Libeccio was armed with two fixed forward-firing wing-mounted 7.7 mm machine-guns, plus a further 7.7. mm weapon in a dorsal turret. The weapons bay accommodated 400 kg (882 lb) of bombs. Power was provided by two 350 kW (470 hp) Piaggio P.VII C 35 radials.

Intended principally for reconnaissance duties with bombing as a secondary role, Regia Aeronautica Ca 310s were pressed into service in North Africa for ground-attack duties for several months after Italy's entry into World War II, but with little success. Twelve Ca 310bis aircraft were bought by Yugoslavia, featuring for the first time an unstepped fully glazed nose section. These had

Gnome-Rhône 9K radial engines and were followed by 15 Ca 311s with more extensive glazing. Some 320 Ca 311s were eventually delivered to the Italian air arm, production terminating in September 1941. The nose glazing distorted visibility and later aircraft were delivered as Ca 311Ms, which reverted to a stepped pilot's cabin.

The Ca 311 retained the same bomb load as the Ca 310, but had a ventral flexibly mounted machine-gun. However the fixed forward-firing armament was reduced to a single 7.7 mm weapon in the port wing. The Piaggio engines were retained, but increased all-up weight resulted in poorer performance. Thirty-nine Ca 312s for export, with 521.6 kW (700 hp) Piaggio P.XVI engines driving three-bladed airscrews, were delivered to the Regia Aeronautica after Belgium and Norway had been overrun.

The Ca 313 and Ca 314 were powered by 521.6 kW (700 hp) Isotta Fraschini Delta RC 35 in-line engines. The Ca 313 received export orders of 200 from France and 300 from Britain in 1939, but the only examples delivered were five French machines. In 1941 Sweden obtained 84 Ca 313 RPB1s, with unstepped fully glazed noses. The same year 120 Ca 313 RPB2s (with stepped cabins) were delivered to the Regia Aeronautica. Armament remained unchanged from that of the Ca 311. The ventral gunner, however, operated his 7.7 mm machine-gun from a bulged position instead of through a simple trapdoor. Maximum speed increased to 435 km/h (270.5 mph), making it 75 km/h (46.5 mph) faster than the Ca 310.

Germany ordered 905 Ca 313G crew trainers from Caproni in 1942. Delivery rate was poor and the trickle dried up in September 1944 after 114 had been completed. The Ca 314 was the last of the line to be built in quantity. It had structural strengthening, the modified stepped nose of the Ca 313G and heavier armament. These changes further increased all-up weight, reducing performance even more. The Italians received 72 Ca 314As for convoy patrol duties, 80 Ca 314B torpedo-bombers and 254 Ca 314C (C for Combattimento) attack-light bombers. The Ca 314C was the most heavily armed, with four fixed forward-firing 12.7 mm SAFAT machine-guns, two in the wing roots and two in a ventral pack,

Caproni-Campini CC.2.

one 12.7 mm Scotti gun in a Delta E dorsal turret and a 7.7 mm Scotti weapon operated from a bulged ventral position. The internal offensive load was boosted to 1,280 kg (2,822 lb).

The Ca 316 was a twin-float development of the Libeccio, strengthened for catapult operations from battleships and cruisers. Fourteen were completed but none operated in their intended role. With 343 kW (460 hp) Piaggio radials, maximum speed was 320 km/h (199 mph).

Data (Ca 314A): *Engines* as above *Wing span* 16.65 m (54 ft 7½ in) *Length* 11.8 m (38 ft 8½ in) *Max T-O weight* 6,618 kg (14,590 lb) *Max level speed* 408 km/h (253.5 mph) *Range* 1,200 km (745 miles)

Caproni-Campini CC.2 (Italy) Officially known as the N.1, the CC.2 was the first Italian jet aircraft to fly when it took off on 28 August 1940 at the hands of Mario di Bernardi. Nevertheless the design was a failure, proving heavy and underpowered. Indeed the power plant was not a turbojet engine as such but a piston engine driving a three-stage variable-pitch fan, forcing air out of a variable-area nozzle at the end of a jet-pipe in which fuel was burned to increase the thrust.

Caproni-Vizzola F.5 (Italy) Single-seat fighter powered by a 626 kW (840 hp) Fiat A-74 RC-38 radial engine. Fourteen built, serving with one Italian squadron during 1942 in the defence of Rome.

Caproni-Vizzola Calif (Italy) In 1969 Caproni-Vizzola began producing a series of Calif sailplanes. The single A-10 was followed by two A-12s, one A-14, one A-15, the A-20 and A-21. The latest versions are the A-21S two-seater (version of the A-14) and the A-21SJ jet-powered version of the A-21, fitted with an 0.90 kN (202 lb st) Microturbo TRS 18 turbojet engine.

Caproni Ca 316.

Caproni-Vizzola F.5 prototype.

Caribe Doman LZ-5 and D-10B (Puerto Rico) Three examples of the LZ-5 utility helicopter (the first flown on 27 April 1953) were followed by the D-10B, a general-purpose helicopter powered by a Lycoming THIO-720-A1A engine derated to 298 kW (400 hp). The single prototype first flew in September 1958.

CARMAM J.P.15-36A Aiglon (France) Single-seat Standard Class sailplane. Twenty-one produced by 1978 in standard and J.P. 15-36AR (retractable nosewheel) versions.

CARMAM 15-38 (France) New single-seat Standard Class sailplane flown in 1978.

CASA C-101 Aviojet (Spain) Construcciones Aeronauticas SA was formed in 1923 and subsequently constructed Breguet XIXs under licence. Among other licence-built aircraft produced during the 1930s and 1940s can be counted the Messerschmitt Bf 109 (as the HA-1109 and HA-1112), two-seat Bf 109 trainers (HA-1110 and HA-1111) and the Heinkel He 111 (C.2111).

The latest product is the Aviojet, a tandem two-seat basic and advanced trainer and light tactical aircraft. Power is provided by a 15.57 kN (3,500 lb st) Garrett-AiResearch TFE 731-2-25 non-afterburning turbofan engine. The first of four prototypes flew on 27 June 1977 and the first of an initial production batch of 60 aircraft for the Spanish Air Force was scheduled for delivery in October 1979.

Data: *Engine* as above *Wing span* 10.6 m (34 ft 9$\frac{3}{8}$ in) *Length* 12.25 m (40 ft 2$\frac{1}{4}$ in) *Max T-O weight* 5,600 kg (12,345 lb) *Max level speed* 676 km/h (420 mph) *Armament* underfuselage attachment for a 30 mm DEFA cannon or 12.7 mm gun pod; six underwing hardpoints for up to 2,000 kg (4,410 lb) of external stores, including cannon, Miniguns, Sidewinder or Maverick missiles, rockets, bombs (incl MK-20 Rockeye laser, MK-82 Snakeye laser, retarded or general-purpose), napalm, etc.

CASA C-101 Aviojet.

CASA C-112 (Spain) Side-by-side two-seat primary trainer; under development.

CASA C.127 (Spain) Licence-built Dornier Do 27As (50); Spanish Air Force designation L-9.

CASA C-201 Alcotan (Spain) Light transport aircraft of 1949 powered by two 372.6 kW (500 hp) ENMA Sirio-VII-A radial engines in 201-B ten-passenger, 201-F navigation/radio/multi-engine/blind-flying training and 201-G bombing/photographic training versions; or by 402 kW (540 hp) Alvis Leonides 503/7 radial engines in the 201-H passenger version. Spanish Air Force designation T.5.

CASA C-202 Halcón (Spain) Twin-engined (ENMA Beta B-41s or Wright R-1820-56 Cyclones) 8–14-passenger light transport aircraft of 1952.

CASA C-207 Azor.

CASA C-207 Azor (Spain) Following the production of ten of the basic C-207-A 30-passenger transport aircraft for the Spanish Air Force (designated T.7A), CASA completed ten C-207-C (T.7B) Azors equipped for cargo carrying.

CASA C-212 Aviocar (Spain) The Aviocar twin-turboprop light utility STOL transport was evolved to perform a variety of military and civil roles, but primarily to replace the mixed fleet of Junkers Ju 52/3m, Douglas DC-3 and Azor transport aircraft formerly in service with the Spanish Air Force.

The prototype first flew on 26 March 1971 and by 1978 a total of 136 production aircraft had been sold. Versions include the C-212A military transport, ordered by the air forces of Indonesia (13), Jordan (3), Portugal (20) and Spain (45 as T.12Bs); C-212AV VIP transport operated by the air forces of Jordan (9) and Spain (5); C-212B photographic survey version delivered to the air forces of Portugal (4) and Spain (6 as TR.12As); C-212C commercial transport accommodating 19 passengers; and C-212E navigation trainer, of which two are operated by the Spanish Air Force. In addition, Aviocars are produced in Indonesia by Nurtanio. A higher-powered, higher-weight version with 645 kW (865 shp) AiResearch TPE

331-10 turboprop engines is under development as the C-212-10.

Data: *Engines* two 559 kW (750 shp) Garrett-AiResearch TPE 331-5-251C turboprops *Wing span* 19.0 m (62 ft 4 in) *Length* 15.2 m (49 ft 10½ in) *Max T-O weight* 6,500 kg (14,330 lb) *Max level speed* 359 km/h (223 mph) *Range* 1,760 km (1,093 miles) *Accommodation* (C-212A) 18 troops, 15 paratroops, 12 stretchers and two medical attendants or 2,000 kg (4,410 lb) of freight, including light vehicles

CASA C-223 Flamingo (Spain) Version of the MBB 223 Flamingo light aircraft produced as a two-seat utility, three–four-seat touring, single-seat aerobatic and agricultural aircraft.

CASA SF-5A and SF-5B (Spain) Licence-built versions of the Northrop F-5A single-seat fighter and F-5B two-seat operational trainer.

Caspar C 32 and C 35 Priwall (Germany) The C-35 of 1928 was an eight-seat biplane airliner powered by a 372.6 kW (500 hp) BMW VI engine. One example flown by Deutsche Luft Hansa. The Ca 32 freighter version was also delivered to the airline in 1929.

Cassutt Special I and II (USA) Single-seat racing monoplanes. The Special I powered originally by a 63.5 kW (85 hp) Continental C85-8F flat-four engine. Plans are available to amateur constructors and by 1979 about 2,000 sets had been sold, including those for the smaller Special II and a sporting version of the Special I with a larger cockpit.

Castel-Mauboussin CM series (France) Aircraft under development by this company in the late 1940s included the CM.10 military glider; CM.100 powered version of the CM.10; CM.101 passenger-carrying version of CM.100 with a retractable landing gear; CM.7, CM.8-15 and CM.18-13 sailplanes; CM.8-15R and CM.8-13R jet-powered gliders; and Mauboussin M.129/48 two-seat light touring and training monoplane.

Caudron C.23 (France) Developed too late for active service during World War I, 54 examples of the C.23 BN2 night bomber were built and equipped Aéronautique Militaire units until February 1920. A large wooden four-bay biplane, it had a single defensive machine-gun position in the extreme nose. The 500 kg (1,102 lb) bomb load was carried under the fuselage. Original power units were two 194 kW (260 hp) Salmson 9Z liquid-cooled engines, although some machines had 149 kW (200 hp) Hispano-Suizas.

Caudron C.59 (France) A 'transitional' trainer which went into large-scale service with the French Aéronautique Militaire in 1923, serving at flying schools for a decade. A two-bay biplane with cockpits for instructor and pupil in tandem, the C.59 was powered by a 134 kW (180 hp) Hispano-Suiza A engine with a radiator under the fuselage between the undercarriage struts. It was intended to follow instruction on low-powered elementary trainers and precede advanced training on modified versions of first-line aircraft. Three C.59s were also used by the Finnish air arm.

Data: *Engine* as above *Wing span* 10.24 m (33 ft 7 in) *Length* 7.8 m (25 ft 7 in) *Max T-O weight*

CASA C-212 Aviocar.

988 kg (2,178 lb) *Max level speed* 170 km/h (105.5 mph)

Caudron C.60 (France) The C.60 was a trainer, differing from the C.59 in having a 97 kW (130 hp) Clerget 9B rotary engine instead of a higher-powered Hispano-Suiza liquid-cooled unit. Rejected by the French authorities, it was offered for export. Thirty were bought by Finland in 1923–24. A further 34 machines were licence-built in Finland during 1927–28. Maximum speed was 20 km/h (12.4 mph) less than the C.59.

Caudron C.61 (France) The C.61 was an eight-passenger biplane airliner of 1921 powered by three 134 kW (180 hp) Hispano-Suiza 8A engines. Twelve were produced, the majority serving on domestic routes in Romania. Some were subsequently re-engined with 194 kW (260 hp) Salmsons and designated C.61*bis*.

Caudron C.81 (France) Enlarged development of the C.61 powered by two 194 kW (260 hp) Salmson CM.9 and one 298 kW (400 hp) Lorraine-Dietrich 12Db engines. Replaced the earlier type on Romanian services.

Caudron C.109 (France) Two-seat light sporting and training parasol-wing monoplane powered by a 30 kW (40 hp) Salmson AD-9 radial engine.

Cassutt Special I.

Caudron C.23.

Caudron

Caudron C.444 Goëland.

Caudron C.635 Simoun.

Caudron C.183 (France) Single example of a seven-seat biplane airliner similar to the C.81.

Caudron C.272 Luciole (France) Built through the 1930s, the Luciole was a two-seat open-cockpit touring biplane. Fifty-one examples were completed, powered by the 71 kW (95 hp) Renault 4 Pb engine. Many other versions followed, terminating with the C.278. Several aircraft survived until well after the end of World War II.

Caudron C.282 Phalene (France) Four-seat light cabin monoplane produced in several versions, including the Super-Phalene with automatic slots and flaps.

Caudron C.440 Goëland series (France) The Goëland appeared in prototype form during 1935 as a handsome cantilever low-wing cabin monoplane with a retractable undercarriage. Originally intended solely as a light transport (accommodating a two-man crew, six passengers and baggage), it remained in production during and after World War II (post-war designation A.A.1). The various designations of the aircraft applied during the production run indicated structural or equipment modifications or variants of the standard two 149 kW (200 hp) Renault 6Q Bengali-Six engines installed. A total of 1,702 Goëlands were constructed.

By September 1939 the C.440 series was in use on a wide scale. Civil machines flew regular services for Air Bleu, Air Afrique and Air France. The 1937 C.445M militarised version was operated by the Armée de l'Air. From June 1940 production of the military variants continued for the Luftwaffe and Vichy regime for use as crew trainers and light transports. Post-war a number of civil operators bought the C.449 version, which was also supplied to the French Air Force and the Aéronavale.

Data (C.445): *Engines* as above *Wing span* 17.6 m (57 ft 8½ in) *Length* 13.68 m (44 ft 10½ in) *Max T-O weight* 3,500 kg (7,716 lb) *Max level speed* 287 km/h (178.5 mph) *Range* 560 km (348 miles)

Caudron C.460 (France) Single-seat cantilever low-wing monoplane racer, built for the 1934 Coupe Deutsch de la Meurthe contest. On 25 December 1934 it set a speed record of 505.848 km/h (314.188 mph).

Caudron C.635 Simoun (France) Developed from a prototype exhibited at the 1934 Paris Salon Aéronautique, the C.630 Simoun series was designed originally as a four-seat tourer or combined mail carrier/air taxi. A smoothly contoured cantilever low-wing cabin monoplane with a

divided undercarriage, featuring single cantilever units with wheel spats, it was produced in a number of versions with a variety of engines. At least 70 were sold to civil operators, the largest user being Air Bleu, which used the type on domestic air mail services. In 1937 the Armée de l'Air ordered the C.635M militarised version with a 164 kW (220 hp) Renault Bengali-Six inverted in-line air-cooled engine. It is thought that no fewer than 435 were ordered, plus another 52 for the French Navy, and were employed on training and liaison duties.

Data (C 635M): *Engine* as above *Wing span* 10.4 m (34 ft 1½ in) *Length* 9.1 m (29 ft 10¼ in) *Max T-O weight* 1,380 kg (3,042 lb) *Max level speed* 300 km/h (186.5 mph) *Range* 1,230 km (764.5 miles)

Caudron C.641 Typhoon (France) Twin-engined high-speed mail-carrier of very similar configuration to the British de Havilland D.H.88 Comet long-distance racing aircraft.

Caudron C.690M (France) Single-seat advanced trainer of 1936 designed by Marcel Riffard and developed from the famous Caudron racers. The C.690 was a single-seat low-wing cabin monoplane with single-strut cantilever main landing gear legs with spatted wheel fairings. Power was provided by a 164 kW (220 hp) Renault 6 Q-05 engine giving a maximum speed of 370 km/h (230 mph). Two prototypes were followed by 17 production C.690Ms for the Armée de l'Air, most being delivered between January 1939 and June 1940. Of these, two were subsequently acquired by the Soviet Union and two by Japan.

Caudron C.714 (France) Single-seat lightweight fighter of 1938 powered by a 335.3 kW (450 hp) Renault 12 Roi-3 inverted in-line engine. Initially rejected by the Armée de l'Air, it was ordered by Finland (80) and Yugoslavia (30). Production began in mid-1939 but only a few C.714s had been delivered by the time fighting against Russia ended in March 1940. The remainder of the fighters were pressed into French service and equipped a few squadrons, including one made up of Polish pilots. Maximum level speed 487 km/h (302.5 mph).

Caudron G.III (France) Developed from the G.II of 1913, the G.III was a two-seat sesquiplane powered by a 59.6 kW (80 hp) Le Rhône, Gnome or Anzani engine mounted in the nose of the short crew nacelle. Originally operated by French squadrons as reconnaissance aircraft over the Western Front and then in less dangerous

Caudron G.III.

theatres of war, the G.III subsequently became a trainer, serving also with the British, Belgian, Italian and American forces.

Caudron G.IV (France) The G.IV was a twin-engined development of the G.III, the two Le Rhône or 74.5 kW (100 hp) Anzani engines mounted either side of the nacelle. This arrangement allowed the installation of one or two machine-guns in the nose of the nacelle. G.IVs served from late 1915 until 1917 as reconnaissance aircraft with French, British and Italian forces; the French and RNAS also using the type as a light bomber carrying a warload of 113 kg (250 lb). Maximum level speed was 130 km/h (81 mph).

Caudron G.VI (France) Much developed version of the G.IV with a conventional fuselage and tail unit replacing the earlier aircraft's open twin booms and very wide tailplane with four vertical surfaces.

Caudron R.4, R.6 and R.11 (France) Entering service in 1916, the R.4 was a conventional but large three-seat reconnaissance and bombing bi-plane powered by two 104.3 kW (140 hp) Hispano-Suiza or Renault engines. Defensive armament comprised Lewis machine-guns in nose and rear cockpits. Found to be under powered, it was used mainly as a reconnaissance type until the arrival in 1918 of the improved R.11. The latter was basically similar but had a reduced wing span, two 134–164 kW (180–220 hp) Hispano-Suiza engines and the R.4's single nosewheel removed. The R.11 proved highly successful during the last months of World War I. The R.6 was a smaller version of the R.4 type, without a nose gunner's position and powered by two 82 kW (110 hp) Le Rhône engines. No less than 750 R.6s were completed for French service.

CCF Norseman (Canada) The Norseman high-wing transport aircraft was first manufactured by Noorduyn Aviation before World War II. It remained in production throughout the war and 746 were delivered to the USAAF as C-64As, together with a few to the US Navy. The first major version was the Norseman Mk V, which was still being produced in the early 1950s as a civil type.

Data: *Engine* one 410 kW (550 hp) Pratt & Whitney R-1340-AN-1 radial *Wing span* 15.75 m (51 ft 8 in) *Length* (landplane/skiplane) 9.86 m (32 ft 4 in), (seaplane) 10.44 m (34 ft 3 in) *Max T-O*

Caudron G.VI.

weight (landplane) 3,357 kg (7,400 lb) *Cruising speed* (landplane) 227 km/h (141 mph) *Range* (landplane) 747 km (464 miles) *Accommodation* crew of two and eight passengers or freight

Century Jetstream III (USA) Version of the Handley Page Jetstream powered by two 626 kW (840 shp) Garrett AiResearch TPE 331-3U-303 turboprop engines.

Cerva (G.I.E.) CE.43 Guépard (France) All-metal version of the Wassmer Super 4/21. Production ended in 1976 after 43 had been completed.

Cessna early designs (USA) Cessna Aircraft Company was founded by Clyde V. Cessna, a pioneer in US aviation, in 1911 and incorporated on 7 September 1927. Prior to the Design No 1 of 1927, Cessna produced eight types, starting with his 1911 Blériot-type monoplane (powered by a 44.7 kW; 60 hp Elbridge engine) and including the Comet, built during the winter of 1916–17 and the first Cessna aircraft to feature a partially enclosed cabin. The Comet was highly successful and completed more than 30 exhibition flights in 1917.

Cessna Model A series (USA) The Type A was the first Cessna production aeroplane and was

CCF Norseman.

Cessna

Cessna Model AW.

Cessna CG-2.

Cessna DC-6B.

available in five models. The AA (14 built) was powered by an 89.4 kW (120 hp) Anzani engine; AC (1 built) with a 97 kW (130 hp) Comet engine; AF (3 built) with a 112 kW (150 hp) Floco/Axelson engine; AS (4 built) with a 93.2 kW (125 hp) Siemens-Halske engine; and the AW (48 built) with a 93.2 kW (125 hp) Warner engine. All were four-seat cantilever high-wing cabin monoplanes. Forty of the AWs were delivered to the Curtiss Flying Service.

Data (AW): *Engine* as above *Wing span* 12.24 m (40 ft 2 in) *Length* 7.52 m (24 ft 8 in) *Max T-O weight* 1,025 kg (2,260 lb) *Max level speed* 209 km/h (130 mph) *Range* 1,050 km (650 miles)

Cessna Model BW (USA) Three-seat version of the AW powered by a 164 kW (220 hp) Wright J-5 engine. Max T-O weight increased to 1,104 kg (2,435 lb). Max level speed 241 km/h (150 mph). Thirteen built before production gave way to DC-6.

Cessna DC-6 (USA) Four-seat version of the BW produced in three versions: the DC-6 of 1929 with a 127 kW (170 hp) Curtiss engine (5 built); DC-6A with a 223.5 kW (300 hp) Wright Whirlwind Nine (22 built); and DC-6B with a 168 kW (225 hp) Wright Seven (22 built from 1929 to 1935).

Cessna CG-2 (USA) During 1930 Cessna produced 84 single-seat gliders, each with a wing span of 10.72 m (35 ft 2 in).

Cessna EC-1 (USA) During 1930 Cessna produced three EC-1 Baby Cessna single-seat lightplanes, each powered by an 18.6 kW (25 hp) Cleone engine.

Cessna EC-2 (USA) Following production of the EC-1, Cessna produced the 22.36 kW (30 hp) E-107A-engined two-seat EC-2.

Cessna C-34 (USA) On 1 January 1934 Cessna re-opened its plant (which had closed during 1933) and began production of the C-34 four-seat cabin monoplane, powered by a 108 kW (145 hp) Warner Super Scarab radial engine. Forty-two were completed.

Cessna C-37 (USA) The 1937 Cessna was the C-37, a four-seat high-wing monoplane of similar configuration to the C-34 but with streamlined wheel fairings and other minor refinements. Forty-six were completed.

Cessna C-38 Airmaster (USA) The 1938 version of the four-seat monoplane, of which 16 were completed.

Cessna C-145 and C-165 Airmaster (USA) In 1938–39 Cessna made the Airmaster available in two basic versions: C-145 and C-165 with a 108 kW (145 hp) and 123 kW (165 hp) Warner Super Scarab radial engine respectively. Both remained four-seaters and, like the earlier models, could be operated as land-, sea- or skiplanes, and as passenger aircraft, freighters or for photographic work. Between 1938 and 1941 Cessna produced 42 C-145s, 34 C-165s, 3 C-165Ds with 130.4 kW (175 hp) Warner engines, and a single example of a special C-165 for General Motors with a 130.4 kW (175 hp) General Motors X-250 engine.

Cessna T-50 and AT-8 (USA) The T-50 of 1939 was a five-seat low-wing cabin monoplane powered by two 168 kW (225 hp) Jacobs L-4MB radial engines. Between 1940 and 1942 a total of 40 were produced for civil use. During 1941 the USAAF received 33 similar aircraft with 220 kW (295 hp) Lycoming R-680-9 radial engines as AT-8s, which were used to train future pilots of multi-engined operational aircraft. A similar type of aircraft with Jacobs engines was also operated under the Commonwealth Air Training Plan in Canada, known as the Crane 1 (640 built).

Cessna AT-17 and UC-78 Bobcat (USA) With America's entry into World War II the number of aircraft needed to train pilots increased greatly and so Cessna produced the AT-17, powered by 182.5 kW (245 hp) Jacobs R-775-9 seven-cylinder air-cooled radial engines. Altogether 450 were completed, followed by 41 AT-17As, 466 AT-17Bs, 60 AT-17Cs and 131 AT-17Ds (AT-17Bs and AT-17Ds delivered after 1 January 1943 were redesignated UC-78Bs and UC-78Cs respectively; see 1945–46 *Jane's*). These later became AT-17Es, Fs, Gs and Hs respectively (the AT-17D not being included in the change of designation).

Following AT-17 production, of which 182 similar Crane 1as were operated under the Commonwealth Air Training Plan, a five-seat personnel transport version was acquired by the USAAF as the UC-78. Both the AT-17 and UC-78 were fitted with Hamilton Standard constant-speed propellers but subsequent series of both models had two-blade fixed-pitch wooden propellers. Otherwise only minor variations in equipment distinguished the various series models. Production of the UC-78 series, which lasted until 1944, covered the construction of 1,004 UC-78s, 2,156 UC-78Bs (UC-78A designation applying to 17 impressed T-50s), and 196 UC-78Cs. These later became UC-78Ds, UC-78Es, and UC-78Fs respectively. All were known under the name Bobcat. In addition 67 UC-78s were acquired from the Air Force by the US Navy and operated as JRC-1s.

Data (UC-78B): *Engines* as above *Wing span* 12.78 m (41 ft 11 in) *Length* 9.98 m (32 ft 9 in) *Max T-O weight* 2,585 kg (5,700 lb) *Max level speed* 314 km/h (195 mph) *Range* 1,207 km (750 miles)

Cessna Model 120 (USA) Between the end of the war and 1950 Cessna produced five new light cabin monoplanes for the civil market. The Model 120, of which 2,171 were completed by 1949, was a side-by-side two-seat cabin monoplane powered by a 63.3 kW (85 hp) Continental C-85-12 flat-four engine. Max level speed was over 193 km/h (120 mph).

Cessna Model 140 and 140A (USA) The Model 140 was identical to the Model 120 but fitted with a 67 kW (90 hp) Continental C-90-12 engine (or the C-85) and had certain refinements including starter, generator and battery. It was also fitted with manually operated all-metal plain-hinge flaps between the ailerons and fuselage. A total of 4,905 were completed by 1949. The Model 140A (526 built) had a wing span of 10.16 m (33 ft 4 in) instead of the usual 10.0 m (32 ft 10 in), but max level speed remained 193 km/h (120 mph).

Cessna Model 150 Commuter and A150 Aerobat (USA) The prototype of the Model 150 flew for the first time in September 1957, receiving FAA Type Approval on 10 July 1958. It was put into production in August 1958 and when its 19-year production run ended in 1977 a total of 23,836 Model 150s had been delivered, including 1,754 aircraft built in France by Reims Aviation as F-150s.

The 1977 American-built Model 150 was announced in standard, Commuter, Commuter II and Aerobat versions. The latter was designed to combine the economy and versatility of the standard Model 150 with aerobatic capability (military customers for the Aerobat including the air forces of Ecuador and Zaïre, 24 and 15 respectively). The Commuter II has the same equipment as the Commuter, plus a second Cessna 300 nav/com, Cessna 300 transponder, true airspeed indicator, emergency locator transmitter and external power socket.

The 1977 versions of the Model 150 have a number of improvements as standard over earlier examples, including a new instrument panel cover (with an energy-absorbing lower panel to increase leg protection); a pre-select flap control; vernier adjustment mixture control; and new interior and exterior styling (the shape of the side cabin windows, rear fuselage and tail unit changing during the production run, but the normal side-by-side seating for two and power plant remaining the same throughout).

Data (1977 Model 150): *Engine* one 74.5 kW (100 hp) Continental O-200-A flat-four *Wing span* 9.97 m (32 ft 8½ in) *Length* 7.29 m (23 ft 11 in) *Max T-O weight* 726 kg (1,600 lb) *Max level speed* 201 km/h (125 mph) *Range* (standard fuel) 629 km (391 miles) *Accommodation* seating for two, plus an optional 'family seat' at rear for two children.

Cessna C-34.

Cessna C-165 Airmaster.

Cessna Model 152 (USA) During 1977 Cessna introduced a new two-seat cabin monoplane to replace the Model 150. Designated Model 152, it differs primarily in having a more powerful engine, an improved 'gull wing' propeller, and power plant installation and cowling changes to reduce engine noise and vibration. Two versions are available: the standard Model 152 and the Model 152/II with a factory-installed electronics and equipment package which includes a Cessna Series 300 nav/com, dual controls, true airspeed indicator, navigation light detectors and other items. By 1978 a total of 1,541 Model 152s had been built, including 19 F-152s constructed by Reims Aviation in France.

Data: *Engine* one 82 kW (110 hp) Lycoming O-235-L2C flat-four *Wing span* 9.97 m (32 ft 8½ in) *Length* 7.34 m (24 ft 1 in) *Max T-O weight* 757 kg (1,670 lb) *Max level speed* 204 km/h (127 mph) *Range* (standard fuel) 769 km (478 miles)

Cessna Model 152 Aerobat (USA) Combines the economy and versatility of the standard Model 152 with aerobatic capability.

Cessna UC-78 Bobcat.

Cessna Model 140.

Cessna Model 120.

Cessna Model A 150 Aerobat.

Cessna Model 170 (USA) Four-seat cabin monoplane powered by a 108 kW (145 hp) Continental C-145-2 flat-six engine. In production from 1948 until 1956, 5,173 aircraft being completed.

Cessna Model 172 Skyhawk (USA) The Skyhawk has been in production since 1956 and by the end of 1978 a total of 30,581 had been produced, excluding 70 Skyhawk Powermatics built in 1963; 630 Reims Rockets (Model R172E, see **Mescalero**) built in France between 1968 and 1976; 1,085 Model R172 Hawk XPs (introduced in June 1976, also produced by Reims Aviation in France as the Model FR172/Reims Hawk XP, and available in two versions with 145.4 kW; 195 hp Continental IO-360-K engines); and T-41 USAF and US Army Mescaleros (described separately).

The Skyhawk is currently available in two versions, the standard aircraft with a 119 kW (160 hp) Lycoming O-320-H2AD flat-four engine and the Skyhawk II with a Series 300 nav/com, dual controls, true airspeed indicator, navigation light detectors and other items of equipment.

Data (landplane): *Engine* as above *Wing span* 10.92 m (35 ft 10 in) *Length* 8.2 m (26 ft 11 in) *Max T-O weight* 1,043 kg (2,300 lb) *Max level speed* 232 km/h (144 mph) *Range* (standard fuel) 1,066 km (662 miles) *Accommodation* seating for four persons, plus baggage space aft of rear seats or an optional foldaway seat in baggage area for one or two children.

Cessna T-41 Mescalero and Model R172E (USA) In July 1964 the USAF ordered 170 earlier-type Model 172s (under the designation T-41A) for basic training of pilots before they pass on to the T-37B jet primary trainer. Others were purchased by the Ecuadorean Air Force (8), Honduran Air Force (5), and Peruvian government (26). Further orders for the T-41A were place by the USAF in 1967. Meanwhile in August 1966 the US Army had ordered 255 aircraft for training and installation support duties as T-41Bs, based on the Cessna Model R172E, a more powerful version of the original Model 172 with a 156.5 kW (210 hp) Continental IO-360-D flat-six engine. The USAF ordered 45 similar aircraft in 1967 as T-41Cs for cadet flight training at the Academy in Colorado, and the Colombian Air Force and USAF subsequently received similar T-41Ds with constant-speed propellers and 28V electrical systems. By the end of 1978 a total of 855 T-41s had been built.

Cessna Model 175 Skylark (USA) Introduced in 1958, the Skylark was produced as a deluxe version of the Skyhawk powered by a 130.4 kW (175 hp) Continental GO-300-E engine. A total of 2,120 were built up to 1962.

Cessna Model 177 Cardinal and Cardinal Classic (USA) In September 1967 Cessna introduced its Model 177, a single-engined four-seat aircraft with a cantilever wing, powered by a 112 kW (150 hp) Lycoming engine, and intended as a luxury addition to its range of single-engined two–four-seaters. Increased engine power was provided subsequently by the installation of the 134 kW (180 hp) Lycoming O-360-A1F6D flat-four engine.

With the introduction of the Cardinal Classic in 1978, Cessna began marketing a luxury aircraft which includes a full complement of flight instruments, engine condition instruments and electronics. A total of 4,070 Model 177/Cardinals had been built by early 1978, including the Cardinal RGs (described separately) and Reims Cardinal RGs built in France.

Data: *Engines* as above *Wing span* 10.82 m (35 ft 6 in) *Length* 8.31 m (27 ft 3 in) *Max T-O weight* 1,134 kg (2,500 lb) *Max level speed* 257 km/h (160 mph) *Range* 1,445 km (898 miles)

Cessna Cardinal RG and RG II (USA) Announced in 1970 as further versions of the Cardinal series with hydraulically retractable tricycle-type landing gears, one 149 kW (200 hp) Lycoming IO-360-A1B6D flat-four engine and a number of different standard and optional items. The RG II is a specially equipped version. By the end of 1978 a total of 1,492 had been built.

Cessna Model 180 Skywagon (USA) The Skywagon first entered production in 1953 as a six-seat cabin monoplane. The two commercial versions available at present are the standard Model 180 Skywagon and the Model 180 Skywagon II, the latter including a factory-installed electronics package. By the end of 1978 a total of 6,019 Skywagons had been built.

Data (landplane): *Engine* one 171.5 kW (230 hp) Continental O-470-U flat-six *Wing span* 10.92 m (35 ft 10 in) *Length* 7.85 m (25 ft 9 in) *Max T-O weight* 1,270 kg (2,800 lb) *Max level speed* 274 km/h (170 mph) *Range* (standard fuel) 1,168 km (725 miles)

Cessna Model 182 and Skylane (USA) The Model 182 entered production in 1956 and remained the basic version of this four-seat cabin monoplane until 1976. The two versions currently available are the Skylane and Skylane II, the latter version incorporating a factory-installed electronics package. A version designated F182 is produced by Reims Aviation in France. By the end of 1978 a total of 17,923 aircraft of the series had been built.

Data: *Engine* as for Model 180 *Wing span* 10.92 m (35 ft 10 in) *Length* 8.57 m (28 ft 1½ in) *Max T-O weight* 1,338 kg (2,950 lb) *Max level speed* 273 km/h (170 mph) *Range* (standard fuel) 1,186 km (737 miles)

Cessna Skylane RG (USA) Newly introduced in 1977, this is a version of the Skylane with a

Cessna Model R172 Hawk XPII.

retractable landing gear, available as the RG and RG II with additional electronics and equipment. Max level speed 296 km/h (184 mph). Total of 879 built by the end of 1978.

Cessna Model 185 Skywagon and U-17 (USA) The prototype of this six-seat cabin monoplane flew for the first time in July 1960 and the first production model was completed in March 1961. It is generally similar to the Model 180 Skywagon, except for the installation of a 224 kW (300 hp) Continental IO-520-D flat-six engine. It is currently available as the standard Model 185 Skywagon and as the Model 185 Skywagon II with a factory-installed electronics package. A total of 3,169 had been completed by late 1978, excluding 497 U-17A/B/C Skywagons ordered by the USAF and built between 1963 and 1973 for delivery to overseas countries under the US Military Assistance Programme.

Cessna A185 AGcarryall (USA) Announced in 1971, the AGcarryall represented a new multi-purpose concept in this specialised category of aircraft. It is intended for use as a demonstrator of spraying techniques; as a runabout for moving people, equipment or cargo when operating in the field; as a backup aircraft for peak seasonal workloads; as an agricultural pilot trainer; and for use by the farmer who requires spraying capability plus transportation.

Based upon the Model 185, the AGcarryall has two seats as standard and optional seating for four additional passengers. It is provided with spraybooms and a 571 litre (151 US gallon) chemical tank. By late 1978 a total of 103 had been built.

Cessna Model 188/T188 AGwagon, AGpickup, AGtruck, AGhusky (USA) The AGwagon was first flown in prototype form on 19 February 1965 as a specialised agricultural aircraft which Cessna decided to develop after an extensive survey into the requirements of the operators of such aircraft. The first two versions were the Model 188 AGwagon 230 with a 171.4 kW (230 hp) Continental O-470-R engine and the Model A188 AGwagon 300 with a 223.5 kW (300 hp) IO-520-D engine.

In 1971 Cessna announced the introduction of new agricultural aircraft based on the earlier AGwagon. Of these, the AGpickup with a similar engine to the AGwagon 230 was discontinued in 1976. The new AGwagon has a similar engine to the Model A188 AGwagon and the AGtruck is generally similar but with a 1,060 litre (280 US gallon) hopper and additional standard equipment. The AGhusky is a turbocharged

Cessna Model 152.

Cessna Model 170B.

Cessna

Cessna Cardinal RG.

Cessna Model 180 Skywagon.

Cessna T-41B Mescalero.

version of the AGtruck, the 231 kW (310 hp) engine providing improved performance at varying operational altitudes.

The 1978 versions of these agricultural aircraft introduced a number of improvements as standard, including a re-engineered night lighting system which saves weight; a remote-mounted oil cooler which simplifies maintenance; a manual spray valve; better access to wings and fuselage to simplify cleaning; and a new exterior styling with polyurethane paint as standard. They are of all-metal construction and have special corrosion proofing, heavy-duty spring Land-O-Matic landing gear and Cessna's Camber-Lift wing to provide better control during low-speed operations. Special attention has been paid to safety features. A total of 3,389 examples of the AGwagon, AGpickup, AGtruck and AGhusky had been built by late 1978.

Data (1978 AGwagon): *Engine* as above *Wing span* 12.41 m (40 ft 8½ in) *Length* 8.0 m (26 ft 3 in) *Max T-O weight* 1,814 kg (4,000 lb) *Max level speed* 243 km/h (151 mph) *Max cruising range* 595 km (370 miles) *Equipment* 757 litre (200 US gallon) hopper, liquid and dry material dispersal control system, etc

Cessna Cardinal.

Cessna Model 190 and 195 Businessliner (USA) Between 1947 and 1954 Cessna built 1,100 Businessliners, four–five-seat cabin monoplanes powered by 179 kW (240 hp) Continental R-670-23 (Model 190); 223.5 kW (300 hp) Jacobs R-755-A2 (Model 195); and 182.5 kW (245 hp) Jacobs R-744-A2 engines (Model 195A).

Cessna LC-126 (USA) Between 1949 and 1952 Cessna built 83 LC-126s, a military variant of the Model 195. The USAF acquired the type under the designation LC-126A, a specially prepared version for Arctic rescue work equipped with interchangeable wheel, float or ski landing gear.

Cessna Model 205 (USA) Between 1962 and 1964 Cessna produced 578 six-seat Model 205/205As, similar to the Model 182 in basic configuration and structure but differing considerably in detail. Power was provided by a 194 kW (260 hp) Continental IO-470-S flat-six engine.

Cessna Model P206 and TP206 Super Skylane (USA) The Super Skylane was a deluxe six-seat version of the Model 206 series. It retained the ability to carry the Super Skywagon's underfuselage cargo pack, but did not have the double loading doors of the U206 and TU206. The P206 was the standard version with a 212.4 kW (285 hp) Continental IO-520-A engine. The TP206 Turbo-System Super Skylane was generally similar but with a 212.4 kW (285 hp) Continental TSIO-520-C turbocharged engine. Between 1964 and 1970 a total of 647 were built.

Cessna Model U206 and Stationair 6 (USA) Cessna subsequently re-named the former U206 Skywagon and TU206 Turbo-Skywagon as the Stationair and Turbo-Stationair, after the original aircraft had entered production in 1964. In 1978 a name change to Stationair 6 and Turbo-Stationair 6 highlighted the six-seat capacity of these cargo/utility aircraft and the considerable differences between them and the Model 185 Skywagon. The Stationair 6 is the standard cargo/utility model with a 224 kW (300 hp) Continental IO-520-F engine and double loading doors. The Turbo-Stationair 6 is similar but has a 231 kW (310 hp) Continental TSIO-520-M turbocharged engine in a modified cowling. A utility version of the Stationair is also available with a single seat for the pilot as standard. Up to five passenger seats can be supplied optionally. A total of 4,820 Model 206 Super Skywagons and Stationairs had been built by the end of 1978.

Data (Stationair 6 landplane): *Engine* as above *Wing span* 10.92 m (35 ft 10 in) *Length* 8.61 m (28 ft 3 in) *Max T-O weight* 1,633 kg (3,600 lb) *Max level speed* 290 km/h (180 mph) *Range* (standard fuel) 1,028 km (639 miles)

Cessna Model 207 and Stationair 7 (USA) In 1969 Cessna announced two new seven-seat versions of the Skywagon utility aircraft. Generally similar to the earlier Model 206 Super Skywagon, the new Skywagon had been 'stretched' to provide improved load-carrying ability while retaining the single engine and operating economy of the Model 206. The first production aircraft flew in January 1969, followed three days later by the first T207 Turbo-Skywagon. In 1978 these models were renamed Stationair 7 and Turbo-Stationair 7; they are powered by a 224 kW (300 hp) Continental IO-520-F and a 231 kW (310 hp) Continental TSIO-520-M turbocharged engine respectively. By the end of 1978 a total of 503 had been built.

Data (Stationair 7): *Engine* as above *Wing span* 10.92 m (35 ft 10 in) *Length* 9.68 m (31 ft 9 in) *Max T-O weight* 1,723 kg (3,800 lb) *Max level speed* 278 km/h (173 mph) *Range* (standard fuel) 871 km (541 miles)

Cessna Model 210, Centurion, Turbo-Centurion and Pressurised Centurion (USA) The original prototype Model 210, which flew in January 1957, followed the general formula of the Cessna series of all-metal high-wing monoplanes, but was the first to have a retractable tricycle landing gear. Later versions of the Model 210 have a fully cantilever wing, the first T210 with the new wing flying on 18 June 1965.

In December 1970 Cessna announced the introduction of two new versions of the Model 210 to be known as Centurion II and Turbo-Centurion II. These differ from the Centurion and Turbo-Centurion by having as standard equipment a factory-installed IFR electronics package which offers a cost saving on electronics equipment, plus a gyro panel, dual controls and other improvements. Two versions of a new Pressurised Centurion were introduced in 1977 powered by a 231 kW (310 hp) Continental TSIO-520-P engine with special high-capacity turbocharger to support the pressurisation system and pressure cabin.

In addition to the Pressurised versions there are four current production versions of the Centurion: the standard Centurion with a 224 kW (300 hp) Continental IO-520-L flat-six engine; Centurion II with additional standard equipment; Turbo-Centurion with a 231 kW (310 hp) Continental

Cessna Skylane RG.

Cessna Model 185 Skywagon.

TSIO-520-R turbocharged engine; and Turbo-Centurion II with additional standard equipment. By the end of 1978 6,612 Model 210s, Centurions, Centurion IIs, Turbo-Centurions and Turbo-Centurion IIs had been built, together with 197 Pressurised models.

Data: *Engine* as above *Wing span* 11.2 m (36 ft 9 in) *Length* 8.59 m (28 ft 2 in) *Max T-O weight* 1,723 kg (3,800 lb) *Max level speed* (Centurion and Centurion II) 325 km/h (202 mph) *Range* (Centurion and Centurion II with standard fuel) 1,973 km (1,226 miles)

Reims-built F182 Skylane II.

Cessna Model 303 (USA) First flown on 17 February 1978, the Model 303 is a lightweight four-seat twin-engined (119 kW; 160 hp Lycoming flat-fours) aircraft. Deliveries to customers were expected to begin in late 1979.

Cessna Model 305/O-1 Bird Dog (USA) First flown in 1949, the Model 305A won a US Army competition for a new two-seat liaison and observation aircraft. Initial production aircraft were Army designated L-19As and among the early deliveries were OE-1s for the US Marine Corps and a number for MAP. Between 1950 and 1963 Cessna produced 3,399 Model 305s but in 1962 the US forces changed the L-19 series designations of their aircraft to O-1. About 17 countries operate Bird Dogs and versions delivered to US forces included the O-1A initial Army version; O-1B USMC version of the O-1A; O-1C USMC version with square-cut fin and 197.5 kW (265 hp) O-470-2 engine; TO-1D US Army instrument training version with an O-470-15 engine and dual controls; O-1D, a modified TO-1D for FAC (Forward Air Control) use by the USAF; O-1E improved US Army version, also licence-built by Fuji of Japan; O-1F, a modified TO-1D for FAC use by the USAF; and O-1G, a modified O-1A for FAC use by the USAF.

Data (O-1E): *Engine* one 159 kW (213 hp) Continental O-470-11 flat-six *Wing span* 10.97 m (36 ft 0 in) *Length* 7.89 m (25 ft 10 in) *Max T-O weight* 1,103 kg (2,430 lb) *Max level speed* 184 km/h (115 mph) *Range* 848 km (530 miles)

Cessna Model 310 and 310 II/U-3 (USA) The Model 310 is a twin-engined five–six-seat cabin monoplane, the prototype of which flew on 3 January 1953. It went into production in 1954. The Turbo-System Model 310 was added in late 1968 and in 1973 Cessna announced two new versions known as the 310 II and Turbo 310 II, which have factory-installed IFR electronics

Cessna A185 AGcarryall.

Cessna AGwagon.

Cessna U206F.

Cessna Model 207.

plus other comfort and convenience features as standard.

The four current models are the standard 310 with two 212.5 kW (285 hp) Continental IO-520-M flat-six engines; 310 II, as for 310 but with additional standard equipment; Turbo-System T310 with two 212.5 kW (285 hp) Continental TSIO-520-B turbocharged engines; and Turbo-System T310 II, as for T310 but with additional standard equipment. In addition the USAF has operated Model 310s since 1957 as light twin-engined administrative liaison and cargo aircraft under the designation U-3 (formerly L-27). Other military operators include the Zaïre Air Force. By the end of 1978 a total of 5,196 aircraft of the series had been built.
Data: *Engines* as above *Wing span* 11.25 m (36 ft 11 in) *Length* 9.74 m (31 ft 11½ in) *Max T-O weight* 2,495 kg (5,500 lb) *Max level speed* (Model 310) 383 km/h (238 mph) *Range* (Model 310) 2,800 km (1,740 miles)

Cessna Model 318/T-37 Tweet (USA) The T-37 was the first jet trainer designed as such from the start to be used by the USAF. The first of two prototype XT-37s flew on 12 October 1954 and the first of an evaluation batch of 11 T-37As flew on 27 September 1955.

A total of 1,272 T-37s had been delivered by the end of 1977, when production ended. In addition to aircraft supplied to the USAF, there have been substantial deliveries to foreign governments by direct purchase or through the Military Assistance Programme.

Three versions were built in quantity: the T-37A initial production version with two 4.1 kN (920 lb st) Continental J69-T-9 turbojets (534 built but converted to T-37B standard by retrospective modification); T-37B with two 4.56 kN (1,025 lb st) Continental J69-T-25 turbojets and other refinements, delivered to the USAF from 1959 and others going to the air forces of Thailand, Chile, Kampuchea and Pakistan and the Federal German government; and T-37C with provision for both armament and wingtip fuel

tanks, ordered by the USAF for supply to foreign countries under MAP.

Cessna Model 318D and 318E/A-37 Dragonfly (USA) The A-37 is a development of the T-37, produced for armed counter-insurgency (COIN) operations from short unimproved airstrips. Two YAT-37D prototypes were produced initially for evaluation by the USAF by modifying existing T-37 airframes. The first flew on 22 October 1963. The two production versions were the A-37A (Model 318D: 39 aircraft produced from T-37B trainers but withdrawn from service in 1974); and A-37B (Model 318E). The latter flew for the first time in September 1967. A total of 577 had been delivered by 1977, when production ended. A-37Bs are operated by five air forces.
Data (A-37B): *Engines* two 12.68 kN (2,850 lb st) General Electric J85-GE-17A turbojets *Wing span* over tip-tanks 10.93 m (35 ft 10½ in) *Length* 8.62 m (28 ft 3¼ in) excl refuelling probe *Max T-O weight* 6,350 kg (14,000 lb) *Max level speed* 816 km/h (507 mph) *Range* 740 km (460 miles) with max payload *Armament* 7.62 mm Minigun in forward fuselage; each wing has four pylon stations – the two inner ones carrying 394 kg (870 lb) each, the intermediate one 272 kg (600 lb) and the outer one 227 kg (500 lb); weapons carried can include bombs, fire bombs, demolition bombs, gun pod, rocket pods or flare launchers

Cessna Model 320 Skyknight (USA) The prototype first flew in 1961 and deliveries of production aircraft began in August 1961. The initial production version of the four–six-seat Skyknight was powered by two 194 kW (260 hp) Continental TSIO-470-D flat-six engines for optimum performance at high altitudes. In 1966 Cessna announced the Turbo-System Executive Skyknight version with two 212.4 kW (285 hp) Continental TSIO-520-B turbosupercharged engines. By the close of production in 1968 a total of 579 Skyknights had been built.

Cessna Model 321/OE-2 (USA) Two-seat reconnaissance monoplane for the USMC powered by a 197.5 kW (265 hp) Continental O-470-2 supercharged engine. Twenty-eight were built between 1955 and 1959.

Cessna Model 336 Skymaster (USA) This unique all-metal four-seat business aircraft resulted from several years of study aimed at producing a twin-engined aeroplane that would be simple to fly, low in cost, safe and comfortable, while offering all the advantages of two engines. The prototype flew for the first time on 28 February 1961 and between 1963 and 1964 a total of 197 were built. Power was provided by two 156.5 kW (210 hp) Continental IO-360-A flat-six engines in pusher and tractor positions.

Cessna Model 337 Skymaster and Skymaster II/O-2 (USA) This four–six-seat business aircraft resulted from the earlier version of the Skymaster and superseded it in production in February 1965. It has increased wing incidence, retractable landing gear and other changes. By the end of 1978 a total of 1,805 had been built, excluding 84 Reims Skymasters built in France. Two versions are currently available as the standard Skymaster with two 156.5 kW (210 hp) Continental IO-360-G flat-six engines and Skymaster II with additional standard equipment.

In addition 544 examples of two military versions (O-2A and O-2B) were delivered to the USAF and Imperial Iranian Air Force for FAC, light strike, training, psychological warfare and liaison duties. O-2s are currently operated in the O-2A version by five air forces.
Data: *Engines* as above *Wing span* 11.63 m (38 ft 2 in) *Length* 9.07 m (29 ft 9 in) *Max T-O weight* 2,100 kg (4,630 lb) *Max level speed* 332 km/h (206 mph) *Range* 2,288 km (1,422 miles)

Cessna Model 340A, 340A II and 340A III (USA) In 1971 Cessna introduced the Model 340 pressurised twin-engined business aircraft. Developed from the Model 310, it had a wing and landing gear generally similar to those of the Model 414, a pressurised fuselage of fail-safe design, a tail unit similar to that of the Model 310

and 212.5 kW (285 hp) Continental TSIO-520-K engines. The Model 340 II followed (with factory-installed electronics as standard) and in 1978 a new Model 340A III was introduced.

Versions of the Model 340 available at the present time are the 340A standard model, 340A II with additional equipment and 340A III with an electronics package. All current models have a number of improvements introduced in 1978. By the end of 1978 a total of 873 Model 340s had been built.
Data: *Engines* two 231 kW (310 hp) turbocharged Continental TSIO-520-Ns *Wing span* 11.62 m (38 ft 1¼ in) *Length* 10.46 m (34 ft 4 in) *Max T-O weight* 2,717 kg (5,990 lb) *Max level speed* 452 km/h (281 mph) *Range* 2,552 km (1,586 miles) *Accommodation* pilot, co-pilot and four passengers, plus up to 422 kg (930 lb) of baggage

Cessna Model 401 (USA) Announced in 1966 as a medium-priced six–eight-seat executive transport powered by two 223.5 kW (300 hp) Continental TSIO-520-E flat-six engines. Between 1967 and 1972 406 were built.

Cessna Model 310 II.

Cessna Model 402, 402 II and 402 III Utililiner and Businessliner (USA) Announced simultaneously with the Model 401, the Model 402 is a ten-seat (optional nine-seat) convertible passenger/freight transport (Utililiner) or six–eight-seat business aircraft (Businessliner). Six versions are currently available with varying standards of equipment. By the end of 1978 a total of 1,092 Model 402s had been built, including 12 for the Royal Malaysian Air Force as multi-engine training (10) and photographic/liaison (2) aircraft.
Data: *Engines* two 224 kW (300 hp) Continental TSIO-520-Es *Wing span* over tip-tanks 12.15 m (39 ft 10¼ in) *Length* 11.0 m (36 ft 1 in) *Max T-O weight* 2,858 kg (6,300 lb) *Max level speed* 424 km/h (264 mph) *Range* 2,280 km (1,417 miles)

Cessna Model 404 Titan (USA) In 1975 Cessna announced that it was developing a new twin-engined business/commuter/cargo aircraft,

Cessna Pressurised Centurion II.

Cessna O-1F Bird Dog.

Cessna A-37B Dragonfly.

Cessna Model 402C.

designated Model 404 Titan. The model number was subsequently deleted, but is included in the heading for reference. Deliveries began in October 1976 and by the end of 1978 a total of 195 had been built.

Eight versions are currently available as the Titan Ambassador, configured to carry eight to ten persons; Titan Ambassador II, as for Ambassador but with additional electronics and equipment; Titan Ambassador III, with equipment of Ambassador II plus heavy-duty brakes and 100A alternators and an electronics package; Titan Courier utility version; Titan Courier II and III, as standard Courier but with electronics and equipment as noted under Ambassador II and III; Titan Freighter cargo version with specially designed cabin walls and ceiling, cargo-handling facilities and a cargo door 1.26 m (4 ft 1½ in) high and 1.24 m (4 ft 1 in) wide; and Titan Freighter II, as standard Freighter but with electronics and equipment of the Ambassador II.
Data: *Engines* two 280 kW (375 hp) Continental GTSIO-520-Ms *Wing span* 14.12 m (46 ft 4 in) *Length* 12.04 m (39 ft 6¼ in) *Max T-O weight* 3,810 kg (8,400 lb) *Max level speed* 430 km/h (267 mph) *Range* 3,402 km (2,114 miles)

Cessna Model P337 Pressurised Skymaster.

Cessna Model 340A.

Cessna Model 411 (USA) Six/eight-seat business aircraft powered by two 253.4 kW (340 hp) Continental GTSIO-520-G flat-six engines. Between 1965 and 1968 a total of 303 were built.
Cessna Model 414A Chancellor (USA) Cessna introduced the pressurised twin-engined Model 414 on 10 December 1969 as a 'step up' aircraft for owners of Cessna or other light unpressurised

Cessna Model 404 Titan.

twins. It combined the basic fuselage and tail unit of the Model 421 with the wing of the Model 402 and had 231 kW (310 hp) turbocharged Continental TSIO-520-N flat-six engines.

In 1978 the basic model was replaced by a similar but much improved version which has the name Chancellor and model designation 414A. Major changes include a new bonded 'wet' wing of increased span, extended nose and baggage area and introduction of an external access door to the tailcone. A total of 677 Model 414 series aircraft have been built, including the three current models of the Model 414A known as the Chancellor, Chancellor II and Chancellor III with varying standards of electronics and equipment.
Data: *Engines* as above *Wing span* 13.45 m (44 ft 1½ in) *Length* 11.09 m (36 ft 4½ in) *Max T-O weight* 3,062 kg (6,750 lb) *Max level speed* 443 km/h (275 mph) *Range* 2,426 km (1,508 miles) *Accommodation* six to eight persons, plus up to 494 kg (1,090 lb) of baggage
Cessna Model 421 Golden Eagle (USA) In 1965 Cessna announced a pressurised twin-engined business aircraft designated Model 421, the prototype of which had flown for the first time on 14 October 1965. Two developed versions of the Model 421 were produced subsequently as the Model 421B Golden Eagle and 421B Executive Commuter, remaining in production until replaced by the Model 421C in 1976. The current versions are the standard Model 421C Golden Eagle, Golden Eagle II and Golden Eagle III with varying standards of electronics and equipment. By the end of 1978 a total of 1,541 Model 421 series aircraft had been built.
Data (Model 421C Golden Eagle): *Engines* two 280 kW (375 hp) turbocharged Continental GTSIO-520-Ls *Wing span* 12.53 m (41 ft 1½ in) *Length* 11.09 m (36 ft 4½ in) *Max T-O weight* 3,379 kg (7,450 lb) *Max level speed* 478 km/h

(297 mph) *Range* 2,755 km (1,712 miles) *Accommodation* six to eight persons, plus up to 680 kg (1,500 lb) of baggage and equipment

Cessna Model 441 Conquest (USA) Eight–eleven-seat pressurised executive transport aircraft powered by two 466 kW (625 shp) Garrett AiResearch TPE 331-8-401S turboprop engines. During 1978 a total of 97 were built.

Data: *Engines* as above *Wing span* 15.04 m (49 ft 4 in) *Length* 11.89 m (39 ft 0¼ in) *Max T-O weight* 4,468 kg (9,850 lb) *Max level speed* 547 km/h (340 mph) *Range* 3,402 km (2,114 miles)

Cessna Model 500 and 501 Citation (USA) In 1968 Cessna announced that it was developing a new eight-seat pressurised executive turbofan aircraft (named Fanjet 500) which would be able to operate from most airfields used by light and medium twin-engined aircraft. After the first flight of the prototype (on 15 September 1969) it was announced that the aircraft's name had been changed to Citation. Between 1971 and 1977 352 were built.

In 1976 Cessna announced a development of the Citation I, differing from the Series 500 by having a wing of increased span and two 9.77 kN (2,200 lb st) Pratt & Whitney JT15D-1A turbofan engines instead of similarly rated JT15D-1s. Two versions of the Citation I are currently available, the standard Citation I and the Citation

I/SP Model 501 certificated to FAR 23 for single-pilot operation. By the end of 1978 127 Citation Is of both versions had been built.

In 1976 Cessna announced the Citation II, introducing several new features including a fuselage lengthened by 1.14 m (3 ft 9 in); an increased-span high-aspect-ratio wing; increased fuel and baggage capacity; and the installation of JT15D-4 turbofan engines rated at 11.12 kN (2,500 lb st). A total of 62 Citation II/IISPs had been built by the end of 1978. A Citation III, powered by 16.24 kN (3,650 lb st) Garrett AiResearch TFE 731-3-100S turbofans, has been developed and deliveries will begin in 1981.

Data (Citation I): *Engines* as above *Wing span* 14.35 m (47 ft 1 in) *Length* 13.26 m (43 ft 6 in) *Max T-O weight* 5,375 kg (11,850 lb) *Cruising speed* 649 km/h (403 mph) *Range* 2,474 km (1,537 miles)

Cessna CH-1 Skyhook and YH-41 Seneca (USA) Cessna entered the helicopter field following its acquisition of the Seibel Helicopter Company. Work on its first helicopter began in 1952 and the test vehicle was developed into the CH-1 of 1954, of which four were built between 1955 and 1957. Further development led to construction of ten YH-41 Seneca four-seat helicopters for the US Army.

Cessna CH-1C Skyhook (USA) Commercial development of the US Army's YH-41, of which 30 were built between 1959 and 1960. Power was provided by a 201 kW (270 hp) Continental FSO-526-A engine.

CFA D-7 Cri-Cri Major (France) Post-World War II version of the Salmson Cri-Cri two-seat training high-wing monoplane powered by a 63.3 kW (85 hp) Salmson 5AQ radial engine and with enclosed tandem cockpits.

CFA Phryganet, Phrygane and Super Phrygane (France) The Phryganet superseded the Cri-Cri Major in production in 1950. It was followed in turn by the four-seat 100.6 kW (135 hp) Salmson 9NC-engined Phrygane and four-seat Super Phrygane with a similarly rated Salmson 7AQ engine.

Champion 7EC Traveler, Traveler Deluxe and TriTraveler (USA) Between 1955 and 1964 Champion Aircraft produced these three two-seat light aircraft, the TriTraveler differing the most by having a tricycle landing gear. Champion-built aircraft followed many thousands of Champions built by Aeronca between 1946 and 1951. (See **Bellanca**)

Cessna Model 441 Conquest.

Cessna Model 414 Chancellor II.

Cessna Model 421 Golden Eagle II.

Cessna Model 500 Citations.

Champion

Champion 7GC Sky-Trac and 7GCB Challenger (USA) Developments of the Traveler series, the three-seat Sky-Trac powered by a 104.3 kW (140 hp) Lycoming O-290-D2B engine and the two-seat Challenger by a 112 kW (150 hp) Lycoming O-320-A2B.

Chance Vought (USA) In April 1939 the Vought-Sikorsky Aircraft Division of United Aircraft Corporation was formed by consolidation of the former Chance Vought and Sikorsky Divisions of United Aircraft. In January 1943 the Chance Vought and Sikorsky Aircraft Divisions of Vought-Sikorsky were reconstituted as separate manufacturing divisions. As a result aircraft produced before and during World War II are listed under **Vought**, with the exception of the F4U Corsair, which remained in production until 1952.

Cessna Citation III.

Interior of a Cessna Citation II.

Chance Vought F4U Corsair (USA) In 1938 – at which time Chance Vought was a division of United Aircraft Corporation (UAC) – the US Navy was seeking a new single-seat fighter suitable for operation from aircraft carriers. Details of the requirement were circulated to US manufacturers and Chance Vought's proposal (then bearing the company identification V-166B) was sufficiently interesting to be selected for prototype construction. A single prototype was contracted for on 30 June 1938, making its first flight on 29 May 1940.

Realising that performance, load-carrying capability and range were essential ingredients of

Champion 7FC TriTraveler.

a carrier-based fighter, Vought set about designing the smallest possible airframe around the most powerful engine then available. The selection of a four-blade propeller meant that the front fuselage had to be kept well clear of the ground. This dictated a tall, stalky landing gear which would be completely unsuitable for carrier landings. The solution to this problem provided the F4U (as designated by the Navy) with a recognition feature *par excellence*: an inverted gull wing. By mounting the main landing gear at the crank of the wing, it was possible to use compact and robust main struts.

Testing of the XF4U-1 prototype soon demonstrated that the Navy had available a fighter faster than anything else in service with the armed forces. On 30 June 1941 the Vought-Sikorsky Aircraft Division of UAC (as the company was then reformed) received a contract for 584 aircraft under the designation F4U-1. What had by then become an honoured name – Corsair – was to be bestowed on this new aircraft, one which was to prove itself the finest carrier-based fighter of World War II.

F4U-1s began to enter service in October 1942, but in order to provide increased fuel capacity the cockpit had been moved further aft to make room for a fuselage fuel tank. When first tested by the Navy it was believed that this adversely affected the pilot's view, to the extent that the Corsair was considered doubtful for carrier operation. Production aircraft were delivered instead to the US Marine Corps for operation from land bases. It was not until 1944, when Corsairs supplied to the Royal Navy under Lend–Lease were being used effectively from carriers, that the US Navy made a serious reappraisal of their suitability for this role. Shortly after, Navy squadrons were given approval to use the Corsair for the task for which it had been designed.

The Corsair was built also by Brewster Aeronautical Corporation and Goodyear Aircraft Corporation to cope with the high production required, under the initial designations of F3A-1 and FG-1 respectively. Both Vought and Goodyear built a number of variants, the last being the F4U-7, of which 90 were built for supply through MAP to the French Aéronavale. By the time that production ended in December 1952 more than 11,000 had been built; of these 2,012 had been supplied to Britain and 370 to the Royal New Zealand Air Force.

Data (F4U-5N): *Engine* one 1,714 kW (2,300 hp) Wright R-2800-32W radial *Wing span* 12.5 m (41 ft 0 in) *Length* 10.21 m (33 ft 6 in) *Max T-O weight* 6,398 kg (14,106 lb) *Max level speed* 756 km/h (470 mph) *Range* 1,802 km (1,120 miles) *Armament* four 20 mm cannon, plus two 1,000 lb bombs underwing

Chance Vought V-173 low-powered full-scale test version of the XF5U-1, a unique experimental heavy fighter of 1946.

Chance Vought F6U-1 Pirate (USA) Single-seat jet fighter, 30 of which were delivered to the US Navy. It underwent its preliminary flight trials at the USAF test base at Muroc, California, where the first of three prototypes flew on 2 October 1946. Production aircraft were powered by one 18.79 kN (4,225 lb st) Westinghouse J34-WE-30A afterburning turbojet engine.

Chance Vought F7U Cutlass (USA) The Cutlass was a swept-wing tailless single-seat carrier-borne fighter which entered service with the US Navy in several versions from 1952. Production ended in December 1955. It was the first production naval aircraft to achieve supersonic flight, the first to release bombs at a speed greater than the speed of sound and the first to be catapulted from a carrier while carrying nearly 5,000 lb of external stores. It was also the first fighter to have incorporated in its design the use of afterburners, full power controls with an 'artificial feel' system and an automatic stabilisation system.

The Cutlass wing, which was of symmetrical section, was fitted with full-span leading-edge slats, air brakes, power-operated irreversible 'ailavators' (combined ailerons and elevators) and vertical fin and rudder surfaces.

Four versions were produced, beginning with 14 F7U-1s for training and operational evaluation for aircraft carrier use. Power was provided by two J34-WE-32 turbojets. The F7U-1s were followed by 180 larger F7U-3s with folding wings, arrester gear and 20.46 kN (4,600 lb st) J46-WE-8A turbojet engines. Armament was increased to four 20 mm cannon and a new type of underfuselage rocket launcher carrying a Mighty Mouse pack. For strike missions two further packs could be carried under the wings. Delivery of production F7U-3s to the Navy began in 1954. In 1955 the F7U-3P variant was produced for photographic reconnaissance duties and 12 were subsequently completed, each featuring an elongated nose to house the camera equipment. The final version of the Cutlass (of which 98 were produced) was the F7U-3M, basically similar to the F7U-3 but with provision for carrying four Sparrow I beam-riding missiles.

Data: *Engines* as above *Wing span* 11.79 m (38 ft

Champion 7GCB Challenger.

Chance Vought F4U Corsairs operating during the Korean War.

Chance Vought F6U-1 Pirate.

Chase

Two Chance Vought F7U-3s being positioned on the steam catapults of USS *Forrestal*.

Chase YC-122 Avitruc.

Chetverikov MDR-6.

8 in) *Length* 13.5 m (44 ft 3½ in) *Max T-O weight* 14,353 kg (31,642 lb) *Max level speed* 1,094 km/h (680 mph) *Range* 1,062 km (660 miles)

Chase YC-122 Avitruc (USA) Twin-engined transport developed from the CG-18A all-metal transport glider of 1946 and accommodating 30 troops, 24 stretchers or cargo. First flown 18 November 1948. Two YC-122A/Bs and nine YC-122Cs built (see **Fairchild C-119 and C-123**).

Chasle YC-12 Tourbillon (France) Single-seat light monoplane. Plans for its construction are available to amateur builders.

Chetverikov ARK-3 (USSR) Twin-engined (M-25s) flying-boat reconnaissance-bomber of World War II.

Chetverikov MDR-4 and MDR-6 (USSR) All-metal long-range reconnaissance and coastal patrol flying-boat of 1938 built as a follow-on to the unsuccessful MDR-4. Major production version was the MDR-6B powered by two 782.5 kW (1,050 hp) Klimov VK-105 engines mounted on the leading edges of the high monoplane wings. Remained in service until the mid-1950s.

Chiang Hung seaplane (China) Two-seat training and three-seat touring seaplane of the late 1920s powered by a 123 kW (165 hp) Wright Whirlwind radial engine.

Chincul-built Pipers (Argentina) This company, a subsidiary of La Macarena SA (Piper's Argentine distributor), concluded an agreement with Piper Aircraft Corporation in 1971 to manufacture a range of Piper products in Argentina. In 1978 the programme included the PA-23-250 Aztec and Turbo Aztec, PA-25-235 Pawnee D, various Cherokees and Navajos, the PA-34-200T Seneca, Pawnee Brave and Tomahawk.

In January 1978 Chincul was flight testing the prototype of a military training aircraft it had developed from the Cherokee Arrow four-seat light aircraft. It has a more powerful 194 kW (260 hp) Lycoming AEIO-540 series flat-six engine; a two-seat cockpit with new canopy; revised internal equipment; and provision for a built-in machine-gun and underwing weapons for armament training.

Chrislea C.H.3 Series 1 Ace and Series 2 Super Ace (UK) The prototype four-seat C.H.3 Series 1 Ace, with a 93 kW (125 hp) Lycoming engine, first flew in August 1946. The production version, as the all-metal Series 2 Super Ace with a 108 kW (145 hp) de Havilland Gipsy Major 10 engine, was relatively unsuccessful (26 built, including Skyjeeps).

Chrislea C.H.3 Series 3 Super Ace (UK) Development of the Super Ace designed originally for military AOP duties.

Chrislea C.H.3 Series 4 Skyjeep (UK) Luxury version of the civil Series 3 Super Ace with enlarged cabin and other improvements, first flown in 1949.

Christen Eagle II (USA) First flown in February 1977, the Eagle II is a two-seat unlimited-class aerobatic biplane powered by one 149 kW (200 hp) Lycoming AEIO-360-A1D flat-four engine. By January 1979 a total of 184 kits of component parts to build the Eagle II had been sold to amateur constructors.

Cicaré C.K.1 (Argentina) Two–three-seat light helicopter first flown in September 1976. Powered

Chrislea C.H.3A.

by one 142–149 kW (190–200 hp) 4C-27 flat-four engine. Work on a pre-series batch of five C.K.1s was under way in 1979.

Cierva Autogiros (UK) Spaniard Don Juan de la Cierva began experiments with autogiros in 1920 with a converted Deperdussin monoplane as the Cierva C.1. It was unsuccessful, as were the C.2 and C.3, which had not resolved the problem of unbalanced lift. The C.4, first flown on 9 January 1923, was successful and was followed by the C.5. With financial help from the Spanish government, Cierva produced the C.6A. This had the fuselage of an Avro 504K fitted with a four-blade articulated rotor, Bristol Fighter ailerons on outriggers and horn-balanced elevators. First flown in May 1924, it was highly successful. In 1926 the Cierva Autogiro Company was formed. A breakaway company was formed subsequently by its founder Mr (later Cdr) Weir, which completed its first Autogiro in June 1933. A Cierva C.6D became the first two-seat Autogiro in the world and on 30 July 1927 Cierva himself became the first passenger to fly in a rotating-wing aircraft.

Cierva Autogiros were built under licence by seven British companies during the 1920s and 1930s (not including Weir); the best-known of these were those produced by Avro as the C.6, C.8, C.9, C.12, C.17, C.19, C.30A and C.30P. On 18 September 1928 a Cierva C.8L Mk II became the first rotating-wing aircraft to fly the English Channel. Between 1934 and 1935 Avro delivered 12 C.30A Autogiros to the RAF as Rota Is (104.3 kW; 140 hp Siddeley Genet Major engine), which operated initially at the army co-operation school at Old Sarum. During World War II a number of civil Autogiros were also impressed into the RAF. In 1934 Cierva succeeded in producing an Autogiro which could take off vertically, without a forward run. (A full description of C.30 and its achievements appears under Autogiro in the 1936 *Jane's*.)

Christen Eagle II.

Cierva W.9 (UK) Two-seat experimental helicopter first flown in 1947. Special design features included jet thrust used for torque compensation instead of a conventional tail rotor.

Cierva W.11 Air Horse (UK) Experimental twin-rotor helicopter with passenger, freight and crop-spraying applications. Designed originally to meet the requirements of Pest Control Ltd for a large crop-dusting helicopter, it first flew on 8 December 1948. Two prototypes were built. Following negotiations with the Cierva Company, the Saunders-Roe Helicopter Division was formed and this helicopter became the Saro-Cierva Air Horse. (See also **Saro Skeeter**)

Cierva CR Twin (UK) Twin-engined light utility helicopter utilising a co-axial contra-rotating rotor system. First flown on 18 August 1969.

Civil Aviation Department HS-2 Mrigasheer and TG-1 Arudhra (India) Current single-seat Standard Class and tandem two-seat advanced training sailplanes.

Civil Aviation Department Revathi Mk II (India) Two–three-seat light aircraft developed from the Revathi Mk I of 1967.

Clément-Bayard airships (France) The first airship was built in 1908 and sold to the Imperial Russian Army, but was destroyed in 1909 during its trials. The Clément-Bayard II flew in 1910 and became the first airship to fly from the Continent of Europe to Great Britain. The small number of subsequent airships were not particularly successful, one being shot down on 24 August 1914 by French troops thinking it to be a German Zeppelin.

Chrislea C.H.3 Series 3 Super Ace.

Chrislea C.H.3 Series 4 Skyjeep.

Cierva C.1.

Clutton-Tabenor

Cierva C.30P Mk II.

Cierva W.9.

Cierva C.4.

Cierva C.19 Mk IV.

Clutton-Tabenor E.C.2 Easy Too (UK) Single-seat all-wooden folding-wing low-wing monoplane still under construction in 1978. Plans will be available to amateur constructors after the conclusion of flight testing.

Clutton-Tabenor FRED and FRED Series 2 (UK) FRED (Flying Runabout Experimental Design) was designed as a powered aircraft that could be flown by any reasonably experienced glider pilot without further training. First flown on 3 November 1963. Plans have been available to amateur constructors since 1970. The Series 2 version has some restyling.

CNNA HL-1 to HL-6 (Brazil) The HL-1 was this company's designation for the Miniz M-11, a two-seat strut-braced high-wing cabin monoplane trainer that closely resembled the Piper Cub, powered by a 44.7 kW (60 hp) Continental A65-8 flat-four engine. It remained in production in HL-1 Series B form until 1950. Following the HL-2 and HL-4, CNNA produced 50 HL-6 two-seat primary training cantilever low-wing monoplanes from 1943, each powered by a 93 kW (125 hp) Lycoming O-290-C flat-four engine. As the HL-6 Series B Caure, it remained in production until 1950.

Coanda turbine (Romania) This was the world's first jet-propelled aircraft to fly, leaving the ground on 10 December 1910. Designed by Henri Coanda, it was an unequal-span biplane powered by a 37.25 kW (50 hp) Clerget piston engine driving a centrifugal air compressor in the nose of the fuselage (delivering a thrust of 2.16 kN; 485 lb).

Coates S.A.III Swalesong (UK) Two-seat light aircraft scheduled to make its first flight in 1979 or 1980. Suitable for homebuilding.

Commonwealth CA-6 Wackett (Australia) Interim two-seat low-wing monoplane trainer for the RAAF, 200 being built during 1941 and 1942 with 130.4 kW (175 hp) Warner Super Scarab engines.

Commonwealth Boomerang (Australia) The Boomerang was a single-seat fighter monoplane incorporating the principal features of the Wirraway, including the rectangular centre-section and tapering outer-section wings, retractable landing gear and tail unit. Designed and produced after the Japanese entered World War II as an emergency measure to strengthen the RAAF, 250 were built between 1942 and 1944 in four versions. Although not as good as the latest Japanese fighters, Boomerangs were successfully operated in New Guinea and elsewhere and also performed ground attack, target marking and reconnaissance duties.

Data: *Engine* one 894 kW (1,200 hp) Pratt & Whitney R-1830-S3C4G Twin Wasp *Wing span* 11.05 m (36 ft 3 in) *Length* 7.77 m (25 ft 6 in) *Max T-O weight* 3,450 kg (7,606 lb) *Max level speed* 476 km/h (296 mph) *Range* 1,500 km (930 miles) *Armament* two 20 mm Hispano cannon and four 0.303 in machine-guns, plus a 500 lb bomb

Commonwealth Wirraway (Australia) During 1936 an Air Board Technical Commission visited the United States and began negotiations to acquire a manufacturing licence from North American for the N.A.33 two-seat general-purpose monoplane. Negotiations were completed in 1937 and the Commonwealth Aircraft Corporation took delivery of an American-built N.A.33 for submission to official test by the RAAF. The Australian development was known as the Wirraway and the prototype flew on 27 March 1939. The first Wirraway was delivered to the RAAF in July 1939 and by the end of production in 1946 a total of 755 had been built.

Originally intended as a trainer, the Wirraway was widely used by the RAAF as an operational type powered by the Australian-built 447 kW (600 hp) Pratt & Whitney S1H1-G Wasp radial engine.

Data: *Engine* as above *Wing span* 13.11 m (43 ft 0 in) *Length* 8.84 m (29 ft 0 in) *Max T-O weight* 2,882 kg (6,353 lb) *Max level speed* 322 km/h (200 mph)

Commonwealth CA-15 (Australia) First flown in March 1946, the Rolls-Royce Griffon 61-powered CA-15 single-seat fighter was designed as a possible successor to the North American Mustang.

Commonwealth CA-17 Woomera (Australia) Designed as a twin-engined bomber/reconnaissance monoplane to replace the Beaufort.

Commonwealth CA-25 Winjeel (Australia) Three-seat basic training monoplane first flown in February 1955 as the production version of the CA-22 prototype Winjeel of 1950. Production of 62 Winjeels for the RAAF was completed in 1958. Power was provided by a 331.6 kW (445 hp) Pratt & Whitney R-985-AN2 Wasp Junior radial engine.

Commonwealth CA-27 Sabre (Australia) The Commonwealth Sabre, the prototype of which flew for the first time on 3 August 1953, was based on the North American F-86F and incorporated a considerable amount of local major redesign to allow it to be powered by the Rolls-Royce Avon turbojet engine. The first 20 aircraft of the production series were Avon-Sabre Mk 30s with imported Avon RA.7 engines and leading-edge slats. The second series of 19 aircraft were Mk 31s with Commonwealth-built engines, slats deleted and wing leading edges extended.

The third version was the Mk 32, which remains in service today with the Air Force of Indonesia. Power is provided by a 33.36 kN (7,500 lb st) Avon 26 engine and has increased underwing armament. Delivery of Mk 32s (72 built) to the RAAF began in 1958 and the final batch of 21 was completed with the latest radar and provision for Sidewinder missiles in addition to the two 30 mm Aden cannon (and optional 500 lb bomb or drop-tanks). Sidewinder capability was retrofitted to earlier Mk 32s. Max level speed of the Mk 32 is 1,125 km/h (700 mph).

Commonwealth CA-28 Ceres (Australia) Single-seat (with provision for a passenger during a ferry flight) agricultural low-wing monoplane, powered by a 447 kW (600 hp) Pratt & Whitney

R-1340-S3H1-G radial engine. Operated successfully in Australia and New Zealand.

Comper C.L.A.7 Swift (UK) Comper Aircraft Company was formed in 1929 to produce the Swift single-seat light monoplane powered by an 89.4 kW (120 hp) de Havilland Gipsy III or Gipsy Major engine. Many remarkable flights were made by Swifts during the 1930s, including a record flight from England to Australia between 31 October and 9 November 1931 by Mr Butler. Comper's Intermediate Trainer, three-seat Mouse, Streak racer (built for the Coupe Deutsch de la Meurthe) and Kite two-seat touring aircraft were prototypes only.

Civil Aviation Department Revathi Mk II.

Comte AC-1 (Switzerland) Single-seat parasol-wing fighter of 1929 powered by a 313 kW (420 hp) Gnome Rhône-built Jupiter engine and built for the Swiss Air Force.

Comte AC-3 (Switzerland) Twin-engined transport and bombing monoplane powered by tandem 447 kW (600 hp) Hispano-Suiza engines.

Comte AC-4 Gentleman (Switzerland) Two–three-seat high-wing cabin monoplane powered normally by a 78.25 kW (105 hp) Cirrus Hermes III engine. Eleven built between 1928 and 1930.

Comte AC-8 (Switzerland) Six-seat high-wing cabin monoplane of 1930. Three built for commercial operations.

Colomban MC 10 Cricri (France) Single-seat ultra-light homebuilt monoplane powered by two modified 160 cc Valmet SM 160J two-stroke engines rated at 8.9 kW (12 hp).

Colonial Skimmer (USA) See **Lake LA-4**

Condor Shoestring (USA) Single-seat Formula One racing monoplane. Plans for its construction are available to amateur builders.

Conroy CL-44-0 (USA) Conversion of the Canadair CL-44 freighter increasing volumetric capacity of the cargo compartment by almost 100%. First flown on 26 November 1969.

Cierva W.11 Air Horse.

Cierva CR Twin.

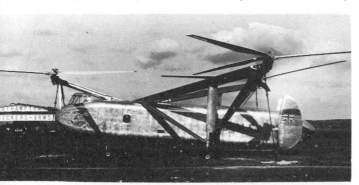

Conroy

Clutton-Tabenor FRED Series 2.

Coates SA.II Swalesong Series I, from which the SA.III has been developed.

Commonwealth CA-6 Wackett.

Commonwealth Boomerangs.

Conroy Stolifter (USA) Extensively modified Cessna Model 337 Super Skymaster, the primary difference being the deletion of the Skymaster's rear-mounted engine and installation of a 428.5 kW (575 shp) Garrett AiResearch TPE 331-25A turboprop in the nose.

Conroy Turbo Albatross (USA) Turboprop-engined conversion of the Grumman HU-16 Albatross amphibian powered by two 1,297 kW (1,740 shp) Rolls-Royce Dart RDa.6 Mk 510s.

Conroy/Douglas Turbo Three (USA) Turboprop conversion of the DC-3 with Dart RDa.6 Mk 510 engines.

Consolidated B-24 Liberator (USA) When in 1939 Consolidated Aircraft Corporation began design of a bomber aircraft intended to be superior to the Boeing B-17, the company could never have imagined that more than 18,000 of these aircraft would be built (as the B-24A to -M for the USAAF and Liberator I to IX for RAF Coastal Command and Bomber Command). The aim of the design team was to achieve better load/range performance than that of the B-17, the basis of the design being a wide-span narrow-chord cantilever wing, mounted high on a deep-section fuselage.

Construction was conventional all-metal, but there were several innovations in addition to the new wing. For the first time on a large aircraft a retractable tricycle-type landing gear was introduced. The bomb bay was deep enough for bombs to be stowed vertically and wide enough to comprise two bays separated by a catwalk providing communication between the flight deck and rear fuselage. Instead of conventional bomb doors, which can affect flight characteristics when open, the bomb bay was closed by roller-shutter-type doors.

The prototype XB-24 flew for the first time on 29 December 1939, by which time the USAAC had ordered seven YB-24s for service trials and others had been ordered by Great Britain and France. These had the same engines as the prototype, but introduced pneumatic de-icing boots for wing and tail unit leading edges. The first production B-24As were delivered in 1941 to the USAAF (and others to Britain as LB-30A trans-

ports for transatlantic ferry flights). During the period of their construction the original prototype was re-engined with turbocharged Pratt & Whitney R-1830-41s, at the same time having the oil coolers mounted on each side of the engine. This was responsible for the unusual elliptical cowlings which, together with the large twin oval endplate fins, made the Liberator easily identifiable.

Subsequent Liberators had increased armament and armour protection. The first major production version was the B-24D, powered by R-1830-43 engines, of which the majority of more than 2,700 built went to the USAAF as bombers. A number were subsequently taken over by the US Navy as PB4Y-1 anti-submarine aircraft. RAF Bomber Command and Coastal Command also received 382 as Liberator III/IIIAs and Vs. The major production version of the Liberator was, however, the B-24J with R-1830-65 engines, making up more than one-third of the total production. These were supplied to the US, British, Canadian and other air forces.

Although the B-24 was deployed alongside the B-17 in Europe, and flew in Africa and the Middle East, its major contribution to America's wartime operations was in the Pacific, where it was first flown in action against the Japanese in January 1942. In Europe it is best remembered for bombing Rome on 19 July 1943 and for a low-level attack by 177 aircraft on the Ploesti oil refineries in Romania on 1 August 1943, a 4,345 km (2,700 mile) round-trip mission from Benghazi in Libya, during which 57 of these eight–ten-crew aircraft were lost. (See also **Consolidated C-87** and **PB4Y-2 Privateer**)

Data (B-24M): *Engines* four 894 kW (1,200 hp) Pratt & Whitney R-1830-65 radials *Wing span* 33.53 m (110 ft 0 in) *Length* 20.47 m (67 ft 2 in) *Max T-O weight* 29,257 kg (64,500 lb) *Max level speed* 483 km/h (300 mph) *Combat range* 3,380 km (2,100 miles) *Armament* ten 0.50 in machine-guns, plus up to 3,992 kg (8,800 lb) bombs

Consolidated B-32 Dominator (USA) The B-32 was the last US heavy bomber to go into

action during World War II, aircraft of this type flying a score or so of sorties before Japan surrendered. It was designed to the same specification as the Boeing B-29, considerably more development being necessary for the B-32. Pressurisation and remote control of the gun turrets were abandoned and the twin-ruddered B-24-type tail was replaced by a very large single fin and rudder on the B-32. The first of three prototypes flew on 7 September 1942. A total of 114 were built, powered by 1,639 kW (2,200 hp) Wright R-3350-23 engines driving Curtiss Electric reversible-pitch four-blade propellers. Armament comprised ten 0.50 in machine-guns and up to 9,072 kg (20,000 lb) of bombs.

Consolidated NY (USA) Two-seat flying and gunnery trainer of the mid-1920s operated by the US Navy in considerable numbers until the end of the 1930s on wheel and float landing gears.

Consolidated PY-1, P2Y and Commodore (USA) In the late 1920s Consolidated won a US Navy competition for a naval patrol flying-boat. Known as the PY-1, it was powered by two 317 kW (425 hp) Pratt & Whitney Wasp engines mounted below the parasol monoplane wing. As a patrol type it was known as the Admiral. With slight modification the aircraft could be used as a 20–32-passenger commercial transport as the Commodore (410 kW; 550 hp Hornet engines), and production Commodores were supplied to several airlines including Pan American Airways.

The P2Y-1 was a development of the PY-1 and between 1932 and 1933 Consolidated produced 23 examples for the US Navy. These differed mainly in having sesquiplane type wings, enclosed accommodation and 428.5 kW (575 hp) R-1820 Cyclone engines. A second production batch of 23 aircraft followed for the Navy as P2Y-3s, with 559 kW (750 hp) R-1820-90 engines mounted on the leading edges of the upper wings instead of below. Eventually, most of the P2Y-1s

were modified to have engines similarly mounted and were redesignated P2Y-2s. In addition a small number of P2Ys were exported, including six to Argentina. Yet a further development of the PY-1 concept was the P3Y-1, which became the PBY Catalina.

Consolidated N2Y (USA) Six Fleet Type 5 biplanes bought by the US Navy to train Curtiss Sparrowhawk pilots. Each aircraft was fitted with apparatus for hooking onto airship trapezes (see **Curtiss Sparrowhawk**).

Consolidated N4Y (USA) Two-seat biplane trainer (Consolidated Series 21-A) of which a small number were acquired by the US Navy and Coast Guard.

Consolidated PB-2A (USA) In 1934 the USAAC ordered 50 examples of the P-30A, a two-seat cantilever low-wing monoplane fighter with a retractable undercarriage and a 521.6 kW (700 hp) Curtiss V-1560-61 engine. These were redesignated PB-2As when in service. Armament comprised two forward-firing and one rear-mounted machine-guns. A ground attack version, known as the A-11, was less successful and only a handful of evaluation aircraft were ordered.

Consolidated PBY Catalina (USA) One of the most successful flying-boats to serve extensively throughout World War II and the most numerous flying-boat in aviation history, the Consolidated Model 28, designed by Isaac Laddon, originated from a US Navy requirement of late 1933. The prototype XP3Y-1, developed from the PY-1/P2Y and flown for the first time on 28 March 1935, introduced some distinctive features. Most important was the parasol wing constructed on the basis of a cantilever wing requiring no supporting structures, although in fact two small I-section struts were mounted between wing and hull on each side. This deletion of the multitudinous struts and bracing wires – seemingly inseparable from flying-boat design until then – offered an immediate improvement in performance. Another new feature was the intro-

Commonwealth Wirraways.

Commonwealth CA-15.

Commonwealth CA-25 Winjeel.

Commonwealth CA-27 Sabre.

Consolidated

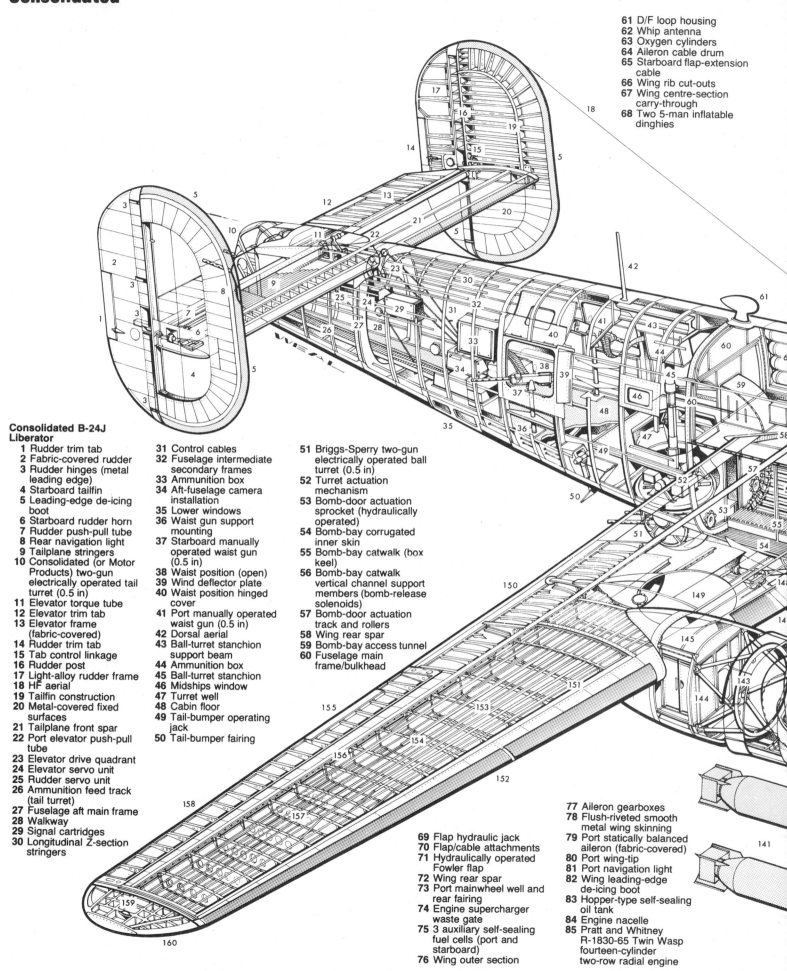

61 D/F loop housing
62 Whip antenna
63 Oxygen cylinders
64 Aileron cable drum
65 Starboard flap-extension cable
66 Wing rib cut-outs
67 Wing centre-section carry-through
68 Two 5-man inflatable dinghies

Consolidated B-24J Liberator

1 Rudder trim tab
2 Fabric-covered rudder
3 Rudder hinges (metal leading edge)
4 Starboard tailfin
5 Leading-edge de-icing boot
6 Starboard rudder horn
7 Rudder push-pull tube
8 Rear navigation light
9 Tailplane stringers
10 Consolidated (or Motor Products) two-gun electrically operated tail turret (0.5 in)
11 Elevator torque tube
12 Elevator trim tab
13 Elevator frame (fabric-covered)
14 Rudder trim tab
15 Tab control linkage
16 Rudder post
17 Light-alloy rudder frame
18 HF aerial
19 Tailfin construction
20 Metal-covered fixed surfaces
21 Tailplane front spar
22 Port elevator push-pull tube
23 Elevator drive quadrant
24 Elevator servo unit
25 Rudder servo unit
26 Ammunition feed track (tail turret)
27 Fuselage aft main frame
28 Walkway
29 Signal cartridges
30 Longitudinal Z-section stringers

31 Control cables
32 Fuselage intermediate secondary frames
33 Ammunition box
34 Aft-fuselage camera installation
35 Lower windows
36 Waist gun support mounting
37 Starboard manually operated waist gun (0.5 in)
38 Waist position (open)
39 Wind deflector plate
40 Waist position hinged cover
41 Port manually operated waist gun (0.5 in)
42 Dorsal aerial
43 Ball-turret stanchion support beam
44 Ammunition box
45 Ball-turret stanchion
46 Midships window
47 Turret well
48 Cabin floor
49 Tail-bumper operating jack
50 Tail-bumper fairing

51 Briggs-Sperry two-gun electrically operated ball turret (0.5 in)
52 Turret actuation mechanism
53 Bomb-door actuation sprocket (hydraulically operated)
54 Bomb-bay corrugated inner skin
55 Bomb-bay catwalk (box keel)
56 Bomb-bay catwalk vertical channel support members (bomb-release solenoids)
57 Bomb-door actuation track and rollers
58 Wing rear spar
59 Bomb-bay access tunnel
60 Fuselage main frame/bulkhead

69 Flap hydraulic jack
70 Flap/cable attachments
71 Hydraulically operated Fowler flap
72 Wing rear spar
73 Port mainwheel well and rear fairing
74 Engine supercharger waste gate
75 3 auxiliary self-sealing fuel cells (port and starboard)
76 Wing outer section

77 Aileron gearboxes
78 Flush-riveted smooth metal wing skinning
79 Port statically balanced aileron (fabric-covered)
80 Port wing-tip
81 Port navigation light
82 Wing leading-edge de-icing boot
83 Hopper-type self-sealing oil tank
84 Engine nacelle
85 Pratt and Whitney R-1830-65 Twin Wasp fourteen-cylinder two-row radial engine

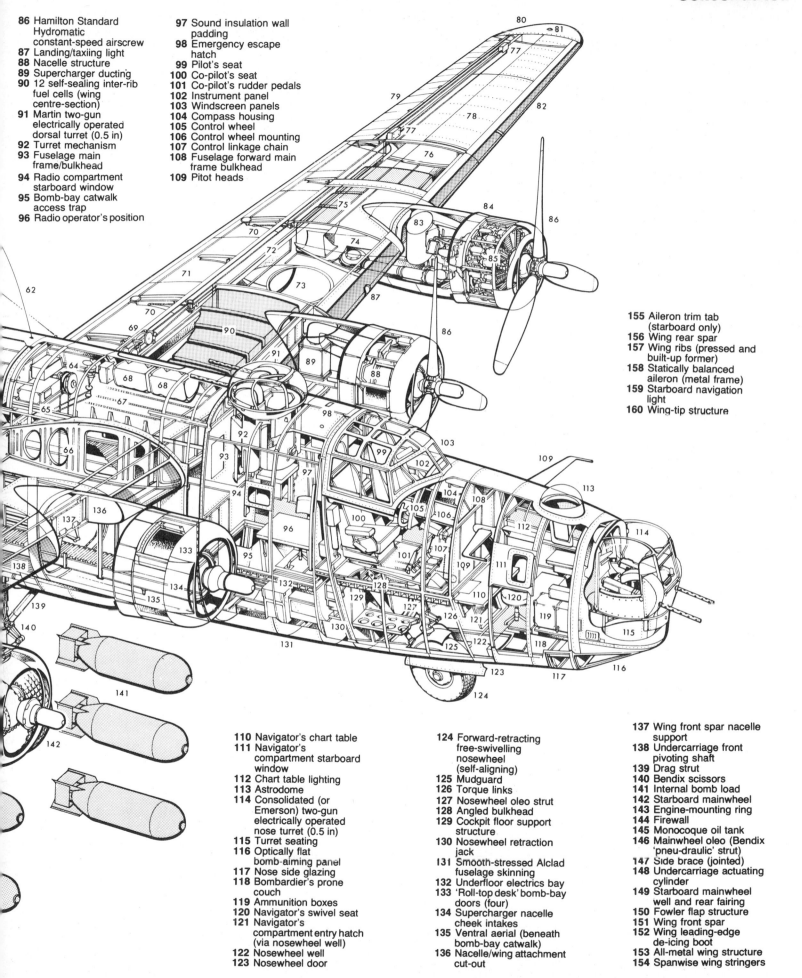

86 Hamilton Standard Hydromatic constant-speed airscrew
87 Landing/taxiing light
88 Nacelle structure
89 Supercharger ducting
90 12 self-sealing inter-rib fuel cells (wing centre-section)
91 Martin two-gun electrically operated dorsal turret (0.5 in)
92 Turret mechanism
93 Fuselage main frame/bulkhead
94 Radio compartment starboard window
95 Bomb-bay catwalk access trap
96 Radio operator's position

97 Sound insulation wall padding
98 Emergency escape hatch
99 Pilot's seat
100 Co-pilot's seat
101 Co-pilot's rudder pedals
102 Instrument panel
103 Windscreen panels
104 Compass housing
105 Control wheel
106 Control wheel mounting
107 Control linkage chain
108 Fuselage forward main frame bulkhead
109 Pitot heads

155 Aileron trim tab (starboard only)
156 Wing rear spar
157 Wing ribs (pressed and built-up former)
158 Statically balanced aileron (metal frame)
159 Starboard navigation light
160 Wing-tip structure

110 Navigator's chart table
111 Navigator's compartment starboard window
112 Chart table lighting
113 Astrodome
114 Consolidated (or Emerson) two-gun electrically operated nose turret (0.5 in)
115 Turret seating
116 Optically flat bomb-aiming panel
117 Nose side glazing
118 Bombardier's prone couch
119 Ammunition boxes
120 Navigator's swivel seat
121 Navigator's compartment entry hatch (via nosewheel well)
122 Nosewheel well
123 Nosewheel door

124 Forward-retracting free-swivelling nosewheel (self-aligning)
125 Mudguard
126 Torque links
127 Nosewheel oleo strut
128 Angled bulkhead
129 Cockpit floor support structure
130 Nosewheel retraction jack
131 Smooth-stressed Alclad fuselage skinning
132 Underfloor electrics bay
133 'Roll-top desk' bomb-bay doors (four)
134 Supercharger nacelle cheek intakes
135 Ventral aerial (beneath bomb-bay catwalk)
136 Nacelle/wing attachment cut-out

137 Wing front spar nacelle support
138 Undercarriage front pivoting shaft
139 Drag strut
140 Bendix scissors
141 Internal bomb load
142 Starboard mainwheel
143 Engine-mounting ring
144 Firewall
145 Monocoque oil tank
146 Mainwheel oleo (Bendix 'pneu-draulic' strut)
147 Side brace (jointed)
148 Undercarriage actuating cylinder
149 Starboard mainwheel well and rear fairing
150 Fowler flap structure
151 Wing front spar
152 Wing leading-edge de-icing boot
153 All-metal wing structure
154 Spanwise wing stringers

Consolidated

Commonwealth CA-28 Ceres.

Condor Shoestring.

duction of stabilising floats which retracted in flight to form the wingtips. Initial trials of the prototype left little doubt that the Navy was about to acquire a significant aircraft. PBY-1s began to enter squadron service in 1937 and by mid-1938 14 squadrons were operational.

Initial export aircraft went to Russia, where the type was built subsequently in large numbers under the designation GST. The RAF acquired a single example for evaluation in 1939 and almost immediately ordered a batch of 50, the first of many to serve with Coastal Command. The name Catalina (adopted first by the RAF) was used later by the USN for the various versions which entered service. The type was also to serve with the RAAF, RCAF, RNZAF and the air arm of the Dutch East Indies. Production as a pure flying-boat ended with the PBY-4, for the last of these was converted to an amphibian with retractable tricycle-type landing gear, under the designation XPBY-5A. Subsequent aircraft had this as standard. Used widely throughout World War II, many amphibious Catalinas remained in service for air-sea rescue for some years after the end of the war.

Comper C.L.A.7 Swift.

Data (PBY-5A): *Engines* two 894 kW (1,200 hp) Pratt & Whitney R-1830-92 radials *Wing span* 31.7 m (104 ft 0 in) *Length* 19.46 m (63 ft 10 in) *Max T-O weight* 16,066 kg (35,420 lb) *Max level speed* 282 km/h (175 mph) *Range* 3,782 km (2,350 miles) *Armament* three 0.30 in and two 0.50 in machine-guns, plus up to 1,814 kg (4,000 lb) bombs

Consolidated PB2Y Coronado (USA) The XPB2Y-1 prototype of the Coronado, ordered in 1936, was first flown in December 1937 and delivered to the US Navy in August 1938. After service trials it served for some time as Flagship of Aircraft, Scouting Force, US Navy. The first PB2Y-2 (the production development) went into service in January 1941. The PB2Y-3 was ordered

Conroy CL-44-O.

in quantity in 1941 and remained in production until 1944 as a long-range patrol-bomber flying-boat.

Many Coronado flying-boats were converted into transports under the designation PB2Y-3R, with military equipment removed, nose and tail turret positions faired over and the four 894 kW (1,200 hp) Pratt & Whitney R-1830-88 Twin Wasp engines replaced by R-1830-92s. Accommodation in this version was for a crew of five (instead of ten) and 44 passengers; 7,257 kg (16,000 lb) of cargo; or 24 passengers and 3,900 kg (8,600 lb) of cargo. A naval ambulance version of the Coronado was also produced as the PB2Y-5H, accommodating 25 stretchers. A total of 210 PB2Y-3s were built, ten of which were acquired by RAF Transport Command for trans-atlantic freight carrying.

Data (PB2Y-3): *Engines* as above *Wing span* 35.05 m (115 ft 0 in) *Length* 24.16 m (79 ft 3 in) *Max T-O weight* 30,344 kg (68,000 lb) *Max level speed* 343 km/h (213 mph) *Range* 1,720 km (1,070 miles) *Armament* eight 0.50 in machine-guns in three power-operated turrets in nose, tail and dorsal positions, plus up to 3,628 kg (8,000 lb) of bombs or depth-charges carried internally and 1,814 kg (4,000 lb) of similar weapons carried under the wings.

Consolidated PB4Y-2 Privateer (USA) The PB4Y-2 was a long-range oversea bomber-reconnaissance development of the PB4Y-1 Liberator. The original contract was placed with Consolidated by the US Navy in May 1943 and work on three prototypes started almost immediately. Four months later, on 20 September, the first prototype flew. It used the same Davis wing and landing gear as the Liberator but was otherwise a new design embodying most of the structural features of its predecessor. The most obvious change was the single fin and rudder. The fuselage forward of the wings was lengthened and armament was rearranged to include a Consolidated nose turret, two Martin dorsal turrets, a Consolidated tail turret and two Erco 'blister'-type waist turrets on the fuselage sides, all with 0.50 in Browning machine-guns. A total of 740

were built. A transport version was also built as the RY-3, of which a small number found their way into US Navy and RAF service.

Consolidated PT series, BT-7, O-17 and TW-3 (USA) Following delivery to the US Army of examples of the 134 kW (180 hp) Wright-powered TW-3 side-by-side two-seat biplane trainer (originated by the Dayton-Wright Company), it produced about 170 PT-1 tandem trainers; 250 similar PT-3/3As with 164 kW (220 hp) Wright J-5 engines; 45 PT-11Ds with 149 kW (200 hp) Lycoming R-680-3 engines; and ten BT-7s with 223.5 kW (300 hp) Pratt & Whitney Wasp Junior engines. In addition a number of PT-3s were built as O-17s for use by the Air National Guard.

Consolidated TBY-2 Sea Wolf (USA) The TBY-2 was the production development of the Vought-designed XTBU-1 torpedo-bomber. Power was provided by a 1,490 kW (2,000 hp) Pratt & Whitney R-2800 engine and accommodation was for a crew of three. Production was cancelled before any aircraft could be delivered to operational units of the US Navy, although 180 had been built.

Consolidated Model 21-A/Courier (USA) Two-seat biplane powered by a 164 kW (220 hp) Wright Whirlwind radial engine. Similar to the US Army's PT-3.

Consolidated Fleet series (USA) Between 1923 (when Consolidated was incorporated) and 1929 the company completed contracts for more than 500 training aircraft, including Husky and Trusty primary training biplanes. During 1928 the factory area was doubled and the Husky Junior two-seat training and sporting biplane was produced, powered by a Warner Scarab engine. The production and marketing of this machine were taken over by Fleet Aircraft Incorporated (a division of Consolidated) and it was renamed the Fleet biplane. It was sold as the Type 1 with the 82 kW (110 hp) Scarab engine and the Type 2 with a 74.5 kW (100 hp) Kinner K-5 engine. During 1929 about 300 Fleet biplanes were produced.

In 1928 the Type 7 and 7A were added to the aircraft in production, both developed from the Husky Junior, the latter with a 93.15 kW (125 hp) Kinner B-5 engine as standard. By 1932 the bi-

planes were known as Consolidated Fleet types. The Fleet 5, 10 and 11 were similar, powered by Kinner K-5, Kinner B-5 and the 119 kW (160 hp) Kinner R-5 engines respectively. Such was the importance of the Fleet trainers that during 1933–34 Consolidated's production centred upon them; ordered for civil use and by several governments. The Type 10G, with a 97 kW (130 hp) de Havilland Gipsy Major engine, was then being produced for the Romanian and Portuguese governments, while Type 10s and 11s were under construction for China and Mexico. Production of the Fleet biplane continued for several more years.

Consolidated Fleetster series (USA) The Fleetster was a high-wing monoplane of Lockheed-like external appearance, powered in its original Type 17 and Type 20 production forms by a 428.5 kW (575 hp) Pratt & Whitney Hornet radial engine. The Type 17 had the wing mounted directly on top of the fuselage and an enclosed cockpit for the pilots located in the leading edge of the wing in front of the six-seat passenger cabin. The Type 20 had a wing attached by a cabane above the fuselage and the open pilot's cockpit was located aft of the wing and five-seat passenger cabin. The latter type was supplied primarily as a mail and express plane and the

Conroy/Douglas Turbo Three.

normal cabin space provided an unusually large hold. One user of the Fleetster was NYRBA, which later became part of Pan American. The Types 17-A and 20-A were similar to the earlier models but were larger (accommodating nine and seven passengers respectively) and powered by a 447 kW (600 hp) Wright Cyclone engine. An operator of the Type 20-A was TWA.

Continental Copters JC-1 Jet-Cat (USA) Special-purpose agricultural aircraft based on the airframe of a Bell JetRanger.

Continental Copters El Tomcat Mk III and Mk V (USA) Each version of the El Tomcat is

Consolidated B-24 Liberators in the Pacific theatre of war.

Convair

Consolidated Commodore.

basically a Bell Model 47G-2 helicopter which has been converted into a specialised single-seat agricultural helicopter. Payload is increased by deletion of unnecessary structure and equipment. The Mk III prototype first flew in April 1965 and was an improved version of the Mk II. A small number of Mk IIIs were followed by Mk IIIAs with Franklin 6V4-200, 6V-335 or 6V-350 engines. The IIIB of 1967 had a still lower and repositioned windscreen, modified glassfibre nose, lower cabin roof and a 6V-350 engine. The Mk IIIC of 1968 was an improved version with a 149–175 kW (200–235 hp) 6V4-200-C32, 6V-335-A or 6V-350A engine. The Mk V entered production in 1968 with a 164 kW (220 hp) Lycoming VO-435-B1A engine, followed by the improved Mk V-A with a 194 kW (260 hp) VO-435-A1F engine and a folding jump-seat to permit carriage of a flagman to distant work sites. The latest version is the 198 kW (265 hp) VO-435-B1A-engined Mk V-B.

Consolidated B-32 Dominator.

Consolidated XPY-1 Admiral prototype.

Convair-Liner 240 and T-29 (USA) The first post-World War II commercial transport designed by Consolidated Vultee was evolved primarily as a DC-3 replacement. The prototype first flew at San Diego on 16 March 1947 and the first licensed aircraft was delivered to American Airlines on 28 February 1948. Altogether 176 were built. Accommodation was provided for 40 passengers. The aircraft was powered by two 1,788 kW (2,400 hp) Pratt & Whitney R-2800-CA18 radial engines.

Military versions of the 240 were produced as the T-29A to E aircrew trainers for navigators and bombardiers; and as the C-131A Samaritan personnel or casualty evacuation transport accommodating 37 passengers or 27 stretchers.

Convair-Liner 340 (USA) Although based on the Convair 240, the 340 was largely a new aircraft with greater wing span (32.11 m; 105 ft 4 in) and area; a longer fuselage for 44 passengers;

Consolidated PB-2A modified into a single-seat fighter. Remained a prototype.

R-2800-CB16 or CB17 engines; greater all-up weight of 21,318 kg (47,000 lb); and many interior design improvements. The first aircraft flew on 5 October 1951 and the first delivery to an airline (United Air Lines) was made on 28 March 1952. A total of 209 had been built by January 1955, when the last two production aircraft were delivered to REAL (Brazil). The USAF also operated 340s as C-131 or VC-131 transports, flying and ECM trainers and for other duties; while the US Navy/Marine Corps received 37 transports as R4Ys.

Convair 440 Metropolitan (USA) The 440 was a development of the 340 with modifications to increase speed by about 8 km/h (5 mph) and to reduce the noise level in the cabin. Special kits were also made available to convert 340s to 440 standard. Accommodation was provided for between 44 and 52 passengers. The prototype first flew on 6 October 1955 and 162 were built before production was phased out in the spring of 1958. A few were also operated by the USAF and US Navy.

Convair (Allison) 580 (USA) Allison was named prime contractor for a conversion under which operators of the Convair 340/440 could have their aircraft modified to 580 standard by having the original engines replaced by 2,794.5 kW (3,750 eshp) Allison 501-D13 turboprops. By January 1968 a total of 123 aircraft conversion had been delivered.

Convair 600/640 (USA) The Convair 600 and 640 were turboprop conversions of the Convair-Liner 240 and 340/440 transports, developed as a joint undertaking by Rolls-Royce of Britain and the Convair division of General Dynamics. Conversion involved replacing the original piston engines with two 2,254 kW (3,025 ehp) Rolls-Royce Dart RDa.10 Mk 542-4 turboprops. With interior modifications, accommodation of the 640 could be raised to 56 passengers.

The first Convair 600 flew on 20 May 1965 and the type first entered service with Central Airlines on 30 November 1965. The 640 first entered service with Caribair on 22 December 1965.

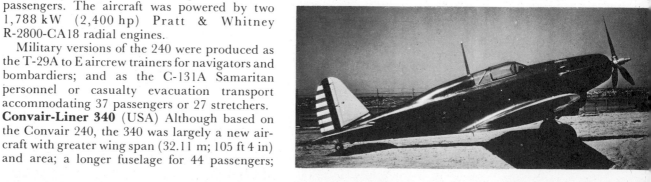

Consolidated PBY
Catalina.

Convair 880 (USA) Announced in April 1956, the Convair 880 was produced as a medium-range jet transport. It was built in two versions: the 880 Model 22 basic model with 49.8 kN (11,200 lb st) General Electric CJ-805-3 turbojet engines, flown for the first time on 27 January 1959; and the 880 Model 22-M with 51.8 kN (11,650 lb st) CJ-805-3B turbojets, power-boosted rudder and four leading-edge slats. The first 880 Model 22-M flew on 3 October 1960. Most 880s had been withdrawn from service by their original operators by 1973, although the type still remains in service today (1980).
Data: *Engines* as above *Wing span* 36.58 m (120 ft 0 in) *Length* 39.42 m (129 ft 4 in) *Max T-O weight* (Model 22-M) 87,540 kg (193,000 lb) *Max cruising speed* 990 km/h (615 mph) *Range* (Model 22-M) 4,630 km (2,880 miles) *Accommodation* 94–110 passengers

Convair 990 Coronado (USA) Announced on 30 July 1958, the 990 (formerly known as the Convair 600) was developed from the Model 880 to meet the specific requirements of American Airlines and was given a longer fuselage and turbofan engines. The first Coronado flew on 24 January 1961. As a result of early testing, Krueger leading-edge flaps were added between the fuselage and the inner engines to increase elevator effectiveness and the outer engine pods were moved rearward to ensure speedier subsidence of vibration induced during test flying. The first 990 delivery was made to American Airlines on 8 January 1962, passenger services beginning on 18 March.

In February 1962 the company completed a speed and range/payload improvement programme for the 990 which led to the redesignation 990A. All aircraft in service were modified to 990A standard, with engine pods extended rearwards to reduce external drag; reduced droop on the wing leading-edge; full-span Krueger flaps in place of the former combination of flaps and slats; and a new fairing at the wing-fuselage juncture. By 1977 the last of the original operators had

Consolidated PB2Y-2
Coronado.

withdrawn their airliners from service, but a number remain flying today with other operators.
Data (990A): *Engines* four 71.17 kN (16,000 lb st) General Electric CJ-805-23B turbofans *Wing span* 36.58 m (120 ft 0 in) *Length* 42.43 m (139 ft 2½ in) *Max T-O weight* 114,760 kg (253,000 lb) *Max cruising speed* 990 km/h (615 mph) *Range* 6,115 km (3,800 miles) *Accommodation* up to 106 passengers

Convair B-36 (USA) Production of the B-36 heavy strategic bomber ceased in August 1954 and, after a service life of 11 years, it was declared obsolete in 1957. Of the 382 built, 95 had been reduced to scrap within a year.

First flown in prototype form on 8 August 1946, the XB-36 prototype was originally fitted with two single main landing gear wheels, but was later equipped with a multi-wheel main gear introduced on the B-36A. The YB-36 production prototype first flew on 4 December 1947. It was followed by the initial production version, the B-36A, powered by six 2,235.6 kW (3,000 hp) Pratt & Whitney R-4360-25 pusher engines mounted in the trailing edges of the wings. Only 22 were built, originally without armament and used for training and type familiarisation. The B-36B, powered by 2,608 kW (3,500 hp) R-4360-41 engines, was fully equipped for combat with full armament. The first flew on 8 July 1948 and the last was delivered to the USAF in December 1951.

The B-36D had the additional power of four General Electric J47 turbojet engines in pairs in pods under the outer wings to supplement the R-4360-41 engines. The prototype, a converted B-36B, first flew on 26 March 1949. With this version the over-target speed increased to more

Transport version of the
Consolidated PB2Y
Coronado with guns
removed.

Consolidated PB4Y-2
Privateer.

Convair

Consolidated PT-1.

Continental Copters El Tomcat IIIB.

Convair-Liner 240.

Convair T-29B.

than 700 km/h (435 mph). It also had snap-action bomb doors instead of the sliding type.

The RB-36D was a long-range strategic reconnaissance version of the B-36D, with 14 cameras in the rear bomb bay. The RB-36E, another strategic reconnaissance version, was a modified B-36A re-engined with R-4360-41s and the J47 jet engines. The fourth production bomber was the B-36F powered by six 2,832 kW (3,800 hp) R-4360-43 engines and J47s, and a long-range reconnaissance version of this model was produced as the RB-36F.

The B-36H had 2,832 kW (3,800 hp) R-4360-53 engines and J47s and incorporated a new two-station flight engineer's panel and improved radar, electronic and night lighting equipment. A long-range reconnaissance version was the RB-36H. The final version was the B-36J, with additional fuel tanks and a strengthened landing gear.

Data (B-36H): *Engines* as above *Wing span* 70.14 m (230 ft 0 in) *Length* 49.4 m (162 ft 1 in) *Max T-O weight* 162,386 kg (358,000 lb) *Max level speed* 700 km/h (435 mph) *Range* 10,943 km (6,800 miles) *Armament* six retractable remotely controlled turrets, each mounting twin 20 mm cannon, plus two 20 mm cannon flexibly mounted in nose and two in radar-controlled tail turret; up to 38,100 kg (84,000 lb) of bombs.

Convair B-58 Hustler (USA) The Hustler supersonic delta-wing bomber stemmed from a USAF design competition which was won in 1949. This 'generalised bomber' study contract examined the feasibility of a manned supersonic bombing system. Another USAF competition resulted in the MX-1964 contract (awarded in August 1952) to produce the B-58 as a flyable bomber under the 'weapon system' management concept which made the company responsible not only for the airframe, but for managing the

development of all B-58 systems with the exception of the engines.

The B-58 carried a crew of three in tandem in individual cockpits. It was designed around the 'minimum size' concept and an important part of the design was the disposable armament and fuel pod which was carried beneath the slender fuselage. In combat the lower component that carried fuel could only be dropped as soon as the fuel became exhausted; the upper component contained both fuel and one of the aircraft's nuclear or conventional weapons. With its weapons dropped the aircraft could then return to base in a 'clean' mode. Interestingly the B-58 was the first aircraft in which the crew had individual escape capsules for emergency use at supersonic speeds.

The first B-58 prototype flew on 11 November 1956. The standard production version was the B-58A, the first eight of which were powered by four General Electric J79-GE-1 turbojet engines and the remainder with 69.4 kN (15,600 lb st) J79-GE-5Bs. A total of 86 were built before production ended in the autumn of 1962. In addition to the genuine tactical B-58As, ten of the 30 service test models were brought up to fully operational standard and eight more were converted into TB-58A advanced trainers. Delivery of the operational B-58A to SAC's 43rd Bombardment Wing at Carswell AFB, Texas, began in December 1959 and the first of three squadrons became operational in August 1960. The B-58 was withdrawn from service in 1970.

Data: *Engines* as above *Wing span* 17.32 m (56 ft 10 in) *Length* 29.49 m (96 ft 9 in) *Max T-O weight* 73,935 kg (163,000 lb) *Max level speed* 2,229 km/h (1,385 mph) *Range* 3,862 km (2,400 miles) *Armament* one General Electric T-171E3 Vulcan 20 mm multi-barrel cannon in flexible mounting in tailcone (radar-directed), plus nuclear or conventional bombs in the pod and under the wings

Convair C-87 (USA) Transport version of the B-24D Liberator. The USAAF received 261 25-passenger C-87s and six C-87As as sleepers for night flights and the RAF received a small number of C-87s.

Convair F-102 Delta Dagger (USA) In very much the same way that Short Brothers built the S.B.5 to serve as a research vehicle for the English Electric Lightning, Convair designed in 1948 an experimental delta-wing research aircraft. Designated XF-92A, it was intended to provide data for the F-92 supersonic fighter which Convair had designed in collaboration with Dr Alexander Lippisch, the German aerodynamicist whose work since 1926 had been concerned mainly with delta wings and tailless aircraft.

When, in 1950, the USAF issued Requests for Proposals for a new interceptor, Convair's submission was basically a scaled-up version of their F-92 design; it was good enough to be awarded a contract for two YF-102 prototypes in November 1951. The first of these flew on 24 October 1953, but was extensively damaged on take-off on 2 November and written off. The second prototype flew on 11 January 1954 but failed, despite extensive work, to attain anywhere near the design maximum speed. It was not until a major engineering redesign introduced an area-ruled fuselage and an advanced Pratt & Whitney J57-P-23 turbojet that during its first flight on 19 December 1954 this new prototype attained a speed of Mach 1.22 and climbed to 16,155 m (53,000 ft).

Entering service in April 1956, F-102As had a fairly active life in USAF squadrons until 1961, when they were steadily transferred to the US Air National Guard; by the end of 1978 all had been withdrawn from service with US armed forces. Some were transferred to the Greek and Turkish air forces, but these had been withdrawn from service by early 1979.

Like the RAF's Lightning, the USAF's Delta Dagger was a complete weapons system, with advanced avionics equipment to ensure that its missiles would be almost 100% certain of making effective interceptions of their targets. This degree of avionics and weapons sophistication meant that, throughout its service life, the F-102A was the subject of almost continuous updating programmes. Interestingly these aircraft had a remarkable safety record during deployment in

Southeast Asia (March 1962 to December 1969): only 15 were lost during this seven-year period, although operated for defence and as escorts for B-52 strategic bombing operations.

A total of 889 F-102As were built, plus 111 TF-102A two-seat trainers with full operational capability. Two QF-102A manned drone aircraft and four PQM-102A RPVs were converted from F-102As in 1974 to represent Soviet MiG-21s during the F-15A Eagle's development programme. Data: *Engine* one 76.5 kN (17,200 lb st) Pratt & Whitney J57-P-23 turbojet with reheat *Wing span* 11.62 m (38 ft 1½ in) *Length* 20.84 m (68 ft 4½ in) *Max T-O weight* 14,187 kg (31,276 lb) *Max level speed* Mach 1.25 *Range* 1,770 km (1,100 miles) *Armament* internal missile bay for weapons including Hughes AIM-26A and AIM-4C Falcon missiles.

Convair F-106 Delta Dart (USA) From early 1949 the USAF's goal was the development and procurement of an ultimate interceptor. They even outlined the requirement under the identity of an Advanced Development Objective (ADO), seeking a supersonic interceptor aircraft which

Convair 440 Metropolitan.

Convair (Allison) 580.

Convair 880.

Convair 990A Coronado.

would be the skeleton, sinew and muscle of a new-technology weapons system, able to deploy lethal missiles against virtually any airborne target.

It was not until 1956 that a further move was made in this direction, when the USAF expressed its need for a Mach 2 interceptor which could operate to an altitude of 21,335 m (70,000 ft) in all weathers. By then Convair had solved its initial problems with the F-102 and its proposal to meet this requirement was basically an improved version of the Delta Dagger under the designation F-102B.

In common with many other 'improvement' programmes, the task was not quite as easy as might have been imagined. Extensive fuselage modifications were necessary to accommodate the chosen Pratt & Whitney J75 turbojet. By the time

Convair

Convair F-102A Delta Dagger.

Convair B-58 Hustler.

that the air intakes had been relocated, the cockpit repositioned, new landing gear provided, and changes in the fin and rudder introduced, Convair had virtually a new aircraft. This is reflected in the USAF's F-106 designation and the new name of Delta Dart.

When the two YF-106A prototypes flew (on 26 December 1956 and 26 February 1957) the USAF were disappointed to learn that maximum speed was approximately 15% lower than the design figure and that acceleration to supersonic speed occupied an excessive time, using masses of fuel that seriously reduced range. It was not until October 1959 that these problems had been resolved sufficiently for aircraft to enter operational service, and it was early in 1961 before the F-106A could be said to have satisfied the USAF's requirements. At that point major modification programmes updated all in-service aircraft to the new common standard.

Since then, continuing modification programmes have ensured that the F-106 has remained in front-line service with the USAF as well as with the Air National Guard. It is anticipated that Delta Darts, of which 277 F-106As and 63 two-seat F-106Bs were built, will remain in front-line service into the early 1980s.

Data: *Engine* one 109 kW (24,500 lb st) Pratt & Whitney J57-P-17 turbojet with reheat *Wing span* 11.67 m (38 ft 3½ in) *Length* 21.56 m (70 ft 8¾ in) *Max T-O weight* 15,876 kg (35,000 lb) *Max level speed* Mach 2.3 *Range* 1,851 km (1,150 miles) *Armament* one 20 mm cannon in modified aircraft, plus one Douglas AIR-2A Genie or AIR-2B Super Genie and four Hughes AIM-4F/G Super Falcon missiles in internal missile bay

Convair L-13 (USA) Two–three-seat braced high-wing monoplane designed for general liaison, observation, photographic and ambulance duties. The L-13A was the production version, of which the USAF ordered 300, powered by the 182.5 kW (245 hp) Franklin O-435-9 flat-six engine. The L-13B was a modified L-13A for operation in sub-zero temperatures. Principal modifications included installation of 40,000 BTU combustion heater and dusting and sealing of all floor and door cracks.

Convair OY Sentinel (USA) Two–three-seat braced high-wing monoplane built for the US Marine Corps from 1943 as a general liaison, artillery spotting and ambulance aircraft. Power was provided by a 138 kW (185 hp) Lycoming engine.

Convair R3YU Tradewind (USA) The R3Y was a long-range tanker-transport flying-boat. Two versions were produced for the US Navy as the R3Y-1 and R3Y-2. The former was first flown on 25 February 1954 and five were built, powered by four 4,098 kW (5,500 shp) Allison T40-A-10 turboprop engines. They were used to carry personnel, cargo or stretchers/sitting casualties. The R3Y-2, of which six were completed, was similar to the earlier version except that the nose section of the hull was hinged to swing upwards to permit direct loading of vehicles or heavy freight, or could be fitted out with 80 demountable seats or 72 stretchers.

Convair XF-92A (USA) First flown on 18 September 1948, the XF-92A was a flying mock-up to test the delta wing configuration, as a phase in the development of the projected XF-92 jet and rocket-powered fighter (see **Convair F-102 Delta Dagger**).

Convair XFY-1 and Lockheed XFV-1 (USA) Experimental VTOL fighters of unusual configuration conceived for a US Navy design competition held in 1950. First flown on 2 August 1954 and March 1954 respectively. Remained experimental types only.

Convair Sea Dart (USA) Experimental delta-winged fighter seaplane, first flown on 9 April 1953. Powered by two Westinghouse J34-WE-42 (XF2Y-1) or J46 (YF2Y-1) turbojet engines. It was the first combat-type aircraft to be equipped with retractable hydroskis, the first delta-winged seaplane and the first seaplane to exceed Mach 1.

Convair Turboliner (USA) The Turboliner was the first turboprop-powered commercial aircraft to fly in the US, first taking to the air on 29 December 1950. Power was provided by two 2,049 kW (2,750 hp) Allison 501 turboprop engines.

Corby CJ-1 Starlet (Australia) Single-seat ultra-light homebuilt aircraft, of which more than 40 have been built or are under construction in Australia, Tasmania and New Zealand.

Cook JC-1 Challenger (USA) Four-seat cabin monoplane powered by a 112 kW (150 hp) Lycoming O-320-E2A flat-four engine.

Cornu helicopter (France) Twin-rotor helicopter of 1907 powered by an 18 kW (24 hp) Antoinette engine (see **Chronology** 13 November 1907).

Cosmic F-23 (USA) Single-seat agricultural aircraft originally marketed as the Funk F-23. Available since 1970 from Cosmic with a 179 kW (240 hp) Continental W-670 radial (F-23A) or 205 kW (275 hp) Jacobs R-755 radial (F-23B).

Couzinet 70/71 (France) Single example of a unique-looking freight- and mail-carrying cantilever low-wing monoplane airliner of 1928, powered by three 484.3 kW (650 hp) Hispano Suiza 12Nb engines. It began regular transatlantic services with Air France in May 1934.

Cox-Klemin TW-2 and XS-1 (USA) Following delivery of three TW-2 tandem two-seat biplane trainers to the USAAS in 1922, Cox-Klemin built six examples of a Bureau of Aeronautics single-seat twin-float scouting biplane for the US Navy as XS-1s for experimental use on board submarines.

CRDA CANT 6 (Italy) The single CANT 6 bomber flying-boat of 1925 was followed by two

Convair R3Y Tradewind.

examples of the civil CANT 6*ter*. These were three-engined biplanes with cabin accommodation for 11 passengers in the forward hull. One was used by the CANT company itself and the other by the Italian airline SISA.

CRDA CANT 7 (Italy) The CANT 7 was a single-engined two-seat flying-boat trainer intended to prepare pilots for commercial flying-boats. Twenty-two were built, mainly for the airline SISA.

CRDA CANT 10 (Italy) The pioneering Italian Adriatic airline SISA utilised at least 15 CANT 10s and CANT 10*ter* single-engined biplane flying-boats on their passenger services. They operated from 1926 right up to 1937. Distinctive single-step 'boats, they had a cabin in the bow for four passengers with the pilot's open cockpit immediately behind. Power was provided by a single 298 kW (400 hp) Lorraine-Dietrich liquid-cooled engine driving a two-bladed pusher propeller.

CRDA CANT 18 (Italy) Two-seat single-engined biplane flying-boat developed from the CANT 7. Incorporated considerable improvements in aerodynamic and hydrodynamic qualities compared with its predecessor. Several were operated by SISA.

Convair F-106A Delta Darts.

Convair XF-92A.

CRDA CANT 22 (Italy) This eight-passenger biplane flying-boat was operated from 1928 by the airline SISA on its routes out of Trieste. Production amounted to about ten aircraft, latter examples as the ten-passenger CANT 22R.1, each with one 380 kW (510 hp) and two 186.3 kW (250 hp) Isotta Fraschini engines in place of the three 149 kW (200 hp) engines of its predecessor. Cruising speed of the CANT 22 R.1 was 140 km/h (87 mph).

CRDA CANT 25 (Italy) Of the world's major military powers between the two World Wars,

Convair L-13.

CRDA CANT

Cornu helicopter.

only Italy persisted with the single-seat fighter flying-boat. An outstanding example was the CANT 25, a slim sesquiplane with a single-step hull, Warren-girder wing bracing and an open cockpit for the pilot just in front of the lower wing leading edge. The prototype was followed by the CANT 25M, which entered service with the Regia Aeronautica in 1931. Powered by a 305.5 kW (410 hp) Fiat A.20 water-cooled engine driving a two-blade pusher propeller, it was armed with two 7.7 mm (0.303 in) Vickers machine-guns fixed in the bow and firing forward.

The CANT 25AR version also went into production. It had conventional wing strutting and folding wings for shipboard stowage. Structural strengthening permitted catapult launching. A number of CANT 25s survived as trainers up to 1940.

Corby CJ-1 Starlets.

Data (CANT 25M): *Engine* as above *Wing span* 12.0 m (39 ft 4½ in) *Length* 8.75 m (28 ft 8½ in) *Max T-O weight* 1,645 kg (3,627 lb) *Max level speed* 242 km/h (150.5 mph)

CRDA CANT 26 (Italy) Light two-seat touring and training biplane powered by a 59.6 kW (80 hp) engine. Entered limited production around 1930.

CRDA CANT 36 (Italy) Two-seat training biplane powered by a 186.3 kW (250 hp) Isotta Fraschini Asso-200 engine.

CRDA CANT Z.501 (Italy) Filippo Zappata's new prototype flying-boat flew on 7 February 1934. It soon established an international reputation when test pilot Mario Stoppani flew it on long-range non-stop flights to East Africa in 1934 and again in July 1935, on each occasion achieving a new world non-stop distance record. The Z.501 was, however, a serious military design intended for maritime long-range reconnaissance duties. Large-scale production was undertaken, with first deliveries to the maritime reconnaissance Squadriglie taken place at the beginning of 1937. Production did not terminate until 1943, by which time 454 aircraft had been delivered to the Regia Aeronautica, plus a small batch to Romania, which operated them from the Con-

Convair Sea Dart.

Cook JC-1 Challenger.

stanza base against the Russians in the Black Sea.

The Z.501 was first blooded with the Italian Aviazione Legionaria supporting the Franco forces in Spain. A unit based in Majorca made a number of bombing raids in addition to carrying out a large number of over-sea patrols. During World War II the Z.501 equipped a large number of Squadriglie and covered thousands of miles in reconnaissance flights over the Mediterranean. The 'Gabbiano' or gull (so named because of its curved parasol wing) was also familiarly known as 'Mamm'aiuto', a colloquial cry 'Mummy! Help!' habitually raised by Italian children in trouble. This was a tribute to its role in rescuing many airmen, not all Italian, brought down at sea. A few Z.501s survived the war and remained operational for a short time after.

The wooden Z.501 had fabric covering on the upper hull and wing. Its single 559 kW (750 hp) Asso 750R or 656 kW (880 hp) Asso XI RC liquid-cooled engine drove a three-bladed tractor propeller. The large engine nacelle housed the cockpit for the flight engineer, who also operated one of the three defensive Vickers 7.7 mm (0.303 in) machine-guns. The other guns were located in semi-enclosed bow and midships positions. Pilot and co-pilot were seated side-by-side in an enclosed cabin. The elliptical horizontal tailplane was strut-braced halfway up the single curved fin and rudder.

Data: *Engine* as above *Wing span* 22.5 m (73 ft 9¾ in) *Length* 14.95 m (49 ft 0½ in) *Max T-O weight* 5,750 kg (12,676 lb) *Max level speed* 275 km/h (171 mph) *Range* 2,600 km (1,615 miles) *Armament* machine-guns as stated above, plus up to 500 kg (1,102 lb) of bombs carried on racks attached to the wing supporting struts, inboard of the stabilising floats

CRDA CANT Z.506 (and Z.509) (Italy) The civil Z.506 prototype (registered I-CANT) was flown for the first time by Mario Stoppani on 19 August 1935. It made an immediate impression with its slim, rounded fuselage and huge twin floats. A low-wing monoplane, it was powered by three 454.5 kW (610 hp) Piaggio Stella radial engines (it had been preceded a month earlier by the slightly larger and heavier Z.505 with 626 kW; 840 hp Isotta Fraschini in-line engines).

The Z.506 was put into production and 37 were built from 1937. They served as VIP transports as well as on regular Ala Littoria Mediterranean routes, carrying 14 passengers. A number remained in wartime service after June 1940, some operating as transports and others as air-sea rescue aircraft. The type captured a number of world seaplane speed, altitude and distance records during 1936–38 (similar records were also set up by the larger Z.509, three of which were built and were intended for Ala Littoria's trans-atlantic postal routes).

The militarised Z.506B was first displayed at the Milan Aeronautical Exhibition in October 1937. It had the same 559 kW (750 hp) Alfa Romeo 126 RC 34 radial engines as the civil production version, but incorporated a raised control cabin and a long ventral gondola. The latter accommodated the bomb load and had glazing at the front for the bomb-aimer and at the rear for the ventral gunner. The prototype established world load-to-height records the following month. Named Airone (Heron), the Z.506B was in production over a six-year period for the Regia Aeronautica. Two prototypes were followed by 322 production machines, which served initially in maritime bomber units, subsequently being passed to the reconnaissance Squadriglie. Many were also converted for air-sea rescue work.

After performing efficiently during World War II and establishing a reputation for reliability and toughness, a number of Z.506Bs remained operational post-war at the Vigna di Valle base. Alongside these military machines remained a single civil Z.506. Interestingly this particular example had been used (bearing ambulance markings) to carry Mussolini to safety from Maddalena to Vigna di Valle on 28 August 1943, just before Italy signed the Armistice with the Allies. Five Z.506Bs had also been delivered to the Spanish Nationalist air arm in late 1938 and the first of a 30-aircraft order for Poland had been completed by August 1939, but was never delivered.

Data (Z.506B): *Engines* as above *Wing span* 26.5 m

CRDA CANT Z.501.

(86 ft 11¼ in) *Length* 19.24 m (63 ft 1½ in) *Max T-O weight* 12,400 kg (27,337 lb) *Max level speed* 364 km/h (226 mph) *Range* 2,745 km (1,705 miles) *Armament* one 12.7 mm Scotti machine-gun in a Caproni-Lanciani Delta E dorsal turret; two side-firing 7.7 mm SAFAT machine-guns and a 7.7 mm SAFAT in ventral position, plus up to 1,100 kg (2,425 lb) of bombs

CRDA CANT Z.1007 (Italy) Following the first flight of the Z.1007 bomber prototype on 11 March 1937, series production was initiated. Thirty-four aircraft had been completed by October 1939, each powered (like the prototype) by three 626 kW (840 hp) Isotta Fraschini Asso IX engines. Unfortunately difficulties were experienced with these aircraft because of their inefficient engines – and not because of the aircraft's largely wooden structure as is sometimes alleged.

Meanwhile the Z.1007*bis* Alcione (Kingfisher) had been developed, powered by three 745 kW (1,000 hp) Piaggio P.XI RC 40 radial engines. During the production run of this version, which amounted to 464 aircraft by the end of 1942, the original large curved single fin and rudder was replaced on some aircraft by oval-shaped twin fins and rudders. Armament included a manually operated dorsal turret with a 12.7 mm machine-gun (in place of the open position on the Z.1007), but later production aircraft had hydraulically operated turrets. Another 12.7 mm gun was operated from a stepped ventral position, while two 7.7 mm machine-guns could be fired through lateral ports either side of the fuselage. A maximum of 1,200 kg (2,645 lb) of bombs could be carried in the internal bay, while up to 1,000 kg (2,204 lb) could be carried on underwing racks.

The Z.1007*bis* was followed by 50 Z.1007*ters*, differing mainly in having three 875.6 kW (1,175 hp) Piaggio P.XIX radial engines, giving a maximum speed of 490 km/h (304.5 mph).

The Alcione first went into action during the second half of 1940. On 29 August ten Alcione bombers flew with the Sicily-based 106° Gruppo attacking Malta, and during the Battle of Britain

Cosmic F-23.

CRDA CANT 25.

Captured CRDA CANT Z.506B.

CRDA CANT Z.1007*bis*.

Cunliffe-Owen O.A.1.

Culver Cadet.

Cunliffe-Owen Concordia.

five operated with the Corpo Aereo Italiano, a largely propaganda unit supporting the Luftwaffe. Thereafter the type served in North Africa, the Mediterranean theatre, Russia, the Balkans and in Italy itself. In general the aircraft gave a good account of itself and was popular with its crews. The standard number of crewmen in each aircraft was five.

Data (Z.1007*bis*): *Engines* as above *Wing span* 24.8 m (81 ft 4½ in) *Length* 18.47 m (60 ft 7¼ in) *Max T-O weight* 13,621 kg (30,029 lb) *Max level speed* 456 km/h (283.5 mph) *Range* 1,795 km (1,115 miles)

CRDA CANT Z.1018 (Italy) The CANT Z.1018 was an advanced bomber designed by Filippo Zappata. The wooden 'flying mock-up' was followed by a definitive all-metal prototype, ten pre-series machines and five examples of the production version. The situation in Italy then halted production in September 1943 and no more of the 800 ordered were completed. A low-wing monoplane with two 1,006 kW (1,350 hp) Piaggio P.XII RC 35 radials, the Z.1018 Leone (Lion) had classic lines with a pointed glazed nose, dorsal gun turret and stepped ventral defensive position.

Armament comprised three 12.7 mm and two 7.7 mm machine-guns and up to 2,000 kg (4,409 lb) of bombs. Maximum level speed was 524 km/h (325.5 mph).

Croses B-EC-9 Paras-Cargo (France) Light cargo transport and utility aircraft for amateur construction.

Croses EAC-3 Pouplume (France) Single-seat tandem-wing biplane with a fixed rear wing and a pivoted forward wing which dispenses with the need for ailerons and elevators. Plans are available to amateur constructors.

Croses EC-6 Criquet (France) Two-seat tandem-wing light aircraft, plans of which are available to amateur constructors.

Croses EC-8 Tourisme (France) Three-seat touring aircraft, generally similar to the standard

wooden Criquet but with an 'all-terrain' landing gear comprising two tandem pairs of main wheels.

Cub Prospector (Canada) Modified version of the Piper L-4B specially produced to meet Canadian requirements.

Culver Dart Model G, Cadet, LFA/LCA and PQ series (USA) The Culver Aircraft Corporation was formed in 1939 to take over from the Dart Manufacturing Corporation the manufacturing and sales rights of the Dart Model G two-seat cabin monoplane. In the following year the company produced the Culver Cadet light cabin monoplane and a version with a retractable landing gear was marketed in two models: the LFA with a 59.6 kW (80 hp) Franklin engine and the

LCA with a 56 kW (75 hp) Continental engine. Production of these models ended when America entered World War II, although many of them were used during the war for Civil Air Patrol service and other civilian duties.

In August 1940 the US government embarked on the task of perfecting the principle of radio control for target use in training air and anti-aircraft gunners. Culver was invited with some 20 other companies to submit designs which could be radio-controlled. The PQ-8 was the first radio-controlled target designed and built for the US Army, followed by the PQ-8A and PQ-14 (all with corresponding TDC-1, TDC-2 and TDC2-1 designations) for the US Navy; all were based on the LFA. The Model V two-seat cabin monoplane of 1946 was completed just before the company went out of business.

Cunliffe-Owen O.A.1 (UK) Improved version of the Burnelli UB-14 airliner, built during 1937–38 and powered by two Bristol Perseus XIV engines. One operated by the French in Africa.

Cunliffe-Owen Concordia (UK) First flown in 1947, this 10–12-seat airliner was powered by two 373 kW (500 hp) Alvis Leonides radial engines. Two built.

Cunningham-Hall PT-6F (USA) Formed in 1928, this company produced several aircraft before World War II. The last was the PT-6F, a two-seat freight-carrying biplane version of the PT-6 powered by a 272 kW (365 hp) Wright R-975E-1 Whirlwind radial engine.

JANE'S
Encyclopedia of Aviation

Volume 3

Aircraft A–Z
Curtiss — Hawker Siddeley

Compiled and edited by Michael J. H. Taylor

Contributors: Bill Gunston, A. J. Jackson, David Mondey,

Malcolm Passingham, John Stroud, Susan H. H. Young

Curtiss

The first Curtiss flying-boat, with Glenn Curtiss (left) and Henry Ford.

Curtiss 18-T.

Curtiss demonstrates his hydroplane to the US Navy.

Curtiss A-3.

Curtiss 18-B and 18-T (USA) Two-seat fighters produced too late to see action with the American forces during World War I. The USAAS received two 18-B biplanes and two 18-T triplanes, while the US Navy received two similar 18-Ts. All were powered by the 298 kW (400 hp) Kirkham K-12 engine.

Curtiss A series (USA) Although the US Army purchased its first aircraft in August 1909 (see **Chronology**), the US Navy took two years longer to acquire an aeroplane in the form of a single Curtiss A-1 hydroplane, having been encouraged by Ely's experiments (see **Chronology** 14 November 1910 and 18 January 1911). The A-1 was a biplane powered by a 56 kW (75 hp) Curtiss pusher engine and with a single main float and stabilising floats under the lower wings. With this aircraft the Navy carried out catapult experiments.

Shortly after the delivery of the A-1 the Navy received the A-2, which was subsequently modified into a flying-boat. Several more aircraft of the general type were received by the Navy, most as seaplanes carrying the new AH designation.

Curtiss A-3 (USA) The A-3A and A-3B were produced for the Army for ground-attack purposes, differing from the O-1B and O-1E observation biplanes in the comprehensive armament fitted. The armament consisted of two 0.30 in Browning machine-guns in the cowling firing through the propeller disc, with two similar guns (one mounted in each bottom plane) firing outside the disc and twin rear-mounted Lewis guns

on a Scarff ring. The two wing guns were arranged so that only the muzzle protruded through the leading edges of the wings, with several hundred rounds of ammunition being carried within the wings. In addition two bomb racks were fitted under the lower wings which could carry 25 lb fragmentation bombs. A total of 76 A-3As and 78 A-3Bs were produced.

Curtiss A-8 and A-12 Shrike (USA) The A-8 prototype attack monoplane appeared in 1931 and was followed by 13 evaluation aircraft which entered USAAC service in the following year. Meanwhile one aircraft had been tested with a Pratt & Whitney Hornet radial engine in place of the normal Curtiss Conqueror in-line. As a result the 46 A-8Bs ordered were cancelled and replaced by an order for a similar number of 514 kW (690 hp) Wright R-1820-37 Cyclone-powered A-12s. They differed also in having redesigned crew accommodation in which the pilot's cockpit and the rear-gunner's semi-cabin were joined by a new upper-deck fairing instead of the A-8's two completely separate cockpits. A-12s remained in service until America entered World War II. Armament comprised four 0.30 in Browning forward-firing machine-guns, one rear-mounted gun and up to 221 kg (488 lb) of bombs.

Curtiss A-18 Shrike (USA) Twin-engined attack aircraft developed from the single A-14 as a replacement for the A-12. Thirteen Y1A-18 evaluation aircraft were built for the USAAC powered by 447 kW (600 hp) Wright Cyclone engines. The A-18 was designed to combine high performance with long range, with particular attention to high performance at low altitude.

Curtiss AT-9 Jeep (USA) Pilot transition trainer powered by two 209 kW (280 hp) Lycoming R-680-9 radial engines. Cabin accommodation for two side-by-side, with provision for two additional seats to the rear. A total of 491 AT-9s and 300 AT-9As produced during World War II.

Curtiss A-25 (USA) USAAC version of the Curtiss SB2C-1 Helldiver, many hundreds of which were ordered; the majority went to the US Marine Corps.

Curtiss B-2 (USA) The NBS-4 Condor was a biplane night bomber developed from the Martin

MB-2 (as built by Curtiss as the NBS-1) and powered by two 447 kW (600 hp) Curtiss Conqueror engines. Only 12 built for the USAAC, delivered from 1929.

Curtiss BT-32 Condor and CT-32 (USA) Not to be confused with the Curtiss B-2 or its 18-passenger Condor airliner development, the Condor was a 15-passenger commercial biplane airliner of the early 1930s, powered by two 529–536.5 kW (710–720 hp) Cyclone radial engines. It enjoyed considerable success and was produced in two versions: for normal daytime flying and as a convertible day- and night-sleeper transport with six compartments, each accommodating two berths/seats. One was used on the Byrd Antarctic Expedition and two were operated by the US Navy as R4Cs. An all-cargo version was produced as the CT-32.

As a military heavy bomber with troop-carrying and ambulance capability, the Condor was supplied to China. Armament comprised five 0.30 in machine-guns and up to 1,800 kg (3,968 lb) of bombs.

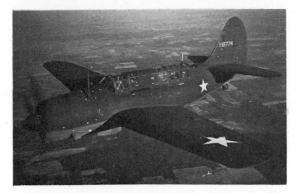

Curtiss A-25.

Curtiss B-2.

Curtiss CW-20 and C-46 Commando (USA) The Commando was evolved from the Curtiss-Wright CW-20 which was originally laid out as a 36-passenger pressurised commercial transport in 1937. The prototype CW-20 first flew on 26 March 1940 and, because the US Army was impressed with its possibilities, authorisation was obtained for the purchase of a large number as cargo transports. In the meantime the prototype was bought, modified and given the Army designation C-55. It was later re-converted for civil use and sold to the British government.

The Army production model of the CW-20, designated C-46, was a redesign not only to suit it to the duties of a military cargo or task-force aircraft but to allow easy large-scale production. It was produced in three large manufacturing plants and was put into widespread use by the US Army Air Transport Command, Air Service

Command and Troop Carrier Command, and by the US Naval Air Transport Command and Marine Corps. The main compartment of the C-46 could accommodate (in addition to general cargo) 40 fully equipped troops, up to 33 stretchers, five Wright R-3350 engines or their equivalent weight of other goods.

Profiting from the experience of the C-46, the Curtiss company in 1944 prepared designs and a mock-up of a commercial version of the aircraft for immediate post-war production. Interestingly, by the end of that year at least two American airlines had ordered the type as the CW-20E. Several hundred of the 3,000 or so Commandos built survived the war and served in a commercial capacity for many years. Even today a number remain operational as commercial freighters.

Data (C-46A): *Engines* two 1,490 kW (2,000 hp) Pratt & Whitney R-2800-51s *Wing span* 32.92 m (108 ft 0 in) *Length* 23.27 m (76 ft 4 in) *Max T-O weight* 25,400 kg (56,000 lb) *Max cruising speed* 301 km/h (187 mph) *Range* 1,883 km (1,170 miles)

Curtiss C-76 Caravan (USA) Twenty-five examples of a twin-engined all-wood assault transport delivered to the USAAF.

Curtiss CR, R2C and R3C racers (USA) See **Schneider Trophy contestants**

Curtiss A-14.

Curtiss AT-9 Jeep.

Curtiss C-46 Commando.

Curtiss Carrier Pigeon cargo aircraft, used on main-line mail and express routes from the mid-1920s.

Curtiss Eagle.

Curtiss CT-32 Condor used on the Byrd Antarctic Expedition.

Curtiss biplane of 1911.

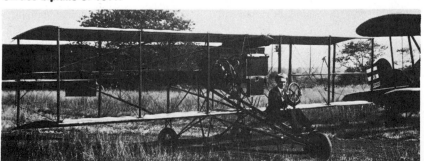

Curtiss CS (USA) The CS biplanes were designed by Curtiss and the US Navy, the first machine being completed in late 1923. The CS-1 (of which six were built) was powered by a 391 kW (525 hp) Wright T-2 engine, while the CS-2 (2 built) used a 436 kW (585 hp) Wright T-3. Both versions were convertible from landplane to twin-float seaplane configurations and could be used for torpedo carrying (with a torpedo under the fuselage in a specially cowled recess), bombing and scouting. Orders for 35 CS-1s and 40 CS-2s went to Martin, which completed them as SC-1s and SC-2s respectively.

Data (SC-2): *Engine* as above *Wing span* (upper) 15.93 m (52 ft 3 in), (lower) 17.25 m (56 ft 6¾ in) *Length* 11.5 m (37 ft 8¾ in) *Max T-O weight* 3,820 kg (8,421 lb) *Max level speed* 169 km/h (105 mph) *Range* 1,640 km (1,020 miles) *Armament* machine-gun over central cockpit, plus one 1,618 lb torpedo

Curtiss biplane and Model D and E (USA) The biplane of 1910 was powered by a 22.35 kW (30 hp) Curtiss four-cylinder pusher engine. It enjoyed considerable success and the first was built for the Aeronautical Society of America by Curtiss and Herring. Glenn H. Curtiss won the Gordon Bennett race in this type. Following Herring's departure from the company, the Curtiss Aeroplane Company was formed, which became the Curtiss Aeroplane and Motor Company in 1916. Meanwhile the US Army had received a military version as the Model D and three improved Model Es. The US Navy also received one or more Model E aircraft as the AH-8.

Curtiss Eagle and Tanager (USA) The Eagle of 1920 (fully described in the *Jane's* of that year) was a triple Curtiss K-6-engined commercial and single Liberty-engined military transport biplane, with cabin accommodation for the crew and six or seven passengers. Curtiss claimed the commercial version to be the first triple-engined aircraft to be designed and built in America. One of three military Eagles purchased by the US Army was configured as a four-stretcher ambulance.

The later single-engined (127 kW; 170 hp Challenger) Tanager accommodated three persons in the cabin, and was similar in many ways to the military Eagle but considerably smaller. It was the winner of the $100,000 Guggenheim Safe Aircraft Competition and featured wingtip (lower) ailerons and full-span (upper wing) leading-edge automatic wing-slots.

Curtiss Model F (USA) The Model F was a two-seat training flying-boat (also used for observation duties) powered by a 74.5 kW (100 hp) Curtiss OX pusher engine mounted between the biplane wings. It is not known how many were built for the US Navy up to 1918, but it is likely to have been in excess of 150, plus others for Russia. The first examples produced carried C designations but these and later production aircraft were redesignated in the AB category. An experimental version of the AB was produced as a triplane with 'K-bar' interplane struts and the engine mounted on the centre wing (see **Chronology** April 1914 and 5 November 1915).

Curtiss F-5L (USA) In 1918 Curtiss began production of 60 F-5L twin 298 kW (400 hp) Liberty-engined patrol flying-boats for the US Navy, based on the Felixstowe F-5 (see **Navy-Curtiss NC**).

Curtiss F6C Hawk (USA) see **P-1/P-6/F6C Hawk**

Curtiss F7C-1 Sea Hawk (USA) Designed as a single-seat shipboard fighter with a 316.5 kW (425 hp) Pratt & Whitney Wasp radial engine, the Sea Hawk differed in many features from the standard F6C Hawk, particularly with regard to the arrangement of the wings, landing gear and equipment. Only a very small number were produced and these were delivered from 1927 for service with the US Marine Corps.

Curtiss F8C/OC and O-1 Falcon (USA) The US Navy's F8C Falcon (not to be confused with the F8C Helldiver) and the USAAC's O-1 Falcon

were based on the same airframe but had a number of important differences, not least of which was the selection of a radial and in-line engine respectively.

The O-1 was designed in 1924 as a two-seat observation biplane with either a Liberty or Packard engine, in accordance with the regulations of the Army Air Service competition. This requirement called for the design of a quickly detachable engine mounting: Curtiss made full use of this in equipping the Falcon with various types of engines to fulfil a number of different Army, Navy, Marine Corps and National Guard requirements. Production for the Army began with ten O-1s, followed by 25 O-1Bs with 324 kW (435 hp) Curtiss D-12 water-cooled engines, and 37 O-1Es.

The O-1Es introduced several minor changes – including a redesigned engine cowling, Frise-type ailerons and horn-balanced elevators – and resembled the 'Conqueror' Falcon which Curtiss produced as a high-powered observation type. The final version was the O-1G, 30 of which were built. Curtiss also produced 66 examples of a Liberty-powered version (similar to O-1B) as the O-11 for the National Guard and ten 447 kW (600 hp) Curtiss Conqueror-engined O-39s. Four O-1Bs were subsequently modified into O-1Cs as a special version for the personal use of high ranking Army officials. The rear cockpit of each machine was upholstered in leather, fitted with a folding table, a special instrument board and a roomy baggage compartment for suitcases and personal effects. Each O-1C also had dual controls.

Navy versions looked very different because of their 320 kW (430 hp) Pratt & Whitney Wasp radial engines. Production began with six

XF8C-1/F8C-1s for the Marine Corps which were intended as two-seat multi-purpose fighters, but were quickly redesignated as OC-1 observation aircraft with combat capability. A further 21 production OC-2s went to the Marine Corps in 1928, while Curtiss delivered examples to China and Nicaragua (joining a selection of other American aircraft including Vought Corsair biplanes).

A third (and usually forgotten) version of the Falcon was the Falcon Mail Plane, a commercial version built in 1928 for National Air Transport – one of the then largest air mail carriers in the United States. Power was provided by a Liberty engine and it carried sufficient fuel for 1,171 km (728 miles).

Data (O-1E): *Engine* as above *Wing span* 11.58 m (38 ft 0 in) *Length* 8.41 m (27 ft 7 in) *Max T-O weight* 1,965 kg (4,332 lb) *Max level speed* 227 km/h (141 mph) *Armament* two forward-firing 0.30 in Browning machine-guns and two rear-mounted Lewis guns

Curtiss Model F, military designation C-2.

Curtiss F7C-1 Sea Hawk.

Curtiss O-1E.

Curtiss F8C/O2C Helldiver (USA) In 1929 Curtiss produced a new version of the Falcon which, while suitable as a shipboard fighter and light bomber, could be dived vertically under full power as a dive bomber. Power was provided by a 335.3 kW (450 hp) Pratt & Whitney Wasp radial engine and the wing span reduced. Following the XF8C-4 prototype (which had its radial engine partially enclosed in a nose fairing) Curtiss produced 25 production F8C-4s to serve with the US Navy on board the USS *Saratoga*, differing in having revised fuselage panels forward of the wings and a narrow-chord ring cowl. These were subsequently transferred to the US Marine Corps, which also received 63 examples of the F8C-5 equipped for land use only and not for carrier operations. These were later redesignated

Curtiss AB-3 catapult-launched from USS *North Carolina*.

Curtiss OC-2.

Curtiss F9C-2 Sparrowhawks.

Curtiss O2C-1.

O2C-1s as observation aircraft with combat capability.

Of the small number of experimental F8Cs built the XF8C-7 deserves mention for having a 428.5 kW (575 hp) Wright Cyclone engine, main wheels and tailwheel covered by streamlined fairings and a canopy for the pilot which was later extended to cover both cockpits.

Data (F8C-5): *Engine* as above *Wing span* 9.75 m (32 ft 0 in) *Length* 7.82 m (25 ft 8 in) *Max T-O weight* 1,802 kg (3,973 lb) *Max level speed* 227 km/h (141 mph) *Armament* two forward-firing 0.30 in Browning machine-guns and two rear-mounted guns, plus one 500 lb and two 116 lb bombs

Curtiss Export Falcon (USA) The Export Falcon was an adaptation of the O-39 Falcon powered by a 521.6 kW (700 hp) Wright Cyclone engine. It was built as a seaplane but could be readily converted into a landplane.

Curtiss F9C-2 Sparrowhawk (USA) The concept of a fighter which could be carried by a larger aircraft and released while airborne to defend the 'motherplane' from enemy attack occupied the talents of many designers throughout the inter-war period and indeed the 1950s. Only once has the concept attained a successful conclusion, with the Sparrowhawk (although in the commercial field of aviation the Short-Maya composite proved that extended range could be achieved by launching a small aircraft from a larger type while airborne).

In 1929 the airships USS *Akron* and *Macon* were designed for the US Navy. Intended to scout

ahead of a fleet, it was clear that a measure of real protection would be required for them if they were to survive under wartime conditions – the success of the Allies in destroying Zeppelins during World War I and the improved performance of fighters and maritime-patrol aircraft by the end of the 1920s highlighted this. To this end Curtiss designed the Sparrowhawk, a small single-seat biplane fighter with a 'skyhook' structure attached to the upper wing to allow it to hook on to the arrester trapeze of an airship (which could lift the aircraft into an internal hangar). As noted under the appropriate entry, the Navy purchased six Fleet 5 light biplanes as N2Ys to train Sparrowhawk pilots. The *Akron* and the Sparrowhawk prototypes first flew in 1931 and in the following year all six production Sparrowhawks were delivered. Meanwhile a prototype had participated in experimental tests using another airship, the USS *Los Angeles* (see **Chronology** 27 October 1931). Trials with the Sparrowhawk and *Akron* began in 1932 (see **Chronology** 29 June 1932) and a period of very successful operation began. Following the demise of *Akron* while flying over the Atlantic (see **Chronology** 3–4 April 1933), the Sparrowhawk (none of which had been lost in the accident) began a second successful period with *Macon* (see **Chronology** 23 June 1933 and 12 February 1935).

Data: *Engine* one 313 kW (420 hp) Wright R-975-E radial *Wing span* 7.77 m (25 ft 6 in) *Length* 6.12 m (20 ft 1 in) *Max T-O weight* 1,256 kg (2,770 lb) *Max level speed* 285 km/h (177 mph) *Range* 590 km (366 miles) *Armament* two forward-firing 0.30 in machine-guns

Curtiss F11C/BFC and BF2C-1 Goshawk (USA) The Goshawk was designed for the US Navy as a modern single-seat shipboard fighter, capable also of carrying bombs. Two prototypes were built: one with a 447 kW (600 hp) Wright R-1510-98 radial engine and the other with a 521.6 kW (700 hp) R-1820-78 Cyclone. The 27 production F11C-2s which followed had the latter engine and served on board USS *Saratoga* from 1934, subsequently being redesignated BFC-2s. Between 1934 and 1935 delivery was made of 28 refined BF2C-1s, naval versions of the Curtiss Hawk III fighter with a manually retractable landing gear of Grumman FF-type. These formed the Fighting Group on board the new aircraft carrier USS *Ranger*, but remained operational for only a very short time.

Curtiss H (America) series (USA) The early history of the *America* is best recorded by quoting from the Curtiss entry in the 1918 *Jane's*: 'In 1914, much attention was paid to flying-boats, and a huge twin-engined machine was built to the order of Mr Wanamaker and designed by Lieut John Porte, RN, the intention being that it should fly the Atlantic. Just before the war this machine was fitted with three engines. Later a big triplane with four 250 hp Curtiss engines was built, and it was reported in American papers that it had been taken over by the British Navy.'

These comments were extremely accurate, although the report fails to mention that the original *America* itself was also taken over by the British Navy. The *America* had been developed via the much smaller aircraft of the A-2/F-types, which had proved the worth of the flying-boat hull in place of the more conventional float arrangement

for sea-going aircraft. The *America*, powered by 67 kW (90 hp) Curtiss OX-5 engines, was delivered to the RNAS the same year along with a second flying-boat. Sixty-two similar aircraft were then ordered by the RNAS as H.4s, powered by 67–112 kW (90–150 hp) engines. These were known as 'America boats' or 'Small Americas' and became operational in 1915 as maritime-reconnaissance types. However the H.4 was not a success and many became trainers.

Collaboration on both sides of the Atlantic resulted in the much improved H.12 or 'Large America' of 1916, the major part of its development being attributed to the ideas of Sqn Cdr John C. Porte, RNAS who subsequently developed it further into the much more successful Felixstowe F.2A type. The US Navy received 20 H.12s with 149 kW (200 hp) Curtiss engines. The RNAS received 71 similar aircraft which were operated from early 1917 with 205 kW (275 hp) Rolls-Royce Eagle I engines, although a number were later fitted with more powerful Eagles. These were successfully used against the U-boat menace in the English Channel and North Sea and could claim their part in destroying the Zeppelin challenge in the air.

The final flying-boat developed from the *America* type to see action during World War I was the H.16, a more refined version of the H.12 with greater span wings, an improved hull with better hydrodynamic qualities and more powerful engines as standard. A total of about 75 H.16s were delivered to Britain during 1918, most of which failed to become operational. These were

fitted with 238.5 kW (320 hp) Rolls-Royce Eagle VIII engines. The US Navy also received Liberty-powered counterparts and with post-war production acquired a total of more than 270 aircraft.

Data (RNAS H.12): *Engines* as above *Wing span* 28.26 m (92 ft 8½ in) *Length* 14.17 m (46 ft 6 in) *Max T-O weight* 4,830 kg (10,650 lb) *Max level speed* 150 km/h (93 mph) *Endurance* 6 h *Armament* three–four machine-guns, plus up to 209 kg (406 lb) of bombs

Curtiss HS-1L and HS-2L (USA) Three-seat 298 kW (400 hp) Liberty-powered anti-submarine and patrol flying-boats of basically similar design, the HS-2L version having increased wing span and carrying heavier bombs. They became the subject of very large orders for the US Navy and were the only aircraft of indigenous design to serve with the Navy in Europe during World War I.

Curtiss America.

Curtiss JN 'Jenny' (USA) A mixture of two earlier aircraft known as the Type J and Type N, conceived respectively by the British designer Mr B. D. Thomas and Glenn Curtiss himself. The JN or 'Jenny' became one of the most widely operated trainers in the world and was the only American mass-produced aircraft to have played a major role during World War I.

Following a relatively small number of early production JN types that entered British and American service, the JN-4 major version was produced. Eventually more than 6,400 were built, serving with the USAAS and US Navy, and in much smaller numbers with the RFC, RNAS and others. It has been calculated that 95% of all aircrew trained in America and Canada during World War I flew in Jennies.

At the Armistice, the vast number of surplus or

Curtiss HS-1L.

Curtiss

Curtiss JN Jennies under construction.

Maj H.A. Dargue poses by his Curtiss Jenny, surrounded by an unfriendly crowd during the Punitive Expedition into Mexico.

Curtiss JN-4D.

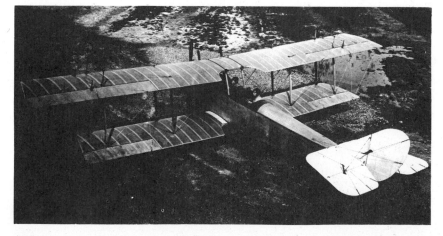

crated and unused Jennies included the latest JN-4Hs. Although a large number of aircraft remained in service with US forces until 1927, many were sold off to civil flying clubs and private pilots. One such aircraft (flown by Ernest C. Hoy) made the first aeroplane crossing of the Canadian Rockies in 1919, while others barnstormed their way into oblivion.

But, despite its gentle nature, the little Jenny had seen action. In March 1916 the Mexican revolutionary Pancho Villa killed 17 people at Columbus, New Mexico. This was the final outrage for the US government and it sent 15,000 soldiers and a squadron of eight Jennies into Mexico to capture Villa. It is a matter of record that the huge force failed in its attempt to catch up with the revolutionaries, but more interesting is that all eight Jennies had to be abandoned after just two months of reconnaissance work; breaking under the strain of operating in the rough terrain and in dust and snow, or being vandalised by Villa's followers.

Data (JN-4D): *Engine* one 67 kW (90 hp) Curtiss OX-5 *Wing span* 13.3 m (43 ft 7½ in) *Length* 8.33 m (27 ft 4 in) *Max T-O weight* 966 kg (2,130 lb) *Max level speed* 121 km/h (75 mph) *Endurance* 2 h 15 min

Curtiss Junior (USA) Two-seat open-cockpit light parasol-wing monoplane powered by a 33.5 kW (45 hp) Szekely pusher engine. Many hundreds were produced for the civil market in the early 1930s.

Curtiss Type L (USA) Civil and military two-seat sea-going triplane of 1916, a small number of which were built with Curtiss engines.

Curtiss MF and Seagull (USA) The MF was produced from 1918 as a modern two-seat training flying-boat for the US Navy, powered by a 74.5 kW (100 hp) Curtiss OXX pusher engine. Just over 100 were produced but the type had an inconspicuous career. A commercial version was also produced as the Seagull.

Curtiss N2C Fledgling (USA) The Fledgling was designed to participate in a competition held by the US Navy to select a new aircraft to serve for both primary and advanced training as either a land- or seaplane. Fourteen other designs were submitted, but the Fledgling was the winner. Two versions were produced: the N2C-1 with a 164 kW (220 hp) Wright J-5 Whirlwind radial engine and the N2C-2 with a 179 kW (240 hp) Wright R-760-94; 31 and 20 being completed respectively. In addition Curtiss produced a commercial version for civilian aircraft schools, powered by a 126.7 kW (170 hp) Curtiss Challenger engine and with the military equipment omitted.

Curtiss N-9 (USA) Seaplane version of the JN-4 Jenny powered by a 74.5 kW (100 hp) Curtiss OX-6 or 112 kW (150 hp) Hispano-Suiza engine and with a greater wing span. A total of 560 were built, serving with the US Navy from 1917 until the mid-1920s and in much smaller numbers with the US Army and RNAS.

Navy-Curtiss NC (USA) The NC flying-boat which achieved fame through the American Transatlantic Flight Expedition of 1919 was not, as is often assumed, specially built for that purpose. The main function of the NCs was to act as 'flotilla leaders' to the Atlantic and the Pacific air forces of the US Navy, which were composed chiefly of F-5L flying-boats. Nevertheless it was for the transatlantic flight that the type is now remembered.

Conceived originally as an anti-submarine aircraft for operation against German U-boats during World War I, with sufficient range to allow direct delivery from America to Europe, the first NC made its maiden flight on 4 October 1918. With the end of the war in November, only ten were eventually built, the first four being allotted to the transatlantic attempt. Each NC carried a crew of five or six. Problems in obtaining spares resulted in the second aircraft (NC-2) being dis-

Curtiss F11C-2 Goshawk.

mantled to serve the other three, and on 8 May 1919 the remaining three set out to begin the attempt (see **Chronology** 8 and 31 May 1919). Data: *Engines* four 298 kW (400 hp) Liberty 12s *Wing span* 38.4 m (126 ft 0 in) *Length* 20.85 m (68 ft 3½ in) *Max T-O weight* 12,925 kg (28,500 lb) *Max level speed* 146 km/h (91 mph) *Normal range* 2,365 km (1,470 miles)

Curtiss O-52 (USA) The O-52 braced high-wing monoplane with a retractable landing gear and enclosed cockpits was delivered to the USAAF for observation and liaison duties, but used as a trainer. More than 200 were built, each with a Pratt & Whitney Wasp engine.

Curtiss P-1/P-6/F6C Hawk (USA) The Curtiss Hawk biplanes (which originated in 1925) represented an important component of the US Army Air Corps' squadrons during the interwar years and, together with the Boeing-built biplanes, equipped many of the Air Corps' first-line squadrons.

Curtiss received in early 1925 a contract for 15 fighter aircraft, these duly becoming the first in the USAAC's new category of fighter (Pursuit) aircraft, thus acquiring the P-1 designation. These aircraft, like the PW-8s which had preceded them, were designed around the almost revolutionary Curtiss D-12 in-line engine, which was the world's first wet sleeve monobloc aero-engine. The potential of this engine was such that it was used to power the Curtiss CR-3 racer which had won the Schneider Trophy Contest in 1923, and was used later as power plant for the RAF's very fast Fairey Fox day bomber.

A single PW-8 had been equipped with tapered and well-staggered biplane wings under the designation XPW-8B. It was this configuration which was chosen for the new P-1 and subsequent variants, the tapered wings providing an easily

recognisable feature. Landing gear was of typical heavy tailskid-type and the pilot's cockpit was well aft of the upper wing. Armament comprised two 0.30 in machine-guns mounted in the engine cowling and firing forward through the propeller disc.

The first ten P-1s were equipped with the Curtiss V-1150-1 (D-12) engine, but the remaining five on the first contract had 373 kW (500 hp) Curtiss V-1400 engines and were designated as P-2 Hawks. Subsequent Hawks had a slightly longer fuselage, but the primary change in succeeding designations concerned the power plant. Thus P-1As were the first with lengthened fuselage, while P-1Bs had V-1150-3 engines. The P-3/-3A designations applied to experimental variants with air-cooled radial engines. Five P-5s were built with turbocharged versions of the V-1150-3 engine, giving much improved performance at 7,620 m (25,000 ft), which represented an altitude above the absolute ceiling of the P-1. They were, however, penalised by poor performance at low levels.

Curtiss F11C-2 Goshawk.

Navy-Curtiss NC-4.

Curtiss O-52.

Competing in the US National Air Races of 1927, a P-1A and P-2 with modified wings and Curtiss Conqueror V-1570 engines took first and second places at respective speeds of 323 km/h (201 mph) and 304 km/h (189 mph). This led to development of the P-6A Hawk, which retained the standard tapered planform wings, but had a more streamlined fuselage and was powered by a V-1570 engine. Variants included the P-6D with turbocharged engine and a much improved P-6E with single-strut main landing-gear units, wheel spats, tailwheel, more streamlined fuselage and V-1570-23 engine.

Curtiss

Curtiss P-3A Hawk.

Curtiss P-36A.

Curtiss P-6Es.

The US Navy also procured Curtiss Hawks in small numbers under the designation F6C, the initial seven F6C-1s (similar to the P-1) entering service in late 1925. Two F6C-2s had strengthened landing gear and arrester hooks: features which were retained in subsequent Navy Hawks. Most extensively built were similar F6C-3s (35) and Pratt & Whitney R-1340 radial-engined F6C-4s (31).

Data (P-6E): *Engine* one 503.5 kW (675 hp) Curtiss V-1570-23 *Wing span* 9.6 m (31 ft 6 in) *Length* 7.06 m (23 ft 2 in) *Max T-O weight* 1,484 kg (3,269 lb) *Max level speed* 319 km/h (198 mph) at sea level *Range* 917 km (570 miles) *Armament* two 0.30 in machine-guns, plus 109 kg (240 lb) of bombs if required.

Curtiss P-36/Hawk 75 (USA) As a single-seat fighter, the P-36 was an intermediate development between the Hawk biplanes and the P-40 Warhawk, using technology gained from the A-8 Shrike. To the USAAC it was seen as a step up from the Boeing P-26, against which it was very advanced. First appearing in 1935, the Wright R-1670-engined prototype was a cantilever low-wing monoplane with a retractable undercarriage, enclosed cockpit and two forward-firing machine-guns. The fuselage and wings were designed to facilitate removal and replacement of any particular section, and the underfuselage was constructed so that a belly-landing would cause the minimum damage to the aircraft.

Put into competition against the similar Seversky P-35, the Hawk 75 (as the P-36 was designated by Curtiss prior to USAAC production orders and the military designation being allotted) was inferior and was not selected. With a change of power plant to a Pratt & Whitney R-1830-13 of similar power to the engine fitted in the Seversky fighter, the Hawk 75 was actually marginally faster and the USAAC placed an order. Delivery of 178 similarly powered P-36As began in the spring of 1938, France also placing an order for the type in an effort to rapidly acquire modern aircraft. But already better, faster and more heavily armed fighters destined for the USAAC were under way and so the P-36s achieved little with the Army, although a much smaller number of four-gun P-36Cs and P-36Gs (with 894 kW; 1,200 hp Pratt & Whitney R-1830-17 and 894 kW; 1,200 hp Wright Cyclone engines respectively) also entered service.

As an export fighter the Hawk 75 was more successful, and among the first orders were those placed by France (originally for 100 H.75A fighters and 173 Pratt & Whitney engines), Norway and Peru. In the event Norwegian fighters were not delivered and many of the French aircraft became British Mohawk IIIs following the capitulation of France. Nevertheless, the first French H.75As arrived in early 1939 and by July all of the first batch had been delivered as H.75A-1s, which became operational with units based in Reims. These were followed by H.75A-2s, -3s and -4s, the last two versions with six guns in each aircraft.

French Hawk 75s first went into action on 8 September 1939 when a number met a formation of German Bf 109Ds. Two invaders were shot down and in the ensuing months the two opposing fighters met many times and proved to be fairly equal. With the Battle of France lost, undelivered French fighters were diverted to Britain, later being joined by Mohawk IVs ordered by the British directly. Not quite good enough for home defence, most were sent to India and the Middle East and remained operational until 1944.

Interestingly, in the mid-1930s Curtiss also produced aircraft of similar general layout to the Hawk 75 as the Model 19R and Model 19L and W, two-seat military trainer and two–three-seat civil cabin monoplanes respectively, both with fixed landing gears.

Data (P-36A): *Engine* one 782.5 kW (1,050 hp) Pratt & Whitney R-1830-13 Twin Wasp *Wing span* 11.36 m (37 ft 3½ in) *Length* 8.77 m (28 ft 9½ in) *Max T-O weight* 2,726 kg (6,010 lb) *Max level speed* 483 km/h (300 mph) *Range* 1,330 km (825 miles) *Armament* two 0.30 in machine-guns, plus optional light bombs

French Curtiss H.75As flying alongside RAF Fairey Battles.

Curtiss P-40 Warhawk (USA) One of the early production Curtiss P-36 aircraft was given an 864.4 kW (1,160 hp) Allison V-1710-19 (C-13) engine (and designated XP-40) instead of the standard R-1830-17 engine. Apart from the essential modifications to the airframe to accommodate the Allison supercharged engine and its coolant radiator and oil cooler, it was the basic airframe of the P-36, free of development problems and ready for immediate production once the USAAC decided it was the aircraft they needed. They did; ordering an initial production batch of 524 P-40s, these acquiring the name Warhawk. On 22 November 1944 the USAAF received the 15,000th Curtiss fighter built for service in World War II. It was a P-40N, the final new production version.

Despite this long production run, the P-40 Warhawk was not an outstanding fighter aircraft. It was, however, rugged and reliable and was used in all theatres of war for a variety of purposes. It was also typical of many early wartime fighters, with armament and engine changes causing the long development progression. Increased armament and equipment needed more power to maintain performance: once this had been achieved, with perhaps a margin of reserve power, more arms or increased armour or fuel tankage again eroded performance.

P-40s served with the RAF as Tomahawks; with Gen Chennault's AVG or 'Flying Tiger' group in China; with the RAAF, SAAF, Soviet Union and Turkish Air Force. Improved P-40D and P-40Es served with the RAF as Kittyhawks, with the RCAF and Soviet Union; and still later versions went to the RNZAF. USAAF usage of the P-40 was mainly in the Middle East and Pacific theatres, but by far the greatest proportion of P-40s built went to Allied nations under Lend–Lease agreements.

Data (P-40N): *Engine* one 1,013 kW (1,360 hp) Allison V-1710-81 *Wing span* 11.38 m (37 ft 3½ in) *Length* 10.16 m (33 ft 3¾ in) *Max T-O weight* 4,014 kg (8,850 lb) *Max level speed* 608 km/h (378 mph) *Range* 386 km (240 miles) *Armament* six 0.50 in machine-guns, plus one 500 lb bomb

Curtiss P-40s being assembled in a factory in China.

Curtiss PW-8 (USA) Single-seat biplane fighter of 1924, 25 of which were acquired by the USAAC with 328 kW (440 hp) Curtiss D-12 engines.

Curtiss R-4 (USA) Two-seat unequal-span biplane powered by a 119 kW (160 hp) Curtiss engine. Ordered by the US Army and RNAS as a reconnaissance type but was overweight and suffered engine trouble. Used in Britain as a bombing trainer.

Curtiss R-6 (USA) Single-seat racing and record-breaking biplane, first flown on 2 October 1922.

Curtiss SB2C Helldiver (USA) The experimental contract for the Helldiver was awarded by the US Navy on 15 May 1939 and the prototype XSB2C-1 first flew on 18 December 1940, although contemporary reports suggest the first flight was made in the previous month. From that date the Helldiver two-seat carrier-borne dive bomber was the subject of constant development. Armour, self-sealing tanks, protected fuel and oil lines, increased armament, a lengthened fuselage and a completely new tail unit with greatly enlarged fixed and moveable surfaces were incorporated in the production SB2C-1, the first of which flew in June 1942. From that date until November 1943 (when the Helldiver first went into action in the Pacific theatre of war) more than 880 design changes were made, some of which were part of the Army-Navy standardisation

Curtiss P-40 Warhawk.

Curtiss P-40 flown by the Flying Tiger volunteer group in China.

Curtiss R-6.

Curtiss SB2C Helldiver.

Curtiss PW-8 in which Russell L. Maughan, USAAS, flew coast-to-coast across the USA in daylight hours on 23 June 1924.

programme to permit the production of an Army version of the Helldiver as the A-25, which later served with the Marine Corps.

As noted above, the first production version was the SB2C-1 (A-25). This version, 978 of which were built by Curtiss, was powered by a 1,267 kW (1,700 hp) Wright R-2600-8 engine driving a three-bladed Curtiss Electric constant-speed propeller. Armament consisted of four 0.50 in machine-guns in the wings and one on a hydraulic mounting in the rear cockpit. Following the experimental XSB2C-2 long-range reconnaissance-bomber seaplane version, delivered in 1943, 1,112 examples of the SB2C-3 were produced with 1,416 kW (1,900 hp) R-2600-20 engines and Curtiss Electric four-bladed propellers. Armament changed to two 20 mm cannon. The SB2C-4 and SB2C-5, more than 3,000 of which were built, were developments of the SB2C-3 with perforated wing flaps and underwing bomb racks under the outer wings for eight 4.5 in rockets.

To supplement Curtiss production, Helldiver contracts were also placed with the Canadian Car and Foundry Company and Fairchild Aircraft, which were terminated in 1945. These were produced as SBWs and SBFs respectively.
Data (SB2C-3): *Engine* as above *Wing span* 15.16 m (49 ft 9 in) *Length* 11.18 m (36 ft 8 in) *Max T-O weight* 6,370 kg (14,042 lb) *Max level speed* 473 km/h (294 mph) *Range* 3,098 km (1,925 miles)

Curtiss SBC (USA) The SBC was a two-seat carrier-borne scout-bomber. Two production versions were developed from the modified biplane prototype of 1935 as the SBC-3 and SBC-4, 257 of which were produced for the US Navy, 45 going to France and five to Britain as Clevelands. The SBC was a single-bay biplane with a tapered upper wing and I-type interplane struts. The fuselage was a metal monocoque structure which housed the retractable landing gear in Goshawk fashion. The former production version was powered by a Pratt & Whitney R-1835-94 Twin Wasp radial engine enclosed in an NACA cowling with controlled flaps, while the SBC-4 major production version had a 708 kW (950 hp) Wright R-1820-34 Cyclone. Many were still operational on US aircraft carriers during the early war years.
Data (SBC-4): *Engine* as above *Wing span* 10.36 m (34 ft 0 in) *Length* 8.37 m (27 ft 5 in) *Max T-O weight* 2,838 kg (6,256 lb) *Max level speed* 378 km/h (235 mph) *Range* 1,376 km (855 miles) *Armament* one forward-firing 0.30 in machine-gun and one rear-mounted 0.30 in gun, plus up to 454 kg (1,000 lb) of bombs

Curtiss SC Seahawk (USA) The development of the Seahawk single-seat shipborne scout and anti-submarine seaplane began in June 1942, when the US Navy Bureau of Aeronautics invited Curtiss to submit proposals for an improved scout seaplane to replace the Kingfisher and Seamew. The Curtiss proposals were submitted on 1 August and on the 25 August a contract was placed for seven aircraft: two experimental models for flight testing and five additional aircraft for equipment and service testing.

The first XSC-1 flew on 16 February 1944 and by 28 April all seven had flown. Following an order for 500 SC-1s, the type entered full production, first becoming operational on USS *Guam*. It was first reported in action with the US Fleet in the pre-invasion bombardment of Borneo in June 1945. A second version of the Seahawk was also produced as the two-seat 1,062 kW (1,425 hp) R-1820-76-engined SC-2, just nine aircraft of the large order being completed before the end of the war.

Data (SC-1): *Engine* one 1,006 kW (1,350 hp) Wright R-1820-62 radial *Wing span* 12.5 m (41 ft 0 in) *Length* 11.08 m (36 ft 4½ in) *Max T-O weight* 4,082 kg (9,000 lb) *Max level speed* 504 km/h (313 mph) *Range* 1,006 km (625 miles) *Armament* two forward-firing 0.50 in machine-guns; plus bombs or depth charges carried under the wings and in the central float, which had bomb doors controllable from the cockpit

Curtiss SOC-1 Seagull.

Curtiss SNC-1, CW-21 and CW-22B (USA) In 1939 the prototype Curtiss CW-21 single-seat lightweight interceptor made its first flight. Looking similar in many ways to the later Chance Vought F4U Corsair, except for having straight wings, it was armed with one 0.30 in and one 0.50 in machine-guns. China ordered 35 with 745 kW (1,000 hp) Wright R-1820-G5 radial engines, most of which were assembled in that country; while the Netherlands East Indies and China ordered examples of the improved CW-21B with four machine-guns, but only the 24 for the Netherlands East Indies were successfully delivered. Maximum level speed of the CW-21B was 505 km/h (314 mph).

The Curtiss Falcon, military-designated SNC-1, was a two-seat advanced trainer monoplane, 305 of which were delivered to the US Navy. It was developed from the CW-22B, which in turn had been developed from the CW-21 type. Powered by a 313 kW (420 hp) Wright R-975-E3

Whirlwind radial engine, the SNC-1's most interesting feature was its landing gear, which retracted backwards into split fairings beneath the wings. SNC-1s were used as gunnery, bombing and instrument trainers from 1941.

Curtiss SOC Seagull (USA) The SOC Seagull was a two-seat scout-observation biplane, of which the US Navy ordered 258 production examples. The first and major production version was the SOC-1, 135 being ordered in 1935 as convertible land- and seaplanes and intended for use on board aircraft carriers, battleships and cruisers. The design allowed the single central float to be interchangeable with a single-strut cantilever land chassis. Power was provided by a 410 kW (550 hp) Pratt & Whitney R-1340-18 Wasp radial engine.

These were followed by 40 SOC-2 landplanes with R-1340-22 engines and SOC-3s with similar landing gears to the SOC-1s. In addition the Naval Aircraft Factory built 64 SOC-3s as SON-1/1As and the US Coast Guard received three SOC-4s. Armament comprised one 0.30 in forward-firing and one rear-mounted Browning machine-guns, plus two 100 lb bombs carried under the lower wings, in each version. Seagulls remained operational throughout World War II.

Curtiss SO3C Seamew (USA) The SO3C was produced as a modern monoplane replacement for the highly successful SOC Seagull biplane; like the earlier aircraft it could be fitted with either a land undercarriage or floats. Delivery to the US

Curtiss CW-21B.

Curtiss SOC-4 Seagull.

Curtiss SO3C-1 Seamew.

Cvjetkovic CA-61R.

Navy began in 1942 with the SO3C-1 version powered by a 387.5 kW (520 hp) Ranger V-770-6 inverted in-line engine. About 800 Seamews were built in several versions but were unsuccessful and were withdrawn from service in 1944. Of the total, about 130 were delivered to the Fleet Air Arm, most being used as trainers but some as Queen Seamew radio-controlled target drones of the type developed and flown in America.

Curtiss June Bug.

Curtiss June Bug, Gold Bug and Golden Flyer (USA) As Director of Experiments for the Aerial Experimental Association (led by Dr Alexander Graham Bell) Glenn Curtiss developed the June Bug, with which he won the Scientific American Trophy (see **Chronology** 4 July 1908). In 1909 Curtiss built the equally successful Gold Bug; followed by the Golden Flyer which set up an official world speed record on 23 August 1909 of 69.821 km/h (43.385 mph). Power was provided by a 37.25 kW (50 hp) Curtiss engine.

Curtiss-Wright X-19A.

Curtiss (Travel Air) 6B (USA) Six-seat commercial cabin monoplane powered by a 223.5 kW (300 hp) Wright J-6 engine.

Curtiss (Travel Air) 12Q and Light Sport and Sport Trainer (USA) Two-seat sporting or training biplanes powered by a 67 kW (90 hp Wright Gipsy, 93 kW (125 hp) Kinner B-5 and 82 kW (110 hp) Warner Scarab engine respectively.

Curtiss (Travel Air) Speedwing A14D (USA) Three-seat open-cockpit sporting biplane powered by a 179 kW (240 hp) Wright R-760-E Whirlwind radial engine.

Curtiss (Travel Air) Speedwing De Luxe B14B (USA) Version of the A14D with a 246 kW (330 hp) R-975-E Whirlwind engine.

Curtiss (Travel Air) Special Speedwing De Luxe B14R (USA) Version of the A14D with a 313 kW (420 hp) Whirlwind engine.

Curtiss Osprey C14B and C14R (USA) Proposed military versions of the B14B and B14R carrying machine-guns and bombs.

Cvjetkovic CA-65.

Curtiss (Travel Air) Sport 16E (USA) Three-seat open-cockpit sporting biplane powered by a 123 kW (165 hp) Wright R-540-E engine.

Curtiss Model 19L and 19W (USA) Side-by-side two-seat all-metal cabin monoplane powered by a 67 kW (90 hp) Lambert R-266 engine (19-L) and two–three-seat version with a 108 kW (145 hp) Warner Super Scarab engine.

Curtiss Model 19R (USA) Tandem two-seat military trainer version of the 19 series powered by a 335.3 kW (450 hp) Wright R-975-E3 radial engine.

Curtiss Sedan (USA) Four-seat cabin monoplane powered by a 134 kW (180 hp) Curtiss Challenger, 156.5 kW (210 hp) Kinner C-5 or 179 kW (240 hp) Wright R-760 engine.

Curtiss-Robertson Robin (USA) The Curtiss-Robertson Aircraft Manufacturing Company, a subsidiary of the Curtiss-Wright Corporation (which was formed in August 1929 by a merger of the Curtiss Aeroplane and Motor Company and Wright Aeronautical Corporation, whose production aircraft built from that date were still known as Curtiss types), was formed in 1928 to undertake the production of the Curtiss Robin three-seat civil high-wing monoplane. Powered by a 134 kW (180 hp) Challenger engine, one Robin remained airborne for more than 420 hours in the summer of 1929 to set a world endurance record. In August 1930 this was bettered by another Robin which stayed up for 647 hours 28 minutes and 30 seconds. A four-seater was also produced as the Robin 4C-1A.

Curtiss-Robertson Kingbird (USA) Eight-seat commercial high-wing monoplane of 1930 powered by two 223.5 kW (300 hp) Wright Cyclone radial engines. One operated by the US Marine Corps.

Curtiss-Reid Rambler (USA) Civil Cirrus-engined light biplane of 1930, a few of which were also sold to the RCAF.

Dassault Super Etendard.

Three prototype Dassault Mirage 2000s fly alongside the larger prototype Super Mirage 4000

de Havilland Mosquito
T.III.

Dassault Mirage F 1
production line.

de Havilland D.H.82A
Tiger Moth.

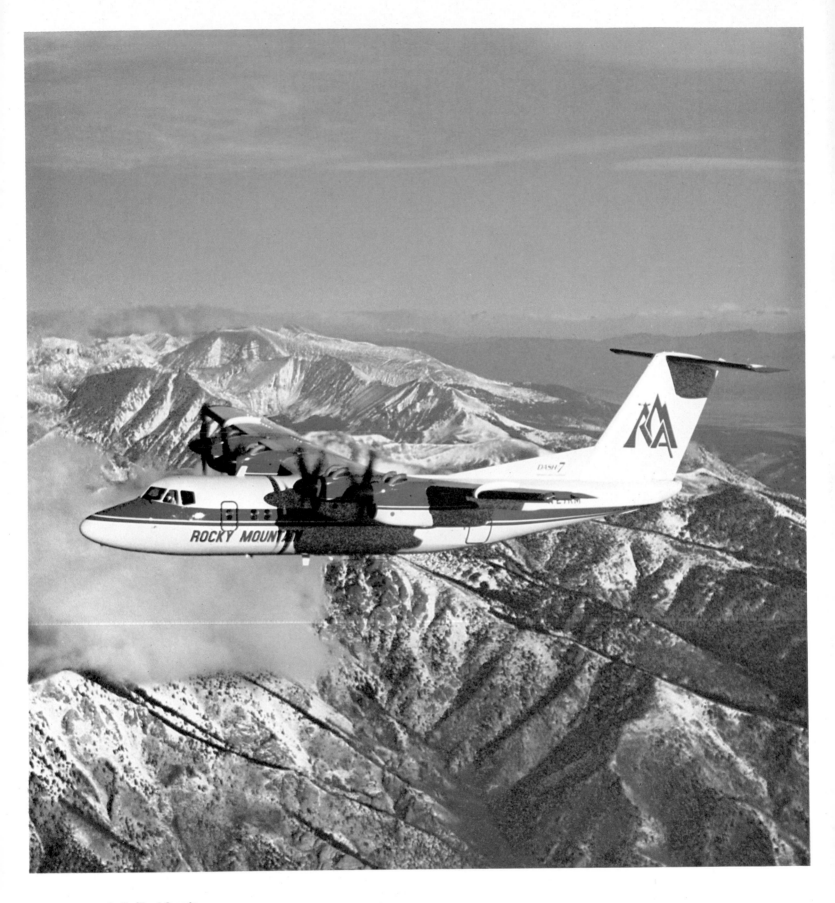

**de Havilland Canada
DHC-7 Dash 7.**

Dornier Do 31E1.

Dornier Do 28D
Skyservant.

Douglas AD-1 Skyraider.

Douglas C-133 Cargomaster.

Curtiss-Wright X-100 and Model 200/X-19A
(USA) Earlier Curtiss-Wright products were usually known as just Curtiss types (see **Curtiss-Robertson Robin** for explanation of mergers). The X-100 is best known as a Curtiss-Wright production and was a VTOL research aircraft built to develop the 'radial lift force' propeller concept. This aircraft made its first STOL flight in March 1960, after which it made successful transitions between vertical and horizontal flight. The X-19A (Model 200) was developed from it, and the first of two aircraft made its maiden hovering flight on 26 June 1964 as a six-seat twin Lycoming-engined aircraft with four propellers mounted in tilting wingtip nacelles. The programme was terminated in 1966.

Cvjetkovic CA-61/61R Mini Ace (USA) Single-seat cantilever low-wing monoplane, plans of which are available to amateur constructors. Non-retractable (CA-61) and retractable (CA-61R) landing gears.

Cvjetkovic CA-65 and CA-65A (USA) Side-by-side two-seat version of CA-61 with a more powerful engine and retractable landing gear. CA-65A is all-metal version. Plans are available to·amateur constructors.

CZL L-60 Brigadyr (Czechoslovakia) Braced high-wing light general-purpose STOL monoplane powered by a 164 kW (220 hp) Praga Doris M208B engine. Large numbers built from later 1950s for military and civil use; the latter including transport (four seats), ambulance (two stretchers and a medical attendant), glider-towing, agricultural, forest patrol and fire-fighting (see **LET** and **Zlin**).

(Swiss Federal Factory) D-3800 series (Switzerland) D-3800 was a licence-built version of the French Morane-Saulnier MS.406 single-seat fighter powered by a 641 kW (860 hp) Hispano-Suiza 12Y-31 engine. Followed by D-3801 version with a 745 kW (1,000 hp) H-S engine and the D-3802 with a 1,112 kW (1,500 hp) H-S engine. About 300 of all versions built for the Swiss Air Force.

Daimler L.6 (Germany) Single-seat biplane fighter of 1918 powered by a 138 kW (185 hp) Daimler D.IIIb engine. Six built.

D'Apuzzo D-260/D-295 Senior Aero Sport (USA) Two-seat sporting biplane powered by a Continental, Lycoming or Ranger engine of between 168–224 kW (225–300 hp). Designed for amateur construction.

D'Apuzzo D-200 Freshman (USA) Single-seat sporting biplane; awaiting completion.

D'Apuzzo D-201 Sportwing (USA) Completely redesigned development of the PJ-260/D-260 Senior Aero Sport series, first flown in 1979.

DAR 4 (Bulgaria) Darjavna Aeroplanna Rabotilnitza produced the DAR 4 four-passenger cabin biplane in 1932, powered by three 108 kW (145 hp) Walter Mars radial engines. Five built.

DAR 6 (Bulgaria) Two-seat training biplane powered by a 63.3 kW (85 hp) Walter Vega or 108 kW (145 hp) Walter Mars engine.

DAR 10F (Bulgaria) Two-seat cantilever low-wing light/dive bomber of 1939 powered by a 708 kW (950 hp) Fiat A.74 RC 38 engine. Small number built for Bulgarian Air Force.

DAS Dalaero (USA) DAS developed several kit modifications to give the Lockheed Lodestar improved performance and safety characteristics to extend its usefulness as a business aircraft.

Dassault Barougan (France) Name given to Dassault Ouragans of the French Air Force which were modified to widen their operational usefulness.

Dassault Etendard IV and Super Etendard (France) The Etendard IV is a single-seat transonic carrier-based strike fighter (IV-M) and tactical-reconnaissance aircraft/tanker (IV-P). The prototype of the IV-M flew on 21 May 1958

Dassault M.D.450 Ouragan.

D'Apuzzo D-260 (2) Senior Aero Sport.

Dassault Falcon D Cargo Jets.

Dassault M.D.311.

and was followed by six pre-production aircraft. The first of 69 production IV-Ms for the French Navy was officially delivered on 18 January 1962. Each IV-M has folding wings, long-stroke undercarriage, fittings for catapulting, deck-arrester hook, retractable refuelling probe, a high-lift system of flaps and Aïda 7 fire control radar. The seventh Etendard served as the prototype IV-P, incorporating nose and ventral camera positions (five OMERA cameras), self-contained navigation system, flight-refuelling nose-probe and a Douglas-designed 'buddy-pack' hose-reel unit. Twenty were ordered for the French Navy.

Dassault is currently producing for the French Navy an uprated version of the Etendard IV-M as the Super Etendard. The airframe and equipment of the new version were expected to be 90% common with those of the earlier aircraft, except for the nav/attack system. In fact the installation of a more powerful 49 kN (11,025 lb st) Atar 8K-50 turbojet and equipment of enhanced capability – together with the adoption of improved aerodynamic features and modern manufacturing techniques – has made the Super Etendard virtually a new aircraft. It is operated as a low- and medium-altitude strike fighter from ships in the class of the French Navy's *Clémenceau* and *Foch*, and has very comprehensive high-lift devices for shipboard use.

Dassault Mercure production line.

The first of two prototypes, a converted Etendard, made its maiden flight on 28 October 1974. Its programme included engine development, followed in 1978 by tests of the Super Etendard's external load-carrying capability and firing trials of the Exocet AM39 anti-shipping missile. It was intended originally to build 100 production aircraft, but the number has been reduced to 71 because of budget limitations. Deliveries began on 28 June 1978 and all are expected to have been delivered by the summer of 1981.

Dassault M.D.320 Hirondelle.

Data (Super Etendard): *Engine* as above *Wing span* 9.6 m (31 ft 6 in) *Length* 14.31 m (46 ft 11½ in) *Max T-O weight* 12,000 kg (26,455 lb) *Max level speed* 1,204 km/h (748 mph) *Radius of action* 650 km (403 miles) *Armament* two 30 mm DEFA cannon; underfuselage attachments for 250 kg bombs and underwing attachments for 400 kg bombs, Magic air-to-air missiles or rocket pods; optionally, one Exocet AM39

Dassault Falcon Cargo Jet (France) Under contract from Pan American Business Jets, Little Rock Airmotive converted a Falcon 20 into a specialised cargo aircraft. The prototype first flew on 28 March 1972. By the summer of that year three were operating with Federal Express Corporation of Little Rock, which subsequently expanded its fleet to 33 Falcon D Cargo Jets. The cargo conversion can be applied to any Mystère-Falcon 20 and is offered on the current Series F aircraft. Basic feature of the conversion is replacement of the standard cabin door by a hydraulically actuated cargo door 1.88 m wide by 1.44 m high (6 ft 2 in × 4 ft 9 in) which opens upwards.

Dassault M.D.311 and M.D.312 (France) Variants of the M.D.315 ordered by the French Air Force. M.D.311 was equipped as a trainer for bombing, navigation and photography, and the M.D.312 was furnished as a six-passenger military-liaison monoplane.

Dassault M.D. 315 Flamant (France) Ten-passenger or freight light general-purpose aircraft designed for service mainly in territories of the French Union. Powered by two 432 kW (580 hp) Renault 12S 02-201 engines. Ordered in quantity during 1947 and 1948.

Dassault M.D.320 Hirondelle (France) Ten or more passenger twin-turboprop executive transport first flown on 11 September 1968. Prototype only.

Dassault M.D.410 Spirale and M.D.415 Communauté (France) Twin-turboprop light transport (M.D.415 – eight passengers, four stretchers, freight, etc) first flown in 1959. Spirale developed as armed multi-purpose military version, but abandoned. Communauté design developed into Spirale III high-wing STOL transport, also abandoned.

Dassault M.D.450 Ouragan (France) The M.D.450 was the first French jet-powered fighter to be ordered in quantity for the French Air Force and its evolution established a notable record in speed of design and construction. The design (to an official interceptor fighter specification) was

Dassault Mirage IV-A.

Milan incorporated a number of technical improvements which greatly increased its capabilities in air-to-ground strike, low-speed handling and operation from short airstrips with steep approaches. The major changes involved the installation of an Atar 9K-50 turbojet engine (70.62 kN; 15,875 lb st) and a high-lift device consisting of two small retractable foreplane surfaces (known as 'moustaches') in the nose. First flight of a fully equipped Milan took place in May 1970. Other modifications included increased external stores-carrying capability, moving-map and head-up displays and an integrated electronic navigation and attack system. Optional features included rocket-assisted take-off and nose folding.

Dassault Mirage III (France) The Mirage III was designed initially as a Mach 2 high-altitude all-weather interceptor capable of performing ground-support missions and requiring only small airstrips. Developed versions include a two-seat trainer, long-range fighter-bomber and reconnaissance aircraft. A total of more than 1,350 Mirage III/5/50s of all types had been ordered by January 1978, including licence-production abroad.

Dassault Milan.

The prototype Mirage III flew for the first time on 17 November 1956 powered by a 44.1 kN (9,900 lb st) Atar 101G turbojet engine with

started in December 1947. Three prototypes were ordered on 1 July 1948, the first flying on 28 February 1949. After successful tests, a pre-production order for 25 aircraft was placed and the first of these flew in November 1950. The first of 350 Ouragans built for the French Air Force flew in December 1951 and 104 were supplied to the Indian Air Force and 12 to Israel (plus 42 ex-French).
Data: *Engine* one 22.67 kN (5,100 lb st) Hispano-Suiza-built Rolls-Royce Nene 104/105 turbojet *Wing span* 13.16 m (43 ft 2 in) *Length* 10.74 m (35 ft 3 in) *Max T-O weight* 6,800 kg (14,991 lb) *Max level speed* 940 km/h (584 mph) *Armament* four 20 mm cannon; provision for 16 rockets or bombs under wings

Dassault Mercure (France) The Mercure is a 120–162-seat twin 68.9 kN (15,500 lb st) Pratt & Whitney JT8D-15 turbofan-engined short-haul transport aircraft, optimised for ranges of 185–2,040 km (115–1,270 miles). Development started in 1967 and the first prototype flew on 28 May 1971. Air Inter ordered ten aircraft, delivery starting in May 1974. A 144–186-seat higher-capacity version was studied as the Mercure 200, to be powered by two SNECMA/General Electric CFM56 turbofans.

Dassault Milan (France) Modified from a French Air Force Mirage III-E, the prototype

Dassault Mirage III-RD.

Dassault Mirage III-B (foreground).

Dassault

Dassault Mirage III-V.

afterburner. Versions produced have included the pre-production III-A with a 58.83 kN (13,225 lb st) Atar 9B turbojet (ten built); III-B tandem two-seat trainer; III-BE tandem two-seat version of III-E; III-C all-weather interceptor and day ground-attack fighter powered by an Atar 9B; III-D tandem two-seat version, built initially in Australia for the RAAF but also built in France (180 ordered by 1978); III-D2Z, generally similar to III-D for South Africa, powered by an Atar 9K-50; III-E long-range fighter-bomber/intruder, lengthened by 30 cm (11.8 in) (523 built by 1978); III-O, version of III-E built under licence in Australia for fighter (III-OF) and attack (III-OA) duties; III-R reconnaissance version of III-E with five OMERA Type 31 cameras in place of radar in nose (153 ordered by 1978); III-R2Z, generally similar to III-R for South Africa but with Atar 9K-50 engine; III-RD, similar to III-R but with improved Doppler navigation system, gyro gunsight and automatic cameras (20 built); and III-S, developed from III-E, with Hughes TARAN electronics fire-control system and armament of HM-55 Falcon missiles.

Dassault Mirage 50.

Data (III-E): *Engine* one 60.8 kN (13,670 lb st with afterburning) SNECMA Atar 9C turbojet *Wing span* 8.22 m (26 ft 11½ in) *Length* 15.03 m (49 ft 3½ in) *Max T-O weight* 13,500 kg (29,760 lb) *Max level speed* Mach 2.2 *Combat radius* 1,200 km (745 miles) *Armament* ground-attack armament consists normally of two 30 mm DEFA cannon in fuselage and two 1,000 lb bombs, or an AS.30 air-to-surface missile under fuselage and 1,000 lb bombs under wings; alternative underwing stores include JL-100 pods, each with 18 rockets, and jettisonable fuel tanks; for interception duties, one Matra R.530 air-to-air missile under fuselage, with optional guns and two Sidewinder missiles

Dassault Mirage 2000.

Dassault Mirage III-V (France) Experimental VTOL fighter development of Mirage III, first flown on 12 February 1965.

Dassault Mirage IV-A (France) The Mirage IV-A is a tandem two-seat delta-wing supersonic bomber which was designed specifically to deliver

Dassault Mirage 5.

a nuclear weapon. Its development and production were undertaken in association with many other companies. The original prototype Mirage IV, which flew for the first time on 17 June 1959, was a scaled-up derivative of the Mirage III fighter, powered by two SNECMA Atar 09 turbojet engines. This aircraft was followed by three pre-production Mirage IVs, the first of which flew on 12 October 1961. Powered by two 62.76 kN (14,110 lb st) Atar 09Cs, this slightly larger aircraft was more representative of the production Mirage IV-A with a large circular radome under its centre-fuselage ahead of the semi-submerged nuclear free-fall bomb.

This first pre-production aircraft was used for bombing trials and development at Colomb-Béchar. The second pre-production Mirage IV was similar and was used to develop the navigation system and for flight-refuelling trials with a Boeing KC-135F Stratotanker. The final pre-production aircraft was a completely operational model with two 70.6 kN (15,873 lb st) Atar 9K-50 engines, full equipment, including flight-refuelling nose-probe and armament. The French Air Force ordered a total of 62 production IV-As for delivery during the 1964–67 period.

Data (IV-A): *Engines* as above *Wing span* 11.85 m (38 ft 10½ in) *Length* 23.5 m (77 ft 1¼ in) *Average T-O weight* 31,600 kg (69,665 lb) *Max level speed* 2,340 km/h (1,454 mph) *Tactical radius* 1,240 km (770 miles) *Armament* one nuclear weapon or 16 × 1,000 lb bombs or four Martel air-to-surface missiles

Dassault Mirage 5 (France) Derived from the Mirage III-E, the Mirage 5 is a single-seat ground-attack aircraft with the full Mach 2+ capability of the Mirage III and its ability to operate from semi-prepared airfields, but with simpler maintenance. The basic VFR version has simplified electronics, greater fuel capacity and much extended stores-carrying capability: seven

carry the full range of operational stores, armament and equipment developed for the Mirage III/5 series. A reconnaissance variant is available and a two-seat training version is projected. Data: *Engine* as above *Wing span* 8.22 m (27 ft 0 in) *Length* 15.56 m (51 ft 0½ in) *Max T-O weight* 13,500 kg (29,760 lb) *Max speed at altitude* Mach 2.2 *Combat radius* 670 km (428 miles)

Dassault Super Mirage 4000.

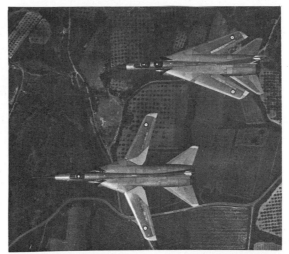

Dassault Mirage G8s.

wing and fuselage attachment points for up to 4,000 kg (8,820 lb) of weapons and 1,000 litres (220 Imp gallons) of fuel. The Mirage 5 is also capable of performing interceptor missions, armed with two Sidewinder air-to-air missiles and 4,700 litres (1,034 Imp gallons) of external fuel. In addition any degree of IFR/all-weather operation can be provided for, with corresponding reductions in fuel or weapons load.

The first Mirage 5 flew in May 1967. Well over 400 production versions have since been ordered by foreign air forces, including Mirage 5-R reconnaissance variants and two-seat Mirage 5-Ds. Data: *Engine* one 60.8 kN (13,670 lb st with afterburning) SNECMA Atar 9C turbojet *Wing span* 8.22 m (26 ft 11½ in) *Length* 15.55 m (51 ft 0¼ in) *Max T-O weight* 13,500 kg (29,760 lb) *Max level speed* (in 'clean' condition with guns installed) Mach 2.2 *Armament* seven attachment points for external loads; normal ground-attack armament consists of two 30 mm DEFA cannon in fuselage and two 1,000 lb bombs or an AS.30 air-to-surface missile under the fuselage and 1,000 lb bombs under the wings; alternative underwing stores include tank/bomb carriers and JL-100 pods, each with 18 × 68 mm rockets and 250 litres (55 Imp gallons) of fuel; in the interceptor role, two Sidewinder missiles can be carried under the wings

Dassault Mirage 50 (France) Retaining the basic airframe of the Mirage III/5 series but powered by the higher-rated SNECMA Atar 9K-50 turbojet (70.6 kN; 15,873 lb st), the Mirage 50 is a multi-mission fighter capable of air-superiority duties with guns and dogfight missiles, air patrol and supersonic interception, and ground attack combined with self-defence capability. It has better take-off performance, higher rate of climb, faster acceleration and better manoeuvrability than the other delta-wing Mirages, yet it can

Dassault Super Mystère.

Dassault Mirage 2000 (France) Under contract from the French government, the Mirage 2000 is being developed as the primary combat aircraft of the French Air Force from the mid-eighties. Although its initial duties will be in the interceptor and air-superiority role, it is expected to be equally suited for reconnaissance, close-support and low-altitude attack missions in areas to the rear of the battlefield.

The choice of a Mirage III/5-type delta-wing design without horizontal tail surfaces resulted from research data which indicated that a delta wing embodying the latest aerodynamic concepts provides the ideal compromise for a relatively small aircraft between structural simplicity, lightweight, high-speed characteristics and the demands of rapid acceleration, high rate of climb and manoeuvrability.

Dassault Mirage F1.

Mirage 2000 performance requirements include a maximum speed of Mach 2.2 at a height of 18,000 m (59,000 ft); low-speed characteristics at least as good as those of the Mirage F.1; rate of climb twice that of the Mirage III, thus permitting it to attack a Mach 3 aircraft penetrating at high altitude approximately five minutes from brake-release; and a 30% better range than the Mirage III after take-off from a 1,200 m (3,940 ft)

Dassault

Dassault Mystère-Falcon 10MER.

strip, enabling it to maintain coverage of a combat area for three times as long.

The first of five prototypes made its maiden flight in March 1978. One prototype will be a two-seat trainer version. Another (which has been funded by the manufacturer) will be used to develop equipment and modifications envisaged for future variants and for export models. Additional airframes are to be built for static and fatigue testing.

Production contracts are expected to finance an initial 127 single-seat and two-seat Mirage 2000s in 'air defence' configuration, with an anticipated requirement of 200 aircraft in this role. The first production model is expected to fly in 1982, with deliveries to the French Air Force beginning at a later date.

Data: *Engine* one 83.4 kN (18,740 lb st with afterburning) SNECMA M53-2 turbofan in prototypes, one 88.3 kN (19,840 lb st with afterburning) in production aircraft *Wing span* (estimated) 9.0 m (29 ft 6 in) *Length* (estimated) 15.33 m (50 ft 3½ in) *Max T-O weight* (combat mission, estimated) 9,000 kg (19,840 lb) *Max level speed* (estimated) over Mach 2.3 *Armament* two 30 mm DEFA cannon; five underfuselage and four underwing attachments for external stores; typical interceptor weapons comprise two Matra Super 530 missiles (inboard) and two Matra 550 Magic missiles under wings (projected strike version would carry up to 5,000 kg; 11,025 lb of external stores, including nuclear weapons)

Dassault Mystère-Falcon 10.

Dassault Super Mirage 4000 (France) A single-seat twin turbofan-engined multi-role combat aircraft under development by Dassault-Breguet, intended primarily for interception and low-altitude penetration attacks on targets a considerable distance from its base. The prototype flew for the first time on 9 March 1979. Information regarding size, weights and performance is generally classified, but installation of two engines of the type fitted in the single-jet Mirage 2000 would give the Super Mirage 4000 a power-to-weight ratio well above 1:1 in an interceptor role.

Features of the aircraft include foreplanes, a blister-type cockpit canopy permitting a 360° field of vision, a large nose radome, and extensive use of composite structures. Aerodynamics are computer-derived, with a rearward CG made possible by a fly-by-wire active control system.

Data: *Engines* two 83.4 kN (18,740 lb st with afterburning) SNECMA M53-2 turbofans *Wing span* 12.0 m (39 ft 4½ in) *Length* 18.7 m (61 ft 4¼ in) *Armament* will include two 30 mm DEFA

Flight deck of a Dassault Mystère-Falcon 20.

cannon and a rail under each outer wing for a Matra 550 Magic air-to-air missile, plus a wide range of air-to-air and air-to-surface weapons

Dassault Mirage F1 (France) Developed initially as a private venture, the prototype Mirage F1 flew for the first time in December 1966 and was followed by three pre-series aircraft. Dimensionally smaller than the Mirage III/5 series aircraft, the F1 has a swept wing with high-lift devices enabling it to take-off and land within 500–800 m (1,600–2,600 ft) at average combat-mission weight. Operation from semi-prepared, or even sod, runways is possible.

The Mirage F1 is intended primarily to perform all-weather interception at any altitude. The F1-C production version carries weapons similar to those of the Mirage III-E and is equally suitable for attack missions, carrying a variety of external stores. Designated F1-A, a ground-attack/air-combat version is also in production with much of the more costly electronic equipment deleted and the consequent space used for an additional fuel tank. Further versions include a two-seat trainer (the F1-B) first flown in May 1976; the F-1E with a more comprehensive nav/attack system, ordered by Libya; and the F-1R reconnaissance version with cameras and electro-optical sensors, 30 of which have been ordered by the French Air Force.

Orders for over 554 aircraft have been placed, including 231 for the French Air Force and 323 for service with the air forces of Ecuador, Greece, Iraq, Kuwait, Libya, Morocco, South Africa and Spain. Deliveries to the French Air Force began officially in 1973. Overseas deliveries started in 1977.

Data (F1-C): *Engine* one 70.6 kN (15,873 lb st with afterburning) SNECMA Atar 9K-50 turbo-

jet *Wing span* 8.4 m (27 ft 6¾ in) *Length* 15.0 m (49 ft 2½ in) *Max T-O weight* 15,200 kg (33,510 lb) *Max level speed* Mach 2.2 *Armament* standard fixed armament of two 30 mm DEFA 553 cannon; two stores attachment pylons under each wing and one under centre fuselage, plus provision for one air-to-air missile at each wing-tip; max external combat load 4,000 kg (8,820 lb)

Dassault Mirage G8 (France) The Mirage G8 was an experimental variable-geometry combat aircraft capable of performing patrol, attack and long-range reconnaissance duties. Two prototypes were ordered by the French government: the first, a tandem two-seater, flew in May 1971 and completed flight testing in July 1973, having explored the complete flight regime in all configurations; the second, a single seat aircraft, flew for the first time in July 1972.

Dassault Mystère IV A and Super-Mystère (France) The first IV A prototype flew on 28 September 1952 and an 'off-shore' order was placed by the USAF, followed by an order for 100 for the French Air Force. In addition 60 were delivered to Israel and 110 to the Indian government, representing a total production of 421 aircraft. Production deliveries began in June 1954. The initial series of 50 aircraft had 27.9 kN (6,280 lb st) Hispano-Suiza Tay turbojet engines, while subsequent aircraft had a 34.25 kN (7,700 lb st) Hispano-Suiza Verdon 350 turbojet.

The Super-Mystère was a successor to the Mystère IV A, with a thinner, more sharply swept (45° as opposed to 38°) wing, improved air intake and better cockpit visibility. The prototype B-1, fitted with a Rolls-Royce Avon Ra.7 engine with afterburner, was flown at Mach 1 in level flight on its fourth test on 3 March 1955, one day after its maiden flight. The 43.1 kN (9,700 lb st) SNECMA Atar 101G turbojet was chosen to power the production version which was designated B-2. The first production B-2 made its maiden flight on 26 February 1957 and delivery of the entire series of 180 aircraft to the French Air Force was completed during 1959. Twelve of these were delivered to the Israeli Air Force.

It was reported in mid-1977 that IAI had begun delivery to the Air Force of Honduras of 12 refurbished Super-Mystère B-2 fighters formerly operated by the Israeli Air Force. Modifications include the installation of a non-afterburning Pratt & Whitney J52-P-8A turbojet engine in place of the French Atar.

Data (Super-Mystère B-2): *Engine* as above *Wing span* 10.51 m (34 ft 5¾ in) *Length* 14.04 m (46 ft 1 in) *Max T-O weight* 10,000 kg (22,046 lb) *Max level speed* 1,195 km/h (743 mph) *Normal range* 965 km (600 miles) *Armament* two 30 mm DEFA cannon and a pack of air-to-air rockets in fuselage; underwing loads of up to 38 rockets in two packs, or two 500 kg bombs, two napalm tanks, 12 air-to-surface rockets or two Matra air-to-air guided missiles

Dassault Mystère-Falcon 10 (France) Basically a scaled-down four–seven-passenger version of the Mystère-Falcon 20, with similar high-lift wing devices to those of the Mystère-Falcon 20F and powered by two 14.4 kN (3,230 lb st) Garrett AiResearch TFE 731-2 turbofan engines. By mid-1978 a total of 148 had been ordered, including two (plus three on option) Mystère-Falcon 10MER aircraft for the French Navy for use as radar trainers for Super Etendard pilots, as well as for communications duties.

Dassault Mystère-Falcon 20 (France) The Mystère-Falcon 20 is a light twin-turbofan executive transport with standard accommodation for eight–ten passengers and a crew of two; an alternative layout offers seats for 14 passengers. The aircraft can be used for a variety of alternative duties including calibration, airline-crew training, cross-country flying, quick-change and cargo, aerial photography and military systems training (Falcon ST).

Dassault

Dayton-Wright Messenger.

The prototype, powered by Pratt & Whitney JT12A-8 turbojet engines, first flew on 4 May 1963. Dassault builds the wings and Aérospatiale the fuselages and tail units of production aircraft, which are marketed in the USA under the name Falcon and elsewhere as Mystère 20s. The first production aircraft flew on 1 January 1965 and by February 1978 sales had reached 429. The basic current version is the Mystère-Falcon 20 Series F. Data (Series F): *Engines* two 20 kN (4,500 lb st) General Electric CF700-2D-2 turbofans *Wing span* 16.3 m (53 ft 6 in) *Length* 17.15 m (56 ft 3 in) *Max T-O weight* 13,000 kg (28,660 lb) *Max cruising speed* 862 km/h (536 mph) *Range* 3,350 km (2,080 miles) *Accommodation* crew of two and 10–14 passengers

Davis DA-3.

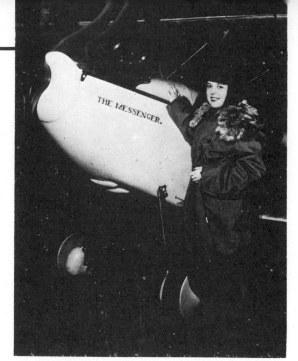

Dassault Mystère-Falcon 20 Series G and Guardian (France) Garrett AiResearch ATF 3-6 turbofan-engined version of the Mystère-Falcon 20. In 1976 it was announced that Falcon Jet Corporation (distributor and support centre for Falcons in the USA) had submitted the lowest tender to meet a US Coast Guard requirement for a medium-range surveillance aircraft known by the project designation HX-XX. Delivery of the 41 Falcon Gs ordered by the Coast Guard as HU-25As began in 1979. To other customers this aircraft is known as the Falcon Guardian.

Dassault-Breguet Mystère-Falcon 50 (France) The Mystère-Falcon 50 is a five–eight-passenger executive transport derived from the Mystère-Falcon 20, powered by three 16.5 kN (3,700 lb st) Garrett AiResearch TFE 731-3 turbofan engines. It has an entirely new wing of supercritical section, adapted to flight at high Mach numbers and embodying efficient high-lift devices. The prototype first flew on 7 November 1976 and by mid-1978 a total of 76 had been ordered. Maximum cruising speed is 889 km/h (552 mph).

Dassault-Breguet/Dornier Alpha Jet (France) The Alpha Jet is a tandem two-seat basic, low-altitude and advanced jet trainer and close-support and battlefield reconnaissance aircraft. Developed jointly by Dassault-Breguet of France and Dornier of Germany, the first of four prototypes flew on 26 October 1973.

The French and German governments have agreed to procure 400 Alpha Jets, 200 each for the Armée de l'Air and the Luftwaffe. By the spring of 1978 firm contracts had been placed for 140 of these (56 Alpha Jet E trainers for France and 84 close-support Alpha Jet As for Germany). In addition Belgium has ordered 16 of the E version, which it designates Alpha Jet 1B, with 17 more on option. The Togolese Air Force has ordered five and the air forces of the Ivory Coast six (with six on option) and Morocco 24.

Dassault-Breguet and Dornier have also teamed with Lockheed-California to enter the Alpha Jet in the US Navy's VTX advanced-trainer competition. Deliveries to the Armée de l'Air began in 1978 and to the Luftwaffe in 1979. Data: *Engines* two 13.24 kN (2,976 lb st) SNECMA/Turboméca Larzac 04-C5 turbofans *Wing span* 9.11 m (29 ft 10¾ in) *Length* (excl nose-probe) 12.29 m (40 ft 3¾ in) *Max T-O weight* 7,250 kg (15,983 lb) *Max level speed* Mach 0.85 at high altitude, 1,000 km/h (622 mph) at low altitude *Combat radius* (max external load for ground attack) 630 km (391 miles) *Armament* for armament training and light close-support missions, can be equipped with an underfuselage detachable pod containing a 30 mm DEFA or 27 mm Mauser cannon, or same pod with a 7.62 mm machine-gun; provision for two hardpoints under each wing, the inner ones each stressed for loads of up to 665 kg (1,466 lb) and the outer for up to 335 kg (738 lb): on these can be carried launchers for 6, 18 or 36 × 68 mm rockets, HE or retarded bombs of 50, 125, 250 or 400 kg; 625 lb cluster dispensers, 690 or 825 lb special-purpose tanks, napalm containers, combined launchers for rockets and 360 lb bombs, practice launchers for bombs or rockets, Dassault-Breguet

Dayton-Wright K.T. Cabin Cruiser.

CC-420 30 mm gun-pods, or drop tanks; provision for carrying Magic or Maverick missiles, target-designation devices or reconnaissance pod; total max payload 2,250 kg (4,960 lb)

Davis DA-2A (USA) Side-by-side two-seat light aircraft, plans of which are available to amateur constructors.

Davis DA-3 (USA) Four-seat scaled-up development of the DA-2A.

Davis DA-5A (USA) Single-seat sporting aircraft, plans of which are available to amateur constructors.

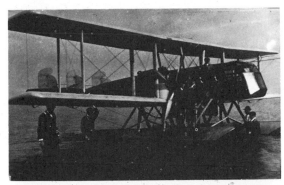

Dayton-Wright K. T. Cabin Cruiser (USA) By February 1919 Dayton-Wright had completed a very large number of Standard J1 trainers and DH-4s. The post-war K.T. was a civil modification of the DH-4 with enclosed seating for three persons.

Dayton-Wright O.W.1 Aerial Coupe (USA) Three-seat cabin biplane derived from the DH-4 and powered by a 134 kW (180 hp) Wright-built Hispano engine.

Dayton-Wright Messenger (USA) Single-seat light aircraft.

Dayton-Wright F.P.2 (USA) Twin-engined forest-patrol biplane developed to satisfy the requirements of the Canadian Forest Service for an aeroplane equipped for aerial photography, mapping, surveying, inspection and timber patrol.

Dayton-Wright RB Racer (USA) Very advanced single-seat cantilever high-wing (variable camber) racing monoplane, built to compete in the 1920 Gordon Bennett Aviation Cup Race. Pilot sat inside the fuselage, with side windows only. Landing gear retracted into fuselage. Powered by one 186.3 kW (250 hp) Hall/Scott Liberty Six. Maximum level speed approximately 320 km/h (200 mph).

Dayton-Wright Chummy and TA-3 (USA) Side-by-side two-seat biplane powered by a Le Rhône engine. Sold as the 59.6 kW (80 hp)

First de Havilland aeroplane, which flew in 1909

Chummy civil aircraft and as the TA-3 to the USAAS, which received ten with more powerful 82 kW (110 hp) engines.

Dayton-Wright TA-5 (USA) Single 149 kW (200 hp) Lawrence-engined trainer acquired by USAAS.

de Havilland aircraft (UK) The first aircraft designed by Geoffrey de Havilland was a 33.5 kW (45 hp)-engined biplane with two pusher propellers which flew once in December 1909. It was followed by a more conventional Farman-type biplane which was bought by the War Office as the F.E.1. The 1911 model was the F.E.2 with an angular nacelle for the pilot. This aircraft underwent a long period of development at the government's works at Farnborough, eventually supporting a flexible forward-firing Maxim machine-gun and a stepped two-seat streamlined crew nacelle of World War I-type. The subsequent aircraft built prior to World War I and up to the D.H.1 were designed by a team led by de Havilland at Farnborough and are known as Royal Aircraft Factory types. Aircraft designed by Geoffrey de Havilland during World War I are covered under Airco (Aircraft Manufacturing Company), up to but not including the D.H.10, which is best known as a de Havilland type.

Dayton-Wright F.P.2.

Dayton-Wright RB Racer.

de Havilland D.H.10A Amiens IIIA.

de Havilland D.H.10 Amiens (and D.H.11) (UK) The D.H.10 was designed as a three-seat heavy bomber and first flew in prototype form on 4 March 1918. Production aircraft were known as Amiens IIIs and IIIAs, powered by two 298 kW (400 hp) Liberty 12 engines mounted between the biplane wings and on the lower wing respectively. Of the total of 1,295 D.H.10s ordered, only just

de Havilland

de Havilland D.H.29.

over 200 were built, of which about eight were in service with the Independent Air Force before the Armistice. Post-war service was also short, remaining operational until 1923 in the UK, in India and Egypt, during which period the Amiens is best remembered as an RAF mail carrier. Unlike the earlier D.H. bombers, the Amiens was not used to any great extent as a civil aircraft.

Interestingly in 1918 the Air Ministry requested a new long-distance day bomber, for which requirement de Havilland produced the D.H.11 Oxford. Although loosely based on the D.H.10, it was of very advanced design. Only half-completed by the Armistice, no great hurry was made to finish it and so it did not fly until 1920. No production was undertaken.

de Havilland D.H.16.

de Havilland D.H.18.

de Havilland D.H.34.

de Havilland D.H.16 (UK) The first purely civilian type produced by the Aircraft Manufacturing Company after World War I, the D.H.16 was built from war-surplus D.H.9A components with a widened fuselage to seat four passengers (in facing pairs) in a glazed cabin. The pilot sat in an open cockpit in front.

In May 1919 the prototype D.H.16 (see below) entered service with Aircraft Transport and Travel Ltd and in July flew to Amsterdam to be demonstrated at the Dutch First Air Traffic Exhibition. On the inaugural day of the London–Paris air service (see **Chronology** 25 August 1919) it flew from Hounslow piloted by Maj Cyril Patterson. Eight more D.H.16s were built, including one for the Buenos Aires–Montevideo cross-river ferry of the River Plate Aviation Company. The remainder were used on the continental routes of AT&T, the last three with 335.3 kW (450 hp) Napier Lion engines. One of these made seven Croydon–Le Bourget return trips in six days in the summer of 1920. The first KLM scheduled service from Croydon to Amsterdam was flown by Capt H. Shaw on 17 May 1920 in D.H.16 *Arras*, on charter from

AT&T. Flight time in extremely bad weather was 2¼ hours.

Only the prototype ditched in the Channel off Brighton on 18 March 1920 when Lieut H. F. Game ran short of fuel. AT&T closed down in the following December and the remaining seven were stored at Croydon; five were broken up in 1922; the other two were used by the de Havilland Aeroplane Hire service on early morning newspaper-delivery flights between Lympne and Ostend. On 5 December 1922 they flew consignments of an Ulster edition of *The Times* from Sealand to Aldergrove on the day of issue.

Data: *Engine* one 238.5 kW (320 hp) Rolls-Royce Eagle VIII *Wing span* 14.17 m (46 ft 6 in) *Length* 9.68 m (31 ft 9 in) *Max T-O weight* 2,155 kg (4,750 lb) *Cruising speed* 161 km/h (100 mph) *Range* 684 km (425 miles)

de Havilland D.H.18 (UK) The D.H.18 was designed and built as an eight-passenger commercial airliner with the pilot in an open cockpit to the rear of the passenger cabin. It is an interesting fact that several aircraft built for passenger carrying during the early 1920s (especially French) had the pilot's cockpit aft of the passenger cabin so that in the event of a crash the pilot would stand the greatest chance of survival and so relate the cause of the accident.

The first D.H.18 to be built began commercial services with Aircraft Transport and Travel (for whom it had been developed) in April 1920 between Croydon and Paris. This aircraft was followed by three D.H.18As and two D.H.18Bs, each powered by a single 335.3 kW (450 hp) Napier Lion engine, all of which were operated initially by Instone Air Line.

On 7 April 1922 one D.H.18A, by then operated by Daimler Airways, was involved in the first air collision between scheduled airliners, colliding with a Farman Goliath (see **Chronology** 7 April 1922). Unfortunately the pilot's seating arrangement did not save his life.

Data: *Engine as above Wing span* 15.62 m (51 ft 3 in) *Length* 11.89 m (39 ft 0 in) *Max T-O weight* 3,380 kg (7,450 lb) *Max level speed* 206 km/h (128 mph) *Range* 644 km (400 miles)

de Havilland D.H.29 (UK) Interesting 12-seat Napier-engined cantilever monoplane transport built for the Air Ministry's Department of Research.

de Havilland D.H.34.

de Havilland D.H.34 (UK) The D.H.34's design resulted from three years of continuous experience with earlier types of D.H. machines on the London (Croydon)–Paris service. In general arrangement it followed the design of the D.H.18, the most important difference being that the pilot's cockpit (with a second seat for a co-pilot/passenger) was moved ahead of the eight-passenger cabin, the latter with a toilet and baggage compartment to the rear. Like the D.H.18, power was provided by a single Napier Lion engine.

A total of 11 D.H.34s were built, of which six were operated by Daimler Airways and four by Instone Air Lines, services by each company starting on 2 April 1922. Seven were eventually taken over by Imperial Airways, including all three D.H.34B modified aircraft with wings of increased span and chord. D.H.34s were generally regarded as the most comfortable passenger-carrying aircraft in regular commercial service during their four years of operation. Cruising speed was 169 km/h (105 mph).

de Havilland D.H.51.

(G-EBFO) for flights to Rangoon and back in 1924–25; and Imperial Airways survey flights to South Africa and Australia, both in 1926. The third D.H.50 inaugurated Imperial Airways' charter section, flown by Capt G. P. Olley.

Fourteen D.H.50As were built with longer cabins, including nine for Australia. One D.H.50A was the first Flying Doctor aircraft, equipped with two stretchers. Others maintained the pioneer air services of West Australian Airways, Australian Aerial Services and QANTAS in the outback and made flights to goldfields with Holdens Air Transport in New Guinea. A single D.H.50 seaplane was also supplied to the RAAF in 1926. This aircraft completed 10,000 miles of ocean flying, piloted by Group Capt R. Williams during a survey flight from Melbourne to the Solomon Islands and back.

In 1926 licences were granted for D.H.50 production overseas: seven were built by QANTAS at Longreach (some with Bristol Jupiter radials as D.H.50Js); three by West Australian Airways at Perth; one by the Larkin Aircraft Supply Company at Melbourne; three by SABCA in Brussels for the Congo services of the Belgian airline Sabena; and seven by Aero in Prague for the Czechoslovakian State Airline, with Czech-built 179 kW (240 hp) Walter W-4 water-cooled engines. The last British-built machine was the D.H.50J 'Pelican' for the North Sea Aerial and General Transport Company's mail service along the Nile from Khartoum to Kisumu, abandoned in 1927 after two river accidents.

de Havilland D.H.50.

de Havilland D.H.50 (UK) A four-passenger taxi biplane with the pilot in an open cockpit behind the cabin, the D.H.50 was first flown in 1923. The prototype immediately gained first prize in the Gothenburg reliability trials and won the King's Cup Race in 1924. Alan J. Cobham earned a knighthood in the second D.H.50

Data: *Engine* one 171.4 kW (230 hp) Siddeley Puma *Wing span* 13.08 m (42 ft 11 in) *Length* 9.27 m (30 ft 5 in) *Max T-O weight* 1,905 kg (4,200 lb) *Cruising speed* 153 km/h (95 mph) *Range* 604 km (375 miles)

de Havilland D.H.53 Humming Bird.

de Havilland D.H.60 Moth.

de Havilland D.H.60X Moth.

de Havilland D.H.60M Moth.

de Havilland D.H.51 (UK) Produced in 1924 to meet the need for a civil two–three-seater of an even more economical type than the D.H.50. It was a very simple biplane powered by a 67 kW (90 hp) RAF 1a air-cooled engine as standard. Three built.

de Havilland D.H.53 Humming Bird (UK) Single-seat very light monoplane produced originally to compete in the Lympne light aeroplane trials of 1923. Fifteen built, two (of eight) acquired by the RAF being used for parasite experiments with the airship R33.

de Havilland D.H.60 Moth (UK) It is not overstating the case to say that the Moth revolutionised aviation and was a direct result of the worldwide surge of enthusiasm for private flying. Although the Humming Bird offered a measure of realistic sport flying, it was too basic to meet the requirement, and yet the D.H.51 was too large. The answer was somewhere between the two and the D.H.60 appeared in 1925 as a scaled-down D.H.51 with an 89.4 kW (120 hp) engine cut in half, reworked and completed as a 44.7 kW (60 hp) ADC Cirrus.

First flown on 22 February 1925, the Moth exceeded expectations and a long series of tests proved that it was eminently suited for school, flying club and private use: it was selected by all the British Flying Clubs formed under the Air Ministry scheme. In addition to the home markets, many civil examples were exported and military models delivered to air forces as tandem two-seat trainers, including those of the UK, Australia, Irish Free State, Sweden, Finland, Japan and Canada.

By the close of production nearly 500 Moths had been built, excluding those licence-built in Australia, Finland and elsewhere. Other engines fitted included the 63.3 kW (85 hp) Cirrus II, 67 kW (90 hp) Cirrus III (as installed in the D.H.60X) and 56 kW (75 hp) Armstrong Siddeley Genet (as the Genet Moth).

The first Moth was flown by (Sir) Alan Cobham from London to Zurich and back in a single day on 29 May 1925; and in 1927 Moths accomplished the London–Cape Town return flight and won the first prize for aerobatics at the Copenhagen International aeroplane meeting. However in 1928 de Havilland produced their own engine for the Moth, the Gipsy, and so the Gipsy Moth was created (see below).
Data (Cirrus I): *Engine* as above *Wing span* 8.84 m (29 ft 0 in) *Length* 7.17 m (23 ft 6 in) *Max T-O weight* 567 kg (1,250 lb) *Max level speed* 146 km/h (91 mph) *Range* 515 km (320 miles)

de Havilland D.H.60G Gipsy Moth (UK) The Gipsy Moth was the outcome of nearly four years and over four million miles of experience with the early versions of the Moth. The main changes were the installation of a 74.5–89.4 kW (100–120 hp) Gipsy I, II or III engine, the split-axle landing gear of the D.H.60X and cleaner lines. Handley Page automatic slots could be fitted if required but were not standard. It remained in production until 1934, by which time it was in worldwide use as a civil and military aircraft for sport flying and training and was built under licence in Australia, France and the USA (see **Chronology** 5–24 May 1930).

de Havilland D.H.60M Moth (UK) Version of the Gipsy Moth with a welded steel-tube fuselage and several minor changes to allow easier maintenance.

de Havilland D.H.60GIII Moth Major (UK) Version of the wooden-airframe Moth with an inverted 89.4 kW (120 hp) Gipsy II engine (known as the Gipsy III) or a 97 kW (130 hp) Gipsy Major.

de Havilland D.H.60T Moth Trainer (UK) This type was a modification of the standard D.H.60M Moth and intended as an economical form of military training aircraft – the first version of the Moth produced solely for military use. It

could be supplied with a variety of military equipment to cover the comprehensive range of possible duties. Powered by an 89.4 kW (120 hp) Gipsy II engine, it had wings of completely new section: these did not detract from the speed and climb of the aircraft, but made the stall less abrupt and the resultant spin slower. The strengthened wing structure allowed the aerobatic C of A for 744 kg (1,640 lb).

Three modifications were made to assure easy and rapid egress in an emergency: the rear flying wires on each side were led forward to the front wing-root fittings, so that no wires were in the way of a person leaving the front cockpit; the cockpits were enlarged and had two doors, those in the front being particularly deep; the exhaust pipe was also led forward and downward at the nose.

Moth Trainers were exported to the air forces of Brazil, China, Egypt, Iraq and Sweden and to the Brazilian Navy.

de Havilland D.H.61 Giant Moth (UK) The Giant Moth was a third generation six–eight-passenger airliner of the type originated with the D.H.18, and was developed to meet an Australian need for a D.H.50 replacement. Powered by a 372.6 kW (500 hp) Bristol Jupiter XIF radial engine, general layout remained similar to the earlier models with an open pilot's cockpit aft of the passenger cabin. Altogether ten were built, serving mainly in Australia and Canada from 1928 until the last crashed in 1938.

de Havilland D.H.66 Hercules (UK) The Hercules was a large commercial biplane designed and constructed to a requirement of Imperial Airways for use on the Cairo–Karachi service. Power was provided by three 313 kW (420 hp) Bristol Jupiter VI air-cooled radial engines, mounted in the nose of the fuselage and on the lower wings. Accommodation was for up to 14 passengers in the large cabin; with Imperial Air-

ways only seven passengers were carried, the remainder of the space being used for mail and freight. Behind the main cabin was a large baggage compartment with separate entrance doors. Pilot and co-pilot sat in an open cockpit high in the nose of the fuselage, forward and above the passenger cabin.

Services with Imperial Airways started in early 1927. Two years later Delhi was added to the route covered by the Hercules. Meanwhile the type had been adopted by West Australian Airways for use on the Perth–delaide service across Australia, which began in April 1929. The Hercules used by this airline had several minor modifications, one of which was an enclosed cabin for the flight crew. Subsequent Imperial Airways' aircraft had this feature as standard and earlier aircraft were so modified.

From 1932 Hercules biplanes were flown to South Africa by Imperial Airways. The last of the 11 aircraft built were two handed over to the South African Air Force in 1934 and declared obsolete in 1943.
Data: *Engines* as above *Wing span* 24.23 m (79 ft 6 in) *Length* 16.92 m (55 ft 6 in) *Max T-O weight* 7,076 kg (15,600 lb) *Max level speed* 209 km/h (130 mph)

de Havilland D.H.61
Giant Moth.

de Havilland D.H.66
Hercules prototype.

de Havilland D.H.75 Hawk Moth (UK) The Hawk Moth was a four-seat braced high-wing monoplane. It was fitted with a 179 kW (240 hp) Armstrong Siddeley Lynx VIA engine as standard or a 223.5 kW (300 hp) Wright Whirlwind, designed for the private owner, taxi work or operating feeder lines on air routes. It was luxuriously equipped, had ample space for the passengers and baggage and allowed exceptional all-round view. Only eight were built, most going to Canada and Australia. Maximum level speed as a landplane was 206 km/h (128 mph).

de Havilland D.H.60T
Moth Trainers.

de Havilland D.H.66 Hercules.

de Havilland D.H.80A Puss Moth.

Prototype de Havilland D.H. 75 Hawk Moth with non-standard engine.

de Havilland D.H.80A Puss Moth (UK) The Puss Moth was a two–three-seat braced high-wing cabin monoplane designed for long-range touring at high speed. First flown on 9 September 1929, the standard power plant for production aircraft was the 89.4 kW (120 hp) Gipsy III engine.

Supplied as a landplane and seaplane, the Puss Moth became extremely popular (despite a number of early fatal accidents) and some 285 were built, including a small number in Canada. One was supplied to the Prince of Wales and another to King Feisal of Iraq. Within the first year of flying Mr C. D. Barnard flew to Malta and back in two days (a flying time of 26½ hours) and to Tangier and back in two days (23 hours). Other notable flights were made by Mr Caspareuthus, who flew from London to Cape Town in 8½ days, and Col The Master of Sempill, who flew a seaplane version across the North Sea from Norway to Scotland while on a touring holiday. These early flights were soon eclipsed by one from England to Tokyo in under nine days by Amy Johnson during July and August 1931; one from England to Cape Town by Jim Mollison in 4 days 17 hours 19 minutes during March 1932; the first solo east–west crossing of the Atlantic by aeroplane, performed by Mollison during 18–19 August 1932; and a flight from Darwin, Australia to Croydon, England in 8 days 9 hours by Mr C. J. Melrose in 1934. These were but a few of the record flights made.
Data: *Engine* as above *Wing span* 11.2 m (36 ft 9 in) *Length* 7.62 m (25 ft 0 in) *Max T-O weight* 930 kg (2,050 lb) *Max cruising speed* 177 km/h (110 mph) *Normal range* 483 km (300 miles)

de Havilland D.H.82A Tiger Moth (UK) de Havilland's famous D.H.82 Tiger Moth could trace a direct line of descent from the equally famous de Havilland D.H.60 Moth of 1925 – the latter being regarded as the type which made possible worldwide development of the flying-club movement. The early Moth was succeeded by several variants of the Moth and Gipsy Moth; examples of the Gipsy Moth, flown by such well-known pilots as (Sir) Francis Chichester, Amy Johnson and J. A. Mollison, will always be remembered in aviation history for pioneering flights between England and Australia.

All of these ancestors were conventional one- or two-seat biplanes with unswept, unstaggered wings. Consequently access to the forward cock-pit of two-seat versions was much restricted by the centre-section struts. This shortcoming was eliminated in the Tiger Moth by resiting the struts forward of the front cockpit, with the result that both wings acquired their characteristic sweep-back to maintain the aircraft's CG in the desired position.

The prototype D.H.82 Tiger Moth flew for the first time on 26 October 1931 and quickly aroused the interest of the RAF – the first for that service being delivered in 1932. By the outbreak of war in September 1939 more than 1,000 were in service with Elementary and Reserve Flying Training Schools. The majority of the RAF's wartime pilots received their elementary training on these aircraft and by the end of the war well over 4,200 had been delivered. In addition almost 3,000 examples were built by manufacturers in Australia, Canada and New Zealand for use in the Commonwealth Air Training Plan; and were used also in South Africa, India and Rhodesia. Last biplane trainer in RAF service, the Tiger

de Havilland D.H.82B Queen Bee (UK) see
D.H.82A Tiger Moth

de Havilland D.H.83 and D.H. 83C Fox Moth
(UK) The Fox Moth first flew on 29 January
1932. Described primarily as a family transport,
but equally suited for joy-riding and with some
conversion could be turned into an ambulance or
adapted for aerial survey and freight carrying
(1.42 m³; 50 cu ft of space with seats removed).
Configured like a small version of the Giant Moth,
it was a biplane with cabin accommodation for
four passengers, the pilot occupying an open
cockpit aft.

de Havilland D.H.80A
Puss Moth *The Hearts
Content*, flown by Jim
Mollison 18–19 August
1932.

Moth remained with Flying Training Command
until 1947 and with the RAFVR until 1951.

One military variant was the radio-controlled
Queen Bee, used in both landplane and floatplane
configurations to provide live target practice for
anti-aircraft gunners. True Tiger Moths were of
composite wood and metal construction, but the
380 Queen Bees supplied to the RAF were all-
wood with fabric covering.

Post-war ex-service Tigers began to come on
the civilian market and were quickly snapped up
by enthusiasts and flying clubs: the supply failing
miserably to meet the demand until 1947 when
large numbers of ex-RAF machines became
available. Even then these superb little aircraft –
regarded worldwide as among the most famous
trainers in aviation history – were to remain in
short supply, for in the early post-war years very
few new lightplanes were available.

Many Tiger Moths were used (especially in
Australia and New Zealand) to pioneer the technique of top-dressing and, later, of crop spraying,
leading to the current worldwide mass-
production of purpose-built agricultural aircraft.
Data (Tiger Moth II): *Engine* one 97 kW (130 hp)
de Havilland Gipsy Major *Wing span* 8.94 m (29 ft
4 in) *Length* 7.29 m (23 ft 11 in) *Max T O weight*
803 kg (1,770 lb) *Max level speed* 175 km/h
(109 mph) at 305 m (1,000 ft) *Cruising speed*
150 km/h (93 mph) *Range* 483 km (300 miles)

de Havilland D.H.82A
Tiger Moth IIs.

de Havilland D.H.82B
Queen Bee.

A valuable feature of the aircraft was that it was
largely composed of standard D.H. components,
large quantities of spares of which were already
available all over the world. The wings, for
instance, were those of the Tiger Moth, while the
tail unit was a combination of Puss Moth and
Gipsy Moth parts, and the nose was a Puss Moth
component. Power was provided by a Gipsy Moth
III or Gipsy Major inverted engine. A total of 98
pre-war Fox Moths were built, numbers of which
were extensively used in Britain and abroad on
feeder routes and communications work. Others
were supplied to the governments of Brazil and
Spain for training in navigation, aerial photography and surveying.

de Havilland D.H.82A
Tiger Moth.

de Havilland D.H.82A
Tiger Moth seaplane.

de Havilland

de Havilland D.H.83
Fox Moth.

de Havilland D.H.85
Leopard Moth.

After World War II the D.H.83C Fox Moth was put into Canadian production for the specific needs of bush operators. The new version was basically the same as the earlier aircraft, but equipped with a 104.5 kW (140 hp) Gipsy Major Ic engine. A variable-pitch propeller was fitted to late production aircraft, of which a total of 52 were built. Other refinements included a sliding Plexiglas canopy over the pilot's cockpit; a larger cabin door for loading freight; improved cabin heating and ventilation; and greater baggage capacity. Improved methods of plywood construction were introduced as a result of experience with the Mosquito.

Data (D.H.83C): *Engine* as above *Wing span* 9.41 m (30 ft 10½ in) *Length* (landplane) 7.85 m (25 ft 9 in) *Max T-O weight* 952 kg (2,100 lb) *Max level speed* 177 km/h (110 mph) *Range* 605–1,207 km (375–750 miles)

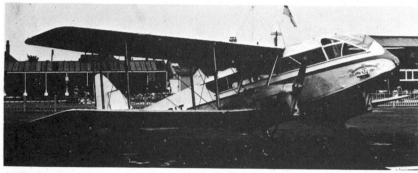

de Havilland D.H.84
Dragon.

de Havilland D.H. 84 Dragon (UK) The Dragon light transport was launched with orders from the Iraqi Air Force and Hillman's Airways, first flying on 24 November 1932. It was a simple wood-and-fabric two-bay biplane with folding wings and non-retractable undercarriage. The engines were two 97 kW (130 hp) de Havilland Gipsy Majors and normal accommodation was for a pilot and six passengers. One hundred and fifteen were built in the UK and they made a major contribution to the establishment of airlines in the British Isles and many other parts of the world.

During World War II 87 were built in Australia as radio and navigation trainers and many of these were later used as civil aircraft.

Data: *Engines* as above *Wing span* 14.43 m (47 ft 4 in) *Length* 10.52 m (34 ft 6 in) *Max T-O weight* 1,905 kg (4,200 lb) *Cruising speed* 175 km/h (109 mph) *Range* 740 km (460 miles)

de Havilland D.H.86A.

de Havilland D.H.85 Leopard Moth (UK) The Leopard Moth was produced in 1934 and on its first public appearance (piloted by its owner Capt Geoffrey de Havilland) won the King's Cup Race at an average speed of 224.52 km/h (139.5 mph). Basically similar in layout to the Puss Moth, it was powered by a 97 kW (130 hp) Gipsy Major engine and had accommodation for three persons. A total of 133 were built.

de Havilland D.H.86 (UK) The D.H.86 'Express Air Liner' was a four-engined (149 kW; 200 hp Gipsy Six) ten-passenger or freight-carrying airliner, first flown on 14 January 1934. It had been designed to comply with the conditions of an Australian government tender for the extension of the Empire Air Route from Singapore to Brisbane. QANTAS, which had submitted a tender using the D.H.86, was successful in getting the contract and a fleet of these machines went into service on that route at the end of 1934.

Similar aircraft (with provision for two pilots sitting side-by-side with a throw-over control column which could be provided with twin controls) also went into service with other companies, including Imperial Airways for their continental services, Jersey Airways, Misr-Airwork, Union Airways of New Zealand and a number of other commercial operators at home and abroad. However the first four aircraft built went to Railway Air Services and Holyman's Airways Pty (Tasmania) and had one-pilot only flight decks.

After 32 aircraft had been built, production changed to the refined D.H.86A version. The final ten of the 62-aircraft production run were D.H.86Bs with auxiliary fins at the extremities of the tailplane and other minor changes. A few D.H.86-series aircraft survived the war and went back into commercial service.

Data (D.H.86B): *Engines* as above *Wing span* 19.66 m (64 ft 6 in) *Length* 14.05 m (46 ft 1¼ in) *Max T-O weight* 4,649 kg (10,250 lb) *Cruising speed* 228 km/h (142 mph) *Range* 724–1,223 km (450–760 miles)

de Havilland D.H.87 Hornet Moth (UK) In 1935 de Havilland introduced the Hornet Moth, a two-seat side-by-side cabin biplane. At the same time it withdrew the Moth from the market. Some early production aircraft had wings which sharply tapered (D.H.87A), but the majority were fitted with the more rectangular wings of the D.H.87B version in 1936. Of the 165 aircraft produced (with Gipsy Major 1 engines) about 12 were still flying in the UK in 1979, plus a few abroad.
Data (D.H.87B): *Engine* one 97 kW (130 hp) de Havilland Gipsy Major 1 *Wing span* 9.73 m (31 ft 11 in) *Length* 7.6 m (24 ft 11½ in) *Max T-O weight* 907 kg (2,000 lb) *Max cruising speed* 169 km/h (105 mph) *Range* 1,002 km (623 miles)

de Havilland D.H.88 Comet (UK) The Comet was specially designed to compete in the England–Australia Air Race. Three were designed, built and tested in eight months, the first flying on 8 September 1934: one (piloted by C. W. A. Scott and T. Campbell Black) won the MacRobertson Trophy and first prize of £10,000 by flying from Mildenhall, Suffolk to Melbourne in 70 hours 54 minutes; another (flown by Cathcart Jones and Waller) was fourth to arrive in Melbourne, 4 days 22 hours after leaving Mildenhall.

Other notable flights were made by the Comet after this race, including from Brussels to Leopoldville (Belgian Congo) and back in 44 hours 40 minutes, London–Lisbon (6 hours 5 minutes) and London–Paris (52 minutes). The last was made with one of two Comets bought by the French government for experimental work in connection with the South Atlantic air mail route. Power for the Comet was provided by two special 171.4 kW (230 hp) Gipsy Six R engines. Maximum level speed 381 km/h (237 mph).

de Havilland D.H.89 Dragon Rapide (UK) The Dragon Rapide was a direct development of the Dragon, employing the same structure but having tapered wings, 149 kW (200 hp) Gipsy Six

engines and a faired-in undercarriage. Known originally as the Dragon Six, it was first flown on 17 April 1934 and remained in production for more than ten years.

Over 700 were built for civil and military customers and served in most parts of the world – playing an important role on air routes in the UK and many parts of the British Commonwealth. The type was produced during World War II as the Dominie radio and navigation trainer. A number of Dragon Rapides were also operated on Fairchild-produced floats by Canadian airlines, produced in Canada by de Havilland's Toronto-based company. It had exceptional airfield performance and a few are still airworthy.
Data: *Engines* as above *Wing span* 14.63 m (48 ft 0 in) *Length* 10.5 m (34 ft 6 in) *Max T-O weight* 2,495 kg (5,500 lb) *Cruising speed* 212 km/h (132 mph) *Range* 933 km (580 miles)

de Havilland D.H. 90 Dragonfly (UK) The Dragonfly was a smaller version of the Dragon Rapide, fitted with two Gipsy Major engines. Like the Rapide it had tapered wings, but differed mainly by having a wooden monocoque fuselage. Accommodation was for a pilot and four passengers. Sixty-seven were built.

de Havilland D.H.91 Albatross (UK) The Albatross was a four-engined (391 kW; 525 hp Gipsy 12) airliner designed for fast and luxurious intercontinental passenger carrying as well as long-range freight and mail transport. The British Air Ministry ordered two examples for experimental operations on the direct route across the North Atlantic. The first made its maiden flight on 20 May 1937. Five were ordered for Imperial Airways with accommodation for 22 passengers, although plans had been made to produce versions with 12 berths for night flying and a 30-

de Havilland D.H.87 Hornet Moth.

de Havilland D.H.89A Dragon Rapide.

de Havilland D.H.88 Comet *Grosvenor House.*

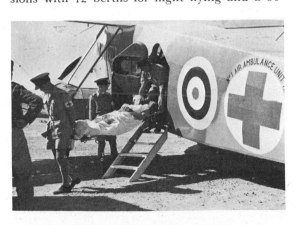

de Havilland D.H.89 Dragon Rapide air ambulance.

de Havilland

de Havilland D.H.90
Dragonfly.

de Havilland D.H.91
Albatross.

de Havilland D.H.93 Don.

de Havilland D.H.94
Moth Minor.

de Havilland D.H.95
Flamingo.

passenger layout. During 1939 the seven Albatross began services to the Continent and India, but with the outbreak of war were used as military transports. Maximum level speed was 362 km/h (225 mph).

de Havilland D.H.93 Don (UK) The Don was designed as an advanced training monoplane, ordered by the Air Ministry and powered by a 391 kW (525 hp) Gipsy King 1 engine. Seats were provided for a pilot and pupil side-by-side with dual controls, while aft were wireless equipment and a rotatable rear gun turret. A Browning machine-gun was installed in the starboard wing and a gun camera in the port. Eight light bombs could be carried on four underwing racks. However the 30 completed aircraft delivered to the RAF were stripped of training equipment and used for communications work.

de Havilland D.H.94 Moth Minor (UK) The Moth Minor was designed as a tandem two-seat cantilever low-wing monoplane replacement for the Moth, powered by a 59.6 kW (80 hp) Gipsy Minor engine. The prototype first flew in June 1937. Just over 100 were built in the UK and Australia with either open cockpits or a hinged coupé superstructure. A number were delivered to the Royal Australian Air Force and British civil

aircraft were impressed into RAF service during World War II.

de Havilland D.H.95 Flamingo (UK) The Flamingo was an all-metal twin-engined (Bristol Perseus) commercial high-wing monoplane, designed to accommodate a crew of three and 12–18 passengers. Only the prototype entered commercial service, flying between the Channel Islands and England; the others completed by the outbreak of World War II going to the RAF as VIP transports. A few more were completed during the war as transports.

de Havilland D.H.98 Mosquito (UK) Most aviation enthusiasts will know the usual stories of de Havilland's 'wooden wonder', the all-wood bomber which was first planned by the company in 1938. It was to carry no defensive armament, relying upon superior speed to evade enemy aircraft. However realisation of a prototype was delayed for one reason and another until the beginning of 1940. This first prototype, of quite unorthodox construction, flew for the first time on 25 November 1940. When demonstrated to official guests at Hatfield, they were astounded to see its fighter-like manoeuvrability and its amazing performance with one engine feathered.

Key to this performance was the lightweight wooden construction: a plywood-balsa-plywood sandwich producing a resilient but light fuselage structure which could accept an enormous amount of punishment, and yet retain its integrity. Power plant comprised two Rolls-Royce Merlin in-line engines, driving constant-speed and fully feathering propellers.

The second and third prototypes were fighter and reconnaissance variants respectively. The Mosquito was to prove that it was more than capable of performing any task, and in the process is remembered as a truly outstanding British aircraft of World War II. There had, of course, been some official misgivings that such an unorthodox aircraft could carry out its combat task and survive in the war skies over Europe. In fact later versions capable of higher performance showed that the original de Havilland concept of an air-

de Havilland Mosquito
PR.34.

craft too fast to be intercepted was correct. Towards the end of the war Mosquito units were averaging one aircraft loss per 2,000 sorties – by far the lowest figure recorded by Bomber Command.

Many Mosquito variants were built within the three bomber/fighter/reconnaissance categories, the first into service being PR aircraft which made their initial daylight sorties over Paris on 20 September 1941. PR Mosquitoes also had the distinction of being the last in RAF front-line service,

being withdrawn in December 1955. Mosquito bombers, which had entered service carrying a 907 kg (2,000 lb) bomb load, were later to carry a 4,000 lb block-buster in a bulged bomb bay. Mosquito fighters were to distinguish themselves in fighter-bomber, anti-shipping and night-fighter roles, and were to destroy some 600 V-1 flying-bombs in the defence of Britain. For reconnaissance duties the Mosquito was the RAF's major long-range aircraft in this category, serving in Europe, Burma and the South Pacific. Including 1,342 Mosquitoes built in Australia and Canada, total construction was 7,781 aircraft when production ended in November 1950.
Data (PR.34): *Engines* two 1,274 kW (1,710 hp) Rolls-Royce Merlin 76s or 113s *Wing span* 16.51 m (54 ft 2 in) *Length* 12.65 m (41 ft 6 in) *Max T-O weight* 11,567 kg (25,500 lb) *Max level speed* 684 km/h (425 mph) *Range* 5,633 km (3,500 miles)

de Havilland D.H.100 Vampire (UK) Perhaps one of the most interesting features of the de Havilland Vampire (as it became known) was the fact that its design began in 1941, not long after the first flight of the first prototype Mosquito.

Designed to satisfy Air Ministry Specification E.6/41 for an interceptor fighter to be powered by the then-developing turbojet engine, the twin-boom configuration of this aircraft was virtually dictated by the chosen power plant. This was because a single turbojet was to provide the total thrust; as this was very limited in early engines, it was necessary to ensure that power loss from the jet tailpipe was restricted to an absolute minimum by keeping the tailpipe as short as possible.

Borrowed from the Mosquito for the cockpit/engine nacelle structure was the plywood-balsa-plywood sandwich form of construction. Like the Mosquito's fuselage, this was built in two half-shells which were joined top and bottom. The monoplane wing was an all-metal structure, incorporating the engine air intakes in the wing roots, split trailing-edge flaps, air brakes and ailerons. The pilot, seated well forward in the central nacelle beneath a three-piece canopy (replaced later by a bubble canopy), had a superb field of view.

de Havilland Mosquito
B.IV about to be armed
with four 500 lb bombs.

de Havilland Vampire F.1.

Powered by a 12 kN (2,700 lb st) de Havilland Goblin turbojet, the prototype Vampire flew for the first time on 20 September 1943. The first production F.1 Vampire made its first flight on 20 April 1945 powered by the same engine as the prototype, as were the next 39 aircraft. Subsequent F.1s had 13.8 kN (3,100 lb st) Goblin Gn.2 engines. Entering service too late to make a contribution to World War II, Vampires began to equip RAF squadrons in mid-1946 and were the second type of jet fighter supplied to it.

Subsequent variants included the F.3 with increased internal fuel capacity and provisions for auxiliary tanks: six of these fighters were the first RAF jet-powered aircraft to achieve a flight across the North Atlantic. The FB.5 close-support fighter/bomber was introduced in 1949 with

de Havilland

de Havilland (D.H.113) Vampire NF.10 night fighter.

de Havilland D.H.104 Dove Series 8.

reduced wing span and long-stroke landing gear to cater for higher landing weights.

FB.9s with more power and improved equipment for operation in tropical conditions entered service with the Far East and Middle East Air Forces in 1952; these were the last RAF single-seat variants. A total of 95 two-seat NF.10 Vampire night-fighters also served in an interim capacity with the RAF from 1951, pending the introduction of Meteor and Venom night fighters.

The last major variant was the Vampire T.11 two-seat trainer, over 800 of which were built. The Royal Navy had a small number of F.20 Sea Vampires, generally similar to the RAF's FB.5, and 74 T.22 two-seat trainers derived from the T.11 (see **Chronology** 3 December 1945). The Dominican Republic and Zimbabwe still operate Vampire fighter-bombers, while Switzerland uses a trainer variant.

Data (FB.9): *Engine* one 14.9 kN (3,350 lb st) de Havilland Goblin D.Gn.3 turbojet *Wing span* 11.58 m (38 ft 0 in) *Length* 9.37 m (30 ft 9 in) *Max T-O weight* 5,620 kg (12,390 lb) *Max level speed* 869 km/h (540 mph) *Range* 1,963 km (1,220 miles) *Armament* four 20 mm cannon, plus up to 907 kg (2,000 lb) bombs on underwing hardpoints

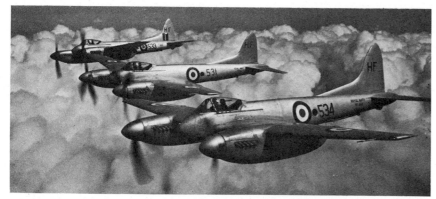

de Havilland Sea Hornet F.20s.

de Havilland D.H.103 Hornet (UK) The twin-engined Hornet fighter was designed to Specification F.12/43 and the first prototype flew on 28 July 1944. It entered production at the end of 1944 and deliveries were made to the RAF from February 1945. Four versions were produced for the RAF as: the Hornet F.1 medium-range single-seat fighter with four 20 mm cannon and provision for carrying two 1,000 lb bombs or two 455 litre (100 Imp gallon) drop tanks; Hornet PR.2 long-range unarmed photographic-

reconnaissance aircraft; Hornet F.3 long-range single-seat fighter with the increased fuel tankage of the PR.2; and Hornet FR.4 with a vertically mounted camera. More than 200 were built. The Hornet was the fastest twin piston-engined operational combat aircraft in the world while in service and the first aircraft to demonstrate a cartwheel manoeuvre. Operated in Malaya in the early 1950s, the type was finally withdrawn from service in 1955.

Data (F.3): *Engines* two 1,512 kW (2,030 hp) Rolls-Royce Merlin 130/131s *Wing span* 13.72 m (45 ft 0 in) *Length* 11.79 m (36 ft 8 in) *Max T-O weight* 9,480 kg (20,900 lb) *Max level speed* 760 km/h (472 mph) *Range* 4,828 km (3,000 miles)

de Havilland D.H.103 Sea Hornet (UK) The Sea Hornet was a naval adaptation of the RAF Hornet. It was fitted with folding wings and had provision for deck arrester and RATO gear. Airdraulic shock-absorber legs replaced the rubber-in-compression legs to eliminate bounce in carrier landings. Three versions were built as: the Sea Hornet F.20 carrier-based medium-range single-seat fighter/reconnaissance/strike aircraft, capable of carrying eight 60 lb rockets, bombs, mines and drop-tanks; Sea Hornet NF.21 carrier-based two-seat night fighter/reconnaissance/strike aircraft fitted with an A.I. radar scanner in a thimble radome in the nose; and Sea Hornet PR.22 carrier-based medium-range photographic-reconnaissance version of the F.20. The F.20 first entered service with No. 801 Squadron, FAA and joined HMS *Implacable* in 1949. A total of 200 Sea Hornets were built.

de Havilland D.H.104 Dove, Devon and Sea Devon (UK) A total of about 540 Dove light transports were built for operation in a variety of roles all over the world. The standard commercial model has accommodation for 8–11 passengers. But variants were designed for survey, pest control, executive and ambulance duties, as well as in Devon C.1 and Sea Devon C.20 light-communications roles with the RAF (and other air forces) and the Royal Navy.

The prototype first flew on 25 September 1945 and production aircraft appeared in many variants. These included the Series 1 standard 8–11-seater with two 253.4 kW (340 hp) Gipsy Queen 70 engines; Series 2 with special executive interior furnishings; Series 4 for RAF as eight-passenger Devon; Series 5 with 283 kW (380 hp) Gipsy Queen 70 Mk 2 engines and 20% increase in payload over an 805 km (500 miles) stage; Series

6, as for Series 5 but with a special executive interior; Series 6A, as for 6 but for US market; Series 6BA with Gipsy Queen 70 Mk 2 engines; Series 7 with 298 kW (400 hp) Gipsy Queen 70 Mk 3 engines, enlarged Heron-type cockpit canopy and AUW of 4,060 kg (8,950 lb), first flown in February 1960; Series 7A, as the Series 7 for US market; Series 8, as for Series 7 but with special five-passenger executive interior; and Series 8A, as for Series 8 for US market and sometimes called the Dove Custom 800.

Data (Series 7 and 8): *Engines* as above *Wing span* 17.4 m (57 ft 0 in) *Length* 11.96 m (39 ft 3 in) *Max T-O weight* 4,060 kg (8,950 lb) *Max cruising speed* 338 km/h (210 mph) *Range* 1,415 km (880 miles)

de Havilland D.H.106 Comet (UK) The Comet was the world's first jet transport to enter service. It resulted from the wartime Brabazon Committee's recommendations for the Type IV North Atlantic turbojet mail plane, which led to numerous studies including a 20-passenger aircraft with three rear-mounted Goblin engines.

The final design emerged as an orthodox low-wing monoplane with 20° leading-edge sweepback and four 19.8 kN (4,450 lb st) de Havilland Ghost centrifugal-flow turbojets buried in the wing roots. Initial accommodation was for 36 passengers in two cabins, pressurised to provide internal pressure equivalent to 2,438 m (8,000 ft) when flying at 12,192 m (40,000 ft). Cruising speed was about 788 km/h (490 mph).

The prototype Comet made its first flight on 27 July 1949. BOAC received a fleet of ten Comet 1s and on 2 May 1952 inaugurated the first passenger services to be operated by turbojet aircraft – on the London–Johannesburg route, covering the 10,821 km (6,724 miles) in 23 hr 34 min. Comets were subsequently introduced on a number of routes, bringing drastic cuts in journey time: such as the reduction from 86 to 33¼ hours between London and Tokyo. Air France and UAT soon began Comet services and there were a number of airline orders for Comet 1s and later models when one broke up near Calcutta exactly a year after its introduction; in January and April 1954 two more suffered inflight structural failure, resulting in the type being withdrawn. The Avon-powered Comet 2s on order for BOAC were strengthened and some delivered to the RAF.

A longer-fuselage long-range Comet 3 had been developed and in the light of the inquiry into the Comet 1 disasters it was redesigned, first flying on

Departure of the first BOAC Comet scheduled passenger flight.

The night shift continues work on the prototype de Havilland D.H.106 Comet.

19 July 1954. It did not go into production but made a round-the-world flight and served as a test vehicle.

In 1957 it was decided that Comets would be reinstated and BOAC ordered 19 Comet 4s. These were powered by 46.71 kN (10,500 lb st) Rolls-Royce Avon 524s, had longer fuselages than the Comet 1 and could carry 60–81 passengers. The first Comet 4 flew on 27 April 1958 and on 4 October BOAC Comets inaugurated North Atlantic jet services (in both directions simultaneously) over the London–New York route – a route for which they did not have adequate range.

From that time Comets took over much of BOAC's network. Other Comet 4s were used by Aerolineas Argentinas, East African Airways and the RAF. From this version were developed the Comet 4B and 4C which first flew on 27 June and 31 October 1959 respectively. The Comet 4B had a 1.98 m (6 ft 6 in) increase in fuselage length, a 2.13 m (7 ft) reduction in span and was intended for high-speed operation over shorter stages. It could carry up to 101 passengers and was not fitted with wing-mounted external fuel tanks. The main operators of Comet 4Bs were British European Airways and Olympic Airways.

The Comet 4C combined the long fuselage of the Comet 4B with the standard Comet 4 wing. This version was ordered by several airlines and went into service in 1960. A total of 112 Comets were built including 74 Series 4 aircraft; and the type was subsequently developed into the RAF Nimrod.

de Havilland D.H.106 Comet 4.

de Havilland

de Havilland Sea Venom F(AW).20/21s.

Data (Comet 1): *Engines* as above *Wing span* 35.0 m (115 ft 0 in) *Length* 28.35 m (93 ft 0 in) *Max T-O weight* 47,627 kg (105,000 lb) *Cruising speed* 788 km/h (490 mph) *Range* 2,816 km (1,750 miles)

de Havilland D.H.108 (UK) First flown on 15 May 1946, this research aircraft was built to investigate stability and control problems arising in aircraft with sweptback wings, and to provide aerodynamic data for the D.H.106 Comet.

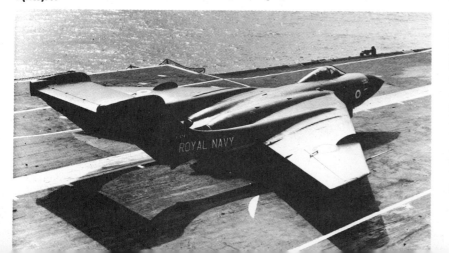

de Havilland D.H.108.

de Havilland D.H.110 Sea Vixen (UK) The Sea Vixen was a two-seat naval day and night all-weather fighter which successfully completed its carrier trials in April 1956. The initial production order for the Royal Navy (placed in January 1955) was followed by further contracts which kept the aircraft in production until 1964. The initial production version was the Sea Vixen F(AW).1, armed with Firestreak missiles and varied loads of air-to-air unguided rockets, bombs and Bullpup air-to-surface missiles.

The first fully developed F(AW).1 flew on 20 March 1957 and the first Royal Navy squadron (No 892) was formed on 2 July 1959. This version subsequently equipped five other squadrons, including No 766 all-weather training and No 899 HQ Squadrons. The Sea Vixen F(AW).2 was basically similar but had changes of equipment, including provision for Red Top missiles, and deeper tailbooms which extended forward of the wing and contained additional fuel tankage. This version entered service in 1964. One hundred and nineteen and 29 examples of the two versions were built.

Data: *Engines* two 44.5 kN (10,000 lb st) Rolls-Royce Avon 208s *Wing span* 15.24 m (50 ft 0 in) *Length* 16.31 m (53 ft 6½ in) *Max T-O weight* (F(AW).1) 15,875 kg (35,000 lb) *Max level speed* 1,038 km/h (645 mph)

de Havilland Sea Vixen F(AW).1.

de Havilland D.H.112 Venom and Sea Venom (UK) The Venom was a straightforward development of the Vampire, designed to accommodate the de Havilland Ghost engine and with aerodynamic refinements enabling it to take full advantage of the increased power. The nacelle and tail assembly were substantially similar to those of the Vampire. However the wings were entirely new, with square tips, very thin section and jettisonable long-range wingtip tanks.

The Venom FB.1 was the first version for the RAF: a day fighter and fighter-bomber with provision for bombs and rockets in addition to the standard four 20 mm Hispano Mk 5 cannon in the nose. The prototype of this version flew for the first time on 2 September 1949. This was followed for the RAF by the Venom NF.2 two-seat night and all-weather fighter; Venom NF.3 development with special combat equipment; and Venom FB.4 with hydraulically operated ailerons and other improvements. Export models of the Venom were also produced, among which the Swedish Air Force received NF.51s (similar to NF.2s).

The Sea Venom was a two-seat naval all-weather fighter which evolved from the NF.2. It had folding wings, catapult and arrester gear. The Royal Navy received the F(AW).20; F(AW).21 improved version with special combat equipment and Martin-Baker ejection seats; and the F(AW).23 with a more powerful Ghost 105 engine. Sea Venoms were also operated by the French Navy which built the NF.52 under licence with a Fiat-built Ghost 48 engine and the Royal Australian Navy which received NF.53s (similar to F(AW).21s). British-operated Venoms and Sea Venoms were withdrawn from operational service in 1962 and 1960 respectively.

Data (FB.1): *Engine* one 21.6 kN (4,850 lb st) de Havilland Ghost 103 turbojet *Wing span* 12.7 m (41 ft 8 in) *Length* 9.7 m (31 ft 10 in) *Max T-O weight* 6,985 kg (15,400 lb) *Max level speed* 1,030 km/h (640 mph)

de Havilland D.H.114 Heron (UK) The Heron was delivered for civil and military service to more than 30 countries. The standard airliner was configured for 14–17 passengers but eight-passenger executive layouts were made available. The prototype (first flown on 10 May 1950) made use of Dove components where possible and, like the Heron Mk 1 production series, had a fixed-tricycle landing gear. Power for all production aircraft was provided by four 186.3 kW (250 hp) Gipsy Queen 30 Mk 2 six-cylinder engines.

The first production aircraft was purchased by New Zealand National Airways, entering service in 1952. The Heron Mk 2 prototype first flew on 14 December 1952 and featured a retractable landing gear and other standard and optional refinements. Nearly 150 Herons were eventually built, some Mk 1s and Mk 2s bearing an A, B, C or D suffix to indicate executive model for the US market, late production examples with greater AUW, and executive models respectively.

Among the military examples sold were four specially equipped Mk 2s which formed the fixed-wing equipment of The Queen's Flight.

Data (Heron Mk 2): *Engines* as above *Wing span* 21.79 m (71 ft 6 in) *Length* 14.78 m (48 ft 6 in) *Max T-O weight* 6,123 kg (13,500 lb) *Cruising speed* 295–307 km/h (183–191 mph) *Range* 1,900–2,500 km (1,180–1,550 miles)

de Havilland Canada DHC-1 Chipmunk (Canada) The Chipmunk two-seat basic trainer was designed and originally built by the Canadian branch of de Havilland. It was selected to replace the Tiger Moth as the standard primary trainer in all RAF Volunteer Reserve flying schools. The RAF version was known as Chipmunk T.10, powered by the 108 kW (145 hp) Gipsy Major 8 engine, and 735 were delivered. Others served with the Royal Canadian Air Force and in Portugal. A civil version of the Chipmunk, powered by a Gipsy Major 10 Mk 2 engine, was also produced as the Mk 21; and in 1958 an agricultural version was produced as the Mk 23.

de Havilland Canada DHC-2 Beaver (Canada) The Beaver was designed as a single-engined STOL utility transport and the prototype flew for

de Havilland Canada Chipmunk T.10s.

the first time in August 1947. Before production of the Mk I version ended 1,657 examples had been built, 968 of which were supplied to the US Air Forces under the designation U-6A (formerly L-20A). Forty-six were acquired by the British Army as the Beaver AL.1. In all, Beaver Mk Is went into civil and military service in 65 countries, some as floatplanes and amphibians.

The single Beaver Mk II, with an Alvis Leonides 502/4 engine, was followed by the Mk III Turbo-Beaver, the prototype of which flew for the first time on 30 December 1963. Sixty Turbo-Beavers were built, 28 of them for the Ontario Department of Lands and Forests. These were provided with wheel/ski landing gears for winter operation and integral fire-bombing floats for summer use. Seventeen other Turbo-Beavers went to Canadian owners and most of the remainder went under US registry. Two were used on Antarctic survey work under British and Australian direction.

Data (Beaver Mk I, unless stated otherwise): *Engine* one 335.3 kW (450 hp) Pratt & Whitney R-985 Wasp Junior; Turbo-Beaver powered by one 431 kW (578 ehp) PT6A-6 or PT6A-20 turboprop *Wing span* 14.64 m (48 ft 0 in) *Length* (landplane) 9.24 m (30 ft 4 in) *Max T-O weight* 2,313 kg (5,100 lb) *Max level speed* 225 km/h (140 mph) *Range* 1,252 km (778 miles) *Accommodation* pilot and seven passengers or freight

de Havilland D.H.114 Heron 1B.

de Havilland Canada DHC-2 Beaver seaplane.

de Havilland Canada

de Havilland Canada DHC-2 Turbo-Beaver.

de Havilland Canada DHC-4 Caribou.

de Havilland Canada DHC-3 Otter (Canada) The Otter flew for the first time on 12 December 1951. It received its Canadian Certificate of Airworthiness as both a landplane and seaplane in November 1952, becoming the first single-engined aircraft to qualify for approval in accordance with ICAO Category D airworthiness requirements. Like the earlier Beaver, the Otter is a STOL utility transport but has accommodation for the pilot and up to ten passengers. All passenger seats are quickly removable for freight carrying. Alternatively 6 stretchers and 4 passengers or 3 stretchers and 7 passengers can be carried.

de Havilland Canada DHC-3 Otter.

A total of 460 were built, including many supplied to the US Army under the designation U-1A. Aircraft of the type accompanied the US Navy's 'Operation Deep-freeze' expedition to the Antarctic in 1956–58. Nine other nations, including the UK, received Otters and Beavers for duty in the Antarctic. The 66 Otters delivered to the RCAF were put into service on search-and-rescue, paratroop-dropping and aerial-photographic duties, while the air forces of at least eight other countries not mentioned above received the type. Commercial operation of the Otter was also widespread.
Data: *Engine* one 447 kW (600 hp) Pratt & Whitney R-1340-S1H1-G *Wing span* 17.69 m (58 ft 0 in) *Length* 12.80 m (41 ft 10 in) *Max T-O weight* 3,629 kg (8,000 lb) *Max level speed* 257 km/h (160 mph) *Range* 1,520 km (945 miles)
de Havilland Canada DHC-4 Caribou (Canada) The Caribou twin-engined all-weather STOL tactical transport was developed with the

de Havilland Canada Buffalo CC-115.

co-operation of the Canadian Department of Defence. The prototype flew for the first time on 30 July 1958. The original DHC-4 Caribou obtained US Type Approval in 1960 at a gross weight of 11,793 kg (26,000 lb). The DHC-4A was approved in 1961 at a gross weight of 12,928 kg (28,500 lb). Five YAC-1 Caribou were delivered to the US Army for evaluation in 1959 and this service subsequently ordered 159 under the designation CV-2 (originally AC-1). Those still in service in 1967 were transferred to the USAF.

Versions delivered to the US Army were the CV-2A (equivalent to DHC-4) and C-7A (formerly CV-2B), equivalent to DHC-4A. The change of designation of the latter version followed transfer to the USAF. Other Caribou were ordered by the air forces of Abu Dhabi, Canada (designated CC-108), Ghana, Taiwan, Kuwait, Zambia, India, Australia, Kenya, Malaysia, Tanzania, Spain and Muscat and Oman, plus the Uganda Police, Thai Police and several airline operators.
The civil version of the Caribou accommodates 30 passengers. The military version carries 32 troops, 26 paratroops, 22 stretchers and four sitting casualties (and 4 attendants), or 3,965 kg (8,740 lb) of freight (including vehicles).
Data (DHC-4A): *Engines* two 1,080 kW (1,450 hp) Pratt & Whitney R-2000-7M2 radials *Wing span* 29.15 m (95 ft 7½ in) *Length* 22.13 m (72 ft 7 in) *Max level speed* 347 km/h (216 mph) *Range* 2,103 km (1,307 miles)
de Havilland Canada DHC-5 Buffalo (Canada) The Buffalo is a developed version of the Caribou with an enlarged fuselage and two General Electric T64 turboprop engines. Five

de Havilland Canada
DHC-7 Dash 7.

evaluation DHC-5s were built initially, the first of which flew on 9 April 1964. Delivery of these to the US Army began in April 1965. Fifteen DHC-5As were delivered to the Canadian Armed Forces in 1967–68. These aircraft are currently designated C-8A (DHC-5) and CC-115 (DHC-5A). Twenty-four Buffalos were delivered to the Brazilian government in 1969–70, 16 to the Peruvian Air Force in 1971–72 and NASA received two as C-8As for experiments with the augmentor wing concept and quiet short-haul research. One CC-115, modified by de Havilland Canada, was loaned to the Canadian Department of Defence for a joint DITC/USAF Air Cushion Landing System development programme.

In 1976 testing was completed of the DHC-5D version of the Buffalo, with a higher gross weight and improved performance. Deliveries of this version have been made to the air forces of Ecuador, Kenya, Mauritania, Togo, Zaïre, Zambia, Oman, Sudan, Tanzania and the United Arab Emirates. Accommodation is for a crew of three and up to 41 troops, 35 paratroops, 24 stretchers and six sitting casualties (and attendants), or 8,164 kg (18,000 lb) of freight.
Data (DHC-5D): *Engines* two 2,336 kW (3,133 shp) General Electric CT64-820-4 turboprops *Wing span* 29.26 m (96 ft 0 in) *Length* 24.08 m (79 ft 0 in) *Max T-O weight* 22,316 kg (49,200 lb) *Max cruising speed* 420 km/h (261 mph) *Range* (max payload) 1,112 km (691 miles)

de Havilland Canada DHC-6 Twin Otter (Canada) First announced in 1964, the Twin Otter is a STOL utility transport powered by turboprop engines. The first of five prototypes flew on 20 May 1965. By June 1978 a total of 613 Twin Otters had been sold to customers in 70 countries for military and civil use, including a version which is being offered as a maritime-surveillance aircraft (an aircraft modified for Greenlandair Charter is used as an ice patrol/maritime-surveillance aircraft). The Twin Otter is also used as a photo-survey aircraft in Switzerland, the Sudan and China, and for geophysical survey.

Deliveries of the current Series 300 version began in the spring of 1969 with the 231st Twin Otter (the first 115 aircraft built as Series 100s with PT6A-20 engines and the next 115 as Series 200s with increased baggage space in lengthened

nose). It is available with a short nose as a floatplane. Ten of the 12 Twin Otters supplied to the Peruvian Air Force were floatplanes. Accommodation is for one or two pilots and 13–20 passengers or up to 1,941 kg (4,280 lb) of freight.
Data (Series 300): *Engines* two 486 kW (652 ehp) Pratt & Whitney Aircraft of Canada PT6A-27 turboprops *Wing span* 19.81 m (65 ft 0 in) *Length* (landplane) 15.77 m (51 ft 9 in) *Max T-O weight* 5,670 kg (12,500 lb) *Max cruising speed* 338 km/h (210 mph) *Range* (with wing tanks) 1,825 km (1,134 miles)

de Havilland Canada DHC-7 Dash 7 and DHC-7R Ranger (Canada) The Dash 7 'quiet-STOL' airliner project was started in 1972. Two pre-production aircraft were built, the first flying on 27 March 1975. The first production Dash 7 flew on 30 May 1977 and by June 1978 12 had been sold, with paid options on another 15. The first to enter service is operated by Rocky Mountain Airways. An all-cargo version of the Dash 7 is designated DHC-7C, while a maritime-reconnaissance version (two of which have been ordered by the Canadian Coast Guard for delivery in 1980) has also been developed.
Data (DHC-7 Dash 7): *Engines* two 835 kW (1,120 shp) Pratt & Whitney Aircraft of Canada PT6A-50 turboprops *Wing span* 28.35 m (93 ft 0 in) *Length* 24.58 m (80 ft 7¾ in) *Max T-O weight* 19,731 kg (43,500 lb) *Max cruising speed* 436 km/h (271 mph) *Range* 2,093 km (1,300 miles) *Accommodation* seats for up to 50 passengers; up to five standard pallets in all-cargo role

Deperdussin monoplane racers (France) see **Schneider Trophy contestants**
Deperdussin TT (France) Two-seat observation and patrol monoplane powered by a 59.6 kW (80 hp) Anzani or Gnome radial engine. Delivered in small numbers from 1912 to the French Army and the RNAS and were used for a short time after the outbreak of World War I. Maximum level speed was a respectable 114 km/h (71 mph).

de Havilland Canada
DHC-6 Twin Otter.

Deperdussin
'Monocoque' racer of
1912, which raised the
world speed record six
times in 1912 while
powered by a 103.4 kW
(140 hp) Gnome rotary
engine.

Dewoitine

Deperdussin TT in early form.

One of two Swiss Dewoitine D.1s.

Dewoitine D.1 and D.9 (France) When the prototype D.1 parasol-wing monoplane first flew on 18 November 1922 it represented a great advance over its single-seat fighter contemporaries. It had an oval-section fuselage of metal construction with a riveted metal-panel covering. The wing was of metal, fabric-covered, and was supported above the fuselage by a streamlined cabane structure and a pair of remarkably short struts either side.

Demonstration models were flown with great effect by test pilots Barbot and Doret. Foreign orders resulted, but delivery to the French Aéronautique Militaire never materialised. Series aircraft had conventional cabane struts and twin radiators attached to the undercarriage struts for the 223.5 kW (300 hp) Hispano-Suiza 8Fb engine. Ansaldo in Italy imported a single example and then built 126 machines under licence as AC.2s. Yugoslavia bought 79 D.1s and Switzerland two. Marcel Doret captured world speed records with the D.1 and later flew his own D.1ter at airshows until 1933. French interest was limited to naval aviation. Some 30 D.1s equipped two fighter escadrilles, one (7C1) operating from the aircraft carrier *Béarn*.

The D.9 was a redesigned D.1 fitted with a 313 kW (420 hp) Gnome-Rhône 9Ab radial engine. Also rejected by France, 150 were built by

Yugoslav Dewoitine D.9.

French Navy Dewoitine D.1s.

Ansaldo as AC.3s for the Aéronautica Militare. Switzerland received three D.1s and ten went to Yugoslavia.

Data (D.9): *Engine* as above *Wing span* 12.24 m (40 ft 1¾ in) *Length* 7.3 m (23 ft 11½ in) *Max T-O weight* 1,333 kg (2,939 lb) *Max level speed* 245 km/h (152 mph) *Range* 750 km (466 miles) *Armament* D.1 and D.9 had two forward-firing machine-guns; Italian AC.3s of 5° Gruppo Aisalto had third machine-gun mounted at an angle on upper wing

Dewoitine D.19 and D.21 (France) Developed from the D.1 and D.9 via the one-off Lorraine-powered D.12, the D.19 parasol-wing monoplane fighter attracted the attention of the Swiss authorities. The original prototype, plus two complete sets of parts, were ordered from Dewoitine's Paris factory. After assembly at the Swiss workshops at Thun, all three aircraft were used for many years as fighter trainers, two aircraft surviving until 1940. Power was provided by a 335.3 kW (450 hp) Hispano-Suiza 12 Jb engine with frontal radiator. Armament comprised a single synchronised 7.7 mm machine-gun.

In 1929 the D.21 appeared. Seven examples were built at the K & W Thun workshops for Argentina, where a further 58 aircraft were subsequently built under licence. Armed with twin machine-guns, the D.21 was powered by a 410 kW (550 hp) Hispano-Suiza 12Gb engine. Czechoslovakia constructed a further 26 D.21s under licence, designated Skoda D.1 and fitted with a Skoda L engine.

Data (Skoda D.1): *Engine* as above *Wing span* 12.24 m (40 ft 1¾ in) *Length* 7.64 m (25 ft 0¾ in) *Max T-O weight* 1,580 kg (3,483 lb) *Max level speed* 270 km/h (168 mph) *Range* 750 km (466 miles)

Dewoitine D.26 (France) Eleven lower-powered versions of the D.27 were built for the Swiss in 1931 as D.26s. Nine D.26s with 186.3 kW (250 hp) Wright 9Qa engines were for gunnery and formation-flying training and the other two, with 223.5 kW (300 hp) Wright Qc engines, for air-combat training. They were not retired until 1948 and then flew as glider-tugs for several years with the Swiss Aero Club.

Dewoitine D.27 (France) Société de Construction Aéronautique E. Dewoitine evolved this single-seat fighter in Switzerland from earlier Dewoitine parasol-wing aircraft. Sixty-five pro-

Swiss Dewoitine D.9.

Orient on its Paris–Saigon route. Power was provided by three 428.5 kW (575 hp) Wright Cyclone radial engines and the aircraft had a trousered fixed landing gear. Several speed-with-load-over-distance world records fell to the D.332 in 1933 and it made many spectacular European flights. However it crashed on the final return stage of the inaugural Paris–Saigon service on 15 January 1935.

Three D.333s followed, each powered by 428.5 kW (575 hp) Hispano-Suiza radial engines and accommodating ten passengers. One was lost in October 1937 while flying the Toulouse–Dakar service with Air France. The others flew in South America on the Buenos Aires–Natal route.

In 1936 the prototype of a new version appeared as the D.338. It was followed by 30 production examples for Air France. These had retractable landing gears, were powered by 484.5 kW (650 hp) Hispano-Suiza V16/17 engines, and each accommodated up to 22 passengers. They were operated on the Paris–Cannes–Damascus–Hanoi and Paris–Dakar routes. Many continued to fly during World War II on government liaison and VIP duties and eight were used for a short time after the war.

Dewoitine D.19.

The D.342 was a one-off development of the D.338, as was the D.620.

Data (D.338): *Engines* as above *Wing span* 29.35 m (96 ft 3½ in) *Length* 22.13 m (72 ft 7¼ in) *Max T-O weight* 11,150 kg (24,582 lb) *Max level speed* 301 km/h (187 mph)

Dewoitine D.21.

duction aircraft (plus the prototype) were acquired by the Swiss Air Arm. Three others were exported to Romania which, along with Yugoslavia, undertook licence production. A Swiss trainer version appeared as the D.26 (see entry). The French used eight D.27s and a strengthened version (D.53) for tests only. Construction was of metal, with only the wings and control surfaces fabric-covered. Flying a D.27, Marcel Doret established a world speed record over a 1,000 km course in November 1927.

Data: *Engine* one 372.6 kW (500 hp) Hispano-Suiza 57 *Wing span* 10.3 m (33 ft 9½ in) *Length* 6.56 m (21 ft 6¼ in) *Max T-O weight* 1,414 kg (3,117 lb) *Max level speed* 298 km/h (185 mph) *Range* 600 km (373 miles)

Dewoitine D.37 series (France) D.37 parasol-wing fighter prototype first flew in 1934. Of 28 production D.371s ordered by Armée de l'Air, ten were sold to the Spanish Republican government during the Civil War, plus 14 D.372s ostensibly for Lithuania. A total of 44 D.373s and D.376s (latter with folding wings for carrier stowage) operated with two French Aéronavale escadrilles until 1940. Power was provided by the 596 kW (800 hp) Gnome-Rhône 14K radial engine. All production was undertaken by the Liore-Olivier firm. French aircraft had four 7.5 mm Darne machine-guns and Spanish Dewoitines twin 0.303 in Vickers guns, later replaced by Soviet PV-1s. The Spanish aircraft gave a good account of themselves during the early part of the Civil War but subsequently fell victim to superior Nationalist fighters.

Data (D.371): *Engine* as above *Wing span* 11.8 m (38 ft 8½ in) *Length* 7.44 m (24 ft 5 in) *Max T-O weight* 1,860 kg (4,101 lb) *Max level speed* 370 km/h (230 mph) *Range* 750 km (466 miles)

Dewoitine D.332, D.333, D.338 and D.342 (France) The single D.332 *Emeraude* was first flown on 11 July 1933 by test pilot Marcel Doret. An all-metal single-spar cantilever low-wing monoplane; it was intended for service with Air

Dewoitine D.27s.

Dewoitine D.500 (France) The first prototype of this single-seat fighter flew on 18 June 1932, piloted by Marcel Doret. D.500 was a monospar cantilever low-wing monoplane with a carefully contoured fuselage and flush-riveted metal skinning. The wide-track fixed undercarriage had independent main units with wheel spats. Cut-

Dewoitine

Dewoitine D.371.

First prototype Dewoitine
D.500.

outs in the wing trailing edge at the junctions with the fuselage permitted good downward visibility. The pilot was seated in an open cockpit and operated two 7.7 mm Vickers guns in the cowling and two 7.5 mm Darne guns in the wings. Power was provided by a 514 kW (690 hp) Hispano-Suiza 12Xbrs engine with a two-bladed propeller. One hundred and two D.500s were built, equipping French Escadrilles de Chasse from 1935. Three were also exported to Venezuela.
Data: *Engine* as above *Wing span* 12.09 m (39 ft 8 in) *Length* 7.74 m (25 ft 4¾ in) *Max T-O weight* 1,710 kg (3,770 lb) *Max level speed* 359 km/h (223 mph) *Range* 850 km (528 miles)

Dewoitine D.501 (France) This aircraft differed from the D.500 in having a 20 mm HS 9 cannon firing through the propeller shaft in place of the two Vickers cowling guns of its predecessor. Like the D.500 and D.510, it was highly manoeuvrable, had effective controls, was stable about all three axes and sturdily built. One hundred and forty-three D.501s went to the Armée de l'Air, which had two-thirds of its first-line fighter units equipped with Dewoitine fighters by mid-1938. Fourteen went to Lithuania, designated D.501Ls.

Dewoitine D.510 (France) The prototype D.501 flew for the first time in August 1934 as a refined version of the D.500. One hundred and eighteen were built. Twenty-four were supplied to China and equipped two squadrons fighting in the Yunan Province. The Japanese bought two machines and Great Britain and the Soviet Union one example each for evaluation. Power was provided by a 641 kW (860 hp) Hispano-Suiza 12Ycrs 'moteur canon' engine. A number were still in French first-line service at the outbreak of World War II. Max speed was 393 km/h (244 mph) at 4,000 m (13,125 ft). Two D.510TH aircraft (originally for Turkey) found their way to the Republican forces during the Spanish Civil War.

Dewoitine D.520 (France) When Emile Dewoitine designed a new fighter to meet the French Air Ministry Programme A23, which in its revised form called for a maximum speed of 520 km/h, he was inspired to give it the designation D.520. The prototype flew for the first time on 2 October 1938 with Marcel Doret at the controls. Performance was disappointing and so the second prototype had wing radiators replaced with a ventral unit and introduced a sliding cockpit hood. The third prototype replaced the tailskid with a tailwheel.

The D.520 had no real rival in France and was ordered in quantity. Main production lines were at the SNCAM Toulouse factories. For the first time in France women joined the workforce and sub-contractors previously outside the aircraft industry were employed. Each aircraft required only half the man-hours needed to build the main French fighter at that time, the MS 406.

The first production aircraft flew on 31 October 1939, but many modifications were required. By the time the German Blitzkrieg was launched only 50 D.520s were with front-line units. By 22 June 1940, 220 were in service. They did well in combat, claiming 77 definite victories against only 34 losses. Vichy units included four Groupes de Chasse and two Aéronavale escadrilles in North Africa. Production restarted for a period by Vichy and then resumed under German supervision. The 891st and last aircraft left the factory in August 1944. Vichy D.520s fought in Syria and in North Africa during the Allied landings. Seventy-five went to the Regia Aeronautica and 100 to Bulgaria, where they flew with the 6th Fighter Regiment. Final operations were with the Free French 'Groupe Doret' against German pockets of resistance in France from November 1944 to May 1945. Post-World War II, a few were converted as D.520 DC two-seat dual-control trainers.

Powered by a supercharged 678 kW (910 hp) Hispano-Suiza 12Y45 engine, the D.520 was armed with an engine-mounted HS-404 20 mm cannon and four wing-mounted 7.5 mm MAC machine-guns. The wing was a single-spar structure with duralumin skinning. Ailerons were fabric-covered and flaps pneumatically operated. The fuselage was an all-metal monocoque structure and the wide-track undercarriage legs retracted inwards into the wing profile.
Data: *Engine* as above *Wing span* 10.2 m (33 ft 5¾ in) *Length* 8.75 m (28 ft 8½ in) *Max T-O weight* 2,780 kg (6,129 lb) *Max level speed* 530 km/h (329 mph) *Range* 1,250 km (777 miles)

DFS 228 (Germany) Single-seat short-range rocket-powered reconnaissance aircraft designed

prised one forward-firing Spandau and one rear-mounted Parabellum machine-gun.

DFW C.V (Germany) The C.V appeared in 1916 as a more powerful development of the C.IV, with balanced control surfaces and other improvements. It was highly manoeuvrable and carried the same armament as the earlier type. It was widely operated on reconnaissance, photographic and artillery co-operation duties until 1918, by which time better aircraft began to replace it on major fronts. However some C.Vs remained operational until the Armistice. After the war a number of C.Vs were used as interim passenger and mail carriers by early airline operators in Germany.

Data: *Engine* one 149 kW (200 hp) Benz Bz.IV *Wing span* 13.27 m (43 ft 6½ in) *Length* 7.87 m (25 ft 10 in) *Max T-O weight* 1,422 kg (3,136 lb) *Max level speed* 156 km/h (97 mph) *Endurance* 3 h 30 min

to have a service ceiling of 22,860 m (75,000 ft). Small number of prototypes and pre-production aircraft built only from 1943 to 1945.

DFS 230 (Germany) Assault glider of World War II accommodating two crew and eight passengers or freight. More than 1,000 built for the Luftwaffe. First reported in Belgium in May 1940.

DFW 1913 types (Germany) Among the pre-World War I aircraft produced by Deutsche Flugzeug Werke were the 1913 monoplane and biplane which used a common fuselage, tail unit, landing gear and 89.4 kW (120 hp) engine. The monoplane won the Prinz Heinrich Preis in 1913 and was operated early in the war.

DFW B.I and B.II (Germany) The swept-wing B.I two-seat (observer forward) reconnaissance and training aircraft operated on the Western and Eastern Fronts during 1914 and 1915. Power was provided by one 74.5 kW (100 hp) Mercedes D.I engine, and it could carry a light gun mounted above the cut-out in the upper wing. It was developed from the single-seat high-speed scout of 1914, which had a similar engine but tapered biplane wings and held all German pre-war cross-country records. The B.II was similar but could be fitted with an 89.4 kW (120 hp) engine and was built mainly for training duties.

DFW C.I and C.II (Germany) Straight-wing developments of the B.I/B.II powered by the 112 kW (150 hp) Benz Bz.III engine. C.I retained crew arrangements of Bs but C.II had observer in rear cockpit with a ring-mounted Parabellum machine-gun. One hundred and thirty C.Is were built.

DFW C.IV (Germany) Much improved reconnaissance and army co-operation biplane of 1916 powered by a 112 kW (150 hp) Benz Bz.III engine. Widely operated by German Army and Navy units until the Armistice. Armament com-

DFW P.1 (Germany) Single example of a four-seat commercial airliner development of a wartime aircraft, powered by a Benz Bz.IV engine. Rear cabin for two passengers was enclosed. Referred to as the Limousine in the 1920 *Jane's*, where it states that it was shown in Holland by a flight to Amsterdam at the time of the Elta Exhibition.

DFW R.I and R.II (Germany) The R.I appeared in 1916 as a large six-crew biplane bomber powered by four Mercedes D.IV engines fitted inside the fuselage and driving two tractor and two pusher propellers. The only R.I built was operated on the Eastern Front during the summer of 1917. The R.II development was powered by 194 kW (260 hp) Mercedes D.IVa engines and only two are thought to have been built. Up to 3,500 kg (7,720 lb) of bombs could be carried.

Interestingly the 1920 *Jane's* states that plans for an eight-engined version were being drawn up when the war ended: a 1,610 kW (2,160 hp) multi-engined giant with a ninth engine fitted for driving a supercharger and for starting the other eight engines. Plans for a 12-passenger commercial airliner version of the R.II were also made after the war and a prototype was at least partially completed.

DINFIA (Argentina) DINFIA was formed in 1957 from the Fábrica Militar de Aviones (Military Aircraft Factory) that was founded in 1927. In

DINFIA IA 35 Huanquero.

DINFIA IA 46 Ranquels.

DINFIA IA 53.

DINFIA IA 38.

DINFIA IA 45 Querandi.

1968 it reverted to its original name, resulting in the early and latest aircraft appearing under the heading FMA.

DINFIA IA 35 Huanquero/Pandora (Argentina) The prototype of the IA 35 first flew on 21 September 1953 and the first of 100 planned production aircraft flew on 29 March 1957. Eventually only 47 were produced for the Argentine Air Force. The first version was an instrument, navigation and photographic trainer, built as the IA 35-Ia with two 484.4 kW (650 hp) IAR 19A El Indio engines. Next came the IA 35-Ib bombing and gunnery trainer/ground-attack aircraft, armed with two fixed forward-firing 7.65 mm machine-guns and underwing attachments for four 50 kg or two 100 kg bombs and two 57 mm or eight 127 mm rockets. The IA 35-II was a light transport for a crew of three and seven passengers, while the IA 35-IV was a reconnaissance version. Later production aircraft were powered by 626 kW (840 hp) IAR 19C engines. The IA 35-III was a prototype ambulance version. A ten-passenger commercial derivative, known as the Pandora, was not put into production.

DINFIA IA 38 (Argentina) First flown on 9 December 1960, the IA 38 was an experimental tailless cargo aircraft.

DINFIA IA 45 Querandi (Argentina) Light Lycoming-engined executive transport, first flown on 23 September 1957. The IA 45B version was a five–six-seater with two 134 kW (180 hp) O-360 pusher engines.

DINFIA IA 46 Ranquel and Super Ranquel (Argentina) The IA 46 light monoplane was designed as a three-seat tourer, easily adaptable for agricultural, glider-towing and pilot-training duties. The prototype first flew on 23 December 1957. The Ranquel was the standard production version with a 112 kW (150 hp) Lycoming O-320-A2B piston engine. The Super Ranquel was similar but had a 134 kW (180 hp) Lycoming O-360-A2A engine.

DINFIA IA 53 (Argentina) The second prototype of this small single-seat (with provision for a second person) agricultural monoplane flew for the first time on 10 November 1966.

Distributor Wing DW-1 (USA) Single-seat agricultural aircraft, first flown on 30 January 1965. Agricultural equipment built into the airframe as an integral part of the aircraft.

Doak VZ-4DA (USA) Experimental VTOL convertiplane, first flown on 25 February 1958.

Dominion Skytrader 800 (USA) Twin-engined (298 kW; 400 hp Lycoming IO-720-B1As) STOL general-purpose transport aircraft, first flown in the spring of 1975. Available in 12-seat, six-seat executive or freight-carrying layouts.

Donnet HB3 (France) Few examples of modified Donnet-Denhaut DD-type flying-boats operated as commercial aircraft during 1920s by Aéronavale.

Donnet-Denhaut DD (France) Small two–three-seat anti-submarine patrol three-bay biplane flying-boat operated by the French Navy and US Navy during World War I. Major version was DD.8 powered by one 149 kW (200 hp) Hispano-Suiza pusher engine.

Dorand AR.1 and AR.2 (France) Two-seat observation biplanes with back-staggered wings. Large numbers built for the Armée de l'Air, with which they served from the spring of 1917 until the beginning of 1918 on the Western and Italian

Fronts. Twenty-two AR.1s and 120 shorter-span AR.2s acquired by the American Expeditionary Force as trainers. Armament comprised one forward-firing Vickers and one or two rear-mounted Lewis machine-guns. After the war examples of each type were used as interim airliners accommodating two or even three passengers. Data (AR.1): *Engine* one 126.7 or 141.6 kW (170 or 190 hp) Renault, (AR.2) 149 kW (200 hp) Renault *Wing span* 12.0 m (39 ft 4½ in) *Length* 9.14 m (30 ft 0 in) *Max level speed* 148 km/h (92 mph)

Dornier Komet II (Germany) Designed in 1920, the Komet II was a five-seat (pilot in open cockpit and four passengers in cabin) monoplane with a thick wing placed on top of the deep box-section fuselage (a full description appears in the 1927 *Jane's*). A small number were built with 134 kW (180 hp) BMW IV engines and were operated from 1922 by Deutsche Luft-Reederei, and Rolls-Royce Falcon-engined examples went to Spain, Colombia, Russia and the Ukraine.

Dornier Komet III (Germany) The Komet III was a larger and more powerful version of the Komet II type, produced in 1924 to provide higher speed and greater capacity for airline services. Accommodation was for a pilot and mechanic side-by-side in front of and below the monoplane wing and six passengers in the cabin. The wing of this Komet was raised above the fuselage on four short struts. Power was provided by a 268 kW (360 hp) Rolls-Royce Eagle IX or 335.3 kW (450 hp) Napier Lion engine. Examples were operated by Deutscher Aero Lloyd and DDL in Europe, were exported to the Ukraine and licence-built in Japan and perhaps Switzerland in civil/military guises (see **Merkur**).

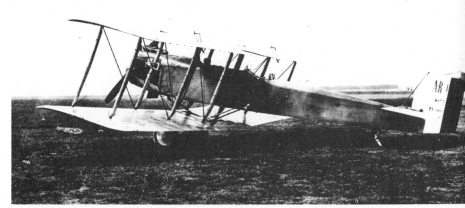

Dorand AR.1.

Royce Falcon III and a 447 kW (600 hp) BMW VI engine respectively. The Delphin L.2 accommodated up to seven passengers (one next to pilot). The L.3 could carry up to 13 and was built in Switzerland by the Aktiengesellschaft für Dornier-Flugzeuge at Altenrhein for over inland water and coastal services.

Dornier Libelle (Germany) In 1920 Dornier produced the Libelle as a two-seat sporting and school flying-boat with a 37.25–56 kW (50–75 hp) engine of the Siemens type, although up to five passengers were occasionally carried. Numbers were sold and operated throughout 1920s.

Dornier Merkur, Do C, Do D and Do T (Germany) The final development of the Komet type was the Merkur, which first flew in February 1925 and was produced from 1926 as a eight–ten passenger airliner powered by a BMW VI engine. It could cruise at 175 km/h (109 mph). Following long-distance overland trial flights, dual controls and adjustable pilot seats were fitted. Deutsche Luft-Hansa received the greatest number with nearly 30 aircraft and these operated from Berlin to Kaliningrad (Königsberg, Lithuania) and elsewhere. A twin-float seaplane version was also produced and Chile received a number as Do C trainers/torpedo-bombers. The Do D was similar to the Do C built for the Yugoslav Naval Air Service, while the Do T was an ambulance derivative of the Merkur.

Dornier Do F (Germany) see **Dornier Do 11**

Dornier Do H Falke (Germany) Prototype single-seat high-performance fighter built in 1922 and expected to be produced in Switzerland and Japan (Kawasaki).

Doak VZ-4DA.

Dornier Merkur operated by Deruluft between Berlin and Moscow in 1927.

Dornier Delphin (Germany) In 1920 Dornier produced the first Delphin commercial flying-boat. It was based upon substantially the same design as the Libelle, from which it differed with regard to the higher form of the fuselage, the enclosed cabin for five or six passengers, and the engine. The first versions, the L.1 and L.1a, were each produced with a high open pilot's cockpit aft of the 138 kW (185 hp) BMW IIIa or 134 kW (180 hp) BMW III engine, but the later L.2 and L.3 versions had seating for two in front of the passenger cabin, separated by a bulkhead. Power for these versions was provided by a 186.3 kW (250 hp) BMW IV or 194 kW (260 hp) Rolls-

Dornier

Italian Dornier Do J Wal I.

Dornier Do R Super-Wal.

Dornier Do X.

Dornier Do J Wal, photographed in 1932.

Dornier Do N (Germany) Night-bomber version of Do F built by Kawasaki of Japan.

Dornier Do R Super-Wal (Germany) Following the removal of the restrictions regarding aircraft building in Germany, Dornier produced the Super-Wal with two separate cabins for a total of

Dornier Do J Wal (Whale) (Germany) The Wal all-metal flying-boat was a direct development of the Gs I of 1919 (which was broken-up) and the uncompleted Gs II. The prototype flew on 6 November 1922. Because of the Allied ban on German construction of this class of aeroplane, production was undertaken by CMASA in Italy with the first aircraft completed in 1923.

The Wal had a broad-beam two-step hull, strut-braced untapered parasol wing, sponsons, single fin and rudder and two engines in tandem above the centre section. Passenger, mail-carrier and military versions were produced with a wide range of engines of 223.6–559 kW (300–750 hp). There were four different wing spans and the maximum weight grew from about 4,000 kg (8,818 lb) to 10,000 kg (22,046 lb). Wals were also built by Piaggio and in Japan, the Netherlands and Spain, and later in Germany. About 300 were built before production ceased in the mid-1930s.

Wals pioneered air services in South America, were widely used in the Mediterranean (with eight–ten seats) and, operating from depot ships, established Luft-Hansa's South Atlantic mail services.

Data (Do J II ten-ton Wal): *Engines* as above *Wing span* 27.2 m (89 ft 2¾ in) *Length* 18.2 m (59 ft 8½ in) *Max T-O weight* 10,000 kg (22,046 lb) *Cruising speed* 183 km/h (114 mph) *Range* 3,600 km (2,236 miles)

21 persons. Initially powered by two 484.4 kW (650 hp) Rolls-Royce Condor engines in tandem and first flown in September 1926, production aircraft usually had four 372.6 kW (500 hp) Bristol Jupiter VIII radials. Super-Wals were licence-built in other countries and were operated commercially by several airlines, including Deutsche Luft-Hansa.

Dornier Do X (Germany) The Do X was built in Switzerland by Aktiengesellschaft für Dornier-Flugzeuge at Altenrhein and first flew on 25 July 1929. It was then by far the largest flying-boat in the world and remained so until World War II: on 21 October 1929 it lifted 150 passengers, a crew of 10 and 9 stowaways. But engine troubles caused considerable problems and the original 12 Siemens-built Bristol Jupiter radials were replaced by 12 Curtiss Conquerors.

Its most notable flight was from Friedrichshafen to New York: beginning on 2 November 1930 and ending on 27 August 1931, it flew via Amsterdam, Calshot (England), Lisbon (where fire damaged a wing), Canary Islands (where the hull was damaged), Bolama (Portuguese Guinea), Cape Verde Islands, Fernando Noronha, Natal (Brazil), Rio de Janeiro and the West Indies.

Two sister ships, the *Umberto Maddalena* and *Alessandro Guidoni*, were also built for Italy.

Data: *Engines* as above *Wing span* 48.0 m (157 ft 5 in) *Length* 40.05 m (131 ft 4 in) *Max T-O weight* 56,000 kg (123,460 lb) *Cruising speed* 190 km/h (118 mph) *Range* 1,700 km (1,055 miles)

Dornier Do 11.

Dornier Do 11, 13 and 23 (Germany) During the late 1920s the German Dornier Metallbauten set up a subsidiary at Altenrhein in Switzerland to build heavy aircraft expressly forbidden under the terms of the Versailles Treaty. The Do P had four engines, the Do Y three, and the Do F was a large twin. All were described as freighters, but their suitability as bombers was obvious. In late 1932 it was boldly decided to put the F into production at the German factory at Friedrichshafen, the designation being changed to Do 11.

The Do 11 had a slim light-alloy fuselage, high-mounted metal wing with fabric covering carrying two 484.4 kW (650 hp) Siemens Sh 22B engines (derived from the Bristol Jupiter), and a quaint retractable landing gear whose vertical main legs were laboriously cranked inwards along the inner wing until the large wheels lay flat inside the nacelles. There was obvious provision for a bomb bay and three gun positions. The first customer was the German State Railways which under the cover of a freight service actually enabled the embryo Luftwaffe to begin training future bomber crews.

It had been planned to deliver 372 Do 11s in 1934 but delays, plus grossly unpleasant handling and structural qualities, led to the substitution first of the short-span Do 11D and then the Do 13 with 559 kW (750 hp) BMW VI water-cooled engines and fixed (often spatted) landing gear. At least 77 Do 11Ds were delivered, some later being passed on to another clandestine air force, that of Bulgaria. The Do 13 was wholly unacceptable, but in September 1934 testing began of a completely redesigned machine called Do 13e with stronger airframe, Junkers double-wing flaps and ailerons and many other changes. To erase the reputation of its forbear this was redesignated Do 23 and in March 1935 production restarted of Do 23F bombers.

No attempt was made to disguise the function of the bomber: the fuselage having a glazed nose for visual aiming of the 1,000 kg (2,205 lb) bomb load housed in vertical cells in the fuselage, and nose, mid-upper and rear ventral positions each being provided with a 7.92 mm MG 15 machine-gun. After building a small number the Dornier plant switched to the Do 23G with the BMW VIU engine cooled by ethylene-glycol. By late 1935

more than 200 had been delivered and these equipped the first five named Fliegergruppen – although about two-thirds of their strength comprised the distinctly preferable Ju 52/3m. Although it played a major part in the formation of the Luftwaffe and continued to the end of World War II to serve in training, trials and research roles, the Dornier Do 23 was not much better than its disappointing predecessors.
Data (Do 23G): *Engines* as above *Wing span* 25.59 m (83 ft 11¾ in) *Length* 18.8 m (61 ft 8 in) *Max T-O weight* 9,200 kg (20,282 lb) *Max level speed* 259 km/h (161 mph) *Range* 1,350 km (840 miles)

Dornier Do 17 (Germany) The Do 17 was less important to the Luftwaffe during World War II than other later types of medium bomber and reconnaissance aircraft, but nevertheless served in one role or another throughout the war. Although originally configured as a commercial high-performance mail and passenger-carrying aircraft for Deutsche Luft-Hansa, it was as a replacement for the stop-gap Junkers Ju 52/3m bomber/transport that the Do 17 'Flying Pencil' is best remembered, and for being the first type of German aircraft shot down by an RAF single-seat fighter during the war (a Hurricane of No 1 Squadron on 30 October 1939).

The first prototype Do 17 made its maiden flight in 1934 and this and later prototypes were tested by Lufthansa, which rejected them because of their cramped accommodation. Following evaluation and development as a bomber, Dornier put the aircraft into production for the Luftwaffe as the Do 17E bomber and F reconnaissance aircraft, each powered by two BMW VI engines and becoming operational from 1937. Within a

Dornier Do 13.

Dornier Do 17Es.

Dornier Do 23G.

Dornier Do 18.

329

Dornier

Dornier Do 24K.

Dornier Do 26 in Luftwaffe service.

Dornier Do 27.

Dornier Do 26 as intended for Luft-Hansa.

year both models were flying missions in Spain. The E and F were followed into production by the Do 17M bomber and P reconnaissance developments with Bramo 323A-1 and BMW 132N engines respectively. A number of Do 17Ps were sent to Spain to supplement the slower and more vulnerable Do 17Fs flying with Nationalist forces. A Do 17 version (essentially similar to the Do 17M) was also exported to Yugoslavia. Following small numbers of Do 17S reconnaissance and Do 17U pathfinder aircraft with Daimler-Benz DB600A engines, the final version appeared as the Do 17Z powered by Bramo 323s.

At the outbreak of World War II the Luftwaffe had about 550 Do 17s in operational condition and the type was immediately used in attacking Poland. On 3 September 1939 the Luftwaffe lost 22 aircraft (four of which were Do 17s), but the overwhelming superiority of the German forces brought a swift end to the campaign. During the Battle of France, French fighters gained a number of important victories over escorted Do 17s, but it was during the Battle of Britain that the Dornier's lack of armour and fire-power was most clearly demonstrated. Although engaged on the Eastern Front, by 1942 most Luftwaffe bomber units had given up their Do 17s and many were thereafter employed on other duties including glider-towing.

Data (Do 17Z-2): *Engines* two 745 kW (1,000 hp) Bramo 323P radials *Wing span* 18.0 m (59 ft 1 in) *Length* 15.8 m (51 ft 10 in) *Max T-O weight* 8,836 kg (19,481 lb) in extended take-off overload condition *Max level speed* 423 km/h (263 mph) *Range* 3,000 km (1,864 miles) *Armament* six MG15 machine-guns, plus up to 1,000 kg (2,204 lb) of bombs (typically 20 × 50 kg)

Dornier Do 18 (Germany) The Do 18 was originally produced as a transatlantic mail-carrying

flying-boat and used on the South Atlantic service of Deutsche Luft-Hansa. It was available in two forms as the Do 18E and Do 18F, with an AUW of 10,000 kg (22,046 lb) and 11,000 kg (24,250 lb) and with larger wings. One Do 18 was redesignated Do 18L when its two 447 kW (600 hp) Junkers Jumo 205s were replaced by 671 kW (900 hp) BMW 132Ns. Do 18s were also operated as reconnaissance and search-and-rescue aircraft by the Luftwaffe, more than 70 being built for this purpose, plus a number of Do 18H trainers.

Data (Do 18E): *Engines* as above *Wing span* 23.7 m (77 ft 9 in) *Length* 19.25 m (63 ft 2 in) *Max T-O weight* 10,000 kg (22,046 lb) *Max level speed* 260 km/h (161.5 mph) *Range* 5,350 km (3,325 miles)

Dornier Do 22 (Germany) Three-seat parasol-wing monoplane of 1938, exported in small numbers to Yugoslavia and Greece and employed in reconnaissance and bombing roles.

Dornier Do 24 (Germany) The Do 24 flying-boat was designed before World War II and series built to order of the Dutch government for use in the East Indies by the Naval Air Service. With licence production in Holland, a total of 37 were operated as Do 24Ks. From May 1940 Do 24s on the production lines were completed under German occupation and these – together with later Do 24Ts and French-built examples – were used by the Luftwaffe as reconnaissance and search-and-rescue aircraft.

The Do 24 was also built under licence in Spain, examples remaining in service into the 1960s. To meet a current need expressed by the Spanish Air Force to replace its Grumman HU-16 Albatross amphibians, Dornier proposed a modern version of the Do 24T as the Do 24A, with retractable landing gear and three Pratt & Whitney Aircraft of Canada PT6A-45 turboprop engines. A production decision has not yet been taken.

Data: *Engines* three 745 kW (1,000 hp) Bramo 323R radials *Wing span* 27.0 m (88 ft 7 in) *Length* 22.0 m (72 ft 2 in) *Max T-O weight* 18,400 kg (40,560 lb) *Max level speed* 340 km/h (211 mph) *Range* 4,750 km (2,950 miles) *Armament* two machine-guns, one cannon, plus up to 600 kg (1,320 lb) of bombs

Dornier Do 26 (Germany) The Do 26 was designed originally for the North Atlantic mail service of Deutsche Luft-Hansa. A four Junkers Jumo-engined flying-boat, it never went into service on the route but was subsequently adapted into a reconnaissance aircraft for the Luftwaffe, carrying an electrically operated bow gun turret with a 23 mm cannon, two side blisters and a rear position for machine-guns.

Dornier Do 27 (Germany) The prototype of this general utility, transport and ambulance light monoplane flew for the first time on 27 June 1955. The first production aircraft flew on 17 October 1956. A total of 680 were built, including 428 ordered for the Federal German Air Force and Army and 50 manufactured under licence by CASA in Spain, as the CASA C.127.
Data (Do 27A-4): *Engine* one 201 kW (270 hp) Lycoming GO-480-B1A6 *Wing span* 12.0 m (39 ft 4½ in) *Length* 9.6 m (31 ft 6 in) *Max T-O weight* 1,850 kg (4,070 lb) *Max level speed* 227 km/h (141 mph) *Range* 1,100 km (685 miles) *Accommodation* seating for five persons or can be used for observation, freight-carrying, ambulance or rescue duties

Dornier Do 28 and Do 28D Skyservant (Germany) First flown in 1959, the Do 28 was basically a twin-engined version of the Do 27 with an

increased wing span. Despite its designation, the Skyservant inherited only the basic configuration of the earlier Do 28, the prototype flying for the first time on 23 February 1966. Sales of this version reached 250 aircraft by 1978, including 101 aerodynamically refined Do 28D-2s for the Federal German Air Force for general duties and 20 to the Navy Air Arm for support duties.
Data (Do 28D-2): *Engines* two 283 kW (380 hp) Lycoming IGSO-540-A1Es *Wing span* 15.55 m (51 ft 0¼ in) *Length* 11.41 m (37 ft 5¼ in) *Max T-O weight* 3,842 kg (8,470 lb) *Max level speed* 325 km/h (202 mph) *Range* 2,950 km (1,830 miles) *Accommodation* pilot and co-pilot/passenger and up to 13 passengers or five stretchers and five sitting casualties/attendants, or freight

Dornier Do 28B-1.

Dornier Do 31E3.

Dornier Do 29 (Germany) Officially sponsored V/STOL research aircraft developed as a much-modified Do 27.
Dornier Do 31E (Germany) Experimental V/STOL transport aircraft, first flown on 10 February 1967. Powered by two Rolls-Royce (Bristol) Pegasus 5-2 vectored-thrust propulsion engines and with removable lift-jet pods at wingtips each housing four Rolls-Royce RB.162-4D turbojets.
Dornier Do 132 (Germany) Prototype five-seat multi-purpose helicopter of early 1970s.
Dornier Do 215 (Germany) Version of the Do 17Z with 857 kW (1,150 hp) Daimler Benz DB 601 engines, ordered by Yugoslavia but operated by the Luftwaffe.

Dornier Do 28D-2.

Dornier Do 215B-4.

Dornier Do 217 (Germany) First flown in August 1938, the Do 217 was a development of the Do 17 and remained in production until the latter part of 1943. The first production version was the Do 217E, which was used during 1940 and 1941 as a bomber and for attacks on convoys. It was powered by two BMW 801A engines and armed with one fixed MG 151 and one flexible MG 151 machine-gun in the nose; one MG 131 in a manually operated dorsal turret; one MG 131 in a lower

Dornier Do 29.

Dornier

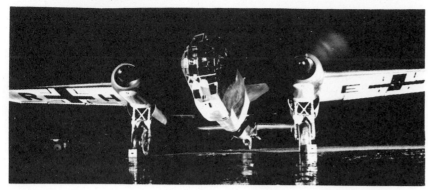

Dornier Do 217E.

Dornier Do 217J-2.

Abandoned Dornier Do 335 Pfeil.

Dornier Do 335A two-seat training version of the Pfeil.

Dornier Do 217K-2.

rearward-firing MG 81 machine-guns in the tail-cone. Like the E and J, the K had BMW 801 engines.

A change of power plant to the Daimler-Benz DB 603 led to the Do 217M, which was otherwise similar to the K and was the latest version of the Do 217 in service at the time of Germany's capitulation. The Do 217N was a night-fighter variant of the M, with armament that could include two or four fixed upward-firing guns.

The final variant of the Do 217 was the P, developed as a very high-altitude bomber and reconnaissance aircraft with a pressurised cabin for the crew of four. First flown in June 1942, this version failed to enter production, as did the further developed Do 317. In total about 1,700 Do 217s were constructed for the Luftwaffe and a few Do 217J night fighters also served with Italy. Data (Do 217M-1): *Engines* two 1,304 kW (1,750 hp) Daimler-Benz DB 603As *Wing span* 19.0 m (62 ft 4 in) *Length* 17.0 m (55 ft 10 in) *Max T-O weight* 16,700 kg (36,815 lb) *Max level speed* 560 km/h (348 mph) *Range* 2,500 km (1,553 miles)

rear-firing position; and two MG 15s in lateral-firing positions.

The E-2 sub-version was similar but had an electrically operated turret, while the E-5 had attachments under the outer wings for two Hs 293 glider bombs for attacking convoys – special equipment for controlling these bombs was installed in the fuselage.

The Do 217J was a night fighter developed from the E, to which it was structurally similar but for having a redesigned solid armoured nose fitted with four 20 mm MG FF cannon and four 7.92 mm MG 17 machine-guns; the upper and lower rear guns of the E-2 were retained. Special night-flying equipment was installed and for some time Js were the standard Luftwaffe night fighter.

The Do 217K was a further development of the E, the distinguishing feature of this version being a redesigned deeper and more rounded nose. The Do 217K-1 was a bomber; but the K-2 with 24.4 m wings was equipped to carry two FX 1400 *Fritz X* radio-controlled armour-piercing bombs for attacking armoured ships. Another novelty in the K was the fitting of a battery of four fixed

Dornier Do 335 Pfeil (Germany) The unusual tandem-engined layout used in the Pfeil was first patented by Dr Claude Dornier in 1937, but it was not until the end of 1942 that permission to build a prototype fighter with tractor and pusher DB 603 engines was given. However the Pfeil was never encountered in operations, although available in small numbers as the Do 335A-1 single-seat fighter (with a maximum speed of 763 km/h; 474 mph), Do 335A-6 two-seat night fighter and Do 335B-series heavy fighter and night fighter towards the end of the war.

Douglas Cloudster.

Douglas DT-1.

Douglas Aircraft Company (USA) The Douglas Aircraft Company was formed in 1921 and from 1928 occupied a factory site at Clover Field, Santa Monica, California. By the end of World War II the company operated further plants at El Segundo (California), Long Beach (California), Tulsa (Oklahoma), Chicago (Illinois), and Oklahoma City (Oklahoma). The products of the company are covered below in order of appearance rather than alphabetically.

Douglas Cloudster (USA) Single example of a Liberty-powered biplane built for an attempt at a non-stop flight across the USA.

excluding five export models delivered to Norway and Peru. The latter had 484.3 kW (650 hp) Wright engines and were operated by the small Naval Air Station at Ancon (20 miles from Lima) which was under the command of US Navy officers on loan to the Peruvian government. Seven DT-2s were also built in Norway under licence.

US Navy DT-2s entered service from 1922 and during their four-year career were experimentally flown from the aircraft carrier USS *Langley*. However several new versions of the DT were developed by fitting new engines into existing DT-2s, the most important of which was the DT-4 bomber with a 484.3 kW (650 hp) Wright T-2, able to carry a bomb load of 748 kg (1,650 lb). Data (DT-2): *Engine* as above *Wing span* 15.24 m (50 ft 0 in) *Length* (floatplane) 11.47 m (37 ft 7½ in) *Max T-O weight* 3,308 kg (7,293 lb) *Max level speed* 161 km/h (100 mph) *Range* 440 km (274 miles)

Production of components for the Douglas Cloudster.

Douglas DT series (USA) The DT-1 appeared in 1921 as a single-seat 298 kW (400 hp) Liberty-powered (with side radiators) torpedo plane. From it was developed the two-seat DT-2, an extremely sturdy single-bay biplane with a 335.3 kW (450 hp) Liberty engine and nose radiator.

The fuselage was of welded steel tubing, braced with tie-rods and provided with stiffening gussets. It was built in three detachable sections: engine section, mid section and tail section, the first two plated with aluminium and the tail with fabric. The vertical tail surfaces had conventional wooden frames, while the horizontal tail surfaces were of steel tubing. The wings were of standard box-beam and built-up rib construction of wood, fabric-covered. The upper wing was made up of three panels, while the lower had the usual two. The undercarriage was remarkable only for having a 3 m (10 ft) wide track, although DT-2s could be fitted with two long wooden floats.

A total of about 80 production DT-2-type aircraft were produced in the USA, most as standard DT-2s for the US Navy but including a small number of SDW-1 scouting floatplanes, but

Douglas World Cruiser (USA) As far as structure was concerned, the DWC was identical to the DT-2. The internal equipment, however, was specially designed for a round-the-world attempt by the US Army Air Service and the saving in weight by deletion of the military load (torpedo with release gear, firing sight, etc) was used to increase the range of the aeroplane to 3,540 km (2,200 miles) by fitting extra petrol and oil tanks – the former totalling 536.25 Imp gallons (644 US gallons; 2,437.8 litres). Able to be fitted with wheel or twin-float landing gears, the all-up weight with the latter was 3,710 kg (8,180 lb). The engine, the improved 313 kW (420 hp) Liberty, offered a weight of less than 0.91 kg (2 lb) per hp. Only four aircraft were built (see **Chronology** 6 and 30 April and 28 September 1924).

Norwegian Douglas DT-2B.

Douglas World Cruisers.

Douglas O-2A.

Douglas M-4.

Douglas M-2.

Douglas O-2 series (USA) The Douglas O-2 series of observation biplanes was among the most successful types of aircraft operated by the USAAC between the wars and also found limited success in the export field.

Designed in 1924 to participate in an Army competition to replace the DH-4B then in service with various squadrons, the prototype followed the general arrangement of the World Cruiser, the principal modifications being a simplified under-carriage (consisting of two oleo legs and two Vees hinged at the centre line of the underside of the fuselage). Petrol tanks for the Liberty engine were carried in the lower wings and could be dropped in an emergency.

From 1925 the USAAC (including Air National Guard) received more than 300 aircraft of the series: starting with a small number of unarmed O-2Bs and 45 armed O-2s, the major production version being the much refined O-2H of 1927 (142 ordered). Many were subsequently modified into two-seat flying and instrument trainers under the designations BT-1s and BT-2s. A small number of O-2Cs were also supplied to Mexico in 1926 to replace ex-USAAS DH-4Bs received during internal troubles in 1924, and two to the USMC as OD-1s. The Canadian govern-

ment received at least one MO-2B three-seat general-purpose biplane with a Wasp engine, for use as a high-altitude photographic aircraft.

Data (O-2H): *Engine* as above *Wing span* 12.19 m (40 ft 0 in) *Length* 9.14 m (30 ft 0 in) *Max T-O weight* 2,040 kg (4,500 lb) *Max level speed* 220 km/h (137 mph) *Range* 824 km (512 miles) *Armament* two forward-firing and one rear-mounted 0.30 in Browning machine-guns

Douglas M series and DAM-4S (USA) Developed from the Douglas Air Mail 1 (a mail-carrying derivative of the O-2 built for the US Post Office), the M-2 was produced to the order of Western Air Express with a compartment of 1.64 m³ (58 cu ft) for up to 454 kg (1,000 lb) of mail, which was 1.83 m (6 ft) long to permit stowage of long packages. This compartment was further provided with two quickly removable seats, enabling two passengers to be carried or for ferrying reserve pilots from one aerodrome to another. Six were operated by Western Air Express over the Salt Lake City–Los Angeles route from 1926. In the same year the US Post Office ordered ten improved M-3s and then 40 M-4s. However the Post Office later stopped flying mail services and these aircraft were sold to a number of air mail contractors in the USA, including National Air Transport and Western Air Express.

The DAM-4S was built as a pilot-training aircraft as well as a mail carrier for National Air Transport, contractors for the Chicago–New York air mail route. The general characteristics were similar to those of the M-4, but there was an additional cockpit aft of the wings and power was provided by a 317 kW (425 hp) Pratt & Whitney Wasp engine.

Data (M-4): *Engine* one 298 kW (400 hp) Liberty *Wing span* 12.09 m (39 ft 8 in) *Length* 8.81 m (28 ft

11 in) *Max T-O weight* 2,253 kg (4,968 lb) *Max level speed* 233 km/h (145 mph) *Range* 1,127 km (700 miles)

Douglas C-1 (USA) The C-1 was a standard cargo and troop (six or eight) transport of the USAAC and followed the lines of the World Cruiser and O-2/M series. First flown in May 1925, ten C-1s were built, followed by the C-1C version of which 17 were ordered in 1927. Principal changes in design included modifications to permit the carriage of four special stretchers for ambulance use, a new tailplane, silencing manifolds on the engine, substitution of metal floors for wooden ones, and a redesigned landing gear.

vided initially by two 391 kW (525 hp) Wright R-1750 engines and subsequently by 428.5 kW (575 hp) R-1820s.

Douglas Dolphin (USA) Developed from the one-off Sinbad operated by the US Coast Guard, the Dolphin was a six–eight-seat amphibian which was originally produced for commercial use. Its outstanding success, both with airlines and private operators, attracted the attention of the US government, with the result that contracts were awarded for the Army, Navy and Coast Guard. The Army received 24 as transports, bearing the designations C-21 and C-26, later becoming OA observation amphibians; while the Navy and Coast Guard received 10 and 13 respectively as RD transports.

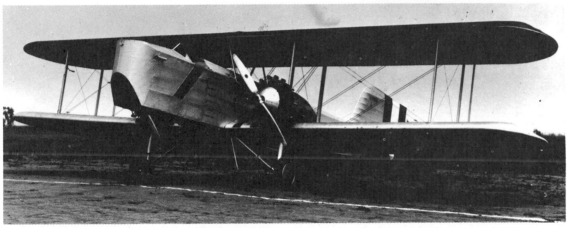

Douglas T2D and P2D (USA) The XT2D-1 prototype was a twin 391 kW (525 hp) Wright Cyclone-engined convertible land- or seaplane designed to fulfil the duties of bombing, torpedo-dropping and scouting and to operate from aircraft carriers. The redesigned T2D-1 entered production in 1927 and 12 were delivered to the US Navy, operating from USS *Langley*. In 1931 the Navy received a new improved version for patrol duties; 18 were produced, embodying up-to-date improvements, 428.5 kW (575 hp) engines and twin fins and rudders. Although first appearing in landplane form, the P2D-1 was usually operated as a twin-float seaplane.

Douglas PD-1 (USA) The PD-1 was developed from a US Navy Bureau of Aeronautics design for a twin-engined coastal-patrol flying-boat. It was a modification of the PN-10 and PN-12 types which were built at the US Naval Aircraft Factory at Philadelphia. Twenty-five PD-1s served throughout the 1930s, latterly as trainers. Power was pro-

Data (C-21): *Engines* two 223.5 kW (300 hp) Wright R-975s *Wing span* 18.29 m (60 ft 0 in) *Length* 13.36 m (43 ft 10 in) *Max T-O weight* 3,891 kg (8,580 lb) *Max level speed* 225 km/h (140 mph) *Range* 885 km (550 miles)

Douglas O-25A.

Douglas O-32A.

Douglas Y10-35.

Douglas O-25 (USA) Following the success of the O-2, Douglas produced a number of prototype developments which culminated in the O-25. Eighty-three production aircraft were produced for the USAAC from 1930 with 447 kW (600 hp) Curtiss V-1570 engines.

Douglas O-32A (USA) Thirty observation aircraft built for the USAAC with 335.3 kW (450 hp) Pratt & Whitney R-1340-3 Wasp radial engines. Subsequently converted into BT-2 trainers. Mexico received 12 similar but Hornet-powered O-2Ms.

Douglas O-38, BT-2 and O2MC (USA) The O-38B was an improved model of the Douglas observation biplane and 63 were delivered to the USAAC and Air National Guard. Power was provided by the 391 kW (525 hp) Pratt & Whitney R-1690-5 Hornet radial engine. Peru received examples of the O-38P with a more streamlined and wider fuselage, while similar E and F versions went to the Air National Guard. The BT-2B and C two-seat trainers were developed from the O-38, as were the O2MCs produced from 1930 for the Chinese government.

Douglas O-43A and O-46A (USA) The O-43A was a two-seat army observation monoplane, 23 of which were delivered to the USAAC during

Douglas DC-1.

Douglas Y1B-7.

1934, following a number of earlier evaluation YO-31s with gull wings. It was a wire-braced parasol-wing monoplane powered by a 503 kW (675 hp) Curtiss V-1570-59 Conqueror engine. Maximum speed was 303 km/h (188 mph) and it could climb to 3,050 m (10,000 ft) in a little over seven minutes. The O-46A followed the O-43A into production for the Army and Air National Guard, 90 being delivered from 1936. Like the O-43A, the O-46A had accommodation for two under canopies and a single-leg-type cantilever landing gear, but was powered by a 540 kW (725 hp) Pratt & Whitney R-1535-7 Twin Wasp Junior engine driving a Hamilton-Standard controllable-pitch propeller.

Data (O-46A): *Engine* as above *Wing span* 13.94 m (45 ft 9 in) *Length* 10.54 m (34 ft 7 in) *Max T-O weight* 3,011 kg (6,640 lb) *Max level speed* 322 km/h (200 mph) *Armament* one forward-firing and one rear-mounted 0.30 in Browning machine-guns

Douglas Y1B-7 and Y1O-35 (USA) Test flown in 1930, the Y1B-7 was the first monoplane bomber to enter USAAC service. Powered by two 503 kW (675 hp) Curtiss V-1570-27 engines, each of the seven evaluation aircraft produced had gull wings, a retractable landing gear and open cockpits for the crew. Five similar observation aircraft were also delivered as Y1O-35s.

Douglas DC-1 (USA) The one and only DC-1 was flown for the first time on 1 July 1933. It had been built to satisfy a requirement of TWA, which had been unable to get hold of early examples of the Boeing 247. It was a 12-passenger airliner and is important as the forerunner of the DC-2 and DC-3. It finally ended its career in Spain in December 1940.

Douglas DC-2 (USA) The Douglas Transport was originally developed for TWA (see above). It entered production in 1933 as the more powerful 529 kW (710 hp) Wright SGR-1820-F3 Cyclone-engined and lengthened (14-seat) DC-2.

The first of 20 ordered by TWA flew on 11 May 1934 and deliveries started soon after. The early DC-2s were so successful that by June 1934 orders for 75 aircraft had been received from airlines in both the US and abroad. Subsequent orders were received from American Air Lines, Eastern Airlines, Pan American Airways and from numerous foreign operators – the first exported DC-2s being flown by KLM in the autumn of 1934.

By September 1935 110 had been ordered and to meet the demand Douglas was producing one aircraft every three days. Such was the importance of the DC-2 that in 1934 Anthony Fokker acquired exclusive European rights to sell the Douglas Transport in Europe. In addition to commercial aircraft, DC-2s were purchased by the US Navy and USAAC and others were impressed into military service during World War II to serve with the Allied forces.

Douglas TBD-1 Devastator (USA) The prototype of the Devastator torpedo bomber flew for the first time on 15 April 1935. It was the first monoplane selected for aircraft-carrier operations, the first of 129 ordered by the US Navy entering service in 1937. Armed with only one forward-firing and one rear-mounted machine-gun (plus a 21 in torpedo or 1,000 lb bomb), it was very vulnerable to enemy attack: heavy losses were suffered in action against the Japanese during the early part of World War II, especially during the Battle of the Coral Sea when the type operated from USS *Lexington* and *Yorktown*, the former being sunk but only after Devastator and Dauntless bombers had sunk the Japanese carrier *Shoho* and severely damaged *Shokaku*. The Battle of Midway, fought between 4 and 7 June 1942, was

the Devastator's last major action: it was relegated to non-combat duties after suffering heavy losses during the battle.
Data: *Engine* one 671 kW (900 hp) Pratt & Whitney R-1830-64 Twin Wasp radial *Wing span* 15.24 m (50 ft 0 in) *Length* 10.67 m (35 ft 0 in) *Max T-O weight* 4,623 kg (10,194 lb) *Max level speed* 332 km/h (206 mph) *Range* 1,152 km (716 miles)

Douglas DC-2.

Douglas B-18 Bolo (USA) The B-18 was a twin-engined bomber adaptation of the Douglas DC-3 transport. The prototype flew for the first time in 1935 and won a USAAC bomber competition in the following year. The original contract for 133 693 kW (930 hp) Wright R-1820-45-engined B-18s was followed by contracts for 237 B-18As (including 20 similar Digby Is for the RCAF) with 742 kW (1,000 hp) Wright R-1820-53 engines, longer and more heavily glazed noses and power-operated dorsal turrets. The Digby Is, like most USAAC B-18As, were subsequently converted into B-18Bs carrying radar in the nose and submarine-detection equipment in a tailcone: they were used for maritime patrol and reconnaissance duties.
Data (B-18A): *Engines* as above *Wing span* 27.28 m (89 ft 6 in) *Length* 17.63 m (57 ft 10 in) *Max T-O weight* 12,550 kg (27,670 lb) *Max level speed* 346 km/h (215 mph) *Armament* 0.30 in machine-guns in nose and dorsal turrets and ventral position, plus bombs

Douglas 8A (USA) The Douglas 8A was basically a development of the Northrop A-17 for export. Between 1939 and 1941 several versions were produced: these included the 8A-1 for Sweden, which became the biggest operator with more than 100 licence-built 8As (as B 5s, with Bristol Mercury XXIV engines); while others were completed for Argentina, Iraq, the Netherlands, Norway (not delivered) and Peru.

Douglas B-18A.

Douglas TBD-1.

Douglas DC-3.

Interior of Douglas DC-3.

with a wide range of Wright Cyclone and Pratt & Whitney Twin Wasp engines ranging in power from 742 to 894 kW (1,000 to 1,200 hp). The aircraft were operated on wheels and skis – one even had floats (the XC-47C-DL) – and there was the XCG-17 experimental troop-carrying glider version. Original US military contracts covered 10,047 aircraft of which more than 9,500 were versions of the C-47 Skytrain with reinforced floor and double doors, and 380 C-53 Skytroopers. The US Navy ordered the DC-3 as the R4D. A wide range of military designations was given to civil aircraft impressed by the services before delivery including C-48, C-49, C-50, C-51, C-52, C-68 and C-84. Many military DC-3s were supplied to the US's allies and the 1,900 plus supplied to the RAF were given the name Dakota – a name which has been widely used in place of the correct DC-3 designation.

Douglas C-47s towing gliders on D-Day.

Douglas DC-3 (USA) One of the world's truly outstanding aeroplanes, the DC-3 resulted from American Airlines' requirement for a sleeper aircraft for its US transcontinental route. The DC-2 fuselage was too small for this, so, reluctantly, in the autumn of 1934 Douglas agreed to build the DST (Douglas Sleeper Transport) as an enlarged DC-2, with lengthened fuselage, increased span and, most important, an increase of 66 cm (26 in) in fuselage width – allowing up to 28 seats or 14 sleeping berths.

The prototype DST, with 633.4–745 kW (850–1,000 hp) Wright Cyclone SGR-1820 engines, made its first flight on 17 December 1935 (not inappropriately the 32nd anniversary of the first powered flight by the Wright Brothers). The type entered service with American Airlines on 25 June 1936 over the New York–Chicago route, with transcontinental sleeper services starting on 18 September. The DC-3/DST soon proved itself and orders grew rapidly, with KLM becoming the first operator outside the US. Including 40 DSTs, 430 DC-3s had been delivered when the USA entered the war – one flew more than 84,000 hours.

The aircraft had such enormous potential that it was ordered in very large numbers by the US armed forces and when production ceased in 1947 Douglas had built 10,654 examples of all civil and military variants; Nakajima and Showa in Japan had built 485 (L2Ds) and about 2,000 had been built in the USSR as PS-84s, but later redesignated Lisunov Li-2s with 742 kW (1,000 hp) Shvetsov engines.

The DC-3 was built in numerous versions and

Workers at the Douglas Long Beach plant pose by the 2,000th DC-3 from their assembly line.

C-47s made such an important contribution to the US war effort that General Eisenhower considered them to be one of the four most significant weapons of World War II. In the China-Burma-India theatre they 'humped' supplies over the Himalayas from India to China and carried airborne troops on all major invasions. Post-war they contributed to the Berlin Airlift, carried supplies and troops into and wounded men out of Korea, and even fought as heavily armed gunships in Vietnam. Many military DC-3s are still in service.

After World War II very large numbers of military DC-3s became surplus and were acquired by most of the world's airlines. In the early post-war years they formed the backbone of most airline fleets, initially with austere interiors but later brought up to much higher standards. Some were equipped to carry as many as 36 passengers but 21–28 was standard. Many others were used for cargo and mail.

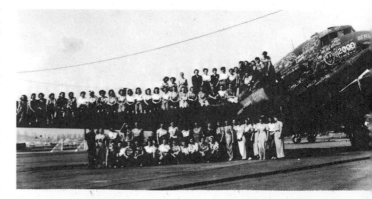

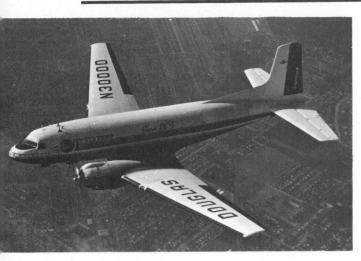

Successful though it was, the DC-3 did not meet post-war ICAO safety standards and a number of dates were set for its withdrawal, but these passed and were forgotten and DC-3s still remain in service after well over 40 years, but reductions have been made in permissible maximum weight.

Various attempts have been made to upgrade the DC-3's performance, including the use of 1,080.5 kW (1,450 hp) Pratt & Whitney R-2000 engines and improved undercarriage doors as on the Hi-Per DC-3, and a number have been fitted with propeller-turbines – but not for normal operation. One was used in the UK as an Armstrong Siddeley Mamba test-bed and BEA operated two Rolls-Royce Dart-powered DC-3s on cargo services to gain experience of the Dart before introduction of the Viscount. In France a DC-3 was fitted with two underwing 1.61 kN (362 lb st) Turboméca Palas turbojets to enhance take-off performance.

Douglas made one attempt to modernise the DC-3, producing the Super DC-3 (DC-3S). Two prototypes were built from a DC-3 and a C-47 and the first flew on 23 June 1949. The aircraft had a new outer wing with 15½° leading-edge sweep and square tips, a new tail unit, strengthened and 99 cm (39 in) longer fuselage to accommodate 30–38 passengers, fully enclosed undercarriage when retracted, and 1,099 kW (1,475 hp) Wright Cyclone R-1820 engines. Capital Airlines bought three. The USAF took the first prototype, as the YC-129 (later YC-47F), but transferred it to the Navy which had 100 of its R4Ds modified to DC-3S standard as R4D-8s, later redesignated C-117D.

Data (DC-3C): Engines as above Wing span 28.96 m (95 ft 0 in) Length 19.63 m (64 ft 5 in) Max T-O weight 12,701 kg (28,000 lb) Cruising speed 274 km/h (170 mph) Range 1,650 km (1,025 miles)

Douglas SBD and A-24 Dauntless (USA) The Dauntless carrier-borne dive bomber and scout went into production in 1940 as the SBD-1, deliveries being to the US Marine Corps. Powered by a 708 kW (950 hp) Wright R-1820-32 engine with a two-speed supercharger, armament comprised two forward-firing 0.50 in machine-guns in the fuselage and one rear-mounted 0.30 in gun for the rear gunner/observer.

The SBD-2 for the Navy was similar except for the revision of the fuel system to two tanks in the centre section and two in the outer wings, deletion of a forward-firing gun, and installation of an automatic pilot. This version entered service on board USS Enterprise and Lexington in late 1941. By December 1941 the SBD-3 was the standard version with the US Fleet. This had a 745 kW (1,000 hp) Wright R-1820-52 engine, a smaller fuel capacity, armour protection and a bullet-proof windscreen, and armament as for SBD-1, although the flexible armament was revised in service to two 0.30 in guns.

Douglas Super DC-3.

Douglas SBD Dauntless.

The SBD-4 was similar to the SBD-3 except for a Hydromatic propeller, installation of a 24 volt electrical system in place of the former 12 volt, and other minor equipment changes. The penultimate version was the SBD-5 with an 894 kW (1,200 hp) Wright R-1820-60 engine; illuminated Mk VIII sight for the fixed guns and Mk IX for the flexible guns in place of the former telescopic and ring sights respectively; increased ammunition and radar installation. The final version was the SBD-6 with a similarly powered Wright R.1820-66 engine and non-metallic self-sealing fuel cells of increased capacity. Sub-variants of these models were also produced as camera-equipped photographic aircraft.

For two years after entering service, the Dauntless fulfilled almost the entire dive-bomber/scout requirements of the US naval forces operating in

Douglas A-24 Dauntless.

Douglas

Douglas A-20 Havoc *Little Hellion* of the 89th Bomb Squadron after crash-landing at an air base in New Guinea.

the Pacific and remained operational throughout the war, some carrying depth charges for anti-submarine patrols.

In 1941 the US Army took delivery of a new version of the Dauntless as the A-24. This was a counterpart of the SBD-3 and differed only from it in minor equipment details and by the deletion of deck-landing gear. The A-24A (SBD-4) and A-24B (SBD-5) followed. Production of the A-24 ceased in November 1943 after several hundred had been built. With the completion of the 5,936th Dauntless on 22 July 1944, production of the SBD ceased. From the end of 1944 the Dauntless was gradually replaced by aircraft of more recent design.

Data (SBD-5): *Engine* as above *Wing span* 12.65 m (41 ft 6 in) *Length* 10.08 m (33 ft 1 in) *Max T-O weight* (as dive bomber) 4,317 kg (9,519 lb) *Max level speed* 410 km/h (255 mph) *Range* 1,794 km (1,115 miles) *Armament* Browning guns as above, plus one 1,000 lb and two 100 lb bombs for dive-bombing or one 500 lb and two 100 lb bombs for scout-bombing missions

Douglas Boston Mk III.

Douglas A-20 Havoc and Boston (USA) The original DB-7 was built as a private venture, produced to the order of the French government. The first production DB-7 flew on 17 August 1939. When France fell the undelivered aircraft outstanding from French contracts were taken over by the British government and given the name Boston. Production for the RAF, USAAF, US Navy and Russia ceased on 20 September 1944 after well over 7,000 had been built. Russia received twice as many as the RAF and only some 800 less than the US Army.

As delivered to the RAF from the French contracts, the Boston I was powered by two Pratt & Whitney R-1830-S3C-4G engines. It was used mainly for training duties, although some were converted for night fighting and given the British name Havoc. The A-20 was the first of the series built to a US Army specification and was powered by two 1,112 kW (1,500 hp) Wright R-2600-7 Cyclone engines with exhaust-driven turbo-superchargers. It was fitted with American armament and equipment.

As the Boston II for the RAF, the A-20 had R-2600-A5B engines and British armament. Those converted into night fighters became Havocs each with a lengthened nose fitted with 12 forward-firing 0.303 in guns, AI radar and other

Douglas DC-4.

special equipment depending on the sub-variant – one carried a high-power searchlight in the nose. As an intruder it carried a crew of three and full armament and bombs.

The A-20A for the USAAC/USAAF was powered by two 1,192 kW (1,600 hp) Wright R-2600-11 engines with integral two-speed superchargers. The A-20B was an experimental development of the A-20A, armed with two 0.50 in guns firing forward, one 0.50 in upper flexible gun, one 0.30 in lower flexible gun, and one 0.30 in gun in the tail of each engine nacelle, firing aft. Nacelle guns were remotely controlled by a foot trigger in the rear compartment. The A-20C was powered by two similarly rated R-2600-23 engines. Armament comprised four fixed guns (two on each side of the transparent nose), two on a flexible mounting in the rear cockpit, and one in the lower rear-firing position – all 0.30 in (A20C) or 0.303 in (British Boston IIIs). Ejector-type exhaust stacks replaced the collector rings used on the earlier models and range was increased by the addition of a self-sealing fuel tank in the forward and rear bomb-bay compartments. Provision was also made on some aircraft to carry a 2,000 lb naval torpedo.

The Boston III was powered by R-2600-A5B engines and carried a crew of four as a bomber. The Boston IIIA was similar but built by Boeing. Some Boston III/IIIAs were fitted as intruders with four 20 mm cannon under the forward fuselage, four 0.303 in guns in the nose, and two 0.303 in guns in the upper flexible position.

Following the experimental XA-20E, with a 37 mm nose cannon and General Electric turrets, the A-20G appeared. This was similar to the A-20C except that the transparent bombardier nose was replaced by a solid nose fitted (in earlier versions) with four 20 mm cannon and two 0.50 in machine-guns and ultimately with six 0.50 in guns. A few also had a single 0.50 in upper

flexible gun, but this was soon replaced by a power-driven turret armed with two 0.50 in guns. Thicker armour for increased crew protection on ground-attack missions was also added.

The A-20H was powered by two 1,267 kW (1,700 hp) R-2600-29 engines and incorporated minor improvements. The A-20J was identical to the later version of the A-20G except that the attack nose was replaced by a moulded-plastic bombardier's nose incorporating bombing controls and flight navigation instruments. One in ten A-20Gs were completed as A-20Js to serve as squadron lead planes. Armament consisted of two 0.50 in machine-guns (one in each side of the transparent nose), two in the power-operated dorsal turret and one in the lower rear firing position.

The A-20K was identical to the A-20H except that the attack nose was replaced by a bombardier's nose, as with the A-20J. The British Boston V was similar. Special US versions of the A-20 appeared as the P-70 night fighter with R-2600-11 engines and armed with four 20 mm cannon mounted in a fairing beneath the fuselage bomb bay; the P-70A conversion of the A-20G with R-2600-23 engines and six 0.50 in machine-guns in a solid nose and dorsal and lower guns; the P-70B development of the P-70A for training, with six 0.50 in 'package' guns and special radar (converted A-20G/Js); the F-3A night photographic-reconnaissance conversion of the A-20J/K; and BD-1/2 target tugs for the US Navy.

Data (A-20G): *Engines* as above *Wing span* 18.68 m (61 ft 3½ in) *Length* 14.63 m (48 ft 0 in) *Max T-O weight* 10,931 kg (24,100 lb) *Max level speed* 523 km/h (325 mph) at 4,420 m (14,500 ft) *Range* (normal combat) 1,650 km (1,025 miles)

Douglas DC-4 (USA) In response to the requirements of five major US airlines, Douglas designed and built the large 52-passenger DC-4, which made its first flight on 7 June 1938. This type was not put into production; instead a smaller unpressurised development was ordered by American, Eastern and United Air Lines. This, too, bore the designation DC-4 and the original aeroplane became the DC-4E. The new aircraft flew on 14 February 1942, by which time the US was at war and all 24 DC-4As built were taken by the armed forces.

The DC-4 had a retractable nosewheel undercarriage and was powered by four 820–1,080 kW (1,100–1,450 hp) Pratt & Whitney Twin Wasps. It was, for its time, an ideal long-range heavy logistic transport with a payload of up to 9,980 kg

(22,000 lb). The military production version was the C-54. A total of 207 C-54As were built, followed by increased-capacity C-54Bs, similar C-54Ds with Pratt & Whitney R-2000-11 radials, C-54Es with convertible cargo/passenger interiors, and C-54Gs with new engines. Nine hundred and fifty-two Skymasters were completed for the USAAF and 211 for the US Navy which designated them as R5D Skymasters.

Used in all theatres of war, none achieved a more impressive record than those operated by the USAAF's Air Transport Command. With this Command C-54s established the first regular transport service across the North Atlantic, averaging for a long period 20 double-crossings per day. One, the VC-54C-DO *Sacred Cow*, served as President Roosevelt's special aircraft and a C-54B-1-DO was used by Prime Minister Winston Churchill.

After the war Douglas built 79 civil DC-4-1009s and many of the military aircraft became available for airline operation – mostly with 44 seats but later with as many as 86. On 7 March 1946 American Airlines was first to introduce DC-4s on US domestic services, between New York and Los Angeles. However in October 1945 American Overseas Airlines had introduced DC-4s on North Atlantic services. Some DC-4s are still in service.

Data (DC-4-1009): *Engines* two 1,080 kW (1,450 hp) Pratt & Whitney R-2000 radials *Wing span* 35.81 m (117 ft 6 in) *Length* 28.6 m (93 ft 10 in) *Max T-O weight* 33,113 kg (73,000 lb) *Cruising speed* 365 km/h (227 mph) *Range* 4,025 km (2,500 miles)

Douglas DC-6B.

Douglas DC-5 (USA) The only Douglas high-wing civil transport, the DC-5 first flew on 20 February 1939. It was powered by two 671 kW (900 hp) Wright Cyclones (later with 820 kW; 1,100 hp Cyclones), had a fully retractable nose-wheel undercarriage, and accommodation for 16–22 passengers.

A few orders were placed, including one for nine by the old British Airways, but only KLM took delivery, with two going to the Netherlands West Indies and two to KNILM. The NWI aircraft later went to KNILM and three helped in the evacuation of civilians from Java, after which they were operated by Australian National Airways and the RAAF.

Douglas F3D-2 Skyknight.

Only five civil DC-5s were built but there were seven R3Ds used by the US Navy and Marine Corps as personnel transports, paratroop transports and cargo aircraft.

Data (DC-5): *Engines* as above *Wing span* 23.77 m (78 ft 0 in) *Length* 18.96 m (62 ft 2 in) *Max T-O weight* 9,072 kg (20,000 lb) *Cruising speed* 325 km/h (202 mph) *Range* 2,575 km (1,600 miles)

Douglas D-558-1 Skystreak.

Douglas B-23 Dragon (USA) The B-23 was a twin 1,192 kW (1,600 hp) Wright GR-2600-engined reconnaissance bomber developed from the earlier B-18A. Defensive armament comprised 0.30 in machine-guns in nose, dorsal and ventral positions and a 0.50 in gun in the tail. Thirty-eight were delivered to the USAAF but were soon relegated to training and transport duties.

Douglas A-26/B-26 Invader (USA) The contract for the prototype XA-26 was placed in June 1941. Actually three experimental models were produced to the basic design: the XA-26 light bomber and attack aircraft; the XA-26A night fighter with 20 mm cannon in a ventral 'package'

and four 0.50 in machine-guns in a remotely controlled upper turret; and the XA-26B attack bomber mounting a 75 mm gun as part of its initial armament.

The XA-26 was flown for the first time on 10 July 1942 and was able to carry approximately twice the bomb load required by the original specification and exceeded every performance guarantee. Tests with these three experimental models culminated in the design of the production A-26B, which carried additional armour protection for the pilot and a closed-in nose armed with six 0.50 in machine-guns. In addition up to ten more guns could be carried in packs mounted underwing and at each side of the nose. Up to 1,814 kg (4,000 lb) of bombs could be carried internally and the underwing hardpoints could accommodate an additional 907 kg (2,000 lb) of bombs, 16 rockets, or extra fuel.

The A-26C, which served as a lead ship, was fitted with a transparent bombardier nose and two forward-firing 0.50 in guns. The FA-26A was a photographic-reconnaissance version. Orders for the A-26D and work on the XA-26F (with an auxiliary General Electric J-31 turbojet engine in the fuselage) were cancelled after VJ Day. However on 26 June 1946 the XA-26F established a new speed-with-payload record over a 1,000 km course of 664 km/h (413 mph). The JT-1 was a stripped version of the Invader for use as a target-tug by the US Navy.

A-26As first went into action in the European theatre of war on 19 November 1944. By the end of production 2,502 Invaders had been built. The designations of the above aircraft were changed to B-26B and B-26C respectively in June 1948 after the original 'Attack' designation was discontinued (at which time the Martin B-26 was no longer in service). Invaders were deployed successfully in the Korean War and against the Viet Cong in South Vietnam. Final variant was the B-26K COIN version of which a prototype conversion had been completed by the On Mark Engineering Company. Improved load carrying and short-field performance allowed up to 14 guns to be carried as standard. About 40 were delivered by On Mark, being re-designated subsequently A-26A under the new 1962 attack category.

Invaders withdrawn from first-line service were used as TB-26B/TB-26C trainers; CB-26B/VB-26B transports; and DB-26C drone launchers/controllers.

Data (A-26C): *Engines* two 1,490 hp (2,000 hp) Pratt & Whitney R-2800-27 or -79 radials *Wing span* 21.34 m (70 ft 0 in) *Length* 15.62 m (51 ft

3 in) *Max T-O weight* 15,876 kg (35,000 lb) *Max level speed* 600 km/h (373 mph) *Range* 2,253 km (1,400 miles) *Armament* six 0.50 in machine-guns, plus up to 1,814 kg (4,000 lb) bombs

Douglas AD Skyraider (USA) Developed to satisfy a US Navy requirement of 1944 for a single-seat carrier-based dive bomber and torpedo carrier, the Douglas AD Skyraider (as it became designated) materialised too late for operational service in World War II. Ordered into production alongside the Martin AM Mauler, which had been developed to meet the same specification, it was to continue in production until 1957; although Martin's aircraft was taken off the production line after 151 had been built.

The Skyraider reflected the navy's wartime experience gained in the Pacific theatre, where it had been proved that the most important requirement for such aircraft was the ability to carry and deliver a heavy load of assorted weapons. Of low-wing monoplane configuration, a big Wright R-3350 radial engine was selected as the most suitable power plant to meet the load-carrying requirement, and this more or less dictated the fuselage proportions. The prototype XBT2D-1 flew for the first time on 18 March 1945. When production terminated 12 years later 3,180 aircraft had been built in many variants.

Although too late for World War II, Skyraiders were successfully deployed in both the Korean War and in Vietnam. Steady development led to the introduction of new power plant and equipment and the AD-5 was one of the most versatile military aircraft in US service. It differed sig-

nificantly from earlier versions by having a wider and lengthened fuselage and providing side-by-side seating for two crew; specially designed quick-change kits were available so that the basic AD-5 could be utilised as a 12-seat transport, as well as for freight-carrying, ambulance and target-towing roles. When the US tri-service designations were rationalised in 1962, AD-1 to AD-7 versions became redesignated from A-1A to A-1J.

In addition to serving with the US Navy, Skyraiders have been operated also by the USAF and with the Royal Navy, French and Vietnamese Air Forces among others.

Data (AD-7): *Engine* one 2,012 kW (2,700 hp) Wright R-3350-26WB radial *Wing span* 15.47 m (50 ft 9 in) *Length* 11.84 m (38 ft 10 in) *Max T-O weight* 11,340 kg (25,000 lb) *Max level speed* 512 km/h (318 mph) at 5,640 m (18,500 ft) *Range* 1,448 km (900 miles) *Armament* four 20 mm cannon, plus up to 3,629 kg (8,000 lb) mixed weapons on external hardpoints

Douglas F4D Skyray.

Douglas C-74 Globemaster I (USA) The Globemaster was a large four-engined transport which, following cancellation of an order for 26 placed by Pan American in 1945, existed only in its military form. The prototype, designated XC-74, made its first flight on 5 September 1945. The original military contract for this aircraft was cut back when the war ended but 14 were completed for the USAAF.

Douglas DC-6 (USA) Built as an enlarged and pressurised DC-4 in order to compete with the Lockheed Constellation, the DC-6 (as the XC-112A) first flew on 15 February 1946. It had a 2.06 m (81 in) longer fuselage than the DC-4, accommodation for 48–52 passengers and was powered by four 1,565 kW (2,100 hp) Pratt & Whitney Double Wasp CA15 engines. American Airlines and United Air Lines introduced the DC-6 on 27 April 1946. A total of 175 DC-6s were built. The windowless DC-6A freighter followed in 1949, powered by 1,788.5 kW (2,400 hp) Double Wasps, with reinforced floor and double cargo doors – 74 were built.

The DC-6A was 1.52 m (5 ft) longer than the DC-6 (101 going to the USAF as C-118A transports). The DC-6B, with accommodation for 54–102 passengers, first flew on 2 February 1951 and also had the longer fuselage. American Airlines introduced DC-6Bs on its US transcontinental services on 29 April 1951. It was one of the finest and most economical piston-engined trans-

Douglas D-558-2 Skyrocket.

Douglas C-124 Globemaster IIs.

Douglas

Douglas X-3.

Douglas DC-7C.

Douglas EB-66E Destroyer.

Douglas EKA-3B TACOS Skywarrior.

ports. It remained in production until 1958 and 288 were built. Many of the DC-6 series were later converted to freighters.

Data (DC-6B): *Engines* as above *Wing span* 35.81 m (117 ft 6 in) *Length* 32.18 m (105 ft 7 in) *Max T-O weight* 48,534 kg (107,000 lb) *Cruising speed* 507 km/h (315 mph) *Range* 4,835 km (3,005 miles)

Douglas D-558-1 Skystreak (USA) Turbojet-powered research aircraft used to obtain in free flight air-load measurements not obtainable in wind tunnels of the time. First flown on 28 May 1947. On 20 August 1947 one of the three Skystreaks built set up a world speed record of 1,030.95 km/h (640.74 mph).

Douglas F3D Skyknight (USA) The Skyknight was a two-seat jet-powered carrier-based all-weather fighter, the prototype of which flew for the first time on 22 March 1948. The first production version for the US Navy was the F3D-1, powered eventually by two 14.46 kN (3,250 lb st) Westinghouse J34-WE-34 engines. Twenty-eight were built, the first flying on 13 February 1950.

The major production version was, however, the F3D-2 for the USMC, first flown on 14 February 1951. A total of 237 were built, each powered

by two 15.12 kN (3,400 lb st) J34-WE-36 engines and with improved air conditioning; wing spoilers for improved lateral control; thicker bullet-proof windscreen; and a new type of automatic pilot. From 1962 Skyknights were redesignated F-10s and remained in service long enough to see action in an electronic-countermeasures role during the Vietnam conflict.

Data (F3D-2): *Engines* as above *Wing span* 15.24 m (50 ft 0 in) *Length* 13.84 m (45 ft 5 in) *Max T-O weight* 12,555 kg (20,680 lb) *Max level speed* 909 km/h (565 mph) *Range* 2,478 km (1,540 miles) *Armament* four forward-firing 20 mm cannon; provision for bombs, rockets, etc underwing.

Douglas D-558-2 Skyrocket (USA) Rocket and turbojet-powered research aircraft, first flown on 4 February 1948 to investigate sweptback wings.

Douglas C-124 Globemaster II (USA) The Globemaster II transport had the ability to load without disassembly 95% of all types of Army Field Force's equipment. It had nose-loading doors with vehicle ramps, a rear cargo hatch with elevator loading and auxiliary floor for double-deck loading. The prototype flew for the first time on 27 November 1949. The first production version was the C-124A powered by four 2,608 kW (3,500 hp) Pratt & Whitney R-4360 20WA engines. This was followed by the major production version, the 2,832 kW (3,800 hp) Ford-built Pratt & Whitney R-4360-63A-engined C-124C, which was fitted with the APS-42 radar in a nose radome. Production ceased on 9 May 1955, by which time 446 Globemasters had been built.

Data (C-124C): *Engines* as above *Wing span* 53.07 m (174 ft 1½ in) *Length* 39.75 m (130 ft 5 in) *Max T-O weight* 88,223 kg (194,500 lb) *Cruising speed* 370 km/h (230 mph) *Range* 10,975 km (6,820 miles)

Douglas F4D Skyray (USA) The Skyray was a single-seat carrier-based jet fighter. It was operated by the US Navy and USMC and was flown by a Navy squadron assigned to the North American Air Defense Command as an all-weather interceptor.

The prototype flew for the first time on 23 January 1951 powered by an Allison J35-A-17 turbojet engine. This and the second prototype were re-engined with the Westinghouse XJ40-WE-6 and then the XJ40-WE-8 with afterburner. With the latter the second prototype set up a world speed record of 1,211.746 km/h (752.9 mph) over a 3 km course on 3 October 1953. The first production F4D-1 Skyray flew on 5 June 1954 with a 60 kN (13,500 lb st) Pratt & Whitney J57-P-2 turbojet engine with afterburning, but after a time this was superseded by the 64.5 kN (14,500 lb st) J57-P-8 engine with afterburning. Delivery of the 419th and last F4D-1 took place on 22 December 1958. In 1962 Skyrays were redesignated F-6As but the type was withdrawn from service two years later.

Data: *Engines* as above *Wing span* 10.21 m (33 ft 6 in) *Length* 13.92 m (45 ft 8¼ in) *Max T-O weight* 12,299 kg (27,115 lb) *Max level speed* Mach 1.05 at 11,000 m (36,000 ft) *Range* 1,930 km (1,200 miles) *Armament* four forward-firing 20 mm cannon, plus up to 1,814 kg (4,000 lb) of bombs, rockets, etc

Douglas X-3 (USA) Turbojet-powered research aircraft first flown on 20 October 1952. It was used to investigate the efficiency of turbojet engines and short-span double-wedge wings and tailplanes, and to collect information on thermodynamic heating at high altitudes and at speeds of up to Mach 3.

Douglas A3D Skywarrior (USA) A US Navy requirement of 1947 led to the eventual procurement of what was then the largest and heaviest aircraft intended for operation from a naval vessel. The potential of turbojet engines combined with nuclear weapons promised a significant aircraft, especially if it possessed good range capability and could be operated from the mobile airfield known as an aircraft carrier.

The Douglas Company's design to satisfy this requirement was for a large monoplane of high-wing configuration with 36° of wing sweepback. Two podded engines were pylon-mounted (one beneath each wing) and a large internal weapons bay was equipped to carry either conventional or nuclear weapons. In the spring of 1949 Douglas received a US Navy contract for two XA3D-1 prototypes powered by 31.14 kN (7,000 lb st) Westinghouse XJ40-WE-3 turbojet engines. The first of these made its maiden flight on 28 October 1952. Deliveries of production aircraft began on

Douglas C-133 Cargomaster.

31 March 1956, but following cancellation of the Wright J40 engine programme these were powered by two 43.15 kN (9,700 lb st) Pratt & Whitney J57-P-6 turbojets.

The 50 A3D-1s which comprised the initial production version were used primarily to investigate the concept for which they had been designed. Five of these aircraft were modified subsequently to serve in an ECM role. Major production version, 164 of which were built, was the A3D-2 with more powerful J57-P-10 engines and changes to the weapons bay to permit the carriage of a wider range of weapons, or to accommodate a flight-refuelling pack and fuel tank to confer long ferry range.

In 1962 the A3D designation was changed to A-3 and the initial A3D-1 Skywarriors became A-3As; main version was the A-3B. Other variants included EA-3B ECM aircraft with four equipment operators accommodated in the weapons bay; RA-3B reconnaissance aircraft; TA-3B to provide training for EA-3B operators; KA-3B flight-refuelling tankers; and EKA-3B TACOS (tanker aircraft/countermeasures or strike).

Data (A-3B): *Engines* two 55.16 kN (12,400 lb st) Pratt & Whitney J57-P-10 turbojets *Wing span*

Druine D.62B Condor.

Douglas F5D-1 Skylancer.

Druine Turbulent.

EAA Acro-Sport I.

Dyke Delta.

22.10 m (72 ft 6 in) *Length* 23.27 m (76 ft 4 in) *Max T-O weight* 37,195 kg (82,000 lb) *Max level speed* 982 km/h (610 mph) *Range* 1,690 km (1,050 miles) *Armament* two 20 mm cannon in radar-controlled rear turret, plus up to 5,443 kg (12,000 lb) weapons carried internally

Douglas DC-7 (USA) Built to provide US transcontinental non-stop service, the DC-7 was a longer-fuselage 60–95-passenger development of the DC-6 series, powered by four 2,442 kW (3,250 hp) Wright Turbo-Compound R-3350 engines. It entered service with American Airlines on the New York–Los Angeles route on 29 November 1953. A total of 110 were built. The DC-7 was followed in 1955 by the longer-range DC-7B of which there were 112.

The ultimate development of the DC-4, DC-6, DC-7 series was the DC-7C (Seven Seas) which entered service with Pan American on the North Atlantic on 1 June 1956. The DC-7C, with longer fuselage and 3.05 m (10 ft) greater span, was designed for non-stop North Atlantic operation in both directions. The engines were 2,534 kW (3,400 hp) R-3350s. The DC-7C inaugurated the true-Polar service of SAS between Copenhagen and Tokyo via Anchorage on 24 February 1957. One hundred and twenty-one were built. Many of the DC-7 series were later converted to freighters.

Data (DC-7C): *Engines* as above *Wing span* 38.86 m (127 ft 6 in) *Length* 34.21 m (112 ft 3 in) *Max T-O weight* 64,864 kg (143,000 lb) *Cruising speed* 571 km/h (355 mph) *Range* 7,410 km (4,605 miles)

Douglas B-66 Destroyer (USA) The B-66 was based on the A3D Skywarrior with design and engineering changes to modify the carrier-based aircraft design into a land-based bomber. The first five aircraft were used for service test only as RB-66As, the first flying on 28 June 1954. The first production bomber (with in-flight refuelling equipment) was the B-66B, first flown on 4 January 1955. Early examples had Allison J71-A-11 turbojet engines, later models 45.37 kN (10,200 lb st) J71-A-13s. Deliveries to the USAF began on 16 March 1956. In February 1956 deliveries began of the RB-66B night photographic-reconnaissance version, followed in May 1956 and June 1957 respectively by the RB-66C all-weather electronics-reconnaissance and WB-66D weather-reconnaissance versions.

Total production was 294 aircraft, the final examples in service being a number of Destroyers modified into EB-66E electronic-warfare aircraft and flown during the Vietnam conflict.

Data (B-66B): *Engines* as above *Wing span* 22.1 m (72 ft 6 in) *Length* 22.91 m (75 ft 2 in) *Max T-O weight* 37,648 kg (83,000 lb) *Max level speed* 1,015 km/h (630 mph) *Range* 2,414 km (1,500 miles) *Armament* two 20 mm cannon in radar-controlled General Electric ball-turret, plus nuclear or conventional bombs

Douglas F5D-1 Skylancer (USA) Development of the Skyray. Four built.

Douglas C-133 Cargomaster (USA) The C-133 was a four-engined transport which – although not much bigger in overall dimensions than the earlier C-124 Globemaster II – could carry payloads equivalent to twice the normal cargo capacity of the C-124. The first production C-133 made its maiden flight on 23 April 1956 and deliveries to the USAF began the following year.

The first version was the C-133A powered by four 4,844 kW (6,500 ehp) Pratt & Whitney T34-P-7WA turboprop engines. A total of 34 were delivered. It was followed by the C-133B powered by 5,589 kW (7,500 eshp) T34-P-9W turboprops and with increased loaded weight and an enlarged main cargo door to permit easier loading of the Atlas ICBM, and Thor and Jupiter IRBMs. Fifteen were delivered to MATS, production ending in April 1961.

All had been withdrawn from service ten years

later, although a few were thereafter used in civil roles.

Data (C-133B): *Engines* as above *Wing span* 54.76 m (179 ft 7¾ in) *Length* 48.0 m (157 ft 6½ in) *Max T-O weight* 129,730 kg (286,000 lb) *Cruising speed* 499 km/h (310 mph) *Range* 6,397 km (3,975 miles) *Accommodation* cargo hold of 368.1 m³ (13,000 cu ft) for vehicles or freight, or up to 200 fully armed troops

Druine Turbi, Turbulent and Condor (France) Roger Druine formed the Druine Company to market plans to amateur builders throughout the world for a number of light aircraft, the best known of which were the single- and two-seat D.31 Turbulent, two-seat D.5 Turbi and D.61/D.62 Condor (see also **Rollason**).

DSK BJ-1b Duster (USA) Latest version of the Duster single-seat sailplane, plans and/or component kits for which are available to amateur constructors.

DSK Airmotive DSK-1 Hawk (USA) Single-seat sporting monoplane, plans of which are available to amateur constructors. Fuselage based on a surplus military drop tank.

DSK Airmotive DSK-2 Golden Hawk (USA) Similar to the Hawk but eliminates the need to acquire a drop tank.

Dufaux triplane (Switzerland) First Swiss aeroplane, built in 1908. Tandem sets of triplane wings and biplane tail unit. The Dufaux II, completed in February 1910, was a much cleaner biplane powered by a 22.4 kW (30 hp) Anzani engine. Later Dufaux aircraft were tested as military types.

Duigan biplane (Australia) Farman-type biplane, said to have been the first Australian-built aeroplane to fly successfully. First flown at Mia-Mia in 1911.

Dunne D.IV (UK) The D.IV was a tailless biplane with swept wings and inherent stability which flew successfully at the Duke of Atholl's estate in Scotland in 1908. It was the culmination of work on inherently stable aircraft that had started in 1905 with gliders and had thereafter been continued in some secrecy on behalf of the British War Office by J. W. Dunne. The Dunne V of 1910 and subsequent aircraft were highly successful and were marketed in the UK and America.

Durand Mk V (USA) Two-seat sporting biplane, planes for which are available to amateur constructors.

Durban Aeriel Mk II (South Africa) First flown in October 1959, the Aeriel Mk II two-seat light monoplane was the first aircraft produced in South Africa, built entirely from local materials except for the Continental C90 engine and propeller. First two production aircraft sold in March 1961.

Duruble RD-03 Edelweiss (France) Two–four-seat light monoplane, plans for which are available to amateur constructors.

du Temple monoplane (France) Monoplane of 17.0 m (55 ft 9½ in) wing span designed by Félix du Temple and powered by one hot-air engine driving a tractor propeller. Made a powered 'hop' in 1874 (see **Chronology** 1874).

EAA Biplane.

Dyke Aircraft JD-2 Delta (USA) Delta-wing four-seat sporting aircraft, plans for which are available to amateur constructors.

EAA Acro-Sport I (USA) Single-seat aerobatic biplane, plans for which are available to amateur constructors. About 800 sets of plans had been sold by January 1979.

EAA Acro-Sport II (USA) Two-seat biplane derived from the Acro-Sport I. Plans are available to amateur constructors.

EAA Biplane (USA) Single-seat sporting biplane, plans for which are available to amateur constructors. More than 7,000 sets of plans had been sold by January 1979.

EAA Nesmith Cougar (USA) Plans for the EAA Nesmith Cougar two-seat sporting monoplane have been discontinued.

EAA Pober P-9 Pixie.

EAA Pober P-9 Pixie (USA) Single-seat lightweight and economical sporting monoplane, plans for which are available to amateur constructors.

Ector L-19 Super Mountaineer.

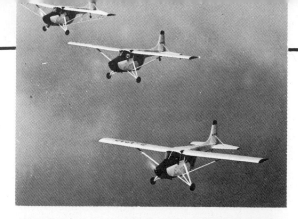

Edgar Percival EP.9s.

EFW C-3604

EKW C-35.

Emair MA-1B.

EAA Super Acro-Sport (USA) Developed version of the Acro-Sport intended for unlimited International Class aerobatic competition at world championship level. Plans are available for amateur construction.

Eagle Helicopter Eagle II (USA) Two-seat lightweight helicopter driven by rotor tip-mounted 'cold jets' supplied with air from a bleed-air compressor.

Ector L-19 Mountaineer and Super Mountaineer (USA) Civil versions of the Cessna L-19 Bird Dog: the Mountaineer with a 159 kW (213 hp) Continental O-470 engine and the Super Mountaineer with a 179 kW (240 hp) Lycoming O-540-A4B5.

Edgar Percival EP.9 and Lancashire Prospector (UK) 201 kW (270 hp) Lycoming GO-480-B1B-engined high-wing monoplane, first flown in prototype form on 21 December 1955. The first aircraft of a production batch of 100 flew on 30 June 1956. Capable of fulfilling passenger (five seats), freighter, agricultural and ambulance roles. Sold to operators in nine countries including Australia, New Zealand, Canada, Germany, Libya, France and Borneo. In 1958 the Lancashire Aircraft Company acquired the design and manufacturing rights of the EP.9 and put it into production as the Prospector.

EFW C-3603 and C-3604 (Switzerland) Two-seat cantilever low-wing ground-attack aircraft. During World War II 144 and 13 were completed of each type for the Schweizerische Flugwaffe, powered by licence-built Hispano-Suiza 12Y 'moteur-canon' engines of 745 kW (1,000 hp) and 932 kW (1,250 hp) respectively (see **F+W C-3605**).

Eiri PIK-20 (Finland) Single-seat Standard Class sailplane. By 1978 149 PIK-20Bs and 100 PIK-20Ds had been delivered.

EKW C-35 (Switzerland) The C-35 was a two-seat close-support sesquiplane fighter based on the Fokker C.V. and fitted with a 656 kW

(880 hp) Hispano-Suiza 12Ycrs 'moteur-canon' engine. Both cockpits were enclosed. Its armament consisted of the 20 mm cannon mounted as part of the engine to fire through the propeller boss, two machine-guns mounted in the lower wings and firing outside the propeller arc, and one machine-gun on a flexible mounting in the rear cockpit.

According to the 1938 *Jane's* maximum speed was 340 km/h (211 mph) at 4,000 m (13,125 ft). It could climb to 5,000 m (16,400 ft) in 8½ minutes and had a service ceiling of 10,000 m (32,800 ft). The Schweizerische Flugwaffe received 88 from 1937.

Elias TA-1 (USA) Biplane trainer of 1921, three of which were acquired for evaluation by the USAAS.

Elias EM (USA) Two-seat combat biplane of 1922. Thirteen built in two versions for the US Navy and USMC with 223.5 kW (300 hp) Hispano or 298 kW (400 hp) Liberty engines.

Ellehammer semi-biplane (Denmark) Crude biplane with a basically triangular lower wing and a gull-type upper wing, developed from his monoplane of 1906. Powered by 15 kW (20 hp) three-cylinder radial engine of own design, driving a tractor propeller via a belt-driven shaft. Lifted from the ground on Lindholm Island for the first time on 16 August 1906.

Ellehammer triplane (Denmark) More successful aeroplane built by J. C. H. Ellehammer which made the first aeroplane flight in Germany on 28 June 1908.

Ellehammer helicopter (Denmark) Twin-rotor helicopter first demonstrated in 1912. First helicopter to incorporate cyclic pitch control.

Ellehammer improved biplane (Denmark) First lifted off the ground on 12 September 1906,

but not credited with the first aeroplane flight in Europe (see **Chronology**). Pendulum seat fitted as a stabilising device.

Elliotts Eon series (UK) During World War II Elliotts of Newbury produced components for several aircraft. After the war it produced the four-seat Newbury Eon cabin monoplane (first flown on 8 August 1947 powered by a 108 kW; 145 hp de Havilland Gipsy Major 10 engine) and the single-seat Olympia Eon high-performance sailplane. The Olympia Eon proved highly popular with clubs and private owners and held British distance and out-and-return records. The company also engaged in the development of the Baby Eon intermediate training sailplane and the Primary Eon ab initio training glider.

Emair MA-1 (Emair 1200) (USA) First flown on 27 July 1969, this single-seat agricultural aircraft was evolved from the Boeing-Stearman Kaydet. It entered production originally as the Agronemair MA-1 Paymaster and by January 1976 25 had been built. This version, with a 447 kW (600 hp) Pratt & Whitney R-1340-AN1 engine, is now available only to special order. The current version is the MA-1B powered by an 895 kW (1,200 hp) Wright R-1820 radial engine, derated to 671 kW (900 hp). By February 1978 24 had been sold.

EMBRAER EMB-110 Bandeirante (Brazil) The Bandeirante is a twin-turboprop light transport and was developed to a Brazilian Ministry of Aeronautics specification for a general-purpose aircraft capable of transport, navigation training, aeromedical evacuation and other duties. The prototype first flew on 26 October 1968 and the first production aircraft on 9 August 1972. By 1978 a total of 187 Bandeirantes of various models had been sold to some 35 operators, including the Brazilian Air Force.

The Bandeirante is available as the EMB-110 12-seat transport (60 operated by the Brazilian Air Force as C-95s); EMB-110B aerial photogrammetric version with electrically operated ventral sliding door permitting the use of aerial cameras (6 operated by the Brazilian Air Force as R-95s); EMB-110B1 quick-change aerial photogrammetric/nine-passenger executive transport (one ordered by Uruguayan Air Force); EMB-110C 15-passenger commercial transport (three operated by Chilean Navy and five by Uruguayan Air Force); EMB-110E seven-passenger executive transport; EMB-110K1 all-cargo version (20 ordered by Brazilian Air Force as C-95As); EMB-110P commercial third-level

EMBRAER EMB-121 Xingu.

commuter version for 18 passengers; EMB-110P1 quick-change version; EMB-110P2 third-level commuter version of K1 carrying 21 passengers; EMB-110S1 geophysical survey version; and EMB-111 maritime patrol version, ordered by the Brazilian Air Force's Coastal Command (12) and the Chilean Navy (6).

Data (EMB-110P2): *Engines* two 559 kW (750 shp) Pratt & Whitney Aircraft of Canada PT6A turboprops *Wing span* 15.3 m (50 ft 2½ in) *Length* 15.1 m (49 ft 6½ in) *Max T-O weight* 5,670 kg (12,500 lb) *Max cruising speed* 417 km/h (259 mph) *Range* 1,900 km (1,180 miles)

EMBRAER EMB-120 Araguaia (Brazil) Longer and more powerful transport version of the 12X (Xingu-type) family, accommodating up to 25 passengers. Powered by two 875 kW (1,173 shp) Pratt & Whitney Aircraft of Canada PT6A-45A turboprops.

EMBRAER EMB-121 Xingu (Brazil) Twin 507 kW (680 shp) Pratt & Whitney Aircraft of Canada PT6A-28 turboprop-powered general-purpose pressurised transport. The prototype flew for the first time on 10 October 1976 and the first production aircraft was delivered the following year to the Copersucar-Fittipaldi Brazilian Formula One racing car team. The Brazilian Air Force operates five as VU-9s. The main cabin accommodates nine passengers.

EMBRAER EMB-123 Tapajós (Brazil) Second version of the 12X series to be developed; intended to have PT6A-45 engines. Design temporarily in abeyance.

EMBRAER EMB-200 and EMB-201 Ipanema (Brazil) The original version of the Ipanema single-seat agricultural aircraft was designed and developed to specifications laid down by the Brazilian Ministry of Agriculture. The EMB-200 prototype first flew on 30 July 1970 and 73 production EMB-200/200As were built. The EMB-201 is a developed version, 188 of which were built between 1974 and 1977. The current version is the EMB-201A, 80 of which had been

EMBRAER EMB-110C Bandeirante.

EMBRAER (Aermacchi) EMB-326GB Xavantes.

EMBRAER

EMBRAER EMB-201 Ipanema.

The Phoenix P.5 Cork, two of which were built during World War I. Phoenix Dynamo Manufacturing Company later became part of English Electric.

EMBRAER EMB-721C Sertanejo.

English Electric P.1A.

EMBRAER EMB-710C Carioca.

built by early 1978 and 24 assembled in Mexico. A glider-towing variant is the EMB-201R (three built for the Brazilian Air Force). A turboprop version of the Ipanema is being studied.

Data (EMB-201A): *Engine* one 224 kW (300 hp) Lycoming IO-540-K1J5D *Wing span* 11.69 m (38 ft 4¼ in) *Length* 7.43 m (24 ft 4½ in) *Max T-O weight* 1,800 kg (3,968 lb) *Max level speed* 230 km/h (143 mph) *Equipment* includes a hopper for 680 litres (149.5 Imp gallons) of liquid or 750 kg (1,653 lb) of dry chemicals

EMBRAER (Aermacchi) EMB-326GB Xavante (Brazil) Licence-built version of the M.B.326GB jet trainer/ground-attack aircraft for the Brazilian Air Force.

EMBRAER-Piper light aircraft programme (Brazil/USA) Piper aircraft built in Brazil by EMBRAER include the EMB-711C Corisco (Piper PA-28R-200 Cherokee Arrow II), EMB-712C Carioquinha (PA-28-181 Cherokee Archer II), EMB-720C Minuano (PA-32-300 Cherokee SIX), EMB-721C Sertanejo (PA-32R-300 Cherokee Lance), EMB-810C Seneca II (PA-34-200T Seneca II) and EMB-820C Navajo (PA-31-350 Navajo Chieftain).

EMBRAER (Piper) EMB-710C Carioca (Brazil) Brazilian licence-built version of the Piper PA-28-235 Cherokee Pathfinder.
Engineering Division USD-9 (USA) Basically a licence-built D.H.9. Only a few built.
Engineering Division B-1A (USA) 223.5 kW (300 hp) Wright-engined development of the Bristol F.2B Fighter. Forty produced after World War I.
English Electric Canberra and Lightning (UK) See **BAC**.

English Electric P.1A (UK) The designation P.1A applied to three research prototypes used in the development of the English Electric Lightning interceptor. The speed of sound was exceeded during the first flight on 4 August 1954. The designation P.1B applied to three operational prototypes.

English Electric Wren (UK) Single-seat ultralight monoplane built to compete in the Lympne light aeroplane trials of October 1923 (see **Chronology** 8 October 1923).

Enstrom Models F-28 and 280 Shark (USA) The F-28 flew for the first time in May 1962 as a three-seat light helicopter. A limited number of production F-28s were built before being superseded by the improved Model F-28A in 1968. Production of the original F-28A version ended in February 1970, although turbocharged and turbine-powered variants had been developed as the F-28B and Model T-28 respectively. In 1971 the Enstrom Helicopter Corporation resumed manufacture of the F-28, having taken over the company from its previous owner the Purex Corporation. The 500th Enstrom helicopter was completed in June 1977. The current versions are the F-28A with a 153 kW (205 hp) Lycoming HIO-360-C1B engine; F-28C with a 153 kW (205 hp) Lycoming HIO-360-E1AD engine with Rajay 301 E-10-2 turbocharger; and F-28F Falcon, a utility version of the F-28C with a 167.7 kW (225 hp) Lycoming engine.

During 1973 an advanced version of the basic F-28A known as the Model 280 Shark was developed. It is generally similar, except for the cabin area, which has improved aerodynamic contours; tail stabilising surfaces that include a small dorsal fin, larger ventral fin with skid, and small fixed horizontal surfaces; and increased fuel capacity. As well as the basic version, the Model 280C is available with a 153 kW (205 hp) Lycoming HIO-360-E1AD engine with Rajay 301 E-10-2 turbocharger.

Latest versions, deliveries of which started in 1979, are the Model 280L Hawk and Model 480 Eagle, four-seat and five-seat helicopters respectively; the latter with an Allison 250-C20B turboshaft engine. Agricultural kits are available for fitment to the F-28C/280C helicopters.

Data (F-28C/280C): *Engine* as above *Main rotor diameter* 9.75 m (32 ft 0 in) *Length* 8.94 m (29 ft 4 in) *Max T-O weight* 998 kg (2,200 lb) *Max cruising speed* 161 km/h (100 mph) *Range* 381 km (237 miles)

Enstrom 280 Shark.

R.E.P. monoplane of 1907.

(Robert) Esnault-Pelterie R.E.P. types (France) R.E.P. tractor monoplanes, usually with their distinctive central fuselage and wingtip-wheel landing gears, appeared from 1908 onwards as single-, two- or three-seaters powered by R.E.P. engines. By 1914 output at the factory was 50 aircraft a year and R.E.P.s were to be found at all major aviation meetings, including that of 22 August 1909 (see **Chronology**).

Etrich Taube (Austria) In November 1909 Igo Etrich made the first flight in Austria in an Austrian-designed and -built aeroplane, at Wiener-Neustadt. It was called the Taube and was a monoplane with bird-like wings. Subsequently produced in refined form as a single- and two-seater, it was built in the greatest numbers as a two-seat military aircraft. By the outbreak of World War I it was in service with the Austro-Hungarian and German air forces. However its

military potential had already been shown when on November 1911 a Taube had carried out the first bombing raid by an aeroplane.

With the outbreak of war in 1914, a Taube piloted by Leutnant von Hiddessen dropped the first bombs to fall on a capital city: five light bombs killed one woman and injured two other persons in Paris on 30 August 1914. From then the Taube was a common raider and flew many missions over England. In Germany it was produced as the Tauben by Rumpler and many other companies, remaining in operational service until 1916.

Data (Rumpler Tauben): *Engine* one 74.5 kW (100 hp) Mercedes D.I. *Wing span* 14.35 m (47 ft 1 in) *Length* 9.85 m (32 ft 4 in) *Max T-O weight* 870 kg (1,918 lb) *Max level speed* 115 km/h (71 mph) *Endurance* 4 h

English Electric Wren.

Etrich Taube.

Evangel 4500-300 (USA) Nine-seat light passenger/cargo STOL transport intended specifically for heavy-duty bush operations. Powered by two 223.5 kW (300 hp) Lycoming IO-540-K1B5 engines. Seven built by 1974.

Evans VP-1 (USA) Single-seat light monoplane, plans for which are available to amateur constructors.

Evans VP-2 (USA) Two-seat development of the VP-1, plans for which are available to amateur constructors.

EWR VJ 101C (Germany) Experimental VTOL aircraft built to provide data for a projected Mach 2 VTOL fighter. Made its first free-hovering flight on 10 April 1963.

Enstrom Model F-28.

Evangel 4500-300.

Evans VP-2.

EWR VJ 101C in hovering flight.

Evans VP-1.

Excalibur Excalibur and Excalibur 800 (USA) Modification of Beechcraft Twin Bonanzas with 283 kW (380 hp) Lycoming IGSO-540-A1A and 298 kW (400 hp) Lycoming IO-720-A1B engines respectively in low-drag nacelles, plus other changes.

Excalibur Queenaire 800 and 8800 (USA) Modification of Queen Air 65 and 80, including installation of two 298 kW (400 hp) Lycoming IO-720-A1B engines.

Explorer PG-1 Aqua Glider (USA) Single-seat homebuilt waterborne glider, plans for which are available to amateur constructors.

Fabre Hydravion (France) First flown on 28 March 1910 for a distance of about 500 m (1,645 ft), the Hydravion was Fabre's first aeroplane to fly (see **Chronology**). It was a tail-first seaplane powered by a 37.25 kW (50 hp) Gnome rotary engine.

Fabrica de Avione SET 7, 7K, 10, XV and 31 (Romania) This important Romanian company built aircraft to the order of the Romanian government. These included the SET 7 two-seat advanced training biplane, specially equipped for wireless and photographic duties (Armstrong Siddeley Jaguar engine); SET 7K two-seat observation derivative of the SET 7 (Gnome-Rhône 7K engine); SET 10 two-seat trainer; SET XV single-seat biplane fighter (Gnome-Rhône 9 Krsd supercharged radial engine, developing 373 kW; 500 hp); and SET 31 two-seat advanced training biplane (Salmson 9Ab radial engine developing 171.4 kW; 230 hp). SET XVs flew alongside licence-built PZL P.11 fighters with the Romanian Army Air Service during the 1930s. A 179 kW (240 hp) Lorraine Mizar-engined SET 31 was flown by Prince Ionel Ghica on his flight from Bucharest to Saigon and back in 1932.

Fábrica Militar de Aviones IA 27 Pulqui and IA 33 Pulqui II (Argentina) The IA 27 was an experimental Rolls-Royce Derwent 5-powered jet fighter, first flown on 9 August 1947. Designed by Emile Dewoitine, it was the first jet aircraft to be designed, built and flown in Latin America. The IA 33 first flew on 27 June 1950 and was the first swept-wing jet fighter of Latin American origin. It was the brainchild of the famous German wartime designer Prof Dipl Ing Kurt Tank.

Fairchild 22 (USA) Tandem two-seat light parasol-wing monoplane powered by a 108 kW (145 hp) Warner Super-Scarab radial engine.

Fairchild 24/Forwarder (USA) The Fairchild 24 first appeared in 1932 as a three-seat commercial cabin monoplane. Refinement of the aircraft continued for several years culminating in 1938 with the four-seat 24J and 24K, powered by 108 kW (145 hp) Warner Super-Scarab and 123 kW (165 hp) Ranger R-690-D3 engines respectively. These were redesignated 24W-9 and 24R-9 in 1939. Meanwhile the US Coast Guard had purchased four examples of an early Ranger-powered version as the J2K in 1936. Because of a shortage of Ranger engines during 1940 and 1941, the 13 GK-1s purchased by the US Navy were powered by 123 kW (165 hp) Warner R-500-7 Super-Scarabs.

The Forwarder was an adaptation of the commercial 24 and was originally produced as a light utility and communications aircraft in 1942 for the RAF as the Argus I, under Lease–Lend. The Argus I (later also adopted by the USAAF as the UC-61) was fitted with a 108 kW (145 hp) Warner R-500-1 Super-Scarab engine. This was followed by the UC-61A (Argus II) with the more powerful 123 kW (165 hp) R-500-7 Super-Scarab.

Early in 1944 the UK-61K appeared for the

USAAF with the 149 kW (200 hp) Ranger L-440-7 inverted engine and was produced from April to November of that year. The sub-types between the UC-61A and K for the USAAF were various commercial models of the 24 bought second-hand for various duties and designated UC-61B (24J with Super-Scarab), UC-61C (24R with Ranger 6-410-B1), UC-61D (Fairchild 51A with Pratt & Whitney R-985), UC-61E (24K with Ranger 6-410-B1), UC-61F (24R with Ranger 6-410-B1), UC-61G (24W with Super-Scarab), UH-61H (24G with Super-Scarab) and UC-61J (24C with Ranger 6-390-D3). A small number of commercial 24R-40s were also given the designation UC-86.

Data (UC-61K): *Engine* as above *Wing span* 11.07 m (36 ft 4 in) *Length* 7.26 m (23 ft 10¼ in) *Max T-O weight* 1,307 kg (2,882 lb) *Max level speed* 200 km/h (124 mph) *Range* (normal) 748 km (465 miles)

Fairchild 24H.

Fairchild PT-19 Cornell.

Fairchild 41 (USA) Four-seat cabin monoplane powered by a 149 kW (200 hp) Wright J-5 Whirlwind radial engine.

Fairchild 42 (USA) Four-seat cabin monoplane powered by a 223.6 kW (300 hp) Wright Whirlwind radial engine.

Fairchild 45 (USA) Five-seat cantilever low-wing cabin monoplane powered by a 238.5 kW (320 hp) Wright R-760 Whirlwind engine. Sold as a commercial aircraft but a few operated by the US Navy as JK-1s during World War II.

Fairchild 51 (USA) see **Fairchild 24**

Fairchild 62/PT-19, PT-23 and PT-26 Cornell (USA) The Fairchild 62 was a tandem two-seat (normally with open cockpits) primary training monoplane, three production versions of which were developed for the USAAF and others. The PT-19 (built by the Fairchild Aircraft Division and the Aeronca Aircraft Corporation) was powered by a 130.4 kW (175 hp) Ranger L-440-1 inverted engine. The PT-23 (built by the Howard Aircraft Corporation and St Louis Aircraft Corporation) was identical in construction to the PT-19B but powered by a 164 kW (220 hp) Continental R-670 radial engine.

The PT-26 was powered by the 149 kW (200 hp) Ranger L-440-7 engine. This version sometimes had sliding cockpit enclosures plus a cabin heater; 12 volt battery (in place of the earlier 24 volt battery); wind-driven generator (in place of the earlier engine-driven type); tubular instead of electrical inter-cockpit communication; landing light in starboard wing; and a blind-flying hood in the rear cockpit (as for PT-19B). As well as serving with the USAAF, it was adopted by the Canadian government as the standard primary trainer for the Commonwealth Air Training Plan and built by Fleet Aircraft in Canada, and was also used by the RAF as the Cornell. Production ceased in 1944 by which time about 7,500 had been completed (see **Fleet Fort**).

Data (PT-26): *Engines* as above *Wing span* 10.97 m (36 ft 0 in) *Length* 8.53 m (27 ft 11⅜ in) *Max T-O weight* 1,243 kg (2,741 lb) *Max level speed* 203 km/h (126 mph) *Range* (normal) 724 km (450 miles)

Fairchild 71 and FC-2 (USA) During 1927–28 Fairchild concentrated production on the FC-2 five-seat high-wing commercial cabin monoplane, powered by a 164 kW (220 hp) Wright Whirlwind engine, and FC-2W with a 317 kW (125 hp) Pratt & Whitney Wasp engine. Both appeared in landplane and seaplane forms. From the FC-2 type Fairchild developed the 71, a seven-seat commercial monoplane that first appeared in 1928–29 powered by a 305.5 kW (410 hp) Pratt & Whitney R-1340-1 Wasp radial engine. A small number of 71s were purchased for Army service (plus a few impressed during World War II) as C-8 photographic and UC-96 transport aircraft. The US Navy also received one landplane. Maximum level speed as a landplane was 222 km/h (138 mph).

Fairchild 78 (USA) see **C-82 Packet and C-119 Flying Boxcar**

Fairchild 22-C7D.

Fairchild PT-26 Cornell.

Fairchild

Fairchild 82, Super-71 and Sekani (Canada)
During 1936 the Fairchild factory in Montreal,
Canada, built 11 Fairchild 82 ten-seat shoulder-
wing commercial transport aircraft (410 kW;
550 hp Pratt & Whitney S3H1 Wasp radial
engine), three going to the government of Venezuela, one to the government of Mexico and the
rest to various Canadian airline operators. Two
other 82s were delivered to the government of
Argentina in 1937. Further orders for the 82 followed. Also during 1936 two Super-71 photographic aircraft were delivered to the Department
of National Defence, Canada (see **Fairchild 71**),
and in the following year the prototype of a twin-
engined general utility monoplane flew for the
first time as the Sekani.

Fairchild A-942 (USA) Ten-seat amphibious
flying-boat of 1936, six of which were ordered by
Pan American Airways. Built in two versions: as
the A-942-A with a 559 kW (750 hp) Pratt &
Whitney S2EG Hornet radial engine and as the
A-942-B with a similarly rated Wright F-52
Cyclone.

Fairchild AT-21 (USA) The AT-21 was
developed from two previous models, the XAT-13
and XAT-14. It was manufactured by Fairchild
and under licence by the Bellanca Aircraft
Corporation and McDonnell Aircraft Corporation as an advanced gunnery crew trainer with
one movable 0.30 in machine-gun in the Plexiglas
nose and two machine-guns in a power-operated
turret aft of the wings. Power was provided by two
387.5 kW (520 hp) Ranger V-770-5 engines. It
was withdrawn from production in 1944 after 175
had been built.

**Fairchild C-82 Packet and C-119 Flying Box-
car** (USA) The original design of the C-82 was
begun in 1941 and the design and mock-up were
approved by the US Army in 1942. The actual
detailed development and engineering, including
the construction and preliminary testing of the
prototype (which flew for the first time on 10
September 1944), took less than 21 months. As
the C-82 Packet twin-engined (1,565 kW;
2,100 hp Pratt & Whitney R-2800s) cargo and
troop transport it was put into production by both
Fairchild and North American Aviation, but at
the end of the war military production was
reduced by 80% and the North American contract cancelled. The C-82 went out of production
in 1948 in favour of the new and improved C-119.

About 220 C-82s were completed for the USAF.
The initial production version of the C-119 was
the C-119B powered by two Pratt & Whitney
R-4360-20 radial engines (rated at 1,975 kW;
2,650 hp at 1,830 m; 6,000 ft). It was followed for
the USAF by the C-119C with 2,608 kW
(3,500 hp) R-4360-20WA engines; C-119F with
similarly rated Wright R-3350-85 Turbo Compound engines and with small lower tailfins
added; and C-119G with R-3350-85 engines, first
flown on 28 October 1952. The last production
C-119 was built in 1955. Production of the C-119
for the USAF and for foreign service under the
Mutual Aid Programme totalled 1,051, excluding
more than 100 R4Q-1s and R4Q-2s (identical to
C-119Cs and C-119Fs) delivered to the US
Marine Corps. Subsequently C-119Bs and
C-119Fs in USAF service were brought up to
C-119C and C-119G standard.

In addition many C-119Gs were later converted into variants such as the AC-119 gunships
and C-119Ks for Ethiopia (with auxiliary turbojet
engines and more powerful piston engines);
C-119F/Gs were converted into C-119Js with
beaver-tail rear doors and ramps; and Indian Air
Force C-119s were converted into C-119 Jet Packs
after the addition of an Orpheus auxiliary turbojet engine in a pod above the centre fuselage to
increase payload and 'hot and high' take-off performance.

Data (C-119K): *Engines* two 2,757 kW (3,700 hp)
Wright R-3350-999 TC18EA2s, plus two
12.68 kN (2,850 lb st) General Electric
J85-GE-17 turbojets *Wing span* 33.3 m (109 ft
3 in) *Length* 26.36 m (86 ft 6 in) *Max T-O weight*
9,070 kg (20,000 lb) *Max level speed* 391 km/h
(243 mph) *Range* 1,595 km (990 miles) *Accommodation* up to 62 troops or freight

Fairchild C-123 Provider (USA) The C-123
troop and cargo transport was designed by the
original Chase Aircraft Company. A production
order for 300 C-123Bs, held by the Kaiser-Frazer

Corporation (which had acquired a majority interest in the Chase company in 1953), was cancelled in June 1953. New bids were asked for, as a result of which production of the C-123B was assigned to Fairchild. The first Fairchild-built C-123B flew on 1 September 1954 and production aircraft entered service with the USAF's 309th Troop Carrier Group in July 1955. Orders totalling more than 300 aircraft were completed by mid-1958, six going to Saudi Arabia and 18 to Venezuela.

In 1955 the prototype C-123B was fitted experimentally with two Fairchild J44 turbojet engines mounted at the wingtips to provide auxiliary power for use in an emergency. As a result ten production aircraft were modified into C-123Js with turbojet engines fitted. Meanwhile a small number of C-123Hs had been produced with wide-track landing gears.

The prototype YC-123H was later experimentally fitted with CJ610 auxiliary turbojet engines and flown on 30 July 1962. Having been tested in South Vietnam as a counter-insurgency aircraft, 183 more C-123Bs were given 12.68 kN (2,850 lb st) General Electric J85-GE-17 auxiliary turbojet engines in underwing pods and designated C-123Ks. Some were further converted to AC-123K 'Spectre' gunships for service during the Vietnam conflict.
Data (C-123K): *Engines* two 1,715 kW (2,300 hp) Pratt & Whitney R-2800-99W radials, plus turbojet engines as noted above *Wing span* 33.53 m (110 ft 0 in) *Length* 23.92 m (76 ft 3 in) *Max T-O weight* 27,215 kg (60,000 lb) *Max level*

speed 367 km/h (228 mph) *Range* 1,666 km (1,035 miles) *Accommodation* up to 61 troops, 50 stretchers and six sitting casualties (plus six attendants), or 6,800 kg (15,000 lb) of freight

Fairchild F-11 Husky (Canada) The Husky was designed as a replacement for the Fairchild 71 and 82 transports which were used extensively for bush-flying in Canada. Although a float, wheel or ski landing gear could be fitted, it was intended primarily as a seaplane with accommodation for six or seven passengers or freight. The prototype first flew from the St Lawrence river near Montreal in June 1946.

Fairchild KR-21 and KR-34 (USA) The KR-21 was a two-seat training biplane, formerly known as the Kreider-Reisner Challenger C-6 prior to the Fairchild Company taking over the Kreider-Reisner Aircraft Company in 1929. The KR-34 three-seat commercial biplane was formerly known as the Challenger C-4.

Fairchild T-31/XNQ-1 (USA) Evaluated by the US Navy and USAF in 1947 as the XNQ-1 and T-31 respectively, this two-seat primary/basic trainer was ordered for both services but was not produced.

Fairchild VZ-5FA (USA) Experimental VTOL aircraft first flown on 18 November 1959.

Fairchild XC-120 Pack-Plane (USA) Experimental prototype detachable-fuselage transport aircraft, first flown on 11 August 1950.

Fairchild Industries F-27 and F-227 (USA) Licence-built versions of the Fokker F.27, of which Fairchild Industries sold 205.

Fairchild Industries (Hiller) FH-1100 (USA) The FH-1100 is a refined development of the OH-5A helicopter which Hiller designed for the US Army's LOH (Light Observation Helicopter)

Troops inside a Fairchild C-119 Flying Boxcar.

Fairchild C-82 Packet.

Fairchild C-119 Flying Boxcar.

Fairchild C-123J Provider.

Fairchild Industries

competition. The prototype OH-5A flew for the first time on 26 January 1963, but the competition was won by Hughes.

The decision to put the FH-1100 into production was announced in February 1965 and the first production helicopter was rolled out in June 1966. About 250 were built for civil and military operation, with normal accommodation for five persons, or the pilot and two stretchers. Military versions have provision for ASW weapons, two weapon packs each containing two 7.62 mm machine-guns or two grenade launchers.

Data: *Engine* one 236.5 kW (317 hp) Allison 250-C18 turboshaft (derated to 174 kW; 233 shp) *Main rotor diameter* 10.79 m (35 ft 4¾ in) *Length of fuselage* 9.08 m (29 ft 9½ in) *Max T-O weight* 1,247 kg (2,750 lb) *Max cruising speed* 204 km/h (127 mph) *Range* 560 km (348 miles)

Fairchild Industries (Pilatus) Porter and Peacemaker (USA) Under licence from Pilatus, Fairchild Industries produced the Porter STOL utility aircraft, the first of which was rolled out on 3 June 1966. Power was provided by a 507 kW (680 shp) Pratt & Whitney Aircraft of Canada PT6A-27 turboprop engine, flat rated to 410 kW (550 shp). A militarised version of the Porter, known as the Peacemaker, was developed for counter-insurgency operations, including transport, light-armed and photographic reconnaissance, leaflet dropping and loudspeaker broadcasting. This version has an underfuselage

hardpoint capable of carrying a 272 kg (600 lb) store, and four underwing hardpoints for up to 636 kg (1,400 lb) of stores.

Fairchild Republic A-10A Thunderbolt II (USA) The first prototype of this single-seat close-support aircraft flew on 10 May 1972. Following evaluation by the USAF against the Northrop A-9A, it was selected for production. An initial order for 22 A-10As, placed in 1974, was followed by further orders. By April 1979 200 had been delivered. All 739 Thunderbolt IIs for the USAF are expected to be delivered by January 1983.

The first operational A-10A wing was the 354th Tactical Fighter Wing, based at Myrtle Beach, South Carolina, deliveries to which began in March 1977. In early 1978 it began to operate A-10As equipped with the Martin Marietta AN/AAS-35 Pave Penny laser target-designation pod, now approved as a standard fit for the aircraft. In August 1977 six A-10As flew to Europe for the first live firing of the aircraft's 30 mm Gatling gun and the anti-armour Maverick air-to-ground missile in the NATO theatre, expending 7.5 tons of conventional 500 lb bombs and 9,000 rounds of 30 mm ammunition during 117 close-support sorties.

Beginning in September 1977 A-10As joined Army Cobra helicopters in California to participate in the Joint Attack Weapon System (JAWS) exercises, designed to develop and evaluate tactical co-ordination between the two types of aircraft. During the exercises the A-10As and helicopters attacked simulated aggressor columns of tanks, armoured personnel carriers and missile launchers supported by artillery and aircraft; evaluations were made of tactics, pilot stress and camouflage effectiveness.

An announcement of the first overseas deployment of the A-10A was made in January 1978. The 81st Tactical Fighter Wing at RAF stations Bentwaters and Woodbridge in the UK received A-10As in early 1979. The Wing (consisting of six squadrons, each of 18 A-10As) will rotate aircraft

in four forward-operating locations in Germany, permitting aircrews and maintenance personnel to receive maximum training in central Europe. Data: *Engines* two 40.3 kN (9,065 lb st) General Electric TF34-GE-100 high-bypass-ratio turbofans *Wing span* 17.53 m (57 ft 6 in) *Length* 16.26 m (53 ft 4 in) *Max T-O weight* 21,500 kg (47,400 lb) *Max combat speed* 722 km/h (449 mph) *Operational radius* 1,000 km (620 miles) *Armament* General Electric GAU-8/A Avenger 30 mm seven-barrel cannon mounted in the nose; plus up to 7,257 kg (16,000 lb) of external stores on eight underwing and three underfuselage pylons: including 28 × 500 lb Mk-82 LDGP or Mk-82 retarded bombs, six 2,000 lb Mk-84 general-purpose bombs, incendiary bombs, 20 Rockeye II cluster bombs, ten AGM-65A Maverick missiles, laser-guided and electro-optically-guided bombs, guns, jammer pods or drop tanks

Fairey IIIA (UK) Fifty two-seat IIIA reconnaissance biplanes built for the RNAS during World War I, each powered by a 186.3 kW (250 hp) Sunbeam Maori II engine. Fourteen built with wheel-type landing gear, the rest with skids (see **Fairey IIID**).

Fairey IIIB (UK) Basically an unequal-span seaplane version of the IIIA, 24 of which were built for the RNAS as patrol bombers (see **Fairey IIID**).

Fairey IIIC (UK) Six of the original order for IIIBs and all of the second batch of IIIBs intended for the RNAS built as IIIC seaplanes for the 1919 North Russian Expedition, combining features of the IIIA and B and powered by the 279.4 kW (375 hp) Rolls-Royce Eagle VIII engine (see below).

Fairey IIID (UK) One of the criticisms of early Fairey aircraft was aimed at their appearance, for they were frequently regarded as being numbered among the most ugly aeroplanes in the air. It was an unkind attitude in an age when it was difficult to attain the sort of performance required by a general-purpose aircraft: one which might be expected to operate from and to a ship at sea, in addition to more conventional use as a landplane or seaplane.

Fairey's IIID, first flown in prototype form in August 1920, derived from the company's F.128 experimental floatplane of 1917. This introduced the Fairey Patent Camber Gear evolved for the Hamble Baby, which was then described as a trailing-edge flap and used to increase the lift of the wings. Today we would regard these aerofoil control surfaces as drooped ailerons, for they were used as ailerons in flight, but could be drooped symmetrically to enhance the lift developed by the normal wing surface. Tested as a two-seat seaplane, the F.128 was known as the Fairey III. With a single frontal radiator behind the propeller and the floats replaced by a wheel landing gear, the designation became Fairey IIIA.

In modified form the designation became Fairey IIIB. These had float landing gear, increased wing area, and ailerons on the upper wing in addition to the Patent Camber Gear on the lower. The IIIC which followed had a performance increase of some 14%, almost entirely due to the installation of a Rolls-Royce Eagle VIII engine. It was regarded as one of the best seaplanes of its day, but it entered service too late to be involved in World War I.

The Fairey IIID benefited from considerable experience with Fairey IIIs in both RFC and RNAS use. The prototype retained the Eagle VIII engine, but of the 207 built for service with the RAF and Fleet Air Arm, 152 were powered by Napier Lion IIB, V or VA engines. A large-span

Fairchild AU-23A Peacemaker.

Full-size mock-up of the Fairchild Republic A-10A's GAU-8/A Avenger cannon.

Fairchild Republic A-10A Thunderbolt II.

Fairey IIIA.

Fairey

Fairey IIIB.

Fairey IIIF.

Fairey IIID used on the Cairo—Cape Town—Cairo flight.

two-bay biplane with constant-chord wings, the IIID was operated as a landplane from shore stations and aircraft carriers, or as a seaplane for catapult launch from warships. In fact, on 30 October 1925, a IIID became the first standard FAA seaplane to be catapulted from a ship at sea.

In landplane form, the IIID was one of the first service aircraft to have oleo-pneumatic (oil/air) shock-absorbers. It was used to record the RAF's first flight from England to South Africa and its first official long-distance formation flight. Led by Wg Cdr C. W. H. Pulford, between 1 March and 21 June 1926 IIIDs completed a flight of almost 22,530 km (14,000 miles), Cairo–Cape Town–Cairo and thence to Lee-on-Solent. At no time throughout the period of almost four months was any delay caused by mechanical failure of any of the aircraft, speaking volumes for the soundness of the basic design of both airframe and engine (see **Chronology** 13 March 1922).
Data: *Engine* one 335.3 kW (450 hp) Napier Lion or 279.4 kW (375 hp) Rolls-Royce Eagle VIII *Wing span* 14.05 m (46 ft 1¼ in) *Length* (land-plane) 10.97 m (36 ft 0 in), (seaplane) 11.28 m (37 ft 0 in) *Max T-O weight* (landplane with Lion engine) 2,290 kg (5,050 lb) *Max level speed* (Eagle engine) 171 km/h (106 mph), (Lion engine) 193 km/h (120 mph) *Range* 885 km (550 miles) *Armament* one forward-firing Vickers gun and one rear-mounted Lewis gun

Fairey IIIF (UK) The success of the Fairey IIID, especially in naval service, encouraged Fairey Aviation in 1925 to begin the development of an improved model. While retaining a very similar two-bay biplane wing and a Napier Lion engine, the fuselage was much more streamlined, the tail unit changed considerably, and the landing gear

much refined by comparison with that of the IIID. First flown on 19 March 1926, the prototype was of three-seat configuration as required for service with the FAA, which was to receive a total of 352 by the time the last one was delivered in September 1932.

Fairey IIIFs for the FAA carried a pilot, observer and wireless operator/gunner. Major change to naval IIIFs was from composite construction in the Mk I and II versions, to an all-metal fabric-covered structure for the Mk III. As neat twin-float seaplanes, IIIFs were catapult-launched for reconnaissance missions from capital ships and cruisers, and the wheeled landing gear versions were to serve on board every British aircraft carrier between 1928 and 1936. A familiar sight at British naval air stations across the world, they were finally declared obsolete in January 1940. Three special IIIFs with increased wing dihedral and automatic pilots, intended as gunnery targets, were known as Fairey Queens.

A total of 215 IIIF Mk IV aircraft served with the RAF between 1927 and 1933 as general-purpose machines, including the role of day bomber with up to 227 kg (500 lb) of bombs carried on underwing racks. The reliability experienced with the IIID encouraged the use of this superior aircraft for a series of long-range flights, led by such well-known personalities as Air Cdre C. R. Sampson, Wing Cdr A. T. Harris and Sqdn Ldr R. S. Sorley. Built in a two-seat configuration for the RAF, they (like those for the FAA) were initially of composite and finally of all-metal construction with fabric covering.
Data: *Engine* one 425 kW (570 hp) Napier Lion XIA *Wing span* (Mk III) 13.96 m (45 ft 9½ in) *Length* (Mk III landplane) 10.36 m (34 ft 0 in), (Mk III seaplane) 11.07 m (36 ft 4 in), (Mk IV) 11.19 m (36 ft 8⅝ in) *Max T-O weight* (Mk III) 2,857 kg (6,300 lb), (Mk IV) 2,740 kg (6,040 lb) *Max level speed* 193 km/h (120 mph) *Max range* (Mk IV) 2,445 km (1,520 miles) *Armament* one forward-firing Vickers machine-gun and one rear-mounted Lewis gun, plus up to 227 kg (500 lb) bombs

Fairey Albacore (UK) The Albacore torpedo-bombing biplane was first flown in prototype form on 12 December 1938. During the spring of 1940 the first production aircraft entered FAA service and for the remainder of that year were flown mainly on coastal patrol, spotter-reconnaissance, minelaying and night-bombing duties. However in the following year Albacores went to sea in HMS *Formidable* and other carriers and from then were active on convoy protection duties in the Baltic and in anti-submarine and other roles in the Mediterranean and elsewhere.

The Albacore was removed from FAA service in late 1943, having never performed its intended role as a Swordfish replacement. It had a more powerful 794 kW (1,065 hp) Bristol Taurus or 842 kW (1,130 hp) Taurus XII 14-cylinder sleeve-valve air-cooled radial engine in the NACA cowling with leading-edge exhaust collector and trailing-edge controllable gills, enclosed cockpits for the crew of two or three, one forward-firing 0.303 in Browning and two rear-mounted 0.303 in Vickers guns on a Fairey high-speed mounting, and hydraulically operated flaps.

The entry in the 1943 *Jane's* sums up the service record of the two types: 'The Albacore is operating both a;oat and ashore. Several land-based Fleet Air Arm squadrons played a brilliant part in the initial stages of the North African campaign and, more recently, other squadrons operating from the British Isles have taken part in night operations against enemy shipping in the English Channel. The Swordfish has a brilliant record during four years of war. It is still in production and performing a multiplicity of duties.'

The last Albacores in operational service were those ex-FAA aircraft taken over by the RCAF and used during the Allied advance into Europe from mid-1944. Production totalled 803 aircraft. Data: *Engine* as above *Wing span* 15.24 m (50 ft 0 in) *Length* (landplane) 12.14 m (39 ft 10 in), (seaplane) 12.91 m (42 ft 5½ in) *Max T-O weight* 4,749 kg (10,460 lb) *Max level speed* 259 km/h (161 mph) *Range* 1,496 km (930 miles) *Armament* machine-guns as above, plus one 1,610 lb torpedo or 908 kg (2,000 lb) of bombs *Accommodation* pilot and gunner as torpedo bomber; pilot, observer and telegraphist/air-gunner as spotter-reconnaissance aircraft

Fairey Barracuda I.

Fairey Barracuda (UK) The Barracuda was the first monoplane torpedo bomber to go into service with the FAA. The original S.24/37 was designed round the Rolls-Royce Exe 24-cylinder X-type engine. Early in the construction stage the power plant was changed to the Rolls-Royce Merlin 30, an engine with many entirely different characteristics. The delay this caused was responsible for retarding the initial production programme. The Merlin-engined prototype first flew on 7 December 1940.

The first prototype Barracuda had an unbraced tailplane in line with the top of the fuselage. During the early trials it was found that when the flaps were in the diving position the disturbed air caused serious tail flutter. To overcome this the tailplane of the second prototype was raised some 1.22 m (4 ft) to clear the wake from the flaps and also to clear the folding wings. The first trials with the repositioned tail unit were made in July 1941 and showed that the trouble had been entirely eliminated.

Fairey Barracuda IIIs.

The Barracuda was first used operationally in September 1941 in raids from HMS *Victorious* on Kirkenes in northern Norway and on Petsamo in Finland. In 1942 Barracudas took part in sweeps over French ports and in the invasion of Madagascar. The first major action in which Barracuda squadrons took part was the successful bombing attack on the German battleship *Tirpitz*

Fairey Albacores.

Fairey

Fairey Battle trainer.

in Alten Fiord, north Norway on 3 April 1944. It was in action against the Japanese for the first time in an attack on enemy installations at Sabang, on the island of Sumatra on 19 April 1944.

Production of the Barracuda ended in 1946, by which time more than 2,500 had been built: as the Barracuda I with a Merlin 30 engine; Barracuda II with a 1,222 kW (1,640 hp) Merlin 32 engine; Barracuda III, similar to the Mk II but with ASV 10 radar equipment in a bulge under the fuselage; and Barracuda V (first flown in June 1945) with a Rolls-Royce Griffon VII engine driving a Rotol four-bladed propeller, increased wing span, larger rudder and fin, generally strengthened structure, no rear armament but one 12.7 mm forward-firing machine-gun.

Data (Barracuda II): *Engine* as above *Wing span* 14.97 m (49 ft 2 in) *Length* 12.34 m (40 ft 6 in) *Max T-O weight* 6,577 kg (14,500 lb) *Max level speed* 367 km/h (228 mph) *Range* 802–1,104 km (500–686 miles) *Armament* two rear-mounted 0.303 in Vickers K machine-guns, plus an 18 in torpedo or up to 680 kg (1,500 lb) of bombs, depth charges, mines or rescue equipment

Fairey Battle.

Fairey Campania.

Fairey Battle (UK) Best remembered as the first RAF aircraft to shoot down a German aircraft during World War II: the rear gunner of a Battle of No 88 Squadron Advanced Air Striking Force shot down a Messerschmitt Bf 109E over France on 20 September 1939. The prototype of this light bomber flew for the first time on 10 March 1936. The Battle was a cantilever low-wing monoplane with a retractable undercarriage, enclosed cockpits for the crew of three and powered by the Rolls-Royce Merlin engine.

It was certainly a major advance over the old Hawker Hart and Hind open-cockpit biplanes it was to replace and was selected as one of the types to be mass-produced for many of the new squadrons forming under the RAF expansion programme of the latter 1930s. Unfortunately advances in aircraft design in the immediate years prior to World War II made the Battle slow and vulnerable, especially as it became clear that the bomber could not hope to outrun even the most mediocre of modern fighters.

Its defensive armament of one forward-firing 0.303 in Browning and one rear-mounted 0.303 in Vickers K was also far from adequate. Nevertheless the RAF was committed to the Battle and by 1938 it had 13 squadrons. With the outbreak of war ten squadrons were sent to

France. The Battle's up-hill task against superior German forces was tackled vigorously and indeed the first VCs won by the RAF during this war were awarded to Battle crews for their actions on 12 May 1940 during an attack on the Maastricht bridges. But the bomber was obsolete and within a short time was withdrawn from operational service, subsequently becoming a trainer and target tug in the UK and in Canada under the Commonwealth Air Training Plan. The type also served with the air forces of Australia, Belgium, South Africa and Turkey. Production totalled more than 2,400 aircraft, many built by Austin Motors.

Interestingly one Battle was fitted with the Fairey P.24 engine and Fairey electrically operated contra-rotating constant-speed propellers – the first propellers of this type to be flight tested in the UK. Between 13 June 1939 and 5 December 1941, the aircraft accumulated about 86 flying hours at the hands of Flt Lieut Christopher Staniland, Mr F. H. Dixon (the company's subsequent chief test pilot) and a number of RAF pilots. It was then shipped to the USA.

Data: *Engine* one 767.5 kW (1,030 hp) Rolls-Royce Merlin I, II, III or V *Wing span* 16.46 m (54 ft 0 in) *Length* 12.9 m (42 ft 4 in) *Max T-O weight* 4,895 kg (10,790 lb) *Max level speed* 388 km/h (241 mph) *Range* 1,690 km (1,050 miles) *Armament* machine-guns as above, plus up to 454 kg (1,000 lb) of bombs

Fairey Campania (UK) The Fairey Campania two-seat seaplane got its name from the ex-Cunard ocean liner *Campania* which the Admiralty had converted into a seaplane carrier during the winter of 1914–15. Production aircraft, powered by a 186.3 kW (250 hp) Sunbeam Maori II or 186.3–257 kW (250–345 hp) Rolls-Royce Eagle engine, entered service in 1917 and eventually operated as armed-reconnaissance aircraft from the carriers *Campania*, *Nairana* and *Pegasus*

EMBRAER EMB-110
Bandeirante.

EMBRAER EMB-201
Ipanema.

Fairchild Industries
F-227.

Fairey Firefly AS.6.

Farman M.F.11
Shorthorn.

Fiat C.R.42.

Fiat G.46.

Fieseler Fi 156 Storch.

Replica Fokker Dr.I.

Gates Learjet 25B.

and from coastal bases until the Armistice, there-after also seeing action in Russia.

A total of about 60 Campanias were built from the contracts placed with Fairey (for 50 aircraft in two batches), Barclay Curle and Company (for 50) and Frederick Sage and Company/Sunbeam Motor Car Company (for 70). Maximum speed was 137 km/h (85 mph).

Fairey F.D.1 (UK) Delta-wing research aircraft powered by a Rolls-Royce Derwent 8 engine and first flown on 12 March 1951.

Fairey Pintail.

Fairey Delta 2 (UK) The Delta 2 was built to investigate the characteristics of flight and control at transonic and supersonic speeds. Two examples were built powered by a Rolls-Royce Avon RA.5 or RA.28 afterburning turbojet engine of 53.4 kN (12,000 lb st) and 57.8 kN (13,000 lb st) respectively. The first made its maiden flight on 6 October 1954. On 10 March 1956 the RA.5-powered aircraft (flown by Peter Twiss) became the first aircraft to set an over-1,000 mph world speed record, with an average of two flights of 1,821 km/h (1,132 mph). The first aircraft was eventually converted into the BAC 221.

Fairey Fawn (UK) Developed from the Pintail, the Fawn was a light bomber and reconnaissance aircraft designed to fill the gap between the de Havilland D.H.9A and Hawker Horsley/Fairey Fox. First flown in prototype form in March 1923, subsequent production Fawns had poor performance and, unlike their Virginia heavy-bomber contemporary, remained in service with the RAF for only a few years. Production amounted to 75 aircraft, made up of five prototype/pre-production aircraft, 50 350 kW (470 hp) Napier Lion II-engined Fawn Mk IIs and 20 Lion V-engined Mk IIIs.

Data (Fawn Mk II): *Engine* as above *Wing span* 15.21 m (49 ft 11 in) *Length* 9.78 m (32 ft 1 in) *Max T-O weight* 2,646 kg (5,835 lb) *Max level speed* 183 km/h (114 mph) *Range* 1,046 km (650 miles) *Armament* one forward-firing Vickers and one rear-mounted Lewis machine-gun, plus up to 209 kg (460 lb) of bombs

Fairey Firefly (UK) The Firefly – which in its prototype form first flew on 22 December 1941 – was produced until the mid-1950s although most of the earlier operational versions remained in use with the Royal Navy, Royal Australian Navy and Royal Netherlands Navy. Reconditioned Firefly 1s were also supplied to the air forces of Ethiopia and Siam during this period; while Firefly target tugs served in Sweden and Denmark.

The Firefly 1 was powered by a 1,483 kW (1,990 hp) Rolls-Royce Griffon 2 or 12 engine driving a Rotol three-bladed propeller. The F.1 was the early two-seat day fighter and was fol-lowed by the FR.1 and 1A standard reconnais-sance fighters (with search radar in a radome under the nose of the fuselage) and the NF.1 night fighter. Each was armed with two 20 mm cannon in each wing. The Firefly T.1 was basically an F.1 converted for use as a deck-landing conversion and instrument-flying trainer. The raised rear cockpit was occupied by the instructor. They were usually unarmed, although a few carried two 20 mm cannon.

The Firefly TT.1 was fitted for towing a glider, banner or sleeve target for ground-to-air or air-to-air firing practice. The Firefly T.2 was an armaments trainer, similar to the T.1 with two 20 mm cannon and provision for carrying bombs, rockets and long-range drop tanks. The Griffon 12-powered Firefly T.3 was a version of the FR.1 intended specifically to train observers, the rear cockpit being equipped with the fullest possible range of radio and radar equipment. The Firefly FR.4 (first flown on 25 May 1945) was powered

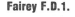

Fairey F.D.1.

Fairey Delta 2.

Fairey

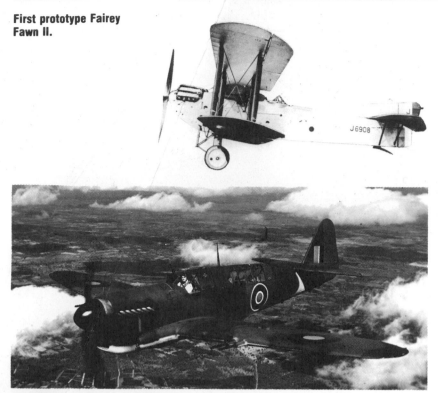

First prototype Fairey Fawn II.

Fairey Firefly F.1.

Fairey Firefly FR.4.

by a Griffon 74 engine driving a Rotol four-bladed propeller and had radiators moved from beneath the nose to leading-edge extensions of the centre-section. The wings were reduced in span and given square tips and the area of the tailfin was increased. Armament was the same as for the Firefly 1 but could also carry two 1,000 lb bombs, 16 × 60 lb rockets or eight heavier rockets, or long-range fuel tanks. A modified version for target-towing was the TT.4.

The similarly powered Firefly 5 was produced in three forms, as the NF, FR and AS, all similar externally to the 4. The FR.5 carried the same radar in the starboard wing nacelle as the 4 and was equipped with beam approach, IFF and communications radio. The NF.5 had the same basic radio plus a radio altimeter and other night-flying equipment. The AS.5 was an anti-submarine version and carried special submarine-detection equipment under the wings and fuselage. The Firefly AS.6 was another anti-submarine aircraft, structurally similar to the 5 but with different operational equipment and no defensive armament.

The Firefly 7 of 1953 was produced in two forms, as the AS and T, although it was used mainly as an anti-submarine training aircraft. Powered by a Griffon engine with a 'chin' radiator, the three-seat anti-submarine aircraft carried the latest detection devices and sonobuoys for tracking a target at sea. A new blister-enclosed rear cockpit accommodated two radar operators and the aircraft had elliptical wings without wing radiators and a new tail unit. The final Firefly variant was the U.8/U.9, designed as new or conversions of earlier aircraft to help with the development of guided missiles and equipped to be used as radio-controlled photographic drones.

Firefly fighters and reconnaissance fighters first went into operational service in late 1943 and were mainly used in the Pacific theatre of war against Japanese forces and targets. Successes on the Western Front included a reconnaissance over the German battleship *Tirpitz* which resulted in the bombing attack by Vought Corsairs and Barracudas on 3 April 1944. Post-war, Fireflies saw action in Korea, flying vast numbers of sorties from British and Australian aircraft carriers, and later in Malaya; finally going out of service in 1956. Firefly production totalled more than 1,700 aircraft of all variants.

Data (Firefly 5): *Engine* one 1,677 kW (2,250 hp) Rolls-Royce Griffon 74 *Wing span* 12.55 m (41 ft 2 in) *Length* 11.56 m (37 ft 11 in) *Max T-O weight* 7,301 kg (16,096 lb) *Max level speed* 618 km/h (386 mph) *Range* 2,090 km (1,300 miles)

Fairey Flycatcher (UK) Built to Air Ministry Specification 6/22, the prototype of what became named the Fairey Flycatcher made its first flight during 1922. A single-seat fighter for first-line service aboard aircraft carriers, it could have interchangeable wheeled, float, or combined wheel/float amphibious landing gear. In this latter form, the ground-contact tread of each wheel was only inches below the undersurface of the float, causing many raised eyebrows as, apparently, a floatplane was to be seen taking off from a grass airfield. Construction was composite with wooden fabric-covered wings and a fuselage of wood and metal with fabric covering.

Some of the nicest people are eccentrics: the Flycatcher seemed to belong in this category, following what appeared to be normal Fairey practice of sacrificing good looks for good performance. The result was an aeroplane which only its designer, or its pilot, could love. Single-bay biplane wings, well-staggered, with pronounced dihedral on the upper wing and a fuselage which appeared to curve upwards to the tail unit, gave the impression that a giant had used this little fighter as a seat. When seen in profile in flight it looked distinctly odd.

But these quirks of configuration (plus Fairey's Patent Camber Gear) provided an aeroplane that was easy to fly, even at low speeds, and yet one which was highly manoeuvrable. No wonder that pilots were enthusiastic about it. Flycatchers remained in service from 1923 until declared

Siddeley Jaguar III or IV *Wing span* 8.84 m (29 ft 0 in) *Length* (landplane) 7.01 m (23 ft 0 in) *T-O weight* (landplane) 1,351 kg (2,979 lb) *level speed* (landplane) 214 km/h (133 mph) *range* (landplane) 500 km (311 miles) *Arman* two Vickers machine-guns; provision for four 20 lb underwing bombs

Fairey Firefly AS.7.

Fairey Fox IA.

obsolete in 1935, during which period 192 were built. Like their contemporary Fairey IIIF, they had the distinction of serving on board all British aircraft carriers of that period. In addition, harking back to World War I procedure, they operated as landplane fighters from a short take-off platform mounted above the gun turrets of capital ships. Their trailing-edge flaps and drooped ailerons provided a steep path of descent which was ideal for carrier landing. One Flycatcher was fitted experimentally with hydraulic brakes which permitted a very short landing run. This was the first FAA aircraft to have such brakes, but they did not then become standard equipment.

Once on deck, they did not have the benefit of folding wings to simplify shipboard stowage. Instead they were designed to be dismantled easily into sections which did not exceed 4.11 m (13 ft 6 in) in length. The training, skill and enthusiasm of deck handling crews made possible such feats as a record of six aircraft landed and stowed in their hangars in only 4 minutes 20 seconds. Landing, of course, was carried out on the main deck. But these little fighters (housed in a forward hangar) could take off from a special tapered runway, only 18.3 m (60 ft) in length, leading directly from their hangar and out over the bows.

Undoubtedly the Flycatcher made an important contribution to the best traditions and practice of naval flying.

Data: *Engine* one 298 kW (400 hp) Armstrong

Fairey Fox (UK) Potentially one of the most exciting aircraft to serve with the RAF in the 1920s, the idea for this high-performance two-seat day bomber almost certainly came to C. R. Fairey (later Sir Richard) in 1923. In that year the Schneider Trophy Contest at Cowes, Isle of Wight was won by an American Curtiss CR-3 racing seaplane at a speed of 285 km/h (177.38 mph), piloted by Lieut David Rittenhouse. Close behind was a second CR-3 flown by Lieut Rutledge Irvine with a speed of 279.16 km/h (173.46 mph). The only other aircraft to complete the 344.69 km (214.18 mile) course was Britain's Supermarine Sea Lion III, powered by a Napier Lion engine which was almost 19% more powerful than the Curtiss D-12 carrying the CR-3 to victory.

Richard Fairey realised that the Curtiss engine, in combination with a Curtiss-Reed propeller, was a most significant factor in this American success. The engine itself was revolutionary: the world's first wet-sleeve monobloc aero-engine; in addition it was of abnormally small frontal area, which meant that a neat streamlined fuselage could be tailored to conform. It took somebody like Fairey to appreciate how important the propeller was to the success of the enterprise. Of comparatively small diameter with forged duralumin blades of thin aerofoil section, it could be rotated at high speed – the blade tips approaching the speed of sound – without any serious loss of efficiency. So fast was the rotational speed that there was no need to interpose an energy-stealing reduction gear between engine and propeller. No reduction gear, small-diameter lightweight propeller blades and (resulting from this latter factor) a shorter landing gear, all produced weight savings that were vitally important to a high-performance aircraft.

Fairey was soon busy negotiating for the licence rights to import and/or build this power plant in Britain, and acquired in short time an engine and propeller for the development of a fast day

Fairey Flycatchers.

Fairey

Fairey Gannet AEW.3.

bomber for the RAF. A prototype was built as a private venture, of single-bay biplane configuration with unequal-span staggered wings. Landing gear, tail unit and fuselage were all typical of Fairey design of that era; the fuselage, of course, was much slimmer than usual. Notable were the considerable efforts made to produce a structure as free from drag as then possible. Even the mounting for the gunner's defensive Lewis gun was of Fairey design, to eliminate the drag induced by the normal Scarff ring.

The prototype was first flown on 3 January 1925. By the time that development was finished, the company was aware that it had produced an aircraft which was aptly named Fox: well able to lead the field and even to make circles round them. Demonstrated in October of that year to Air Chief Marshal Sir Hugh Trenchard, its performance was so impressive that a complete squadron of aircraft was ordered into production. Strict budgets of that time (which became tighter as the 1930s approached) limited procurement to 28 aircraft. When issued to No 12 Squadron (in August 1926) they proved to be some 80 km/h (50 mph) faster than the Fairey Fawns which they superseded, and were able to show an embarrassingly clean pair of heels to any contemporary fighter. At a later period some of these aircraft were re-engined with the Rolls-Royce Kestrel and redesignated Fox IAs, remaining operational until 1931.
Data: *Engine* one 357.7 kW (480 hp) Curtiss D-12 *Wing span* 11.58 m (38 ft 0 in) *Length* 9.5 m (31 ft 2 in) *Max T-O weight* 1,867 kg (4,117 lb) *Max level speed* 251 km/h (156 mph) *Range* 805 km (500 miles) *Armament* one Vickers and one Lewis machine-gun, plus up to 209 kg (460 lb) of bombs

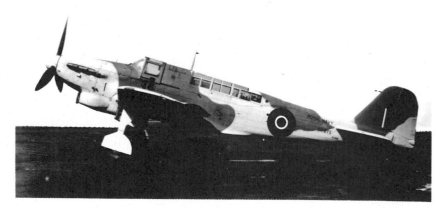

Fairey Fulmar II.

Fairey Fulmar (UK) The Fulmar was a two-seat Fleet fighter armed with eight 0.303 in Browning machine-guns, four in each wing. It was unusual for a two-seater in having no rear-mounted gun for the observer/radio operator. The prototype flew for the first time on 4 January 1940 and by the latter part of the same year early production Mk Is were firmly in action. A total of 250 853 kW (1,145 hp) Rolls-Royce Merlin VIII-powered Mk Is were built, followed by 350 969 kW (1,300 hp) Merlin 30-powered Mk IIs. During its career, which lasted until the end of the war, it performed many roles including those of escort fighter, convoy protection and reconnaissance,

Fairey Gordon II in the Sudan.

but with the introduction of the faster Supermarine Spitfire its main carrier-borne day-fighter role was substituted for the less demanding night-fighter role.
Data (Mk I): *Engine* as above *Wing span* 14.14 m (46 ft 4½ in) *Length* 12.27 m (40 ft 3 in) *Max T-O weight* 4,445 kg (9,800 lb) *Max level speed* 450 km/h (280 mph) *Range* 1,288 km (800 miles)
Fairey Gannet (UK) Built to the requirements of a carrier-based anti-submarine warfare (ASW) aircraft, Fairey's prototype was known initially as the Type Q. It flew for the first time on 19 September 1949. This and the second prototype were of two-seat configuration, but the third prototype (which first flew on 10 May 1951) was more representative of production aircraft with three cockpits to accommodate the pilot (forward), observer/navigator (centre), and radio-radar operator (aft). Of all-metal stressed-skin construction, this large mid-wing monoplane had mechanically folding wings to facilitate carrier stowage.

Aptly named Gannet, for its deep fuselage was able to swallow and carry all its major strike weapons internally, this was very much a 'first and last' aircraft. An outstanding feature was its Armstrong Siddeley Double Mamba turboprop engine, comprising two turbine engines with individual co-axial contra-rotating propellers; it was the first aircraft in the world to fly with such a power plant. Either engine could be shut down independently and its propeller feathered so that the aircraft could cruise economically on patrol. When power was needed for take-off and combat, both engines were available.

It was also the first aircraft in FAA service to combine the 'hunter/killer' role for ASW. Previously, a 'hunter' aircraft had located the target for

a 'killer' to attack, but the problems posed by communication and rendezvous clearly reduced efficiency. The Gannet enabled a specialist team to work together. As mentioned above, it was able to carry its major strike weapons internally, the first British-built operational naval aircraft with such capability. Up to 16 air-to-surface rockets could be carried beneath the wings.

The first operational squadron was formed on 17 January 1955. AS.1 and AS.4 aircraft, as well as T.2 and T.5 trainers, served with the FAA until gradually superseded by Whirlwind helicopters from 1958. On 1 February 1960 the Gannet AEW.3 early-warning variant began to enter service, having a more powerful Double Mamba engine and a large radome mounted beneath the fuselage. Its pilot was accommodated in a forward cockpit and the two radar operators were seated within the fuselage. A total of 44 of these were built, the later examples by Westland Aircraft which took over the Fairey factories in 1960. The AEW.3s which went to sea aboard HMS *Ark Royal* in the summer of 1970 were the last Fairey-designed first-line aircraft to serve with the FAA. Data (AS.4): *Engine* one 2,262 kW (3,035 ehp) Armstrong Siddeley Double Mamba 101 double turboprop *Wing span* 16.56 m (54 ft 4 in) *Length* 13.11 m (43 ft 0 in) *Max T-O weight* 8,891 kg (19,600 lb) *Max level speed* 481 km/h (299 mph) *Range* 1,065 km (662 miles) *Armament* weapons bay for two homing torpedoes, parachute mines, depth charges, or other weapons; provision for 16 underwing rockets

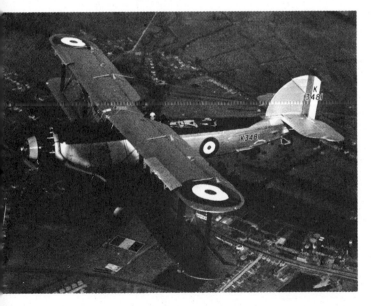

Fairey Gordon and Seal (UK) The Fairey Gordon was almost identical to the Fairey IIIF, except for having a 391 kW (525 hp) Armstrong Siddeley Panther IIA radial air-cooled engine in place of the Napier Lion water-cooled engine. It was a medium-range day bomber with a forward-firing Vickers machine-gun mounted on the left side of the fuselage and a rear-mounted Lewis gun. Up to 209 kg (460 lb) of bombs could be carried and a prone bombing position was provided in the fuselage.

The prototype flew for the first time in 1930 and

Fairey Gyrodyne.

a total of 163 were built for the RAF, including a small number of trainers. Compared to the IIIF, the Gordon offered a considerable increase in speed, due mainly to the increased efficiency of the engine and a lighter AUW. In addition to the production Gordon Is, 24 refined Gordon IIs were built for the RAF and about 90 IIIFs were brought up to Gordon standard. They remained operational until 1938. A number were also exported, production examples going to China and Brazil, while RAF types were passed to Egypt and New Zealand.

The Seal was the Fleet Air Arm version of the Gordon and was operated as a three-seat spotter-reconnaissance biplane. Items of equipment unique to the Seal were a tailwheel, wheel brakes, catapult points, flotation gear, slinging gear and an arrester hook, enabling it to be used from aircraft carriers and as a seaplane from warships. Marginally slower than the Gordon because of the naval equipment, plus an increased bomb load, 90 were delivered to the FAA between 1933 and 1935 (the 91st Seal ordered but thought not to have been delivered).

Seals were also sold to Peru, Latvia (stated to be Gordons in the 1936 *Jane's*), Argentina and Chile. Late in their career a number of Seals passed into RAF service, remaining operational in Ceylon during the early years of World War II. Data (Gordon I): *Engine* as above *Wing span* 13.94 m (45 ft 9 in) *Length* 11.19 m (36 ft 8½ in) *Max T-O weight* 2,674 kg (5,905 lb) *Max level speed* 233 km/h (145 mph) *Range* 965 km (600 miles)

Fairey Gyrodyne and Jet Gyrodyne (UK) The Gyrodyne was an experimental four–five-seat helicopter which incorporated several new principles in design: the usual control and anti-torque rotor was dispensed with, its functions taken over by a conventional propeller on the stub wing; the

Fairey Seal.

Fairey Jet Gyrodyne.

Modified prototype Fairey Hendon with three Fairey Gordons to the rear.

Fairey Long-Range Monoplane J9479.

First of the production Fairey Hendon bombers.

offset tractor propeller allowed the aircraft to be flown as an autogyro. Powered by a 391 kW (525 hp) Alvis Leonides radial engine, the Gyrodyne flew untethered for the first time on 7 December 1947. The second Gyrodyne was modified subsequently into the Jet Gyrodyne with tip-jet rotor drive.

Fairey Hamble Baby (UK) The Hamble Baby is one of the lesser-known aircraft that took an active part in World War I, despite the fact that the RNAS received more than 100 as single-seat anti-submarine seaplanes and a further 74 as Hamble Baby Convert landplane trainers from 1917. The majority of Hamble Babies/Converts were powered by the 97 kW (130 hp) Clerget rotary engine.

Fairey Hendon (UK) Twin 447 kW (600 hp) Rolls-Royce Kestrel VI-engined cantilever low-wing monoplane heavy night bomber, 14 of which were operated by the RAF from 1937 until just before the outbreak of World War II.

Fairey Long-Range Monoplane (UK) In 1926 a proposal was made that the RAF should attempt a non-stop flight to India. This would not only be operationally significant, but enormously prestigious to the service if successful. It would at the same time establish a new world long-distance record. The chosen vehicle for this attempt was the Hawker Horsley, then entering RAF service as a day and torpedo-bomber.

A production example was modified with strengthened landing gear to carry the additional weight of an extra 3,955 litres (870 Imp gallons) of fuel accommodated in new wing and fuselage tanks. On 20 May 1927 Flt Lieut C. R. Carr (later Air Marshal Sir Roderick) and Flt Lieut L. E. M. Gillman took off for India, only to be forced down in the Persian Gulf after completing 5,504 km (3,420 miles): a new long-distance record that was beaten in less than 24 hours when Charles Lindbergh landed at Paris after his 5,778 km (3,590 miles) solo flight across the North Atlantic. Two later but unsuccessful attempts were made with the Horsley.

Consequently the Air Ministry decided to obtain a purpose-built long-range aircraft to make a new attack on the record: the Fairey Long-Range Monoplane was the result. A clean, high-wing cantilever monoplane of low wing loading, it was of composite construction and fabric-covered. The high-efficiency wing, which incorporated a triangulated-tube internal bracing system devised by Hollis Williams, also contained tanks for more than 4,546 litres (1,000 Imp gallons) of fuel. In this aircraft (J9479) Sqd Ldr A. G. Jones-Williams and Flt Lieut N. H. Jenkins flew from Cranwell, Lincolnshire to Karachi, recording the first non-stop flight between Britain and India, but failing to beat the world long-distance record. This aircraft was lost in a second long-range attempt, resulting in the construction of a new aircraft which differed only in detail and by the addition of an autopilot.

In this, during the period 6–8 February 1933, Sqd Ldr Gayford (with Flt Lieut G. E. Nicholetts as navigator) flew non-stop from Cranwell to Walvis Bay, South West Africa, creating a world long-distance record of 8,544 km (5,309 miles). Such was the speed of progress that only six months later this record was captured by France. Data: *Engine* one 425 kW (570 hp) Napier Lion XIA *Wing span* 24.99 m (82 ft 0 in) *Length* 14.78 m (48 ft 6 in) *Max T-O weight* 7,258 kg (16,000 lb) *Cruising speed* 177 km/h (110 mph) *Range* over 8,047 km (5,000 miles)

Fairey Rotodyne (UK) The Rotodyne was an experimental VTOL transport convertiplane. It was powered by two 2,236 kW (3,000 hp) Napier Eland N.E.L.3 turboprop engines mounted in

Fairey Rotodyne.

tractor configuration on the stub wings and pressure jets on the rotor-blade tips. The Rotodyne Y prototype flew for the first time on 6 November 1957. On 5 January 1959 it established a world speed record for rotorcraft with a speed of 307.22 km/h (190.9 mph) over a closed circuit of 100 km. Although the Rotodyne could carry a pilot, co-pilot and 40 passengers, the proposed production Rotodyne Z was designed to carry 54–70 passengers.

Fairey Seafox (UK) The Seafox was a light two-seat (the rear cockpit enclosed) reconnaissance catapult seaplane, best remembered for its invaluable service throughout the action against the *Admiral Graf Spee* during the Battle of the River Plate in December 1939, having flown from the Royal Navy cruiser HMS *Ajax*. A total of 64 Seafox biplanes were built for the FAA, each powered by a 294.4 kW (395 hp) Napier-Halford Rapier VI 16-cylinder air-cooled engine.

Fairey Swordfish (UK) It could be argued, with some conviction, that if Fairey Aviation had designed and built only this one type of aircraft – 2,391 of which were to be constructed eventually – its name, and that of the magnificent Swordfish, would remain forever inscribed in the pages of naval aviation history. One flaw in the argument is that without Fairey's very considerable experience in the construction of naval aircraft, the Swordfish would never have materialised.

It evolved via a rather small private-venture biplane, identified as the TSR.I (*Torpedo-Spotter-Reconnaissance*). When this was lost in an accident (on 11 September 1933) a new and larger TSR.II was built. This became the Swordfish prototype, first flown on 17 April 1934. It was obviously of Fairey parentage: a two-bay unequal-span staggered biplane of metal construction, with wings, fuselage, tail unit and control surfaces fabric-covered, it was powered by a

Bristol Pegasus radial engine. The wings could be folded for carrier stowage; these had ailerons on all four wings and Handley Page slots in the leading edge of the upper wing. Landing gear was massive and the wheels were provided with pneumatically operated brakes; if desirable an interchangeable float landing gear could be fitted. The fuselage was suitably stressed for catapult launching and arrested landings, and equipped with arrester gear.

Armament comprised a fixed synchronised Vickers machine-gun, firing forward through the propeller disc; a Lewis or Vickers machine-gun on a Fairey high-speed mounting in the rear cockpit; and an 18 in torpedo or a 1,500 lb mine carried beneath the fuselage, between the main landing gear. This was a large and useful area for the carriage of a variety of cargo unspecified by the Air Ministry, including a barrel of beer. One regular visitor to an Oxfordshire RAF station in the early days of the war would land, unstrap his bicycle from beneath the landing gear, and cycle off.

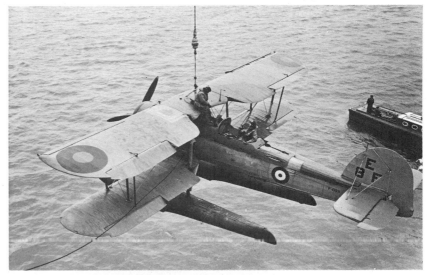

Fairey Swordfish seaplane.

Falconar AMF-S14.

But this Fairey biplane, undoubtedly of archaic appearance, had guts and character in plenty. Its superb handling qualities, even at low speeds and in gusty weather conditions, earned it both respect and affection from its pilots. It was these characteristics which kept it in front-line service for the whole of World War II (outstaying the Fairey Albacore which was designed to supersede it), carrying it gloriously to D-day to strafe the enemy with underwing rockets.

Known affectionately as the 'Stringbag' – which well describes its appearance during hectic

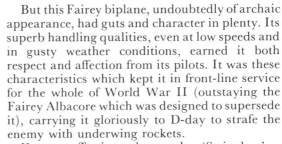

Fairey Swordfish.

Falconar 121 Teal.

Henry Farman III.

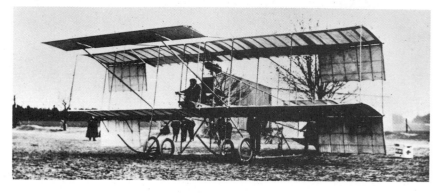

Grahame-White's Henry Farman being erected for the *Daily Mail* £10,000 London—Manchester race.

ment as above, plus up to 680 kg (1,500 lb) bombs disposed under fuselage and underwing, plus (Mk II aircraft) eight 60 lb air-to-surface rockets instead of torpedoes or bombs

Falconar AMF-S14 (Canada) Two-seat sporting and touring high-wing cabin monoplane, plans of which were available to amateur constructors until 1971.

Falconar 121 Teal (Canada) Two-seat light amphibian, first flown in 1967.

Fanaero-Chile Chincol (Chile) Two-seat primary military trainer, first flown on 14 December 1955. Fifty built for the Chilean Air Force.

Voisin-Farman I (France) First flown on 30 September 1907, the Voisin-Farman I was a 37.25 kW (50 hp) Antoinette-powered boxkite-type biplane with a wing span of 10.2 m (33 ft 5½ in) and a maximum speed of 67 km/h (42 mph). Having set officially recognised speed and distance records with this aircraft on 26 October 1907 – 52.7 km/h (32.746 mph) in a closed circuit and 0.77 km (0.478 miles) respectively – Henry Farman remained in the air for more than one minute on 9 November 1907 (see **Chronology** 13 January 1908).

periods of utilisation – these aircraft were involved in practically every naval occasion recorded in the history of World War II; space will allow only some highlights. On 11 April 1940 Swordfish aircraft flying from HMS *Furious* made the first co-ordinated torpedo attack launched from a carrier to be recorded in the history of naval warfare. Two days later a catapult-launched Swtrdfish from HMS *Warspite* sank the German submarine U-64, the first destroyed by an aircraft of the FAA in the war. In May 1940 these aircraft began mine-laying operations in enemy-held Channel ports, and following the defeat of France in June of that year immobilised the French battle-cruiser *Dunkerque* at Oran, preventing its use by Axis forces. On the night of 11 November 1940 aircraft from the carriers *Eagle* and *Illustrious* attacked the Italian fleet in Taranto harbour, severely damaging the battleships *Cavour*, *Duilio* and *Italia*, the cruiser *Trento*, the destroyers *Libeccio* and *Pessango*, and sinking two auxiliary vessels. Swordfish were involved in the sinking of the German battleship *Bismarck*; sank the first submarine ever to be destroyed by an aircraft at night; and sank the U-752 by rocket fire.

But success must be tempered by glorious failure: the FAA will remember forever the six Swordfish (commanded by Lieut-Cdr Esmonde) which were destroyed while attempting to prevent the escape of the German battleships *Gneisenau*, *Prinz Eugen* and *Scharnhorst* through the English Channel on 12 February 1942. Only five of the 18 crew members survived and Lieut-Cdr Esmonde was awarded a posthumous VC – the first ever awarded to a member of the Fleet Air Arm.

Data (Swordfish I): *Engine* one 514 kW (690 hp) Bristol Pegasus IIIM.3 or 559 kW (750 hp) Pegasus XXX *Wing span* 13.87 m (45 ft 6 in) *Length* (landplane) 11.07 m (36 ft 4 in) *Max T-O weight* 4,196 kg (9,250 lb) *Max level speed* 224 km/h (139 mph) *Range* 1,658 km (1,030 miles) *Arma-*

Henry Farman III (France) One of the most important aeroplanes of the 'pioneering age', the Henry Farman III was the first aeroplane in the world to have fully effective ailerons. It was built by Farman after Gabriel Voisin had sold a specially improved Voisin ordered by him to J. T. C. Moore-Brabazon. Powered initially by a 37.25 kW (50 hp) Vivinus and later a Gnome rotary piston engine, it won the Grand Prix for distance at the Reims meeting (see **Chronology** 22 August 1909) and set a number of height and distance records between 1909 and 1911. The success of the Model III led Farman to build further aeroplanes for sale. Indeed both competitors in the *Daily Mail* London—Manchester air race of 1910 flew Farmans.

Farman F.40.

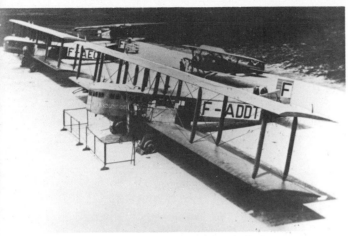

Maurice Farman (France) Brother of Henry Farman, Maurice never achieved the personal fame of Henry but nevertheless set up a factory to build his aircraft soon after Henry had established a company in 1908. One of the best remembered Maurice Farman types was the 1910 two-seater, flown by two famous pilots Tabuteau and Fourny to set up a series of records for distance flown in a closed circuit between 28 October 1910 and 11 September 1912, ranging from 465.72 km (289.38 miles) to 1,010.9 km (628.14 miles).

Farman F.40 (France) As noted above, Henry and Maurice Farman set up separate factories to build aeroplanes. In 1912 they combined and opened a factory at Billancourt in January. Although the H.F.20 series and M.F.7 Longhorn/M.F.11 Shorthorn aircraft are credited to Henry and Maurice separately, all subsequent types appeared as just Farmans built by Avions H. et M. Farman.

The jointly designed F.40 was inevitably dubbed 'Horace' Farman by the British. It had a robust curved nacelle for its two crew members supported on struts between the upper and lower wings. The tailplane and landing gear were developed by Henry. Power was provided by a variety of engines, including a 100.6 kW (135 hp) and 119 kW (160 hp) Renault. Armament could include a single machine-gun operated by the observer as a reconnaissance type, light bombs or Le Prieur rockets mounted on the interplane struts for attacking enemy balloons. F.40s and variants served in Russia, with the French forces and the RNAS.

Farman F.50 (France) The twin 186.3 kW (250 hp) Lorraine-powered F.50 Bn 2 was a two–three-seat night bomber. Its fuselage accommodated the pilot in a cockpit level with the wing leading edge, a gunner in a nose cockpit, and the third cockpit amidships. It equipped night-bomber escadrilles F.110 and F.114 in 1918. After the Armistice two were modified for passenger carrying with the fuselage behind the pilot's cockpit built up to contain a cabin for four–five passengers. These were operated by the airline CGEA. Maximum level speed as a bomber was 150 km/h (93 mph).

Farman F.50.

Retouched photograph of the interior of a Farman F.60 Goliath airliner.

Farman F.60 Goliath (France) The two FF.60 bomber prototypes of 1918 heralded the start of a great family of passenger airliners and night bombers which dominated European aviation for the next decade. However the design formula remained fairly constant with equal-span biplane wings and a conventional monoplane-type tail unit. The landing-gear legs had trousered fairings and each supported twin wheels. Immediately above each leg was an engine set in a large nacelle on the lower wing, with minimal clearance between the propeller and the slab-sided fuselage. Bomber versions invariably had gunners' cockpits in the nose and amidships, while the pilot and co-pilot/navigator were seated in tandem in open cockpits. Commercial transport Goliaths had a nose cabin for four passengers and an aft cabin for

Farman F.121 Jabiru.

Farman

Farman F.166 seaplane.

Farman F.166 landplane.

Farman F.220 *Le Centaure*.

Farman F.168 seaplane.

Thirty-six F.60 bombers (with Salmson engines and cut-down noses) served with the French 21ème and 22ème Régiments d'Aviation and 24 square-nosed Jupiter-powered Goliaths equipped naval escadrilles 6R1, 6B1 and 6B2, following tests with a passenger type. These could be mounted on twin floats (with stabiliser floats under the lower wings) as an alternative to the normal wheel-type landing gear. Russia purchased sufficient F.62s to equip two units which formed the embryo of its new heavy bomber force; Japan and Italy bought a single example each for testing; and Poland acquired 32 F.68 bombers. Export bombers – like the 42 F.63s for the French Army and a large batch of F.65s for the French Navy – each had a 'balcony'-type nose-gunner's cockpit with a 'step' below.

Data (F.60 with Salmson engines): *Engines* as above *Wing span* 26.5 m (86 ft 10 in) *Length* 14.33 m (47 ft 0 in) *Max T-O weight* 4,770 kg (10,515 lb) *Cruising speed* 120 km/h (75 mph) *Range* 400 km (248 miles) *Accommodation* normally 12, but up to 25 passengers could be carried

eight, separated by a raised open cockpit for the two pilots under the leading edge of the upper wing.

About 60 commercial Goliaths were built in several versions with Salmson, Renault, Lorraine, Gnome-Rhône-built Jupiter, Armstrong Siddeley Jaguar and Farman engines, among the most important being those powered by 171.4 kW (230 hp) Salmson Z.9 radial engines operated by Air Union. Several flew with other airlines including the Farman airline, and indeed it was this company that started the world's first regular international passenger service, beginning on 22 March 1919 between Paris and Brussels. Of course this had not been the first international passenger service by an airline between European capital cities, this being officially recognised as the Farman flight between Paris and London on 8 February 1919 carrying military personnel. However the latter was not the start of a sustained or civil passenger service and as such does not conflict with the Paris–Brussels 'first'. Versions operated by the Farman airline included the Renault-powered F.61 and Gnome-Rhône-built Jupiter-powered F.63*bis* (see also **Chronology** 7 April 1922). Six passenger-carrying Goliaths were also built under licence in Czechoslovakia, two going to the air force.

Farman F.70/73 (France) Unequal-span wooden biplane with accommodation for six passengers immediately behind the open pilot's cockpit. At least 14 223.5 kW (300 hp) Renault 12Fe-powered F.70s were built and used by various French airlines (plus one Polish operator) from 1922. Most were converted into F.73s in 1927 with the installation of 283 kW (380 hp) Gnome-Rhône 9A radial engines. The F.130 was a military bomber variant.

Farman F.121 Jabiru (France) The nine-passenger F.3X (as the F.121 was also known) with huge high-mounted wings, deep slab-sided fuselage and four 134 kW (180 hp) Hispano-Suiza 8Ac engines in tandem pairs, won the 1923 French Grand Prix des Avions Transports and 500,000 francs. Four flew on the Farman airline's Paris–Brussels–Amsterdam route from 1926 and Danish Air Lines used a few between Amsterdam and Copenhagen. Four even uglier F.4X six-passenger aircraft followed, each with three uncowled 223.5 kW (300 hp) Salmson Az.9 engines, two engines mounted (as before) above the landing gear on the lower stub wings and one in the upper fuselage nose. These served with Compagnie Internationale de Navigation

Aérienne (formerly CFRNA) along with the more attractive Caudron 81s and Potez 32s (a full description appears in the 1926 *Jane's*).

Interestingly military Jabirus also appeared as prototype heavy bombers and escort fighters with stepped noses, each carrying twin Lewis guns on a Scarff ring in a nose cockpit and light bombs in a fuselage bay. Heavier bombs or a torpedo could be carried under the fuselage.

Farman F.160 Goliath series (France) The F.160 was an attempt (made in 1928) to modernise the original Goliath design. Externally little difference was apparent apart from increased tail-fin area. The F.160, F.161 and F.165 were night bombers, the former capable of carrying a 1,500 kg (3,307 lb) load. The F.162, F.166, F.167 and F.168 were naval torpedo-bombers, convertible as landplanes or seaplanes. A number of French Navy F.167s and F.168s remained operational until 1937 when they gave way to LeO biplanes. The sole civil version was the F.169 which was tested with a new landing gear.

The F.160 and F.161 were powered by 372.6 kW (500 hp) Farman 12WE engines, while the F.162 and F.163 had Salmsons and the remainder up to 372.6 kW (500 hp) Gnome-Rhône-built Jupiter engines.

Farman F.170 Jabiru (France) The wood-and-fabric F.170 was basically a single-engined version of the F.121 Jabiru with a thick strut-braced high wing. Its 372.6 kW (500 hp) Farman 12WE water-cooled engine drove a four-bladed propeller. The open pilot's cockpit was in the top of the fuselage immediately in front of the wing leading edge. Below the wing was the eight-passenger cabin. The F.170*bis* was of mixed construction and carried nine passengers. Eighteen of both versions were built for the Farman airline.

Farman F.180 'Oiseau Bleu' (France) Intended for a 1927 transatlantic attempt, the F.180 was a two-bay unequal-span biplane with a narrow-track undercarriage, enclosed cabin for the crew of two and two 372.6 kW (500 hp) Farman 12WE water-cooled engines in tandem in the upper wing driving four-bladed propellers. For short ranges 25 passengers were accommodated in the long cabin, or the aircraft could provide 17 passenger seats or 12 sleeping berths. Three or more were built for Farman European routes.

Farman F.190 series (France) The F.190 was a strut-braced high-wing cabin monoplane built in

a number of variants between 1928 and 1931. Of over 100 completed, about 30 served with airlines, principal users being Farman, Air Union and Air Orient. Accommodation was provided for the pilot and four passengers. Power plant was a single 171.4 kW (230 hp) Gnome-Rhône Titan 5Ba uncowled radial engine. Six other types of engine were fitted and type numbers ranged up to F.197.

Farman F.200 (France) Two-seat light touring and training monoplane fitted with an 89.4 kW (120 hp) Salmson or similar Hispano-Suiza or Lorraine engine. Its selling price was £770.

Farman F.202 (France) Similar to the F.200 but available as an open-cockpit three-seater or two-seat cabin monoplane.

Farman F.220–F.224 (France) The F.220.01 Bn4 was an experimental thick section high wing heavy bomber, powered by four Hispano-Suiza in-line engines in tandem pairs mounted on lower stub wings braced to the main wings. This prototype flew for the first time on 26 May 1932. It was followed by the F.221.01 with 596 kW (800 hp) Gnome-Rhône L4Kbrs radials and armed with three manually operated gun turrets in nose, dorsal and ventral positions. Ten F.221 Bn5-series bombers (some later converted into F.222s) were followed by 11 F.222s with retractable undercarriage. The final bomber version was the F.222.2, 24 of which were built during 1937–8 with redesigned front fuselage sections and dihedral on the outer wing sections. The last 16 machines had 685.6 kW (920 hp) engines. Escadre GB II/15 operated F.221s from November 1936, then F.222s from April 1937. These were the largest bombers to serve in France between the world wars. After the outbreak of World War II the bombers flew leaflet raids over Germany, but night bombing raids during May and June 1940 led to three losses.

The improved F.223 had a more streamlined fuselage, slimmer wings, simplified strutting and twin fins and rudders. Originally fitted with radial engines, eight were re-engined during

Farman F.221.

Farman F.2233, a re-engined (Hispano-Suiza 12Y50/51s) F.223.

Farman F.500 Monitor I.

Farman F.222 prototype.

Farman H.F.20s at Farnborough, England, in July 1915.

1939–40 with 820 kW (1,100 hp) Hispano-Suiza water-cooled 12Y50/51s. After June 1940 a number of F.222 and F.223 bombers were used as military transports.

Civil passenger/mailplane versions of the F.220 family included *Le Centaure*, the converted F.220.01, four F.2200s and a single F.2220 – all with in-line engines and intended for the South Atlantic service. Six radial-engined F.224s, with new deep fuselages for 40 passengers, were rejected by Air France and subsequently went to the Armée de l'Air. The F.2231 and F.2232 were civil equivalents of the F.223 bomber; the F.2231 made a spectacular flight to South America in November 1937 piloted by Paul Codos.

Three F.2234s built during 1938–9 had the thin tapering wings of the F.223 and F.2231/2, but featured a new streamlined fuselage with a pointed nose section. All were requisitioned by the French Navy in September 1939. One (*Jules Verne*) made the first Allied air raid on Berlin in June 1940. After the French collapse in June 1940 these three machines were returned to Air France. *Le Verrier* was shot down in the Mediterranean on 27 November 1940.

Data (F.222): *Engines* as above *Wing span* 36.0 m (118 ft 1¼ in) *Length* 21.57 m (70 ft 9¼ in) *Max T-O weight* 18,700 kg (41,226 lb) *Max level speed* 325 km/h (202 mph) *Range* 1,200 km (745 miles) *Armament* machine-guns as above, plus up to 4,430 kg (9,771 lb) of bombs

Farman H.F.20 mounting a forward-firing machine-gun.

Faucett F-19.

Farman F.230 (France) Light open-cockpit two-seat cantilever low-wing monoplane powered by a 30 kW (40 hp) Salmson radial engine. Held several world records for its class for speed, height, duration and distance in a straight line and closed circuit.

Farman F.231–F.238 (France) This type of two-seat cantilever low-wing monoplane was similar to the F.230 but was of somewhat larger dimensions and could be fitted with a variety of engines: the type 231 had a 71 kW (95 hp) Renault; the 232 a 74.5 kW (100 hp) Michel; the 233 a 71 kW (95 hp) de Havilland Gipsy; the 234 a 71 kW (95 hp) Salmson; the 235 a 74.5 kW (100 hp) Hispano-Suiza; the 236 a 74.5 kW (100 hp) Renault; and the 238 an 89.4 kW (120 hp) de Havilland Gipsy III. The Type 231 held world landplane and seaplane records.

Farman F.300–F.310 (France) The Farman Type 300 was an eight-passenger commercial monoplane. The various designations of the series indicated the type and number of engines fitted, which could range from one to three: the Type 301 was powered by three 171.4 kW (230 hp) Salmson 9Abs; the 302 by one 484.4 kW (650 hp) Hispano-Suiza 12Nb; the 303 by three 171.4 kW (230 hp) Gnome-Rhône Titans; the 304 by three 223.5 kW (300 hp) Lorraines; the 305 by one 283 kW (380 hp) Gnome-Rhône-built Jupiter and two Titans; the 306 by three 179 kW (240 hp) Lorraine 7Mes; and the 310 seaplane by three 171.4 kW (230 hp) Salmson 9Abs.

The Farman line was by far the largest operator with 12 aircraft, which constituted nearly half its fleet in 1931. Air Orient operated four and a few others were in service with other airlines.

Farman F.355 and F.356 (France) The F.355 was a two-seat cabin monoplane powered by an 89.4 kW (120 hp) Renault engine. The F.356 was a very successful open-cockpit version which held 18 world records for its class.

Farman F.390 (France) Basically a four-seat version of the F.190 powered by a 112 kW (150 hp) Farman radial engine.

Farman F.430 and F.431 (France) Four examples only of a six-seat twin-engined commercial transport similar in appearance to the de Havilland Dragon.

Farman F.500 Monitor (France) Two-seat primary trainer, first flown on 11 July 1952 and developed in collaboration with M. Stampe. Further developed versions included the all-metal Monitor II (which won the 1953 competition for primary trainers meeting the SALS/SFASA requirement), Monitor III and Stampe-Renard S.R.7B.

Farman H.F.20 (France) The two-seat H.F.20 was in service with the French and Belgian military in 1913 and was basically a refined Shorthorn. Power was provided by a 59.6 kW (80 hp) Gnome rotary engine driving a pusher propeller. With the outbreak of World War I the type was used also by the British air services for scouting and light bombing but achieved only marginal success as a reconnaissance type and then trainer.

By substituting the Gnome for a Le Rhône engine of similar power it was hoped to extend the aircraft's capabilities, but the resulting H.F.21 was obsolete. In a final attempt to rectify the tremendous lack of power the H.F.27 was developed with a 104.3 kW (140 hp) or 119 kW (160 hp) Canton-Unné engine – as fitted to the equally light but far more successful early Voisin types. The resulting aircraft was sufficiently promising to be deployed on secondary war fronts.

Farman M.F.7 (France) From 1912 the Maurice Farman-designed M.F.7 served with the French military as well as with many civil and military flying schools in France, Britain and elsewhere in Europe. It was an unequal-span biplane usually fitted with a 52 kW (70 hp) Renault engine driving a pusher propeller. Characteristic of the design was the prominent frontal elevator which led to the nickname 'Longhorn'. Next to the French – who used it initially for reconnaissance duties with seven escadrilles and later for training – the best customers were the RFC and RNAS who received a large number from France and others licence-built in the UK for training duties.

Farman M.F.11 (France) During 1914 and 1915 the M.F.11 (developed from the M.F.7) formed the first-line equipment of some 40 French reconnaissance escadrilles, plus six RFC and two RNAS squadrons. It had a single horizontal tailplane and twin triangular rudders in place of the biplane tail unit of the M.F.7. The crew nacelle was of improved aerodynamic form and the M.F.7's front elevator was eliminated. The relatively short landing-gear skids earned the M.F.11 the nickname 'Shorthorn'. Power was provided by a Renault or De Dion engine in the 59.6–97 kW (80–130 hp) range. Large-scale production in France was supplemented by licence production in Italy (by SIA) and the UK.

When relegated to training duties in late 1915 (having served on the Western Front, in the Dardanelles and Mesopotamia), the M.F.11 had proved one of the most numerically important Allied aircraft. The seaplane variant was designated M.F.11H, examples of which were sold to Russia as well as being operated by the RNAS. Data: *Engine* as above *Wing span* 16.15 m (53 ft 0 in) or 16.3 m (53 ft 5¾ in) *Length* 9.35 m (30 ft 8 in) *Max T-O weight* 810 kg (1,786 lb) *Max level speed* 100 km/h (62 mph) *Endurance* 3 h 45 min *Armament* one forward-firing Lewis or Hotchkiss machine-gun on some aircraft, plus up to 130 kg (287 lb) of bombs

Faucett F-19 (Peru) Cia de Aviacion Faucett S.A. was the oldest aeronautical concern in Peru and operated airlines and a factory for manufacture, repair and maintenance. The F-19 eight-seat high-wing transport was developed for its own airlines and a number were also sold to the government. Power was provided by a 652 kW (875 hp) Pratt & Whitney Hornet engine in landplane form and 447 kW (600 hp) Wasp in seaplane form. Production ended in 1947.

Fauvel AV.44 (France) Two–three-seat tailless monoplane, plans of which are available to amateur constructors.

Fauvel AV.50 (61) Lutin (France) Single-seat tailless monoplane, examples of which are under construction by amateur builders.

Fauvel AV.45.

Fauvel AV.361, AV.45/AV.451 and AV.222 (France) Single-seat general-purpose sailplane, single-seat tailless motor glider and two-seat motor glider respectively, plans of which are available to amateur constructors.

FBA flying-boats (France) Franco-British Aviation was based in Paris. It had been founded in 1913–14 by Lieut Jean de Conneau, French Navy (better known as André Beaumont, winner of the Paris–Rome, Circuit-European and Circuit of Britain races) and M. Schreck of the French Wright Company, to work to patents pertaining to the Donnet-Lévêque and Artois flying-boats. What was achieved was a series of small coastal patrol and anti-submarine high-speed flying-boats that were widely operated by all the Allied naval air services for fighting over water until the Armistice. The Italian aircraft continued to fly until 1922.

The earliest examples of FBA military flying-boats found their way into Austrian and Danish service before the outbreak of World War I, but in very small numbers. Large-scale production for the French, Italian and British (RNAS) began with the Types A, B and C, entering service from 1915 and powered by 59.6–74.5 kW (80–100 hp) Gnome Monosoupape or 97 kW (130 hp) Clerget pusher engines. Unlike other services the RNAS employed its FBAs mainly as trainers from the start.

The major version was the Type H, which was produced in very large numbers in France and under licence by several Italian manufacturing companies. A three-seater, with the flight crew side-by-side and a nose gunner, French aircraft were powered by 112 kW (150 hp) or 127 kW (170 hp) Hispano-Suiza or occasionally 119 kW (160 hp) Lorraine engines; while the 982 built in Italy had the 127 kW (170 hp) Hispano-Suiza or

F + W C-3605.

FBA

Felixstowe F.2A.

Felixstowe F.3.

FFA AS.202 Bravo.

**Fiat A.S.1 photographed
during the 1929
International Tourist
Challenge.**

more commonly 134 kW (180 hp) Isotta-Fraschini V-4B or 112 kW (150 hp) Isotta-Fraschini engine. Type Hs also served with the Belgian Navy and a very small number with the RNAS.

The final wartime version was the Type S powered by a 149 kW (200 hp) Hispano-Suiza and operated by the French. This was the fastest version and could carry a useful 100 kg (220.5 lb) bomb load.

Data (Type H): *Engine* one 134 kW (180 hp) Isotta-Fraschini V-4B *Wing span* 14.55 m (47 ft 8¾ in) *Length* 10.2 m (33 ft 5½ in) *Max T-O weight* 1,400 kg (3,086 lb) *Max level speed* 140 km/h (87 mph) *Range* 600 km (373 miles) *Armament* one Revelli machine-gun, plus bombs

FBA 17 (France) Like the wartime FBA series, the FBA 17 (sometimes referred to as the Schreck FBA 17 after its designer) was an unequal-span flying-boat biplane with a single-step hull. Pilot and observer were accommodated side-by-side in open cockpits. The prototype flew for the first time in April 1923 and by 1930 229 production aircraft had been built, each powered by a single 112 kW (150 hp) or 134 kW (180 hp) Hispano-Suiza 8A engine driving a pusher propeller. Production was made up of 37 HMT2 two-seat amphibians, 3 four-seat HT4 transport/touring aircraft, 141 HE2 two-seat trainers and 10 HL2s for catapult launching. Most were for the French Navy but a few were exported to Poland and others were used as civil types. Nine FBA 171/172 flying-boats followed. Maximum speed 162 km/h (101 mph).

FBA 19 (France) Three-seat bombing amphibious flying-boat, first flown in April 1924. Developed into HMB2 reconnaissance aircraft. Third variant produced as the HMT3 commer-

cial transport, one of which was operated by Air Union from 1925. Powered by one 261 kW (350 hp) Hispano-Suiza tractor engine. Maximum speed 175 km/h (101 mph). Often referred to as the Schreck FBA 19 after its designer (see **FBA flying-boats**).

FBA 21 HMT (France) Commercial development of he FBA 19, accommodating the pilot, mechanic and four passengers, plus 130 kg (286 lb) of mail or freight. Powered by one 372.6 kW (500 hp) Hispano-Suiza, 335.3 kW (450 hp) Lorraine or 313 kW (420 hp) Gnome-Rhône-built Jupiter engine.

FBA 290 (France) Four-seat cabin amphibious flying-boat powered by a 223.5 kW (300 hp) Lorraine Algol engine driving a pusher propeller.

FBA 310 (France) Two-seat cabin amphibious flying-boat powered by an 89.4 kW (120 hp) Lorraine pusher engine mounted above the high monoplane wing.

F + W C-3605 (Switzerland) Turboprop conversion of the EKW C-3603 fighter-bomber which has been in Swiss Air Force service since 1942 and 144 of which were built up to 1944. The prototype conversion flew for the first time on 19 August 1968 and 23 more aircraft were subsequently converted; delivery of these was completed in January 1973. Power is provided by the 820 kW (1,100 hp) Lycoming T53-L-7 turboprop engine. C-3605s are used as two-seat target-towing aircraft.

Felixstowe F.2A, F.3 and F.5 (UK) In 1914 Lieut J. C. Porte, Royal Navy, went to America to take part in the development of the Curtiss *America* flying-boat see entry), in which an attempt at crossing the Atlantic was to be made. However, although the *America* had been completed, Porte returned to England in August following the outbreak of World War I, where he joined the RNAS.

Porte began to develop the Curtiss type of flying-boat at the Felixstowe station for possible use by the RNAS, concentrating mainly on improving the hydrodynamic qualities of the hull.

The first Felixstowe type was the F.1 (based on the Curtiss H.4), four of which were produced. The F.2 followed (designed around the Curtiss H.12) with a Porte hull and Curtiss wings and tail unit. Superior in every way to the H.12, it was produced in 1917 as the F.2A. It was one of the finest aircraft of the war and was widely operated as an anti-submarine patrol flying-boat until the Armistice. Armament comprised typically a Scarff ring mounting in the nose for one or two Lewis guns; a single Lewis gun on a pillar mounting at each of two beam positions; and one or two Lewis guns in a dorsal position aft of the wings. In addition two 104 kg (230 lb) bombs could be carried under the lower wings. Nearly 100 F.2As were completed before the Armistice and the aircraft's fine performance and manoeuvrability also made it an effective multi-seat attack and anti-Zeppelin type.

The F.3 was a development of the F.2A, with some of the former aircraft's agility being sacrificed for longer range and heavier bomb load. Approximately the same number of F.3s were built as the slightly smaller F.2As, but served in the Mediterranean as well as from British stations. Post-war deliveries to the RAF were made as the F.5 and this became the standard reconnaissance type for several years, but was inferior to both the F.2A and F.3. A Liberty-powered variant went into production in America as the F.5L and the Japanese Navy received a small number. One company that produced F.5s, Gosport Aircraft, attempted to market a version as the Gosport G.5 for use as a passenger, mail or freight carrier, or for firefighting and transport duties in Canada and the USA, initially under the direction of Porte who had joined the staff in 1919.
Data (F.2A): *Engines* two 257 kW (345 hp) Rolls-Royce Eagle VIIIs *Wing span* 29.13 m (95 ft 7½ in) *Length* 14.09 m (46 ft 3 in) *Max T-O weight* 4,536 kg (10,978 lb) *Max level speed* 193 km/h (95 mph) *Endurance* 6 h

FFA AS.202 Bravo (Switzerland) Following an agreement with SIAI-Marchetti of Italy, FFA is engaged in production and development of the Bravo light two–three-seat trainer and sporting aircraft. Power is provided by a 134 kW (180 hp) Lycoming AEIO-360-B1F engine in the

AS.202/15 initial production version (32 ordered by 1978); while the AS.202/18A aerobatic version has a 134 kW (180 hp) Lycoming (72 ordered by 1978). Production aircraft serve with the air forces of Iraq, Morocco, Oman and Uganda. In 1978 the AS.202/26A training and aerobatic version made its first flight, powered by a 194 kW (260 hp) Lycoming engine.

FFA P-16 (Switzerland) Single-seat strike fighter of the late 1950s, five of which were built.

Fiat 7002 (Italy) General-purpose helicopter first flown on 26 January 1961. Main rotor was 'cold-jet' type.

Fiat A.120 (Italy) Two-seat parasol-wing reconnaissance monoplane of the early 1930s.

Fiat A.P.R.2 (Italy) Twin-engined 12-passenger commercial airliner of 1935 powered by two 522 kW (700 hp) Fiat A.59R supercharged radial engines. One operated by Avio-Linee Italiane.

Fiat A.S.2.

Fiat B.R.G.

Fiat A.S.1 (Italy) Two-seat parasol-wing monoplane trainer of 1928 powered by a 63.3 kW (85 hp) Fiat A.50 or Walter engine. Built for the Italian Air Force. Much cleaner looking and faster A.S.2 developed from it in early 1930s.

Fiat B.R.G. (Italy) Triple-engined transport looking somewhat similar to the Farman F.121.

Fiat B.R. and B.R.1 to 3 (Italy) The B.R. appeared in 1919 and was used by the Italian Air Force for several years as a bombing and long-range reconnaissance biplane. Development of an improved version (as the B.R.1) began in June 1923 and was at first limited to redesigning the B.R. to incorporate modifications suggested during its years of service. This included the ability to carry a large bomb or torpedo under the fuselage, necessitating a divided landing gear. Power was provided by a 522 kW (700 hp) Fiat A.14 engine. The prototype, carrying a 1,500 kg payload, set up a record by reaching a height of 5,516 m (18,097 ft) on 23 December 1924. Although not inferior to the B.R., the B.R.1 was not much of an

Fiat B.R.

Fiat B.R.1.

Fiat B.R.2.

improvement except for giving the crew a better view by virtue of the 5° wing stagger. The lower wings were also of reduced span and had slight dihedral.

The B.R.2 of 1925 was powered by an 812 kW (1,090 hp) Fiat A.25 engine, giving the aircraft a maximum speed of 240 km/h (149 mph), compared to the B.R.'s 200 km/h (124 mph) but similar to the B.R.1's. The similarity of speeds of the B.R.1 and 2 is explained by the fact that the former had a AUW of 3,920 kg (8,642 lb) and the latter 4,196 kg (9,250 lb). Late production B.R.2s also incorporated Handley Page slotted wings. The final production version was the B.R.3, which was heavier than the B.R.2, had a marginally lower speed, but served as a bomber and then weapons trainer until 1940.

Fiat B.R.20 Cicogna.

Fiat C.R.1. B.R.20 *bis*.

Data (B.R.3): *Engine* as for B.R.2 *Wing span* 17.3 m (56 ft 9 in) *Length* 10.55 m (34 ft 7½ in) *Max T-O weight* 4,350 kg (9,590 lb) *Max level speed* 230 km/h (143 mph) *Range* 750 km (466 miles) *Armament* one forward-firing and one rear-mounted 7.5 mm Darne machine-guns, plus bombs

Fiat B.R.20 Cicogna (Italy) The B.R.20 cantilever low-wing medium bomber appeared in

Fiat B.R.3.

1936. A number of the initial production aircraft delivered to the Regia Aeronautica were operated in Spain by the Italian Aviazione Legionaria in support of the Nationalists during the Civil War, while others were delivered for actual Spanish use. However operational service in Spain against the latest Russian-supplied Republican fighters and during Italy's campaign in Albania, led to the need for some fundamental revisions. Consequently the B.R.20M and B.R.20*bis* versions were produced with improved visibility, provision of a 12.7 mm gun in place of one of the 7.7 mm guns and other changes.

By June 1940, when Italy entered the war, the Regia Aeronautica had about 220 Cicognas in service, most of which were immediately available for action and indeed began attacks on Malta on their first full day of war. A major blow to Italy's war effort came when Marshal Italo Balbo (leader of the 1931/33 Atlantic flights), was killed over Tobruk within a month, shot down by Italian guns. During October and November 1940 daylight raids were made on the UK, but these met with heavy opposition from RAF Hurricanes and Spitfires and within a short time even night attacks from bases in Belgium ended. Cicognas fought also in Greece, Libya, Yugoslavia and on the Russian Front.

By the time Italy surrendered to the Allies in September 1943 only one in seven of about 600 Cicognas built were still in service. Also worthy of mention are the 85 Fiat B.R.20s supplied to the Japanese Army. Although these received the Allied code name *Ruth*, they were never used operationally during World War II. A small number of bombers also served in Venezuela.

Data (B.R.20M): *Engines* two 745 kW (1,000 hp) Fiat A.80 RC-41 radials *Wing span* 21.56 m (70 ft 8¾ in) *Length* 16.173 m (53 ft 0¾ in) *Max T-O weight* 10,100 kg (22,267 lb) *Max level speed* 430 km/h (267 mph) *Range* 3,000 km (1,864 miles) *Armament* one 12.7 mm and three 7.7 mm machine-guns in nose, dorsal and ventral positions; plus 1,600 kg (3,527 lb) of bombs.

Fiat C.R.1 (Italy) The C.R.1 biplane – 240 of which were ordered for the Regia Aeronautica to equip 12 first-line fighter squadrons – was the first fighter of indigenous design to serve with the new air force. Powered by a 223.5 kW (300 hp) Hispano-Suiza engine, the C.R.1 was operational from 1925 until 1930.

Data: *Engine* as above *Wing span* 8.95 m (29 ft 4½ in) *Length* 6.24 m (20 ft 5½ in) *Max T-O weight* 1,155 kg (2,546 lb) *Max level speed* 270 km/h (168 mph) *Range* 650 km (404 miles) *Armament* two forward-firing 7.7 mm Breda-SAFAT machine-guns

Fiat C.R.20*bis*.

9.8 m (32 ft 2 in) *Length* 6.7 m (21 ft 11 in) *Max T-O weight* 1,487 kg (3,278 lb) *Max level speed* 250 km/h (155 mph), (C.R.20) 276 km/h (171.5 mph) *Range* 500 km (310 miles) *Armament* two forward-firing 7.7 mm machine-guns

Fiat C.R.25 (Italy) Twin-engined multi-seat fighter and attack monoplane of 1939, powered by 626 kW (840 hp) Fiat A.74 RC-38 engines. Ten built, later being used as transports

Fiat C.R.20 (Italy) With the exception of the C.R.32, the C.R.20 was Fiat's most successful inter-war fighter: more than 670 being built for the Regia Aeronautica and for export to Austria, Hungary and Paraguay. The prototype appeared in 1926 and, although powered by a 298 kW (400 hp) Fiat A.20 engine, was only slightly faster than the C.R.1 because of its larger dimensions and considerably heavier weight. Nevertheless, what it lacked in speed it more than made up for in manoeuvrability and structural strength. Interestingly like the C.R.1 it was an unequal-span biplane, but had the shorter-span wings as the lower and not upper planes.

Production covered several versions, including the initial version; C.R.20B two-seat trainer; C.R.20*bis* with a divided landing gear and other changes; C.R.20*AQ* high-altitude fighter; C.R.20 *Asso* with a 335.3 kW (450 hp) Isotta-Fraschini engine; and the twin-float C.R.20 *Idro*. After being flown against tribesmen in Libya and Abyssinia the C.R.20 was retired from service.

Data (C.R.20 *Asso*): *Engine* as above *Wing span*

Fiat C.R.1.

Fiat C.R.20 *Idro*.

Fiat C.R.30 (Italy) Designed as a replacement for the C.R.20, the C.R.30 was a workmanlike biplane fighter armed with two 7.7 mm or 12.7 mm Breda-SAFAT machine-guns and powered by a 447 kW (600 hp) Fiat A.30 RA engine. The first prototype flew on 5 March 1932. One of the prototypes won the speed contest at the 1932 Zurich International Fighter Competition, averaging 340 km/h (211 mph). The two-seat C.R.30B training version won a Romanian international competition in the following year. One hundred and twenty-one C.R.30s were ordered for the Regia Aeronautica, deliveries starting in 1934, while export versions went to Austria and Hungary to replace their C.R.20s. Italian C.R.30 fighters served only until 1937, a promising career cut short by another Fiat fighter, the C.R.32.

Fiat C.R.25.

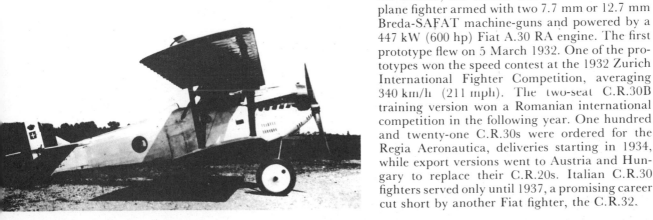

Fiat C.R.20.

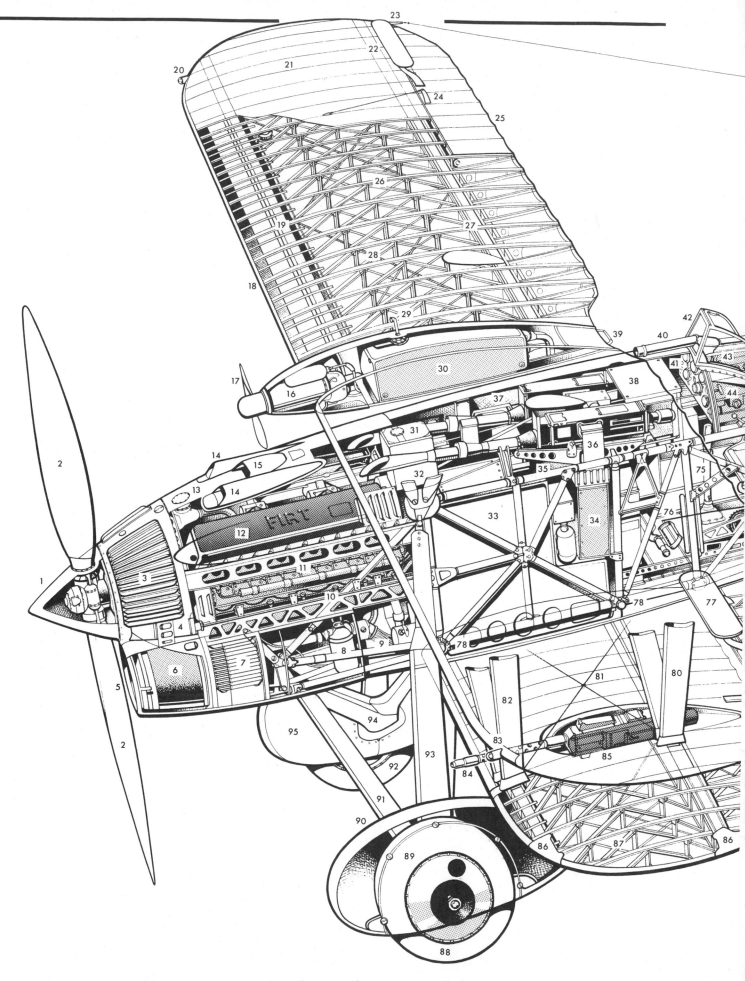

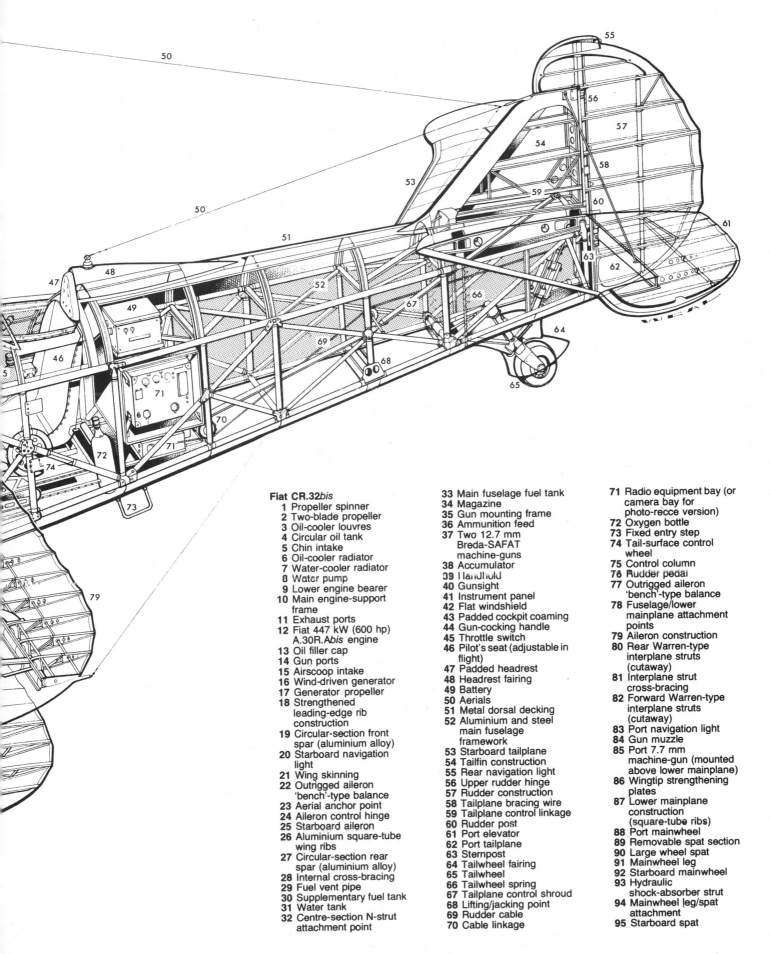

Fiat CR.32*bis*

1 Propeller spinner
2 Two-blade propeller
3 Oil-cooler louvres
4 Circular oil tank
5 Chin intake
6 Oil-cooler radiator
7 Water-cooler radiator
8 Water pump
9 Lower engine bearer
10 Main engine-support frame
11 Exhaust ports
12 Fiat 447 kW (600 hp) A.30R.A*bis* engine
13 Oil filler cap
14 Gun ports
15 Airscoop intake
16 Wind-driven generator
17 Generator propeller
18 Strengthened leading-edge rib construction
19 Circular-section front spar (aluminium alloy)
20 Starboard navigation light
21 Wing skinning
22 Outrigged aileron 'bench'-type balance
23 Aerial anchor point
24 Aileron control hinge
25 Starboard aileron
26 Aluminium square-tube wing ribs
27 Circular-section rear spar (aluminium alloy)
28 Internal cross-bracing
29 Fuel vent pipe
30 Supplementary fuel tank
31 Water tank
32 Centre-section N-strut attachment point

33 Main fuselage fuel tank
34 Magazine
35 Gun mounting frame
36 Ammunition feed
37 Two 12.7 mm Breda-SAFAT machine-guns
38 Accumulator
39 Handhold
40 Gunsight
41 Instrument panel
42 Flat windshield
43 Padded cockpit coaming
44 Gun-cocking handle
45 Throttle switch
46 Pilot's seat (adjustable in flight)
47 Padded headrest
48 Headrest fairing
49 Battery
50 Aerials
51 Metal dorsal decking
52 Aluminium and steel main fuselage framework
53 Starboard tailplane
54 Tailfin construction
55 Rear navigation light
56 Upper rudder hinge
57 Rudder construction
58 Tailplane bracing wire
59 Tailplane control linkage
60 Rudder post
61 Port elevator
62 Port tailplane
63 Sternpost
64 Tailwheel fairing
65 Tailwheel
66 Tailwheel spring
67 Tailplane control shroud
68 Lifting/jacking point
69 Rudder cable
70 Cable linkage

71 Radio equipment bay (or camera bay for photo-recce version)
72 Oxygen bottle
73 Fixed entry step
74 Tail-surface control wheel
75 Control column
76 Rudder pedal
77 Outrigged aileron 'bench'-type balance
78 Fuselage/lower mainplane attachment points
79 Aileron construction
80 Rear Warren-type interplane struts (cutaway)
81 Interplane strut cross-bracing
82 Forward Warren-type interplane struts (cutaway)
83 Port navigation light
84 Gun muzzle
85 Port 7.7 mm machine-gun (mounted above lower mainplane)
86 Wingtip strengthening plates
87 Lower mainplane construction (square-tube ribs)
88 Port mainwheel
89 Removable spat section
90 Large wheel spat
91 Mainwheel leg
92 Starboard mainwheel
93 Hydraulic shock-absorber strut
94 Mainwheel leg/spat attachment
95 Starboard spat

Fiat

Fiat C.R.30.

Fiat C.R.32 flying with Nationalist forces during the Spanish Civil War.

Data: *Engine* as above *Wing span* 10.5 m (34 ft 5½ in) *Length* 7.83 m (25 ft 8¼ in) *Max T-O weight* 1,895 kg (4,178 lb) *Max level speed* 350 km/h (217 mph) *Range* 850 km (528 miles)

Fiat C.R.32 (Italy) Though a thoroughbred stemming from a series of Caccia Rosatelli designs, the C.R.32 reflected the continuing wish of the Italian Regia Aeronautica fighter pilots to sacrifice almost every other feature for outstanding manoeuvrability and all-round pilot view, and as a result was fundamentally obsolete even at the time of its design. Aerodynamically and structurally it was almost identical to the C.R.30. One might have expected it to be designated as a mere sub-type of the earlier machine, but in fact, despite close similarity, the airframe was completely new and had reduced dimensions and greater strength, making it virtually indestructible by the most violent flight manoeuvres. Structure was a mixture of steel tube and strip and light alloy, most of the covering being fabric.

The engine was again just a refinement of that used in the C.R.30, a Fiat A.30 RA*bis* V-12 water-cooled of 447 kW (600 hp), driving a two-bladed propeller with fixed-pitch metal blades. The same W-type Warren strut bracing was used between the unequal-size wings, the upper planes

Fiat C.R.32*ter*.

having 'park bench' ailerons. The sturdy, spatted landing gear had brakes, allowing a tailwheel to be used, and the fin was larger than that of the C.R.30. Equipment and armament, however, were unchanged: two 12.7 mm Breda-SAFAT machine-guns in the top decking of the fuselage ahead of the cockpit, which was placed aft out of reach of the gun breeches.

The first of these extremely nimble and tough fighters flew in 1933 and after rapid flight trials went into large-scale production. By 1935 more than 350 had been delivered and production continued with the C.R.32*bis* with two 7.7 mm Breda-SAFAT guns added above the lower wings, with ammunition boxes inside the wing. The 32*bis* also had a rack under the fuselage for either one bomb of 100 kg or two of 50 kg . More than 300 of this type were built. This was the chief fighter of the Aviación Legionaria sent to Spain to fight for the Nationalists. So impressed were the Spaniards that they obtained a licence and made a large number as the Hispano Aviación HA-132L Chirri.

About a further 100 were made of the 32*ter*, with minor changes. Total Italian production was brought to 1,212 with the final sub-type, the 32 *quater*. This had no wing guns and instead had slightly more fuel and oxygen, and better radio. Some were fitted with exhaust shrouds for use as night fighters, which along with ground attack comprised the type's main role in World War II. Appreciable numbers of various sub-types were sold to Chile, Hungary, Paraguay and Venezuela.

Data (C.R.32): *Engine* as above *Wing span* 9.5 m (31 ft 2 in) *Length* 7.46 m (24 ft 5½ in) *Max T-O weight* 1,865 kg (4,111 lb) *Max level speed* 375 km/h (233 mph) *Range* 750 km (466 miles)

Fiat C.R.42 (Italy) The C.R.42 was the last biplane fighter to enter service with the Regia Aeronautica. It was in fact a sesquiplane powered by a 626 kW (840 hp) Fiat A.74 RC-38 engine – a power plant widely used in Italy during the late 1930s and found also in the G.50, C.R.25, R.S.14 and Macchi C.200. It was produced as insurance against the failure of the more radical G.50 Freccia and indeed could have shown a clean pair of heels to all but the fastest versions of the other great biplane of the period, the Gloster Gladiator.

The prototype flew for the first time in 1939, and along with orders for the Regia Aeronautica, Fiat received substantial contracts from Belgium, Sweden and inevitably Hungary. Production ended in 1942 after 1,781 had been built in several versions. These included the initial C.R.42; the C.R.42*bis* with twin 12.7 mm Breda-SAFAT machine-guns; the C.R.42*ter* four-gun fighter; and C.R.42AS fighter-bomber. These served as day and night fighters, bomber escorts and fighter-bombers, performing their best work in North Africa.

Data (C.R.42): *Engine* as above *Wing span* 9.7 m (31 ft 10 in) *Length* 8.26 m (27 ft 1½ in) *Max T-O weight* 2,295 kg (5,060 lb) *Max level speed* 450 km/h (280 mph) *Range* 775 km (481 miles) *Armament* one 12.7 mm and one 7.7. mm forward-firing machine-guns (see above)

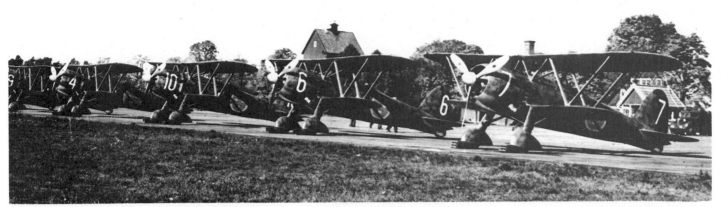

Fiat G.2 Mk II (Italy) Single example of an eight-seat cantilever low-wing commercial transport aircraft of 1932, powered by three 97 kW (130 hp) Fiat A.60 four-cylinder engines. Operated on domestic routes by Avio-Linee Italiane.

Fiat G.8 (Italy) Two-seat dual-control biplane of 1934 for touring and flying/aerobatic training, powered by a 100.6 kW (135 hp) Fiat A.54 engine. Operated by the Italian Air Force until 1950.

Fiat G.12 (Italy) The series of G.12 civil and military transport monoplanes stemmed from the G.12C 14-passenger commercial airliner for Avio-Linee Italiane of 1940. Powered by three 596 kW (800 hp) Fiat A.74 RC-42 engines, three entered service. The basically similar cargo version, the G.12 Gondar, did not enter commercial service but instead was used by the Regia Aeronautica as the G.12T military transport, serving in small numbers from 1941 until the end of the war. The G.12 GA of 1942 was designed as a civil airliner capable of operating a 10,000 km (6,210 mile) route to South America, but neither this nor the LGA version was flown commercially. Similarly the G.12RT models for the Rome–Tokyo–Rome service were not used for their intended purpose.

In 1946 Fiat was engaged in the production of 20 G.12s and sought permission from the Allied control authorities to build a further 12 or 14, some for export to South America. These included the G.12CA 18-passenger version with Alfa Romeo 128 engines; the G.12L 22-passenger commercial transport with Fiat A.74 RC-42 engines; G.12LA with 641 kW (860 hp) Alfa Romeo 128 RC.18 engines; G.12LB with 604 kW (810 hp) Bristol Pegasus 48 engines; and the G.12LP with 793.6 kW (1,065 hp) Pratt & Whit-

ney R-1830-S1C3G engines. G.12Ls and LBs entered service with Italian airlines and the air force received G.12Ls, LAs and LPs, some of which were used as aircrew trainers.

Data (G.12T): *Engines* as above *Wing span* 28.6 m (93 ft 10 in) *Length* 20.1 m (65 ft 11½ in) *Max T-O weight* 15,000 kg (33,069 lb) *Max level speed* 390 km/h (242 mph) *Range* 2,300 km (1,429 miles)

Fiat G.18 (Italy) First flown in 1935, the G.18 was a cantilever low wing commercial airliner accommodating 18 passengers. Three G.18s, each eventually powered by two 521.6 kW (700 hp) Fiat A.59 engines, went into service with Avio-Linee Italiane, together with six G.18Vs with 745 kW (1,000 hp) Fiat A.80 engines.

Fiat G.46 (Italy) Two-seat trainer of 1948 produced in five major versions with 145.3–160 kW (195–215 hp) Alfa 115 or 186.3 kW (250 hp) de Havilland Gipsy Queen 30 engines. More than 300 built for the Italian and Argentine air forces.

Fiat G.49 (Italy) Two-seat trainer powered by a 410 kW (550 hp) Alvis Leonides or 447 kW (600 hp) Pratt & Whitney R-1340-S3H1 engine.

Fiat

Fiat G.50 Freccia.

Fiat G.82.

Fiat G.55 Centauro.

Fiat G.212 in Avio-Linee Italiane service.

Fiat G.212 Aula Volante.

Fiat G.50 Freccia (Italy) Contemporary of the Macchi C.200 Saetta fighter, but attaining a considerably lower maximum speed with the same 626 kW (840 hp) Fiat A.74 RC-38 engine. The G.50 began life with all the modern features expected of a fighter in the latter 1930s. The prototype flew for the first time on 26 February 1937. It entered production in the following year and one squadron was sent to Spain to fight in the Civil War.

In the Regia Aeronautica G.50s replaced C.R.32s and by June 1940 about 100 were in service. Approximately 280 G.50s were built, followed by 450 G.50*bis* fighters with the troublesome transparent sliding canopy removed and the rear fuselage decking remodelled to produce an extremely neat open cockpit with greatly improved vision for the pilot. Other refinements included armour protection for the pilot. Underpowered and poorly armed with just two 12.7 mm Breda-SAFAT machine-guns, the Freccia was no match for opposing fighters on the Western Front and consequently spent most of its career in North Africa, the Mediterranean area and Greece. A two-seat training version was designated G.50B. Fighters were exported to Finland and elsewhere, Finnish aircraft carrying the usual swastika.
Data: *Engine* as above *Wing span* 10.9 m (35 ft 9 in) *Length* 7.8 m (25 ft 7 in) *Max T-O weight* 2,706 kg (5,966 lb) *Max level speed* 472 km/h (293 mph) *Range* 1,000 km (621 miles)

Fiat G.55 Centauro (Italy) Having tested a G.50 with a 745 kW (1,000 hp) Daimler-Benz DB 601 in-line engine, the possibilities of a new fighter of refined form based on the G.50 were apparent. Replacement of the radial engine with an in-line allowed better streamlining and the much more powerful 1,099 kW (1,475 hp) licence-built Daimler-Benz DB 605A selected for the new aircraft meant that a fighter of truly international performance could be developed. Coupled with improved armament of either four 12.7 mm Breda-SAFAT machine-guns and a 20 mm MG 151 cannon or two machine-guns and three cannon, the resulting G.55 of 1942 was without question one of the best fighters produced in Italy during World War II.

However only about 100 were delivered during the war and most of these served with pro-German forces. After the war the G.55 went back into production as the G.55A single-seat operational advanced trainer, armed with four

12.7 mm machine-guns and racks for two 100 kg bombs, and G.55B two-seat dual-control aerobatic trainer. Post-war aircraft went into Italian, Argentine, Egyptian and Syrian service. From the post-war variants was evolved the G.59 (see below).
Data: *Engine* as above *Wing span* 11.85 m (38 ft 10½ in) *Length* 8.37 m (27 ft 5½ in) *Max T-O weight* 3,710 kg (8,179 lb) *Max level speed* 620 km/h (385 mph) *Range* 1,650 km (1,025 miles)

Fiat G.59 (Italy) The G.59 was a single- or two-seat advanced military trainer, based on the G.55 but powered by a Rolls-Royce Merlin engine of 842 kW (1,130 hp). Armament for the single-seater varied between two and four 12.7 mm machine-guns, plus up to 160 kg (350 lb) of bombs or rockets; while the two-seater had provision for one 7.7 mm gun. Production aircraft were delivered to the Italian Air Force and certain foreign air forces.

Fiat G.80 and G.82 (Italy) On 10 December 1951 the prototype of a de Havilland Goblin 35-

powered two-seat jet trainer made its first flight as the G.80-1B. The production development, fully equipped for day or night training, was the G.80-3B. Ten G.80-3Bs went into Italian Air Force service, followed by the production version proper, the 24 kN (5,400 lb st) Rolls-Royce Nene-powered G.82.

Fiat G.212 (Italy) First flown on 19 January 1947, the G.212 was a three-engined transport aircraft developed from the G.12. Two civil versions were produced as the 26–34-passenger G.212CP Monterosa and the G.212TP Monviso freight carrier. Both were powered by three 782.5 kW (1,050 hp) Pratt & Whitney R-1830-S1C3-G Twin Wasp radial engines, but only the passenger version entered service with Avio-Linee Italiane and other operators in small numbers.

A G.212 was also used as the presidential aeroplane, while a second was used by the Ministry of Defence. A military version also entered service with the Italian Air Force College as the G.212 Aula Volante (Flying Classroom), fitted out with 22 seats and tables, each with the necessary radio instructional equipment. For bombing training a gondola for a pupil and instructor was mounted beneath the fuselage. Instructional photographic equipment was also fitted.

Fiat R.2 (Italy) Two-seat reconnaissance biplane powered by a 223.5 kW (300 hp) Fiat A.12*bis* engine. Maximum level speed 175 km/h (109 mph).

Fiat R.22 (Italy) Two-seat reconnaissance biplane of 1926 fitted with a 410 kW (550 hp) Fiat A.22 engine. Basically a two-seat version of the CR.20 incorporating the Warren-type interplane bracing common on Fiat biplanes.

Fiat R.S.14 (Italy) Torpedo-bombing and reconnaissance twin-float seaplane of 1938, powered by a 626 kW (840 hp) Fiat A.74 RC-38 engine. A total of 152 built for service during World War II but were somewhat overshadowed by CANT and Savoia-Marchetti aircraft. By the Italian Armistice of 1943 only a small number remained in service. Maximum level speed 390 km/h (242 mph).

Fieseler F.2 Tiger (Germany) Two-seat aerobatic and sporting biplane powered by a 313 kW (420 hp) Walter Pollux engine.

Fieseler F.5 (Germany) Two-seat light monoplane with trailing-edge flaps and a cantilever landing gear, powered by a Hirth H.M.60 or H.M.60R engine.

Fieseler F.97 (Germany) Four-seat cabin monoplane, built for the 1934 Challenge de Tourisme International.

Fieseler Fi 156 Storch used by Rommel.

A captured Fieseler Fi 156 Storch in RAF markings with a Vultee Vigilant (rear).

Fieseler Fi 156 Storch (Germany) First flown in 1936, the Storch was developed specifically for slow-speed flying and for take off from and landing in restricted spaces. It was used throughout World War II on various military duties, the Fi 156A-1 being the first production type; the Fi 156C-1 serving as a staff transport; the Fi 156C-2 as a short-range reconnaissance aircraft; and the Fi 156D as an ambulance. Other sub-types were used for general-purpose and army co-operation duties. During the occupation of France, the Fi 156 was built by the Morane-Saulnier company at its Puteaux factory, while others were produced in Mraz, Czechoslovakia.

A total of 2,549 Fi 156s were built. Serving on virtually every front, the Storch is best remembered for rescuing Benito Mussolini from the hotel where he was being held in the Gran Sasso mountain range on 12 September 1943.

Data (Fi 156C-3): *Engine* one 179 kW (240 hp) Argus As 10C *Wing span* 14.25 m (46 ft 9 in) *Length* 9.9 m (32 ft 5½ in) *Max T-O weight* 1,326 kg (2,920 lb) *Max level speed* 175 km/h (109 mph) *Range* 380 1,010 km (236–628 miles) *Armament* one 7.9 mm MG 15 machine-gun *Accommodation* pilot and one or two passengers; the five-passenger Fi 256 enlarged version, developed during the occupation at the Morane-Saulnier factory, was abandoned

Fieseler Fi 167 (Germany) Two-seat torpedo-bombing and reconnaissance biplane of 1938 developed to serve on the German aircraft carrier *Graf Zeppelin*.

Fiat R.S.14 prototype.

Fike Model E.

Firestone Model 45.

Fike Model D (USA) Single- or two-seat light high-wing monoplane (Continental A65 engine), plans for which are available to amateur constructors.

Fike Model E (USA) Single- or two-seat light high-wing monoplane (Continental C85 engine), plans for which are available to amateur constructors.

Firestone Model 45 (USA) Under the designation XR-9B, this two-seat helicopter was developed by G & A Aircraft in co-operation with the US Army Air Force's Air Technical Service Command. The prototype flew in 1944. A civil variant was also produced as the GA-45D. Development of the helicopter ended in 1947.

Fisher P-75 Eagle (USA) First flown in September 1943, the Eagle was an unusual-looking single-seat fighter, powered by a 1,937 kW (2,600 hp) Allison V-3420-19 engine. Thirteen prototypes and P-75A production aircraft were built for the USAAF. It made use of components from the Curtiss P-40, Vought F4U and Douglas A-24.

Flanders B.2.

Flaglor Scooter (USA) Ultra-light sporting monoplane, plans of which are available to amateur constructors.

Flanders B.2 (UK) Single example of a Gnome-powered biplane of 1912; subsequently used by the RNAS after being impressed in 1914.

Flanders F.4 (UK) Single example of an aeroplane taken on charge by the British Army's Central Flying School. Army number 239.

Flaglor Scooter.

Fleet Models 1 and 2 (USA) Fleet Aircraft was formed to market the Fleet biplane, originally

known as the Consolidated Husky Junior. As the Model 1 it was powered by an 82 kW (110 hp) Warner Scarab engine and as the Model 2 by a 74.5 kW (100 hp) Kinner. Both versions were two-seat open-cockpit biplanes.

Fleet PT-6 (USA) Basically a militarised version of the Fleet Model 2, 15 of which were purchased by the USAAC.

Fleet Model 50, Finch and Fort (Canada) Formed in 1930, this company took over complete world rights from Consolidated Aircraft for the Fleet Trainer. It also developed the Model 50K twin-engined freighter and the Model 60 two-seat advanced training monoplane, known as the Fort. Only 90 Forts were produced for the Commonwealth Air Training Plan, production ending in favour of the Fairchild M-62 or Freshman. The Fleet Trainer (known by this company as the Finch) was used for primary training in the Commonwealth Air Training Plan and the original order for 400 was completed in 1940 – many months ahead of schedule. A further contract for 202 followed, each powered by a 93 kW (125 hp) Kinner B-5 radial engine.

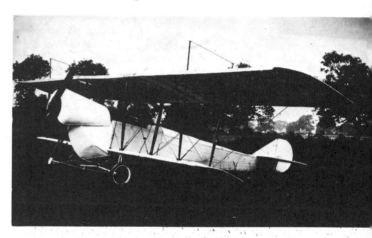

Fleet Model 80 Canuck (Canada) First post-war design, produced as a two-seat high-wing light cabin monoplane. Power was provided by a 63.3 kW (85 hp) Continental C-85-12J radial engine. Production ended in 1947.

Fleet Super V (Canada) Conversion of the Beechcraft Bonanza.

Fleetwings Sea Bird (USA) Four-seat high-wing amphibious flying-boat powered by a 223.5 kW (300 hp) Jacobs L-5 radial engine.

Fleetwings Model 23/BT-12 (USA) Two-seat basic training monoplane powered by a 335.3 kW (450 hp) Pratt & Whitney R-985-25 radial engine. Twenty-five delivered to the USAAF as the BT-12.

Fleetwings Model 33 (USA) Two-seat light training monoplane powered by a 97 kW (130 hp) Franklin 6AC-298 engine.

Fletcher FBT-2 (USA) Two-seat primary training monoplane of 1941 powered by a 212.4 kW (285 hp) Wright R-769E-1 radial engine. Sliding Plexiglas canopy covered tandem cockpits.

Fletcher FL-23 (USA) Two-seat observation, reconnaissance and liaison monoplane entered in a USAF/AGF competition of 1950, but was eliminated.

Fletcher FD-25 Defender and FD-25A (USA)
Prototype single-seat light ground-support
monoplane of 1953 powered by a 168 kW
(225 hp) Continental E-225-8 engine. FD-25A
was a two-seat version for ground support,
liaison, observation, gunnery control, instrument
or flight training.

Fletcher FU-24 (USA) Designed primarily for
agricultural top-dressing work in New Zealand,
where 100 were assembled initially. The prototype flew for the first time in July 1954, followed
by the first production aircraft five months later.
Power was provided by a 168 kW (225 hp) or
179 kW (240 hp) Continental O-470 engine. In
1960 the company became known as Flair Aviation. Meanwhile in 1957 Air Parts of New Zealand had acquired the Australasian sales rights
for the FU-24. In 1964 it acquired all manufacturing and sales rights and marketed the aircraft with
a 194 kW (260 hp) Continental IO-470-D engine
as the FU-24 basic agricultural and five-seat version and the FU-24A six-passenger and cargo-
carrying version. The FU-24 is available today as
the Aerospace Fletcher FU-24-950.

Flight Dynamics Flightsail VII (USA) Two-
seat lightweight homebuilt amphibian.

Fabrica Militar de Aviones (FMA) (Argentina)
see also **IA** and **DINFIA**

FMA Ae C.1, C.2 and C.3 (Argentina) The Ae
C.1 was a 112 kW (150 hp) Armstrong Siddeley
Mongoose or 104 kW (140 hp) Genet-Major-
engined three-seat touring monoplane. The
123 kW (165 hp) Wright-engined C.2 was a two-
seat training derivative of 1932, while the C.3 of
1934 was a two-seat training and touring version
of the C.2 with a Genet-Major engine. C.3s were
supplied to civil flying schools.

FMA Ae.M.O.1 (Argentina) Two-seat military
training monoplane with a 179 kW (240 hp)
Wright Whirlwind engine. Twelve produced for
the Argentine Army, delivered in July 1934.

Fletcher FD-25 Defender.

FMA Ae.MB.2 (Argentina) Cantilever low-wing
light bombing and reconnaissance monoplane
powered by a 530.5 kW (712 hp) Wright
CR-1820 engine. Fifteen built, production ending
in 1936.

FMA Ae.T.1 (Argentina) Five-seat cabin monoplane of 1933 powered by a 335 kW (450 hp)
Lorraine W engine. First commercial aeroplane
produced in Argentina.

FMA El Boyero (Argentina) Light two-seat
cabin high-wing monoplane of 1939, powered by
a 37.25 kW (50 hp) Continental A-50 or 48.4 kW
(65 hp) Continental A-65 engine.

FMA IA.50 Guarani I and II (Argentina) The
Guarani I light transport first flew in prototype
form on 6 February 1962 and utilised about 20%
of the structural components of the IA.35 Huanquero. Power was provided by two 633.4 kW
(850 hp) Turboméca Bastan IIIA turboprop
engines. The Guarani II was developed from it
and the prototype flew for the first time on 23
April 1963. It was placed in production for the
Argentinian Air Force for communications,
photographic (with the Military Geographic
Institute) and executive transport duties, while
the Navy received one as a staff transport. A total
of 41 G.11s were built.
Data (G.II): *Engines* two 693 kW (930 shp) Turboméca Bastan VIA turboprops *Wing span*
19.59 m (64 ft 3¼ in) *Length* 15.3 m (50 ft 2½ in)
Max T-O weight 7,750 kg (17,085 lb) *Max level
speed* 500 km/h (310 mph) *Range* 2,575 km
(1,600 miles) *Accommodation* 10–15 passengers,
paratroops, six stretchers and two attendants or
other specialised interiors

FMA IA.58 Pucará (Argentina) Twin-
turboprop counter-insurgency aircraft designed
to meet an Argentinian Air Force requirement.

Fleet Model 80 Canuck.

Fletcher FU-24A.

Flight Dynamics Flightsail VII.

FMA Ae.C.2.

FMA Ae.M.0.1.

Known originally as the Delfin, the first powered prototype made its maiden flight on 20 August 1969. An initial order for 30 aircraft was placed, the first flying on 8 November 1974. Early aircraft serving with the II Escuadron de Exploration y Ataque at Reconquista air base were deployed operationally in 1976 against armed groups in north-west Argentina. A further 15 Pucarás were ordered in 1977 but the Air Force has an eventual requirement for 100 of these aircraft. The purchase of four aircraft was under consideration in 1977 by the Mauritanian Islamic Air Force. An IA.58B version of the Pucará is being studied for the Argentinian Air Force with two 30 mm cannon in a redesigned and strengthened fuselage. Data (IA.58): *Engines* two 761 kW (1,022 ehp) Turboméca Astazou XVI G turboprops *Wing span* 14.5 m (47 ft 6¾ in) *Length* 14.25 m (46 ft 9 in) *Max T-O weight* 6,800 kg (14,991 lb) *Max level speed* 500 km/h (310 mph) *Range* 3,042 km (1,890 miles) *Armament* two 20 mm Hispano HS-804 cannon and four 7.62 mm FN-Browning machine-guns, plus up to 1,620 kg (3,571 lb) of external stores including gun and rocket pods, bombs or auxiliary fuel tanks

FMA IA.62 (Argentina) Primary trainer for the Argentinian Air Force. Under development.

FMA Ae.M.B.1, prototype of the Ae.M.B.2.

Focke-Achgelis Fa 223 (Germany) With the first free flight of the Focke-Wulf Fw 61 on 26 June 1936, Germany had gained a world lead in the development of a practical helicopter. However the Fw 61 was not of much use, being unable to carry anything more than a pilot. In August 1940 a commercial development made its first free flight as the Fa 266. It had two large rotors driven through reduction gearing by a 745 kW (1,000 hp) BMW 323 engine. Its AUW was about 3,900 kg (8,600 lb), but more importantly it had a useful payload of about 800 kg (1,764 lb). The helicopter was redesignated Fa 223 Drache soon after and further developed as a military aircraft. During 1942 it was evaluated successfully as a military type and initial production aircraft were ordered. However Allied bombing of factories prevented all but a few Fa 223s from becoming operational, although three were used as transports by Luft-transportstaffel 40. The much more ambitious Fa 284 (with two BMW 801 engines) was never completed.

Focke-Achgelis Fa 330 Bachstelze (Germany) The Fa 330 was a man-lifting rotor kite, specially developed for use by ocean-going IX-type U-boats as an observation post. A free-turning three-bladed rotor was mounted on a vertical pylon attached to a simple framework on which there was a seat for the pilot/observer. The kite was connected to the U-boat by cable and winch and maintained altitude by being towed by the surfaced submarine. The pilot communicated to the submarine by telephone. With this rotor kite an altitude of about 122 m (400 ft) could be achieved. However the Fa 330 was not liked by submarine crews or pilots as it took too long to recover and so delayed submerging in an emergency.

Focke-Wulf A.16 (Germany) Three–four-passenger monoplane, the general outlines of which were reminiscent of those of the Dornier Komet II, while the wing was somewhat similar to the Taube type. A total of 24 A.16s were built in several versions, early types being fitted with 56 kW (75 hp) Siemens, 67 kW (90 hp) Junkers L.1a or 89.4 kW (120 hp) Mercedes engines. It was used in the northern part of Germany for joy-riding and occasional passenger work (including with Deutsche Luft-Hansa). It was also used to transport newspapers by Berliner Lokal-Anzeiger from Berlin to Hannover, Bremen, etc.

Focke-Wulf A.17 Möwe (Germany) Nine-passenger commercial cabin monoplane of 1928 powered by a 313 kW (420 hp) Gnome-Rhône

Jupiter 9Ab radial engine. Ten operated by Deutsche Luft-Hansa.

Focke-Wulf A.20, A.20a and A.23 Habicht (Germany) Single-engined four-passenger cabin monoplanes of 1927–28, only a handful of which were built.

Focke-Wulf A.21 Photo (Germany) Modification of the A.17 adapted for photographic and air survey work. Cabin equipped with photographic equipment, including dark room.

Focke-Wulf A.29 Möwe (Germany) Nine-passenger commercial cabin monoplane of 1929 powered by a 447 kW (600 hp) BMW VI engine. Small number operated by Deutsche Luft-Hansa.

Focke-Wulf A.32 Bussard (Germany) Six-passenger commercial cabin monoplane of 1930 powered by a 209–231 kW (280–310 hp) Junkers L.5 engine. Small number operated by Deutsche Verkehrsflug, but from 1931 the financial crisis caused some suspension of scheduled services.

Focke-Wulf A.33 Sperber (Germany) Four-seat taxi and touring cabin monoplane powered by a 108 kW (145 hp) Walter Mars engine. Very small number built during 1930.

Focke-Wulf A.38 Möwe (Germany) Refined version of the Möwe powered by a 380 kW (510 hp) Siemens-built Jupiter VI engine. Four purchased by Deutsche Luft-Hansa, bringing the total number of Möwes operated by this company to 18.

Focke-Wulf A.43 Falke (Germany) Three-seat express passenger-carrying cabin monoplane of 1932 powered by a 164 kW (220 hp) Argus As. 10 engine.

Focke-Wulf A.47 (Germany) Two-seat parasol-wing monoplane produced as a prototype meteorological observation aircraft.

Focke-Wulf C-19 (Germany) German version of the British-built Autogiro C-19 Mk IV powered by a 74.5 kW (100 hp) Siemens Sh.14 engine.

Focke-Wulf F-19 Ente (Germany) Twin-engined tail-first (canard-type) cabin monoplane demonstrated in the Netherlands, England and Belgium in 1931.

Focke-Wulf Fw 44 Stieglitz (Germany) Two-seat biplane produced from 1933 and used as a primary trainer by the Luftwaffe and exported. Powered by a 112 kW (150 hp) Siemens Sh.14A engine.

Focke-Wulf Fw 56 Stosser (Germany) Single-seat parasol-wing monoplane powered by a 179 kW (240 hp) Argus As.10C engine and first flown in 1933. Developed as a fighter for the Luftwaffe and exported to Austria and Hungary, it

later became an advanced flying, radio, gunnery and bombing trainer, remaining in production until 1940.
Data: *Engine* as above *Wing span* 10.5 m (34 ft 5½ in) *Length* 7.65 m (25 ft 1½ in) *Max T-O weight* 996 kg (2,195 lb) *Max level speed* 278 km/h (171 mph) *Range* 460 km (286 miles)

FMA IA.50 Guarani II.

FMA IA.58 Pucara.

Focke-Wulf Fw 58 Weihe (Germany) The Weihe was first flown in 1935 as an advanced training, light transport and communications aircraft for the Luftwaffe, powered by two 179 kW (240 hp) Argus As.10C engines. However before the outbreak of World War II Deutsche Luft-Hansa received eight as six-passenger commercial transports. Armament in the military training version comprised a gunner's turret in the nose (which could be replaced by a metal cone for blind-flying instruction) and an aft gun position. The turret had space for an instructor and pupil for machine-gun and bomb-aiming training. Two seats side-by-side were provided in the cockpit for flying training, while a bomb trap with sights in a further compartment was provided for bombing instruction.

Focke-Achgelis Fa 330 Bachstelze under test by the RAF.

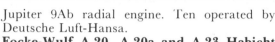

Focke-Wulf Fw 61 (Germany) The Fw 61 was the world's first truly successful helicopter, flying for the first time on 26 June 1936. It had a normal aeroplane fuselage and tail unit and was powered by a 119 kW (160 hp) Siemens-Halske Sh.14A engine mounted in the nose. Two three-bladed rotors were mounted on the tips of inclined steel-tube outrigger pylons. Piloted by Ewald Rohlfs, it established several FAI-recognised records for helicopters during 1937, including 122.553 km (76.151 miles) covered in a closed circuit, a duration of 1 hour 20 minutes and 49 seconds, and other records for distance flown in a straight line, speed over a 20 km course, and height. In 1938

Focke-Wulf

Focke-Wulf F-19 Ente.

Hanna Reitsch flew the Fw 61 from Stendal to Berlin, flying forwards, backwards and sideways. Maximum level speed was about 145 km/h (90 mph).

Focke-Wulf Fw 44 Stieglitz biplanes.

Focke-Wulf Fw 56 Stossers.

Focke-Wulf Fw 187 Zerstörer (Germany) Twin-engined fighter, three of which were built and used operationally.

Focke-Wulf Fw 189 Uhu (Germany) The Uhu was first flown in July 1938 and entered service with the Luftwaffe from 1940 as a short-range reconnaissance and army co-operation aircraft. Armament comprised four 7.9 mm machine-guns and two or four 50 kg bombs. The central crew nacelle, projecting rearwards between the twin tailbooms, was extensively glazed and provided excellent all-round vision for the crew of three. Operated mainly on the Eastern Front, the Uhu remained in production until 1944, by which time nearly 850 aircraft had been completed, including a number of purpose-built five-seat trainers. However, because of the low speed of the aircraft, its use was subsequently restricted to less active duties, such as evacuation of wounded, radio training and communications.
Data (Fw 189A): *Engine* two 335.3 kW (450 hp) Argus As.410A-1s *Wing span* 18.4 m (60 ft 5 in)

Length 12.0 m (39 ft 4 in) *Max T-O weight* 3,950 kg (8,708 lb) *Max level speed* 344 km/h (214 mph) *Range* 690 km (430 miles)

Focke-Wulf Fw 190 (Germany) Although to the end of World War II it was made in smaller numbers than the Bf 109, the type it was intended to replace, the Fw 190 was by far the better all-round aircraft and in many ways the most advanced combat machine to go into action in quantity in the war. It was extremely small and compact, yet had a large and powerful radial engine installed in an extremely attractive way to give lower drag than in earlier radial installations. The all-metal structure was of outstanding strength, and with little difficulty was locally reinforced to clear the aircraft for use with extremely heavy loads of guns, ammunition and bombs – including the SC1800 bomb of 3,968 lb and the large LTF 5b torpedo. Though its original mission had been air combat, by 1943 the Fw 190 had largely replaced the Ju 87 and other types as the Luftwaffe's standard tactical attack and close-support aircraft, with large numbers also deployed in such roles as reconnaissance and missions against heavy bombers.

There is little doubt that Kurt Tank, who led the project staff in the spring of 1938, was influenced by the Hughes racer which had set a speed record in America. He followed the same layout with slim fuselage, extremely small wing and tall landing gear with very wide track. The first prototype (powered by the BMW 139 engine in an advanced totally enclosed cowl with cooling airflow admitted through the large ducted propeller spinner) began taxi trials in May 1939 and flew on 1 June, although it remained completely unknown to British Intelligence. Considerable changes followed with various further prototypes, including discarding of the ducted spinner, addition of a cooling fan, change to the slightly larger but more powerful 1,192 kW (1,600 hp) BMW 801C engine, repositioning of the beautifully enclosed cockpit further back (for centre of gravity reasons, despite the poorer forward view on the ground, but reducing temperature around the pilot's feet and making room for guns in the top decking), and in the late summer of 1940, a larger wing and tailplane.

Early Fw 190A-1 fighters were delivered from June 1941, with four 7.92 mm MG 17 machine-guns. The A-2 replaced the inner-wing guns with two of the new high-velocity MG 151/20 cannon, and the A-3 added two 20 mm MG FF cannon outboard to make it the most heavily armed single-engined fighter of its day. In 1942 the A-3 was met in force by the RAF, which at first thought the Luftwaffe was using captured Curtiss H.75 Hawks, but the new machine outperformed the Spitfire VB and for more than a year dominated the sky over north-west Europe.

Fantastic profusion of Fw 190A sub-types followed with numerous schemes of armament and other devices including air-to-surface and air-to-air missiles, 21 cm mortars, upward or downward tubes for rockets for destroying bombers or tanks, various anti-ship weapons, and equipment for night fighting. There were long-range variants with large overwing tanks, a tandem dual trainer and a ramming model with armoured leading edges.

The most important tactical versions were the 190F, a heavily armed and armoured battlefield version with more than 20 sub-versions, and the G-series of long-range attack aircraft with auto-pilot and extra fuel. After two years of development via the 190B and C series, most fitted with the DB 603 liquid-cooled inverted-V engine, delivery began in the autumn of 1944 of the first of the 'long-nose' 190s, the D-9 (called Dora 9 by its pilots). Despite the fact that, for reasons of availability, this had the Jumo 213A-1 bomber engine, of 1,323.5 kW (1,776 hp), it could out-perform the previous models and was often judged superior to the P-51D or late-model Spitfires. By this time almost all Fw 190 versions had changed the rifle-calibre guns in the top deck-ing for 13 mm MG 131s, and the D-9 usually also carried just two MG 151s inboard plus heavy bomb loads. Some D models had a 30 mm MK 108 firing through the spinner, and the heaviest armament comprised five 30 mm guns, a firepower unmatched by any other fighter of the day. From this outstanding machine was derived the Ta 152, described separately. Total Fw 190 production was 20,001 and in 1945–6 the French SNCAC group built 64 with the designation NC 900.

Data (Fw 190A-8): *Engine* as above *Wing span* 10.5 m (34 ft 5½ in) *Length* 8.96 m (29 ft 4¾ in) *Max T-O weight* 4,900 kg (10,802 lb) *Max level speed* (clean) 657 km/h (408 mph) *Range* 800 km (497 miles)

Focke-Wulf Fw 200 Condor (Germany) Designed originally as a 26-passenger airliner for Deutsche Luft-Hansa, the first prototype Condor made its maiden flight in July 1937. Various pre-production and Fw 200B-series production aircraft were operated as commercial transports by Deutsche Luft-Hansa, Det Danske Luftfartselskab and a Brazilian operator from the latter half of 1938, the B version powered by four 648.3 kW (870 hp) BMW 132H engines. With the outbreak of World War II, Luft-Hansa's Condors were impressed into the Luftwaffe as transports, while a small number being built for the Japanese Army (including a maritime reconnaissance conversion) were also taken over.

Interest in the Condor as an interim reconnaissance bomber for the Luftwaffe led to contracts for the Fw 200C, starting with a small number of pre-production aircraft of basically commercial type. The Fw 200C-1 introduced the long bomb-bay gondola beneath the fuselage, slightly offset to starboard. This contained a bomb aimer's position at the forward end and gun positions at both the forward and aft ends. The guns were placed on hemispherical mountings with restricted movement. Total defensive armament comprised, according to sub-variant, one 7.9 mm machine-gun, 15 mm or 20 mm cannon in a power-operated turret above the pilot's cabin, one 13 mm machine-gun in an aft dorsal position, two–four 7.92 mm machine-guns for lateral fire, one 20 mm cannon in the nose of the gondola and

Focke-Wulf Fw 58 Weihe.

Focke-Wulf Fw 61.

one 7.92 mm or 13 mm machine-gun or 20 mm cannon in the tail of the gondola. Power was provided by four BMW 132H-1 engines in the Fw 200C-1 and C-2 versions and 700.5 kW (940 hp) Bramo Fafnir 323R-2s in the C-3 and later air-craft. A total of 263 production aircraft were built.

Operated in small numbers against Allied shipping during 1940, as well as for maritime reconnaissance and mine-laying duties, the Condor really came into its own in 1941. From then until the summer of 1944 it was used extensively against convoys and for U-boat co-operation. However, as early as 1943 purpose-designed maritime reconnaissance aircraft began replacing the Condor, whose activities had been somewhat curtailed by the introduction of Allied CAM merchant ships carrying expendable Hurricane fighters, long-range Beaufighters and Liberators. Thereafter the Condor reverted to transport duties. Interestingly, in the early stages of the war experiments had been made to use the Condor as a barrage-balloon destroyer, while a few special Condors were delivered for the use of Hitler and his staff.

Data (Fw 200C-3): *Engines* as above *Wing span* 33.0 m (108 ft 3 in) *Length* 23.8 m (78 ft 3 in) *Max T-O weight* 22,700 kg (50,045 lb) *Max level speed* 384 km/h (240 mph) *Range* 4,440 km (2,759 miles) *Armament* as above, plus a normal bomb load of 1,500 kg (3,307 lb)

Focke-Wulf Fw 189A Uhu.

Focke-Wulf

Focke-Wulf S-2 (Germany) Side-by-side two-seat parasol-wing trainer of the late 1920s powered by a 59.6 kW (80 hp) Siemens Sh.11 radial engine.

Focke-Wulf S-24 Kiebitz (Germany) Two-seat light biplane powered by a 44.7 kW (60 hp) Siemens engine.

Focke-Wulf Fw 190s.

Focke-Wulf Fw 190D-9.

Focke-Wulf Ta 152 (Germany) Following the success of the so-called 'long-nosed Fw 190' (Fw 190D), Kurt Tank redesigned the aircraft to meet a Luftwaffe requirement for a high-altitude interceptor based on an airframe already in production. Structurally there was little difference between the Ta 152A and its predecessor. The wings were of slightly greater area and differed in plan form from those of the Fw 190 and the nose was cleaned up to give a smoother fuselage top line. Hydraulic instead of electric operation was used for the landing gear and flaps. After the Jumo 213A-powered Ta 152A had been abandoned, the Jumo 213E-powered Ta 152B appeared. This had a maximum speed of 685 km/h (426 mph) at 11,225 m (36,825 ft) but only a few were produced.

The first version of the Ta 152 to go into series production and service was the Ta 152H, a high-altitude fighter and reconnaissance aircraft with extended wings, a pressurised cockpit and powered by a Jumo 213E-1 engine with an MW 50 power-boost to provide 1,528 kW (2,050 hp). By the end of the war about 150 had been delivered. Meanwhile production of the Ta 152C was being organised, powered by a 1,714 kW (2,300 hp) Daimler-Benz DB 603LA engine with an MW 50 power-boost. This version could attain 747 km/h (464 mph) at 10,680 m (35,040 ft), but none reached operational status.

Data (Ta 152H-1): *Engine* as above *Wing span* 14.5 m (47 ft 7 in) *Length* 10.7 m (35 ft 1½ in) *Max T-O weight* 5,220 kg (11,508 lb) *Max level speed* 760 km/h (472 mph) *Range* 2,000 km

Focke-Wulf Fw 200 Condor maritime reconnaissance aircraft.

(1,243 miles) *Armament* one 30 mm MK 108 cannon and two 20 mm MG 151 cannon

Focke-Wulf Ta 154 (Germany) Twin-engined two-seat aircraft designed to meet a specification for a night/bad-weather day fighter with a high maximum speed and duration for 2¾ hours. The first experimental prototype was produced in mid-1943. Only 24 built.

Fokker Fokker aircraft built up to the 1918 Armistice are listed under Germany and follow the single entry on the Fokker B.III built in Austria-Hungary. After the end of World War I Anthony Fokker smuggled some D.VII fighters and components into Holland and set up a new factory in his native country. Aircraft built in Holland follow those under Germany and go right up to date with the latest types produced by Fokker-VFW. The final aircraft covered under Fokker are those built in America by Atlantic Aircraft Corporation (a subsidiary of the Fokker Aircraft Corporation) and include the Universal, Super Universal and F-10, all primarily developed for the American market (see also **Atlantic Aircraft**).

Fokker B.III (Austria-Hungary) Single-seat fighter biplane powered by a 74.5 kW (100 hp) Oberursel rotary engine. Deliveries were made to the Austro-Hungarian forces in 1916 and the type was licence-built in Budapest.

Fokker A series (Germany) A.I, A.II and A.III were the service designations of the production Fokker M.8 two-seat artillery-spotting monoplane, M.5L and M.5K single-seat scouting monoplanes. Each was powered by a 59.6 kW (80 hp) Oberursel rotary engine. Used by Germany and Austria-Hungary until mid-1915.

Fokker D.I (Germany) Single-seat fighter biplane of 1916 powered by an 89.4 kW (120 hp) Mercedes D.III engine and armed with a single Spandau machine-gun. Developed with the D.II as an Eindecker replacement, it was only 11 km/h (7 mph) faster than the E.III and lacked the manoeuvrability of the monoplane. Only a small number were built and these served briefly on the Western and then Eastern Fronts (see **Fokker D.V**).

Fokker D.II (Germany) Contemporary reports (such as those found in the 1918 edition of *Jane's*) suggest that the D.II was heavily influenced by French Nieuport and Morane types and indeed many similarities can be found. The upper wing was attached to a low cabane structure of Nieuport type, and almost touched the top of the fuselage to an extent that the leading edge of the centre section of the wing was raised to permit use of the offset machine-gun. The fuselage, elevators and landing gear were of the latest Morane type. Consequently some concern was expressed by Allied authorities that it could be confused with British and French aircraft. Basically the D.II was similar to the D.I but had shorter-span wings and a longer fuselage. Power was provided by a 74.5 kW (100 hp) Oberursel U.I rotary engine. The lighter weight of the D.II gave it the same maximum level speed as the D.I on less power and was flown from the early part of 1916 as an escort fighter (see **Fokker D.V**).

Fokker D.III (Germany) Basically a D.II with the wings of a D.I and powered by a 119 kW (160 hp) Oberursel U.III rotary engine. Despite the extra power a maximum speed of only 160 km/h (99.5 mph) was achieved. Nevertheless fairly large numbers of D.IIs and D.IIIs were delivered to the German and Austro-Hungarian forces and the Dutch government. These flew on the Western Front at a time when most of the earlier monoplanes were only operational on the Eastern Front (see **Fokker D.V**).

Fokker D.IV (Germany) Only a small number of D.IV fighters were produced, powered by the 119 kW (160 hp) Mercedes D.III engine and combining new greater-span wings with the D.III fuselage. Overall performance was almost identical to the D.III, which restricted production (see **Fokker D.V**).

Fokker D.V (Germany) The D.V was by far the best version of the D.I to D.V series of single-seat fighters despite reverting to the 74.5 kW (100 hp) Oberursel U.I engine. The upper wing had slight sweepback, the forward section of the fuselage was rounded to fair-in the engine which was enclosed in a neat circular cowling, and a propeller spinner was fitted. Approximately two-thirds of the 565 D.I to D.Vs built were of this version but were used mainly for training duties from the autumn of 1916.

Data: *Engine* as above *Wing span* 8.75 m (28 ft 8½ in) *Length* 6.05 m (19 ft 10 in) *Max T-O weight* 565 kg (1,246 lb) *Max level speed* 170 km/h (105.5 mph) *Endurance* 1 h 30 min *Armament* one or two Spandau forward-firing machine-guns

Fokker D.VI (Germany) For the January 1918 fighter competition Fokker entered two new aircraft, the D.VI and the D.VII. The D.VII became a legend in its own lifetime, while the D.VI is barely remembered. Yet the D.VI was a very able fighter with a maximum speed of 196 km/h (122 mph), achieved on the small 82 kW (110 hp) Oberursel UR.II engine. It was also a 'safe' design, marrying the engine and cowling, fuselage, tail unit and landing gear (with the characteristic aerofoil-section axle) of the Dr.I with new biplane wings. The result was a light and highly manoeuvrable fighter of reliable configuration. However, despite its qualities, it had not the overall performance of the D.VII and so production was limited: 52 going into German service as a fighter and advanced trainer and seven going to the Austro-Hungarian forces.

Focke-Wulf Ta 152H-1.

Focke-Wulf Ta 154.

Fokker D.VII (Germany) The D.VII is not only remembered as the finest German single-seat fighter of World War I but as the aircraft with which Anthony Fokker established a new factory in Holland after the war. This subsequently produced such stalwarts of commercial aviation as the F.III and F.VIIb-3m. As mentioned above, the D.VII (designed by Reinhold Platz) was produced for the first single-seat fighter competition of 1918 and was rushed into immediate production to supplement the outmatched Albatros D.Vs and Fokker Dr.I triplanes then equipping the Air Service. Indeed production of the D.VII became so important that the new D.VI was quickly taken off the production lines and the Albatros Werke was ordered to abandon production of its own type to make room for expanded production of the Fokker fighter.

Fokker D.I.

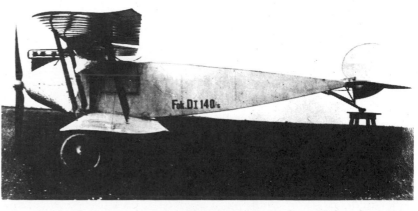

Fokker D.II.

Fokker D.V.

Fokker D.VI.

Fokker D.IV.

D.VIIs became operational from April 1918 and were soon in combat against the latest aircraft from the Allied camp. Faster and with a higher service ceiling than the Sopwith Camel, the D.VII was only truly matched by the British Sopwith Snipe and French Spad XIII. It was while flying a Spad XIII that the Allied 'Ace of Aces' Frenchman Capitaine René Paul Fonck shot down four D.VIIs, an Albatros D.V and a two-seater on 26 September 1918. By the autumn of 1918 more than 40 Jastas flew the D.VII, which was the final wartime mount of many famous pilots including Rudolph Berthold and Hermann Göring. By the Armistice nearly 800 had been delivered, although by no means all were operational.

Such was the importance of the fighter that, along with Zeppelin airships, the Versailles Peace Treaty made special provision for the handing over of all examples to the Allies. Anthony Fokker had other ideas and managed to smuggle a number of these (plus components) into his native country of Holland, where he set up a new factory to put the D.VII back into production for the Royal Netherlands Air Force. He also sold ex-German aircraft to Belgium and Switzerland. From the D.VII Fokker developed several post-war fighters and general-purpose aircraft. One such aircraft was the D.XI which, ironically, he found impossible to sell to the Dutch as they were more than satisfied with their D.VIIs.
Data: *Engine* one 138 kW (185 hp) BMW IIIa or 119 kW (160 hp) Mercedes D.III *Wing span* 8.9 m (29 ft 2¼ in) *Length* 6.95 m (22 ft 9¾ in) *Max T-O weight* 904 kg (1,993 lb) *Max level speed* 200 km/h (124 mph) *Endurance* 1 h 30 min *Armament* two forward-firing Spandau machine-guns
Fokker D.VIII (Germany) This was the last Fokker single-seat fighter to go into production during World War I and the fastest German fighter of the war. Having test flown a D.VII with its lower wings removed, Reinhold Platz designed a new parasol-wing fighter based around the small but reliable 82 kW (110 hp) Oberursel U.II rotary engine. It was basically a Dr.I with a D.VII-type vertical tail and a completely new thick and tapered wing. Having taken part in the April 1918 fighter competition, it entered production as the E.V or Eindecker V. Early production aircraft were evaluated under combat conditions in August, but although the general reaction was favourable they were found to suffer from a weak wing structure and several crashed as a result. Production of the D.VIII resumed after some modification of the design but too late to bring a change to Germany's fortune. Massive deployment of the D.VIII on the Western Front took place during the final three weeks of the war and it seems likely that Air Service and naval fighter Jastas flew about 100 by the Armistice.

Development of the D.VIII had not been completely in vain and the basic parasol-wing layout was immediately employed in new post-war commercial types, as noted in the 1920 *Jane's*: 'During the past winter months the chief designer of the Fokker Works, Herr Reinhold Platz, produced a new commercial model, by enlargement of the last Fokker war scout, namely, the Parasol D.VIII.' This aircraft was in fact the prototype F.II.
Data: *Engine* as above *Wing span* 8.4 m (27 ft 6¾ in) *Length* 5.86 m (19 ft 2¾ in) *Max T-O weight* 562 kg (1,239 lb) *Max level speed* 204 km/h (127 mph) *Endurance* 1 h 30 min *Armament* two forward-firing Spandau machine-guns

Fokker Dr.I (Germany) The Dr.I triplane is probably the best known of all German fighters of World War I. This is mainly because it was while flying a triplane that the top-scoring fighter pilot of the war Manfred von Richthofen ('The Red Baron') met his death. However the Dr.I was prominent during an era when most of the remaining experienced German aces were killed.

In February 1917 the Sopwith Triplane entered service with the RNAS. It was a highly manoeuvrable fighter, capable of outperforming the early Albatros and other contemporary German fighters then operational. As a matter of some urgency several manufacturers tried to copy the Sopwith Triplane layout. One can only speculate whether the Fokker Dr.I was the result of the Triplane or whether it was the result of original thought. What is known is that the prototype appeared with cantilever wings requiring no bracing wires or interplane struts. Unfortunately flight testing revealed that the wings vibrated in a most dangerous manner, forcing the use of conventional interplane struts. The struts and other subsequent modifications had the result of curtailing performance but nevertheless production fighters, originally known as F.Is, entered service in August 1917.

Pilots took quickly to the aircraft and consequently it has not been properly established whether it was genuine structural weakness of the wings or pilot concern that led to the Dr.I's temporary suspension from duty from October to December of that year. Full-scale operations resumed thereafter and until the arrival of the Fokker D.VII it was one of the main German fighters. It was credited with a good rate of climb and German authorities claimed that it could climb to 4,500 m (14,760 ft) in 17 minutes. Perhaps its main shortcoming was its lack of high-altitude performance. Reference to this was made in the 1918 *Jane's* : 'This machine is obviously copied from the Sopwith Triplane, and is a German attempt to produce a small quickly-manoeuvrable machine, apparently specially for fighting at lower altitudes, owing to the fact that the very high-powered Albatros chasers with their heavy fixed-cylinder engines are, in spite of their high speed, at a distinct disadvantage in the type of rough-and-tumble fight between a number of aeroplanes at the same time, which is commonly known by the RFC as a dog fight. The Albatros seems to depend for its effect on one rush, generally in the form of a dive from above, but it is unable to spin round, or loop, or turn in the same small radius which is possible to the light and lower-powered British fighting machines. Hence, the introduction by the Germans of this new triplane.'

Data: *Engine* as above *Wing span* 7.2 m (23 ft 7½ in) *Length* 5.77 m (18 ft 11 in) *Max T-O weight* 585 kg (1,290 lb) *Max level speed* 166 km/h (103 mph) *Endurance* 1 h 30 min *Armament* two forward-firing Spandau machine-guns

Fokker E series (Germany) On 19 April 1915 a most significant event happened that was to change the whole course of World War I: Frenchman Lieut Roland Garros, flying a Morane-Saulnier Type L, was shot down by anti-aircraft fire and landed behind German lines. More importantly, despite the badly burnt state of the Morane, it was discovered to be fitted with a Hotchkiss machine-gun which was fixed to fire through the propeller arc, any bullets that would have hit and damaged the propeller being deflected away by steel wedges attached to the blades. With this arrangement Garros had, in fact, shot down three German aircraft.

Grasping the importance of the concept that a fighter pilot could perform best by aiming the aircraft at the enemy rather than a flexibly mounted gun, Fokker was approached by the German authorities to produce a similar arrangement for a German aircraft. Having been supplied with a Parabellum MG 14 gun, Anthony

Fokker

Fokker E.III.

Fokker and Heinrich Luebbe produced a mechanical synchronising gear that timed the bullets to shoot through the propeller arc between the turning blades. This interrupter gear did away with the need for deflector wedges. Interestingly a similar gear had been patented before the war by Franz Schneider. The whole set-up was mounted on a Fokker M.5K monoplane, which became an M.5K/MG, and was demonstrated with great effect. Initial production monoplanes carrying an LMG.08 Maxim-type machine-gun or Spandau and fitted with the interrupter gear were designated E.Is (Eindecker or Monoplane Is), powered by 59.6 kW (80 hp) Oberursel rotary engines. E.Is were followed by 74.5 kW (100 hp) Oberursel-powered E.IIs and E.IIIs (the main production version) and a small number of heavy and fairly unsuccessful 119 kW (160 hp) Oberursel-powered E.IVs, totalling about 400 aircraft.

Fokker Spider.

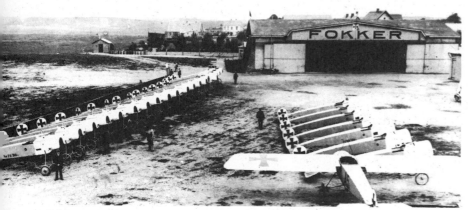

Fokker monoplane fuselages awaiting wings and engines.

Eindeckers appeared on the Western Front in the autumn of 1915 and, until their activities were curtailed by the de Havilland D.H.2 and Royal Aircraft Factory F.E.2b, enjoyed a winter of unparalleled success. The so-called 'Fokker scourge' saw a period of near-total German air supremacy, with the slow, badly armed and over-stable B.E.2c becoming its favourite prey. Both of Germany's first renowned fighter aces, Oswald Boelcke and Max Immelmann, flew Eindeckers, and for Immelmann it was to be also his last mount, falling victim to an F.E.2b of No 25 Squadron, RFC on 18 June 1916. Within a year the only Fokker monoplanes flying on active service were on the Eastern Front.

Data (E.III): *Engine* as above *Wing span* 9.52 m (31 ft 2¾ in) *Length* 7.3 m (23 ft 11¼ in) *Max T-O weight* 635 kg (1,400 lb) *Max level speed* 142 km/h (88 mph) *Endurance* 2 h 45 min

Fokker C.II.

Fokker M.7 and W.4 (Germany) The M.7 was a two-seat unarmed sesquiplane of 1915, a small number of which were supplied with land undercarriages to the German Navy. A single twin-float variant was the W.4.

Fokker M.16Z (Germany) Two-seat armed reconnaissance biplane of 1915 powered by a 149 kW (200 hp) Austro-Daimler engine. Thirty delivered to the Austro-Hungarian Air Service.

Fokker Spider (Germany) Single- or two-seat 'stick and string' monoplane, about 18 of which were built between 1912 and 1913 by Fokker-Aeroplanbau at Johannisthal, near Berlin. Gave way to the Morane-type monoplane in 1913.

Fokker F.B.II, B.II and B.III (Netherlands) The F.B.II was an amphibious flying-boat of the early 1920s powered by a 335.3 kW (450 hp) Napier Lion engine mounted in pusher configuration on the upper wing. Accommodation was provided for a flight crew of two, nose and dorsal gunners. It had been produced for the Navy. The similar B.II was a smaller two-seat flying-boat powered by a 268 kW (360 hp) Rolls-Royce Eagle IX tractor engine. The 1924 *Jane's* shows a B.II in Dutch military markings. The B.III was an improved F.B.II.

Fokker B.IV (Netherlands) Six-passenger amphibious flying-boat of about 1930.

Fokker C.I, C.II and C.III (Netherlands) The C.I was developed from the D.VII as two–three-seat touring and commercial biplane with military applications. A number of C.Is were operated by the Netherlands Army Air Service for artillery spotting and reconnaissance duties and by the Navy as trainers. The C.II and C.III were two-seat variants of basically similar type. Two-seat training derivatives became S types (see entry).

engines as the Bristol Jupiter, Pratt & Whitney Wasp and Hornet and Armstrong Siddeley Jaguar. New water-cooled engines included the Hispano 12X and Rolls-Royce Kestrel, and the MLD (Naval Air Force) in the East Indies used the Napier Lion. Most of the later Norwegian models had the Pegasus radial.

Fokker C.VD.

Fokker C.IV (Netherlands) Two-seat general-purpose biplane, forerunner of the C.V and able to be fitted with wings of different spans. Operated by the Netherlands Army Air Service and Netherlands East Indies Air Service as reconnaissance aircraft, powered by 298 kW (400 hp) Liberty and 335.3 kW (450 hp) Napier Lion engines respectively. Those exported included seven to the US Army as CO-4s and others to Russia (see **D.XI**). A twin-float seaplane version was also produced as the C.IV-W and exports included a number to Argentina.

Fokker C.V (Netherlands) Although Anthony Fokker's reputation ensured good sales for his Amsterdam-based company, no other military product between the World Wars quite equalled the worldwide acceptance of his C.V. A classical single-engined biplane of mixed construction in the Fokker tradition, with welded steel-tube fuselage and wooden wings, it scored by being robust, adaptable, pleasant to fly and exceptionally simple to maintain. A special point in its favour was that it was offered with wings of different span and area, all possible kinds of landing gear and engines of almost every make offering powers of 261–544 kW (350–730 hp).

Based upon the C.IV, the first C.V flew in May 1924 and went into production with constant-chord wings of three sizes, the C.VA having 37.5 m² (403.6 sq ft), the C.VB 40.8 m² (139.2 sq ft) and the C.VC 46.1 m² (496.2 sq ft). Engines included the 298 kW (400 hp) Liberty, and BMW, Lorraine or Hispano. Growing numbers of these were built for the LVA (Dutch Air Force) and export. (Fokker later complained that the C.V was so trouble-free that none came back for overhaul, leading to shortage of work in the factory.)

Fokker C.VE with ski landing gear.

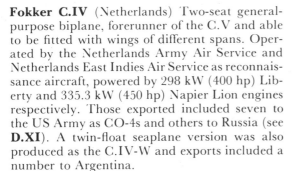

Fokker C.VI.

Total production of the C.V is not known, although it exceeded 1,000. Most were used for almost all military roles including bombing, fighting, reconnaissance, army co-operation, utility transport and even polar exploration. Various versions were made under licence in Italy (Meridionali), Denmark, Hungary, Sweden, Norway and Switzerland. The Swiss EKW C-35 was based on the C.V, and this outstanding tough and serviceable machine served as a pattern for many other military aircraft of the inter-war era, especially those built in smaller nations. Several hundred C.Vs of various types were in service with many air forces in 1939, including 28 with the LVA when that country was invaded on 10 May 1940.

Data (C.VE, larger wing): *Engine* as above *Wing span* 15.3 m (50 ft 2¼ in) *Length* (typical, varied with engine) 9.42 m (30 ft 11 in) *Max T-O weight* 2,220 kg (4,900 lb) *Max level speed* (typical) 255 km/h (158 mph) *Range* 850 km (528 miles) *Armament* one forward-firing and one rear-mounted machine-gun, plus small bombs

Fokker C.VI (Netherlands) Similar to the C.V and used by the Netherlands Army Air Force as an artillery-spotting aircraft. Powered by a 261 kW (350 hp) Hispano-Suiza or 287 kW (385 hp) Armstrong Siddeley Jaguar engine.

Fokker C.VEs.

In 1926 a new series introduced a cleaner fuselage and tapered wing without overhanging ailerons. The C.VD had wing area of 28.8 m² (310 sq ft), and the C.VE 39.3 m² (423 sq ft). A further change was a revised universal engine-mounting structure able to accept such radial

Fokker C.X.

Fokker

Fokker C.VII-W (Netherlands) Light-reconnaissance and advanced-training seaplane powered by a 164 kW (220 hp) Armstrong Siddeley Lynx engine. Operated by the Dutch Navy as a trainer.

Fokker C.VIII and C.VIII-W (Netherlands) Three-seat long-range reconnaissance aircraft of similar parasol-wing type, but powered by a 447 kW (600 hp) Hispano-Suiza 12Lb and 335.3 kW (450 hp) Lorraine-Dietrich engine respectively as a landplane for the Netherlands Army Air Service and seaplane for the Naval Air Service and East Indies Naval Air Service.

Fokker C.IX (Netherlands) 447 kW (600 hp) Hispano-Suiza-powered reconnaissance and training biplane operated during the 1930s by the Netherlands Army Air Service.

Fokker C.X (Netherlands) The C.X was designed as a fighter-reconnaissance and light-bombing biplane to replace the very successful C.V. Armament comprised one or two fixed 7.9 mm guns firing through the propeller arc and one rear-mounted gun on a movable mounting. Two racks, each for 200 kg (441 lb) of bombs (two 100 kg, four 50 kg, eight 25 kg or twelve 16 kg), were attached to the lower wings. Production orders were few: ten open-cockpit C.Xs, powered by 484.4 kW (650 hp) Rolls-Royce Kestrel V engines, delivered to the Netherlands East Indies Air Service in 1937, followed by five similarly powered C.Xs with open cockpits and 15 with

sliding cockpit enclosures to the Netherlands Army Air Service. Finland received four of the latest-type C.Xs with powerful 622 kW (835 hp) Bristol Pegasus XXI radial engines replacing the neater in-line engines, and went on to licence-build a further 35. Dutch and Finnish C.Xs saw action during the conflicts that followed.

Data (Kestrel engine): *Engine* as above *Wing span* 12.0 m (39 ft 4 in) *Length* 9.2 m (30 ft 2 in) *Max T-O weight* 2,250 kg (4,960 lb) *Max level speed* 320 km/h (199 mph) *Range* 830 km (516 miles)

Fokker C.XI-W (Netherlands) Two-seat shipboard reconnaissance seaplane powered by a 559 kW (750 hp) Wright SR-1820-F2 Cyclone engine. Operated by the Naval Air Service.

Fokker C.XIV-W (Netherlands) Two-seat training and light-reconnaissance seaplane operated by the Naval Air Service. Powered by one 335.3 kW (450 hp) Wright Whirlwind engine.

Fokker D.X (Netherlands) Parasol-wing fighter, ten of which were delivered to Spain.

Fokker D.XI (Netherlands) First flown in 1923, the D.XI was a further development of the wartime D.VII, powered by a 223.5 kW (300 hp) Hispano-Suiza engine and with sesquiplane wings, a new tail unit and landing gear. Later the same year it was displayed at the International Air Exhibition in Sweden, but despite a maximum speed of 225 km/h (140 mph) was unable to generate sufficient interest to convince the Dutch government that it should replace its D.VIIs with D.XIs.

However the D.XI had considerable export success. The Red Air Force received 125 fighters which later flew alongside 50 D.XIIIs and approximately 25 C.IVs and were used widely as trainers for German aircrew. Others went to Argentina, Romania, Spain, Switzerland and the USA, the latter comprising three Curtiss-engined aircraft which were designated PW-7s by the US Army. More importantly the D.XI gave Fokker the basis on which to develop more successful aircraft.

Data: *Engine* as above *Wing span* 11.68 m (39 ft 4 in) *Length* 7.0 m (22 ft 11½ in) *Max T-O weight* 1,250 kg (2,755 lb) *Max level speed* 225 km/h (140 mph) *Armament* two forward-firing machine-guns

Fokker D.XIII (Netherlands) First flown on 12 September 1924, the D.XIII was a single-seat fighter developed from the famous D.VII. It was of sesquiplane layout powered by a 335.3 kW (450 hp) Napier Lion engine. Cooling was by side radiators that could be drawn into the fuselage and oil cooling was by means of movable louvres in the engine cowling. Fifty were acquired by Russia and used predominantly by German pilots from 1927. Maximum level speed was 265 km/h (165 mph).

Fokker D.XIV (Netherlands) Interesting prototype single-seat open-cockpit cantilever low-wing fighter of the mid-1920s.

Fokker D.XVI (Netherlands) First flown in 1929, the D.XVI was a single-seat fighter based largely on the C.V and powered by an Armstrong Siddeley Jaguar engine enclosed in a Townend ring. Only 20 were built, most going to the Army Air Service but a few to Hungary and China. Maximum level speed was 320 km/h (199 mph).

Fokker D.XVII (Netherlands) Larger development of the D.XVI with a new landing gear and other refinements and powered by a 443.4 kW (595 hp) Rolls-Royce Kestrel or Hispano-Suiza 12Xbrs engine. Some of the 11 production aircraft built for the Netherlands Army Air Service were of this version, but a number were produced as D.XVII-As, an almost identical but air-cooled version with an Armstrong Siddeley Panther air-cooled radial engine. Armament comprised twin Vickers machine-guns. Maximum level speed with the Hispano-Suiza engine was 376 km/h (234 mph).

Fokker D.XXI (Netherlands) First flown on 27 March 1936, the D.XXI was a neat single-seat cantilever low-wing fighter with standard armament of four 7.9 mm machine-guns (two in the wings and two in the fuselage). Other armament combinations available were two 7.9 mm machine-guns in the fuselage and two 20 or 23 mm shell-firing guns underwing or four 7.9 mm guns in the wings plus two in the fuselage. The enclosed cockpit had a Plexiglas screen with side windows and the landing gear was of fixed cantilever type with aluminium sheet fairings.

The Dutch government ordered 36 production aircraft with 618.5 kW (830 hp) Mercury VII or VIII radial engines, which entered service from 1938. The Finnish Air Force also received 100 D.XXIs with Mercury or Pratt & Whitney Twin Wasp engines, most of which were licence-built at the State Aircraft Factory at Tampere. Interestingly the SAF also produced a two-seat advanced trainer of its own design called the Pyry, which was very similar to the D.XXI but with a Wright R-975-E3 radial engine of about half the power of the Twin Wasp. The Danish Air Force also received 13 D.XXIs (ten licence-built at the Royal Army Aircraft Factory at Klovermarksvej, Copenhagen) which were operated by one squadron. These were powered by 480.7 kW (645 hp) Mercury VI-S engines.

Finnish fighters played an important role during the Winter War with Russia and conflicts thereafter, while Dutch aircraft were active throughout the Five-Day War with Germany (10–15 May 1940). On one action alone on the first day of the German invasion of Holland, Dutch D.XXIs intercepted 55 Ju 52/3m transports and shot down between 37 and 39 of them, while others managed to destroy Bf 109s when faced with equal numbers.

Fokker D.C.1 (Netherlands) Two-seat fighter-reconnaissance biplane of 1924 designed on the lines of the C.IV but with a Napier Lion engine. Armament comprised two forward-firing and two rear-mounted machine-guns (one on a Scarff ring and one firing down through the floor). Ten were built for the Netherlands East Indies Air Service.

Fokker DC-1.

Fokker F.VIIa.

Fokker F.II (Netherlands) During the winter months of 1918–19 Reinhold Platz designed a commercial aircraft based on the configuration of the D.VIII fighter. It was, of course, enlarged and statements were issued to the effect that it would be capable of flying from Berlin to Petrograd with six persons in seven hours. This first aircraft eventually crashed. A new prototype was built (138 kW; 185 hp BMW engine) and this flew for the first time in October 1919. A small number of production F.IIs were completed in Holland and Germany and were operated by KLM and others from 1920. Most F.IIs flown on the London–Amsterdam route and elsewhere in Europe during 1921 were built in Germany and several German airlines flew the type at one time or another. However apart from the initial production aircraft, the largest number of F.IIs completed were built in Germany during the mid-1920s, all going to Deutsche Luft-Hansa.

Fokker F.III (Netherlands) The F.III was a six-seat commercial airliner based on the F.II,

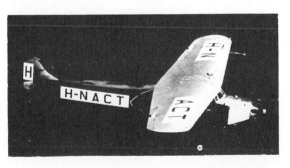

Fokker F.VIIa.

Fokker

Fokker F.VIIb/3m in RAF markings, with Stieger Monospar wing.

normally powered by one 179 kW (240 hp) Armstrong Siddeley Puma, 268 kW (360 hp) Rolls-Royce Eagle or 186.3 kW (250 hp) BMW IV engine (a full description appears in the 1925 *Jane's*). It was produced in Holland and Germany and first entered service with KLM in April 1921. It was used in regular service on the London–Amsterdam, the Hamburg–Bremen–Amsterdam–Rotterdam services of KLM, and also on the service between Danzig and Memel. Other operators included Deutsche Luft-Hansa and Deutscher Aero Lloyd, while the F.IIIs of Malert were the first aircraft operated by this Hungarian airline, beginning in July 1923.

Fokker F.IV/A-2 and T-2 (Netherlands) Only two F.IVs were built, powered by 298 kW (400 hp) Liberty engines. Both went to the USA to be evaluated by the Army, one becoming the A-2 ambulance and the other the T-2. The latter made the first non-stop crossing of the US by aeroplane during 2 and 3 May 1923 (see **Chronology**).

Fokker F.VII (Netherlands) Eight-passenger airliner based on the F.III. Five were built for KLM and were used on regular services in Holland, Poland and Switzerland. An F.VII type was also used by Mr C. D. Barnard when he flew from Karachi to London in 4½ days. Normal power plant was a 268 kW (360 hp) Rolls-Royce Eagle IX. A military version with internal bomb racks and other armament was produced as the F.VII.M.

Fokker F.VIIa and F.VIIb (Netherlands) The F.VIIa and F.VIIb were versions of the F.VII, the former with a wing area of 58.2 m² (626 sq ft) and the latter of 67.6 m² (727.6 sq ft). The F.VIIa was put into production as an eight-passenger or cargo-carrying airliner powered normally (as for KLM) by a 335.3 kW (450 hp) Gnome-Rhône-built Jupiter VI engine, although a number appeared with a 298 kW (400 hp) Packard Liberty (as for the USA), 335.3 kW (450 hp) Lorraine-Dietrich (as for Poland) and other types of engine.

The first F.VII-3m built was used by Lieut Cdr Richard E. Byrd, US Navy and Floyd Bennett on the first aeroplane flight over the North Pole (see **Chronology** 9 May 1926). Others achieved the record flight from Amsterdam to Batavia and back in 19 days (Lieut Koppen); San Francisco to Honolulu (Lieuts Maitland and Hegenberger, US Army); across the Atlantic (Cdr Byrd); first flight across the Pacific from San Francisco to Australia (Kingsford Smith and Ulm); and across the Atlantic as a seaplane (Miss Earhart and Mr Stulz).

Several different types of engine were fitted to F.VII-3ms, including three 164 kW (220 hp) Wright Whirlwinds and Armstrong Siddeley Lynx. The F.VIIb-3m differed from the F.VIIa-3m in having a larger wing with a straight inner trailing edge and a higher operating weight.

Data: *Engines* as above *Wing span* 19.3 m (63 ft 4 in) *Length* 14.5 m (47 ft 7 in) *Max T-O weight* (Lynx engines) 4,100 kg (9,038 lb) *Max level speed* 190 km/h (118 mph)

Fokker F.VIII (Netherlands) The F.VIII was a development of the F.VII, produced originally for KLM and accommodating up to 15 passengers. Power was provided initially by two 335.3 kW (450 hp) Gnome-Rhône-built Jupiter VI engines. Production remained limited but a few also served with the Hungarian airline Malert.

Fokker F.VIII.

Fokker F.VIIb/3m *Southern Cross*.

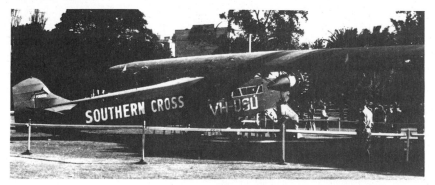

Fokker F.VIIa-3m and F.VIIb-3m (Netherlands) First flown on 4 September 1925, the F.VII-3m was a three-engined version of the F.VII and was, during its lifetime, one of the most widely known commercial aircraft in use in the world. It was originally produced for use in America and, apart from being used in commercial work, was chosen for several noteworthy flights.

Fokker F.IX.

Fokker F.IX (Netherlands) Three-engined 20-passenger airliner of 1929, two of which were built for KLM. Also built under licence by Avia as F-39 bomber for the Czech and Yugoslav air forces.

Fokker F.XI Universal (Netherlands) see **Fokker** (USA)

Fokker F.XII (Netherlands) Sixteen-passenger airliner of 1930, ten going into service with KLM and a few others with DDL and Aktiebolaget Aerotransport. KLM aircraft were powered by three 317 kW (425 hp) Pratt & Whitney Wasp engines.

Fokker F.XVIII (Netherlands) Fourteen-seat airliner of 1932 powered by three 328 kW (440 hp) Pratt & Whitney Wasp engines. Five were built for KLM. The normal accommodation of seven passengers on each side of the central gangway was reduced on KLM's route to the East to six chairs, two for an engineer and navigator and four for passengers.

Fokker F.25 Promotor.

Fokker F.25 Promotor (Netherlands) Four-seat twin-boom cabin monoplane, a post-war design powered by a 141.5 kW (190 hp) Lycoming O-435-A engine.

Fokker F.XXXVI (Netherlands) Four-engined 32-passenger airliner of 1934. One built and operated by KLM.

Fokker F.XXXVI.

Fokker F.XX (Netherlands) Single (but important) example of a three-engined 12-seat high-speed aircraft, featuring undercarriage legs that could be drawn into the engine nacelles.

Fokker F.XXII (Netherlands) Twenty-two-passenger airliner of 1935 powered by four 380 kW (510 hp) Pratt & Whitney Wasp T1D1 engines mounted in the leading edges of the wings. Four built, three for KLM and one for Aktiebolaget Aerotransport.

Fokker G.I (Netherlands) Twin 618.5 kW (830 hp) Bristol Mercury VIII-engined heavy-fighter and ground-attack monoplane, featuring twin booms and a central nacelle for a crew of three. Thirty-six G.Ias were delivered to the Netherlands Army Air Service from 1938, nearly two-thirds of which were serviceable when Germany invaded Holland, together with 12 two-seat Pratt & Whitney Twin Wasp Junior-powered G.Ibs ordered by Spain but not delivered. Armament of the G.Ia comprised eight 7.9 mm machine-guns in the nose and one in the conical turret in the tail of the nacelle and fired by the observer (plus bombs). Maximum level speed was 475 km/h (295 mph) with Mercury engines and 431 km/h (268 mph) with Twin Wasp Juniors. A few G.Is were subsequently used as fighter-trainers by the Luftwaffe.

Fokker F.XVIII.

Fokker F.XX.

Fokker G.Ias.

Fokker S.I (Netherlands) Biplane trainer developed from the C.I.

Fokker S.II (Netherlands) Similar to the S.I, with side-by-side seating for two. Designed to be powered by an engine in the 59.6–89.4 kW (80–120 hp) range, including a Mercedes, Renault, Curtiss, Benz, Gnome or Oberursel type. Became the standard trainer with the Netherlands Army Air Service.

Fokker F.XXII.

Fokker

Fokker S.11s.

Fokker S.14 Mach-Trainers.

Fokker T.IV.

Fokker S.III (Netherlands) Tandem two-seat biplane trainer operated by the Naval Air Service (MLD). Power was provided by an 89.4 kW (120 hp) Mercedes engine.

Fokker S.IV (Netherlands) Tandem two-seat trainer powered by a 97 kW (130 hp) Armstrong Siddeley Mongoose radial engine. Became the standard trainer of the 1930s with the Netherlands Army Air Service, later being joined by the S.IX and Koolhoven F.K.51 and F.K.56.

Fokker S.IX (Netherlands) Tandem two-seat biplane trainer of Tiger Moth appearance, first flown in 1937. More than 50 delivered to the Netherlands Army Air Service and Naval Air Service.

Fokker S.11 and S.12 Instructor (Netherlands) Two-seat basic trainer of the 1950s, powered by a 141.5 kW (190 hp) Lycoming O-435A engine. The S.12 was a nosewheel landing gear version. The S.11 entered service in the Netherlands, Israel, Brazil and Italy. The Italian Macchi company built the S.11 under licence as the M.416 and 100 were built at Fokker's Brazilian factory, which also constructed 50 S-12s.

Fokker S.14 Mach-Trainer (Netherlands) Rolls-Royce Derwent-powered two-seat jet trainer. Mach-Trainer Mk II was powered by a Rolls-Royce Nene engine. Fifty Mach-Trainers were constructed by the Fokker company in Brazil for the Brazilian Air Force.

Fokker T.IV (Netherlands) Large torpedo-bombing and reconnaissance seaplane of 1927 with thick shoulder-mounted monoplane wings and open cockpits for the two pilots (side-by-side), nose and dorsal gunners. Eleven 335.3 kW (450 hp) Lorraine-Dietrich W-powered T.IVs

Fokker S.12.

went into service with the Netherlands East Indies Navy and a few Rolls-Royce Eagle-powered aircraft with the Portuguese Navy. In 1935 the East Indies Navy received 12 improved T.IVas powered by 574 kW (770 hp) Wright SR-1820-F2 Cyclone engines and featuring a new enclosed cockpit for the pilots, nose and dorsal gun turrets and a ventral gun position. Surviving T.IVs were subsequently brought up to this standard. These remained operational until the Japanese invasion. Maximum level speed 260 km/h (161.5 mph).

Fokker T.V (Netherlands) Modern twin 689.3 kW (925 hp) Bristol Pegasus XXVI-engined cantilever mid-wing monoplane medium bomber, 16 of which equipped one squadron of the Netherlands Army Air Service from 1938. Not all remained operational in May 1940. Maximum level speed 417 km/h (259 mph).

Fokker T.VIII-W (Netherlands) Twin 618.5 kW (830 hp) Bristol Mercury XI-engined reconnaissance and torpedo-bombing seaplane, 11 of which entered service with the Dutch Navy shortly before the German invasion. Armament comprised one fixed forward-firing machine-gun and one similar gun on a flexible mounting for the observer, plus a torpedo or bombs. Five more were completed during the occupation for the Luftwaffe. Maximum level speed 358 km/h (222.5 mph).

Fokker-VFW F.27 Friendship (Netherlands) The most successful of all the twin-turboprop medium-range transports has been the Fokker F.27, even though the Soviet Union mas have produced more Antonov An-24s. It wa Fokker's first post-war transport and flew for the first time on 24 November 1955. It is a high-wing pressurised monoplane powered by two Rolls-Royce Dart engines, and is in service in most parts of the world in a number of versions. Accommodation ranges from 28 to 60 seats, and there are freighter, mail, passenger/cargo, troop-carrying and calibration models. In many areas of the world it

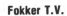
Fokker T.V.

aircraft. Two have been delivered to the Peruvian Navy and three (for search-and-rescue duties) to Spain.

Fokker-VFW F.28 Fellowship (Netherlands) The F.28 first flew on 9 May 1967 as a jet successor to the F.27. It is a low-wing monoplane with 16° of wing sweep to achieve good slow-speed handling and is currently powered by two 44 kN (9,900 lb st) Rolls-Royce R.B.183-2 Spey Mk 555-15H turbofans. It has a T-tail and an unusual feature is the split rear-fuselage air-brakes.

Fokker-VFW F.27 Friendship.

replaced the DC-3 and proved capable of operating from small rough aerodromes and in all climates.

The Friendship was also produced in the US by Fairchild as the F-27 and later by Fairchild Hiller as the FH-227 (with a 2 m; 6 ft 7 in longer fuselage). The first example to enter service was a Fairchild-built aircraft which began work with West Coast Airlines on 28 September 1958. The first Amsterdam-built F.27 to go into operation was flown over the Dublin–Glasgow route by Aer Lingus on 15 December 1958.

The standard engine now fitted to the Series 200, 400, 500 and 600 versions is the 1,596 kW (2,140 shp) Dart R.Da.7 Mk 532-7R. Maximum take-off weight has risen from 18,370 kg (40,500 lb) for the Series 100 to 20,410 kg (45,000 lb) for the current aircraft. By July 1978 a total of 675 Friendships had been built.
Data: *Engines* as above *Wing span* 29.0 m (95 ft 2 in) *Length* 23.56 m (77 ft 3½ in) *Max T-O weight* 20,410 kg (45,000 lb) *Normal cruising speed* 480 km/h (298 mph) *Range* (Mk 400) 1,935 km (1,203 miles)
Fokker-VFW F.27 Maritime (Netherlands) Medium-range maritime patrol version of the Friendship intended for customers who do not require a more sophisticated long-range patrol

Fokker T.VIII-W.

The Series 1000 aircraft entered service with Braathens SAFE Air Transport on 28 March 1969 and by the end of 1978 more than 150 had been sold to airlines in Europe, Africa, Asia, Australia and the Americas. Original accommodation was for 55–79 passengers, but the slightly larger Series 3000 and 4000 now in production can accommodate 65 and 85 passengers at normal seat pitch.

The F.28 has proved extremely successful, operating on unprepared and short runways, and in many places is the only jet type to operate. It is the only jet transport to be allowed to use Stockholm's Bromma Airport where noise abatement rules are very strict.

There are proposals for a Super F.28 version for 110–125 passengers.
Data (F.28 Series 4000): *Engines* as above *Wing span* 25.07 m (82 ft 3 in) *Length* 29.61 m (97 ft 1¾ in) *Max T-O weight* 32,200 kg (71,000 lb) *Max cruising speed* 843 km/h (523 mph) *Range* 1,852 km (1,151 miles)
Fokker TA-1 (USA) Similar to the C-2A. Three were supplied to the US Marine Corps for use in Nicaragua as bombing/cargo/ambulance/attack monoplanes.

Fokker-VFW F.28 Series 1000 Fellowship.

Fokker

Ford 5-AT-C5 Tri-motor
with twin-float landing
gear.

Ford 5-AT Tri-motor.

Interior of a National Air
Transport Ford Tri-motor.

Fokker C-2 and C-2A (USA) see **Atlantic Aircraft Corporation**

Fokker F-11-A Flying Yacht (USA) Six-passenger amphibious flying-boat powered by a 317 kW (425 hp) Pratt & Whitney Wasp engine mounted above the monoplane wing in pusher configuration.

Fokker F.10 (USA) Sometimes referred to as Super-Trimotors, the F.10 and F.10-A were 12-passenger refined variants of the Fokker F.VII-3m, each powered by three 317 kW (425 hp) Pratt & Whitney Wasp radial engines. Sixty-five F.10s and 59 F.10-As were built, and these were used widely by American Airways, Pan American Airways, Western Air Express (first three) and other operators.

Data (F.10-A); *Engines* as above *Wing span* 24.16 m (79 ft 3 in) *Length* 15.24 m (50 ft 0 in) *Max T-O weight* 5,942 kg (13,100 lb) *Cruising speed* 193 km/h (120 mph) *Range* 1,230 km (765 miles)

Fokker Universal (USA/Netherlands) The Universal (as designed in America) was a four-passenger high-wing cabin monoplane powered by a 223.5 kW (300 hp) Wright J-6 Whirlwind engine. The pilot and co-pilot sat initially in an open cockpit in the leading edge of the wing. The Universal was subsequently refined to include an enclosed cockpit for the pilots. In 1928 the main Dutch Fokker company produced its own version of the Universal (as the F.XI Universal) which was similar to the American refined version but powered by a 179 kW (240 hp) Lorraine engine. Only three were produced.

Fokker Super Universal (USA) Five–six-passenger cabin monoplane produced as a larger version of the Universal. Power was provided by three 317 kW (425 hp) Pratt & Whitney Wasp engines. Production totalled 123 aircraft.

Data: *Engines* as above *Wing span* 15.4 m (50 ft 7 in) *Length* 11.15 m (36 ft 7 in) *Max T-O weight* 2,392 kg (5,270 lb) *Cruising speed* 190 km/h (118 mph) *Range* 1,183 km (735 miles)

Fokker F.14 (USA) Single 391 kW (525 hp) Pratt & Whitney Hornet-engined six-passenger and mail carrier with a parasol wing and an open pilot's cockpit aft. Operated by Western Air Express.

Fokker F.32 (USA) As the first four-engined commercial airliner to be built in the USA, the Fokker F.32 flew for the first time in 1929. Power was provided by four 391 kW (525 hp) Pratt & Whitney Hornet radial engines mounted in tandem pairs, one on each side of the fuselage below

the high monoplane wing. Accommodation provided for 30 passengers and two pilots. Ten examples were built and entered service on the Western Air Express line between Los Angeles and San Francisco. They also played an important part in the continuation of mail and passenger routes from the Pacific Coast to New York City.

Data: *Engines* as above *Wing span* 30.18 m (99 ft 0 in) *Length* 21.29 m (69 ft 10 in) *Max T-O weight* 10,200 kg (22,500 lb) *Cruising speed* 193 km/h (120 mph)

Folland Gnat (UK) see **Hawker Siddeley Gnat**

Ford Tri-motor (USA) The original Stout Metal Airplane Company was purchased in August 1925 by Henry Ford and the aeroplane factory became a division of the Ford Motor Company. In the following year this company produced a three-engined commercial monoplane developed from the single-engined Stout Pullman, designated the Ford 3-AT. Power was provided by three 149 kW (200 hp) Wright J-4 Whirlwind engines. From the 3-AT was developed the 4-AT, an 11-passenger airliner which flew for the first time on 11 June 1926. Production quickly got under way and by 1929 the factory had to be

expanded to produce four Tri-motors (of all versions) a week.

A total of 78 4-ATs were eventually completed, powered by 223.5 kW (300 hp) Wright J-6 or Pratt & Whitney Wasp Junior engines. The 4-AT was joined on the production lines by the 14–15-passenger 5-AT, with 313 kW (420 hp) Wasps, and the 13-passenger 7-AT, with one Wasp and two J-6 engines. The single 484.4 kW (650 hp) Hispano-Suiza-engined freighter version (known as the 8-A) was not a success. From 1930 production gradually declined, ceasing completely in 1933. The 'Tin Goose', as it was nicknamed, was also used as a military transport. The US Navy received nine of the 4-AT and 5-AT versions from 1927, while the USAAC received 13.
Data (4-AT-E): *Engines* as above *Wing span* 22.56 m (74 ft 0 in) *Length* 15.19 m (49 ft 10 in) *Max T-O weight* 4,598 kg (10,130 lb) *Cruising speed* 172 km/h (107 mph) *Normal range* 917 km (570 miles)

Found FBA-2A seaplane.

Found FBA-2C.

seaplane in the following year. The production version was the FBA-2C, the first two of which were ordered by Georgian Bay Airways of Ontario and flew in 1962. Production totalled 34 aircraft, completed in 1967. Power was provided by a 186.3 kW (250 hp) Lycoming O-540-A1D engine.

Fornaire F-1A Aircoupe.

Found Centennial 100 (Canada) Six-seat utility transport aircraft powered by a 216 kW (290 hp) Lycoming IO-540-G engine. First flown on 7 April 1967.

Fornaire Execta, Expediter and Explorer (USA) In April 1955 Fornaire purchased the manufacturing rights for the Ercoupe and marketed it originally as the F-1 Aircoupe. The company then offered three new versions of the aircraft, the luxurious and fully equipped Execta, lesser-equipped Expediter and low-priced Explorer.

Fouga C.M. 170 Magister and C.M. 175 Zephyr (France) see **Aérospatiale**

Fouga C.M. 88-R Gemeaux (France) First flown on 6 March 1951, the Gemeaux was an experimental twin-fuselage aircraft used as a test-bed for Turboméca turbojet engines.

Found FBA-1A (Canada) First flown on 13 July 1949, the FBA-1A was a four-seat cabin monoplane powered by a 104.3 kW (140 hp) de Havilland Gipsy Major engine.

Found FBA-2 (Canada) The prototype of this five-seat utility transport aircraft flew for the first time on 11 August 1960. It was converted into a

Found Centennial 100.

Fournier RF-6B (France) Two-seat aerobatic monoplane powered by a 74.5 kW (100 hp) Rolls-Royce Continental O-200-A engine. Forty had been completed by early 1978.

Foxjet ST600-S/8 (USA) Six-seat twin-turbofan (3.56 kN; 800 lb st Williams Research WR44-800) transport aircraft, first flown in 1979. Firm orders for 73 aircraft had been received by mid-1978.

Frakes Turbine Mallard (USA) Grumman Mallard fitted with two Pratt & Whitney Aircraft of Canada PT6A-27 turboprop engines.

Frakes/Grumman Turbo-Cat (USA) Modified Grumman Ag-Cat powered by a 559 kW (750 shp) Pratt & Whitney Aircraft of Canada PT6A-34 turboprop engine.

Frakes Mohawk 298 (USA) As Mohawk 298s, Frakes Aviation updated a fleet of Nord 262s serving Allegheny Airlines' commuter operators. Modifications included the fitting of 875.5 kW

Fouga C.M.88-R Gemeaux.

Frakes Turbine Mallard.

(1,174 ehp) Pratt & Whitney Aircraft of Canada PT6A-45 free-turbine turboprop engines. All nine 25-passenger conversions had been completed by 1978.

Frankfort Cinema and TG-1A (USA) Two-seat glider produced before the outbreak of World War II as the civil Cinema and delivered to the USAAF from 1941 as the TG-1A.

Frederick-Ames EOS (USA) Single-seat light sporting monoplane, kits of parts of which will be made available to amateur builders.

Friedrichshafen F.F.29 (Germany) Pre-war designed two-seat 89.4 kW (120 hp) Mercedes D.II-powered coastal patrol and bombing twin-float seaplane of conventional biplane layout. Thirty-four built, serving with the German Navy as F.F.29s and F.F.29As during early months of World War I.

Friedrichshafen 1913 model and F.F.31 (Germany) In 1913 Friedrichshafen produced an amphibious pusher biplane with a central float straddled by wheels, underwing and tail stabilising floats. The crew of two sat in a central nacelle. Two developed examples were produced for the Navy in 1915 as twin-float F.F.31s, each carrying a Parabellum machine-gun in the nose of the nacelle.

Civil conversion of a Friedrichshafen F.F.49C.

Friedrichshafen F.F.33, F.F.39 and F.F.49 (Germany) Friedrichshafen was the first German aircraft company to devote itself almost exclusively to the manufacture of seaplanes (although this trend was broken with the G bombers of 1916) and was one of the two chief contractors to the German Navy, the other being Brandenburg (lesser types from Sablatnig and Gotha). The F.F. series was also built under licence by LFG, Sablatnig and Travemünde. In all more than 25 different models were produced, eight alone under the F.F.33 designation, one as the F.F.34 and two as F.F.49s.

The F.F.33 (of which only a handful were built) was virtually identical to the F.F.29 (except for the floats) and was followed in late 1914 by the F.F.33B, powered by a 119 kW (160 hp) Maybach engine and with the seating reversed so that the observer occupied the rear cockpit (armed with a machine-gun). The F.F.33E was another reconnaissance version (with bombing capability) powered by a 112 kW (150 hp) Benz Bz.III engine. It was the first Friedrichshafen aircraft to employ the characteristic extra ventral tail fin and balanced rudder and some were provided with a wireless. The floats of the version had increased in length so much that during the production run the tail float was abandoned.

A total of between 160 and 190 F.F.33Es were built. The last reconnaissance version was the F.F.33J, a direct successor of the E, especially seaworthy and powered by a 112 kW (150 hp) Benz engine. It was employed on board the raider cruiser *Wolff* and, when superseded by 149 kW (200 hp)-powered seaplanes, was employed as the F.F.33S naval trainer.

The F.F.33F was another derivative of the F.F.33 type but of reduced dimensions to improve controllability, and was the first German naval fighting scout. A further improvement was the F.F.33H with a shortened fuselage and redesigned ailerons and floats, aiming to reduce head resistance. It also featured a new cabane and provision of load struts between the floats, duplicating the cable wiring so that the gunner could fire between the propeller arc and the inner set of struts without fear of destroying the aircraft if the cable wiring was accidentally shot through. The F.F.33L was a further development of the H, powered by a Benz or Mercedes engine and was used for fighting, representing a compromise between performance and seaworthiness. For scouting the F.F.33 type was further developed into the F.F.39C of 1917 (14 built), with increased dimensions to suit a 149 kW (200 hp) Benz engine and the wings given increased stagger.

As a replacement for the F.F.33J, the F.F.39C type was improved as the F.F.49C and was in service for the last two years of war. It satisfied German demands for a seaplane with a speed of 140 km/h (87 mph) and a climb to 2,000 m (6,560 ft) in 25 to 30 minutes – although it did most of its flying at low altitudes. It was often used to rescue ditched crews, but on one occasion the crew of an F.F.49C were rescued after a week of drifting at sea. The F.F.49B was identical but for the adoption of the front observer's cockpit to carry an aiming device, as this version was used as a light bomber. Production of the F.F.49

amounted to 240 aircraft, all but a few as F.F.49Cs. A small number were operated by Deutsche Luft-Reederei, DDL and others as commercial seaplanes after the war. Friedrichshafen seaplanes performed extremely well in service over the North Sea and elsewhere and were reported as faster than British types. Development was also continuous.

Data (F.F.49C): *Engine* as above *Wing span* 17.15 m (56 ft 3¼ in) *Length* 11.65 m (38 ft 2¾ in) *Max T-O weight* 2,135 kg (4,707 lb) *Max level speed* 140 km/h (87 mph) *Endurance* 5 h 30 min *Armament* one forward-firing Spandau and one rear-mounted Parabellum machine-gun

Friedrichshafen F.F.34 (Germany) Prototype twin-boom pusher seaplane powered by a 179 kW (240 hp) Maybach engine. Subsequently converted into the F.F.44.

Friedrichshafen F.F.35 (Germany) First twin-engined (112 kW; 150 hp Mercedes) G-class seaplane. Prototype only.

Friedrichshafen F.F.40 (Germany) Experimental model with twin-tractor propellers driven by a single 179 kW (240 hp) Maybach engine, which was satisfactory but for the excessive weight of the transmission gears.

Friedrichshafen F.F.41 (Germany) From the experience of G-class landplane bombers, a naval torpedo bomber was developed as the F.F.41A with two 112 kW (150 hp) Benz engines. It proved seaworthy but only nine were completed.

Friedrichshafen F.F.43 (Germany) Prototype single-seat fighter with the pilot's eyes level with the upper wing.

Friedrichshafen F.F.48 (Germany) Two-seat fighting seaplane with an endurance of 5½ hours. Power was provided by a 179 kW (240 hp) Maybach engine. Armament comprised one fixed and one flexibly mounted machine-gun (forward firing of the latter between the propeller arc and the inner strut sets was possible if required). Three built.

Friedrichshafen F.F.53 (Germany) Three examples of a 194 kW (260 hp) Mercedes-powered torpedo bomber.

Friedrichshafen F.F.59C (Germany) To provide the scouting seaplane with improved facilities for defence, the F.F.59C had wing struts placed further apart and wiring removed for safe forward firing of the rear-mounted machine-gun.

Friedrichshafen F.F.60 (Germany) Four-engined triplane mounted on two huge floats. Prototype only.

Friedrichshafen F.F.64 (Germany) Last seaplane built by this company during World War I and designed as a result of the *Wolff* raider. Power was provided by a 119 kW (160 hp) Mercedes D.III engine. Three were built, which could be hoisted on board ship and were easily dismountable.

Friedrichshafen G series (Germany) Although Friedrichshafen was a major producer of seaplanes, it also built a series of large and usually twin pusher-engined landplane bombers for use as night raiders from bases on the Western Front. The prototype G.I was developed into the more powerful ⅜149 kW; 200 hp Benz Bz.IV) G.II of 1916, which went into limited production and

service. However its offensive load of just 450 kg (992 lb) and range were not adequate for major attacks on British and other strategic targets, and so the G.III was developed: a much larger aircraft carrying the normal crew of three but with an offensive load of 1,500 kg (3,307 lb). Power for the G.III was provided by two 194 kW (260 hp) Mercedes D.IVa engines.

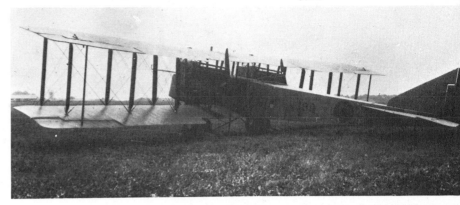

Captured Friedrichshafen G.III.

Friedrichshafen G.IIIa.

During 1917 Friedrichshafen concentrated on the production of the G.III and G.IIIa (with a biplane instead of conventional monoplane-type tail unit), with many others being built under contract by Daimler and Hansa. It is not known how many G.IIIs and G.IIIas were built in total, but more than 330 were produced by the sub-contractors.

The final version was the G.IV of 1918, which was basically similar to the G.IIIa but had a slightly shorter wing span, a modified and rounded fuselage nose and D.IVa engines mounted in tractor configuration.

Data (G.III): *Engines* as above *Wing span* 23.75 m (77 ft 11 in) *Length* 12.8 m (42 ft 2 in) *Max T-O weight* 3,940 kg (8,686 lb) *Max level speed* 135 km/h (84 mph) *Endurance* 5 h *Armament* two–three Parabellum machine-guns in nose and rear dorsal positions, plus bombs

Fuji FA-200 Aero Subaru (Japan) First flown on 12 August 1965, the Aero Subaru is a four-seat light monoplane, currently produced in three versions with 119–134 kW (160–180 hp) Lycoming engines. Between 1968 and 1977 a total of 274 were completed, but production continues against firm orders only.

Fuji LM and KM series (Japan) The Fuji LM-1 Nikko was built under licence as a version of the Beechcraft Mentor, but with a wider centre fuselage to accommodate four persons for liaison duties with the JGSDF. The LM-2 was produced as a conversion of the LM-1 powered by a 254 kW

Fuji

Fuji FA-200 Aero Subaru.

Funk Model B.2.

GAF Nomad.

GAF Nomad
Search Master L.

Fuji T1A.

(340 hp) Lycoming IGSO-480-A1F6 engine (with optional fifth seat). The KM-2 two–four-seat primary trainer is similar in appearance to the LM-2 and was built for the JMSDF (IGSO-480-A1C6 engine).

The latest and most important version of the series is the KM-2B (a modification of the KM-2) combining the airframe and power plant with the two-seat cockpit installation of the Beechcraft T-34A Mentor. The first KM-2B was flown on 26 September 1974 and deliveries to the JASDF began in 1978. A total of 54 KM-2Bs are expected to be purchased by the JASDF as T-3s.

Data (KM-2B): *Engine* one 254 kW (340 hp) Lycoming IGSO-480-A1A6 *Wing span* 10.0 m (32 ft 10 in) *Length* 8.03 m (26 ft 4¼ in) *Max T-O weight* 1,510 kg (3,329 lb) *Max level speed* 377 km/h (234 mph) *Range* 965 km (600 miles)

Fuji T1A and T1B (Japan) First flown in 1958, the T1A is an intermediate trainer powered by a 17.8 kN (4,000 lb st) Bristol Siddeley Orpheus 805 turbojet engine. Forty were built for the JASDF, delivery ending in May 1963. The T1B version was first flown in 1960. Twenty-two were built for the JASDF, each powered by an Ishikawajima-Harima J3-IHI-3 turbojet engine.

Fuji/Rockwell Commander Model 700 (Japan/USA) Design and development of the FA-300 began in Japan in 1971. It is currently proceeding as a collaborative venture between Fuji and Rockwell International (see **Rockwell**).

Fulton Model FA-2 Airphibian (USA) First flown on 7 November 1946, the FA-2 was a two-seat roadable monoplane comprising two main detachable sections, a coupé-type car (thought suitable for the road and with two seats) and a wing/rear fuselage/tail-unit section.

Funk F-23 (USA) see **Cosmic F-23**

Funk Model B (USA) Two-seat light cabin monoplane of 1941 powered by a 56 kW (75 hp) Lycoming engine.

Funk Model B-85-C (USA) Produced after World War II as an updated version of the Model B to resume production. Power was provided by a 63.3 kW (85 hp) Continental C85-12 engine.

GA (UK) see **General Aircraft**

GAF Nomad (Australia) The Nomad is a twin-turboprop utility aircraft. The first of two Model N2 prototypes flew on 23 July 1971 and five production versions have been announced. The original short-fuselage civil version (N22B) is intended primarily as a STOL utility aircraft for short/medium-range transportation of up to 13 passengers and/or cargo. It is also used as an air ambulance, for geophysical survey and for aerial photography.

The Mission Master is a short-fuselage military version, in service in Australia, Papua New Guinea, the Philippines and Indonesia. This ver-

sion is employed . for maritime surveillance, forward-area support and surveillance, and as a light military transport for personnel and equipment.

The N24A is the designation of the current version of the limited-production lengthened-fuselage N2 (six delivered to the Northern Territory Aeromedical Service) with improved performance. It entered production in 1978 and offers seating for up to 17 passengers. The Search Master B is the basic version of a maritime patrol variant, equipped with a 46 cm (18 in) forward-looking flat-plate scanner in a nose radome, 12 of which were ordered for the Indonesian Navy. The more sophisticated Search Master L has a 92 cm (36 in) Litton LASR-2 (AN/APS-504) 360° revolving scanner in an undernose 'guppy' radome. By early 1978 more than 70 Nomads of all versions had been sold.

Data: *Engines* two 298 kW (400 shp) Allison 250-B17B turboprops *Wing span* 16.46 m (54 ft 0 in) *Length* (N22B) 12.56 m (41 ft 2½ in), (N24A) 14.36 m (47 ft 1¼ in) *Max T-O weight* (N22B) 3,855 kg (8,500 lb) *Normal cruising speed* 311 km/h (193 mph) *Range* 1,352 km (840 miles)

Garland Linnet (UK) Two-seat light monoplane (67 kW; 90 hp Continental C90-F engine), built as a version of the French Piel C.P.301 Emeraude.

Gatard Statoplan AG 02 Poussin (France) Single-seat ultra-light monoplane, plans for which are available to amateur constructors.

Gatard Statoplan AG 04 Pigeon (France) Two–three-seat high-wing monoplane, first flown in 1976.

Gates Learjet 24 series (USA) The Learjet 24 superseded the Learjet 23 and deliveries began in March 1966. A total of 80 were built, after which the more powerful Learjet 24B and then Learjet 24D entered production – the latter with two 13.12 kN (2,950 lb st) General Electric CJ610-6

turbojet engines (the Learjet 24C was a lighter-weight lower-cost version of the 24D).

The current versions of the Learjet 24 series are the 24E and 24F, with Century III modifications which incorporate a cambered wing and other changes to reduce stall and approach speeds and balanced field lengths. The Learjet 24E is powered by two engines of 24D type, while the 24F has two 13.8 kN (3,100 lb st) CJ610-8As. The 24E's maximum take-off weight is also restricted to 5,850 kg (12,900 lb) to offer reduced runway requirements.

Data (Learjet 24F): *Engines* as above *Wing span over tip-tanks* 10.84 m (35 ft 7 in) *Length* 13.18 m (43 ft 3 in) *Max T-O weight* 6,123 kg (13,500 lb) *Max operating speed* 877 km/h (545 mph) *Range* 2,512 km (1,561 miles) *Accommodation* two seats on flight deck, plus up to six passengers in cabin

Gates Learjet 25 series (USA) First flown on 12 August 1966, this version is 1.27 m (4 ft 2 in) longer than the Series 24 aircraft and accommodates up to eight passengers in the cabin. Factory-installed thrust reversers for the CJ610-8A engines are optional on the 25D variant. Two Learjet 25Bs supplied to the Peruvian Air Force are each fitted with an underbelly pack containing two Wild RC-10 aerial survey

Gates Learjet 25B.

Gates Learjet 24D.

Gates Learjet

Gates Learjet 35.

Gee-Bee Model Y Senior
Sportster.

Gates Learjet 36.

Gemini capsule.

cameras. Maximum cruising speed of the Learjet 25D is 859 km/h (534 mph). The Learjet 25F is a longer-range version of the basic Learjet 25 and entered production in 1970. With four passengers and maximum fuel (45 minutes reserve) it has a range of 3,060 km (1,902 miles).

Gates Learjet 28 and 29 Longhorn (USA) Displayed for the first time in September 1977, the prototype of the 28/29 series was shown to be generally similar to the Learjet 25D. The Model 28 accommodates a crew of two and ten passengers and the Model 29 a crew of two and eight passengers. Production deliveries began in late 1978.

Gates Learjet 35 and 36 (USA) Generally similar in basic configuration to the other members of the Learjet family of executive aircraft, the Learjet 35 and 36 are slightly larger in size than the 25B. Identified as the Learjet 35 Transcontinental and Learjet 36 Intercontinental, each is powered by two 15.6 kN (3,500 lb st) AiResearch TFE 731-2 turbofan engines. The 1976 Learjet 35A and 36A versions introduced (as standard) Century III improvements and engine synchronisers. The Learjet 35A accommodates a crew of two and eight passengers and the 36A two crew and six passengers. Maximum range of the latter with four passengers is 5,071 km (3,151 miles).

Gates Learjet 54, 55 and 56 Longhorn (USA) Gates Learjet announced in 1977 its decision to develop a new series of business jets. Power plant will compromise two Garrett AiResearch TFE 731-3 turbofan engines, each rated at 16.24 kN (3,650 lb st), mounted in pods on each side of the fuselage aft of the wings. Each model will have a much more spacious 'stand-up' cabin. Deliveries are expected to begin in 1980.

Gee-Bee (Granville Aircraft Corporation) Sportster and Senior Sportster (USA) High-performance single and two-seat braced low-wing monoplanes of 1930 respectively, powered by a 70.8 kW (95 hp) Menasco B-4, 93 kW (125 hp) Menasco C-4, 70.8 kW (95 hp) Cirrus, 100.6 kW (135 hp) Ranger or 82 kW (110 hp) Warner Scarab engine in the Sportster and 160 kW (215 hp) Lycoming, 179 kW (240 hp) Wright J-6, 223.5 kW (300 hp) Pratt & Whitney Wasp Junior, 298 kW (400 hp) Wasp or 156.5 kW (210 hp) Kinner engine in the Senior Sportster.

Gee-Bee (Granville Aircraft Corporation) Super-Sportster (USA) For the 1933 National Air Races, the 1932 596 kW (800 hp) Pratt & Whitney Wasp-engined Gee-Bee Super-Sportster single-seat racing aeroplane was fitted with a 670.7 kW (900 hp) Pratt & Whitney Hornet supercharged engine. In the Wasp-engined Super-Sportster James Doolittle won the 1932 Thompson Trophy Race at an average speed of 406.5 km/h (252.6 mph) and on 23 September 1932 put the world landplane speed record up to 473.5 km/h (294.2 mph). While competing in the Bendix Trophy Race the Hornet-engined Super Sportster had an accident and the pilot/owner (Russell Boardman) was killed. Nevertheless it is the best remembered of all the Gee-Bee racing aircraft and was little more than a huge engine fitted to a minimum airframe.

Gemini spacecraft (USA) The Gemini was a two-astronaut conical spacecraft comprising a re-entry module and adapter module. The former was based on the single-astronaut Mercury capsule but was of increased size to provide a 50% increase in cabin volume. Two unmanned and ten manned Gemini launches were made between April 1964 and November 1966.

Genairco Biplane (Australia) Three-seat biplane of the early 1930s powered by an 85.7 kW (115 hp) Cirrus-Hermes II or similar engine. A four-seat version with fully enclosed accommodation was produced as the Cabin Biplane.

General Aircraft Cygnet (UK) The Cygnet was the first light all-metal stressed-skin civil aircraft to be produced in the UK and was a two-seat cabin monoplane powered by a de Havilland Gipsy Major, Cirrus Major or Menasco engine.

General Aircraft Hamilcar glider.

General Aircraft Hamilcar (UK) The Hamilcar was a military tank- or vehicle-carrying glider, originally designed to carry the Tetrarch tank or two Universal carriers. It was later adapted to carry a great variety of military loads, for which its spacious main freight compartment was 7.77 m (25 ft 6 in) long, 2.44 m (8 ft) wide and 2.29 m (7 ft 6 in) high. The nose of the fuselage was hinged to open for easy loading. The full-size prototype flew on 27 March 1942 and 390 production Hamilcar Is were built, towed by Halifax, Lancaster and Stirling bombers. The Hamilcar X designation applied to 22 Mk I aircraft each fitted with two Bristol Mercury 31 engines to assist take off.

General Aircraft Hotspur (UK) The original Hotspur I glider was intended for use as a small troop transport and had a wing span of 18.75 m (61 ft 6 in). The Hotspur II and III had wing spans of 14.0 m (45 ft 10¾ in) and became the production versions, used as the standard trainers of the Glider Pilot Regiment. The main difference between the two production types was in the flying controls and instruments, the Mk III aircraft having a complete duplication for each pilot.

General Aircraft Monospar Universal (UK) Four-seat twin-engined (67 kW; 90 hp Pobjoy Niagara III radials) cabin monoplane.

General Avia (Procaer) F15F (Italy) Four-seat light monoplane powered by a 149 kW (200 hp) Lycoming IO-360-A1B1 engine and derived from the Procaer F15E Picchio.

General Avia F.600 Canguro (Italy) Twin-engined (231 kW; 310 hp Lycoming TIO-540-A2C) freight, ambulance and general-utility transport, first flown in late 1978.

General Aviation GA-15 and GA-43 (USA) In the summer of 1931 the former Fokker Aircraft Corporation was taken over in its entirety by the General Aviation Corporation, and the name was changed to The General Aviation Manufacturing Corporation. Although a merger with North American Aviation in 1933 subsequently ended

aircraft production under the name of General Aviation or GA, two important aircraft carry the name, the GA-15 and GA-43. The former was a twin-engined flying-boat developed for the US Coast Guard. Five were delivered from 1932, each powered by two 313 kW (420 hp) Pratt & Whitney Wasp engines and subsequently designated PJ-1/2s. The GA-43 was a ten-passenger commercial aircraft powered by a 521.6 kW (700 hp) Wright R-1820 Cyclone engine and produced in landplane and twin-float seaplane forms. The latter was specially developed (as the GA-43-J) for SCADTA for its services in Colombia, South America.

General Aircraft Cygnet II.

General Dynamics F-111 and FB-111 (USA) Winner of an exceptionally large and prolonged evaluation contested by Boeing-Wichita for the USAF TFX (Tactical Fighter Experimental) requirement, intended to replace virtually all the 'Century-series' fighter-bombers. The F-111 also had to be designed as a carrier-based US Navy fighter with 'maximum commonality' – a new concept insisted upon by the Secretary of Defense to save money. The prototype F-111A flew on 21 December 1964, but soon exhibited engine compressor-stall problems. These were the first of many difficulties which ended with the F-111A entering USAF service in 1967 with considerably shorter range than planned, despite a very large increase in internal fuel capacity. Instead of the 1,350 planned, the USAF bought only 141 of the A model, with two 82.3 kN (18,500 lb st) afterburning Pratt & Whitney TF30-P-1 or -3 engines,

General Aircraft Hamilcar X carrying a self-propelled Bofors gun on a Morris vehicle.

General Aircraft Hotspur II.

Cockpit of a General Aircraft Monospar Universal.

General Aircraft Monospar Universal.

and these were used not as fighters but as very useful all-weather precision bombers. By far the most important feature of this aircraft, transcending even its variable-geometry swing-wings (the first in service in the world) with limits of 26° to 72.5°, was the all-weather navigation and weapon-delivery avionics, which include the first TFR (terrain-following radar) able to make the aircraft fly automatically at the lowest safe height to evade enemy radar and missiles.

The next version was to have been the Navy F-111B (developed jointly with Grumman), but this suffered such difficulty that in 1968 it was abandoned. The F-111C is a version with long-span wings and strengthened landing gear, 24 of which were supplied to the RAAF after a delay of ten years. The F-111D has Mk II avionics of much more advanced type, which caused severe cost and serviceability problems, but 96 aircraft still serve with one Tactical Fighter Wing. The 20th Tactical Fighter Wing in England is equipped with the F-111E, similar to the A but with enlarged inlets for the more powerful TF30 engine that was never fitted. The best tactical version of the F-111 is the F, equipping the 48th TFW in England; this has two 111.5 kN (25,100 lb st) TF30-P-100 engines and simplified avionics.

USAF Strategic Air Command planned to buy 210 FB-111A strategic bombers to replace early B-52 models and the B-58s, but cost escalation reduced the number to 76, 60 of which equip two SAC bomb wings. This has the wing and landing gear of the C and can carry four SRAM missiles externally and two internally or heavy loads of conventional bombs. Like all versions it has a receptacle for Flying Boom inflight refuelling. For several years a much improved FB-111H was planned, but this will not now be built, and total production of all versions was thus limited to 562 – the last being delivered in November 1976. The planned RF-111A reconnaissance version flew in prototype form in 1967, but after development costing $118 million never went into production; in 1979 a different reconnaissance pallet was being developed for the RAAF. The last version is the EF-111A, rebuilt from existing aircraft to carry the same ECM/jamming system as the Navy EA-6B Prowler but without the need for two operators. Conversion of EF models for Tactical Air Command was expected to begin in 1979.
Data (F-111F): *Engines* as above *Wing span* (max sweep) 9.74 m (31 ft 11½ in) *Length* 22.4 m (73 ft 6 in) *Max T-O weight* 45,360 kg (100,000 lb) *Max level speed* (clean, high altitude) 2,335 km/h (1,450 mph) *Range* 4,707 km (2,925 miles)

General Dynamics F-16 (USA) The F-16 is a single-seat lightweight air-combat fighter (F-16A) and two-seat fighter/trainer (F-16B). It was designed to compete in the Lightweight

General Dynamics CCV YF-16 (USA) Modified prototype F-16 as a testbed for a control configured vehicle (CCV) programme.

General Dynamics/Martin RB-57F .(USA) Conversion of Martin B-57 tactical bombers into reconnaissance aircraft with the designation RB-57F. Standard engines were replaced by two 80 kN (18,000 lb st) Pratt & Whitney TF33-P-11 turbofans, plus 14.68 kN (3,300 lb st) Pratt & Whitney J60-P-9 auxiliary turbojets underwing. Deliveries began in 1964.

Construction of an early F-111 development and flight test aircraft.

General Dynamics FB-111A.

Fighter (LWF) prototype programme: of the proposals submitted by five companies only General Dynamics and Northrop were awarded contracts to build two prototypes each as YF-16s and YF-17s respectively. The first YF-16 flew on 20 January 1974. In January 1975 the Secretary of the USAF announced that the F-16 had been selected and authorised for full-scale engineering development. The original YF-16 requirement for an air-superiority day fighter was expanded to give equal emphasis to the air-to-surface role, including provision of all-weather radar and navigation capabilities, making the F-16 a true multi-role fighter. Eight single-seat and two two-seat pre-production aircraft were then ordered. The first development F-16A flew on 8 December 1976.

The USAF has indicated its intention to procure a total of 1,388 operational F-16s, but in practice this figure is likely to be cut substantially. The NATO countries of Belgium, Denmark, the Netherlands and Norway have also selected the F-16 to replace their current Lockheed F-104s, with initial orders of 116, 58, 102 and 72 respectively. Production of the F-16 began in 1978 and the first aircraft off the production lines flew in August of that year. Delivery of 60 aircraft to the USAF was planned by the end of 1979.

Data (F-16A): *Engine* one 111.2 kN (25,000 lb st) Pratt & Whitney F100-PW-100(3) turbofan *Wing span* (over missile launchers) 9.45 m (31 ft 0 in) *Length* 14.52 m (47 ft 7¾ in) *Max T-O weight* 10,335–14,968 kg (22,785–33,000 lb) *Max level speed* above Mach 2 *Radius of action* 925 km (575 miles) *Armament* General Electric M61A-1 20 mm multi-barrel cannon and one infra-red air-to-air missile at each wingtip; one underfuselage and six underwing hardpoints for additional stores up to a possible maximum weight of 6,894 kg (15,200 lb)

General Dynamics F-16A.

General Model G1-80 Skyfarer (USA) Two-seat cabin monoplane of 1940; only the second aeroplane certified by the US Civil Aeronautics Board as 'characteristically incapable of spinning'.

German Bianco-Macchi M.B.308 (Argentina) First flown in February 1959, this three-seat cabin monoplane was a licence-built version of the Macchi M.B.308.

Giffard dirigible (France) World's first piloted and powered dirigible to fly, on 24 September 1852. Powered by a steam engine developing about 2.24 kW (3 hp) and driving a large three-bladed propeller, it flew from the Paris Hippodrome to Trappes, about 27 km (17 miles).

Glaser-Dirks DG-100 and DG-200 (Germany) The DG-100 single-seat Standard Class sailplane is currently built under licence in Yugoslavia by Elan. Production in both countries totalled 105 by late 1978. The DG-200 is an improved model with wing flaps and was developed for unlimited international competition.

General Dynamics F-111C.

General Dynamics/Martin RB-57F.

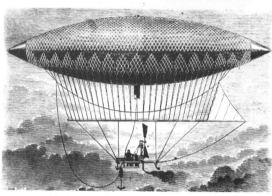

Giffard dirigible.

Glasflügel Kestrel, Hornet, Mosquito and Mosquito B (Germany) The Kestrel single-seat high-performance Open Class sailplane was known originally as the 17-metre Libelle and by the end of 1978 129 had been delivered. The Hornet is a derivative of the Club Libelle and is a single-seat Standard Class sailplane, 88 of which had been delivered by the end of 1978. The Mosquito is a single-seat 15-metre Contest Class sailplane, 100 of which had been delivered by January 1979. The Mosquito B (60 delivered) differs in having GRP ailerons, no fuselage/wing fairings, reduced wing span and slimmer horizontal tail surfaces.

Globe Model BTC-1 (USA) Twin-engined (Jacobs L-6) eight-seat commercial monoplane of about 1940.

Globe Swift (USA) Following the prototype Swift Model GC-1 (that was awarded an Approved Type Certificate in 1942), the Swift Model GC-1A and GC-1B were put into production after World War II as two-seat light cabin monoplanes powered by a Continental C85 and C125 engine respectively.

Glaser-Dirks DG-200A Acroracer.

Gloster E.28/39 (UK) On 12 April 1937 Frank Whittle started the world's first turbojet aircraft engine, developed from his original ideas and produced by a company known as Power Jets Ltd. In March of the following year the Air Ministry issued a contract for a single engine and subsequently awarded Gloster a contract to produce the necessary airframe and further develop the aircraft under the specification E.28/39. Although the contract was seen as representing the operational requirements of a high-altitude interceptor, this aspect was not stressed, the main concern being to give special attention to the many new features associated with the installation of the turbojet engine.

The E.29/39 was a cantilever low-wing monoplane of all-metal construction with the single engine located in the fuselage aft of the pilot's cockpit. Air that passed through the nose orifice was channelled to pass each side of the cockpit to the engine. The aircraft flew for the first time on 15 May 1941 at Cranwell, piloted by Flt Lieut P. E. G. Sayer. Subsequent development saw modifications made to the engine and airframe. The E.28/39 programme resulted in the development of the twin-engined Meteor fighter (see entry).

Data: *Engine* one 3.83 kN (860 lb st) Power Jets W.1 turbojet *Wing span* 8.84 m (29 ft 0 in) *Length* 7.72 m (25 ft 3¾ in) *Max T-O weight* 1,678 kg (3,700 lb) *Max level speed* 544 km/h (338 mph)

Gloster Gambet (UK) Single-seat carrier-borne fighter biplane, first flown in February 1928. The only production models were those licence-built in Japan for the Imperial Japanese Navy, which received 50 Nakajima A1N1s and 100 A1N2s, powered by 317 kW (425 hp) Bristol Jupiter VI and 387.5 kW (520 hp) Nakajima Kotobuki 2 radial engines respectively. Maximum level speed of the A1N2 was 241 km/h (150 mph).

Gloster Gamecock (UK) One of the first biplane fighters with which the RAF began to re-equip in 1923 was the Gloster Grebe. This aircraft (together with Armstrong Whitworth Siskin IIIs) superseded the Sopwith Snipes which had proved to be so dominant in the closing stages of World War I. The Grebes were popular with their pilots because of their speed and manoeuvrability, but detested by ground crews because of the unreliability of their Armstrong Siddeley Jaguar IV radial engines.

The Grebe was followed into service by the Gloster Gamecock, one more in the long line of fighters which the renowned H. P. Folland designed for the RAF. In fact the Gamecock started life as an improved Grebe with a Bristol Jupiter IV engine, and in 1924 a Grebe II prototype was ordered with this power plant. Shortly afterwards two more aircraft were ordered, one with the improved Jupiter VI engine. Almost 18 months of development flying were completed before 30 of these aircraft were ordered by the Air Ministry as Gamecock Is.

Gamecocks entered service with No 43 Squadron in March 1926, but it was soon discovered that, despite excellent handling characteristics, they suffered from wing and tail flutter and spinning problems. In a period of 19 months there were 22 accidents, eight of which were fatal. Later modifications more or less cured the problem. The Gamecock remained in service until mid-1931, being remembered with affection by its pilots. In its Mk II form it also became standard equipment in the Finnish Air Force, and the type put up the fastest time in the Sassoon Cup Race for three years running. A few Gamecocks found their way to South Africa.

Data: *Engine* one 317 kW (425 hp) Bristol Jupiter VI radial *Wing span* 9.08 m (29 ft 9½ in) *Length* 5.99 m (19 ft 8 in) *Max T-O weight* 1,244 kg (2,742 lb) *Max level speed* 233 km/h (145 mph) *Range* 523 km (325 miles) *Armament* two forward-firing Vickers machine-guns

Globe Swift Model GC-1B.

Gloster Gauntlet (UK) The somewhat embarrassing situation caused by the introduction into service of the Fairey Fox day bomber (see entry), made it imperative that the Air Ministry should replace the Gamecocks and Siskins equipping its fighter squadrons. It was essential that the aircraft chosen for this task should be manoeuvrable, considerably faster than anything then in service, and because increasing speeds meant that defender and attacker would be in contact for shorter periods, much heavier fire power was needed.

Such a requirement posed considerable problems to the British aircraft industry, with such companies as Armstrong Whitworth, Boulton & Paul, Bristol, Hawker and, of course, Gloster, all keen to secure what it was believed would be a worthwhile contract. Specifications F.9/26 and F.20/27 remained unfulfilled; and F.7/30 calling for a 402 km/h (250 mph) four-gun fighter seemed initially even more unlikely to be attained. Gloster's first submission had been an improved version of the all-metal Goldfinch, and with the progression of time this design had been subjected to several permutations of airframe innovations and differing engines. When, in 1933, Gloster's SS.19B demonstrated a maximum speed of 346 km/h (215 mph) during tests at Martlesham Heath, it was ordered into production under the name Gauntlet I.

During the period 1935 to 1937 Gauntlets were the fastest fighters in RAF service, partially replaced by Gladiators and Hurricanes in 1938 and finally ousted by Spitfires in 1939. Aircraft produced from 1935, after Hawker Aircraft had taken over the Gloster company, were constructed according to Hawker production methods, bringing changes to wing spar and

fuselage structure. These differing aircraft were designated Gauntlet II.

Last open-cockpit biplane in RAF service, the Gauntlet equipped 14 squadrons at its peak period of usage. It was during this same period that a very different performance was given under most secret conditions when (in November 1936) three of No 32 Squadron's Gauntlets intercepted a civil airliner under the guidance of an experimental ground-radar installation at Bawdsey Manor, Suffolk. Thus the Gauntlet has the distinction of carrying out the world's first radar-controlled interception.

Data (Mk I): *Engine* one 480.7 kW (645 hp) Bristol Mercury VIS2 radial *Wing span* 9.99 m (32 ft 9½ in) *Length* 7.98 m (26 ft 2 in) *Max T-O weight* 1,792 kg (3,950 lb) *Max level speed* 370 km/h (230 mph) *Range* 740 km (460 miles) *Armament* two forward-firing Vickers machine-guns

Glasflügel Mosquito B.

Gloster E.28/39.

Gloster-built Gambet.

Gloster Gladiator/Sea Gladiator (UK) An improved version of the high-performance Gauntlet, the Gladiator represented the pinnacle of biplane development in Britain. With the Gloster SS.37, H. P. Folland endeavoured to satisfy the requirement of the Air Ministry's F.7/30 specification which the Gauntlet had failed to meet – although this latter aircraft was undoubtedly the best offering of the British aircraft industry at that time. However the Gauntlet's maximum speed was some 32 km/h (20 mph) below the F.7/30 requirement, which also called for an offensive armament of four machine-guns.

One of the Gloster Gamecock IIs flown by the Finnish Air Force.

Gloster Gauntlets in 1938.

Gloster Gauntlet in Danish service.

RAF Gloster Gladiator.

Clearly the Gauntlet represented a close approach to the requirement and Folland decided that aerodynamic improvements of the basic Gauntlet fuselage (together with installation of a more powerful engine) should prove adequate for the Gloster design to be ordered into production. It had been intimated by the Air Ministry that submissions for the F.7/30 requirement which were powered by the new Rolls-Royce Goshawk evaporative-cooled engine would receive favourable consideration. This meant that of the seven other contenders for this contract, five were designed to utilise the Goshawk. When this engine failed, it eliminated most of Gloster's competitors. Folland, however, pinned his hopes on the Bristol Mercury ME.30 radial which was then promising a power output of some 521.6 kW (700 hp). But it was not available when the prototype SS.37 was nearing completion and the first

flight, on 12 September 1934, was made with a 395 kW (530 hp) Mercury IV.

Early tests, following the prototype's first flight, showed that the target maximum speed was in sight. On 1 July 1935 the Air Ministry ordered 23 aircraft, as Gladiators, one going to Greece. These were powered by the 618.5 kW (830 hp) Bristol Mercury IX. Other improvements included an enclosed cockpit with a sliding canopy and a redesigned tail unit.

Gladiators first entered service with No 72 Squadron in early 1937. But despite the aura of glamour and invincibility which always seems to be associated with these aircraft, it is an undeniable fact that they were virtually outdated at that time – a biplane in a monoplane era. The early Gladiator Is were followed by an improved Gladiator II in 1938 powered by the Bristol Mercury VIIIA engine. Other improvements comprised the addition of a battery and electric starter and the inclusion of a full blind-flying instrument panel.

Production also included 60 Sea Gladiators for the FAA. Generally similar to the Gladiator II, they differed by being equipped for catapult launch and deck landing – although not intended for operational use from carriers – and carried an inflatable dinghy in a fairing beneath the lower wing centre-section. Of the total 747 Gladiators which were built, almost 30% were exported, serving with the armed forces of Belgium, China, Finland, Greece, Iraq, Irish Republic, Latvia, Lithuania, Portugal, Norway and Sweden. In addition some aircraft transferred from the RAF operated with Egyptian and South African forces.

When World War II started the Gladiator – which at the peak of its deployment was flown by 29 home and 11 overseas squadrons – had largely been superseded. Nevertheless many remained in RAF service until early 1945 and were the last biplane fighters to serve with both the RAF and Royal Navy.

Many of the stirring stories of Gladiator operations must be regarded as apocryphal: in truth it was the courage of its pilots rather than its ability as a fighter which notched up its successes. But it cannot be denied that the Gladiator was a classic biplane with superb handling characteristics. The 'communications' Gladiator of one RAF station had an almost unbelieveable performance in the hands of the unit's chief flying instructor. Time

and again he could produce an impeccable and accurate side-slip landing, a demonstration not only of his skill, but of the controllability and manoeuvrability of this beautiful aeroplane.

Data (Gladiator II): *Engine* one 618.5 kW (840 hp) Bristol Mercury VIIIA/VIIIAS radial *Wing span* 9.83 m (32 ft 3 in) *Length* 8.36 m (27 ft 5 in) *Max T-O weight* 2,155 kg (4,750 lb) *Max level speed* 402 km/h (250 mph) *Range* 660 km (410 miles) *Armament* two forward-firing Browning machine-guns, plus two additional Brownings mounted beneath the lower wings

Gloster Grebe (UK) In 1923 Gloster built a two-seat private-venture research aircraft which became known as the Grouse, to carry out flight evaluation of new and special biplane wings. Simultaneously a single-seat version was built. When demonstrated to Air Ministry officials, its performance was considered to be so impressive that three prototypes were ordered. The first of these became the Grebe prototype which, following evaluation, was ordered into production under the designation Grebe II. This differed from the two-seat version by having a more powerful Jaguar IV engine (instead of a Jaguar III) and several other modifications.

The Grebe entered service in October 1923 with the RAF's No 111 Squadron, and total production numbered 113 aircraft, including a small number of two-seat dual-control trainers. The Grebe was found to have wing flutter problems, resulting in the addition of outward-sloping Vee

struts to brace the overhang of the upper wing. Two Grebes were modified during 1926 with special release attachments on the top surface of the upper wing. This allowed them to be carried into the air beneath the keel of the British rigid airship R-33, and used for launching experiments.

Grebes remained in service until their replacement by Armstrong Whitworth Siskins in mid-1928.

Data: *Engine* one 298 kW (400 hp) Armstrong Siddeley Jaguar IV radial *Wing span* 8.94 m (29 ft 4 in) *Length* 6.17 m (20 ft 3 in) *Max T-O weight* 1,151 kg (2,538 lb) *Max level speed* 261 km/h (162 mph) *Range* 644 km (400 miles) *Armament* two forward-firing Vickers machine-guns

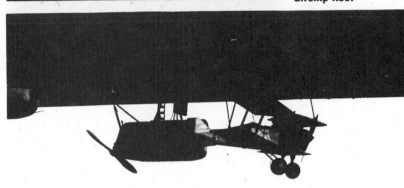

Gloster Javelin (UK) The Javelin was the first twin-engined delta-wing aircraft and the first British aircraft to be designed for the specific operational role of all-weather fighter. Five prototypes were built, the first flying initially on 26 November 1951. The first production Javelin F(AW).1 flew for the first time on 22 July 1954 and entered service with RAF Fighter Command in 1956.

Nine versions of the Javelin were produced, the first 40 as F(AW).1s with two 36.92 kN (8,300 lb st) Bristol Siddeley Sapphire ASSa.6 turbojet engines. Armament comprised four 30 mm Aden guns in the wings. Equipment to aid fulfilment of the all-weather capability included dual UHF communication transceivers, ADF, Gee radar, ILS and IFF, and AI.17 radar to enable the aircraft to seek its prey in adverse weather or at night.

Versions which followed the Mk 1 into service were the F(AW).2 with equipment changes and US-designed radar installed in a nose of reduced length (first production aircraft flown on 25 April 1956); T.3 dual-control trainer with a fuselage lengthened to 18.59 m (61 ft), no nose radar and an 'all-flying' tail; F(AW).4 with an 'all-flying'

Gloster Gladiator in Finnish service.

First production Gloster Grebe II.

Gloster Grebe beneath airship R33.

Cockpit of a Gloster Gladiator.

Gloster

Gloster Javelin F(AW).9s.

tail; F(AW).5 with a new wing with increased internal fuel capacity (first production aircraft flown on 24 August 1956); F(AW).6, similar to the Mk 5 but with equipment changes (first production aircraft flown on 15 January 1957); F(AW).7 with 48.93 kN (11,000 lb st) Sapphire 203/204 engines, two 30 mm Aden guns and four Firestreak air-to-air missiles (first production aircraft flown on 9 November 1956; modified into F(AW).9s); F(AW).8, similar to the Mk 7 but with US radar, drooped leading edge and Sperry autopilot (first flown on 9 May 1958); and F(AW).9, basically a reheat version (59.56 kN; 13,390 lb st each with reheat) of the Mk 7 with provision for flight refuelling.

Almost 400 Javelins were built for the RAF, remaining in operational service during a decade in which far more potent and complex aircraft were being developed as integrated weapons systems. Javelins were operational until mid-1967 with the RAF overseas.

Data (F(AW).9): *Engines* as above *Wing span* 15.85 m (52 ft 0 in) *Length* 17.3 m (56 ft 9 in) *Max T-O weight* 19,473 kg (42,930 lb) *Max level speed* 998 km/h (620 mph) *Range* 1,497 km (930 miles) *Armament* two 30 mm Aden guns, plus four Firestreak air-to-air missiles, or four rocket packs

Gloster Mars series (UK) Designed by H. P. Folland, the Mars I or 'Bamel' was a single-seat racing biplane: the greater part of the fuselage, landing gear and tail unit being constructed from components similar to those used in the well-known Nieuport Nighthawk, which the company took over in 1920. The Mars II was a single-seat fighter powered by a 171.4 kW (230 hp) Bentley B.R.II engine. Thirty were delivered to the Japanese Navy as Sparrowhawk Is.

A similar two-seat training and general-purpose derivative was built as the Mars III, the Japanese Navy receiving ten as Sparrowhawk IIs. The Mars IV was practically a Mars II, fitted with hydrovanes and emergency flotation gear. Ten were delivered to the Japanese Navy as Sparrowhawk IIIs. The Mars VI was a high-performance single-seat fighter, fitted with a 242 kW (325 hp) Armstrong Siddeley Jaguar engine. All Mars VIs were conversions of Nieuport Nighthawks, and the Greek Army Air Force received 25. The final version was the Mars X, known to the Fleet Air Arm as Nightjar. The FAA received 22 as carrier-borne fighters, generally similar to the Mars VI version as they were constructed from Nighthawk airframes (see **Nieuport Nighthawk**).

Gloster Meteor (UK) The Meteor was designed to meet Specification F.9/40, the first such British specification to be issued for a combat aircraft using turbojet engines. The eight original F.9/40 airframes were used to test several different types of British gas turbines including the Rover-built Power Jets W2B, the parent design of the Rolls-Royce Welland with which the Meteor I was fitted; the Metropolitan Vickers F.2/1, the first British axial-flow unit to fly (13 November 1943); the Halford H.1, the predecessor to the de Havilland Goblin; and the Rolls-Royce Trent, the first turboshaft engine to fly. Actually the 6.67 kN (1,500 lb st) Halford-engined F.9/40 was the first version of the Meteor to fly (on 5 March 1943) as the W2B engines (4.45 kN; 1,000 lb st) installed in another F.9/40 in July 1942 were not ready for flying until June 1943.

The first production version of the Meteor (the F.1) was powered by two 7.56 kN (1,700 lb st) Rolls-Royce Welland 1 turbojet engines and had a cockpit canopy that was side-hinged. Only 20 of this first version were built, first going to No 616 Squadron, RAF and were used on operational sorties against German V-1 flying-bombs. The F.3 followed the Mk 1 into production and was the first quantity production version. The standard engines were two 8.9 kN (2,000 lb st) Rolls-Royce Derwent 1s, although the first 15 Mk 3s were fitted with Wellands. Sliding cockpit hoods were standard and provision was made for a long-range fuselage drop tank. The last 15 were fitted with the lengthened engine nacelles standardised on the Mk 4. A few were used operationally in Germany during the closing stages of World War II. The Meteor was the only Allied jet-propelled aircraft to go into operational service during this

Gloster Mars I or Bamel.

war, but it never met a German Messerschmitt Me 262 in combat.

Post-war types began with the F.4, the first example flying on 12 April 1945. Power was provided by two Derwent 5 engines and the wing span was reduced to 11.33 m (37 ft 2 in) to improve the rate of roll. Other features included long engine nacelles, pressure cabin, and fittings for bombs and rocket projectiles. An aircraft of this version set up world speed records on 7 November 1945 and 7 September 1946 of 975 km/h (606 mph) and 991 km/h (616 mph) respectively. The Meteor T.7 was a two-seat training version of the Mk 4, with the forward fuselage lengthened by 0.76 m (30 in) to accommodate tandem cockpits under a continuous canopy. No armament was carried. The first T.7 flew on 19 March 1948.

Many variants were built subsequently, including the F.8 (the major production version, first flown on 12 October 1948 and the only British jet fighter used operationally during the Korean War, flown by the RAAF), which established international point-to-point records on London–Copenhagen, Copenhagen–London and London Copenhagen–London in 1950 and in the following year set up a new international speed record over a 1,000 km (621 mile) closed circuit of 822.2 km/h (510.9 mph); FR.9 fighter-reconnaissance version of the Mk 8; PR.10 unarmed version for high-altitude reconnaissance; NF.11 two-seat night fighter, the design of which was undertaken by Armstrong Whitworth and first flown in May 1950; and NF.12, 13 and 14 night fighters (night-fighter production by Armstrong Whitworth totalling 547 aircraft). British production of the Meteor totalled about 3,550 aircraft, more than 1,100 of which were F.8s. Conversions included the TT.20 high-speed target-towing Meteor and U.15, 16 and 21 radio-controlled drones developed by Flight Refuelling Ltd. Meteors were also exported in considerable numbers for service with the armed forces of Argentina, Australia, Belgium, Brazil, Denmark, Ecuador, Egypt, France, Israel, the Netherlands and Syria.
Data (F.8 at Max T-O weight as indicated): *Engines* two 15.57 kN (3,500 lb st) Rolls-Royce Derwent 8 turbojets *Wing span* 11.33 m (37 ft 2 in) *Length* 13.59 m (44 ft 7 in) *Max T-O weight* (internal fuel only) 7,100 kg (15,675 lb) *Max level speed* 956 km/h (592 mph) *Range* 1,143 km (710 miles) *Armament* four Hispano 20 mm cannon

Glowiński monoplane (Poland) Blériot-type monoplane with a triangular-section fuselage and powered by an 18.6 kW (25 hp) Anzani engine. It made the first officially recognised controlled aeroplane flight in Poland in 1911.

Goodyear World War II production (USA) During this war the Corporation produced upwards of 200 airships for the US Navy, including L-type trainers and K and M patrol craft, completing the programme in April 1944. It also built F4U Corsair fighters under FG designations, delivered to the US Navy from April 1943, and produced a development (too late for use in the war) as the F2G-1.

Gloster Sparrowhawk I.

Goodyear GA-2 Duck (USA) Three-seat amphibious flying-boat powered by a 108 kW (145 hp) Franklin engine mounted in pusher configuration above the fuselage.

Goodyear commercial airships (USA) Goodyear had built a total of 303 airships by 1979, 261 of which were constructed under contract for the US Navy and Army and included the USS *Akron* and *Macon*. The remaining 42 have been commercial airships, the first of which was the *Pilgrim*, launched in 1925.

Goodyear currently operates four non-rigid airships for public relations and sales promotion activities: *America*, *Columbia IV*, *Europa* and *Mayflower*. *Europa* is based near Rome, the other three in the USA. The newest of the four is the *Mayflower*, constructed during 1978 and erected at Houston, Texas where it was flown for the first time that November. It has a gross volume of 5,740 m³ (202,700 cu ft) and an envelope surface area of 2,006 m² (21,600 sq ft). The envelope is made of two-ply Neoprene-coated Dacron and is helium filled. On each side is a four-colour sign containing 3,780 lamps to flash static or animated messages. Power is provided by two 157 kW (210 hp) Continental IO-360-D engines.

Gloster Mars X.

Gloster Meteor F.8s.

Goodyear GA-2 Duck packed for transportation.

Gloster Meteor NF.11s.

Gotha G types (Germany) The G types (excluding the G.I.) were large landplane bombers of conventional layout, designed to supplement and later take over from the Zeppelin airships the role of long-range heavy bombing. However, despite the legend G types built for themselves, they were not alone among larger German bombers: interestingly Gotha built the first experimental three-engined giant biplane for Count Zeppelin that was developed into the Staaken-type bomber.

The G.II and G.III were basically 1916 types powered by two 164 kW (220 hp) Benz and 194 kW (260 hp) Mercedes D.IVa engines respectively. The full description of the early Gotha bombers that appears in the 1918 *Jane's* mentions armament comprising three machine-guns. In fact the G.II and G.III were armed with two Parabellum guns, one in the nose and a second aft of the wings. However the description was undoubtedly based on a G.III, which introduced a special plywood-lined tunnel in the rear fuselage and a V-shaped opening in the top decking to allow the dorsal gun to be sighted and fired downwards through the fuselage when required: thus making the aircraft appear to have three

guns. Although the normal offensive load was six bombs, a total of 14 could be carried.

The G.IV and G.V became operational in numbers from early 1917 and were the main versions of the Gotha G types, numbers also going to the Austro-Hungarian forces. The G.IV (also produced by LVG and Siemens-Schuckert) was used in the first mass attack on England, when 21 Gothas raided Folkestone, Shorncliffe and elsewhere on 25 May 1917, killing about 95 people and injuring many others. On 13 June 14 Gothas attackedLondon for the first time and caused the worst casualties (of an air raid) of the war, with 162 people being killed and 432 injured. The heavy casualties suffered among the civilian population of England by these raids forced the return of aircraft from France to defend the cities, and such was their success that the last big raid on England during daylight hours was carried out on 12 August. Both the G.IV and G.V were powered by two 194 kW (260 hp) Mercedes D.IVa engines, mounted as pushers.

The night raids on England, following the daylight raids, brought the Gothas new problems. Because of their size and relatively low power, take-off and landing had always been somewhat hazardous. At night it was positively dangerous and, although British home defence fighters were having their share of success, accidents during landing were putting more Gothas out of action than Allied guns. It is worth recording here that the first Gotha to be shot down at night was claimed by two Sopwith Camels of No 44 Squadron, RAF in early 1918. In an effort to reduce landing mishaps Gotha produced the G.Vb, basically a G.V with two pairs of wheels under each engine and a twin tail assembly. Attrition, nevertheless, remained high and by May 1918 the night attacks on England had ended.

A major shift in design approach brought about the G.VII and subsequent G.VIII, G. IX and G.X (possibly a trainer or reconnaissance version)· none of which was built in any numbers. All were smaller, lighter and had shorter rounded noses which did away with the forward gun position. Their design was a deliberate attempt to increase speed, fighting power and altitude to meet the threat of the latest high-speed Allied fighters (a write-up on these appears in the 1920 *Jane's*). Power for the G.VII to G.X was provided by two Mercedes D.IVa, 182.6 kW (245 hp) Maybach Mb.IV and Mercedes D.III or 134 kW (180 hp) BMW IIIa engines respectively.

Interestingly it appears that no Gothas were converted into makeshift airliners post-war.

Data (G.IV): *Engines* as above *Wing span* 23.72 m (77 ft 10 in) *Length* 11.86 m (38 ft 11 in) *Max T-O weight* 3,625 kg (7,992 lb) *Max level speed* 140 km/h (87 mph) *Range* 500 km (311 miles) *Armament* two Parabellum machine-guns, plus up to 500 kg (1,102 lb) of bombs

Gotha G.I and U.W.D. (Germany) The G.I was an unusual-looking biplane with its wings and fuselage arranged in a similar manner to that chosen by Fairey for its Heyford bomber many years later. The first G.I flew in July 1915 and a small number entered service. Power was provided by two 112 kW (150 hp) Benz Bz.III engines mounted on the lower wing. A single Mercedes D.III-engined example of a seaplane version was also completed as the U.W.D. (Ursinus Wasser Doppeldecker, or Oscar Ursinus-designed float biplane).

Gotha Go.145 (Germany) Two-seat primary and advanced training biplane, first flown in February 1934. Power was provided by a 179 kW (240 hp) Argus As.10C engine. About 10,000 were built in Germany and under licence in Spain and Turkey.

Gotha Go.146 (Germany) Twin 149 kW (200 hp3 Hirth-engined four-seat cabin monoplane. Only a small number constructed.

Gotha Go.149 (Germany) Single-seat advanced-training monoplane powered by a 179 kW (240 hp) Argus As.10C engine.

Gotha Go.242 and Go.244 (Germany) The Go.242 was a high-wing twin-boom monoplane glider with a central fuselage accommodating 23

Gotha G.V.

Wrecked Gotha Go.242.

Goupy I.

Gotha L.E. type.

spring of 1915, this was a prototype tractor-engined high-speed seaplane. It became the favourite mount of the commander of the Holtenau naval air station, Capt Langfeld, who kept it for his private use, even when appointed commanding officer of the naval air station in Constantinople (see 1920 *Jane's*).

Gotha W.D.7 (Germany) Following the Gotha F

– the first twin tractor-engined twin-float seaplane ordered by the German Navy (89.4 kW; 120 hp Mercedes) – the W.D.7 was produced as a twin-engined seaplane based on the Ursinus pattern, with twin fins and rudders above a one-piece elevator. A small number were built and employed mainly as trainers in the art of torpedo dropping.

Gotha W.D.8 (Germany) The 179 kW (240 hp) Maybach-engined W.D.8 was the first German high-speed seaplane, ordered in the spring of 1915. According to the 1920 *Jane's* production was not entered into until two years later, but it is likely that the production aircraft were of a different type.

Gotha W.D.9 (Germany 119 kW (160 hp) Mercedes D.III-engined seaplane, a few of which were delivered to the Turkish Naval Air Service.

Gotha W.D.11 (Germany) The results obtained with large seaplanes encouraged the Imperial Naval Office to commence the building of torpedo-carrying seaplanes, the Gotha works turning out the models 11 and 14. The former had the usual tandem seating with the observer in the nose of the fuselage forward of the biplane wings.

fully equipped troops. It was used extensively from 1942, towed by Ju 52 or He 111 aircraft. The Go. 244 was a powered version of the Go.242 with two French-built Gnome-Rhône 14M engines installed in nacelles which virtually formed continuations of the tail booms.

Gotha L.D.1a-L.D.7 (Germany) Designs of 1914–15 produced as unarmed two-seat reconnaissance biplanes. The 74.5 kW (100 hp) L.D.1a, L.D.2 and L.D.4 were used in small numbers at the beginning of World War I.

Gotha L.E. types (Germany) Taube-type monoplanes used as unarmed scouts at the beginning of World War I. Major production version was the L.E.3, 80 of which were built.

Gotha W.D.1 and W.D.2 (Germany) Gothaer Waggonfabrik, situated in the middle of Germany, was the only large German aircraft manufacturer not to have a seaplane branch of their own as such, but was a major contractor to the German Navy besides being a supplier to the Turkish Naval Air Service. In 1914 the Gotha works arranged with the city of Rostock to have a plant and sheds erected near Breitling, which were used when preparing for the Warnemünde seaplane competition. When war broke out this plant was taken over by the Navy and formed the nucleus of the air station. Gotha took up the limited production of the Ursinus twin-engined (112 kW; 150 hp Benz Bz.III) biplane as a two-seat coastal patrol floatplane for the German Navy and Turkey (details of construction can be found in the 1920 *Jane's*).

Gotha W.D.3 (Germany) Twin-boom pusher-engined (119 kW; 160 hp Daimler) twin-float seaplane, ordered as a prototype in the spring of 1915 by the Imperial Naval Office.

Gotha W.D.5 (Germany) Also ordered in the

Power was provided by two 119 kW (160 hp) Mercedes D.III engines, providing a maximum speed of 120 km/h (74.5 mph). It could climb to 1,500 m (5,000 ft) in 20 minutes. Only 13 were built. Armament comprised a machine-gun and 725 kg (1,600 lb) torpedo.

Gotha W.D.12 (Germany) This was the next step in improving the German naval seaplane, cutting head resistance with the aim of getting high speed for patrol missions from the 119 kW (160 hp) Mercedes D.III engine. A small number were delivered to Turkey. Maximum level speed was 141 km/h (88 mph) – see the 1920 *Jane's* for full details. Interestingly seaplanes were sent to Turkey by railway to Herkulesbad, Hungary, erected there and flown with spare parts across Romania and Serbia to Lom-Polanka, Bulgaria, from where they could be transported to Constantinople.

Gotha W.D.13 (Germany) Basically a development of earlier types, powered by a 112 kW (150 hp) Benz Bz. III engine. A number were delivered to Turkey during 1917.

Gotha W.D.14 (Germany) The W.D.14 was a later model of the W.D.11 type with increased dimensions and powered by two 149 kW (200 hp) Benz Bz.IV engines in tractor configuration. The beam of the fuselage was further increased to enable side-by-side seating for the pilot and observer and machine-guns were provided in nose and dorsal positions. This model was further improved by the provision of folding wings. The torpedo was carried below the fuselage and a special dropping gear was provided.

Altogether 66 were produced: being used for mine-laying both on the French and English coasts and against the Russian naval forces, and as transports during the raid on Krisland for the occupation of the island of Oesel, landing machine-gun detachments who went on to occupy the surrounding small islands. For mine-laying the torpedo gear was replaced by mine racks, and special drop tanks could be carried for long-distance patrol flights over the North Sea (11 to 12 hours endurance).

Data: *Engines* as above *Wing span* 25.5 m (83 ft 8 in) *Length* 14.45 m (47 ft 5 in) *Max T-O weight* 4,640 kg (10,230 lb) *Max level speed* 126 km/h (78 mph)

Gotha W.D.15 (Germany) Highest-powered and last single-engined (194 kW; 260 hp Mercedes D.IVa) type to be built for the German Navy. Only prototypes were delivered.

Gotha W.D.20 (Germany) Similar to the W.D.14, powered by 149 kW (200 hp) Benz Bz.IV engines. Prototypes only.

Gotha W.D.22 (Germany) Four-engined (in tandem pairs) long-range patrol seaplane. Prototypes only.

Gotha W.D.27 (Germany) Improved version of the W.D.22. Prototypes only.

Goupy I and II (France) The Goupy I was the first full-size triplane to fly, on 5 September 1908. Power was provided by a 37.25 kW (50 hp) Renault engine. The more important Goupy II was powered by an 18 kW (24 hp) REP engine and flew for the first time on 9 March 1909. This aircraft is generally recognised as the first successful tractor-engined biplane to fly.

Gourdou-Leseurre 430/432/521/633 (France) The Gourdou-Leseurre firm carried out a considerable amount of experimental work in the sphere of dive-bombing during the 1930s in conjunction with the French Navy. The G.L.430 B1 was an adaptation of the standard G.L.32 C1 fighter. Two prototypes were built, differing from the fighter in having strengthened wing bracing and

Gourdou-Leseurre 810Hy being towed back to ship after launching.

provision for a 50 kg (110 lb) bomb under the fuselage – launched in a dive by means of a 'fork' release to avoid hitting the propeller.

Four G.L.432 BP1 aircraft followed. They had faired headrests for the pilot, a wide-track divided undercarriage and provision for a 150 kg (331 lb) bomb under the fuselage. A single machine-gun was fixed in the port wing.

Single examples of two developments were built. The G.L.633 was a reinforced and modified G.L.32 C1 which served with the Republicans in the Spanish Civil War, while the G.L.521 had a new taller vertical tailplane and a 559 kW (750 hp) Gnome-Rhône 9Kfr radial in place of the 313 kW (420 hp) engine which powered all the other G.L. dive bombers.

Data (G.L.432 BP1): *Engine* as above *Wing span* 12.2 m (40 ft 0¼ in) *Length* 7.6 m (24 ft 11¼ in) *Max T-O weight* 1,535 kg (3,384 lb) *Max level speed* 300 km/h (186.5 mph)

Gourdou-Leseurre 810Hy (France) The L2 prototype armed-reconnaissance and attack aircraft flew for the first time in 1927, followed in 1928 by six pre-production L3s. These were low-wing monoplanes of mixed construction, fabric-covered, and had twin-float landing gears with a multiplicity of struts. The crew of three were provided with tandem cockpits. Armament comprised one fixed forward-firing 7.7 mm Vickers machine-gun and twin Lewis guns (in the centre cockpit of the L2 and rear cockpit of the L3), plus two 75 kg (165 lb) G2 bombs. Twenty-four production G.L.810Hys were delivered from 1931, stressed for catapult launching; followed by 20 G.L.811Hys with dual

Gourdou-Leseurre Type A.

controls and folding wings; 29 G.L.812Hys; and 13 G.L.813Hys with enlarged and rounded vertical tail assemblies. All were powered by single 313 kW (420 hp) Gnome-Rhône 9Ac radial engines. Flown from battleships, cruisers and the seaplane carrier *Commandant Teste*, production aircraft remained in front-line service until 1937, although some were reactivated with the outbreak of World War II.

Data (G.L.810Hy): *Engine* as above *Wing span* 16.0 m (52 ft 6 in) *Length* 10.49 m (34 ft 5 in) *Max T-O weight* 2,290 kg (5,049 lb) *Max level speed* 195 km/h (121 mph)

Gourdou-Leseurre 832Hy (France) The G.L.831Hy prototype was followed by 22 production G.L.832Hy ultra-light two-seat catapult twin-float seaplanes, each powered by a 171.4 kW (230 hp) Hispano-Suiza 9Qb radial engine and with folding wings. Armament comprised one 7.7 mm Lewis gun on a flexible mounting for the observer. G.L.832Hys embarked on French cruisers and colonial sloops, as well as equipping Escadrilles 8S2 (French West Indies) and 8S4 (Levant).

Gourdou-Leseurre Type B/ET-1 (France) The G.L. Type A was a prototype single-seat parasol-wing fighter built to the French Programme of 1 November 1917. With a 134 kW (180 hp) Hispano-Suiza 8Ab liquid-cooled engine it reached 242 km/h (150.3 mph) at 1,000 m (3,281 ft). The Type B had reinforced wing strutting and was armed with twin synchronised Vickers machine-guns. Produced as the Type B2 (later G.L.21) and revised B3 (or G.L.22 C1). Fifty of both versions were built, exported to Estonia, Finland, Latvia and Czechoslovakia. The B6 aerobatic variant was flown by G.L. test pilot Jerome Cavalli between 1931 and 1939.

The G.L. ET or ET-1 was an unarmed G.L.22, 30 flying with the French Army and Navy, the latter operating from the carrier *Béarn*. The G.L.22 ET-2 or B5 was an experimental two-seat trainer. Three civil single-seaters, painted red, white and blue respectively, performed aerobatic displays as 'Escadrille Tricolore' during 1923. An experimental series of G.L.23 single-seaters had the enlarged wing of the G.L.22.

Data (B2/G.L.21): *Engine* as above *Wing span* 9.4 m (30 ft 10 in) *Length* 6.5 m (21 ft 4 in) *Max T-O weight* 880 kg (1,940 lb) *Max level speed* 230 km/h (143 mph)

Government Factories 45MN Zolja, Type 451 and 452 (Yugoslavia) The Zolja was Yugoslavia's first jet-powered aircraft and was followed by five experimental light jets: the S-451M, 452-2, J-451MM Strsljen, S-451MM Matica and T-451MM Strsljen II, all equipped for military training and research roles.

Government Factories Type 214-D (Yugoslavia) Twin-engined (447 kW; 600 hp Wasp) bombing and aircrew trainer of the 1950s.

Government Factories Type 522 (Yugoslavia) Two-seat advanced trainer powered by a 447 kW (600 hp) Pratt & Whitney R-1340-AN-1 Wasp radial engine.

Government Factories C-3 Trojka (Yugoslavia) Two-seat light monoplane powered by a

Graf Zeppelin I photographed in the USA in 1929 beside Goodyear airship *Volunteer*.

44.7 kW (60 hp) Walter Mikron II engine. Designed for and winner of a competition as a light trainer suitable for use by national flying clubs and schools.

Government Factories S-49 (Yugoslavia) The S-49 was the first Yugoslavian-designed combat aircraft to be produced in series and was basically a redesign of the Yak-9. It was developed through the S-49A, fitted with a Russian VK-105 (Hispano-Suiza 12Y type) engine, to the S-49C with a 1,118 kW (1,500 hp) Hispano-Suiza 12Z. Armament comprised two 12.7 mm machineguns and one 20 mm cannon. Maximum level speed was approximately 620 km/h (385 mph).

Government Workshops H.F. XX-02 (Chile) Two-seat trainer of the early 1950s powered by a 130.4 kW (175 hp) Ranger L-440-1 engine.

Graf Zeppelin I and II (Germany) The *Graf Zeppelin I* was built from funds from the German government and public subscription and was launched in 1928. Designated LZ127, it was 236.22 m (755 ft) long and powered by five 410 kW (550 hp) Maybach engines. Its successful career began with a journey to the USA, the return flight setting up a record of just 71 hours and 7 minutes. Of the many notable flights that followed (until it was broken up in its shed at Frankfurt in March 1940) can be counted a trans-Siberian flight – the first non-stop flight across Russia; a survey of the Arctic in 1929; and a flight to South America in July 1930 which inaugurated regular services by DELAG.

The *Graf Zeppelin II* was the last of the German rigid airships, flying for the first time on 14 September 1938. Designated LZ130, it was 245 m (803 ft) long and powered by four 894.25 kW (1,200 hp) Mercedes-Benz engines. It made only a few flights (the last on 20 August 1939) and was broken up with LZ127, having been grounded following the *Hindenburg* tragedy.

Great Lakes Sport Trainer Model 2T-1A.

Grahame-White Type X Aerobus (UK) Five-seat pusher biplane flown by Grahame-White at Hendon during 1913 as a commercial joy-riding aircraft. Power was provided by a 74.5 kW (100 hp) Green engine.

Grahame-White Type XI (UK) Two-seat military biplane normally powered by a 74.5 kW (100 hp) Gnome Monosoupape engine (see **Type XIII** below).

Grahame-White Type XIII (UK) Built

Graf Zeppelin I over its shed.

Grahame-White

Baby Great Lakes.

originally with floats for the Circuit of Britain seaplane race, it was rebuilt after the outbreak of World War I as a fast landplane of exceptionally modern design. Powered by a 74.5 kW (100 hp) Gnome Monosoupape engine.

Grahame-White Type XV (UK) Two-seat 59.6 kW (80 hp) pusher-engined biplane trainer widely operated by the RNAS during the early part of World War I.

Grahame-White Baby (UK) In 1911 Grahame-White Aviation handled the British agency for the US Burgess aeroplane known as the Baby. A development of the Baby became the New Baby. It is worth noting that in 1913 the firm became an agency for Morane-Saulnier and built a number of monoplanes for the War Office.

Great Lakes Sport Trainer Model 2T-1 (USA) The Sport Trainer biplane was produced with Cirrus, Ensign and Menasco engines by the original Great Lakes Company (founded on 2 January 1929), and was one of the most popular light aircraft manufactured in the US. Distributors and dealers were located in all important centres in the USA and in several foreign countries. Variants included the 2T-1A Type A standard and Type B de luxe (Cirrus-powered), and 2T-1E Type A and B de luxe (Ensign-powered) models.

During the 1960s the name re-emerged as the Great Lakes Aircraft Company and this company began selling plans and materials for the construction of a scaled-down Sport Trainer known as the Baby Great Lakes. Subsequently plans and material kits were also marketed for a full-size Sport Trainer, later to be reduced only to certificated components and materials. In 1973 the Sport Trainer was put back into production and more than 100 had been built by 1978. The final version was the 2T-1A-2 powered by a 134 kW (180 hp) Lycoming AEIO-360-B1G6 engine. Maximum level speed of this two-seat version is 212 km/h (132 mph)

Grigorovich I-2.

Great Lakes BG-1 (USA) The BG-1 was a two-seat carrier-based dive-bomber, 60 of which were delivered to the US Marine Corps and US Navy from 1934. Power was provided by a 559 kW (750 hp) Pratt & Whitney R-1535 radial engine and armament comprised one forward-firing and one rear-mounted machine-gun, plus bombs.

Great Lakes BG-1.

Both cockpits were enclosed by sliding canopies. All BG-1s had been relinquished before America entered World War II. Maximum speed was 303 km/h (188 mph).

Great Lakes Model 61/XSG-1 (USA) Interesting prototype Pratt & Whitney Wasp Senior-engined observation amphibious flying-boat of 1932, built for the US Navy. Enclosed compartment for the gunner/observer in the rear end of the engine nacelle.

Great Lakes TG (USA) Designation of the Martin T3M/T4M torpedo bomber built by this company from 1928.

Grega GN-1 Aircamper (USA) Modernised version of the Pietenpol Aircamper, plans of which are available to amateur constructors.

Grigorovich I-2 (USSR) Dmitri P. Grigorovich became technical director of the State Aircraft Factory No 1 (GAZ No 1) in 1923 and in the following year produced the I-1 biplane fighter. Although the I-1 was highly manoeuvrable, it lacked the all-round performance expected of a modern fighter, coupled with cooling problems.

From the basic I-1 design Grigorovich and his design team produced the I-2 powered by a similar M-5 engine (298 kW; 400 hp Liberty copy). Following flight tests and refinement of the design, the fighter entered production in 1926 as the I-2*bis*. Although construction often left much to be desired, the I-2*bis* was the first single-seat fighter to go into quantity production in Russia (more than 200 built) and to become operational with the Red Air Force.

Data: *Engine* as above *Wing span* 10.8 m (35 ft 5¼ in) *Length* 7.32 m (24 ft 0¼ in) *Max T-O weight* 1,575 kg (3,472 lb) *Max level speed* 235 km/h (146 mph) *Range* 600 km (373 miles) *Armament* two forward-firing 7.62 mm machine-guns

General Dynamics F-111.

Gloster Gladiator.

Gloster Meteor F.8.

Great Lakes Sport Trainer
Model 2T-1A.

Grumman A-6E Intruders.

Grumman E-2C Hawkeye.

Grumman EA-6B Prowler.

Grumman F-14A Tomcat.

Grumman F9F Panther.

Grumman J2F-6 Duck.

Grigorovich IZ and PI-1 (USSR) The IZ was a single-seat low-wing monoplane fighter powered by a 335.3 kW (450 hp) M-22 engine. Armament comprised one machine-gun and two cannon. From the IZ was evolved the improved PI-1, the prototype of which flew for the first time in 1934. Power was provided by a 533 kW (715 hp) M-25 engine and armament comprised a machine-gun and two 75 mm APK cannon. An open cockpit was provided and the landing gear retracted into underwing nacelles.

Production aircraft for the Red Air Force initially retained the armament of the prototype but in later aircraft two 20 mm ShVAK cannon were standardised. The lighter cannon did away with the PI-1's last advantage over other Soviet fighters and was quickly superseded. Maximum level speed was 435 km/h (270 mph).

Grigorovich M.9 (Russia) Two-seat 112 kW (150 hp) Canton-Unné-powered armed reconnaissance flying-boat of World War I, flown by the Russian Navy.

Grigorovich TSh-2 (USSR) The TSh-2 was a conventional but heavily armed two-seat ground-attack biplane of 1931, powered by a 410 kW (550 hp) M-17 engine. Only ten were built.

Grob Astir, Twin Astir and Speed Astir II (Germany) The Astir sailplane is currently produced in two versions, as the single-seat Standard Astir (Standard Class) and Club Astir (Club Class). The Twin Astir is essentially a tandem two-seat development of the Standard Astir, while the Speed Astir II is a single-seat Open Class sailplane. By 1978 more than 550 Astirs had been delivered, together with 120 Twin Astirs (excluding the Twin Astir Trainer with non-retractable monowheel). Deliveries of the Speed Astir II began in 1979.

Grigorovich TSh-1, prototype of the TSh-2.

Grumman A-6 Intruder (USA) The A-6A Intruder (originally known as the A2F-1) was conceived as a carrier-borne low-level attack bomber equipped specifically to deliver nuclear or conventional weapons on targets completely obscured by weather or darkness. Later versions currently equip 17 operational US Navy/Marine Corps squadrons, and three readiness training squadrons.

The A-6A initial production version of the Intruder entered service in February 1963 and is no longer in use. The A-6B conversion of the A-6A to provide Standard ARM missile capability, and the A-6C conversion provided with improved night-attack capability using forward-looking infra-red sensors and a low-light-level television camera, are no longer operational.

The current versions are the EA-6A, which retains partial strike capability but is equipped primarily to support strike aircraft and ground forces by suppressing enemy electronic activity and obtaining tactical electronic intelligence within a combat area (27 built, including six A-6As modified into EA-6As); EA-6B Prowler, described separately; KA-6D Intruder, a flight refuelling tanker capable also of controlling aircraft for air-sea rescue operations or day-bomber operations (62 completed from A-6As); A-6E Intruder, an advanced conversion of the A-6A with multi-mode radar and an IBM computer similar to that first tested in the EA-6B (squadron deployment began in 1972 and a total procurement of 318 is planned); A-6E/TRAM target-recognition and attack multi-sensor version of the A-6E, deployment of which began recently; and

Grigorovich PI-1.

Grumman A-6E Intruder.

Grumman KA-6D Intruder.

CCW A-6A circulation-control-wing experimental aircraft, under development for the US Navy. Data (A-6E): *Engines* two 41.4 kW (9,300 lb st) Pratt & Whitney J52-P-8A turbojets *Wing span* 16.15 m (53 ft 0 in) *Length* 16.69 m (54 ft 9 in) *Max T-O weight* 27,397 kg (60,400 lb) *Max level speed* 1,043 km/h (648 mph) *Range* 3,096 km (1,924 miles) *Armament* five weapon attachment points for up to 8,165 kg (18,000 lb) of external stores; typical loads are 30 × 500 lb bombs or three 2,000 lb general-purpose bombs plus two 1,135 litre (300 US gallon) drop-tanks

Grumman AF Guardian (USA) Originally designated the XTB3F-1 (G-70), this aircraft was designed as a torpedo bomber with a composite power plant consisting of an R-2800-34W piston engine in the nose and a Westinghouse 19XB-2B turbojet engine in the rear fuselage. During evaluation trials considerable modifications were made to change its role to anti-submarine: in 1949 two new prototypes incorporating all the changes were built (carrying the designations XTB3F-1S and XTB3F-2S) the former equipped as a submarine hunter and the latter as a killer.

Grumman AF-2S and
AF-2W Guardians.

Both types were ordered by the US Navy under the respective designations AF-1S and AF-2S, but before completion of the first AF-1S its designation was changed to AF-2W. The AF-2S Guardian (G-82) carried one 2,000 lb torpedo, two 1,600 lb depth charges or two 2,000 lb bombs internally, while a similar load could be carried externally. In addition a searchlight was carried under the port wing and a radar scanner under the starboard. The AF-2W carried a large search and early-warning radome beneath the forward fuselage. In 1952–53 the AF-3S version was produced with additional submarine detection gear. Production of the Guardian ended in March 1953. Data: *Engine* one 1,788.5 kW (2,400 hp) Pratt & Whitney R-2800-48W radial *Wing span* 18.49 m (60 ft 8 in) *Length* 13.21 m (43 ft 4 in) *Max T-O weight* (approx) 11,340 kg (25,000 lb) *Max level speed* (approx) 507 km/h (315 mph) *Range* (approx) 2,414 km (1,500 miles)

Grumman C-1 Trader (USA) General-utility version of the S-2 Tracker, designed to accommodate nine passengers or 1,587 kg (3,500 lb) of cargo and operate as a COD (Carrier On-board Delivery) aircraft to and from aircraft carriers of the US Navy. The first C-1A flew in January 1955 and 87 were built, four of which were converted into EC-1As with special electronic countermeasures equipment. The C-1A could also be used for all-weather operational carrier training. Power was provided by two 1,136.4 kW (1,525 hp) Wright R-1820-82WA piston engines. No longer in service.

Grumman E-1B Tracer (USA) The Tracer (formerly known as the WF-2) was a modification of the Trader for airborne early-warning and fighter-direction duties. Suitable for all-weather operation, it was equipped with a long-range antenna housed in a large radome and served on board aircraft carriers. The prototype was flown for the first time on 1 March 1956 and 64 production aircraft followed, entering service with the Atlantic Fleet in early 1960.

Grumman E-2 Hawkeye (USA) The Hawkeye

was evolved as a carrier-borne early-warning aircraft, but is suitable for land-based operations from unimproved fields. The prototype flew for the first time on 21 October 1960, since when four versions have been built.

The E-2A (formerly known as the W2F-1) was the initial production version and flew for the first time on 19 April 1961. Delivery of 62 to the US Navy began on 19 January 1964. The E-2B version, which flew for the first time in February 1969, differs from the E-2A by having a Litton Industries L-304 micro-electronic general-purpose computer and reliability improvements. A retrofit programme updated all operational E-2As to this standard.

The E-2C first flew in January 1971 and 41 had been delivered by the end of 1977. Firm orders exist for a total of 47 aircraft, with procurement of 36 more by the end of 1985. Israel has four and in 1979 Japan released funds for the first four of an eventual total of about 15 for the JASDF. The E-2C has an advanced radar that is capable of detecting airborne targets anywhere in a three-million-cubic-mile surveillance envelope. It first entered service with the US Navy in November 1973 and went to sea on board USS *Saratoga* in late 1974. A training version is designated TE-2C.

Teams of Hawkeyes are able to maintain patrols on naval task force defence perimeters in all weathers, at an operating height of about 9,150 m (30,000 ft). They are capable of detecting and assessing any threat from approaching high-Mach-number enemy aircraft over ranges approaching 480 km (300 miles). The radar also monitors movements of enemy ships and land vehicles. It enables each E-2C to track, automatically and simultaneously, more than 250 targets and to control more than 30 airborne interceptions. To make this possible highly sophisticated equipment is carried by the aircraft, including a Randtron Systems AN/APA-171 antenna system housed in a 7.32 m (24 ft) diameter saucer-shaped rotodome mounted above the rear fuselage of the aircraft.

Data (E-2C): *Engines* two 3,661 kW (4,910 ehp) Allison T56-A-425 turboprops *Wing span* 24.56 m

Grumman E-1B Tracer.

(80 ft 7 in) *Length* 17.55 m (57 ft 7 in) *Max T-O weight* 23,541 kg (51,900 lb) *Max level speed* 602 km/h (374 mph) *Endurance* 6 h 6 min

Grumman EA-6B Prowler (USA) The EA-6B is an advanced electronics development of the EA-6A. Except for a 1.37 m (4 ft 6 in) longer nose section and large fin pod, the external configuration of this version is the same as that of the basic A-6A. The longer nose section provides accommodation for a total crew of four, the two additional crewmen being necessary to operate the more advanced ECM equipment. Deliveries of production aircraft began in January 1971 and the total programme is expected to cover the supply of 96 aircraft (including four prototypes and one R & D aircraft) to equip US Navy and Marine Corps squadrons. Ten US Navy squadrons were equipped with the Prowler in mid-1977.

Data: *Engines* two 50 kN (11,200 lb st) Pratt & Whitney J52-P-408 turbojets *Wing span* as for A-6E *Length* 18.11 m (59 ft 5 in) *Max T-O weight* 29,483 kg (65,000 lb) *Max level speed* 1,048 km/h (651 mph) *Range* 1,769 km (1,099 miles)

Grumman F2F and F3F (USA) Developed from the FF-1, the XF2F-1 prototype single-seat carrier-borne biplane fighter made its first flight just a few months after deliveries began of the earlier type. In terms of performance it was a great improvement over naval fighters then operational and so the US Navy ordered it into

Grumman E-2C Hawkeye.

Grumman F2F-1.

Grumman EA-6Bs.

48 km/h (30 mph) faster than the F3F-1. Altogether a total of 216 F2F/F3Fs were produced, remaining operational until the latter part of 1939.

It is of interest to note that a modified F2F-type biplane, with a 745 kW (1,000 hp) Wright R-1820-G1 engine, was sold to the Aviation Manager of the Gulf Refining Company as the G-22 aerobatic aircraft.

Data (F2F-1): *Engine* as above *Wing span* 8.69 m (28 ft 6 in) *Length* 6.53 m (21 ft 5 in) *Max T-O weight* 1,701 kg (3,750 lb) *Max level speed* 381 km/h (237 mph) *Range* 1,207–1,585 km (750–985 miles) *Armament* two 0.30 in Browning machine-guns, plus provision for two 116 lb bombs

production. The F2F-1 production version was powered by the 484.4 kW (650 hp) Pratt & Whitney R-1535-72 radial engine, had a neat cockpit canopy which was faired into the rear fuselage and retained the type of retractable landing gear used on the FF-1.

Soon after all F2F-1s had been delivered, Grumman produced a new prototype, the XF3F-1, which flew for the first time in March 1935. This version was slightly larger and production aircraft entered service in the following year. F3F-1s and later F3F-2s were powered by 484.4 kW (650 hp) R-1535-84 and 559 kW (750 hp) Wright Cyclone engines respectively, although in general construction they were identical to the F2F-1. Maximum level speed of the F3F-2 was 434.5 km/h (270 mph), a clear

Grumman F-4F Wildcat (USA) In 1931 a very young American aviation manufacturing company – Grumman Aircraft Engineering Corporation – received its first contract from the US Navy for a carrier-based fighter of biplane configuration. Under the designation FF (fighter) or SF (scout), they marked the beginning of an association which seems certain of remaining unbroken for at least a half-century. In that period some remarkable naval aircraft have originated from Grumman, earning the trust and respect of those who have flown them in peace and war.

The company's first carrier-based fighter of monoplane configuration was designed to meet a US Navy requirement which originated in 1935, but it was not until July 1936 that the Navy ordered this aircraft, under the designation XF4F-2. In its developed service form it was to prove an outstanding naval fighter of World War II, but when first evaluated against a competing design from the Brewster Aeronautical Corporation, it failed to be selected for production, despite being some 16 km/h (10 mph) faster than the Brewster design.

To overcome the shortcomings of the XF4F-2, a new prototype was built with a more powerful two-stage supercharged engine, and airframe revisions which increased wing span and brought changes to wingtips and tail surfaces. In this form the XF4F-3 flew for the first time on 12 February 1939.

The Wildcat was first ordered by the US Navy in 1939 and the F4F-3, F4F-4 and F4F-7 (a special long-range photographic-reconnaissance version of the F4F-4) were all built by the Grumman company. Concurrently the British Martlet (later renamed Wildcat) Mks I to IV were Grumman-built.

In 1942 the manufacture of the Wildcat was transferred to the Eastern Aircraft Division of the General Motors Corporation. The first FM-1 Wildcat, assembled from parts supplied by Grumman, flew on 1 September 1942. By 11 April 1944 the Eastern Aircraft Division had produced its 2,500th Wildcat. The FM-1, fitted with a Pratt & Whitney R-1830-86 engine, was virtually the same as the F4F-4 (Wildcat IV). The FM-2 (Wildcat VI), which went into production in 1943, was fitted with a Wright R-1820-56 engine of greater power but lower weight than the previous unit, had a redesigned tail unit with a taller fin and rudder and had the oil coolers removed from the under surface of the centre-section to the cowling, which was revised in shape. The removal of the oil coolers permitted the installation of universal racks under the inner wings for bombs or auxiliary fuel tanks.

Altogether nearly 8,000 Wildcats were built, three-quarters by the Eastern Division. These were used operationally by the US Navy on a wide scale in the Pacific (FM-2s in particular serving as light escort carrier fighters), participating in the battles of the Coral Sea and Midway, and were used extensively in the attack on Guadalcanal. Although somewhat inferior to the Japanese Zero, the rugged Wildcat proved invaluable in the early stages of the war in the Pacific, until gradually replaced by more effective fighters from 1943, although the type remained in first-line service until the end of the war. British Martlets initially replaced Sea Gladiators and, like their US Navy counterparts, remained operational until the end of the war.
Data (F4F-4): *Engine* one 894 kW (1,200 hp) Pratt & Whitney R-1830-86 radial *Wing span* 11.58 m (38 ft 0 in) *Length* 8.79 m (28 ft 10 in) *Max T-O weight* 3,607 kg (7,952 lb) *Max level speed* 512 km/h (318 mph) *Range* 1,239 km (770 miles) *Armament* six forward-firing 0.50 in machine-guns, plus two bombs
Grumman F6F Hellcat (USA) It is probably true to say that the Hellcat was designed in the spring of 1942, as important changes to the XF6F-1 and XF6F-2 prototypes led to the XF6F-3, which flew for the first time on 26 June 1942 (sometimes stated to be August). Large-scale production of the F6F-3 began at the end of that year and the Hellcat was first reported in action with a US Carrier Task Force in an attack on Marcus Island on 1 September 1943, flying from USS *Yorktown*.

The F6F-5 differed from its predecessor by having a redesigned engine cowling, improved windshield, new ailerons, strengthened tail surfaces, additional armour behind the pilot and a waxed high-gloss skin finish. It could also carry two 454 kg (1,000 lb) bombs under the centre-section or drop-tanks, and was equipped to carry rocket projectiles and search radar as the F6F-5E. Night-fighter (F6F-5N) and photographic-reconnaissance (F6F-5P) versions were also in service.

The F6F-5K was a long-range radio-controlled pilotless drone conversion of the Hellcat. The modification was undertaken by the Naval Aircraft Modification Unit at Johnsville. Several were used in the Bikini operations.

The F6F-5 was the last operational version of the Hellcat, which was finally withdrawn from production in November 1945. The 10,000th Hellcat was delivered to the US Navy in March 1945 and final production amounted to 12,275. Interestingly the Hellcat was the only US aircraft designed and built (see above) after Pearl Harbor to be produced in this quantity and proved one of the most significant fighters flown in World War II, achieving a major victory against the Japanese in the Battle of the Philippine Sea. It was also flown by the Royal Navy as the Hellcat I and II.
Data (F6F-5): *Engine* one 1,490 kW (2,000 hp) Pratt & Whitney R-2800-10W radial *Wing span* 13.06 m (42 ft 10 in) *Length* 10.24 m (33 ft 6⅝ in) *Max T-O weight* 5,774–6,991 kg (12,730–15,413 lb) *Max level speed* 597 km/h (371 mph) *Range* 1,520 km (945 miles) *Armament* four 0.50 in machine-guns and two 20 mm cannon or six machine-guns (three in each outer wing), up to six underwing rockets, and up to 907 kg (2,000 lb) of bombs carried beneath the fuselage
Grumman F7F Tigercat (USA) Very different from the Grumman 'cats' which had preceded it, the F7F Tigercat (as it became known) was designed as a twin-engined fighter-bomber for operation from the then new Midway class of aircraft carriers displacing 45,000 tons. In fact it was not until 1945 that F7F-4Ns were delivered equipped with arrester gear and suitable for carrier operations. In spite of its size, speed and tricycle

Grumman

Grumman F4F-3 Wildcat.

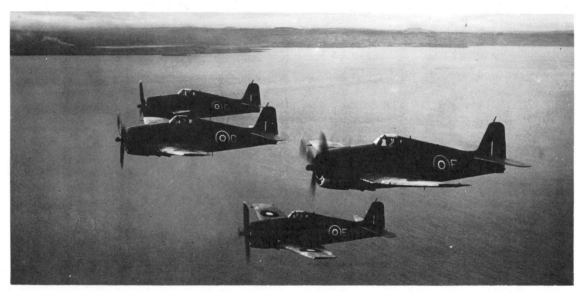

Grumman Hellcat Is.

Grumman F7F-3N Tigercat.

Tigercat. Other variants included F7F-3 single-seat day fighters, similar to the -1, and -3N and -4N two-seat night fighters (a full list of versions, with descriptions, appears in the 1947 *Jane's*). Tigercats were developed too late for operational deployment in World War II, and while small numbers served post-war with the Marine Corps, these were soon displaced by first-generation jet-powered fighters/fighter-bombers.

Data (F7F-3): *Engines* two 1,565 kW (2,100 hp) Pratt & Whitney R-2800 radials *Wing span* 15.7 m (51 ft 6 in) *Wing span* (folded) 9.52 m (31 ft 2½ in) *Length* 13.82 m (45 ft 4 in) *Max T-O weight* 11,666 kg (25,720 lb) *Max level speed* 687 km/h (427 mph) *Range* 1,623–1,931 km (1,015–1,200 miles) *Armament* four 20 mm cannon or four

landing gear, the Tigercat also operated successfully from carriers of the *Essex* class.

The prototype XF7F-1, which flew for the first time in December 1943, had been designed for a close-support role. To provide high performance and the capability to carry a heavy weapon load, it was powered by two 1,565 kW (2,100 hp) radial engines mounted in underwing nacelles. Deliveries of single-seat land-based production F7F-1s to the US Marine Corps began in April 1944, but only small numbers entered service before production of a two-seat night fighter was initiated – this having the designation F7F-2N

0.50 in machine-guns, plus zero-length rocket projectiles, torpedoes or up to 1,818 kg (4,000 lb) of bombs on underwing racks

Grumman F8F Bearcat (USA) Last in the line of single-seat single-engined fighters to originate from the F4F Wildcat, the Bearcat had the distinction of being one of the most successful piston-engined aircraft to serve with the US Navy. The provision of significantly more power than the R-2800 engine of the F6F Hellcat was impractical, so the design team concentrated upon producing a smaller lightweight aircraft which would ensure the performance required of a carrier-based interceptor.

The prototype XF8F-1 flew for the first time on 27 November 1943, confirming at once that Grumman had produced a high-performance fighter, and deliveries of F8F-1s to the first operational squadron began in May 1945. Variants included F8F-1B with cannon armament; F8F-1N night fighter with redesigned powerplant section and revised radio and radar equipment; F8F-2 with an 1,863 kW (2,500 hp) R-2800-E engine, fin and rudder height increased by 30.5 cm (12 in) to improve directional stability (made a controlled climb from take-off to 3,050 m; 10,000 ft in 92 seconds); F8F-2N night fighter; and F8F-2P photo-reconnaissance aircraft. Entering service too late for operational deployment in World War II, ex-US Navy Bearcats were used by the French Armée de l'Air and the Royal Thai Air Force, playing a significant role in the conflict in Indo-China.

Data (F8F-1): *Engine* one 1,565 kW (2,100 hp) Pratt & Whitney R-2800-34W radial *Wing span* 10.92 m (35 ft 10 in) *Length* 8.61 m (28 ft 3 in) *Max T-O weight* 5,875 kg (12,947 lb) *Max. level speed* 678 km/h (421 mph) *Range* 1,778 km (1,105 miles) *Armament* four 0.50 in machine-guns

Grumman F9F Cougar (USA) The Cougar was a swept-wing development of the earlier G-79 Panther. The fuselage was similar but the wings and tailplane were swept at 35°. First flown in prototype form on 20 September 1951, the initial production version was the F9F-6 armed with four 20 mm cannon and powered by a 32.25 kN (7,250 lb st) Pratt & Whitney J48-P-8 turbojet engine. The F9F-6P was an unarmed photographic-reconnaissance version with a longer nose to accommodate K-17 and tri-metrogon cameras. Next came the F9F-7, similar to the previous version except that it was powered by a 28.25 kN (6,350 lb st) Allison J33-A-16A engine.

The first production F9F-8 flew on 18 January 1954. Powered by J48-P-8 engine, it was a development of the F9F-6 with increased speed and range. Movable leading-edge slats were replaced by fixed cambered leading-edge extensions outboard of the wing fences. Total internal fuel capacity was increased by 530 litres (140 US gallons). A photographic-reconnaissance version (the F9F-8P) flew for the first time on 21 August 1955 and had an extended nose for the cameras. The F9F-8 went out of production in 1957.

The final version of the Cougar was the F9F-8T two-seat fighter-trainer, first flown on 4 April 1956. Production of this version ended on the last day of 1959 after 399 had been built. Total production of the Cougar was 1,985 aircraft. Many F9F-8Ts were flown operationally in Vietnam.

Data (F9F-8T, later TF-9J): *Engine* one 37.81 kN (8,500 lb st) Pratt & Whitney J48-P-8A turbojet *Wing span* 10.51 m (34 ft 6 in) *Length* (incl nose-probe) 14.78 m (48 ft 6 in) *Normal T-O weight* 9,344 kg (20,600 lb) *Max level speed* 1,135 km/h (705 mph) *Range* 1,610 km (1,000 miles) *Armament* two nose-mounted 20 mm cannon, plus underwing racks for two 1,000 lb bombs, or six HVAR rockets, or four Sidewinder air-to-air missiles and two drop-tanks

Grumman F9F Panther (USA) The original layout of this single-seat carrier-based fighter provided for the installation of four wing-mounted Westinghouse 19XB-2B (Navy J30) axial-flow jets. But this arrangement was abandoned in favour of one fuselage-mounted high-powered turbojet engine before prototype construction began, a change prompted by the successful tests conducted by the Navy in December 1946 with two imported Rolls-Royce Nene engines.

The first prototype XF9F-2 was powered by an imported Nene engine and flew for the first time on 24 November 1947. The second prototype was similarly fitted, but the third (the XF9F-3) had an

Grumman F8F-1 Bearcats.

Allison J33 engine. Production aircraft were divided between Nene and Allison-powered models, the former engines licence-built by Pratt & Whitney as J42s.

The first production F9F-2, powered by a 22.24 kN (5,000 lb st) J42-P-6, flew for the first time on 24 November 1948. The 20.46 kN (4,600 lb st) J33-A-8-powered prototype flew for the first time on 15 August 1948 and a total of 418 of both versions were built. However the F9F-2 proved to be the better version and the F9F-3s were re-engined to F9F-2 standard. The F9F-4 (73 of which were ordered originally) was powered by an Allison J33-A-16 engine, but none was completed and the contracts were combined with those for more than 580 27.80 kN (6,250 lb st) Pratt & Whitney J48-P-4/6A-engined F9F-5s (which flew for the first time on 21 December 1949). The F9F-5P was a photographic-reconnaissance version with a longer camera nose.

Panthers are remembered in US Navy history as their first jet fighter to be used in combat, introduced into the Korean War on 3 July 1950, as well as for recording a victory against an enemy jet aircraft, a MiG-15, on 9 November 1950.

Data (F9F-5): *Engine* as above *Wing span* 11.58 m (38 ft 0 in) *Length* 11.84 m (38 ft 10 in) *Max T-O weight* 8,491 kg (18,720 lb) *Max level speed* 932 km/h (579 mph) *Range* 2,092 km (1,300 miles) *Armament* four 20 mm cannon in nose; provision for 5 in rockets, 500 lb bombs, napalm bombs, etc

Grumman F11F Tiger (USA) The Tiger single-seat fighter flew for the first time in prototype form on 30 July 1954 – less than 15 months after receipt of a letter of intent from the US Navy. The production version was the F11F-1. A small

Grumman F9F-8 Cougar.

Grumman

Grumman F9F-8T Cougar.

number of pre-production aircraft, each with a Wright J65-W-6 turbojet engine with afterburner, were followed by 39 production aircraft (ordered with J65-W-4 afterburning engines), two of which were modified to F11F-1F standard with 66.72 kN (15,000 lb st) General Electric J79-GE-7 afterburning engines. One of the F11F-1Fs attained a speed of 1,963 km/h (1,220 mph) and set a short-lived height record on 18 April 1958 of 23,449 m (76,932 ft).

A further contract for J65-W-18-engined Tigers placed for the US Navy brought the total number of F11F-1s built to about 200, but these were gradually phased out of first-line service from 1959. Those which remained in second-line service when the tri-service designations became rationalised in 1962 were redesignated F-11A.

Interestingly the 1958–59 *Jane's* mentions that the F11F-1F was selected for the JASDF, 300 of which were going to be built under licence by Mitsubishi between 1959 and 1962. This did not materialise. The designation F11F-1FT applied to a projected two-seat training version.

Data: *Engine* one 46.71 kN (10,500 lb st, with afterburning) Wright J65-W-18 turbojet *Wing span* 9.64 m (31 ft 7½ in) *Length* 13.69 m (44 ft 11¼ in) *Max T-O weight* 10,921 kg (24,078 lb) *Max level speed* 1,207 km/h (750 mph) *Range* 2,044 km (1,270 miles) *Armament* four 20 mm cannon and four Sidewinder or air-to-ground missiles

Grumman F9F-5 Panther.

Grumman F-14 Tomcat (USA) In the late 1960s the US Navy identified a requirement for a new carrier-based fighter, known originally as the VFX. Five aerospace companies received requests for proposals in June 1968 and the submissions of Grumman and McDonnell Douglas were selected for final consideration. In early 1969 Grumman's proposal was chosen for development and production (under the designation F-14A) and given the name Tomcat.

The aim of the VFX requirement was to produce a small, lightweight aircraft of high performance. Not only had it to be superior to the McDonnell Douglas F-4 Phantom II all-weather fighter which was in service with the Navy, but it was required also to offer a significant performance advance over then current Soviet combat aircraft. Three primary missions were detailed for the F-14A: fighter sweep/escort, defence of carrier task forces, and secondary attack of tactical ground targets. The first is concerned with clearing contested airspace of enemy fighters and protecting the task force, with backing from AEW aircraft, communication networks and surface ships; the second to be achieved by standing patrol or deck-launched intercept (DLI) operations; the third mission relies upon ECM and escort-fighter support.

To provide such potential from a carrier-based aircraft was no easy task and, not surprisingly, the F-14 is of unique configuration. To obtain optimum performance for deck operations – as well as for Mach 2 plus high-speed capability – a variable-geometry wing was chosen. This has 20° sweep in the fully forward setting, ranging to 68° fully swept, and with an oversweep position of 75° for carrier stowage. To ensure optimum setting of the wing throughout the flight regime, it is controlled automatically by a Mach sweep programmer, thus relating wing sweep to altitude and Mach number. This system can, if necessary, be turned over to manual control. Other design features include small foreplanes which extend automatically at supersonic speeds, manoeuvring slats and flaps, and twin outward-canted fins and rudders. Power plant comprises two turbofan engines with afterburning: their air intakes have movable programmed ramps to provide the correct airflow to each engine under all flight conditions.

The first prototype was lost in a non-fatal accident on its first flight. It was not until 24 May 1971 that a successful first flight was made with the second prototype, and flight testing was able to begin. US Navy contracts were awarded for 12 research and development aircraft, followed by 26 production F-14As. The Navy is expected to procure eventually a total of 390 examples, these including the 12 R & D aircraft. Carrier trials in June 1972 were followed by initial deployment with the fleet in October 1972.

Flown by a crew of two, who are seated on zero-zero rocket ejection seats, the F-14A Tomcat is a formidable multi-role fighter. Its avionics include a Hughes AN/AWG-9 weapons-control system to obtain optimum performance for the missiles and bombs which it can carry, and ECM equipment is provided to give maximum protection against the all-seeing eyes of enemy radar and radar-guided weapons.

Data: *Engines* two 93 kN (20,900 lb st, with afterburning) Pratt & Whitney TF30-P-412A turbofans *Wing span* (unswept) 19.55 m (64 ft 1½ in), (swept) 11.65 m (38 ft 2½ in) *Length* 18.89 m (61 ft 11 in) *Max T-O weight* 33,724 kg (74,348 lb) *Max level speed* Mach 2.4 *Armament* one General Electric M61A-1 Vulcan 20 mm cannon, and four to six missiles; maximum external weapon load, comprising a mix of missiles and bombs, of up to 6,577 kg (14,500 lb)

Grumman FF-1 and SF-1 (USA) In 1928 the US Navy aircraft carrier *Langley* participated in an exercise in which it made a surprise attack on the naval base of Pearl Harbor. The irony of this exercise aside, it proved two things: firstly that the US Navy appreciated that the base would be a prime target for any enemy during a major Pacific war; secondly that the aircraft carrier was one of the major offensive weapons of the future. As a result of this thinking USS *Lexington* and *Saratoga*

Grumman FF-1.

were completed in 1927 and subsequently commissioned to bring the Navy's carrier force to three.

In 1931 the XFF-1 prototype two-seat carrier-based biplane fighter flew for the first time. It was of advanced design with enclosed cockpits (the canopy made up of telescoping sections) and a landing gear that retracted into well-type recesses in the forward fuselage sides (almost identical with that used previously on the Dayton-Wright racing monoplane of 1920). During 1933 production FF-1s were delivered, each powered by a single 559 kW (750 hp) Wright R-1820-78 radial engine, followed in 1934 by similar but R-1820-84-powered SF-1 scouts. FF-1s and SF-1s totalled 60 aircraft, sufficient to equip the *Lexington*. These remained on board until 1936, when they were replaced by F2Fs. Thereafter the fighters were converted into FF-2 dual-control trainers.

In addition to US Navy aircraft, Turkey received 40 FF-1s and the RCAF 15 as Goblin 1s, all built by the Canadian Car and Foundry Company under licence. The Turkish fighters had by far the most interesting service life, being passed over to the Republican forces during the Spanish Civil War, with whom they fought for a time with other obsolete aircraft against well-equipped Nationalist forces. These were the only American-designed aircraft to fight in Spain. Another irony, only matched by that mentioned above, is that a single FF-1 was sold to Japan, a country that learned quickly the lessons in carrier operations taught throughout the inter-war period by unsuspecting nations.

Data (Goblin 1): *Engine* as for FF-1 *Wing span*

Grumman F-14A Tomcat.

Grumman F11F-1s.

Grumman

Grumman J4F-1 Widgeon. 10.52 m (34 ft 6 in) *Length* 7.47 m (24 ft 6 in) *Max T-O weight* about 2,177 kg (4,800 lb) *Max level speed* 340 km/h (211 mph) *Range* 1,041–1,480 km (647–920 miles) *Armament* three 0.30 in Browning machine-guns

Grumman JF/J2F Duck (USA) Nine versions of this aeroplane were built for the US Navy and Coast Guard, the first appearing for the Navy in 1933 as the JF-1, powered by a 521.6 kW (700 hp) Pratt & Whitney R-1830 Twin Wasp engine. This was followed by the JF-2 Coast Guard version, powered by a 559 kW (750 hp) Wright Cyclone radial, and the JF-3. A number of JF-2s were also delivered to Argentina. By the beginning of 1941 about 115 JF and J2F-1 to J2F-4 Ducks were in service as general/utility amphibians for photographic, target-towing, scouting and rescue work. These were followed by J2F-5s and J2F-6s, the latter produced in 1944 by the Columbia Aircraft Corporation of Valley Stream, Long Island, under licence from Grumman, bringing the total number of JF/J2Fs built to over 600.

Data (J2F-6): *Engine* one 670.7 kW (900 hp) Wright R-1820-54 radial *Wing span* 11.89 m (39 ft 0 in) *Length* 10.36 m (34 ft 0 in) *Max T-O weight* 3,492 kg (7,700 lb) *Max level speed* 306 km/h (190 mph) *Range* 1,255 km (780 miles)

Grumman J2F Duck.

Grumman J4F Model G-44 Widgeon (USA) The Widgeon was a military utility version of the four–five-seat commercial Model G-44 amphibian. It first went into service with the US Coast Guard as the J4F-1 in 1941 and as the J4F-2 with the US Navy in the following year. It also served with the USAAF (as the OA-14) and with the RCAF and Royal Navy as the Gosling. Production totalled more than 200 aircraft. In 1946 the G-44A appeared incorporating a number of improvements, including a deeper bow, step vents to improve hydrodynamics and modified internal equipment. SCAN of France built 40 aircraft after the war, most of which had their 149 kW (200 hp) Ranger L-440-5 engines replaced by 223.6 kW (300 hp) Lycoming R-680s. In addition McKinnon Enterprises converted more than 70 Widgeons into Super Widgeon executive transports powered by two 201 kW (270 hp) Lycoming GO-460-B1D engines.

Grumman JRF-5.

Data (Super Widgeon): *Engines* as above *Wing*

span 12.19 m (40 ft 0 in) *Length* 9.47 m (31 ft 1 in) *Max T-O weight* 2,500 kg (5,500 lb) *Max cruising speed* 290 km/h (180 mph) *Range* 1,600 km (1,000 miles)

Grumman JRF/Model G-21A Goose (USA) The G-21A eight-seat commercial amphibian flew for the first time in June 1937 and was Grumman's first aircraft produced for the private and commercial market. It proved outstandingly successful and 20 were delivered prior to 1 October 1938, when many more were on order. However most of the 300 or so aircraft built went into military service, the US Navy receiving initially JRF-1s and the US Coast Guard JRF-2s in 1939–40.

Further series included JRF-1A aircraft, fitted for target towing and photography; JRF-3 fitted with anti-icing equipment and autopilot for use in northern waters by the US Coast Guard; JRF-4, a development of the JRF-1; JRF-5 (OA-9) for the USAAF and fitted for photography; and the JRF-6B navigational trainer. JRF-5s also served with the RCAF and the JRF-5 and -6 with the RAF as the Goose. Production of the JRF ceased in September 1945, but the type continued to serve as a general/utility amphibian with the US Navy and Coast Guard.

After the war McKinnon Enterprises began a conversion programme, replacing the original 335.3 kW (450 hp) Pratt & Whitney R-985-AN-6 engines with four 253.4 kW (340 hp) Lycoming GSO-480s and incorporating other refinements to produce executive transports. This programme was superseded by the turboprop-powered G-21C, D and G Turbo-Goose conversions, initiated in 1966. The latter is the current version, powered by two 507 kW (680 shp) Pratt & Whitney Aircraft of Canada PT6A turboprop engines.

Data (G-21G Turbo-Goose): *Engines* as above *Wing span* 15.49 m (50 ft 10 in) *Length* 12.07 m

(39 ft 7 in) *Max T-O weight* 5,670 kg (12,500 lb) *Max operating speed* 391 km/h (243 mph) *Range* 2,575 km (1,600 miles) *Accommodation* pilot and up to 11 passengers

Grumman C-2A Greyhound (USA) Derivative of the E-2A Hawkeye, designed specifically to deliver cargo to air groups deployed on aircraft carriers of the US Navy. First flown in prototype form on 18 November 1964, production deliveries to the US fleet began in 1966. Power is provided by two 3,018 kW (4,050 ehp) Allison T56-A-8A turboprops and there is accommodation for up to 39 troops, 20 stretchers and four attendants, or freight.

Grumman OV-1 Mohawk.

Grumman OV-1 Mohawk (USA) First flown in 1959, the Mohawk is a two-seat observation aircraft. Delivered to the US Army as the OV-1A initial production version with T53-L-3 engines and equipped for day and night reconnaissance; JOV-1A with provision for bombs, rockets and 0.50 in machine-guns on hardpoints; OV-1B with APS-94 side-looking airborne radar and internal camera; OV-1C with AAS-24 infra-red mapping sensor and internal camera, and powered by T53-L-3 engines; OV-1D with side-looking airborne radar, infra-red or other sensors, new cameras and powered by T53-L-7 engines; and RV-1C/D, OV-1C/Ds modified for electronic reconnaissance. The EV-1 is a planned conversion of OV-1Bs to electronic-surveillance aircraft with AN/ALQ-133 radar target locator systems. Data (OV-1D): *Engines* two 1,043 kW (1,400 shp) Lycoming T53-L-701 turboprops *Wing span* 14.63 m (48 ft 0 in) *Length* 12.5 m (41 ft 0 in) *Max T-O weight* (SLAR) 8,214 kg (18,109 lb) *Max level speed* (SLAR) 465 km/h (289 mph) *Range* (SLAR) 1,520 km (944 miles)

Grumman S-2 Tracker (USA) The Tracker is a twin 1,136.4 kW (1,525 hp) Wright R-1820-82WA-powered carrier-based anti-submarine search and attack aircraft, produced originally for the US Navy but currently also in

service with the air forces and navies of several countries.

The prototype flew for the first time on 4 December 1952 and more than 1,000 S-2s were delivered by Grumman. The initial production version was designated S-2A (CP-121, formerly CS2F-1 for the Canadian version). Next came the S-2B with new anti-submarine detection equipment; the TS-2B trainer; S-2C with enlarged bomb bays to house two homing torpedoes (most converted to US-2C or RS-2C); S-2D with improved anti-submarine equipment, wider cockpit and longer range; S-2E with improved anti-submarine equipment; S-2F with uprated submarine detection equipment; S-2G, early version uprated with a Martin Marietta kit; US-2A/C, S-2A/C converted for target towing; US-2B utility/transport conversion of the S-2B; RS-2C, S-2C converted for photo-reconnaissance/ survey work; AS-2D, S-2D modified for night

Grumman C-2A Greyhound.

Grumman CS2F-1 Trackers.

Grumman TB Avengers.

Grumman U-16 Albatross anti-submarine amphibians.

attack; and E-1B Tracer, which is covered under a separate entry.

Data (S-2E Tracker): Engines as above *Wing span* 22.13 m (72 ft 7 in) *Length* 13.26 m (43 ft 6 in) *Max T-O weight* 13,222 kg (29,150 lb) *Max level speed* 426 km/h (265 mph) *Armament* fuselage bay for 60 echo-sounding depth charges; one Mk 101 or Mk 57 nuclear depth bomb or equivalent store in bomb bay; six underwing pylons for torpedoes, 5 in rockets, etc; 32 sonobuoys in nacelles

Grumman TB Avenger (USA) Grumman's association with the US Navy began with a small contract placed in 1931. By the time the Navy contracted two prototype XTBF-1 torpedo-bombers in 1940, the company had already gained considerable experience of designing and building naval aircraft. The choice of a powerful radial engine meant that the fuselage was of the rather portly barrel shape that is associated with Grumman aircraft of the era. However a requirement for a crew comprising pilot, gunner and radar operator, plus up to 907 kg (2,000 lb) of bombs and defensive armament, required much greater wing area and, consequently, a longer fuselage, which produced an artificially sleek appearance.

The prototype was delivered for evaluation in 1941. The TBF-1 initial series version went into production the same year and it began to go into service with the US Navy as a replacement for the TBD early in 1942. It was first reported in action in the Battle of Midway in June 1942.

The Avenger was latterly produced solely by the Eastern Aircraft Division of General Motors (under the designation TBM), the first being assembled from parts supplied by Grumman and flown on 11 November 1942. By December 1943 all production of the Avenger by Grumman had ceased. When all production ended a total of more

Grumman Mallard.

than 9,830 Avengers had been built. Grumman-built aircraft included TBF-1s (1,267 kW; 1,700 hp Wright R-2600-8 radial engine); TBF-1Cs each with two 0.50 in wing guns; and TBF-1Bs supplied to Britain and the RNZAF. Eastern's versions included TBM-1s, TBM-1Cs, TBM-3s (major production version) and TBM-4, the latter representing the final wartime version with a Wright R-2600-20 engine and strengthened airframe, but was a prototype only. TBM-1s and -3s served with the Royal Navy as Avenger IIs and IIIs respectively.

Following on from the TBM-3E anti-submarine variant produced immediately post-war, many Avengers were subsequently completely rebuilt in US Navy establishments into TBM-3W (search) and TBM-3S (attack) aircraft for anti-submarine duties. The former had a large radome replacing the underbelly which housed the torpedo or bomb bay and ventral gun position in the original TBM-3. Other Avengers were converted for target-towing, COD (Carrier On-board Delivery) and similar non-combat roles.

Data (TBM-3E): Engine one 1,416 kW (1,900 hp) Wright R-2600-20 radial *Wing span* 16.51 m (54 ft 2 in) *Length* 12.49 m (40 ft 11½ in), (TBF-1) 12.19 m (40 ft 0⅛ in) *Max T-O weight* 8,117 kg (17,895 lb), (TBF-1, normal) 7,047 kg (15,536 lb) *Max level speed* 444 km/h (276 mph), (TBF-1) 447 km/h (278 mph) *Range* 1,625 km

(1,010 miles) *Armament* one 0.30 in and three 0.50 in machine-guns, plus up to 907 kg (2,000 lb) of weapons in bomb bay, comprising one short torpedo, one 2,000 lb bomb, one 1,600 lb armour-piercing bomb, four 500 lb bombs or equivalent weight of smaller bombs, a smoke-screen tank, drop-tank, tow target and equipment

Grumman Mallard (USA) The Mallard eight–ten-seat amphibian was developed just after World War II as a commercial aircraft, similar in layout to the Goose and Widgeon but larger and powered by two 410 kW (550 hp) Pratt & Whitney R-1340-S3H1 radial engines.

Grumman U-16 Albatross (USA) The prototype of this general/utility amphibian flew in October 1947 and the Albatross entered military service in July 1949. More than 450 were built, after which conversion of existing airframes produced new versions.

The HU-16A was the initial production version, built for the USAF for search-and-rescue duties under the original designation SA-16A. The majority were subsequently modified to have greater wing spans and increased empty and all-up weights as HU-16Bs (formerly SA-16Bs). The HU-16C/D are US Navy versions, 135 of which were ordered as UF-1s. Fifty-one were subsequently modified as UF-2s, all UFs later being redesignated HU/LU/TU-16C and HU-16D. HU-16E is the latest US Coast Guard designation for UF-1G/UF-2Gs and ex-USAF SA-16As. A special ASW version of the HU-16B, able to perform anti-submarine duties – with a nose radome, retractable MAD and ECM and capable of carrying depth charges – has also been developed.

Data (HU-16B): *Engines* two 1,062 kW (1,425 hp) Wright R-1820-76A or -76B radials *Wing span* 29.46 m (96 ft 8 in) *Length* 19.18 m (62 ft 10 in) *Max T-O weight* 17,010 kg (37,500 lb) *Max level speed* 379 km/h (236 mph) *Range* 4,587 km (2,850 miles) *Accommodation* crew of three–five and 22 passengers or 12 stretchers

Grumman (General Dynamics) EF-111A (USA) A programme to convert General Dynamics F-111As into EF-111A electronic-warfare prototypes to provide ECM jamming coverage for air-attack forces was initiated in 1972–73. USAF plans envisage the conversion of 42 F-111Fs into ECM jamming aircraft. The production contract for the first six was signed in 1979.

Gulfstream American Cheetah.

Grumman American Tr.2 (USA) Similar to the AA-1A but produced in small numbers as an advanced trainer and sporting aircraft.

GST Catalina (USSR) Russian State Aircraft Factory-built version of the American Consolidated PBY Catalina powered by two 745 kW (1,000 hp) Shvetsov ASh-621R radial engines.

Gulfstream American AA-1 and T-cat (USA) Designed originally as a specialised trainer version of the American Aviation AA-1 American Yankee, the prototype AA-1A Trainer first flew on 25 March 1970. In 1973 this aircraft was redesignated as the AA-1B Trainer. The 1977 version was the AA-1C, still marketed under the company name of Grumman American. In the following year American Jet Industries (AJI) announced that it had purchased the 80% holding in Grumman American Aviation Corporation held by Grumman Corporation and the company thereafter became known as Gulfstream American. Production of the AA-1C two-seat trainer/utility monoplane (87.75 kW; 115 hp Lycoming O-235-C2C engine) and the T-cat, basically similar but with dual controls and additional equipment, has now ended.

Gulfstream American Tiger.

Gulfstream American Lynx (USA) Generally similar to the AA-1C, intended as an advanced-trainer and sporting aircraft. Production has now ended.

Gulfstream American AA-5A and Cheetah (USA) Four-seat cabin monoplanes, each powered by one 112 kW (150 hp) Lycoming O-320-E2G engine. The AA-5A is the standard version (formerly known as the Traveler) and the Cheetah is the de luxe version with additional equipment (formerly known as the Traveler de luxe).

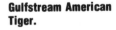

Grumman American Tr.2.

Gulfstream American AA-5B and Tiger (USA) The AA-5B standard version and the Tiger de luxe version are more powerful derivatives of the AA-5A with increased fuel capacity. Power is provided by the 134 kW (180 hp) Lycoming O-360-A4K engine. The 1,000th Tiger was delivered in November 1978.

Gulfstream American GAC 159-C Gulfstream I Commuter and Grumman Gulfstream I (USA) The Grumman American Gulfstream I was designed as a 19-seat executive aircraft and marketed from 1958 to 1969. A total of 200 had been built when production was terminated in favour of the twin-turbofan Gulfstream II. Gulfstream American acquired the tooling and fixtures for Gulfstream I production when it purchased the former company (see **AA-1** entry above) in September 1978. During the first half of 1979 Gulfstream American conducted marketing and engineering studies to determine the feasibility of putting into production a 32–38-seat commuter version of the twin-turboprop G-159 Gulfstream I. Design changes planned for the Gulfstream I Commuter include lengthening the

speed 936 km/h (581 mph) *Range* 6,025 km (3,744 miles) *Accommodation* crew of two or three and 19 passengers; large baggage compartment with a capacity of 907 kg (2,000 lb)

Gulfstream American Gulfstream III (USA) Grumman (now Gulfstream) American announced the resumption of the Gulfstream III programme in 1978. It differs from the Gulfstream II primarily in having redesigned wings with 'winglets' at the tips, a lengthened fuselage and increased fuel capacity combined with an increase of some 18% in fuel economy and efficiency. A prototype (converted from a production Gulfstream II) flew for the first time in November 1979. Deliveries of production aircraft were expected to begin in mid-1980.

Data: *Engines* as for Gulfstream II *Wing span* 23.72 m (77 ft 10 in) *Length* 25.27 m (82 ft 11 in) *Max T-O weight* 30,935 kg (68,200 lb) *Max cruising speed* Mach 0.85 *Max range* 7,495 km (4,660 miles)

Grumman Gulfstream I.

Gulfstream American Cougar.

fuselage by 2.90 m (9 ft 6 in). As a first stage, Gulfstream American was lengthening the fuselage of an existing Gulfstream I in the summer of 1979.

Gulfstream American Gulfstream II (USA) The first production Grumman American Gulfstream II flew on 2 October 1966. Deliveries of more than 240 had taken place by 1 January 1979 (from September 1978 as Gulfstream American Gulfstream IIs), including a single Gulfstream II operated by the US Coast Guard under the designation VC-11A. Two other Gulfstream IIs were converted as flying simulators for the Space Shuttle Orbiter vehicle. Production was due to end in December 1979, after the sale of 256 aircraft.

Data: *Engines* two 50.7 kN (11,400 lb st) Rolls-Royce Spey Mk 511-8 turbofans *Wing span* 20.98 m (68 ft 10 in) *Length* 24.36 m (79 ft 11 in) *Max T-O weight* 29,711 kg (65,500 lb) *Max cruising*

Grumman American Gulfstream II.

Gulfstream American GA-7 and Cougar (USA) Four-seat lightweight cabin monoplanes, each powered by two 119.3 kW (160 hp) Lycoming O-320-D1D engines and produced as basic and de luxe versions respectively. Delivery of production aircraft began in February 1978.

Gulfstream American Super Ag-Cat and Grumman American Ag-Cat (USA) The prototype of the original Ag-Cat agricultural biplane flew for the first time on 27 May 1957. Series production was undertaken by Schweizer under sub-contract from Grumman. First deliveries were made in 1959 and 2,280 Ag-Cats (including 2,250 of the A and B models) had been built by 1 January 1979.

The Super Ag-Cat (first certificated in 1966) was basically a higher-powered version of the Ag-Cat. The four current models are the Super Ag-Cat B/450 basic version, powered by a

335.5 kW (450 hp) Pratt & Whitney R-985 radial engine; Super Ag-Cat B/525, with a 391.5 kW (525 hp) Continental/Page R-975 radial; Super Ag-Cat C/600, with a 447.5 kW (600 hp) Pratt & Whitney R-1340 radial; and the Turbo Ag-Cat D, available in three versions from 1979 with a 507 kW (680 shp) PT6A-15 engine and a 1,893 litre (500 US gallon) hopper/tank, 559 kW (750 shp) PT6A-34 engine and a 634 kW (850 shp) PT6A-41 engine.

Gulfstream American Hustler Model 500 (USA) Formerly known as the AJI Hustler Model 500, the prototype of this twin-engined business/utility aircraft flew for the first time on 11 January 1978 and had accumulated more than 250 hours' flying by mid-1979.

Gulfstream American Peregrine 600 (USA) Two-seat military trainer based on the Hustler 500 design and powered by a 13.34 kN (3,000 lb st) Pratt & Whitney Aircraft of Canada JT15D-5 turbofan engine. Under development.

Gyrodyne Rotorcycle (USA) Under contract from the US Navy, this company produced a simple one-man co-axial portable helicopter known as the RON-1 Rotorcycle, intended for use by the USMC for observation, liaison and small-unit tactical manoeuvres.

Haefeli DH 1 and DH 2 (Switzerland) Pusher- and tractor-engined observation biplanes respectively of 1916, a very small number of which were built for the Swiss Fliegertruppe.

Haefeli DH 3 (Switzerland) Two-seat reconnaissance and light bombing biplane, 110 of which were delivered to the Swiss Fliegertruppe between 1917 and 1927, remaining in service as a trainer until the mid-1930s. Armament comprised two machine-guns, plus bombs, and power was provided by an 89.4 kW (120 hp) Argus-SLM or 112 kW (150 hp) Hispano engine. DH 3s were also flown on an experimental passenger and mail service between Zurich and Bern.

Grumman American Ag-Cat B.

Haefeli DH 3.

HAL HA-31 Mk II Basant.

Haefeli DH 5 and DH 5A (Switzerland) The DH 5 was a standard two-seat general-purpose biplane of the Swiss Fliegertruppe, entering service as a DH 3 replacement from 1922. Powered by a 149 kW (200 hp) Winterthur engine, it remained in service throughout the remaining inter-war years, latterly as a trainer. Altogether 60 were built, each armed with two forward-firing and one rear-mounted machine-guns. The DH 5 was followed by 22 examples of the improved DH 5A, powered by a 164 kW (220 hp) engine and incorporating a fuselage constructed of metal tubing.

Along with a single-seat fighter developed from the Fokker D.VII and designated M.7, Haefeli developed the M.8, an improved version of the DH 5 powered by a 223.5 kW (300 hp) Hispano-Suiza engine. Capable of 217 km/h (135 mph) compared to 187 km/h (116 mph) for the DH 5, it failed to enter production.

HAL HA-31 Mk II Basant (India) Single-seat agricultural and utility aircraft, flown for the first time on 30 March 1972 (preceded by the Mk I prototype of 1969). A pre-production batch of 20 Mk II Basants followed, the first eight going to the

Gyrodyne Rotorcycles.

HAL

HAL HJT-16 Mk IA Kiran.

HAL HAOP-27 Krishak Mk 2.

HAL Kiran Mk II.

HAL HF-24 Marut.

Indian Ministry of Food and Agriculture in June 1974. By the beginning of 1979 36 production aircraft had been completed. The basic aircraft is intended primarily for aerial application of pesticides and fertilisers, but can be used for aerial survey, fire/patrol duties and cloud seeding. Power is provided by a 298 kW (400 hp) Lycoming IO-720-C1B engine.

HAL HAOP-27 Krishak Mk II (India) First flown in November 1959, the Krishak Mk II is a two–three-seat air observation post or ambulance, powered by a 168 kW (225 hp) Rolls-Royce Continental O-470-J engine. Sixty-eight were built and these serve with the Indian Army.

HAL HF-24 Marut (India) Development of the Marut single-seat ground-attack fighter was started in 1956. The prototype Mk I, powered by two 21.57 kN (4,850 lb st) Bristol Orpheus 703 turbojet engines, flew for the first time on 17 June 1961. One hundred and twenty-nine Mk Is were built, together with 18 Mk IT tandem two-seat trainers.

Data: *Engines* as above *Wing span* 9.0 m (29 ft 6¼ in) *Length* 15.87 m (52 ft 0¾ in) *Max T-O weight* 10,925 kg (24,085 lb) *Max level speed* 1,083 km/h (673 mph) *Armament* four 30 mm Aden Mk 2 guns in nose and a retractable pack of 50 SNEB 68 mm air-to-air rockets; attachments for four 1,000 lb bombs, napalm tanks, Type 116 SNEB rocket packs, clusters of T10 air-to-surface rockets, or other stores

HAL HJT-16 Mk I Kiran (India) Two-seat turbojet-powered basic trainer, flown for the first time in prototype form on 4 September 1964. A total of 24 pre-production Mk Is were delivered to the Indian Air Force from March 1968. By 1 January 1979 a total of 119 Mk Is and 25 Mk IAs (with underwing hardpoints for weapons as standard) had been produced to meet the require-

ments of both the Air Force and Navy. Total requirement is for 190 aircraft. Power is provided by one 11.12 kN (2,500 lb st) Rolls-Royce Viper 11 turbojet engine.

HAL Kiran Mk II (India) Version of the Kiran suitable for armament-training or counter-insurgency duties; under development.

HAL HPT-32 (India) Two–three-seat fully aerobatic basic trainer or four-seat liaison aircraft, currently under development for the Indian Air Force. Power is provided by a 194 kW (260 hp) Lycoming AEIO-540-D4B5 engine.

HAL HT-2 (India) All-metal basic trainer which entered production in 1953. About 160 built, mostly for the Indian Air Force, Indian Navy and Indian Civil Aviation Training Centre. Twelve were sold to the Ghana Air Force and single examples were presented to Indonesia and Singapore. Power was provided by a 115.5 kW (155 hp) Blackburn Cirrus Major III engine.

HAL HUL-26 Pushpak (India) Built as an inexpensive ultra-light training aircraft for Indian flying clubs, the Pushpak was first flown in prototype form on 28 September 1958. One hundred and fifty had been delivered by early 1969, each powered by a 67 kW (90 hp) Continental C90-8F engine.

HAL Ajeet prototype.

Halberstadt CL.II.

HAL Ajeet (India) The Hawker Siddeley Gnat light fighter and fighter bomber was built under licence by HAL between 1962 and 1974. The Ajeet was designed as a Mk II version of the Gnat with improved performance characteristics and equipment. The last two Gnat Mk I aircraft were converted as prototypes for the Ajeet; the first of these was flown on 5 March 1975. By mid-January 1979 a total of 23 (of approximately 80 then on order) production Ajeets had been completed.
Data: *Engine* one 20 kN (4,500 lb st) Rolls-Royce Orpheus turbojet *Wing span* 6.73 m (22 ft 1 in) *Length* 9.04 m (29 ft 8 in) *Max T-O weight* 4,170 kg (9,195 lb) *Max level speed* 1,152 km/h (716 mph) *Combat radius* (with two 500 lb bombs) 204 km (127 miles) *Armament* two 30 mm Aden Mk 4 cannon; four underwing hardpoints able to carry two 500 lb bombs, four Arrow Type 122 pods each containing 18 × 68 mm rockets, or two drop-tanks
HAL Ajeet Trainer (India) Tandem two-seat trainer version of the Ajeet, retaining combat capability. Under development.
HAL Light Helicopter (India) High-performance light helicopter, under development for the Indian Air Force, Army and Navy.
Halberstadt C.V (Germany) Developed from the C.III, the C.V was unusual for a new aircraft entering service in mid-1918 in that it was not a combat type but a photographic-reconnaissance biplane, produced to make long-range flights over enemy positions, often unescorted and against fierce fighter opposition. Powered by a 164 kW (220 hp) Benz Bz.IV engine, it was not particularly fast (maximum speed 170 km/h; 106 mph) and often had to rely on its forward-firing Spandau and rear-mounted Parabellum machine-guns to get itself out of trouble. Its importance, how-

ever, was highlighted with the final Allied advance (not with the German advance of spring 1918 for which it had been envisaged), reflected by the fact that no less than four companies had the C.V in production. After the war the Swiss Air Force and others flew C.Vs as trainers.
Data: *Engine* as above *Wing span* 13.6 m (44 ft 8½ in) *Length* 6.9 m (22 ft 8 in) *Max T-O weight* 1,365 kg (3,009 lb) *Max level speed* 170 km/h (106 mph) *Endurance* 3 h 30 min
Halberstadt CL.II and CL.IV (Germany) The CL.II was produced to meet a new German specification calling for a small and light two-seat aircraft capable of escorting reconnaissance types and performing ground-attack duties when required. It became operational in mid-1917 and immediately went into action with considerable success. As the CL.II's 119 kW (160 hp) Mercedes D.III engine gave a speed of only 165 km/h (102.5 mph), the CL.IIa was produced, powered by a 138 kW (185 hp) BMW engine. However series production of the CL.IIa was cut short by the appearance of the much refined CL.IV which introduced major changes to the airframe but reverted to the original type of engine. Although smaller and lighter than the CL.II, with improved aerodynamics, maximum speed was disappointingly the same as for the earlier type, although rate of climb and manoeuvrability were improved upon. All three types were operational for the March 1918 offensive but, as this crumbled, were used increasingly for attacks on advancing Allied ground forces. After the Armistice a number of CL.IVs were operated on commercial services between German cities, each carrying two passengers.
Data (CL.II): *Engine* as above *Wing span* 10.77 m (35 ft 4 in) *Length* 7.3 m (23 ft 11½ in) *Max T-O weight* 1,133 kg (2,498 lb) *Max level speed* 165 km/h

HAL HPT-32 prototype.

Halberstadt

Halberstadt CL.IV.

Halberstadt D.II.

Hamilton Nomair.

(102.5 mph) *Endurance* 3 h *Armament* one or two forward-firing Spandau and one rear-mounted Parabellum machine-guns, plus light bombs

Halberstadt D types (Germany) D-type single-seat fighters never gained the war record or reputation of the Halberstadt two-seaters, but nevertheless were good enough to allow the company the boast 'cherished of the premier aviators of the war'. The rather angular D.I was used operationally from early 1916, powered by a 74.5 kW (100 hp) Mercedes D.I engine. It displayed many of the design features that were characteristic of the whole D series, including the early Morane-type of tapering fuselage and strut-braced vertical tail. Like the Fokker Eindeckers which the D types were expected to replace, armament comprised a single Spandau machine-gun. The D.I was followed by the 89.4 kW (120 hp) Argus As.II-powered D.Ia; D.II with an 89.4 kW (120 hp) Mercedes D.II (first with wing dihedral); D.III with an Argus As.II; 112 kW (150 hp) Benz Bz.III-powered D.IV; and Argus As.II-powered D.V of 1917.

The main production versions were the D.II and D.III, although it is thought that not more than 100 or so were built. A few also went to Turkey. During the summer of 1916 D types were particularly active over the British sector of the Western Front, judged by the number destroyed in comparison with 'kills' on the French front.

The 1918 *Jane's* gives a lengthy description of a D.III based on information gained from No 234, captured from the Germans and later flown by the RFC in British markings. In brief, the upper wing was slightly larger than the lower, which had a span of 7.85 m (25 ft 9 in). The wings were set at a dihedral angle, were washed out and noticeably staggered (0.45 m; 1 ft 6 in). The ailerons, on the upper wing only, projected slightly. Wing chord was 1.56 m (5 ft 1½ in). The rudder and elevators were built entirely of metal tubing, the ribs in the elevators having internal 'zig-zag' brac-

ing. The fuselage was constructed of wood, with hollow spars. Armament, which normally comprised a single Spandau, was increased to two guns on later examples, with 1,300 rounds of ammunition. From 1917 the D types were totally obsolete on the Western Front but continued to serve for a while in Macedonia and Palestine.

Data (D.III): Engine as above *Wing span* 8.8 m (28 ft 10½ in) *Length* 7.3 m (23 ft 11½ in) *Max T-O weight* 770 kg (1,698 lb) *Max level speed* 145 km/h (90 mph) *Endurance* 1 h 30 min

Hall PH series (USA) Twin Wright R-1820 Cyclone-engined patrol and rescue flying-boats: nine PH-1s going to the US Navy in 1932 and 14 PH-2s and -3s to the US Coast Guard a few years later. Two interesting experimental aircraft built by Hall were the XP2H four-engined patrol and bombing biplane flying-boat and the XPTBH-2 twin-engined torpedo-bombing seaplane.

Hollmann HA-2M Sportster (USA) Two-seat gyroplane normally powered by a 112 kW (150 hp) Lycoming O-320 engine driving a pusher propeller. By early 1979 more than 50 were under construction by amateur builders.

Hamilton Nomair (USA) Two-seat military trainer or five-seat light transport, produced as a conversion of the ex-USAF North American T-28A.

Hamilton Westwind II STD (USA) 'Stretched' version of the Beech 18 providing accommodation for up to 17 passengers. Power is provided by two 626 kW (840 hp) Pratt & Whitney Aircraft of Canada PT6A-34 turboprops, each derated to 470 kW (630 ehp), as standard.

Hamilton Westwind III (USA) Utility eight-passenger/cargo commuter airliner conversion of the Beech Model 18, powered by two 432 kW (579 ehp) Pratt & Whitney Aircraft of Canada PT6A-20 turboprops as standard. Prototype flew for the first time in 1963.

Hamilton Westwind IV (USA) Latest conversion of the Beech Model 18, generally similar to the Westwind III but with the fuselage lengthened by 0.76 m (2 ft 6 in) and available with six alternative power plants and a large cargo door.

Handley Page H.P.42 (UK) Commercial aviation got off to a slow start in the years immediately following World War I, and it was not until the mid-1920s that the pioneering civil airlines began to push out tentative long-range routes. In Britain the pace had been set by such companies as Air-

Hamilton Westwind II
STD.

craft Transport and Travel, British Marine Air Navigation Company, the Daimler Airways, Handley Page Transport and the Instone Air Line. Air Transport and Travel (Britain's first airline) ceased operations on 17 December 1920; the remaining four companies formed the building blocks from which Imperial Airways was created on 1 April 1924.

To Imperial Airways fell the task of establishing British commercial air transport on an economic basis, and with government backing it became possible – at least in a modest way – to begin the procurement of new aircraft and the survey and inauguration of air routes to link the British Empire. Needing more capacity than was provided by its 18–20-seat Armstrong Whitworth Argosy or 14-seat Handley Page W.10 aircraft, Imperial Airways acquired from the latter a total of eight aircraft designed specifically for use on the European and eastern sections of the Empire air routes.

Large biplanes, with a maximum wing loading of less than 48.2 kg/m² (10 lb/sq ft), they were of all-metal construction except for the aerofoil surfaces and aft fuselage, which were fabric-covered. The unequal-span biplane wings were devoid of flying and landing wires, braced instead by massive Warren girder struts, and having ailerons and Handley Page slots only on the upper wing. The tail unit was also of biplane configuration, with triple fins and rudders, and the heavy landing gear was of fixed-tailwheel type. Power plant comprised four supercharged Bristol Jupiter engines, two mounted on the upper wing and one on each side of the fuselage on the lower wing. All

four engines were kept as near as possible to the aircraft's centreline, to minimise the problems of asymmetric flight in the event of an engine failure.

For the first time in any British airliner the crew were accommodated inside the aircraft, in a compartment high in the fuselage nose which we would now call a flight deck. Within the main cabins – fore and aft of the wing area where the engine noise originated – passengers were provided with completely new standards of comfort and spaciousness. Those intended originally for eastern use (on the Indian and South African routes) carried six (later 12) passengers in the forward cabin and 12 in the rear, with space for 14.16m³ (500 cu ft) of baggage and mail amidships. The four equipped for the European routes (based at Croydon) carried 18 passengers forward, 20 aft and had 7.08 m³ (250 cu ft) of baggage space.

Handley Page H.P.42 *Helena.*

The prototype flew first in November 1930. It was equipped subsequently for long-range service (H.P.42E, 'E' for Eastern) and named *Hannibal*. First of the H.P.42W ('W' for Western) for the European services was delivered in September 1931 and named *Heracles*. The remainder of this family of 1930s 'Jumbo' airliners had the names *Hadrian, Hanno, Helena, Hengist, Horatius* and *Horsa*. Remembered nostalgically in the early history of Imperial Airways, it was an unforgettable sight to see one climbing majestically away from Croydon or floating in on those enormous wings. Anthony Fokker once commented that H.P.42s had built-in headwinds, but their cruising speed of around 161 km/h (100 mph), excellent handling at low speeds and robust structure ensured that they were able to boast a decade of fatal-

Handley Page H.P.42 *Heracles.*

accident-free flight before being withdrawn from civil airline service on 1 September 1939.

Data: *Engines* (H.P.42W) four 413.6 kW (555 hp) Bristol Jupiter XFBMs, (H.P.42E) four 365 kW (490 hp) Bristol Jupiter XIFs *Wing span* 39.62 m (130 ft 0 in) *Length* 27.36 m (89 ft 9 in) *Max T-O weight* (H.P.42W) 13,381 kg (29,500 lb), (H.P.42E) 12,701 kg (28,000 lb) *Max level speed* (H.P.42W) 204 km/h (127 mph), (H.P.42E) 193 km/h (120 mph) *Cruising speed* (both) 153–169 km/h (95–105 mph) *Range* 805 km (500 miles)

Handley Page H.P.75 Manx (UK) First flown on 24 August 1943 to investigate the problems associated with tailless aircraft.

Handley Page H.P.75 Manx.

Handley Page H.P.88.

Handley Page H.P.88 (UK) First flown on 21 June 1951, it was built to investigate the flight characteristics of the crescent wing for use in larger form on the H.P. Victor bomber.

Handley Page H.P.115 (UK) Aerodynamic research aircraft, first flown on 17 August 1961 and powered by an 8.45 kN (1,900 lb st) Bristol Siddeley Viper 9 turbojet engine.

Handley Page O/100 (UK) The first successful H.P. monoplane was the Type E of 1911 which (as noted in *Jane's* of the time) flew successfully over London from Barking to Brooklands and was one of the first serious attempts in England to obtain inherent stability. It is also remembered for its likeness to the German Taube. The G/100 biplane which followed was somewhat similar and was taken over by the Navy at the outbreak of war and used for instructional flying.

Such was Handley Page's beginning. The development of the O/100 thereafter is best explained by quoting from the 1918 *Jane's*: 'The War Office then entrusted the firm with the making of machines of the B.E. type. A new type of biplane on an ambitious scale was being perfected when the War broke out. It was to have been equipped with a 200 hp Salmson engine. The firm . . . since then have been engaged on the production of giant machines with multiple engines. Lest it be supposed that the giant type is entirely a product of the War, it should be pointed out that the firm had conducted frequent experiments with big machines before Europe was thrown into a world-wide conflict. The results of these searches were placed before the Admiralty, who requested the immediate construction of a large experimental machine as suggested by the specifications. The first machine designed and built for the Admiralty, left the ground at 1.51 pm on December 18th [1915]. In July 1916 an O/100 took 20 passengers to a height of 7,000 ft over London. In August the first squadron was formed by RNAS at Dunkirk.'

From a purely factual standpoint, when (in December 1914) the British Admiralty indicated a requirement for a maritime patrol aircraft which was to be powered by two engines, carry six 112 lb bombs, and have a maximum speed of at least 116 km/h (72 mph), Handley Page lost little time

Handley Page H.P.115.

in producing a design. When it was shown to Cdre Murray Sueter, who was then Director of the Air Department of the Admiralty, he intimated to Frederick Handley Page that he wanted a 'bloody paralyser' to hit the enemy where it would hurt most.

Accepting this comment at its face value, Handley Page revised the design, increasing its size and introducing more powerful engines. Designated O/100, it was then the largest aeroplane which had been built in Britain and its construction posed many new problems. Of biplane configuration with unequal-span wings, the two engines were mounted between the wings, just outboard of the fuselage. This latter structure was of square-section cross-braced construction, and the tail unit of biplane structure. Landing gear comprised a large tailskid and twin wheels on each main unit. Accommodation was initially in an enclosed cabin with bullet-proof glass and armour plate for the protection of the crew. Features were folding wings, ground-adjustable tailplane incidence and engines mounted in armoured nacelles.

O/100s probably entered service in November rather than August 1916. Operations began in the following year, and (as noted in *Jane's*) one flew from London to the Middle East, via Paris, Rome and the Balkans. After an overhaul it bombed Constantinople and returned safely (9 July), although one engine had been put out of action by a chance shot while over the city. Later it attacked Adrianople and other Turkish and Bulgarian towns on many occasions. Used primarily as night bombers on the Western Front, O/100s later equipped the first bomber squadron of the RAF's Independent Force.

Data: *Engines* two 198 kW (266 hp) Rolls-Royce Eagle IIs *Wing span* 30.48 m (100 ft 0 in) *Length*

19.16 m (62 ft 10¼ in) *Max T-O weight* (approx) 6,350 kg (14,000 lb) *Max level speed* (approx) 137 km/h (85 mph) *Armament* up to five flexibly-mounted Lewis machine-guns, plus 16 × 112 lb bombs

Handley Page O/400 (UK) Operational experience with the O/100s showed that certain changes were desirable, especially to the fuel system. In the original layout each engine had its own armoured fuel tank contained within the armoured nacelle which housed the engine, restricting the amount of fuel which could be carried. The modified fuel system consisted of two fuselage tanks and two gravity-fed tanks installed in the leading edge of the upper wing's centre-section. Wind-driven pumps supplied fuel direct to the engines, as well as to the gravity-fed tanks. Removal of the fuel tanks from the nacelles allowed them to be shortened and a new inter-plane strut to be fitted immediately aft of each nacelle.

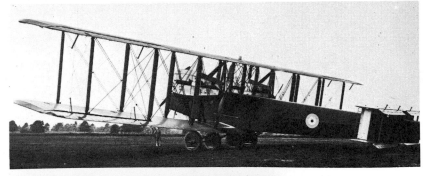

Other improvements included the provision of a compressed-air engine-starting system, with a crank handle for manual start in the event of pressure loss, and changes to the rear gun position and central fin. In this new configuration this variant of the O/100 was redesignated O/400. An initial contract for 100 of these aircraft was awarded to Handley Page in August 1917.

Production deliveries of O/400s began in the spring of 1918, but it was not until 9 August 1918 that No 97 Squadron, which was equipped with these aircraft, joined the Independent Force and began operations. As numbers built up it became possible to launch heavier and more frequent raids: on the night of 14–15 September 1918 an attack by 40 Handley Pages was launched against

Handley Page 0/100.

Handley Page 0/400s go into action.

Prototype Handley Page V/1500.

Handley Page V/1500 flying in the USA.

Handley Page Halifax GR. VI.

Handley Page Hampden I built in Canada and later converted into a torpedo bomber.

enemy targets. It was also during September that O/400s began to use newly developed 1,650 lb bombs for the first time.

A single O/400 also played an important role during the final offensive in Palestine, bombing HQs and communications and doing the work of a squadron of smaller machines. The outward flight of this aircraft from Britain to Egypt was important in its own right (see **Chronology** 28 July and 8 August 1918). After the Armistice the bomber returned to Cairo and from there flew to Delhi and Calcutta (see **Chronology** 12 December 1918).

A total of 700 O/400s were ordered, and about 400 were delivered before the Armistice. In the US 1,500 of these aircraft were ordered from Standard Aircraft Corporation, with power plant comprising two 261 kW (350 hp) Liberty 12-N engines, but of this total only 107 were delivered to the US Army Air Service before signature of the Armistice brought contract cancellation. A number of British-built O/400s were delivered post-war to China.

Data: *Engines* (standard) two 268 kW (360 hp) Rolls-Royce Eagle VIII *Wing span* 30.48 m (100 ft 0 in) *Length* 19.16 m (62 ft 10¼ in) *Max T-O weight* 6,060 kg (13,360 lb) *Max level speed* 157 km/h (97.5 mph) *Range* about 1,205 km (750 miles) *Armament* up to five flexibly mounted Lewis guns, plus up to 907 kg (2,000 lb) of bombs

Handley Page V/1500 (UK) Ordered as an experimental bomber in the summer of 1917, the large four-engined V/1500 was envisaged for the purpose of bombing Berlin from bases in England and was designed to carry five tons of crew and disposable load. The Armistice intervened before the weather was sufficiently favourable for the three machines delivered to fly to the German capital. Power for each aircraft was provided by four 279.5 kW (375 hp) Rolls-Royce Eagle VIIIs mounted in tandem pairs.

The first long flight of a V/1500 was from England to India (see **Chronology** 13 December 1918), which included one stretch of 1,285 km (800 miles) over water and another non-stop stage of 1,610 km (1,000 miles) from Cairo to Baghdad.

Handley Page Halton.

In London a V/1500 lifted 41 passengers to a height of nearly 2,440 m (8,000 ft) the same year. Other worthy flights are recorded in the 1920 *Jane's*.

Handley Page Halifax and Halton (UK) Second of Britain's four-engined bombers to enter service with the RAF, the Halifax owed its origin to the Air Ministry Specification B.13/36 which called for a medium bomber fitted with two of the Rolls-Royce Vulture 24-cylinder X-type engines then under development. When it was realised that the Vulture engine would not be available in sufficient numbers, the design was changed to take four Rolls-Royce Merlin engines. As a result, the designed loaded weight increased from 11,930 kg (26,300 lb) to 18,145 kg (40,000 lb).

The prototype Halifax flew for the first time on 25 October 1939, 22 months after construction began. It was fitted with four Merlin X engines, had a loaded weight of 24,950 kg (55,000 lb) and a maximum speed of 450 km/h (280 mph). The production Halifax I flew in October 1940 and delivery to squadrons began the following month. On 11–12 March 1941 Halifaxes made their first operational attack.

The Halifax was the subject of steady development and was in continuous service with the RAF during World War II. Many versions appeared, beginning with the initial Halifax I, armed originally with eight 0.303 in machine-guns, two in a Boulton Paul nose turret, four in a Boulton Paul tail turret and two hand-operated beam guns. Later a Boulton Paul Hudson-type two-gun turret was introduced in the mid-upper position in place of the beam guns.

The Halifax II was basically similar to the Mk I but was powered by four Rolls-Royce Merlin XX engines. Sub-variants of the Mk II were the Series I and IA, an interim model with the nose turret removed and replaced by a fairing (Series I); and a cleaned-up version with Merlin XXII engines, symmetrical transparent plastic nose fitted with one centrally mounted 0.303 in hand-held gun, a Boulton Paul Defiant-type four-gun mid-upper turret, the W/T mast removed and the aerial attached directly to the top of the D/F loop, new-type Morris block radiators, improved flame-dampers, lower astrodome, retractable tailwheel and a smooth-finish paint scheme (Series IA). The latter served as a tug for the Hamilcar glider.

The Halifax III was powered by four 1,203.5 kW (1,615 hp) Bristol Hercules XVI radial engines. A later modification introduced to this version an increased wing span of 31.75 m (104 ft 2 in) (from 30.12 m; 98 ft 10 in), which became standard in all production aircraft. The

ventral gun was often replaced by an HS2 radar scanner for blind bombing.

The Halifax IV was an experimental version for testing new engine mountings, while the Mk V introduced a Dowty (instead of Messier) landing gear. The Halifax VI was powered by four 1,341.4 kW (1,800 hp) Bristol Hercules 100 engines in circular self-contained nacelles, but was otherwise similar to the Mk III except for better performance. When supply of Hercules 100 engines was found to be temporarily insufficient, a number of Halifaxes were fitted with Hercules XVIs as Mk VIIs.

The Mk VIII and IX were modified versions of the Halifax specially produced for RAF Transport Command, stripped of military equipment and fitted for carrying 11 passengers, up to 16 troops, freight or ambulance equipment. A large boat-shaped pannier fitted in the bomb bay was capable of carrying 3,629 kg (8,000 lb) of freight. Mk VIIIs and IXs joined earlier A-type transport conversions.

The Halifax (6,176 of which were built for RAF Bomber Command, Coastal Command and Transport Command) shared with the Lancaster the lion's share of the bombing offensive against Germany. It took part in the first 1,000-bomber raid against Cologne on the night of 30–31 May 1942, followed soon after by major attacks on Essen and then Bremen. It was also responsible for the destruction of many of Germany's V-1 launching sites and enjoyed considerable success as a special-duties aircraft for dropping agents into occupied Europe and for radio counter-measures. In the Middle East it performed good work against the Afrika Korps. The type was finally withdrawn from first-line service in 1952.

To make available as soon as possible a high-speed long-range civil transport to serve as an interim type until the Hermes was ready, Handley Page produced the Halton, a civil conversion of the Halifax bomber for use by airline operators. It was generally equivalent to the C.VIII but with accommodation for ten passengers. Haltons were supplied initially to BOAC for operation on the UK–Cairo–Karachi and UK–West Africa routes. Data (Halifax VI): *Engines* as above *Wing span* 31.75 m (104 ft 2 in) *Length* 21.82 m (71 ft 7 in) *Max T-O weight* 30,844 kg (68,000 lb) *Max level speed* 502 km/h (312 mph) *Range* 2,028 km (1,260 miles) *Armament* nine 0.303 in Browning machine-guns, plus up to 6,577 kg (14,500 lb) of bombs

Handley Page Hereford.

Handley Page Hampden (UK) Handley Page's H.P.52 (later named Hampden) was to share with the Wellington and Armstrong Whitworth Whitley the major portion of Bomber Command's early raids over Germany in World War II.

Unorthodox in appearance because of its deep fuselage and slender tailboom, it was to earn the nicknames 'Flying Panhandle' and 'Tadpole'. Unorthodox or not, it was faster than both the Wellington and Whitley but, like a number of British bomber aircraft, suffered heavy losses when deployed against German targets by day, largely on account of inadequate defensive armament. Temporarily grounded while this deficiency was rectified, they returned to operational service with twin Vickers K-type machine-guns in dorsal and ventral turrets, armour protection and flame-dampers for the exhausts.

By early 1940 they were back in service again but, of course, operating by night. Of conventional all-metal stressed-skin construction, the Hampden's thick-section mid-set monoplane

Handley Page

Handley Page Harrow.

wings tapered both in chord and thickness. Handley Page slots on the leading edge of the wing outer panels, plus trailing-edge flaps, made possible a low landing speed. Somewhat cramped accommodation was provided for a crew of four.

Hampdens notched up a number of 'firsts' for Bomber Command: the first mine-laying operations; together with Whitleys dropped the first bombs of World War II on the German mainland; took part in the first attack on Berlin; and added their numbers to the first 1,000-bomber raid on Cologne. By mid-September 1942 they were withdrawn from Bomber Command operations as new and more effective aircraft became available, but continued for some time to support Coastal Command's anti-shipping operations in the capacity of a torpedo bomber. One squadron operated the type until relieved by Bristol Beaufighters in late 1943.

Data: *Engines* two 730 kW (980 hp) Bristol Pegasus XVII radials *Wing span* 21.08 m (69 ft 2 in) *Length* 16.33 m (53 ft 7 in) *Max T-O weight* 8,508 kg (18,756 lb) *Max level speed* 426 km/h (265 mph) *Range* 3,200 km (1,990 miles) *Armament* six 0.303 in machine-guns and up to 1,814 kg (4,000 lb) of bombs

Handley Page Hereford (UK) The Hereford was basically a Hampden powered by 711.7 kW (955 hp) Napier Dagger VIII engines. Trouble with the engines resulted in only 100 Herefords being built and these were operated as trainers for bombing crews.

Handley Page Harrow (UK) The 1939 *Jane's* states: 'In 1936 the Hampden high-performance medium bomber and Harrow heavy bomber were ordered in quantity for the Royal Air Force. By the end of 1937 the Harrow contract had been completed.' Although this is essentially correct, a total of 100 Mk I and Mk II Harrows were ordered in August 1935, differing in having two 618.5 kW (830 hp) Bristol Pegasus X and 689.3 kW (925 hp) Pegasus XX engines respectively.

Not to be confused with the Harrow two-seat general-purpose torpedo bomber of 1926, the Harrow bomber was a cantilever high-wing monoplane with a fixed divided-type landing gear and a twin fin and rudder-type tail unit. Enclosed accommodation was provided for a normal flight crew of four, who were also expected to man the nose turret, tail turret and mid-upper gun position.

With the arrival of the Wellington, Harrows were converted into 20-troop or freight-carrying transports, although a number performed mine-laying duties during the early part of World War II.

Data (Mk II): *Engines* as above *Wing span* 26.95 m (88 ft 5 in) *Length* 25.04 m (82 ft 2 in) *Max T-O weight* 10,432 kg (23,000 lb) *Max level speed* 322 km/h (200 mph) *Range* 2,011-2,961 km (1,250-1,840 miles) *Armament* machine-guns as noted above, plus up to 1,361 kg (3,000 lb) of bombs

Handley Page Hastings (UK) The Hastings was a general-purpose long-range transport flown by the RAF and RNZAF. Its roles included those of freighter, paratroop-transport, ambulance, troop-carrier, supply-dropper, jeep-carrier and glider-tug.

The initial production version was the C.1, first flown on 25 April 1947 and powered by four Bristol Hercules 101 engines. All C.1s were subsequently modified to Mk 2 standard and redesignated C.1As. The C.2 was powered by four Hercules 106 engines, had the tailplane lowered to the centreline of the fuselage and increased in area, extra fuel tanks, and the crew rest station

Handley Page Hastings C.1s.

replaced by an air-quartermaster post. The Hercules 737-powered C.3 was similar to the Mk 2 and four were supplied to the RNZAF. The final version was the C.4, a VIP version of the Mk 2 with accommodation for four VIPs and staff. Four were delivered to RAF Transport Command, bringing the total number of Hastings operated by the RAF up to 147. The last Hastings were withdrawn from service in 1968.

Data (C.2): *Engines* four 1,248 kW (1,675 hp) Bristol Hercules 106s *Wing span* 34.44 m (113 ft 0 in) *Length* 24.89 m (81 ft 8 in) *Max T-O weight* 36,287 kg (80,000 lb) *Max level speed* 560 km/h (348 mph) *Range* 6,840 km (4,250 miles) *Accommodation* 30 paratroops with supplies, 32 stretchers plus 28 sitting casualties, 50 fully equipped troops, or freight

Handley Page Hermes 4.

Handley Page Herald Model 101.

Handley Page H.P.R.7 Herald (UK) The prototype Dart-engined Herald made its first flight on 11 March 1958 and the first production Herald Series 100 flew on 30 October 1959. The Series 100 accommodated between 38 and 47 passengers. The Series 200 was the main production version with a forward fuselage 1.07 m (42 in) longer than that of the Series 100. Accommodation was provided for 50–56 passengers.

The Series 300 (a modified Series 200 developed to meet US airworthiness requirements) was followed by the Series 400 military transport with a side loading door and accommodation for 50 troops, paratroops, 24 stretchers or freight, eight of which went to the Royal Malaysian Air Force. The projected Series 500 was followed by the Dart 532/9 turboprop-engined Series 600.

The final two versions were the Series 700 long-range version of the Series 600, accommodating up to 60 passengers or 52 passengers and baggage over 1,980 km (1,230 mile) stages, and the Series 800 military version of the 700.

Data (Series 200): *Engines* two 1,568.6 kW (2,015 ehp) Rolls-Royce Dart Mk 527 (RDa.7) turboprops *Wing span* 28.88 m (94 ft 9 in) *Length* 23.01 m (75 ft 6 in) *Max T-O weight* 19,500 kg (43,000 lb) *Max cruising speed* 443 km/h (275 mph) *Range* 2,830 km (1,760 miles)

Handley Page Hermes 4 (UK) The Hermes 4 was the first British post-war airliner built to modern standards to go into service; 25 were delivered to BOAC for use on its Commonwealth routes, services beginning in August 1950. Normal accommodation was for 40 passengers, but alternative seating arrangements provided for a maximum of 74. Originally powered by four 1,565 kW (2,100 hp) Bristol Hercules 763 radial engines, all were subsequently re-engined with 1,583.5 kW (2,125 hp) Hercules 773s and were thereafter known as Hermes 4As.

Handley Page Heyford (UK) First flown in prototype form in mid-1930, the Heyford was the last of the RAF's long-range biplane night bombers. It was powered in Mk I form by two 391.2 kW (525 hp) Rolls-Royce Kestrel IIIS

Handley Page Heyford Mk IA.

Handley Page

Handley Page Hinaidi.

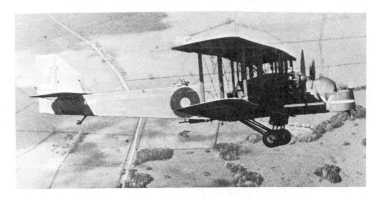

engines and in the Mk II and Mk III by 428.5 kW (575 hp) Kestrel VIs. The Heyford was an equal-span biplane with staggered wings: the upper wing centre-section rested on top of the fuselage, while the lower was positioned well below the fuselage, connected to the under-fuselage by N-type struts. The inner interplane struts supported the engine mountings. An interesting feature of the design was that bombs of various sizes were carried inside the thickened centre-section of the lower wing, each bomb being carried in a separate cell closed by spring doors. The fixed landing gear comprised two large wheels faired into the lower wing.

King George V about to inspect a Handley Page Heyford during the Jubilee Review of 1935.

Handley Page Marathon T.11.

A total of 124 Heyfords were built, made up of 38 Mk Is and IAs, 1 intermediate Mk IA/II, 16 Mk IIs and 71 Mk IIIs – these figures being adjusted to take into account changes made from the original production orders. Heyfords served with heavy-bomber squadrons from 1933 to 1939, giving way to more modern monoplanes of World War II-type.

Data (Mk II/III): *Engines* as above *Wing span* 22.86 m (75 ft 0 in) *Length* 17.68 m (58 ft 0 in) *Max T-O weight* 7,598 kg (16,750 lb) *Max level speed* 228 km/h (142 mph) *Range* 1,480 km (920 miles) *Armament* three machine-guns on screened rotatable mountings above the forward bomb-aimer's post, dorsal position and ventral cylindrical retractable 'dustbin' turret; up to 1,588 kg (3,500 lb) of bombs

Handley Page Hyderabad, Hinaidi and Clive (UK) The Hyderabad was basically a W.8 airliner built for the Air Ministry as a heavy night bomber. Powered by two 335.3 kW (450 hp) Napier Lion engines, it had a maximum speed of 175 km/h (109 mph) and carried an offensive load of 500 kg (1,100 lb). Production for the RAF

amounted to just 39 aircraft, three of which were later converted into Hinaidis.

The Hinaidi followed the Hyderabad into RAF service and 12 Mk Is and 33 Mk IIs were built, six of the Mk Is originally being ordered as Hyderabads but built as Hinaidis (not converted after completion). These served from 1930. The RAF also received three examples of the troop-transport version known as the Clive (formerly Chitral). Each could accommodate 17 fully armed troops, or equivalent freight; folding seats being provided on both sides of the cabin and racks for the rifles. Two gun positions were retained (nose and dorsal). The first Clive was later civil registered G-ABYX and named *Youth of Australia* (subsequently *Astra*).

Data (Hinaidi II): *Engines* two 343 kW (460 hp) Bristol Jupiter VIIIs *Wing span* 22.86 m (75 ft 0 in) *Length* 18.03 m (59 ft 2 in) *Max T-O weight* 6,570 kg (14,486 lb) *Max level speed* 196 km/h (122 mph) *Armament* three machine-guns in nose, dorsal and ventral positions, plus up to 658 kg (1,450 lb) of bombs carried internally or under lower wings

Handley Page Jetstream (UK) See **BAe Jetstream**

Handley Page Marathon 1 (UK) The Marathon was designed by Miles Aircraft as an 18–22-passenger medium-range feeder-line aircraft and manufacture was undertaken by Handley Page after it acquired the production rights. Examples were delivered to West African Airways Corporation (six) and the Union of Burma Airways (three). Thirty Marathons were also ordered for the RAF as advanced navigation trainers under the designation T.11, but two were sold to Japan. RAF aircraft entered service in 1953. Power was provided by four 253.4 kW (340 hp) de Havilland Gipsy Queen engines.

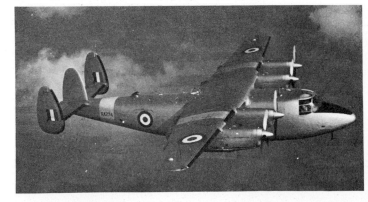

Handley Page Victor (UK) With the intention that the RAF should provide Britain's strategic nuclear deterrent, design work began at Handley Page in 1947 on a long-range four-engined medium bomber that would be able to carry nuclear or conventional weapons internally. The Victor was the last of three V-bombers (named by Sir Winston Churchill) to enter RAF service, preceded by the Valiant and Vulcan.

All three designs were, to some degree, unconventional, for the requirement to carry a heavy payload of weapons at high speed/altitude over long-ranges was not easy to satisfy at a time when turbine power plants were still very limited in thrust. The Handley Page design was a cantilever mid-wing monoplane with leading-edge sweepback which varied from root to wingtip, calling this configuration a 'crescent' wing (see **H.P.88**). The tail unit (in T-tail configuration) had all-swept surfaces, and the structure of this all-metal aircraft was conventional throughout. Unusual features included an eight-wheel bogie for each of the main landing-gear units, and hydraulically operated air brakes on each side of, and a large braking parachute stowed in, the tail cone.

The first prototype made its maiden flight on 24 December 1952. The first production B.1s, each with four 48.93 kN (11,000 lb st) Bristol Siddeley Sapphire turbojets began to enter RAF service with No 232 Operational Conversion Unit in November 1957. The first Victor squadron (No 10) became fully operational at Cottesmore in the spring of 1958. Formation of the planned total of four Victor B.1 squadrons was completed early in 1960. B.1A aircraft had ECM and other equipment changes.

B.2 Victors began to enter RAF service (initially with No 139 Squadron) in February 1962. These had more powerful engines, increased wing span, enlarged air intakes, and introduced a 'Window' dispenser pod on the trailing edge of each wing. No 139 Squadron was the first to become operational with the Blue Steel nuclear stand-off bomb in February 1964. Victor squadrons were subsequently specified for low-altitude in addition to high-altitude attack.

Following the B.2's entry into service, Mk 1 aircraft were converted to BK.1 and BK.1A flight-refuelling tankers. Victor B(SR).2 strategic-reconnaissance aircraft entered service with No 543 Squadron at RAF Wyton in the autumn of 1965. These aircraft had the capability to radar map an area of up to 1,942,490 km² (750,000 sq miles) during a six-hour period. All Mk 2 versions have since been converted to K.2 tankers, with the first delivered to the RAF on 8 May 1974. This is the only version currently operational with the RAF.
Data (B.2): *Engines* four 91.63 kN (20,600 lb st) Rolls-Royce Conway RCo 17 Mk 201 turbojets *Wing span* 36.58 m (120 ft 0 in) *Length* 35.03 m (114 ft 11 in) *Max T-O weight* (approx) 79,379 kg (175,000 lb) *Max level speed* Mach 0.92 (1,062 km/h; 660 mph) at 12,190 m (40,000 ft) *Range* 7,403 km (4,600 miles) *Armament* Blue Steel air-to-surface strategic missile, or 35 × 1,000 lb bombs, or nuclear free-fall weapons

Handley Page Victor B.2s.

Handley Page W.8, W.9 and W.10 (UK) The Handley Page W.8B (three of which were originally operated by Handley Page Transport and then from 1924 by Imperial Airways on its London–Paris service) was a refinement of the original W.8. The latter flew for the first time on 2 December 1922 and had been modelled on the wartime Handley Page bombers. Twelve passenger seats were provided in two rows in a well-glazed cabin, while the pilot and co-pilot sat in an open cockpit in the nose of the fuselage. Unlike the W.8, which was powered by 335.3 kW (450 hp) Napier Lion IB engines, the W.8Bs each had two 268 kW (360 hp) Rolls-Royce Eagle VIII engines. The last W.8B was retired in 1932 (a full description of the W.8B appears in the 1926 *Jane's*).

In addition to the British-operated W.8Bs, one was built and exported to Belgium, where SABCA licence-built three more for Sabena. Handley Page also delivered a single example of

Handley Page W.8.

Handley Page W.8F Hamilton.

Hannaford Rose Parakeet.

Handley Page W.9A Hampstead.

Hannover CL.II.

the W.8E, with two 171.4 kW (230 hp) Siddeley Puma and one nose-mounted 268.3 kW (360 hp) Rolls-Royce Eagle IX engines. Eight were subsequently licence-built in Belgium.

The final new W.8 version was the W.8F Hamilton. This was similar to the W.8E and in the words of the 1926 *Jane's* 'is a modification of the well-known W.8 type which has been designed specially with a view to producing a machine which shall be as nearly as it is possible to make it immune from involuntary landings caused by engine stoppage. These machines are to be used in the Belgian Congo, and it will readily be understood that absolute freedom from involuntary landings is of the very first importance for service in such a country. The machine itself is, except for the power plant, practically a standard W.8B. The nose of the fuselage ahead of the cabin has naturally been considerably modified. One of these machines in 1925 completed a flight from Brussels to the Belgian Congo, a distance of 7,000 miles, piloted by Lt Thieffry, of the Belgian Army, accompanied by Mécanicien De Bruycker.'

It can be seen from this write-up that *Jane's* did not make a distinction between the W.8E and F. In fact Imperial Airways received only one W.8F, followed by one W.9A Hampstead and four W.10s (the last retired in 1933). The Hampstead was powered by three 287 kW (385 hp) Siddeley Jaguar and then 335.3 kW (450 hp) Bristol Jupiter VI engines and had a 5.31 m (17 ft 5 in) long, 1.35 m (4 ft 5 in) wide and 1.78 m (5 ft 10 in) high passenger cabin for 14 persons. The W.10s each had two 335.3 kW (450 hp) Napier Lion IIB engines and featured a new type of rudder, fitted with a balance of the inset-hinge type, instead of

the earlier horn-balance arrangement. An interesting detail was the use of an entirely metallic structure for the engine mountings, replacing the usual wooden bearers.

Data (W.10): *Engines* as above *Wing span* 22.86 m (75 ft 0 in) *Length* 18.08 m (59 ft 4 in) *Max T-O weight* 6,250 kg (13,780 lb) *Max level speed* 180 km/h (112 mph) *Range* 805 km (500 miles) *Accommodation* 14 passengers

Hannaford Rose Parakeet (USA) In 1948 the Hannaford Aircraft Company acquired the manufacturing rights for the Parakeet single-seat low-powered light biplane from the Rose Aeroplane and Motor Company and made it available in three versions, with engines of 30–63.3 kW (40–85 hp).

Hannover CL.II, CL.III and C.V (Germany) Hannoversche Waggonfabrik designed its first aircraft in about the middle of World War I. It soon became well known for its introduction of the distinctive biplane-tailed two-seat escort fighters and ground-attack aircraft; a design feature which reduced the blind tail field-of-fire of the rear gunner.

The CL.II was a 134 kW (180 hp) Argus As.III-engined biplane. The rear-gunner's cockpit was raised above the height of the pilot's cockpit to give an excellent firing circle, aided by the low positioning of the upper wing and (as mentioned above) the short vertical tail. Production totalled nearly 440 aircraft, followed by more than 600 119 kW (160 hp) Mercedes D.III-engined CL.IIIs and CL.IIIas, the majority as the latter type powered by the Argus As.III and with new ailerons and rounder horizontal tail surfaces. The C.V, only a few of which were built, was produced as a faster version powered by a 138 kW (185 hp) BMW IIIa engines. It appeared with both the

traditional biplane and a more conventional monoplane tail unit and I-type interplane struts. However C.Vs were not delivered in time for operational service in the war but, according to a report made by the German Technical Department, were superior in speed and climb to any of their scouts then built.

Post-war the company traded as Hawa and produced several enclosed limousine-type commercial aircraft based on the military types. The F.3 was based on the unsuccessful military CL.IV and carried two passengers. The F.10 was a 164 kW (220 hp) Benz-powered three-seat triplane.
Data (CL.IIIa): *Engine* as above *Wing span* 11.7 m (38 ft 4½ in) *Length* 7.58 m (24 ft 10½ in) *Max T-O weight* 1,080 kg (2,380 lb) *Max level speed* 165 km/h (102.5 mph), (C.V) 195 km/h (121 mph) *Endurance* 3 h *Armament* one forward-firing Spandau and one rear-mounted Parabellum machine-gun

Hanriot HD-1 (France) The first single-seat scout designed for Hanriot by Pierre Dupont, the HD-1 was constructed of wood and duralumin, with fabric covering except for the forward fuselage which had metal sheeting. Powered by an 89.4 kW (120 hp) Le Rhône 9J rotary engine, the HD-1 was a lightly built and highly manoeuvrable unequal-span biplane with a marked stagger and considerable dihedral on the upper wing.

The prototype flew in June 1916 and displayed good flying qualities. However production was not undertaken for France, the authorities preferring the new Spad VII with its liquid-cooled engine and twin synchronised machine-guns as against the rotary engine and single weapon of the Hanriot. The Belgian Air Arm did order the HD-1, 125 being delivered by the end of World War I. One Belgian escadrille used the HD-1 until 1926. Italy was also interested in the HD-1 and sent a commission to France, which ordered the scout in 1916. A total of 831 were built in France and no fewer than 901 under licence by Macchi-Nieuport in Italy. By 1918 16 of 18 operational Italian fighter squadriglie were equipped with the HD-1. It remained in first-line service until 1925. Interestingly the Italian aces Piccio, Baracca and Scaroni, and the Belgian ace Willy Coppens, gained most of their victories while flying the HD-1.

Post-war a number of Italian HD-1s were used as sporting aircraft. Switzerland bought 16 machines in 1921 and in 1923 Paraguay acquired three of the type.
Data: *Engine* as above *Wing span* 8.51 m (27 ft 11 in) *Length* 6.01 m (19 ft 8½ in) *Max T-O weight* 695 kg (1,532 lb) *Max level speed* 184 km/h (114.5 mph) *Endurance* 2 h 30 min

Hannover CL.IIIa.

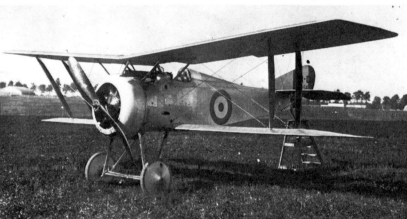

Hanriot HD-1.

Hanriot HD-2 (France) The HD-2 originated as a seaplane version of the HD-1. The prototype had two short main floats and a third under the tailplane. The production HD-2 had enlarged main floats which did away with the need for a tail float, and enlarged vertical tail surfaces. Power was provided by a 97 kW (130 hp) Clerget 9B rotary engine and armament comprised twin 7.7 mm Vickers machine-guns.

A number saw active service as scouts at the Dunkirk naval air station during 1918. The US Navy also purchased ten which were subsequently converted into landplanes for experimental take-offs from turret platforms on board battleships. Similar tests were conducted in France with two converted HD-2s (redesignated HD-2Cs) which also carried out deck-landing trials on board the French aircraft carrier *Béarn*.

Hanriot HD-3 (France) Two-seat fighter and reconnaissance biplane of 1917 powered by a 194 kW (260 hp) Salmson SA 9Z engine. Small number built before the end of the war.

Hawa F.6.

Hawa F.10.

Hanriot

Hanriot HD-2 experimentally mounted on the gun platform of a US Navy battleship.

Two-seat fighter version of the Hanriot HD-3.

Hanriot HD-14.

Photographic reconnaissance version of the Hanriot HD-3.

Hanriot HD-14 (France) The HD-14 'avion école' (primary trainer) was built in vast numbers and was an equal-span biplane powered by a 59.6 kW (80 hp) Le Rhône rotary engine. Hanriot produced more than 2,000, 1,925 going to the French Aéronautique Militaire as HD-14 EP2s. It was also exported and licence-built in Belgium and Japan (as the Ki-1). Fifty HD-14S ambulance aircraft were operated by France during anti-Rif operations in Morocco during 1931.

Hanriot HD-17 and HD-41H (France) The HD-17 was basically a twin-float version of the HD-14. Production aircraft, built from 1923, served with French Navy flying schools. Power was provided by a 97 kW (130 hp) Clerget 9B engine. A number were also exported to Estonia and Latvia. The HD-41H was a development of the HD-17 powered by an 89.4 kW (120 hp) Salmson 9Ac engine and with water-steerable

floats. Twelve were exported to Greece and Portugal.

Hanriot HD-19 (France) The prototype of this 134 kW (180 hp) Hispano-Suiza-engined trainer flew for the first time in 1923. Hanriot built 31 production examples, one for export to Japan, and 55 were licence-built in Poland.

Hanriot HD-28 (France) The HD-28 was basically an export version of the HD-14. Three hundred were licence-built by the Samolot company for Polish military service (200), national aero clubs (84) and for ambulance duties (16).

Hanriot HD-32 (France) Developed in 1924 from the HD-14, powered by a 59.6 kW (80 hp) Le Rhône rotary engine and with reduced wing span, modified tailplane and simplified mixed construction. Used in quantity by the French and exported, licence production being undertaken in Poland and Yugoslavia.

Hanriot H-16 (France) Two-seat parasol-wing monoplane of 1934 powered by an 89.4 kW (120 hp) Renault 4Pdi engine. Fourteen produced as primary trainers, followed by 29 H-16-1 observation/liaison aircraft, all for the Armée de l'Air.

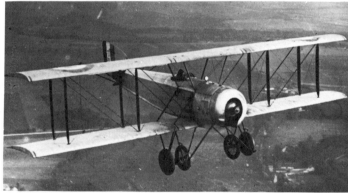

Hanriot H-43 series (France) The H-43 prototype training and general-purpose biplane was powered by a 194 kW (260 hp) Salmson engine. It had a rounded-section fuselage and staggered wings. The H-431 initial production version was powered by a 171.4 kW (230 hp) Lorraine Mizar engine and featured a slab-sided fuselage, straight wings and a revised vertical tail. The H-433 and H-436 models followed, powered by Salmson 9Ab engines. On 10 May 1940 75 Hanriot biplanes were still in French service. Total H-43 production was more than 160 aircraft, including 12 H-438s built for Peru.

Hanriot H-170, H-180 and H-190 series (France) Designed by Montlaur, the prototype H-180 was a three-seat touring monoplane, built mainly of duralumin. First flown in June 1934, it was the progenitor of a large family of aircraft which differed mainly in power plant. The H-180 series all had Renault engines, H-170s Salmsons and H-190s Regniers. Equipment variations permitted the basic design to be adapted for a variety of military and civil roles. The strong structure permitted aerobatics, with the high-mounted wing V-strut braced and stub lower wings attached to the fuselage. Aft of the enclosed cabin was an open cockpit for a second pilot or

gunner. After tests the trousered landing gear of the prototype was replaced by slim cantilever strut units attached to the stub wings, and the vertical tailplane was enlarged.

The major production version was the H-182, for military two-seat light observation (A2) or training (ET2) duties. In 1936 it equipped the Cercles Aériens Régionaux, training weekend reserve fliers. A total of 346 H-182s were built. Only 46 of all other versions were completed, including ten radio-equipped H-175s (130.4 kW; 175 hp Salmson) for liaison duties and six H-185s (104.3 kW; 140 hp Renault), both for the French Navy, seven H-172N civil touring aircraft and nine H-192N trainers (Regnier Bo 1) for the Bourges flying school.

The type also flew in Spain during the Civil War, and 50 H-182s were exported to Turkey in 1939. No less than 172 H-182s were found on Vichy aerodromes by occupying German troops in 1942.

Hanriot H-232 (France) The H-232.2 was a smooth-contoured mid-wing monoplane with considerable dihedral. It had a retractable landing gear and was powered by two 164 kW

(220 hp) Renault 6Q engines. Accommodation was provided for a pupil and instructor in tandem. Thirty-two of 40 aircraft ordered had been completed by 1940 and these were used by the French as advanced trainers. However only three of 22 ordered by Finland were delivered.

Hansa-Brandenburg C.I (Germany/Austria-Hungary) The C.I was one of the early designs of Ernst Heinkel, who had previously worked for LVG and Albatros. It was a general-purpose biplane capable of successfully performing light-bombing, reconnaissance and artillery-observation duties. The company, although based in Germany, was run by an Austrian; this may have been why many were built by Phönix and Ufag in Austria-Hungary for military service. Production aircraft appeared in many different series and with varied power plants, including

119 kW (160 hp) Mercedes D.III and Austro-Daimler, 149 kW (200 hp) Hiero, 164 kW (220 hp) Benz and other engines. Entering service in 1916 the C.I type remained operational until the Armistice. Interestingly a number of C.Is operated a national and international air mail service during the final months of the war. Maximum speed with the Austro-Daimler engine was 140 km/h (87 mph).

Hansa-Brandenburg CC (Germany) The CC was a distinctive-looking single-seat flying-boat fighter of 1916, with biplane wings and unusual cross-star-type interplane struts. Production aircraft were built in limited numbers for the German and Austrian navies, powered by 112 kW (150 hp) Benz Bz.III and 138 kW (185 hp) Hiero or 149 kW (200 hp) Austro-Daimler engines mounted as pushers respectively. Armament comprised one or two forward-firing machine-guns.

Hansa-Brandenburg D.I (Germany/Austria-Hungary) The D.I, best remembered as the 'Star Strutter' because of its interplane strut arrangement, was designed in Germany but produced by Phönix and Ufag in Austria-Hungary. It entered service in autumn 1916. Armed with one Schwarzlose machine-gun, the fighter could manage 187 km/h (116 mph) on its 119 kW (160 hp) Austro-Daimler engine.

Hansa-Brandenburg D and FD (Germany) The Type D was a conventional two-seat unarmed tractor biplane of 1914, powered by an 82 kW (110 hp) Benz Bz.II engine. The FD was basically a refined D, powered by a Bz.III engine. A total of 27 Ds and FDs were produced for German and Austro-Hungarian use.

Hanriot HD-14S Sanitaire air ambulance.

Hanriot HD-17.

Hanriot HD-16 prototype.

Hanriot HD-433.

Hansa-Brandenburg

Hanriot H-232.

Prototype Hanriot H-180.

Hanriot H-182.

Hansa-Brandenburg FB (Germany) Single 119 kW (160 hp) Austro-Daimler-powered sesquiplane flying-boat of 1915, operated in small numbers by the German and Austro-Hungarian navies as an armed observation type.

Hansa-Brandenburg G.I (Germany/Austria-Hungary) Twelve examples of a twin 119 kW (160 hp) Austro-Daimler-powered biplane bomber built in Austria-Hungary.

Hansa-Brandenburg GW (Germany) Twin-float torpedo-bombing biplane of 1916, powered by two 119 kW (160 hp) Mercedes D.III engines. Twenty were built for the German Navy.

Hansa-Brandenburg D.I 'Star Strutter'.

Hansa-Brandenburg KDW (Germany) The KDW was produced as an interim twin-float biplane fighter to protect naval seaplane bases from attack. Only 58 were produced, powered by Benz Bz.III, Maybach Mb.III or Mercedes D.III engines in the 112–119 kW (150–160 hp) range. Armament comprised one or two forward-firing Spandau machine-guns. Maximum level speed was 170 km/h (105.5 mph).

Hansa-Brandenburg W, NW and GNW (Germany) The first of these two-seat twin-float reconnaissance and usually unarmed patrol biplanes was the Benz Bz.III-powered Type W of 1914, 27 of which were delivered to the German Navy. The NW and GNW of the following year were basically refined and more powerful versions with Mercedes D.III engines, nearly 50 of which were built.

Hansa-Brandenburg W.11 (Germany) Prototype development of the KDW powered by a 149 kW (200 hp) Bz.IV engine.

Hansa-Brandenburg W.12, W.13, W.19, W.27 and W.32 (Germany) The success of British flying-boats in raiding German coastal naval bases caused great concern to the German Navy, whose only logical response was to fit floats to existing fighters in an attempt to hold the fort while purpose-built seaplane fighters were being developed.

The first Hansa-Brandenburg fighter to comply was the W.12 biplane of early 1917. Its 'gap-filling' fuselage was raised towards the rear and the vertical tail was positioned below the horizontal surfaces, both features incorporated to reduce blind spots for the rear-gunner. This layout was especially favoured by the chief commander of the Austrian Air Force, Col Uzelac. Production aircraft, 146 of which were built, were powered by 112 kW (150 hp) Benz Bz.III or 119 kW (160 hp) Mercedes D.III engines. Armament comprised one or two forward-firing Spandau and one rear-mounted Parabellum machine-guns. The W.12 was fast, manoeuvrable and well designed and afforded real protection for the naval bases.

The success of the W.12 led Hansa-Brandenburg to develop the concept throughout the war, and indeed the Finnish government continued development into the 1920s with its IVL A-22. W.13 to W.18 covered a range of biplane or triplane flying-boats and a single-seat seaplane fighter, only the first of which had any real success, built in limited numbers as the Type K for the Austro-Hungarian Navy. However the W.19 reverted to the W.12 configuration, but was considerably larger and therefore heavier and powered by a 194 kW (260 hp) Maybach Mb.IV engine. W.19s entered service in January 1918 but were slower than the W.12s by nearly 10 km/h (6 mph). Fifty-five were built and these served until the Armistice.

The final biplanes of the series were the W.27 and W.32, only prototypes of which were completed. These were slightly shorter in length than the W.12 and could easily be identified by their heavily staggered wings and single I-type interplane and centre-section struts.

Data (W.12): *Engine* as above *Wing span* 11.2 m

Handley Page H.P.R.7
Herald.

Hawker Hart.

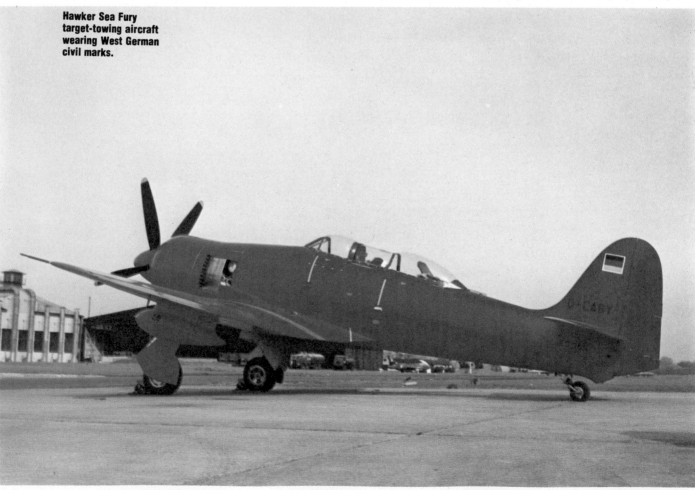

Hawker Sea Fury
target-towing aircraft
wearing West German
civil marks.

Hawker Hurricane IIC.

Hawker Siddeley
Buccaneer S.2Bs.

**Hawker Siddeley Gnat in
Finnish service.**

Hawker Sea Hawk FGA.4.

Hawker Hunter FGA.9s.

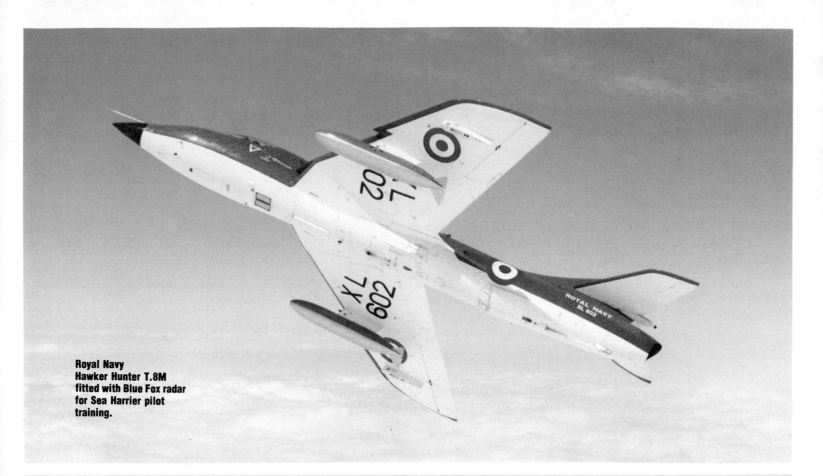

Royal Navy
Hawker Hunter T.8M
fitted with Blue Fox radar
for Sea Harrier pilot
training.

(36 ft 9 in) *Length* 9.65 m (31 ft 8 in) *Max T-O weight* 1,465 kg (3,230 lb) *Max level speed* 160 km/h (99.5 mph) *Endurance* 3 h 30 min

Hansa-Brandenburg W.29 and W.33 (Germany) These were basically monoplane developments of the W.12 and W.19 respectively, similar except for the new wings and minor details. Their impact after entering service from April 1918 can be best summed up by quoting from the 1920 *Jane's*: 'The final Brandenburg monoplane sea fighter is well known by appearance, and scored heavily during the last months of the war, when its activities would have asked for trouble from some superior opponent.' That this report mentions only one type of monoplane reflects the fact that of about 100 W.29/W.33s built, three-quarters were of the former type. Interestingly the Armistice prevented more than a handful of a new version of the W.29, with a 138 kW (185 hp) Benz Bz.IIIa engine, from being completed.

Post-war W.29s were flown by the Danish Air Force, while 310 were built under licence in Japan by Aichi (150) and Nakajima (160). As noted in the W.12 entry, a new version of the W.33 was also developed in Finland.

Data (W.29): *Engine* as above *Wing span* 13.5 m (44 ft 3½ in) *Length* 9.35 m (30 ft 8 in) *Max T-O weight* 1,470 kg (3,241 lb) *Max level speed* 175 km/h (109 mph) *Armament* as for W.12

Harlow PJC-2 and PC-5A (USA) The PJC-2 was a four-seat cabin monoplane of all-metal construction, fitted with a retractable landing gear. Power was provided by a 108 kW (145 hp) Warner Super-Scarab engine. Production ended in late 1941. Four were impressed into USAAF service as UC-80s. The PC-5A was a two-seat training version of the PJC-2, powered by a

123 kW (165 hp) Super-Scarab engine. PC-5As were built under licence in India by HAL.

Harmon 1-2 Mister America (USA) Single-seat lightweight sporting monoplane, plans for which are available to amateur constructors.

Harrison (Fairchild) F-11-2 Husky (Canada) Conversion of the Husky powered by a 410 kW (550 hp) Alvis Leonides radial engine.

Hatz CB-1 biplane (USA) Two-seat lightweight biplane, plans for which are available to amateur constructors.

Hawker P.1052 (UK) Rolls-Royce Nene-powered research aircraft built to investigate the controllability and stability of sweptback wings at low speeds. First flown on 19 November 1948.

Hawker Audax (UK) Early experience with the Hart day bomber in squadron service left little doubt that it would prove suitable for adaptation to fulfil a variety of roles. One of the first involved fairly minor changes to satisfy an Army co-operation requirement, with the RAF needing a replacement for lower-performance but highly successful Armstrong Whitworth Atlas and Westland Wapiti aircraft. For this role the Hart was provided with a message pick-up hook and other equipment changes.

About 652 Audax biplanes were ordered for the RAF, including those purchased by South Africa and those transferred to Malaya for the Straits Settlement Volunteer Air Force. Others were constructed for Persia (with Bristol Pegasus and Pratt & Whitney Hornet engines), Iraq, Canada, Singapore and Egypt – the latter with Armstrong Whitworth Panther X engines and supplied to

Hansa-Brandenburg KDW.

Hansa-Brandenburg W.12.

Hansa-Brandenburg W.33.

Hansa-Brandenburg NW.

481

Hawker

Harmon 1-2 Mister America.

Harrison (Fairchild) F-11-2 Husky.

Hawker P.1052.

Hatz CB-1 biplane.

allow Egypt to share with Britain the defence of Egypt, the Sudan and the Canal zone under the terms of the Anglo-Egyptian Treaty.

RAF Audaxes entered service in 1932 and some based overseas were still flying in 1941–42. This fact is verified from records kept by British Aerospace, which state that an Audax squadron was used as fighter cover at the Digboi air station in north east Assam, India in 1942. However most of the remaining Audaxes were operated during the early war years as Hotspur glider tugs and trainers, 18 having previously been converted into Hart Specials.

Data (Audax I): *Engine* one 399 kW (535 hp) Rolls-Royce Kestrel IB or de-rated 428 kW (575 hp) Kestrel X *Wing span* 11.35 m (37 ft 3 in) *Length* 9.02 m (29 ft 7 in) *Max T-O weight* 2,023 kg (4,460 lb) *Max level speed* 272 km/h (169 mph) *Range* 845 km (525 miles) *Armament* one forward-firing Vickers and one rear-mounted Lewis machine-guns, plus one 112 lb bomb, two small practice bombs or other stores under each lower wing

Hawker Dankok (UK/Denmark) Hawker Woodcocks built under licence in Denmark with 287 kW (385 hp) Armstrong Siddeley Jaguar IV engines for the Naval Air Service.

Hawker Dantorp (UK) Name given by the Royal Danish Naval Air Service to Armstrong Siddeley Leopard-powered Hawker Horsleys.

Hawker Demon (UK) When the Hawker Hart day bomber entered service in January 1930, its performance was so outstanding that it was then, in terms of speed, able to outfly all other aircraft in RAF service. Procurement of fighters with even better performance was following the RAF's between-wars pattern of 'slow-but-sure', but it seemed sensible to the decision makers to put into service a two-seat fighter version of the Hart. This might have marginally better performance than the bomber, and would certainly provide additional fire-power from the rear cockpit.

Accordingly two prototypes were prepared for evaluation by modification of Hart bombers. These were each powered by a 417.3 kW (560 hp) fully supercharged Rolls-Royce Kestrel engine. Each was equipped with two synchronised forward-firing Vickers machine-guns and had the coaming of the rear cockpit modified to provide a maximum field of fire for the Lewis gun operated by the observer/air gunner. Known as Hart Fighters, these were evaluated and a small batch of six was ordered.

In 1932 the fighter received the name Demon. A total of 305 Demons were built, made up of the prototypes/pre-production aircraft, 77 with Kestrel IIS engines (seven as instructional airframes and one fitted with a 477 kW; 640 hp Kestrel VI engine under the Hawker report number 475), 155 with 436 kW (585 hp) Kestrel VI engines and those for Australia (see below). From late 1936 aircraft coming from the Boulton Paul production line were equipped with a hydraulically operated shield in the aft cockpit and were known as Turret Demons. The segmented metal shield was provided to give the gunner some protection from the slipstream. Many earlier aircraft were modified retrospectively to this standard. In addition to aircraft supplied to the RAF, a total of 64 were produced for the Royal Australian Air Force which procured them as army co-operation fighters each fitted with bomb racks, a message-retrieving hook and other equipment.

As a fighter with the RAF the Demon was

finally superseded from late 1938 by the Blenheim IF, but a few were used as target tugs until replaced by the Hawker Henley.

Data (Demon): *Engine* one 391 kW (525 hp) Rolls-Royce Kestrel IIS *Wing span* 11.35 m (37 ft 3 in) *Length* 8.99 m (29 ft 6 in) *Max T-O weight* 2,023 kg (4,460 lb) *Max level speed* 293 km/h (182 mph) *Range* 604 km (375 miles) *Armament* two forward-firing Vickers and one rear-mounted Lewis machine-guns, plus light bombs carried underwing

Hawker Audax.

Hawker Fury (UK) Certainly the fastest and aesthetically one of the most elegant biplanes to enter service with the RAF, the Fury was evolved from an un-named interceptor-fighter prototype which subsequently managed a level speed of more than 322 km/h (200 mph). Because the Air Ministry changed the official specification for a new fighter to include an in-line rather than radial engine, Hawker developed the supercharged Rolls-Royce Kestrel F.XIS/D.XII S-engined Hornet. Later renamed Fury, it was evaluated against the beautiful Fairey Fantôme (first flown on 16 January 1930). Emerging the winner, production of the Fury I began: the first 333 km/h (207 mph) aircraft flying for the first time on 26 March 1931.

Altogether 118 were completed for the RAF with 391 kW (525 hp) Kestrel IIS engines. In addition, Hawker Fury number 401, powered by an Armstrong Siddeley Panther IIIA engine and flown on 5 August 1932, was exported to Norway, 16 Pratt & Whitney Hornet-powered Furies went to Persia, three Furies to Portugal and six Hispano-Suiza 12-engined aircraft to Yugoslavia.

Fury Is first went to No 43 Squadron, RAF in mid-1931. Interestingly a Fury I won the coveted speed contest for military aircraft flying over a triangular course at the Zurich international meeting and in 1934 a number of RAF aircraft were sent to Canada to take part in the Centennial celebrations in Toronto.

On 13 April 1932 the private-venture Intermediate Fury made its first flight, basically as a refined Fury I. After further modification it re-emerged with a 477 kW (640 hp) Kestrel VI engine, with semi-evaporative cooling, flying for the first time in this form on 1 October 1933. With this engine it achieved a staggering 370 km/h (230 mph). British Aerospace records suggest that this biplane was re-engined in 1934 with a Goshawk III and flown on 17 October of that year, subsequently receiving a later Goshawk engine. More importantly on 3 May 1933 the experimental High Speed Fury flew for the first time. Initially it was powered by a Kestrel engine, with which it became the fastest of all Furies by attaining a speed of 394 km/h (245 mph); later it was fitted with a 518 kW (695 hp) Goshawk.

In 1934 it was decided that a Fury I should be fitted with a Kestrel VI with composite cooling, modified fuel and oil systems and streamlined wheel spats as the Fury II. This was first flown on 20 August 1935. Twenty-three production Fury IIs were built by Hawker with increased fuel capacity, followed by 89 from General Aircraft, six of which were delivered to the South African Air Force. Fury IIs entered RAF service in 1937 as an interim measure pending the delivery of greater numbers of monoplane fighters, remaining operational in their designed role until 1939. Exports were made to Yugoslavia (ten which, according to the *Jane's* of the time, had supercharged Kestrel XVI engines developing 555 kW; 745 hp and were fitted with single-leg cantilever landing gears and internally sprung wheels), Persia (six with Bristol Mercury engines), and Spain (three with 514 kW; 690 hp Hispano-Suiza 12Xbrs engines and first flown on 7 April 1936).

Hawker Audax built for Persia.

Hawker Dankok.

Hawker Dantorp seaplane.

Persian Hawker Fury I.

Australian Hawker Demon.

Hawker Turret Demon.

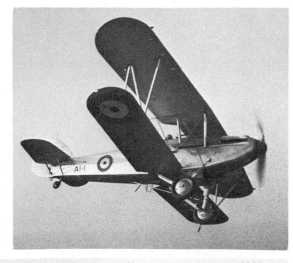

When introduced into service Fury Is were the RAF's first fighters able to exceed 322 km/h (200 mph) in level flight and gave good account of themselves during exercises. They were reliable, highly manoeuvrable and light on the controls and were most popular with their pilots. Fury IIs were even more impressive but were obsolete by the late 1930s and were retired not a moment too soon.

Data (Fury II): *Engine* as above *Wing span* 9.14 m (30 ft 0 in) *Length* 8.15 m (26 ft 8¾ in) *Max T-O weight* 1,642 kg (3,620 lb) *Max level speed* 359 km/h (223 mph) *Range* 418–435 km (260–270 miles) *Armament* two forward-firing Vickers machine-guns

Hawker Fury and Sea Fury (UK) The Fury was designed to conform to Specification F.2/43 and was developed from the Tempest. A light version of the Tempest to Specification F.6/42 had been projected at the end of 1942, but in January 1943 it was decided to produce a completely new design, which was later named the Fury.

The Fury used the same high-speed aerofoil section which had been specially developed for the Tempest to delay the compressibility effects first encountered with the Tornado and Typhoon. The wing consisted of two Tempest outer sections bolted together on the fuselage centreline, instead of being attached to the sides of the fuselage as on the Tempest. The monocoque fuselage and tail unit were completely new structures.

The first Bristol Centaurus 12-engined prototype flew for the first time on 1 September 1944. It was subsequently re-engined with a Centaurus 15. Although two other Centaurus-engined prototypes were built, the second to fly (on 27 November 1944) was powered by a Rolls-Royce Griffon 85 engine driving two Rotol three-bladed co-axial contra-rotating propellers. One of the Griffon-engined prototypes was subsequently re-engined with a Napier Sabre VII driving a five-bladed propeller, and flown in June 1946. A second Sabre-engined Fury was also flown.

With the end of the World War II approaching, the RAF cancelled its order for the Fury. However other nations were interested in the type and production began with 30 Centaurus-engined Fury 1s ordered for the Iraqi Air Force in 1946. Thereafter two Fury Trainers, each with a second separate cockpit introduced immediately aft of the fighter cockpit (first flown on 15 January 1948), were delivered to Iraq, together with another batch of 25 Fury 1s and Trainers. The Fury FB.60 and 61 were single-seat and two-seat Furies for Pakistan, the single Trainer having a 'tunnel' enclosure over the two cockpits.

The Sea Fury was a naval counterpart of the Fury conforming to Specification N.7/43. Production aircraft were derived from the three prototype 'Hooked' Furies, with various degrees of navalisation including folding wings and arrester gear. The first prototype to fly made its maiden flight on 21 February 1945. Fifty Sea Fury F.10s were ordered for the Royal Navy, each powered by an 1,841 kW (2,470 hp) Bristol Centaurus 18 eighteen-cylinder two-row radial sleeve-valve air-cooled engine. The F.10 was followed by the FB.11, which was similar but embodied all the small internal modifications introduced progres-

Data (FB.11): *Engine* as above *Wing span* 11.7 m (38 ft 4¾ in) *Length* 10.57 m (34 ft 8 in) *Max T-O weight* (normal) 5,602 kg (12,350 lb) *Max level speed* 724 km/h (450 mph) at 6,100 m (20,000 ft) *Range* (internal fuel only) 1,127 km (700 miles) *Armament* four 20 mm British Hispano Mk 5 cannon; racks below wings for two 500 lb or 1,000 lb bombs, 12 × 7.62 cm (3 in) or 12.7 cm (5 in) rockets or four rockets with 180 lb heads

Hawker Hardy (UK) The Hardy was a two-seat general-purpose biplane developed from the Hart. Production aircraft were built by Gloster Aircraft. The first 37 were powered by 391.2 kW (525 hp) Rolls-Royce Kestrel IB engines, the remaining ten by more powerful Kestrel Xs. These served with the RAF, latterly as a communications type, until 1941.

Hawker High Speed Fury.

sively in the first 50 airframes. The Royal Navy received a total of 615 (with provision for rocket-assisted take-off, or RATO), which remained operational until replaced by Sea Hawks, having seen action during the Korean War. Others were delivered to the navies of Canada and Australia.

The Sea Fury T.20 was a two-seat trainer version for the Royal Navy, based on the F.10. One 20 mm cannon was deleted from each wing to allow for the installation in the wings of equipment displaced from the fuselage by the second cockpit. Bombs and rockets or long-range drop tanks could be carried beneath the wings as on the FB.11 fighter bomber. The Sea Fury FB.51 was similar to the FB.11 but had Dutch language instruments and other minor changes for service with the Royal Netherlands Navy. Deliveries from Hawker were supplemented by production under licence by Fokker in the Netherlands. In addition Pakistan received 93 Sea Furies and five trainers and Egypt 12. The Sea Fury was the last piston-engined fighter to be built in quantity in the UK, and its career climaxed with the sale by Hawker of reconditioned aircraft to several countries, including Cuba and Burma.

Hawker Fury prototype.

Hawker Fury FB.11.

Hawker Hart (UK) The outstanding performance of the Fairey Fox day bomber (see entry), undoubtedly came as something of a shock both to Fairey's competitors and the Air Ministry. As a result the Air Ministry Specification 12/26 for a new light bomber required an improvement upon the performance of the Fox.

Hawker's submission for this requirement, which eventually became known as the Hart, was evolved in conjunction with Rolls-Royce, and when submitted in late 1926 proved sufficiently attractive for construction of a prototype to be authorised. Sidney Camm's design utilised what became known in later years as 'Hawker's patent metal construction system', a lightweight and robust structure with fabric covering. From Rolls-Royce came a new engine – known then as the F.XI, a development of the Falcon engine – which had weight-saving six-cylinder monoblocs instead of individual cylinders.

Hawker Fury II.

Spanish Hawker Fury II.

485

Hawker

Hawker Hardy.

The airframe design was that of an uncluttered single-bay biplane, the fuselage nicely streamlined, very much a conventional Hawker tail unit, and robust fixed landing gear with tailskid. The biplane wings were of unequal span, the lower wing of constant chord and with a straight leading edge. The upper wing, however, was slightly swept back – a useful recognition feature – and incorporated the ailerons and Handley Page leading-edge slots.

Hawker Hart day bomber.

The prototype was flown for the first time in late June 1928 in the hands of Flt Lt Bulman and was subsequently flown in competitive evaluation against the Avro Antelope and Fairey Fox II. With superior performance of the Hart confirmed, 15 pre-production aircraft were ordered initially for development and familiarisation, and the first 12 of these entered service with the RAF's No 33 (Bomber) Squadron in late 1929 or January 1930 (records differ) and one was sent

Swedish Hawker Hart.

for trials in India. Once again, as with the Fairey Fox which was introduced into service in 1926, a new day bomber was to cause acute embarrassment to the fighter squadrons.

In RAF service the Hart was to prove itself one of the most adaptable aircraft of its era, resulting in a number of variants. These included the Hart Trainer (483 built, not including conversions of other models); Hart C communications aircraft; and tropicalised versions known as the Hart India and Hart Special. A version was built for the Royal Navy, serving both with wheeled and float landing gear, and this was designated Hawker Osprey. In addition Harts were built for overseas customers which included Estonia, Sweden (also licence-built 42 Pegasus-engined Harts) and Yugoslavia, while ex-RAF aircraft eventually went to South Africa, Egypt and Southern Rhodesia.

Harts remained in service with the RAF on the North-West Frontier in India until displaced by Bristol Blenheims in 1939. Some Royal Navy Ospreys were used for target towing and training until 1940, but so far as is known the last in operational service was a Hart used by the South African Air Force well into World War II. Most extensively built between-wars British military aircraft, a total of 952 had been constructed when production ended in 1937, with Armstrong Whitworth, Gloster and Vickers acting as sub-contractors.

Hawker records also refer to a civil-registered Hart, first flown on 15 September 1932 and known as the Hart II. This was powered in succession by a Kestrel IIS, Kestrel VI and Kestrel XVI, with the latter having an all-up weight of 2,109 kg (4,649 lb). It was used for demonstrations at air displays and for taking air-to-air photographs of Hawker aircraft, accumulating 627 flying hours in these roles from August 1933. Data (Hart bomber): *Engine* one 391.2 kW (525 hp) Rolls-Royce Kestrel IB *Wing span* 11.35 m (37 ft 3 in) *Length* 8.94 m (29 ft 4 in) *Max T-O weight* 2,102 kg (4,635 lb) *Max level speed* 296 km/h (184 mph) *Range* 756 km (470 miles) *Armament* one forward-firing 0.303 in Vickers machine-gun and one rear-mounted Lewis gun, plus normally two 250 lb bombs

Hawker Hartbees (UK) The Hartbees was another development of the Hart produced to a South African Air Force requirement for a two-seat general-purpose aircraft. Sixty-five were built under licence at the Aircraft and Artillery Depot at Roberts Heights, joining four Hawker-built aircraft. These remained in service throughout World War II, ending their time as trainers.

Hawker Hector (UK) The Hector was developed as a two-seat army co-operation biplane based around a Hind-type fuselage, tail unit and landing gear and married to unswept biplane wings. A total of 178 were built for the RAF, entering service in 1937. These were stationed in the UK. Only a handful of Hectors were ever flown in anger, raiding German positions in occupied France in May 1940. Power was provided by a 600 kW (805 hp) Napier Dagger IIIMS 24-cylinder H-type air-cooled and supercharged engine, giving a maximum speed of 301 km/h (187 mph).

Hawker Henley (UK) The Henley was designed as a two-seat·high-performance light bomber. The prototype first flew in March 1937. Despite its promise, its role was changed to that of target towing. Four hundred were ordered, but only 100 Merlin II and 100 Merlin III-engined Henleys were built at the Gloster works. According to Hawker records two Henleys were used as engine test beds for Vulture and Griffon engines and one was tropicalised.

Hawker Hind (UK) The rapidly changing world of the 1930s forced the British government to take stock of its defences in relation to the growing military capability of Germany. In 1933 Winston Churchill warned Parliament of Germany's latest path and by 1935 expansion programmes for the British armed forces had been agreed. The Hind light bomber was one of the types produced for quick delivery to the RAF, based on the Hart and therefore needing little new development, although a number of improvements were introduced as the result of long experience with the Hart.

The first prototype was in fact a modified Hart and first flew on 12 September 1934 at Brooklands. Production covered no less than 528 aircraft, although with the delivery of modern monoplane bombers a number of the final Hinds on the production lines for the RAF were completed as dual-control trainers, a new role which many were eventually to fulfil. Records show that from even the first batch of 20 Hinds, General Aircraft was later to convert nine into trainers. Nine foreign users of the Hind (new and ex-RAF aircraft) included Latvia, New Zealand, Persia and South Africa.

Data: *Engine* one 477 kW (640 hp) Rolls-Royce Kestrel V *Wing span* 11.35 m (37 ft 3 in) *Length* 9.02 m (29 ft 7 in) *Max T-O weight* 2,403 kg (5,298 lb) *Max level speed* 301 km/h (187 mph) *Range* 692 km (430 miles) *Armament* one forward-firing Vickers Mk III or V machine-gun and one rear-mounted Lewis gun, plus two 250 lb bombs as standard

Hawker Horsley (UK) The Horsley was produced for the RAF as a bomber and torpedo bomber, entering service in these roles in 1927 and 1928 respectively after severe competitive tests against the Westland Yeovil, Bristol Berkeley and Handley Page Handcross. The Greek

Hawker Hartbees.

Naval Air Service also received six in 1928, and it was licence-built in Denmark as the Dantorp (military designation H.M.III). In total 121 Horsleys were built, most powered by 499 kW (670 hp) Rolls-Royce Condor IIIA geared engines and with all-metal airframes, although early production aircraft were of wooden and then mixed construction. In its class, it had an excellent performance. Apart from its speed and climb, it possessed the manoeuvrability of a scout and the aerodynamic design was such that the machine could be flown 'hands off' for periods of more than five minutes. The range, of course, varied according to the mixed load of bombs and fuel, and day or night operations were possible.

The excellent range and load-carrying ability of the Horsley made it suitable for very-long-distance flying: a special Horsley was produced with extra fuel tanks with a view to carrying out RAF training for duration and non-stop long-distance work. In fact the Horsley made three long-distance flights. The first was carried out by Flt Lt Carr as pilot and Flt Lt Gillman as navigator, who had expected to cover more than 6,440 km (4,000 miles) from Cranwell to India. However during 20–21 May 1927 they covered a distance of 5,502 km (3,419 miles), landing short near Bandar Abbas on the Persian Gulf because of problems with the oil system. A second effort by Carr and Flt Lt Mackworth ended after one hour's flying; while a third attempt by Carr and Fl Officer Dearth ended in Austria, alighting in the River Danube. For the attempts 5,000 litres (1,100 Imp gallons) of fuel were carried in seven tanks and it is a remarkable fact that, with an overload of nearly 200% of the structure weight, the Horsley could land safely.

Data (Mk II): *Engine* as above *Wing span* 17.3 m (56 ft 9 in) *Length* 11.66 m (38 ft 3 in) *Max T-O weight* 4,205 kg (9,270 lb) *Max level speed* 203 km/h (126 mph) *Armament* one forward-firing Vickers

Hawker Hart Trainer.

Hawker Hector.

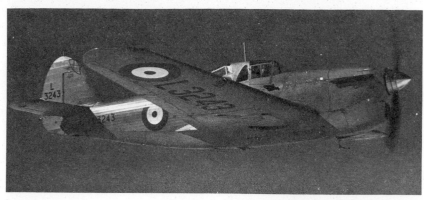

Hawker Henley.

Hawker Horsley specially prepared for an attempt on the world distance record.

Hawker Hunter F.1.

Hawker Hinds.

machine-gun and one rear-mounted Lewis gun, plus one 2,150 lb torpedo or bombs

Hawker Hunter (UK) In late 1946 Hawker initiated the design of this aircraft under the identity P.1067, hoping that it would prove sufficiently attractive to be accepted by the Ministry of Supply as a replacement for the Gloster Meteor. In fact, this brainchild of Sydney Camm and the company's design team was to represent, in later squadron service, the peak of development of the subsonic jet fighter. In January 1948 Hawker tendered this design for approval and in June of that year three prototypes were ordered. One was to be powered by an Armstrong Siddeley Sapphire, two by the new Rolls-Royce Avon – the engine around which the P.1067 had been designed.

Construction of the first prototype began in late 1949 and it flew for the first time on 20 July 1951. This and the second prototype were powered by Avons; the third had the Armstrong Siddeley Sapphire. The first production Hunter F.1 was flown on 16 May 1953. Of all-metal stressed-skin construction, the mid-set monoplane wing had 40° sweepback, and all controls were powered. Fuselage was of conventional construction: built in three sections, with an air brake fitted beneath the underside of the rear fuselage. Landing gear was of tricycle type, hydraulically retractable, and the engine was mounted in the centre-fuselage section with intake ducts in the wing roots.

Hunter F.1s (Avon 104 or 107) entered RAF service with No 43 Squadron in July 1954, and total construction of this version amounted to 139 aircraft. In squadron service trouble was encountered with gun firing at high altitude, causing surging and a tendency for the engine to 'flame out', resulting in an altitude restriction for gun

firing. The F.2 Sapphire Mk 101-powered Hunter suffered none of these gun-firing problems, but only 45 were built. The F.4 was an improved variant of the F.1 with increased internal fuel capacity and underwing hardpoints for a variety of weapons and drop-tanks. Of the 365 built, the final 209 had modified Avon 115 engines which eliminated the gun-firing surge problem, and most of the earlier aircraft with Avon 113s were modified retrospectively. The Sapphire Mk 101-powered F.5 introduced the structural improvements of the F.4.

A further developed F.4 had the designation F.6, and this introduced the more powerful Avon 203-series engine and improved flying controls (374 built). Those constructed later in the production run had extended or 'dog-tooth' leading-edge panels and provision for four pylons under the wings for a greater range of external stores. This version entered service in late 1956 and eventually equipped all RAF day-fighter squadrons in Europe. Some F.4s were given similar wing leading-edge modification.

Other versions included the T.7 RAF and T.8 Navy two-seat trainers (wider fuselage to accommodate a new cockpit); F(GA).9 ground-attack variant of the F.6 with a more powerful Avon 207 engine, a tail-stowed parachute deployable for short-field landing, and provisions to carry two 1,045.5 litre (230 Imp gallon) drop-tanks; FR.10 fighter-reconnaissance camera-equipped aircraft generally similar to the F(GA).9; and the GA.11 conversion of the F.4 which served with the Royal Navy as a single-seat advanced trainer.

Hunter production totalled 1,985 aircraft, including those manufactured by Aviolanda and

Fokker in Holland, and Avions Fairey and SABCA in Belgium under the American 'off-shore' purchasing arrangements. Export aircraft (some of which were refurbished) were supplied to Chile, Denmark, India, Iraq, Jordan, Kuwait, Lebanon, Peru, Qatar, Rhodesia, Saudi Arabia, Singapore, Sweden and Switzerland.

Mention must be made of the single Hunter 3, with an Avon R.A.7R which developed 42.7 kN (9,600 lb st) with reheat. In this aircraft (on 7 September 1953) Sqdn Ldr Neville Duke established a new world absolute speed record of 1170.96 km/h (727.6 mph) over a 3 km course (a full description of all the Hunter variants appears in the 1961–62 and 1964–65 editions of *Jane's*).
Data (F.4): *Engine* one 44.5 kN (10,000 lb st) Rolls-Royce Avon 203 or 207 turbojet *Wing span* 10.26 m (33 ft 8 in) *Length* 13.98 m (45 ft 10½ in) *Max T-O weight* 7,756 kg (17,100 lb) *Max level speed* Mach 0.95 at 10,970 m (36,000 ft), 1,150 km/h (715 mph) at S/L *Armament* four 30 mm Aden guns, plus 1,000 lb bomb, multiple rocket launchers, napalm bombs or practice bomb carriers on inboard pylons; drop-tanks or rocket launchers on outboard pylons
Hawker Hurricane (UK) Few British aircraft have attained the special niche in the history of the RAF which is accorded to the Hawker Hurricane, sharing with the Supermarine Spitfire the brunt of air defence during the Battle of Britain in

August–September 1940. One of the significant statistics of the Hurricane's contribution to this hard-fought battle was the fact that these aircraft destroyed more enemy aircraft than the combined total of all other defence systems, air or ground. Even that factor must be equated with the information that at the beginning of the battle (on 8 August 1940) approximately 65% more Hurricanes than Spitfires (2,309 to 1,400) had been delivered to the RAF's Fighter Command. Perhaps, in the final analysis, such figures can be regarded as more controversial than revealing. The fact remains that this combination of machines and courageous pilots was enough to deny the Luftwaffe access to the daylight skies over Britain without unacceptable loss.

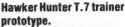

Hawker Hunter F.4.,

Hawker Hunter T.7 trainer prototype.

The family tree of the Hurricane can be traced back to a 'Fury monoplane' proposal of 1933, then to be powered by the Rolls-Royce Goshawk evaporative-cooled power plant. Instead it was decided in early 1934 to adapt this design to incorporate the new PV.12 engine which Rolls-Royce had developed – and which was the direct forbear of the famous Merlin. From that time the airframe/engine combination bore so little relation to the Fury that it then became identified as the 'Interceptor Monoplane'.

This finalised design was submitted to the Air Ministry in 1934, and in the following year a prototype was ordered to Specification F.36/34. On 6 November 1935, powered by a 767 kW (1,029 hp) Merlin 'C' engine, the Hurricane took to the air for the first time. Although of cantilever monoplane configuration, its construction was typical of the Fury from which it stemmed, and even its wings were fabric-covered in early Mk Is, with a metal leading edge and trailing-edge flaps. The tailwheel-type landing gear had hydraulically retractable main units of wide track. Armament of production Mk Is comprised four 0.303 in Browning machine-guns in each wing, making this the RAF's first eight-gun fighter.

Early tests of the prototype confirmed the predicted performance, and an initial order for 600 placed in June 1936 was followed by one for 1,000 additional aircraft in November 1938. The first

Hawker Hurricane Is of 111 Squadron, RAF.

Hawker

Hawker Hurricane IIC fighter-bomber under construction.

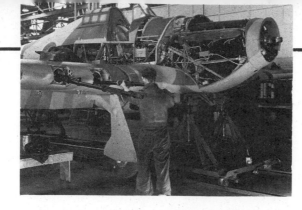

Hawker Tempest II.

Hawker Osprey I.

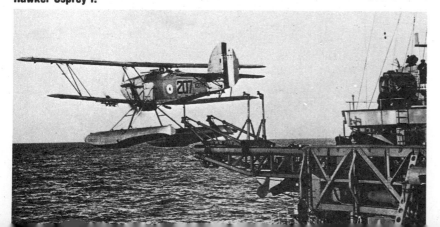

production aircraft flew in October 1937 and Hurricane Is began to enter service in December 1937, first with No 111 Squadron. In early February 1938 Britain's breakfast-time newspaper readers almost choked on their toast when headlines assured them that, during the night, No 111 Squadron's commanding officer (Sqdn Ldr J. Gillan) had flown his Hurricane from Edinburgh to Northolt at an average speed of 657 km/h (408 mph), assisted by a tail wind!

Subsequent Hurricane versions included the Mk IIA with Merlin XX and eight guns; Mk IIB with 12 guns; and Mk IIC with four 20 mm cannon. Mk IIDs with two 40 mm Vickers 'S' guns and two 0.303 in guns (plus additional armour for low attack) were used extensively in the Western Desert. The final production version was the Mk IV with a wing able to accept armament comprising two Browning machine-guns plus two 40 mm guns, or eight rocket projectiles, or two 250 lb or 500 lb bombs, or long-range fuel tanks. The Hurricane V (only two built) was powered by a Merlin 27 or 32 engine, while Hurricane Xs, XIIs and XIIAs were produced in Canada by the Canadian Car and Foundry Company with Packard 28 or 29 engines. A total of 12,780 Hurricanes were built in Britain, plus 1,451 in Canada.

Sea Hurricanes joined the Royal Navy in January 1941 and became the first carrier-based British single-seat monoplane fighter when taken to sea by HMS *Furious* in July 1941. Under the 'Catfighter' scheme, Sea Hurricane IAs were equipped for catapult launch from the decks of CAM merchant ships (catapult-equipped merchantmen) to counter the threat posed by Germany's Focke-Wulf Fw 200 Condors, introduced in the spring in 1941. Only the Mk IA was specially built. The approximate figure of 800 Sea Hurricanes which entered service included 50 Mk IAs and about 750 conversions of Mk II and Canadian-built aircraft.

In addition to the Hurricanes already mentioned, more than 4,000 were supplied to other air forces, including Belgium, Canada, Egypt, Eire, Finland, India, Persia (now Iran), Poland, Portugal, Romania, South Africa, the Soviet Union, Turkey, and Yugoslavia.

Data (IIC): *Engine* one 883 kW (1,185 hp) Rolls-Royce Merlin XX, later increased to 954 kW (1,280 hp) *Wing span* 12.19 m (40 ft 0 in) *Length* 9.75 m (32 ft 0 in) *Max T-O weight* 3,742 kg (8,250 lb) *Max level speed* 538 km/h (334 mph) *Range* (standard fuel) 740 km (460 miles) *Armament* four 20 mm cannon, plus two 250 lb or two 500 lb bombs underwing

Hawker Nimrod (UK) The Nimrod was basically the FAA version of the Fury single-seat interceptor fighter. In general arrangement and construction it was almost identical to the Fury and was fitted with a 440 kW (590 hp) Rolls-Royce Kestrel IIS supercharged engine (later replaced by the Kestrel V on Mk IIs). It was, of course, strengthened for catapulting and carried more comprehensive equipment and extra fuel.

The Nimrod, like all other Hawker products of the period, embodied the Hawker-patented system of metal construction, all but the first three stainless steel Mk IIs being built of ordinary steel and duralumin. Apart from simplicity of construction, this system allowed maintenance and repairs, if necessary, to be undertaken by unskilled labour and with the simplest of materials. Armament comprised two forward-firing Vickers machine-guns, plus optional light bombs; equipment included a wireless, oxygen apparatus, hoisting gear and electrical equipment.

A total of 54 Mk Is and 27 Mk IIs were produced for the FAA, plus a handful for export to Japan, Denmark and Portugal.

Data (MkI) *Engine* as above *Wing span* 10.22 m (33 ft 6¼ in) *Length* 8.23 m (27 ft 0 in) *Max T-O weight* 1,834 kg (4,043 lb) *Max level speed* 291 km/h (181 mph)

Hawker Osprey (UK) The Osprey was a two-seat naval fighter-reconnaissance biplane, developed from the Hart but with additional strengthening for catapult launching, folding wings for storage on board ship and naval equipment.

The first prototype flew in 1930 and was eventually followed by 37 Osprey Mk I, 14 Mk II, 52 Mk III and 26 Mk IV production aircraft; the Mk IIs later being modified into Mk IIIs with Fairey Reid propellers and other refinements. A small number of the genuine Mk IIIs were constructed of stainless steel, one of which, according to Hawker records, was exhibited in skeleton form at the 1932 Paris Show. Standard power plant for

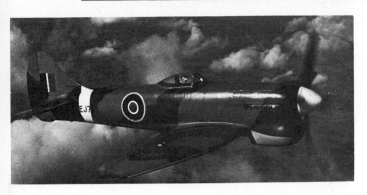

The prototype Sea Hawk flew in 1947. It was eventually followed by the Rolls-Royce Nene 101-powered Sea Hawk F.1, 35 of which were built for the Royal Navy by Hawker and 60 by Armstrong Whitworth. The Mk 2 version was similar but had powered ailerons. It was first flown in February 1954 and 40 were delivered. There followed 116 Sea Hawk FB.3 fighter-bombers, 97 F(GA).4s with additional ground-attack capability, the Sea Hawk FB.5 with uprated Nene 103 engines (about 50 converted

Hawker Tempest V.

Hawker Sea Hawk F.1 on board HMS *Eagle*.

the Mk Is, IIs and IIIs was the 423.3 kW (568 hp) Rolls-Royce Kestrel IIMS, giving a maximum speed of 257 km/h (160 mph) as a landplane. Seaplane Ospreys had twin floats, although an interesting but unsuccessful experiment was carried out with one aircraft fitted with a central main float and wingtip stabilising floats. The Mk IV was powered by a 477 kW (640 hp) Kestrel V engine.

Ospreys entered service with the FAA in 1932 and eventually flew from aircraft carriers, cruisers and other warships. In 1934 one RAF squadron took delivery of four Ospreys for communications work, and in the same year HMS *Sussex* went to Melbourne as part of the Centenary celebrations carrying an Osprey. By mid-1935 several ships of the Second Cruiser Squadron of the Home Fleet had been issued with Ospreys and the new cruiser *Ajax* had received two for service with the Mediterranean Command. These remained in service until 1939 (see **Hart**).

Meanwhile the Swedish vessel *Gotland* had received Mercury-powered Ospreys, known as Nohabs. These remained operational as naval co-operation aircraft alongside Heinkel He 5s until 1940. Three Ospreys were also delivered to Portugal and Spain, although it is uncertain whether the Spanish aircraft was among the 57 machines sent by Britain to the Republican Air Force during the Civil War.

Data (Mk IV landplane): *Engine* as above *Wing span* 11.28 m (37 ft 0 in) *Length* 8.94 m (29 ft 4 in) *Max T-O weight* 2,254 kg (4,970 lb) *Max level speed* 279 km/h (173 mph) *Armament* one forward-firing Vickers machine-gun and one rear-mounted Lewis gun

Hawker (Armstrong Whitworth) Sea Hawk (UK) The Sea Hawk single-seat naval fighter was designed and initially produced by Hawker Aircraft Ltd. Development and series production of this aircraft were the responsibility of Armstrong Whitworth from 1953.

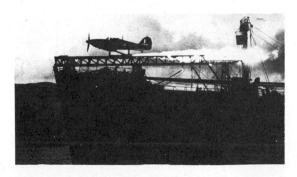

from Mk 3s), 86 new (plus some converted) Sea Hawk F(GA).6s, 22 Sea Hawk Mk 50s for the Royal Netherlands Navy (similar to Mk 6 but with American radio equipment; modified in 1959 to carry Sidewinder missiles), 34 Sea Hawk Mk 100 close-support strike fighters for the Federal German Navy, and 34 Sea Hawk Mk 101 long-range radar reconnaissance fighters for the Federal German Navy. In addition, two squadrons of F(GA).6s were acquired by the Indian Navy for service on the aircraft carrier *Vikrant*; this service subsequently also received 22 ex-RN F(GA).4/6s and 28 ex-German aircraft. Of the 434 Sea Hawks produced for the Royal Navy, plus those for foreign service, only about 30 aircraft, serving on the *Vikrant*, remained in 1980.

Data (F(GA).6): *Engine* one 24 kN (5,400 lb st) Rolls-Royce Nene 104 turbojet *Wing span* 11.89 m (39ft 0in) *Length* 12.09m (39 ft 8 in) *Max T-O weight* 7,348 kg (16,200 lb) *Max level speed* 964 km/h (599 mph) *Combat radius* 370 km (230 miles) *Armament* four 20 mm cannon, plus provision for bombs, rockets or Sidewinder missiles.

Hawker Tempest (UK) The performance of the Typhoon was such that speeds of around 805 km/h (500 mph) could be attained in a dive. It was, therefore, numbered among the high-performance aircraft of World War II which began to be affected by the problems of compressibility, with the accelerated airflow over the cambered upper surface of the wing beginning, locally, to approach the speed of sound. It was in April 1941 that discussions were opened between Hawker and the Ministry of Aircraft Production on the subject of Typhoon development. Proposals for a Typhoon Mk II included the installation of a Sabre IV engine of higher power and driving a four-bladed propeller, improved view and a cleaned-up tail.

Hawker Hurricane Ia being launched from a CAM ship.

Hawker

Hawker Sea Hawk Mk 100s in German Marineflieger markings.

Hawker Nimrod I seaplane.

Hawker proposals (submitted in August 1941) included the suggestion that the Typhoon Mk II should have thin elliptical wings of 12.8 m (42 ft) span and 27.9 m² (300 sq ft) area, with a 15% thickness/chord ratio at the root and 10% at the tip. The introduction of a new thin-section wing made it necessary to reduce the amount of fuel carried in the wings and an extra bay was inserted in the fuselage behind the engine to accommodate an additional fuel tank. The lengthening of the fuselage called for increased fin area.

Owing to the delay in the production of the Sabre IV engine, it was decided to complete the prototype Typhoon II with a Sabre II engine. However, because the Mk II had become a completely different aeroplane both in external appearance and in construction, permission was sought and granted to change its name to Tempest.

In June 1942 it was proposed that six Tempest prototypes should be completed: one with a Sabre VI (Tempest I); two with Centaurus (Tempest IIs); one with a Rolls-Royce Griffon 2B (Tempest III); one with a Griffon 61 (Tempest IV); and one with a Sabre III (Tempest V). Owing to heavy commitments Hawker could not undertake to build more than three and the Mks I, II and V were chosen. The Tempest V prototype first flew on 2 September 1942, and the first production aircraft appeared on 25 June 1943; this version was chosen with the Sabre II, a well-tried power unit available in quantity.

The Tempest V first entered RAF service in April 1944, and was the only version to be used operationally during World War II. Early utilisation was largely in the train-busting role, but their high speed made them an ideal interceptor of V-1 flying-bombs, which were launched against London from 13 June 1944. In just under three months Tempest Vs destroyed more than one-third of the RAF's total of 1,771 V-1s. Later, with the 2nd TAF in Europe, they not only made a valuable contribution in the close-support role, but claimed the interception and destruction of 20 Messerschmitt Me 262 jet-powered aircraft.

The Tempest VI was a tropicalised version of the Mk V with a 1,714 kW (2,300 hp) Sabre V engine. This entered RAF service post-war, as did the Tempest II with Bristol Centaurus power plant. This latter version, 450 of which were built, was the RAF's last single-seat piston-engined

fighter bomber. It was largely replaced by the de Havilland Hornet during 1948, but a few squadrons still flew Tempests until 1951, including several squadrons in Germany.

Towards the end of 1948 ex-RAF Tempest IIs were supplied also to the air forces of India and Pakistan. Many Mk V and Mk VI aircraft were converted subsequently to serve as TT.5 or TT.6 high-speed target tugs.

Data (Mk II): *Engine* one 1,882 kW (2,525 hp) Bristol Centaurus V or VI *Wing span* 12.5 m (41 ft 0 in) *Length* 10.49 m (34 ft 5 in) *Max T-O weight* 6,010–6,412 kg (13,250–14,125 lb) *Max level speed* 711 km/h (442 mph) *Range* 1,352 km (840 miles) *Armament* four forward-firing British Hispano Mk 5 20 mm cannon, plus two 500 lb or 1,000 lb bombs or air-to-ground rockets mounted underwing

Hawker Tomtit (UK) Two-seat training biplane powered by an Armstrong Siddeley Mongoose III radial engine. Small number built for the RAF, for civil registration and for export to Canada and New Zealand.

Hawker Typhoon (UK) Air Ministry Specification F.18/37 was concerned with the design and development of two advanced interceptor fighters: one with a Rolls-Royce Vulture engine was identified initially as the R (Rolls-Royce) type fighter; the second, with a Napier Sabre engine, was known as the N (Napier) type. Prototypes of both were built, the first designated as the Hawker Tornado, but development problems with the Vulture caused this programme to be abandoned.

The Sabre-engined N-type fighter prototype flew for the first time on 24 February 1940, but after the collapse of France in June was stopped to enable Hawker to devote its maximum effort to the production of the Hurricane. This caused considerable delay in the introduction of the

Hawker Nimrod I.

Typhoon, work on which was not resumed until later in 1940. The first production Typhoon flew on 26 May 1941. This was, in profile, a very Hurricane-looking low-wing monoplane, with retractable tailwheel-type landing gear. Construction combined what had become traditional Hawker with stressed-skin techniques. The one very un-Hurricane-like feature was the chin-fairing for the ventral radiator.

Typhoon IA production aircraft began to enter RAF service in September 1941, and went into action in the summer of 1942. Initial usage proved a great disappointment, with unsatisfactory high-altitude performance, inferior rate of climb

and frequent engine breakdowns. When structural failure of the tail unit caused a number of fatal accidents it was suggested that the Typhoon should be withdrawn from service. Fortunately its superb low-level performance ensured that fast action was taken to overcome the shortcomings, and introduction of the Sabre II engine brought improved reliability.

Typhoon IAs were armed with 12 × 0.303 in Browning machine-guns, but the bomb-dropping, cannon-firing or rocket-firing Typhoon IBs became 'train-busters' *par excellence* and, with the invasion of Europe, proved to be a valuable component of the 2nd Tactical Air Force. Utilised on a 'cab-rank' system, under which Typhoons on standing patrol could be called in from the ground for tactical close support of army formations, they decimated the enemy's Panzer divisions. Indeed, the Typhoon's fire-power was sometimes compared with that of a broadside from a cruiser, and was sufficient to penetrate the most heavily armoured tanks.

A total of 3,330 Typhoons were produced for the RAF, but by the end of 1945 none remained in front-line service.
Data (Typhoon IB): *Engine* one 1,625.5 kW (2,180 hp), 1,639.4 kW (2,200 hp), or 1,684 kW (2,260 hp) Napier Sabre IIA, IIB or IIC *Wing span* 12.67 m (41 ft 7 in) *Length* 9.73 m (31 ft 11 in) *Max T-O weight* 6,010 kg (13,250 lb) *Max level speed* 663 km/h (412 mph) *Range* (internal fuel) 821 km (510 miles) *Armament* four wing-mounted 20 mm Hispano cannon, and under-wing racks for two 500 lb or 1,000 lb bombs or eight air-to-ground rockets (with 60 lb high explosive or 25 lb armour-piercing warheads)
Hawker Woodcock (UK) H. G. Hawker Engineering Co was formed from the voluntary liquidation of the famous Sopwith company. The

Woodcock – along with the Duiker reconnaissance and fighting parasol-wing monoplane and the Cygnet light aeroplane built for the 1924 Lympne trials (see **Chronology**, 8 October 1923 for the first trials) – was one of the new company's first products and indeed its first single-seat fighter for the RAF. Built as one of the replacements for the Snipe, it was an orthodox single-bay biplane of wood and metal construction, possessing exceptional flying qualities if not speed. Power was provided by a 298 kW (400 hp) Bristol Jupiter IV radial engine.

A total of 62 (out of 67 ordered) were produced for the RAF, entering service from May 1925. During its career (which lasted until 1928) it was used for night-flying training and never suffered an accident of any description. Differential ailerons gave adequate control and the wide landing gear facilitated landings by day or night. The Woodcock was also licence-built in Denmark as the Dankok (see entry, page 634).
Data: *Engine* as above *Wing span* 9.91 m (32 ft 6 in) *Length* 7.98 m (26 ft 2 in) *Max T-O weight* 1,351 kg (2,979 lb) *Max level speed* 230 km/h (143 mph) *Endurance* 3 h 30 min *Armament* two forward-firing Vickers machine-guns
Hawker Siddeley Dove, Heron and Sea Vixen (UK) see **de Havilland**
Hawker Siddeley Andover (UK) The Andover is the RAF's short/medium-range rear-loading military transport version of the BAe (Hawker

Siddeley) 748 turboprop airliner. Production of the 748 Series 2 included aircraft for the Queen's Flight and others for Support Command as Andover CC.2s, some of which now fly with the RNZAF as C.1s. The RAF also operates six E.3s for flight checking and calibration duties. Military versions of the 748 currently serve with the air forces of 17 countries (see **BAe 748**).
Hawker Siddeley Buccaneer (UK) The Buccaneer, designed originally by Blackburn Aircraft to meet an Admiralty requirement for a high-speed aircraft able to deliver a nuclear weapon at low level, was identified originally as the Blackburn N.A.39. The prototype flew for the first time on 30 April 1958, and S.1 production aircraft began to enter service with the Royal Navy in March 1961. Power plant of the S.1 comprised two 31.6 kN (7,100 lb st) de Havilland Gyron Junior 101 turbojets.

Hawker Typhoon IB.

Hawker Woodcock.

Hawker Siddeley

Hawker Siddeley Buccaneer S.2A.

In January 1962 – by which time the Blackburn Company had been absorbed into the Hawker Siddeley organisation – a Rolls-Royce Spey-engined development was ordered by the Navy. A pre-production prototype, converted from an S.1, flew for the first time on 17 May 1963 and production S.2s began to enter Navy service in March 1965. In October of that year an S.2, crewed by Cdr G. Higgs and Lieut Cdr A. Taylor, covered the distance of 3,138 km (1,950 miles) from Goose Bay, Labrador to Lossiemouth, Scotland without the aid of flight refuelling.

In 1968 the RAF decided to acquire Buccaneers to fill the enormous gap that had been left in its planned force of long-range strike/reconnaissance aircraft. This situation had arisen from the termination of the development programme of the BAC TSR.2 tactical-strike aircraft, the cancellation of the 50 F-111K variable-geometry strike aircraft on order from General Dynamics in the US, and the withdrawal of France from partnership in the AFVG (Anglo-French Variable-Geometry) combat aircraft. A total of 43 S.2B Buccaneers were ordered, these being new production examples with the capability to launch Martel air-to-ground missiles, and most Royal Navy S.2s were transferred to the RAF as aircraft carriers were withdrawn from service. Production of the new aircraft ended in 1977, and S.2A (without Martel), S.2B (with Martel) Buccaneers were in RAF service in 1979. Those still remaining with the Navy were designated S.2C without and S.2D with Martel capability. Sixteen aircraft similar to

Hawker Siddeley Gnat of the Red Arrows aerobatic team.

the S.2 were supplied to the South African Air Force as S.50. They differ by having a 35.6 kN (8,000 lb st) retractable rocket engine in the rear fuselage to enhance take-off performance.

A high-performance aircraft for low-level missions, the Buccaneer is of mid-wing monoplane configuration. The wing has graduated sweep-back and both it and the all-moving T-tail have a boundary-layer control (BLC) system. For carrier stowage the wings and nose-cone folded and to reduce length the easily recognisable tail-cone (which consists of two sideways-opening air brakes) could be made to disappear by extending the air brakes. Advanced avionics integrated with weapon-delivery electronics provide a comprehensive weapon system for the Buccaneer's strike role.

Data (S.2B): *Engines* two 49.4 kN (11,100 lb st) Rolls-Royce RB.168 Spey Mk.101 turbofans *Wing span* 13.41 m (44 ft 0 in) *Length* 19.33 m (63 ft 5 in) *Max T-O weight* 28,123 kg (62,000 lb) *Max level speed* Mach 0.85 (1,038 km/h; 645 mph) at 60 m (200 ft) *Range* (strike mission) 3,700 km (2,300 miles) *Armament* max weapons load of 7,257 kg (16,000 lb) comprising nuclear or conventional weapons, bombs, rockets, Bullpup or Martel missiles, carried in weapons bay and on underwing pylons

Hawker Siddeley Gnat (UK) Development of the Gnat single-seat lightweight fighter was started by the former Folland Aircraft Ltd as a private venture in 1951. The first Gnat fighter prototype, powered by a Bristol Siddeley Orpheus turbojet engine, flew for the first time on 18 July 1955. Production Gnat Mk 1 fighters were supplied subsequently to the Ministry of Aviation (6), India (25, plus 15 sets of components), Finland (12) and Yugoslavia (2). In addition the Gnat fighter was produced under licence in India between 1962 and 1974. A developed version, known as the Ajeet, is currently in production in India (see entry).

On 31 August 1959 the prototype Gnat Trainer with tandem cockpits flew for the first time. Its primary role was that of advanced-flying training, but it was given the ability to carry a wide range of external stores for armament instruction and emergency tactical operations. As the Gnat T.1, it entered service with the RAF, subsequently becoming the mount of the Red Arrows Aerobatic Team.

Data (fighter): *Engine* one 20.1 kN (4,520 lb st) Bristol Siddeley Orpheus 701 turbojet *Wing span* 6.75 m (22 ft 2 in) *Length* 9.06 m (29 ft 9 in) *Max T-O weight* 3,010–4,020 kg (6,650–8,885 lb) *Max level speed* Mach 0.98 *Normal endurance* 1 h 30 min *Armament* two 30 mm Aden cannon, plus bombs or rockets underwing

Hawker Siddeley P.1127 Kestrel (UK) Experimental V/STOL tactical fighter, first flown (tethered) on 21 October 1960. Was developed into the Harrier (see entry).

JANE'S
Encyclopedia of Aviation

Volume 4

Aircraft A–Z
Heinkel — Norman Thompson

Compiled and edited by Michael J. H. Taylor

Contributors: Bill Gunston, A. J. Jackson, David Mondey,

Malcolm Passingham, John Stroud, Susan H. H. Young

Heinkel

Heinkel HD 28.

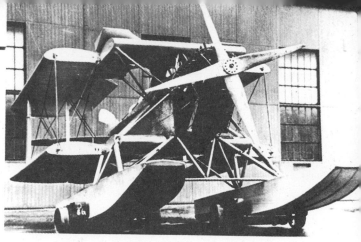

Heinkel HE 1 (Germany/Sweden) Three-seat low-wing monoplane floatplane designed by Ernst Heinkel but produced under licence in Sweden for the Navy as the Svenska S.1 of 1923, powered by the 179 kW (240 hp) Maybach Mb IVa or Siddeley Puma engine.

Heinkel HE 2 (Germany/Sweden) The Heinkel HE 2 represented an improvement on the HE 1 and underwent considerable testing before it was licence-built in Sweden as the Svenska S.2 for the Swedish Navy and for export to Finland and possibly other countries. A two-seater, it was normally powered by a 268.3 kW (360 hp) Rolls-Royce Eagle IX engine, although a 223.6 kW (300 hp) Hispano-Suiza, 298 kW (400 hp) Liberty or similar engine could be fitted. Maximum level speed was 185 km/h (115 mph).

Heinkel HE 4 and HE 5 (Germany/Sweden) Three-seat reconnaissance monoplanes of 1926, developed from the HE 1 and powered by 268.3 kW (360 hp) Rolls-Royce IX and 335.3 kW (450 hp) Napier Lion engines respectively. Both types were licence-built in Sweden for the Navy by Svenska.

Heinkel HE 5b.

Heinkel HE 3 and HE 18 (Germany) The HE 3 was a cantilever low-wing monoplane of the type originated by Dr Junkers, but was of wooden construction and had seating for three as a school or touring aircraft. Powered by a 55.6 kW (75 hp) Siemens-Halske radial engine, it was readily convertible from a twin-float seaplane to a landplane, the two landing gears forming completely braced structures which could be interchanged by releasing and securing two fastenings only. The wings could also be detached. It won the first prize in its class at the 1923 Gothenburg meeting. As a landplane and seaplane respectively, maximum speeds were 150 km/h (93 mph) and 145 km/h (90 mph).

The HE 18 was a two-seat development of the HE 3, featuring a fuselage constructed from steel tubes and spruce wings with full-span slotted ailerons. Maximum level speed was 140 km/h (87 mph).

Heinkel HE 8 (Germany) The HE 8 was a two/three-seat reconnaissance floatplane powered by a 335.3 kW (450 hp) Armstrong Siddeley Jaguar radial engine. It was a development of the earlier Napier Lion-engined HE 5. The Danish Naval Air Service received at least 22 under the designation H.M.II, many remaining operational throughout the 1930s. Maximum level speed was 218 km/h (135 mph). Armament comprised a rear-mounted machine-gun.

Heinkel HD 42B.

Heinkel HE 12 and HE 58 (Germany) The HE 12 was a two-seat twin-float commercial seaplane designed for catapulting and powered by a 372.6 kW (500 hp) BMW-built Pratt & Whitney Hornet radial engine. Aft of the rear cockpit was a mail and cargo compartment, the floor of which was constructed from corrugated light metal. Only one was built, operated by Deutsche Luft-Hansa (see **Chronology** 22 July 1929).

The single HE 58 was built for use on *Bremen*'s sister ship *Europa*: a slightly larger aircraft but powered by a similar engine and with side-by-side instead of tandem seating. Maximum speeds of the HE 12 and HE 58 were 215 km/h (133.5 mph) and 204 km/h (127 mph) respectively.

Heinkel HD 17 (Germany) Two-seat reconnaissance biplane of 1926 powered by a 335.3 kW (450 hp) Napier Lion engine.

Heinkel HD 21 (Germany) The HD 21 appeared in 1924 and was a tandem three-seat biplane suitable for basic training at flying schools. The front cockpit under the upper wing was often faired over for training. It was constructed of spruce and powered by a 74.5 kW (100 hp) or 89.4 kW (120 hp) Mercedes engine. Maximum speed was 145 km/h (90 mph).

Heinkel HD 22 (Germany) Two-seat general-purpose or sporting biplane of 1926, powered by a BMW IV or Junkers L-5 engine.

Heinkel HD 23 and HD 28 (Germany) Single-seat shipboard biplane fighter (447 kW; 600 hp BMW VI) and three-seat reconnaissance biplane (335.3 kW; 450 hp Bristol Jupiter VI) respectively, examples of each going to Japan.

Heinkel HD 24 and HD 36 (Germany) Two-seat basic training biplanes of 1928 powered by 171.4 kW (230 hp) BMW IV and 119 kW (160 hp) Mercedes D.III engines respectively.

Heinkel HD 25 (Germany) This was a two-seat twin-float reconnaissance biplane of 1928, powered by a 335.3 kW (450 hp) Napier Lion engine. It was stressed for catapulting. A few served with the Japanese Navy.

Heinkel HD 26 (Germany) Single-seat twin-float biplane of 1928 powered by a 223.6 kW (300 hp) Hispano-Suiza engine. A few went to the Japanese Navy.

Heinkel HD 29 and HD 32 (Germany) Following on from the HD 21, Heinkel produced the HD 29 and HD 32 in 1926. These were basically similar, powered by either a 56 kW (75 hp) or 74.5 kW (100 hp) Siemens engine. Several HD 32s took part in the 1925 'Deutscher Rundflug', one of which was fitted with a Bristol Lucifer engine.

Heinkel HD 37 and HD 38 (Germany) Single-seat biplane fighters of 1928, differing only in having a wheeled landing gear and twin floats respectively. Power was provided by 559 kW (750 hp) BMW VI engines. One hundred and forty-five HD 37Cs were licence-built in Russia from 1932 and HD 38Ds were produced in Germany for the Reichswehrministerium.

Heinkel HD 35 (Germany) Development of the HD 21, normally used as a three-seat school type but equally suited to touring. Powered by an 89.4 kW (120 hp) Mercedes engine.

Heinkel HD 39 and HD 40 (Germany) The HD 39 was produced during 1926 to the order of *B.Z. am Mittag* (Berlin's most widely read newspaper) for the purpose of operating a newspaper delivery service between Berlin and Hamburg, Köln, Bremen, Hannover, Frankfurt, Dresden, Leipzig, etc. Power was provided by a 164 kW (220 hp) BMV IV engine. In the following year the larger HD 40 was delivered, able to carry four–six passengers and cargo. Power was provided by a 447 kW (600 hp) BMW VI engine.

Heinkel HD 42 (Germany) The HD 42 was designed as a two-seat twin-float biplane for training and sporting use. The prototype first flew on 3 March 1931 powered by a BMW Va engine. The initial production version was the HD 42A, 32 of which went to the German Navy as trainers, powered by 223.5 kW (300 hp) Junkers L-5 engines. The next version was the HD 42B, powered by the L-5-G engine. In total 44 were produced, all strengthened for catapulting and used as trainers and reconnaissance aircraft. The final version was the HD 42C, similar to the HD 42B but with the 283 kW (380 hp) L-5-Ga engine. Some were armed with a machine-gun. A number of HD 42s remained in service as trainers until 1944.

Heinkel He 45 (Germany) The He 45 was the first of Heinkel's combat aircraft proper for the Third Reich. At the time of its appearance the general practice of using HD designations for Heinkel Doppeldeckers (biplanes) and HE designations for Heinkel Eindeckers (monoplanes) was dropped in favour of He designations.

Appearing in 1931, the He 45 was a two-seat general-purpose biplane powered by a 559 kW (750 hp) BMW VI engine. Early production examples were employed mainly as trainers, but subsequent aircraft produced by Heinkel, Gotha,

Heinkel He 51s.

Focke-Wulf and BFW were used by the Luftwaffe for reconnaissance and light bombing duties. Production totalled 512 aircraft.

Data (He 45C): *Engine* as above *Wing span* 11.5 m (37 ft 8¾ in) *Length* 10.6 m (34 ft 9½ in) *Max T-O weight* 2,745 kg (6,051 lb) *Max level speed* 290 km/h (180 mph) *Range* 1,200 km (746 miles) *Armament* one forward-firing 7.9 mm MG 17 and one rear-mounted MG 15 machine-guns, plus up to 300 kg (661 lb) of bombs

Heinkel He 46 (Germany) The He 46 of 1931 was a two-seat armed reconnaissance and army co-operation parasol-wing monoplane, powered in its production form by a 484.4 kW (650 hp) Bramo 322B radial engine. It was one of the main types chosen for the Luftwaffe expansion programme, initiated well before Germany's official announcement of the Air Force's existence. Nearly 480 He 46s were produced, remaining operational with the Luftwaffe on the Eastern Front until 1943. It also served with the Bulgarian and Hungarian Air Forces, and had previously been used by the Nationalist forces during the Spanish Civil War.

Data: *Engine* as above *Wing span* 14.0 m (45 ft 11¼ in) *Length* 9.5 m (31 ft 2 in) *Max T-O weight* 2,300 kg (5,071 lb) *Max level speed* 260 km/h (162 mph) *Range* 1,050 km (653 miles) *Armament* one rear-mounted MG 15 machine-gun, plus 20 × 10 kg bombs

Heinkel He 59.

Heinkel

Luft-Hansa Heinkel He 70.

Heinkel He 50 (Germany) The He 50 was a 484.4 kW (650 hp) Bramo 322B-engined single-seat dive-bomber and two-seat reconnaissance biplane of 1931, production examples of which went into Luftwaffe service and were exported to China and Japan. Luftwaffe He 50As remained operational on the Eastern Front until 1944. Maximum level speed was 235 km/h (146 mph) and armament comprised one forward-firing 7.9 mm MG 17 or one rear-mounted MG 15 machine-gun (dive-bomber and reconnaissance types respectively), plus up to 500 kg (1,102 lb) of bombs.

Heinkel He 60.

Heinkel He 63.

Heinkel He 51 (Germany) Ernst Heinkel, chief designer of Hansa Brandenburg for a number of years, was responsible for the creation of several significant seaplanes which were built by that company during World War I. Following liquidation of Hansa Brandenburg, Heinkel built a series of seaplanes in Sweden, ostensibly for Svenska. In fact this was a ruse to circumvent the ban on all construction of military aircraft in Germany which had been imposed under the terms of the Versailles Treaty.

Following establishment of the new military regime in Germany, Heinkel began the design and construction of aircraft in a factory located at Rostock. There (in 1932) he completed the prototype of a biplane fighter which had the company designation He 49A. A generally similar aircraft with floats, instead of wheel landing gear, was identified as the He 49B. The He 49A design was submitted to the German Air Ministry, which ordered ten pre-production aircraft under the designation He 51, and it was this which became the first single-seat fighter to serve with the new, and then still secret, Luftwaffe.

The He 51 was of composite construction and unequal-span single-bay biplane configuration. The single seat for the pilot was in a cockpit just aft of the wings, and a cut-out in the centre-section of the upper wing was made to enhance the pilot's field of view. Power plant comprised a BMW 12-cylinder in-line engine, and adoption of a minimum cowled section provided a bluff, square look to the fuselage nose. Wheel landing gear of the He 51A was neat and functional, that of the He 51B remarkably clean for a float installation.

Delivery of the first of the He 51A-0 pre-production aircraft began in late 1933, and the type was among those which were sent to take part in the Spanish Civil War in support of the Nationalists. The first batch of aircraft sent to Spain comprised six He 51As and 20 Junkers Ju 52/3ms: these were virtually the foundation aircraft of the Condor Legion. Combat in Spain soon showed that the He 51 was an inferior fighter, but they proved valuable in a close-support role. Because of this they were still in service at the beginning of World War II, being used for a

Spanish Heinkel He 70.

variety of non-combatant duties until 1943. Production versions for the Luftwaffe were the He 51A and He 51C; floatplanes which served with the German Navy had the designation He 51B. Data (He 51A): *Engine* one 559 kW (750 hp) BMW VI *Wing span* 11.0 m (36 ft 1 in) *Length* 8.4 m (27 ft 6¾ in) *Max T-O weight* 1,900 kg (4,189 lb) *Max level speed* 330 km/h (205 mph) *Range* 390 km (242 miles) *Armament* two forward-firing 7.9 mm MG 17 machine-guns

Heinkel He 55 (Germany) The He 55 appeared in 1929 and was a two-seat shipboard flying-boat with foldable equal-span single-bay wings and strengthened for catapulting. Power was provided by a 447 kW (600 hp) Siemens radial engine mounted in a streamlined nacelle and supported on struts above the front cockpit and well forward of the wings. More than 40 were delivered to Russia, where they were given the designation KR-1. Maximum level speed was 194 km/h (120.5 mph).

Heinkel He 56 (Germany) Two-seat reconnaissance biplane of 1932, subsequently developed by Aichi into the E3A1 or Navy Type 15 Reconnaissance Seaplane, which remained in service until Japan's entry into World War II.

Heinkel He 59 (Germany) The He 59 first appeared in 1931 and was a large twin-float biplane powered by two 492 kW (660 hp) BMW VI engines. It was produced in limited numbers as a two- or four-seat reconnaissance and torpedo bomber, although numbers were operated as aircrew and armament trainers and for air-sea rescue. In the latter role it survived into World War II. Maximum level speed was 240 km/h (149 mph).

Heinkel He 60 (Germany) The He 60 entered production in 1933 as a two-seat short-range armed reconnaissance biplane and trainer, powered by a 492 kW (660 hp) BMW VI engine. In its twin-float reconnaissance configuration for catapulting from warships, it remained in service until 1939. It was replaced by the Arado Ar 196. Maximum level speed was 225 km/h (140 mph).

Heinkel He 61 (Germany) Two-seat reconnaissance biplane of 1932 powered by a 492 kW (660 hp) BMW VI engine. A few were exported to China.

Heinkel He 62 (Germany) Two-seat reconnaissance biplane of 1932, a few of which were exported to Japan.

Heinkel He 100V8.

Heinkel He 63 (Germany) Two-seat biplane trainer of 1932 powered by a 179 kW (240 hp) Argus As 10C engine. Ten built.

Heinkel He 64 (Germany) Two-seat sporting and training monoplane powered by a 112 kW (150 hp) Argus As 8R inverted engine. Both cockpits were completely enclosed by a glazed coupé top. Small number were built. Maximum level speed 245 km/h (152 mph).

Heinkel He 70 and He 170 (Germany) The He 70 was produced as a commercial and military high-performance monoplane, powered by a 469.5 kW (630 hp) or 559 kW (750 hp) BMW VI engine. It first flew on 1 December 1932 as a commercial type, accommodating a pilot, navigator and four passengers (an additional folding seat for a passenger was provided behind the pilot). Aft of the passenger cabin was a baggage compartment. The low cantilever wings tapered in chord and thickness and were of spruce construction, planked with plywood. The fuselage was an oval duralumin monocoque, and the landing gear was retractable. Deutsche Luft-Hansa received 14 aircraft, although actual production of the passenger-carrying variants was 28.

Meanwhile the He 70's military potential had not gone unnoticed and, following the delivery to the Luftwaffe of a number of He 70Ds for communications duties, the He 70E and He 70F appeared as three-seat light-bombing and reconnaissance aircraft respectively. Only the F entered production, numbers serving with the Luftwaffe and going to the Condor Legion and the Nationalist forces in Spain during the Civil War. The production total of nearly 300 military He 70s included 18 He 170As exported to Hungary during 1937–38, each of these powered by a 678 kW

Heinkel He 72 Kadet.

Heinkel He 111V2.

Heinkel

Captured Heinkel He 111H.

Heinkel He 111H-6 torpedo-bomber.

(910 hp) Gnome-Rhône 14K Mistral Major radial engine and armed with two 7.8 mm Gebauer machine-guns for defence.

Data (He 70F): *Engine* as above *Wing span* 14.8 m (48 ft 6½ in) *Length* 12.0 m (39 ft 4½ in) *Max T-O weight* 3,460 kg (7,628 lb) *Max level speed* 360 km/h (224 mph) *Range* (with auxiliary fuel tank) 1,400 km (870 miles) *Normal range* 800 km (497 miles)

Heinkel He 72 Kadet (Germany) Appearing in 1933, the He 72 was a two-seat open-cockpit bi-plane for training and aerobatics, usually powered by a 112 kW (150 hp) Siemens Sh.14a radial

engine. Large numbers were produced for the Luftwaffe and for civil flying schools. Maximum speed was 180 km/h (112 mph).

Heinkel He 74 (Germany) Produced as an armed single-seat advanced-training and light-fighter sister to the He 72, the He 74 was powered by a 179 kW (240 hp) Argus As 10C engine. Only a handful were built.

Heinkel He 100 (Germany) Designed as a replacement for the very successful Messerschmitt Bf 109, the He 100 failed to win production orders. Nevertheless the 12 He 100D-1s built were eventually flown by Luftwaffe pilots as home-defence fighters. Power was provided by a Daimler-Benz DB 601 engine. On 30 March 1939 He 100V8 set a new world absolute speed record of 746.604 km/h (463.917 mph) at the hands of Flugkapitän Hans Dieterle.

Heinkel He 111 (Germany) Like a number of German aircraft which were designed and built in the 1930s, the He 111 was planned from the beginning for a dual-purpose role. The first was in a legitimate civil capacity, during which the engines and airframe would be developed to good standards of reliability, or modified as necessary to attain such high standards. The second role was for military usage by the Luftwaffe which, at the period when a number of Germany's most successful wartime aircraft were being designed and/or developed, was still a clandestine organisation.

The prototype – an all-metal low-wing monoplane powered by two 447 kW (600 hp) BMW VI in-line engines – flew for the first time on 24 February 1935. The wings were of semi-elliptical planform, fitted with hydraulically operated

Heinkel He 111Z Zwilling towing an Me 321 Gigant glider.

trailing-edge flaps, the tailwheel-type retractable landing gear also being hydraulically actuated. Very clean in appearance, the prototype (in bomber configuration) was able to accommodate an internal bomb load of 1,000 kg (2,205 lb), and was armed with three machine-guns in nose, dorsal and ventral positions. Flight testing proved that, like some British bomber aircraft of the period, its performance equalled or even bettered that of contemporary fighters.

The second prototype was completed as a civil transport and was handed over to Luft-Hansa following the termination of early testing. Subsequently, this aircraft reverted to being used by the Luftwaffe for secret high-altitude reconnaissance missions. Many such missions were flown prior to the outbreak of World War II, both by military and civil aircraft, so that long before wartime operational missions were flown, the Luftwaffe had acquired very detailed documentation of a vast number of important targets.

The fourth prototype was completed as a civil airliner with accommodation for ten passengers in two cabins. Named *Dresden*, it was delivered to Luft-Hansa on 10 January 1936 and given the full glare of press publicity. Six production airliners, He 111Cs named *Breslau, Karlsruhe, Köln, Königsberg, Leipzig,* and *Nürnberg,* entered service from the summer of 1936.

He 111B-1 production bombers began to enter Luftwaffe service in late 1936 and, like many German military aircraft of that period, were blooded first in the Spanish Civil War, gaining valuable experience. In the case of the He 111 it proved somewhat misleading: since its performance was superior to that of opposing fighter aircraft, it could operate unescorted. Similar tactics, when used against British Hurricanes and Spitfires, proved costly and from that time their deployment over Britain was mainly in the role of a night bomber. The mauling by British fighters meant that, as development progressed, He 111s became more heavily armed. Many had 20 mm cannon and as many as seven machine-guns.

Most extensively built version was the He 111H, with considerably more than 5,000 built before production ended in 1944. Power plant of this version comprised two Junkers Jumo engines, with power ranging from 752.6 kW (1,010 hp) for the Jumo 221A to 1,323.5 kW (1,776 hp) in the Jumo 213A-1s installed in the final production He 111H-23 paratroop carrier. Other roles fulfilled by this exceptional aircraft included torpedo-bomber, launch platform for Hs 293 glider bombs and V-1 flying-bombs, path finding using

Y-Geräte, glider-tug, and with two aircraft 'twinned' (He 111Z Zwilling, with a fifth engine at the new joining centre-section) operated as a tug for the Messerschmitt Me 321 Gigant (Giant) glider.

A remarkable aircraft of long life – which speaks well for the excellence of its basic design – examples of Spanish-built aircraft (constructed by CASA post-war) remained in use for crew training into 1970.

Data (He 111H-16): *Engines* two 1,006 kW (1,350 hp) Junkers Jumo 211F-2 in-lines *Wing span* 22.6 m (74 ft 1¾ in) *Length* 16.4 m (53 ft 9¾ in) *Max T-O weight* 14,000 kg (30,865 lb) *Max level speed* 435 km/h (270 mph) *Range* 1,950 km (1,212 miles) *Armament* one 13 mm MG 131, one MG 81 twin-gun, one MG FF cannon, plus a bomb load of up to 2,000 kg (4,409 lb)

Heinkel He 112B-Os, thirty of which were built for evaluation against the Messerschmitt Bf 109. Many of these were flown in 1938 by Nationalist forces fighting in Spain.

Heinkel He 114A-2s.

Heinkel He 114 (Germany) The He 114 was a two-seat reconnaissance seaplane, originally intended for catapult operations from ships of the German Navy. Power was provided by a BMW 132 engine. A limited number were produced and served into the war as coastal-patrol and reconnaissance aircraft. A few were also exported to Romania and Sweden. Maximum level speed 335 km/h (208 mph).

Heinkel He 115 (Germany) the first prototype He·115 flew in early 1938 and in March set eight world speed records. As a result orders were placed for the German naval air arm by Sweden and Norway, eventually totalling more than 300 aircraft. These were used as reconnaissance, torpedo-carrying and mine-laying seaplanes. The

Heinkel

Heinkel He 115B-1/R-2.

**Heinkel He 162A-2
Salamander.**

He 115 was the first German aircraft adapted to carry the magnetic mine.
Data (He 115B): *Engine* two 671 kW (900 hp) BMW 132Ns *Wing span* 23.15 m (75 ft 10 in) *Length* 17.38 m (57 ft 0 in) *Max T-O weight* 9,100 kg (20,062 lb) *Max level speed* 350 km/h (217 mph) *Range* 2,100 km (1,305 miles) *Armament* two 7.9 mm MG 15 machine-guns, plus an 800 kg torpedo or 1,000 kg (2,205 lb) of bombs
Heinkel He 116 (Germany) Long-range mail and freight-carrying airliner of 1937, powered by four 179 kW (240 hp) Hirth HM 508 engines. A small number were built, operators including Deutsche Luft-Hansa and Manchuria Airtransport.

Heinkel He 116.

Heinkel He 118 (Germany) see **Junkers Ju 87**
Heinkel He 162 Salamander (Germany) Popularly known as the 'Volksjäger' (People's Fighter) but best remembered by the name Salamander, the He 162 turbojet-powered single-seat fighter was designed to employ as little strategic material as possible, which by 1944 was in short supply.

Design work on the fighter started on 23 September 1944 and the first prototype flew on 6 December 1944. On the second flight the leading edge of the wing collapsed and the prototype broke up in the air. This did not seriously hinder the development programme and, after modifications were made to the wings, the He 162

went into large-scale production in widely dispersed assembly plants, many underground. However only 116 He 162As had been completed by Germany's capitulation and few were operational.
Data (He 162A): *Engine* one 7.83 kN (1,760 lb st) BMW 003-1 or -2 turbojet *Wing span* 7.2 m (23 ft 7¾ in) *Length* 9.05 m (29 ft 8½ in) *Max T-O weight* 2,700 kg (5,953 lb) *Max level speed* 840 km/h (522 mph) *Range* 220–1,000 km (137–621 miles) *Armament* two 20 mm MG 151 cannon
Heinkel He 170 (Germany) see **Heinkel He 70**
Heinkel He 176 (Germany) Single-seat experimental aeroplane powered by a 5.89 kN (1,324 lb st) Walter HWK-R1 203 rocket motor (see **Chronology** 15 June 1939).

Heinkel He 177 Greif (Germany) Four years of development preceded the first production orders for the He 177, the first prototype of which had flown in November 1939. It was a heavy bomber, introducing an entirely new type of power plant in which four Daimler-Benz 12-cylinder inverted engines were grouped together in pairs, each pair driving a single propeller. Many prototypes were built, most of which displayed obvious shortcomings including dangerous diving characteristics, landing gear and structural weaknesses, and problems associated with the engines including persistent crankshaft torsional vibration, lubrication and propeller troubles: two prototypes broke up in the air and at least one caught fire.

Following a brief period of use as an emergency transport aircraft on the Eastern Front, during which time several caught fire and so earned the nickname 'Flaming Coffin', the Greif began its operational career in October 1943 on anti-convoy and U-boat co-operation duties. It took part (sub-types A-3 and A-5) in attacks on England in January 1944, known as the 'Little Blitz', but as the war progressed was used to a greater extent as a missile carrier for anti-shipping duties. As the end of the war approached fewer and fewer Greifs remained operational: shortages of fuel and trouble with the engines grounding large numbers.

Although a small number of twin-finned He 177Bs were built in early 1944, most of the 1,160 or so Greifs produced were A-series types, although it is doubtful whether more than about 200 became fully operational in all respects. The He 177A-0 was the pilot production model, powered by two DB 606 engines (made up of four DB 601s). Armament comprised two 13 mm MG 131s in dorsal and tail positions, one 7.9 mm MG 81 in the nose, two 7.9 mm MG 81s in a ventral

Captured Heinkel He 177 Greif.

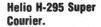

Heinkel He 280.

position facing aft and a 20 mm MG FF cannon firing forward from a 'chin' position, plus 48 × 70 kg, ten 500 kg, six 1,000 kg, or two 2,500 kg bombs. The He 177A-1 was similar except for defensive armament, while the He 177A-3 had two DB 610 power units (four DB 605 engines), airframe changes and was equipped to carry two Hs 293 glider missiles. The final major version, the He 177A-5, was equipped to carry three Hs 293, two Hs 294 or two PC 1400 Fritz X (armour-piercing) radio-controlled missiles.

Data (He 177A-5): *Engines* two 2,198 kW (2,950 hp) Daimler-Benz DB 610A-1s and B-1s (see text) *Wing span* 31.44 m (103 ft 1¾ in) *Length* 22.0 m (72 ft 2 in) *Max T-O weight* 31,000 kg (68,343 lb) *Max level speed* 488 km/h (303 mph) *Range* 4,000–5,500 km (2,485–3,418 miles) *Armament* three 7.9 mm MG 81J and three 13 mm MG 131 machine-guns, two 20 mm MG 151 cannon, plus bombs or missiles

fuel, was developing about 4.89 kW (1,100 lb st). In Britain the world's first turbojet aircraft engine had been bench-run on 12 April 1937. Of particular interest is the fact that the work of von Ohain and Whittle was entirely independent.

The He 178 was designed to utilise von Ohain's power plant. It was a shoulder-wing monoplane of composite construction. The engine was mounted in the fuselage, with a nose air-intake duct passing beneath the pilot's seat and a long tailpipe discharging from the fuselage tailcone. Retractable tailwheel-type landing gear was installed. A research aircraft only, the He 178 was donated to the Air Museum in Berlin where it was destroyed during a wartime air raid.

Data: *Engine* one HeS 3b turbojet of about 5.34 kN (1,200 lb st) *Wing span* 7.2 m (23 ft 7½ in) *Length* 7.48 m (24 ft 6½ in) *Max T-O weight* 1,998 kg (4,405 lb) *Cruising speed* 580 km/h (360 mph)

Heinkel He 178.

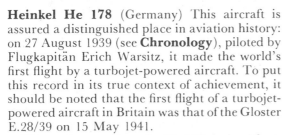

Heinkel He 178 (Germany) This aircraft is assured a distinguished place in aviation history: on 27 August 1939 (see **Chronology**), piloted by Flugkapitän Erich Warsitz, it made the world's first flight by a turbojet-powered aircraft. To put this record in its true context of achievement, it should be noted that the first flight of a turbojet-powered aircraft in Britain was that of the Gloster E.28/39 on 15 May 1941.

The engine to power the He 178 derived from the pioneering research work of Dr Hans Pabst von Ohain who (together with his assistant Max Hahn) had been employed by Ernst Heinkel in March 1936 and provided with the necessary facilities to continue the development of his work. By September 1937 a hydrogen-fuelled demonstration engine was being run on the bench, and in March 1938 his HeW 3 engine, using petrol as

Helio H-295 Super Courier.

505

Heinkel

Helio Stallion Model
550A.

Heinkel He 219 Uhu (Germany) The He 219 was designed in 1940–41 as a high-altitude and high-performance twin-engined interceptor but was modified into a specialised night fighter. The first prototype flew in 15 November 1942 and production aircraft went into service in the summer of 1943. It is believed that about 290 of all versions were built.

Data (He 219A-7): *Engines* two 1,416 kW (1,900 hp) Daimler-Benz DB 603Gs *Wing span* 18.5 m (60 ft 8 in) *Length* 15.5 m (50 ft 11¾ in) *Max T-O weight* 15,300 kg (33,731 lb) *Max level speed* 670 km/h (416.5 mph) *Range* 2,000 km (1,243 miles) *Armament* two 20 mm MG 151 machine-guns, four 30 mm MK 108 and two 30 mm MK 103 cannon *Accommodation* two crew

Heinkel He 280 (Germany) Single-seat jet-propelled fighter developed in parallel to the Messerschmitt Me 262. Prototypes only.

Helio Courier, Super Courier, Strato Courier and Trigear Courier (USA) The Helioplane

Four or Courier prototype was derived from the Koppen-Bollinger two-seat lightplane (an extensively rebuilt Piper Vagabond, first flown in 1949) and production aircraft appeared in 1954. The improved five-seat H-391B Courier was followed by the H-392 Strato Courier, intended mainly for high-altitude photographic work, and the six-seat Courier Model H-250 of 1964. The latter was generally similar to the Super Courier (see below), except for having a 186.3 kW (250 hp) Lycoming O-540-A1A5 flat-six engine. The original H-395 and H-395A versions of the Super Courier six-seat light STOL personal, corporate and utility monoplane appeared from 1958. Three were supplied to the USAF for evaluation, under the designation L-28A. Further substantial orders were received subsequently, some aircraft being assigned to Tactical Air Command for counter-insurgency duties.

The final commercial versions of the Courier to be produced were the Super Courier Model H-295 with a non-retractable tailwheel landing gear and the Trigear Courier Model HT-295 with a non-retractable tricycle-type landing gear. The prototype H-295 flew for the first time on 24 February 1965. Production deliveries of the Trigear Courier began in 1974.

USAF Super Couriers were produced in three versions: the U-10A standard version with a Lycoming GO-480-G1D6 engine and 227 litres (60 US gallons) of fuel; the U-10B long-range version with twice the internal fuel capacity and paratroop doors as standard; and the U-10D improved long-range version, with provision for an aerial camera and sound broadcasting equipment. Military Couriers are currently operated by Peru and Super Couriers by the USAF (more than 100 of all versions acquired) and Thailand.

Data (U-10B): *Engine* one 220 kW (295 hp)

Helwan HA-300.

Lycoming GO-480-G1D6 *Wing span* 11.89 m
(39 ft 0 in) *Length* 9.45 m (31 ft 0 in) *Max T-O
weight* 1,542 kg (3,400 lb) *Max level speed* 269 km/h
(167 mph) *Range* 1,062 km (660 miles) *Accommodation* pilot and five passengers or freight

Helio Stallion Model H-550A (USA) Design of
the turboprop Stallion 8–10-seat general-utility
STOL transport was started in July 1963 and the
prototype first flew on 5 June 1964. Construction
of the first production version (the Model
H-550A) began in 1966. This had full-span automatic leading-edge slats, an augmented lateral
control system, slotted flaps to enhance STOL
performance, and a crash-resistant cabin structure. An armed version was also produced with
the USAF designation AU-24A for armed reconnaissance, COIN operations, close air support
and other special missions including forward air
control. A small number of AU-24As were supplied to Cambodia by the USAF.

Helitec (Sikorsky) S-55T (USA) Turbine-powered conversion of the Sikorsky S-55, fitted
with a 626 kW (840 shp) Garrett-AiResearch
TSE 331-3U-303 turboshaft engine (derated to
485 kW; 650 shp).

Helwan Al-Kahira (Egypt) Name given to the
Hispano HA-200 Saeta tandem two-seat
advanced trainer built under licence in Egypt.

Helwan HA-300 (Egypt) Prototype supersonic
jet fighter, first flown in March 1964.

Hendy Heck (UK) Last product of the Hendy
Company, completed in 1934 as a two-seat high-performance cabin monoplane. Preceded by the
Hobo and Model 302 (entered in the King's Cup
Air Race of 1930). In 1935 the Heck was flown in
record time from Cape Town (South Africa) to
Lympne (England). A small number were produced by Parnall Aircraft.

Henschel Hs 123 (Germany) Designed as an
interim dive bomber until an aircraft of the Junkers Ju 87 class was available for squadron service,
the prototype single-seat Hs 123 biplane first flew
in 1935. Hs 123A-1 production aircraft entered
Luftwaffe service from October of that year. In
the following year a number were evaluated in
Spain as an element of the Nationalist forces
fighting in the Civil War. These proved particularly successful for ground attack. With the outbreak of World War II many Hs 123s were still in
first-line service with the Luftwaffe as ground-attack aircraft and these participated in the campaigns against Poland, Belgium, France and then
Russia – where they continued to operate until the
middle of 1944.
Data: *Engine* one 656 kW (880 hp) BMW 132Dc
radial *Wing span* 10.5 m (34 ft 5¼ in) *Length*
8.33 m (27 ft 4 in) *Normal T-O weight* 2,217 kg
(4,888 lb) *Max level speed* 341 km/h (212 mph)
Range 860 km (534 miles) *Armament* two 7.9 mm
MG 17 machine-guns, plus one 250 kg bomb as a
dive bomber or four 50 kg bombs, 92 anti-personnel bombs or two cannon for ground-attack
role

Henschel Hs 126 (Germany) Adequate information of an enemy's positions, reserves, movements and supplies has long been a vital factor in
war. Before the outbreak of World War II Germany's Col-Gen Baron von Fritsch had predicted: 'The next war will be won by the military
organisation with the most efficient photographic
reconnaissance.' It is not surprising, therefore,
that Germany made special efforts to have adequate photo-reconnaissance aircraft with which to
fight the coming war.

One of the most important in the early years of
the war was the Henschel Hs 126 short-range
reconnaissance aircraft: the first all-metal aircraft
of this type to enter service with the Luftwaffe.
This evolved from the earlier Hs 122 design of
1935, but the Hs 126 was developed to offer
improved performance and handling characteristics. Of parasol-wing configuration with an absolute minimum of supporting and bracing struts, it
had a strut-braced tail unit and tailwheel-type
landing gear with streamlined cantilever main-gear struts. Initial production Hs 126A-1s were

Hendy 302.

Henschel Hs 123.

Henschel Hs 126.

Henschel Hs 129.

Heston A.2/45.

Hiller Model 12E-L3.

Heston Phoenix Series II.

into service on the Russian Front in 1942. The original Hs 129A was fitted with two Argus As 410A 12-cylinder inverted-Vee air-cooled engines driving Argus automatic controllable-pitch propellers. This was later superseded by the Hs 129B series with two French-built 492 kW (660 hp) Gnome-Rhône 14M 04/05 radial engines driving Ratier propellers.

The Hs 129B-1 and B-2 were the major production variants, the latter fitted to carry a drop-tank. Some were equipped experimentally with the SG 113A recoilless gun installation: a battery of six

powered by the 656 kW (880 hp) BMW 132Dc radial engine. Accommodation was provided for a pilot and observer/gunner.

At the beginning of the war the Hs 126 was in service with most of the Luftwaffe's army co-operation reconnaissance units, used for both day and night sorties over battle areas. Used extensively and successfully at the beginning of the Russian campaign, they were later to meet severe opposition and often could be operated only with fighter escort. By early 1943 they were almost completely superseded by more advanced types, thereafter being used as glider tugs and for training.

Data (Hs 126B-1): *Engine* one 633.4 kW (850 hp) BMW Bramo-Fafnir 323A-1 or Q-1 radial *Wing span* 14.5 m (47 ft 6¾ in) *Length* 10.85 m (35 ft 7¼ in) *Max T-O weight* 3,090 kg (6,812 lb) *Max level speed* 311 km/h (193 mph) *Range* 700 km (435 miles) *Armament* one forward-firing 7.9 mm MG 17 machine-gun and one rear-mounted MG 15 machine-gun, plus ten 10 kg bombs carried in two fixed containers in place of camera, when required

Henschel Hs 129 (Germany) The Hs 129 was designed solely for ground attack and first went

75 mm smooth-bore tubes, each 1.6 m (5 ft 3 in) long, mounted in the fuselage at an angle slightly beyond the vertical to fire downwards and rearwards. The weapon was intended for use against tanks and was triggered automatically when the aircraft flew over a tank at low altitude. A total of more than 800 Hs 129s were built.

Data (Hs 129B-2): *Engines* as above *Wing span* 13.5 m (44 ft 6 in) *Length* 9.75 m (31 ft 11¾ in) *Max T-O weight* 5,250 kg (11,574 lb) *Max level speed* 408 km/h (254 mph) *Normal range* 560 km (345 miles) *Armament* one 20 mm MG 151 cannon and one 7.9 mm MG 17 machine-gun on each side of the fuselage nose and firing forward, and one 30 mm MK 101 cannon under the fuselage. As an alternative to the 30 mm cannon, the Hs 123B-1/R3 carried a battery of four 7.9 mm MG 17 machine-guns. Some models carried a total of 350 kg (772 lb) of bombs in place of the 30 mm cannon or four 7.9 mm guns

Henson Aerial Steam Carriage (UK) The model Steam Carriage of 1847 (see **Chronology**) was followed by a designed full-size version with a wing span of 45.72 m (150 ft 0 in) and powered by one 22.35 kW (30 hp) Henson steam engine driving two pusher propellers.

Heston Type 5 Special (UK) 1,714 kW (2,300 hp) Napier Sabre-engined racing aircraft, first flown on 12 June 1940. Although designed to establish a new world speed record, it made a forced landing because of cooling problems and was destroyed.

Heston A.2/45 (UK) Prototype two-seat air observation post powered by a 179 kW (240 hp) de Havilland Gipsy Queen 33 engine mounted as a pusher.

Heston Phoenix (UK) Five-seat braced high-wing cabin monoplane of 1935 with a retractable landing gear and powered by a 149 kW (200 hp) de Havilland Gipsy Six engine.

Hiller YH-32s.

Hiller UH-12/Model 360 and H-23 Raven (USA) Originally built as the Model 360, this light utility helicopter was later known as the UH-12 while produced under the company name United Helicopters and subsequently just Model 12 under Hiller Aircraft parentage. Commercial variants began with the Model 12 powered by one 133 kW (178 hp) Franklin 6V4-178-B33 piston engine, followed by 149 kW (200 hp) or 156.5 kW (210 hp) Franklin-engined Models 12A, B and C. The latter was the first to introduce the 'goldfish-bowl' canopy.

The initial versions of the Model 12E were the 12E-L3 and 12E-SL3 with 227.5 kW (305 hp) VO-540-C2B and 235 kW (315 hp) TIVO-540-

A2A turbocharged engines respectively. The Model E4 also featured a lengthened fuselage to accommodate a pilot and a rear bench seat for three passengers, and introduced stabilising tail surfaces. The H-23 Raven was the military version of the UH-12, produced under several designations for the US forces, including OH-23B and OH-23G. Examples were also exported, but few remain operational today.

In January 1973 Hiller Aviation acquired from Fairchild Industries (which had amalgamated with Hiller) the design rights, production tooling and spares of the Hiller 12E and has put it back into production as the three-seat UH-12E basic model with a 253.5 kW (340 hp) Lycoming VO-540 piston engine and the four-seat UH-12E-4 turbine version with a 298 kW (400 shp) Allison 250-C20 turboshaft engine (derated to 224 kW; 301 shp). Altogether more than 2,200 aircraft of the whole series have been completed.

Data (UH-12E): *Engine* as above *Main rotor diameter* 10.8 m (35 ft 5 in) *Length of fuselage* 8.69 m (28 ft 6 in) *Max T-O weight* 1,270 kg (2,800 lb) *Cruising speed* 145 km/h (90 mph) *Range* 346 km (215 miles)

Hiller Model E4.

Hiller HJ-1 Hornet (USA) Two-seat ramjet-powered helicopter, 12 of which were produced for the US Army and three for the US Navy under the designations YH-32 and HOE-1 respectively.

Hiller X-18 (USA) Experimental tilt-wing convertiplane, first flown as a conventional aeroplane on 24 November 1959. Power was provided by two 4,359 kW (5,850 eshp) Allison T40-A-14 turboprop engines, driving six-bladed Curtiss-Wright contra-rotating propellers, plus a Westinghouse J34 turbojet engine. Data provided by the X-18 was used in the development of the XC-142A tilt-wing aircraft.

Hiller H-23F Raven.

Fairchild (Hiller) FH-1100/OH-5A (USA) See **Fairchild Industries**

Hill Hummer (USA) Single-seat ultra-light monoplane, plans and kits of parts for which are available to amateur constructors.

Hindenburg

Hispano HA-43 (Spain) Two-seat advanced trainer powered by a 290.6 kW (390 hp) Armstrong Siddeley Cheetah 27 radial engine. Produced in 1947 for the Spanish Air Force.

Hispano HA-100 Triana (Spain) Two-seat advanced-flying and armament trainer produced to replace the Spanish Air Force's HS-42 and HA-43 trainers. First post-war Hispano aircraft designed under the direction of Willi Messerschmitt. The first prototype flew on 10 December 1954. An initial batch of 40 HA-100-E1s were ordered.

Hindenburg (Germany) LZ 129 or *Hindenburg* is the best remembered of all Zeppelin airships because of its tragic end on 6 May 1937 when it caught fire at Lakehurst, New Jersey (USA) with the loss of 35 lives out of a total of 97 crew and passengers. Launched in 1936, it was 245 m (804 ft) long and powered by four 894 kW (1,200 hp) Mercedes Benz engines. Prior to the accident it had made 62 flights, 36 of which were ocean crossings.

Hiro G2H1 (Japan) Twin-engined medium bomber, eight of which were built from 1935 for the Japanese Navy.

Hirtenberg HS.9 (Austria) Two-seat touring and training parasol-wing monoplane of 1935 powered by a 93 kW (125 hp) Siemens Sh.14a (HS.9) or de Havilland Gipsy Major engine (HS.9A). Maximum level speed was 190 km/h (118 mph). Other Hirtenberg types that were not series produced included the HS.10 three-seat light cabin monoplane; HA.11 twin-engined amphibious flying-boat; HAM.11 military version of the HA.11; HV.12 twin-engined light commercial transport; HM.13 single-engined two-seat general-purpose military biplane; HV.15 twin-engined 4–6-seat commercial monoplane; HM.15 military version of the HV.15; and HS.16 single-seat military training monoplane.

Hispano HA-200 Saeta and HA-220 Super Saeta (Spain) First flown in 1955, the Saeta is an advanced flying and instrument trainer and is currently operated by the air forces of Spain (designated E.14) and Egypt. The HA-200A was the initial production version for Spanish service, powered by two 3.92 kN (880 lb st) Turboméca Marboré IIA turbojet engines and armed with two 7.62 mm machine-guns and underwing rockets. The HA-200B is similar but armed with one 20 mm cannon. This version was produced for Egyptian service, being built in Spain and under licence in Egypt as the Al-Kahira. The improved HA-200D for Spanish use has uprated equipment and heavier armament.

The HA-220 Super Saeta was first flown in 1970 and is a single-seat specialised ground-attack version powered by two 4.71 kN (1,058 lb st) Marboré VI turbojet engines. It is operated by the Spanish Air Force as the C.10-C. Data (HA-220 Super Saeta): *Engines* as above *Wing span* (over tip-tanks) 10.93 m (35 ft 10 in) *Length* 8.97 m (29 ft 5 in) *Max T-O weight* 3,700 kg (8,157 lb) *Max level speed* 700 km/h (435 mph) *Range* 1,700 km (1,055 miles) *Armament* can be equipped with a variety of guns, rockets and bombs on two underfuselage and four underwing attachments

Hispano HA-1109 Buchón (Spain) Messerschmitt Bf 109 built under licence in Spain by Hispano and fitted with an Hispano HS-12Z or Rolls-Royce Merlin engine (a full list of versions appears in the 1957–58 *Jane's*).

Hispano HS-42 (Spain) First flown in March 1947, this was a two-seat advanced trainer powered by one 290.6 kW (390 hp) Armstrong Siddeley Cheetah 25 engine. Produced for the Spanish Air Force.

Hitachi T.2 (Japan) Two-seat light training sesquiplane of the early 1940s powered by one 134 kW (180 hp) Jimpu 3 radial engine.

Hitachi T.R.1 (Japan) Twin 179 kW (240 hp) Kamikaze 5A radial-engined six-seat commercial monoplane of the early 1940s.

Hönningstad 5A Finnmark (Norway) Twelve-passenger (plus two crew) amphibious flying-boat, first flown in September 1949. Power was provided by two 447 kW (600 hp) Pratt & Whitney Wasp R-1340-S1H1 radial engines mounted in the leading edges of the wings. One built which was operated by VLS.

Hopfner HA-1133 (Austria) Four-seat twin-engined amphibious flying-boat of the early 1930s.

Hopfner HS-528 (Austria) School and sporting parasol-wing monoplane of latter 1920s powered by a 44.7 kW (60 hp) Walter engine.

Hopfner HS-829 and HS-932 (Austria) The HS-829 was a school and sporting light parasol-wing monoplane powered by an 82 kW (110 hp) Walter Venus or similar engine. The HS-932 was a more powerful and modernised development of the previous type of two-seater.

Hopfner HS-1033 (Austria) Three-seat cabin monoplane developed from the HS-932. Power was provided normally by a 97 kW (130 hp) de Havilland Gipsy Major. The Hopfner Company operated a taxi and joy-riding service with aircraft of its own design.

Hopfner HV-3 (Austria) Single example of a four-passenger high-wing commercial monoplane of 1927 powered by a 171.4 kW (230 hp) Hiero engine and very similar in appearance to the Fokker F.III. Operated on commercial services between Vienna and Munich.

Hopfner HV-428 (Austria) Four-seat commercial monoplane powered by a 179 kW (240 hp) BMW IV engine.

Hopfner HV-628 (Austria). Single example of a six-seat commercial cabin monoplane of 1928 powered by a 171.4/223.6 kW (240/300 hp) Walter Castor radial engine. Operated by Aero St Gallen.

Hovey Whing Ding II (WD-II) (USA) Single-seat ultra-light biplane, plans of which are available to amateur constructors: more than 6,000 sets sold by 1979.

Howard 250, 350 and 500 (USA) The Howard Aero 250 and 350 were conversions or re-manufactured examples of the Lockheed PV-1 Ventura for sale as executive transports, powered by two 1,006 kW (1,350 hp) Wright R-1820-56A and 1,863 kW (2,500 hp) Pratt & Whitney R-2800 CB-17 engines respectively. The Howard 500 was produced as a new aircraft, although

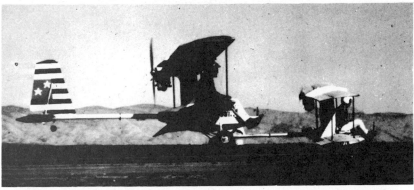

Hovey Whing Ding IIs.

retaining the general lines and power plant of the Model 350. First flown in September 1959, it was a pressurised 10–14-passenger aircraft. The first production example flew on 15 March 1960.

Howard DGA-8 (USA) A 1936 four-seat commercial version of *Mr Mulligan*, an aircraft which won the 1935 Bendix Trophy Race from Los Angeles to Cleveland.

Howard DGA-9 (USA) A 1937 model of the DGA-8 powered by a 212.4 kW (285 hp) Jacobs L-5 engine instead of the former aircraft's 238.5 kW (320 hp) Wright R-760-E2 engine. Success of these aircraft resulted in the formation of the Howard Aircraft Corporation.

Howard 500.

Howard DGA-11 and DGA-12 (USA) Versions of the DGA-9 with 335.3 kW (450 hp) Pratt & Whitney Wasp Junior and 223.6 kW (300 hp) Jacobs L-6 engines respectively.

Howard DGA-15 and Nightingale (USA) The DGA-15 was designed as a four–five-seat cabin monoplane powered by a 261 kW (350 hp) Wright R-760-E2 (DGA-15W), 335.3 kW (450 hp) Pratt & Whitney Wasp Junior (DGA-15P) or 223.6 kW (300 hp) Jacobs L-6 engine (DGA-15J). During 1943 the company ceased production of commercial aircraft to manufacture the DGA-15 for the US Navy as a

Howard DGA-3 *Pete* racer with a 67 kW (90 hp) Wright Gipsy engine.

Howard DGA-15P seaplane.

Huff-Daland AT-1, TA-2, TA-6 and TW-5 (USA) In 1921 the USAAS received three Huff-Daland TA-2 biplane trainers powered by 74.5 kW (100 hp) Anzani engines. These were followed by a single 149 kW (200 hp) Lawrence J-1-powered TA-6 and five 134 kW (180 hp) Wright-Hispano E-2-powered TW-5 trainers. In 1924 Huff-Daland delivered 11 more TW-5s, all being redesignated AT-1s (see also **Keystone**).

Hughes H-1 (USA) Hughes Aircraft was founded in 1935. The H-1 was its first product and was a single-seat racing monoplane powered by a 522/745 kW (700/1,000 hp) Pratt & Whitney R-1535-SA1G Twin Wasp Junior radial engine.

Hughes XF-11.

Wasp Junior-engined four-seat personnel transport (GH-1); ambulance (GH-2 and GH-3); and instrument trainer (NH-1). In addition the US Army acquired a number of civil aircraft as UC-70As (DGA-12), UC-70Bs (DGA-15J), UC-70Cs (DGA-8) and UC-70Ds (DGA-9). Military versions were known as Nightingale.

HTM FJ-Skytrac and Skyraider (Germany) Lightweight multi-purpose helicopters, the former two-seater received German certification in 1969 and the latter four-seater first flew in 1974. Production ceased because of financial difficulties.

Huff-Daland HN-1, HN-2 and HO-1 (USA) The HN-1 and HN-2 were two-seat training biplanes powered by 134 kW (180 hp) Wright-Hispano E-2 and 149 kW (200 hp) Lawrence J-1 engines respectively. Three of each type were delivered to the US Navy in 1923, together with three HO-1 observation derivatives.

On 13 September 1935 Howard Hughes set a speed record in the H-1 of 567.115 km/h (352.388 mph).

Hughes XF-11 (USA) Prototype long-range photographic-reconnaissance aircraft designed during World War II but not completed until the summer of 1946.

Hughes XH-17 (USA) Experimental helicopter designed to prove the pressure-jet propulsion system. First flown on 23 October 1952.

Hughes XV-9A (USA) Research helicopter utilising a hot-cycle propulsion system. First flown in November 1964.

Hughes H-4 Hercules (USA) The 180-ton Hercules was the largest flying-boat ever built and made just one flight at the hands of Howard Hughes on 2 November 1947, covering a distance of about 1.6 km (1 mile) over Los Angeles Harbor, California. Powered by eight 2,236 kW (3,000 hp) Pratt & Whitney R-4360 engines, it had a wing span of 97.54 m (320 ft).

Hughes Model 269 and Model 300 (USA) Following reorganisation of Hughes Tool Company as the Summa Corporation in the early 1970s, its former Aircraft Division became known as Hughes Helicopters.

Design and development of the Model 269 two-seat helicopter began in 1955 and the first of two prototypes flew in October of the following year. Five pre-production Model 269As for the US Army were evaluated as YHO-2HU command and observation helicopters. Deliveries to commercial customers began in October 1961. The Model 269A was selected by the US Army in mid-1964 as a light helicopter primary trainer and 792 were built under the designation TH-55A Osage.

Hughes XH-17.

Heinkel He 111.

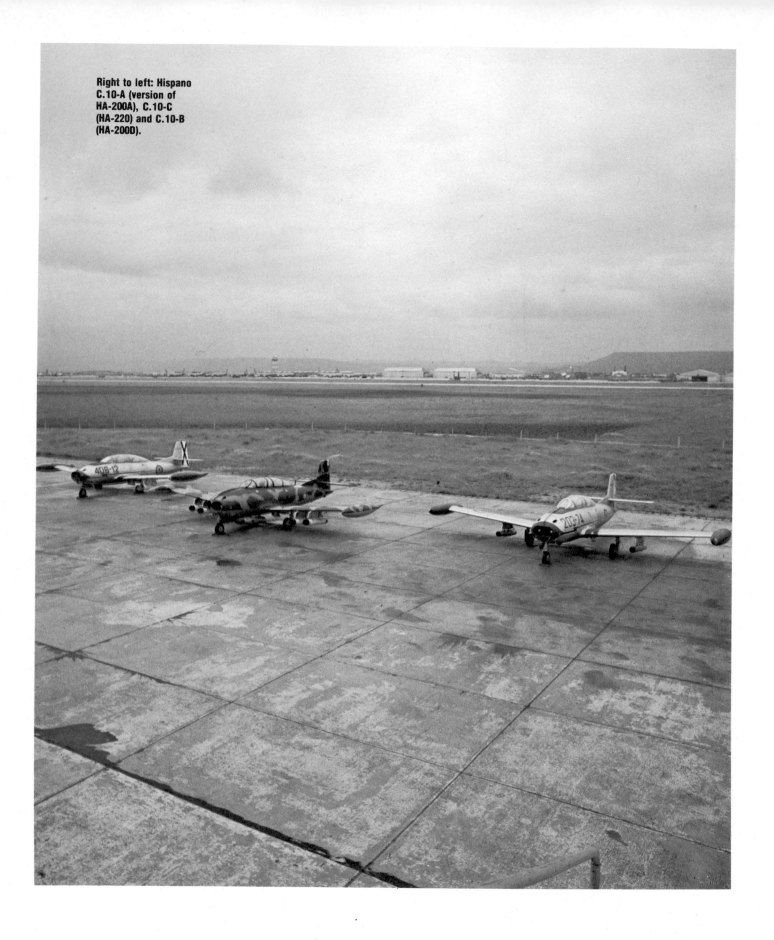

Right to left: Hispano
C.10-A (version of
HA-200A), C.10-C
(HA-220) and C.10-B
(HA-200D).

Howard DGA-15P.

Hunting Pembroke C(PR).1.

IAI Kfir.

Ilyushin Il-2 Shturmovik.

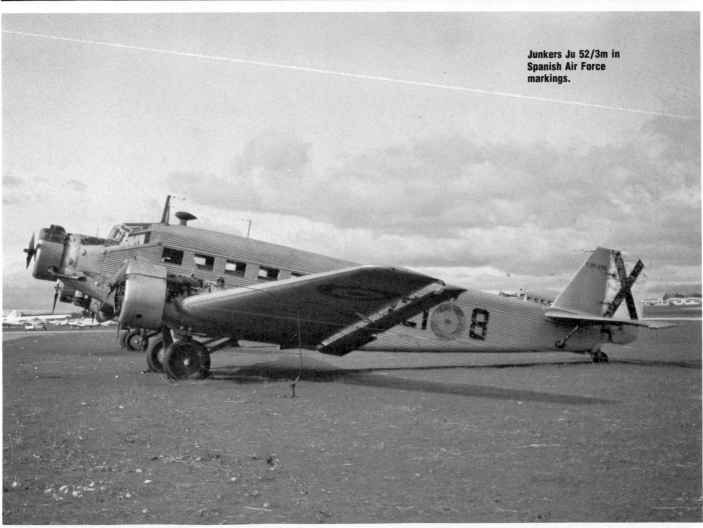

Junkers Ju 52/3m in Spanish Air Force markings.

Junkers Ju 88D-1.

Kamov Ka-26.

Let Super Aero 45.

The Model 300 was developed originally as the Model 269B. Production began in 1964 and those delivered from 1967 were fitted with quiet tail rotors (QTR). The Model 300C is the current production version with improvements to allow a 45% increase in payload. The first production example flew in December 1969 and more than 550 had been delivered by January 1979. It is also manufactured in Italy by BredaNardi. A specially equipped Model 300C is available for police patrol and is known as the Sky Knight.

Following the research that produced a modified version of the OH-6A known as 'The Quiet One', Hughes used similar techniques to develop a quiet version of the Model 300 as the Model 300CQ. In this configuration emission of audible sound is 75% less than with earlier models, and the necessary modifications can be fitted to existing 300Cs.

Data (Model 300C): *Engine* one 142 kW (190 hp) Lycoming HIO-360-D1A *Main rotor diameter* 8.18 m (26 ft 10 in) *Length overall* 9.4 m (30 ft 10 in) *Max T-O weight* 930 kg (2,050 lb) *Max cruising speed* 169 km/h (105 mph) *Range* 370 km (230 miles) *Accommodation* three persons, plus 45 kg (100 lb) of baggage.

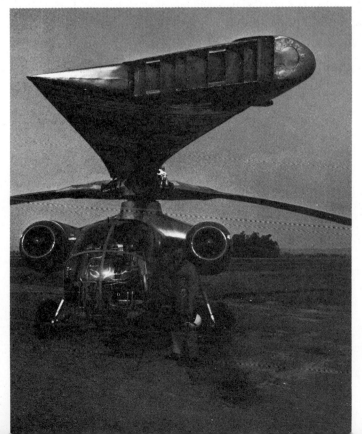

Hughes OH-6 Cayuse, Model 500M and Model 500M-D Defender (USA) Military versions of the Model 500 operated as light observation, anti-submarine and multi-mission helicopters. The US Army received 1,434 examples under the designation OH-6A, all delivered by August 1970. In 1971 Hughes announced a modified version known as 'The Quiet One', claimed to be the world's quietest helicopter. The Model 500M is an uprated version of the OH-6A which is available to foreign customers. Deliveries began to the Colombian Air Force in April 1968 and examples are currently in service with Japan, Argentina, Denmark, Spain, Mexico and the Philippines. Those delivered to the Spanish Navy for ASW duties have AN/ASQ-81 MAD and can carry two Mk 44 torpedoes.

Hughes XV-9A.

Hughes Model 269As under construction.

The Model 500M-D Defender is a multi-role version of the Model 500D, suitable for training, command and control, scout, light-attack, anti-submarine, troop or casualty transport and logistical support missions. It can carry up to seven people or two stretchers and a crew of two. Four versions are currently available as the 500M-D Standard Scout, able to carry a variety of alternative weapons including 14 × 2.75 in rockets and either a 7.62 mm Minigun, a 40 mm grenade launcher, a 7.62 mm chain gun or a 30 mm chain gun; 500M-D/TOW anti-tank version armed with four TOW missiles; 500M-D Quiet Advanced Scout with added quietening kit and Martin Marietta mast-mounted sight; and 500 M-D/ASW for anti-submarine warfare and surface-search missions.

The Model 500M-D is the subject of a building programme in South Korea. By June 1979 a total of 75 Scouts and 25 TOW-equipped Defenders had been delivered, with the local content progressing from assembly to full manufacture; another 48 were then in production. Israel has ordered 30 of the TOW version from the USA and

Hughes XV-9A hot-cycle rotor system.

Hughes Model 300.

Hughes Model 500M-D Defender.

Hughes OH-6A.

Kenya was to receive 32 Defenders. The Taiwanese Navy has also received 12 Defenders equipped with search radar and torpedoes.

Data (OH-6A Cayuse): *Engine* one 236.5 kW (317 shp) Allison T63-A-5A turboshaft *Main rotor diameter* 8.03 m (26 ft 4 in) *Length of fuselage* 7.01 m (23 ft 0 in) *Overload max T-O weight* 1,225 kg (2,700 lb) *Max cruising speed* 241 km/h (150 mph) *Normal range* 611 km (380 miles)

Hughes Model 500 and Model 500C (USA) First flown in prototype form in 1963, the Model 500 is the standard commercial version powered by one 236.5 kW (317 shp) Allison 250-C18A turboshaft engine (derated to 181 kW; 243 shp). The Model 500C is similar except for the installation of a 298 kW (400 shp) engine for improved hot-day/altitude performance. RACA of Argentina, BredaNardi of Italy and Kawasaki of Japan are building Model 500/500Cs under licence. Maximum cruising speed of the Model 500C is 232 km/h (144 mph) and accommodation provides for a pilot and four passengers or freight.

Hughes Model 500D (USA) First flown in 1974, the Model 500D is similar in size and general appearance to the Hughes Model 500C, but differs in having a 313 kW (420 shp) Allison 250-C20B engine plus the modifications applied to 'The Quiet One'. A small T-tail introduced to this model gives greater flight stability in both high and low-speed regimes, as well as better handling characteristics in abnormal manoeuvres. Maximum cruising speed is 258 km/h (160 mph) and accommodation provides for a pilot and two passengers on the forward bench seat and two–four passengers seated in the aft compartment of the cabin.

Hughes YAH-64 (USA) This is a prototype armed helicopter designed to meet the US Army's requirement for an Advanced Attack Helicopter (AAH) capable of undertaking a full day/night/adverse weather anti-armour mission and of fighting, surviving and 'living with' troops in a front-line environment.

The first prototype flew in 1975 and in December 1976 the type was selected winner of the competition against the Bell YAH-63. Delivery of the first production AH-64 is planned for December 1982, with production of the expected 536 aircraft extending until 1989.

Data: *Engines* two 1,145 kW (1,536 shp) General Electric T700-GE-700 turboshafts, derated for normal operations *Main rotor diameter* 14.63 m (48 ft 0 in) *Length of fuselage* 15.06 m (49 ft 5 in) *Max T-O weight* 8,006 kg (17,650 lb) *Max level speed* 309 km/h (192 mph) *Max range* 611 km (380 miles) *Armament* flexible armament consists of a Hughes-developed XM230E1 30 mm chain gun mounted in an underfuselage turret, four underwing hardpoints on which can be carried up to 16 Hellfire anti-tank missiles or up to 76 × 2.75 in folding-fin rockets, or a combination of both

Hunting Percival P.56 (UK) The P.56 Provost trainer was designed by Percival Aircraft prior to it becoming part of the Hunting Group in 1954. It was designed to Specification T.16/48 to meet RAF requirements. Three prototypes were built: two fitted initially with Armstrong Siddeley Cheetah 18 engines and one with an Alvis Leonides. The first (Cheetah-engined) prototype flew on 23 February 1950. As a result of comprehensive trials, the Leonides-engined P.56 was selected for production as the standard RAF two-seat basic trainer under the designation Provost T.1. Some 461 Provosts had been built by 1960, including T.51s supplied to the Eire Air Corps; T.52 armed version for the Rhodesian Air Force; and T.53 armed version for the Eire Air Corps, the Burma Air Force, the Iraqi Air Force and the Sudan Air Force.

Data: *Engine* one 410 kW (550 hp) Alvis Leonides Mk 126 *Wing span* 10.72 m (35 ft 2 in) *Length* 8.74 m (28 ft 8 in) *Max T-O weight* 1,995 kg (4,400 lb) *Max level speed* 322 km/h (200 mph) *Endurance* 4 h

Hunting P.66 Pembroke (UK) The Pembroke prototype first flew in November 1952 as a military six–ten-seat communications and light-transport aircraft developed from the Percival Prince. Because the company name was changed to Hunting Aircraft in 1957, the Pembroke is best known as the Hunting Pembroke.

Two versions were produced for the RAF: the Pembroke C.1 communications and transport aircraft; and the Pembroke C(PR).1 aerial photography aircraft. Both remained operational in 1979, although the C.1s have had their wings re-sparred to prolong their service life. Export versions were also produced for the Belgian Air Force, Royal Swedish Air Force, Royal Danish Air Force, Finnish Air Force, West German Air Force and Sudanese Air Force. Only those exported to Sweden remain operational
Data (C.1): *Engines* two 402–417 kW (540–560 hp) Alvis Leonides Mk 127s *Wing span* 19.66 m (64 ft 6 in) *Length* 14.02 m (46 ft 0 in) *Max T-O weight* 6,125 kg (13,500 lb) *Max level speed* 360 km/h (224 mph) *Range* 1,850 km (1,150 miles) *Accommodation* crew of two and eight passengers or freight

Hunting P.66 Sea Prince (UK) Developed from the Percival Prince, three versions of the Sea Prince were built for the Royal Navy. The C.1 communications aircraft was similar to the civil Prince Series II but with extra equipment. Four were delivered, one of which was used by Flag Officer (Air) Home and another by the naval staff with the British Joint Services Mission in Washington, DC. The C.2 was an improved version with increased disposable load. Accommodation was provided for a crew of two and eight passengers. Three were delivered. The T.1 was a training version for instruction in navigation and anti-submarine warfare and featured an extended nose. Forty-two T.1s were delivered between 1951 and 1954.

Hughes Model 500M-D/ASW Defender.

Hughes Model 500D.

Hughes YAH-64.

Hunting P.84 Jet Provost (UK) see **BAC Jet Provost**

Hunting President (UK) Development of the Pembroke for the civil market, made available as a six-passenger executive transport, 12-passenger feeder airliner or for air survey, photographic, freighter and air ambulance roles.

Hurel-Dubois H.D.10, H.D.31, H.D.32 and H.D.34 (France) Avions Hurel-Dubois was formed to develop and put into practice the theories of M. Hurel regarding the advantages of using wings of high-aspect ratio. The company's first product was the H.D.10, an experimental monoplane powered by a single engine. As a result of the trials the French government ordered two twin-engined aircraft of the same general configuration. The first (the H.D.31) flew on 29

Hughes Model 500C.

Instituto Aerotecnico (I.Ae)

Hunting Percival Provost T.1s.

Hunting President.

Hurel-Dubois H.D.10.

December 1953; the second (the H.D.32) on 11 February 1955. The latter entered very limited production, with SNCASE being responsible for the manufacture of major components and final assembly. The H.D.34 was a development of the H.D.32, specially adapted as a photographic aircraft meeting the requirements of the Institut Géographique National. Eight were built, the first flying on 26 February 1957.

Instituto Aerotecnico (I.Ae) D.L.22 (Argentina) Two-seat advanced trainer powered by a 335.3 kW (450 hp) I.Ae 16 El Gaucho engine. The D.L.22-C was basically similar but fitted with a 354 kW (475 hp) Armstrong Siddeley Cheetah 25 engine.

I.Ae 24 Calquin (Argentina) The Calquin, which flew for the first time in June 1946, was the first twin-engined (782.5 kW; 1,050 hp Pratt & Whitney R-1830-SC-G Twin Wasp) aircraft to be designed and built in Argentina. It was of all-wood construction with a likeness to the British de Havilland Mosquito and intended as an attack bomber. One hundred were built and the type remained operational until about 1960.

Data: *Engines* as above *Wing span* 16.3 m (53 ft 5¾ in) *Length* 12.0 m (39 ft 4½ in) *Max T-O weight* 7,200 kg (15,873 lb) *Max level speed* 440 km/h (273 mph) *Armament* four 20 mm cannon, plus up to 800 kg (1,764 lb) of bombs

I.Ae 27 Pulqúi 1 (Argentina) First jet-powered aircraft to be designed, built and flown in Latin America. Designed by M. Emilio Dewoitine, it flew for the first time on 9 August 1947. Power for the experimental fighter was provided by a 15.57 kN (3,500 lb st) Rolls-Royce Derwent 5 turbojet engine.

Hunting Pembroke C.1.

I.Ae 30 Nancú (Argentina) Prototype single-seat fighter powered by two 1,516.5 kW (2,035 hp) Rolls-Royce Merlin engines. First flown in July 1948.

I.Ae 31 Colibri (Argentina) Tandem two-seat light trainer powered by a Blackburn Cirrus Major 3 or de Havilland Gipsy Major 10 engine.

IAI 101, 102 and 201 Arava (Israel) The Arava was designed to fulfil the need for a light transport with STOL performance and rough-field landing capabilities. The first prototype to fly took to the air on 27 November 1969. The IAI 101 civil-transport version was certificated by the FAA in 1972. The IAI 102, based on the IAI 101, accommodates 20 passengers in airline-standard configuration, although VIP configurations for up to 12 passengers, all-cargo and medical clinic for flying doctor services are available; together with versions for mapping, mining research, rainmaking and bridge construction, as flying laboratories for agriculture and health ministries, and for supplying oil-prospecting units.

The IAI 201 is the military transport version, although in 1977 it was announced that a version suitable for maritime surveillance duties had also been developed. The IAI 202 is a modified version of the Arava, first flown in 1976. It is longer, has a fully 'wet' wing fitted with endplate surfaces ('winglets') and a boundary layer fence just inboard of each tip. Power for this version is provided by two 559 kW (750 shp) Pratt & Whitney Aircraft of Canada PT6A-36 turboprop engines.

Sales of the Arava had reached more than 80 by 1979, six civil 102s having been sold to customers in Argentina and the remaining aircraft to military customers in Israel, Bolivia, Ecuador, Guatemala, Honduras, Mexico, Nicaragua and Salvador.

Data (IAI 201): *Engines* two 559 kW (750 shp) Pratt & Whitney Aircraft of Canada PT6A-34 turboprops *Wing span* 20.96 m (68 ft 9 in) *Length* 13.03 m (42 ft 9 in) *Max T-O weight* 6,903 kg (15,000 lb) *Max cruising speed* 319 km/h (198 mph) *Range* 1,306 km (812 miles) *Armament* optional 0.50 in Browning machine-gun pack on each side of fuselage, above a pylon for a pod containing six 82 mm rockets. Provision for aft-firing machine-gun

IAI 1123 Westwind (Israel) Israel Aircraft Industries acquired all production and marketing rights for the Rockwell-Standard Corporation (formerly Aero Commander) Jet Commander business jet transport. Deliveries as the 1123 Westwind were made to customers in Israel, the USA, Canada, the German Federal Republic, Mexico and Panama. Production ended in 1976 after about 36 aircraft. Power was provided by two 13.79 kN (3,100 lb st) General Electric CJ610-9 turbojet engines.

IAI 1124 Westwind I (Israel) The 1124 is a longer-range version of the Westwind, the first of two modified 1123 Westwind prototypes flying on 21 July 1975. A total of 74 had been sold by the end of 1978. Aircraft from c/n 240 onwards are designated Westwind I. Major changes from the original 1124 are a 317 kg (700 lb) increase in fuel load and an increase of approximately 5% in cabin useful volume by relocation of some avionics and by lowering the floor in the toilet/lavatory compartment.

A maritime-reconnaissance version of the 1124 has also been produced as the Sea Scan, the first operational aircraft being delivered to the Israeli Navy in early 1978. Several versions are available, equipped for specific operational requirements. High-altitude search range and endurance are 4,500 km (2,795 miles) and more than eight hours respectively.

Data (civil Westwind I): *Engines* two 16.46 kN (3,700 lb st) Garrett AiResearch TFE 731-3-1G turbofans *Wing span* 13.65 m (44 ft 9½ in) *Length* 15.93 m (52 ft 3 in) *Max T-O weight* 10,659 kg (23,500 lb) *Max level speed* 872 km/h (542 mph) *Range* more than 3,983 km (2,475 miles) *Accommodation* two pilots and up to ten passengers in pressurised cabin

I.Ae 24 Calquin.

IAI 201 Arava.

IAI Kfir and Kfir-C2 (Israel) Following the manufacture of the Nesher, IAI developed a more extensively modified and further improved version of the same airframe, powered by a General Electric J79 afterburning turbojet engine. A prototype of the Kfir was flown in 1973.

The Kfir utilises a basic airframe similar to that of the Dassault Mirage 5, the main changes being a shorter but larger-diameter rear fuselage to accommodate the J79 engine; an enlarged and flattened undersurface to the forward portion of the fuselage; introduction of four small fuselage airscoops, plus a larger dorsal airscoop in place of the triangular dorsal fin, to provide cooling air for the afterburner; and a strengthened landing gear, with long-stroke oleos. Several internal changes have also been made. Intended for both air-defence and ground-attack roles, the Kfir retains the standard Mirage fixed armament of two

Hurel-Dubois H.D.32s.

IAI 1123 Westwind.

IAI 1124 Westwind I.

government. A similar order from Taiwan – for 50 Kfir-C2s for the Chinese Nationalist Air Force – was granted US approval in 1978.

Data (Kfir-C2): *Engine* one 79.62 kN (17,900 lb st, with afterburning) General Electric J79-J1E turbojet *Wing span* 8.22 m (26 ft 11½ in) *Length* approx 16.35 m (53 ft 7¾ in) *Max combat T-O weight* 14,600 kg (32,188 lb) *Max level speed* over Mach 2.3 *Combat radius* 370–1,300 km (230–807 miles) according to mission *Armament* two 30 mm DEFA 552 cannon. For interception duties, one Rafael Shafrir 2 infra-red homing air-to-air missile under each outer wing. Ground-

30 mm DEFA cannon and can carry a variety of external weapons including the Rafael Shafrir 2 air-to-air and Luz-1 air-to-surface missiles. Two squadrons of the Israeli Air Force were equipped with this initial Kfir-C1 version.

In 1976 the first public demonstration took place of the modified Kfir-C2, by which time it was already in service with the Air Force. The most significant changes from the original Kfir are the addition of non-retractable, sweptback canard surfaces just aft of the engine air intakes, a small strake on each side of the extreme nose, and an extended wing leading edge created by increasing the chord on approximately the outer 40% of each half-span. The Kfir-C2 is the principal production version, both for the Israeli Air Force and for export. The modifications (which are reportedly being retrofitted to existing Kfirs) were designed to improve the aircraft's dogfighting manoeuvrability at the lower end of the speed range and to enhance take-off and landing performance.

A two-seat trainer version of the Kfir-C2 was scheduled to fly for the first time in 1979. Approximately 150 Kfirs and Kfir-C2s were believed to have been built by the spring of 1979. Twenty-four were ordered in 1976 by the Ecuadorean Air Force, but this order was later vetoed by the US

attack version can carry two 1,000 lb bombs, four 500 lb bombs, or a Rafael Luz-1 or similar air-to-surface missile under fuselage, and two 1,000 lb or six 500 lb bombs (conventional or 'concrete dibber' type) under wings. Alternative external stores may include IMI rocket pods, napalm, Shrike, Maverick or Hobos missiles, or droptanks

IAI Nesher (Israel) Following the French embargo on the delivery of Dassault Mirage 5 fighters to Israel, the decision was taken in Israel to manufacture aircraft of generally similar design to the Mirage. As an interim step to the Kfir, IAI undertook responsibility for manufacturing spares for the Mirage III-CJ fighters operated by the Israeli Air Force and for putting into production an aircraft named the Nesher. This comprised a locally built airframe, similar to that of the Mirage III/5, fitted with an Atar 9C afterburning turbojet and Israeli electronics and equipment. The prototype flew for the first time in September 1969 and deliveries of production aircraft began in 1972. About 40 Neshers are said to have taken part in the October 1973 war.

IAR 37, 38 and 39 (Romania) To replace French-built aircraft of 1920s type then in first-line service with the Romanian Air Force, IAR produced the Model 37 three-seat biplane light bomber in 1938. It was powered by a 648.3 kW (870 hp) IAR-built French Gnome-Rhône 14K radial engine. A two-seat reconnaissance variant was also produced as the Model 38, while the Model 39 was another bomber type.

IAR 80 and 81 (Romania) The IAR 80 single-seat cantilever low-wing monoplane fighter first flew in prototype form in 1938 and embodied many components of the PZL P-24E which the company had manufactured under licence. The new fighter went into production in 1941 and

IAI 1124 Sea Scan.

entered squadron service with the Romanian Air Force in the following year. It is thought that between 120 and 125 were built, excluding a small number of developed IAR 81 fighter-bombers, each able to carry two 100 kg bombs or rocket projectiles underwing.

Having signed the Axis Tripartite Pact on 23 November 1940, Romania assisted Germany in the invasion of the Balkans and Russia, and IAR 80s fought alongside their German counterparts. Having been overrun by Russian forces, Romania accepted a peace offer from the Allies on 24 August 1944 and on the following day declared war on Germany. IAR 80s and 81s remained operational until replaced by Russian fighters in 1949.

Data (IAR 80): *Engine* one 700.5–764 kW (940–1,025 hp) IAR-built Gnome-Rhône 14K radial *Wing span* 10.0 m (32 ft 10 in) *Length* 8.16 m (26 ft 9½ in) *Max T-O weight* 2,286–2,485 kg (5,040–5,478 lb) *Max level speed* 510–550 km/h (317–342 mph) *Range* 950 km (590 miles) *Armament* two 20 mm cannon and four 7.7 mm machine-guns

ICA-Brasov IAR-821 (Romania) Single-seat light crop-spraying and dusting monoplane. Production began in 1968. Powered by one 223.6 kW (300 hp) Ivchenko AI-14RF radial engine.

ICA-Brasov IAR-821.

ICA-Brasov IAR-822B (Romania) Tandem two-seat version of the IAR-822 for training, glider-towing and agricultural-training duties.

ICA-Brasov IAR-823 (Romania) Two–five-seat training and touring cabin monoplane powered by a £16 kW (290 hp) Lycoming IO-540-G1D5 flat-six engine. The first production aircraft flew in 1974 and by mid-1979 about 50 had been delivered to the Romanian Air Force and Romanian flying clubs.

ICA-Brasov IAR-824 (Romania) Six-seat light multi-purpose aircraft, first flown in 1971. Power is provided by a 216 kW (290 hp) Lycoming IO-540-G1D5 flat-six engine. Production status is uncertain.

ICA-Brasov IAR-827 (Romania) Single–two-seat agricultural aircraft powered by a 298 kW (400 hp) Lycoming IO-720-DA1B flat-eight engine. Developed from the all-metal IAR-826 with increased payload, more powerful engine and improved flying and operating characteristics.

ICA-Brasov IS-24 (Romania) Six-seat light executive and utility aircraft of 1971, the design of which was based upon the prototype IS-23A.

ICA-Brasov IAR-822 and IAR-826 (Romania) Utility/agricultural single/two-seat monoplanes of mixed and all-metal construction respectively. Power for each is provided by one 216 kW (290 hp) Lycoming IO-540-G1D5 flat-six engine. No longer in production.

IAI Kfir.

ICA-Brasov IAR-823.

IAI Kfir-C2s.

ICA-Brasov IS-28B2.

ICA-Brasov

ICA-Brasov IS-28M2.

ICA-Brasov IS-28 – IS-33 (Romania) Current sailplanes and motor gliders, including the IS-28B2 high-performance training sailplane; IS-28M two-seat motor glider; IS-29 single-seat Standard Class and Open Class sailplane (various wing spans available); IS-30 Open Class sailplane developed from the IS-28B2; IS-31, version of the IS-29 with 20 m wings and interconnected flaps and ailerons; IS-32 18 m Open Class development of the IS-28B2; and IS-33, a version of the IS-29 type with 150 kg (300 lb) water ballast tanks, estimated to have the best glide ratio of 41.5 at 114 km/h (71 mph).

Ikarus S.M and I.O (Yugoslavia) This company was formed in 1923 and became the largest aircraft undertaking in Yugoslavia. It began with the design and construction of a number of training flying-boats, known as the Ikarus S.M., fitted with 89.4 kW (120 hp) Mercedes engines. These proved very successful. Later a military-type I.O with an engine of 335.3 kW–447 kW (450–600 hp) was put into production. In 1926 the company acquired a licence to build the Potez 25 and later the Avia B.H.33.

Ikarus IK-2 (Yugoslavia) In 1935 the company designed and built an all-metal prototype single-seat high-wing monoplane fighter known as the IK-1. The aircraft was fitted with a 641 kW (860 hp) Hispano-Suiza engine and was reported to have a maximum speed of over 400 km/h (248 mph). A development of this was the IK-2 powered by a 641 kW (860 hp) Hispano-Suiza 12Ycrs 'moteur-canon' engine which had a built-in 20 mm HS-404 cannon. Two 7.92 mm Darne machine-guns completed the armament. Twelve were built for the Air Force, delivered in 1937. The eight remaining were used as ground-attack aircraft during the German invasion of 6–17 April 1941. Two later designs that failed to enter production were the low-wing IK-3 fighter and twin-engined multi-seat Orkan fighter and medium bomber.

Ilyushin DB-3.

Ilyushin DB-3F/Il-4.

Ilyushin DB-3 and Il-4 (USSR) While at TsAGI in the 1920s, Sergei Vladimirovich Ilyushin (son of peasant workers living in the village of Diliavili in the Vologda district) designed the first successful post-Revolution Soviet glider. In 1934 he designed the record-breaking TsKB-26 low-wing transport, modelled on the American Douglas DC-2, which eventually became the DB-3 bomber.

Following on from the unsuccessful DB-2 bomber prototype of 1936, the DB-3 (TsKB-26) bomber appeared in the following year and was accepted for production as the DB-3 (TsKB-30) long-range bomber. In retrospect it can be seen as being in roughly the same class as the German Heinkel He 111. Production aircraft entered service with the Red Air Force in 1937 and were the first operational aircraft to bear the name Ilyushin.

The first DB-3s were powered by two 570 kW (765 hp) M-85 engines, but these were superseded by two 715 kW (960 hp) M-86s which gave a further increase in performance. The high speed, long range, manoeuvrability and reasonable offensive capability of the bomber ensured widespread service and indeed the type was used against Finland during the Winter War that started on 30 November 1939 and later against German forces during the invasion that began in June 1941.

Continuous development of the bomber led to the DB-3F which featured a restyled forward fuselage (incorporating a lengthened and more pointed glazed nose and housing a manually operated 7.62 mm machine-gun) and an improved dorsal gun turret. It was normally powered by two 820 kW (1,100 hp) M-88 radial engines. With the change in the military designation system, the DB-3 became the Il-4. A later version of the Il-4 had 1,192 kW (1,600 hp) M-82 engines which gave a maximum speed of only 370 km/h (230 mph), although bomb load increased to 2,700 kg (5,952 lb) – as described in the 1947 *Jane's*. But the DB-3F variant remained the major production bomber and was still being built in 1944.

On 8 August 1941 Il-4s carried out the first Soviet bombing raid on Berlin. The type was later also used successfully as a torpedo bomber in the Baltic area and elsewhere, carrying an 18 in torpedo. During the final months of the war the Il-4 took on the less hazardous roles of glider towing and aircrew training.

Data (DB-3F variant): *Engines* as above *Wing span* 21.39 m (70 ft 2 in) *Length* 14.3 m (47 ft 7 in) *Max T-O weight* 10,050 kg (22,156 lb) *Max level speed* 445 km/h (277 mph) with M-87A engines, 425 km/h (264 mph) with M-88s *Range* 4,000 km (2,485 miles) *Armament* three 7.62 mm ShKAS machine-guns in nose, dorsal and ventral positions, plus up to 2,500 kg (5,511 lb) of bombs, a torpedo or mine

Ilyushin Il-2 (single-seater).

Ilyushin Il-4.

Ilyushin Il-2 Shturmovik (USSR) Though seemingly an ordinary and unexciting machine with superficial close similarity to Britain's Fairey Battle (which proved a disaster), the Il-2 was almost certainly built in larger numbers than any other single type of aircraft. Output averaged 1,200 per month during most of World War II, to give a total of approximately 36,000. When the Il-10 developed version is added the total is reported to amount to 42,330.

Designed as an armoured ground-attack and anti-tank aircraft, the prototype (designated BSh-2 from Bronirovanni Shturmovik, armoured attacker) flew for the first time on 30 December 1939. It looked like a larger edition of one of the single-seat fighters of the period and was powered by an AM-35 engine. Apart from the wooden rear fuselage it was all-metal, and the area round the engine and cockpit was actually constructed from 700 kg (1,542 lb) of steel armour, offering excellent protection against fire from the ground. On 12 October 1940 the TsKB-57 took to the air with the more powerful 967 kW (1,300 hp) M-38 engine. This improved machine led to the Il-2 which was just getting into service when the Germans invaded in June 1941.

Armament of the original Il-2 was two 20 mm ShVAK and two 7.62 mm ShKAS guns firing ahead, plus eight 82 mm rockets and four 100 kg (220 lb) bombs. The need for rear protection resulted in a second crew member being added to man a rear gun, usually a 12.7 mm BS, and the forward guns were changed to the hard-hitting 20 or 37 mm VYa, and sometimes two of each. Bomb load went up to 600 kg (1,323 lb), including

PTAB armour-piercing bombs. The Shturmovik's weapons could pierce all German armoured vehicles, even the Tiger tank being vulnerable when attacked from the rear. Swarms of these tough aircraft are judged by the Soviet Union to have played the dominant role in air warfare on the Eastern Front. Il-2s remained in operational service in the Soviet Union and with the Air Forces of Czechoslovakia and Poland into the 1950s. Indeed Stalin commented that the Il-2 was 'as essential to the Soviet Army as air and bread'.

Data: *Engine* (from 1942) one 1,192 kW (1,600 hp) AM-38F *Wing span* 14.6 m (47 ft 11 in) *Length* 11.6 m (38 ft 1 in) *Max T-O weight* (two-seat Il-2M3) 5,872 kg (12,947 lb) *Max level speed* 434–452 km/h (270–281 mph)

Ilyushin Il-2 (two-seater).

Ilyushin Il-4 (USSR) see **Ilyushin DB-3**

Ilyushin Il-10 Shturmovik (USSR) The Il-10 was a direct development of the Il-2, differing mainly in being powered by a 1,490 kW (2,000 hp) AM-42 engine. As noted in the 1949-50 *Jane's*, 'His [Ilyushin] best known product of the War 1941–45 was the famous Il-2 Shturmovik which was in squadron service as a single-

Ilyushin Il-10s.

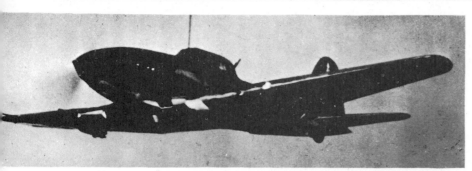

Illyushin Il-10.

seater at the time of the 1941 German invasion of the Soviet Union. This series of low-wing monoplanes brought Ilyushin the award of *Hero of Soviet Labour* in 1941 and 150,000 roubles as a *Stalin Prize* in 1945 for the redesign, the Il-10 two-seater'.

The Il-10 saw little service during World War II but was used in action in Korea in 1950, flown by airmen of the Korean People's Democratic Republic. Armament of the Il-10 included four rocket projectiles under each wing (see Il-2).

Ilyushin Il-12 (USSR) Known in the West under the NATO reporting name *Coach*, the Il-12 twin-engined transport aircraft first flew in 1944. It entered service with the Soviet Air Force as a troop/paratroop or freight transport and for glider towing. It also went into commercial service with Aeroflot, CSA of Czechoslovakia and LOT of Poland. Very few Il-12s remained flying in 1979.

Data: *Engines* two 1,323 kW (1,775 hp) ASh-82FNV radials *Wing span* 31.67 m (103 ft 11 in) *Length* 21.31 m (69 ft 10¾ in) *Max T-O weight* 17,250 kg (38,030 lb) *Max cruising speed* 350 km/h (217 mph) *Range* 1,250–3,000 km (777–1,865 miles) *Accommodation* 27–32 passengers

Ilyushin Il-14 (USSR) First flown in 1953, the Il-14 was developed from the Il-12 and is known in the West under the NATO reporting name *Crate*. Many thousands were produced in the Soviet Union, East Germany and Czechoslovakia (as the Avia 14). The Il-14 basic version with normal accommodation for 28 passengers was followed by the Il-14M and Il-14P. The former has a fuselage lengthened by 1.0 m (3 ft 3¼ in) and accommodates up to 32 passengers, while the latter seats 26 passengers, has improved performance and an AUW of 16,500 kg (36,376 lb). A large number of M and P versions were converted into Il-14T freighters. Civil Il-14s remain flying in the Soviet Union, China, Cuba and Mongolia, while military examples are operated by about 26 countries.

Data (Il-14M): *Engines* two 1,416 kW (1,900 hp) Shvetsov ASh-82T radials *Wing span* 31.67 m (103 ft 11 in) *Length* 22.34 m (73 ft 3½ in) *Max T-O weight* 17,250 kg (38,030 lb) *Max level speed* 415 km/h (258 mph) *Range* 1,508 km (937 miles)

Ilyushin Il-18 (USSR) Known also under its NATO reporting name *Coot*, the Il-18 is a four-engined passenger transport aircraft. The prototype (named *Moskva*) flew for the first time on 4 July 1957 and production models entered service with Aeroflot in 1959. Production is believed to have exceeded 700 aircraft, more than 100 of which were exported for use by commercial airlines. Military operators include the Air Forces of Afghanistan, Algeria, Bulgaria, China, Czechoslovakia, Poland, the Soviet Union, Syria and Yugoslavia, mostly in comparatively small numbers.

An anti-submarine derivative, the Il-38, is described separately. Another specialised mili-

Ilyushin Il-12.

Ilyushin Il-14.

tary variant is the ECM or electronic intelligence aircraft known to NATO as *Coot-A*.

Versions of the Il-18 commercial transport are the Il-18V standard version for Aeroflot, powered by four 2,993 kW (4,000 ehp) Ivchenko AI-20K turboprops and accommodating 90–110 passengers; Il-18E developed version with four 3,169 kW (4,250 ehp) AI-20M engines and accommodating 110–122 passengers; and the Il-18D, generally similar to the Il-18E but with additional fuel capacity to increase range to 3,700–6,500 km (2,300–4,040 miles).

Data: (Il-18E) *Engines* as above *Wing span* 37.4 m (122 ft 8½ in) *Length* 35.9 m (117 ft 9 in) *Max*

Ilyushin Il-18.

Ilyushin Il-28T torpedo-bomber.

cially adapted for use by Aeroflot between Sverdlovsk and Novosibirsk for a brief period of operation from early 1956, carrying cargo associated with newspapers.

Data (Il-28): *Engines* as above *Wing span* 21.45 m (70 ft 4½ in) *Length of fuselage* 17.65 m (57 ft 11 in) *Max T-O weight* 21,000 kg (46,297 lb) *Max level speed* 900 km/h (559 mph) *Range* (with max bomb load) 2,260 km (1,404 miles) *Armament* two 20 mm cannon in nose and two 23 mm cannon in tail turret; bomb load of 2,040 kg (4,500 lb)

Cockpit of an Ilyushin Il-18.

T-O weight 61,200 kg (134,925 lb) *Max cruising speed* 675 km/h (419 mph) *Range* 3,300–5,200 km (1,990–3,230 miles)

Ilyushin Il-28 and Il-20 (USSR) First flown in 1948, the Il-28 (NATO reporting name *Beagle*) still remains operational today with the air forces of about 12 countries (including the USSR) as a four-seat tactical aircraft powered by two 26.47 kN (5,950 lb st) Klimov VK-1 turbojet engines. Those operated by the larger air forces have been adapted from tactical bombers for specialised tasks such as reconnaissance (Il-28R), electronic countermeasures, and training (Il-28U with a second cockpit forward and below the standard canopy); although Chinese-built Il-28s may carry nuclear weapons.

The Il-20 was a civil version of the Il-28, spe-

Ilyushin Il-28U.

Ilyushin Il-38 (USSR) Known by NATO as *May*, the Il-38 is an anti-submarine maritime-patrol development of the Il-18 airliner. It has a lengthened fuselage fitted with an undernose radome, a MAD tail 'sting', other specialised electronic equipment and a weapon-carrying capability.

The Il-38 is a standard shore-based maritime-patrol aircraft of the Soviet Naval Air Force, operating widely over the Atlantic and Mediterranean. More recently Il-38s of the Soviet Navy have operated over the Indian Ocean from an airfield in the People's Democratic Republic of Yemen.

In 1975 the Indian Navy ordered an initial batch of four Il-38s, delivery of which began in 1977. Maximum range 7,240 km (4,500 miles).

Ilyushin Il-28s.

Ilyushin

Ilyushin Il-20.

Ilyushin Il-38.

Aeroflot's Moscow–Havana route in 1974 and have taken over progressively all of the airline's long-distance routes. A variant announced in 1978 is the Il-62MK with a strengthened wing for longer airframe life. Its engines are derated to 107.9 kN (24,250 lb st); max T-O weight is increased to 167,000 kg (368,170 lb); and accommodation is for 195 passengers.

Ilyushin Il-76T (USSR) First flown in prototype form on 25 March 1971, the Il-76T (NATO

Ilyushin Il-62 (USSR) Known by NATO as *Classic*, the Il-62 is a four-turbofan-engined long-range airliner. It accommodates up to 186 passengers and was designed to fly on ranges equivalent to Moscow–New York with more than 150 passengers and reserve fuel. Aeroflot introduced the airliner on its Moscow–Montreal service on 15 September 1967 as a replacement for the Tu-114. Services to New York began in July 1968, since which time it has been introduced on other routes, including to Paris and Tokyo. Production is reported to have totalled 125 by December 1976, including exports.
Data: *Engines* four 103 kN (23,150 lb st) Kuznetsov NK-8-4 turbofans *Wing span* 43.2 m (141 ft 9 in) *Length* 53.12 m (174 ft 3½ in) *Max T-O weight* 162,000 kg (357,150 lb) *Normal cruising speed* 820–900 km/h (510–560 mph) *Range* 6,700–9,200 km (4,160–5,715 miles)

Ilyushin Il-76T.

reporting name *Candid*) is a high-performance pressurised heavy transport of conventional layout, powered by four 117.7 kN (26,455 lb st) Soloviev D-30KP turbofan engines. Nominal task of the Il-76T is to transport 40 tonnes of freight for a distance of 5,000 km (3,100 miles) in less than six hours, as a replacement for the An-12. It can take off from short unprepared airstrips and began operations in Siberia, the north of the Soviet Union and Far East, where operation of other types of transport is difficult. It thereafter entered service on Aeroflot's Moscow–Japan route.

As a military transport the Il-76 has been in service with the Soviet Air Force since 1974, and is superseding the An-12 as the standard equipment of Transport Aviation units, with about 100 currently in first-line squadrons. The military Il-76 has a turret mounting two guns at the tail. A version has also been evaluated as a flight-refuelling tanker for the *Backfire* supersonic strategic bombers of the Soviet Air Force and Naval Air Fleet. It will soon enter service in this role. Military Il-76s have also been exported, including to Iraq, Czechoslovakia and Poland.
Data: *Engines* as above *Wing span* 50.5 m (165 ft 8 in) *Length* 46.59 m (152 ft 10½ in) *Max T-O weight* 170,000 kg (374,785 lb) *Cruising speed* 750–800 km/h (466–497 mph) *Max range* 6,700 km (4,163 miles)

Ilyushin Il-62.

Ilyushin Il-62M/MK (USSR) The Il-62M is a developed version of the Il-62 with no dimensional changes to the airframe, but fitted with four 112.8 kN (25,350 lb st) Soloviev D-30KU turbofan engines, increased fuel capacity for a 10,000 km (6,215 miles) range and other minor changes. Production models entered service on

Ilyushin Il-86 (USSR) Known by NATO as *Camber*, the Il-86 is a four-turbofan-engined wide-bodied passenger transport aircraft accommodating up to 350 passengers. The first of two prototypes flew on 22 December 1976. It was announced subsequently that the airliner would be in Aeroflot service in time to carry visitors from Prague, Sofia and Berlin to the 1980 Olympic Games in Moscow.

The Il-86 is likely to be used also by the Soviet Air Force and the evolution of an AWACS version has been suggested as a possibility by Western observers.

Data: *Engines* four 127.5 kN (28,660 lb st) Kuznetsov NK-86 turbofans *Wing span* 48.06 m (157 ft 8¼ in) *Length* 59.54 m (195 ft 4 in) *Max T-O weight* 190,000–206,000 kg (418,875–454,150 lb) *Normal cruising speed* 900–950 km/h (560–590 mph) *Range* 4,600 km (2.858 miles)

IMAM Ro.10 (Italy) Licence-built Fokker F.VII-3m.

IMAM Ro.30 (Italy) Three-seat reconnaissance and army co-operation cabin biplane developed from the Romeo Ro.1 and powered by a 410 kW (550 hp) Piaggio-built Jupiter engine.

IMAM Ro.37 (Italy) The Ro.37 biplane was first flown on 6 November 1933 as a reconnaissance and attack aircraft to replace the Fokker C.Vs built under licence as Ro 1s. Two versions went into production as the 410 kW (550 hp) Fiat A.30-engined Ro.37/A.30 and 417 kW (560 hp) Piaggio P.IX-engined Ro.37*bis*. A total of 637 aircraft were built by 1939.

Ro.37s were operated during the Italian invasion of Abyssinia and with the Italian Aviazione Legionaria in Spain during the Civil War. During World War II the 296 aircraft remaining in front-line service were operated in East and North Africa, against Greece and then in the Balkans. Exported Ro.37s went to Afghanistan, Austria, Ecuador, Hungary and Uruguay.

IMAM Ro.41 (Italy) The Ro.41 of 1935 was designed as a single-seat biplane fighter powered by a 290.6 kW (390 hp) Piaggio P.VII C.45 supercharged radial engine. It could also be supplied as a two-seat advanced trainer with dual controls. A number went into service with the Regia Aeronautica.

IMAM Ro.43 and Ro.44 (Italy) The Ro.43 two-seat reconnaissance biplane and the Ro.44 single-seat fighter were both developed from the Ro.37*bis* and were powered by the 521.6 kW (700 hp) Piaggio P.X.R. radial engine. The wings of each aircraft were designed to fold for easy stowage on board ship and the landing gear comprised a large central float and two underwing stabilising floats. In the event only the two-seater was widely operated at sea, the fighter being used mainly from coastal stations. When Italy became involved in World War II 105 Ro.43s and 30 Ro.44s had been delivered, but these were obsolete and were little used.

Data (Ro.44): *Engine* as above *Wing span* 11.6 m (38 ft 0½ in) *Length* 9.71 m (31 ft 10½ in) *Max T-O weight* 2,220 kg (4,894 lb) *Max level speed* 320 km/h (199 mph) *Armament* two 12.7 mm and two 7.7 mm machine-guns

Ilyushin Il-86.

IMAM Ro.57 (Italy) Designed as a twin-engined (626 kW; 840 hp Fiat A.74 RC-38) fighter, the Ro.57 entered service in small numbers with the Regia Aeronautica in 1942 as a fighter-bomber because of its comparatively low speed of 500 km/h (310.5 mph) and poor manoeuvrability. From the Ro.57 was developed the Ro.57*bis*, evolved from the start as a fighter bomber and dive bomber. Although it was similarly powered, two 20 mm cannon were added to the 12.7 mm machine-guns and dive-brakes were installed. Carrying up to a 500 kg (1,102 lb) bomb under its fuselage, this version was fairly successful but had faded from the scene before the Italian Armistice of September 1943.

IMAM Ro.37.

IMAM Ro.37bis.

IMAM Ro.63 (Italy) Because of Italy's change of fortune in 1943, only the prototype Ro.58 twin-engined fighter bomber and five examples of the Ro.63 708 kW (950 hp) Hirth HM 508D-engined liaison and ambulance monoplane were produced.

IMCO

IMAM Ro.41.

IMAM Ro.57.

IMAM Ro.43.

IMAM Ro.44.

IMCO CallAir A-9.

IMCO CallAir A-9 (USA) The A.9 single-seat agricultural aircraft was developed from the CallAir series of agricultural aircraft following IMCO's purchase of CallAir Inc in 1962 (see **Rockwell Quail Commander** and **AAMSA Quail**).

IMPA Tu-Sa (Argentina) First flown on 17 April 1943, the Tu-Sa was built for flying-club use but after a number of accidents the type was withdrawn from service. A total of about 25 were built.

Indraéro Aéro 110 (France) Two-seat light training biplane of the 1950s powered by a 33.5 kW (45 hp) Salmson 9ADB engine in the prototype and a 56 kW (75 hp) Minié 4.DC.32 in the production model ordered by the S.ALS.

INTA H.M. series (Spain) Sometimes referred to as AISA types, the Instituto Nacional de Técnica Aeronaútica (INTA) designed the H.M.1 two-seat primary training monoplane, H.M.5 single-seat advanced training monoplane and the H.M.9 two-seat glider tug – all of which were built by AISA and produced and put into service in 1943. In 1945 the H.M.2 two-seat training cabin monoplane was completed, followed in 1947 by the prototypes of the H.M.3 two-seat training seaplane and the H.M.7 four-seat touring cabin monoplane.

Interceptor 400 (USA) The Type Certificate for the Interceptor 400 was transferred to a corporate entity named Prop-Jets Inc in 1977. It was seeking finance in early 1979 to put the aircraft into production (see **Aero Commander 200**).

International F-17 Sportsman and F-18 Air-Coach (USA) During the brief period that the International Aircraft Corporation existed, it produced the F-17 three-seat biplane and the F-18 six-seat cabin biplane.

Interstate S-1A Cadet (USA) First flown in 1940, the Cadet was a two-seat light cabin monoplane powered by a 48.4 kW (65 hp) Continental A65 engine. Following America's entry into World War II the type was (at the request of the US Army authorities) developed into a light liaison and observation monoplane powered by an 85.7 kW (115 hp) Franklin flat-four engine. Two hundred and fifty were delivered under the designation L-6 Grasshopper. Maximum level speed was 167 km/h (104 mph) and range 870 km (540 miles). A modern derivative of the Cadet is currently being built by the Arctic Aircraft Company as the Arctic Tern.

IPE KW 1b 2 Quero Quero II (Brazil) Single-seat training glider, 24 production examples of which had been built by April 1979.

534

Isaacs Fury II.

Isaacs Fury and Fury II (UK) The original Fury single-seat ultra-light homebuilt aircraft (representing a Hawker Fury fighter of the 1930s) first flew in 1963. The Fury II re-stressed and re-engined version appeared in 1967 and plans are available to amateur constructors.

Isaacs Spitfire (UK) Single-seat sporting aircraft, plans of which are available to amateur constructors.

Issoire (Siren) D 77 Iris and E 78 Silène (France) Single-seat training sailplane and side-by-side two-seat training sailplane respectively.

Italia (N2) and Norge (N1) (Italy) *Italia* and *Norge* were sister airships, both built by SCA and launched in 1924. Each was powered by three 186.3 kW (250 hp) Maybach engines, was 106 m (347 ft 10 in) long and had a maximum speed of 113 km/h (70 mph). (See **Chronology** 11–14 May 1926 and 23 May 1928).

IVL A-22 (Finland) Basically a licence-built version of the German Hansa-Brandenburg W.33 powered by a 223.5 kW (300 hp) Fiat A.12*bis* engine. A total of 122 were produced and these served as reconnaissance seaplanes between 1922 and 1936.

IVL Kotka (Finland) Built in the latter 1920s for Finnish Air Force service, the Kotka was a Bristol Jupiter-powered two-seat bombing and reconnaissance biplane capable of operating on a wheel or twin-float landing gear.

Jamieson J (USA) Four-seat light cabin monoplane, first flown in December 1958 as a larger development of the J-2-L-1 Jupiter of the 1940s. Small number of production aircraft built, each powered by a 112 kW (150 hp) Lycoming O-320-A3C engine.

Janowski J-1B Don Kichot (Poland) Single-seat ultra-light monoplane, plans for which are available to amateur constructors.

Javelin Wichawk (USA) Two–three-seat sporting biplane. Plans, wing ribs and fuel tanks are available to amateur constructors.

Jean St-Germain Raz-Mut (Canada) Single-seat ultra-light monoplane, component parts for which are available in kit form to amateur constructors.

Jeffair Barracuda (USA) Two-seat all-wooden sporting monoplane, plans for which are available to amateur constructors.

Jodel D.9 and D.92 Bébé (France) Single-seat light monoplane powered by an 18.6 kW (25 hp) Poinsard and a modified Volkswagen motorcar engine respectively. Plans are available to amateur constructors.

Jodel D.11 and D.119 (France) Two-seat light monoplanes powered by a 33.5 kW (45 hp) Salmson and a 67 kW (90 hp) Continental engine

Norge.

Italia.

Jamieson J.

Janowski J-1B Don Kichot.

Javelin Wichawk.

respectively. Plans are available to amateur constructors. Like other Jodel aircraft, these have also been commercially manufactured.

Jodel D.112 Club (France) Dual-control version of the D.9 fitted normally with a 48.5 kW (65 hp) Continental engine. Plans are available to amateur constructors.

Jodel D.112 Club.

Junkers A 20 (Germany) The A 20 was first flown in 1923 as a fast two-seat open-cockpit low-wing monoplane for carrying mail and freight. Having been passed by the Commission Aéronautique Inter-Allié for production, it was produced as the A 20L landplane and A 20W twin-float seaplane in Germany and Sweden, normally powered by 119 kW (160 hp) Mercedes D.IIIa and 164 kW (220 hp) Junkers L.2 engines respectively. More than 30 were built, serving

Junkers A 50, a two-seat sporting monoplane built in limited numbers from 1929.

mainly with Deutsche Luft-Hansa of Germany and Ad Astra Aero of Switzerland, although some found their way into military service.

Junkers A 35 (Germany) Basically a developed version of the A 20 powered by a 208.7–231 kW (280–310 hp) Junkers L.5 engine. The 24 or so aircraft produced included a number of A 20s brought up to this standard and those built under licence in Sweden. A military derivative was produced in Sweden as the R 53, armed with two forward-firing and two rear-mounted machine-guns.

Junkers CL.I (Germany) The CL.I carried the Junkers designation J 10 and was a two-seat ground-attack and escort monoplane, skinned with the typical corrugated metal. Power was provided normally by a 134 kW (180 hp) Mercedes D.IIIa engine. Forty-seven had been delivered by the end of World War I, including three CLS.I floatplanes to the Navy. Post-war a coupé conversion of the CL.I became Junkers' first commercial type, operating its Dessau–Weimar service in 1919.

Junkers D.I (Germany) The D.I (Junkers J 9) was a single-seat cantilever monoplane fighter, first flown in prototype form on 10 March 1918. Production totalled just 41 aircraft, these becoming the first ever operational all-metal combat planes (full structural details appear in the 1920 edition of *Jane's*). Power was provided normally by a 138 kW (185 hp) BMW IIIa engine, giving a maximum speed of 185 km/h (116 mph). Interestingly the first detailed information on the D.I to reach the Allies came from an abandoned specimen discovered at Evère, near Brussels.

Junkers F 13 (Germany) The F 13 was the world's first purpose-built all-metal commercial aircraft to enter service and was basically a development of the wartime J 10 (CL.I). First flown on 25 June 1919, it was a four-passenger monoplane (plus two crew in an open and later enclosed cockpit), powered as a prototype by a single 119 kW (160 hp) Mercedes D.IIIa engine. Initial production aircraft were fitted with the 138 kW (185 hp) BMW IIIa engine, giving way subsequently to the 231 kW (310 hp) Junkers L.5. Interestingly the first F 13 built was still flying regularly in 1939, giving joy-rides in Berlin.

Production of the F 13 continued until 1932, by which time no less than 322 had been built in

provided by Mercedes D.IIIas, Junkers J.2s, or two J.2s and a Napier Lion engine. Accommodation was for a crew of three and nine passengers.

Although the G 23 was the 'official' German version of the aircraft – built according to the limitations of the Versailles Treaty and approved by the Commission Inter-Allié for service in Germany – the G 24 that appeared in 1925 became the major production version of the design. It differed in the engines fitted (normally three 231 kW; 310 hp Junkers L.5s or one L.5 and two 171.4 kW; 230 hp Junkers L.2as); these made it heavier and faster. By the autumn of 1925 it was the major European version, 56 eventually being built.

On 24 July 1926 three G 24s left Berlin and flew to Peking and back, arriving in Berlin on 26 September; the object was to examine the possibilities of Deutsche Luft-Hansa opening a regular service across Asia. In March 1927 a G 24 with Junkers L.2a engines (piloted by Herr Röder and carrying a 2,000 kg load) flew 1,018 km in 7 hours 52 minutes, setting up world duration, speed and distance records. Eventually a number of G 24s were converted into F 24s (see entry).

From the G 24 was developed a military

some 60–70 variants. The operator of the largest number of F 13s was undoubtedly Deutsche Luft-Hansa which received approximately 15% of all those built. Others went into civil and military service in at least ten European and several South American countries, in addition to the USA, Russia and elsewhere.

Data: *Engine* as above *Wing span* 17.75 m (58 ft 2¾ in) *Length* 9.6 m (31 ft 6 in) *Max T-O weight* 1,730 kg (3,814 lb) *Cruising speed* 140 km/h (87 mph) *Endurance* 5 h

Junkers F 24 (Germany) Appearing in 1928 the F 24 was simply a single-engined conversion of the G 24 with the wing-mounted engines removed. Eleven were produced, nine operated by Deutsche Luft-Hansa.

Junkers G 23, G 24 and K 30/R-42 (Germany) Preceding the F 24, the G 23 was the first all-metal three-engined commercial transport monoplane in the world, nine of which were built in Germany and Sweden. It first went into service with AB Aerotransport on its Malmö–Hamburg–Amsterdam route from 15 May 1925. Power was

bomber version known as the K 30. Powered by three L.5s, it had two open dorsal gunners' cockpits, each armed with two Lewis guns, and a retractable ventral 'dustbin' with a further gun. Bombs were carried under the wings. As the R-42, the bomber entered production in Sweden, Russia and Turkey.

Data (G 24 landplane): *Engines* as above *Wing span* 29.9 m (91 ft 1 in) *Length* 15.7 m (51 ft 6 in) *Max T-O weight* 6,500 kg (14,330 lb) *Max level speed* 200 km/h (124 mph) *Range* 1,300 km (808 miles)

Junkers G 31 (Germany) The G 31 was a three-engined (335.3 kW; 450 hp Gnome-Rhône Jupiter or 391.2 kW; 525 hp BMW-built Pratt & Whitney Hornet) enlarged development of the G 24, accommodating 12–15 passengers in three compartments. Alternatively the design allowed for each compartment to be fitted with sleeping bunks for night flying. The first G 31 appeared in 1926 and a total of 15 were built, operators including Deutsche Luft-Hansa. Maximum level speed and cruising speed were 200 km/h (124 mph) and 170 km/h (106 mph) respectively.

Junkers

Junkers F 24.

Junkers G 38
Generalfeldmarschall
von Hindenburg.

Junkers J 1 and J.I (Germany) At Dolberitz on 12 December 1915 the first flight was made of a prototype all-metal monoplane, the J 1. This was the first Junkers aircraft to be built and was powered by an 89.4 kW (120 hp) Mercedes D.II engine. Dubbed 'Tin Donkey', initial troubles were quickly overcome and by January 1916 it proved to have excellent speed despite the use of metal for skinning. As a result in the autumn an order was placed for an experimental armoured aircraft. This appeared as the Junkers J 4 and first flew in February 1917.

The J 4, unlike the J 1, was a biplane, and its workmanlike appearance gave rise to the nickname 'Furniture Van'. Powered by a 149 kW (200 hp) Benz Bz.IV engine, the J 4 went into production as the J.I, entering service in the summer of 1917. Although heavy to fly, it proved a first-class low-level reconnaissance and close-support aircraft and was well liked by crews. Production totalled 227, each armed with two forward-firing Spandau and one rear-mounted Parabellum machine-guns, plus light bombs, etc. Data: *Engine* as above *Wing span* 16.0 m (52 ft 6 in) *Length* 9.1 m (29 ft 10¼ in) *Max T-O weight* 2,175 kg (4,795 lb) *Max level speed* 155 km/h (96 mph) *Endurance* 2 h

Junkers J 1.

Junkers G 38 (Germany) The G 38 was a most remarkable aircraft. It was a huge all-metal monoplane with a wing span of 44.0 m (144 ft 4 in) and powered in its final form by four 559 kW (750 hp) Junkers Jumo 204 engines. Accommodation provided for three passengers in each of two cabins in the wing roots, two passengers in the fuselage nose and a further 26 passengers in the main cabins. Only two were built: the first was named *Deutschland* (flying on 6 November 1929) and the second *Generalfeldmarschall von Hindenburg*. Both served with Deutsche Luft-Hansa. The first crashed in 1936 but the second carried on flying until destroyed in an RAF raid in 1940. Cruising speed was 208 km/h (129 mph).

Junkers Ju 46 (Germany) One 484.4 kW (650 hp) BMW 132E-engined side-by-side two-seat commercial floatplane of 1932, five of which were built for Deutsche Luft-Hansa as mail and freight-carrying monoplanes.

Junkers Ju 52 (Germany) Not to be mistaken for the three-engined Ju 52/3m (although it can be considered the prototype), the Ju 52 was first flown on 13 October 1930 as a single-engined freight-carrying all-metal commercial transport. Only five were built.

Junkers Ju 52/3m (Germany) Built in larger numbers than any other European transport aircraft before or since, this extremely robust machine combined exceptional qualities of payload, STOL and all-round utility that resulted in a very long active life. The original prototype (flown in May 1932) was a Ju 52 redesigned to be powered by three engines. Most early civil examples had the 447 kW (600 hp) BMW Hornet engine, made under Pratt & Whitney licence; but the vast bulk of later sub-types had the derived engine known as the BMW 132, rated at 507–618.5 kW (680–830 hp).

Junkers G 38.

Junkers H 21 (USSR) Built at the Junkers factory at Fili, near Moscow, the H 21 was a two-seat parasol-wing armed-reconnaissance monoplane powered by a 138 kW (185 hp) BMW IIIa engine. Armament comprised one or two forward-firing and one rear-mounted machine-guns. About 100 were built, entering service with the Red Air Force from 1924.

Like the original single-engined Ju 52, the tri-motor transport had a structure wholly of light alloy with corrugated skin and a very large cantilever wing with patented 'double wing' flaps and ailerons giving great lift at low airspeeds. The fixed landing gear was almost unbreakable and on a few examples had spats; float-seaplane and ski versions were not uncommon. In World War II the vast numbers of Luftwaffe transports (more than 90% of which were of this basic type) changed landing gear to suit the local terrain and climate.

The Ju 52/3m was by far the leading European civil airliner of the 1930s, seating 15 to 17 in single seats each side of the central aisle. It carried more than 75% of Luft-Hansa's Europe-wide traffic in the 1930s, the airline using at least 120. Exported civil models had Wasp, Hornet and Pegasus engines, and a small number in Germany had Jumo diesels. In 1935 the first 3mg3e bombers reached the Luftwaffe, with 1,500 kg (3,307 lb) of bombs and MG 15 machine-guns in a dorsal cockpit and ventral 'dustbin'. In 1936 about half the total production (450) of this model were serving as transports or bombers with the Condor Legion in Spain.

Total production of all models was about 4,845 on German account, 575 of which were completed before 1940. German plants then made a further 2,659, the rest comprising output by Amiot for the Luftwaffe. The latter was continued post-war by the AAC which delivered 400 by 1947 with the designation AAC.1. A further 170 were built by CASA in Spain. More than 3,500 served with the Luftwaffe, nearly all in the transport role with the popular names 'Tante Ju' (Auntie Ju) and 'Iron Annie'. The most-produced wartime types were the 3mg5e, 7e, 8e and 14e, though differences were confined to such features as armament, loading arrangements, autopilot, glider couplings and crew armour. There were several non-transport versions, such as the g6eMS with a degaussing ring for exploding mines. After 1945 BEA used a fleet on internal services and the Spanish T.2B version was not withdrawn until 1975. One of the last, with the Swiss Air Force, was still active in 1979.

Data (g7e): *Engines* three 618.5 kW (830 hp) BMW 132T-2 radials *Wing span* 29.25 m (95 ft 11½ in) *Length* (landplane) 18.9 m (62 ft 0 in) *Max T-O weight* 11,030 kg (24,317 lb) *Max level speed* 286 km/h (178 mph) *Range* 1,300 km (808 miles)

Junkers Ju 52/3m.

Junkers H 21.

Junkers Ju 60 and Ju 160 (Germany) The Ju 60 was a six-passenger airliner of 1932 powered by a 447 kW (600 hp) BMW-built Pratt & Whitney Hornet C radial engine. Only four were produced for Deutsche Luft-Hansa.

In June 1934 the first Ju 160 flew. This was basically a refined version of the Ju 60 with many improvements to the airframe: the most obvious of which were a redesigned cockpit and the use of smooth metal for skinning. Production of the Ju 160 totalled 48 aircraft, about half of which were operated by Deutsche Luft-Hansa.

Junkers Ju 86 (Germany) The Ju 86, best remembered as a bomber and later a high-altitude reconnaissance aircraft, began life as a commercial airliner, first flying on 4 November 1934. From 1936 Ju 86s began operating a number of Deutsche Luft-Hansa's domestic services, each aircraft accommodating ten passengers or freight. Other users included South African Airways and AB Aerotransport. The engines fitted to the commercial models varied considerably but those of Luft-Hansa had 447 kW (600 hp) Junkers Jumo 205Cs.

Junkers J.I.

South African Airways Junkers Ju 86s.

Junkers Ju 87D-1.

From 1935 until 1938 Junkers also produced military variants of the Ju 86 for the Luftwaffe and for export. The Ju 86A was the first bomber type, used essentially for evaluation under squadron conditions. Next came the Ju 86D, powered also by Jumo 205C-4 engines but with refinements to improve longitudinal stability. By the autumn of 1938 the Luftwaffe had nearly 160 Ju 86A/Ds in service, together with a much smaller number of BMW 132-powered Ju 86Es and Ju 86Gs. Prior to the introduction of the wartime-reconnaissance versions this was the height of the Ju 86's career with the Luftwaffe. From this point on Ju 86s were relegated to transport and training roles.

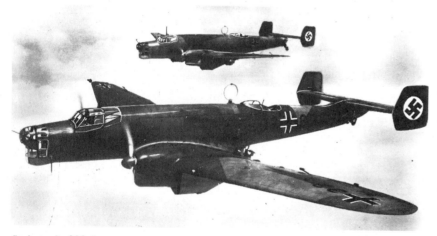

Junkers Ju 86A-1s.

Meanwhile the bomber, like the airliner, had proved fairly successful as an export product with the air forces of Sweden (also licence-built), Chile, Hungary and Portugal. Also, with the outbreak of war, all South African Airways' Ju 86 airliners were impressed by the South African Air Force as transports.

Swedish Junkers Ju 86.

The fact remained that the Ju 86 was not a good bomber and it appeared that its first line career was to end. Even *Jane's* of 1939 noted: 'It may be rated as an obsolete type.' However Junkers produced a new reconnaissance version with an increased wing span, a pressurised cabin for the crew and powered by two Jumo 207 engines. This became the Ju 86P and was well received by the Luftwaffe. From 1940 a number of successful very high-altitude missions were flown over Britain, then on the Eastern Front. Its success can be measured by the fact that the 1943–44 *Jane's* states that 'the Ju 86P appeared in 1942', indicating that the aircraft was able to carry out missions in complete secrecy and without fear of interception. But this situation was not to last long. In the summer of 1942 three Ju 86Ps were shot down by Spitfires over the Mediterranean at heights of 12,190 m (40,000 ft) and over. The interception by an RAF Spitfire VC flown by G. W. H. Reynolds in August was made at a staggering

15,090 m (49,500 ft) – the highest interception ever made by an unpressurised aircraft and with the pilot not wearing a pressure suit.

The possibility that Allied aircraft would eventually manage to intercept the Ju 86P led Junkers to produce the Ju 86R, the final version of the aircraft with a wing span of 32.0 m (105 ft) and powered by 745 kW (1,000 hp) Jumo 207B-3 engines. Design service ceiling was 14,000 m (45,925 ft). Few were produced.

Data (Ju 86P): *Engines* as above *Wing span* 25.6 m (84 ft 0 in) *Length* 16.46 m (54 ft 0 in) *Max T-O weight* 10,400 kg (22,928 lb) *Max level speed* 360 km/h (223.5 mph) *Range* 1,750 km (1,087 miles) *Armament* one 7.9 mm MG 17 machine-gun, plus four 250 kg bombs as a bomber

Junkers Ju 87 (Germany) Remembered as the 'Stuka', the Ju 87 was an ugly cranked-wing dive-bomber and ground-attack aircraft. For a plane that was to blast its way through Europe during the first months of World War II, it is ironic that the first prototype made its maiden flight in the spring of 1935 powered by a Rolls-Royce Kestrel V engine. Evaluated against the Arado Ar 81, Hamburger Ha 137 and Heinkel He

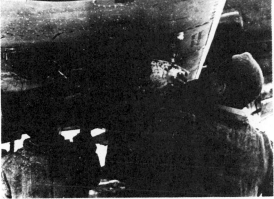

Italian Junkers Ju 87s.

Arming a Junkers Ju 87.

118, the Ju 87 was, perhaps surprisingly, judged winner; although Heinkel found solace in the interest shown for the He 118 by Japan.

Sent to Spain for battle evaluation with the Condor Legion (like so many other Luftwaffe combat aircraft), the Ju 87 found little opposition from the poorly equipped and 'stretched' Republican forces. As a result few changes were made to the design and Ju 87As and Bs were mass produced for the Luftwaffe, Italy and other countries. Power was provided by Jumo 210C and much more powerful 211D engines respectively.

The designation Ju 87C was applied to an experimental deck-landing development of the B-1 intended for use from the aircraft carrier *Graf Zeppelin*, which was never completed. This version was stressed for catapulting and fitted with a jettisonable landing gear for emergency alighting in the sea.

The Ju 87D was developed from the B and R, the latter being similar to the B but with provision for external fuel tanks under the wings in place of bombs to increase range. The D differed considerably, having a Jumo 211J engine with induction cooling, redesigned cowling and cockpit enclosure, and provision for carrying up to a 1,800 kg (3,960 lb) warload. Coolant radiators were mounted under the wings and additional armour was fitted. Several sub-variants were produced, originally as dive bombers but later for specialised ground-attack work, often by night. The Ju 87D-4, for example, had provision for mounting two jettisonable weapons containers (each with six MG 81 machine-guns) for service on the Eastern Front. Later versions of the D introduced increases in the wing span and armament.

The Ju 87G was an anti-tank version fitted with long- and short-span wings, without dive brakes and carrying two 37 mm BK (Flak 18) guns under the wings. The final version was the Ju 87H, a dual-control trainer corresponding to the D-1,

D-3, D-5, D-7 and D-8. Production of all versions of the Ju 87 amounted to more than 5,700 aircraft.

During its early wartime campaigns the Ju 87 proved able to 'Blitzkrieg' its way through Poland, France and other countries. It received a reputation far in excess of its actual abilities, made clear when opposed by RAF fighters during the Battle of Britain. Against a well-equipped defence force the Ju 87 was shown to be slow and poorly armed, proving an easy target for the RAF. With destruction the obvious outcome, Ju 87s were begrudgingly withdrawn from the fray but continued to serve until the end of the war on the Eastern Front, in North Africa and elsewhere. Data (Ju 87D-1): *Engine* one 1,043.3 kW (1,400 hp) Junkers Jumo 211J-1 *Wing span* 13.8 m (45 ft 3½ in) *Length* 11.5 m (37 ft 8¾ in) *Max T-O weight* 6,585 kg (14,517 lb) *Max level speed* 410 km/h (255 mph) *Range* 1,000 km (621 miles) *Armament* two forward-firing 7.9 mm MG 17 and two rear-mounted 7.9 mm MG 81 machine-guns, plus one 250 kg, 500 kg, 1,000 kg or 1,800 kg bomb under the fuselage and four 50 kg, two 250 kg or two 500 kg bombs under wings

Junkers Ju 88 prototype.

Junkers Ju 88 (Germany) The Ju 88 became the Luftwaffe's 'maid of all work' and production eventually totalled 14,980 aircraft. It was first flown in prototype form as a bomber on 21 December 1936 and by the beginning of 1939 approximately 50 were in service. During World War II the basic design was adapted for a wide variety of duties and was still in production when hostilities ended, having served throughout the entire period of the European war.

The initial version was the Ju 88A bomber, produced in a large number of sub-variants. The

One of ten Italian Junkers Ju 87s captured by the RAF after landing near Allied forces. The pilots accused German ground crews of only half-filling their tanks.

Junkers

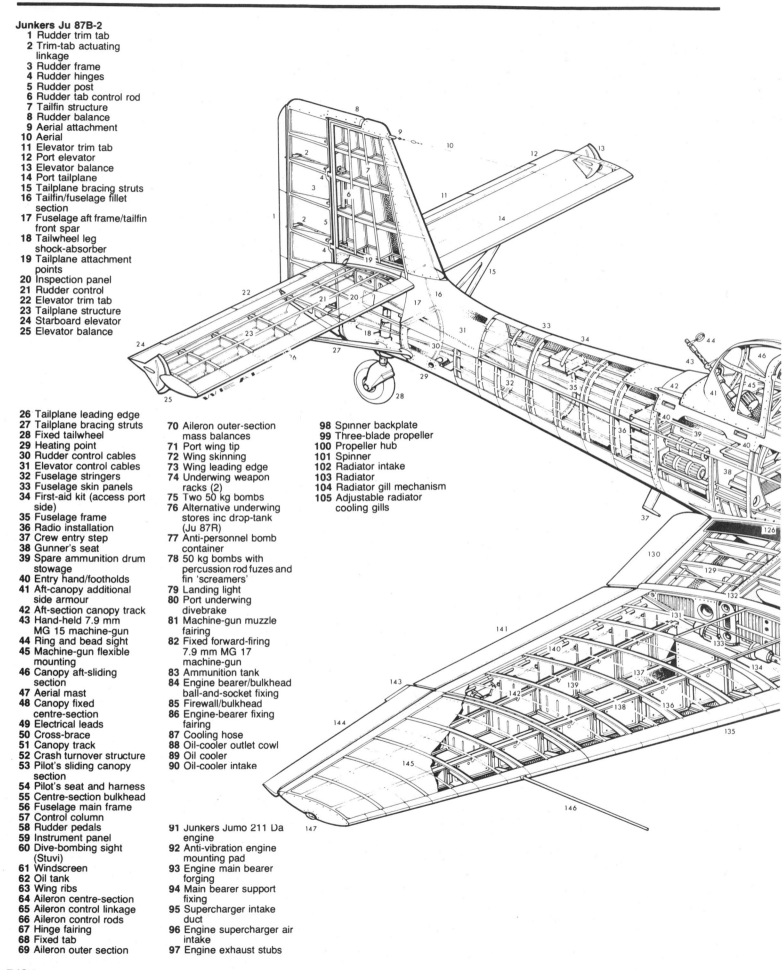

Junkers Ju 87B-2
1 Rudder trim tab
2 Trim-tab actuating linkage
3 Rudder frame
4 Rudder hinges
5 Rudder post
6 Rudder tab control rod
7 Tailfin structure
8 Rudder balance
9 Aerial attachment
10 Aerial
11 Elevator trim tab
12 Port elevator
13 Elevator balance
14 Port tailplane
15 Tailplane bracing struts
16 Tailfin/fuselage fillet section
17 Fuselage aft frame/tailfin front spar
18 Tailwheel leg shock-absorber
19 Tailplane attachment points
20 Inspection panel
21 Rudder control
22 Elevator trim tab
23 Tailplane structure
24 Starboard elevator
25 Elevator balance

26 Tailplane leading edge
27 Tailplane bracing struts
28 Fixed tailwheel
29 Heating point
30 Rudder control cables
31 Elevator control cables
32 Fuselage stringers
33 Fuselage skin panels
34 First-aid kit (access port side)
35 Fuselage frame
36 Radio installation
37 Crew entry step
38 Gunner's seat
39 Spare ammunition drum stowage
40 Entry hand/footholds
41 Aft-canopy additional side armour
42 Aft-section canopy track
43 Hand-held 7.9 mm MG 15 machine-gun
44 Ring and bead sight
45 Machine-gun flexible mounting
46 Canopy aft-sliding section
47 Aerial mast
48 Canopy fixed centre-section
49 Electrical leads
50 Cross-brace
51 Canopy track
52 Crash turnover structure
53 Pilot's sliding canopy section
54 Pilot's seat and harness
55 Centre-section bulkhead
56 Fuselage main frame
57 Control column
58 Rudder pedals
59 Instrument panel
60 Dive-bombing sight (Stuvi)
61 Windscreen
62 Oil tank
63 Wing ribs
64 Aileron centre-section
65 Aileron control linkage
66 Aileron control rods
67 Hinge fairing
68 Fixed tab
69 Aileron outer section

70 Aileron outer-section mass balances
71 Port wing tip
72 Wing skinning
73 Wing leading edge
74 Underwing weapon racks (2)
75 Two 50 kg bombs
76 Alternative underwing stores inc drop-tank (Ju 87R)
77 Anti-personnel bomb container
78 50 kg bombs with percussion rod fuzes and fin 'screamers'
79 Landing light
80 Port underwing divebrake
81 Machine-gun muzzle fairing
82 Fixed forward-firing 7.9 mm MG 17 machine-gun
83 Ammunition tank
84 Engine bearer/bulkhead ball-and-socket fixing
85 Firewall/bulkhead
86 Engine-bearer fixing fairing
87 Cooling hose
88 Oil-cooler outlet cowl
89 Oil cooler
90 Oil-cooler intake
91 Junkers Jumo 211 Da engine
92 Anti-vibration engine mounting pad
93 Engine main bearer forging
94 Main bearer support fixing
95 Supercharger intake duct
96 Engine supercharger air intake
97 Engine exhaust stubs

98 Spinner backplate
99 Three-blade propeller
100 Propeller hub
101 Spinner
102 Radiator intake
103 Radiator
104 Radiator gill mechanism
105 Adjustable radiator cooling gills

106 Bomb crutch pivot
107 Engine main bearer lower support strut
108 Ventral bomb shackle
109 Vent
110 Bomb crutch (extended)
111 Port mainwheel
112 Alternative main bomb load inc: 500 kg SC-type fragmentation bomb
113 500 kg SC-type semi-armour-piercing bomb
114 500 kg PC-type 'Pauline' armour-piercing bomb
115 Starboard mainwheel
116 Mainwheel spat
117 Axle fork/spat fixing lugs
118 Axle fork
119 Aerodynamic siren fairing (capped)
120 Undercarriage leg
121 Torque link
122 Machine-gun muzzle fairing
123 Undercarriage leg/wing front spar fixing
124 Inboard leading edge

125 Main spar centre-section carry-through
126 Wing-root entry/maintenance walkway
127 Wing tank fuel filler cap
128 Starboard wing fuel tank
129 Wing ribs
130 Starboard aileron inboard section
131 Outboard wing section attachment rib
132 Wing join capping strip
133 Ball-and-socket spar fixings
134 Starboard wing MG 17 machine-gun
135 Leading-edge panels
136 Nose ribs

137 Outer wing fuel tank position (Ju 87R)
138 Wing front spar
139 Wing ribs
140 Aileron control rods
141 Starboard aileron centre-section
142 Wing rear spar
143 Fixed tab
144 Starboard aileron outboard section
145 Wing skinning panels
146 Pitot head
147 Starboard navigation light

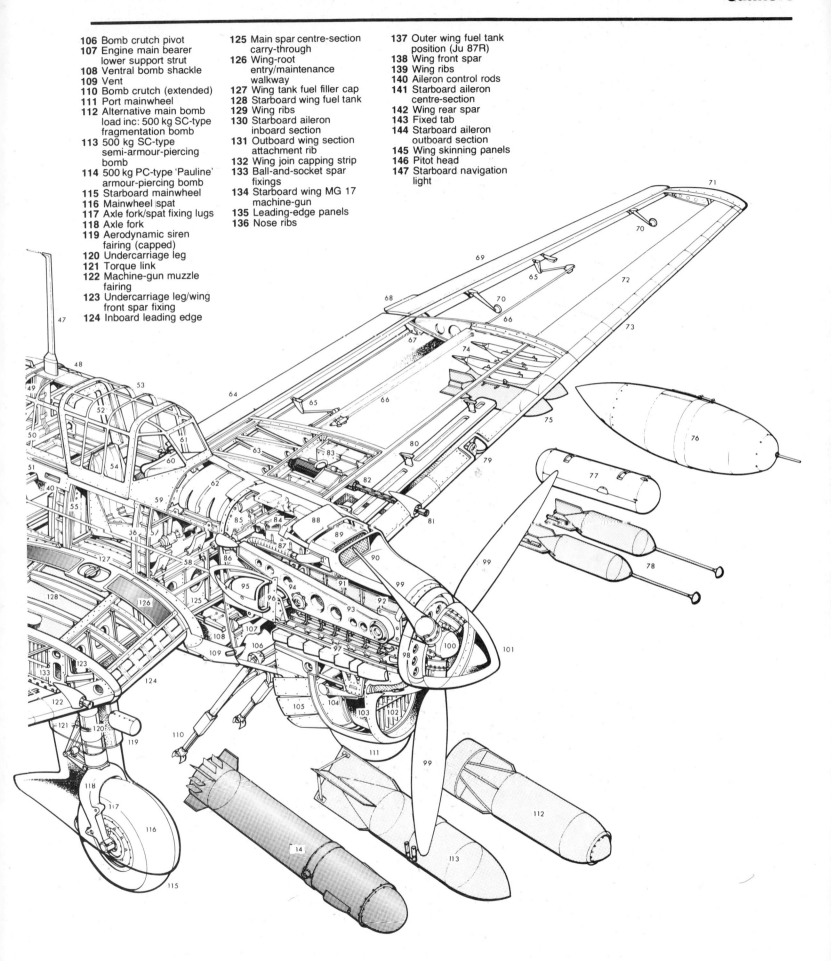

Junkers Ju 88A.

Junkers Ju 88P-2.

Junkers Ju 88C-6.

Junkers Ju 88G-7.

width. An interesting model was the A-13, a ground-attack aircraft with increased armour, no dive brakes, an automatic pull-out device or precision bomb sight and fitted with a special anti-personnel bomb installation. The A-14, A-16 and A-17 were a bomber (with a built-in cable cutter and other refinements), dual-control trainer and a torpedo-bomber respectively.

Ju 88A-1 was powered by Jumo 211B-1 or 211G engines and armed with four 7.9 mm MG 15 machine-guns plus 2,500 kg (5,511 lb) of bombs. This was followed by the A-2 with special fittings for catapult-assisted take-off; the A-3 trainer with dual controls and duplicate instruments; and the A-4 with Jumo 211F, 211J-1 or 211J-2 engines, increased wing span of 20.0 m (65 ft 8 in) and a typical armament of one 13 mm MG 131 and five 7.9 mm MG 81 machine-guns and 3,000 kg (6,614 lb) of bombs. The Ju 88A-5, powered by Jumo 211Gs, had the wing span and bomb load of the A-4 but was otherwise similar to the A-1. It was also the first version to have the option of a balloon-cable cutter. The A-6 had a balloon-cable fender and balloon-destroying gear; while the A-7 was a dual-control trainer based on the A-5. The A-8 was similar to the A-6.

Following a few Ju 88Bs fitted with BMW 801 engines and generally regarded as one of the forerunners of the Ju 188, Junkers produced the Ju 88C series as day and night fighters. Power was provided by Jumo 211B, 211G, 211J and BMW 801 engines. Variants covered C-1 to C-7, the first 'Zerstörers' armed normally with three 7.9 mm MG 17 machine-guns, one 20 mm MG FF cannon and a further two MG FF cannons in an underfuselage pack. Armament for the C-6 included a 'Schräge Musik' mounting in which

two MG 151 guns were fixed in the fuselage to fire obliquely upward and forward.

The Ju 88D was a specialised long-range reconnaissance version; while the Ju 88G was produced in several variants as a night fighter with BMW 801D, 801G, Jumo 213A or 213E engines. The Ju 88H – originally projected in bomber, fighter and reconnaissance forms – had a longer fuselage. However most Hs were used as the lower component of the Mistel composite.

The final versions of the Ju 88 were the P, S and T. The P was a ground-attack aircraft produced in very limited numbers. Originally mounting a 75 mm cannon, this proved unsuccessful and was replaced subsequently by two 37 mm and then one 50 mm BK 5 cannon. The S was built in three sub-variants as a bomber, originally powered by BMW 801G engines with GM-1 power-boost and later with Jumo 213As. The final version was the Ju 88T, similar to the Ju 88S but for photographic-reconnaissance duties.

The Ju 88A-9 was the first tropical version (based on the A-1), carrying water containers, sun blinds, shotgun and rifle, rucksacks, sleeping bags, etc for desert operation. The A-10 and A-11 were also tropical versions. The A-12 was a trainer version of the A-5 with increased cockpit

Data (Ju 88A-4): *Engines* two 998.5 kW (1,340 hp) Junkers Jumo 211Js (see above) *Wing span* 20.0 m (65 ft 8 in) *Length* 14.3 m (47 ft 1½ in) *Max T-O weight* 14,000 kg (30,865 lb) *Max level speed* 470 km/h (292 mph) *Normal range* 2,500 km (1,553 miles)

Junkers Ju 90 (Germany) Forty-passenger commercial airliner of 1937 powered by four 618.5 kW (830 hp) BMW 132H engines. Eleven delivered to Luft-Hansa during 1938, most of which later passed to the Luftwaffe as troop transports.

Interior of a Junkers Ju 90.

Junkers Ju 90.

Junkers Ju 90 fuselage under construction.

Junkers Ju 188 (Germany) The Ju 188 was a development of the Ju 88. It had a redesigned nose, new wings of greater span with pointed tips, and heavier armament.

The first major versions were the Ju 188E and Ju 188F of 1941, which entered service before the Ju 188A and were bombing and reconnaissance types respectively. Power for these was provided by 1,267 kW (1,700 hp) BMW 801D and G engines. Next came the Ju 188A which had been held up by the slow delivery of the 1,323.5 kW (1,776 hp) Jumo 213A engines. One version of the A was adapted to carry two torpedoes. The Ju 188D was a reconnaissance sister to the A fitted with the same engines and armament.

Projected versions of the Ju 188 included the C

bomber (with a remotely controlled tail turret); G (development of the C); H reconnaissance aircraft (developed from the C); R night fighter; and the T photographic reconnaissance aircraft with a pressure cabin. The only other version to enter service was the Ju 188S, a three-seat high-altitude bomber powered by Jumo 213E engines and with a pressurised crew cabin. The priority for low-level attack aircraft caused an abrupt end to Ju 188S production, all remaining airframes being converted into unpressurised aircraft mounting a 50 mm BK 5 cannon. More than 1,000 Ju 188s of all versions were built.

Data (Ju 188A): *Engines* as above *Wing span* 22.0 m (72 ft 2 in) *Length* 14.95 m (49 ft 0½ in) *Max T-O weight* 14,530 kg (32,033 lb) *Max level speed* 520 km/h (323 mph) *Range* 2,500 km (1,550 miles) *Armament* one 20 mm MG 151 cannon in nose, one 20 mm MG 151 cannon in dorsal turret, one 13 mm MG 131 machine-gun in dorsal position, and one 13 mm MG 131 gun or twin 7.9 mm MG 81 guns in lower rear-firing position; up to 3,000 kg (6,614 lb) of bombs

Junkers Ju 188F-1.

Junkers Ju 252 and Ju 352 Herkules (Germany) The Ju 252 was a transport aircraft powered by three 1,051 kW (1,410 hp) Junkers Jumo 211 engines. It had been designed to replace the Ju 52/3m but only 15 were produced. The Ju 352 development was based on wood in order not to use strategic materials. Power was provided by three 894 kW (1,200 hp) Bramo 323R-2 engines. Production of this version totalled 43 or 44.

Junkers Ju 352 Herkules.

Junkers Ju 288 (Germany) In spite of its numerical similarity, the Ju 288 was not a development of the Ju 88 or Ju 188. It was designed as a twin-engined (Daimler-Benz DB 610) medium bomber and was test flown in 1940. Development was slow but a long series of prototypes had been completed by 1943.

Junkers Ju 290.

Junkers K 37.

Junkers Ju 290 (Germany) The Ju 290 was originally designed as a development of the Ju 90 transport and was test flown in 1941. Subsequent development was undertaken to enable it ultimately to supersede the Fw 200C for long-range over-sea anti-shipping and U-boat co-operation work, but it failed to achieve this. Nevertheless seven versions of the A series were produced as transport (A-1 with BMW 801D engines), reconnaissance (A-2, A-3 and A-5), transport (A-6), reconnaissance-bombing (A-7), and reconnaissance (A-8) aircraft – the latter with provision for carrying two Hs 293 anti-shipping glider missiles. Production totalled about 55 aircraft.

The Ju 290B was a projected heavily armed long-range bomber. It was followed by the Ju 290C reconnaissance and transport aircraft, Ju 290D long-range bomber and Ju 290E night bomber: all of which failed to enter production. Data (Ju 290A-8): *Engines* four 1,192.3 kW (1,600 hp) BMW 801L-2 radials *Wing span* 42.0 m (138 ft 0 in) *Length* 28.2 m (92 ft 6 in) *Max T-O weight* 45,000 kg (99,207 lb) *Max level speed* 450 km/h (280 mph) *Range* 6,060 km (3,766 miles) *Armament* three 20 mm MG 151 cannon and two 7.9 mm MG 81 machine-guns, plus two Hs 293 glider missiles

Junkers Ju 388.

Junkers Ju 388 (Germany) The only version of this Ju 188 development to enter production before the end of the war was the Ju 388L reconnaissance aircraft, a small number of which were built. Power was provided by two 1,349 kW (1,810 hp) BMW 801TJ engines.

Junkers Ju 390 (Germany) Six-engined (BMW 801E) development of the Ju 290, test flown in 1943 as a large transport aircraft. Failed to become operational during the war.

Junkers K 16 (Germany) The K 16 of 1922 was a small three-seat (two passenger) cabin monoplane powered by a 41–83.5 kW (55–112 hp) Siemens & Halske or 74.5 kW (100 hp) Bristol Lucifer engine. Only a small number were built, being used for aerial survey and photographic work as well as passenger carrying with a few airline operators.

Junkers K 37 (Sweden) This aircraft first appeared in 1927 as a twin-engined mailplane. At the Junkers factory in Sweden it was developed into the K 37 three-seat general-purpose military aircraft armed with two Vickers machine-guns and three Lewis guns as a fighter; two quicker-firing machine-guns and three Lewis guns as a chaser; and guns and bombs as a reconnaissance bomber. From the K 37 donated to Japan was developed the Mitsubishi Ki-2.

Junkers K 39 (Sweden) Prototype only of a three-seat reconnaissance bomber.

Junkers K 43 (Sweden) Three-seat single-engined reconnaissance and bombing monoplane developed from the W 33/W 34 and available in landplane and seaplane form. Exported to Colombia and Finland.

Junkers K 47 (Sweden) The K 47 was a high-performance two-seat fighter of 1928 powered by a Bristol Jupiter or Mercury radial engine. A few were exported to China.

Junkers K 53 (Sweden) This was a military fighter-reconnaissance development of the A 20 postal aircraft powered by a 231 kW (310 hp) Junkers L.5 engine. A few went into service in Sweden from 1926, while others were built at the Junkers factory in Russia for the Red Air Force and for export to Turkey.

seat monoplane intended for high-performance aerobatic and competition flying. Plans are available to amateur constructors.

Jurca M.J.7 and M.J.77 Gnatsum (France) Scale replica for amateur construction of the North American P-51 Mustang fighter. Its name 'Gnatsum' is 'Mustang' reversed. Two-thirds scale and three-quarters scale respectively.

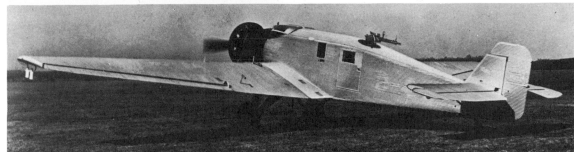

Junkers W 33 and W 34 (Germany) Cantilever low-wing transport aircraft of 1926, usually powered by 231 kW (310 hp) Junkers L.5 and 313 kW (420 hp) Gnome-Rhône Jupiter engines respectively. Except for the engines and the cockpits (open in the W 33 and enclosed in the W 34), the two types were virtually identical and could be operated as landplanes or seaplanes. Each had two pilots sitting side-by-side and a large freight compartment which was entered from the side door and communicated with the cockpit. Some W 34s had this compartment fitted for six passengers. A total of 199 W 33s were produced, together with a large number of E 34s. Production ended in 1934.

Data (W 34 landplane): *Engine* as above or similar *Wing span* 17.75 m (58 ft 2¾ in) *Length* 10.27 m (33 ft 8 in) *Max T-O weight* 2,700 kg (5,953 lb) *Cruising speed* 175 km/h (109 mph) *Range* 850 km (528 miles)

Jurca M.J.7S Solo (France) Intended as a single-seat advanced trainer, basically similar to the M.J.7 Gnatsum.

Jurca M.J.8 and M.J.80 1-Nine-0 (France) Three-quarters and full-size representations of the Focke-Wulf Fw 190 respectively. Plans for the M.J.8 are available to amateur constructors.

Jurca M.J.9 One-Oh-Nine (France) Prototype three-quarters scale representation of a Messerschmitt Bf 109.

Jurca M.J.10 Spit (France) Single-seat three-quarters scale representation of a Supermarine Spitfire which can be modified into a two-seater. Plans are available to amateur constructors.

Jurca M.J.12 Pee-40 (France) Three-quarters scale representation of a Curtiss P-40.

Jurca M.J.14 Fourtouna (France) Small single-seat racing aircraft of unorthodox configuration.

Kaiserlicht Werft floatplanes (Germany) A small number of two-seat KW floatplanes were operated by the German Navy during World War I, each powered by a 119 kW (160 hp) Benz Bz.III engine.

Kalinin AK-1, K4 and K5 (USSR) The AK-1 was a four-seat high-wing monoplane of 1923–24, a single example of which was operated by Dobrolet for a brief time on the Moscow–Kazan service. The AK-1 was one of 16 types that Konstantin Kalinin helped design, two others being the K4 of 1928 and the K5 of 1929. The K4, powered by a BMW IV engine, entered very limited production and was operated as a six-passenger airliner by Dobrolet and Ukrvozduchput, the two

Jurca M.J.2 and M.J.20 Tempête (France) Single-seat light monoplanes, plans for which are available to amateur constructors.

Jurca M.J.3H Dart (France) Single-seat sporting monoplane, plans for which are available to amateur constructors.

Jurca M.J.5 Sirocco (France) Tandem two-seat monoplane developed from the Tempête as a potential club training and touring aircraft. It is fully aerobatic when flown as a two-seater. Plans are available to amateur constructors.

Jurca M.J.5 Sirocco (Sport Wing) (France) Special version of the Sirocco with increased wing span.

Jurca M.J.51 Sperocco (France) Tandem two-

Kaman

Kaman SH-2F Seasprite.

Kaman H-43B Huskie.

companies becoming Dobroflot in 1929. The K5 was an eight-passenger development of the K4, usually powered by a 391 kW (525 hp) M-15 engine. In 1932 Plant C.H. (formerly Kalinin) received an order for 120 K5s, which entered service with Dobroflot in the following year. It is likely that total production was double this figure.

Of interest are the K6 single-engined mail-carrying parasol-wing monoplane, the K7 and the K9 two-seat light monoplane. The giant K7 was reportedly tested in 1933 and had accommodation for 128 passengers. Late the same year it met with disaster, resulting in heavy loss of life.

Data (K5): *Engine* as above *Wing span* 20.5 m (67 ft 2½ in) *Length* 15.7 m (51 ft 6 in) *Max T-O weight* 3,500 kg (7,716 lb) *Max level speed* 198 km/h (123 mph)

Kaman H-2 Seasprite (USA) The prototype Seasprite helicopter flew for the first time on 2 July 1959 and many versions were produced subsequently for the US Navy. From 1967 all of the original UH-2A/B Seasprites were converted progressively to UH-2C twin-engined configuration, with two 932 kW (1,250 shp) General Electric T58-GE-8B turboshafts in place of the former single T58. They have since undergone further modification under the US Navy's important LAMPS (Light Airborne Multi-Purpose System) programme to provide helicopters for ASW (Anti-Submarine Warfare) and ASMD (Anti-Ship Missile Defence) operations. Therefore versions which no longer remain in service or that have been converted to later standards include the UH-2A, B, C, HH-2C and YSH-2E.

Versions of the Seasprite still operated in 1979 were the HH-2D, three aircraft without LAMPS modifications assigned to Coast and Geodetic Survey work, being upgraded to SH-2F standard, NHH-D test aircraft assigned to the circulation control rotor (CCR) programme; SH-2D LAMPS version for ASW, ASMD and a utility role, being upgraded to SH-2F standard; and the SH-2F further developed Mk I LAMPS version with Kaman's 101 rotor, increased-strength landing gear, shortened wheelbase, and twin 1,007 kW (1,350 shp) General Electric T58-GE-8F turboshaft engines – deployment of which began in September 1973 (87 delivered by 1979).

Data (SH-2F): *Engines* as above *Main rotor diameter* 13.41 m (44 ft 0 in) *Length overall* 16.03 m (52 ft 7 in) *Normal T-O weight* 5,805 kg (12,800 lb) *Max*

level speed 265 km/h (165 mph) *Normal range* 679 km (422 miles) *Armament* one or two Mk 44 or Mk 46 ASW homing torpedoes carried on auxiliary fuel tank mounts on each side of the fuselage; eight Mk 25 marine flares/smoke markers (US Navy tests have proved the Seasprite suitable as a platform for firing air-to-surface missiles, guns and rockets)

Kaman H-43 Huskie (USA) First flown in 1956, the Huskie helicopter was produced in several versions for crash-rescue, firefighting, liaison and utility roles. The OH-43, UH-43 and HH-43A piston-engined variants of the original H-43 design, with twin intermeshing rotors, were ordered by the US Navy and USAF (the US Navy OH-43Ds originally designated HOK-1s) and were used during the Korean War.

The HH-43B was the initial turbine-powered production version with a T53-L-1B turboshaft engine (derated to 615 kW; 825 shp). HH-43Bs served with the USAF and in Burma, Colombia, Morocco, Pakistan and Thailand. The HH-43F was a development of the HH-43B, 40 of which were built for the USAF and 17 were acquired by Iran. The QH-43G was produced as a drone development of the HH-43F for the US Navy. Very few Huskies remain operational today.

Data (HH-43F): *Engine* one 857.5 kW (1,150 shp) Lycoming T53-L-11A turboshaft (derated to 615 kW; 825 shp) *Main rotor diameter* (each) 14.33 m (47 ft 0 in) *Length of fuselage* 7.67 m (25 ft 2 in) *Max T-O weight* 4,150 kg (9,150 lb) *Max level speed* 193 km/h (120 mph) *Range* 811 km (504 miles) *Accommodation* pilot, two fully clothed firefighters and 454 kg (1,000 lb) of firefighting and rescue gear. Alternative accommodation for a pilot, co-pilot and ten passengers; or pilot, four stretchers and a medical attendant

Kamov Ka-10 (USSR) Single-seat light utility helicopter powered by one 41 kW (55 hp) AI-4G engine driving two contra-rotating three-bladed rotors. Twelve examples were built for testing during 1950 (NATO reporting name *Hat*). A later modification was the Ka-10M with twin fins and rudders, several of which were demonstrated during 1950.

Kamov Ka-15 (USSR) Known to NATO as *Hen*, the Ka-15 was a two-seat general-purpose helicopter powered by a 205 kW (275 hp) AI-14V radial engine driving two contra-rotating three-bladed rotors. First reported in 1956, some were supplied to State Collective Farms for agricultural purposes. Others served with the Soviet Navy as ship-based anti-submarine helicopters. A variant, known as the Ka-15M, was flown by Aeroflot with two external panniers for stretchers.

Kamov Ka-18 (USSR) Known to NATO as *Hog*, the Ka-18 was a four-seat development of the Ka-15. It flew for the first time in mid-1957 and went into production for passenger, freight- and mail-carrying, geographic-survey and agricultural duties. An ambulance version carried a stretcher in the cabin. Maximum level speed was 150 km/h (93 mph).

Kamov Ka-20 (USSR) Known to NATO as *Harp*, the Ka-20 was first shown in public in the 1961 Soviet Aviation Day fly-past. It was a specialised anti-submarine helicopter following the familiar Kamov formula of two three-bladed co-axial contra-rotating rotors, pod and boom fuselage, multi-fin tail unit and four-wheel landing gear. Power was provided by two small turboshaft engines. A radome under the nose housed a search radar, while a further blister-fairing under the tail-boom housed more equipment. Main armament comprised a pair of air-to-surface missiles (see **Ka-25**).

Kamov Ka-22 Vintokryl (USSR) Experimental large twin-turboprop convertiplane shown in public during the 1961 Soviet Aviation Day display.

Kamov Ka-25 and Ka-25K (USSR) The prototype of the Ka-25 military helicopter was first shown in public in the Soviet Aviation Day fly-past over Tushino Airport, Moscow in July 1961. It was allocated the NATO reporting name *Harp*, but this was changed to *Hormone* for the production versions, about 460 of which were built in 1966–75. Nine are also operated on coastal anti-submarine duties by the Syrian Air Force and others by India and Yugoslavia.

In its ship-based anti-submarine version, the Ka-25 operates from the cruisers of the *Kresta* and *Kara* classes, the carrier/cruiser *Kiev* and the helicopter carrier/cruisers *Moskva* and *Leningrad* — each of which accommodates about 18 aircraft. It has a search-radar installation in an undernose radome, while other equipment includes a towed magnetic anomaly detector, dipping sonar housed in a compartment at the rear of the cabin, and an electro-optical sensor.

Kamov Ka-10M.

Kamov Ka-18.

Kamov Ka-15.

Kamov Ka-20.

Kamov Ka-22 Vintokryl.

Kamov Ka-25.

Kamov Ka-25K.

used widely on Aeroflot's air-ambulance services and is suitable for many other applications, including cargo and passenger transport, forest firefighting, mineral prospecting, pipeline construction and laying transmission lines.

The space aft of the pilots' cabin (between the main landing-gear units and under the rotor transmission) is able to accommodate a variety of interchangeable payloads. For agricultural work the chemical hopper (capacity 900 kg; 1,985 lb) and dust-spreader or spraybars are fitted in this position. This equipment is quickly removable and can be replaced by a cargo/passenger pod accommodating six persons with provision for a seventh in the co-pilot's seat. Alternatively the Ka-26 can be operated with either an open platform for hauling freight or a hook for slinging bulky loads at the end of a cable or in a cargo net. Data: *Engines* as above *Main rotor diameter* (each) 13.0 m (42 ft 8 in) *Length of fuselage* 7.75 m (25 ft 5 in) *Max T-O weight* 3,250 kg (7,165 lb) *Max cruising speed* 150 km/h (93 mph) *Max range with auxiliary tanks* 1,200 km (745 miles)

As well as serving as an anti-submarine and missile-guidance aircraft, the Ka-25 fulfils a variety of other military roles. Only two versions may be identified at present by NATO reporting names *Hormone-A* (basic anti-submarine version) and *Hormone-B* (special electronics variant able to acquire targets for ship-launched missiles).

The Ka-25K (also carrying the NATO reporting name *Hormone*) is a commercial flying-crane variant of the Ka-25, first shown in public in 1967. Instead of the undernose radome of the ASW version, it has a removable gondola giving an exceptional field of view for the occupant.

Kamov Ka-25 *Hormone-A*s on board *Moskva*.

Kamov Ka-26 with cargo/passenger pod attached.

Data (Ka-25K): *Engines* (Ka-25 and Ka-25K) two 671 kW (900 shp) Glushenkov GTD-3 turboshafts *Main rotor diameter* (each) 15.74 m (51 ft 8 in) *Length of fuselage* 9.83 m (32 ft 3 in), (Ka-25, estimated) 9.75 m (32 ft 0 in) *Max T-O weight* 7,300 kg (16,100 lb) *Max level speed* 220 km/h (137 mph) *Range* 650 km (405 miles) *Armament* (Ka-25) enclosed weapons bay for ASW torpedoes, nuclear depth charges and other stores. Some armed with newly developed 'fire-and-forget' air-to-surface missiles

Kamov Ka-26 (USSR) Known to NATO as *Hoodlum*, the Ka-26 is a twin 242.5 kW (325 hp) M-14V-26 radial-engined light helicopter which entered large-scale service as an agricultural aircraft in the Soviet Union in 1970 – being used primarily over orchards and vineyards. It is also

Karhumäki Karhu 48B (Finland) Four-seat cabin monoplane of the early 1950s powered by a 141.6 kW (190 hp) Lycoming O-435A flat-six engine.

Kawanishi Navy E7K (Japan) First flown on 6 February 1933, the Kawanishi Type J was a three-seat twin-float biplane designed by Eiji

Sekiguchi. It was an immediate success and was placed in production for the Japanese Navy for ship-based (catapult-launched) and shore-based operations as the E7K1 Type 94 Reconnaissance Seaplane. It was a single-bay equal-span biplane with a liquid-cooled 559 kW (750 hp) Hiro 91 engine. The wings folded for shipboard stowage.

Although its qualities in flight and on the water were excellent, the E7K1 had a rather poor maximum speed, as a result of which Kawanishi modified one machine to take a 633.4 kW (850 hp) Mitsubishi Zuisei radial engine. Performance was much improved and the new version went into service in 1938 as the E7K2 Type 94 Model 2. Both versions were in first-line service for a variety of duties during the early part of the war in the Pacific. Production totalled 530 and lasted until 1941.

Data (E7K2): *Engine* as above *Wing span* 14.0 m (45 ft 11¼ in) *Length* 10.5 m (34 ft 5½ in) *Max T-O weight* 3,300 kg (7,275 lb) *Max level speed* 275 km/h (171 mph)

Kawanishi Navy E15K1 (Japan) Six prototypes of this remarkable high-speed reconnaissance seaplane were built in 1942. A two-seat low-wing cantilever monoplane with the Kawanishi designation K10, it originally featured ingenious retractable wingtip floats with inflatable top sections, but these were discarded during development and replaced by fixed cantilever units. Only nine production E15K1 'Siun' floatplanes were completed, retaining the same type of jettisonable central float of the prototypes. The intention was to discard the drag-inducing float when necessary to avoid interception, but six aircraft were lost soon after being put into service as a result of failure of the jettisoning mechanism. Powered by a 1,378.6 kW (1,850 hp) Kasei 24 radial engine, the E15K1 (coded *Myrt* by the Allies) reached 561 km/h (348.5 mph) with the float detached (93 km/h; 57.8 mph faster than in normal configuration).

Kawanishi Navy H3K1 (Japan) The Short S.15 or K.F.1 was a biplane flying-boat powered by three 633.4 kW (850 hp) Rolls-Royce Buzzard engines. It was built for Kawanishi who re-assembled it and sold it to the Japanese Navy for maritime-reconnaissance duties in 1930. Four more examples were built by Kawanishi under the designation H3K2 or Type 90-II Flying-Boat.

Kawanishi Navy H6K (Japan) The H6K1 prototype flew for the first time on 14 July 1936. Designed by Yoshio Hashiguchi and Shizuo Kikuhara, it represented a marked improvement over previous Japanese flying-boat designs. A parasol-wing monoplane, it was powered by four 626 kW (840 hp) Nakajima Hikari 2 radial engines, had an enclosed cabin for the flight crew, and defensive machine-gun positions in the nose and bow and in a manually operated tail turret set behind the twin fin and rudder tail assembly. Series-built aircraft were known as the Type 97 Flying-Boat; a total of 217 of all versions up to the H6K5 being built. These included 38 transport versions, some of which operated with Japan Air Lines on Pacific routes pre-World War II. The main production maritime-reconnaissance version was the H6K4 with four 797.4 kW (1,070 hp) Mitsubishi Kinsei radials. Offensive load comprised two 800 kg torpedoes or 1,000 kg (2,205 lb) of bombs carried on racks attached to the underwing struts.

The H6K (Allied code name *Mavis*) had outstanding performance compared with its foreign contemporaries, but by 1942 proved an easy prey to Allied fighters in the Pacific.

Data (H6K4): *Engines* as above *Wing span* 40.0 m (131 ft 2¾ in) *Length* 25.63 m (84 ft 1 in) *Max T-O weight* 21,500 kg (47,400 lb) *Max level speed* 340 km/h (211 mph) *Range* 4,100 km (2,550 miles)

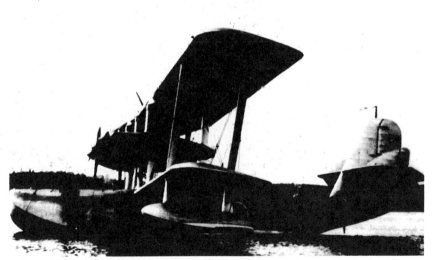

Kawanishi Navy H3K2.

Kawanishi Navy H8K (Japan) Code-named *Emily* by the Allies, the H8K is acknowledged as the world's finest four-engined flying-boat of World War II. Designed by Kikuhara, the prototype flew initially on 31 December 1940. Hydrodynamic qualities left something to be desired, but after modification to the keel the aircraft went into production and service as the Type 2 Flying-Boat, reaching first-line units in 1942. Power was provided by four 1,379 kW (1,850 hp) Mitsubishi Kasei 22 radials. A high-wing cantilever monoplane with a deep slab-sided hull, it carried a normal crew of ten. Armament comprised one 20 mm Type 99 cannon in bow, dorsal and tail turrets and in two beam blisters, plus four 7.7 mm machine-guns on flexible mountings and an offensive load of 2,000 kg

Kawanishi

Kawanishi Navy H6K4.

Kawanishi Navy H6K5.

(4,409 lb) of bombs or two 800 kg torpedoes, or an equivalent weight of depth charges.

Japan's industrial potential limited production to 131 maritime bomber-reconnaissance machines plus 36 Seiku H6K2-L transports, which could carry up to 64 troops. These served throughout World War II in the Pacific, proving very effective and difficult to destroy even towards the end when Allied fighters enjoyed total air superiority.

Data (H8K2): *Engines* as above *Wing span* 38.0 m (124 ft 8 in) *Length* 28.13 m (92 ft 3½ in) *Max T-O weight* 32,500 kg (71,650 lb) *Max level speed* 467 km/h (290.2 mph) *Max range* 7,180 km (4,461 miles)

Kawanishi Navy N1K1 (Japan) The first K 20 prototype flew for the first time in May 1942. It was a tubby mid-wing monoplane with a central main float and wingtip stabilising floats. During development the retractable wingtip floats and contra-rotating propellers – both advanced features – were discarded. Ninety-seven production machines were built between 1943 and 1944

Series of photographs showing a Kawanishi Navy H8K2 being shot down in July 1944.

as single-seat fighters carrying the Japanese Navy designation N1K1. Armed with two 20 mm cannon and two 7.7 mm machine-guns and powered by a 1,088 kW (1,460 hp) Kasei radial, the N1K1 was named Kyofu by the Japanese and coded *Rex* by the Allies. It reached a maximum 489 km/h (304 mph) but saw only limited service in Borneo and over the homeland.

Kawanishi Navy N1K1-J and N1K2-J (Japan) A landplane fighter development of the N1K1, the N1K1-J appeared in 1942. Power plant selected was the Nakajima Homare radial which gave considerable trouble. Nevertheless the design was promising and further prototypes were followed by more than 1,420 series N1K1-J and N1K2-J fighters (known to the Allies as *George*). Most N1K1-J machines were armed with two fuselage-mounted 7.7 mm machine-guns, two 20 mm cannon in the wings and two more cannon in underwing gondolas. The N1K2-J had four wing-mounted cannon.

The inherited mid-wing configuration of the N1K1-J resulted in a long stalky undercarriage which caused many problems. It was discarded in favour of a low-mounted wing in the N1K2-J which was able to utilise a more conventional and tougher undercarriage. The second external change was a fin and rudder of enlarged area. The Shiden (Japanese name for N1K1-J) and Shiden-Kai (N1K2-J) became the Navy's principal land-based fighter and fighter bomber (the latter role with up to 1,000 kg; 2,205 lb of bombs). Experienced Shiden pilots did well against their main US Navy opponent, the F6F Hellcat.

Data (N1K2-J): *Engine* as above *Wing span* 12.0 m (39 ft 4½ in) *Length* 9.35 m (30 ft 8 in) *Max T-O weight* 4,860 kg (10,714 lb) *Max level speed* 595 km/h (369.5 mph) *Range* more than 1,700 km (1,056 miles)

Kawasaki Army Type 87 (Japan) The first twin-engined bomber to be built in series in Japan, the Type 87 was in fact a licence-built Dornier Do N, the work of Dr Richard Vogt. Total production amounted to 28 aircraft. An all-metal parasol-wing monoplane, it was powered by two 372.6 kW (500 hp) BMW VI engines. Open cockpits were provided for the pilot and nose and dorsal gunners. Armament was three light machine-guns and up to 1,000 kg (2,205 lb) of bombs. In 1931 the Type 87 was used in action against the Chinese during the Manchurian Incident, but with limited success.

Kawasaki Army Type 88 (Japan) The prototype KDA-2 reconnaissance aircraft and light bomber flew for the first time in February 1927. Designed by Dr Vogt (by then Kawasaki's chief designer), it was a single-bay, unequal-span two-seat biplane with I-type wing-bracing struts and powered by a 372.6 kW (500 hp) BMW VI liquid-cooled engine with a frontal radiator. It proved successful and was placed in large-scale production, 710 having been completed by 1931. A number were adapted to take additional streamlined fuel tanks beneath the forward fuselage, giving an increased range of 1,200 km (746 miles).

The need for a specialised light bomber led to the development of an improved version, the Type 88-II, with smooth nose contours and radiator relocated below the nose. It also had a fin and rudder of entirely new design. It was placed

Kawasaki

Kawasaki Army Type 88.

in production in 1929 and 407 were built. Both the Kawasaki Type 88-I and Type 88-II were extensively used during the fighting in Manchuria and China during the early 1930s.

Data: *Engine* as above *Wing span* 15.0 m (49 ft 2 in) *Length* (Type 88-I) 12.8 m (42 ft 0 in), (Type 88-II) 12.38 m (40 ft 3½ in) *Max T-O weight* (Type 88-II) 3,100 kg (6,834 lb) *Max level speed* 210 km/h (130.5 mph) *Endurance* 6 h *Armament* three machine-guns, plus a normal offensive load of 200 kg (441 lb) of bombs

Kawasaki Army Type 92 Fighter (Japan) The KDA-5 was a single-seat fighter biplane with a basic structure of metal. The wings were braced either side with single I-struts and the undercarriage was of split-axle type. Power was provided by a 447 kW (600 hp) BMW VI engine, uprated to 559 kW (750 hp) in production machines. Five prototypes were followed by 180 Type 92 Model 1 production aircraft and 200 slightly modified Model 2 machines. Deliveries were completed in 1934 and the Type 92 participated in the fighting during the Manchurian and Chinese incidents. Armed with two 7.7 mm machine-guns, the Type 92 was manoeuvrable and had a maximum speed of 320 km/h (199 mph).

Kawasaki Army Ki-3 (Japan) The two-seat Ki-3 was the last Vogt design to go into production for the Japanese Army. Three prototypes, tested in 1933, were followed by 243 production aircraft built up to March 1935 (40 built by Tatchikawa).

Powered by a single 596 kW (800 hp) Ha 2 liquid-cooled engine with nose radiator, the Ki-3 was known as the Type 93 Light Bomber in Army service. It was an unequal-span biplane braced either side by a single contoured I-strut. The fixed

Kawasaki Ki-10.

wide-track divided undercarriage could be fitted with wheel spats. Armament comprised one fixed 7.7 mm synchronised machine-gun installed in the engine cowling and another weapon of the same calibre on a Scarff-type mounting over the rear cockpit. Up to 500 kg (1,102 lb) of bombs were carried on underwing racks.

The Ki-3 was in front-line service in the fighting with China until relegated to supply-dropping missions to isolated troops during 1939.

Data: *Engine* as above *Wing span* 13.0 m (42 ft 8 in) *Length* 10.0 m (32 ft 9½ in) *Max T-O weight* 3,100 kg (6,834 lb) *Max level speed* 260 km/h (161.5 mph)

Kawasaki Army Ki-10 (Japan) Four Ki-10 single-seat fighter prototypes made their appearance in the spring of 1935, designed by Takeo Doi (who had succeeded Richard Vogt as Kawasaki's chief designer). The Ki-10 was selected in competition with Nakajima's Ki-11 low-wing monoplane, the Japanese Army preferring the Ki-10 biplane's manoeuvrability to its opponent's slightly superior speed.

Production Ki-10-I aircraft were powered by the 633.4 kW (850 hp) Kawasaki Ha-9-IIa liquid-cooled engine, 300 of which were built between 1935 and 1937 and went into service as the Army Type 95 Fighter. They featured biplane wings of unequal span, braced by N-struts and with ailerons on the upper wing only. The divided undercarriage had wheel spats. The all-metal structure was alloy sheet and fabric-covered. Armament comprised two synchronised 7.7 mm Type 89 machine-guns. The improved Type 95 Model 2 had increased wing span and length, and vertical tail surfaces of greater area. This version remained in production until December 1938, 280 being completed. Meanwhile during 1936–7 three experimental variants, incorporating modifications to improve performance, were tested but rejected for production.

The Ki-10 had excellent dogfighting qualities and proved itself during the second Chinese incident. It took part in the fighting against Russian forces at Nomonhan, although by then (1939) it was largely outclassed. The Ki-10 was coded *Perry* by the Allies.

Data (Ki-10-I): *Engine* as above *Wing span* 9.55 m (31 ft 4 in) *Length* 7.2 m (23 ft 7½ in) *Max T-O weight* 1,650 kg (3,638 lb) *Max level speed* 400 km/h (248.5 mph) *Range* 1,000 km (621 miles)

Kawasaki Army Ki-32 (Japan) The Ki-32 light bomber was an all-metal mid-wing monoplane powered by a single 708 kW (950 hp) Ha-9-IIb liquid-cooled engine. Its wide-track fixed cantilever undercarriage featured open-sided wheel fairings. Wing and tail surfaces were finely tapered. The two-man crew were accommodated beneath a long raised canopy. Armament comprised one fixed cowling 7.7 mm Type 89 machine-gun and another of the same type on a flexible mounting operated by the observer. An internal bomb bay accommodated a 300 kg (661 lb) offensive load, supplemented by 150 kg (330.5 lb) of bombs on external racks.

Eight 1937 prototypes were followed by 846 series aircraft built up to May 1940 and designated Army Type 98 Light Bomber. They saw extensive war service in China, flying with seven Sentais during 1938–9 and participated in the fierce fighting over the Khalkin Gol and at Nomonhan against Soviet forces during 1939. Among the Type 98's final operational sorties were successful bombing raids on Hong Kong prior to its surrender in December 1941. The type was coded *Mary* by the Allies.

Data: *Engine* as above *Wing span* 15.0 m (49 ft 2½ in) *Length* 11.64 m (38 ft 2¼ in) *Max T-O weight* 3,762 kg (8,294 lb) *Max level speed* 423 km/h (263 mph) *Range* 1,350 km (839 miles)

Kawasaki Army Ki-45 Kai (Japan) The first Ki-45 twin-engined fighter prototype made its maiden flight in January 1939 – nearly two years after an official Army specification had appeared calling for such an aircraft. Designer Takeo Doi was then only at the beginning of his troubles and after the building and testing of eight more Ki-45 prototypes, the need emerged for a simplified design suitable for mass production. Three Ki-45 Kai prototypes (test-flown during 1941) were followed by 12 development aircraft. Only in early 1942 did quantity production as the Army Type 2 two-seat fighter begin.

The Ki-45 Kai had aesthetically attractive lines. The slim, oval fuselage of the original Ki-45 was retained, but the wings and horizontal tail-plane acquired straight contours instead of the original elliptical configuration. Of all-metal construction, the Ki-45 Kai had two 782.5 kW (1,050 hp) Nakajima Ha-25 close-cowled radial engines. The main undercarriage legs retracted backwards into the nacelles.

The Model A fighter went into service in August 1942 with the home-based 5th Sentai. A specialised attack version replaced the fixed nose mounted 20 mm Ho 5 cannon and two 12.7 mm Type 1 machine-guns of the Model A with a 37 mm Type 98 cannon in a ventral tunnel and a 20 mm Ho 3 cannon. The observer retained his 7.92 mm Type 98 machine-gun on a flexible mounting. The need for an effective night fighter led to production of the Model C from April 1944. This had a 37 mm Ho 203 cannon in the ventral tunnel and two obliquely mounted forward-firing 20 mm Ho 5 cannon on top of the fuselage.

Kawasaki Army Ki-45 Kai.

Captured Kawasaki Army Ki-45 Kai.

All the versions of the Ki-45 Kai were popular with their crews. The Model B scored some successes against Allied shipping and the Model C destroyed a number of American Liberators in the south-west Pacific and Superfortresses over the home islands. Named Toryu by the Japanese, the Ki-45 Kai was coded *Nick* by the Allies. Total production was 1,701, including prototypes and evaluation machines.

Data (Model A): *Engine* as above *Wing span* 15.02 m (49 ft 3¼ in) *Length* 10.6 m (34 ft 9¼ in) *Max T-O weight* 5,276 kg (11,632 lb) *Max level speed* 547 km/h (340 mph) *Range* 1,500 km (932 miles)

Kawasaki Army Ki-48 (Japan) During 1939 nine Ki-48 prototypes and evaluation aircraft were extensively tested by the Japanese Army. As a twin-engined light bomber (Allied code name *Lily*) it entered operational service in Northern China during the autumn of 1940, designated Army Type 99. Its high speed and good serviceability won much praise; it was not until it encountered serious air opposition from the British and Americans during the Pacific war that the weaknesses of the design became obvious.

Defensive armament of three 7.7 mm machine-guns in nose, dorsal and ventral step positions was increased in the late production Model IIc aircraft by a single 12.7 mm weapon. Bomb load of the Model II (1,411 built) was doubled to 800 kg (1,764 lb), but was still inadequate. Originally powered by two 708 kW (950 hp) Ha-25 radial engines these were replaced in Model II aircraft by 857 kW (1,150 hp) HA-115s. Production

Kawasaki Army KI-32s.

Kawasaki

Kawasaki Army Ki-48s.

Kawasaki Army Ki-61 in Chinese Air Force markings.

Kawasaki Army Ki-61-I.

totalled 1,977 aircraft of all versions, many being relegated to night attacks and finally to Kamikaze operations as the war approached the Japanese home islands.

Data (Model II): *Engines* as above *Wing span* 17.45 m (57 ft 3 in) *Length* 12.75 m (41 ft 10 in) *Max T-O weight* 6,750 kg (14,881 lb) *Max level speed* 505 km/h (314 mph) *Range* 2,400 km (1,491 miles)

Kawasaki Ki-55 (Japan) Advanced trainer, powered by a 335.3 kW (450 hp) Hitachi Ha.13A radial engine.

Kawasaki Army Ki-56 (Japan) Developed from the Lockheed 14 transport built by the Kawasaki Company under licence, the Ki-56 had an enlarged fuselage incorporating a large freight loading door in the port rear-fuselage side. Powered by two 671 kW (900 hp) Ha-26-II radial engines, two prototypes were followed by 119 series-built machines designated Army Type 1 Freight Transport (assembled between 1941 and 1943). Widely used in the Pacific war, the Ki-56 was coded *Thalia* by the Allies.

Kawasaki Army Ki-61 (Japan) When it first appeared in action in April 1943, the Kawasaki Army Type 3 'Hien' (production version of the Ki-61 single-seat fighter known to the Allies as *Tony*) was confused with the German Bf 109F. It was in fact an original design by Takeo Doi. The first of 11 prototypes flew in December 1941 and 2,654 production Ki-61-I aircraft plus 137 Ki-61-IIs were built up to the end of the Pacific war in 1945. The Ki-61 was an important part of the Japanese Army's aircraft inventory but, like other in-line-engined Japanese types, it had a relatively poor serviceability record due to problems with its 820 kW (1,100 hp) Ha-40 engine (replaced by the 1,118 kW; 1,500 hp Ha-140 in the Ki-61-II).

Nevertheless the all-metal low-wing Ki-61 proved popular with its pilots who acquitted themselves well in action over New Guinea, Formosa (Taiwan), the Philippines, Okinawa and finally over the Japanese homeland. It had sleek lines, and the initial armament of two fuselage-mounted 12.7 mm Ho-103 machine-guns and two wing-mounted 7.7. mm Type 89s was increased in later Ki-61-I aircraft to two 20 mm cannon in the wings and two 12.7 mm machine-guns; changing to four 12.7 mm machine-guns and finally to four 20 mm cannon. The Ki-61 Kai and Ki-61-II Kai had external racks for two 250 kg (551 lb) bombs.

Data (Ki-61-Ib): *Engine* as above *Wing span* 12.0 m (39 ft 4½ in) *Length* 8.75 m (28 ft 8½ in) *Max T-O weight* 3,250 kg (7,165 lb) *Max level speed* 592 km/h (368 mph) *Range* 1,900 km (1,180 miles)

Kawasaki Army Ki-100 (Japan) Late in 1944, 275 airframes for Kawasaki Ki-61-II fighters lay unused due to lack of engines resulting from the destruction by USAAF Superfortresses of the company's aeroengine factory. The skilled Kawasaki engineers rapidly adapted them to take the 1,118 kW (1,500 hp) Ha-122-II radial engine in place of the original in-line power plant. The first conversion flew in February 1945. First production aircraft was in fact the fourth Ki-100 to take to the air. The type went into service as the Army Type 5 Fighter Model 1A and proved very successful operating with home-defence units. All 275 airframes were completed as Model 1As and 118 Ki-100-Ib fighters were built from scratch. Each featured a cut-down fuselage aft of the cockpit. Two Ki-100-II high-altitude fighter prototypes were built before the Japanese surrender.

Data (Ki-100-Ib): *Engine* as above *Wing span* 12.0 m (39 ft 4½ in) *Length* 8.82 m (28 ft 11¼ in) *Max T-O weight* 3,500 kg (7,716 lb) *Max level speed* 580 km/h (360.5 mph) *Range* 2,000 km (1,243 miles)

Kawasaki Army Ki-102 (Japan) Developed from the Ki-45 Kai via the experimental Ki-96 fighter, the first of three Ki-102 prototypes flew in March 1944. Twenty evaluation aircraft followed. Production was initiated and the first series-built machines were rolled out towards the end of 1944. They went into service as the Army Type 4 Assault plane or Ki-102b, resembling the Ki-45 Kai externally but having an angular fin and rudder, pointed nose and retractable tailwheel.

The two-man crew and fuel tanks had armour protection. Armament comprised a 57 mm Ho-141 nose cannon, two 20 mm Ho-5 forward-firing cannon in the lower forward fuselage and a single 12.7 mm Ho-103 machine-gun operated by the observer. Two 250 kg bombs could be carried. A total of 215 were built up to July 1945, some participating in the battle for Okinawa. Twenty-six earlier aircraft were modified as Ki-102a high-altitude fighters and two as Ki-102c night fighters equipped with radar. Allied code name for the Ki-102b was *Randy*.

Data (Ki-102b): *Engines* two 1,118 kW (1,500 hp) Mitsubishi Ha.112-II radials *Wing span* 15.57 m (51 ft 1 in) *Length* 11.45 m (37 ft 6¾ in) *Max T-O weight* 7,300 kg (16,094 lb) *Max level speed* 580 km/h (360.5 mph) *Range* 2,000 km (1,243 miles)

Kawasaki Ki-108 (Japan) Pressurised high-altitude fighter developed from the Ki-102. Four built.

Kawasaki C-1 (Japan) The C-1 medium-sized troop and freight transport was designed to meet a JASDF requirement for a replacement for its former fleet of Curtiss C-46s. The first flying prototype took off for the first time on 12 November 1970 and the first production aircraft was delivered in December 1974. By early 1978 24 production C-1s had been delivered, including two long-range aircraft with an additional 4,732 litre (1,250 US gallon) wing centre-section fuel tank. Three more long-range C-1s were ordered thereafter and further production is anticipated.

Future derivatives of the C-1 under study in 1979 included an electronic warfare version, a minelaying version and an improved tactical transport version with an extended fuselage.

Data: *Engines* two 64.5 kN (14,500 lb st) Mitsubishi (Pratt & Whitney) JT8D-M-9 turbofans *Wing span* 30.6 m (100 ft 4¾ in) *Length* 29.0 m (95 ft 1¾ in) *Max T-O weight* 45,000 kg (99,210 lb) *Max level speed* 806 km/h (501 mph) *Range* 1,300–3,353 km (807–2,084 miles) *Accommodation* crew of five, plus up to 60 troops, 45 paratroops, 36 stretchers and attendants, or 11,900 kg (26,235 lb) of freight

Kawasaki KH-4 (Japan) Four-seat light general-purpose helicopter powered by a 201 kW

Kawasaki KH-4.

(270 hp) Lycoming TVO-435-D1A flat-six engine. Based on the Bell Model 47G-3B, the prototype first flew in August 1962. A total of 211 production examples were built up to mid-1975 for civil and military use. Maximum level speed is 169 km/h (105 mph).

Kawasaki P-2J (Japan) The P-2J was developed to meet a JMSDF requirement for a new anti-submarine aircraft to replace its P2V-7 Neptunes in service during the 1970s. Work on the conversion of a standard P2V-7 to the P-2J prototype began in mid-1965 and it flew for the first time on 21 July 1966.

The first production aircraft was flown on 8 August 1969 and a further 81 P-2Js were built, the last delivered in 1979. One has been converted to UP-2J configuration for target-towing duties. Three further conversions are planned.

Data: *Engines* two 2,282 kW (3,060 ehp) Japanese-built General Electric T64-IHI-10E turboprops, plus two 15.2 kN (3,417 lb st) Ishikawajima J3-IHI-7D turbojets *Wing span* 29.78 m (97 ft 8½ in) *Length* 29.23 m (95 ft 10¾ in) *Max T-O weight* 34,019 kg (75,000 lb) *Max cruising speed* 402 km/h (250 mph) *Range* 4,450 km (2,765 miles)

Kawasaki P-2J.

Kawasaki (Boeing Vertol) KV-107/II and KV-107/IIA (Japan) Kawasaki has extensive rights to manufacture and sell the Boeing Vertol 107 Model II helicopter. The first KV-107 to be built under the agreement flew for the first time in May 1962.

In 1965 Kawasaki obtained worldwide sales rights of the KV-107 from the Boeing Company's Vertol Division. An improved model, the KV-107/IIA, is available in any of the KV-107/II forms powered by two 1,044 kW (1,400 shp) General Electric CT58-140-1 or Ishikawajima-Harima CT58-IHI-140-1 turboshaft engines (max continuous rating 932 kW; 1,250 shp), which give improved performance during VTOL and in 'hot and high' conditions.

Parachuting from an early Kawasaki C-1.

Kawasaki KV-107/II.

Kellett KD-1B.

Versions of the KV-107/II and IIA so far announced are the KV-107/II-1 basic utility helicopter (none yet built); KV-107/II-2 basic airline helicopter (11 built;) KV-107/II-3 mine-countermeasures (MCM) helicopter for the JMSDF, with extended-range fuel tanks, towing hook and cargo sling (nine ordered, all of which were delivered in 1975, including seven KV-107/IIA-3s with uprated power); KV-107/II-4 tactical cargo/troop transport for the JGSDF, with foldable seats for 26 troops or 15 casualty stretchers (57 delivered by March 1979, including one with VIP interior for Cabinet use, the latest 16 as KV-107/IIA-4s with uprated power); KV-107/II-5 long-range search-and-rescue helicopter for the JASDF (27 delivered by early 1979, including eight uprated KV-107/IIA-5s); KV-107/II-6 de luxe transport (none yet built); KV-107/II-7 de luxe VIP version with 6–11 seats; KV-107/IIA-17 long-range passenger and cargo transport version for the Tokyo Metropolitan Police Department; KV-107/IIA-SM-1 firefighting version for the Saudi Arabian government (four delivered by early 1979); and KV-107/IIA-SM-2 rescue and aeromedical version for the Saudi Arabian government (two delivered).

Data (commercial KV-107/II-2): *Engines* two 932 kW (1,250 shp) General Electric CT58-110-1 or Ishikawajima-Harima CT58-IHI-110-1 turboshafts *Main rotor diameter* 15.24 m (50 ft 0 in) *Length of fuselage* 13.59 m (44 ft 7 in) *Max T-O weight* 9,706 kg (21,400 lb) *Max level speed* 253 km/h (157 mph) *Range* 175 km (109 miles), (KV-107/IIA with max fuel) 1,097 km (682 miles)

Kawasaki-Dornier types (Japan/Germany) During 1925 Kawasaki obtained licences to construct the Dornier Komet, BMW engine and the Vincent Andre radiator. Komets were supplied to the Tozai-Teiki-Kokukai as a commercial transport for use on the service between Tokyo and Osaka. Following this, several Kawasaki-Dornier Do F bombers were delivered to the Japanese Army Air Service.

Keleher Lark-1B (USA) Single-seat sporting monoplane, plans for which are available to amateur constructors.

Kellett K-3 Autogiro (USA) The Kellett Autogiro Corporation held a licence to build the Cierva autogiro and undertook development of the type from 1929. The K-3, one of which went with Admiral Byrd on the 1933 Antarctic expedition, was a side-by-side two-seat aircraft powered by a 156.5 kW (210 hp) Kinner radial engine. Rotor diameter was 12.34 m (40 ft 6 in) and wing span 7.92 m (26 ft 0 in).

Kellett K-4 Autogiro (USA) Two-seat autogiro powered by a 156.5 kW (210 hp) Continental R-670 radial engine. Wing span 7.49 m (24 ft 7 in).

Kellett KD-1 Autogiro (USA) Following considerable research and development in connection with the Direct-Control Wingless Autogiro, Kellett produced the KD-1 which was similar to the British C-30 Autogiro and was completed in late 1934. It was demonstrated to the US Army and Navy as well as civil authorities. In May 1935 it made the first landing on the roof-top of a building with air mail during the opening ceremony of the new Philadelphia post office. One was bought by the US Army as the YG-1, its first rotary-winged aircraft.

Kellett KD-1A Autogiro (USA) Two-seat direct-control wingless autogiro built for commercial purposes. It represented a considerable improvement over the KD-1. Powered by a 167.7 kW (225 hp) Jacobs L-4-MA radial engine. One purchased by the US Army as the YG-1A.

Kellett KD-1B and YO-60 Autogiro (USA) Single-seat direct-control wingless autogiro operated in an air-mail shuttle service by Eastern Airlines between Camden Airport, Philadelphia and the roof of the Philadelphia post office. Maximum level speed was 209 km/h (130 mph). Seven were purchased by the US Army as YG-1Bs; one subsequently being modified into the XR-2 and another as the XR-3. In 1943 the company completed delivery to the USAAF of seven more autogiros, six as YO-60s. On completion of this order it abandoned the manufacture of autogiros.

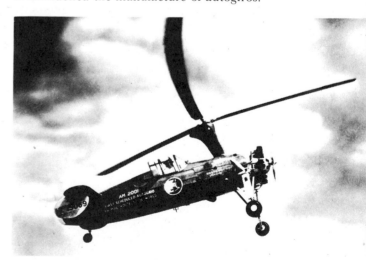

Kellett XH-8 and XH-10 (USA) Kellett produced the XR-8 and XR-10 helicopters for the USAAF/USAF, delivered 1943–45 and June 1948 respectively. These became XH-8 and XH-10 respectively.

Kellett XH-17 (USA) Kellett development of a very large heavy-lift helicopter powered by a jet rotor system: Kellett served in the role of subcontractor to the Hughes Aircraft Company which had purchased the prime contract from Kellett in August 1948 (see **Hughes XH-17**).

Keystone Y1B-4.

Keystone bombers (USA) On 8 March 1927 Huff-Daland Airplanes Inc became the Keystone Aircraft Corporation. Keystone bombers formed the backbone of the USAAC's heavy offensive force for nearly a decade. Although the first aircraft of the series was delivered in 1927, they were still being produced in large numbers in the early 1930s. Indeed during 1931 and early 1932 Keystone delivered more than 100 bombardment biplanes to the USAAC. In the following year Keystone maintained bomber production, supplemented by amphibians and patrol flying-boats for the US Navy.

As a replacement for the Martin NBS-1 biplane bombers, Keystone delivered in August 1927 nine LB-1s, each powered by a single 566.7 kW (760 hp) Packard 2A-2540 engine. Known to Keystone as the Cyclops, the LB-1 was a development of the XLB-1 Pegasus prototype powered by a 596 kW (800 hp) Packard 1A-2540 engine (see 1927 *Jane's* for full details). With a change of USAAC policy from single-engined to twin-engined bombers, Keystone delivered the original XLB-5 Pirate. This decision was no doubt influenced by the successful flight testing of the XLB-5 Pirate which in 1926 had proved capable of maintaining altitude for half an hour on one engine only, and it had 'the ideal' bombing fuselage, developed by Air Corps engineers. This was followed by ten Liberty-powered LB-5s and one XLB-3, the latter with a triple fin and rudder tail unit. Twenty-four 313 kW (420 hp) Liberty-powered LB-5As were then produced, each with twin fins and rudders, plus one 391 kW (525 hp) Wright R-1750-1 Cyclone-engined XLB-6.

Production continued with 17 Cyclone-powered LB-6 and 18 391 kW (525 hp) Pratt & Whitney R-1690-3 Hornet-powered LB-7 Panthers. Experimental installation of different engines in LB-6s and LB-7s led to a number of one-off types, including the LB-9, LB-10, LB-11 and LB-12. However series production began again with 36 B-3As, featuring a lengthened fuselage and a conventional single fin and rudder tail unit. Power for the B-3As was provided by Hornet engines similar to those fitted to the LB-6, as also

powered five service-test Y1B-4s. Twenty-seven B-5As and six Y1B-6s, with 391 kW (525 hp) Cyclones, followed 25 428.5 kW (575 hp) Hornet-powered B-4As. Finally came 39 428.5 kW (575 hp) Wright R-1820-1 Cyclone-powered B-6As, making a grand total of well over 200 bombers built in the series.

Although generally similar to earlier versions, it is worth remarking on the accommodation for the B-6A. A crew of five was carried with a gunner's and bomber's cockpit in the nose fitted with a gun-mounting above and a bomb-sighting and -dropping compartment below. Pilots' cockpit, with accommodation for two side-by-side, was in front of the wings. Under the centre-section was carried the standard Air Corps internal bomb rack for 975 kg (2,150 lb) of bombs. Midway between the wings and the tail was the aft gunner's position armed with twin Lewis guns above and one Lewis gun below; with the wireless operator's compartment in the fuselage.

Of the Keystone bomber force, only 120 aircraft served in the USA, the rest being deployed in Hawaii, the Philippines and around the Panama Canal. Interestingly a number of the bombers took part in the National Air Races and also performed occasionally as makeshift mail carriers.

Data (B-3A): *Engines* as above *Wing span* 22.76 m (74 ft 8 in), (B-6A) 22.78 m (74 ft 9 in) *Length* 14.88 m (48 ft 9½ in) *Max T-O weight* 5,875 kg (12,950 lb), (B-6A) 6,048 kg (13,334 lb) *Max level speed* 183 km/h (114 mph), (B-6A) 195 km/h (121 mph) *Normal range* 1,385 km (860 miles), (B-6A) 1,328 km (825 miles) *Armament* three 0.303 in Browning machine-guns, plus 975–1,134 kg (2,150–2,500 lb) of bombs

Keystone NK-1 Pup (USA) Two-seat trainer, 16 of which were delivered to the US Navy in 1930.

Keystone PK-1 (USA) Eighteen 428.5 kW (575 hp) Wright Cyclone-powered examples of an all-metal development of the Naval Aircraft Factory PN-12 flying-boat, delivered to the US Navy in 1931.

Keystone Air Yacht (USA) Six-passenger cabin amphibious biplane powered by one 391 kW

Klemm Kl.107B.

Koolhoven F.K.40.

Klemm KL.25.

(525 hp) Wright Cyclone engine mounted in the leading edge of the upper wing.

Keystone Commuter (USA) Four-seat cabin flying-boat powered by a 223.6 kW (300 hp) Wright J-6 engine.

Keystone OL-9 (USA) High-speed amphibian powered by a 317 kW (425 hp) Pratt & Whitney R-1340-4 Wasp engine. Twenty-six delivered to the US Navy (see **Loening OL**).

Keystone Patrician (USA) Twenty-passenger cabin monoplane fitted with three 391 kW (525 hp) Wright Cyclone engines. Began trials in November 1928. The first Patrician was thoroughly service-tested in a return trip to the Pacific coast and on a month's charter to the Colonial Air Transport, with whom it was placed on the scheduled passenger run between Boston and New York.

Keystone Pathfinder (USA) Ten-passenger commercial cabin biplane powered by three 164 kW (220 hp) Wright J-5 Whirlwind radial engines. The first Pathfinder was used by the West-Indian Aerial Express of Santo Domingo.

Keystone Pronto (USA) Three-seat general-utility commercial biplane powered by a 164 kW (220 hp) Wright J-5 Whirlwind engine. Number supplied to Peru.

Kungl. Flygförvaltningens Flygverkstad J.22 (Sweden) Owing to the difficulty of purchasing aircraft from abroad during World War II and the fact that the small Swedish aircraft industry was fully engaged, the Swedish Air Board undertook the design and construction of a single-seat fighter. Its design was supervised by Mr Bo Lundberg; production was handled by the Royal Air Board Aircraft Factory (FFVS) at Ulvsunda.

Powered by a 782.5 kW (1,050 hp) Swedish-built Pratt & Whitney R-1830 Twin Wasp radial engine, armament comprised two 13.2 mm and two 7.9 mm machine-guns in the J.22A version and four 13.2 mm guns in the J.22B. A total of 198 were produced, deliveries starting in 1943. The J.22 remained operational until 1952.

Data: *Engine* as above *Wing span* 10.0 m (32 ft

10 in) *Length* 7.8 m (25 ft 7 in) *Max T-O weight* 2,858 kg (6,300 lb) *Max level speed* 575 km/h (357 mph) *Range* 1,250 km (777 miles)

Kharkov KhAI-1 (USSR) M-22-powered seven-seat commercial monoplane operated by Aeroflot for a few years from 1934.

Kingsford Smith PL-7 and KS-3 Cropmaster (Australia) In 1955 the company began the construction of a prototype agricultural biplane which became known as the PL-7 Tanker. It flew for the first time on 21 September 1956. Following this the KS-3 was developed as a conventional low-wing agricultural aircraft powered by a Warner Super Scarab engine. From the end of the 1950s the company concentrated on an Auster aircraft modernisation and re-engining programme, producing the Bushmaster (J-5G Cirrus Autocar with a 134 kW; 180 hp Lycoming O-360); Kingsmith (Autocar J/1 with a 112 kW; 150 hp Lycoming O-320); Auster J/5G Super Autocar (with a 168 kW; 225 hp Continental O-470); and an E.P.9 conversion.

Kinner Envoy (USA) Enlarged version of the Playboy with the cabin accommodating four people. Power was provided by a 276 kW (370 hp) SC-7 radial engine. In 1935 the US Navy ordered three Envoys as personnel transports, designated RK-1s.

Kinner Playboy (USA) Two-seat cabin monoplane powered by a 119 kW (160 hp) Kinner R-5 Series II engine.

Kinner Sportster (USA) Two-seat open-cockpit light monoplane powered by a 74.5 kW (100 hp) Kinner K-5 or 93 kW (125 hp) B-5 engine.

Kinner Sportwing (USA) Refined version of the Sportster powered by a 119 kW (160 hp) Kinner R-5 Series II engine.

Klemm Kl.25 (Germany) see **British Aircraft Swallow** and **Eagle**

Klemm Kl.31 (Germany) Four-seat light cabin monoplane of 1933 powered by a 112 kW (150 hp) Siemens Sh.14a or similar engine.

Klemm Kl.32 (Germany) Three-seat light cabin monoplane of 1933 powered by a Siemens Sh.14a or similar engine.

Klemm Kl.35B and Kl.35D (Germany) The Kl.35B was a two-seat light monoplane with either open or enclosed cockpits. Power was provided by a 74.5 kW (100 hp) Hirth H.M.504A-2 engine. It held several international records for aircraft with engines of 6.5 litres capacity as a landplane and seaplane (listed in the 1939 *Jane's*) and many were built for the home market and for export. It was also built in Sweden under licence.

560

Koolhoven

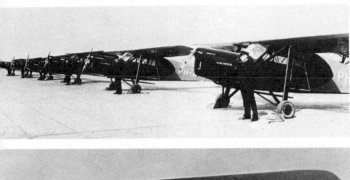

Kokusai Army Ki-76 (Japan) A strut-braced high-wing cabin monoplane inspired by the Fieseler Storch but fitted with Fowler instead of slotted flaps. The Japanese claimed that it had higher STOL qualities than the German machine. Power was provided by a 231 kW (310 hp) Ha-42 radial engine. It is believed that several hundred were built between 1941 and 1944. They were used mainly in conjunction with artillery units and were designated Army Type 3 Command Liaison Plane. They received the Allied code name *Stella*. A few were used for anti-submarine coastal-patrol duties carrying two 60 kg (132 lb) depth charges. In the latter role a number were embarked on the Army's only aircraft carrier during 1943.

Koolhoven F.K.26 (Netherlands) Small commercial aircraft operated by the British Aerial Transport Company (BAT) on its short-lived London–Birmingham and London–Amsterdam services (see BAT F.K.26).

Koolhoven F.K.30 (Netherlands) Small two-seat sporting monoplane fitted with Armstrong Siddeley Genet, Walter or Siemens Sh.11 engine in the 41–44.7 kW (55–60 hp) range.

Koolhoven F.K.43s.

Koolhoven F.K.46.

Koolhoven F.K.48.

Koolhoven F.K.50.

The Kl.35D was a 59.6 kW (80 hp) Hirth H.M.60R-engined version, produced as a trainer for the Luftwaffe (which had received numbers of the earlier types).

Klemm Kl.36 (Germany) Four-seater specially designed to compete in the 1934 Challenge de Tourisme International.

Klemm Kl.105 (Germany) Two-seat light monoplane of 1938 powered by a 37.25 kW (50 hp) Zundapp Z.9-92 or similar engine.

Klemm Kl.107 (Germany) Similar to the Kl.105 but fitted with a 74.5 kW (100 hp) Hirth engine. Only six had been built for the Luftwaffe when the factory was destroyed completely during World War II. In 1955 a new prototype of the Kl.107 was completed. Following this a prototype Kl.107B was built which flew for the first time on 4 September 1956 with a 112 kW (150 hp) Lycoming O-320-A2A engine. A number of production Kl.107Bs were built.

Knoller C.I and C.II (Austria-Hungary) Two-seat observation biplanes of 1916 powered by 119 kW (160 hp) or 138 kW (185 hp) Austro-Daimler engines.

Knowles Duet (UK) Two-seat light monoplane, plans for which are available to amateur constructors.

Kocherghin DI-6 (USSR) Two-seat (rear cockpit enclosed) biplane fighter of 1935 powered by a 533 kW (715 hp) M-25 radial engine. Armament comprised four forward-firing 7.62 mm ShKAS machine-guns and a similar rear-firing gun. Used against the Japanese in Mongolia in 1939. Maximum level speed 385 km/h (239 mph).

Kokusai Army Ki-59 (Japan) A high-wing light transport powered by two 335.3 kW (450 hp) Ha-13a radial engines. A number were operated as commercial feeder-line transports, but 59 military examples (each accommodating ten troops or freight) went into service in 1941 as the Army Type 1.

Koolhoven F.K.31 (Netherlands) The F.K.31 was a two-seat parasol-wing general-purpose aircraft powered by a 298 kW (400 hp) Bristol Jupiter radial engine. It was designed in three forms: as an Avion de Chasse with fuel for two hours; an Avion de Combat with fuel for four hours; and as an Avion de Corps d'Armée with fuel for six hours. Each version carried a pilot and observer/rear-gunner. Armament for the interceptor/fighter versions was two forward-firing and two rear-mounted machine-guns, while the observation variant carried a fifth gun firing downwards.

Produced for the Dutch Air Force (LVA) during 1924 and 1925, it was found to be too slow – with a maximum speed of only 235 km/h (146 mph) in the combat versions and 218 km/h

Koolhoven

Koolhoven F.K.51s.

Koolhoven F.K.52.

Koolhoven F.K.53.

Koolhoven F.K.50B.

(135.5 mph) as an observation type. Therefore many were passed on to the Netherlands East Indies Army Air Service. A few were also licence-built in France by M. Louis de Monge, powered by Gnome-Rhône-built Jupiters.

Koolhoven F.K.33 (Netherlands) Ten-seat twin Armstrong Siddeley Puma-engined commercial transport aircraft produced to the order of KLM for use on its Amsterdam–Paris, London and Malmö services.

Koolhoven F.K.40 (Netherlands) Four–six-seat cabin monoplane powered by a 171.4 kW (230 hp) Gnome-Rhône Titan or 223.5 kW (300 hp) Pratt & Whitney Wasp Junior engine. Operated by KLM.

Koolhoven F.K.41 (Netherlands) Three-seat cabin monoplane powered by a Cirrus III or Cirrus Hermes engine.

Koolhoven F.K.42 (Netherlands) Two-seat training and touring monoplane powered by a Cirrus Hermes engine.

Koolhoven F.K.43 (Netherlands) Four-seat cabin monoplane powered by a 97 kW (130 hp) de Havilland Gipsy Major engine.

Koolhoven F.K.46 (Netherlands) Two-seat training biplane powered by a 97 kW (130 hp) de Havilland Gipsy Major engine. A light version, powered by a 70.8 kW (95 hp) Walter Minor 4 engine, was also produced as the F.K.46L; while the F.K.46S was a specially adapted version for aerobatics.

Koolhoven F.K.48 (Netherlands) Six-passenger commercial cabin monoplane of 1934 powered by two 97 kW (130 hp) de Havilland Gipsy Major engines. One example was operated by KLM on its Rotterdam–Eindhoven service.

Koolhoven F.K.49 (Netherlands) Twin-engined survey aircraft with a 5.8 m³ (205 cu ft) cabin suitable for placing cameras or adaptable for carrying four stretchers as an ambulance or for general-purpose military duties. Power was provided by two 227 kW (305 hp) Ranger V-770.B-4 engines. The Turkish government received the type.

Koolhoven F.K.50 (Netherlands) Three F.K.50 high-performance commercial monoplanes were built, all delivered to Alpar of Switzerland. Power was provided by two 313 kW (420 hp) Pratt & Whitney Wasp Junior T1B engines and accommodation was for eight passengers (six in chairs and two on a bench seat at the rear of the cabin). A military version, carrying a crew of four and 1,000 kg (2,205 lb) of bombs, was projected as the

F.K.50B powered by Bristol Mercury VIII engines.

Koolhoven F.K.51 (Netherlands) Two-seat advanced training biplane powered by a 261 kW (350 hp) Armstrong Siddeley Cheetah IX engine. Sixty-eight built for the LVA and Dutch Navy, some going to the Netherlands East Indies. A number were assigned as artillery spotters.

Koolhoven F.K.52 (Netherlands) Two-seat Bristol Mercury VIII-engined general-purpose biplane built to the order of the Netherlands government.

Koolhoven F.K.53 Junior (Netherlands) Two-seat light touring monoplane powered by a 46 kW (62 hp) Walter Mikron II engine.

Koolhoven F.K.58 (Netherlands) The F.K.58 was a single-seat fighter with a retractable landing gear, enclosed cockpit and powered by an 805 kW (1,080 hp) Hispano-Suiza 14AA radial (F.K.58) or Gnome-Rhône 14N/16 engine (F.K.58A). Armament comprised four 7.5 mm machine-guns. Fifty were ordered by France and the LVA ordered 40 with Bristol Taurus engines, but only 18 F.K.58s and F.K.58As were delivered, all to France. These were flown by Polish pilots during the Battle of France on local defence duties. Maximum level speed was 504 km/h (313 mph) and it could climb to 5,000 m (16,400 ft) in just over six minutes.

Kraft K-1 Super Fli (USA) Single-seat aerobatic monoplane, plans for which are available to amateur constructors.

Kress triplane (Austria) In 1901 Wilhelm Kress flight-tested a twin-hulled tandem triplane-winged seaplane. As it began to take off an attempt was made to change direction and the aircraft capsized (see **Chronology** 1901).

Kyushu Navy E9W1 (Japan) Hitachi Amakaze-powered reconnaissance aircraft carried by submarine, known by the Allies as *Slim*.

Kyushu Navy K11W (Japan) A total of 798 examples of this single-engined mid-wing crew trainer was built as the Navy Operations Trainer 'Shiragiku' between 1942 and 1945. They were intended to train aircrew for Mitsubishi G3M bombers. Pilot and radio-operator/gunner were seated above the wing, protected by a continuous transparent canopy. The instructor, navigator and bomb aimer were accommodated in a cabin under the wing. Power was provided by a 384 kW (515 hp) Hitachi Amakaze 21 radial engine. Most aircraft produced were of the K11W1 version, although a few all-wood K11W2s were also completed.

Data (K11W1): *Engine* as above *Wing span* 15.0 m (49 ft 3 in) *Length* 10.24 m (33 ft 7 in) *Max T-O weight* 2,800 kg (6,173 lb) *Max level speed* 230 km/h (143 mph).

Kyushu Navy Q1W (Japan) Twin-engined low-wing anti-submarine aircraft, 153 examples of which were built between 1943 and 1945: the majority were the all-metal Q1W1 version, but a few were Q1W2s with wooden rear fuselages. Named 'Tokai' by the Japanese, the type saw little service. It was coded *Lorna* by the Allies. Power was provided by two 454.5 kW (610 hp) Hitachi Tempu 31 radial engines giving a maximum speed of 320 km/h (199 mph).

KZ KZ I (Denmark) Kramme & Zeuthen's first product was the KZ I single-seat light monoplane of 1937.

KZ KZ II (Denmark) Pre-war two-seat light open-cockpit (Sport), cabin (Kupe), and military training (KZ II Trainer) monoplane, powered by a 67 kW (90 hp) Cirrus Minor engine. The latter was supplied to the Danish Air Force as a primary trainer.

KZ KZ III (Denmark) Two-seat cabin monoplane produced for domestic, European and overseas markets.

KZ KZ IV (Denmark) Six-seat cabin monoplane powered by two 97 kW (130 hp) de Havilland Gipsy Major engines. Two flown commercially from the late 1940s.

KZ KZ VII Lark.

KZ KZ VII Lark (Denmark) Four-seat cabin monoplane powered by a 93 kW (125 hp) Continental C125 engine. Produced for the same markets as the KZ III.

KZ KZ VIII (Denmark) Single-seat advanced trainer and aerobatic monoplane.

KZ KZ X (Denmark) AOP monoplane powered by a 108 kW (145 hp) Continental C145-2 engine. Twelve ordered by the Danish Army.

Laister-Kauffman TG-4 (USA) Two-seat training glider, 150 of which were delivered to the USAAF during World War II.

LAK LAK-9 Lietuva (USSR) Single-seat Open Class sailplane.

Lake LA-4 (USA) Four-seat amphibian powered by a 134 kW (180 hp) Lycoming O-360-A1A engine. Developed from the original Colonial C-2 Skimmer IV after the company purchased the manufacturing rights to the aircraft. Developed versions included the LA-4, 4A, 4P, 4S and 4T.

Lake LA-4.

Lake LA-4-200 Buccaneer (USA) The Buccaneer is the latest production version of the LA-4. It is basically similar to the earlier LA-4 versions (946 of all versions had been built by the beginning of 1979) but is powered by a 149 kW (200 hp) Lycoming IO-360-A1B engine.

Data: *Engine* as above *Wing span* 11.58 m (38 ft 0 in) *Length* 7.6 m (24 ft 11 in) *Max T-O weight* 1,220 kg (2,690 lb) *Max cruising speed* 241 km/h (150 mph) *Max range* 1,327 km (825 miles)

Koolhoven F.K.58.

Lancashire Aircraft

Lake LA-4-200 Buccaneer.

Langley Aerodrome.

Lancashire Aircraft Prospector (UK) See **Edgar Percival.**

Landgraf Model H-2 Helicopter (USA) Experimental single-seat twin-rotor helicopter powered by a Pobjoy R radial engine. First flown on 2 November 1944. In 1945 the company received a contract from the US Army for development of the helicopter.

Langley Aerodrome (USA) The full-size *Aerodrome* was a tandem-wing aeroplane powered by a 38.75 kW (52 hp) Manly radial engine driving two 2.67 m (8 ft 9 in) propellers. Wing span was 14.63 m (48 ft 0 in). (See **Chronology** August 1901, 7 October 1903 and 8 December 1903).

On board the houseboat with the full-size Langley Aerodrome.

Langley Monoplane (USA) First product of the Langley Aircraft Corporation was a twin 48.4 kW (65 hp) Franklin 4AC-176-engined cantilever low-wing four-seat cabin monoplane of 1940–41, of moulded plastic and plywood construction.

Lapan XT-400 (Indonesia) Twin-engined light STOL transport, first flown in 1980.

Larkin KC-3 Skylark (USA) Two-seat light twin-boom monoplane, plans and material kits for which are available to amateur constructors.

Latécoère 8 (France) Single 223.6 kW (300 hp) Renault-powered five-passenger commercial biplane of 1921. It is believed that it was used on Lignes Aériennes Latécoère's Moroccan services.

Latécoère 14 (France) See **Latécoère 17.**

Langley Monoplane.

Latécoère 15 (France) In the 1920s Lignes Aériennes Latécoère (succeeded by Aéropostale company) pioneered air routes from Toulouse across North Africa to Dakar. After connection by ship, other aircraft of South American associated companies connected Natal in Brazil to Buenos Aires. There is no firm evidence that earlier Latécoère designs operated on these lines, but the Laté 15 – a gawky, parasol-wing monoplane with two 205 kW (275 hp) Lorraine Dietrich engines and cabin accommodation for four–six passengers – flew over the Toulouse–Casablanca sector. At least 10 were built during 1925–6.

Latécoère 17.

Mermoz, Dabry and Gimie) of 3,173 km (1,971.6 miles) in a straight line from St Louis (West Africa) to Natal (Brazil).

Latécoère 28/9 (France) Three-seat high-wing bomber, three of which were delivered to Venezuela. Power was provided by a 484.4 kW (650 hp) Hispano-Suiza 12Nb engine.

Latécoère 28-1.

Latécoère 17 (France) The whole France–Brazil Aéropostale route (with the aid of ships from Dakar to Natal) was opened in early 1928. At least two Laté 14s were followed by approximately 20 Laté 17s. The latter was a single-engined parasol-wing monoplane with a rounded metal fuselage (fabric-covered) accommodating four passengers plus baggage and mail. Most were powered by a 223.6 kW (300 hp) Renault 12Fc engine, although some were fitted with a Gnome-Rhône-built Jupiter.

Latécoère 21 (France) A single example of the Laté 21 four-passenger commercial parasol-wing flying-boat was followed by approximately five Laté 21*bis* (redesigned hull and tailplane) and one Laté 21*ter* (Farman engines). Power for the Laté 21 and 21*bis* was provided by twin 313 kW (420 hp) Gnome-Rhône Jupiter 9Ab engines mounted in tandem. All were operated by Aéropostale on its Marseilles–Algiers route.

Latécoère 25 (France) The Laté 25 was basically a Laté 17 with increased wing span powered by a Renault or Jupiter 9Ab engine in the 335.3–372.6 kW (450–500 hp) range. A few were fitted with Handley Page automatic slots. More than 50 were built, operated by Aéropostale and by subsidiary Brazilian and Argentinian companies.

Latécoère 26 (France) The Laté 26 (about 70 were built during 1928–30 mainly for Aéropostale) was primarily a mailplane, although it accommodated two passengers. The crew sat in tandem open cockpits. Power was provided by a 335.3 kW (450 hp) Renault 12Ja engine in the Laté 26.2R and a 372.6 kW (500 hp) Renault 12Jb in the Laté 26.6R.

Latécoère 28 (France) The Laté 28 was a handsome single-engined commercial high-wing monoplane accommodating eight passengers in a long cabin. About 50 were built: operated by Aéropostale from 1930 in several versions on routes to Africa and South America. Power was provided by a 372.6 kW (500 hp) Renault 12Jb (Laté 28-0 and 28-1), 372.6 kW (500 hp) Hispano-Suiza 12Lbr (Laté 28-3 floatplane) and 484.4 kW (650 hp) Hispano-Suiza 12Nb engine (Laté 28-5 floatplane).

Nineteen speed-with-load-over-distance, closed circuit with load and endurance records were established with Laté 28-3 and 28-5 landplanes (5) and floatplanes (14). The Laté 28-3 is also remembered for an outstanding flight (by

Latécoère 32 (France) Slightly larger than the Laté 21 but with the same parasol wing with sponsons, the Laté 32 was powered by two 372.6 kW (500 hp) Farman 12We engines. At least eight were built during 1927–28, five becoming Laté 32-3s when re-engined with Hispano-Suiza 12Hbrs engines of similar power. Used by Aéropostale on its Toulouse–Algiers mail service, although the aircraft could be converted to accommodate four passengers.

Latécoère 290 (France) The Laté 290 was a naval development of the Laté 28. Two prototypes were followed by 40 production aircraft built during 1933–34. Each powered by a single 484.4 kW (650 hp) Hispano-Suiza 12Nbr engine, these were normally operated with twin metal floats. Armament comprised twin machine-guns in a manually operated dorsal turret and a torpedo or two 150 kg bombs. Production aircraft were flown by Escadrilles 1T1 and 4T1 of the French Aéronavale.

Latécoère 28-6, a transport version of the Laté 28 delivered to Aviacion Nacional Venezolana.

Latécoère 290.

Latécoère

Latécoère 298s.

Latécoère 298 (France) A multi-purpose twin-float seaplane, the prototype Laté 298.01 first flew on 8 May 1936. Intended missions included torpedo bombing; horizontal or shallow dive bombing (with two bombs of up to 150 kg each); long-range reconnaissance (with extra 535 litre; 118 Imp gallon fuel tank); night reconnaissance; and smokescreen laying. A cantilever low-wing monoplane with an all-metal oval-section stressed-skin fuselage, the production Laté 298A was powered by a 656 kW (880 hp) Hispano-Suiza 12Ycrs engine and had a crew of three accommodated under a glazed canopy. The Laté 298B version had folding wings for shipboard stowage. Armament comprised two fixed 7.5 mm Darne wing guns and a third Darne machine-gun on a flexible mounting at the rear of the crew canopy. The Laté 298D had a fourth crew member, and the 'one-off' unsuccessful Laté 298E had a ventral observation gondola.

Latécoère 300.

Some 110 Laté 298s of all versions had been built by 25 June 1940 and a further 20 Laté 298Fs (with MAC instead of Darne weapons and two additional 7.7 mm machine-guns for ventral 'under-tail' defence) were built for the French Vichy regime.

Latécoère 298.

The first naval escadrilles to equip with the type were T2 at Saint-Raphaël and T1 at Berre in February and March 1939 respectively. Escadrilles HB1 and HB2 on the seaplane carrier *Commandant Teste* re-equipped with Laté 298Bs in April and July the same year. From then on the type saw widespread service, flying overland in shallow dive-bombing attacks during the May–June 1940 'Blitzkrieg' on France and subsequently continuing to operate – mainly on reconnaissance missions – with both the Vichy and Free French forces. Several captured aircraft were used for liaison duties by the Germans. A number of Laté 298s continued into the post-World War II period with the French Aéronavale.
Data: *Engine* as above *Wing span* 15.5 m (50 ft 10¼ in) *Length* 12.56 m (41 ft 2½ in) *Max T-O weight* 4,800 kg (10,582 lb) *Max level speed* 290 km/h (180 mph) *Range* 2,200 km (1,367 miles)
Latécoère 300 series (France) The Latécoère 300 flew for the first time in 1931 and then had to be rebuilt after sinking. It was flown again in 1932 as the *Croix du Sud* parasol-wing monoplane flying-boat with four 484.4 kW (650 hp)

Hispano-Suiza 12NBr water-cooled engines in tandem pairs. On 31 December 1933 it achieved an international record by covering 3,679 km (2,285 miles) non-stop.

Thereafter it operated the Air France South Atlantic mail service between Dakar and Natal, until it was lost at sea with pilot Jean Mermoz on the 24th crossing on 7 December 1936.

Three civil Laté 301s and three military Laté 302s were built during 1935–6, incorporating changes made to the Laté 300 in 1935, including increased wing dihedral and enlarged tail surfaces. Laté 302s had 693 kW (930 hp) Hispano-Suiza 12Ydrs engines. The first Laté 301 was lost but the remaining two maintained a South Atlantic service until World War II.

The all-metal two-step hull accommodated a four-man crew with sleeping accommodation, mail load and most of the fuel. Naval Laté 302s had machine-gun posts in bow and two beam positions, as well as two in the engine nacelles. Bomb load was 300 kg (661 lb). Laté 302s equipped Escadrille E4 at Berre, joined by the last civil but militarised Laté 301 in August 1939. These were used during the early part of World War II to patrol from Dakar (West Africa) and continued to do so after the German Armistice, until prevented by lack of spares.
Data (Latécoère 302): *Engines* as above *Wing span* 42.8 m (144 ft 5 in) *Length* 26.15 m (85 ft 9½ in) *Max T-O weight* 24,000 kg (52,911 lb) *Max level speed* 240 km/h (149 mph)
Latécoère 380/381 (France) The first prototype of the Laté 380 parasol-wing flying-boat flew for the first time in 1930. Having established six world seaplane records in September 1931 – including three speed-with-load-over-distance and a closed circuit distance-with-load

(2,208.42 km; 1,372.25 miles) – it entered service with Aéropostale on the South Atlantic mail route. A second prototype followed.

Three Laté 381 maritime-reconnaissance flying-boats were also produced in 1934, which entered service with Escadrille 3E3 at Saint-Raphaël. Each Laté 381 had three defensive positions, each armed with twin 7.62 mm machine-guns. A bomb load of 300 kg (661 lb) was carried on underwing racks.

Data: *Engines* two 507 kW (680 hp) Hispano-Suizas *Wing span* 31.4 m (103 ft 0¼ in) *Length* 18.5 m (60 ft 8¼ in) *Max T-O weight* 9,280 kg (20,459 lb) *Max level speed* 200 km/h (124 mph)

Latécoère 500/501 (France) The Laté 500 flying-boat, powered by three 298 kW (400 hp) Hispano-Suiza 12Jb engines, flew for the first time in mid-1931. It had been built to serve the South Atlantic mail route but was scrapped due to poor flying qualities. The eight-passenger Laté 501 flew in April 1932. Powered by Hispano-Suiza 12Jbr engines of similar power, it was used on Mediterranean passenger routes.

Latécoère 631.

March 1940. The remaining aircraft of the series performed Atlantic patrols with Escadrilles E6 and E12. One Laté 523 had been lost in September 1939, a second was scuttled in June 1940; and the Laté 521 was demobilised in August of that year. The surviving Laté 523 was grounded in August 1942, having flown with Escadrille 4E out of Dakar since June 1941. The Laté 521 and 522 were destroyed at Berre by retreating Germans in August 1944.

Data (Laté 523): *Engines* as above *Wing span*

Latécoère 521.

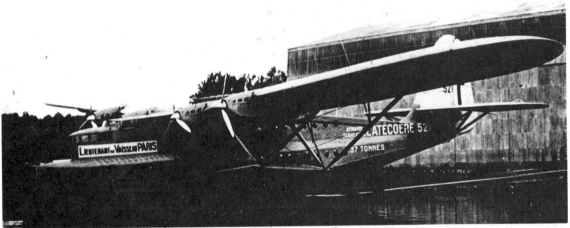

Latécoère 521 series (France) The Laté 521 was an outsized flying-boat with strut-braced high wings and short stub sponsons. Named *Lieutenant de Vaisseau Paris*, it was powered by six 641 kW (860 hp) Hispano-Suiza 12Ycrs engines (inboard engines mounted as tandem pairs) and flew for the first time on 17 January 1935. A total of 76 passengers could be accommodated on the two decks of the two-step hull. Unfortunately it sank in a storm on its inaugural flight to the USA, but was salvaged and rebuilt with 484.4 kW (650 hp) Hispano-Suiza 12Nbr engines. It subsequently established seaplane load-over-distance and load-to-height records in 1937.

The Laté 522 (powered by six 671 kW; 900 hp Hispano-Suiza 12Y37 engines) appeared in April 1937 but World War II prevented a regular transatlantic service. Both the Laté 521 and 522 were impressed into French Navy service on 1 September 1939, three naval Laté 523s having already been delivered between January and October 1938. These were armed with five 7.5 mm Darne machine-guns and carried up to 1,200 kg (2,645 lb) of bombs. Maximum endurance was an excellent 33 hours.

The Laté 522 returned to passenger service in

49.3 m (161 ft 9 in) *Length* 31.6 m (103 ft 8 in) *Max T-O weight* 42,000 kg (92,594 lb) *Max level speed* 260 km/h (161.5 mph)

Latécoère 631 (France) The prototype Laté 631 flew for the first time on 4 November 1942. It was a graceful high-wing monoplane flying-boat powered by six 1,192 kW (1,600 hp) radial engines. Accommodation was provided for 46 passengers in two- or four-berth cabins. However this aircraft was confiscated by the Germans during the occupation of France.

Three Laté 631s were built after the war and inaugurated transatlantic services to Fort de France on 26 July 1947. One was lost on 1 August

Latécoère 631.

Lavochkin La-5.

1948 and the type was subsequently withdrawn from the service. It is believed that eight aircraft were eventually built. The Société France-Hydro operated one on cargo services in French Equatorial Africa for three years, but it crashed: after which all remaining Laté 631s were broken up.

Latham H.B.3 (France) Two Latham prototype three-seat bomber-reconnaissance flying-boats were tested between 1924 and 1926 in the French Navy's H.B.3 classification. This resulted in 18 production aircraft being ordered, each powered by two 283.2 kW (380 hp) Gnome-Rhône-built Jupiter radial engines. These served with Navy Escadrilles 4R1 and 5R1, with which they remained operational until 1929. Armament comprised twin machine-guns in bow and midship gunners' positions, plus up to 400 kg (882 lb) of bombs. Eight Lorraine-powered flying-boats were also sold to Poland.

Latham 47.

Latham 47 R3B4 (France) Produced as a replacement for the H.B.3 type, the two prototype Latham 47s first appeared in 1928. Production flying-boats, powered by tandem-mounted 447 kW (600 hp) Hispano-Suiza 12Lbs engines and designated R3B4s, entered service with the French Navy in 1929, but were withdrawn in the following year.

Laverda Falco and Super Falco (Italy) Originally produced by Aerfer. See **Aeromere** and **Sequoia 8FL**.

Lavochkin LaGG-1 and LaGG-3 (USSR) Designed by Lavochkin, Gorbunov and Gudkov, the I-22 or LaGG-1 single-seat fighter flew for the first time in March 1939. Power was provided by

Lavochkin LaGG-3.

an M-105P engine and armament comprised one 20 or 23 mm Shpitalny-Vladimirov cannon and two 12.7 mm Beresin machine-guns. Although placed in production (entering squadron service in 1940), the LaGG-1 was quickly superseded by an improved and lightened version of the same aircraft, designated LaGG-3. The construction of the LaGG-3 was described by the Russians at the time as 'revolutionary'. Of virtually all-wood construction, the wings, fuselage and tail unit were covered by plastic-bonded diagonal plywood strips, the plastic bonding being used as an adhesive and as an impregnating medium. Power was provided by the M-105PF engine and several armament combinations were introduced during the production run, which lasted until mid-1942. In addition to guns and cannon, the aircraft could be used as a fighter bomber, carrying bombs or six 25 kg RS-82 rocket-propelled fragmentation bombs on special guide rail-type racks under the wings.

Although rugged, the LaGG-3 was underpowered and lacked the manoeuvrability of some other fighters, but nevertheless performed well as a fighter and fighter bomber to the end of the war. It is perhaps best remembered as an escort fighter for the Ilyushin Il-2 ground-attack aircraft.

Data (LaGG-3): *Engine* one 820 kW (1,100 hp) M-105PF *Wing span* 9.8 m (32 ft 1¾ in) *Length* 8.87 m (29 ft 1¾ in) *Max T-O weight* 3,200 kg (7,055 lb) *Max level speed* 560 km/h (348 mph) *Normal range* 650 km (404 miles)

Lavochkin La-5 and La-7 (USSR) After the LaGG-3 had been completed, the LaGG design committee broke up and in 1941–42 Lavochkin produced the radial-engined La-5. This light all-wood single-seat fighter was first used in large numbers during the Battle of Stalingrad. From ground level to 3,660 m (12,000 ft) it proved aerobatically superior to the German Messerschmitt Bf 109F and Focke-Wulf Fw 190A fighters. The title of Hero of Socialist Labour was conferred on Semyon Lavochkin for this successful design. The original La-5 power plant of one 1,192 kW (1,600 hp) ASh-82A radial engine was replaced by a higher-power ASh-82FN engine in the La-5FN of 1943. This also featured structural improvements, the most noticeable of which were the cutting down of the aft fuselage top decking and improvements to the shape of the engine cowling.

Taking advantage of the improved performance of the La-5FN with the ASh-82FN engine, Lavochkin redesigned the La-5 and produced the La-7 in 1943. As a result of his work Lavochkin was awarded a Stalin Prize of 100,000 roubles. By the end of the war the La-7 was in service in greater numbers than any other type, except for the Yak-3. Powered by a 1,323 kW (1,775 hp) ASh-82FN engine and supporting an extra 20 mm ShVAK cannon, it had a maximum speed of 680 km/h (422 mph).

La-7s entered service in the latter half of 1944. Prototypes also appeared of the La-7R version with a small rocket motor in the tail to boost 'dash' speed to more than 740 km/h (460 mph). In 1946 a two-seat trainer version of the La-7 appeared, also suitable for reconnaissance and liaison duties. The La-7 fighter remained in service post-war, also serving with the Czechoslovakian Air Force. More than 5,700 La-7s were built, about half the number of La-5s completed.

Data (La-5FN): *Engine* as above *Wing span* 9.8 m (9 ft 1¾ in) *Length* 8.5 m (27 ft 10¾ in) *Max T-O weight* 3,360 kg (7,407 lb) *Max level speed* 647 km/h (402 mph) *Range* 765–850 km (475–528 miles) *Armament* two 20 mm ShVAK cannon, plus up to 150 kg (331 lb) of bombs

Lavochkin La-9.

Lavochkin La-9 fitted experimentally with two underwing turbojet engines.

Lavochkin La-9 and La-11 (USSR) In 1946 Lavochkin switched from wood to metal construction and his first all-metal fighter design, the La-9, entered service as a replacement for the La-7. On the 3 April 1947 Soviet Aviation Day Display, a large number of La-9s took part, numerous examples carrying an experimental athodyd (or ramjet) engine under each wing as well as at least one La-9 with rocket boosters. Normal power was provided by a 1,378 kW (1,850 hp) ASh-82 FNV engine, giving a speed of 690 km/h (429 mph). Armament comprised four 23 mm cannon. La-9s

were also operated by other nations friendly to the Soviet Union and some were identified among the fighters escorting formations of Tu-2s of the Chinese Air Force in Korea in December 1951, a number of which were shot down by USAF fighters.

The La-11 was a revised longer-range version of the La-9 and was the final piston-engined fighter to come from the Lavochkin stable. It incorporated technical improvements and was armed with three 23 mm cannon. The first evidence of its existence was obtained in the summer of 1949 when an aircraft of the type crash-landed in Sweden. The pilot (a young Russian lieutenant) requested political asylum and the aircraft was returned to the USSR.

Lavochkin La-15 (USSR) Lavochkin's first turbojet-powered fighter, which entered production for the Soviet Air Force in 1948. Power was provided by a 15.57 kN (3,500 lb st) RD-500 engine and armament comprised two 23 mm cannon, bombs and rockets. NATO gave the aircraft the reporting name *Fantail*.

Lavochkin La-7.
Lavochkin La-7R.

Lavochkin La-15.

Lavochkin La-150, which unsuccessfully rivalled the Yak-17.

Leduc 0.10 carried by its SE 161 Languedoc motherplane.

Lawson L-2 and L-4 (USA) Eighteen-seat twin Liberty-powered and larger triple Liberty-powered airliners of 1920 and 1922 respectively, both built for the Lawson Air Line. The latter was provided with berths, shower bath, etc for the night service between New York and Chicago, but had an accident on its first trial flight.

Lear Jet 23 (USA) Small twin-jet (12.7 kN; 2,850 lb st General Electric CJ610-1) executive transport, first flown on 7 October 1963. Accommodation for a crew of two and seven passengers. One hundred and four delivered before being superseded by the Model 24D (see **Gates Learjet**).

Lear Jet 23.

Leduc 0.21.

Lebed 12.

Leduc 0.22.

Lebed 11, 12 and 13 (USSR) The Lebed 11 of 1915 was a two-seat unarmed reconnaissance biplane powered by a 112 kW (150 hp) Canton-Unné engine. A small number were produced before being superseded by the Lebed 12, with reduced wing span and armed with one or two machine-guns. This version could also carry a light offensive load of 90 kg (200 lb) of bombs. A total of 214 were built up to 1917. The Lebed 13 development of the 12 remained a prototype only.

Lederlin 380-L (France) Two-seat light aircraft, plans for which are available to amateur constructors.

Leduc 0.10, 0.21 and 0.22 (France) Experimental aircraft powered by ramjet (or athodyd) engines. The 0.10 first flew on 21 April 1949. The

0.21 first flew on 16 May 1953 and the 0.22, designed as a prototype Mach 2 interceptor, first flew on 26 December 1956.

Lefebvre MP.205 Busard (France) Single-seat racing monoplane, plans for which are available to amateur constructors.

Let L-13 Blanik (Czechoslovakia) Training sailplane for all categories from elementary to 'blind' flying and for high-performance flight. It is fully aerobatic when flown solo and capable of aerobatic manoeuvres when carrying a passenger. More than 2,600 had been sold by the end of 1978, when production terminated.

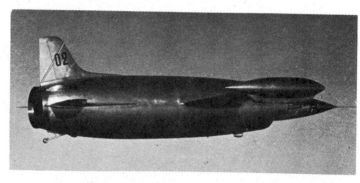

Let L-40 Meta-Sokol (Czechoslovakia) Four-seat light training and sporting monoplane, the standard version powered by a 104 kW (140 hp) Walter M332 engine. Two hundred were built up to the end of 1961.

Let L-200 Morava (Czechoslovakia) Twin-engined (156.5 kW; 210 hp M337) light business and taxi monoplane accommodating four or five persons. First flown on 8 April 1957. More than 1,000 were built in three versions, the L-200D being introduced in 1962.

Let L-410 Turbolet (Czechoslovakia)

Design of the L-410 twin-turboprop light transport began in 1966 and the first prototype flew on 16 April 1969. The L-410A initial passenger/cargo production version, powered by 533 kW (715 ehp) Pratt & Whitney Aircraft of Canada PT6A-27 engines, entered service with the Czechoslovak domestic operator Slov-Air in 1971. The L-410AF is the aerial-photography/survey version and the L-410M is a 17-passenger version (deliveries started in 1976). From 1979 the standard production version has been the L-410UVP, most of which are being supplied to Aeroflot.

Data (L-410UVP): *Engines* two 544 kW (730 ehp) Walter M 601 B turboprops *Wing span* 19.49 m (63 ft 11¼ in) *Length* 14.47 m (47 ft 5½ in) *Max T-O weight* 5,700 kg (12,566 lb) *Max cruising speed* 365 km/h (227 mph) *Max range* 1,040 km (646 miles) *Accommodation* standard accommodation for 15 passengers; alternative layouts for 14 parachutists, 12 firefighters, six stretchers and five sitting casualties (plus medical attendant), or all cargo

Let Mraz M.1 Sokol (Czechoslovakia) Three-seat sporting, training, touring and air-taxi cabin monoplane powered by a 78.25 kW (105 hp) Walter Minor 4-III engine.

Let Mraz M.2 Skaut (Czechoslovakia) Two-seat training and touring monoplane powered by a 56 kW (75 hp) Praga D engine.

Let Mraz M.3 Bonzo (Czechoslovakia) Four-seat cabin monoplane powered by a 119 kW (160 hp) Walter Minor 6-III engine.

Let Aero 145 and Super Aero (Czechoslovakia) The Aero 145 was produced as a development of the widely exported twin 78.25 kW (105 hp) Walter Minor 4-III-engined Super Aero. Powered by two 104.3 kW (140 hp) M332 engines, it was designed to accommodate four or five persons in the air-taxi configuration. Production ended in the early 1960s.

Let Z-37 Čmelák (Czechoslovakia) The prototype of this agricultural aircraft flew for the first time on 29 June 1963. Additional applications for the production Z-37 include mail and cargo transport during the winter season. Power is provided by a 234.7 kW (315 hp) M462RF radial engine. Production ended in 1975 after 600 examples had been produced.

Let Z-37-2 Sparka (Czechoslovakia) Two-seat conversion trainer model of the Čmelák, produced to train pilots in the operation of agricultural aircraft.

Let L-40 Meta-Sokol.

Let L-410M Turbolet.

Let L-200A Morava.

Let Mraz M.1C Sokol.

Let Aero 145.

Side-facing photographer's seat in the glazed nose of a Let L-410AF Turbolet.

Letord

Letord 1 to 7 (France) Between 1916 and 1919 a series of twin-engined Le Père designs were built at the Letord factory, Meudon. Many went into service as A3-category long-range reconnaissance aircraft carrying a three-man crew. Defensive armament comprised twin machine-guns in bow and midships cockpits and aerial cameras were carried. Their secondary role was long-range bomber escort. Most widely used were the Let.1 of 1916 (175 built) and the Let.5 of 1918. The former had two 112 kW (150 hp) Hispano-Suiza 8A engines and the latter two 179 kW (240 hp) Lorraine-Dietrich 8Bs. Like the Let.2, the Let.4 and Let.7 were also built in quantity; they were twin-engined unequal-span biplanes with large single-fin-and-rudder tail assemblies and twin-wheel main undercarriage units. They could be distinguished by their rounded noses and consid-

erable negative wing stagger. A total of 1,500 of all versions were ordered, but the exact number built is not known. The Let.9 night bomber was a very different design, but was too late to go into wartime production.

Data (Let.1): *Engines* as above *Wing span* 18.0 m (59 ft 0¾ in) *Length* 11.15 m (36 ft 7 in) *Max T-O weight* 2,450 kg (5,401 lb) *Max level speed* 148 km/h (92 mph)

Letov L-101 and L-290 Orel (Czechoslovakia) The L-101 was a twin Argus As.410-powered 12-passenger feeder-line commercial monoplane produced immediately after World War II. The L-290 Orel was a four-engined (BMW 801) 44–48 passenger airliner produced after the war as a civil development of the Junkers Ju 290. Neither type entered service.

Letov S-1 and S-2 (Czechoslovakia) The S-1 was the first military aircraft to be designed (by Alois Smolik) and built in Czechoslovakia. A total of 90 were produced from 1919 as SH-1s (164 kW; 220 hp Hiero L engine); SM-1s (194 kW; 260 hp Maybach Mb.IVa engine); and S-2s (Mb.IVa engine). An SM-1 type was also produced as a commercial biplane with a fully enclosed cabin to the rear of the pilot's open cockpit (full details of the SM-1 appear in the 1920 *Jane's*). Armament comprised three machine-guns and up to 120 kg (264.5 lb) of bombs. Maximum level speed of the SM-1 was 195 km/h (121 mph).

Letov S-4 (Czechoslovakia) Single-seat biplane fighter of 1922 powered by a 149 kW (200 hp) Hispano-Suiza 8Ba engine.

Letov S-6 (Czechoslovakia) Two-seat reconnaissance bomber of 1923 powered by a 194 kW (260 hp) Maybach Mb.IVa engine.

Letov S-10 (Czechoslovakia) Licence-built Hansa-Brandenburg aircraft of 1923.

Letov S-16 series (Czechoslovakia) The S-16 two-seat reconnaissance bomber first appeared in 1926 powered by a Skoda-built 335.3 kW (450 hp) Lorraine-Dietrich engine. Armament comprised one forward-firing Vickers machine-gun and twin rear-mounted Lewis guns, plus up to 600 kg (1,323 lb) of bombs. The quickly detachable engine mounting permitted the installation of any engine of similar power or type; production aircraft, built first for export to Latvia (S-16) and Turkey (S-16T) and in 1928 for the Czechoslovak Air Force, only varied in having Hispano-Suiza 50 (S-16L) and the standard Lorraine-Dietrich engines. Production of the S-16 of all types totalled just over 150 aircraft.

Using the detachable mounting to its full potential, Letov produced the S-116 (335.3 kW; 450 hp Skoda L); S-216 (358 kW; 480 hp Walter-built Jupiter); S-316 (335.3 kW; 450 hp Hispano-Suiza 12N); S-416 (372.6 kW; 500 hp Breitfeld-Danek BD-500); S-515 (596 kW; 800 hp Isotta-Fraschini Asso); S-616 (of 1930 with a 447 kW; 600 hp Hispano-Suiza 12Nbr); S-716 (Skoda L); S-816 (410 kW; 550 hp Praga ES); and S-916 (Lorraine-Dietrich). A seaplane version of the S-16 was also produced for Yugoslavia as the S-16J with long duralumin single-step floats.

Data (S-16, unless otherwise stated): *Engine* as above *Wing span* 15.3 m (50 ft 3 in) *Length* 10.22 m (33 ft 6 in) *Max T-O weight* 2,280 kg (5,026 lb) *Max level speed* 230 km/h (143 mph), (S-816) 225 km/h (140 mph), (S-516) 276 km/h (171.5 mph) *Cruising range* 800–1,000 km (497–621 miles)

Letov S-18 (Czechoslovakia) Biplane trainer of 1925 flown by the Czechoslovak and Bulgarian air forces.

Letov S-19 (Czechoslovakia) Four-passenger commercial biplane of 1924 powered by a 194 kW (260 hp) Maybach Mb.IVa or Walter W-IV engine. Seven operated by CSA.

Letov S-20 and S-21 (Czechoslovakia) The S-20 was a single-seat biplane fighter of 1926 powered by a 223.5 kW (300 hp) Skoda-built Hispano-Suiza 8Fb engine. A total of 95 S-20s were produced (most as S-20Ms with slimmer fuselages) including 20 ordered by Lithuania. Armament comprised two forward-firing Vickers machine-guns with 800 rounds of ammunition. Maximum level speed was 256 km/h (159 mph).

The S-21 of the same year was an unarmed training version of the S-20 powered by a 134 kW (180 hp) Hispano-Suiza 8Aa engine. A small number were produced.

Letov S-31 (Czechoslovakia) Single-seat biplane fighter of 1929 powered by a Walter-built Jupiter engine. A development of 1933 was the S-231 powered by a Bristol Mercury IV engine.

Letov S-32 (Czechoslovakia) Five-passenger

Letov S-20.

commercial monoplane of 1932 powered by three 108 kW (145 hp) Walter Mars engines. Five operated by CSA.

Letov S-39 (Czechoslovakia) Two-seat light sporting monoplane of 1931 powered by a 41 kW (55 hp) Walter Polaris or 55.6 kW (75 hp) Pobjoy R radial engine.

Letov S-228 (Czechoslovakia) Two-seat observation and light bombing biplane of 1931 powered by a 372.6 kW (500 hp) Gnome-Rhône-built Mercury VII engine. Production aircraft delivered to Estonia.

Letov S-239 (Czechoslovakia) Two-seat light sporting monoplane of 1933 powered by a 63.3 kW (85 hp) Walter Minor engine.

Letov S-328 and S-528 (Czechoslovakia) Like the S-228, these aircraft were direct developments of the Walter Castor-powered S-28 of 1929. With the experience of the excellent S-228 behind it, Letov produced a modified version of the same aircraft for Czech service as an observation and light bombing biplane, designated S-328. Power was provided by the more powerful 387.5 kW (520 hp) Walter-built Pegasus II.M-2 radial engine, giving a maximum speed 35.5 km/h (22 mph) faster than the previous version. The prototype appeared in 1932 and in 1934 the type was ordered for the Czechoslovak Army Air

Letov S-328.

Levasseur P.L.2 AT.2.

Force, deliveries starting in the following year. A total of nearly 460 were produced, including a small number of two-seat night-fighter variants. These remained operational throughout the remaining 1930s. After the German occupation many S-328s were passed to Slovak and Bulgarian squadrons. Armament comprised two forward-firing and two rear-mounted machine-guns, the latter on a Skoda mounting. Provision was made for carrying 120 kg or smaller bombs under the lower wings.

The S-528 of 1935 was basically similar to the S-328, but was powered by a 596 kW (800 hp) Walter-built Gnome-Rhône 14Krsd Mistral Major engine. Only a very small number were built. Maximum bomb load was increased from 350 kg (772 lb) to 400 kg (882 lb).

Data (S-328): *Engine* as above *Wing span* 13.71 m (44 ft 11¾ in) *Length* 10.36 m (34 ft 0 in) *Max T-O weight* 2,640 kg (5,820 lb) *Max level speed* 280 km/h (174 mph) *Range* 700 km (435 miles)

Levasseur P.L.2 (France) Inspired by Blackburn designs and intended in production form to equip the first French aircraft carrier *Béarn*, the P.L.2 AT.1 prototype was first displayed at the 1921 Paris Salon Aéronautique. Nine production AT.2s followed, each powered by a 432 kW (580 hp) Renault 12Ma engine. No defensive armament was carried, but the offensive load was a 670 kg 400DA-type torpedo or two 225 kg bombs. Flotation bags of British design were installed, inflatable when an emergency required a 'put down' on water. The P.L.2s served for two

years on the *Béarn* from 1926, but suffered engine troubles which forced early scrapping.

Data: *Engine* as above *Wing span* 15.15 m (49 ft 8½ in) *Length* 11.0 m (36 ft 1 in) *Max T-O weight* 3,652 kg (8,051 lb) *Max level speed* 180 km/h (112 mph) *Range* 700 km (435 miles)

Levasseur P.L.4 (France) Carrier-borne three-seat reconnaissance biplane of 1926 powered by a 335.3 kW (450 hp) Lorraine water-cooled engine. Thirty-nine modified production aircraft were built between 1928 and 1931, equipping Escadrille 7R1 (later 7S1) on board *Béarn*. An interesting feature of the design was the landing gear which could be jettisoned for an emergency ditching, while the underfuselage was hull-shaped and floats were attached to the lower wings ('avion marin').

Levasseur P.L.5, P.L.6 and P.L.9 (France) The P.L.5 was a two-seat sesquiplane fighter ('avion marin'), of which four prototypes and 20 production aircraft were delivered to Aéronavale Escadrille 7C1 in 1927 for service on board the carrier *Béarn*. Power was provided by a 335.3 kW (450 hp) Lorraine 12Eb engine. Only a single example of the P.L.6 landplane variant was produced. A lower-powered naval trainer development of the P.L.5 was the P.L.9, six of which were built.

Levasseur P.L.7 (France) The P.L.7 was produced as a torpedo bomber for service with Escadrille 7B1 on board the aircraft carrier *Béarn*. It was an unequal-span biplane powered in prototype form by a 410 kW (550 hp) Farman engine. The 1930 initial production version standardised the 18.0 m (59 ft 0¾ in) span upper wing with rounded tips, and ten were built as three-seaters. After testing on board *Béarn*, a second production batch of 30 aircraft was ordered, featuring upper wings of reduced span with downward-folding outer sections to fit the lifts of the carrier. Both series were 'avions marins'. Armament comprised two 7.7 mm machine-guns mounted in the rearmost cockpit, plus a single 670 kg (1,474 lb) torpedo or 550 kg (1,212 lb) of bombs.

After two P.L.7s had been lost due to structural collapse, all were grounded in June 1931. The engine bearers and cabane struts were reinforced and three-bladed metal propellers fitted to the production aircrafts' 447 kW (600 hp) Hispano-Suiza engines. Following re-delivery in 1933 the

Levasseur P.L.5.

Levasseur P.L.7.

P.L.7s only remained on the carrier until the following year – when they were put ashore – but returned for a third time in 1936, thereafter serving until World War II.

Data (final form): *Engine* as above *Wing span* 16.5 m (54 ft 1½ in) *Length* 11.68 m (38 ft 3¾ in) *Max T-O weight* 3,950 kg (8,708 lb) *Max level speed* 170 km/h (106 mph) *Range* 650 km (404 miles)

Levasseur P.L.10 (France) Carrier-borne three-seat reconnaissance aircraft armed with one forward-firing 7.7 mm and two rear-mounted machine-guns. Twenty-nine production aircraft built, serving in board *Béarn* from 1930 to 1936.

Levasseur P.L.14 (France) Reconnaissance seaplane version of the P.L.7. Thirty were produced, initially as landplanes, subsequently serving as seaplanes at the Berre naval air station with Escadrille 7B2. Following the structural troubles with the P.L.7s, the P.L.14s were refitted with wheel landing gears, four thereafter serving on board *Béarn* from 1935 to 1937 (see **P.L. 15**).

Levasseur P.L.15.

Levasseur P.L.15 (France) Built from the start as a seaplane, the twin-float P.L.15 eliminated the deep 'avion marin' fuselage of the P.L.14 and had slim contours. The prototype and 16 production aircraft equipped Escadrille 7B2 on board the seaplane carrier *Commandant Teste* from 1933. Like the P.L.14s, these performed several roles, including bombing, torpedo-dropping and long-range reconnaissance (with four-man crew and extra fuel tanks to increase range to 1,500 km; 932 miles).

In 1938 the aircraft went into reserve, but were hurriedly withdrawn from retirement in September 1939 to form Escadrille 3S6 for coastal-patrol duties along the Bay of Biscay. The type later won fame by sinking a German U-boat on 30

October 1939. As with the P.L.14 power was provided by a 484.4 kW (650 hp) Hispano-Suiza 12 engine.

Data: *Engine* as above *Wing span* 18.0 m (59 ft 0¾ in) *Length* 12.85 m (42 ft 2 in) *Max T-O weight* 4,350 kg (9,590 lb) *Max level speed* 190 km/h (118 mph)

Levasseur P.L.101 (France) Carrier-borne armed-reconnaissance biplane developed from the P.L.10. Power was provided by a 484.4 kW (650 hp) Hispano-Suiza 12 engine. Thirty were produced to replace P.L.10s with Escadrille 7S1 on board *Béarn*.

Georges Lévy G.L.40 HB2 (France) Numerically less important than the FBA flying-boats, the Georges Lévy HB2 of November 1917 was the most efficient of several types of two–three-seat flying-boats operated for coastal patrol by the French Navy during 1917–18. It was an unequal-span biplane, with a distinctive bow and curved fin and rudder. Power was provided by a 223.6 kW (300 hp) Renault 12Fe water-cooled engine, driving a two-bladed pusher propeller. Pilot and observer sat side-by-side in open cockpits just in front of the lower wing, while the bow cockpit had a machine-gun on a flexible mounting. Up to 200 kg (441 lb) of bombs were carried. G.L.40 HB2s remained in post-war service with the French Navy. Six were also exported to Belgium and 12 to Finland. Belgian aircraft were operated by SNETA as commercial flying-boats in the Congo from 1920.

Levasseur P.L.14.

Georges Lévy G. L. 40 HB2 in Finnish service.

Armament comprised as standard a rear-mounted Parabellum machine-gun as a reconnaissance aircraft, increased with a forward-firing Spandau for escort duties. Four light bombs could also be carried under the fuselage, attached to bomb clips with jaw-type release gear.

Data: *Engine* as above *Wing span* 10.3 m (33 ft 10 in) *Length* 7.7 m (25 ft 3 in) *Max T-O weight* 1,310 kg (2,888 lb) *Max level speed* 165 km/h (102.5 mph) *Endurance* 4 h

LFG Roland D.I, D.II and D.III (Germany) The D-type single-seat fighters incorporated in design many of the innovations of the C.II. The fuselages were again of monocoque construction,

Georges Lévy G.L.40 HB2 operated by SNETA in the Congo, 1923.

Data: *Engine* as above *Wing span* 18.5 m (60 ft 8¼ in) *Length* 12.4 m (40 ft 8¼ in) *Max T-O weight* 2,350 kg (5,181 lb) *Max level speed* 150 km/h (93 mph) *Range* 435 km (270 miles)

Lévy-Le Pen (France) Alternative designation for the Georges Lévy G.L.40 flying-boat, M. Le Pen being the designer.

LFG Roland C.II (Germany) Aircraft produced by Luft Fahrzeug Gesellschaft (LFG) were normally known as Roland types after their designer. The C.II, nicknamed 'Walfisch' (Whale), was a high-performance general-purpose biplane, considerably smaller than other German two-seaters of the 1916–17 period. The most interesting feature of the aircraft was its monocoque fuselage which was round in section and so deep that windows were let into the flanks to aid downward vision. Both sets of wings were attached directly to the fuselage, enabling the pilot to have a clear view over the top of the upper wing. Several hundred C.IIs were built powered normally by the 119 kW (160 hp) Mercedes D.III engine.

consisting of very small longerons round which were placed bands of crossed veneer – in the manner of the Deperdussin – the whole forming a single multi-ply structure, reinforced with layers of thin fabric. The six layers of wood and the fabric had a total thickness of only 1½ mm. To enable the wings to be attached directly to the fuselage in C.II fashion, the normal wing gap forward of the pilot's cockpit was built up, while the lower wings attached to fixed fuselage/wing-root projections to avoid 'live' fittings and enable a cleaner join. The engine and the twin Spandau machine-guns were cowled inside the forward fuselage, the whole retaining its rounded appearance by the use of a large propeller spinner.

The first fighter (the D.I) was powered by a 119 kW (160 hp) Mercedes D.III engine and entered service in 1917. Production of this version was limited, allowing for rapid deployment of the refined D.II which had better vision for the pilot because of its slimmed-down wing gap structure and cut-down cockpit sides. The D.IIa was similar to the D.II but had a 134 kW (180 hp) Argus As.III engine. However none of the fighters was particularly good and squadron shortages were normally made up with Albatros types. With the D.III LFG attempted to improve the design, the most obvious changes being the use of cabane struts to support the upper wing and a tail fin of increased area. The D.III proved inferior to Albatros fighters and the few built were employed mainly in secondary roles (a full description of the D.II appears in the 1918 *Jane's*, details for which were obtained from a machine captured by the French).

LFG Roland C.II.

576

Data (D.II): *Engine* as above *Wing span* 8.94 m (29 ft 4 in) *Length* 6.93 m (22 ft 9 in) *Max T-O weight* 950 kg (2,094 lb) *Max level speed* 170 km/h (105.5 mph) *Endurance* 2 h

LFG Roland D.VI (Germany) The D.VI was the last fighter from the LFG stable to go into operational service during World War I, although it was followed by several new prototypes. It differed in virtually every respect from the earlier D.I–D.III series and indeed enjoyed considerable success with the Air Service and Navy.

Powered by a 119 kW (160 hp) or 134 kW (180 hp) Mercedes engine in its D.VIa and 149 kW (200 hp) Benz Bz.IIIa in its D.VIb production versions, it had a 'boat-built' fuselage comprising longitudinal wooden strips which formed a robust and very streamlined structure. Cabane struts were used to support the upper wing and (for the first time on an LFG fighter) horn-balanced ailerons were fitted to the upper wings. If it had one problem it was the time needed in construction, which prevented any great numbers from serving during the last months of the war.

Data (D.VIb): *Engine* as above *Wing span* 9.4 m (30 ft 10 in) *Length* 6.3 m (20 ft 8¾ in) *Max T-O weight* 860 kg (1,896 lb) *Max level speed* 182 km/h (113 mph) *Endurance* 2 h *Armament* two forward-firing Spandau machine-guns

LFG V 13 and V 130 Strela (Germany) In the first few years after the Armistice LFG produced a number of commercial monoplanes and biplanes; most of which were operated in ones or twos, remained prototypes, were used for experimental purposes, or were built for competition flying.

Among the more successful was the Strela four-passenger cabin biplane. The initial version was the V 13, mounted on large twin floats and suitable for a Benz, Mercedes or BMW engine in the 134–194 kW (180–260 hp) class. Range with four passengers was 400 km (249 miles), but with two was increased to 865 km (538 miles). A very small number were produced for commercial use. From the V 13 was developed a landplane version as the V 130 Strela. At least seven were built. The V 13s first served on Luft-Fahrzeug's Hamburg–Stettin–Danzig and Stettin–Swinemünde–Stralsund services, later operated in conjunction with Luftverkehr Pommern. These and the V130s eventually served with Deutsche Luft-Hansa (details of many other types can be found in the 1926 *Jane's*).

LFG V 20 Arkona (Germany) Four-passenger commercial low-wing monoplane fitted with twin floats and powered by a 112 kW (150 hp) Benz or 138 kW (185 hp) BMW IIIa engine. A small number were used by Luft-Fahrzeug on the services mentioned under the V 13/V 130 entry above.

LFG V 101 Jasmund (Germany) Although Luft-Fahrzeug expected to operate its seaplane routes in North Germany with V 59s from 1926 (in conjunction with Luftverkehr Pommern), it is believed that the V 59 was abandoned in favour of the V 101 – an all-metal version of the V 20 and flown alongside Strela and Arkona types. Power was normally provided by a 138 kW (185 hp) BMW IIIa engine.

LFIL-Reghin RG-6 (Romania) Two-seat light monoplane powered by a 56 kW (75 hp) Praga D engine. Produced from the later 1950s for the national sports flying organisation AVSAP. A single-seat fully aerobatic development, powered by a 78.25 kW (105 hp) Walter Minor engine, was designated RG-6c.

LIBIS KB-6D Matajur (Yugoslavia) Two-seat light training and sporting aircraft, first flown in June 1952. Power was provided by a 101.3 kW (136 hp) Régnier 4L00 engine.

LFG Roland D.I.

LIBIS KB-6T Matajur.

LIBIS KB-6T Matajur (Yugoslavia) Three-seat development of the KB-6D powered by a 119 kW (160 hp) Walter Minor 6-III-J engine. Produced mainly for Yugoslav flying clubs.

LIBIS KB-11 Branko (Yugoslavia) Four-seat light monoplane intended for business and air-taxi operations. First flown in December 1959. Power was provided by a 134 kW (180 hp) Lycoming O-435-1 engine.

LFG Roland D.VIb.

Lioré et Olivier

LIBIS KB-11 Branko.

Lioré et Olivier 20s.

Lioré et Olivier 7/3.

Lioré et Olivier 7 (France) Evolved from the twin-engined ground-attack LéO 5 prototype, the LéO 7 of 1922 was intended for bomber-escort or multi-seat combat duties. Following the solitary LéO 7/1, which made a crash landing, some 20 examples of the modified LéO 7/2 were built. These were three-seat unequal-span biplanes powered by 223.6 kW (300 hp) Hispano-Suiza liquid-cooled engines. The observer/gunner was seated in a nose cockpit, while the pilot and radio operator/rear gunner sat close together in tandem immediately below a 'cut-out' in the upper wing and had armour protection. The LéO 7/3 (12 of which went to the French Navy) had a more rounded nose with a cut back observation position beneath. The main and tailwheel spats were much enlarged, containing buoyancy bags in the event of an emergency landing at sea. The LéO 7/2 served briefly at Metz and the LéO 7/3 at Saint-Raphaël.
Data (LéO 7/2): *Engines* as above *Wing span* 18.6 m (61 ft 0¼ in) *Length* 11.25 m (36 ft 11 in) *Max T-O weight* 3,000 kg (6,614 lb) *Max level speed* 203 km/h (126 mph)

Lioré et Olivier 12 (France) Intended as a two-seat night bomber, the prototype LéO 12 flew for the first time in June 1924. A three-bay equal-span biplane, it was constructed largely of duralumin (with fabric covering) and had two 298 kW (400 hp) Lorraine liquid-cooled engines. It featured a blunt nose, a gunner's cockpit amidships and trousered independent main landing-gear legs. Three other LéO 12s were built, one

later being converted into a 12-passenger transport and operated by a LéO subsidiary, L'Aéronavale. In 1925 the sole LéO 122 appeared, the true prototype of the LéO 20. It differed from the LéO 12 in having a nose-gunner's 'balcony' and Jupiter radial engines. One LéO 12 was subsequently converted into the fully enclosed LéO 123 used by the French Air Ministry for experimental work.

Lioré et Olivier 20 (France) The true prototype of the LéO 20 night bomber was the LéO 122, in turn developed from four evaluation LéO 12 bombers. The LéO 20 Bn3 three-bay equal-span biplane was the backbone of French night-bomber escadrilles until replaced by the Bloch 200 in 1935. About 100 machines were still airworthy when World War II broke out.

First production machines were delivered in 1927 to 21ème and 22ème Regiments d'Aviation at Nancy and Chartres. Total production for French military aviation amounted to 311 aircraft, and seven LéO 20s were exported to Brazil. Of mixed construction, the LéO 20 was powered by two uncowled 313 kW (420 hp) Gnome-Rhône radial engines. In the extreme nose was a gunner's cockpit, with a glazed bomb-aimer/navigator's 'balcony' below and slightly to the rear. Pilot was located in an open cockpit in front of the wing, behind which was the dorsal gunner with a twin-gun mounting. A fifth machine-gun was carried in a retractable ventral turret.
Data: *Engines* as above *Wing span* 22.25 m (73 ft 0 in) *Length* 13.81 m (45 ft 3¾ in) *Max T-O weight* 5,460 kg (12,037 lb) *Max level speed* 198 km/h (123 mph) *Range* 1,000 km (621 miles)

Lioré et Olivier 21 (France) Two examples of the commercial LéO 21 appeared in 1926, each accommodating 18 passengers in a deep fuselage. These were operated by Air Union, serving the Paris–London route from July 1927. When each was subsequently re-engined with two 335.3 kW (450 hp) Renault 12Jas, they became LéO 212s; one also being further modified into a flying restaurant for 12 passengers. In 1928 the LéO 213 appeared with improved accommodation for 12 passengers. Eleven were built, serving Air Union's regular Paris–London route. Nine aircraft were bought by the Armée de l'Air in October 1934 as transports for 20 troops.
Data: *Engines* as above *Wing span* 23.43 m (76 ft 10½ in) *Length* 15.95 m (52 ft 4 in) *Max T-O weight* 5,700 kg (12,566 lb) *Max level speed* 190 km/h (119 mph)

Lioré et Olivier 206 (France) Four-engined developments of the LéO 20 included the LéO 203, 206, 207, 208 (with retractable undercarriage) and the H-204 twin-float seaplane. The only version to see service was the LéO 206, first flown in 1932. Open cockpits were retained for the crew, but power was provided by four 261 kW (350 hp) Gnome-Rhône Kd radial engines mounted in tandem pairs. A long ventral gondola contained the bomb bay, with a ventral gunner's position at the rear. The 37 LéO 206s built were based at Chartres, Reims and in Morocco. Nicknamed 'Caravelle', 29 were still flyable in September 1939.

relegated to transport and liaison duties (a number flown in these roles by the Luftwaffe). Twenty-seven LéO 451s were ceded to Italy in 1941 but saw little service.

There were numerous experimental conversions of the basic design. Several examples remained in use in secondary roles for several years following the end of the Second World War.

Data: *Engines* as above *Wing span* 22.52 m (73 ft 10½ in) *Length* 17.17 m (56 ft 4 in) *Max T-O weight* 11,398 kg (25,128 lb) *Max level speed* 480 km/h (298.5 mph) *Range* 1,675 km (1,040 miles)

Lioré et Olivier 451s.

Lioré et Olivier 451 (France) The LéO 45.01 B4 – designed by Jean Mercier to Armée de l'Air Programme A21(1934) – first flew on 16 January 1937. It was an all-metal low-wing monoplane powered by two radial engines. The wings had considerable dihedral and the streamlined elliptical monocoque fuselage had a pointed and fully glazed nose. The landing gear was fully retractable. Accommodation provided for a pilot in an enclosed cockpit, behind which was the radio operator's panel and below the retractable ventral gun turret.

Production LéO 451s had two 849.5 kW (1,140 hp) Gnome-Rhône 14N 48/49 or 38/39 radial engines in specially designed Mercier cowlings. Despite excellent performance, construction of the type was slow. Only five LéO 451s were on first-line strength by 3 September 1939. When France collapsed in June 1940 only 452 of some 1,700 ordered had been delivered. A number of modifications were incorporated during series production, the principal being a totally redesigned fin and rudder assembly. Armament included a fixed 7.5 mm MAC 1934 nose machine-gun, another gun of the same type flexibly mounted in the ventral gondola, and a somewhat troublesome 20 mm HS-404 on a special mounting in the dorsal position. Maximum bomb load – carried in fuselage and wing bomb bays – was 2,400 kg (5,291 lb).

The LéO 451s were used initially for long-range reconnaissance missions, then for daylight bombing during the Battle of France and in night raids on Italian targets during June 1940. A further 225 were ordered by the French Vichy regime, the type serving in French overseas territories, later

Lioré et Olivier H-13 series (France) The LéO H-13 was an equal-span biplane flying-boat powered by two 112 kW (150 hp) Hispano-Suiza engines driving two-bladed tractor propellers. The pilot was accommodated in an open cockpit behind the wings, in front of which was the four-passenger cabin. Twenty-five were produced, three as H-13A amphibians. These were operated on several Mediterranean routes, starting with the Antibes–Ajaccio (Corsica) service of Aéronavale. The sole H-13*bis* (1934) was a navalised variant. Two H-132s were followed by four H-133s, each with a single 223.6 kW (300 hp) Renault engine. Two H-13s were subsequently modified to H-134s, each powered by a single 335.3 kW (450 hp) Lorraine engine.

Seven H-135 amphibians were acquired by the Polish Navy for reconnaissance and training duties, and the prototype H-136 was followed by 12 production aircraft for the French Navy, each with the pilot's cockpit in front of the wings, bow and midships gunners' positions. Production of all the H-13 versions totalled 52 aircraft.

Data: *Engines* as above *Wing span* 16.0 m (52 ft 6 in) *Length* 11.5 m (37 ft 8¾ in) *Max T-O weight* 2,564 kg (5,653 lb) *Max level speed* 160 km/h (99.5 mph)

Lioré et Olivier H-25 series (France) Developed from the LéO 20, the 1928 prototype had a new tailplane and liquid-cooled Hispano-Suiza engines. The second aircraft was sold to Romania and three LéO 253 landplane bombers (built in 1931) went to Brazil.

The LéO H-254 was the first naval variant with an interchangeable wheel or twin-float landing gear. It retained the open cockpits of the earlier

Lioré et Olivier

Lioré-Olivier H-25
prototype.

Lioré-Olivier H-25
prototype.

**Lioré-Olivier H-257bis
landplane.**

versions and the 'balcony'-type nose-gunner's cockpit. The single supercharged H-255 followed, which established several altitude records for seaplanes. Four LéO H-256s had engines with reduction gear, while the single LéO H-257 was the prototype for a series of 60 H-257bis delivered to the French Navy from 1935. These had enclosed cabins for the flight crew, a bow gun position and revised bomb-aimer's position. The dorsal gun position remained open and a retractable ventral turret was fitted. Armament comprised four 0.303 in Lewis or 7.7 mm Darne machine-guns, plus a 670 kg torpedo or up to 600 kg (1,323 lb) of bombs. Power was provided by two 648.3 kW (870 hp) Gnome-Rhône 14Kfrs radial engines.

Twenty-six 484.4 kW (650 hp) Hispano-Suiza-powered H-258s were produced as stop-gaps pending the delivery of the H-257bis. The solitary H-259 was powered by 641 kW (860 hp) Hispano-Suiza engines with variable-pitch propellers.

LéO H-257bis and H-258s equipped a number of naval escadrilles flying neutrality patrols during the Spanish Civil War and anti-submarine patrols during World War II. Some even carried out attacks on land targets during the German Blitzkrieg of May 1940.
Data (LéO H-257bis): *Engines* as above *Wing span* 25.5 m (83 ft 8 in) *Length* 17.54 m (57 ft 6¾ in)

Max T-O weight 9,380 kg (20,679 lb) *Max level speed* 250 km/h (155.5 mph) *Range* 1,500 km (932 miles)

Lioré et Olivier H-43 (France) Built to a French Navy requirement of 1933, the prototype H-43 first flew in December 1934. It was a three-seat twin-float monoplane armed with two machine-guns. The 20 production aircraft were not delivered until 1939 by which time the type was totally obsolete.

Lioré et Olivier H-47 (France) Intended for Air France's South Atlantic route, the prototype H-47 flew for the first time in July 1936 but was lost in March of the following year. Five strengthened production flying-boats were delivered during 1938–39 but were requisitioned by the Navy at the outbreak of World War II. Power was provided by four 641 kW (860 hp) Hispano-Suiza 12Y34 engines mounted in tandem pairs.

Lioré et Olivier H-49 (France) See **Sud-Est SE 200**

Lioré et Olivier H-190 series (France) The H-190 was a single-engined flying-boat of wooden construction. Twenty-nine initial production aircraft were built (including five H-190Ts), each accommodating six passengers. These had the pilot's cockpit aft of the biplane wing. All subsequent production aircraft had the pilot's cockpit forward of the wings. The postal H-198 variant (nine built) was powered by a 357.7 kW (480 hp) Jupiter radial engine and reinforced for catapult launching from transatlantic liners. All had been withdrawn from service by 1933.

The LéO H-194 of 1926 became famous for making a three-month African cruise covering 28,000 km (17,400 miles). Two examples of the twin tandem-engined LéO H-199 were completed, together with 16 examples of a naval variant of the series designated H-193S, used for coastal-patrol duties.
Data (LéO H-193S): *Wing span* 16.0 m (52 ft 6 in) *Length* 12.5 m (41 ft 0 in) *Max T-O weight* 3,185 kg (7,022 lb) *Max level speed* 170 km/h (105.5 mph)

Lioré et Olivier H-242 (France) Fourteen H-242 flying-boats went into service from 1932 with Air Union (soon to be Air France) on Mediterranean routes – each aircraft bearing the name of a French-controlled Mediterranean port. Powered by four 313 kW (420 hp) Gnome-Rhône 7Kd radial engines mounted in tandem pairs above the high cantilever wing, each had an enclosed pilot's cockpit and cabin accommodation for 15 passengers. Robust aircraft, they survived on regular routes until 1939, most falling into Italian hands in 1940.

Lioré et Olivier H-246 (France) Twenty-six-passenger flying-boat designed for Air France's Mediterranean routes. Power was provided by four Hispano-Suiza 12X liquid-cooled engines mounted in the leading edge of the high monoplane wing. The prototype was followed by six production aircraft in 1939, five of which operated the Marseille–Algiers route. The sixth had a glazed bow and defensive armament and was used as a military reconnaissance aircraft during 1939–40.

Lipnur LT-200 (Indonesia) Two-seat light aircraft based on the Pazmany PL-2. Powered by one 112 kW (150 hp) Lycoming O-320-E2A engine. It was expected that about 30 would be built initially for the Indonesian Air Force, Civil Flying School and flying clubs (see also **Angkatan**).

Lisunov Li-2 (USSR) Soviet licence-built version of the Douglas DC-3 operated widely during World II and after by air forces and airlines. Power was provided by two 745 kW (1,000 hp) Shvetsov ASh-621R radial engines.

Lloyd C types (Austria-Hungary) The Lloyd series of two-seat reconnaissance and training biplanes began before the outbreak of World War I with the C.I. At the 1914 Vienna meeting it was flown by Oberlieut Bier (former director of Deutsche Flugzeug Werke) to an altitude of more than 6,150 m (20,200 ft), at the same time or on a separate occasion setting an altitude record while carrying three persons. During the war Lloyd aircraft were standardised in the Austro-Hungarian Air Service, the C.Is giving way to 108 kW (145 hp) Hiero-powered C.IIs, 119 kW (160 hp) Austro-Daimler-powered C.IIIs and C.IVs, and 138 kW (185 hp) Austro-Daimler or 149 kW (200 hp) Benz-powered C.Vs, operated until the end of the war. Production of all versions totalled about 400 aircraft. Several interesting experimental aircraft were also built during the war by Lloyd.

Data (C.III): *Engine* as above *Wing span* 14.0 m (45 ft 11½ in) *Length* 9.0 m (29 ft 6½ in) *Max T-O weight* 1,380 kg (3,042 lb) *Max level speed* 134 km/h (83 mph) *Endurance* 3 h 30 min *Armament* one rear-mounted Schwarzlose machine-gun

Lockheed C-5A Galaxy (USA) In October 1965 Lockheed was selected prime contractor for a new very large logistics transport for Military Airlift Command (then MATS) and the designation C-5A and name Galaxy were assigned. Initial construction began in August 1966 and the first flight was made on 30 June 1968. Contracts were placed subsequently covering the manufacture of 81 C-5As for the USAF and delivery of these was completed in May 1973. The Galaxy remains the largest aeroplane in the world.

In early 1978 Lockheed received a USAF contract to manufacture two new sets of C-5A wings of a design intended to reduce stress and increase service life to 30,000 hours. Apart from the moving surfaces, these wings are of virtually new design. One set is for ground testing and one for flight trials in 1980. If these tests are successful it is planned to fit them to the 77 Galaxies still in operational service with the USAF, beginning in 1982.

Data: *Engines* four 182.4 kN (41,000 lb st) General Electric TF39-GE-1 turbofans *Wing span* 67.88 m (222 ft 8½ in) *Length* 75.54 m (247 ft 10 in) *Max T-O weight* 348,810 kg (769,000 lb) *Max level speed* 919 km/h (571 mph) *Range* (max payload) 6,033 km (3,749 miles) *Accommodation* normal crew of five, with rest area for 15 people (relief crew, couriers, etc) at front of upper deck. Basic version has seats for 75 troops on rear part of upper deck. Provision for 270 troops on lower deck, but aircraft is employed primarily as a

Lloyd experimental observation biplane of World War I, with the observer occupying a cockpit high in the nose of the fuselage.

Lioré-Olivier H-246.

Lisunov Li-2.

Lockheed

Lockheed C-5A Galaxy.

Lockheed C-5A Galaxy.

freighter. Typical freight loads include two M-60 tanks or 16 × ¾ ton lorries; or one M-60 and two Bell Iroquois helicopters, five M-113 personnel carriers, one M-59 2½ ton truck and an M-151 ¼ ton truck; or 10 Pershing missiles with tow and launch vehicles; or 36 standard 463L load pallets. Visor-type upward-hinged nose and loading ramp permit straight-in loading into front of hold under flight deck.

Lockheed C-130 Hercules (USA) Following a decision to equip the USAF with turboprop transport aircraft able to carry outsize cargo economically over long ranges, two types emerged from the resulting design competition: the Lockheed C-130 and the much larger, longer-range Douglas C-133.

Lockheed received an initial contract for two YC-130 prototypes on 11 July 1951 and the first of these made its maiden flight on 23 August 1954.

The first production C-130A flew on 7 April 1955. These aircraft (named Hercules) began to enter service with Troop Carrier Command and Tactical Air Command in December 1956.

As the primary requirement was to carry cargo, the wing was mounted high on the fuselage so that its carry-through structure would cause the minimum loss of internal capacity. In the same way the main landing gear was kept on the outside of the fuselage, with the struts and wheels retracting into external fairings. Access to the main cargo hold was from the rear with a large hydraulically operated ramp making easy the direct on-loading of military vehicles, or simplifying the handling of general cargo. Once the load was aboard the ramp was raised, forming the undersurface of the rear fuselage. Power plant of the C-130A comprised four Allison T56-A-1A or -9 turboprop engines mounted in nacelles at the wing leading edge.

Second major version was the C-130B which differed from the original C-130A by having increased fuel capacity, uprated landing gear and more powerful Allison engines. The first of these entered service with Tactical Air Command on 12 June 1959 and 230 were built before production ended. The requirement for increased range brought about production of 503 C-130Es with additional fuel capacity. The current production version in 1979 was the C-130H, well over 500 of which had been ordered.

Apart from its basic transport role, the Hercules has proved to be particularly adaptable for a range of differing tasks, leading to a large number of variants of each version. C-130As included a single test example AC-130A gunship; two GC-130A (later DC-130A) drone carrier/launch/control aircraft; JC-130As for the tracking of missiles and spacecraft, seven of which were reconverted to AC-130A gunship configuration; and RC-130A mapping aircraft.

Variants of the C-130B include US Coast Guard HC-130B search and rescue aircraft; and NC-130B for short take-off and landing (STOL) research; RC-130Bs similar to RC-130As; and 17 WC-130Bs for weather reconnaissance and research.

Lockheed C-130K Hercules, designated C.1 by the RAF.

Lockheed L-100 Hercules.

Lockheed CP-140 Aurora (USA) Special version of the Lockheed P.3 Orion for the Canadian Armed Forces, combining the airframe, power plant and basic aircraft systems of the Orion with the avionics systems and data-processing capability of the US Navy's carrier-based Lockheed S-3A Viking. Delivery of 18 aircraft will be completed between May 1980 and March 1981.

Lockheed C-141 StarLifter (USA) With the aim of increasing significantly the strategic airlift capability of the USAF, the specification SOR-182 (Specific Operational Requirement 182) was issued in 1960. Intended to provide

Lockheed Hercules W.2, operated by the RAF for weather reconnaissance.

C-130E variants have included AC-130E gunships; DC-130E drone launch and control aircraft; special-duty US Coast Guard EC-130E; three HC-130E SAR aircraft for the Coast Guard; and weather reconnaissance WC-130Es for the USAF.

C-130H variants include long-range SAR HC-130Hs; JC-130Hs to retrieve re-entering space capsules; a drone launch and recovery DC-130H; and KC-130H tankers.

Other Hercules versions include the C-130D with wheel/ski landing gear for operation in snow-bound areas; C-130F assault transport; KC-130F assault transport/tanker; HC-130N for space capsule retrieval; HC-130P helicopter-refuelling tanker; EC-130Q US Navy Command communication aircraft; KC-130R tanker; and LC-130R wheel/ski landing gear transport. More than 1,500 examples of the Hercules have been built. In addition Lockheed build a lengthened-fuselage civil counterpart under the designation L-100. The designations L-100-50 and L-400 Twin Hercules apply to two projected new versions, the former a 'stretched' L-100 and the latter a twin-engined derivative of the C-130.

Data (C-130H): *Engines* four 3,362 kW (4,508 ehp) Allison T56-A-15 turboprops *Wing span* 40.41 m (132 ft 7 in) *Length* (except HC-130H) 29.79 m (97 ft 9 in) *Max T-O weight* 79,379 kg (175,000 lb) *Max level speed* 621 km/h (386 mph) *Range with max payload* 4,002 km (2,487 miles) *Armament* (gunship versions) has included a variety of 7.62 mm, 20 mm, 40 mm and 105 mm guns

Lockheed CP-140 Aurora.

global-range airlift for MATS (subsequently MAC) as well as high-speed strategic deployment for US Strike Command, Boeing, Douglas, General Dynamics/Convair and Lockheed all made submissions. It was announced on 13 March 1961 that the Lockheed-Georgia Company had been chosen as winners of the design contest. On 16 August 1961 construction of an initial batch of five C-141As was contracted and the first of these aircraft made its initial flight at Marietta on 17 December 1963 (the 60th anniversary of the first powered flight made by the Wright brothers).

Design of the fuselage was somewhat similar to that of the C-130 Hercules, with a rear loading door, but to provide the high-speed characteristics required by Strike Command, the monoplane wing (mounted in a high-wing configuration) had 25° sweepback and carried four turbofan engines mounted in underwing pods. Tricycle-type landing gear consisted of a twin-wheel nose unit, each main unit comprising a four-wheel bogie.

C-141A StarLifters (as the type was named)

Prototype Lockheed
YC-141B StarLifter
undergoing
flight-refuelling tests.

Lockheed C-141A
StarLifter.

began to enter service with MATS in October 1964 and by the summer of 1965 had started regular operational flights across the Pacific to Vietnam, maintaining virtually a daily service.

C-141A StarLifters carried a crew of four to six and could accommodate 154 troops, 123 paratroops, 80 stretchers and 16 sitting casualties, or cargo. Some aircraft were modified to carry a Minuteman intercontinental ballistic missile in its special container: a load totalling 39,103 kg (86,207 lb). However operational deployment showed that C-141As were often loaded considerably below their maximum permissible weight, although the cargo hold was physically full. This resulted in a C-141A being modified by having the fuselage lengthened by 7.11 m (23 ft 4 in) and the inclusion of flight-refuelling equipment. This flew for the first time on 24 March 1977. It is planned to convert the existing 277 C-141As to this new C-141B StarLifter standard by July 1982.
Data (C-141A): *Engines* four 9,525 kg (21,000 lb st) Pratt & Whitney TF33-P7 turbofans *Wing span* 48.74 m (159 ft 11 in) *Length* 44.2 m (145 ft 0 in) *Max T-O weight* 143,607 kg (316,600 lb) *Max level speed* 919 km/h (571 mph) *Cruising speed* 797 km/h (495 mph) *Range* (with 32,136 kg; 70,847 lb payload) 6,566 km (4,080 miles)

Lockheed F-80A Shooting
Star.

Lockheed F-80 Shooting Star (USA) In June 1943 Lockheed was instructed to proceed with the design and development of a new single-seat fighter, utilising as its power plant a British de Havilland H-1 turbojet. This was undoubtedly an exciting project for Lockheed, for the first US-built turbojet-powered aircraft – the Bell XP-59A prototype – had made its maiden flight less than nine months earlier. At that time the tempo of American aircraft production had got into high gear and C. L. ('Kelly') Johnson, leader of Lockheed's design team, used his genius and enthusiasm to such effect that the project details had been completed within a week.

The design proved acceptable to the USAAF. It was a low-wing cantilever monoplane with a knife-edge laminar-flow wing section; engine within the rear fuselage; air intakes on each side of the fuselage forward of the wing leading edge; and retractable tricycle-type landing gear. Equally attractive was the company's proposal to complete an initial prototype within 180 days and little time was lost in awarding contracts for three prototypes and 13 service trials aircraft. Work on the first prototype began in August 1943 and just 143 days later (on 9 January 1944) this aircraft flew for the first time.

Service designation of the prototype was XP-80. Its power plant was a 13.34 kN (3,000 lb st) de Havilland H-1 turbojet, predecessor of the Goblin and supplied to the USA in July 1943. Unfortunately plans for this engine to be built by the Allis-Chalmers Company in America went awry, so the next two prototypes each had a 16.68 kN (3,750 lb st) General Electric I-40 turbojet. This was a larger and more powerful engine than the intended Allis-Chalmers J36, involving redesign which included increased span and length, a taller fin and strengthened landing gear. The exercise cost five months, for it was not until 10 June 1944 that the first of these two XP-80As was flown.

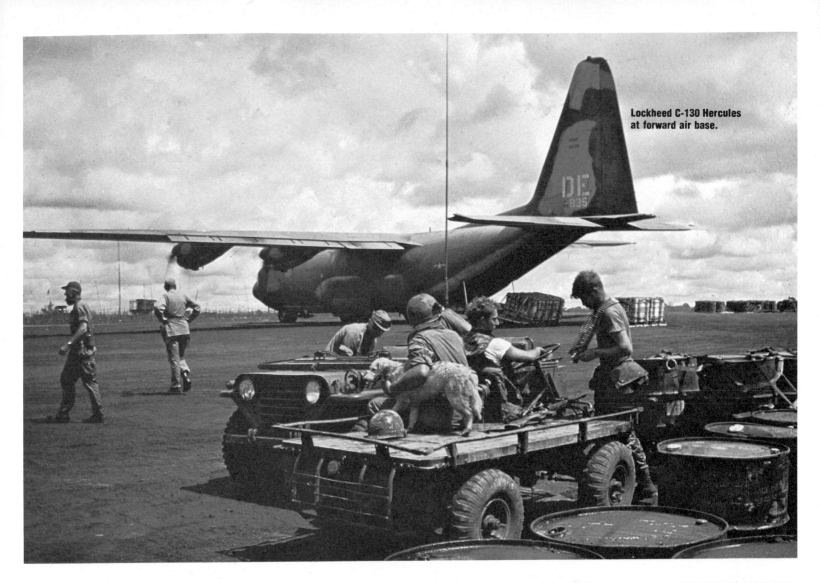

Lockheed C-130 Hercules at forward air base.

Lockheed C-141B StarLifter about to be refuelled by a KC-135 tanker.

**Prototype Lockheed
L.188 Electra.**

Lockheed P-3 Orion.

Lockheed PV-1 Ventura.

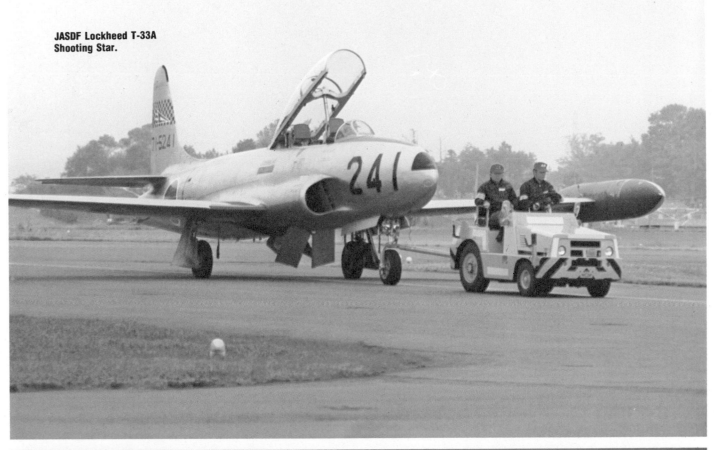

JASDF Lockheed T-33A
Shooting Star.

Lockheed S-3A Viking.

**Lockheed Super
Constellation flying over
New York.**

LTV-Hiller-Ryan XC-142A.

LVG C.VI.

The YP-80A service trials aircraft, powered by Allison-developed General Electric J33s, began to equip USAAF units in October 1944 but were too late to see operational service in World War II. The name allocated (Shooting Star) was indicative of the excitement generated by these new turbine-powered aircraft, able to demonstrate speeds of 160–240 km/h (100–150 mph) higher than those of the best piston-engined fighters. Because of such performance, war-end contract cancellations did not eliminate the P-80 (changed to F-80 in 1948), but ensured that production continued to re-equip USAAF first-line squadrons – beginning in December 1945.

Production P-80As had wingtip tanks and provision for bombs, rockets and fuel tanks to be carried beneath the wings, plus six 0.50 in guns mounted in the fuselage nose. P-80Bs which followed had a more powerful engine, thinner wing section, stronger bulkheads in the nose section to support greater fire-power, stainless steel armoured engine compartment and provisions for JATO. Final version was the P-80C (RF-80C unarmed photographic reconnaissance subvariant), with a still more powerful engine and increased underwing weapons capability.

Lockheed F-94C Starfire.

The Shooting Star has an established place in USAAF/USAF history: its first operational jet-powered aircraft, one of which set a world speed record of 1,003.91 km/h (623.8 mph) on 19 June 1947. Soon after (in 1950) they were used in combat during the Korean War and an F-80C, flown by Lieut Russell J. Brown on 8 November 1950, achieved the first air-combat victory between two jet-powered fighters, destroying a Mikoyan MiG-15 of the Chinese People's Republic Air Force. For Korea, F.80s were adapted to carry two 500 lb and four 260 lb fragmentation bombs or two 1,000 lb bombs plus eight rockets or four 40 US gallon napalm bombs.

Variants have included reconnaissance RF-80s, QF-80A and QF-80F drones, and one F-80C was converted as a prototype two-seat trainer (see **Lockheed T-33**).

Data (F-80C): *Engine* one 20.46 kN (4,600 lb st) Allison J33-A-23 turbojet *Wing span* 12.17 m (39 ft 11 in) *Length* 10.52 m (34 ft 6 in) *Max T-O weight*

7,646 kg (16,856 lb) *Max level speed* 933 km/h (580 mph) *Cruising speed* 707 km/h (439 mph) *Range* 2,221 km (1,380 miles) *Armament* six 0.50 in guns, rockets, bombs and napalm bombs

Lockheed F-94 Starfire (USA) Third member of Lockheed's F-80 family, the F-94 Starfire was evolved to satisfy a requirement for a two-seat all-weather radar-equipped fighter. It was evolved from the two-seat T-33, trainer and originally used many of the main components and the production facilities of its predecessor. The prototypes were converted T-33s, each with a new 26.69 kN (6,000 lb st) Allison J33-A-33 turbojet, radar equipment installed in the fuselage nose and suitably equipped accommodation for the radar operator in the rear cockpit. Armament of four 0.50 in guns was retained in the forward fuselage.

Deliveries of production F-94As began in June 1950. These incorporated the wings, landing gear and centre fuselage of the T-33, with a new nose and rear fuselage (former to house the radar and the latter for the afterburner installation). All hydraulic, electric and control systems were similar to those of the F-80C. The F-94As were followed in 1951 by F-94Bs which differed in having square wingtips with centrally mounted Fletcher tip-tanks of larger capacity and improved shape, raised to the wing centre-line, and a revised hydraulic system. Final version was the F-94C with a thinner wing, longer nose, swept horizontal tail surfaces, larger vertical surfaces, a more powerful engine, and the radome centred in the fuselage nose and surrounded by a ring of 24 air-to-air rockets housed in firing tubes, faired by a retractable shield. Two pods (one mounted on each wing) could together accommodate 24 more rockets. A total of 544 kg (1,200 lb) of electronic equipment included automatic locating, tracking and firing instruments, Westinghouse autopilot, Sperry Zero-Reader, ILS, etc. A total of 854 production Starfires were built. The USAF's first turbojet-powered all-weather interceptor, the type served primarily with Air Defense Command for national defence.

Data (F-94C): *Engine* one 38.92 kN (8,750 lb st, with afterburning) Pratt & Whitney J48-P-5 or

Checking the cameras in a Lockheed RF-80 Shooting Star.

Lockheed

Lockheed F-104Js and two-seat F-104DJs of the JASDF.

Lockheed F-104Gs in Luftwaffe service.

Lockheed L.10A Electra.

-5A turbojet *Wing span* 12.93 m (42 ft 5 in) *Length* 13.56 m (44 ft 6 in) *Max T-O weight* 10,977 kg (24,200 lb) *Max level speed* 941 km/h (585 mph) at 9,145 m (30,000 ft) *Range* 1,931 km (1,200 miles) *Armament* up to 48 air-to-air rockets

Lockheed F-104 Starfighter (USA) Lockheed's C. L. ('Kelly') Johnson has designed some really exciting aircraft, but the company's Model 83 (which originated in late 1952) must qualify as outstanding when the state of the art at that time is taken into account. Lockheed were aware that USAF experience in Korea had shown the need for an air-superiority fighter able to operate from forward airfields and climb rapidly from the ground to engage in high-level combat. The Model 83 was designed to fulfil these roles, and in formulating his design 'Kelly' Johnson attempted to keep it as cheap, small and readily maintainable as possible. Tendered to the USAF as an unsolicited proposal, it was necessary for competitive bids to be received and the USAF notified a formal requirement for such an aircraft in late 1952.

Submissions were received from North American and Republic; but as both of these companies were already heavily involved in fighter development and production, Lockheed's proposal was selected cautiously: two XF-104 prototypes being ordered for development and testing. The first of these flew on 28 February 1954, followed by test and evaluation aircraft. It was not until 26 Janu-

ary 1958 that the first production F-104As began to enter service – as interceptors – with Air Defense Command's 83rd Fighter Interceptor Squadron.

These production aircraft appeared quite revolutionary to those seeing them for the first time: with but a token monoplane wing mid-set on the fuselage – this latter assembly wrapped tightly round a powerful turbojet engine – needle-nosed and T-tailed. Able to demonstrate a level speed of around 2,250 km/h (1,400 mph) and to climb to a height of 25 km (15.15 miles) in about 4.5 minutes, it is not surprising that the Press dubbed the Starfighter the 'missile with a man in it'.

F-104As (170) and multi-mission F-104Cs (77) served with the USAF, as well as F-104B (26) and F-104D (21) two-seat operational-trainer counterparts of the A and C respectively. Major construction, however, was in Europe: following development by Lockheed of the multi-mission F-104G, more than 1,000 came from production lines in Belgium, Germany, Holland and Italy to equip the air forces of those nations. Similar versions were built under licence in Canada and Japan. Lockheed also built 179 F-104Gs for export or for supply to friendly nations through the Military Assistance Program.

Final production line was that of Aeritalia SpA in Turin, Italy which built 205 Starfighters for the Italian Air Force and 40 for Turkey. These multi-role combat aircraft have the designation F-104S and have extended production of this outstanding (and sometimes controversial) aircraft for a period of 20 years.

Interestingly a Starfighter – built from non-serviceable ex-military aircraft components by American Darryl Greenamyer over a ten-year period – was without doubt the fastest and most complex 'homebuilt' aircraft ever completed. With this aircraft – known as the Red Baron F-104RB Starfighter – he raised the world speed record over a 3 km low-level course to 1,590.45 km/h (988.26 mph) on 24 October 1977. Unfortunately the F-104RB was lost in an accident in 1978.

Data (F-104S): *Engine* one 79.62 kN (17,900 lb st, with afterburning) General Electric J79-GE-19 turbojet *Wing span* 6.68 m (21 ft 11 in) *Length* 16.69 m (54 ft 9 in) *Max T-O weight* 14,061 kg (31,000 lb) *Max level speed* Mach 2.2 *Cruising speed* 982 km/h (610 mph) *Range* 1,247 km (775 miles) *Armament* one 20 mm M-61 Vulcan cannon and up to 1,814 kg (4,000 lb) external weapons. Two Sparrow or Sidewinder missiles can be carried in an interceptor role

Lockheed L.10 Electra (USA) Lockheed enjoyed considerable success with its Vega, Orion and Air Express commercial aircraft, but by the beginning of the 1930s it was clear that a new and modern replacement was needed if the company was to have continued success. Its answer came in the form of the L.10 Electra, a high-speed twin-engined all-metal cantilever low-wing airliner accommodating ten passengers or freight. Appearing after the Boeing Model 247 and the Douglas DC-1/DC-2, the Electra first flew in February 1934 and entered service with Northwest Airlines in August of that year.

Several versions were produced including the 298 kW (400 hp) Pratt & Whitney R-985 Wasp Junior-engined L.10A; 313 kW (420 hp) Wright Whirlwind-powered L.10B; and 335.3 kW (450 hp) Pratt & Whitney R-1340 Wasp-engined L.10E. During 1935 41 Electras were delivered and the company recorded its most profitable year ever. In 1937 the 100th Electra was delivered to Poland. Lockheed built a total of 148 Electras, most of which were used by airlines but a few went to the USAAC, US Navy and US Coast Guard as the C-36/C-37, R2O and R3O respectively.

Data (L.10A): *Engines* as above *Wing span* 16.76 m (55 ft 0 in) *Length* 11.76 m (38 ft 7 in) *Max T-O weight* 4,763 kg (10,500 lb) *Max level speed* 325 km/h (202 mph) *Range* 1,416 km (880 miles)

Lockheed L.12 Electra (USA) In 1936 the new Lockheed L.12 Electra made its appearance. It was smaller than the L.10 but much faster. Power was provided by two Wasp Junior or Whirlwind engines and six passengers were carried. Like the L.10, the L.12 had considerable success and sales included a few to the USAAC and US Navy as C-40s and JOs respectively.

Lockheed L.14 Super Electra (USA) The L.14 was a larger and refined version of the Electra powered by two 559 kW (750 hp) Pratt & Whitney Hornet or 566.4 611 kW (760 820 hp) Wright Cyclone engines. Accommodation was provided for 12 passengers. Innovations included the use of Fowler flaps which increased area by sliding back 1.07 m (42 in) in streamlined guides fitted between the ailerons and the fuselage, and baggage holds below the floor of the cabin and in the nose.

The first L.14 flew on 29 July 1937, by which time more than 30 had already been ordered. In addition to L.14s ordered for commercial service, Lockheed received an order for 250 L.14s from

Lockheed L.14 Super Electra.

Britain and 50 from Australia as military reconnaissance bombers. These became Hudsons (see entry).

Interestingly in 1938 Mr Howard Hughes and a crew of four flew a circuit of the Northern Hemisphere in an L.14 in 3 days 19 hours and 8 minutes. This flight of 23,804 km (14,791 miles) began in New York on 10 July and took in Paris, Moscow and other major cities before ending back in New York on 14 July.

Data (Hornet engines): *Engines* as above *Wing span* 19.96 m (65 ft 6 in) *Length* 13.47 m (44 ft 2½ in) *Max T-O weight* 7,938 kg (17,500 lb) *Max level speed* 393 km/h (244 mph) *Range* 3,315 km (2,060 miles)

Lockheed L.12 Electra.

Lockheed L.18 Lodestar (USA) First flown on 21 September 1939, the L.18 was a direct development of the L.14 and accommodated a crew of three and 14 passengers. It first entered service in March 1940 with Mid-Continent Airlines and eventually more than 600 were built for commercial and military service. By the end of World War II more than a dozen airlines in four continents were still flying the type.

During World War II the Lodestar was widely adapted for service transport use by the USAAF and US Navy. Military versions were the C-56, a USAAF model for executive or general personnel transport duties, also delivered to Britain as the Lodestar I; R5O-1, the US Navy equivalent of the C-56; C-57 for the USAAF with differences in engines and cabin installations; C-59 for the USAAF with R-1690 Hornet engines and carrying 14 passengers, supplied to Britain (as the Lodestar IA) and other countries under the Defence Aid programme; R5O-2, the US Navy equivalent of the C-59; R5O-3 US Navy executive

Lockheed L.18 Lodestars.

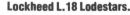

Lockheed

Lockheed C-60 Lodestars towing troop-carrying gliders.

transport, accommodating a crew of four and six passengers; C-60 for the USAAF's Defence Aid programme (used by Britain as the Lodestar II), fitted with Wright R-1820-87 Cyclone engines and accommodating 18 fully armed troops; R5O-4, -5 and -6 US Navy equivalents of the C-60, accommodating 4–7 passengers, 14 passengers and 18 troops respectively; and the single C-66 for the USAAF Defence Aid programme, accommodating 11 passengers.

Data (C-56, Lodestar I): *Engines* two 745.2 kW (1,000 hp) Wright R-1820 Cyclone radials *Wing span* 19.96 m (65 ft 6 in) *Length* 15.19 m (49 ft 9⅞ in) *Max T-O weight* (standard) 7,938 kg (17,700 lb) *Max level speed* 417 km/h (259 mph) *Range* 3,041 km (1,890 miles)

Lockheed L.188 Electra (USA) The Electra was designed as a short/medium-range airliner powered by four 2,794.5 kW (3,750 eshp) Allison Model 501 turboprop engines. The first prototype flew on 6 December 1957. The initial order 'off the drawing board' for 35 Electras was received in 1955 from American Airlines, who later sold five to Varig of Brazil. Subsequent orders were placed by 12 airlines and a handful of other customers, including Eastern Air Lines, National Airlines,

Lockheed L.188 Electra.

Braniff International Airways, KLM, Qantas, Garuda Indonesian Airways and Northwest Orient Airlines.

The first airline to inaugurate Electra services was Eastern Air Lines (on 12 January 1959), followed by American Airlines (on 23 January 1959).

Data: *Engines* four Allison Model 501-D13s (see above), later 3,018 kW (4,050 eshp) Model 501-D15s *Wing span* 30.18 m (99 ft 0 in) *Length* 31.81 m (104 ft 6½ in) *Max T-O weight* 52,664 kg (116,000 lb) *Cruising speed* 652 km/h (405 mph) *Range* 4,458–5,570 km (2,770–3,460 miles) *Accommodation* 44, 65, 66 or 88 passengers

Lockheed L-1011 TriStar (USA) Following extended market research, Lockheed began the design of a wide-body short/medium-range airliner under the identity of Lockheed Model 28S. Influenced by the expressed requirements of American Airlines, Lockheed began discussions with other domestic operators to establish the greatest common area of requirement. In the process the company's initial design changed from a two- to three-engined layout and the Rolls-Royce RB.211 turbofan was selected because of its promised economy. In its final design stage the Model 28S became designated L-1011 and given the name TriStar.

Construction of the prototype began in March 1969 and it flew for the first time on 16 November 1970. Production examples of the basic L-1011-1 TriStar were delivered to Eastern Airlines and TWA in April 1972 and the first scheduled revenue flight was made on 26 April 1972. Since that time a number of longer-range versions have entered service and some new versions had been proposed in mid-1979. By early December 1978 a total of 156 aircraft had been delivered to 12 major airlines and orders (208) and options (80) totalled 288 by early May 1979.

Of conventional fail-safe light-alloy construction, the TriStar has a cantilever monoplane wing which features powered low-speed (outboard) and high-speed (inboard) ailerons, hydraulically actuated double-slotted Fowler trailing-edge flaps, leading-edge slats, and six spoilers on the upper surface of each wing. Fuselage and tail unit are conventional structures (the tail unit having powered controls) but are designed to accommodate the third engine in the rear fuselage at the base of the fin. The other two engines are pylon-mounted in pods beneath the wing. Landing gear (retractable tricycle-type) has twin wheels on the nose unit and twin-wheel units in tandem on each main unit. Operated by a crew of 13, standard accommodation of the L-1011-1 is for 256 mixed-class passengers, with a maximum of 400 in a high-density seating arrangement.

Developed versions in current service include the longer-range L-1011-100, L-1011-200 and L-1011-250; and the shorter-fuselage extended-range L-1011-500 which has standard and maximum passenger accommodation of 246 and 300 passengers respectively. Proposals include the short/medium-range L-1011-400A with the shortened fuselage of the -500 and accommodation for 251 passengers; a multi-purpose version of that

Lockheed L-1011 TriStar.

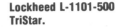
Lockheed L-1101-500 TriStar.

extended forward to accommodate the retractable landing gear. Power was provided by a heavily modified 156.5 kW (210 hp) Continental flat-six engine. The YO-3A was deployed in Vietnam for more than a year.

Lockheed P-2 Neptune (USA) The first US Navy contract for two XP2V-1 Neptune maritime-reconnaissance bombers was placed in April 1944. The first prototype flew in 1945. From then Lockheed received contracts for the P2V-1 to P2V-7 versions which were subsequently redesignated in the P-2 category.

aircraft designated L-1011-400A MP; the even shorter-fuselaged L-1011-600 to accommodate 174–200 passengers over short/medium ranges; and an advanced-technology version of that same aircraft designated L-1011-600A.

In 1979 Lockheed were flying the original prototype under the name Advanced TriStar. This is equipped with several advanced-technology features which are being flight tested and evaluated for possible inclusion in current production or projected versions. Potentially the most important of these features are wingtip extensions which have been found to reduce drag to the extent that fuel savings in the order of 3% can be expected from modified aircraft.

Data (L-1011-500): *Engines* three 222.42 kN (50,000 lb st) Rolls-Royce RB.211-524B turbofans *Wing span* 47.35 m (155 ft 4 in) *Length* 50.05 m (164 ft 2½ in) *Max T-O weight* 224,982 kg (496,000 lb) *Max cruising speed* 898 km/h (558 mph) *Range with max passengers* 9,653 km (5,998 miles)

Lockheed O-3A and Q-Star (USA) Faced with the military requirement for a quiet observation aircraft, Lockheed developed the two-seat Q-Star. Two QT-2s flew in August 1967 and were fitted subsequently with night sensors and taken to Vietnam for evaluation under operational conditions.

Potential of the Q-Star was such that Lockheed produced the refined YO-3A version for the US Army, still based on the Schweizer SGS 2-32 sailplane but with low wings and the wing roots

Lockheed P-2H Neptune.

The current versions in operational service are the P-2E (formerly P2V-5) which introduced the glazed nose, MAD tailboom, Julie/Jezebel ASW systems, etc, and later fitted with auxiliary underwing turbojets; SP-2E, as for the P-2E but with modernised equipment; P-2H, the first version to introduce auxiliary underwing turbojets and incorporating equipment and detail changes; and the SP-2H, as for the P-2H but with modernised equipment. These serve with the Argentinian Navy (P-2H), Australian Air Force (SP-2H), Brazilian Air Force (P-2E), French Navy (P-2H), JMSDF (P-2H, and Kawasaki P-2J see entry), Netherlands Navy (SP-2H), Portuguese Air Force (SP-2E) and the US Navy (SP-2H).

Data (P-2H): *Engines* two 2,608 kW (3,500 hp) Wright R-3350-32W piston engines and two 15.12 kN (3,400 lb st) Westinghouse J 34 turbojets *Wing span over tip tanks* 31.65 m (103 ft 10 in) *Length* 27.94 m (91 ft 8 in) *Max T-O weight* 36,240 kg (79,895 lb) *Max level speed* 648 km/h (403 mph) *Max range* (with ferry tanks) 5,930 km (3,685 miles) *Armament* provision for 16 × 5 in rocket projectiles under wings. Weapon load of 3,630 kg (8,000 lb) – carried internally – may consist of bombs, depth charges or torpedoes. Provision for optional dorsal turret with two 0.50 in machine-guns

Prototype Lockheed Advanced TriStar.

Lockheed L-1011-500 TriStar

1 Radome
2 VOR localiser aerial
3 Radar scanner dish
4 ILS glideslope aerial
5 Front pressure bulkhead
6 Curved windscreen panels
7 Windscreen wipers
8 Instrument panel shroud
9 Rudder pedals
10 Cockpit floor level
11 Ventral access door
12 Forward underfloor radio and electronics bay
13 Pitot tubes
14 Observer's seat
15 Captain's seat
16 First officer's seat
17 Overhead panel
18 Flight engineer's station
19 Cockpit roof escape hatch
20 Air-conditioning ducting
21 Forward galley units
22 Starboard service door
23 Forward toilet compartments
24 Curtained cabin-divider
25 Wardrobe
26 Forward passenger door
27 Cabin attendant's folding seat
28 Nose undercarriage wheel bay
29 Ram-air intake
30 Heat exchanger
31 Nose undercarriage leg strut
32 Twin nosewheels
33 Steering jacks
34 Nosewheel doors
35 Air-conditioning plant, port and starboard
36 Cabin window panel
37 Six-abreast first-class seating, 24 seats
38 Forward underfloor freight hold
39 Forward freight door
40 VHF aerial
41 Curtained cabin-divider
42 Overhead stowage bins
43 Nine-abreast tourist-class seating, 222 seats
44 Baggage/freight containers, twelve LD3 containers forward
45 Fuselage frame-and-stringer construction
46 Wing-root fillet
47 Taxiing lamp
48 Bleed-air system ducting
49 Escape chute and liferaft stowage
50 Mid-section entry door
51 Centre-section galley units
52 Fuselage centre-section construction
53 Wing centre-section carry-through structure
54 Dry bay
55 Centre-section fuel tanks, capacity 8,060 US gal (30,510 litres)
56 Floor beam construction
57 Fuselage/front spar attachment main frame
58 Anti-collision lights

59 Starboard inboard fuel tank bay, capacity 7,985 US gal (30,226 litres)
60 Thrust-reverser cascade, open
61 Starboard engine nacelle
62 Nacelle pylon
63 Fixed portion of leading edge
64 Fuel surge box and boost pump reservoir
65 Fuel system piping
66 Outboard fuel tank bay, capacity 3,806 US gal (14,407 litres)
67 Pressure refuelling connections
68 Screw jack drive shaft
69 Slat screw jacks
70 Leading-edge slat segments, open
71 Extended wing-tip fairing
72 Starboard navigation light
73 Wing-tip strobe light
74 Static dischargers
75 Starboard active-control aileron
76 Aileron hydraulic jacks
77 Fuel jettison pipe
78 Outboard spoilers
79 Outboard spoilers/speedbrakes
80 Flap screw jacks
81 Flap track fairings
82 Outboard double-slotted flap, down
83 Inboard aileron
84 Inboard double-slotted flap, down
85 Flap vane
86 Inboard spoilers/speedbrakes
87 Fuselage/rear spar attachment main frame
88 Cabin trim panels
89 Pressure floor over wheel bay
90 Hydraulic reservoirs
91 Centre-section service bay
92 Main undercarriage retracted position
93 Hydraulic flap-drive motors

94 Cabin floor panels
95 Seat attachment rails
96 Overhead air-conditioning ducting
97 Fuselage frame-and-stringer construction
98 Cabin ceiling panelling
99 Overhead stowage bins
100 Rear cabin seating
101 Cabin roof lighting panels
102 Noise-attenuating intake fairing
103 Centre engine intake
104 Intake duct support structure
105 Aft galley units
106 Rear toilet compartments (5)
107 Rear pressure dome
108 Tailplane centre-section
109 Variable-incidence tailplane hydraulic jacks
110 Intake S-duct
111 Intake de-icing air supply
112 Sloping fin spar bulkhead
113 Starboard tailplane
114 Starboard elevator
115 HF aerial
116 Fin construction
117 Fin leading edge
118 VOR aerial
119 Rudder mass balance
120 Static dischargers
121 Rudder construction
122 Rudder hydraulic jacks
123 Engine bleed-air system
124 Centre engine pylon mounting
125 Tail fairing

126 Detachable engine cowlings
127 Centre engine installation
128 Geared elevator hinge control
129 Port elevator
130 Elevator balance weights
131 Tailplane tip fairing
132 Tailplane construction
133 Moving tailplane-sealing fairing
134 Pratt & Whitney 720 shp auxiliary power unit
135 Rear cabin door
136 Aft electronics bay
137 Underfloor cargo compartment

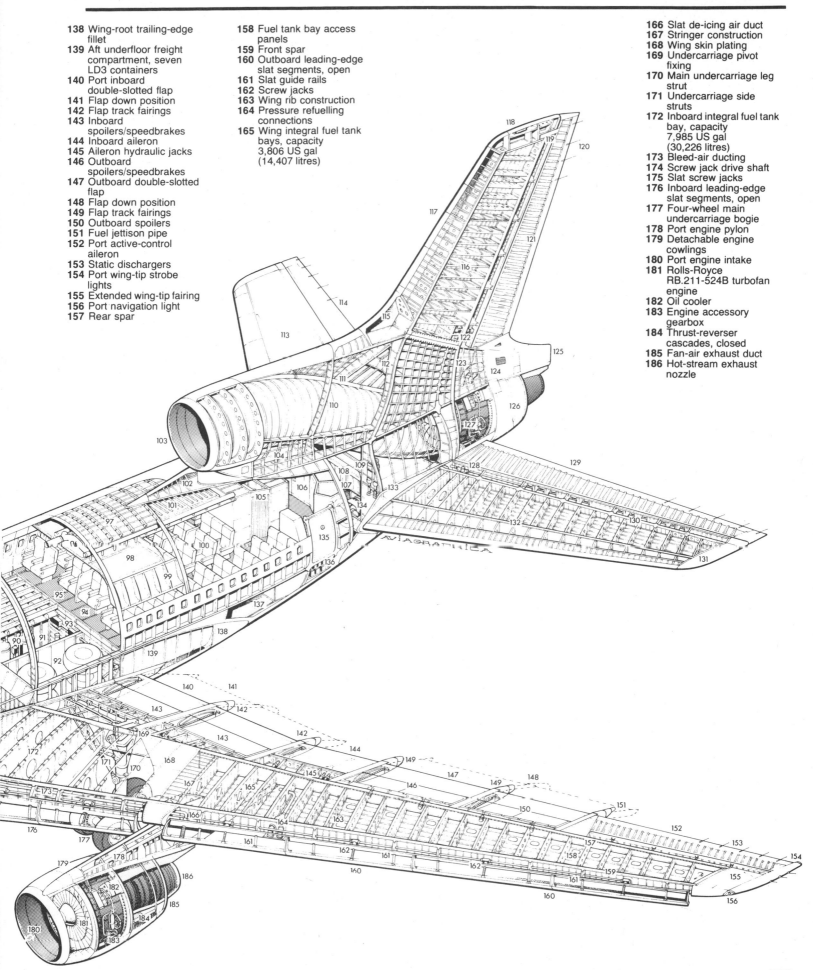

138 Wing-root trailing-edge fillet
139 Aft underfloor freight compartment, seven LD3 containers
140 Port inboard double-slotted flap
141 Flap down position
142 Flap track fairings
143 Inboard spoilers/speedbrakes
144 Inboard aileron
145 Aileron hydraulic jacks
146 Outboard spoilers/speedbrakes
147 Outboard double-slotted flap
148 Flap down position
149 Flap track fairings
150 Outboard spoilers
151 Fuel jettison pipe
152 Port active-control aileron
153 Static dischargers
154 Port wing-tip strobe lights
155 Extended wing-tip fairing
156 Port navigation light
157 Rear spar

158 Fuel tank bay access panels
159 Front spar
160 Outboard leading-edge slat segments, open
161 Slat guide rails
162 Screw jacks
163 Wing rib construction
164 Pressure refuelling connections
165 Wing integral fuel tank bays, capacity 3,806 US gal (14,407 litres)

166 Slat de-icing air duct
167 Stringer construction
168 Wing skin plating
169 Undercarriage pivot fixing
170 Main undercarriage leg strut
171 Undercarriage side struts
172 Inboard integral fuel tank bay, capacity 7,985 US gal (30,226 litres)
173 Bleed-air ducting
174 Screw jack drive shaft
175 Slat screw jacks
176 Inboard leading-edge slat segments, open
177 Four-wheel main undercarriage bogie
178 Port engine pylon
179 Detachable engine cowlings
180 Port engine intake
181 Rolls-Royce RB.211-524B turbofan engine
182 Oil cooler
183 Engine accessory gearbox
184 Thrust-reverser cascades, closed
185 Fan-air exhaust duct
186 Hot-stream exhaust nozzle

Lockheed P-3 Orions.

Lockheed YP-38 Lightnings.

Lockheed Orion (USA) In April 1958 it was announced that Lockheed had won a US Navy competition for an 'off-the-shelf' ASW aircraft with a developed version of the civil Electra four-turboprop airliner. Named the Orion, production continued in 1979 and a list of the many variants built can be found below:

P-3A Initial production version for US Navy with 3,356 kW (4,500 ehp, with water-alcohol injection) Allison T56-A-10W turboprop engines. First P-3A flew on 15 April 1961. Deliveries of 157 to US Navy began on 13 August 1962 to replace the P-2 Neptune. Three P-3As were also supplied to Spanish Air Force.

WP-3A Weather-reconnaissance version of P-3A. Four delivered to US Navy during 1970 to re-equip squadrons previously flying WC-121Ns.

P-3B Follow-on production version with 3,661 kW (4,910 ehp) Allison T56-A-14 turboprop engines which do not need water-alcohol injection. USN contracts covered 124 P-3Bs. In addition, five P-3Bs were delivered to the Royal New Zealand Air Force in 1966, ten to the Royal Australian Air Force during 1968 and five to Norway in the spring of 1969. USN P-3Bs were modified retrospectively to carry Bullpup missiles. Others became EP-3Bs.

P-3C Advanced version using a Univac digital computer. First flight of this version was made on 18 September 1968 and the P-3C entered service in 1969. A total of 143 of this version had been delivered to the US Navy by early 1978. Under a programme designated P-3C Update, new electronics and software were developed to enhance the effectiveness of this aircraft. A prototype with this equipment was handed over to the US Navy on 29 April 1974 and the first production aircraft was delivered in January 1975. All subsequent production aircraft for the US Navy have this equipment. Ten P-3Cs with Update modifications have been delivered to the Royal Australian Air Force. Japan has ordered 45 P-3Cs, four of which will be assembled and 38 licence-built in Japan by Kawasaki. The US Navy and Lockheed have continued with a further electronics improvement programme for the P-3C.

RP-3D One P-3C was reconfigured during manufacture for a five-year mission to map the Earth's magnetic field (under Project Magnet), controlled by the US Naval Oceanographic Office.

WP-3D Two aircraft equipped as airborne research centres ordered by the US National Oceanic and Atmospheric Administration. Equipped to carry out atmospheric research and weather modification experiments.

EP-3E Ten P-3As and two EP-3Bs were converted to EP-3E configuration to replace Lockheed EC-121s. Identified by large canoe radars on upper and lower surfaces of fuselage and ventral radome forward of wing.

P-3F Six aircraft – similar to the US Navy's P-3Cs – for Iran. Delivery was completed in January 1975.

By the beginning of 1979 Lockheed-California had delivered 483 P-3s of all versions.

Data (P-3C): *Engines* four 3,661 kW (4,910 ehp) Allison T56-A-14 turboprops *Wing span* 30.37 m (99 ft 8 in) *Length* 35.61 m (116 ft 10 in) *Max T-O weight* 64,410 kg (142,000 lb) *Max level speed* 761 km/h (473 mph) *Mission radius* 3,835 km (2,383 miles) *Armament* bomb bay can accommodate a 2,000 lb MK 25/39/55/56 mine, three 1,000 lb MK 36/52 mines, three MK 57 depth bombs, eight MK 54 depth bombs, eight MK 43/44/46 torpedoes or a combination of two MK 101 nuclear depth bombs and four MK 43/44/46 torpedoes. Ten underwing pylons for torpedoes, 500 lb/1,000 lb/2,000 lb mines and rockets. Max total weapon load includes six 2,000 lb mines under wings and a 3,290 kg (7,252 lb) internal load made up of two MK 101 depth bombs and four MK 44 torpedoes

Lockheed P-38 Lightning (USA) The P-38 was the only American fighter built before World War II to be still in production on VJ Day. Developed through many successively improved versions, the Lightning was used in all US combat zones as a high- and low-altitude fighter, fighter escort, bomber, photographic-reconnaissance aircraft, low-level attack and rocket fighter, and smoke-screen layer.

Allison V-1710-33 engines which had proved to be underpowered in the XP-38 prototype.

P-38Ds in US service differed from the original P-38 by introducing self-sealing tanks and tail-unit revisions to overcome buffeting. P-38Es had armament changes and were followed by the P-38F with more powerful engines and underwing racks (between engines and fuselage nacelle) for drop-tanks or weapons: late production examples introduced Fowler-type flaps which had a 'droop' setting to enhance manoeuvrability. P-38Gs had more powerful engines, as did the P-38H and -38J – the latter introduced an improved cooling system and powered ailerons. Most extensively built version was the P-38L (3,923), equipped to carry rocket projectiles beneath the outer-wing panels. Some P-38Js were converted to serve as two-seat 'Pathfinders'; some P-38Ls as P-38M night fighters or TP-38L two-seat trainers; and other versions included F-4 and F-5 photo-reconnaissance aircraft.

The Lightning is remembered especially as a long-range escort for Eighth Air Force bombers making deep-penetration daylight attacks on targets in Germany, as well as for the long-range interception and destruction of the Mitsubishi G4M1 (*Betty*) bomber carrying Japan's Admiral Isoroku Yamamoto (see **Chronology** 18 April 1943).

Data (P-38L): *Engines* two 1,099 kW (1,475 hp) Allison V-1710-111/113s *Wing span* 15.85 m (52 ft 0 in) *Length* 11.53 m (37 ft 10 in) *Max T-O weight* 9,798 kg (21,600 lb) *Max level speed* 666 km/h (414 mph) *Cruising speed* 467 km/h (290 mph) *Range* (internal fuel) 724 km (450 miles) *Armament* one 20 mm and four 0.50 in guns, plus up to 726 kg (1,600 lb) of underwing weapons

Lockheed P-38L Lightning.

Lockheed P-38M Lightning.

The first aeroplane developed from the start as a military type by Lockheed, the P-38 was designed to meet an Air Corps specification issued in 1936. The XP-38 prototype flew for the first time on 27 January 1939 and the first YP-38 service-evaluation aircraft of a limited procurement order for 13 was delivered to the USAAF in March 1941.

The P-38D was the first version of the Lightning to go into service in the war – an aircraft of this mark was the first American fighter to shoot down an enemy aeroplane, flying over Iceland a few minutes after the US declared war on Germany. The P-38L was the last fighter version to see combat service, which took in the final stages of the Pacific War. Two P-38L Lightnings escorting a Boeing Fortress were actually the first Allied fighters to land on Japanese soil after the surrender.

Built in large numbers throughout the war (the 1945–46 *Jane's* states 9,923 delivered to the USAAF), the Lightning – as the type was first named by the RAF – appeared in 18 variants. The RAF, however, received only three of 143 aircraft similar to the P-38D which followed the P-38 into production – their performance being unacceptable to the RAF. This resulted from the fact that Lockheed were not permitted to export aircraft with turbocharged engines, making it necessary to install the unsupercharged 775 kW (1,040 hp)

Lockheed Ventura I.

Lockheed PV, B-34, B-37 Ventura (USA) The Ventura – a military development of the Lodestar transport – was originally designed and built to the order of the British government. First British contracts were placed with the Vega Aircraft Corporation in 1940 and the first Ventura I flew on 31 July 1941. Mk Is entered RAF service as medium bombers in 1942, defensively armed with two 0.50 in and two 0.303 in machine-guns in the nose, two or four 0.303 in guns in a Boulton Paul dorsal turret and two 0.303 in guns in a rear-firing ventral position. Power was provided by two 1,378.6 kW (1,850 hp) Pratt & Whitney R-2800-S1A4G engines. One hundred and eighty-eight were built.

Final assembly of Lockheed P-38 Lightnings.

Lockheed PV-2 Harpoons.

The Ventura II and IIA followed for the RAF, powered by 1,490.4 kW (2,000 hp) R-2800-31 engines. These versions were also built by Vega but under American contracts and incorporated detail changes, mainly in armament and equipment. These were supplied to Bomber Command under Lease–Lend, carrying the US designation B-34. Many were flown also by the USAAF, plus a few by the US Navy as PV-3s.

With R-2600-13 engines, Lockheed began producing the Ventura III (US designation O-56, later B-37) for the RAF, but only 18 were delivered. The final version was the PV-1, produced mainly for the US Navy as a patrol bomber with a closed-in nose for two fixed 0.50 in machine-guns. The remainder of gun armament was as for the B-34. The bomb bay was adapted to accommodate bombs, depth charges or a torpedo and fuel capacity was increased. A total of 1,600 PV-1s were built, 388 of which were delivered to Coastal Command, RAF, under Lease–Lend as Ventura IVs or GR.Vs, which saw widespread service with several Commonwealth air forces. Total

Lockheed PV-1.

Ventura/B-34/PV production amounted to 2,475 aircraft (see **Lockheed PV-2 Harpoon**).

Data (PV-1): *Engines* as above *Wing span* 19.96 m (65 ft 6 in) *Length* 15.77 m (51 ft 9 in) *Max T-O weight* more than 14,061 kg (31,000 lb) *Max level speed* 502 km/h (312 mph) *Range* 1,609–2,672 km (1,000–1,660 miles) *Armament* machine-guns as above, plus up to 1,360 kg (3,000 lb) of bombs, depth charges or a torpedo

Lockheed PV-2 Harpoon (USA) The Harpoon was a development of the Ventura PV-1. It had wings of greater span (22.84 m; 75 ft 0 in), constant taper and with rounded wingtips; a new rectangular tailplane with new fins and rudders; a larger bomb bay which completely enclosed the torpedo; and five 0.50 in machine-guns in the nose, a Martin dorsal turret and a power-operated mounting in a rear-firing ventral position. Engines were as for the PV-1.

Lockheed S-3A/US-3A Viking (USA) In early 1954 the US Navy introduced into service the Grumman S-2 Tracker: its first ASW aircraft to combine the hunter-killer role which had been performed far less efficiently by two machines. The undoubted success of this category of aircraft meant that by the mid-1960s the USAF was formulating its requirements for a more advanced design to replace the Tracker which – by the time its successor had been developed to the in-service stage – was likely to have been operational for about 20 years.

The Navy's design competition (initiated in 1967) attracted submissions from General Dynamics, Grumman, McDonnell Douglas, North American Rockwell and Lockheed-California in conjunction with LTV Aerospace. It was Lockheed which was awarded a $461 million contract on 4 August 1969 for construction and development of their design, allocated the designation S-3A. Lockheed announced immediately that this aircraft would be developed in partnership with Vought Aeronautics who would be responsible for design and production of the wings, engine pods, landing gear and tail unit; and with the Univac Federal System Division of Sperry Rand who would develop an advanced computer to process the data necessary for its operational role. Lockheed was to co-ordinate the entire effort, design and build the fuselage, assemble the aircraft and integrate its electronics system.

Lockheed S-3A Viking.

A conventional shoulder-wing monoplane, the S-3A's wings have advanced high-lift features to provide excellent low-speed handling; its fuselage is built to withstand the stresses of catapult launching and arrested landing; and for carrier stowage wings, fin and rudder can be folded hydraulically. Power · plant comprises two pylon-mounted, economical turbofan engines. Avionics for its specialist role include a wide range of advanced sonobuoys, MAD, forward-looking infra-red, passive ECM, and the Univac 1832A digital computer. Accurate navigation is ensured by an INS, Doppler, Tacan and UHF/DF; good communications by HF and UHF systems; and to simplify all-weather operation, the S-3A has an automatic carrier-landing system. Weapons which can be deployed from a large weapons bay include MK-36 destructors, MK-46 torpedoes, MK-82 bombs, MK-54 or -57 depth bombs, or MK-55 mines. Underwing hardpoints can accommodate mines, cluster bombs, rocket pods, flares, practice bombs and auxiliary fuel tanks.

A prototype S-3A flew first on 21 January 1972 and production aircraft (then named Viking) began to enter service on 20 February 1974. All 187 S-3As on order had been delivered before the end of 1978. The prototype of a carrier on-board delivery aircraft (designated US-3A) flew for the first time on 2 July 1976. With all ASW equipment deleted such an aircraft would have an all-cargo capacity of 1,701 kg (3,750 lb) or could accommodate six passengers and 1,275 kg (2,810 lb) of cargo.

Data (S-3A): *Engines* two 41.26 kN (9,275 lb st) General Electric TF34-GE-2 turbofans *Wing span* 20.93 m (68 ft 8 in), (folded) 8.99 m (29 ft 6 in) *Length* 16.26 m (53 ft 4 in), (folded) 15.06 m (49 ft 5 in) *Max T-O weight* 23,831 kg (52,539 lb) *Max level speed* 834 km/h (518 mph) *Cruising speed* 686 km/h (426 mph) *Range* 3,706 km (2,303 miles)

Lockheed SR-71A (USA) The USAF's SR-71A two-seat strategic-reconnaissance aircraft originates from the remarkable Lockheed A-11, detail design of which began in 1959. Almost certainly intended to follow into service the Lockheed U-2 (see entry), the A-11 derived from the design team led by C. L. ('Kelly') Johnson. Four A-11s were ordered, the first being flown on 26 April 1962.

Three were later modified into YF-12A interceptors, entering service for evaluation in 1964. They were capable of speeds in excess of Mach 3 and of sustained supersonic flight at heights of up to 24,385 m (80,000 ft). Consequently construction was largely of titanium to maintain structural integrity, for as a result of kinetic heating, localised skin temperatures of up to about 427°C (800°F) could be reached. To retard as much as possible the effects of such heating, these aircraft were finished in a high-heat-emissive black paint, leading to the name Blackbird.

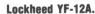

Lockheed SR-71A.

The fourth A-11 (ordered on the original contract) was subsequently redesignated YF-12C. From it was developed the SR-71A reconnaissance aircraft, the first of which flew on 22 December 1964. The readily recognisable configuration of this aircraft results from extensive wind-tunnel testing to evolve a minimum-drag fuselage providing maximum speed while keeping kinetic heating to the minimum; and to maintain the best possible handling characteristics at supersonic, take-off (about 370 km/h; 230 mph) and landing (about 278 km/h; 173 mph) speeds.

Power plant comprises two 144.6 kN (32,500 lb st, with afterburning) Pratt & Whitney turbojets. The 36,287 kg (80,000 lb) of special fuel for these engines – which is contained within upper-fuselage and inner-wing tanks – acts as a heat sink for the entire aircraft, fuel temperature

Lockheed YF-12A.

Lockheed

Lockheed T2V-1 Seastar.

being raised to 320°C (608°F) before being injected into the engines. Highly complex air intakes with computer-controlled fail-safe systems are essential to ensure that smooth airflow to the engines is maintained over the enormous forward speed range of 0–3,200 km/h+ (0–2,000 mph+), at the upper limit of which the engines are virtually operating as turbo-ramjets.

SR-71As began to enter USAF service in January 1966 and it is believed that as many as 31 may have been built. They have the capability to survey an area of 155,400 km² (60,000 sq miles) within an hour and in 1976 established a closed-circuit speed record of 3,367.221 km/h (2,092.294 mph); a world absolute speed record of 3,529.56 km/h (2,193.17 mph); and a sustained-altitude record of 25,929.031 m (85,069 ft).

Data: *Engines* two 144.6 kN (32,500 lb st, with afterburning) Pratt & Whitney JT11D-20B by-pass turbojets *Wing span* 16.94 m (55 ft 7 in) *Length* 32.74 m (107 ft 5 in) *Max T-O weight* 77,111 kg (170,000 lb) *Max level speed* more than 3,219 km/h (2,000 mph) at 24,000 m (78,740 ft) *Range* (at Mach 3 with internal fuel) 4,800 km (2,982 miles)

Lockheed TV-2.

Lockheed TO, TV, T2V Seastar (USA) In 1948 the US Navy acquired 50 Lockheed F-80Cs (see entry) from the USAF for operation as advanced trainers, these subsequently becoming designated TO-1 and later TV-1. During 1949 an initial contract was placed with Lockheed for 26 TO-2s (later TV-2s), generally similar to the USAF's T-33A (see entry). Total procurement of this version for the US Navy and Marine Corps amounted to 699 examples, these later becoming designated T-33B. Aircraft modified subsequently for guidance and control of missiles and targets were designated TV-2D (later DT-33B), and as drones or control aircraft TV-2KD (DT-33C). Final version was the improved Lockheed L-24S with a more powerful engine and a number of changes to improve low-speed handling characteristics. When these began to enter service in 1956 the designation T2V-1 (later T-1A) was allocated and they were named Seastar.

Data (T2V-1): *Engine* one 27.13 kN (6,100 lb st) Allison J33-A-24 or -24A turbojet *Wing span* 13.06 m (42 ft 10 in) *Length* 11.75 m (38 ft 6½ in) *Max T-O weight* 7,167 kg (15,800 lb) *Max level speed* 933 km/h (580 mph) *Range* 1,561 km (970 miles)

Lockheed T-33A Shooting Star (USA) Lockheed's P-80 Shooting Star (see entry) has its own special niche in USAAF/USAF history. From it evolved a lengthened-fuselage two-seat trainer version, designated originally TF-80C. The first of these flew on 22 March 1948. In addition to the fuselage 'stretch', a second cockpit in tandem was provided with dual controls, the transparent canopy was extended to cover both cockpits and the armament of the F-80 was deleted.

A total of 128 TF-80Cs were built before the designation was changed to T-33A in May 1949. Adopted as the USAF's standard jet trainer, it remained in production for a further ten years. A total of 649 were also built for service with the US Navy and Marine Corps under the designation TV-2, later T-33B. Total production amounted to 5,691 aircraft (including those for the Navy): 1,058 for supply to friendly nations under the Military Assistance Program and the balance to the USAF. T-33As were also licence-built in Canada (656 as the Silver Star, with Rolls-Royce Nene engine) and Japan (210). Variants included small numbers modified as DT-33A drone directors and AT-33A armed close-support aircraft.

Lockheed T-33A Shooting Stars.

Data (current aircraft): *Engine* one 23.13 kN (5,200 lb st) Allison J33-A-35 turbojet *Wing span* 11.85 m (38 ft 10½ in) *Length* 11.51 m (37 ft 9 in) *Max T-O weight* 6,550 kg (14,440 lb) *Max level speed* 965 km/h (600 mph) *Range* 2,165 km (1,345 miles) *Armament* (AT-33) two 0.50 in machineguns

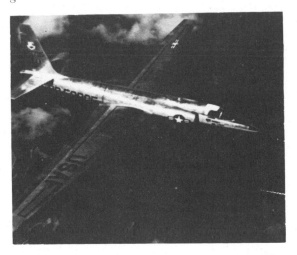

Lockheed U-2 (USA) Development of the U-2 began in the spring of 1954 to meet a joint CIA/USAF requirement for a high-altitude strategic reconnaissance and special-purpose research aircraft. It took place in the Lockheed 'Skunk Works' at Burbank, California, where – after acceptance of the design in late 1954 – two prototypes were hand-built in great secrecy by a small team of engineers. The aircraft's true purpose was cloaked under the USAF U-for-Utility designation U-2, and the first flight took place on or about 1 August 1955.

At about the same time US President Dwight D. Eisenhower was proposing his 'Open Skies' policy, one of mutual East/West aerial reconnaissance of territories. President Eisenhower hoped that his policy would reduce tension between East and West, thus preventing the growth of the nuclear arms race. Unfortunately the Soviet Union would have nothing to do with this proposal. Consequently 'Kelly' Johnson's new 'spy plane' assumed greater importance. The prototypes were followed by production of about 48 single-seat U-2As and U-2Bs with differing power plant, and five two-seat U-2Ds. Some -2Bs were converted later to U-2D standard. An additional batch of 12 U-2Rs was ordered in 1967. A new version, known as the TR-1, is currently in pro-

duction as a tactical-reconnaissance aircraft, equipped with a variety of electronic sensors. This version will be deployed mainly in Europe.

The requirement for high altitude and long range posed enormous problems: the former needed an aircraft with low wing loading, the latter large quantities of heavy fuel to confer the necessary range. Therefore the U-2 is of very lightweight construction, dispensing with conventional landing gear and pressurisation to save extra weight, and having wings of large area. Landing gear is of bicycle type with single wheels fore and aft, and balanced on the ground by wing-tip 'pogos' – a strut and wheel device which drops away when the U-2 becomes airborne – was selected. The pilot is accommodated on a lightweight seat, dressed in a semi-pressure suit with his head enclosed in an astronaut-type helmet, and forced to breathe pure oxygen for his survival. A medium-powered turbojet is adequate to lift this lightweight aircraft, and long range is possible by shutting it down and gliding for long periods.

In addition to photo and electronic reconnaissance, U-2s were used for weather reconnaissance, high-altitude research, measurement of radiation levels, and for the tracking and recovery of space capsules. They were used for reconnaissance during the Cuban crisis, in Vietnam and during the Arab–Israeli conflict.

Data (U-2B): *Engine* one 75.62 kN (17,000 lb st) Pratt & Whitney J75-P-13 turbojet *Wing span* 24.38 m (80 ft 0 in) *Length* 15.11 m (49 ft 7 in) *Max T-O weight* 7,189 kg (15,850 lb) *Max level speed* 850 km/h (528 mph) at 12,190 m (40,000 ft) *Cruising speed* 740 km/h (460 mph) *Range* about 6,437 km (4,000 miles)

Lockheed XV-4A Hummingbird (USA) Two-seat VTOL research aircraft, first flown as a conventional aircraft on 7 July 1962.

Lockheed XV-4A
Hummingbird in vertical
(upper) and horizontal
flight.

Lockheed

Lockheed XFV-1.

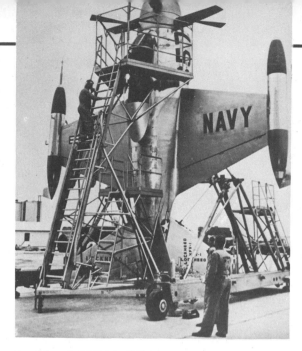

Lockheed C-69 Constellation.

Lockheed Air Express.

Lockheed Altair.

Lockheed XFV-1 (USA) Experimental VTOL 'tail-sitting' fighter, first flown in March 1954.

Lockheed Air Express (USA) Designed to the specification of Western Air Express for use on its air mail routes, the Air Express differed from the Vega in that the monoplane wing was raised above the fuselage in parasol fashion on four struts and the pilot was seated aft of it in an open cockpit. Four passengers were accommodated in the cabin and power was provided by a 317 kW (425 hp) Pratt & Whitney Wasp radial engine. By 1931 Air Express passenger and mail-carrying monoplanes were being built only to special order.

Lockheed Altair (USA) The Altair was basically similar to the Orion, except that it was arranged as a two-seat high-performance mail-carrying or sporting monoplane. With the same engine as the Orion, the Altair had similar performance.

Lockheed Constellation and Super Constellation (USA) In June 1939 Lockheed began the design of an airliner to satisfy a Transcontinental & Western Air – later Trans-World Airlines (TWA) – requirement for a transcontinental airliner with a 5,633 km (3,500 miles) range and 2,722 kg (6,000 lb) payload capability. By then the company had already gained considerable experience of the design and construction of civil airliners, although in a much smaller category. Consultation with Pan American Airways also brought orders. Busy with military contracts, the company was not restrained by cash limitations and was able to face the design and development of their Model 49 with confidence.

Construction of a prototype began in 1940 – the first of nine aircraft ordered by TWA. But before this was completed the US became involved in World War II. Thus TWA's L-49s – in common with all other transports in production at the time of Japan's attack on Pearl Harbor – were commandeered by the USAAF. The prototype flew for the first time on 9 January 1943 as a military aircraft. It borrowed features from several earlier aircraft. New features included hydraulically powered controls and a thermal de-icing system

for wing- and tail-unit leading edges. Power plant comprised four 1,639.4 kW (2,200 hp) Wright R-3350-35 Duplex Cyclone radial engines, driving three-bladed fully feathering and reversible propellers. The Constellation (when taken into civil use) was the first airliner to use reverse pitch to reduce the length of its landing run.

A total of 22 Model 49s were produced for the USAAF: TWA's initial nine plus 13 of later civil orders. Designated C-69 in Air Force service, they were sold back to the airlines after about 12 months' use in Air Transport Command. Orders for C-69Cs (43 passengers and 6 crew) and C-69Ds (63 passengers and 6 crew) were cancelled at the war's end and these were completed as Lockheed Model L-049s for supply to airlines: TWA receiving its first on 1 October 1945 and flying the first transatlantic proving flight on 3–4 December of that year – from Washington via Gander and Shannon to Paris. ATC number 763 was granted by CAB on 11 December 1945.

In airline use the L-049 Constellation was improved steadily through a series of variants. It was followed by the L-649 with more powerful engines and the L-749 with strengthened landing gear and greater fuel capacity. The next stage in development led to the L-1049 Super Constellation with lengthened fuselage, strengthening for higher gross weight, increased fuel capacity and more powerful engines. The first prototype Super Constellation (a conversion of the original C-69

Lockheed Constellation.

speed 607 km/h (377 mph) at 5,670 m (18,600 ft) *Cruising speed* 520 km/h (323 mph) at 6,100 m (20,000 ft) *Range* with max payload 8,690 km (5,400 miles)

Lockheed Hudson, A-28/29/AT-18 and PBO
(USA) The Hudson was originally built to the order of the British government as a military conversion of the L.14 transport. The first Hudson flew on 10 December 1938. Production lasted from 1939 until June 1943, thousands being built and delivered to the British, Australian, New Zealand, Canadian, Netherlands, Chinese and US forces.

prototype) flew for the first time on 13 October 1950. First in commercial service (on 15 December 1951) was one owned by Eastern Air Lines. This version could accommodate 71 first-class or 95 coach-class passengers (14 delivered to Eastern and ten to TWA during 1951–52). A number of improved variants followed – the last and most important being the L-1649A Starliner, regarded as the ultimate development of the piston-engined civil airliner.

L-749 Constellations served with the USAF as C-121A, VC-121A and VC-121B (all later designated PC-121A) passenger transports; and L-1049 Super Constellations were in use by both the USAF and US Navy under a variety of C-121 and R7V designations respectively. (A full list of variants appears in the 1957–58 *Jane's*.)

Data (L-1649A): *Engines* four 2,533.6 kW (3,400 hp) Wright R-3350-988TC18EA-2 turbo-compound radials *Wing span* 45.72 m (150 ft 0 in) *Length* (with weather radar) 35.41 m (116 ft 2 in) *Max T-O weight* 70,760 kg (156,000 lb) *Max level*

Lockheed EC-121M Warning Star, a version of the Super Constellation used by the USAF for early-warning and control missions.

US Navy equivalent of the USAF's RC-121 was the Lockheed WV-2 Warning Star AEW aircraft.

Six versions of the Hudson were delivered to the British government, the majority of which arrived by air across the Atlantic. The Hudson I was powered by two 745.2 kW (1,000 hp) Wright GR-1820-G102A Cyclone engines driving Hamilton-Standard two-position propellers. It first entered service with Coastal Command, RAF in mid-1939. The Hudson II was similar to the Mk I but had Hamilton-Standard Hydromatic constant-speed propellers fitted.

The Hudson III represented the first major revision, having 894 kW (1,200 hp) GR-1820-G205A Cyclone engines with Hydromatic propellers and a retractable rear-firing ventral gun position. Large numbers of the Hudson IIIAs were delivered to the RAF under Lease–Lend (resulting in the use of the USAAF designation A-29) with 894 kW (1,200 hp) Wright

Lockheed Constellations.

Lockheed Super Constellation.

Lockheed

Lockheed Hudson.

R-1820-87 Cyclone engines. Like earlier Hudsons, the Mk III was basically a maritime-patrol bomber and reconnaissance aircraft, but A-29As were fitted with benches for troop carrying. A-29/29As were also used by the USAAF and by the US Navy (as PBO-1s).

Powered by two Pratt & Whitney R-1830-SC3G Twin Wasp engines, the Hudson IV was produced for the RAAF, but a small batch was diverted to the RAF. These had the ventral gun removed but received a D/F loop aerial in a transparent blister. The Hudson V for the RAF had R-1830-S3C4G engines driving Hamilton-Standard two-position propellers and a retractable ventral gun (as fitted to the Mk III). The final version was the Hudson VI (designated A-28 by the USAAF) which was convertible to troop transport or cargo carrier with the turret removed.

Lockheed Orion.

After withdrawal from combatant service with the RAF, USAAF and US Navy, the Hudson continued to be used for miscellaneous duties, including transport, air/sea rescue, training, target-towing, etc. As a trainer for air gunners, the USAAF operated a special version with a Martin dorsal turret as the AT-18.

The Hudson III was the first aeroplane to be fitted to carry the British-developed Mk I airborne lifeboat. This lifeboat was first used operationally in May 1943 by an RAF air/sea-rescue squadron to rescue the crew of a downed bomber in the North Sea.

Lockheed Orion.

Data (Hudson VI): *Engines* as above *Wing span* 19.96 m (65 ft 6 in) *Length* 13.51 m (44 ft 4 in) *Max T-O weight* 8,391 kg (18,500 lb) *Max level speed* 443 km/h (275 mph) *Range* 3,476 km (2,160 miles) *Armament* two forward-firing 0.303 in Browning machine-guns, two 0.303 in

Lockheed JetStar II.

Browning guns in a Boulton Paul dorsal turret, two 0.303 in Browning guns on beam mountings one each side of fuselage, and one 0.303 in Browning gun in a retractable prone position beneath fuselage. Up to 635 kg (1,400 lb) of bombs or depth charges

Lockheed JetStar (USA) First flown on 4 September 1957, the JetStar is a jet-powered utility transport with normal accommodation for a crew of two and eight or ten passengers. The standard power plant is four 14.68 kN (3,300 lb st) Pratt & Whitney JT12A-8 turbojet engines. By mid-1973 162 JetStars had been delivered, including five to the USAF Communications Service as C-140As for inspecting worldwide military air-navigation aids and 11 VC-140B transports for operation by the special air missions wing of MAC.

The current version is the JetStar II, first flown in production form on 18 August 1976. This version uses an airframe generally similar to that of the earlier JetStar but with detail changes in configuration and equipment. By January 1979 a total of 31 JetStar IIs had been built.

Data (JetStar II): *Engines* four 16.5 kN (3,700 lb st) Garrett-AiResearch TFE 731-3 turbofans *Wing span* 16.6 m (54 ft 5 in) *Length* 18.42 m (60 ft 5 in) *Max T-O weight* 20,185 kg (44,500 lb) *Max level speed* 880 km/h (547 mph) *Range* 5,132 km (3,189 miles)

Lockheed Orion (USA) The Orion was one of the mainstays of the Lockheed company during the early 1930s and attempts were made to fit the latest types of engine to keep it up to date. However, with the arrival of the Electra, the Orion was only built to special order.

It was a cantilever low-wing monoplane with a retractable landing gear. Power was provided normally by a Wright Cyclone or Pratt & Whitney Wasp radial engine in the 391.2–410 kW (525–550 hp) class. Behind the engine was an enclosed cockpit for a pilot which projected above the top lines of the fuselage but was streamlined into it; behind it was the passenger cabin for six persons. Orions were operated by Varney Air Transport in America and in Europe by Swissair on its Zurich–Munich–Vienna route

Data (Orion 9D): *Engine* one 410 kW (550 hp) Pratt & Whitney S1D1 Wasp radial *Wing span* 13.05 m (42 ft 10 in) *Length* 8.48 m (27 ft 10 in) *Max T-O weight* 2,449 kg (5,400 lb) *Max level speed* 364 km/h (226 mph) *Cruising range* 1,207 km (750 miles)

Lockheed 'Project Stealth' (USA) In the so-called 'Skunk Works' at Burbank, Lockheed-California is reported to be building a single-seat reconnaissance/strike aircraft. Its primary feature is low radar, infra-red and optical signatures. The aircraft is said to be powered by two 53.4 kN (12,000 lb st) turbojet engines and is believed to have flown for the first time in 1977.

Lockheed Vega and Speed Vega (USA) Lockheed Aircraft Corporation had many ups and downs in its early years. It was founded in 1916 by the brothers Allan and Malcolm Loughead who called their first venture the Loughead Aircraft Manufacturing Company. This was liquidated in 1921; but five years later the Lockheed Aircraft Company of Hollywood was formed, its most famous product in the period 1925–32 being the Vega monoplane.

Designed originally by John K. Northrop (later the founder of Northrop Aircraft Inc), the Vega was developed progressively by Lockheed until, at the beginning of the 1930s, it represented one of the most advanced light transports of its day. Key to its success lay in its clean lines – the cantilever monoplane wing free from struts and bracing wires, as was its tail unit. The fuselage – like so many of that era – was circular in section (dictated by the radial engine) and tapered in neat streamline form back to the tail unit. The only major drag-inducing features were the heavy non-retractable tailwheel-type landing gear and uncowled engine; but later production aircraft had streamlined wheel spats and a neat NACA-design engine cowling. Apart from the landing-gear structure – which included oleo-pneumatic shock-absorber struts – the Vega was almost entirely of wooden construction.

Most advanced of the various models that were built was the seven-seat Vega 5-B, used from its first appearance for many record-breaking flights. Among the best known of these one should record *Winnie Mae* in which (between 23 June and 1 July 1931) Wiley Post, with Harold Gatty as navigator, completed a record-breaking round-the-world flight in 8 days 15 hours 51 minutes. Almost two years later – this time flying *Winnie Mae* alone – Wiley Post accomplished the first solo round-the-world flight (between 15–22 July 1933) in 7 days 18 hours 49 minutes. During the period 20–21 May of the previous year Amelia Earhart completed a solo west–east crossing of the North Atlantic (the first by a woman) in the Vega 5-B *Little Red Bus*.

When the record-breakers had moved on to newer aircraft, the Vega was able to carry on with

Lockheed Vega.

the light-transport role for which it had been designed. A total of 141 were built between 1925–32; many of these served with American airlines which have now grown into major companies. Three examples also served with the USAF, each having separate designations – Y1C-12, Y1C-17 and UC-101.

A modified version of the Vega was also produced as the Speed-Vega, powered by a supercharged Pratt & Whitney Wasp engine and with new wire-braced single-strut landing-gear legs.

Data (5-B): *Engine* one 335.3 kW (450 hp) Pratt & Whitney R-1340 Wasp radial *Wing span* 12.5 m (41 ft 0 in) *Length* 8.38 m (27 ft 6 in) *Max T-O weight* 1,935 kg (4,265 lb) *Max level speed* 290 km/h (180 mph) *Cruising speed* 249 km/h (155 mph) *Range* (standard aircraft) 1,110 km (690 miles)

Lockspeiser LDA-01 (UK) Prototype single 119 kW (160 hp) Lycoming-engined general-utility aircraft with the strut-braced main wings at the rear.

Lockspeiser LDA-01.

Loening Air Yacht (USA) In 1928 the Loening Aeronautical Engineering Corporation became a division of the Keystone Aircraft Corporation. The Air Yacht – produced during the 1920s by Loening for commercial and military operation – had no relation to the later Keystone Air Yacht, with the exception that both were flying-boat types. The Loening Air Yacht was powered by a single Liberty engine, mounted as a pusher. It accommodated four passengers. Eight or nine were produced in 1923 for the USAAS as S-1s, intended to be used as communications aircraft between island bases. Three commercial Air Yachts were of special interest as they were built for the New York–Newport Air Line.

Loening Air Yacht.

Loening M-8.

Loening M-8 (USA) In 1918 Loening produced a two-seat strut-braced high-wing monoplane fighter powered by a Wright-built Hispano-Suiza engine developing 223.6 kW (300 hp). Performance was excellent and large production contracts were placed by the US Navy and Army, but were cancelled with the end of World War I. However performance was such that the Navy re-ordered about 54 M-8 landplanes and M-8-1S twin-float seaplanes as armed observation aircraft for post-war service. Maximum level speed was 233 km/h (145 mph). (A full description of the M-8 – and its performance in the 1920 Pulitzer Trophy Race – can be found in the 1922 *Jane's*.)

Loening OA and OL series (USA) The Loening OA and OL designations cover a series of amphibians produced mainly for the US Navy as observation aircraft. The last in the series (the OL-9) was built by Keystone and can be found under that heading.

Quoting from the 1926 *Jane's*: 'For the first time, the ordinary tractor type biplane has been

Early Liberty-powered Loening amphibian used by the US Coast Guard. Purchased in 1926, it was the Coast Guard's first aeroplane.

Loening M-8.

so modified, so that the machine is capable of landing on either land or water, with ability to start from or alight on either, at a moment's notice. No extra floats or other devices are used, as the new design obtains its amphibious characteristics by the shape of the main fuselage body itself, the bottom of which is shaped like a flying-boat hull. To this is attached a folding landing gear, an ingenious device, which is operated by an electric motor.'

Powered by Liberty engines, the first nine production aircraft went to the USAAC as COA-1s in 1924–25; followed eventually by 42 OA-1As, OA-1Bs, OA-1Cs and 358 kW (480 hp) Wright V-1460-powered OA-2s. The US Navy received from Loening 17 328 kW (440 hp) Packard-powered OL-1s, Liberty-powered OL-2s, Packard-powered OL-3s and Liberty-powered OL-4s; plus 28 Packard-powered OL-6s, 20 317 kW (425 hp) Pratt & Whitney Wasp-engined OL-8s and 20 carrier-borne OL-8As. The OL-8s had a maximum speed of 200 km/h (124 mph). This version was ordered after successful catapult trials of a standard Loening amphibian and deployed on US Navy battleships. By the end of production Loening amphibians were being operated by the USAAC, US Navy and Marine Corps, and the US Coast Guard.

Navy OL-2s were used successfully on the MacMillan Expedition of 1925 where 9,700 km (6,000 miles) of Arctic flying were covered by Cmdr Byrd and his men in less than 12 days' flying. These same planes were subsequently sent to Cuba where they completed a hydrographic survey for the US Navy Department. During the summer of 1926 the US Navy used the type to map Alaska by air. At the end of the same year the USAAC began a 32,200 km (20,000 mile) Pan-American flight round South America with five of its Loenings.

Data (OL-8): *Engine* as above *Wing span* 13.72 m (45 ft 0 in) *Length* 10.74 m (35 ft 2¾ in) *Max T-O weight* 2,383 kg (5,253 lb) *Max level speed* 200 km/h (124 mph) *Range* 1,046 km (650 miles)

Loening PW-2 (USA) Experimental pursuit monoplane of 1920 based on the M-8 and tested by the Air Service Engineering Division at McCook Field. Ten built, most with the Wright-built Hispano-Suiza engine of the M-8.

Lohner B types (Austria-Hungary) Two-seat unarmed reconnaissance biplane produced from before World War I until 1917. Powered by Austro-Daimler or other engines in the 63.3–119 kW (85–160 hp) range.

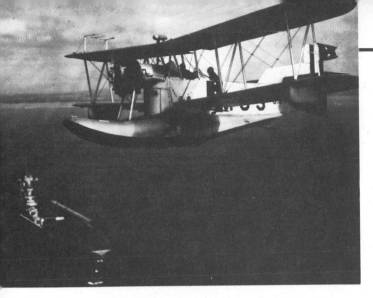

indication of the major contribution the series made to the air war. Indeed several hundred were built as maritime patrol and reconnaissance aircraft, in addition to the training variant. The first major version was the Type E, a limited number of which were built with 63.3 kW (85 hp) Hiero engines. Next came the major production version, the Type L, powered by a 119 kW (160 hp) Austro-Daimler engine. A photographic-reconnaissance version of the L was the Type R; while the Type K was an unarmed trainer.

Data (Type L): *Engine* as above *Wing span* 16.2 m (53 ft 1¾ in) *Length* 10.24 m (33 ft 7 in) *Max T-O weight* 1,700 kg (3,748 lb) *Max level speed* 105 km/h (65 mph) *Endurance* 4 h *Armament* one Schwarzlose machine-gun, plus up to 200 kg (441 lb) of bombs

Loening OA-1As used on the Pan-American flight round South America.

Lohner C.I (Austria-Hungary) Armed version of the B types powered by a 119 kW (160 hp) Austro-Daimler engine and carrying one rear-mounted machine-gun. Maximum level speed 137 km/h (85 mph).

Lohner E, L, R and S (Austria-Hungary) Quoting from the 1920 *Jane's*: 'As Herr Igo Etrich had already given up the manufacture of his "Taube" line at the outbreak of war, Lohner remained the only Austrian manufacturer of international note. His flying-boats and the Italian copy of them have been extensively used by both belligerents in the lower Adriatic Sea, which was a smooth water field for the flying-boat type. After the war, commercial Lohner flying-boats have been employed for mail service in the Ukraine, and have in converted editions been sold for joy-riding purposes to Switzerland and elsewhere, the low Austrian exchange rate affording a strong inducement to buyers.'

Such was the overall career of the Lohner flying-boats; but this write-up failed to give a clear

Loire 46 (France) The all-metal Loire 46 represented a radical redesign of the earlier Loire 43 and 45 prototypes. It was a gull-wing strut-braced single-seat fighter monoplane with the typical open cockpit and fixed, spatted landing gear of the era. The NACA-cowled 596 kW (800 hp) Gnome-Rhône 14Kcs radial engine drove a three-bladed propeller. The Loire 46 prototype flew for the first time in September 1934, followed by five evaluation machines. These proved to have an excellent climb rate and diving speed. As a result, 60 aircraft were ordered for the Armée de l'Air, each armed with four 7.5 mm MAC machine-guns, plus two racks for light bombs. They equipped the 6ème Escadre at Chartres from mid-1936, subsequently being relegated to the Cazaux gunnery school. Five Loire 46s were sent to Spain in September 1936, serving briefly with the Republican forces.

Cockpit of a Lohner C.I.

Data: *Engine* as above *Wing span* 11.8 m (38 ft 8½ in) *Length* 7.76 m (25 ft 5½ in) *Max T-O weight* 2,100 kg (4,630 lb) *Max level speed* 368 km/h (228.7 mph) *Range* 860 km (534 miles)

Loire 46.

Loire 130.

Loire 70 (France) A three-engined (two tractor, one pusher) high-wing monoplane flying-boat designed for long-range maritime reconnaissance. The prototype flew for the first time in December 1933. Modified series-built aircraft (with a crew of eight) had a glazed observer's position in the bow and six machine-guns mounted in two lateral bow positions, one in a turret forward of the flight cabin, one in a dorsal turret and two in lateral midships hatches. Bomb load was 600 kg (1,323 lb). Only seven production machines were built, each powered by three 551.4 kW (740 hp) Gnome-Rhône 9 Kfr radials. These were operated by Escadrille E7 out of Karouba (North Africa) until August 1940.

Loire 102 (France) Four-engined long-distance commercial flying-boat ordered by Air France.

Loire 130 (France) The first prototype of this robust strut-braced high-wing monoplane flying-boat flew on 19 November 1934. Production totalled at least 126 aircraft, including 30 built in 1941 for the French Vichy regime. Intended for a variety of roles, it was stressed for catapult launching. The 536.5 kW (720 hp) Hispano-Suiza 12Xirs liquid-cooled engine was carried above the centre section on a pair of N-type struts and drove a three-bladed Ratier pusher propeller. A crew of three was carried and armament comprised single 7.7 mm Darne machine-guns in bow and dorsal positions. Offensive load was made up of two 75 kg bombs or SM depth charges carried under the wings (which folded for shipboard stowage). The type remained operational until 1945.

Data: *Engine* as above *Wing span* 16.0 m (52 ft 6 in) *Length* 11.3 m (37 ft 1 in) *Max T-O weight* 3,396 kg (7,487 lb) *Max level speed* 222 km/h (138 mph)

Loire 210 (France) Using the fuselage of the Loire 46 landplane fighter, the Loire 210 was a cantilever low-wing monoplane with an open pilot's cockpit. It featured a generously braced, large single main float and two wingtip stabilising

Loire 210.

floats. Designed as a catapult-launched fighter seaplane, the prototype flew in March 1935. Development was prolonged and an order placed in 1937 for 20 aircraft was not fulfilled until mid-1939. Powered by a 730 kW (980 hp) Hispano-Suiza 9Vbs radial engine and armed with four 7.5 mm machine-guns, the Loire 210s performed badly, reaching only 315 km/h (195.7 mph). They served for only three months with Escadrilles HC 1 and HC 2 of the French Navy, being withdrawn in November 1939.

Loire-Gourdou-Leseurre 32.C1 (France) Test flown in 1925, the LGL32.01 fighter performed well and quantity production for the French Aéronautique Militaire followed. Delivered from 1928, some 380 were eventually in first-line service with 14 escadrilles de chasse plus two escadrilles (3C1 and 3C2) of the Aéronautique Maritime, serving for six years.

The fuselage, tailplane and wing spars were of metal-alloy construction which resulted in a light and manoeuvrable fighter. It had a strut-braced parasol wing and was armed with two Vickers 0.303 in machine-guns in the upper forward fuselage decking. Power was provided by an uncowled 313 kW (420 hp) Gnome-Rhône Jupiter radial engine. However defects soon became apparent; its obsolescent narrow-track undercarriage which retained a single axle and 'sandows' (primitive rubber shock-absorbers) finally giving way to a divided wider-track undercarriage with Messier shock absorbers on late production aircraft. The poor forward and upward visibility for the pilot remained a problem.

The LGL32.C1 was exported to Romania (50 aircraft), Turkey (12) and Japan (one). Three pre-series machines had been used for demonstrations to win these foreign contracts, but interestingly failed to gain orders from Spain. In August 1936, however, the Spanish Republican government obtained a batch (perhaps 12) of obsolete LGL32.C1s from France under a secret agreement. The Basques in northern Spain purchased via SFTA (a French 'cover' company) 12 more examples – this time specially manufactured and fitted with the revised undercarriage. They flew from January to October 1937. In that time they achieved the sinking of the Nationalist battleship *España*, each aircraft carrying two 100 kg bombs.

Data: *Engine* as above *Wing span* 12.2 m (40 ft 0¼ in) *Length* 7.55 m (24 ft 9¼ in) *Max T-O weight* 1,376 kg (3,034 lb) *Max level speed* 237 km/h (147.5 mph) *Range* 500 km (311 miles)

Loire-Nieuport 401 and 411 (France) The Loire-Nieuport 40 single-seat dive-bomber prototype was first tested in 1938. It was developed into the LN-401 for the French Navy and LN-411 for the Armée de l'Air (with a 514 kW; 690 hp Hispano-Suiza 12Xcrs engine). For dive bombing, the rearward-retracting main wheels and tailwheel were locked in the down position, their large fairings acting as dive-brakes. The low wing was of cranked type, with considerable dihedral on outer sections. Stability problems led to fitting auxiliary end-plate fins to the horizontal tailplane.

Not all of 120 LN-401s and 411s ordered were

delivered, but all those built went to the Navy (four escadrilles) and were operated against the Germans and Italians during May and June 1940. Armament comprised one 20 mm HS-404 cannon and three machine-guns, plus up to 225 kg (496 lb) of bombs.

Data: *Engine* as above *Wing span* 14.0 m (45 ft 11¼ in) *Length* 9.76 m (32 ft 0¼ in) *Max T-O weight* 2,850 kg (6,283 lb) *Max level speed* 320 km/h (199 mph) *Range* 1,200 km (746 miles)

Lombardi F.L.3 (Italy) At the end of 1947 AVIA (Azionaria Vercellese Industrie Aeronautiche) was taken over by Lombardi. The original company had produced 400 F.L.3 two-seat light monoplanes before 1942 and after the war production was resumed by AVIA and then Lombardi (a further 100 or so built by 1948). Power was provided by a 63.3 kW (85 hp) Continental engine.

Lombardi L.M.5 Aviastar (Italy) Two-seat light cabin monoplane powered by a 44.7 kW (60 hp) CNA D4 engine.

Loring R-1, R-2 and R-3 (Spain) The R-1 was the company's first design to enter production, 30 having been ordered as reconnaissance biplanes for the Spanish Army Air Service. Later developments were the R-2 and R-3, also produced for the Spanish Army Air Service – the latter powered by a 447 kW (600 hp) Hispano-Suiza engine and armed with machine-guns and optionally 40 × 11 kg or eight 50 kg bombs.

Lübeck-Travemünde F.2 (Germany) Two-seat reconnaissance seaplane, 17 of which were operated by the German Navy during World War I.

Lublin R-XI (Poland) E. Plage & T. Laskiewicz, known under the name Lublin (location of the factory), produced in 1930 a single example of a Wright J-5 Whirlwind-engined six-seat commercial monoplane.

Lublin R-XIII (Poland) Two-seat army co-operation, light reconnaissance and advanced training monoplane of 1931, powered by a 164 kW (220 hp) Skoda-built Wright J-5 Whirlwind, 283 kW (380 hp) Mors or similar engine. From 1932 about 300 R.XIIIs were built for the Polish Air Force and Navy, a large number of which remained operational in September 1939. Navy aircraft were operated as R-XIII*ter hydro* twin-float seaplanes. Armament comprised one rear-mounted Vickers machine-gun and a message-retrieving hook was fitted below the fuselage.

Data: *Engine* one 164 kW (220 hp) Skoda-built Wright J-5 Whirlwind *Wing span* 13.25 m (43 ft 6 in) *Length* 8.2 m (26 ft 11 in) *Max T-O weight* 1,290 kg (2,840 lb) *Max level speed* 177 km/h (110 mph), (seaplane) 175 km/h (109 mph) *Endurance* 4 h

Lublin R-XIV (Poland) Two-seat advanced training, aerobatic training and liaison monoplane powered by a 164 kW (220 hp) Wright J-5 Whirlwind engine.

Los Angeles **moored to Patoka.**

Los Angeles (USA) The *Los Angeles* rigid airship was built for the US Navy by the Zeppelin company and delivered to the US on 15 October 1924. Powered by five 298 kW (400 hp) Maybach engines, it was approximately 200 m (656 ft) long and had a cubic capacity of about 70,000 m³ (2,472,000 cu ft). Maximum level speed was 109 km/h (68 mph). It was finally retired in 1932, having taken part in the parasite fighter experiments connected with the Curtiss Sparrowhawk. It was finally broken up in 1940 (see **Chronology** 27 October 1931).

LTV-Hiller-Ryan XC-142A (USA) Four-engined experimental tilting-wing transport aircraft, first flown as a conventional aircraft on 29 September 1964. It made its first hovering flight on 29 December the same year and on 11 January 1965 made two transitions from hovering to horizontal flight.

Lublin R-XVI and R-XVIB (Poland) The R-XVI was a four-passenger high-wing commercial transport aircraft of 1932 powered by a Skoda-built 164 kW (220 hp) Wright J-5 Whirlwind engine. It failed to enter production; but an ambulance version – arranged to accommodate two stretchers and with a wash stand with running water and a large cabin door – was produced in small numbers for the Polish Red Cross. The type won first prize at the 1933 International Medical Aviation Congress at Madrid.

Lucas L5 (France) Two-seat light monoplane, first flown in 1976.

Luscombe Phantom (USA) The first product of this company was the Phantom two-seat high-wing cabin monoplane, powered by a 108 kW (145 hp) Warner Super Scarab engine. It was very similar in appearance to the Monocoupe D-145, but was entirely of metal construction and

Luscombe

Luscombe Phantom.

Luscombe Fifty.

Luscombe T8F Observer.

Luscombe Model 8A Silvaire.

Luscombe Model 8E Silvaire.

The Model 8A Silvaire was produced as a two-seat light cabin monoplane powered by a 48.4 kW (65 hp) Continental A-65-8 engine. From it was developed the Model 8A-2 with more standard equipment; Model 8B with a 48.4 kW (65 hp) Lycoming engine; Model 8C with a 56 kW (75 hp) Continental A-75; Model 8D with two 45.4 litre (12 US gallon) tip tanks; Model 8E with a 63.3 kW (85 hp) Continental C-85-12 engine; Model 8F with a 67 kW (90 hp) Continental C-90 engine; four-seat Sedan with a 123 kW (165 hp) Continental E-165 engine; and the Model 8A Sky Pal, a version of the Model 8F with a Continental C-65 engine. Many thousands of aircraft of the series were built.

Data (Model 8F Special): *Engine* as above *Wing span* 10.67 m (35 ft 0 in) *Length* 6.1 m (20 ft 0 in) *Max T-O weight* 635 kg (1,400 lb) *Max level speed* 206 km/h (128 mph)

Luscombe Model 10 (USA) Single-seat enclosed-cabin low-wing monoplane powered by a 48.4 kW (65 hp) Continental engine.

Luscombe T8F Observer and Silvaire Sprayer (USA) Tandem two-seat cabin monoplane and agricultural aircraft respectively, each powered by a 67 kW (90 hp) Continental C-90 engine.

LVG B.I, B.II and B.III (Germany) In 1912, having hitherto chiefly produced Farman-type box kites, Luft Verkehrs Gesellschaft engaged the Swiss engineer Franz Scheider. His first design for the company was a Nieuport-type monoplane but his second was a robust biplane which subsequently became a standard unarmed scouting aircraft with the German Air Service. It secured the top three places in the 1914 Prince Henry flight and was subsequently put into production by LVG and built under licence by Otto in Munich and Schütte-Lanz. From the outbreak of World War I until about 1917, the biplane – in B.I and B.II versions with 74.5 kW (100 hp) Mercedes D.I or 82 kW (110 hp) Benz engines – served as a reconnaissance and then training aircraft. The B.III appeared in 1917 as a trainer only.

LVG C.I, C.II and C.IV (Germany) From the B.I and B.II were developed in 1915 the C.I and C.II armed reconnaissance aircraft, powered by 112 kW (150 hp) Benz Bz.III and 119 kW (160 hp) Mercedes D.III engines respectively. At the height of their service some 250 were in operational use, later production C.IIs adding a forward-firing Spandau machine-gun to the observer's Parabellum gun. Other duties

---

designed for quantity production. A total of 125 were built. Maximum level speed was 270 km/h (168 mph).

Luscombe Fifty (USA) Similar to the Phantom but powered by a 37.25 kW (50 hp) Continental A-50 engine.

Luscombe Sixty-Five (USA) Similar to the Fifty but powered by a 48.4 kW (65 hp) Continental A-65 engine.

Luscombe Ninety (USA) Two-seat cabin monoplane powered by a 67 kW (90 hp) Warner engine.

Luscombe Model 8 Silvaire (USA) In 1937 Luscombe introduced the Silvaire series, production of which was suspended from 1942 until the end of World War II. Immediately after VJ Day production resumed.

included bombing: on 28 November 1916 a C.II, piloted by Deck Offizier P. Brandt, dropped six light bombs near Victoria Station – the first bombs to be released from an aeroplane on London. Following the unsuccessful C.III, LVG produced the C.IV, similar to the C.II but powered by a 164 kW (220 hp) Mercedes D.IV engine. The 1918 *Jane's* states that the LVG types were not as fast as the contemporary Rumpler IV, had inferior rates of climb and lower service ceilings. *Data (C.II): Engine* as above *Wing span* 12.85 m (42 ft 2 in) *Length* 8.1 m (26 ft 7 in) *Max T-O weight* 1,400 kg (3,086 lb) *Weight empty* 845 kg (1,863 lb), (C.IV) 900 kg (1,984 lb) *Max level speed* 130 km/h (80.5 mph) *Endurance* 4 h

LVG C.V and C.VI (Germany) The C.V and C.VI were among the most widely operated aircraft of 1917 and 1918, and production of the latter alone (that first appeared in February 1918) is believed to have been nearly 1,100, with a monthly output of 175 aircraft. Both versions were powered by 149 kW (200 hp) Benz Bz.IV engines driving Garuda Type V propellers. The C.VI had a cleaner appearance and most of its refinements were aimed at improving the pilot's and observer's vision. However plain ailerons replaced the C.V's horn-balanced ailerons, the radiator was relocated, the engine was uncowled and the tailplane increased in area. Roles included reconnaissance and bombing (a full description appears in the 1918 *Jane's*).

Post-war C.Vs and C.VIs were used as interim commercial transports. From the C.VI was developed the K.I or Kurier-Express (a two-seater with an endurance of up to 12 hours for passenger or mail carrying), the P.I limousine and the W.I seaplane. The single example of the LVG C.VIII (built during the war) was also operated post-war by Deutsche Verkehrsflug. *Data (C.VI): Engine* as above *Wing span* 13.0 m

(42 ft 7¾ in) *Length* 7.45 m (24 ft 5⅓ in) *Max T-O weight* 1,310 kg (2,890 lb) *Max level speed* 170 km/h (105.5 mph) *Endurance* 3 h 30 min *Armament* one forward-firing Spandau and one rear-mounted Parabellum machine-guns, plus 115 kg (253 lb) of bombs

LVG C.II.

LVG C.VI operated commercially by DLR.

LVG P.I.

LWD Junak (Poland) Two-seat basic trainer designed by Dipl Ing T. Sołtyk to meet the requirements of Polish flying schools. The prototype Junak 1 flew for the first time on 22 February 1948. The Junak 2 initial production version was powered by a 119 kW (160 hp) Polish-built M11FR engine. It was followed by the Junak 3 with a tricycle instead of tailwheel landing gear.

LWD Szpak-4A and -4T (Poland) Two-seat aerobatic trainer and four-seat touring monoplane respectively, each powered by a 112 kW (150 hp) Bramo Sh.14 radial engine.

LWD Zak-1, -2 and -3 (Poland) Two-seat enclosed-cockpit trainer (56 kW; 75 hp Walter Mikron II engine), open-cockpit trainer (37.25 kW; 50 hp Continental A-50), and two-seat enclosed-cockpit trainer (48.4 kW; 65 hp Walter Mikron I) respectively.

Captured LVG C.V.

LWD Junak 3.

LWS.3 Mewa.

Macchi L.3.
Macchi M.5.

Macchi L.2 and L.3 (Italy) The L.2 of 1916 was basically a developed L.1 powered by a 119 kW (160 hp) Isotta-Fraschini V.4B engine. The production version of the L.2 was the L.3 or M.3 which appeared in April 1916 and remained operational as a reconnaissance-bomber and later trainer until 1924. A few were also flown commercially post-war. A total of 200 were built.

Data (L.3/M.3): *Engine* as above *Wing span* 15.95 m (52 ft 4 in) *Length* 10.25 m (33 ft 7½ in) *Max T-O weight* 1,350 kg (2,976 lb) *Max level speed* 145 km/h (90 mph) *Range* 450 km (279 miles)

LWS.3 Mewa (Poland) Two-seat reconnaissance and army co-operation monoplane. Only a few had been built by the time of the German invasion in 1939 and none had been delivered to the Polish Air Force. A Bulgarian development of the Mewa was produced during the war for the Bulgarian Air Force, powered by a 641 kW (860 hp) Fiat A.74 RC engine.

LWS.4 Zubr (Poland) First flown in March 1936, the Zubr bomber stemmed from an aborted commercial transport project and was an ugly, heavy and ill-conceived aircraft. It was powered by two 507 kW (680 hp) Polish-built Pegasus VIII radial engines driving three-bladed Hamilton-Standard controllable-pitch propellers. A bomb-aiming compartment was positioned in the lower nose with a twin machine-gun turret above. Defensive armament was completed with dorsal and ventral machine-gun positions. Bombs could be carried in the internal bay and also externally – up to a maximum of 1,000 kg (2,205 lb). Only 16 were built for the Polish Air Force. Maximum level speed was 380 km/h (236 mph).

Macchi M.5 (Italy) From the earlier two-seaters Macchi developed the M.5 single-seat flying-boat fighter: a much smaller aircraft normally powered by a V.4B engine although some later examples had a 186.3 kW (250 hp) Isotta-Fraschini V-6 fitted. It entered production for Italian naval squadrons in 1917 and 240 were built, a few also serving with the US Navy.

Data (V-6 engine): *Engine* as above *Wing span* 9.7 m (31 ft 10 in) *Length* 8.0 m (26 ft 3 in) *Max T-O weight* 1,081 kg (2,383 lb) *Max level speed* 205 km/h (127.5 mph) *Range* 600 km (373 miles) *Armament* two forward-firing Fiat machine-guns

Macchi M.7 (Italy) With a wing span of 9.95 m (32 ft 7¾ in) and powered by a V-6 engine, the M-7 appeared in 1918. Only three had been received into service by the Armistice. Delivery of a small number continued post-war and these remained in service until 1928.

LWS.4 Zubr.

LWS RWD-14 Czapla (Poland) Designed by RWD, the Czapla army co-operation monoplane first appeared in 1935. Sixty-five were produced by LWS for the Polish Air Force, each powered by a 313 kW (420 hp) Mors II engine. Armament comprised two 7.7 mm Vickers machine-guns, plus light bombs. Maximum level speed was 247 km/h (153 mph).

Macchi L.1 (Italy) In 1915 Macchi produced its first flying-boat in the form of the two-seat L.1. Power was provided by a 112 kW (150 hp) Isotta-Fraschini V.4A engine mounted between the biplane wings as a pusher. This was no more than a copy of the Lohner Type L of Austro-Hungarian origin, a captured example of which had been taken to the Macchi works across land.

Macchi M.7.

Macchi M.8 (Italy) The M.8 appeared in 1917 and from then until the Armistice 57 were built for Italian service and a few for the US Navy. It was basically a 'cleaned-up' M.3 for coastal patrol and anti-shipping duties, powered by a V.4B engine and defensively armed with one machine-gun. Maximum level speed was 162 km/h (100.5 mph).

Military version of the Macchi M.18.

Macchi M.18 (Italy) Developed from the Macchi M.8 and M.9, the M.18 was a post-World War I maritime patrol flying-boat powered as a prototype by a 141.6 kW (190 hp) Isotta-Fraschini V.4B engine and as a production aircraft by a 186.3 kW (250 hp) Isotta-Fraschini Asso. The wings folded for storage. In addition to the military type, three civil variants were produced as a dual-control trainer, an open-cockpit passenger or mail carrier and a saloon type with accommodation for four persons in an enclosed cabin. Production of the civil variants totalled 70 aircraft.
Data (Military M.18): *Engine* as above *Wing span* 15.8 m (51 ft 10 in) *Length* 9.75 m (31 ft 11¾ in) *Max T-O weight* 1,780 kg (3,924 lb) *Max level speed* 187 km/h (116 mph) *Range* 1,000 km (621 miles) *Armament* one forward-firing machine-gun, plus bombs

Macchi M.19 (Italy) See **Schneider Trophy contestants**

Macchi M.8.

Macchi M.9.

Macchi M.9.

Civil version of the Macchi M.18 (foreground) with M.3.

Macchi M.9 (Italy) In 1918 Macchi produced the M.9 reconnaissance and bombing flying-boat, a 223.6 kW (300 hp) Fiat A.12*bis*-engined development of the M.8. It is believed that about 16 were completed before the Armistice, with a further 14 built after. These remained operational until 1924. The M.9*bis* was a four-passenger cabin version of the M.9, a handful of which were flown commercially in Switzerland.

Macchi M.12 (Italy) This was a twin-boom reconnaissance and bombing flying-boat of 1918, powered by a 335.3 kW (450 hp) Ansaldo engine. It was later used in connection with the Schneider Trophy.

Macchi M.13 (Italy) See **Schneider Trophy contestants**

Macchi M.16 (Italy) Strange single-seat float-plane powered by a 22.35 kW (30 hp) Anzani engine. Three purchased by the US Navy as experimental communications aircraft.

Macchi

Macchi MB.308.

Macchi M.24 (Italy) Construction began in 1923 of a new twin-engined flying-boat, defensively armed with machine-guns in nose and aft positions and suitable for torpedo carrying. The engines, 216 kW (290 hp) Fiat A.12*bis*, were mounted in tandem on struts between the biplane wings. A civil variant was also designed. In 1924 the design was modified, involving adding extensions to the lower wings to make them equal in span to the upper and fitting 298 kW (400 hp) Lorraine engines. In late 1925 a flying-boat of this type flew from Varase across the Alps to Amsterdam, Copenhagen, Stockholm, Leningrad and back to Varase.

As the M.24*bis*, the extended-wing version entered production in about 1926. Powered by two Lorraine or 372.6 kW (500 hp) Isotta-Fraschini engines, it was produced as a bomber and torpedo carrier for military service and as a six-passenger (plus two crew) airliner for commercial use. Among the commercial operators was the Società Anonima Aero Expresso which used a number on its Brindisi–Athens–Constantinople route.

Data (military version): *Engines* as above *Wing span* 22.0 m (72 ft 2 in) *Length* 14.63 m (48 ft 0 in) *Max T-O weight* 5,500 kg (12,125 lb) *Max level speed* 185 km/h (115 mph) *Range* 700 km (435 miles)

Macchi M.24 with propellers removed.

Macchi M.39 (Italy) Twin-float racing seaplane built for and winner of the 1926 Schneider Trophy Contest (see **Schneider Trophy contestants**).

Macchi M.41 (Italy) Single-seat flying-boat fighter of 1927 powered by a 313 kW (420 hp) Fiat A.20 engine.

Macchi M.41.

Macchi M.52 (Italy) Twin-float racing seaplane built for the 1927 Schneider Trophy Contest (see **Schneider Trophy contestants**).

Macchi M.67 (Italy) Twin-float seaplane built for the 1929 Schneider Trophy Contest (see **Schneider Trophy contestants**).

Macchi MB.308 (Italy) Two-seat light cabin monoplane of the latter 1940s produced for the Italian Air Force and for civil use. Power was provided by a 63.3 kW (85 hp) C-85 or 67 kW (90 hp) C-90 Continental engine.

Macchi MB.320 (Italy) Six-seat cabin monoplane of 1949 powered by two 134 kW (180 hp) Continental E-185 engines. Only six built, three operated by East African Airways.

Macchi MB.326 (Italy) See **Aermacchi MB 326**

Macchi Parasol (Italy) The Parasol of 1913 was a single-seat shoulder-wing monoplane powered by a 59.6 kW (80 hp) Gnome rotary engine. Before the outbreak of World War I the type set up new Italian records. The Army Air Service received about 42 which were flown on artillery-observation duties until 1916. Maximum level speed was 125 km/h (77.5 mph).

Macchi Santa Maria (Italy) Licence-built Lockheed LASA 60 light monoplane.

Macchi MC.72 (Italy) First flown in June 1931, the MC.72 was a single-seat twin-float seaplane built originally to compete in the 1931 Schneider Trophy Contest. It was unable to take part because of defects in its experimental engine; but development enabled the aircraft to set a world speed record on 10 April 1933 of 682.078 km/h (423.822 mph), followed by others in the same year and in 1934.

Macchi MC.94 (Italy) Designed as a commercial amphibian, the prototype MC.94 flew for the first time in 1935 while powered by two 574 kW (770 hp) Wright SGR-1820-F air-cooled radial engines. Accommodation was provided for two pilots in the fully enclosed cockpit, 12 passengers in the cabin with a toilet to the rear, baggage in an aft compartment and marine gear in a nose compartment. The first five production MC.94s (without the retractable wheels of the prototype which swung forward into streamlined casings in the leading edges of the wings) were similarly powered. The only other production aircraft were six similar flying-boats with 596 kW (800 hp) Alfa Romeo 126 RC.10 engines. All MC.94s served initially with Ala Littoria.

Meanwhile in 1937 the MC.94 prototype set up several international records. These are listed as they appeared in the 1938 *Jane's*:

Height, carrying 1,000 kg (2,200 lb) of commercial load: 6,432 m (21,097 ft), put up on 15 April 1937.
Speed over 1,000 km (621 miles): 256.51 km/h (159.29 mph), put up on 6 May 1937.
Speed over 2,000 km (1,242 miles): 248.957 km/h (154.60 mph), put up on 6 May 1937.
Speed over 1,000 km (621 miles), carrying 500 kg (1,100 lb) and 1,000 kg (2,200 lb) of commercial load: 257.138 km/h (159.682 mph), both put up on 9 May 1937.

Macchi MC.100 (Italy) Developed from the MC.94, the MC.100 was a 26-passenger flying-boat powered by three Alfa Romeo 126 RC.10 engines. Three were delivered to Ala Littoria.

Macchi MC.200 Saetta (Italy) In 1936 Macchi and Fiat faced the problem of designing new single-seat cantilever low-wing fighters around the relatively low-powered Fiat A.74 RC.38 engine, rated at only 626 kW (840 hp). Not surprisingly the resulting fighters looked somewhat alike and both flew in prototype form in 1937 (the MC.200 on 24 December). Superior airframe design by Macchi's team, led by Mario Castoldi, resulted in the faster of the two aircraft, although by European standards the MC.200 was not a true match for the latest types from Germany, Britain and France. Interestingly both Macchi and Fiat subsequently got round the lack of power by using German engines in their follow-up aircraft. But for the present the Regia Aeronautica ordered the MC.200 into production as one of the replacements for the C.R.32.

When Italy entered World War II more than 150 MC.200s had been delivered, although the final number produced was nearer 1,000, most flown with open cockpits. The A1 and A2 versions were basically similar, except that the A2 had strengthened wings to allow the carriage of 50 kg, 100 kg or 160 kg bombs.

First used in action against Malta, MC.200s later turned their attention to Greece, Russia and North Africa – first meeting real opposition in the form of Hawker Hurricanes. The type was finally withdrawn from service in 1947.

Data: *Engine* as above *Wing span* 10.58 m (34 ft 8½ in) *Length* 8.19 m (26 ft 10½ in) *Max T-O weight* 2,328 kg (5,132 lb) *Max level speed* 503 km/h (312.5 mph) *Range* 870 km (540 miles) *Armament* two 12.7 mm Breda-SAFAT machine-guns.

Macchi MC.202 Folgore (Italy) The MC.202

Macchi MC.202 Folgore.

was a development of the MC.200. As mentioned above, the availability of a German-designed engine for the new fighter offered a great improvement in performance and the prototype Folgore was no more than a Saetta installed with an 801 kW (1,075 hp) Daimler-Benz 601A engine, flying for the first time on 10 August 1940.

Production Folgores entered service with the Regia Aeronautica in 1941, the first examples being powered by German-built engines and armed with two 12.7 mm machine-guns. Thereafter Folgores were fitted with DB 601s built under licence in Italy as Romeo R.A.1000 RC.41-Is, rated at 894 kW (1,200 hp). Production totalled about 1,500 aircraft.

Data (Romeo-built engine): *Engine* as above *Wing span* 10.58 m (34 ft 8½ in) *Length* 8.85 m (29 ft 0½ in) *Max T-O weight* 2,937 kg (6,475 lb) *Max level speed* 600 km/h (373 mph) *Range* 765 km (475 miles) *Armament* two 12.7 mm and two 7.7 mm Breda-SAFAT machine-guns

Prototype Macchi MC.200 Saetta.

Macchi MC.202 Folgore.

Macchi MC.205V Veltro.

Macchi MC.205V Veltro (Italy) The Veltro was basically a Folgore powered by a 931.5 kW (1,250 hp) Fiat R.A.1050 RC.58 Tifone engine – a licence-built Daimler-Benz DB.605. First flown as a prototype on 19 April 1942, production aircraft entered service in the following year but saw little action before the Italian surrender to the Allies. Armament comprised two 20 mm cannon and two 12.7 mm machine-guns, plus bombs if required. Maximum level speed was 642 km/h (399 mph).

plane of 1925 (about 20 built, most with the 223.6 kW; 300 hp Hispano-Suiza water cooled engine); M.F. 10 two-seat advanced training seaplane; M.F.11 three-seat reconnaissance biplane (399 kW; 535 hp Armstrong Siddeley Panther engine); and M.F.12 primary training biplane.

MacCready *Gossamer Condor* during one of its practice flights.

MacCready Gossamer Condor (USA) The Condor was a 29.26 m (96 ft 0 in) wing span single-seat man-powered aircraft which (on 23 August 1977) won the £50,000 Kremer Prize by becoming the first aircraft propelled entirely by a man to complete a figure-of-eight flight around two pylons half a mile apart. The pilot was Bryan Allen.

MacCready Gossamer Albatross (USA) The Albatross was a 28.6 m (93 ft 10 in) wing span single-seat man-powered aircraft which (on 12 June 1979) won the £100,000 Kremer Prize by making the first crossing of the English Channel by an aircraft propelled entirely by a man. The pilot was Bryan Allen.

MacDonald S-20 (USA) Single-seat light sporting monoplane, plans for which are available to amateur constructors.

Martin 2-0-2 prototype.

MacDonald S-20.

Manchuria Hayabusa (Manchuria) Six-passenger commercial monoplane powered by a 343 kW (460 hp) Nakajima Kotobuki radial engine.

Mann Egerton Type B (UK) Ten examples built for the RNAS during 1916 of an improved version of the Short 184 seaplane, powered by a 167.7 kW (225 hp) Sunbeam engine.

Marinens Flyvebatfabrikk M.F.8, M.F.9, M.F.10, M.F.11 and M.F.12 (Norway) From 1915 this establishment licence-built several types of military aircraft, including the Hansa Brandenburg W.33 reconnaissance seaplane. Aircraft of its own design included the M.F.8 two-seat training biplane; M.F.9 single-seat fighter sea-

Marsh/Rockwell S2R-T Turbo Thrush (USA) Turbine-powered version of the piston-engined Rockwell Thrush Commander, powered by a derated Garrett-AiResearch TPE 331-1-101 turboprop engine. The first production conversion was handed over in September 1976.

Martin 2-0-2 (USA) First flown on 22 November 1946, the Martin 2-0-2 was a 36–42-passenger airliner powered by two 1,788.5 kW (2,400 hp) Pratt & Whitney R-2800-CA18 Double Wasp radial engines. Thirty-one production aircraft were built, first entering service in 1947 with Northwest Airlines (which received 25) and Linea Aerea Nacional of Chile (4). Cruising speed was 460 km/h (286 mph). The 2-0-2A was a re-engined version of the 2-0-2, 12 of which were leased to TWA pending delivery of 4-0-4s. These were fitted with R-2800-CB16 engines.

Martin 4-0-4.

Martin 4-0-4 (USA) A development of the 2-0-2, the 4-0-4 was 1 m (3 ft 3 in) longer and was pressurised. One hundred and three were ordered, 60 for Eastern Air Lines, 41 for TWA and two for the US Coast Guard. Power was provided by two 1,788.5 kW (2,400 hp) Pratt & Whitney R-2800-CB16 Double Wasp radial engines. Deliveries began in the autumn of 1951.

Data: *Engines* as above *Wing span* 28.42 m (93 ft 3 in) *Length* 22.73 m (74 ft 7 in) *Max T-O weight* 19,800 kg (43,650 lb) *Cruising speed* 450 km/h (280 mph) *Range* 1,738–4,184 km (1,080–2,600 miles)

Martin Maryland IIs.

Martin 130 China Clipper (USA) The Martin 130 was a large four-engined monoplane flying-boat designed for transoceanic services. Three were built for Pan American Airways in 1935 and on 21 October 1936 began operating over the Pacific from San Francisco to Manilla, Philippine Islands. Two were impressed by the US Navy in 1942.

The hull was of advanced design and the result of exhaustive testing of models. Lateral buoyancy was provided by stub wings or 'seawings' instead of the conventional sponsons or outboard stabilising floats. Accommodation was provided for a crew of four and 36–48 daytime passengers or 18 sleeping bunks for night flying.

Data: *Engines* four 618.5 kW (830 hp) Pratt & Whitney R-1830-S1A4G Twin Wasp radials *Wing span* 39.62 m (130 ft 0 in) *Length* 27.62 m (90 ft 7½ in) *Max T-O weight* 23,587 kg (52,000 lb) *Cruising speed* 262 km/h (163 mph) *Range* (with 2,188 kg; 4,824 lb payload) 5,150 km (3,200 miles)

Martin 156 (USA) Large four-engined flying-boat developed for Pan American Airways for transoceanic passenger (up to 46) and mail carrying. Power was provided by 745 kW (1,000 hp) Wright GR-1820-G2 Cyclone radial engines.

Martin 167 Maryland (USA) The Model 167 three-seat attack bomber was designed for use by the USAAC and first flew as the XA-22 prototype in early 1939. The French government placed the only pre-war order, but with the fall of France these aircraft were diverted to the RAF as Maryland Is. The RAF eventually received 225 Maryland Is and IIs, most of which were used as reconnaissance bombers in the Mediterranean and North African theatres. Some were flown by South African Air Force units under RAF command.

Data: *Engines* two 782.5 kW (1,050 hp) Pratt & Whitney R-1830 Twin Wasp radials *Wing span* 18.69 m (61 ft 4 in) *Length* 14.22 m (46 ft 8 in) *Max T-O weight* 7,516 kg (16,571 lb) *Max level speed* 443 km/h (275 mph) *Range* 2,092 km (1,300 miles) *Armament* four forward-firing 0.303 in Browning machine-guns, two Vickers guns in a dorsal turret and a rear-firing ventral position. Bomb load of 567 kg (1,250 lb) carried internally. For attack duties special racks and chutes for small fragmentation bombs could be installed in the bomb bay in place of the normal racks

One of the last Martin 4-0-4s in commercial service.

Martin Baltimore IIIA.

Martin A-30 Baltimore (USA) The Model 187 was designed in 1940 to meet the tactical requirements of the British and French governments as a medium bomber to supersede the Model 167 Maryland which was then being built for France. When France fell the British government took over the French contracts for both aircraft.

Six versions of the Baltimore (British name) are listed in the 1945–46 *Jane's* as having been supplied to the RAF, but it is usually accepted that the Mk VI general-reconnaissance version did not enter service as a separate type. Until

Martin 130 *China Clipper.*

Martin

Martin Baltimore V.

Martin AM-1 Mauler on board USS _Kearsarge_.

Martin AM-1 Mauler (USA) Designed as a single-seat attack bomber, the first prototype Mauler flew as the XBTM-1 on 26 August 1944. Delivery to US Navy squadrons began in early 1948 but production was restricted to 149 aircraft. These were subsequently replaced by Skyraiders. Data: _Engine_ one 2,235.6 kW (3,000 hp) Pratt & Whitney R-4360-4 Wasp Major radial _Wing span_ 15.26 m (50 ft 0 in) _Length_ 12.55 m (41 ft 2 in) _Max T-O weight_ 10,054–13,154 kg (22,166–29,000 lb) _Max level speed_ 591 km/h (367 mph) _Range_ 2,090 km (1,300 miles) _Armament_ four 20 mm cannon, plus three 2,200 lb torpedoes and 12 × 5 in rockets, bombs or mines on 15 attachment points

Lease–Lend was introduced, the Baltimore was built to British contracts. Thereafter it was ordered by the US government as the A-30 light attack bomber. It was engaged exclusively on operations in the Mediterranean area with the RAF and Allied Air Forces operating under RAF command. It was never used operationally by the USAAF. Production ceased in May 1944, by which time 1,575 had been delivered to the RAF.

The Baltimore I and II were each powered by two 1,192 kW (1,600 hp) Wright GR-2600-A5B radial engines. Both carried up to 907 kg (2,000 lb) of bombs and had four forward-firing 0.303 in wing guns, four guns in the lower fuselage aft of the wings firing to the rear and one or two

Martin B-10s photographed in 1934.

ventral guns; but the Mk I had a single Vickers gun on a flexible mounting in the rear cockpit and the Mk II had twin Vickers guns. The Mk III and Mk IIIA were similar to the Mk II except for having Boulton Paul power-operated turrets in place of the previous rear-cockpit dorsal armament. The Mk IV introduced a Martin electrically operated turret armed with two 0.50 in guns and the Mk V had four 0.50 in wing guns, two 0.50 in guns in a Martin turret and a single 0.50 in gun in a flexible rear-firing ventral position. It differed also in having two 1,267 kW (1,700 hp) Wright GR-2600-A5B5 engines.

Data (Mk V): _Engines_ as above _Wing span_ 18.69 m (61 ft 4 in) _Length_ 14.78 m (48 ft 6 in) _Max T-O weight_ 12,633 kg (27,850 lb) _Max level speed_ 515 km/h (320 mph) _Range_ 1,577 km (980 miles)

Martin YB-12 fitted with floats.

Martin B-10 and B-12 (USA) The Martin Model 139 was a twin-engined mid-wing monoplane bomber developed from the experimental Model 123 of 1932. During 1934 48 Model 139s were delivered to the USAAC. Fifteen were fitted with 503 kW (675 hp) Wright R-1820 Cyclone engines as YB-10s and 33 with 577.5 kW (775 hp) Pratt & Whitney R-1690 Hornet engines as YB-12s and B-12As, a number of which were later converted into twin-float seaplanes for coastal patrol duties.

Development of the Model 139 led to numerous improvements being made, including the installation of 551.4 kW (740 hp) SGR-1820-G3 Cyclone engines, a Sperry automatic pilot and the addition of wing flaps, constant-speed propellers, de-icers and numerous structural and maintenance refinements. During 1935 and 1936 103 of the

Martin AM-1 Mauler.

improved aircraft (B-10Bs) were delivered to the USAAC.

On 1 July 1936 the bomber was released for export and was subsequently ordered by six foreign governments, the Netherlands East Indies alone receiving 120 Model 139Ws and Model 166s with 670.7 kW (900 hp) Cyclone engines. The latter aircraft introduced improved aerodynamics and performance characteristics and featured a continuous cockpit enclosure instead of the previous separate enclosures.

Data (Model 166 with Cyclone engines): *Engines* as above *Wing span* 21.39 m (70 ft 2¼ in) *Length* 13.47 m (44 ft 2¼ in) *Max T-O weight* 6,983 kg (15,395 lb) *Max level speed* 418 km/h (260 mph) *Range* 3,347 km (2,080 miles) *Armament* one 0.303 in Browning machine-gun in nose turret and two in rear-cockpit dorsal and ventral positions. Up to 1,025 kg (2,260 lb) of bombs

Martin B-26 Marauder (USA) The projected design data for the Model 179 Medium Bomber were accepted by the USAAC on 5 July 1939 and the first Marauder flew on 25 November 1940.

The flow of production Marauders began on 25 February 1941 and by the end of 1944 more than 5,150 had been delivered. The Marauder first went into action in the Australian theatre in April 1942.

The B-26 initial production version was powered by two 1,378.6 kW (1,850 hp) Pratt & Whitney R-2800-5 radial engines and carried a defensive armament of five 0.50 in machine-guns in the nose, dorsal turret and tail. Normal bomb load was 907 kg (2,000 lb) but up to 2,631 kg (5,800 lb) could be carried in the tandem bomb bays. The B-26A was similar to the earlier version except for having R-2800-39 engines and minor changes. Similar Marauder Is were delivered to the RAF and SAAF in 1942 under Lend–Lease.

The B-26B corresponded to the Lend–Lease Marauder IA and II and was produced in more than one form. Power was provided by R-2800-5 or 1,490.4 kW (2,000 hp) R-2800-41/-43 engines and tail armament was increased to two guns. From B-26B-10 (Marauder II) the wing span was increased from 19.81 m (65 ft 0 in) to 21.64 m (71 ft 0 in); the area of the vertical tail surfaces was also increased; and armament raised to include one fixed and one flexible gun in the nose, four 'package' guns on the sides of the forward fuselage, two guns in the Martin dorsal turret, two flexible waist guns, one ventral-tunnel gun and two tail guns. The front bay could carry two 2,000 lb bombs on special carriers and use of the rear bomb bay was discontinued. The crew was increased from five to seven. The B-26B variants were the most produced of the series.

The B-26C (Marauder II) was the same as the B-26B-10 types but built at the Martin Omaha plant. The single experimental B-26D with exhaust-heated surface de-icing equipment and the single B-26E special stripped model were followed by the B-26F and G (Marauder III). These were similar to the B-26C except for having the incidence of the wings increased by 3½°, no provision for carrying a torpedo, and 11 guns fitted.

Preparing to arm a Martin B-26 Marauder.

Martin B-26G Marauder.

Martin B-26s with paint removed to increase speed.

Martin

Martin BM-2.

Certain examples of earlier B-26s were stripped of armament and adapted for training and general utility duties, particularly high-speed target-towing. These were originally known as AT-23s but were subsequently redesignated TB-26s. A number of TB-26Gs were also built. The designations JM-1 and JM-2 applied to stripped versions of the B-26C and B-26G respectively, used by the US Navy for target-towing and other general utility duties. The JM-1P was equipped for photographic reconnaissance.
Data (B-26B/C, with R-2800-43 engines): *Engines* as above *Wing span* 21.64 m (71 ft 0 in) *Length* 17.75 m (58 ft 3 in) *Max T-O weight* 17,327 kg (38,200 lb) *Max level speed* 462 km/h (287 mph) *Range* 1,931 km (1,200 miles)

Martin B-57B.

Martin MB-1.

Martin B-57 (USA) Tandem two-seat light tactical-bombing (B-57) and reconnaissance (RB-57) versions of the English Electric Canberra built under licence in the USA. The B-57A initial bomber version was modelled on the Canberra B.2 except for its engines and equipment. The B-57B two-man intruder version introduced the tandem 'blister' canopy and a wing span of 19.51 m (64 ft 0 in). It had eight 0.50 in machine-guns in the wings, underwing stores pylons and a rotating bomb-bay door. Subsequent versions and conversions (see **General Dynamics**) were produced for electronics-warfare, target-towing and night-interdiction duties. B-57s remain operational with the USAF and as the B-57B with the Pakistan Air Force.

Martin BM-1.

Martin BM-1 and BM-2 (USA) Delivered to the US Navy from the latter half of 1931, the BM-1 and BM-2 were all-metal specialised shipboard tandem two-seat dive-bombing biplanes. They were powered by 428.5 kW (575 hp) Pratt & Whitney R-1690-44 Hornet radial engines. Production amounted to just 32 aircraft. Maximum level speed was 230 km/h (143 mph). They were the first US Navy aircraft capable of carrying a 1,000 lb bomb in a terminal-velocity vertical dive and of recovering from the dive without dropping the bomb.

Martin MB and NBS-1 (USA) The Glenn L. Martin Company was organised during World War I and produced the first successful twin-engined aeroplane of American design, as the W.F. Night Bomber or 'Seven Ton' bomber. As it is generally accepted that the first bomber built for the USAAS was the MB-1 (first flown on 15 April 1918), the view can be taken that the W.F. and MB-1 are one and the same. Contemporary reports state that the W.F. was converted into the passenger and cargo-carrying Commercial type. Again it is known that one of the ten MB-1s was so converted, although a drawing of the Commercial made in 1921 shows a rounded-nose aircraft with folding outer-wing sections, single-wheel landing-gear units and open cockpit for the pilots, while the MB-1-type Commercial was actually produced with an enclosed cockpit. Nevertheless as features of the Commercial were subsequently to be found on the improved MB-2 bombers, including the revised single- instead of double-wheel landing gear units, it can be taken that the W.F. Commercial and MB-1-type Commercial or T-1 were the same aircraft. All but one of the remaining MB-1s were produced as bombers or

Martin PBM Mariners.

Martin Marietta X-24A.

Max Holste M.H.1521
Broussard.

Single-seat fighter (foreground), two-seat (top) and reconnaissance versions of the McDonnell F-101 Voodoo.

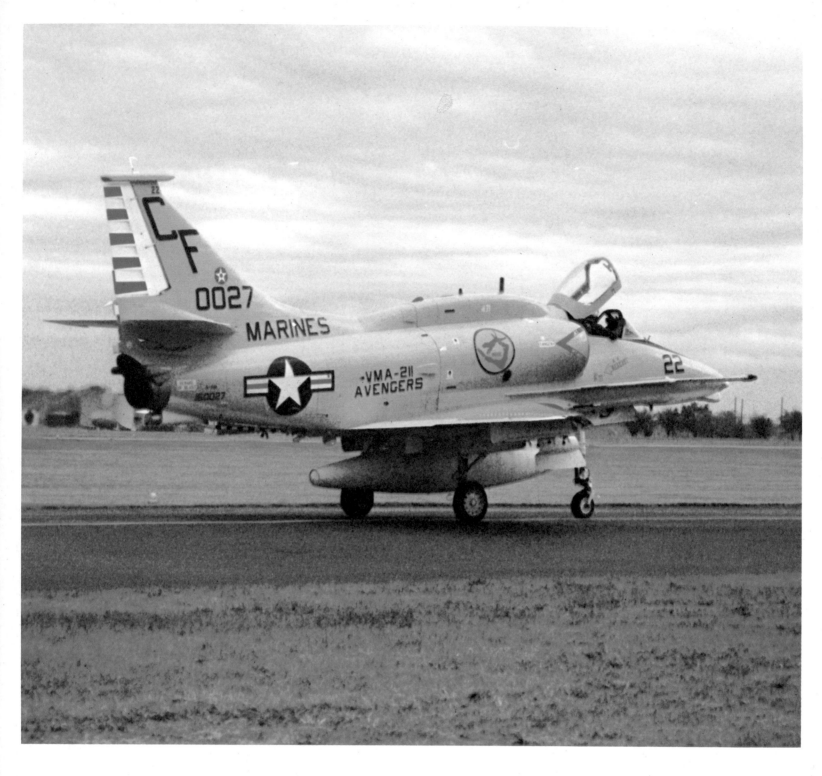

**McDonnell Douglas A-4M
Skyhawk II.**

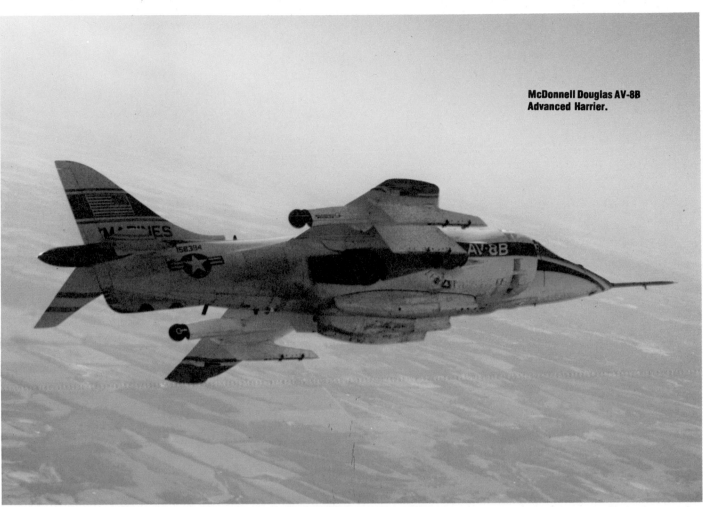

McDonnell Douglas AV-8B
Advanced Harrier.

McDonnell Douglas C-9A
Nightingale.

**McDonnell Douglas
DC-10.**

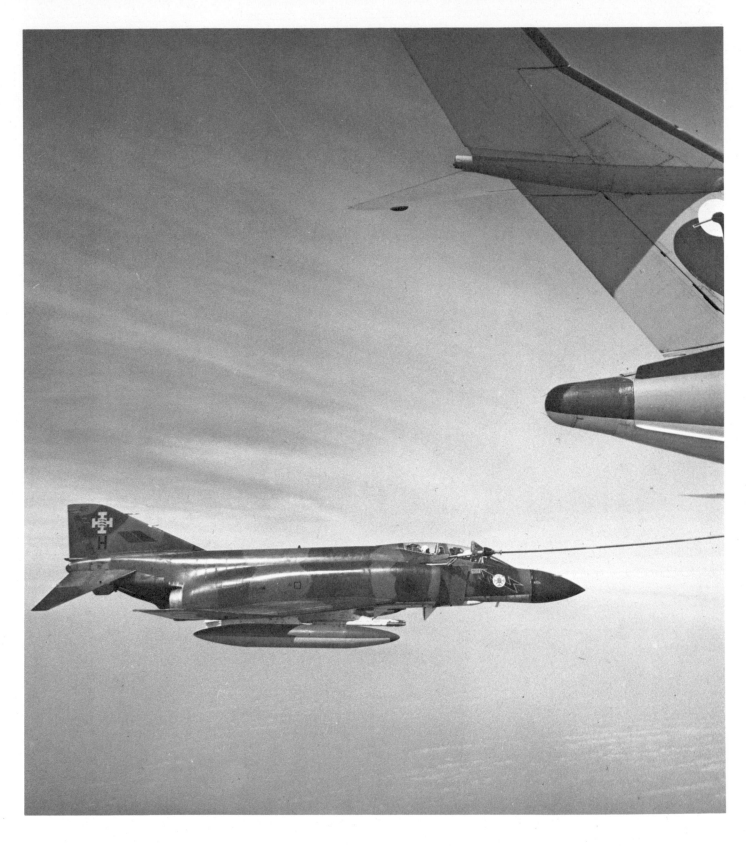

**RAF McDonnell Douglas
Phantom FGR.2.**

**Prototype McDonnell
Douglas F-18 Hornet.**

July 1921, other MB bombers and flying-boats destroyed a submarine, cruiser and destroyer. *Data (MB-2): Engines* as above *Wing span* 22.6 m (74 ft 2 in) *Length* 13.0 m (42 ft 8 in) *Max T-O weight* about 5,443 kg (12,000 lb) *Max level speed* 159 km/h (99 mph) *Range* 901 km (560 miles) *Armament* five 0.30 in machine-guns in nose, dorsal and ventral positions, plus up to 907 kg (2,000 lb) of bombs (see text)

Martin MO-1 (USA) Cantilever shoulder-wing observation monoplane powered by a Curtiss D-12 engine. Thirty-six delivered to the US Navy.

Martin P3M-1 and P3M-2 (USA) Production versions of the Consolidated PY-1 long-range patrol flying-boat (Martin Model 120), first flown in 1929. Only nine built, with two 317 kW (425 hp) Pratt & Whitney R-1340-38 Wasp and two 402.4 kW (540 hp) Pratt & Whitney R-1690-32 Hornet engines respectively. Maximum level speed of the P3M-2 (as guaranteed by Martin) was 185 km/h (115 mph). Alighting speed was 96.5 km/h (60 mph). The P3M-2 version also featured an enclosed cockpit.

Martin T-1 with an enclosed cockpit and fuselage windows.

Martin NBS-1.

Martin MO-1.

observation aircraft, followed by four more military MB-1s for US Government air mail services. A further two were produced as torpedo bombers for the US Navy, which designated them MTB-1s.

As an interim stage between the MB-1 and the later MB-2, Martin produced the MT-1 extended-wing torpedo bomber, eight of which were operated by the US Marine Corps. The MB-2 itself was powered by 313 kW (420 hp) instead of 298 kW (400 hp) Liberty engines and had the wing span of the MT-1 and the landing gear of the Commercial. One hundred and thirty were produced by four manufacturers, a large number as short-range NBS-1 night bombers. Bombs were carried in racks in a compartment in the fuselage, or, in the case of large bombs, on special racks or chocks directly under the fuselage. Interestingly one MB-2, fitted with superchargers, attained an altitude of about 8,077 m (26,500 ft) while carrying a pilot and three observers. A contemporary report states that, had it not been for the extreme cold and lack of fuel, a still greater altitude could have been reached. MB/NBS-1 bombers were eventually replaced in service by Keystone types.

The MB-2 is best remembered as the aircraft with which Brig-Gen William 'Billy' Mitchell demonstrated the effectiveness of the bomber by sinking the stationary ex-German warship *Ostfriesland*. During the same demonstrations on 21

Martin P3M-1.

Martin PM-1 and PM-2 (USA) Martin-built examples of the Naval Aircraft Factory PN biplane patrol flying-boat, powered by two 391 kW (525 hp) Wright R-1750 and 410 kW (550 hp) Wright R-1820 Cyclone radial engines respectively. Based on the PN-12 and carrying the Martin Model number 122, they were of all-metal construction and carried wireless-receiving and -sending apparatus, together with a Bellini-Tosi wireless direction finder.

Martin P3M-2 with open cockpits.

Martin P4M-1 Mercator (USA) Designed as a long-range patrol aircraft for the US Navy, the Mercator (Martin Model 219) was powered by

One of six Martin MB-1s produced for postal services.

Martin

Martin PM-1, with single fin and rudder.

Martin PM-2, with twin fins and rudders.

Martin P4M-1 Mercators.

French Navy Martin P5M-2 Marlin.

Martin P6M-2 SeaMaster.

Martin P5M-1 Marlins.

and was delivered to the Navy in December of that year. A number of air-sea rescue versions of the P5M-1 were delivered to the US Coast Guard in the autumn of 1953 as P5M-1Gs.

The P5M-2 (145 built) had two R-3350-32W or -32WA engines, the main external changes being the introduction of a 'T' tail and increased wing span. It also had a lower bow chine line to reduce spray damage to the propellers and a rearrangement of much of the interior equipment for greater operational comfort and convenience. The first P5M-2 flew in August 1953 and was delivered to the Navy on 23 June 1954. Ten were also supplied to the French Navy under MDAP. Modernisation of the aircraft led to the designations P5M-1S and P5M-2S, fitted with MAD gear, Julie active echo-sounding and Jezebel passive sonobuoy detection equipment. The type went out of operational use in 1966.

Data (P5M-2): *Engines* as above *Wing span* 36.03 m (118 ft 2¼ in) *Length* 30.66 m (100 ft 7¼ in) *Max T-O weight* (ASW mission) 34,761 kg (76,635 lb) *Max level speed* 404 km/h (251 mph) *Range* 3,300 km (2,050 miles) *Armament* bomb bays in engine nacelles for various types of offensive stores, including four torpedoes, four 2,000 lb bombs, smaller bombs or mines

two Pratt & Whitney R-4360-20A Wasp Major radial engines and two 17 kN (3,825 lb st) Allison J33 turbojet engines. A production order for 19 was authorised under the 1947 Naval Appropriations Bill and final assembly of the first production aircraft began in April 1949. This contract was completed in September 1950.

Martin P5M Marlin (USA) The P5M (Martin Model 237) was the first twin-engined flying-boat to be developed for the US Navy for anti-submarine warfare after the war. P5M-1 and -2 were the main versions produced. The P5M-1 was powered by two 2,422 kW (3,250 hp) Wright R-3350-36WA or 2,533.7 kW (3,400 hp) R-3350-32WA Turbo Compound engines and featured a low-mounted tailplane. The first of 114 production P5M-1 Marlins flew on 22 June 1951

Martin P6M-2 SeaMaster (USA) The SeaMaster was a four-jet swept-wing high-performance flying-boat of advanced design. Its two primary functions were expected to be mine laying and photographic reconnaissance, but with combat capability. The first of two XP6M-1 prototypes flew on 14 July 1955 and the first of six pre-production YP6M-1s on 20 January 1958. An

order for 24 production P6M-2s (with Pratt &
Whitney J75 turbojets) was reduced to 18 in 1957
and later to 3 – the first of which flew on 17
February 1959. It was intended to use four
YP6M-1s and P6M-2s to form an operational
evaluation squadron.

Max T-O weight 27,350 kg (60,300 lb) *Max level
speed* over 314 km/h (195 mph) *Range* 3,700 km
(2,300 miles) *Armament* six or eight 0.50 in
machine-guns in nose and amidships turrets, plus
up to 1,814 kg (4,000 lb) of bombs or depth
charges

Martin PBM-3 Mariner.

Martin PBM Mariner (USA) The XPBM-1 prototype flying-boat patrol bomber was originally
ordered by the US Navy in 1936. Before it was
built, a quarter-size prototype (Model 162A) was
constructed and flown. The full-size aircraft was
flown for the first time in February 1939.

The production PBM-1 – fitted with two
1,192 kW (1,600 hp) Wright R-2600-6 radial
engines, a dihedral tail and retractable wingtip
floats – was ordered in 1938 and 20 of these went
into Navy service in 1941. A single XPBM-2 was
ordered at the same time as a long-range version
specially strengthened for catapult take-off.

The PBM-3, with two 1,267 kW (1,700 hp)
Wright R-2600-12 engines, was ordered in quantity in 1940 and deliveries began in 1942. In this
version the crew was increased from seven to nine,
the armament was revised and the fuel capacity
increased. The retractable wingtip floats of the
PBM-1 were replaced by fixed floats. In 1942 the
PBM-3 was adopted also as a naval transport
carrying 20 passengers or 3,629–4,082 kg
(8,000–9,000 lb) of cargo (PBM-3R). Twenty-six
PBM-3B patrol bombers were also used by RAF
Coastal Command, delivered under Lend–Lease.
At the end of the war a specialised anti-submarine
version was also developed as the PBM-3S.

The final two production versions of the
Mariner were the PBM-5 and PBM-5A, powered
by 1,565 kW (2,100 hp) R-2800-22 and
R-2800-34 engines respectively. The last
PBM-5A was delivered to the US Navy in April
1949. This version was basically an amphibious
version of the PBM-5 and ended its career as a
general utility aircraft.
Data (PBM-5A): *Engines* as above *Wing span*
35.97 m (118 ft 0 in) *Length* 24.33 m (79 ft 10 in)

Martin S.

Martin S (USA) Two-seat observation floatplane
powered by a 93 kW (125 hp) Hall-Scott A-5
engine. Fourteen operated by the US Army and
two by the US Navy from 1915.
Martin T and TT (USA) Tandem two-seat
dual-control training seaplanes, 17 of which were
delivered to the US Army from 1914.

Martin T3M-1.

Martin T3M, T4M and Great Lakes TG (USA)
During 1924 and 1925 the Martin Works were
engaged in the production of SC torpedo bombers
for the US Navy (see **Curtiss**). As an improvement Martin designed and built the T3M-1, 24 of
which were ordered by the US Navy as torpedo-
carrying, bombing and scouting biplanes.
Deliveries were made in 1926. These differed from
the SCs mainly in the rearrangement of the seating and equipment, the substitution of an all-
welded fuselage for a partly welded and partly
riveted construction, and the installation of a
428.5 kW (575 hp) Wright T-3B engine.

The T3M-1 was followed into production by
the T3M-2, a contract for 100 being placed in
March 1927. It employed a welded chrome
molybdenum steel-tube fuselage, wooden wing
structure and duralumin tail surfaces. The bombing compartment was retained in the forward part

Martin PBM-5 Mariner
with search radar above
the fuselage.

Martin

Martin Marietta X-24A.

Martin Marietta X-24B.

Martin XPB2M-1.

Martin JRM-1 Mars.

Martinsyde F.4 Buzzard.

of the fuselage but the seating arrangement was in tandem instead of side-by-side. Power was provided by a 544 kW (730 hp) Packard 3A-2500 engine.

The new T4M-1 could be rapidly converted, like the earlier types, from landplane to seaplane form and vice versa, and was particularly suited for aircraft carrier use. Power was provided by a 391 kW (525 hp) Pratt & Whitney R-1690-24 Hornet radial engine. Wing span was reduced from 17.25 m (56 ft 7 in) to 16.15 m (53 ft 0 in), a new balanced rudder was fitted and the rear cockpit was reshaped and supported a small windscreen. The US Navy received 102 T4M-1s, most of which served as carrier-borne aircraft with wheel landing gears.

The final aircraft of the series were 40 TG-1s and TG-2s built by Great Lakes and powered by 410 kW (550 hp) Pratt & Whitney R-1690-28 Hornet and 428.5 kW (575 hp) geared Wright R-1820-86 Cyclone engines respectively. The TG-2 reverted to the old-style raised rear-gunner's cockpit but with a small windscreen. Data (T3M-2): *Engines* as above *Wing span* 17.25 m (56 ft 7 in) *Length* 12.6 m (41 ft 4 in) *Max T-O weight* (landplane) 4,310 kg (9,503 lb), (seaplane) 4,581 kg (10,101 lb) *Max level speed* 195 km/h (121 mph) *Range* 589–1,215 km (366–755 miles) *Armament* one rear-mounted 0.30 in machine-gun, plus a torpedo or bombs

Martin JRM Mars (USA) The Mars was originally built as an experimental patrol bomber with the designation XPB2M-1. It flew for the first time in July 1942. It was subsequently modified as a cargo transport flying-boat and redesignated XPB2M-1R

The JRM was the production development of the XPB2M-1R. An order for 20 was placed as the result of the successful performance of the prototype with the US Navy Air Transport Services. The first of the new 'boats was completed in the summer of 1945. The US Navy contract was later reduced to five aircraft. The fourth JRM-1 was delivered in the summer of 1946; the fifth (JRM-2), with an improved power-plant installation, in the autumn of 1947. Subsequently JRM-1s were converted to JRM-2 standard and redesignated JRM-3s.
Data (JRM-2): *Engines* four 2,236 kW (3,000 hp) Pratt & Whitney R-4360 Wasp Major radials, (JRM-1) four 1,565 kW (2,100 hp) Wright R-3350-8 Duplex-Cyclone radials *Wing span* 60.96 m (200 ft 0 in) *Length* 36.65 m (120 ft 3 in) *Max T-O weight* 74,842 kg (165,000 lb) *Max level speed* 383 km/h (238 mph)

Martin Marietta X-23A and X-24 (USA) The X-23A was a small unmanned lifting-body research vehicle built to prove the aerodynamic characteristics of the basic design. From it was developed the SV-5P (piloted low-speed test aircraft), designated X-24A by the USAF. This made its first rocket-powered flight on 19 March 1970. In 1972 the X-24A was stripped down and rebuilt as the X-24B, the previous 'bulbous wedge-shaped' fuselage giving way to a new triangular cross-section with the flat-side underneath. The X-24B flew for the first time on 1 August 1973 and made its final powered flight on 23 September 1975.

Martinsyde F.4 Buzzard (UK) The Buzzard was a 223.6 kW (300 hp) Hispano-Suiza-engined biplane fighter of 1918. None of the small number

636

of aircraft built became operational before the Armistice. Most were passed to other air forces post-war. Maximum level speed was 233 km/h (145 mph).

Martinsyde S.I. Scout (UK) In late 1914 the firm produced a small but fast biplane scout powered by a 59.6 kW (80 hp) Gnome rotary engine. Although inferior to other types in service, the S.I was a limited success in its role and played an important part in the air war in 1915 until the increased speed of German aircraft rendered it obsolete. Thereafter it became a trainer. In all about 60 were produced, superseded on the production lines by the Elephant. Maximum level speed was 140 km/h (87 mph).

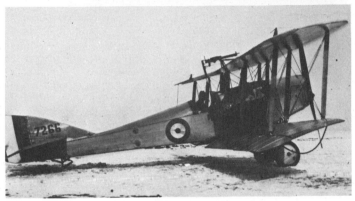

Martinsyde Elephant (UK) The 1922 *Jane's* lists the Elephant as a scouting type and indeed it was as a long-range fighter and escort that the aircraft was originally conceived. The prototype G.100 of 1915 crashed after just over 43 flying hours, but production of a small number of G.100s and 270 Elephants followed. Powered by an 89.4 kW (120 hp) and then a 119 kW (160 hp) Beardmore engine, the Elephant proved inadequate as a fighter when it entered service in 1916. Its endurance, however, made it an ideal light high-speed bomber and reconnaissance aircraft and it was in these roles that the type served into 1917. In addition to serving on the Western Front, a number were despatched to Palestine and Mesopotamia. In mid-1917 an Elephant was flight tested with a radiator taken from a German aircraft.
Data (119 kW; 160 hp engine): *Engine* as above *Wing span* 11.58 m (38 ft 0 in) *Length* 8.08 m (26 ft 6 in) *Max T-O weight* 1,100 kg (2,424 lb) *Max level speed* 167 km/h (104 mph) *Endurance* 4 h 30 min *Armament* two forward-firing Lewis machine-guns, plus up to 118 kg (260 lb) of bombs (one Elephant tested with a Lewis gun mounted on the upper wing)

Maule M-4 Rocket.

Mauboussin M.123, M.124, M.128 and M.129 (France) The M.123 was a two-seat light open-cockpit monoplane developed from the Corsaire (44.7 kW; 60 hp Salmson engine), first built in series by Fouga in 1937. The M.124, M.128 and M.129 were based on similar airframes but had different engines – a 63.3 kW (85 hp) Salmson 5AP, 74.5 kW (100 hp) Mathis G.4R and a 52 kW (70 hp) Minie 4DO engine respectively. The M.124 also had enclosed cockpits.

Mauboussin M.200 (France) Single-seat high-performance monoplane powered by an 85.7 kW (125 hp) Régnier engine. In May 1939 this aircraft put up speed records for light aeroplanes with engines of 2–4 litre capacity of 274.223 km/h (170.394 mph) and 255 km/h (158.45 mph) over 100 km and 1,000 km respectively.

Maule M-4 Jetasen and Rocket (USA) Four-seat light monoplanes, the prototype of which flew for the first time on 8 September 1960. Production began in 1962 and lasted until 1975. Four versions were produced as the basic M-4 Jetasen (108 kW; 145 hp Continental O-300-A); de luxe M-4 Astro-Rocket (134 kW; 180 hp Franklin 6A-335-B1A), M-4 Rocket (156.5 kW; 210 hp Continental IO-360-A); and M-4 Strata-Rocket (164 kW; 220 hp Franklin 6A-350-C1).

Maule M-5 Lunar Rocket (USA) Four-seat light monoplane first flown on 1 November 1971. Currently available in five versions as the M-5-180C (134 kW; 180 hp Lycoming O-360-C1F); M-5-210C (156.5 kW; 210 hp Continental IO-360-D); M-5-210TC (cargo version with a 156.5 kW; 210 hp Lycoming TO-360-C1A6D); M-5-235C (175 kW; 235 hp Lycoming O-540-J1A5D); and Maule Patroller (civil patrol version of Lunar Rocket).

Martinsyde S.I Scout.

Martinsyde G.100.

Maule M-5 Lunar Rocket.

Mayo Composite.

Max Holste M.H.53.

Max Holste M.H.250
Super Broussard.

Max Holste M.H.1521
Broussard.

Max Holste M.H.52 (France) Two-seat touring (M.H.52) and training (M.H.52/E) monoplane powered by a 112 kW (150 hp) Potez 4D or similar engine.

Max Holste M.H.53 (France) Similar to the M.H.52 but fitted with a tailwheel landing gear and powered by a 100.6 kW (135 hp) de Havilland Gipsy Major 10 engine.

Max Holste M.H.250 Super Broussard (France) Prototype twin-engined light high-wing transport which flew for the first time on 20 May 1959. Accommodation was for up to 23 persons.

Max Holste M.H.1521 Broussard (France) Six-seat light utility transport and liaison aircraft, the prototype of which flew for the first time on 17 November 1952. Alternative interior layouts provide for two stretchers and two sitting casualties or attendants. Powered by the 335 kW (450 hp) Pratt & Whitney R-985-AN-1 radial engine, production aircraft went into wide-scale service with civil and military operators; military versions still being flown today by the French Air Force and the air forces of 11 other countries.

Data: *Engine* as above *Wing span* 13.75 m (45 ft 1¼ in) *Length* 8.65 m (28 ft 4½ in) *Max T-O weight* 2,700 kg (5,953 lb) *Max level speed* 270 km/h (168 mph) *Range* 1,200 km (745 miles)

Mayo Composite (UK) The Mayo Composite Company was formed in 1935 to handle the world rights of the Composite Aircraft invented and patented by Maj R. H. Mayo. The composite (better known as the Short-Mayo Composite) comprised an Empire flying-boat, named *Maia*, above which was carried the much smaller Mayo

twin-float seaplane, named *Mercury*. The composite was completed in late 1937 and the first separation of the aircraft was made on 6 February 1938 after exhaustive tests with the separate components. Following satisfactory trials and passing through the Marine Aircraft Experimental Establishment at Felixstowe, the composite was handed over to Imperial Airways (see **Chronology** 6 February and 21–22 July 1938).

Data (*Mercury*): *Engines* four 283 kW (380 hp) Napier-Halford Rapier VIs *Wing span* 22.25 m (73 ft 0 in) *Length* 15.52 m (50 ft 11 in) *Max T-O weight* 9,435 kg (20,800 lb) *Max level speed* 341 km/h (212 mph) *Cruising endurance* 21 h 30 min

MBB 223 Flamingo (Germany) The MBB (originally SIAT) Flamingo was the winner of a German competition for a standard club and training aircraft. It flew for the first time on 1 March 1967. Two versions were produced: the basic two-seat 223A1 utility version intended primarily for training airline pilots and the 223K1 single-seat fully aerobatic version. Production of the two versions totalled 50 aircraft by January 1972. Manufacture was later transferred to CASA in Spain.

MBB BO 105 (Germany) The prototype of this five-seat light utility helicopter flew for the first time in 1967. The original production version was the BO 105C powered by two 298 kW (400 shp) Allison 250-C20 turboshaft engines. This is no longer available. The current models are the BO-105CB powered by two 313 kW (420 shp) Allison 250-C20B engines and the standard production model since 1975; BO 105CBS with increased seating or cargo capacity in a 0.25 m (9¾ in) longer fuselage, available in five-seat executive or six-seat high-density configurations; BO 105D, a variant supplied to the UK with modified equipment; BO 105L, deliveries of which began in 1980; BO 105M (VBH) liaison and observation helicopter for the German Army, with uprated engines and transmission (227 ordered to replace Alouette IIs); and the BO 105P (PAH-1) anti-tank version, with outriggers able to carry six Hot missiles; procurement of 212 PAH-1s by the German Army began in 1979.

Data (BO 105CB): *Engines* as above *Main rotor diameter* 9.84 m (32 ft 3½ in) *Length overall* 11.86 m (38 ft 11 in) *Max T-O weight* 2,300 kg (5,070 lb) *Max cruising speed* 245 km/h (152 mph) *Range* 656 km (408 miles) *Accommodation* five persons or pilot and two stretchers or freight

MBB BO 208C Junior (Germany) Two-seat light aerobatic monoplane powered by a 74.5 kW (100 hp) Rolls-Royce Continental O-200-A engine. Licence-built version of the Malmö MFI-9 Junior, for which MBB acquired production rights. The first MBB-built Junior flew in 1962. By April 1968 170 had been completed in Germany, by which time German and Swedish production had totalled about 250 aircraft.
Data: *Engine* as above *Wing span* 8.02 m (26 ft 4 in) *Length* 5.79 m (19 ft 0 in) *Max T-O weight* 630 kg (1,390 lb) *Max level speed* 230 km/h (143 mph) *Range* 1,000 km (621 miles)

MBB BO 209 Monsun (Germany) Two-seat light touring, training, aerobatic and glider- or banner-towing monoplane, more than 100 of which were built up to February 1972. Three versions were produced as the BO 209-150 with a 112 kW (150 hp) Lycoming O-320-E1C, -E1F or -E2C engine; BO 209-160 with a 119 kW (160 hp) Lycoming IO-320-D1A fuel-injected engine; and the BO 209S trainer with non-retractable nose-wheel and a 97 kW (130 hp) Rolls-Royce Continental O-240 engine.

MBB BO 209 Monsun.

MBB BO 105D.

MBB BO 105 carrying six Hot missiles.

Data (BO 209-160): *Engine* as above *Wing span* 8.4 m (27 ft 6¾ in) *Length* 6.6 m (21 ft 7¾ in) *Max T-O weight* 820 kg (1,807 lb) *Max level speed* 274 km/h (170 mph) *Range* 1,200 km (745 miles)
MBB HFB 320 Hansa (Germany) The Hansa was intended primarily as a 7–12-seat executive transport/feeder-liner, but was available as a freighter and for a variety of military and civil duties, including pilot/navigator training, calibration, aerial survey, and target flying and towing. The first prototype flew on 21 April 1964 and the first production Hansa in February 1966. The initial production series of 50 aircraft were each powered by two General Electric CJ610-1 turbojets (first 15), two CJ610-5s (16th to 35th) and two 13.79 kN (3,100 lb st) CJ610-9 turbojets (36th onward). The German Air Force operates the type as a transport, flight calibration and ECM aircraft.
Data (latest models): *Engines* as above *Wing span over tip-tanks* 14.49 m (47 ft 6 in) *Length* 16.61 m (54 ft 6 in) *Max T-O weight* 9,200 kg (20,280 lb) *Max cruising speed* 825 km/h (513 mph) *Range* 2,370 km (1,472 miles)

MBB HFB 320 Hansa.

MBB/Aérospatiale PAH-2 (Germany/France) Anti-tank helicopter projected for the German and French Armies.
MBB/Kawasaki BK 117 (Germany/Japan) Multi-purpose eight–ten-seat helicopter powered by two 447 kW (600 hp) Avco Lycoming LTS 101-650B-1 turboshaft engines. First flown in prototype form on 13 June 1979. Deliveries of production aircraft will begin in late 1981.
McCarley Mini-Mac (USA) Single-seat limited aerobatic monoplane, plans for which are available to amateur constructors.

MBB BO 208 Junior.

McCarley Mini-Mac.

McCulloch

McDonnell F2H-2 Banshee.

McCulloch 4E (USA) Tandem-rotor light helicopter built as a four-seat development of the JOV-3, MC-4 and YH-30 helicopters. Certificated by the FAA in 1962.

McCulloch J-2 (USA) Two-seat light autogyro, first flown in 1962. Deliveries of production aircraft began in 1970 and by early 1972 a total of 83 had been built. Power was provided by a 134 kW (180 hp) Lycoming O-360-A2D engine.

McCulloch MC-4.

McCulloch J-2.

McDonnell F2H Banshee (USA) The original contract for the design and construction of the XF2H-1 single-seat naval fighter was placed by the US Navy in March 1945. The first prototype flew on 11 January 1947 and the first production order for the F2H-1 was placed in May 1947. As the Banshee, it finally went out of production in 1953 after a total of 892 production aircraft of all versions had been delivered to the US Navy and Marine Corps. During 1955 the Royal Canadian Navy received 39 F2H-3 Banshee all-weather fighters, the delivery being fulfilled by the US Navy.

The first production model was the F2H-1 powered by two 13.34 kN (3,000 lb st) Westinghouse J34-WE-22 engines. The first flew on 10 August 1949 and 56 were built. The F2H-1 was followed by the F2H-2 with two 14.01 kN (3,150 lb st) J34-WE-34 engines and a lengthened fuselage to accommodate extra fuel. This was the major production version and included 14 F2N-2N night fighters and 58 F2H-2P photographic-reconnaissance aircraft.

The F2H-3 long-range all-weather fighter had an extra section inserted in mid-fuselage to accommodate two additional fuel tanks. Search radar was positioned in the nose and the cannon armament was placed further aft in the fuselage sides. A new tailplane with slight dihedral was fitted and the aircraft had 'probe-drogue' flight-refuelling equipment (later fitted to all F2H-2s).

The final model was the F2H-4, production of 150 being completed on 30 October 1953. Power was provided by two 16.01 kN (3,600 lb st) J34-WE-38 engines.
Data (F2H-2): *Engines* as above *Wing span* 13.67 m (44 ft 10 in) *Length* 12.24 m (40 ft 2 in) *Max T-O weight* 10,120 kg (22,312 lb) *Max level speed* over 917 km/h (570 mph) *Range* 2,374 km (1,475 miles) *Armament* four forward-firing 20 mm cannon

McDonnell F3H Demon (USA) The Demon was a single-seat carrier-based fighter which equipped 12 US Navy squadrons on board seven carriers in 1959. The prototype XF3H-1 flew for the first time on 7 August 1951. In August 1952 the US Navy placed an order for 150 F3H-1s to be powered by the Westinghouse J40-W-22 turbojet. During development the weight of the F3H-1 was increased from 9,980 kg (22,000 lb) to 13,150 kg (29,000 lb) to meet the all-purpose fighter requirement and a higher thrust engine (J40-W-24) was specified in place of the original power unit. This engine, however, did not come up to expectations, resulting in the F2H-1 being underpowered. Consequently the last 90 of the original order were re-ordered as F3H-2s with 63.39 kN (14,250 lb st, with afterburning) Allison J71-A-2 engines. Of the 56 F3H-1s built, 21 early production aircraft were retained for use as ground trainers and 29 were modified to take the J71 engine and converted to the later standard.

Three versions of the F3H-2 Demon were built. The F3H-2N with a J71-A-2 engine was the standard night and all-weather fighter and the first production version. Armament comprised four

McDonnell F3H-2N Demons.

20 mm cannon and various types of external stores, including the Sidewinder infra-red homing missile and nuclear weapons. The F3H-2M was the day-fighter missile-carrier version, armed with four cannon and four Sparrow III missiles. The F3H-2P was the photographic-reconnaissance version. The 519th and last production F3H was completed in November 1959. Data (F3H-2N): *Engine* as above *Wing span* 10.77 m (35 ft 4 in) *Length* 17.96 m (58 ft 11 in) *Max T-O weight* 15,377 kg (33,900 lb) *Max level speed* 1,170 km/h (727 mph) *Normal range* 2,414 km (1,500 miles)

McDonnell F-101 Voodoo (USA) The Voodoo was built as a supersonic twin-jet fighter for the USAF. It was developed from the XF-88 and XF-88A experimental twin-jet long-range penetration fighters which underwent successful evaluation during 1949–50.

The first production version of the Voodoo was the F-101A powered by two 64.5 kN (14,500 lb st, with afterburning) Pratt & Whitney J57-P-13 turbojet engines. The first F-101A flew on 29 September 1954, exceeding Mach 1. Deliveries began in May 1957. Intended originally as a long-range escort fighter for Strategic Air Command, it was no longer needed in this role when the B-36 bomber was superseded by the B-52 Stratofortress. Accordingly the F-101A was adapted for multi-purpose interceptor/fighter-bomber duties and supplied to Tactical Air Command. Armament comprised four 20 mm M-39E cannon, plus three Hughes GAR-1 Falcon missiles and 12 rockets.

The RF-101A was the long-range photographic-reconnaissance version of the F-101A, while the F-101B was powered by two 66.2 kN (14,880 lb st, with afterburning) J57-P-55 engines as a two-seat long-range interceptor for USAF Air Defense Command and the RCAF – the latter receiving the first of 66 on 24 July 1961. Armament comprised two Genie unguided air-to-air nuclear missiles and three Falcon missiles or bombs.

The F-101C was similar to the F-101A but was strengthened for low-level fighter-bomber operations. A pylon and crutch for atomic weapons was fitted under the fuselage between two 1,705 litre (450 US gallon) external fuel tanks. The 20 mm cannon armament was retained. Deliveries were made to USAF Tactical Air Command.

The final version built as such was the RF-101C, a long-range photographic version of the F-101C. A few were subsequently acquired by the Chinese Nationalist Air Force. Production of the Voodoo ended in March 1961 with the delivery of the last F-101B. Of the total of 807 Voodoos built, 327 were of the F/RF-101A/C single-seat series. The designation RF-101G and RF-101H refer to uprated RF-101A and RF-101C versions.

The Canadian Armed Forces still operate the CF-101B and CF-101F, the latter a dual-control trainer similar to the USAF's TF-101B; while the RF-101C, F-101B/TF-101B continue to serve in the USA.

Data (F-101B): *Engines* as above *Wing span* 12.09 m (39 ft 8 in) *Length* 20.55 m (67 ft 5 in)

McDonnell CF-101B Voodoo.

McDonnell RF-101A Voodoo.

Max T-O weight 21,090 kg (46,500 lb) *Max level speed* 1,963 km/h (1,220 mph) *Range* 2,495 km (1,550 miles)

McDonnell FH-1 Phantom (USA) The McDonnell Aircraft Corporation was incorporated on 6 July 1939 and in September 1941 received its first contract for an aircraft of its own design, covering the experimental XP-67 for the USAAF. In January 1943 the company received its first Navy contract to design and build the XFD-1 Phantom carrier-based fighter.

Two XFD-1 prototypes were built, the first of which flew on 26 January 1945. In March 1945 McDonnell received an order for the redesignated FH-1 Phantom, the company's first production contract for an aircraft of its own design. Sixty FH-1s were eventually produced (see **Chronology** 21 July 1946).

Data: *Engines* two 7.1 kN (1,600 lb st) Westinghouse J30-WE-20 turbojets *Wing span* 12.42 m (40 ft 9 in) *Length* 11.82 m (38 ft 9 in) *Max T-O weight* 5,164 kg (12,035 lb) *Max level speed* 810 km/h (505 mph) *Combat range* 1,105 km (690 miles) *Armament* four forward-firing 0.50 in machine-guns. Eight zero-length rocket launchers could be fitted under the wings

McDonnell FH-1 Phantoms.

McDonnell

McDonnell Douglas A-4E
Skyhawk carrying a
tanker pack.

McDonnell XF-85 Goblin (USA) Small single-seat jet-propelled parasite interceptor fighter designed to be carried in the forward bomb bay of a B-36 bomber and to be launched and picked up by a release and hook-on 'trapeze' technique. It was first flown on 23 August 1948, but remained an experimental type only.

McDonnell XF-85 Goblin.

McDonnell Douglas A-4M
Skyhawk IIs.

McDonnell XF-88B.

McDonnell XF-88B (USA) Designed for research into supersonic propeller design, the XF-88B flew for the first time on 14 April 1953. Power was provided by two Westinghouse J34 turbojets and a nose-mounted Allison XT38 turboprop engine.

McDonnell XV-1.

McDonnell XV-1 (USA) Experimental convertiplane powered by a Continental R-975-19 piston engine and McDonnell rotor-tip pressure jets. The first transition from vertical to horizontal flight was made on 29 April 1955.

McDonnell Douglas A-4 Skyhawk (USA) Designed to provide the US Navy and Marine Corps with a simple low-cost lightweight attack and ground support aircraft, the Skyhawk was based on experience gained during the Korean

McDonnell Douglas A-4S
Skyhawk.

War. Since the initial requirement called for operation by the US Navy, special design consideration was given to flight characteristics and size for aircraft carrier operations.

Construction of the XA4D-1 prototype began in September 1953 and the first flight took place on 22 June 1954. Power was provided by a 32 kN (7,200 lb st) Wright J65-W-2 turbojet engine. A total of 1,845 examples of the early A-4A to E versions was built. By the end of production in 1979, 2,405 Skyhawk attack aircraft and 555 trainers had been built. The type currently serves also with the air forces of Argentina, Australia, Israel, Kuwait, New Zealand and Singapore.

Current versions of the Skyhawk are the A-4F single-seat attack bomber powered by a 41.37 kN (9,300 lb st) Pratt & Whitney J52-P-8A engine and with improved take-off performance and improved electronics in a dorsal hump; A-4G, a version of the A-4F for Australia; A-4H, an Israeli version with Rafael MAHAT lightweight analogue weapons-delivery system; A-4K, a slightly modified version of the A-4F for New Zealand; A-4KU, similar to the A-4M for Kuwait; TA-4F/G/H/K/KU, tandem two-seat trainer versions for the US Navy, Royal Australian Navy, Israel, New Zealand and Kuwait respectively; TA-4J, a simplified version of the TA-4F for the US Navy with a J52-P-6 or P-8A engine and equipment deletions; A-4L, a modified A-4C with an uprated engine, bombing computing system and electronics relocated in a fairing hump aft of the cockpit as on the A-4F; A-4M Skyhawk II, an improved A-4F with a

50 kN (11,200 lb st) J52-P-408 engine and many other improvements; A-4N Skyhawk II, the export version of the A-4M; A-4P/A-4Q, revised A-4Bs for the Argentinian Air Force and Navy; A-4S, revised A-4B for Singapore; TA-4S two-seat trainer version of the A-4S with stepped cockpits; A-4Y, an uprated A-4M for the USMC with a new head-up display, redesigned cockpit and Hughes Angle Rate Bombing System; and the OA-4M, a new forward air control version for the USMC, converted from the TA-4F.

Data (A-4M Skyhawk II): *Engine* as above *Wing span* 8.38 m (27 ft 6 in) *Length* (excl flight-refuelling probe) 12.27 m (40 ft 3¼ in) *Max T-O weight* 11,113 kg (24,500 lb) *Max level speed* (with 1,814 kg; 4,000 lb of bombs) 1,038 km/h (645 mph) *Max ferry range* 3,225 km (2,000 miles) *Armament* provision for several hundred variations of military load, carried externally on one under-fuselage rack, capacity 1,588 kg (3,500 lb); two inboard underwing racks, capacity of each 1,020 kg (2,250 lb); and two outboard underwing racks, capacity of each 450 kg (1,000 lb). Weapons that can be deployed include nuclear or HE bombs, air-to-surface and air-to-air rockets, Sidewinder infra-red missiles, Bullpup air-to-surface missiles, ground-attack gun pods, torpedoes, countermeasures equipment, etc. Two 20 mm Mk 12 cannon in wing roots standard. DEFA 30 mm cannon available as optional on international versions

McDonnell Douglas AV-8B Advanced Harrier (USA) After it had been found that there was insufficient common ground on an Advanced Harrier to suit both the British and US governments, McDonnell Douglas took over development to meet the requirements of the US Navy and Marine Corps. Essentially the objective of the Advanced Harrier programme is to evolve a version which would virtually double the aircraft's weapon payload/combat radius without too much of a departure from the existing Harrier airframe.

The USMC has stated a requirement for 336

Advanced Harriers. Initially McDonnell Douglas and the USMC modified two AV-8As as prototype YAV-8Bs. The first flew on 9 November 1978. The first full-scale development aircraft is scheduled to fly in mid-1981.

McDonnell Douglas DC-8 (USA) The second type of American jet transport to be built, the prototype DC-8 flew for the first time on 30 May 1958. Its configuration was the same as the Boeing 707's, but the wing was swept back only 30° at quarter chord.

The first version was the Series 10 basic domestic aircraft with four pod-mounted 57.83 kN (13,000 lb st) Pratt & Whitney JT3C-6 turbojets and maximum seating for 176 passengers. The DC-8-10 entered service with Delta Air Lines and United Air Lines on 18 September 1959.

The DC-8-10 was followed by the Series 20 for use from hot/high-altitude airports, with 70.28 kN (15,800 lb st) JT4A engines; the Series 30 intercontinental version with JT4A-9s; the similar Series 40 with 77.85 kN (17,500 lb st) Rolls-Royce Conway R.Co.12 bypass engines; and the Series 50 with Pratt & Whitney JT3D turbofans.

There were numerous versions of each series, including the -50CF convertible passenger/cargo aircraft with reinforced floor and large cargo door, and the -50AF windowless freighter which could carry a 42,161 kg (71,900 lb) payload 4,440 km (2,760 miles). The DC-8 saw worldwide airline service and 294 of the standard versions were built.

The basic aeroplane had been designed with growth potential and its tall undercarriage and upswept rear fuselage allowed for considerable stretch. Taking advantage of this, Douglas built three main versions of stretched aircraft. First was the Model 61 for the longer and busier US domestic routes. This retained the standard wing but 11.23 m (36 ft 10 in) was added to the fuselage, giving a maximum of 259 seats. The -61 flew on 14 March 1966 and entered service with United Air

McDonnell Douglas DC-8-63.

McDonnell Douglas TA-4S Skyhawk.

McDonnell Douglas AV-8B Advanced Harrier.

McDonnell Douglas DC-8-30.

McDonnell Douglas

Lines in February 1967. The -62 for longer range had 1.83 m (6 ft) added to the span but the fuselage was only 2.03 m (6 ft 8 in) longer than the standard DC-8. This version went into service with SAS on 22 May 1967. The -63 combined the long fuselage of the -61 with the bigger wing of the -62 and was designed for transatlantic operation. It first flew on 10 April 1967 and entered service with KLM. Convertible passenger/cargo and all-cargo versions of the Series 60 were produced and 262 DC-8-60s were built, to give a DC-8 total of 556 when production ceased in 1972.

A series of DC-8 four-turbofan transports were announced in the spring of 1979. The Series 71, 72 and 73 are, respectively, re-engined Series 61, 62 and 63 aircraft with CFM56 or Pratt & Whitney JT8D-209 engines. The first customer was United Air Lines which is having 30 DC-8-61s converted to Series 71 standard, with 98.1 kN (22,050 lb st) CFM56 engines. Deliveries will begin in 1981. Data (Super 63): *Engines* four 84.51 kN (18,000 lb st) Pratt & Whitney JT3D-7 turbofans *Wing span* 45.23 m (148 ft 5 in) *Length* 57.1 m (187 ft 5 in) *Max T-O weight* 158,760 kg (350,000 lb) *Cruising speed* 965 km/h (600 mph) *Range* 8,820 km (5,480 miles)

McDonnell Douglas DC-9 (USA) By far the most successful of all the twin-jet transports, the DC-9 was announced by Douglas in April 1963 as its second commercial jet airliner. The first order was placed by Delta Air Lines in May of that year.

The basic DC-9-10 first flew on 25 February 1965. Powered by Pratt & Whitney JT8D turbofans, it could accommodate a maximum of 90 passengers. It entered service on 8 December 1965. To ensure good low-speed handling, wing sweep was kept to 24° at quarter chord. The -10 series was followed by the -30 with 1.2 m (4 ft) increase in span, 4.57 m (15 ft) increase in length and seating for up to 115. It entered service with Eastern Air Lines on 1 February 1967 and soon proved the most popular version.

Two special versions were designed for SAS:

the -40 with an extra 1.82 m (6 ft) added to the fuselage and seats for up to 125 passengers; and the short-field -20 which combined the -10 fuselage and -30 wings and had 90 seats. The -40 entered service in March 1968 and the -20 in January 1969. These were followed by the -50 which was 8.89 m (29 ft 2 in) longer than the basic DC-9 and could carry up to 139 passengers. The -50 first flew on 17 December 1974 and entered service with Swissair on 24 August 1975.

The first DC-9 had been powered by 53.38 kN (12,000 lb st) engines and had a maximum take-off weight of 35,244 kg (77,700 lb), but the -50 had 71.17 kN (16,000 lb st) engines and a maximum weight of 54,885 kg (121,000 lb).

Cargo and mixed-configuration models were produced. Some military versions were built as the C-9A Nightingale aeromedical evacuation type, the C-9B Skytrain II logistic transport and the VC-9C VIP transport. By the spring of 1979 more than 1,000 DC-9s had been ordered, by which time the 900th had been delivered. Before the end of 1978 DC-9s had flown more than 17 million hours, with 118 aircraft each having exceeded 30,000 hours.

Due to enter service in 1980 is the DC-9-80 with 82.3 kN (18,500 lb st) JT8D-209 turbofans, a further increase in length, up to 172 seats and a maximum weight of 63,503 kg (140,000 lb). A Super 80SF short-field version is also under consideration, based on the DC-9-40.

Data (DC-9-30): *Engines* initially two 62.3 kN (14,000 lb st) Pratt & Whitney JT8D-7 turbofans; JT8D-9, JT8D-11, JT8D-15 and JT8D-17 are options *Wing span* 28.47 m (93 ft 5 in) *Length* 36.37 m (119 ft 3½ in) *Max T-O weight* 54,885 kg (121,000 lb) *Max cruising speed* 907 km/h (564 mph) *Range* 2,148 km (1,335 miles)

McDonnell Douglas DC-10 (USA) The DC-10 was the second of the wide-bodied transports and the first with three engines. Its final configuration was largely governed by American Airlines' requirement for a 250-passenger aeroplane capable of operating non-stop between Chicago and the US West Coast and which could use LaGuardia's runways and have New York–Chicago capability with full payload.

Powered by three 178 kN (40,000 lb st) General Electric CF6-6 turbofans (one mounted at the base of the fin), the DC-10 made its first flight on 29 August 1970. It went into service with Ameri-

McDonnell Douglas
DC-10-30CF.

can Airlines on the Los Angeles–Chicago route on 5 August 1971. Basic layout is for 270 passengers. The Series 15 is basically similar, but with 206.8 kN (46,500 lb st) General Electric CF6-45B2 engines. Four were ordered by Aeromexico and Mexicana in the summer of 1979.

Developed from the DC-10-10 was the -30 long-range intercontinental model with 218 kN (49,000 lb st) CF6-50A, 227 kN (51,000 lb st) -50C or -50H engines or 233.5 kN (52,500 lb st) -50C1 engines. The span of this model was increased by 3.05 m (10 ft) and an additional twin-wheel undercarriage unit was added because of the increased weight. This version went into service with Swissair on the North Atlantic on 15 December 1972.

Similar to the -30 is the -40 (originally designated -20) which was built for Northwest Airlines. This is powered by 220 kN (49,400 lb st) Pratt & Whitney JT9D-20s or 236 kN (53,000 lb st) JT9D-59A turbofans. The -40 entered service on 16 December 1972.

CF (convertible cargo/passenger) and F (freighter) models have been produced with reinforced floors and large cargo doors. The KC-10A tanker-cargo development has been ordered by the USAF.

There have been a number of studies for development of the DC-10, including a twin-engined version, but the most likely addition to the family is a stretched aeroplane. By September 1979 McDonnell Douglas had received firm orders for 346 DC-10s, by which time the total DC-10 fleet had carried 233 million passengers. Data (DC-10-30): *Engines* as above *Wing span* 50.41 m (165 ft 4½ in) *Length* 55.5 m (182 ft 1 in) *Max T-O weight* 259,450 kg (572,000 lb) *Max cruising speed* 908 km/h (564 mph) *Range* 7,413 km (4,606 miles)

McDonnell Douglas F-4 Phantom II (USA) Generally judged the leading all-round combat aircraft of the entire 1960s, this large and extremely capable aircraft was developed as a private venture by McDonnell Aircraft in 1954–57 – at first despite official disinterest by the US Navy. It passed through two major phases,

McDonnell Douglas F-4B
Phantom II.

including the AH-1 multi-role attack aircraft, before finally being ordered as the F4H-1 all-weather fighter. The prototype flew on 27 May 1958. It soon demonstrated unprecedented performance on the power of its two General Electric J79 afterburning turbojets which were installed in fully variable ducts with both inlet and nozzle areas and profiles infinitely adjustable for Mach 2-plus speeds.

The first production version was the F-4A (under the 1962 designation system) with tandem seats for pilot and radar-intercept officer and a broad fuselage carrying four Sparrow air-to-air missiles recessed into the underside. The type was carrier-equipped and the thin but large wing had blown flaps and blown drooped leading edges. Volume production began with the F-4B with raised cockpits and canopy and a much larger nose to house the Westinghouse APQ-72 radar. Eventually this variant – which with the A set more world records for speed, climb and height than any other aircraft in history – gave way to the F-4J with AN/AWG-10 pulse-Doppler fire-control system, more powerful engines (J79-GE-10 rated at 79.6 kN; 17,900 lb st), slatted tail and drooping ailerons. The Navy/Marine models include the S which is a modified F-4J with structural strengthening to increase operational life and other changes.

In March 1962 the USAF decided that the F-4 had such unparalleled qualities that it should be adopted for 16 of the 23 wings then in Tactical Air Command. The first USAF model was the 'minimum change' F-4C with inflight-refuelling-boom receptacle instead of the Navy probe, rear cockpit configured for a second rated pilot, larger wheels and high-capacity brakes, and different inertial-navigation and weapon-delivery avionics. Next came the completely redesigned RF-4C multi-sensor reconnaissance aircraft packed with radars, cameras and other sensors, ECM (electronic countermeasures) and special communications, but without armament. The Marines bought the RF-4B.

McDonnell Douglas
DC-10-40.

Guided under radar control by a B-66 Destroyer (bottom), four McDonnell Douglas F-4B Phantom IIs attack targets in Vietnam.

McDonnell Douglas F-4K Phantom II prototype.

McDonnell Douglas F-4G Advanced Wild Weasel.

In 1964, when the USAF had received over 1,000 F-4s, permission was granted for a version tailored to the USAF's needs, and this quickly matured as the F-4D. It had numerous improvements – especially to mission avionics – and the radar was the APQ-109. In most D models the prominent secondary fairing under the nose for the AAA-4 infra-red detector is absent. Large numbers of Cs and Ds flew in SE Asia in 1966–73, suffering many stall/spin losses caused by harsh manoeuvres with heavy ordnance load (never considered when the 'fighter' was designed). The answer was a completely new wing, but before this could be introduced production had switched to the F-4E. This had extra power (J79-GE-17 of -10 rating), extra rear-fuselage tank, slotted tailplane, zero-zero seats and many other changes – as well as a completely new solid-state AN/APQ-120 radar with smaller flat dish in a more pointed nose. A last-minute modification was to fit the long-awaited internal gun, a 20 mm M61 being added under the nose, fed by a 640-round drum immediately to the rear.

From June 1972, when several hundred E models had been delivered, the new wing came into production. It has since been fitted as a rebuild to large numbers of USAF, Navy and Marines aircraft. The main change is to delete the droops and blowing system, add thicker skins and fatigue straps on the main spar, and fit a new leading edge with large hydraulic slats which extend automatically in violent manoeuvres or at low airspeeds. The folding outer wings are also new. Not only is safety improved but combat manoeuvrability is considerably enhanced. No new USAF version emerged, but all variants have been greatly updated with defensive avionics, target-acquisition and weapon-aiming systems and additional sensors and advanced weapons.

Among many export versions are the Luftwaffe's RF-4E multi-sensor reconnaissance version of the E and F-4F simplified fighter; the Royal Navy's Phantom FG.1 with Rolls-Royce Spey turbofans of 91.25 kN (20,515 lb st, with afterburning) and many other changes; the derived RAF Phantom FGR.2 (both British versions carry Sky Flash instead of Sparrow); and the Japanese-assembled F-4EJ. The F-4G Advanced Wild Weasel is an ECM platform carrying the APR-38 sensing and jamming system with a large fin-top aerial array and provision for Shrike, Standard ARM or HARM anti-radar missiles.

Production of the Phantom ended with the 5,057th US-built aircraft in mid-1979. McDonnell Douglas attempted to prolong production with the proposed F-4T air-superiority version without ground-attack capability.

Data (F-4E): *Engines* two 79.6 kN (17,900 lb st) General Electric J79-GE-17 turbojets *Wing span* 11.77 m (38 ft 7½ in) *Length* 19.2 m (63 ft 0 in) *Max T-O weight* 28,030 kg (61,795 lb) *Max level speed* (clean, high altitude) 2,414 km/h (1,500 mph) *Combat radius* 795–1,266 km (494–786 miles)

McDonnell Douglas F-15 Eagle (USA) In 1969 it was announced that McDonnell Douglas had been selected as prime airframe contractor of a new air-superiority fighter for the USAF. The contract called for the design and manufacture of 20 aircraft for development testing, these to comprise 18 single-seat F-15As and two TF-15A two-seat trainers, with production scheduled at a rate of one aircraft every other month.

First flight of the F-15A was made on 27 July 1972 and the first flight of a two-seat TF-15A trainer (designated subsequently F-15B) on 7 July 1973. Eagles delivered from mid-1979 are to F-15C and F-15D standard which provides for an additional 907 kg (2,000 lb) of internal fuel and the ability to carry FAST Packs (Fuel And Sensor Tactical Packs) which contain extra fuel and can accommodate avionics. The first F-15C flew on 26

McDonnell Douglas F-15A
Eagle.

minated and instead versions of the General Dynamics YF-16 and Northrop YF-17 light-weight fighter prototypes were investigated. As a result of this review McDonnell Douglas teamed with Northrop to propose a derivative of the YF-17 to meet the Navy's requirement, with McDonnell Douglas as the prime contractor. Identified as the Navy Air Combat Fighter (NACF), this received the designation F-18 Hornet when selected for further development.

In 1976 it was announced that full-scale development had been initiated by the US Navy.

McDonnell Douglas F-15A Eagle.

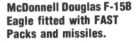

McDonnell Douglas F-15B Eagle fitted with FAST Packs and missiles.

February 1979. By 1 July 1979 a total of 444 Eagles had been delivered. It is planned to procure 749 for the USAF by 1983, including the 20 R & D models. Thirty-five were ordered under an initial contract from the Israeli Air Force and 60 by Saudi Arabia. The JASDF plans to purchase 100 F-15Js, all except eight of which will be licence-built in Japan with Mitsubishi as the prime contractor.

Designed specifically as an air-superiority fighter, the F-15A Eagle has proved equally suitable for air-to-ground missions without degradation of its primary role. It is able to carry a variety of air-to-air and air-to-ground weapons.
Data (F-15A): *Engines* two 111.2 kN (25,000 lb st) Pratt & Whitney F100-PW-100 turbofans *Wing span* 13.05 m (42 ft 9¾ in) *Length* 19.43 m (63 ft 9 in) *Max T-O weight* 25,401 kg (56,000 lb) *Max level speed* more than Mach 2.5 *Ferry range* more than 4,631 km (2,878 miles) *Armament* provision for carriage and launch of a variety of air-to-air weapons over short and medium ranges, including four AIM-9L Sidewinders, four AIM-7F Sparrows and a 20 mm M61A-1 six-barrel gun. Five weapon stations allow for the carriage of up to 7,257 kg (16,000 lb) of bombs, rockets or additional ECM equipment

McDonnell Douglas F/A-18 Hornet (USA) In 1974 the US Department of Defense accepted a proposal from the US Navy to study a low-cost lightweight multi-mission single-seat carrier-based fighter, then identified as the VFAX. In August of that year the VFAX concept was ter-

McDonnell Douglas Hornet prototype.

The first Hornet made its maiden flight on 18 November 1978; the second flew on 12 March 1979 and five aircraft had flown by mid-year. The first batch of nine production Hornets was authorised in Fiscal Year 1979. The F-18 is due to become operational in 1982.

A total of 1,377 Hornets (including the 11 development aircraft) are planned for construction by the end of the 1980s, as the Hornet is required to replace both USN and US Marine Corps F-4 Phantoms for primary missions of fighter escort and interdiction. About 7% of those built will be two-seat trainers, and the attack version of the Hornet will replace the Navy's A-7 Corsair II aircraft in the mid-1980s, under the designation A-18. This is identical to the F-18 except that FLIR and a laser tracker – which are being developed as part of the Hornet programme – will replace fuselage-mounted Sparrows for attack missions.
Data: *Engines* two 71.2 kN (16,000 lb st) General Electric F404-GE-400 low-bypass turbofans *Wing span* 11.43 m (37 ft 6 in) *Length* 17.07 m (56 ft 0 in) *Max T-O weight* 21,319 kg (47,000 lb) *Max level speed* more than Mach 1.8 *Combat radius* 1,019 km (633 miles) *Armament* nine external weapon stations with a combined capacity of 8,165 kg (18,000 lb) of mixed ordnance. These comprise two wingtip stations for AIM-9 Sidewinder air-to-air missiles; two outboard wing stations for an assortment of air-to-ground or air-

First McDonnell Douglas F-15C Eagle.

McDonnell Douglas

to-air weapons, including AIM-7 Sparrows; two inboard wing stations for external fuel tanks or air-to-ground weapons; two nacelle fuselage stations for Sparrows or Martin Marietta sensor pods; and a centreline fuselage station for external fuel or weapons. An M61 20 mm six-barrel gun is mounted in the nose

McDonnell Douglas YC-15 (USA) Two prototypes of the YC-15 advanced military STOL transport were built as contenders for the USAF's AMST prototype fly-off programme – to compete for orders against the Boeing YC-14. The programme was terminated for economic reasons in 1978.

McKinnon Goose and Turbo-Goose (USA) see **Grumman Goose**

McKinnon Super Widgeon (USA) see **Grumman Widgeon**

MDG Midgy-Club (France) Two-seat light biplane of the late 1940s powered by a 48.4 kW (65 hp) Continental A65 engine.

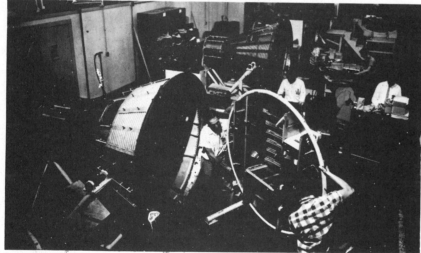

Mercury capsule (USA) Following a design competition for which 12 companies submitted proposals, McDonnell was awarded a NASA contract on 13 February 1959 to design and develop the capsule which was to be used in the Project Mercury manned spacecraft programme.

The original order covered the manufacture of 12 capsules, delivery beginning in the summer of 1960. Subsequent contracts increased the order to 20. Some were used in the test of the vehicle and its booster system. Others were used for the suborbital piloted flights down the Atlantic missile range which preceded the full orbital flights achieved in 1962 (see **Chronology** 20 February 1962 onwards).

The capsule was 2.74 m (9 ft) long and meas-

ured 1.89 m (6 ft 2½ in) in diameter. The main cabin section was constructed of inner and outer nickel-alloy shells, seam-welded together. The blunt curved end was the leading face during orbital flight and consisted of a single piece of beryllium which acted as a heat sink to protect the capsule from extreme thermal conditions during re-entry. It was coated in layers of heat-resistant plastics substance which were burned away to reduce structural heating by the ablative technique. The pilot sat reclined on a replaceable couch, contoured to his individual shape, with his back against the curved face.

Meridionali/Agusta EMA 124 (Italy) Three-seat light helicopter of 1970 derived from the Bell Model 47.

Messerschmitt Bf 108 Taifun (Germany) Four-seat cabin monoplane designed originally as the M 37 by the Bayerische Flugzeugwerke company (which became Messerschmitt in 1935) for the 1934 Challenge de Tourisme Internationale. Production as the Bf 108 Taifun began in 1934.

Operated by the Luftwaffe during World War II as a communications and personnel transport. Power was provided by a 179 kW (240 hp) Argus As.10C (Bf 108B version).

Messerschmitt Bf 109 (Germany) It would take rather more than a Solomon to judge which was the best of the fighter aircraft used by the combatant nations during World War II. But as it is virtually impossible to arrive at a fair basis of comparison – having regard to a number of variables – it is safe to say that the Bf 109 (designed by Willy Messerschmitt) was not only one of the great fighter aircraft of the war, but almost certainly the most famous of all German aircraft ever built. If numbers constructed was the criterion, it would have been in first or second place, for it has been estimated that about 35,000 were built, which is not far short of the total production figure estimated for Russia's Ilyushin Il-2 Shturmovik.

Design of the Bf 109 was initiated by Bayerische Flugzeugwerke in late 1933, following issue by the Reichsluftfahrtministerium (RLM) of a specification for a monoplane fighter to replace the Arado Ar 68 and Heinkel He 51 in Luftwaffe service. The need was not then urgent, but the RLM believed that by competitive evaluation and with reasonable time available for development, they would have a worthwhile fighter when the moment came for it to enter operational service. Submissions were made by Arado, Bayerische Flugzeugwerke, Focke-Wulf and Heinkel: those of the second and last companies were selected for construction and evaluation, with each initially to build ten examples. Heinkel's He 112 was the first to fly (in the summer of 1935) but it was the Bf 109 (first flown in mid-September 1935) that was to be built in very large numbers. Strangely both of these prototypes made their first flight under the power of a Rolls-Royce Kestrel in-line engine, as the Junkers Jumo 210 in-line engine – around which both had been designed – was not available in time.

First production version to enter service with the Luftwaffe was the Bf 109B-1 powered by a 473.2 kW (635 hp) Jumo 210D engine, followed by the 109B-2 with a 477 kW (640 hp) Jumo 210E and later with a 499 kW (670 hp) Jumo 210G. A single-seat fighter of all-metal construction, the Bf 109 was a cantilever low-wing monoplane, the wing having automatic leading-edge slots, large slotted trailing-edge flaps, and ailerons which drooped when the flaps were right down. The main landing-gear units were retractable but most versions had a non-retractable tailwheel. The tail unit was conventional, but the tailplane was braced by struts until a tailplane of cantilever structure was introduced with the Bf 109F.

Bf 109B-2s and variants of the Bf 109C were flown by the Condor Legion in the Spanish Civil War. The Daimler-Benz DB 600 engine was introduced in the Bf 109D version: more than 200 of these being in service with the Luftwaffe at the outbreak of war. It was followed into service by the Bf 109E with 820 kW (1,100 hp) DB 601A engine. In addition to production for the Luftwaffe, some 300 examples of this type were exported. The Bf 109E was the principal version

Messerschmitt Bf 108 Taifun.

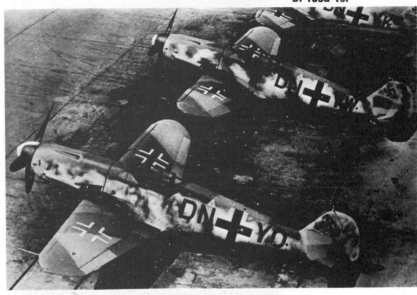

Messerschmitt Bf 109G-1s.

Messerschmitt Bf 109E-4/N Trop.

used in the Battle of Britain and was followed by the Bf 109F with an 894.2 kW (1,200 hp) DB 601N or 969 kW (1,300 hp) DB 601E engine. Considered to represent the peak of development of this superb aeroplane, the Bf 109F had much cleaner aerodynamic lines, introducing the unbraced tailplane and retractable tailwheel.

Most extensively built version was the Bf 109G which was inferior in performance to the version which had preceded it, although introducing a more powerful Daimler-Benz engine. Despite the effects of strategic bombing by the Allies, Bf 109Gs were still being produced in very large numbers right up to the end of hostilities in Europe. Last versions to see limited use were the increased-span Bf 109H and a refined version of the Bf 109G, designated Bf 109K. Production of the Bf 109 continued in Czechoslovakia and Spain during early post-war years, and some Czech-built S-99s were used in a training role until 1957 (a full description of the Bf 109 appears in the 1945–46 *Jane's*).

Messerschmitt

Data (Bf 109G-6): *Engine* one 1,099–1,490.4 kW (1,475–2,000 hp) Daimler-Benz DB 605 *Wing span* 9.92 m (32 ft 6½ in) *Length* 8.84 m (29 ft 0½ in) *Max T-O weight* 3,150–3,678 kg (6,945–8,109 lb) *Max level speed* 621 km/h (386 mph) *Normal range* 563 km (350 miles) *Armament* one 30 mm MK 108 or 20 mm MG 151 cannon, two 13 mm MG 131 machine-guns, and two 20 mm MG 151 cannon (optional). One 250 kg, four 75 kg or 50 kg, or 96 2 kg bombs could be carried

Messerschmitt Bf 110C-5.

Messerschmitt Bf 110E-2/N.

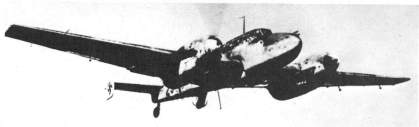

Messerschmitt Bf 110 (Germany) Second of the important fighters designed by Willy Messerschmitt, the Bf 110 originated from a Reichsluftfahrtministerium requirement of 1934 for a long-range escort fighter or heavily armed Zerstörer (destroyer). Of cantilever low-wing monoplane configuration, this two-seat fighter had an oval-section fuselage, long glazed canopy, high-mounted tailplane with endplate fins and rudders, retractable landing gear, and power plant comprising two Daimler-Benz DB 600 in-line engines. When the prototype flew for the first time on 12 May 1936, it was able to demonstrate a most satisfactory turn of speed. However further testing showed that the Bf 110 might face problems in combat, for despite its high speed, its manoeuvrability left much to be desired.

Pre-production Bf 110A-0s were powered by two 454.5 kW (610 hp) Junkers Jumo 210B engines, bringing a deterioration in performance.

Messerschmitt Bf 110G-4.

Early production Bf 110Bs had similar engines of increased power. Only a small number of this version were built before 820 kW (1,100 hp) DB 601A engines became available and these powered a much-improved Bf 110C. Unfortunately for the Luftwaffe, it had not been possible to evaluate the Bf 110 in the Spanish Civil War, with the result that when Bf 110Cs escorted the bomber units that devastated Poland at the beginning of World War II, it was believed that they had acquired a valuable new weapon. Perhaps this belief was strengthened when, just before Christmas 1939, Bf 109s and 110s destroyed 12 of a force of 22 Wellingtons which were making a reconnaissance of Heligoland Bight.

Bf 110Cs and longer-range Bf 110Ds were, therefore, launched confidently against Britain in the summer of 1940. But even before the Battle of Britain had reached a peak, it was clear that the Bf 110 was no match for the RAF's highly manoeuvrable single-seat fighters. Indeed it was so vulnerable that this 'escort' fighter was unable to operate in British airspace by daylight unless it was itself escorted.

Despite its failure in this role, the Bf 110 was to prove a most valuable and successful night fighter until more advanced aircraft entered the scene in the latter stages of the war. Bf 110Es with DB 601N engines and Bf 110Fs with DB 601E engines formed the nucleus of such operations. Considerable success was gained by these aircraft in conjunction with Würzburg radar, the pilots being directed by ground controllers into an interception position.

The three-seat night-fighter Bf 110F was followed into production by a series of Bf 110Gs with DB 605B engines, the early versions serving as fighter bombers. However the four-seat Bf 110G-4a, -4b, -4c, and -4d variants were provided with differing airborne radar installations for operation as night fighters. Final production version was the Bf 110H, generally similar to the Bf 110G but equipped with heavier armament. It is worth recording a significant factor in favour of the Bf 110, so often dismissed as a complete failure. During early 1944 almost 60% of the entire German night-fighter force was composed of variants of the Bf 110. A total of about 6,000 of these aircraft was built before production ended.

Data (Bf 110G-4c): *Engines* two 1,099 kW (1,475 hp) Daimler-Benz DB 605B-1s *Wing span* 16.26 m (53 ft 4 in) *Length* 13.0 m (42 ft 10 in) *Max T-O weight* 10,024 kg (22,100 lb) *Max level speed* 550 km/h (342 mph) *Normal range* 900 km (559 miles) *Armament* two 30 mm MK 108 cannon, two 20 mm MG 151 cannon and two 7.9 mm MG 81 machine-guns (Bf 110G-4/R3), or two 20 mm MG 151 cannon, four 7.9 mm MG 17 and two MG 81 machine-guns

Messerschmitt M.18, M.20, M.24 and M.28
(Germany) Five- or seven-passenger, ten-passenger, eight- or ten-passenger, and high-speed mail-carrying commercial aircraft respectively, produced between 1926 and 1931 (see **BFW**).

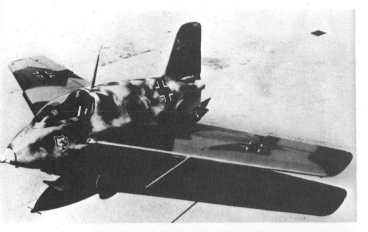

Messerschmitt Me 163 Komet (Comet) (Germany) Few aircraft (if any) can have been as hair-raising to fly as the Messerschmitt Me 163 Komet. The first production examples were delivered to a new fighter wing, JG 400, in May 1944, but it was not until 16 August of that year that these revolutionary aircraft had their first (unsuccessful) brush with an Allied bomber stream. Their development can be said to have originated from work begun in 1933 by Dr Alexander Lippisch at the German Gliding Research Institute (DFS) at Darmstadt, being based on the Lippisch-designed DFS 194. Dr Lippisch and his staff were transferred to Messerschmitt's works at Augsburg in January 1939.

In early 1940 the DFS 194 was equipped with a rocket motor at Peenemünde. After test flights by Heini Dittmar had confirmed speeds of up to 550 km/h (342 mph) on the power of a single 2.94 kN (661 lb st) Walter motor, there was sufficient interest to initiate development. In 1941 the first Me 163 prototype was being tested in gliding flight and shortly after was fitted with a 7.35 kN (1,653 lb st) Walter RII-203 rocket motor. Speeds of up to 915 km/h (569 mph) were achieved (limited by the volume of liquid propellants carried) and to gain some idea of the speed potential, this aircraft was towed to a high altitude before being released. Flown under power, a speed of over 1,000 km/h (620 mph) was attained before the engine had to be throttled back because the aircraft was becoming uncontrollable.

Operational Me 163Bs were powered by the 16.67 kN (3,748 lb st) Walter 109-509A-2 rocket motor. Each had mid-set monoplane wings of wooden construction and the fuselage was a semi-monocoque all-metal structure. Landing gear comprised a tailwheel, jettisonable mainwheel trolley and a central underfuselage skid which was extended for landing.

Produced too late and in only small numbers (about 360 examples), they were in service in the defence of the Reich early in 1945 but had no significant impact upon the constant streams of Allied bombers attacking Germany. In theory their high speed and initial rate of climb of about 3,600 m (11,800 ft)/minute should have made them a potent interceptor, despite the enormous hazards of training pilots and using these rocket-planes operationally. Had they enjoyed a longer period of development before introduction into service in the closing stages of the war, the story might have been very different.

The slightly larger Me 163C development – with aerodynamic refinements, pressurised cockpit and blister-type canopy, and more powerful Walter 109-509C rocket motor – was built only in prototype and pre-production form. It did not enter service, although it was almost ready for delivery to Luftwaffe squadrons at the time of the German surrender. With this version, endurance was increased from eight–ten minutes to twelve minutes; this could be extended by periods of gliding.

**Messerschmitt
Me 163B-1 Komet.**

**The instrument panel of a
Messerschmitt Me 163
Komet.**

Data (Me 163B-1): *Engine* one 16.67 kN (3,748 lb st) Walter 109-509A-2 rocket motor *Wing span* 9.32 m (30 ft 7 in) *Length* 5.69 m (18 ft 8 in) *Max T-O weight* 4,309 kg (9,500 lb) *Max level speed* 960 km/h (596.5 mph) *Range* 80 km (50 miles) *Armament* two 30 mm MK 108 cannon with ammunition carried in two boxes under a detachable fairing in the fuselage. Up to 24 rockets underwing, or four vertically discharged rockets within the wings

Messerschmitt Me 210 and Me 410 Hornisse
(Germany) Almost from the earliest moments of its service trials the Bf 110 had been found to lack one essential characteristic of a fighter – good manoeuvrability. The Me 210 (which originated

**Messerschmitt
Me 209V1, powered by a
Daimler-Benz DB 601ARJ
engine. It set an absolute
world speed record of
755.138 km/h (469.220
mph) on 26 April 1939.**

Messerschmitt Me 210V13.

Messerschmitt Me 262V6.

Messerschmitt Me 262A-2a.

in 1937) was designed as a superior twin-engined multi-purpose aircraft to replace the Bf 110. The outcome was similar to that of several other projects in aviation history: the Bf 110 long outlived the aircraft intended to replace it.

Somewhat similar in appearance to the Bf 110 in original prototype form, when first flown on 2 September 1939 it was found to be so unstable that the twin fin/rudder tail unit (borrowed from its predecessor) was replaced by a more conventional large single fin and rudder. Despite this and other modifications, stability was still very marginal. Although introduced into operational service in Me 210A, B and C versions from early 1941, most were being replaced within two years.

The Me 410 Hornisse was developed in 1942 to replace the Me 210 and was essentially similar to the late-production examples of this latter aircraft. In addition to embodying in its design all the modifications incorporated into the Me 210 – including the new cockpit canopy, lengthened fuselage and wing leading-edge slots – it introduced Daimler-Benz DB 603A engines. Initial tests were carried out with aircraft converted from Me 210As and these were followed by a true Me 410 prototype which flew for the first time at the end of 1942.

Messerschmitt Me 410 Hornisse.

Demonstrating far more attractive characteristics than those of its forerunner, the Me 410 was ordered into production and some 1,100 were built before construction came to an end in September 1944. Versions included the Me 410A-1 high-performance light bomber; A-1/U-2 fighter conversion of the A-1; A-2 destroyer; and A-3 photo-reconnaissance aircraft; similar B-1, B-2 and B-3 versions; B-5 torpedo bomber; and B-6 anti-shipping strike aircraft. A number of variants of the foregoing were built, but several projected versions failed to enter production.
Data (Me 210A-1): *Engines* two 820 kW (1,100 hp) Daimler-Benz DB 601A in-lines *Wing span* 16.4 m (53 ft 9½ in) *Length* 11.2 m (36 ft 9 in) *Max T-O weight* 8,100 kg (17,857 lb) *Max level speed* 620 km/h (385 mph) *Range* 2,400 km (1,491 miles) *Armament* two 20 mm MG 151 cannon and two 7.9 mm MG 17 machine-guns

Messerschmitt Me 262.

Data (Me 410A-1/U-2): *Engines* two 1,304 kW (1,750 hp) Daimler-Benz DB 603A in-lines *Wing span* 16.4 m (53 ft 9½ in) *Length* 12.4 m (40 ft 8¼ in) *Max T-O weight* 10,670 kg (23,523 lb) *Max level speed* 624 km/h (387.5 mph) *Range* 2,330 km (1,448 miles) *Armament* two 7.9 mm MG 17 machine-guns, two MG 131 machine-guns and four 20 mm MG 151 cannon

Messerschmitt Me 262 (Germany) What would have been the outcome of the war in Europe if in 1940 the potential of Messerschmitt's Project 1065 had been appreciated by high authority? If a crash programme had been originated to put this turbojet-powered aircraft into service at a much earlier date, would the Luftwaffe have regained the initiative of the first two years of World War II?

Unfortunately the answers are not clear cut and there is no space here to discuss the pros and cons. It must suffice that the Me 262 (as the P.1065 became designated) was the world's first turbojet-powered aircraft to enter operational service – at Juvincourt, France on 10 July 1944. By then, however, the end of hostilities in Europe was only ten months away: the lack of a real plan for the deployment of these aircraft and the

inadequacy of tactics to gain full benefit of their speed advantage could not be rectified in so short a time – especially under the chaotic conditions existing in Germany and with dwindling supplies of fuel (see **Chronology** 24 August 1944).

Messerschmitt's P.1065 design had originated as early as 1938 when the Reichsluftfahrtministerium had requested the company to design a twin-engined fighter able to utilise the new turbojet engines being developed in Germany. After inspection of the mock-up, three prototypes were ordered on 1 June 1940. But because the engines to power the Me 262 had not been developed sufficiently, the first prototype flew initially with piston engines. It was not until 18 July 1942 that the first flight with all-turbojet power was recorded. (The Heinkel 280, which did not enter production, had flown before the Me 262, on 2 April 1941, so becoming the world's first twin-engined jet.)

Of conventional all-metal stressed-skin construction, the wing had moderate sweepback, long-span ailerons, trailing-edge flaps, and full-span automatic leading-edge slots. The engines were mounted beneath the wing to preclude a complex wing-spar structure and the landing gear was of retractable tailwheel type. The fifth prototype introduced a non-retractable nosewheel unit and the sixth was the first to have a fully retractable tricycle-type landing gear.

First major version was the Me 262A-1a Schwalbe (Swallow) interceptor, armed with four 30 mm MK 108 cannon mounted in the nose. It was powered by two 8.825 kN (1,984 lb st) Junkers Jumo 109-004B-1 eight-stage axial-flow turbojets. A number of variants were built with differing armament. The other major version was the Me 262A-2a Sturmvogel (Stormbird) bomber. This was produced at the insistence of Adolf Hitler – a decision which caused considerable overall production delays. It carried, in addition to the standard MK 108 armament, one 1,000 kg, two 500 kg or two 250 kg bombs. As with the

Messerschmitt Me 323 Gigant.

Schwalbe, there were a number of variants, mainly for armed or unarmed reconnaissance.
Data (Me 262A-1a): *Engines* two 8.825 kN (1,984 lb st) Junkers Jumo 109-004B-1 or 004B-4 turbojets *Wing span* 12.5 m (41 ft 0⅛ in) *Length* 10.61 m (34 ft 9¾ in) *Max T-O weight* 7,045 kg (15,531 lb) *T-O run with two auxiliary rockets* 600 m (1,969 ft) *Max level speed* 868 km/h (539 mph) at 7,000 m (22,975 ft) *Range* 1,050 km (652 miles)

Messerschmitt Me 321/Me 323 Gigant (Germany) Before going to war in 1939 Germany had explored and developed the use of parachute and airborne troops, thus ensuring that man-made barricades (such as the Maginot Line or Albert Canal) or natural barriers (such as the Kithirai Channel) would provide no hindrance to gaining a strong foothold in desirable territory. Early deployment of airborne forces had shown the need for gliders of greater capability than, for example, the DFS 230s used to capture the Belgian fort of Eben-Emael. There were many advantages in using gliders as opposed to free-fall paratroops: the unit was not dispersed and troops did not need often precious moments to disentangle themselves from shroud lines or a billowing parachute.

Consequently Junkers and Messerschmitt competed in 1940 to design and develop a very large transport glider suitable for the delivery of men or materials. Junkers' Ju 322 Mammut (Mammoth) spanned 62.0 m (203 ft 5 in) and would have accommodated more than 100 fully equipped troops, but when tested proved to be unstable and was cancelled by the Reichsluftfahrtministerium. On the other hand Messerschmitt's Me 321 was a most successful design of braced high-wing configuration and with construction of welded steel tube, wood and fabric. The pilot was perched high on the fuselage in a single-seat cockpit, adjacent to the wing's leading edge. Access to the main cabin was via large clamshell doors in the nose or by doors on each side of the rear fuselage. A payload of 22,000 kg (48,502 lb) could be carried.

The Me 321 V1 prototype flew first in March

Messerschmitt Me 262s lined up near the Obertraubling assembly plant, which had been bombed by the USAAF.

Messerschmitt Me 264, designed as a long-range bomber capable of attacking America. Remained a prototype only.

Messerschmitt P.1101, an experimental jet fighter capable of having its wings set at different angles of sweepback. It was never completed but influenced the post-war development of the Bell X-5.

1941 and Me 321A-1 production aircraft entered service in May of that year. The later Me 321B-1 had a crew of three and defensive armament of four 7.9 mm MG 15 machine-guns. Me 321s (some 200 built) were towed usually by a trio of Bf 110Cs or by the unusual five-engined Heinkel He 111Z. Rocket units could be used to assist take-off from rough fields.

The Me 323 was, in effect, a powered version of the Me 321, basically similar except for strengthening and the installation of engines in nacelles of the same type as those designed for the Bloch 175: four in the original prototype and six in subsequent prototype and production aircraft (about 200 built). Versions included the Me 323D, E and F (plus variants), with a variety of engines, defensive armament and fuel capacity. They were no easy machines to fly, often needing rocket or towing assistance to get them airborne. Slow and vulnerable – despite heavy defensive armament – they suffered severe losses when ferrying supplies to the Afrika Korps in the closing stages of the North African campaign.

Data (Me 323E): *Engines* six 849.5 kW (1,140 hp) Gnome-Rhône 14N 48/49 radials *Wing span* 55.0 m (180 ft 5¼ in) *Length* 28.46 m (93 ft 4¼ in) *Max T-O weight* 45,000 kg (99,208 lb) *Cruising speed* 218 km/h (135.5 mph) *Range* 1,100 km (684 miles) *Armament* normal armament provided for five 13 mm MG 131 machine-guns, but this could be increased to seven MG 131s and two 20 mm MG 151 cannon

MFI MFI-10 Vipan.

Meteor FL.55.

Mignet Pou du Ciel.

Meteor FL.53 (Italy) Two-seat trainer and tourer powered by a 44.7 kW (60 hp) CNA D4 or 48.4 kW (65 hp) Continental A65 engine.

Meteor FL.54 (Italy) Three-seat version of the FL.53 powered by a 63.3–67 kW (85–90 hp) Continental engine.

Meteor FL.55 and FL.55B (Italy) Four-seat versions of the FL.54, each powered by a 97-112 kW (130–150 hp) Lycoming engine. Could be adapted for agricultural work. The F.55B was basically similar to the FL.55 but had a combination wheel-ski landing gear for operation in mountainous regions. This version was chosen in 1956 to equip a Swiss mountain rescue organisation, accommodating a stretcher optionally.

Meteor Bis (Italy) Three-seat light cabin monoplane powered by an 82 kW (110 hp) Meteor Alfa 2 engine.

Meteor Super (Italy) Similar to Bis but fitted with a 164 kW (220 hp) Meteor Alfa 4 engine.

Meyers OTW-160 (USA) Two-seat light training biplane powered by a 119 kW (160 hp) Kinner R-56 engine. Delivered to flying schools operating under the CAA War Training scheme during World War II.

Meyers MAC 125 and MAC 145 (USA) Two-seat light cabin monoplanes of the latter 1940s powered by 93 kW (125 hp) or 108 kW (145 hp) Continental engines respectively.

Meyers 200 (USA) The Meyers 200 four-seat cabin monoplane flew for the first time on 8 September 1953. An advanced turbine-powered development of the 200C version is currently produced as the Prop-Jets Interceptor 400.

Meyers 200D (USA) Four-seat cabin monoplane currently produced with a 212.5 kW (285 hp) Continental IO-520 flat-six engine. Maximum level speed is 346 km/h (215 mph).

MFI MFI-9 Junior (Sweden) First flown on 10 October 1958, the Junior was a two-seat light aerobatic monoplane produced by MFI (Malmö) and MBB (see entry).

MFI MFI-10 Vipan (Sweden) Four-seat cabin monoplane of 1961 powered by a 119 kW (160 hp) Lycoming O-320 engine.

Mignet H.M.310 Estafette (Brazil) Designed by Henri Mignet, designer of the 'Pou du Ciel' or 'Flying Flea' of the 1930s, the Estafette was a two-seat light aircraft powered by a 67 kW (90 hp) Continental A90-12F engine. It retained the tandem heavily staggered 'slot' or 'gap' effect wings of his earlier type.

Mignet Pou du Ciel (France) The famous 'Sky Louse' or 'Flying Flea' single-seat light monoplane powered by a 12.7 kW (17 hp) Aubier & Dunne 540 cc engine. Widely built in the 1930s. The wing was hinged to a steel-tube pylon over the nose of the fuselage and was tilted fore-and-aft by cables to give longitudinal control.

Mikoyan-Gurevich MiG-1, MiG-3 and MiG-5 (USSR) The MiG designation was formed from the initials of the designers Artem I. Mikoyan and Mikhail I. Gurevich. The MiG-1 was designed as a single-seat high-altitude fighter and flew for the first time on 5 April 1940 as the I-61 prototype. Power was provided by an 894 kW (1,200 hp) AM-35A engine. Armament comprised one 12.7 mm and two 7.7 mm machine-guns mounted in the nose. This fighter and a longer-range derivative (known as the MiG-3 and incorporating many improvements, including an enclosed cockpit) were operational with the Soviet Air Force at the time of the German invasion (the MiG-1 shown above has a non-standard enclosed cockpit).

In combat the MiGs proved excellent at high altitude, but were far from satisfactory at lower levels and were quickly dropped as production types – some 2,100 being built in total. Captured German documents indicated that armament of the MiG-3 was similar to the MiG-1's, although many carried six special guide-rail-type racks under the wings for 25 kg rocket-propelled fragmentation bombs; but it is known that a large number of aircraft were retrofitted with two more 12.7 mm machine-guns under the wings.

The MiG-5, which did not enter quantity production, was a twin-engined escort fighter.
Data (MiG-3): *Engine* as above *Wing span* 10.3 m (33 ft 9 in) *Length* 8.16 m (26 ft 8¾ in) *Max T-O weight* 3,350 kg (7,385 lb) *Max level speed* 640 km/h (398 mph) *Range* 1,250 km (777 miles)

Mikoyan-Gurevich MiG-9 (USSR) Nothing much was heard of the designers Mikoyan and Gurevich following the MiG-3 until after the end of World War II. However at the 1946 Soviet Aviation Day Display at Tushino Airport, a novel three-seat tail-first light monoplane was demonstrated as the Utka (Duck). But the designers had been hard at work on one of their most important aircraft to date, the MiG-9. This was a single-seat straight-wing fighter originally known as the I-300. It was powered by two 7.83 kN (1,760 lb st) RD-20 turbojet engines mounted in the fuselage and fed with air from a divided intake in the nose. Armament comprised one 37 mm N-37 cannon projecting from the intake and two undernose 23 mm cannon. The first flight was made on 24 April 1946.

The I-300 or MiG-9 represented a completely new aircraft and the designers received a Stalin Prize. Having ironed out the problems, production was initiated and the type was among the first jet-propelled fighters to go into squadron service with the Soviet Air Force. A number were also based in East Germany, although by the early 1950s the type was considered obsolete. The fighter was given the NATO reporting name *Fargo*.
Data: *Engines* as above *Wing span* 10.0 m (32 ft 9¾ in) *Length* 9.75 m (32 ft 0 in) *Max T-O weight* 5,070 kg (11,178 lb) *Max level speed* 910 km/h (565 mph)

Mikoyan-Gurevich MiG-15 (USSR) After the war the Soviet Union suffered from lack of gas-turbine experience and designed its first generation of jet aircraft to use engines of basically German origin. The picture was transformed by the supply from Britain of the latest Rolls-Royce Nene, which immediately went into production at No 45 production factory in Moscow, designated RD-45 after the factory. The design bureau of Mikoyan and Gurevich immediately used the new engine in the I-310 fighter prototype, flown with a Rolls-built Nene 2 on 30 December 1947. It was by far the best of several designs built to a 1946 specification.

After intensive testing the type went into production in early 1948 as the MiG-15 (NATO *Fagot*), well ahead of any other Mach 0.9-plus all-swept aircraft other than the F-86 which was roughly similar in timing. After the first batches the engine switched to the RD-45F rated at 22.26 kN (5,005 lb st). Armament comprised a 37 mm N-37 with 40 rounds and two 23 mm NS-23KM each with 80 rounds, all mounted under the nose. The aircraft was of advanced conception but extremely simple and well-adapted to primitive environments. Internal fuel totalled 1,460 litres (321 Imp gal), augmented by two underwing drop-tanks. There were no avionics other than an HF radio and a homing receiver

MiG

Mikoyan-Gurevich
MiG-15*bis*

1 Bifurcated engine air
    intake
2 Landing light (moved to
    port wing root on later
    production aircraft)
3 Combat camera fairing
4 Accumulator
5 Radio transmitter
6 Radio receiver
7 Armoured-glass
    windscreen
8 Gyro gunsight
9 Starboard electrics
    control panel
10 Ejection seat
11 Aft-sliding canopy (open
    position)
12 VHF blade antenna
13 Wing fence
14 Slipper-type drop-tank
    (247.5 litres/54.4 Imp gal
    capacity)
15 Pitot pressure head
16 Compass unit
17 Starboard navigation
    light
18 Starboard aileron
19 Main fuel tank
20 Rear fuselage
    attachment joint
21 Engine bearers
22 Klimov VK-1 turbojet
23 Control rods
24 Rear fuselage frames
25 Fin mainspar
26 Rudder balance weight
27 Rudder (upper section)
28 Tail navigation light
29 Elevator trim tab
30 Port elevator
31 Single-spar tailplane
32 Jetpipe fairing
33 Airbrake (partly
    extended)
34 Walkway
    (rubber-coated)
35 Split landing flap
36 Trim-operating
    mechanism
37 Aileron-operating rods
38 Trim tab
39 Port aileron
40 Port rear spar
41 Port navigation light
42 Mainspar
43 Rib
44 Attachment for slipper
    tank
45 Inward-retracting main
    undercarriage member
46 Mainspar branch
47 Twin air channel
48 Wing centre-section
49 Fuel tank
50 Canopy jettison knob
51 Control column
52 Radio altimeter
53 Port air duct
54 Gun pack (shown
    cable-lowered for
    servicing)
55 Ammunition tank
56 Twin 23 mm NS-23
    cannon
57 Single 37 mm N-37
    cannon
58 Forward-retracting
    nosewheel
59 Nosewheel doors
60 Blast protection panel

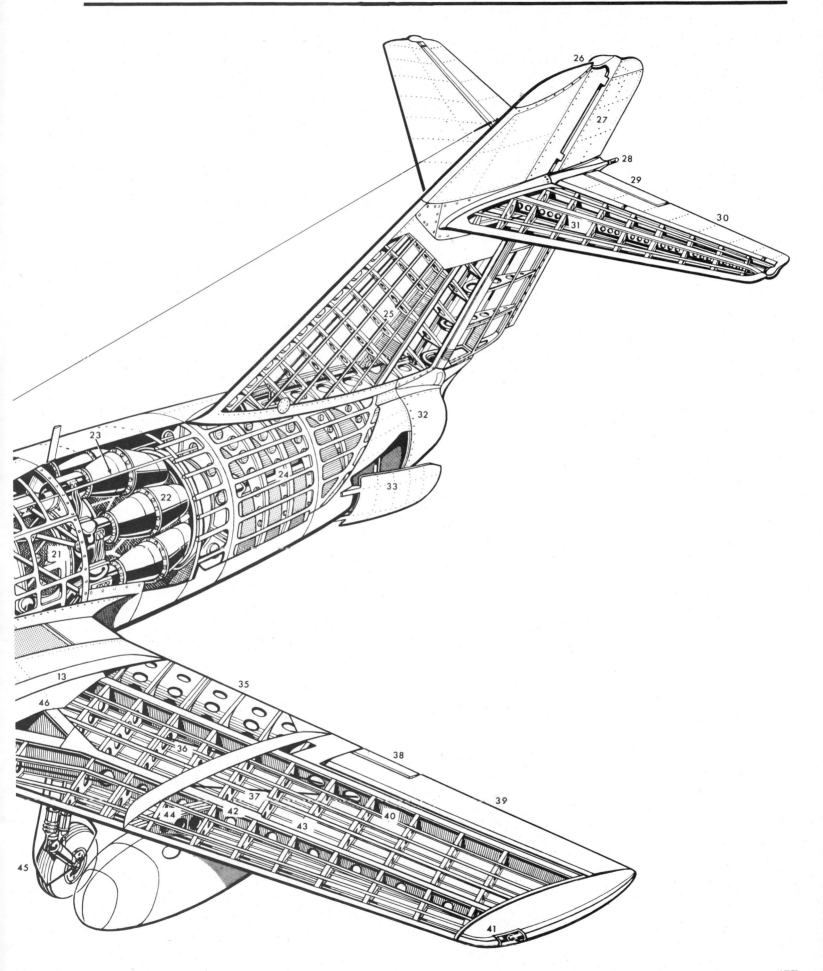

Polish Air Force LIM-1/MiG-15s.

Mikoyan-Gurevich MiG-15UTI.

Mikoyan-Gurevich MiG-17s (MiG-15UTIs in background).

Mikoyan MiG-19 carrying *Alkali* missiles.

and the gunsight was copied from the British GGS Mk 2. Production under licence was begun in Poland as the LIM-1 and in Czechoslovakia as the S-102.

In 1950 the MiG-15*bis* replaced the earlier model, with a 26.48 kN (5,952 lb st) VK-1 engine (a Soviet development of the Nene), reduced structure weight and much augmented avionics. Polish and Czech versions were designated LIM-2 and S-103. Later variants included the MiG-15UTI dual-control tandem trainer (NATO *Midget*); MiG-15P all-weather interceptor with Izumrud radar; MiG-15S*bis* high-altitude model with reduced armament and other changes; and MiG-15*bis*R with a vertical camera as well as full armament.

Early versions entered service in 1948 and large numbers (over 1,000) were supplied to China and North Korea, entering combat in 1951. No Allied fighter could stay with it and even the technically superior F-86 had inferior climb, ceiling and high-altitude turn radius. Many thousands of all versions were built, though basic deficiencies in stability and handling in violent manoeuvres caused production in the Soviet Union to switch by 1953 to the completely redesigned MiG-17. Nevertheless the MiG-15 remained an invaluable aircraft for air forces with little jet experience, being supplied to at least 18. Nearly all these countries still use the UTI trainer.

Data: *Engine* as above *Wing span* 10.08 m (33 ft 0¾ in) *Length* 11.05 m (36 ft 3¼ in) *Max T-O weight* 5,700 kg (12,566 lb) *Max level speed* 1,075 km/h (668 mph) *Range* 1,860 km (1,155 miles)

Mikoyan-Gurevich MiG-17 (USSR) Known to NATO as *Fresco*, the MiG-17 was a development of the MiG-15 which it began to supersede in production in 1953. In addition to Soviet production, it was built in Poland, Czechoslovakia and China, and was supplied to the air forces of many countries. Indeed, today 25 countries other than the Soviet Union still operate the type as a fighter and ground-attack aircraft.

The initial production model was the *Fresco-A* single-seat interceptor powered by a 26.48 kN

(5,952 lb st) VK-1 turbojet and with rear-mounted dive brakes. The *Fresco-B* was similar but had the dive brakes forward near the wing trailing edge. The MiG-17F or *Fresco-C* was the most widely used day-fighter version, powered by an afterburning VK-1A turbojet (33.14 kN; 7,450 lb st) and with underwing fuel tanks. The MiG-17PF or *Fresco-D* was produced as the all-weather version and entered large-scale service; its limited all-weather interceptor capability came from a radar positioned in a central bullet in the air intake. A non-afterburning version of the D was given the reporting name *Fresco-E*.

Data (MiG-17F): *Engine* as above *Wing span* 9.6 m (31 ft 6 in) *Length* 11.36 m (37 ft 3¼ in) *Max T-O weight* 6,069 kg (13,379 lb) *Max level speed* 1,145 km/h (711 mph) *Max range* (external tanks and bombs) 1,400 km (870 miles) *Armament* one 37 mm N-37 and two 23 mm NR-23 cannon

Mikoyan MiG-19/F-6/A-5 (USSR/China) The I-350 prototype of the MiG-19 first flew in September 1953. The initial production day fighter began to enter service with the Soviet air defence force in early 1955, but before long an all-moving tailplane replaced the elevators of early production aircraft. At the same time three 30 mm guns replaced the original armament of a 37 mm and two 23 mm cannon, which had been standard on all MiG jets from the earliest MiG-9; and an attachment was added under each wing for a bomb or an air-to-surface rocket. This new version was designated MiG-19S (for Stabilisator).

With the adoption in 1957 of the Tumansky R-9 axial-flow turbojet as the standard engine, the MiG-19SF was produced. At the same time another version appeared with limited all-weather capability as the MiG-19PF, supporting a small Izumrud radar scanner inside its engine

Max level speed 1,452 km/h (902 mph) Combat radius 685 km (425 miles) Armament three 30 mm NR-30 cannon. Underwing attachments for two air-to-air missiles, two rockets of up to 212 mm calibre, two packs of eight air-to-air rockets, two 250 kg bombs, drop-tanks or other stores

air intake and a ranging unit in the intake lip. The later MiG-19PM differed from the PF in having four first-generation *Alkali* radar-homing missiles instead of guns.

In the Soviet Union the MiG-19 was phased out of production by the end of the 1950s, making way for expanded MiG-21 production. However in 1958 a licence to build the MiG-19 had been agreed with China but, following delivery of knocked-down MiGs for Chinese construction, relations between the two countries deteriorated. Nevertheless the MiG-19 construction went ahead under the Chinese designation F-6 (MiG-19S), the first of which flew in December 1961. F-6s became the standard equipment of the Chinese Air Force of the People's Liberation Army from mid-1962.

Production of the F-6 was stepped up from about 1966 and it is thought that several thousand have been built, including counterparts of the MiG-19PF and SF. China has developed a number of variants of its own design. One is a tactical reconnaissance aircraft, while the TF-6 is a trainer version and the A-5 (formerly referred to as the F-9 and F-6 *bis*) a strike fighter with different appearance because of its pointed nose radome between the semi-circular side air intakes. The span of the A-5 has also been increased to about 10.2 m (33 ft 5 in). Maximum level speed of this version is estimated to be close to Mach 2.

Versions of the MiG-19 and F-6 are currently operational with the air forces of about 12 countries. NATO reporting names for the MiG-19 and A-5 are *Farmer* and *Fantan-A*.
Data (MiG-19SF, built as the F-6): *Engines* two 31.9 kN (7,165 lb st) Klimov RD-9B turbojets *Wing span* 9.0 m (29 ft 6¼ in) *Length* 12.54 m (41 ft 1¾ in) *Max T-O weight* 8,700 kg (19,180 lb)

Mikoyan MiG-21 (USSR) The MiG-21 air-superiority fighter was developed on the basis of experience of air combat in the Korean War and eventually became the most widely used fighter in the world. The E-5 prototype flew for the first time in 1955 and the initial production version (NATO *Fishbed-A*) was built in only limited numbers. Power was provided by a Tumansky R-11 turbojet engine rated at 50 kN (11,240 lb st, with afterburning). Armament comprised two 30 mm NR-30 cannon. Meanwhile the Soviet Union had developed the K-13 (NATO *Atoll*) infra-red homing air-to-air missile and two pylons for two K-13s were fitted to the more powerful MiG-21F. The F became known to NATO as *Fishbed-C* and was a short-range clear-weather fighter (one 30 mm cannon only) powered by a 56.4 kN (12,676 lb st, with afterburning) Tumansky R-11. The large number of variants that followed are listed below for convenience:

MiG-21PF (*Fishbed-D*) Basic model of the second series, produced as a limited all-weather version powered by a 58.4 kN (13,120 lb st, with afterburning) R-11 engine.
Fishbed-E Basically similar to the C but with a broader fin and provision for a GP-9 underbelly pack housing a GSh-23 twin-barrel 23 mm gun. Identified in 1964.
MiG-21FL Export version of the late-model MiG-21PF series with the broader fin and provision for the gun pod. About 200 were initially assembled and later built under licence in India by HAL, with the Indian Air Force designation

Chinese-built F-6 in Pakistan Air Force markings.

Mikoyan MiG-21F *Fishbed-C* of the Indian Air Force.

Mikoyan MiG-21PFM *Fishbed-F*.

Chinese-built A-5 strike fighters.

Mikoyan MiG-21MF
Fishbed-Js.

Type 77. Powered by an R-11-300 turbojet rated at 60.8 kN (13,668 lb st, with afterburning). Identified in 1966.

MiG-21PFS or MiG-21PF(SPS) Similar to D but with SPS as standard production installation.

MiG-21PFM (*Fishbed-F*) Successor to the interim PFS embodying all the improvements introduced progressively on the PF and PFS. Leading edge of the fin extended forward, small dorsal-fin fillet eliminated, sideways-hinged canopy and other refinements. R2L radar of the FL. Built in Czechoslovakia.

Analogue Standard PF fitted with scaled-down Tu-144 'ogee' delta wings for aero-dynamic flight testing and development prior to the prototype airliner being completed.

Fishbed-G Experimental STOL version of the PFM with a pair of vertically mounted lift-jet engines in a lengthened centre-section.

MiG-21PFMA (*Fishbed-J*) Multi-role version basically similar to the PFM but with a deeper dorsal fairing containing fuel tankage above the fuselage. Provision for the GP-9 underbelly gun pack as an alternative to the centreline fuel tank. Four underwing pylons (instead of the former two) for a variety of ground-attack weapons and stores, as an alternative or supplementary to two or four air-to-air missiles. Missiles can include *Advanced Atoll* and *Atoll*. Later production aircraft can have the GSh-23 gun installed inside the fuselage.

MiG-21M Generally similar to the PFMA with the internal gun pack. Built in India as the Type 88.

MiG-21R (*Fishbed-H*) Tactical reconnaissance version basically similar to the PFMA. External pod for forward-facing or oblique cameras, infra-red sensors or ECM devices, and fuel. Suppressed antenna at mid-fuselage and optional ECM equipment in wingtip fairings.

MiG-21MF (*Fishbed-J*) Similar to the PFMA

Mikoyan MiG-21
Fishbed-G.

but powered by a Tumansky R-13-300 turbojet of lighter weight and higher performance. Entered service with the Soviet Air Force in 1970.

MiG-21RF (*Fishbed-H*) Tactical reconnaissance version of the MF.

MiG-21SMT (*Fishbed-K*) Similar to the MF except for having a deep dorsal spine to provide maximum fuel. Able to carry ECM equipment in small removable wingtip pods. Deliveries to Warsaw Pact countries began in 1971.

MiG-21bis (*Fishbed-L*) Third-generation multi-role air-combat/ground-attack version with updated avionics and generally improved construction standards.

MiG-21bis (*Fishbed-N*) Advanced version of the L with a Tumansky R-25 engine, further improved avionics and increased radar detection range. Standard equipment of the Soviet Air Force for several years.

MiG-21U (*Mongol*) Two-seat training version.

MiG-21US (*Mongol-B*) Similar to the U but with provision for SPS flap-blowing. Retractable periscope for instructor in the rear seat.

MiG-21UM (*Mongol-B*) Two-seat trainer counterpart of the MF with the R-13 engine and four underwing stores pylons.

E-33, E-66, E-66A, E-66B and E-76 Prepared record-breaking versions of the MiG-21 series.

Data (MiG-21MF): *Engine* one 64.73 kN (14,550 lb st, with afterburning) Tumansky R-13-300 turbojet *Wing span* 7.15 m (23 ft 5½ in) *Length* 15.76 m (51 ft 8½ in) *Max T-O weight* 9,400 kg (20,725 lb) *Max level speed* Mach 2.1 *Max low-level speed* Mach 1.06 *Range* (internal fuel) 1,100 km (683 miles) *Armament* one twin-barrel 23 mm GSh-23 gun in belly pack. Four underwing pylons for weapons or drop-tanks

Mikoyan MiG-21U
Mongol.

Mikoyan MiG-23 (USSR) The prototype of this variable-geometry air-combat fighter was first shown to the public in 1967. Initial deliveries of pre-series aircraft to the Soviet Air Force were made in 1970 and deployment in large numbers began in 1973. It has been estimated that more than 1,500 MiG-23s of all versions (including the related MiG-27) had been delivered by the spring of 1979. Others have been supplied to the air forces of Bulgaria and Czechoslovakia, and exported (with lower equipment standard) to Algeria, Cuba, Egypt, Ethiopia, Iraq, Libya and Syria.

Several production versions of the MiG-23 have been built (NATO reporting name *Flogger*), as the MiG-23S (*Flogger-B*) single-seat air-combat fighter which is rapidly displacing the MiG-21 as the primary air-to-air tactical aircraft of the Soviet Air Force – deployed in both forward areas and the interior of the USSR and capable of tracking and engaging targets flying below its own altitude; MiG-23U (*Flogger-C*) tandem two-seat operational trainer and combat aircraft; MiG-23S (*Flogger-E*) export version of the *Flogger-B*, without an undernose laser rangefinder or Doppler navigation equipment and armed with *Atoll* missiles and a GSh-23 gun; *Flogger-F* export counterpart of the Soviet Air Force's MiG-27 (*Flogger-D*) ground-attack/interdictor version; and MiG-23S (*Flogger-G*), similar to *Flogger-B* but with a much smaller dorsal fin and absence of operational equipment, perhaps produced in small numbers as an aerobatic display aircraft.

Early production aircraft were powered by a Tumansky R-27 turbofan rated at 100 kN (22,485 lb st, with afterburning). This power plant continues in use in the MiG-23U, but the current MiG-23S and MiG-27 have a Tumansky R-29B turbojet.
Data (MiG-23S): *Engine* one 112.8 kN (25,350 lb st, with max afterburning) Tumansky R-29B turbojet *Wing span* (spread) 14.25 m (46 ft 9in), (swept) 8.17 m (26 ft 9½in) *Length* 16.8 m (55 ft 1½ in) *Max T-O weight* (estimated) 12,700–15,000 kg (28,000–33,050 lb) *Max level speed* Mach 2.3 *Combat radius* 960 km (600 miles) *Armament* one 23 mm GSh-23 twin-barrel gun in fuselage belly pack, with large flash eliminator around muzzles. One pylon under centre-fuselage, one under each engine air-intake duct and one under each fixed inboard wing panel for rocket packs, air-to-air missiles of the *Apex* and *Aphid* types or other external stores
Mikoyan MiG-25 (USSR) Development of the MiG-25 (NATO reporting name *Foxbat*) was initiated to counter the threat of the USAF's Mach 3 North American XB-70 Valkyrie

strategic bomber. When the bomber programme was cut back to a research project in 1961, work on the MiG-25 continued with increased emphasis on the reconnaissance potential of the design.

First indication that the prototype had flown came in April 1965 with a Soviet claim that a twin-engined aircraft designated E-266 had set a 1,000 km closed-circuit speed record of 2,320 km/h (1,441.5 mph), carrying a 2,000 kg payload. On 5 October 1967 the E-266 set a speed record in level flight of 2,981.5 km/h (1,852.61 mph) over a 500 km closed circuit. Other records followed: on 17 May 1975 the E-266M (uprated power plant) climbed to 25,000 m in 2 minutes 34.2 seconds; 30,000 m in 3 minutes 9.7 seconds; and 35,000 m in 4 minutes 11.3 seconds. The current absolute height record was set by the E-266M on 31 August 1977 when it climbed to 37,650 m (123,524 ft).

Four MiG-25 reconnaissance aircraft were deployed with Soviet Air Force units in Egypt in the spring of 1971: between the autumn of that year and the spring of 1972 they were despatched in pairs from Cairo West airfield on at least four occasions to carry out high-speed reconnaissance missions off the Israeli coastline or down the full length of the Israeli-occupied Sinai Peninsula. Phantom II interceptors sent up by the Israeli Air Force failed to make contact with the MiGs, which remained in Egypt until September 1975. In 1977 MiG-25 reconnaissance aircraft were based in the Soviet Union and in Syria. Operators in 1979 were reported to include the Algerian and Libyan Air Forces.

On 6 September 1976 a MiG-25 was flown from the Soviet air base of Sikharovka to Japan by a defecting pilot. Examination showed that it was constructed mainly of steel, with titanium only in places subjected to extreme heating. ECM standards were high. Of particular interest was the aircraft's high-quality airborne computer which,

Mikoyan MiG-23S *Flogger-B.*

Mikoyan MiG-25R *Foxbat-B.*

Nose of the Mikoyan MiG-25U *Foxbat-C.*

Mikoyan

Mikoyan MiG-27
Flogger-D.

WSK-Swidnik SM-1.

Mil Mi-4.

Mil Mi-1s.

in conjunction with a ground-based flight-control system, enabled the interceptor to be vectored automatically on to its target over long ranges.

Five variants of the MiG-25 are known: the MiG-25 (*Foxbat-A*) basic interceptor with a large radar in the nose and armed with four air-to-air missiles; MiG-25R (*Foxbat-B*) basic-reconnaissance version with five camera windows and various flush dielectric panels aft of a very small dielectric nosecap for radar; MiG-25U (*Foxbat-C*) trainer version with a new nose containing a separate cockpit with an individual canopy forward of the standard cockpit; MiG-25R (*Foxbat-D*), generally similar to *Foxbat-B* but with a larger SLAR (side-looking airborne radar) dielectric panel and no cameras; and the E-266M experimental aircraft which holds the records mentioned earlier.

Data (*Foxbat-A*, estimated): *Engines* two 107.9 kN (24,250 lb st, with afterburning) Tumansky R-31 (R-266) single-shaft turbojets *Wing span* 13.95 m (45 ft 9 in) *Length* 22.3 m (73 ft 2 in) *Max T-O weight* 36,200 kg (79,800 lb) *Max level speed* (with missiles) Mach 2.8, (*Foxbat-B*) Mach 3.2 *Max combat radius* 1,300 km (805 miles) *Armament* four air-to-air missiles. May include two infra-red and two radar-homing *Acrid*s. More usually two *Apex* and two *Aphid* missiles

Mikoyan MiG-27 (USSR) Ground-attack version of the MiG-23, known to NATO as *Flogger-D*. It differs from the MiG-23 in important respects, including fixed air intakes and a fixed nozzle. The forward part of the fuselage is completely redesigned with a sharply tapered nose incorporating a small sloping window covering a laser range-finder and marked-target seeker. Additional armour has been fitted on the flat sides of the cockpit. A six-barrel 23 mm Gatling-type underbelly gun replaces the GSh-23 and there are five pylons for external stores, including tactical nuclear weapons and, probably, the air-to-surface missile known to NATO as *Kerry*. Maximum level speed at height is Mach 1.75 and at S/L Mach 0.95. Maximum weapon load is 3,000 kg (6,610 lb).

New Mikoyan fighter (USSR) Reports have suggested that a new air-superiority fighter – looking somewhat like and in the same class as the projected Northrop F-18L – is in the advanced flight-testing stage.

Mil Mi-1 and WSK-PZL Swidnik SM-1 (USSR/Poland) Known to NATO as *Hare*, the Mi-1 was the first helicopter to go into series production in the Soviet Union. The first prototype flew in September 1948. Many production aircraft were built for civil and military use, the principal versions being the Mi-1T three-seater; Mi-1 Moskvich improved transport for Aeroflot; Mi-1NKh general-purpose helicopter capable of accommodating two stretcher panniers or mail containers, agricultural equipment, etc; and the Mi-1U dual-control trainer. Mi-1s remain operational in several Eastern bloc, African, Asian and Middle Eastern countries.

The WSK-PZL Swidnik SM-1 was produced in Poland when that country took over production of the Mi-1 in 1955. Several versions were built, including the SM-1WS ambulance and SM-1WSZ dual-control trainer.

Data (SM-1W): *Engine* one 429 kW (575 hp) LiT-3 (Polish-built AI-26V) *Main rotor diameter* 14.35 m (47 ft 1 in) *Length of fuselage* 12.1 m (39 ft 8½ in) *Max T-O weight* 2,460 kg (5,425 lb) *Max level speed* 170 km/h (106 mph) *Max range* 600 km (370 miles) *Accommodation* pilot and three passengers or freight

Mil Mi-2 (USSR) See **PZL-Swidnik Mi-2**

Mil Mi-4 (USSR) The Mi-4 is basically the Soviet equivalent of the American Sikorsky S-55. About 3,500 were built for civil and military use up to 1969, first entering service in 1953. The military version (still flown in 26 countries) can accommodate up to 14 troops, freight or a vehicle of the GAZ-69 command truck size in the transport role (NATO *Hound-A*) – the large rear clam-shell doors allowing easy loading of bulky items of

equipment. In addition new versions have recently appeared carrying the NATO reporting names *Hound-B* and *-C*, intended as specialised ASW and ECM aircraft respectively, the latter fitted with communications jamming equipment.

Civil versions of the Mi-4 were built in three main versions: the basic Mi-4 cargo-carrying version; the Mi-4P passenger-carrying or ambulance (eight stretchers) version; and the Mi-4S agricultural version. The helicopter is also produced in China.

Data: *Engine* one 1,268 kW (1,700 hp) Shvetsov ASh-82V *Main rotor diameter* 21.0 m (68 ft 11 in) *Length of fuselage* 16.8 m (55 ft 1 in) *Max T-O weight* 7,800 kg (17,200 lb) *Max level speed* 210 km/h (130 mph) *Range* (with eight passengers) 400 km (250 miles)

Mil Mi-6 (USSR) First announced in 1957, the Mi-6 (NATO *Hook*) was then the largest helicopter flying anywhere in the world. From it were evolved the Mi-10 and Mi-10K. Five Mi-6s are reported to have been built for development testing, followed by an initial pre-series of 30 and subsequent manufacture of some 800 for military and civil use. Six were supplied to the Indonesian Air Force; many others have since been delivered to the Bulgarian, Egyptian, Iraqi, Syrian and Vietnamese air forces and to the government of Peru.

Data: *Engines* two 4,101 kW (5,500 shp) Soloviev D-25V (TV-25M) turboshafts *Main rotor diameter* 35.0 m (114 ft 10 in) *Length of fuselage* 33.18 m (108 ft 10½ in) *Max T-O weight* 42,500 kg (93,700 lb) *Max level speed* 300 km/h (186 mph) *Range* (with external tanks and 4,300 kg; 9,480 lb payload) 1,050 km (652 miles) *Accommodation* crew of five and 65 passengers, 41 stretchers and two medical attendants or freight *Armament* a few Mi-6s are fitted with a gun in the nose

Mil Mi-8 (V-8) (USSR) This turbine-powered helicopter was shown in public for the first time in 1961. Since then nearly 6,000 Mi-8s (NATO *Hip*) have been delivered for military and civil use. With Mi-24s, they form the standard equipment of Soviet tactical helicopter regiments, in a variety of forms – some carrying extremely heavy weapon loads. Military Mi-8s have also been supplied to the Afghan, Algerian, Anguilla, Bangladesh, Bulgarian, Czechoslovak, Egyptian, Ethiopian, Finnish, East German, Hungarian, Indian, Iraqi, North Korean, Laotian, Libyan, Malagasy, Pakistani, Peruvian, Polish, Romanian, Sudanese, Syrian, Vietnamese, North Yemen, South Yemen and Yugoslav armed forces.

The commercial Mi-8 is in service with Aeroflot for transport and air ambulance duties. It is operated by this airline in support of Soviet activities in the Antarctic, standard Mi-8s being used there for ice patrol and reconnaissance, for rescue operations, and for carrying supplies and equipment to Vostok Station, near the South Pole. The three civil versions are the Mi-8, carrying 28 passengers; Mi-8T utility transport for internal or external freight or 24 passengers; and the Mi-8 Salon, a de luxe version for 11 passengers.

Data: *Engines* two 1,118.5 kW (1,500 shp) Isotov TV2-117A turboshafts *Main rotor diameter* 21.29 m

Mil Mi-6 operated by Aeroflot.

Military version of the Mil Mi-6.

(69 ft 10¼ in) *Length of fuselage* 18.31 m (60 ft 0¾ in) *Normal T-O weight* 11,100 kg (24,470 lb) *Max T-O weight* 12,000 kg (26,455 lb) *Max level speed* 260 km/h (161 mph) *Range* 480 km (298 miles) *Accommodation* crew of two and 28–32 passengers, 12 stretchers and a medical attendant, or freight *Armament* military versions can be equipped with a great variety of weapons, including a flexibly mounted 12.7 mm machine-gun in the nose and a triple rack for anti-tank missiles, bombs and rocket pods on each side of the fuselage

Mil Mi-8.

Mil Mi-10 (USSR) Known to NATO as *Harke*, the Mi-10 is a flying-crane development of the Mi-6 and was first demonstrated in public in 1961, having had its maiden flight in the previous year. The tall long-stroke quadricycle landing gear enables the helicopter to taxi over a load it is to carry and to accommodate loads as bulky as a

Mil Mi-10.

Mil Mi-10K.

Mil Mi-24 Hind-A.

Mil V-12.

Mil Mi-14 (V-14).

prefabricated building. Use can be made of interchangeable wheeled cargo platforms which are held in place by hydraulic grips. A closed-circuit TV system (with cameras scanning forward and downward) is used to observe the payload and main landing gear, touchdown being by this reference. The TV system replaced the retractable undernose 'dustbin' fitted originally.

About 55 Mi-10s are believed to have been delivered by 1977. Some have been exported to Iraq.

Data: Engines two 4,101 kW (5,500 shp) Soloviev D-25V turboshafts *Main rotor diameter* 35.0 m (114 ft 0 in) *Length of fuselage* 32.86 m (107 ft 9¾ in) *Max T-O weight* 43,700 kg (96,340 lb) *Max level speed* 200 km/h (124 mph) *Range* (with platform payload of 12,000 kg; 26,455 lb) 250 km (155 miles) *Accommodation* main cabin can be used to carry 28 passengers or freight. External sling gear as standard equipment for up to an 8,000 kg (17,635 lb) load *Max payload on a platform* (incl platform) 15,000 kg (33,070 lb)

Mil Mi-10K (USSR) First displayed publicly in March 1966, the Mi-10K is a development of the Mi-10 with a number of important design changes. Most apparent of these are a reduction in the height of the landing gear and a more slender tail-rotor support structure. Maximum slung payload is 11,000 kg (24,250 lb). Provision is made for an additional rearward-facing cockpit gondola under the nose of the fuselage to allow a pilot to control the helicopter in hovering flight, while having an unrestricted view of cargo loading, unloading and hoisting.

Mil Mi-14 (V-14) (USSR) Known to NATO as *Haze*, this is a shore-based anti-submarine helicopter derived from the Mi-8, and is in standard service with the Soviet Navy as a replacement for the Mi-4. About 50 are believed to have

been delivered by 1977, with production continuing as a rate of 25 per year.

Mil Mi-24 (USSR) Known to NATO as *Hind*, the Mi-24 is a high-performance assault helicopter. Deliveries of all models are believed to exceed 1,000, with production continuing at a rate of 30 a month. Full regiments of Mi-24s are based in the USSR and East Germany and numbers have been supplied to the forces of Afghanistan, Libya and East Germany.

Five versions of the Mi-24 are known: the *Hind-A* heavy assault helicopter with a large enclosed flight deck for the crew of four and auxiliary wings with three weapon stations each for heavy armament, supplemented by a large-calibre machine-gun in the nose; *Hind-B*, which is believed to have preceded the A but was not built in large numbers, with four weapon stations; *Hind-C*, generally similar to the A but without nose gun and undernose blister fairing, and no missile rails at wingtips; *Hind-D*, basically similar to the late model A, but with the front fuselage completely redesigned for a primary gunship role, with tandem stations for the weapons operator and pilot (with individual canopies) and undernose four-barrel Gatling-type large-calibre machine-gun in a turret plus wing armament; and *Hind-F*, a variant reported to be based in East Germany in 1979, with armament of six anti-tank missiles. Other developments reported in 1979 were the introduction on some *Hind*s of a 30 mm Gatling-type nose gun and a laser seeker.

Data (estimated): Engines two 1,118.5 kW (1,500 shp) Isotov turboshafts *Main rotor diameter* 17.0 m (55 ft 9 in) *Length overall* 17.0 m (55 ft 9 in) *Normal T-O weight* 10,000 kg (22,000 lb) *Max level speed* more than 322 km/h (200 mph) *Armament* (*Hind-A*) one 12.7 mm machine-gun in nose. Rails for Swatter anti-tank missiles under endplate pylons at wingtips. Four underwing pylons for rocket pods (each 32 × 57 mm rockets), special

Messerschmitt Bf 108
Taifun.

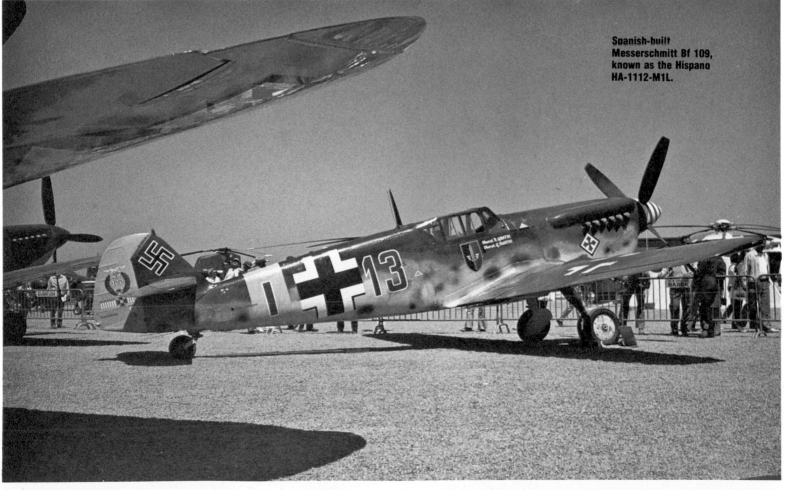

Spanish-built
Messerschmitt Bf 109,
known as the Hispano
HA-1112-M1L.

Messerschmitt Me 262.

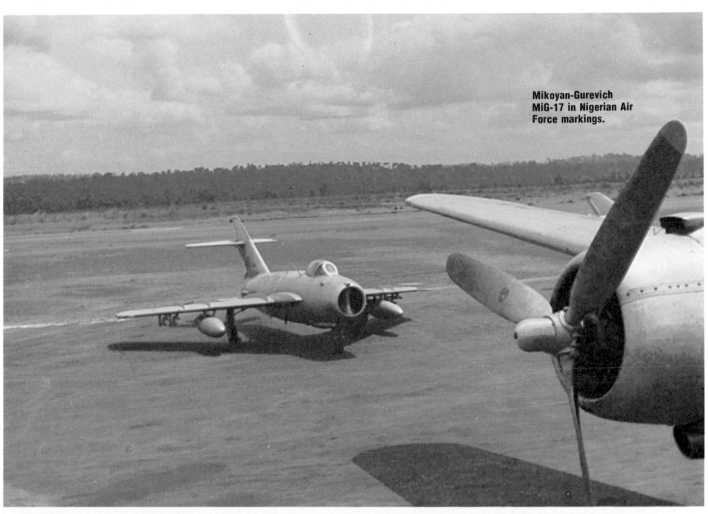

Mikoyan-Gurevich MiG-17 in Nigerian Air Force markings.

Mikoyan MiG-23S.

Mil Mi-8.

**Mitsubishi A6M5
Zero-Sen.**

Morane-Saulnier MS.230.

Nieuport 24*bis*.

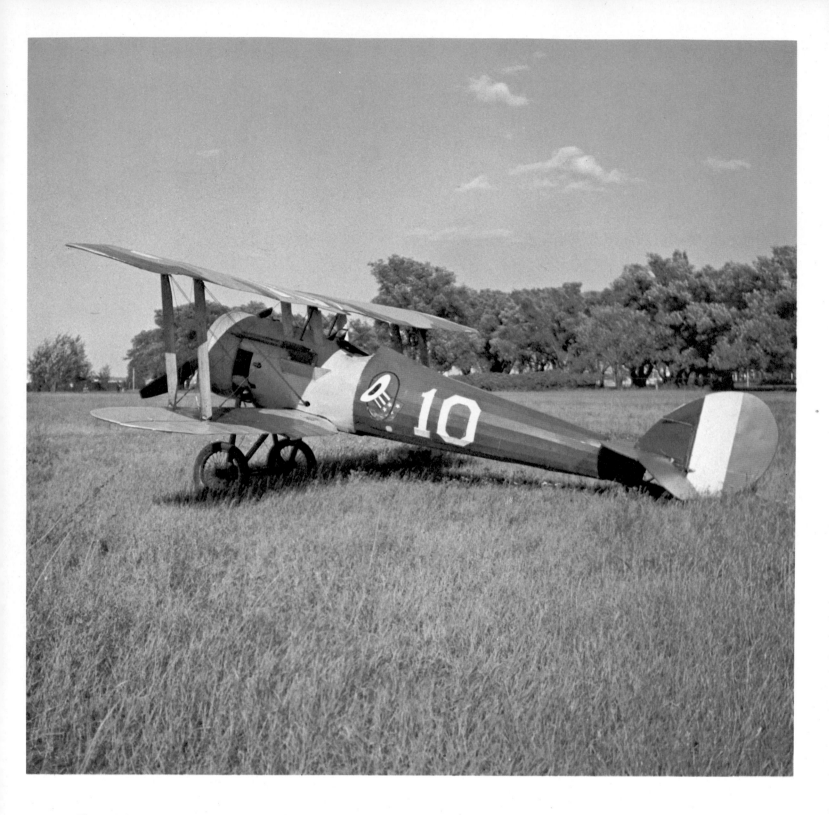

Nieuport 28.

bombs, or other stores. Entering service is a tube-launched 'fire-and-forget' anti-tank missile which homes on targets illuminated by a laser designator (NATO *Spiral*)

Mil V-12 and Halo (USSR) The V-12 was a heavy general-purpose helicopter (known to NATO as *Homer*) capable of accommodating missiles and other payloads compatible with those of the Antonov An-22 fixed-wing transport. Power was provided by four 4,847 kW (6,500 shp) Soloviev D-25VF turboshaft engines. The first confirmation of its existence was given in 1969 when it was stated that it had set a number of payload-to-height records which exceeded by some 20% the records established by the Mi-6 and Mi-10K. It is believed that *Homer* remained a prototype only.

In 1979 reports were made of a new heavy-lift helicopter that was being tested in prototype form. This carries the NATO reporting name *Halo*. It is believed to have a single main rotor and clamshell rear loading doors. Total power output of the engines may be in the 18,650 kW (25,000 shp) range.

Mil naval helicopter (USSR) A new ASW and reconnaissance helicopter is being developed for the Soviet Navy for deployment in the mid-1980s.

Miles M.2 Hawk (UK) Two-seat light touring and training monoplane of 1929 powered in its original form by a 67 kW (90 hp) Cirrus III engine. Fifty-five were built.

Miles M.2 Hawk Major (UK) The Hawk Major made its appearance in July 1934 and the first of the type (flown by Flt Lieut T. Rose) took second place in the race for the King's Cup. A standard Hawk Major two-seat light monoplane was entered for the Handicap Section of the Mac-Robertson Race from England to Australia, becoming the fifth aircraft to complete the course. Power was provided by a 97 kW (130 hp) de Havilland Gipsy Major engine. Sixty-four were built.

Miles M.2 Hawk Trainer (UK) This aircraft of 1934 had the wider cockpits of the de luxe Hawk Major but without the special interior finish. It was approved for use at the RAF Reserve Training School, operated by Phillips & Powis Aircraft. Twenty-five were built.

Miles M.3 Falcon Major and Falcon Six (UK) Three-seat light cabin monoplanes powered by a 97 kW (130 hp) de Havilland Gipsy Major and 149 kW (200 hp) de Havilland Gipsy Six engine respectively. A total of 36 was built.

Miles M.5 Sparrowhawk (UK) The Sparrowhawk was intended as a high-performance aircraft for the private owner and was placed on the market with a 97 kW (130 hp) de Havilland Gipsy Major engine and Miles split trailing-edge flaps at £970. It differed from the standard Hawk in having wings with an area of 12.82 m² (138 sq ft) instead of 15.7 m² (169 sq ft) and a new faired single-strut landing gear. Five were built in 1935.

Miles M.7 Nighthawk (UK) The Nighthawk was intended primarily to provide complete instruction in flying, navigation, cloud flying, etc, but could also be supplied as a four-seat cabin monoplane for the private owner or for feeder-line

Miles M.2 Hawk.

Miles M.2X Hawk Trainer.

Miles M.7A Nighthawk.

use. The standard engine was a 149 kW (200 hp) de Havilland Gipsy Six. Six were built.

Miles M.9A Master I (UK) In January 1939 large extensions to the Miles factory were completed and opened by the Secretary of State for Air. These were necessary to cope with a large contract for the Master I high-speed advanced training monoplane: a two-seater powered by a 536.5 kW (720 hp) Rolls-Royce Kestrel 30 engine. Nine hundred were built.

Miles M.11 Whitney Straight (UK) First flown in mid-1936, the Whitney Straight was a side-by-side two-seat light cabin monoplane powered by a 97 kW (130 hp) de Havilland Gipsy Major engine. Fifty were built.

Miles M.14 Magister (UK) The Magister was a two-seat primary-training monoplane based on the Hawk Trainer. While in production it was the only monoplane in Great Britain to be approved

Miles M.9A Master I.

Miles

Miles M.11A Whitney Straight.

Miles M.14A Magister.

Miles M.25 Martinet.

Miles M.27 Master III.

Miles M.17 Monarch.

Miles M.19 Master II with experimental rocket installation.

Miles M.38 Messenger 2A.

674

by the Air Ministry for ab initio instruction of RAF pilots and was used by RAF training establishments in England and overseas. Power was provided normally by a 97 kW (130 hp) de Havilland Gipsy Major engine, although a 100.6 kW (135 hp) Blackburn Cirrus Major was also fitted. A total of 1,293 was built between 1937 and 1941, some being exported.
Data: *Engine* as above *Wing span* 10.31 m (33 ft 10 in) *Length* 7.5 m (24 ft 7½ in) *Max T-O weight* 845 kg (1,863 lb) *Max level speed* 233 km/h (145 mph) at 305 m (1,000 ft)

Miles M.16 Mentor (UK) Three-seat Gipsy Six-powered cabin monoplane, 45 of which were operated by the RAF as trainers and communications aircraft.

Miles M.17 Monarch (UK) Two–three-seat light cabin monoplane derived from the Mentor but powered by a 97 kW (130 hp) de Havilland Gipsy Major engine. Eleven built in 1938.

Miles M.19 Master II (UK) Soon after the outbreak of World War II, the prototype Master II flew for the first time. It was based on the Master I but powered by a 648.3 kW (870 hp) Bristol Mercury XX radial engine. Production amounted to approximately 1,800 aircraft, a number of which

were sent to South Africa. Master IIs were also acquired by the air forces of Egypt, Portugal and Turkey. One Master II was used in connection with rocket experiments.
Data: *Engine* as above *Wing span* 11.89 m (39 ft 0 in) *Length* 9.0 m (29 ft 6 in) *Max T-O weight* 2,410 kg (5,312 lb) *Max level speed* 391 km/h (243 mph) *Range* 632 km (393 miles)

Miles M.25 Martinet (UK) Two-seat target-towing monoplane based on the Master and powered by a Bristol Mercury XX or XXX radial engine. The prototype flew for the first time on 24 April 1942 and more than 1,700 were built for the RAF.

Miles M.27 Master III (UK) The Master III was a further development of the Master series, powered by a 615 kW (825 hp) Pratt & Whitney R-1535-SB4G Wasp Junior radial engine. A total of 602 was built. Maximum level speed was 372 km/h (231 mph).

Miles M.33 Monitor (UK) The Monitor was a twin 1,304 kW (1,750 hp) Wright R-2600-31 Cyclone-powered target-towing monoplane, first flown on 5 April 1944. Twenty were built for the Royal Navy as TT.IIs, intended to simulate dive-bombing attacks on ships. A 7.4 kW (10 hp) hydraulic winch was installed in the fuselage (driven by the starboard engine) allowing operation of targets at more than 483 km/h (300 mph). Maximum level speed was 579 km/h (360 mph).

Miles M.38 Messenger (UK) The Messenger four-seat cabin monoplane was a development of the prototype M.28 and was converted during the

war to meet the requirements of Specification 17/43 for use as an Air Observation Post by the Army. The prototype flew for the first time on 12 September 1942. Power for production aircraft was provided by a 104.3 kW (140 hp) de Havilland Gipsy Major or 115.5 kW (155 hp) Blackburn Cirrus Major III engine. About 80 Messengers were produced, 21 going to the RAF and most of the remainder to private owners.

Miles M.50 Queen Martinet (UK) In 1942 Miles Aircraft was asked to consider the development of a radio-controlled aircraft to replace the de Havilland Queen Bee biplane target. Two projects (M.47 and M.49) were tendered, but subsequently it was decided to use a standard Martinet converted as a target. Sixty-five were produced, 43 by the end of 1945.

Miles M.52 (UK) The Miles M.52 was a supersonic flight research aircraft which would have been the first manned aircraft to fly faster than the speed of sound had the project not been abandoned in 1946.

Miles M.57 Aerovan (UK) The Aerovan flew for the first time in January 1945 and was a freight, passenger (six or nine) or ambulance monoplane. Power was provided by two 115.5 kW (155 hp) Blackburn Cirrus Major engines. The main cabin was 3.73 m (12 ft 3 in) long, the hinged rear section of the fuselage allowing a vehicle to be driven into the cabin. Maximum level speed was 204 km/h (127 mph). Forty-eight Aerovans were built.

Miles M.60 Marathon (UK) The Marathon was designed to Specification 18/44 to meet the

Miles M.60 Marathon.

requirements of the Brabazon Type V class for a medium-range feeder-line aircraft. The first flight of the prototype was made at Woodley Aerodrome on 19 May 1946. This aircraft was fitted with a third central fin and rudder but the second prototype had them removed. However production aircraft again featured a triple vertical tail. Power was provided by four 246 kW (330 hp) de Havilland Gipsy Queen 71 engines.

Twenty-five Marathons were ordered for BEA, but this order was later reduced and then cancelled altogether. Although a number of aircraft did go into commercial airline service as 18–22-passenger transports, most of the 42 Marathons built were passed to the RAF for use as navigation trainers.

Miles M.50 Queen Martinet.

Miles M.65 Gemini (UK) The Gemini was a four-seat cabin monoplane developed from the M.38 Messenger. It used a similar fuselage, wings and tail unit, except that only twin fins and rudders were fitted. The prototype flew for the first time on 26 October 1945 with a fixed landing gear. Production aircraft (about 170 built) had retractable landing gears.

Miles M.52.

Data: *Engines* two 74.5 kW (100 hp) Blackburn Cirrus Minor IIs *Wing span* 11.02 m (36 ft 2 in) *Length* 6.78 m (22 ft 3 in) *Max T-O weight* 1,361 kg (3,000 lb) *Max level speed* 241 km/h (150 mph) *Range* 1,320 km (820 miles)

Miller WM-2 (USA) Single-seat sport monoplane, plans for which are available to amateur constructors.

Miles M.57 Aerovan 4.

Miller WM-2.

Mini-Hawk TH.E.01.

Mini-Hawk TH.E.01 Tiger-Hawk (USA) Single-seat lightweight monoplane, plans and kits for which are available to amateur constructors.

Mitsubishi Army Type 92 (Japan) Bearing the company designation 2MR8, this two-seat parasol-wing reconnaissance monoplane was used against the Chinese in Manchuria during the later stages of the fighting which terminated in 1933 with the establishment of the Japanese state of Manchukuo. A total of 230 was built. Armament could comprise up to four 7.7 mm machine-guns. Power was provided by a single 354 kW (475 hp) Mitsubishi Type 92 radial engine, giving a maximum speed of 220 km/h (136.5 mph).

Mitsubishi Army Type 92.

Mitsubishi Army 2MB1.

Mitsubishi A5M2a.

Mitsubishi Navy 1MF (Japan) A compact single-seat biplane design by Herbert Smith, the 1MF1 was accepted for Japanese Navy service in 1921 under the designation Navy Type 10 Carrier Fighter. A total of 138 of several versions was completed by the time production terminated in 1928. The Type 10-2 or 1MF3 had the 223.6 kW (300 hp) Hispano-Suiza engine as the first production version, but utilised twin Lamblin radiators instead of the original frontal type. It was a Type 10-2 which made the first successful take-off by a Japanese-built aircraft from the aircraft carrier *Hosho*, in February 1923. Armament comprised two 7.7 mm machine-guns.
Data (1MF3B): *Engine* as above *Wing span* 8.84 m (29 ft 0 in) *Length* 6.88 m (22 ft 7 in) *Max T-O weight* 1,135 kg (2,502 lb) *Max level speed* 225 km/h (140 mph)

Mitsubishi Navy 1MT1 (Japan) Another Herbert Smith design, the 1MT1 was a single-seat triplane torpedo bomber intended for carrier operations. Twenty were built, going into service briefly in 1923 as the Navy Type 10 Carrier Attacker.

Mitsubishi Army 2MB1 (Japan) The 2MB1 was basically a longer-range Army version of the Navy B1M torpedo bomber, powered by a 335.3 kW (450 hp) Hispano-Suiza engine. Armament comprised forward-firing, dorsal and ventral 7.7 mm machine-guns and 500 kg (1,102 lb) of bombs. It entered limited production

as the Type 87 Light Bomber in 1927. Another development of the B1M may have been the MC-1 four-passenger commercial transport.

Mitsubishi Navy 2MR (Japan) Designed by Herbert Smith, the prototype 2MR was completed in January 1921. The following year the 2MR1 version went into Navy service as the Type 10 Carrier Reconnaissance Aircraft. Power was provided by a 223.6 kW (300 hp) Hispano-Suiza engine. The 159 aircraft manufactured up to 1930 appeared in many versions. Armament could comprise up to four 7.7 mm machine-guns and 90 kg (198 lb) of bombs. Civilianised Type 10s were in use right through the 1930s.

Mitsubishi Navy 2MT (Japan) See **Mitsubishi Navy B1M.**

Mitsubishi A5M (Japan) Because of the complexity of the specification that eventually produced the Zero-Sen, the little A5M fighter, with its two forward-firing 7.7 mm machine-guns, fixed landing gear and usually open cockpit, remained a standard carrier-borne fighter with the Japanese Navy for nearly a year after Pearl Harbor.

The A5M prototype flew for the first time on 4 February 1935 while powered by a 410 kW (550 hp) Nakajima Kotobuki 5 radial engine. Although maximum speed was considered excellent, the inverted-gull wings were not well received and were replaced on the second prototype by straighter wings. The second aircraft also had a more powerful engine fitted. The aircraft entered production with a 436 kW (585 hp) Kotobuki 2 engine as the Navy A5M1 or Type 96 Model 11 Carrier Fighter.

During the production run, when nearly 1,000 A5Ms were built, several changes took place. The A5M2s introduced a 454.5 kW (610 hp) Kotobuki 2 engine, while the A5M4 had a 529 kW (710 hp) Kotobuki 41. The only version with an enclosed cockpit was the A5M2b.

Flown in action during the late 1930s against Chinese and Russian opposition, the A5M acquitted itself well but was obsolete by 1941. Under the Allied code system the A5M was named *Claude*.
Data (A5M4): *Engine* as above *Wing span* 11.0 m (36 ft 1 in) *Length* 7.56 m (24 ft 9½ in) *Max T-O weight* 1,670 kg (3,682 lb) *Max level speed* 440 km/h (273.5 mph) *Range* 1,200 km (746 miles) *Armament* two 7.7 mm machine-guns, plus two 30 kg bombs

Mitsubishi A6M Zero-Sen (Japan) By far the most famous and widely used Japanese aircraft in history, the Zero-Sen gained its name from the fact that it was put into production in 1940 – Japanese year 5700 – and thus was also desig-

nated Navy Fighter Type 00. The Allies called it the *Zero*, a name which stuck after the official reporting code name had been promulgated as *Zeke*.

A design team led by the legendary Jiro Horikoshi met a most difficult Navy specification in 1938: this demanded not only speed of 500 km/h and armament of two cannon and two machine-guns, but also carrier compatibility, tankage for extremely long range and manoeuvrability not inferior to that of the amazingly nimble A5M, which the new fighter was to replace. The prototype flew on 1 April 1939, and 15 swept away all opposition during service trials in China from July 1940. Full reports by the American Volunteer Group (which fought these aircraft) were ignored and when the type was met in force at Pearl Harbor it was a terrible shock. Over 400 A6M2s and clipped-wing A6M3s were by that time in use; with drop-tanks and refined long-range cruise procedures they covered such immense distances that the Allies estimated the number to be at least twice as many. Matched by scattered and generally inferior Allied machines, the Zero-Sen gained total ascendancy, the Japanese regarding it as invincible.

After the Battle of Midway in 1942, Allied opposition steadily gained the upper hand. The A6M's light construction often collapsed under the fire of an F6F or F4U and little could be done. The A6M5 had individual exhaust stacks giving higher speed from the same 842 kW (1,130 hp) Nakajima Sakae 21 engine, and the wing racks could carry two heavier bombs of 60 kg. The 5b had one of the machine-guns replaced by a heavy 12.7 mm weapon; and the 5c and all later versions had the 20 mm wing guns augmented by two 13.2 mm guns, often with a third in the fuselage. Nakajima built 6,217 *Zeros* of several versions out of the total production of 10,937. It also designed and built 327 of a float-seaplane version (A6M2-N, called *Rufe* by the Allies). The only other notably different variant was the A6M2-K, the most numerous of several tandem dual trainer developments.

From 1942 the A6M had been intended for replacement by the A7M Reppu, but the continued non-appearance of the new fighter resulted in prolonged A6M updating. In late 1944 a boosted Sakae engine was fitted to the A6M6c and at the end of the war a few A6M8cs were delivered with 1,162.5 kW (1,560 hp) Kinsei engines. By this time most of the surviving A6Ms had been converted as Kamikaze suicide attackers.

Data (A6M5): *Engine* as above *Wing span* 11.0 m (36 ft 1 in) *Length* 9.06 m (29 ft 8½ in) *Max T-O weight* 2,744 kg (6,050 lb) *Max level speed* 570 km/h (354 mph) *Range* 1,570 km (976 miles)

Mitsubishi A7M Reppu (Japan) First flown in May 1944, the Reppu (Hurricane) was designed as a higher-powered development of, and a replacement for, the Zero-Sen. However none had become operational before VJ Day.

Mitsubishi Navy B1M (Japan) Following on his association with the Mitsubishi company, Herbert Smith designed the 2MT1 two-seat biplane torpedo bomber which flew for the first time in

January 1923. It went into Japanese Navy service as the Type 12 carrier-borne attack aircraft and was followed by the 2MT2 and 2MT3 variants. The redesigned Type 13-2 was designated B1M2. The final version, the Type 13-3 or B1M3, had the firm's designation 3MT2 and was a three-seater. Total production was 354 and the type served into the 1930s, 32 flying from the aircraft carriers *Kaga* and *Hosho* during the Shanghai Incident in 1932. An aircraft from *Kaga* was lost during the famous air encounter when American volunteer pilot Robert Short lost his life while flying for the Chinese. The B1M was powered by a 335.3 kW (450 hp) Napier Lion or Hispano-Suiza engine according to version.

Data (B1M1): *Engine* as above *Wing span* 14.75 m (48 ft 5 in) *Length* 9.8 m (32 ft 1 in) *Max T-O weight* 2,700 kg (5,952 lb) *Max level speed* 210 km/h (130 mph) *Endurance* 2 h 30 min *Armament* three 7.7 mm machine-guns, plus one or two 240 kg torpedoes

Mitsubishi Navy B2M (Japan) Bidding to secure an order to replace their B1M, Mitsubishi again turned to a British designer, and Blackburn's G. E. Petty produced the prototype 3MR4 in Britain. Development in Japan followed and proved rather prolonged. As a result the series aircraft (known as the B1M1 or Navy Type 89-1) did not go into service until 1932. It was an equal-span two-bay biplane introducing a largely metal structure and a strongly made wide-track landing gear. The B2M2 or Type 89-2 appeared in 1934. It retained the original 484.3 kW

Mitsubishi

(650 hp) Hispano-Suiza liquid-cooled engine, but had a redesigned angular fin and rudder assembly. Production spanned five years from 1931 and both versions flew in action against the Chinese. Total production was 200 aircraft.

Mitsubishi Navy B5M1 (Japan) Mitsubishi's Ka-16 was a three-seat cantilever low-wing monoplane with a fixed and spatted landing gear, intended for carrier operations as a bomber or torpedo bomber. The crew were housed under a long glazed canopy. Production was undertaken as the Mitsubishi Navy Type 97-2 Carrier Attacker, intended largely as a back-up design for the Nakajima B5N1. With the success of the B5N1, production of the B5M1 ended with the 125th aircraft. The B5M1 saw operational service during World War II, but only from land bases. The 745.2 kW (1,000 hp) Mitsubishi Kinsei 43 radial gave a maximum 382 km/h (237.5 mph).

Mitsubishi C5M (Japan) See **Mitsubishi Ki-15**

Mitsubishi F-1.

Mitsubishi F-1 (Japan) Design of the FS-T2-Kai (later redesignated F-1) began in 1972 following the JASDF's decision to develop a single-seat close-support fighter from the T-2 supersonic trainer. First flown in prototype form on 3 June 1975, the F-1 was subsequently chosen for production. Orders for 59 aircraft had been placed by July 1978 of an anticipated total order for about 70. The first production aircraft flew on 16 June 1977 and was delivered to the JASDF on 26 September 1977. Twenty-six had been delivered by March 1979.

Data: *Engines*, *wing span* and *length* as for T-2 (see entry) *Max T-O weight* 13,674 kg (30,146 lb) *Max level speed* similar to T-2 *Combat radius* 278–556 km (173–346 miles) *Armament* single JM-61 multi-

Mitsubishi G3M.

Mitsubishi Navy F1M2.

678

barrel 20 mm cannon. One underfuselage and four underwing hardpoints for 250, 500 or 750 lb bombs, up to a maximum of 2,721 kg (12 × 500 lb bombs). The underwing stations can each carry rocket pods. For air-to-air combat, four AIM-9 Sidewinder missiles can be carried

Mitsubishi Navy F1M2 (Japan) The Ka-17 was evolved by designer Joji Hattori. The four prototypes built to a 10-Shi (1935) specification were designated F1M1. After a protracted development programme, the F1M2 production version was evolved, powered by a 652 kW (875 hp) Mitsubishi Zuisei radial engine. This entered service during 1940 under the designation Type O Observation Seaplane (Allied code name *Pete*). A total of 1,114 aircraft was built, flying from seaplane tenders and cruisers as well as from shore bases. In addition to performing reconnaissance and patrol work, F1M2s flew numerous support operations over Pacific island beaches.

The F1M2 was an impressive biplane with gracefully tapering wings braced by single I-struts. Great care was given to streamlining the fuselage. The radio-operator/gunner (armed with a 7.7 mm Type 92 machine-gun) was protected by a distinctive extended glazed windscreen. The pilot operated two fixed forward-firing 7.7 mm guns, and two 60 kg bombs could be carried underwing.

Data: *Engine* as above *Wing span* 11.0 m (36 ft 1 in) *Length* 9.5 m (31 ft 2 in) *Max T-O weight* 2,550 kg (5,622 lb) *Max level speed* 370 km/h (230 mph)

Mitsubishi G3M (Japan) On 7 December 1941 aircraft from a Japanese carrier force attacked the American naval base at Pearl Harbor, announcing in spectacular fashion that Japan had entered World War II. On 10 December 1941 a force of 60 Mitsubishi G3M2 and 26 G4M1 medium bombers of the Imperial Japanese Navy Air Force flew from bases in French Indo-China to attack several ships of the Royal Navy that had been spotted by a C5M2 (Mitsubishi Ki-15) patrol aircraft and submarine. HMS *Repulse* and *Prince of Wales* were sunk with great loss of life after a major battle.

Although this action is the best-remembered exploit of the G3M (Navy Type 96 Torpedo Bomber) or *Nell* as it was code-named by the Allies, the aircraft remained operational throughout the war as a bomber and later also as the L3Y ten-passenger transport aircraft. The first prototype (powered by two 447 kW; 600 hp Hiro Type 91 radial engines) flew in July 1935.

Production eventually began with the G3M1 powered by two 615 kW (825 hp) Kinsei 2 or 678 kW (910 hp) Kinsei 3 engines. The G3M1 was quickly superseded by the improved G3M2 variants powered by 745.2 kW (1,000 hp) Kinsei 42 or 45 engines, and later still by the G3M3 with 969 kW (1,300 hp) Kinsei 51 engines. About 1,050 aircraft of all versions were built.

Data (G3M2): *Engines* as above *Wing span* 25.0 m (82 ft 0¼ in) *Length* 16.45 m (53 ft 11¾ in) *Max T-O weight* 8,000 kg (17,636 lb) *Max level speed* 368 km/h (230 mph) *Normal range* 2,600 km (1,615 miles) *Armament* up to one 20 mm cannon and four 7.7 mm machine-guns, plus 1,000 kg (2,205 lb) of bombs or an 800 kg torpedo

Mitsubishi G4M (Japan) Developed from the G3M, the G4M (Navy Type 97 Torpedo Bomber), or *Betty* as it was known to the Allies, flew for the first time in October 1939. Following production of a small number of specially prepared but unsuccessful G6M1 escort-fighter variants, the G4M1 entered production as a medium bomber. This was the major production version, amounting to half of the 2,400 or so G4Ms built. Power was provided by two 1,140 kW (1,530 hp) Mitsubishi Kasei engines. It was while flying in a G4M1 that the Japanese naval Commander in Chief, Admiral Isoroku Yamamoto, was killed (see **Chronology** 18 April 1943).

The two major faults with the G4M were its lack of defensive armament and armour protection around vital areas such as fuel tanks. In combat it appeared all too easy to turn the bomber into a fireball, which led to the nickname 'flying lighter'. In response Mitsubishi developed the G4M2, a higher-powered version with increased armour and a cannon-armed dorsal turret in place of the previous half-blister position with one light machine-gun. Power was provided by two 1,341 kW (1,800 hp) Kasei 21 radial engines. Later variants of the G4M2 series (and the G4M3) had Kasei 25 or 27 engines.

Right up to the end of the war G4Ms remained prime targets for Allied fighters, some of the heaviest losses occurring during the so-called 'Marianas Turkey Shoot' of mid-1944. As mentioned under the Yokosuka Ohka entry, the G4M2e variant was the main carrier for the rocket-powered suicide aircraft, although again the bomber found it difficult to approach US naval vessels close enough to launch the limited-range Ohkas without being intercepted and destroyed by US Navy fighters.

Data (G4M2a): *Engines* two 1,378.5 kW (1,850 hp) Mitsubishi Kasei 25 radials *Wing span* 25.0 m (82 ft 0¼ in) *Length* 19.6 m (64 ft 4¾ in) *Max T-O weight* 12,500 kg (27,558 lb) *Max level speed* 440 km/h (273 mph) *Range* 1,920–6,000 km (1,193–3,728 miles) *Armament* one 7.7 mm machine-gun and four 20 mm cannon, plus up to 1,000 kg (2,205 lb) of bombs or an 800 kg torpedo

Mitsubishi G4M carrying an Ohka suicide aircraft.

Captured Mitsubishi J2M Raiden.

Mitsubishi J2M Raiden (Japan) Known to the Allies as *Jack*, the Raiden (Thunderbolt) was a single-seat land-based fighter. The first prototype flew on 20 March 1942 while powered by a Kasei 13 radial engine. The initial production version was the J2M2 powered by a 1,378.5 kW (1,850 hp) Kasei 23a engine and armed with two 7.7 mm machine-guns in the fuselage and two 20 mm cannon in the wings. Production of this version amounted to 155 aircraft, approximately one-third of all Raidens built before the end of the war. The only other version built in significant numbers was the J2M3. The four-cannon J2M5 was the fastest version, the Kasei 26a engine giving a maximum speed of 615 km/h (382 mph).

Data (J2M2): *Engine* as above *Wing span* 10.8 m (35 ft 5 in) *Length* 9.7 m (31 ft 10 in) *Max T-O weight* over 3,200 kg (7,055 lb) *Max level speed* 600 km/h (372 mph) *Range* 1,050 km (652 miles)

Captured Mitsubishi G4M2a.

Mitsubishi

Mitsubishi J8M Shusui.

Mitsubishi Ki-2-I.

Mitsubishi J8M Shusui (Japan) Rocket-powered single-seat interceptor based on the German Messerschmitt Me 163 Komet. Prototypes only.

Mitsubishi Navy K3M (Japan) The K3M was designed by Joji Hattori as a single-engined crew trainer for the Japanese Navy. It was a high-wing strut-braced monoplane with a fixed landing gear. Pilot and gunner were accommodated in open cockpits and there was a cabin under the wing for the remaining three crew members, including the instructor. The Navy was impressed with the performance of the four K3M1 prototypes and production was initiated as the Type 90-1 Crew Trainer. Three hundred and seventeen K3M2s, with 253.4 kW (340 hp) Hitachi radial engines, were followed by 301 K3M3s with 432.2 kW (580 hp) Nakajima Kotobukis. Production did not end until 1941. Code-named *Pine* by the Allies, the K3M was very successful as a trainer and proved useful in a liaison role.

Mitsubishi Navy K3M2s carrying surrender markings.

Mitsubishi Karigane I, the civil version of the Ki-15.

Mitsubishi Army Ki-1 (Japan) Based on a Junkers design, the Ki-1 was a cantilever low-wing monoplane with a fixed landing gear and twin fins and rudders. As the Army Type 93 Heavy Bomber it was flown against the Chinese during the mid-1930s. Power was provided by two 700.5 kW (940 hp) Mitsubishi Ha-2-2 in-line engines. Armament comprised 7.7 mm machine-guns in nose and dorsal positions and in a retractable ventral turret. Bomb load was up to 1,000 kg (2,205 lb). The Ki-1 Model 2 had improved fuselage contours and a trousered streamlined landing gear. Total production of both versions was 118. Maximum speed of the Ki-1 was 220 km/h (136.5 mph).

Mitsubishi Army Ki-2 (Japan) In contrast to the Ki-1, the Ki-2 was a successful design. Developed from the Junkers K-37, it was a three-seat low-wing light bomber, with a fixed landing gear and powered by two 424.8 kW (570 hp)

Mitsubishi Ki-1-II.

Nakajima Kotobuki radial engines. Single 7.7 mm machine-guns were mounted in nose and dorsal positions, and it carried a bomb load of 500 kg (1,102 lb). The original production version went into service from 1934, designated Army Type 93 Twin-engined Light Bomber. One hundred and thirteen were built.

In 1937 the radically redesigned Model 2 or Ki-2-II appeared with an enclosed pilot's cabin and a manually operated gun turret in the nose. An internal bomb bay accommodated a 300 kg (662 lb) offensive load and power was provided by two 559 kW (750 hp) Ha-8 radials. A retractable undercarriage was also introduced. Sixty-one Model 2s were completed during 1937–8. A record-breaking variant of the Model 2 was named *Ohtori*, which made a long-distance flight to Bangkok in December 1936, built to the order of the *Asahi* newspaper.

Data (Model 1): *Engines* as above *Wing span* 19.96 m (65 ft 5¾ in) *Length* 12.6 m (41 ft 4 in) *Max T-O weight* 4,645 kg (10,240 lb) *Max level speed* 225 km/h (140 mph)

Mitsubishi Army Ki-15 (Japan) The prototype of this two-seat cantilever low-wing cabin monoplane flew in May 1936. Eleven months later the civil-registered Kamikaze (Divine Wind) made a record flight from Tokyo to London in just over 51 hours flying time. The same year the Ki-15 type went into production as the Army Type 97. The rakish Ki-15 had a fixed, spatted cantilever landing gear and a single 410 kW (550 hp) Nakajima Ha-8 radial in a long-chord cowling. It proved a great success during the fighting in China.

Performance was increased with the Model 2 (Ki-15-II), which went into service in 1939 powered by a 670.7 kW (900 hp) Ha-26-I radial. The long range (2,400 km; 1,491 miles for the original version) enabled reconnaissance missions deep into Chinese territory. Army Ki-15s remained supreme until the arrival of the twin-engined Ki-46. The Japanese Navy was also attracted by the design and ordered 20 C5M1s with 652 kW (875 hp) Mitsubishi Zuisei radials; followed in 1940 by 30 C5M2s with 708 kW (950 hp) Naka-

jima Sakei power plants. A C5M2 operating from Indo-China on 10 December 1941 located the ill-fated British capital ships HMS *Prince of Wales* and *Repulse*.

The Ki-15/C5M was code-named *Babs* by the Allies. Production for the Army totalled 439.
Data (Ki-15-II): *Engine* as above *Wing span* 12.0 m (39 ft 4½ in) *Length* 8.7 m (28 ft 6½ in) *Max T-O weight* 2,480 kg (5,467 lb) *Max level speed* 510 km/h (317 mph)

Mitsubishi Army Ki-20 (Japan) Long-range heavy bomber developed from the Junkers G 38 commercial transport as the Army Type 92. Six were built but proved totally unsuccessful.

early aircraft were converted as transports and redesignated MC-21.
Data (Ki-21-IIb): *Engines* as above *Wing span* 22.5 m (73 ft 9¾ in) *Length* 16.0 m (52 ft 6 in) *Max T-O weight* 9,710 kg (21,407 lb) *Max level speed* 485 km/h (302 mph) *Range* 2,175 km (1,351 miles)

Mitsubishi Army Ki-30 (Japan) Code-named *Ann* by the Allies, this all-metal cantilever mid-wing monoplane went into service as the Army Type 97 Light Bomber in 1938, subsequently seeing widespread action in China and then in the early months of the Pacific War. It achieved a formidable reputation with effective attacks on enemy troops and strong points. The two-man crew were housed under a long raised canopy and it had a fixed, spatted cantilever landing gear. The 633.4 kW (850 hp) Mitsubishi Ha-6 radial engine gave a maximum speed of 432 km/h (268.5 mph). When production ceased in 1941 704 Ki-30s had been completed. Armament comprised two 7.7 mm machine-guns and 300 kg (661 lb) of bombs carried internally.

Mitsubishi Ki-46 (Japan) Code-named *Dinah* by the Allies, the Ki-46 is one of the less memorable Japanese aircraft of the Pacific War because of its HQ-reconnaissance role. However it was among the most successful aircraft to serve with the Japanese forces and for a time its very high performance gave it immunity from attack.

The prototype Ki-46 flew for the first time in November 1939, powered by two 633.4 kW (850 hp) Mitsubishi Ha-26-I engines. The first of more than 1,700 production aircraft were similarly powered; but the Ki-46-II major production version had two 784.5 kW (1,050 hp) Mitsubishi Ha-102 engines fitted, increasing speed by about 65 km/h (40 mph).

Mitsubishi Army Ki-21 (Japan) Known to the Allies as *Sally*, the Ki-21 was the most important Japanese Army bomber built between 1938 and 1944. The first of eight prototype and test aircraft flew on 18 December 1936. A total of 2,064 Ki-21s was eventually built, the first entering service during 1938 as the Army Type 97 Heavy Bomber.

The Model 1 was defensively armed with just three 7.7 mm machine-guns and power was provided by 633.4 kW (850 hp) Nakajima Ha-5Kai radial engines. Despite its good performance, it suffered some losses against indifferent Chinese opposition during the Sino-Japanese conflict that began again in 1937. Armament was subsequently increased by the addition of a tail 'stinger' gun and beam guns.

By the time of Pearl Harbor in December 1941, the new Model 2 equipped most bomber units, powered by 1,080.5 kW (1,450 hp) Mitsubishi Ha 101 radials. The larger nacelles of these engines enabled the main undercarriage wheels to be fully retracted. In its Ki-21-IIb version the bomber featured a large dorsal turret housing a 12.7 mm Type 1 machine-gun. The maximum bomb load for all versions of the Ki-21 was an unimpressive 1,000 kg (2,205 lb).

The Ki-21 served in every theatre of war where the Japanese Army was engaged. A number of

The final production version was the Ki-46-III powered by 1,118 kW (1,500 hp) Ha-112-II engines, giving a maximum level speed of 640 km/h (397.5 mph). Reconnaissance Ki-46-IIIs had a reshaped and more heavily glazed pilot's cockpit which merged into the nose of the fuselage. The 607 production Ki-46-IIIs included a number of -KAI interceptors, specially prepared with one 37 mm cannon and two 20 mm cannon or 12.7 mm machine-guns. The Ki-46-IV was a turbo super-charged version of the III.
Data (Ki-46-II): *Engines* as above *Wing span* 14.7 m (48 ft 3 in) *Length* 11.0 m (36 ft 1 in) *Max T-O weight* 5,050 kg (11,133.5 lb) *Max level speed* 595 km/h (370 mph) *Range* 2,880 km (1,790 miles) *Armament* one 7.7 mm machine-gun or none

Mitsubishi

Mitsubishi Ki-51.

Mitsubishi Army Ki-51 (Japan) Drawing on the experience gained with the Ki-30, the Mitsubishi design team developed two Ki-51 prototypes which flew in the summer of 1939. Intended specifically for ground-attack work, they dispensed with an internal bomb bay and were thus able to adopt a low-wing layout. The two crew members were seated closer together under a shorter canopy, thus ensuring better co-ordination. Power was provided by a 708 kW (950 hp) Mitsubishi Ha-26-II radial engine in a long-chord cowling. Production lasted until July 1945, a total of 2,385 machines being built. Armament comprised two wing-mounted 7.7 mm machine-guns (replaced by 12.7 mm weapons in late production aircraft) and a flexibly mounted 7.7 mm gun. The bomb load carried externally was up to 200 kg (441 lb).

Mitsubishi Ki-67-Ib Hiryu.

Going into service as the Type 99, the Ki-51 proved adaptable and saw widespread service in the Far East theatres of war. Incorporated in the design was provision for tactical-reconnaissance equipment and the type was often used for such duties. With the desperate situation that faced Japan by 1945, a number were expended on Kamikaze missions, carrying a 250 kg bomb. Interestingly several Ki-51s captured by Indonesian Nationalist forces were used against the Dutch during the second half of 1945. The Ki-51 was code-named *Sonia* by the Allies.
Data: *Engines* as above *Wing span* 12.1 m (39 ft 8½ in) *Length* 9.21 m (30 ft 2½ in) *Max T-O weight* 2,920 kg (6,437 lb) *Max level speed* 424 km/h (263.5 mph) *Range* 1,060 km (658.5 miles)

Mitsubishi Army Ki-57 and MC-20 (Japan) The MC-20 was an 11-passenger commercial airliner powered by two 633.4 kW (850 hp) Kinsei engines. From the MC-20 was evolved the military 12–20-troop Ki-57 or Type 100 Transport Plane Model 1, known to the Allies as *Topsy*. About 500 Ki-57s were built in two versions: the Ki-57-I with 633.4 kW (850 hp) Ha-5 engines and the Ki-57-II with 782.5 kW (1,050 hp) Ha-102 engines.

Mitsubishi Army Ki-57.

Mitsubishi Army Ki-67 Hiryu and Ki-109 (Japan) There were two major versions of the Ki-67 or *Peggy*, to give it its Allied code name: the standard bomber carrying a crew of seven, a bomb load of 800–1,600 kg (1,764–3,528 lb) or a torpedo and defensive armament of one 20 mm cannon and four 12.7 mm machine-guns; and a special three-seat model which was used for suicide attacks on Allied shipping. For suicide missions defensive armament was removed, the nose and tail were faired in, side blisters removed and a long rod projecting from the nose of the aircraft fitted to trip a switch to explode two 800 kg bombs on impact with the target. About 700 Ki-67s were built.

Developments of the basic Ki-67 included the Ki-109 interceptor, carrying a 75 mm cannon, a small number of which were operated fairly unsuccessfully against Boeing B-29 bombers of the USAAF.
Data (Ki-67): *Engines* two 1,431 kW (1,920 hp) Mitsubishi Ha-104 radials *Wing span* 22.5 m (73 ft 9¾ in) *Length* 18.7 m (61 ft 4¼ in) *Max T-O weight* 13,765–13,850 kg (30,346–30,534 lb) *Max level speed* 540 km/h (335 mph) *Range* 3,800 km (2,361 miles)

Mitsubishi MU-2 (Japan) The MU-2 is a twin-turboprop STOL utility transport, the basic design of which was begun in 1960. Prototype construction began in 1962 and the first aircraft was flown on 14 September 1963. By March 1979 total orders for the MU-2 (all versions) had reached 570, including 524 for export and 46 for Japanese customers.

The two current versions are the Marquise, basically similar to the MU-2N but with AiResearch TPE 331-10-501M turboprop engines, four-bladed propellers and increased fuel capacity (7 built by 1979); and the Solitaire, basically similar to the MU-2P but with AiResearch TPE 331-10-501M turboprop engines, rated in this installation at 495.5 kW (665 shp) each (3 built by 1979).
Data (Marquise): *Engines* two 533 kW (715 shp) Garrett-AiResearch TPE 331-10-501M turboprops *Wing span over tip-tanks* 11.94 m (39 ft 2 in) *Length* 12.02 m (39 ft 5 in) *Max T-O weight* 5,250 kg (11,575 lb) *Max cruising speed* 571 km/h (355 mph) *Range* 2,584 km (1,606 miles) *Accommodation* pilot and co-pilot/passenger and seven–nine passengers

Mitsubishi MU-300 Diamond I (Japan) First flown on 29 August 1978, the Diamond I is a prototype twin-turbofan business aircraft powered by 11.1 kN (2,500 lb st) Pratt & Whitney Aircraft of Canada JT15D-4 engines.

Mitsubishi T-2 (Japan) The T-2 was the first supersonic aircraft developed by the Japanese aircraft industry. It is a twin-engined two-seat jet trainer designed to meet the requirements of the JASDF. The first XT-2 prototype took to the air on 20 July 1971 and flew supersonically for the first time in level flight (Mach 1.03) during its 30th flight on 19 November 1971.

Production orders have been placed for 73 T-2s: 31 T-2 advanced trainers, 40 T-2A combat trainers, and two as prototypes for the F-1 close-support fighter version, described separately. Fifty-two of the T-2/2As had been delivered by March 1979.

Data: *Engines* two 32.5 kN (7,305 lb st, with after-burning) Rolls-Royce Turboméca Adour turbofans *Wing span* 7.88 m (25 ft 10¼ in) *Length* 17.84 m (58 ft 6¼ in) *Max T-O weight* 9,805 kg (21,616 lb) *Max level speed* Mach 1.6 *Ferry range* 2,593 km (1,610 miles) *Armament* (combat trainer version) one Vulcan JM-61A-1 multi-barrel 20 mm cannon in lower fuselage. Attachment point on underfuselage centreline and two under each wing for drop-tanks or other stores. Wingtip attachments for air-to-air missiles

Mitsubishi Hinazuru (Japan) Japanese licence-built version of the Airspeed Envoy.

MKEK Models 1 to 7 (Turkey) In 1952 MKEK took over the Turk Hava Kurumu (THK) factory. The THK-15 two-seat trainer became the MKEK Model 1; the projected THK-16 small twin-jet trainer became the MKEK Model 2; the THK-5 twin-engined light ambulance became the MKEK Model 5; the THK-5A twin-engined six-seat transport became the MKEK Model 5A; the THK-14 two-seat sailplane became the MKEK Model 6; and the THK-2 single-seat aerobatic trainer became the MKEK Model 7. In addition MKEK produced the Model 4 two-seat

primary trainer, examples of which were delivered to the Turkish Air Force and presented to the Royal Jordanian Air Force.

Monnett Sonerai and Sonerai II (USA) Single-seat Formula V racing aircraft and two-seat high-performance sporting aircraft respectively, plans and component parts for which are available to amateur constructors.

Mooney 201 (M20J) and Executive (USA) Four-seat cabin monoplane powered by a 149 kW (200 hp) Lycoming IO-360-A3B6D engine. Faster development of the now discontinued Executive (M-20F). A total of 763 had been built by 1 December 1978. Maximum level speed 325 km/h (202 mph).

Mooney M-10 Cadet (USA) See **Alon**

Mooney M-18 Mite (USA) Single-seat light monoplane, the first product of the company and originally powered by an 18.6 kW (25 hp) Crosley engine. Two new production versions were developed as the M-18LA (48.4 kW; 65 hp Lycoming O-145 engine) and the M-18C (48.4 kW; 65 hp Continental A-65 engine).

Mooney Chaparral (USA) Updated version of the Super-21 which flew for the first time in July 1963. Four-seat cabin monoplane powered by a 149 kW (200 hp) Lycoming IO-360-A1A engine.

Mooney Mark 21, Master and Super-21 (USA) In 1954 Mooney began production of the Model M-20 four-seat light monoplane. Soon the M-20A (Lycoming O-360-A) had superseded the M-20 (Lycoming O-320) and by 1964 the current versions comprised the Mark 21 (M-20C), Master (M-20D) and Super-21 (M-20E, see **Mooney Ranger**)

Mooney Mark 22 (USA) Five-seat light monoplane powered by a 231 kW (310 hp) Lycoming TIO-541-A1A engine.

Mooney Ranger (USA) The Ranger (first flown in 1961) is the current name of the Super-21 (see above). Power is provided by a 134 kW (180 hp) Lycoming O-360-A1D engine. By the end of 1978 2,191 Rangers had been built.

Data: *Engine* as above *Wing span* 10.67 m (35 ft 0 in) *Length* 7.06 m (23 ft 2 in) *Max T-O weight* 1,168 kg (2,575 lb) *Max level speed* 272 km/h (169 mph) *Range* 1,410 km (876 miles)

Mitsubishi MU-2L (foreground) and MU-2M.

Mitsubishi MU-300 Diamond I.

Mooney 201 (M20J).

Mooney Chaparral.

Mitsubishi T-2.

Mooney Statesman (USA) This model (M-20G) was introduced in 1968 and was basically similar to the Mark 21 (M-20C), except for having the longer fuselage of the Executive and two additional passenger windows, plus other refinements. By mid-January 1970 183 had been delivered.

Mooney Ranger.

Mooney Statesman.

Mooney Turbo Mooney 231 (USA) The Turbo Mooney (M-20K) first flew in 1976 and is generally similar to the Ranger except for having a 156.5 kW (210 hp) Continental TSIO-360-GE turbocharged engine and increased wing span. Maximum level speed is 338 km/h (210 mph).

Morane-Saulnier Type AC (France) Appearing in the autumn of 1916, the Type AC was a single-seat shoulder-wing scout with a circular cross-section fuselage and a long headrest fairing. Triangular fins and rudders were positioned above and below the fuselage. Armament comprised a single synchronised Vickers 0.303 in machine-gun. Power was normally provided by a closely cowled 82 kW (110 hp) Le Rhône 9J rotary. Some 30 Type ACs were built, two going to the RFC and the rest to French units.

Morane-Saulnier Type AI (France) Tested in August 1917, the Type AI was produced in three main versions: the MoS 27C1 and Mos 29C1 were fighting scouts usually powered by single 112 kW (150 hp) Gnôme Monosoupape 9N engines – the former having a single Vickers synchronised 0.303 in machine-gun and the latter twin guns; the MoS 30E1 was an unarmed lower-powered single-seat trainer.

The basic design was a parasol-wing monoplane with complex strut-bracing providing considerable strength. The forward fuselage was of metal construction and the rear of spruce, the whole tapering to a point at the rear behind the tailplane.

It is believed some 1,300 were built. The single-seat scouts served briefly with French

Morane-Saulnier Type BB.

Morane-Saulnier Type AC (military XXIII).

escadrilles MS 156, 158 and 161 in early 1918, being withdrawn in mid-May after allegations of structural weakness. The MoS 30E1 was used by the AEF in France for training. Small numbers were also exported. The type continued to serve after the war as a military trainer, although others were disposed of on the civilian market.

Data (MoS 27C1): *Engine* as above *Wing span* 8.5 m (27 ft 11 in) *Length* 5.65 m (18 ft 6½ in) *Max T-O weight* 421 kg (926 lb) *Max level speed* 225 km/h (140.5 mph)

Morane-Saulnier AR (France) First flown in 1915, the AR was a two-seat parasol-wing monoplane constructed largely of wood with fabric covering. About 400 were built after World War I (when it was known as the MS.35), mainly as intermediate trainers in three principal versions: MS.35R with a 59.6 kW (80 hp) Le Rhône 9c rotary engine; MS.35A with an Anzani engine; and MS.35C with a Clerget 9B engine. The MS.35EP2 served with French Aéronautique Militaire 'Ecoles de Pilotage' up to 1929. Other military users were Poland (60), Argentina, Belgium, Brazil, Guatemala, Romania, Soviet Union (30) and Turkey. A number also went to civil users.

Morane-Saulnier Types BB and BH (France) The BB of 1915 was a two-seat short-span biplane powered by a 59.6 kW (80 hp) or 82 kW (110 hp) Le Rhône rotary engine with a circular cowling and large spinner. A Lewis gun was spigot-mounted over the rear cockpit and a fixed machine-gun fired forward from the top of the upper wing. Most served with the French Army for artillery observation duties, although three RFC squadrons were briefly equipped with the type. The BH was an experimental variant with a Hispano-Suiza water-cooled engine.

Morane-Saulnier Types G and H (France) The Type G was a two-seat mid-wing monoplane for civil and military use. Built in 1912, the GA variant had a 44.7 kW (60 hp) Le Rhône rotary engine and the GB a 59.6 kW (80 hp) Gnome. Ninety-four were delivered to the French Army during 1913–14. The Type H was a single-seat equivalent, 76 going into French military service in 1913.

Morane-Saulnier Types L and LA (France) The two-seat Type L (popularly known as the Morane Parasol) appeared in 1913 powered by a 59.6 kW (80 hp) rotary engine. The original L had lateral control by wing warping, but the LA was fitted with ailerons. Fifty aircraft built for Turkey were requisitioned in August 1914 and equipped French escadrilles MS 23 and MS 26. Eventually some 600 went to the French Army.

Others were supplied to the RFC, RNAS and to Russia. Sub-Lieut Warneford – flying from the RNAS Station at Dunkerque in a Type L – destroyed German Army Zeppelin LZ37 over Belgium on 6/7 June 1915 by flying overhead and dropping small bombs onto the airship's envelope, setting it on fire (see **Chronology**).

The original armament – earning the Type L the optimistic French title 'Morane de Chasse' – was a rifle, carbine or Lewis gun carried by a crew member. Even so several German aircraft fell to Type Ls during the next few months. It was while flying a Type L fitted with an experimental machine-gun mounting that Roland Garros was forced to land behind enemy lines on 1 April 1915 (see **Chronology**).

Data: *Engine* as above *Wing span* 10.3 m (33 ft 9½ in) *Length* 6.32 m (20 ft 9 in) *Max T-O weight* 680 kg (1,499 lb) *Max level speed* 115 km/h (71.5 mph)

Morane-Saulnier Types N, I and V (France) A single-seat shoulder-wing scout, the Type N was designed in 1914 and was known to the French as the 'Monocoque' (a misnomer) and to the British as 'Bullet'. Power was provided by a 59.6 kW (80 hp) Le Rhône rotary engine. Twenty-four were used by the RFC and a smaller number by the French. Armament was a single light-calibre fixed machine-gun. Four examples of the 82 kW (110 hp) Le Rhône-powered Type I variant were also acquired by Britain, together with 12 Type V scouts. A considerable number of Type Is and Type Vs were also supplied to Russia.

Morane-Saulnier Type P (France) A total of 565 Morane-Saulnier Type P two-seat parasol-wing monoplanes was built from 1916. It had a carefully faired round-section fuselage of entirely new design and a large spinner for its 82 kW (110 hp) Le Rhône 9J rotary engine. Alternatively designated MoS 21, it was intended largely for reconnaissance duties. Armament comprised a 7.7 mm forward-firing machine-gun fixed above the wing and another on a ring mounting over the rear cockpit. Most were used by the French from 1917, although some were supplied to the RFC.

Morane-Saulnier Type T (France) The Type T was a large unequal-span biplane powered by two 59.6 kW (80 hp) Le Rhône rotary engines in streamlined nacelles between the biplane wings. Ailerons were fitted to the top wing only. One hundred Type Ts were ordered by the French Army in 1916 as three-seat reconnaissance aircraft.

Morane-Saulnier MS.35 (France) Post-World War I designation of the Morane-Saulnier AR (see entry).

Morane-Saulnier MS.43 (France) Following the single MS.42, 79 MS.43 robust two-seat unequal-span intermediate training biplanes were built for the French Aéronautique Militaire – flown between 1924 and 1929. Power was provided by the 134 kW (180 hp) Hispano 8Ab liquid-cooled engine. One machine used by the US Military Attaché in Paris during 1929.

Morane-Saulnier MS.129 and MS.130 (France) The prototype MS.130 trainer flew for the first time in 1926 and represented a considerable advance over previous Morane parasol-wing

Morane-Saulnier Type N.

trainers. The swept-back wing was strut-braced (instead of wire-braced) and was an 'autostable' design with a thick section, both surfaces being convex. Wing spars were of dural tube but the rest of the basic structure was of wood. Wings, tailplane and circular-section fuselage were all covered with fabric.

A total of 145 MS.130s was built, most going to the French Navy, although 26 were delivered to civil operators and 15 were exported to Brazil. The 171.4 kW (230 hp) Salmson Ab radial replaced the 134 kW (180 hp) Hispano-Suiza of the earlier MS.129, 15 of which went to civil users.

Data (MS.130): *Engine* as above *Wing span* 10.7 m (35 ft 1¼ in) *Length* 6.94 m (22 ft 9¼ in) *Max T-O weight* 1,165 kg (2,568 lb) *Max level speed* 210 km/h (130.5 mph)

Morane-Saulnier MS.138 (France) Developed from the MS.35 and first flown in 1927, the MS.138 was a basic trainer (178 built). Most flew with the French Aéronautique Militaire, remaining in use until 1935; others were exported to Denmark and Greece. Thirty-three more were civil registered. It was a two-seat wire-braced parasol-wing monoplane, largely of wooden construction but with metal wing spars. All surfaces were fabric covered. Power was provided by a 59.6 kW (80 hp) Le Rhône 9c rotary engine.

Morane-Saulnier MS.147 (France) Developed from the MS.138 with a redesigned wing and an 89.4 kW (120 hp) Salmson 9Ac radial engine. One hundred and nine were built, mainly for export – 30 alone going to Brazil.

Morane-Saulnier MS.149 (France) The MS.149 represented an interim stage between the MS.138 and MS.130. It had the wing of the MS.130 but retained the wire wing bracing of the earlier aircraft. Power was provided by a 74.5 kW (100 hp) Lorraine 5Pa radial engine. Fifty-six were supplied to the French Navy, serving until 1935.

Morane-Saulnier MS.225 (France) Developed from the MS.121 'Jockey' fighter and the MS.221/MS.224 prototypes, the MS.225 was an all-metal parasol-wing monoplane. It was

Morane-Saulnier MS.130.

Morane-Saulnier

Morane-Saulnier MS.317.

Morane-Saulnier
MS.405 C1.

Morane-Saulnier MS.225.

powered by a 372.6 kW (500 hp) Gnome-Rhône 9Kbrs radial engine. Seventy-four were built during 1932–34: three were exported to China, 15 went to the French Aéronavale (Escadrille 3C1), and the balance went to the Armée de l'Air, serving with GC I/7 and GC I/42 until 1937. Armament comprised twin 7.5 mm machine-guns.

Nine MS.225s flew with the Dijon-based 'Patrouille Aérobatique' and five more (with modified tailplanes) with the national display team 'Patrouille de l'Ecole de l'Air'. One-off variants included the MS.226 modified for carrier experiments.

Data: *Engine* as above *Wing span* 10.56 m (34 ft 7¾ in) *Length* 7.24 m (23 ft 9 in) *Max T-O weight* 1,581 kg (3,485 lb) *Max level speed* 328 km/h (204 mph) *Range* 950 km (590 miles)

Morane-Saulnier MS.229 (France) This was a variant of the MS.230 parasol-wing basic trainer. It differed largely in having a 141.6 kW (190 hp) Hispano-Suiza 8Ac liquid-cooled engine. Two examples were bought by Switzerland in 1931, one being converted the following year to take a Wright 9Qa radial.

Morane-Saulnier MS.230 (France) Designed to meet a 1928 French Air Ministry Programme, the prototype MS.230 flew for the first time in February 1929. Because of its excellent flying and aerobatic qualities, more than 1,000 were eventually built: used by the Armée de l'Air as an observation, gunnery and advanced pilot-training aircraft, as well as for target-towing. A number also served with French naval aviation. All but 77 were built by the parent company, 59 of the remainder constructed pre-war by SFAN and 18 post-war by Levasseur. Several MS.230s were also privately owned, while others were used by commercial flying schools. In addition 20 were exported to Romania, 25 to Greece, nine to Brazil and nine to Belgium.

Variants of the MS.230 included the MS.233 with a Gnome-Rhône Titan engine (22 built in France and 16 by OGMA in Portugal); the MS.234 special aerobatic single-seater flown by Michel Detroyat; and the MS.236 (built under licence by SABCA in Belgium with a Lynx engine).

Data (MS.230): *Engine* one 171.4 kW (230 hp) Salmson 9Ab *Wing span* 10.7 m (35 ft 1¼ in) *Length* 6.7 m (22 ft 10¾ in) *Max T-O weight* 1,150 kg (2,535 lb) *Max level speed* 205 km/h (127.5 mph)

Morane-Saulnier MS.315 (France) Lighter than the MS.230, the MS.315 was a primary trainer with a 100.6 kW (135 hp) Salmson 9Nc

radial engine and a redesigned fin and rudder. Four 1933 prototypes were followed by 346 production aircraft for French military use, 33 being completed after World War II. Production included five civil MS.315/2s. A number of pre-war aircraft were operated after the war for target-towing, fitted with 164 kW (220 hp) Continental engines and redesignated MS.317.

Morane-Saulnier MS.405 and MS.406 (France) Entered for the Armée de l'Air single-seat fighter Programme of 1934, the MS.405 prototype flew for the first time on 8 August 1935. Good performance and excellent flying qualities made it a natural successor to the D.500 series, but complexity of construction led to its redesign to suit it for mass production. By the time production had started, all technical advantage had been lost.

Fifteen MS.405 C1s were built, largely for design development. The first production MS.406 C1 flew on 29 January 1939 but was outmoded compared with fighters already in service in Britain and Germany. Nevertheless 572 MS.406 C1s had been delivered by the outbreak of World War II. Deliveries had risen to 1,080 when France collapsed in June 1940. The most important French fighter during the Battle of France, it gave a reasonable account of itself. Thirty were also exported to Finland, 30 to Turkey and two to Switzerland. Thirty-six aircraft captured by the Germans were supplied to Croatia in 1942 and 20 others to Finland. Interestingly the latter were powered by captured Soviet M-105 engines.

The MS.406 C1 was a cantilever low-wing monoplane with a bulky fuselage. Construction was of metal with 'Plymax' (plywood and aluminium) covering, except for the rear fuselage, tailplane and moving control surfaces which were fabric covered. The landing-gear wheels retracted inwards and an archaic tailskid was standard. Armament comprised one 20 mm HS-9 or HS-404 cannon which fired through the hollow propeller shaft of the 641 kW (860 hp) Hispano-Suiza 12Y31 engine, augmente by two wing-mounted 7.5 mm MAC 1934 machine-guns.

Data (MS.406 C1): *Engine* as above *Wing span* 10.61 m (34 ft 9¾ in) *Length* 8.17 m (26 ft 9¾ in) *Max T-O weight* 2,540 kg (5,600 lb) *Max level speed* 488 km/h (303 mph) *Range* 800 km (497 miles)

Morane-Saulnier MS.470 'Vanneau' (France) The MS.470.01 intermediate trainer prototype flew for the first time in December 1944. An all-metal cantilever low-wing monoplane, the MS.470 housed the crew in tandem under a glazed canopy. It had an inward-retracting landing gear, the wheels of which turned through 90° to lie partially exposed under the fuselage in case of a wheels-up landing. Five hundred production aircraft were built: 230 MS.472s (477 kW; 640 hp Gnome-Rhône 14M radial); 70 MS.474s (navalised version of MS.472); and 200 MS.475s (641 kW; 860 hp liquid-cooled Hispano-Suiza 12Y45). The MS.477 and MS.479 were experimental variants with 432.2 kW (580 hp) Renault 12SO2 and 611 kW (820 hp) SNECMA 14X-04 engines respectively.

Morane-Saulnier MS.500 Criquet (France) During World War II the Morane-Saulnier factory was a major producer of the Fieseler Fi.156 liaison aircraft. Post-war production continued as the MS.560 Criquet with the original Argus As 410C engine fitted. Two other versions of the Criquet were the MS.501 (Renault 6Q engine) and the MS.502 (Salmson 9Abc), the latter being produced in quantity. The Criquet saw considerable service with the Armée de l'Air and Aéronavale.

Morane-Saulnier MS.570 and MS.571 (France) The MS.571 was a three–four-seat version of the MS.570 two-seat touring and training monoplane, powered by the same 104.3 kW (140 hp) Renault 4Pei engine.

Morane-Saulnier MS.733 Alcyon (France) The MS.730 and MS.732 prototypes flew in 1949 and 1951 respectively. Three-seat all-metal low-wing monoplanes with long glazed crew canopies, they were intended for basic training. The landing gear of the MS.730 was fixed, while that of the MS.732 retracted rearwards. The MS.733.01 prototype flew for the first time in 1951 and had an outward-retracting undercarriage. Two hundred production aircraft went to the Armée de l'Air (130), Aéronavale (40) and for export (including 15 to Cambodia). Some French machines (carrying a light machine-gun) were used as gunnery trainers. In 1956 some were redesignated MS.733A and were operated on counter-insurgency duties in Algeria, armed with machine-guns and anti-personnel bombs.

Data: *Engine* one 171.4 kW (230 hp) Potez 6D *Wing span* 11.28 m (37 ft 0 in) *Length* 9.32 m (30 ft 7 in) *Max T-O weight* 1,670 kg (3,682 lb) *Max level speed* 260 km/h (161.5 mph)

Morane-Saulnier MS.760 Paris.

Morane-Saulnier MS.760 Paris (France) Developed from the experimental MS.755 Fleuret two-seat jet fighter trainer of 1953, the prototype MS.760 flew for the first time on 29 July 1954. Designed primarily as a four-seat high-speed communications aircraft, it was also easily adaptable for training and other duties. A total of 219 production aircraft was built: the Armée de l'Air receiving 31, Aéronavale 19, Argentina 88 (76 built under licence) and Brazil 48.

Data: *Engines* two 3.91 kN (880 lb st) Turboméca Marboré II turbojets *Wing span* 10.15 m (33 ft 3 in) *Length* 10.05 m (33 ft 0 in) *Max T-O weight* 3,375 kg (7,440 lb) *Max level speed* 650 km/h (404 mph) *Range* 1,500 km (932 miles) *Armament* in weapon-training role could comprise two 7.5 mm machine-guns and two 50 kg bombs or four 3.5 in rockets

Morane-Saulnier MS.500 Criquet.

Myasishchev M-4 (USSR) Known to NATO as *Bison*, the M-4 is a long-range reconnaissance bomber operated by the Soviet Air Force and Navy. The prototype first flew in about 1954 and three versions are currently operational. The *Bison-A* is a long-range reconnaissance bomber with internal bomb bays for free-fall nuclear or conventional weapons. Up to 50 have been modified into flight-refuelling tankers. *Bison-B* is the maritime-reconnaissance version, with a solid nose replacing the glazed nose of the A and fitted with a large superimposed flight-refuelling probe.

Morane-Saulnier MS.733A Alcyon.

Myasishchev M-4 *Bison-C.*

Myasishchev M-52 Bounder.

It also has underfuselage blister fairings over electronic equipment and armament is reduced by the removal of the aft gun turrets above and below the fuselage. *Bison-C* is similar to B except for having a large search radar faired into a longer nose, aft of the centrally mounted flight-refuelling probe.

Data (*Bison-A*): *Engines* four 85.3 kN (19,180 lb st) Mikulin AM-3D turbojets *Wing span* 50.48 m (165 ft 7½ in) *Length* 47.2 m (154 ft 10 in) *Max T-O weight* 158,750 kg (350,000 lb) *Max level speed* 901 km/h (560 mph) *Unrefuelled range* (with 4,535 kg; 10,000 lb of bombs) 11,265 km (7,000 miles) *Armament* ten 23 mm guns in twin-gun turrets above fuselage, fore and aft of wings, under fuselage, fore and aft of weapon bays, and in tail. Three weapon bays in centre fuselage for free-fall nuclear or conventional weapons

Myasishchev M-52 (USSR) Prototype supersonic strategic bomber of about 1958, known to NATO as *Bounder*. Powered by four 127.5 kN (28,660 lb st) D-15 turbojets, the inner two having afterburning. Estimated maximum level speed 2,000 km/h (1,243 mph). Proved to have a limited range and so was adapted for experimental work.

Muegyetemi Sportrepulo Egyesulet Gerle 12 and 13, and M-19, M-21 and M-24 (Hungary) The Gerle 12 was a two-seat training or sporting biplane powered by a 97 kW (130 hp) Weiss Manfred Sp.III engine. The Gerle 13 was another sporting aircraft, this time powered by an Armstrong Siddeley Genet Major engine. One Gerle 13 made two important flights in 1933: the first from Budapest through Italy, France, Spain, North Africa, Egypt, Palestine, Turkey, Greece, Italy and back to Budapest; and the other from Budapest through Northern Europe to England and back to Budapest.

The M-19, also of the 1930s, was a light cabin monoplane powered by a 97 kW (130 hp) Gipsy Major engine. The M-21 was a 119 kW (160 hp)

Nakajima A2N1.

Mudry CAP 20L.

Siemens Sh.14A-powered single-seat advanced-training and aerobatic biplane, while the M-24 was another two-seat cabin monoplane powered by a 74.5 kW (100 hp) Hirth HM.504 engine and with a retractable landing gear.

Mudry CAP 10B, CAP 20L and CAP 21 (France) The CAP 10 was originally developed by CAARP and the prototype first flew in August 1968. The current CAP 10B is a two-seat light monoplane intended for training, touring and aerobatics. Power is provided by a 134 kW (180 hp) Lycoming IO-360-B2F engine. Ninety CAP 10s had been built by May 1979, including 30 for the French Air Force (more have since been ordered, plus 6 for the French Navy).

The CAP 20L first flew in 1976 and is a lightweight development of the CAP 20. It is a single-seat aerobatic light monoplane powered by a 149 kW (200 hp) Lycoming AIO-360-B1B engine.

The CAP 21 is a new single-seat aerobatic competition aircraft, first displayed at the 1979 Paris Air Show. Power is provided by an AIO-360-B1B engine.

Muniz M-7 and M-9 (Brazil) Two-seat light primary training biplane (M-7) and two-seat advanced training biplane (M-9) of the 1930s, powered by a 97 kW (130 hp) de Havilland Gipsy Major and a 149 kW (200 hp) Gipsy Six engine respectively.

Muniz M-11 (Brazil) see **CNNA**

Muniz Casmuniz 52 (Brazil) The Casmuniz 52 was a twin-engined (138 kW; 185 hp Continental E-185) five-seat cabin monoplane, the first all-metal twin-engined aircraft to be built in Brazil. The prototype underwent flight tests to obtain certification in 1955.

Nakajima Navy A1N (Japan) Licence-built Gloster Gambet single-seat fighter powered by a Bristol Jupiter VI radial engine. It entered service with the Japanese Navy as the Type 3 Carrier Fighter.

Nakajima Navy A2N (Japan) The stylish and robust NY prototype single-seat carrier-borne fighter biplane was flight tested in early 1930. It featured elliptical wingtips and a divided wide-track and spatted landing gear. Ailerons were fitted to both upper and lower wings and power was provided by a 372.6 kW (500 hp) Nakajima Kotobuki radial engine enclosed by a Townend ring cowl.

The NY went into production as the Navy Type 90 Carrier Fighter or A2N. The first two production versions, the A2N1 and A2N2, had no upper wing dihedral, but the A2N3 introduced dihedral to both wings. Armament comprised two

Nakajima B6N1 Tenzan.

forward-firing 7.7 mm Vickers machine-guns. A2Ns were operated over Shanghai with the resumption of hostilities between Japan and China in July 1937, flying from the carrier *Kaga*.

Production of the A2N types totalled 106 single-seaters and 66 similar A3N1 two-seat trainers. Maximum level speed of the A2N1 was 325 km/h (202 mph).

Nakajima Navy A4N1 (Japan) Developed as a stop-gap type prior to the introduction of low-wing monoplane single-seat fighters, the Japanese Navy's A4N1 owed a great deal to its 1930 pre-decessor, the A2N. Power was provided by a 574 kW (770 hp) Nakajima Hikari radial engine in a long-chord cowling and the aircraft could carry a jettisonable underwing auxiliary fuel tank for extended range. A tailwheel replaced the A2N's tailskid. In general, however, it represented only a minimal advance over the earlier type. Entering service in 1935 as the Type 95 Carrier Fighter, the A4N1 (company designation YM) was popular with the Navy's traditionalists who preferred the biplane for its manoeuvrability. Two hundred and twenty-one were built, remaining in first-line service until 1939. Maximum speed was 352 km/h (218.5 mph)

Nakajima AT (Japan) The AT was an all-metal ten-seat commercial monoplane, specially designed for operation on Japanese air routes. By mid-1941 three were in regular use in Manchukuo and five others were under construction for the Tokyo–Hsinking and Tokyo–Tienstin services. Power was provided by two 343 kW (460 hp) Nakajima Kotobuki IIB radial engines.

When Japan became involved in World War II the aircraft was taken over as a military type, designated Ki-34 or Type 97 Transport. It was code-named *Thora* by the Allies. Later production aircraft had 484.4 kW (650 hp) Ha-1B engines. Approximately 350 of all versions were built.

Nakajima Navy B5N (Japan) The prototype of this cantilever low-wing monoplane torpedo bomber flew for the first time in early 1937, powered by a 574 kW (770 hp) Nakajima Hikari 3 nine-cylinder radial engine. With a maximum speed of 360 km/h (224 mph), it was a first-class aircraft and was ordered into production as the B5N1, entering service as the Type 97 Torpedo Bomber.

With the introduction of the improved 760 kW (1,020 hp) Nakajima Sakae 11-powered B5N2 or Type 97 Model 3 in 1940, some B5N1s were relegated to training duties, although a sufficient number remained operational in December 1941 to take a major part in the Pearl Harbor attack. Production of the B5N totalled about 1,200 aircraft. A number were later employed as anti-

submarine aircraft. The Allied code name for the B5N was *Kate*.

Data (B5N2): *Engine* as above *Wing span* 15.5 m (50 ft 10½ in) *Length* 10.3 m (33 ft 9½ in) *Max T-O weight* 4,100 kg (9,039 lb) *Max level speed* 380 km/h (236 mph) *Range* 980 km (609 miles) *Armament* two forward-firing 7.7 mm and one or two rear-mounted 7.7 mm machine-guns, plus 500 kg of bombs or an 800 kg torpedo

Nakajima Navy B6N Tenzan (Japan) Designed as a replacement for the B5N, the B6N Tenzan (Heavenly Mountain) entered service in 1944 as the Carrier Attack Plane. The original production version was the B6N1 powered by a 1,393.5 kW (1,870 hp) Nakajima Mamoru II (Protector) 14-cylinder radial engine. Problems with this engine led to the introduction of the major version, the B6N2 with a Mitsubishi Kasei 25 14-cylinder engine developing 1,147.6 kW (1,540 hp) at 5,500 m (18,050 ft). Production of both versions totalled nearly 1,270 aircraft.

Code-named *Jill* by the Allies, the B6N also performed reconnaissance duties and, like so many other types, ended its career in Kamikaze attacks.

Data (B6N2 torpedo bomber): *Engine* as above *Wing span* 14.9 m (48 ft 10 in) *Length* 10.85 m (35 ft 7½ in) *Max T-O weight* 5,210–5,650 kg (11,486–12,455 lb) *Max level speed* 480 km/h (298 mph) *Range* more than 1,450 km (900 miles) or 3,680 km (2,287 miles) in a reconnaissance role *Armament* one forward-firing 7.7 mm machine-gun in the wing and one 7.7 mm gun in the rear cockpit. A ventral floor hatch position was also provided. One 800 kg torpedo or six 100 kg bombs

Nakajima Navy C6N Saiun (Japan) The Saiun (Painted Cloud) entered service in 1944 as the C6N1 or Carrier Reconnaissance Plane Model 12, powered by a 1,490.4 kW (2,000 hp) Nakajima Homare 21 18-cylinder radial engine. It was code-named *Myrt* by the Allies. Performance was excellent and so defensive armament was restricted to one rear-mounted 7.9 mm machine-gun. The cameras were mounted in the middle cockpit. It was also used as a torpedo-carrier, the

Nakajima B5N1.

Nakajima C6N1 Saiun.

Nakajima

Nakajima Navy J1N1-C Gekko.

torpedo being attached beneath the fuselage and offset to starboard. For this role a crew of two instead of three was accommodated. A third and unexpected role performed by the Saiun was that of night fighter (C6N1-S), armed with two forward-firing 20 mm cannon and used to intercept USAAF B-29 Superfortress bombers. About 460 C6N1s were built.

Data: *Engine* as above *Wing span* 12.5 m (41 ft 0 in) *Length* 11.1 m (36 ft 6 in) *Max T-O weight* 5,260 kg (11,597 lb) *Max level speed* 624 km/h (387 mph) *Range* 4,640 km (2,883 miles)

Nakajima Navy E2N1 (Japan) A twin-float V-strut sesquiplane, this two-seater went into Japanese Navy service in 1927 as the Type 15 Reconnaissance Seaplane. Power was provided by a 223.6 kW (300 hp) Hispano-Suiza engine. Production totalled 77 aircraft.

Nakajima Navy E4N2 (Japan) The E4N2 (or NJ as it was designated by the Nakajima company) closely resembled the US Navy's Vought Corsair biplane. It was a two-seat biplane with a single main float and twin wingtip floats. A total of 152 was built, and the type went into service in 1930 as the Type 90-2 Reconnaissance Seaplane. A landplane version was known as the E4N2-C. Power was provided by a single 335.3 kW (450 hp) Nakajima Kotobuki radial engine.

Nakajima Navy E8N1.

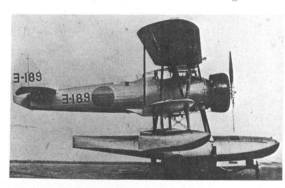

Nakajima Army G8N1 Renzan.

Nakajima Navy E8N1 (Japan) An outstanding design by Kishiro Matsuo, the Nakajima MS biplane won a Navy design competition in 1933 for a two-seat reconnaissance catapult seaplane. It had sweptback wings with rounded tips, a delicately tapered tailplane and a large single main float and two wingtip floats. Power was provided by a 432.2 kW (580 hp) Kotobuki engine.

As the Navy Type 95 Reconnaissance Seaplane the E8N1 entered service in 1935, 755 eventually being built. It was widely operated from cruisers and battleships, as well as from seaplane tenders and shore bases. It was still operational in December 1941 when it was code-named *Dave* by the Allies. Maximum level speed was 300 km/h (186.5 mph).

Nakajima Army G5N1 Shinzan (Japan) This aircraft, Japan's first operational four-engined bomber, was originally designed by Mitsubishi as the G5M1 but was not successful. It was modified by Nakajima and put into production as the G5N1 or Type 2 Land Attack Plane Model 11, but only a handful were built and these became transports. The Shinzan (Mountain Recess) was known to the Allies as *Liz*.

Nakajima Army G8N1 Renzan (Japan) Prototype four-engined bomber code-named *Rita* by the Allies.

Nakajima Navy J1N Gekko (Japan) This twin-engined two-seat monoplane was originally developed as a reconnaissance aircraft and became operational in this role in 1943 as the Type 2 Land Reconnaissance Plane or J1N1-C. In mid-1943 it was modified as a night fighter and, after a number of converted aircraft were deployed, deliveries began of a purpose-built night fighter as the J1N1-S Gekko, armed with four 20 mm Type 99 cannon. Four hundred and seventy J1N1 production aircraft were built. The Allied code name for the type was *Irving*.

Data: *Engines* two 760 kW (1,020 hp) Nakajima Sakae 21 radials *Wing span* 17 m (55 ft 8½ in) *Length* 12.2 m (39 ft 11½ in) *Max T-O weight* more than 7,250 kg (15,983 lb) *Max level speed* 533 km/h (331 mph) *Range* more than 2,175 km (1,351 miles) *Armament* (reconnaissance type) one 20 mm cannon and two 7.7 mm machine-guns in nose fired by the pilot, and two tandem dorsal turret mountings, each fitted with two 7.7 mm guns and remotely controlled by the radio operator. Provision for one 7.7 mm tunnel gun beneath the radio operator's compartment

Nakajima Army Ki-4 (Japan) Tested in 1934, the Ki-4 unequal-span biplane went into Army service in 1935 as the Type 94 Direct Co-operation Aircraft. A wide-track landing gear guaranteed operational efficiency from unprepared strips. Power was provided by a 447 kW (600 hp) Nakajima Ha-8 Hikari radial engine, giving a maximum speed of 300 km/h (186.5 mph). Armament comprised four 7.7 mm machine-guns and up to 50 kg (110 lb) of light bombs. As an army co-operation type it was used widely in China between 1935 and 1940, but was thereafter relegated to supply and liaison duties. Production totalled 516 aircraft.

Nakajima Army Ki-4.

Nakajima Army Ki-27 (Japan) Known to the Allies as *Nate*, the Ki-27 was the first fighter to enter service with the Japanese Army Air Force with a cantilever low wing, and the first with a fully enclosed cockpit. First flown in prototype form on 15 October 1936, the Ki-27 was rushed immediately into production and entered service the following year as the Army Type 97 Fighter. It took part in the fighting in Manchuria in 1938 and remained one of the main single-seat fighters of the early Pacific War years. Nearly 3,400 were built, each powered by the 529 kW (710 hp) Nakajima Ha-1b radial engine.
Data: *Engine* as above *Wing span* 11.3 m (37 ft 1 in) *Length* 7.53 m (24 ft 8½ in) *Max T-O weight* 1,790 kg (3,946.3 lb) *Max level speed* 460 km/h (286 mph) *Normal range* 545 km (339 miles) *Armament* two forward-firing 7.7 mm machine-guns, plus two 100 kg bombs
Nakajima Ki-34 (Japan) See **Nakajima AT** (*Thora*).

Nakajima Army Ki-44 Shoki.

Nakajima Army Ki-49-II Donryu.

Nakajima Army Ki-43 Hayabusa (Japan) Designed as a replacement for the Ki-27, the Ki-43 appeared in prototype form in 1939. As the Army Type 1 Fighter, it entered service in 1941 with a 708 kW (950 hp) Nakajima Ha-25 radial engine fitted, giving a maximum speed just 35 km/h (22 mph) faster than the earlier fighter. In 1942 production was supplemented by the Ki-43-II series, powered by the 857 kW (1,150 hp) Nakajima Ha-115 radial engine, the Ki-43-IIb variant featuring a reduced wing span. The final production model was the further improved Ki-43-IIIa, only a small number of which had been built by the end of the war. Production totalled about 5,900 aircraft, nearly half built by Tachikawa. The Allied code name for the Ki-43 was *Oscar*.
Data (Ki-43-IIb): *Engine* as above *Wing span* 10.86 m (35 ft 7 in) *Length* 8.9 m (29 ft 3 in) *Max T-O weight* 2,640 kg (5,820 lb) *Max level speed* 533 km/h (331 mph) *Range* 1,600–1,760 km (994–1,094 miles), which could be increased by use of jettisonable underwing fuel tanks *Armament* two 12.7 mm machine-guns, plus two 250 kg bombs
Nakajima Army Ki-44 Shoki (Japan) Known as *Tojo* by the Allies and as Shoki (Formidable) by the Japanese, the Ki-44 was very like a small version of the P-47 Thunderbolt, although the first prototypes appeared well before the American type in the summer of 1940. Similarity of design was due entirely to the use of a large radial engine, chosen mainly because it was less vulnerable in combat than the cleaner-looking liquid-cooled in-line engine that required a radiator. As

Nakajima Army Ki-43-II Hayabusa.

the Army Type 2 Fighter it entered service in 1942, initially getting a cool reaction from pilots, who disliked its heavy handling qualities. However this was compensated by excellent speed and rate of climb, attributes which enabled it to make a major contribution as a home-defence fighter during the late stages of the war.
Data (Ki-44-IIb): *Engine* one 1,080.5 kW (1,450 hp) Nakajima Ha-109 Type 2 radial *Wing span* 9.45 m (31 ft 0 in) *Length* 8.8 m (28 ft 10 in) *Max T-O weight* 2,770 kg (6,106.5 lb) *Max level speed* 605–615 km/h (376–383 mph) *Range* 1,300 km (808 miles) *Armament* four 12.7 mm machine-guns
Nakajima Army Ki-49 Donryu (Japan) Donryu (Dragon Swallower) was a twin-engined heavy bomber which entered service in early 1942 as the Army Type 100. Power for most of the 800 production aircraft built was provided by two 1,080.5 kW (1,450 hp) Nakajima Ha-109 Type 2 radial engines. Armament comprised one 20 mm cannon in a dorsal turret, two 7.9 mm or 12.7 mm machine-guns in the nose and tail turrets, and three 7.9 mm machine-guns in two waist positions and one aft-firing ventral position, plus 1,000 kg (2,205 lb) of bombs. The Allied code name for the bomber was *Helen*. A number were later employed on suicide missions.
Data (Ki-43-II): *Engines* as above *Wing span* 20.3 m (66 ft 7 in) *Length* 16.2 m (53 ft 1½ in) *Max T-O weight* 10,680 kg (23,545 lb) *Max level speed* 490 km/h (304.5 mph) *Range* 2,400 km (1,491 miles)
Nakajima Army Ki-84 Hayate (Japan) The first prototype Ki-84 single-seat fighter flew in March 1943 and was eventually followed by a

Captured Nakajima Ki-84-1a Hayate.

**Nakajima Army Ki.43-I
Hayabusa**

1 Starboard navigation
   light
2 Wing tip
3 Starboard
   fabric-covered aileron
4 Aileron actuating linkage
5 Aileron control rod
6 Control rod connecting
   fittings
7 Aileron tab
8 Flap outer cable drum
9 Flap travel
10 Flap control cables
11 Radio mast
12 Light-alloy wing skinning
13 Starboard undercarriage
   fairing
14 Gun-port fairings
15 Nose ring
16 Annular radiator/cooler
17 Two-blade two-pitch
   metal propeller

18 Spinner
19 Starter dog
20 Supercharger air intake
21 Intake fairing
22 Nakajima Ha-25 (Type
   99) 14-cylinder two-row
   radial engine
23 Cowling gills
24 Exhaust collector ring
25 Exhaust outlet
26 Engine lower bearers
27 Oil regulator valve
28 Oil pressure tank
29 Engine accessories
30 Engine upper bearers
31 Cowling gill controls
32 Two 0.303 in (7.7 mm)
   Type 89 machine-guns
33 Gun gas outlet
34 Cartridge link ejection
   chute

35 Fireproof (No 1)
   bulkhead
36 Ammunition magazine
   (500 rpg)
37 Cartridge ejection chute
38 Gun breech fairing
39 Telescopic gunsight
40 One-piece curved
   windscreen
41 Radio aerial
42 Aft-sliding cockpit
   canopy
43 Turnover structure
44 Seat back
45 Seat adjustment rails
46 Seat pan
47 Throttle quadrant
48 Instrument panel
49 Control column
50 Rudder pedals
51 Underfloor control
   linkage
52 Seat support frame
53 Control cable and rod
   bearings

54 Oxygen cylinders
55 Rudder cable pulleys
56 Transceiver
57 Type 96 Hi-3 radio
58 Receiver unit
59 Transmitter unit
60 Anti-vibration mounting
   slings
61 Fuselage construction
   break
62 Inspection/access panel
63 Fuselage stringers
64 Fuselage structure
65 Frame
66 Fuselage upper
   longeron
67 Elevator control cables
68 Fuselage skinning
69 Tailwheel shock strut
70 Tail unit attachment
71 Fin root fairing
72 Starboard tailplane
73 Elevator balance

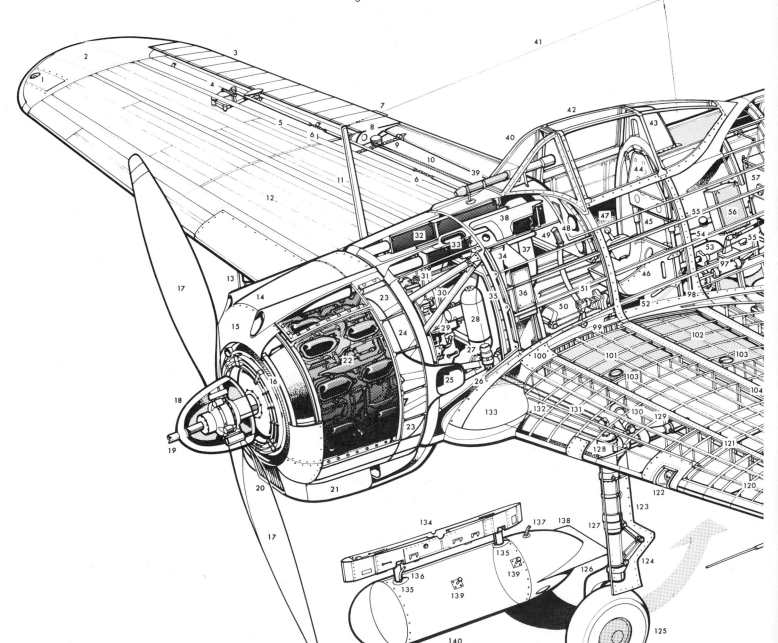

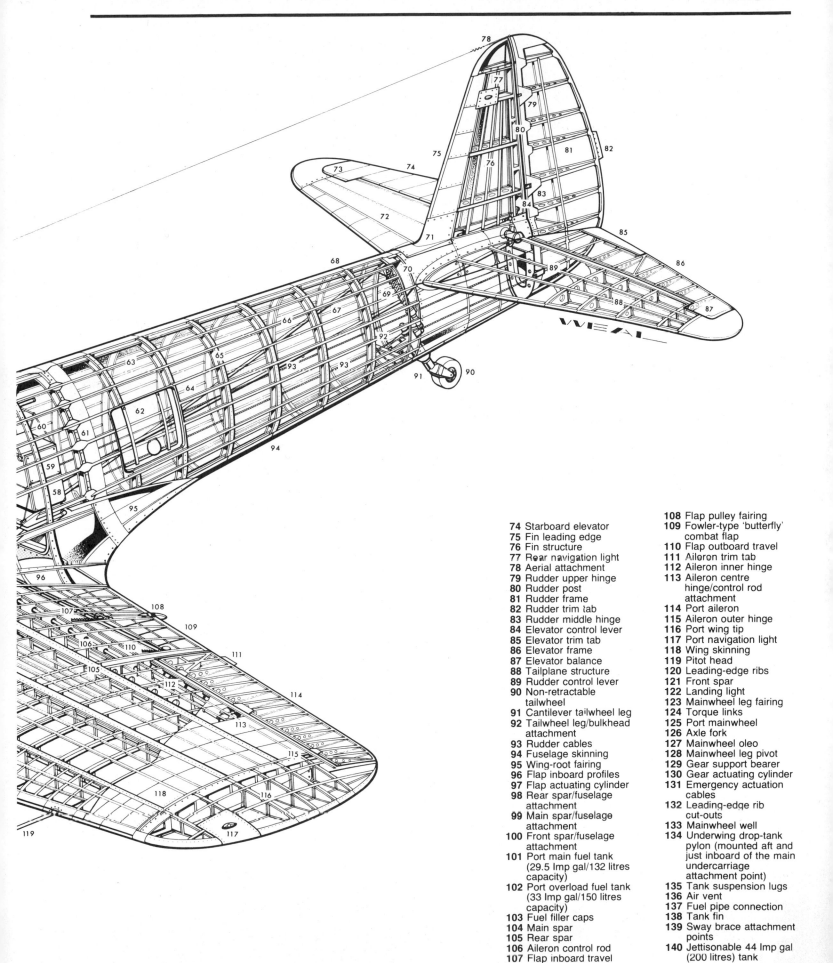

74 Starboard elevator
75 Fin leading edge
76 Fin structure
77 Rear navigation light
78 Aerial attachment
79 Rudder upper hinge
80 Rudder post
81 Rudder frame
82 Rudder trim tab
83 Rudder middle hinge
84 Elevator control lever
85 Elevator trim tab
86 Elevator frame
87 Elevator balance
88 Tailplane structure
89 Rudder control lever
90 Non-retractable tailwheel
91 Cantilever tailwheel leg
92 Tailwheel leg/bulkhead attachment
93 Rudder cables
94 Fuselage skinning
95 Wing-root fairing
96 Flap inboard profiles
97 Flap actuating cylinder
98 Rear spar/fuselage attachment
99 Main spar/fuselage attachment
100 Front spar/fuselage attachment
101 Port main fuel tank (29.5 Imp gal/132 litres capacity)
102 Port overload fuel tank (33 Imp gal/150 litres capacity)
103 Fuel filler caps
104 Main spar
105 Rear spar
106 Aileron control rod
107 Flap inboard travel
108 Flap pulley fairing
109 Fowler-type 'butterfly' combat flap
110 Flap outboard travel
111 Aileron trim tab
112 Aileron inner hinge
113 Aileron centre hinge/control rod attachment
114 Port aileron
115 Aileron outer hinge
116 Port wing tip
117 Port navigation light
118 Wing skinning
119 Pitot head
120 Leading-edge ribs
121 Front spar
122 Landing light
123 Mainwheel leg fairing
124 Torque links
125 Port mainwheel
126 Axle fork
127 Mainwheel oleo
128 Mainwheel leg pivot
129 Gear support bearer
130 Gear actuating cylinder
131 Emergency actuation cables
132 Leading-edge rib cut-outs
133 Mainwheel well
134 Underwing drop-tank pylon (mounted aft and just inboard of the main undercarriage attachment point)
135 Tank suspension lugs
136 Air vent
137 Fuel pipe connection
138 Tank fin
139 Sway brace attachment points
140 Jettisonable 44 Imp gal (200 litres) tank

Nakajima

Nakajima Army Ki-115 Tsurugi.

Nakajima-built Breguet 36.

NAMC YS-11 geological survey aircraft.

Nakajima Army Type 91.

huge number of pre-production aircraft to speed up development, testing and evaluation. Production proper began in the spring of 1944. By the end of the war no less than 3,380 full-production Ki-84s or Type 4 Fighters had been built. The Hayate (known to the Allies as *Frank*) was a most formidable fighter, able also to carry two 250 kg bombs or a larger number of small bombs for ground-attack missions. Early armament of two 12.7 mm machine-guns in the fuselage and two 20 mm cannon in the wings was increased to four 20 mm cannon, and later still to two 30 mm and two 20 mm cannon.

Data (Ki-84-I): *Engine* one 1,416 kW (1,900 hp) Nakajima Ha-45 radial *Wing span* 11.3 m (36 ft 10¼ in) *Length* 9.92 m (32 ft 6½ in) *Max T-O weight* more than 3,600 kg (7,937 lb) *Max level speed* 625 km/h (388 mph) *Range* 1,700 km (1,056 miles)

Nakajima Army Ki-115 Tsurugi (Japan) Purpose-built suicide aircraft looking like a short-span fighter. None were used operationally.

Nakajima Akatsuki (Japan) Twin-engined six-seat commercial monoplane of the latter 1930s, used by the Manchuria Aviation Company.

Nakajima commercial types (Japan) In addition to the commercial types already covered, Nakajima produced a number of original and licence-built aircraft between the two world wars, including the P-1 single-seat high-performance mail-carrying biplane, the Douglas DC-2, the Breguet Br 36 and the Fokker Universal.

Nakajima Army Type 91 (Japan) Developed from the 1927 NC single-seat fighter prototype, the Type 91 was a parasol-wing monoplane which was evolved through six consecutive development

aircraft. Much modified and greatly strengthened, the Type 91 had rounded wingtips, an elliptical horizontal tailplane of advanced design and a wide-track divided landing gear. Its 335.3 kW (450 hp) Nakajima-Bristol Jupiter engine was enclosed in a Townend ring cowl. Intended primarily as an air-superiority fighter, the Type 91 had an outstanding rate of climb and reached a maximum speed of 300 km/h (186.5 mph). Production terminated in 1934 with the 450th machine. Type 91s fought in Manchuria until the province was conquered in 1933, by which time it was the principal Army fighter. Armament comprised two Vickers 7.7 mm machine-guns.

Data: *Engine* as above *Wing span* 11.0 m (36 ft 1⅛ in) *Length* 7.0 m (22 ft 11½ in) *Max T-O weight* 1,500 kg (3,307 lb) *Max level speed* 300 km/h (186.5 mph) *Range* 600 km (373 miles)

NAMC YS-11 (Japan) The first prototype of this twin-turboprop short/medium-range transport aircraft flew for the first time on 30 August 1962, and the first production aircraft flew on 23 October 1964. Deliveries to airline operators began in March 1965. By May 1967 35 had been delivered against orders for 76 aircraft placed by seven airlines and three other operators, which included seven for the Japan Self-Defence Force.

Four major versions were produced: the YS-11-100 basic transport, accommodating 60 passengers; YS-11A-200 passenger version of the YS-11A, with increased payload (1,350 kg; 2,970 lb); YS-11A-300 mixed traffic version, accommodating 46 passengers and with 15.3 m³ (540 cu ft) of cargo space; and the YS-11A-400 all-cargo version, with 81 m³ (2,860 cu ft) of space, reinforced floor and a large cargo door.

The JASDF and JMSDF currently operate several versions of the aircraft as the YS-11-103/105 VIP transports (JASDF); YS-11-112 cargo transport (JMSDF); YS-11A-206 radar-equipped anti-submarine training aircraft (JMSDF); YS-11A-218 passenger transport (JASDF); YS-11A-305 mixed passenger/cargo transport (JASDF); YS-11A-400 all-cargo transport (JMSDF); YS-11A-402 all-cargo transport (JASDF); and YS-11E electronic-warfare training version (JASDF).

Data (YS-11A-200): *Engines* two 2,280 kW (3,060 ehp) Rolls-Royce Dart RDa.10/1 Mk 542-10K turboprops *Wing span* 32.0 m (104 ft 11¾ in) *Length* 26.3 m (86 ft 3½ in) *Max T-O weight* 24,500 kg (54,010 lb) *Max cruising speed* 469 km/h (291 mph) *Range* (with bag tanks) 3,215 km (2,000 miles)

Nardi F.N.305 (Italy) Fast two-seat light monoplane of 1935 with a retractable landing gear, powered by a 134 kW (180 hp) Fiat A.70 radial engine. Produced for flying training, pursuit training and aerobatics. A number were delivered to the Italian Air Force.

Nardi F.N.310 (Italy) Four-seat cabin version of the F.N.305, able to be equipped also as an air ambulance for one stretcher and an attendant.

Nardi F.N.315 (Italy) A 1938 development of the F.N.305 powered by a 194 kW (260 hp) Hirth HM.508C engine. Could be equipped as a two-seat touring or advanced training aircraft or as a single-seat aerobatic or fighter trainer. Flown by the Italian Air Force and exported to several countries.

Nardi F.N.333 (Italy) First post-war product, originally built as a three-seat twin-boom light amphibian. First flown on 4 December 1952 powered by a 108 kW (145 hp) Continental engine mounted as a pusher in the wing trailing edge. A four-seat production-standard aircraft was produced in 1956, powered by a 179 kW (240 hp) Continental O-470-H engine. Production aircraft proper were produced by SIAI-Marchetti from 1962 as the Riviera (as the North Star for the US market) powered by an IO-470-P engine.

lant tank for lift-off.

Orbiter's main tasks are to place satellites into orbit, retrieve satellites from orbit, and repair and service satellites in orbit. It could also be used for short-duration scientific and applications missions; for space rescue; as a tanker for space refuelling; as an orbiting research laboratory or reconnaissance vehicle; and for support of orbiting space stations. The first orbital mission is scheduled to be flown by the second Orbiter (*Columbia*) in the first half of 1981. The first Orbiter is named *Enterprise* (see **Chronology**).

Naval Aircraft Factory N3N (USA) Tandem two-seat primary training biplane powered by a 175 kW (235 hp) Wright R-760-2 engine. Operated by the US Navy on wheeled and float landing gears from 1936 until 1960.

Naval Aircraft Factory PN series (USA) Developments of the F-5L (or PN-5 as it became) biplane flying-boat, powered by two 391 kW (525 hp) Wright R-1750D radial engines in the PN-12 variant of 1928.

Naval Aircraft Factory PT-1 and PT-2 (USA) Twin-float patrol and torpedo-carrying biplanes of 1922. Thirty-three PT-1s and PT-2s were completed for the US Navy from components of earlier Curtiss aircraft.

Naval Aircraft Factory TG series (USA) Armament training biplane of 1922 produced for the US Navy. The landing gear comprised one large central float and two stabilising floats under the lower wings.

Naval Aircraft Factory TS-1 (USA) Biplane fighter of 1922 which was delivered to the US Navy as initial equipment of the new aircraft carrier USS *Langley* and for operation as a twin-float fighter from other types of warship. Power was provided by a 149 kW (200 hp) Wright J-4 radial engine and armament comprised one forward-firing 0.30 in Browning machine-gun. Maximum level speed was 198 km/h (123 mph). A few examples of several refined versions were subsequently produced.

Navion Rangemaster G and H (USA) Five-seat light monoplanes of 1974 and 1976 respectively, the latter powered by a 212.5 kW (285 hp) Continental IO-520 engine.

NASA Space Shuttle (USA) The Space Shuttle is the first re-usable space vehicle, consisting basically of two stages: a booster and an Orbiter. The Orbiter has a delta wing and looks very like a conventional aeroplane, but powered by rocket engines. The liquid propellants for these engines are carried in a large external jettisonable tank which will be attached to the Orbiter at lift-off. Two large solid-propellant jettisonable boosters will be mounted on opposite sides of the propel-

NDN

Neiva T-25 Universals.

Neiva Paulistinha 56-C.

NDN 1 Firecracker.

NDN 1 Firecracker (UK) Two-seat civil and military training and sporting aircraft, first flown on 26 May 1976. Power is provided by a 194 kW (260 hp) Lycoming AEIO-540-B4D5 engine.

Neiva N621 Universal and N622 Universal II (Brazil) Two–three-seat basic trainers powered by a 224 kW (300 hp) Lycoming IO-540-K1D5 and a 298 kW (400 hp) Lycoming IO-720 engine respectively. Operated by the Brazilian Air Force as a basic trainer and light reconnaissance/attack aircraft (two 7.62 mm machine-guns in pods attached to underwing hardpoints) under the designations T-25 (N621) and T-25A (N622). Ten N621s also delivered to the Chilean Army but transferred to the Air Force.

Neiva Campeiro (Brazil) Two-seat light monoplane developed from the Paulistinha 56 but with a 112 kW (150 hp) Lycoming O-320-A engine. Small number operated by the Brazilian Air Force for liaison, training, observation and rescue duties under the designation L-7.

Neiva Lanceiro (Brazil) Civil development of the Neiva Regente. First production aircraft flew in September 1973. Production ended in 1975.

Neiva Paulistinha 56 (Brazil) Two-seat light monoplane, the final two production versions being the 56-C and 56-D with a 67 kW (90 hp) Continental C-90-8F/12F and 112 kW (150 hp) Lycoming O-320-A1A engine respectively.

Neiva Regente (Brazil) Four-seat light monoplane of 1961 powered by a 134 kW (180 hp) Lycoming O-360 engine. Ordered for the Brazilian Air Force as the C-42 utility and L-42 liaison and observation aircraft.

Neukom S-4A Elfe 15 (Switzerland) Single-seat Standard Class sailplane.

Nieuport Type VIM monoplane (France) One of the first true military aircraft, the Type VIM monoplane was a 37.25 kW (50 hp) or 59.6 kW (80 hp) Gnome rotary-engined scout. It was developed from the Nieuport Type IIN of 1911 which had set a world speed record of 119.76 km/h (74.415 mph) at Châlons on 11 May of that year. Other early Nieuports included the IV and HG. The two-seat Type VIG was followed by the Type VIM, which entered military service in France, Italy (licence-built by Macchi), Russia (licence-built) and Great Britain (RNAS). Monoplanes were flown on the Western Front until 1915.
Data: *Engine* as above *Wing span* 10.97 m (36 ft 0 in) *Length* 7.8 m (25 ft 7 in) *Max T-O weight* about 660 kg (1,455 lb) *Max level speed* 114 km/h (71 mph)

Nieuport 10 (France) Originally designed as a racing aircraft to compete in the Gordon Bennett Trophy race, the Nieuport 10 was a neat biplane of advanced design. With the outbreak of war it was modified into a two-seat military aircraft, primarily for reconnaissance. However some examples were fitted with a gun above the upper wing for fighting duties, with the observer forward to stand and fire the gun. From 1915 it was flown by the air services of France, Great Britain, Belgium and Italy – being licence-built in the latter country as the Macchi-Nieuport Ni 10. Power was provided by a 59.6 kW (80 hp) Le Rhône or Anzani engine. Maximum level speed was 142 km/h (88 mph).

Nieuport 11 and 16 (France) The Type 11 was the first true Nieuport fighter, derived also from the Gordon Bennett racer design but featuring accommodation for a pilot only and armed as standard with a forward-firing Lewis machine-gun above the upper wing. Nieuport 11s were delivered to the air services of France, Great Britain (RNAS and RFC), Holland, Belgium, Russia and Italy – many hundreds being licence-built in the latter country alone as the Macchi-Nieuport Ni 11 *Bébé*. With the D.H.2 and F.E.2b, Nieuport 11s put an end to the so-called 'Fokker Scourge' and helped establish the reputations of several of the better-remembered aces of World War I.

From the Nieuport 11 was derived the Type 16, a higher-powered derivative with an 82 kW (110 hp) Le Rhône rotary engine. Only limited numbers were produced, these serving with the French, Belgian and British air services. Some were employed as anti-airship/balloon types, armed with Le Prieur rockets.
Data (Nieuport 11): *Engine* one 59.6 kW (80 hp) Le Rhône rotary *Wing span* 7.55 m (24 ft 9 in) *Length* 5.8 m (19 ft 0¼ in) *Max T-O weight* 480 kg (1,058 lb) *Max level speed* 155 km/h (96 mph) *Endurance* 2 h 30 min

Nieuport HG.

Many outdated Nieuport 17s were eventually delivered to the American Expeditionary Force as single-seat trainers, and it was as a trainer that the Nieuport 21 was evolved. Most were built with 59.6 kW (80 hp) Le Rhône engines.

The Nieuport 23 was basically similar to the 17 but had the machine-gun mounted on the cowling over the engine.

Data (Nieuport 17): *Engine* as above *Wing span* 8.2 m (26 ft 11 in) *Length* 5.95 m (19 ft 7 in) *Max T-O weight* 560 kg (1,235 lb) *Max level speed* 175 km/h (109 mph) *Endurance* 2 h

Nieuport 24 and 27 (France) Although the Nieuport 24 prototype was a converted Type 23 (previously updated from a Type 17*bis*), it represented a significant change in design. The most obvious new feature was the round sides to the fuselage which now merged neatly with the cowling over the 89.4 kW (120 hp) Le Rhône rotary engine. Two production versions were built: the Type 24 and the Type 24*bis*, differing in having a fin and rudder and a fin only respectively. These were flown by France, Great Britain, Belgium, Italy and America: the 261 acquired by the AEF being used as trainers. Armament comprised a Vickers and a Lewis machine-gun (or one or the other) mounted on the engine cowling and/or above the wing.

Nieuport 12 (France) The Nieuport 12 was closely related to the Type 10, although larger, heavier and powered by an 82 kW (110 hp) or 97 kW (130 hp) Clerget rotary engine. Production was undertaken in France and Britain, some late examples featuring the first use of a synchronised forward-firing Vickers machine-gun on a Nieuport biplane. Most Type 12s served on the Western Front and elsewhere only until 1916, then many were converted into Nieuport 83 trainers.

Data: *Engine* as above *Wing span* 9.0 m (29 ft 7½ in) *Length* 7.3 m (23 ft 11½ in) *Max T-O weight* 920 kg (2,028 lb) *Max level speed* 155 km/h (96 mph) *Endurance* 3 h

Nieuport 14 (France) Slow two-seat day bomber of 1916 powered by a 112 kW (150 hp) Hispano-Suiza engine. Not successful.

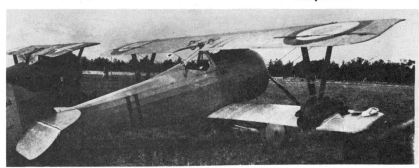

The Nieuport 27 was similar to the 24, differing only in having more rounded wingtips and vertical tail, and a revised landing gear. Armament comprised one synchronised Vickers machine-gun. Type 27s were used by France, Great Britain, Italy and America: again the AEF using its 120 aircraft as trainers.

Data (Nieuport 24): *Engine* as above *Wing span* 8.2 m (26 ft 11 in) *Length* 5.8 m (19 ft 0¼ in) *Max T-O weight* 550 kg (1,212 lb) *Max level speed* 177 km/h (110 mph) *Range* 250 km (155 miles)

Nieuport 28 (France) First flown in prototype form in June 1917, the Nieuport 28 was a completely new design, benefiting greatly from experience with the Nieuport 27. Like the earlier aircraft, its fuselage was of rounded section, although more heavily tapered towards the tail. The 119 kW (160 hp) Gnome Monosoupape rotary engine was fully cowled. New wings replaced the previous sesquiplane type, braced by parallel instead of Vee struts. Armament comprised twin synchronised Vickers guns. Most of the production aircraft built went to American Expeditionary Force squadrons, becoming the first Nieuport to be flown by the AEF as a combat type. The AEF received 298. On 14 April 1918,

Nieuport 17, 21 and 23 (France) The Type 17 was undoubtedly the finest single-seat fighter to come from the Nieuport stable during World War I and was the mount of many aces. It was while flying a Nieuport 17 with No 60 Squadron that William Avery Bishop won his VC on 2 June 1917, subsequently accumulating 72 kills to become the second highest-scoring British and Empire pilot of World War I.

Powered by an 82 kW (110 hp) Le Rhône rotary engine, the Nieuport 17 was a fast-climbing and highly manoeuvrable fighter armed with a single forward-firing Lewis machine-gun over the upper wing or by a synchronised Vickers gun, or both. It was flown into action by pilots of France, Belgium, Great Britain, Russia and Italy; and in its more powerful 17*bis* form (97 kW; 130 hp Clerget) by those of France and Romania.

Nieuport

Nieuport-Delage NiD 62 C1s (foreground), NiD 29s (background).

Nieuport 28s of the 94th Pursuit Squadron became the first AEF aircraft to see combat: two of its pilots shooting down two German aircraft (see **Chronology**). However before the end of the war SPAD XIIIs had generally replaced the Nieuports, but work had already begun on the still slimmer Type 29 (see entry). Post-war a number of Nieuport 28s passed into civil use.
Data: Engine as above *Wing span* 8.0 m (26 ft 3 in) *Length* 6.5 m (21 ft 3¾ in) *Max T-O weight* 625 kg (1,378 lb) *Max level speed* 196 km/h (122 mph) *Range* 400 km (248.5 miles)

Nieuport 28.

Nieuport-Delage NiD 29 C1s.

Nieuport Nighthawk (UK) Single-seat fighter originally produced by Nieuport & General Aircraft. Taken over by Gloster in 1920 (see **Gloster Mars**).

Nieuport-Delage NiD 29 (France) This single-seat fighter flew in prototype form for the first time on 21 August 1918. By the mid-1920s it was the principal fighter of the French, Italian, Japanese and Belgian air arms.

Still under development at the end of World War I, the NiD 29 emerged as a two-bay equal-span biplane fitted with ailerons on the lower wings only. Armament comprised the standard twin Vickers machine-guns. A second prototype reached an altitude of 9,123 m (29,931 ft) on 14 June 1919. In 1920 it was ordered into quantity production, forming the sole equipment of the 1er and 3ème Regiments de Chasse by the end of 1923. Eventually several hundred NiD 29s went to the French Aéronautique Militaire. In 1926 a unit of modified NiD 29s operated as bombers against the Riffs in Morocco, carrying individual loads of 60 kg (132 lb) of bombs.

However Japan was the country which used the greatest number of NiD 29s. The Nakajima company built no fewer than 608 between 1923 and 1932. They equipped fighter units of the Imperial Japanese Army Air Service under the designation Ko-4. In September 1931 the first Nieuport-equipped unit arrived in Shenyang, Manchuria to support the Japanese campaign; others followed

and remained there until 1933. With little air opposition, they were employed mostly as ground-attack aircraft and on troop-support duties.

Licence production in Italy as the Macchi-Nieuport Ni 29 began in 1924. Ultimately 175 were built for the Regia Aeronautica. Belgium followed up the purchase of 20 French-built NiD 29s with licence-production of 88 by SABCA. Other countries to use the fighter were Spain (30), Sweden and Argentina.

Back in 1919 the modified NiD 29V racer had won the Coupe Deutsch at an average speed of 266.4 km/h (165.5 mph) and also the Grand Prix de Monaco, followed later by the 1920 Gordon Bennett Trophy. On 10 and 20 October the racer raised the world speed record to 296.694 km/h (184.357 mph) and 302.529 km/h (187.982 mph) respectively, and on 30 October 1923 also gained the height record by attaining an altitude of 11,145 m (36,565 ft).

Throughout its career the NiD 29 captured headlines, as on 27 May 1927 when a mock dogfight was staged over Le Bourget between fighters piloted by the celebrated NiD 29V pilot Sadi Lecointe and Charles Lindbergh of trans-atlantic fame.
Data: Engine one 223.6 kW (300 hp) Hispano-Suiza 8Fb *Wing span* 9.7 m (31 ft 10 in) *Length* 6.5 m (21 ft 4 in) *Max T-O weight* 1,192 kg (2,628 lb) *Max level speed* 226 km/h (140.5 mph) *Range* 580 km (360 miles)

Nieuport-Delage NiD 30T (France) Six–eight-passenger commercial biplane powered by a 335.3 kW (450 hp) Renault engine. Several were operated between Paris and London during 1919–29 by Compagnie Générale Transaériennes, replacing Breguet types. This company operated in association with AT & T.

Nieuport-Delage NiD 39 (France) In the early 1920s Nieuport-Delage designed and built a new two-passenger cabin biplane as the NiD 38, powered as standard by a 134 kW (180 hp) Hispano-Suiza 8Ad engine. From it was developed the generally similar NiD 39, built in two versions with the Hispano-Suiza engine (NiD 390) or a 164 kW (220 hp) Armstrong Siddeley Lynx (NiD 391). A total of 26 aircraft of both versions was built for commercial service from 1927.

Nieuport-Delage NiD 42 C1 (France) The original aircraft was a single-seat parasol-wing fighter with Y-form wing struts. A racing variant designated NiD 42S, powered by a 447 kW (600 hp) Hispano-Suiza engine, set up new speed-over-distance records during 1924–25. After a two-seat version with a lower 'stub' wing was displayed at the 1924 Paris 'Salon', two single-seat prototypes were tested in 1926. Twenty-five evaluation aircraft, built to the same sesquiplane formula, were bought by the French Aéronautique Militaire. Armament comprised two 7.7 mm machine-guns.

Nieuport-Delage NiD 52 C1 (France) The 1927 prototype was developed from the NiD 42 and was of all-metal construction except for fabric covering on its upper wing. It won the 1928 Spanish government fighter competition, resulting in 91 aircraft being licence-built by Hispano Aviacion (Guadalajara) between 1929 and 1936. Thirty-four additional machines were delivered by Nieuport. Armament comprised two 0.303 in Vickers machine-guns and power was provided by a 372.6 kW (500 hp) Hispano-Suiza 12Hb in-line engine. At the outbreak of the Spanish Civil War in July 1936, six squadrons were still equipped with NiD 52 C1s. These were flown by Republican and Nationalist pilots.

Nieuport-Delage NiD 62 C1 (France) Appearing at the same time as the NiD 52 prototype, the NiD 62 retained the earlier aircraft's 372.6 kW (500 hp) Hispano-Suiza 12Hb engine but had a wooden monocoque fuselage (on the lines of the NiD 42) and an enlarged tailplane. Armament comprised the usual twin machine-guns. A total of 265 examples was ordered for the French Aéronautique Militaire between 1928 and 1929, followed by 50 for the Aéronautique Navale. In 1929 three aircraft were fitted with floats to train proposed Schneider Trophy contestants.

The lighter Hispano-Suiza 12Md engine, driving a metal instead of a wooden propeller, was fitted to the NiD 622, ordered into production in 1930. Other modifications included full-span ailerons. Two hundred and sixty NiD 622s went to the air force and 62 to the navy. The first reached the 31ᵉᵐᵉ Régiment at Le Bourget aerodrome in the summer of 1931. By the following year French fighter defence relied almost entirely on Nieuports.

In 1933 Peru received 12 NiD 626s. With an Hispano-Suiza 12Mdsh engine, fitted with a Szydlowski-Planiol supercharger and Lamblin radiators, the NiD 629 was the next production version. The antiquated landing gear of the earlier versions gave way to a modern Messier type with oleo-pneumatic shock-absorbers. Fifty were ordered, going into service in 1935, by which time they were already obsolete.

NiD 62-series aircraft still equipped reserve fighter units when World War II broke out. On 10 May 1940 143 of all versions were still on charge with the Armée de l'Air.

Data (NiD 62): *Engine* as above *Wing span* 12.0 m

Nipper Mk III.

(39 ft 4½ in) *Length* 7.5 m (24 ft 7¼ in) *Max T-O weight* 1,795 kg (3,957 lb) *Max level speed* 270 km/h (168 mph) *Range* 500 km (311 miles)

Nieuport-Delage NiD 641 (France) Six-seat and mail-carrying commercial high-wing monoplane of 1930 powered by a 179 kW (240 hp) Lorraine 7Ma Mizar radial engine. A small number entered service with Société de Transports Aériens Rapides.

Nipper Mk III and IIIA (UK) Single-seat ultralight monoplanes powered by a 1.5 litre Rollason Ardem and 1.6 litre Ardem engine respectively (41 kW; 55 hp as the Ardem XI). Plans are available to amateur constructors.

Nippon Ki-59 (Japan) Twin-engined transport aircraft of 1939, 59 of which were built for the Japanese Army. Received the Allied code name *Theresa*.

Nippon Ki-76.

Nippon Ki-76 (Japan) Fieseler Storch-type liaison aircraft of 1941 powered by a 209 kW (280 hp) Hitachi engine. Received the Allied code name *Stella*.

Nippon Ki-86 (Japan) Licence-built Bücker Jungmann biplane trainer. Received the Allied code name *Cypress*.

Nippon Ku-7 Manazuru (Japan) Military transport glider known to the Allies as *Buzzard*. Later tested as a powered aircraft with two 708 kW (950 hp) Mitsubishi Ha-26 engines as the Ki-105 Ohtori.

Nippon Ku-8 (Japan) A 14–20-troop or cargo-transport glider developed from the Ki-59. Received the Allied code name *Gander*. First-known example was discovered on Luzon after the invasion of the Philippines.

Nieuport-Delage NiD 622.

Nord 500.

Noorduyn

Nord 1500 Griffon II.

Noorduyn C-64 Norseman (Canada) See **CCF Norseman.**

Nord 262 (France) See **Aérospatiale N.262.**

Nord 500 (France) VTOL research aircraft intended primarily to evaluate the principles of the tilt-duct concept. First flown (tethered) in July 1968.

Nord N.C.853 (France) Two-seat light training monoplane designed by the Société Nationale de Constructions Aéronautiques de Centre and first flown in April 1948. Production taken over by SNCAN (Nord) in 1949. Powered by a 56 kW (75 hp) Minié 4.DC.32 engine.

Nord N.C.856 (France) Development of the N.C.853 placed in production by Nord for the French Army as a two–three-seat artillery observation and liaison monoplane. Powered by a 100.6 kW (135 hp) Régnier 4 LO4 engine. The N.C.856-H and N.C.856-N were three-seat seaplane and four-seat civil derivatives of the N.C.856-A military version.

Nord 1101 Noralpha (France) Four-seat cabin monoplane produced after World War II, powered by a 179 kW (240 hp) Renault 6Q10 engine.

Nord 1203/II Norécrin II.

Nord 1201, 1203 Norécrin and 1203/II Norécrin II (France) Development of the Norécrin light cabin monoplane began in 1943 and the prototype first flew in December 1945 as the two-seat Nord 1200. The first production model was the three-seat Nord 1201 powered by the 104.3 kW (140 hp) Renault 4POI engine, later replaced by a 100.6 kW (135 hp) Régnier 4 LO4 and designated Nord 1203. In 1948 the Norécrin was made into a four-seater, the Norécrin II.

Nord 1221 Norélan (France) Two–three-seat training monoplane, first flown in June 1948. Powered by a 134 kW (180 hp) Mathis 8G-20.

Nord 1402 Noroit (France) Maritime reconnaissance and rescue amphibious flying-boat, first flown as the Nord 1400 prototype in January 1949. Powered by two 1,192 kW (1,600 hp) Gnome-Rhône 14R25 engines. Four pre-production aircraft followed by 20 production Nord 1402 Noroits, each of the production aircraft powered by two 1,565 kW (2,100 hp) SFECMAS 12 H engines (Jumo 213As).

Nord 1402 Gerfaut 1A and 1405 Gerfaut II (France) The Gerfaut II was a development of the

Gerfaut 1A, which was the first high-powered jet delta-wing aircraft to fly in France (15 January 1954), powered by a 43.15 kN (9,700 lb st) SNECMA Atar 101G turbojet with afterburner. The Gerfaut II first flew on 17 April 1956 and on 16 February 1957 established a number of time-to-height records from a standing start, including a climb to a height of 6,000 m in 1 minute 17 seconds and to 9,000 m in 1 minute 34 seconds. The Gerfauts were used to collect data for a high-speed fighter design.

Nord 1500 Griffon (France) Experimental aircraft built to test a new airframe design embodying a combination turbojet-ramjet propulsion unit. First flown on 20 September 1955. Re-engined, it became the Griffon II.

Nord 1601 (France) Experimental aircraft built to investigate the stability of swept wings, the effects of sweepback on high-lift devices and other aerodynamic problems at high subsonic speeds. Flown for the first time on 24 January 1950.

Nord 2501 Noratlas (France) Short/medium-range troop/paratroop (45) and freight (up to 6,800 kg; 14,990 lb) transport powered by two 1,520 kW (2,040 hp) SNECMA-built Bristol Hercules 738 or 758 radial engines. First flown in 1950, Noratlas twin-boom transports are currently flown by the air forces of France, Chad, Greece and Niger.

Data: *Engines* as above *Wing span* 32.5 m (106 ft 7½ in) *Length* 21.96 m (72 ft 0½ in) *Max T-O weight* 22,000 kg (48,500 lb) *Max level speed* 405 km/h (251 mph) *Range* (with 5,000 kg; 11,025 lb payload) 2,500 km (1,550 miles)

Nord 3202/3212 (France) Two-seat basic trainers, each powered by a 179 kW (240 hp) Potez 4-D32 engine. Prototype first flew in April 1957 and production aircraft were delivered from July 1959 (see also **Aérospatiale 3202-B1B**).

Nord 3400 (France) Two-seat observation and casualty-evacuation monoplane, first flown in January 1958. Powered by a 194 kW (260 hp) Potez 4-D34 engine. Production aircraft delivered to the French Army from July 1959.

Norman Thompson N.T.4 (UK) Reconnaissance and anti-submarine flying-boat of World War I powered by two 104.3 kW or 149 kW (140 or 200 hp) Hispano-Suiza engines. Fifty were ordered, but it is not known whether any from the final batch of 20 were delivered to the RNAS.

Nord 2501 Noratlas.

JANE'S
Encyclopedia of Aviation

Volume 5

Aircraft A–Z
North American — Zlin

Compiled and edited by Michael J. H. Taylor

Contributors: Bill Gunston, A. J. Jackson, David Mondey,

Malcolm Passingham, John Stroud, Susan H. H. Young

North American AJ Savage (USA) The Savage was a large composite-powered carrier-borne attack bomber capable of carrying an atomic bomb. Three versions were produced for the US Navy: the AJ-1 with two 1,788.5 kW (2,400 hp) Pratt & Whitney R-2800-44W piston engines and a 20.5 kN (4,600 lb st) Allison J33 turbojet in the rear fuselage, first flown in May 1949; AJ-2 with R-2800-48 piston engines and a J33, a higher tailfin and a tailplane without dihedral; and the AJ-2P photographic-reconnaissance version of the AJ-2, first flown in 1952. Production totalled 140 aircraft of all versions. These remained operational until 1959, when some were converted into refuelling tankers. Maximum level speed was 758 km/h (471 mph).

North American AT-6 Texan/Harvard and NA-16 series (USA) The AT-6 first appeared in 1938 and was similar to and eventually replaced the BC-1A basic-combat trainer when the BC classification was abandoned. But the BC-1A itself was only one of a very large number of aircraft that stemmed from the NA-16 of 1935.

Originally designed as a basic trainer for the USAAC, the NA-16 was a cantilever low-wing monoplane powered by a 298 kW (400 hp) Wright Whirlwind engine. The two tandem cockpits were open and the fixed landing-gear legs were trousered. Following selection by the Army, the prototype was modified to near production standard, with a hastily fitted long cockpit enclosure, a revised landing gear and a long-chord cowling round the 447 kW (600 hp) Pratt & Whitney R-1340 Wasp engine.

Production aircraft for the US services and for export to many countries were built under a wide range of NA, NJ, BC and BT designations. They were used as combat trainers, basic trainers, general-purpose aircraft and bombers. They featured a wide range of engines, fixed or retractable landing gears and varying cockpit enclosures

(one BT-9 being modified into the NA-22 with open cockpits and a 167.7 kW; 225 hp Wright R-760 engine).

The first model to introduce the AT Texan (advance trainer) designation was the NA-59 ordered for the USAAC. As the NA-66 or Harvard II it was supplied to the air forces of Canada, Great Britain and New Zealand, following the Harvard I (NA-49) previously supplied to Britain and Canada. The AT-6A (US Navy SNJ-3) was powered by a Pratt & Whitney R-1340-49 engine and had a removable aluminium fuel tank. It was also built under licence in Canada by Noorduyn Aviation as the Harvard IIB, 2,485 going to the RAF alone and those supplied to the USAAC becoming AT-16s. The AT-6B was fitted with an R-1340-AN-1 engine.

The AT-6C (SNJ-4 and Harvard IIA) differed in being redesigned to eliminate the use of aluminium-alloy and high-alloy steels. The wings, centre-section, fin, rudder, elevators, ailerons, flaps, etc, were made of spot-welded low-alloy steel; the side panels of the forward fuselage and the entire rear fuselage, tailplane, floor boards, etc, were of plywood – introducing a weight saving of 566 kg (1,246 lb). However fear of shortages of strategic materials proved groundless and the normal structure was later reverted to. The AT-6D (SNJ-5 and Harvard III), nearly 4,400 of which were built, retained the R-1340-AN-1 engine but had no photographic equipment fitted. The final production version was the AT-6F, most going to the US Navy as SNJ-6s.

In post-war USAF service, Texans were redesignated under the T-6 classification, new versions being produced by modification. Today Texans/Harvards are still flown as basic trainers and light attack aircraft by the air forces of 22 countries, although no longer in the USA. Among the purpose-built combat aircraft based on the AT-6 were the NA-50 and NA-68 single-seat fighter-bombers, built for Peru and Siam respect-

ively. The latter were retained for the USAAF as P-64 trainers.

Data (T-6G): *Engine* one 410 kW (550 hp) Pratt & Whitney R-1340-AN-1 radial *Wing span* 12.8 m (42 ft 0 in) *Length* 8.99 m (29 ft 6 in) *Max T-O weight* 2,548 kg (5,617 lb) *Max level speed* 341 km/h (212 mph) *Normal range* 1,400 km (870 miles) *Armament* (optional) underwing attchments for light bombs and rockets

North American B-25 Mitchell (USA) Built in larger numbers than any other American twin-engined bomber, the Mitchell was tough, extremely noisy, but hard-hitting and highly versatile. It stemmed from the NA-40 prototype flown in January 1939. Completely redesigned with much more powerful engines, it met a revised US Army specification for a medium bomber with 1,089 kg (2,400 lb) bomb load and went into production without any further prototype. The first B-25 Mitchell flew on 19 August 1940. Powered by 1,006 kW (1,350 hp) Wright R-2600-9 Cyclone 14 engines, it had a tricycle landing gear and shoulder-high wings passing above the bomb bay whose capacity was actually 1,361 kg (3,000 lb). Three 0.30 in guns were aimed from nose and waist positions and there was an 0.50 in gun in the cramped position in the extreme tail.

The B-25A introduced armour and self-sealing tanks, and the B dispensed with the tail gun but added two 0.50 in turrets, above and below the fuselage. In April 1942 Jimmy Doolittle led 16 on a daring raid from the carrier *Hornet* against

Tokyo. The C had more fuel and external bomb racks. The D was similar but made at a new factory at Kansas City. These early versions were widely supplied to the Soviet Union, RAF, Netherlands, China and Brazil.

Operations in the Pacific led to totally different ideas, with the emphasis on forward-firing guns as well as bombs for attacks on shipping. Field modifications of C and D models added four 0.50 in guns in the nose (the bombardier station being removed) and four in side packages. The B-25G had an Army 75 mm gun loaded by hand with 21 rounds, with two 0.50 in guns for sighting and flak suppression and four 0.50 in package guns added later. The H had the 75 mm plus 14 × 0.50 in guns, four in the nose, four in packages, two in waist bulges and two each in dorsal and new tail turrets. The most numerous of all was the J, 4,318 of which were built, with normal bomb/mine/torpedo load of 1,814 kg (4,000 lb), 13 × 0.50 in guns, and a glazed nose. The corresponding attack version had an eight-gun nose.

Other wartime versions included the F-10 unarmed reconnaissance and mapping aircraft, and the PBJ-1H and PBJ-1J (corresponding to the B-25H and JP) of the Marine Corps. Post-war variants were numerous, including the CB-25 transport and TB-25J, K, L and M trainers, all rebuilds. Total production amounted to 9,816. These fine aircraft served with every Allied air force in World War II and with numerous countries post-war – some remaining nominally operational well into the 1970s.

Data (B-25J): *Engines* two 1,378.6 kW (1,850 hp) Wright R-2600-29 Cyclone radials. *Wing span* 20.6 m (67 ft 7 in) *Length* 16.1 m (52 ft 11 in) *Max T-O weight* 18,960 kg (41,800 lb) *Max level speed* 443 km/h (275 mph) *Range* 2,052 km (1,275 miles)

North American B-45 Tornado (USA) The XB-45 was the first American multi-jet heavy aircraft to fly, making its maiden flight at Muroc on 17 March 1947. Production comprised 96 B-45A light tactical bombers each powered by

North American B-45 Tornado.

North American T-6s used during the Korean War for spotting targets and directing heavily armed fighters to their objectives.

North American Mitchell IIs (B-25Cs).

North American TB-25K Mitchell.

North American RB-45C Tornado being refuelled from a Superfortress tanker.

four 22.24 kN (5,000 lb st) General Electric J47 turbojet engines and entering service in 1948; ten 23.1 kN (5,200 lb st) J47-engined B-45C tactical support bombers; and 33 RB-45C high-altitude photographic-reconnaissance aircraft. Fourteen B-45As were subsequently modified into high-speed target tugs to tow a Chance-Vought 6.1 m (20 ft) span all-metal target glider. Maximum level speed of the B-45C was 932 km/h (579 mph).

North American F-82 Twin Mustang (USA) see **North American P-51 Mustang**
North American F-86 Sabre (USA) The first swept-wing transonic jet to be built and – with the MiG-15 – the first to enter service. The XP-86 was originally planned as a conventional aircraft but was delayed for a year in 1945–6 to take advantage of German research into swept wings and tails. The first NA-140 prototype XP-86 flew on 1 October 1947, with all surfaces swept at 35°. Despite the undeveloped TG-180 axial turbojet of 16.7 kN (3,750 lb st), the new fighter demonstrated extraordinary speed, and during 1947 was first dived faster than sound. Handling was faultless and pilot view well-nigh perfect. Features included hydraulically boosted flight controls, large full-span leading-edge slats which were unlocked for low speeds, tricycle landing gear and large speed brakes on each side of the rear fuselage.

The production P-86A (later F-86A), named Sabre, first flew on 20 May 1948 and entered service with the 1st and 4th Fighter Groups of the new US Air Force in 1949. Armament comprised six 0.5 in guns in the sides of the nose. The production engine was the 22.24 kN (5,000 lb st) TG-190, redesignated General Electric J47. In September 1948 a standard F-86A broke the world speed record at 1,080 km/h (671 mph).

The next model was the F-86E with 23.1 kN (5,200 lb st) J47-GE-13 engine and many improvements, including a 'flying tail' in which elevator movement resulted in instant augmentation by the tailplane as well giving more powerful control in the pitching plane. Underwing racks carried two 1,000 lb bombs, drop-tanks or octets of rockets. The E was the most numerous model of the Korean War and, thanks to superior pilot training and experience, achieved a marked superiority over the MiG-15 despite having marginally inferior flight performance.

In August 1950 Canadair flew the first of 1,815 Sabres made under licence as the CL-13. The first batches corresponded to the F-86E and 430 of these were supplied to give the RAF a modern fighter in 1952–3. Subsequently Canadair fitted the locally produced Orenda engine, with ratings of 28.27 or 32.36 kN (6,355 or 7,275 lb st), giving what many pilots judged the best Sabres of all. Commonwealth Aircraft in Australia built the Sabre (initially based on the F-86E) with the 33.36 kN (7,500 lb st) Rolls-Royce Avon 26 and two 30 mm Aden guns. Much later another licensed manufacturer was Mitsubishi in Japan, where 300 were assembled from imported parts.

The Japanese pattern aircraft was the F-86F, similar to the E apart from a 26.56 kN (5,970 lb st) J47-GE-27 engine and new leading edge without slats but with extended chord and

North American F-100C
Super Sabres.

small fences. This wing resulted in higher landing speed and other penalties but gave fractionally better high-altitude manoeuvrability. The most numerous of all versions was a totally new aircraft, originally to have been the F-95A but finally called F-86D. This was a much heavier all-weather interceptor with afterburning J47-GE-17 or -33 rated at 34 kN (7,650 lb st), the enlarged fuselage being crammed with the large, complex and troublesome Hughes E-4 lead-collision-course fire-control system, with APG-37 radar in the nose above the inlet duct. This automatically steered the aircraft to fire a battery of 24 Mighty Mouse spin-stabilised rockets from a retractable tray to strike hostile aircraft not from the usual rear but from the side. Total production of this pioneer single-seat all-weather interceptor was 2,504.

The F-86K was produced for NATO air forces, with most D features but armament of four 20 mm M-24 cannon and simpler fire control tailored to traditional pursuit interceptions. North American built 120, and 221 were assembled by Fiat in Italy. From 1956 the USAF had 827 F-86Ds remanufactured as F-86L interceptors with later avionics and a new long-span wing with extended chord but also having slats – a wing also fitted to the final F-86F-40, the last batch of F-86Fs. The ultimate USAF version was the completely redesigned F-86H tactical attack fighter with 39.7 kN (8,920 lb st) General Electric J73-GE-3E engine, four 20 mm M-39 revolver cannon and heavy external weapon loads. Two Sabres were rebuilt as tandem dual TF-86 trainers.
Data (F-86F): *Engine* one 26.56 kN (5,970 lb st) General Electric J47-GE-27 turbojet *Wing span* 11.91 m (39 ft 1 in) *Length* 11.44 m (37 ft 6½ in) *Max T-O weight* 9,350 kg (20,610 lb) *Max level speed* 1,105 km/h (687 mph) *Range* 1,485 km

(925 miles) *Armament* six 0.50 in Browning machine-guns in nose. Provision for two Sidewinder missiles, two 1,000 lb bombs or eight rockets under wings

North American F-100 Super Sabre (USA) First of the 'Century fighters', the prototype F-100 flew on 25 May 1953. The initial production version was the F-100A, a single-seat day fighter powered by a 43.15 kN (9,700 lb st) J57-P-7 or P-39 engine. Armament comprised four 20 mm M-39E cannon plus external stores on six underwing hardpoints. The RF-100A was a photo-reconnaissance conversion of the F-100A with a deeper camera-carrying front fuselage.

The F-100C appeared in 1954 as a single-seat fighter bomber with strengthened wings, up to 3,402 kg (7,500 lb) of bombs on eight underwing hardpoints, in-flight refuelling capability and 75.62 kN (17,000 lb st, with afterburning) Pratt & Whitney J57-P-21A turbojet engine. The similar F-100D introduced design refinements, including a taller fin, and could be armed with four Sidewinder or two Bullpup missiles, or 3,402 kg (7,500 lb) of external weapons in addition to its standard four 20 mm cannon. The final version built was the F-100F, a lengthened tandem two-seat operational trainer and tactical attack aircraft, armed with two 20 mm cannon and capable of carrying 2,722 kg (6,000 lb) of external stores.

Super Sabres remain operational in Denmark, Taiwan, Turkey and the USA.
Data (F-100D): *Engine* as above *Wing span* 11.81 m (38 ft 9 in) *Length* 16.54 m (54 ft 3 in) *Max T-O weight* 15,800 kg (34,832 lb) *Max level speed* 1,390 km/h (864 mph) *Range* (with two external tanks) 2,410 km (1,500 miles)

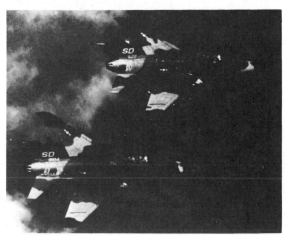

North American F-107A (USA) Experimental advanced fighter-bomber development of the F-100 Super Sabre.
North American FJ Fury (USA) The XFJ-1 marked the entry of North American into the field of jet-propelled military aircraft. The first prototype flew on 27 November 1946. Thirty production

North American F-86D Sabre.

North American F-86F Sabres flown by the JASDF.

North American F-100 Super Sabres flying over Vietnam.

North American F-86H Sabre.

North American

North American F-107A.

North American F-107A.

North American FJ-1 Fury.

North American P-82D
Twin Mustang.

North American Mustang
in RAAF service.

North American P-51A
Mustang.

chase test results on the P-40 from Curtiss), the Mustang became the pre-eminent long-range escort fighter of World War II and in many respects the greatest all-round combat aircraft. The design took full advantage of advances in technique since the inception of most of its rivals and incorporated a neat wide-track landing gear; ducted coolant radiator under the rear fuselage which gave reduced drag (and sometimes positive thrust); laminar-flow wing section, again giving reduced drag; and a very efficient structure. The result was an aircraft no larger than its rivals but which had two to four times the internal fuel capacity.

FJ-1 single-seat fighters were delivered to the US Navy, featuring straight wings and a 17.8 kN (4,000 lb st) Allison J35-A-5 turbojet engine. After being used for jet familiarisation, these were transferred to Naval Air Reserve units.

Although carrying FJ Fury designations, the next series of single-seat fighters for the US Navy were swept-wing aircraft based on the F-86 Sabre. The first was the FJ-2, first flown in prototype form on 14 February 1952. Production FJ-2s were powered by the General Electric J47-GE-2 turbojet engine and were basically navalised F-86Es. FJ-3 and FJ-4 variants followed, powered by Wright J65-W-2/W-4/W-16A engines, bringing the total number of swept-wing Furies built by 1958 to 1,115.

Data (FJ-4): *Engine* one 34.25 kN (7,700 lb st) Wright J65-W-16A turbojet *Wing span* 11.92 m (39 ft 1 in) *Length* 11.07 m (36 ft 4 in) *Max T-O weight* 10,750 kg (23,700 lb) *Max level speed* 1,094 km/h (680 mph) *Combat range* 2,390 km (1,485 miles) *Armament* four 20 mm cannon, plus four Sidewinder missiles or bombs

North American O-47 (USA) Two-seat observation monoplane of 1935 powered in its O-47A production form by a 726.6 kW (975 hp) Wright R-1820-49 radial engine. A total of 238 O-47A/Bs was delivered to the USAAC. The O-47 formed the basis for the Texan (see entry).

North American P-51 Mustang (USA) Quickly designed in the summer of 1940 to meet a request by the British Purchasing Commission (which doubted the company's ability and insisted it pur-

The prototype flew on 26 October 1940, and the first Mustang I for the RAF flew on 1 May 1941. Deliveries began in October 1941 and for the first time the RAF judged an American fighter outstanding in all respects, except performance at high-altitude – a shortcoming of the 857 kW (1,150 hp) Allison V-1710-F3R engine. Armament comprised two 0.50 in guns under the engine, two more in the wings and four 0.303 in guns – all with an exceptional supply of ammunition. At low altitude the speed of 628 km/h (390 mph) was considerably greater than that of any other RAF fighter, but the low-blown engine caused most of the 620 supplied to be used for army co-operation and photographic work. The Mk IA had four 20 mm cannon and the Mk II racks for two 500 lb bombs. By 1942 the USAAF had awoken to the type's exceptional qualities and bought large numbers, beginning with the P-51 (four cannon), A-36A (dive bomber) and F-6A (tactical reconnaissance).

By late 1942 the high-blown Merlin engine was being tested in Mustang airframes in separate efforts by Rolls-Royce and North American – the speed leaping to around 710 km/h (440 mph). In 1943 large-scale deliveries began of the P-51B (built at Los Angeles) and P-51C (built at Dallas), both powered by the 1,133 kW (1,520 hp) Packard V-1650-3 – one of the first US variants of the Merlin. Armament was only four 12.7 mm guns, but fuel capacity was increased and provision was made for two drop-tanks or two 1,000 lb bombs. Almost 4,000 of these models were made, those of the RAF being designated Mustang III and often having a frameless bulged hood instead of the side-hinged original. The USAAF photo version was the F-6C. In 1944 numerous improvements resulted in the P-51D (Packard V-1650-7), most of which had six 0.50 in guns, a teardrop sliding canopy and extra dorsal fin. No fewer than 6,502 were made at Los Angeles and 1,454 at Dallas – the latter also built 1,337 P-51Ks with Aeroproducts propeller. In 1945 production switched to the lighter and more advanced P-51H, fastest production Allied fighter, but only 555 had been made (bringing the overall total to 15,586) at VJ Day.

There were many post-war versions, beginning with the Twin Mustang built as the F-82E escort, F-82F and F-82G night fighters – having APS-4 or SCR-720 radar in a pod hung on the centre-section between two P-51 fuselages of revised form, with Allison engines and longer rear sections. In 1961 development began of rebuilt or developed versions of the P-51D for COIN (counter-insurgent) warfare, some being produced with either one or two seats and a choice of engines by Cavalier Aircraft. The Mustang was also made under licence by Commonwealth Aircraft in Australia. Large numbers served with air forces all over the world until the 1970s and a handful survived into 1979.

Data (P-51D): *Engine* as above *Wing span* 11.29 m (37 ft 0½ in) *Length* 9.81 m (32 ft 2½ in) *Max T-O weight* 5,206 kg (11,600 lb) *Max level speed* 703 km/h (437 mph) *Range* 1,529–3,347 km (950–2,080 miles)

North American T-2 Buckeye (USA) see **Rockwell**

North American T-28B Trojan.

North American XB-70A Valkyrie.

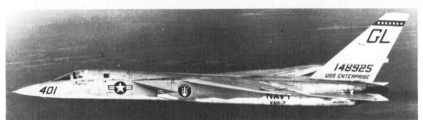

North American A-5A Vigilante.

North American T-28 Trojan (USA) First flown in 1949, the Trojan was put into production as the T-28A two-seat basic trainer for the USAF. Power was provided by a 596 kW (800 hp) Wright R-1300-1 radial engine. The T-28B was the initial US Navy version fitted with a 1,062 kW (1,425 hp) Wright R-1820-86 engine and a two-piece sliding canopy (as fitted to late production T-28As). Two further T-28 versions were produced: the T-28C with deck-arrester gear; and the T-28D, a converted T-28A with a 1,062 kW (1,425 hp) R-1820-56S engine and strengthened airframe for light-attack duties. An attack-trainer version was designated AT-28D. A licence-built version was also made in France as the Fennec.

T-28 Trojans are still operated by the air forces of 16 countries.

Data (T-28A): *Engine* as above *Wing span* 12.23 m (40 ft 1 in) *Length* 9.76 m (32 ft 0 in) *Max T-O weight* 3,068 kg (6,759 lb) *Max level speed* 461 km/h (288 mph) *Max range* 1,612 km (1,008 miles)

North American T-39 Sabreliner (USA) Aircrew trainer, pilot-proficiency/administrative-support and transport aircraft operated by the USAF and US Navy (see **Rockwell**).

North American X-15A (USA) The X-15A was a high-performance research aircraft used to provide date about heating, stability, control and the problems of re-entry into the atmosphere. It was flown faster and higher than any other manned aircraft, achieving a speed of Mach 6.72 or 7,297 km/h (4,534 mph) and an altitude of 107,960 m (354,200 ft). After 199 flights the X-15 programme was terminated in 1968. Power was provided by a 253.6 kN (57,000 lb st) Thiokol (Reaction Motors) XLR99-RM-2 single-chamber throttleable liquid-propellant rocket motor.

North American T-39A Sabreliner.

North American X-15A after launch from its motherplane.

North American

North American XB-70A Valkyrie (USA)
First flown on 21 September 1964, the Valkyrie was designed as a Mach 3 strategic bomber to replace the USAF's B-52. When the bomber programme was abandoned, it became an aerodynamic research aircraft (see **MiG-25**).

North American Rockwell A-5 Vigilante (USA) The Vigilante was designed as a Mach 2 carrier-based attack aircraft capable of carrying nuclear or conventional bombs. The first prototype flew on 31 August 1958 and 57 production A-5A attack aircraft were delivered to the US Navy, becoming operational on board USS *Enterprise* in February 1962. The other major version of the Vigilante was the RA-5C, a reconnaissance type of which more than 90 were built as new; most of the A-5As were subsequently converted to this standard.
Data (RA-5C): *Engines* two 79.44 kN (17,859 lb st, with afterburning) General Electric J79-GE-10 turbojets *Wing span* 16.15 m (53 ft 0 in) *Length* 23.35 m (76 ft 7¼ in) *Max T-O weight* 30,300 kg (66,800 lb) *Max level speed* 2,228 km/h (1,385 mph) *Range* 4,830 km (3,000 miles) *Armament* variety of weapons – including thermonuclear bombs – accommodated underwing

Northrop A-17 (USA) In 1933 Northrop produced the 2-C two-seat attack monoplane which eventually resulted in modified A-17s being ordered for the USAAC. Power was provided by a

559 kW (750 hp) Pratt & Whitney R-1535 Twin-Wasp Junior radial engine enclosed in an NACA cowling. A fixed cantilever landing gear was standard. In 1938 a second order for 100 A-17As was completed for the USAAC and production was started on an additional order for 29. The A-17A version featured a 615 kW (825 hp) R-1535 engine and a retractable landing gear. However a large number of the A-17As were transferred to SAAF squadrons and the RAF during the early war years, becoming known as Nomads.

Meanwhile in 1934 the British Air Ministry had purchased an example of the 2-E for test and 150 similar aircraft were ordered by China. In 1937 the Bristol Aeroplane Company also acquired an A-17 for use as a flying test-bed for the Bristol Hercules engine. Northrop made other pre-war exports: the Bristol-powered 8A-2 going to Sweden (also licence-built); the 626 kW (840 hp) Wright Cyclone-powered 8A-2 to Argentina; the 783 kW (1,050 hp) Pratt & Whitney R-1830-engined 8A-3N to the Netherlands; the 745.2 kW (1,000 hp) GR-1820G Cyclone-powered 8A-3P to Peru; and the 8A-4 to Iraq. The 895 kW (1,200 hp) Cyclone-engined 8A-5s ordered by Norway were delivered to Canada following Norway's occupation, while similar aircraft ordered by Peru were impressed by the USAAF as A-33s.
Data (A-17A): *Engine* as above *Wing span* 14.54 m (47 ft 8½ in) *Length* 9.87 m (31 ft 8½ in) *Max T-O weight* 3,375–3,425 kg (7,440–7,550 lb) *Max level speed* 354 km/h (220 mph) *Range* 1,175 km (730 miles) *Armament* five 0.30 in machine-guns, four in the leading edges of the wings and one flexibly mounted in the rear-gunner's cockpit; plus four 100 lb or 20 smaller bombs or chemicals for smoke-screen laying

Northrop BT-1 (USA) The BT-1 was a two-seat carrier-borne dive-bomber of similar lines to the Army A-17A. The US Navy received 53 from 1938.

Northrop C-125 Raider and Pioneer (USA) The Northrop Pioneer was built as a 40-passenger commercial transport aircraft, powered by three 596 kW (800 hp) R-957 Cyclone engines. From it was developed the C-125 Raider for the USAF, 23

of which were built with 894 kW (1,200 hp) Wright R-1820-99 engines: 13 as C-125A assault transports and ten as C-125B Arctic rescue aircraft.

Northrop F-5 (USA) This lightweight tactical export fighter and fighter bomber is similar in design and construction to the T-38 Talon trainer but utilises a higher-rated version of the J85 engine. Its design began in 1955 and the prototype flew for the first time on 30 July 1959.

The production single-seat version was the F-5A; those for Canada, the Netherlands, Norway and Spain being designated CF-5A, NF-5A, F-5G and SF-5A respectively. The RF-5A was built as a photographic-reconnaissance version of the F-5A; while the F-5B is the tandem two-seat operational or trainer version with the 20 mm nose guns deleted. Fifteen countries still operate the F-5. Data (F-5A): *Engines* two 18.15 kN (4,080 lb st, with afterburning) General Electric J85-GE-13 turbojets *Wing span* 7.7 m (25 ft 3 in) *Length* 14.38 m (47 ft 2 in) *Max T-O weight* 9,379 kg (20,677 lb) *Max level speed* 1,488 km/h (925 mph) *Range* 2,232 km (1,387 miles) *Armament* two Sidewinder missiles on wingtip launchers and two 20 mm Colt-Browning M-39 guns in the fuselage nose. A bomb of more than 2,000 lb or a high-rate-of-fire gun pack can be suspended from the underfuselage pylon, while four underwing hardpoints can carry missiles, rockets, gun packs, etc

Northrop F-5 Tiger II (USA) The F-5E single-seat light tactical fighter was selected in November 1970 by the US government as the winner of a competition to determine the International Fighter Aircraft (IFA) which was to succeed Northrop's F-5A aircraft.

The first F-5E made its maiden flight on 11 August 1972. USAF Tactical Air Command, with assistance from Air Training Command, was assigned responsibility for training pilots and technicians of user countries. First deliveries of the F-5E (to the USAF's 425th Tactical Fighter Squadron) were made in the spring of 1973. Twenty aircraft had been supplied for the USAF

Northrop F-5E Tiger II.

training programme by the end of September 1973 and deliveries to foreign countries began in late 1973. The 1,000th F-5E was delivered to the Republic of Korea in August 1979, when production of the F-5E and two-seat F-5F was continuing. Customers to date include the USAF (112 F-5Es), US Navy (10 F-5Es and 3 F-5Fs), Brazil, Chile, Republic of China, Iran, Jordan, Kenya, South Korea, Malaysia, Saudi Arabia, Singapore, Sudan, Switzerland, Thailand and the Yemen Arab Republic.

In addition to their use as tactical fighters, F-5Es are operated by the USAF and US Navy in the 'aggressor' role, to simulate 'enemy' aircraft at major air-combat training schools in the USA, England and the Philippines.

Northrop F-5As.

The F-5E is the standard production version which is also produced under licence by AIDC in Taiwan. Brazilian Air Force F-5Es have a large dorsal fin to accommodate an ADF antenna. The F-5F is the tandem two-seat version of the F-5E with a fuselage lengthened by 1.08 m (3 ft 6½ in).

In 1978 Northrop announced receipt of US government approval for a company-funded development and flight demonstration programme of an RF-5E specialised reconnaissance version of the F-5E. This has a modified forward fuselage with quick-change capabilities to accommodate a wide variety of reconnaissance equipment. Both day and night photo missions were demonstrated during the subsequent test programme. Modification of a production F-5E made possible the first flight of the RF-5E prototype in January 1979.

Northrop F-5B.

Data (F-5E): *Engines* two 22.24 kN (5,000 lb st, with afterburning) General Electric J85-GE-21A turbojets *Wing span* 8.13 m (26 ft 8 in) *Length* 14.68 m (48 ft 2 in) *Max T-O weight* 11,193 kg

Northrop F-18L prototype multi-role land-based fighter, counterpart of the US Navy's McDonnell Douglas Hornet.

Northrop

Northrop P-61 Black Widow.

Northrop F-89H Scorpion.

(24,676 lb) *Max level speed* Mach 1.63 *Combat radius* (max fuel) 2,483 km (1,543 miles) *Armament* two AIM-9 Sidewinder missiles on wingtip launchers. Two 20 mm M-39A2 cannon mounted in fuselage nose. Up to 3,175 kg (7,000 lb) of mixed ordnance can be carried on one underfuselage and four underwing stations, including M129 leaflet bombs; MK-82 GP and Snakeye 500 lb bombs; MK-36 destructors; MK-84 2,000 lb bomb; BLU-1, -27 or -32 U or F napalm; LAU-68 (7) 2¾ in rockets; LAU-3 (19) 2¾ in rockets; CBU-24, -49, -52 or -58 cluster-bomb units; and SUU-20 bomb and rocket packs

Northrop F-89 Scorpion (USA) The F-89 was a twin-jet two-seat all-weather fighter of fairly conventional straight-wing design. Power was provided by Allison J35 engines for all the production versions, mounted externally in nacelles on the sides of the lower fuselage. Comprehensive radar and night/bad-weather equipment was fitted. The XF-89 prototype made its first flight on 16 August 1948. The first production version was the F-89A, powered initially by 21.8 kN (4,900 lb st) afterburning Allison J35-A-21 engines which were later replaced by more powerful -21As. Armament comprised six nose-mounted 20 mm cannon. The F-89D major production version introduced rocket armament as a replacement for the cannon. This comprised 104 2¾ in folding-wing air-to-air rockets carried in permanently mounted wingtip pods. The final production version was the F-89H fitted with new electronic equipment to allow the aircraft to launch Hughes Falcon air-to-air missiles. The F-89J designation was applied to earlier F-89s brought up to F-89H standard. Production of all versions of the Scorpion totalled 1,050 aircraft.

Northrop F-15A Reporter.

Data (F-89D): *Engines* two 35.6 kN (8,000 lb st, with afterburning) Allison J35-A-35 turbojets *Wing span* 18.19 m (59 ft 8 in) *Length* 16.41 m (53 ft 10 in) *Max T-O weight* 19,160 kg (42,240 lb) *Max level speed* 982 km/h (610 mph) *Range* 1,408 km (875 miles)

Northrop N-3PB.

Northrop N-3PB (USA) Three-seat patrol-bomber seaplane powered by a 708 kW (950 hp) Wright GR-1820-G205A Cyclone radial engine. Twenty-four were ordered by the Norwegian government, delivered in early 1941 and operated with a squadron of the Royal Norwegian Air Force serving with RAF Coastal Command.

Northrop P-61 Black Widow (USA) The Black Widow night fighter was built to a USAAF specification issued in 1940. Development began in 1940 and an order for two XP-61s was placed in January 1941. The first flew on 26 May 1942.

The P-61A and P-61B first production versions were generally similar, although the early P-61As had two Pratt & Whitney R-2800-10 (B Series) engines fitted, while later P-61As and P-61Bs had 1,490.4 kW (2,000 hp) R-2800-65 (C Series) engines – both with two-stage superchargers. Only the first 37 P-61As were fitted with the dorsal turret. Provision for external auxiliary tanks was made on late P-61Bs.

The P-61C was fitted with R-2800-73 engines with single-stage superchargers, driving new Curtiss Electric propellers with paddle-type blades. These also had slatted airbrakes on upper and lower surfaces of the outer wings. The XP-61D, XP-61E and XP-61F were prototypes only; while a small number of P-61G weather-reconnaissance aircraft were produced from P-61Bs. Production of all versions totalled 691 aircraft.

Data (P-61B): *Engines* as above *Wing span* 20.12 m (66 ft 0 in) *Length* 15.11 m (49 ft 7 in) *Max level speed* 603 km/h (375 mph) *Range* 1,609 km (1,000 miles) *Armament* four 20 mm cannon and four 0.50 in machine-guns

Northrop F-15A Reporter (USA) Photographic-reconnaissance aircraft developed from the Black Widow. Two prototypes were completed in January and February 1945 and 175 were ordered for the USAAF. In the event only 36 were produced.

Northrop T-38A Talon.

Northrop T-38 Talon (USA) Two-seat super-sonic trainer powered by two 17.13 kN (3,850 lb st, with afterburning) General Electric J85-GE-5 turbojet engines. Currently operated by the air forces of Germany, Taiwan and the USA.

Northrop X-4 Bantam (USA) Jet-powered research aircraft, first flown on 15 December 1948 and used to investigate the stability and flight characteristics of aircraft of swept-back, tailless configuration at subsonic speeds.

Northrop XP-79B, an experimental flying-wing combat aircraft of 1945 designed to ram the tails of enemy aircraft.

Northrop X-4 Bantam.

Northrop Beta (USA) Two-seat open-cockpit light monoplane powered by a 119 kW (160 hp) Menasco engine.

Northrop Delta (USA) Passenger-carrying version of the Gamma, accommodating a pilot and eight passengers or two pilots and six passengers. Thirty-two were built from 1933, two going to Pan American Airways and TWA.

Northrop Gamma (USA) Designed as a single-seat freight-carrying all-metal monoplane, normally powered by a single Wright SR-1820-F or Pratt & Whitney Hornet engine. Sixty-one were built from 1932.

Northrop/NASA HL-10, M2-F2 and M2-F3 (USA) Lifting-body research vehicles, first flown on 22 December 1966 (unpowered), 12 July 1966 (unpowered) and 25 November 1970 (powered) respectively. The M2-F3 was the M2-F2 completely dismantled and rebuilt in slightly different form, powered (as for the HL-10 and M2-F2) by a 35.6 kN (8,000 lb st) Thiokol XLR 11 rocket engine.

Nyeman R-10 (USSR) Originally produced as a six-passenger civil transport aircraft, featuring a low monoplane wing and a retractable landing gear. Many were operated on domestic services. Its high performance led to the development of a

Northrop N-9M, scale model of the XB-35.

Northrop XB-35 and YB-49 (USA) Piston and turbojet-engined flying-wing heavy bombers respectively. The first XB-35 flew on 25 June 1946, following earlier trials with a twin-engined flying-scale model. Fourteen YB-35s were ordered, of which three were to be converted to YB-49 eight-jet and YRB-49A six-jet form. An order for 30 production B-49s was cancelled in 1949.

Northrop Alpha (USA) Six-passenger all-metal cabin monoplane powered by a 317 kW (425 hp) Pratt & Whitney Wasp radial engine.

Northrop Delta.

Northrop XB-35.

First Northrop Gamma.

Northrop HL-10.

Oberlerchner Job 15.

On Mark Marksman.

Orenco (Ordnance Engineering Corporation) Model A, a two-seat primary trainer built as the company's first product. Orenco's most successful aircraft was the Model D fighter (223.5 kW; 300 hp Hispano engine), 50 of which went to the US Army.

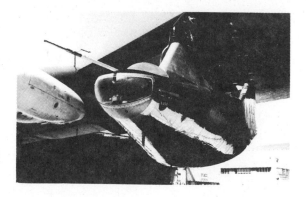

Northrop M2-F2 under the wing of its B-52 motherplane.

light bombing version (designated KhAI-5) armed with two forward-firing and one rear-mounted 7.62 mm ShKAS machine-guns and normally 400 kg (882 lb) of bombs. Large number (perhaps 500) completed for the Air Force, each powered by a 559 kW (750 hp) M-25V engine. They were operational from 1937 until 1941. Maximum level speed was 360 km/h (224 mph).

Oberlerchner Job 15 (Austria) Four-seat light monoplane of 1960 suitable for touring, training or glider-towing. Production aircraft initially powered by a 100.6 kW (135 hp) Lycoming O-290 engine, but superseded by a 112 kW (150 hp) Lycoming O-320 engine as the Job 15-150.

On Mark Marksman and Musketeer (USA) Six–eight-passenger executive transport conversions of the World War II Douglas B-26 bomber, produced with a pressurised and unpressurised fuselage respectively.

Osprey (Pereira) GP3 Osprey II (USA) Two-seat lightweight amphibian, plans for which are available to amateur constructors.

PacAero Learstar, Nomad and Tradewind (USA) The Nomad was produced as a civil and military utility conversion of the North American T-28A trainer. The Learstar of 1954 was a high-speed long-range custom-equipped executive version of the Lockheed Model 18-56 Lodestar, while the Tradewind was a conversion of the Beechcraft Model 18.

Packard-Le Père LUSAC-11 and LUSAC-21 (USA) The LUSAC-11 was a single-seat fighter of 1918 powered by a 317 kW (425 hp) Liberty 12 engine. Only 30 had been built by the Armistice, when orders for nearly 3,500 were cancelled. The 313 kW (420 hp) Bugatti 16-powered LUSAC-21 appeared after the war but remained a prototype.

Panavia Tornado (UK/Germany/Italy) The Tornado is a twin-engined two-seat supersonic variable-geometry aircraft capable of fulfilling the agreed operational requirements of its three sponsoring countries. It is intended for close air support/battlefield interdiction; interdiction/counter-air strike; air superiority; interception/air defence; naval strike; and reconnaissance.

The 809 aircraft to be produced for the participating nations will comprise 671 operational aircraft plus 138 dual-control trainers with full-operational capability.

The RAF is to have 385 Tornadoes, 220 of which will be of the interdictor/strike version and 165 of the air-defence version. These are due to become operational with Strike Command in 1982 and will initially replace Vulcans and Buccaneers of nine squadrons in the overland strike and reconnaissance roles. Later the air-defence version will succeed the Phantom; and finally the Tornado will replace the Buccaneer for maritime-strike tasks. Some two-thirds of the RAF's front-line aircraft will eventually be Tornadoes.

The Luftwaffe is to receive 212 Tornadoes to

replace the Lockheed F-104G in battlefield inter-diction, counter-air and close air support roles. The 112 Tornadoes for the German Navy will be used for strike missions against sea and coastal targets, and for reconnaissance.

The Italian Air Force will use 54 of its 100 Tornadoes to replace F-104G and G91R aircraft in the air-superiority, ground-attack and recon-naissance roles. The remainder will be kept in reserve, except for 12 which will be equipped as dual-control trainers.

The first prototype Tornado flew in Germany on 14 August 1974. Other prototypes followed, and by 1979 all six pre-production Tornadoes had flown. By June 1979 prototype and pre-series Tornadoes had accumulated a total of 2,750 hours' flying in more than 2,200 flights.

Data (interdictor/strike version): *Engines* two 71.2 kN (16,000 lb st, with afterburning) Turbo-Union RB.199-34R-04 turbofans *Wing span* (spread) 13.9 m (45 ft 7¼ in), (swept) 8.6 m (28 ft 2½ in) *Length* 16.7 m (54 ft 9½ in) *Max T-O weight* 26,490 kg (58,400 lb) *Max level speed* above Mach 2 *Radius of action* 1,390 km (863 miles) *Armament* two 27 mm IWKA-Mauser cannon, plus armament with emphasis on the ability to carry advanced non-nuclear wepons on three under fuselage attachments and up to four swivelling hardpoints beneath the outer wings, to a maximum of 7,257 kg (16,000 lb). Among the weapons already specified for, or suitable for carriage by, the Tornado are the Sidewinder, Sky Flash, Sparrow and Aspide air-to-air missiles; A.S. 30, Martel, P3T and Kormoran air-to-surface mis-siles; napalm; BL 755 600 lb cluster bombs; 1,000 lb bombs; and 'smart' or retarded bombs.

Parker Teenie Two (USA) Single-seat light monoplane, plans and a kit of parts for which are available to amateur constructors.

Parnall Panther (UK) Two-seat carrier-borne spotter and reconnaissance biplane of 1917 pow-ered by a 171.4 kW (230 hp) Bentley B.R.2 engine. One hundred and fifty served with the FAA from 1919 until 1926.

Packard-Le Père LUSAC-11.

Parnall Plover (UK) Single-seat carrier-borne fighter biplane of 1922, ten of which served with the FAA during 1923–24. Power was provided by a 324 kW (435 hp) Bristol Jupiter IV engine.

Partenavia P.48-B Astore, P.52 Tigrotto and P.55 Tornado (Italy) Two-seat high-wing monoplane of 1952, three-seat low-wing mono-plane of 1953 and high-performance two-seat competition and touring monoplane respectively.

PacAero Nomad.

First production Panavia Tornado GR.1 interdictor/strike aircraft.

Panavia Tornado F.2 air-defence variant.

Parker Teenie Two.

Partenavia P.57 Fachiro (Italy) Designed as a simple and inexpensive two–four-seat high-wing monoplane suitable for touring and general-purpose flying (P.57-1 four-seater), side-by-side two-seat touring (P.57-2) and tandem two-seat military observation and liaison duties (P.57-3).

First flown in November 1958, the Fachiro II-f was developed from the lower-powered Fachiro, fitted with a 134 kW (180 hp) Lycoming O-360-A2A engine.

Partenavia P.59 Jolly (Italy) Two-seat cabin monoplane, first flown in 1960.

PacAero Tradewind.

Partenavia

Parnall Panther.

Partenavia P.57 Fachiro II-f.

Partenavia P.68R.

Partenavia P.68 Observer.

Partenavia P.66C-160 Charlie.

Partenavia P.64 Oscar (Italy) The prototype of the P.64 Oscar flew for the first time on 2 April 1965. Design of an improved version of the Oscar four-seat light aircraft was started in 1966 and the prototype P.64B Oscar-180 flew in 1967. Seventy-three had been built by February 1974. Power was provided by a 134 kW (180 hp) Lycoming O-360-A1A engine. A version known as the RSA 200 was licence-built in South Africa. A second version was produced as the Oscar-200 powered by a 149 kW (200 hp) IO-360-A1B engine (16 built by February 1974).

Partenavia P.66B Oscar (Italy) By February 1974 Partenavia had built 107 Oscar-100 two-seaters with the 85.7 kW (115 hp) Lycoming O-235-C1B engine and 79 Oscar-150 three-seaters with 112 kW (150 hp) O-320-E2A engines.

Partenavia P.66C-160 Charlie (Italy) Two–four-seat basic training aircraft built as an improved version of the P.64/P.66 Oscar series, powered by a 119 kW (160 hp) Lycoming O-320-H2AD engine. Deliveries began in 1977.

Partenavia P.68 Victor (Italy) First flown on 25 May 1970, the Victor was designed as a six–seven-seat twin-engined transport to supplement the Oscar series. The P.68B is a developed version

and by mid-1979 approximately 190 Victors had been delivered, more than 100 for export. Power is provided by two 149 kW (200 hp) Lycoming IO-360-A1B6 engines. Maximum level speed is 322 km/h (200 mph). A version with a retractable landing gear has been flight tested as the P.68R.

Partenavia P.68RTC (Italy) Variant of the P.68B with a retractable landing gear and 156.5 kW (210 hp) Lycoming TIO-360 turbocharged engines.

Partenavia P.68C (Italy) Improved version of the P.68B with a lengthened nose, oleo-type nosewheel strut, single integral fuel tank in each wing and other refinements. A version with a retractable landing gear has been built as the P.68C-R, and a version with two 156.5 kW (210 hp) TIO-360-C1A6D turbocharged engines is the P.68C-TC.

Partenavia P.68 Observer (Italy) Version of the P.68 with a forward and downward view for the crew equal to that of a helicopter, with a new Plexiglas nose, cockpit and associated structures. Ordered by the German and other police departments.

Partenavia/Aeritalia AP.68TP (Italy) Turbine-engined version of the P.68R (known originally as the P.68 Turbo) being developed in association with Aeritalia. The prototype flew on 11 September 1978 powered by two 246 kW (330 shp) Allison 250-B17B turboprop engines.

Payne Knight Twister KT-85 (USA) Single-seat light biplane suitable for engines in the 63.5–67 kW (85–90 hp) range. Plans are available to amateur constructors.

Payne Knight Twister.

Payne Knight Twister.

Percival (UK) see also **Hunting Percival**
Percival P.40 Prentice (UK) Three-seat basic trainer, first flown in prototype form on 31 March 1946. Prentice T.1 became the standard RAF basic trainer, powered by a 187 kW (251 hp) de Havilland Gipsy Queen 32 engine. Also supplied to Argentina, India and the Lebanon. Licences also acquired by companies in Argentina and

Pazmany PL-1 Laminar.

Payne Knight Twister SKT-125 (USA) Developed version of the KT-85 with increased wing area and a 93 kW (125 hp) Lycoming engine. Plans are available to amateur constructors.

Payne Knight Junior KT-75 (USA) Basically similar to the KT-85 but with tapered wings of larger area.

Pazmany PL-1 Laminar (USA) Two-seat light monoplane, plans for which are available to amateur constructors. Standard power plant is a 71 kW (95 hp) Continental C-90-12F engine. The PL-1B is a version built in Taiwan powered by a 112 kW (150 hp) Lycoming O-320 engine.

Pazmany PL-2 (USA) Developed version of the PL-1, plans for which are available to amateur constructors.

Pazmany PL-4A.

India. The Prentice T.3 version was delivered to the Indian Air Force, powered by a 257 kW (345 hp) de Havilland Gipsy Queen 71 engine.

Percival P.50 Prince (UK) The Prince, designed mainly for feeder-line and executive travel, first flew on 13 May 1948. The Series I had an all-up weight of 4,831 kg (10,650 lb) and was powered by two 387.5 kW (520 hp) Alvis Leonides 501/4 engines. The Series II and Series III had all-up weights of 4,990 kg (11,000 lb), the latter powered by two 410 kW (550 hp) Alvis

Pazmany PL-2.

Pazmany PL-4A (USA) Single-seat lightweight sporting monoplane powered by a modified 1,600 cc Volkswagen motorcar engine. Plans are available to amateur constructors.

PDQ Aircraft Products PDQ-2 (USA) Single-seat lightweight sporting aircraft, plans for which are available to amateur constructors (more than 2,000 sets sold).

Pemberton-Billing P.B.25 (UK) Pusher-engined (74.5 kW; 100 hp Gnome or 82 kW; 110 hp Clerget) biplane of 1916, 20 of which were built as scouts for the RNAS.

PDQ Aircraft Products PDQ-2.

Percival

104.3 kW (140 hp) de Havilland Gipsy Major Series II and 152.8 kW (205 hp) Gipsy Six Series II engines respectively. The Q-6 was also chosen for service with the RAF as a communications aircraft under the name Petrel.

Percival Proctor (UK) Before World War II the Percival Vega Gull was chosen by the Air Ministry for conversion to service use. Officially named the Proctor, it served as a navigational and radio trainer with the RAF and Royal Navy, and also

Percival P.50 Prince Series I.

Leonides 24 (502/4) engines. Accommodation was provided for 6–12 passengers (according to layout), freight, or four stretchers and two medical attendants. A photographic-survey version was also produced as the P.54 Survey Prince IIIA.

Data (Series III): *Engines* as above *Wing span* 17.07 m (56 ft 0 in) *Length* 13.06 m (42 ft 10 in) *Max T-O weight* as above *Max level speed* 368 km/h (229 mph) *Range* 1,451 km (902 miles)

Percival Gull (UK) Three-seat cabin monoplane of the early 1930s powered by a 97 kW (130 hp) de Havilland Gipsy Major engine. Superseded by the similar Gull Major and the Gipsy Six-engined Gull Six.

Percival Mew Gull.

Percival Mew Gull (UK) Single-seat high-speed monoplane powered by a 149 kW (200 hp) de Havilland Gipsy Six engine. The 1938 King's Cup Race was won by a Mew Gull flown by Mr A. Henshaw at an average speed of 380.2 km/h (236.25 mph), and another came second. In February 1939 Mr Henshaw flew a Mew Gull from Gravesend, England to Cape Town, South Africa and back in 4 days 10 hours 15 minutes, lowering the previous record by 1 day 6 hours 45 minutes.

Percival Q-6.

Percival Petrel, Q-4 and Q-6 (UK) The Q-4 and Q-6 were light twin-engined six–seven-seat cabin monoplanes of the latter 1930s, powered by

performed dual-control training and four-seat liaison duties. More than 1,000 were eventually delivered to the services.

The Proctor I was a communications type for the RAF and ATA with side-by-side seats and dual controls, and a third seat to the rear. The Navy received the Proctor IA radio and navigational trainer fitted for three crew (including a radio operator on a rotatable rear seat) and with a D/F loop aerial on top of the cabin. The Proctor II and IIA were RAF and Royal Navy radio and navigational trainers respectively, with the radio operator seated beside the pilot. The Proctor III was produced in three forms for the RAF: as a three-seat communications type without dual controls; radio trainer with the rear seat positioned to the port side and a small radio set alongside; and the Series 2 radio trainer with

Percival Gull Six.

in 1938 as a two-seat fighter, then dive bomber, only later being standardised as a light bomber. Initial production aircraft were powered by two 820 kW (1,100 hp) Klimov M-105R engines, but from 1943 these were replaced by 976 kW (1,310 hp) M-105PFs as the Pe-2M. Other versions included the Pe-2R reconnaissance aircraft and the Pe-3, the latter being a purpose-built and refined long-range fighter and reconnaissance model derived from the adapted Pe-2V fighter. After the war the aircraft carried the reporting name *Buck*.

Data: *Engines* as above *Wing span* 17.16 m (56 ft 3 in) *Length* 12.6 m (41 ft 4 in) *Max T-O weight* 8,520 kg (18,783 lb) *Max level speed* 540 km/h (335.5 mph) *Range* 1,200 km (745.5 miles) *Armament* initially four 7.62 mm machine-guns or two 12.7 mm and two 7.62 mm guns, plus 1,000 kg (2,205 lb) of bombs

seating for two (radio operator facing aft) and a D/F loop on top of the cabin.

The final production version was the Proctor IV, built from 1943 as a radio trainer for the RAF and featuring a larger, heavier and completely redesigned fuselage which was fully equipped for night flying and carried the largest type of radio transmitter and receiver as used on operational aircraft. Many were subsequently converted into four-seat communications aircraft with dual controls. The projected Proctor V version did not enter service.

Post-war a large number of Proctors were demilitarised and sold off, although the type remained in service with the RAF as a communications aircraft until 1955.

Data (Proctor IV): *Engine* one 155 kW (208 hp) de Havilland Gipsy Queen II *Wing span* 12.04 m (39 ft 6 in) *Length* 8.59 m (28 ft 2 in) *Max T-O weight* 1,588 kg (3,500 lb) *Max level speed* 253 km/h (157 mph) *Max range* 1,255 km (780 miles)

Percival Vega Gull (UK) Four-seat light cabin monoplane developed from the Gull and first flown in 1935. Power was provided by a 149 kW (200 hp) de Havilland Gipsy Six engine. Many were sold to private owners before a specialised version was developed for the RAF and Royal Navy as the Proctor, which followed 14 Vega Gull IIIs delivered to the RAF as communications aircraft in 1938.

Petlyakov Pe-2 (USSR) The Pe-2 proved to be one of the finest and most versatile Soviet aircraft of World War II, perhaps ranking with the German Junkers Ju 88 for sheer adaptability. Indeed, although deployed widely from 1941 as a bomber and ground-attack aircraft, it had been conceived

Petlyakov Pe-2s.

Petlyakov Pe-2.

Petlyakov Pe-8 (USSR) Credited as a design by Andre Tupolev in the 1945–46 *Jane's* because of its TB-7 air force designation, this four-engined heavy bomber was the work of Petlyakov and carried the design designation ANT-42. The first prototype flew on 27 December 1936. Production Pe-8s were well armed, carrying two 7.62 mm machine-guns in a spherical nose turret, two machine-guns or a 20 mm cannon in a dorsal turret, one hand-operated 12.7 mm machine-gun in the rear of each inboard engine nacelle under the wing trailing edge and a 20 mm cannon in a tail turret, plus up to 4,000 kg (8,003 lb) of bombs stowed internally.

Initially the Pe-8 was powered by four 820 kW (1,100 hp) M-105 engines and entered service in this form in 1940. The 1941 model had 1,080.5 kW (1,450 hp) Mikulin AM-35As fitted. During the production run (which lasted until

Percival Proctor I.

Petlyakov Pe-2.

Petlyakov Pe-8.

PFA Luton L.A.4a Minor.

PFA Currie Wot.

1944) several other engines were installed either experimentally or as a standard type, including the 967 kW (1,300 hp) AM-38, 1,304 kW (1,750 hp) M-82 and a diesel engine.

On the night of 21 July 1941 German bombers attacked Moscow for the first time. As a reprisal Soviet Il-4 bombers made their first attack on Berlin on the night of 7 August. The resulting damage was minimal but it cleared the way for further attacks. In the spring of 1942 the Soviet ADD or Long-Range Aviation was formed, using the Pe-8 as its main component. Pe-8 raids on Germany began in July 1942 with small numbers of aircraft attacking Königsberg and then Berlin and elsewhere. However these were not very successful and extremely heavy losses were endured. Although Pe-8s remained operational as bombers until the end of the war, a number were converted into transports.

Data: *Engines* as above *Wing span* 40.0 m (131 ft 3 in) *Length* 24.5 m (80 ft 6 in) *Max T-O*

weight approximately 28,600–33,300 kg (63,050–73,400 lb) *Max level speed* 448 km/h (278 mph) *Range* 4,000 km (2,845 miles) with a 2,000 kg (4,410 lb) bomb load

PFA Currie Wot (UK) The Popular Flying Association is responsible for marketing plans for several aircraft, one of which is the Currie Wot single-seat fully aerobatic light biplane.

PFA Druine D31 Turbulent (UK) Single-seat ultra-light monoplane, plans for which are available to amateur constructors.

PFA Luton L.A.4a Minor (UK) Single-seat light monoplane, plans for which are available to amateur constructors.

Pfalz A.I, A.II and E.III (Germany) Prior to World War I the Pfalz company, founded by the brothers Everbusch, built a military aircraft of similar appearance to the Ago pusher, powered by a 74.5 kW (100 hp) Rapp engine. This aircraft carried out an African flight between Swakopmund and Karibib. The next Pfalz military type was the A.I. Developed from the French Morane-Saulnier Type L, the A.I and later A.II were two-seat unarmed reconnaissance monoplanes that served with the German and Austrian forces for the first year or so of World War I. Power was provided by a 59.6 kW (80 hp) and 74.5 kW (100 hp) Oberursel rotary engine respectively. With the synchronised machine-gun of the Fokker E fitted, the A.II became the single-seat E.III fighter.

Pfalz D.III (Germany) Pfalz's first attempt at producing a modern high-powered single-seat fighter biplane, the D.III entered service in 1917 powered by a 119 kW (160 hp) Mercedes D.III engine. Armament comprised the usual twin forward-firing Spandaus. Although useful as a supply aircraft for German units needing replacements, it was considered inferior to other types. Nonetheless several hundred were built. For the last months of the war the D.IIIa became available, basically a refined D.III with a more-powerful 134 kW (180 hp) Mercedes D.IIIa engine.

Data (D.III): *Engine* as above *Wing span* 9.4 m (30 ft 10 in) *Length* 6.95 m (22 ft 9½ in) *Max T-O weight* 932 kg (2,055 lb) *Max level speed* 165 km/h (103 mph) *Range* 250 km (155 miles)

Pfalz D.VIII (Germany) Single-seat biplane fighter of 1918 powered by a 119 kW (160 hp) Siemens-Halske Sh.III rotary engine. Small number had been delivered by the Armistice.

Pfalz D.XII (Germany) Arriving too late and in too few numbers to make a great impression on the 'air war' during the final months of World War I, the Pfalz D.XII was nevertheless an excellent single-seat fighter. Its only fault – if it can be judged as that – was that its maximum speed of 170 km/h (105.5 mph) was on the low side compared to the equally new Fokker D.VII. Power was provided by a 134 kW (180 hp) Mercedes D.IIIa engine and armament comprised the standard Spandaus. The number built is not known but it is unlikely to have exceeded 100.

Pfalz Dr.I (Germany) During the German triplane period – which came to a rather abrupt end with the death of von Richthofen – the Pfalz works

turned out the Dr.I, often stated to have used a triplane copy of the Nieuport wing arrangement. A far cleaner looking triplane than the Fokker type, it was powered by a Siemens-Halske Sh.III rotary engine. Only a handful were built in 1917.

Pfalz E.I, E.II, E.IV and E.V (Germany) Of similar appearance to the Fokker Eindecker, the Pfalz E series were operational during the same period and were flown with and without machine-gun armament for scouting and reconnaissance duties. The main variants were the E.I and E.II with 59.6 kW (80 hp) and 74.5 kW (100 hp) Oberursel rotary engines respectively, although the E.IV had a 119 kW (160 hp) engine fitted and the E.V a 74.5 kW (100 hp) Mercedes D.I.

Phönix C.I (Austria-Hungary) The Phönix works turned out 1,084 aeroplanes of 22 different types during World War I, starting with licence-built Albatros two-seaters, passing next to Brandenburg types and ending with aircraft of its own design.

The C.I was an ugly but functional two-seat armed-reconnaissance and general-purpose biplane, which became standardised equipment of the Austro-Hungarian air arm from 1917. In addition to reconnaissance it undertook artillery directing by wireless and, in an emergency, contour fighting and bombing (four 12 kg or two 25 kg bombs). It was on a C.I that the observer Leut Barwig brought down the leading Italian fighter pilot Maj Baracca. A total of 110 was built, powered by the 171.4 kW (230 hp) Hiero engine: the first delivered on 2 March 1917 and the last on 1 October 1918. Armament comprised one forward-firing and one rear-mounted Schwarzlose machine-guns.

Phönix D.I, D.II and D.III (Austria-Hungary) Appearing soon after the C.I, the prototype D.I single-seat fighter biplane bore little similarity to the reconnaissance aircraft and first flew with a 149 kW (200 hp) Austro-Daimler engine installed. The two initial production versions entered service with the air arm and navy the same year as the D.I and D.II (balanced elevators), each powered by the 149 kW (200 hp) Hiero engine and armed with two Schwarzlose machine-guns. Maximum speed was good, but the fighters had two faults – neither critical but nevertheless undesirable – being over-stable and structurally on the weak side.

As manoeuvrability was the very life-blood of fighters of 1917–18, a new version was produced in 1918 as the Type 9 or D.III which featured ailerons on all wings and was powered by a 171.4 kW (230 hp) Hiero engine (a full description appears in the 1920 *Jane's*). The first of 158 built was supplied on 15 March 1918 and the last on 4 November 1918. It was undoubtedly the stability of the Phönix rather than its speed that led to a number of the earlier versions being used

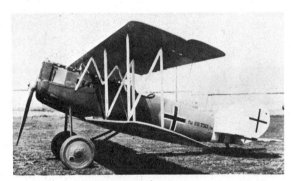

Piaggio

Phönix D.III.

as photographic-reconnaissance aircraft. A number of D.IIIs found their way into Swedish service after the war.

Data (D.III): *Engine* as above *Wing span* 9.8 m (32 ft 5 in) *Length* 6.85 m (22 ft 5¾ in) *Max T-O weight* 805 kg (1,775 lb) *Max level speed* 180 km/h (112 mph) *Endurance* 2 h

Piaggio P-6ter (Italy) Twin-float two-seat reconnaissance biplane of the early 1930s, powered by a 313 kW (420 hp) Fiat A-20 engine and designed for catapulting. Another reconnaissance seaplane designed by Piaggio in the early 1930s was the P-10, a three-seater powered by a Jupiter engine.

Piaggio P-11 and P-12 (Italy) Blackburn Lincock and Segrave respectively, built under licence.

Piaggio P.32.

Piaggio P.108B.

Piaggio P.50.

Piaggio P.108B (Italy) In 1938 the P.50 prototype four-engined bomber appeared which had been designed as the heavy partner to the Piaggio P.32 twin-engined medium bomber (which remained a prototype). From the P.50 was evolved the P.108, the prototype first flying in 1939. The only version to enter operational service was the P.108B, 163 of which were delivered to the Regia Aeronautica from 1942. Each P.108B was armed with eight 12.7 mm Breda-SAFAT machine-guns, four of which were mounted in pairs in two turrets – one in each outer engine nacelle and remotely controlled from two revolving power-operated domes in the roof of the fuselage. These staggered control positions contained the master control and gun-sight for their respective turrets. A bomb load of 3,500 kg (7,716 lb) could be carried or substituted by three 18 in torpedoes. Interestingly one experimental P.108A was fitted with a 102 mm cannon as an anti-shipping aircraft.

P.108Bs were flown in the Mediterranean area – making several attacks on Gibraltar – and on the Eastern Front. It is well recorded that Bruno Mussolini was killed during a raid on Gibraltar, but the 1941 *Jane's* states that he was killed while flying the prototype which was destroyed in an accident.

Data: *Engines* four 1,118 kW (1,500 hp) Piaggio P.XII RC 35 radials *Wing span* 32.0 m (105 ft 0 in) *Length* 22.29 m (73 ft 1½ in) *Max T-O weight* 29,885 kg (65,885 lb) *Max level speed* 420 km/h (261 mph) *Range* 3,520 km (2,187 miles)

Piaggio P.136 (Italy) More than 80 P.136 five-seat light amphibians were built as one of the company's first post-war products, 23 of which were supplied to the Italian Air Force for use as flying-boat trainers and for air-sea rescue duties. Power was provided by two 201 kW (270 hp) Lycoming GO-480-B (P.136-L-1) or 253.4 kW (340 hp) Lycoming GSO-480 geared and supercharged (P.136-L-2) engines.

Piaggio P.148 and P.149 (Italy) In September 1950 Piaggio began development of the P.148 primary trainer and in less than six months the prototype had been certificated. Production examples became standard trainers with the Italian Air Force. Power was provided by the 141.6 kW (190 hp) Lycoming O-435-A engine.

The P.149D was a development of the P.148 and was designed to incorporate many of the same structural components. The prototype first flew in

Piaggio P.136.

radar-equipped search, surveillance and coastal-patrol aircraft (for the South African Air Force as the Albatross); and four P.166-DL2s.

The current version is the ten-seat P.166-DL3 powered by two 438 kW (587 shp) Avco Lycoming LTP 101-600 turboprop engines, first flown on 3 July 1976. Ten production aircraft are being built. Maximum level speed is 417 km/h (259 mph).

Piaggio P.148.

July 1953 and two years later the type was chosen for liaison and basic training duties for the German Air Force. Seventy five were supplied to Germany by Piaggio and the type was also built under licence there. Accommodation was provided for five, reduced to two for aerobatic flying. Today P.149Ds are flown by the air forces of Germany and Uganda.

Data (P.149D): *Engine* one 201 kW (270 hp) Lycoming GO-480 *Wing span* 11.12 m (36 ft 5¾ in) *Length* 8.78 m (28 ft 9½ in) *Max T-O weight* 1,680 kg (3,704 lb) *Max level speed* 309 km/h (192 mph) *Range* 1,095 km (680 miles)

Piaggio P.166 (Italy) Thirty-two examples of the P.166 twin-engined light transport were produced together with 51 P.166M general-purpose military counterparts (for the Italian Air Force); five P.166B Portofinos; two P.166Cs; 20 P.166S

Piaggio PD-808 (Italy) The PD-808 is a six–ten-seat light utility jet aircraft which was intended for both civil and military use. The first prototype flew on 29 August 1964. Four versions were produced for the Italian Air Force as the PD-808 VIP six-seater for government and military VIP transport duties; PD-808 TA nine-seat transport and navigation trainer; PD-808 ECM electronic-countermeasures version; and the PD-808 RM radio-calibration version that is equipped for medium- and high-altitude calibration of navigation aids.

Data (VIP): *Engines* two 14.95 kN (3,360 lb st) Rolls-Royce Viper Mk 526 turbojets *Wing span over tip tanks* 13.2 m (43 ft 3½ in) *Length* 12,85 m (42 ft 2 in) *Max T-O weight* 8,165 kg (18,000 lb) *Max level speed* 852 km/h (529 mph) *Range* 2,128 km (1,322 miles)

Piaggio P.149D.

Piaggio P.166-DL3.

Piasecki PV-3 Rescuer (USA) In March 1956 the Piasecki Helicopter Corporation became known as the Vertol Aircraft Corporation, later still Boeing-Vertol. Prior to this Piasecki produced several important helicopters for civil and military use which, although final production of a number was completed by Vertol, are listed as Piasecki types.

On 11 April 1943 Piasecki flew the PV-2, only the second American-built helicopter to be flown publicly. On 1 February 1944 the company was

Piaggio P.166M.

Piasecki

Piaggio PD-808.

Piasecki PV-2.

Piasecki HRP-2.

Piasecki HRP-1 (PV-3).

Piasecki H-21 Workhorse (USA) The Workhorse was a derivative of the HRP-2 and was eventually supplied to the USAF, US Army, French Navy, Royal Canadian Air Force and the West German Defence Force.

The YH-21 first flew on 11 April 1952, powered by an 857 kW (1,150 hp) Wright R-1820-103 engine. The USAF ordered 38 production H-21A Arctic-rescue helicopters which had demonstrated the ability to operate in temperatures down to minus 65°F/18°C (six for Canada under MAP).

The next version to be ordered was the H-21B powered by a similar engine rated at 1,062 kW (1,425 hp). Designed as a troop (20) and cargo transport capable of performing assault airlift, transport of troops and equipment, and rescue and evacuation (12 stretchers) missions, the additional equipment available included a readily removable armour kit for the protection of certain areas of the aircraft. The USAF received 163 examples. The US Army version of the H-21B was the H-21C Shawnee which had an external hook for an 1,814 kg (4,000 lb) slung load. The Army received 334 by early 1959. Meanwhile in August 1957 an H-21C had set up a closed-circuit distance record for helicopters of 1,929.7 km (1,199.07 miles), for which it had been fitted with three additional fuel tanks. Another H-21C in the same month made a non-stop flight from San Diego to Washington, during which it was refuelled in flight four times by a U-1A Otter tanker aircraft.

awarded a contract by the US Navy for the development and construction of a large tandem-rotor helicopter. The PV-3 prototype 'Flying Banana' (Navy-designated XHRP-1) was flown successfully in March 1945 and an initial service test order for ten transport helicopters was placed in June 1946, followed by a repeat order for ten more. The first HRP-1 was completed on 15 August 1947 and HRP-1s eventually served with the US Navy, Marine Corps and Coast Guard. Power was provided by a 447 kW (600 hp) Pratt & Whitney R-1340-AN-1 Wasp engine and accommodation allowed for two pilots and eight passengers, six stretchers, rescue equipment or freight. Maximum level speed was 167 km/h (104 mph).

A much refined version of the HRP-1 was developed for the Navy as the PV-17 (Navy designation HRP-2). This formed the basis for the H-21 Workhorse/Shawnee.

The final version was the H-21D experimental helicopter, an H-21C fitted under a US Navy/Army contract with two General Electric T58 turboshaft engines and flown in September 1957. Data (H-21B/C): *Engine* as above *Rotor diameter* (each) 13.56 m (44 ft 6 in) *Length overall* 26.31 m (86 ft 4 in) *Max T-O weight* 6,033 kg (13,300 lb) *Max level speed* 211 km/h (131 mph)

Piasecki HUP Retriever and H-25A Army Mule (USA) The single-engined tandem-rotor Retriever was designed to meet the requirements of the US Navy for shipboard operation, including carrier planeguard duty, rescue, observation and inter-ship and ship-to-shore utility transport duties. In July 1954 the 339th and final HUP-type helicopter was delivered to the US Navy. Others served with the US Army, Royal Canadian Navy and French Navy.

The initial production version was the HUP-1 powered by a 391.2 kW (525 hp) Continental R-975-34 engine. Deliveries to the Navy began in 1949. Next came 165 HUP-2s powered by the 410 kW (550 hp) Continental R-975-42 engine – all with autopilot (first tested on the prototype XHJP-1) which allowed elimination of the tail-stabilising surfaces used on the HUP-1. A derivative was the HUP-2S fitted with anti-submarine sonar equipment. It was the first interim ASW helicopter to go into service. The HUP-3 was the Navy's medical-evacuation and light cargo helicopter, basically an Army H-25A. In 1962 the HUP-2 and 3 were redesignated UH-25B and C respectively.

The H-25A was the US Army version of the HUP-2, incorporating hydraulic boost on all controls, strengthened all-metal-clad cabin floor with cargo tie-down fittings and special modifications to facilitate loading and unloading stretcher patients. Seventy were ordered for the Army.

Data (HUP-2): *Engine* as above *Rotor diameter* (each) 10.67 m (35 ft 0 in) *Length overall* 17.35 m (56 ft 11 in) *Max T-O weight* 2,608 kg (5,750 lb) *Max level speed* 169 km/h (105 mph) *Range* 547 km (340 miles)

Piel Super Diamant (France) Three–four-seat version of the Emeraude, plans for which are available to amateur constructors.

Piel Emeraude and Super Emeraude (France) Two-seat light monoplanes, plans for which are available to amateur constructors. There have been several factory-built versions, but these are no longer available.

Piel CP.70/750 Beryl (France) Two-seat aerobatic monoplanes developed from the Emeraude, plans for which are available to amateur constructors.

Piel CP.80 (France) Single-seat racing aircraft, plans for which are available to amateur constructors.

Piel CP.90 Pinocchio (France) Smaller single-seat development of the basic Emeraude, intended for aerobatic and general sport flying. Plans are available to amateur constructors.

Piel CP.1320 (France) Three-seat light monoplane, plans for which are available to amateur constructors.

One of two Piasecki YH-16 Transporter helicopters built for evaluation by the USAF.

Piel CP.301B Emeraude.

Piel CP.500 (France) Five-seat 'push and pull' staggered tandem-wing light aircraft, to be powered by two 112–119.5 kW (150–160 hp) Lycoming O-320 engines.

PIK PIK-3, PIK-5, PIK-7, PIK-13 and PIK-20 (Finland) PIK (the Flying Club of the Helsinki University of Technology) was established in 1931 and has produced several types of sailplanes and powered aircraft over the years. All the types listed in the heading are sailplanes: of particular interest are the PIK-3a and -b which were accepted as standard types for Finnish gliding clubs; and the PIK-13, designed and constructed for the 1954 World Championships. The PIK-20 single-seat 15-metre Contest Class sailplane first flew in 1973 and remains in production today in its current D version, produced by EIRI.

Piasecki VZ-8P Airgeep, an experimental VTOL aircraft and ground vehicle developed for the US Army.

PIK PIK-15

PIK PIK-11, PIK-15 and PIK-19 (Finland) The PIK-11 was the first powered aeroplane to be built by the club and flew in 1953. The PIK-15 Hinu was a two-seat glider-towing aircraft. The similar PIK-19 was intended for series production but did not achieve this.

Pilatus P-2 (Switzerland) The P-2 first flew in 1945 as a trainer for operation from high-altitude airfields, fitted with night-flying, radio and oxygen equipment. The initial 27 aircraft were built for the Swiss Air Force as pilot trainers; the final 26 as weapons and observer trainers. It remains operational today. Power is provided by a 346.5 kW (465 hp) Argus As.410 engine.

Piel CP.80.

Pilatus P-3 (Switzerland) The P-3 first flew in 1953 and remains operational today with the air forces of Brazil and Switzerland as a primary and advanced trainer, including aerobatics, night flying, instrument and blind flying, and weapon training. Power is provided by a 194 kW (260 hp) Lycoming GO-435-C2A engine.

Pilatus P-4 (Switzerland) Designed as a five-seat cabin monoplane to be powered by a 179 kW (240 hp) engine.

Pilatus PC-6 Porter and Turbo-Porter, and AU-23A Peacemaker (Switzerland) The PC-6 Porter is a single-engined multi-purpose utility aircraft with STOL characteristics permitting operation from unprepared strips under harsh environmental and terrain conditions. It can be converted rapidly from a pure freighter to a passenger transport and can be adapted for a great number of different missions including supply-dropping, ambulance, aerial survey and photography, parachuting, crop-spraying, water-bombing and target-towing; as well as operation from soft ground, snow, glacier or water; and long-range operations.

The first PC-6 prototype flew on 4 May 1959. Several production variants have been produced over the years, beginning with the PC-6 Porter basic version powered by a 253 kW (340 hp) Lycoming GSO-480-B1A6 engine. This has been followed by the PC-6/350 Porter with a 261 kW (350 hp) Lycoming IGO-540-A1A engine; PC-6/A Turbo-Porter, a series of turboprop-powered versions with Turboméca Astazou engines of 390–427 kW (523–573 shp); PC-6/B Turbo-Porter, a series with Pratt & Whitney Aircraft of Canada PT6A turboprops of 410 kW (550 shp); PC-6/C Turbo-Porter, a series with AiResearch TPE 331 turboprops of 429 kW (575 shp); and the AU-23A Peacemaker, a

Data: *Engine* as above *Wing span* 10.4 m (34 ft 1½ in) *Length* 9.75 m (32 ft 0 in) *Max T-O weight* 2,700 kg (5,952 lb) *Max cruising speed* 500 km/h (310 mph) *Range* 1,500 km (932 miles) *Armament* can be carried for tactical training

PIK PIK-20E motor glider, based on the PIK-20D sailplane.

Pilatus SB-2 (Switzerland) Four–six-seat cabin monoplane, first flown in 1944 and put into service by a Swiss transport company.

Piper J-3 Cub (USA) Originally the Taylor Aircraft Co, it was reorganised and renamed the Piper Aircraft Corporation in 1937. Sales of the Cub by the old and new companies for 1936 and 1937 represented about one-third of the total aircraft sold in the US. The standard engine was the 30 kW (40 hp) Continental A-40-4, although 37.25 kW (50 hp) Continental A-50-5, Lycoming O-145, Menasco M-50, Franklin AC-150 and Lenape Papoose, and later 48.4 kW (65 hp) Continental, Lycoming and Franklin engines were available. No less than 14,125 were built as two-seat light monoplanes, excluding 5,687 48.4 kW (65 hp) Continental O-170-3-powered L-4 and 97 kW (130 hp) Lycoming O-290-3-powered L-14 (three-seat) Army liaison aircraft and 100 US Navy HE ambulance aircraft.

Piper J-4 Cub Coupé (USA) Two-seat light monoplane powered by a 37.25 kW (50 hp), 48.4 kW (65 hp) or 56 kW (75 hp) engine (including the 56 kW; 75 hp Continental A-75-8). A total of 1,250 was built from 1938.

Pilatus PC-6/B1 Turbo-Porter agricultural aircraft.

Pilatus P-2.

Pilatus P-3.

specialised version of the Turbo-Porter developed by Fairchild (USA) for counter-insurgency duties and powered by a 485 kW (650 shp) AiResearch TPE 331-1-101F turboprop engine. Agricultural versions of the Turbo-Porter have also been developed for liquid spraying and dusting; the necessary equipment for this being easily removable when not required to permit the use of the aircraft for other work.

Data (current PC-6/B2-H2 Turbo-Porter): *Engine* one 410 kW (550 shp) Pratt & Whitney Aircraft of Canada PT6A-27 turboprop *Wing span* 15.13 m (49 ft 8 in) *Length* 10.9 m (35 ft 9 in) *Max T-O weight* 2,770 kg (6,100 lb) *Max cruising speed* 259 km/h (161 mph) *Range* 1,036 km (644 miles) *Accommodation* ten persons, seven persons and freight, or pilot and freight

Pilatus PC-7 Turbo-Trainer (Switzerland) Fully aerobatic two-seat training aircraft fitted with a 410 kW (550 shp) Pratt & Whitney Aircraft of Canada PT6A-25A turboprop engine. Suitable for basic, transition and aerobatic training and, with suitable equipment installed, for IFR and tactical training. Customers by early 1979 included the Swiss Air Force, Bolivia, Burma, Guatemala and Mexico.

Fairchild (Pilatus) AU-23A Peacemaker.

Pilatus PC-7 Turbo-Trainers.

Piper J-3C-65 Cub.

Piper PA-12 Super Cruiser.

Piper J-5 Cruiser (USA) Three-seat light monoplane powered by a 56 kW (75 hp) Continental A-75-8 engine. 1,394 were built from 1940.

Piper J-5C Super Cruiser (USA) Similar to the Cruiser but with a 74.5 kW (100 hp) Lycoming engine. Ten built in 1941.

Piper PA-11 Cub Special (USA) Two-seat light cabin monoplane powered by a 48.4 kW (65 hp) Continental A-65-8 or 67 kW (90 hp) Continental engine. 1,428 were built from 1947.

Piper PA-12 Super Cruiser (USA) Similar to the Cruiser but with a 74.5 kW (100 hp) Lycoming engine. 3,758 were built from 1945.

Piper L-4s operated in the China/Burma theatre during World War II.

Piper J-4 Cub Coupé.

Piper PA-14 Family Cruiser (USA) Four-seat cabin monoplane powered by an 85.7 kW (115 hp) Lycoming O-235-C1 engine. 232 were built from 1948.

Piper PA-15 and PA-17 Vagabond (USA) The PA-15 was a low-priced two-seat cabin monoplane with a 48.4 kW (65 hp) Lycoming engine. The Vagabond was a two-seat training version of the PA-15 with a similarly rated Continental A-65 engine. 585 were built from 1948.

Piper PA-16 Clipper (USA) Four-seat version of the PA-15 powered by an 85.7 kW (115 hp) Lycoming O-235-C1 engine. 726 were built from 1949.

Piper PA-16 Clipper.

Piper PA-18 Super Cub (USA) Two-seat light cabin monoplane powered by a 67 kW (90 hp) or 71 kW (95 hp) Continental C-90 (Super Cub 95), 93 kW (125 hp) O-290-D (Super Cub 125), 100.6 kW (135 hp) Lycoming O-290-D (Super Cub 135) or 112 kW (150 hp) Lycoming O-320 (Super Cub 150) engine. 5,435 PA-18 Super Cubs were built between 1949 and the end of 1978, excluding 716 93 kW (125 hp) Lycoming-engined L-21 and 972 67 kW (90 hp) Continental C-90-8F-engined L-18 Army liaison aircraft and 243 PA-18Ts for flying schools.
Data (latest version with Lycoming O-320 engine): *Wing span* 10.76 m (35 ft 3½ in) *Length* 6.86 m (22 ft 6 in) *Max T-O weight* 794 kg (1,750 lb) *Max cruising speed* 185 km/h (115 mph) *Range* 742 km (461 miles)

Piper PA-18A Super Cub (USA) Version of the Super Cub 135, specially developed for agricultural duties but adaptable for normal use. 2,650 built from 1952.

Piper PA-19 Super Cub (USA) Version of the Super Cub modified for the Army Ground Forces Liaison Aircraft competition. One only.

Piper PA-20 Pacer (USA) Four-seat cabin monoplane fitted with a 93 kW (125 hp) Lycoming O-290-D or 100.6 kW (135 hp) Lycoming O-290-D2 engine. 1,119 were built between 1950 and 1955.

Piper Stinson (USA) General utility or light freighter version of the Voyager. 325 were built between 1948 and 1950.

Piper PA-22 Tri-Pacer (USA) Special version of the PA-20 with a nosewheel landing gear and interconnected rudder and aileron control so that the aircraft could be flown by wheel or rudder pedals alone. 7,668 were built between 1951 and 1963 with Lycoming engines in the 93–112 kW (125–150 hp) range.

Piper PA-22 Colt (USA) Low-cost side-by-side two-seat sporting and training monoplane powered by an 80.5 kW (108 hp) Lycoming O-235-C1B engine. 1,827 were built between 1961 and 1964.

Piper PA-23 Apache 150 (USA) Four-seat cabin monoplane powered by two 112 kW (150 hp) Lycoming O-320 engines. 1,231 were built between 1954 and 1957.

Piper PA-23 Apache 160 (USA) Four–five-seat cabin monoplane powered by two 119 kW (160 hp) Lycoming O-320B engines. 816 were built between 1958 and 1962.

Piper PA-23 Apache 235 (USA) Four–five-seat cabin monoplane powered by two 175 kW (235 hp) Lycoming O-540-B1A5 engines. Introduced swept tail surfaces. 119 built between 1962 and 1966.
Data: *Engines* as above *Wing span* 11.33 m (37 ft 1¾ in) *Length* 8.41 m (27 ft 7 in) *Max T-O weight* 2,177 kg (4,800 lb) *Max level speed* 325 km/h (202 mph) *Range* 1,905 km (1,185 miles)

Piper PA-23 Aztec 250 (USA) Six-seat executive transport powered by two 186.3 kW (250 hp) Lycoming IO-540-C4B5 engines. The Aztec F and Turbo Aztec F are the current versions, the latter powered by two TIO-540-C1A engines fitted with the AiResearch turbocharging system 4,575 had been built by the end of 1978.
Data (Turbo Aztec F): *Engines* as above *Wing span*

11.37 m (37 ft 3½ in) *Length* 9.51 m (31 ft 2½ in) *Max T-O weight* 2,360 kg (5,200 lb) *Max level speed* 407 km/h (253 mph) *Range* 2,120 km (1,317 miles)

Piper PA-24 Comanche 180 (USA) The first version of the four-seat Comanche, with a 134 kW (180 hp) Lycoming O-360-A1A engine. 1,143 were built between 1958 and 1967.

Piper PA-24 Comanche 250 (USA) As for the Comanche 180 but powered by a 186.3 kW (250 hp) Lycoming O-540 engine. 2,537 were built between 1958 and 1965.

Piper PA-24 Comanche 260 (USA) As for the Comanche 180 but powered by a 194 kW (260 hp) Lycoming IO-540 engine. First flown on 24 May 1956. 1,028 built from 1964, including the Turbo Comanche with a turbocharged engine.

Piper PA-24 Comanche 400 (USA) A 298 kW (400 hp) version of the Comanche. 148 were built between 1964 and 1968.

Piper PA-17 Vagabond.

Piper PA-18 Super Cub.

Instrument panel of a Piper Tri-Pacer.

Piper PA-22 Colt.

Piper PA-18A Super Cub.

Piper PA-20 Pacer and PA-22 Tri-Pacer.

Piper

Piper PA-23 Apache 160.

Interior of a Piper Apache 235.

Piper PA-23 Aztec 250.

Piper PA-25 Pawnee 235 (USA) More powerful version of the Pawnee 150 with a 175 kW (235 hp) derated Lycoming O-540-B2B5 engine. 3,650 built since 1962.

Data (Pawnee D): *Engine* as above *Wing span* 11.02 m (36 ft 2 in) *Length* 7.53 m (24 ft 8½ in) *Max T-O weight* 1,315 kg (2,900 lb) *Max level speed* 177–200 km/h (110–124 mph)

Piper PA-25 Pawnee 260 (USA) Version of the Pawnee with a 194 kW (260 hp) Lycoming O-540-E engine. 634 built since 1967.

Piper PA-28 Cherokee 140 (USA) Original version of the Cherokee two-seat sporting and training monoplane powered by a 104.4 kW (140 hp) Lycoming engine. Superseded in 1965 by the Cherokee 140-4, powered by a 112 kW (150 hp) Lycoming O-320 engine and convertible into a full four-seater. The 140-4 was itself superseded by the Cherokee 140B. Some 10,086 Cherokee 140-series aircraft have been built.

Data (Cherokee 140-4): *Engine* as above *Wing span* 9.14 m (30 ft 0 in) *Length* 7.1 m (23 ft 3½ in) *Max T-O weight* 975 kg (2,150 lb) *Max level speed* 229 km/h (142 mph) *Range* 1,350 km (839 miles)

Piper PA-28 Cherokee 150 (USA) Original four-seat Cherokee powered by a 112 kW (150 hp) Lycoming O-320-A2A engine. 300 were built between 1961 and 1967.

Piper PA-24 Comanche 260.

Piper Turbo Aztec F.

Piper PA-25 Pawnee 150 (USA) Initial production version of the Pawnee single-seat agricultural monoplane powered by a 112 kW (150 hp) Lycoming O-320 engine. 731 were built between 1959 and 1963.

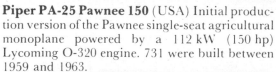

Piper PA-28 Cherokee 160 (USA) Four-seat cabin monoplane powered by a 119 kW (160 hp) Lycoming O-320-D2A engine. 810 built from 1961.

Piper PA-28 Cherokee 180/181 (USA) Four-seat cabin monoplane with a 134 kW (180 hp) Lycoming O-360-A3A engine. 8,201 built from 1962.
Data: *Engine* as above *Wing span* 9.14 m (30 ft 0 in) *Length* 7.16 m (23 ft 6 in) *Max T-O weight* 1,089 kg (2,400 lb) *Max level speed* 245 km/h (152 mph) *Range* 1,360 km (845 miles)

Piper PA-28 Cherokee 235 (USA) Four-seat cabin monoplane, first flown on 9 May 1962. Power is provided by a 175 kW (235 hp) Lycoming O-540-B4B5 engine. The Cherokee 235 retains the basic layout of the Cherokee 180 (see **Pathfinder**).

Piper PA-28 Cherokee Arrow (USA) Announced in June 1967, the PA-28-180R Cherokee Arrow is generally similar to the OA-28-180 Cherokee D but has a retractable landing gear. It has been made available with a 134 kW (180 hp) Lycoming IO-360-B1E engine as the Arrow I (1,161 built); 149 kW (200 hp) IO-360-C1C engine as the larger PA-28-200R Arrow II (2,850 built); and a 149 kW (200 hp) IO-360-C1C engine and the increased wing span of the Archer II as the PA-28R-201 Arrow III (491 built).

Piper PA-28R-201T Cherokee Turbo Arrow III (USA) As for the Cherokee Arrow III but with a 149 kW (200 hp) Continental TSIO-360-F turbocharged engine. 793 built from 1976 until the end of 1978.

Piper PA-28RT-201 Arrow IV (USA) Introduced for 1979, this aircraft derives from the Cherokee Arrow II which was generally similar to the Cherokee Archer II. Powered by a 149 kW (200 hp) Lycoming IO-360-C1C6 engine. The Turbo Arrow IV has a similarly rated Continental TSIO-360-F turbocharged engine.
Data (Arrow IV): *Engine* as above *Wing span* 10.67 m (35 ft 0 in) *Length* 7.62 m (25 ft 0 in) *Max T-O weight* 1,247 kg (2,750 lb) *Max level speed* 282 km/h (175 mph) *Range* 1,334 km (829 miles)

Piper PA-28-151 Cherokee Warrior (USA) New four-seat version of the Cherokee series introduced in 1974 and powered by a 112 kW (150 hp) Lycoming O-320-E2D engine. 1,899 have been built.

Piper PA-28-161 Warrior II (USA) The 1977 version of the Cherokee Warrior, first flown on 27 August 1976. Power is provided by a 119 kW (160 hp) Lycoming O-320-D3G engine. 1,223 had been built by the end of 1978.
Data: *Engine* as above *Wing span* 10.67 m (35 ft 0 in) *Length* 7.25 m (23 ft 9½ in) *Max T-O weight* 1,054 kg (2,325 lb) *Max level speed* 233 km/h (145 mph) *Range* 1,176 km (731 miles)

Piper PA-25 Pawnee D.

Piper PA-28 Cherokee Arrow.

Piper PA-28RT-201 Arrow IV.

Piper PA-28 Cherokee 140.

Piper PA-28 Cherokee 180.

Piper PA-28 Cherokee 235.

Piper

Piper PA-28-151 Cherokee Warrior.

Piper PA-28-235 Cherokee Pathfinder.

Piper PA-28-181 Archer II.

Piper PA-28-201T Turbo Dakota.

Piper PA-30 original version of the Twin Comanche.

Piper PA-28-235 Cherokee Pathfinder (USA) Four-seat cabin monoplane basically similar to the Cherokee 235. Power is provided by a 175 kW (235 hp) Lycoming O-540-B4B5 engine. 2,094 were built by Piper (including Cherokee 235s), but production has been transferred to EMBRAER in Brazil.

Piper PA-28-181 Archer II (USA) In 1972 Piper introduced the Cherokee Challenger as a successor to the Cherokee 180. In 1974 this was superseded by the Cherokee Archer with the same basic airframe and power plant but introducing many new equipment and avionics options. In 1976 this aircraft was redesignated PA-28-181 Cherokee Archer II and in 1978 had the tapered wings of the Warrior II fitted. Power is provided by a 134 kW (180 hp) Lycoming O-360-A4M engine.

Piper PA-28-236 Dakota and PA-28-201T Turbo Dakota (USA) The Dakota was introduced in 1978 with a 175 kW (235 hp) Lycoming O-540-J3A5D engine. The Turbo Dakota was introduced in 1979 as a low-cost four-seat turbocharged aircraft with the fixed landing gear of the standard Dakota. Power is provided by a 149 kW (200 hp) Continental TSIO-360-FB turbocharged engine. 65 Dakotas had been built by the end of 1978.

Piper PA-30 Twin Comanche (USA) The original four-seat Twin Comanche was first flown on 7 November 1962 as a replacement for the Apache H. In 1968 the Twin Comanche C was announced with a number of improvements. It was the final version built. By 1971 a total of 1,998 Twin Comanches had been produced. The PA-30C Turbo Twin Comanche had two 119 kW (160 hp) IO-320-CIA engines fitted.
Data: *Engines* two 119 kW (160 hp) Lycoming IO-320-Bs *Wing span* 10.97 m (36 ft 0 in) *Length* 7.67 m (25 ft 2 in) *Max T-O weight* 1,690 kg (3,725 lb) *Max level speed* 330 km/h (205 mph) *Range* 1,930 km (1,200 miles) *Accommodation* four seats, with option for two more

Piper PA-31 Navajo (USA) Six–eight-seat corporate and commuter airline transport, first flown in September 1964. Powered by two 231 kW (310 hp) Lycoming TIO-540-A2C engines. 1,180 had been built by the end of 1978.
Data: *Engines* as above *Wing span* 12.4 m (40 ft 8 in) *Length* 9.94 m (32 ft 7½ in) *Max T-O weight* 2,948 kg (6,500 lb) *Cruising speed* 399 km/h (248 mph) *Range* 1,973 km (1,226 miles)

Piper PA-31-325 Navajo C/R (USA) Identical to the Navajo but with contra-rotating engines

and nacelle compartments. Power is provided by one 242.5 kW (325 hp) Lycoming LTIO-540-F2BD and one TIO-540-F2BD. 251 had been built by the end of 1978.

Piper PA-31P Pressurised Navajo (USA) Announced in 1970 as a pressurised version of the Navajo. 248 had been built by the end of 1978.

Piper PA-31-350 Chieftain (USA) Announced in September 1972, the Chieftain is a lengthened version of the Navajo powered by 261 kW (350 hp) Lycoming TIO-540-J2BD and LTIO-540-J2BD engines. 1,051 had been built by the end of 1978.
Data: *Engines* as above *Wing span* 12.4 m (40 ft 8 in) *Length* 10.55 m (34 ft 7½ in) *Max T-O weight* 3,175 kg (7,000 lb) *Cruising speed* 409 km/h (254 mph) *Range* 1,761 km (1,094 miles)

Piper PA-31T-1 Cheyenne I (USA) Introduced in 1978, the Cheyenne is a low-cost version of the established Cheyenne PA-31T which has now been redesignated Cheyenne II. Power is provided by two 372.6 kW (500 shp) Pratt & Whitney Aircraft of Canada PT6A-11 turboprop engines. 16 had been built by the end of 1978.

Piper PA-31T Cheyenne II (USA) The PA-31T prototype flew for the first time on 20 August 1969. Following the introduction of the low-cost Cheyenne I and the 6–11-seat Cheyenne III, the original version was redesignated Cheyenne II. Accommodation is for six–eight persons. Power is provided by two 462 kW (620 ehp) Pratt & Whit-

ney Aircraft of Canada PT6A-28 turbo-props. 284 had been built by the end of 1978.
Data: *Engines* as above *Wing span* 13.01 m (42 ft 8¼ in) *Length* 10.57 m (34 ft 8 in) *Max T-O weight* 4,082 kg (9,000 lb) *Cruising speed* 524 km/h (326 mph) *Range* 2,020 km (1,255 miles)

Piper PA-32 Cherokee SIX (USA) The prototype PA-32 Cherokee SIX flew for the first time on 6 December 1963 as a six-seater with an option for a seventh. The 1969 SIX B introduced increased cabin space. Two versions were available in 1978: the Cherokee SIX 260 with a 194 kW (260 hp) Lycoming O-540-E engine and the SIX 300 with a 224 kW (300 hp) Lycoming IO-540-K1G5D engine. Only the SIX 300 continued in production in 1980. 1,493 SIX 260s and 2,108 SIX 300s had been built by the end of 1978.
Data (SIX 300): *Engine* as above *Wing span* 9.99 m (32 ft 9½ in) *Length* 8.45 m (27 ft 8¾ in) *Max T-O weight* 1,542 kg (3,400 lb) *Max level speed* 289 km/h (179 mph) *Range* 1,548 km (962 miles)

Piper PA-32R-300 Lance (USA) First flown on 30 August 1974 as the Cherokee Lance, this six–seven-seater is powered by a 224 kW (300 hp) Lycoming IO-540-K1G5 engine. 1,137 had been built by the end of 1978.

Piper PA-32RT-300 Lance II (USA) The 1978 version of the Lance with a T-tail. Power is provided by an IO-540-K1G5D engine. 328 had been built by the end of 1978.
Data: *Engine* as above *Wing span* 9.99 m (32 ft 9½ in) *Length* 8.62 m (28 ft 3½ in) *Max T-O weight* 1,633 kg (3,600 lb) *Max level speed* 307 km/h (191 mph) *Range* 1,613 km (1,002 miles)

Piper PA-32RT-300T Turbo Lance II (USA) Identical to the Lance II except for the installation of a 224 kW (300 hp) Lycoming TIO-540-S1AD turbocharged engine, giving a maximum speed of 351 km/h (218 mph). 305 had been built by the end of 1978.

Piper PA-34 Seneca II (USA) In 1971 Piper announced a new six–seven-seat twin-engined light aircraft as the Seneca. The 1975 version was redesignated Seneca II. Power is provided by two 149 kW (200 hp) Continental TSIO-360-E turbocharged contra-rotating engines. 2,606 had been built by the end of 1978.
Data: *Engines* as above *Wing span* 11.85 m (38 ft 10¾ in) *Length* 8.69 m (28 ft 6 in) *Max T-O weight* 2,073 kg (4,570 lb) *Max level speed* 361 km/h (225 mph) *Range* 1,129 km (701 miles)

Piper PA-31-325 Navajo C/R.

Piper PA-31P Pressurised Navajo.

Piper PA-32 Cherokee SIX 300.

Piper PA-31-350 Chieftain.

Piper PA-34 Seneca.

Piper PA-42 Cheyenne III (USA) A 6–11-seat corporate and commuter airline transport, produced as the latest version of the Cheyenne family. The first production aircraft flew in May 1979 powered by two 507 kW (680 shp) Pratt & Whitney Aircraft of Canada PT6A-41 turboprops.

Piper PA-42 Cheyenne III.

Chincul-built Piper PA-36 Pawnee Brave.

Piper PA-36 Pawnee Brave 285 (USA) More powerful and larger version of the single-seat Pawnee agricultural aircraft with increased capacity for liquid or dry chemicals. Power is provided by a 212.5 kW (285 hp) Teledyne Continental Tiara 6-285-C engine. 372 have been built.

Piper PA-36 Brave 300 and 375 (USA) Current versions of the Pawnee Brave powered by a 224 kW (300 hp) Lycoming IO-540-K1G5 and 279.5 kW (375 hp) Lycoming IO-720-D1CD engines respectively. By the end of 1978 244 Brave 300s and 70 Brave 375s had been built.

Piper PA-44-180 Seminole (USA) Lightweight four-seat cabin monoplane introduced in 1978. Power is provided by two 134 kW (180 hp) Lycoming O-360-E1AD/LO-360-E1AD contra-rotating engines. 183 had been built by the end of 1978.
Data: *Engines* as above *Wing span* 11.75 m (38 ft 6⅝ in) *Length* 8.41 m (27 ft 7¼ in) *Max T-O weight* 1,723 kg (3,800 lb) *Max level speed* 311 km/h (193 mph) *Range* 1,631 km (1,013 miles)

Piper Aerostar 600/601/601P (USA) Design of this aircraft was started by the Ted Smith Aircraft Co in November 1964 and the first 600/601 prototype flew in October 1967. The current models are the 600A with two 216 kW (290 hp) Lycoming IO-540-K1J5 engines; the 601B with 216 kW (290 hp) IO-540-S1A5 turbocharged engines and increased wing span; and the 601P with higher flow-rate turbochargers. By the end of 1978 190 Model 600s, 135 Model 601s and 259 Model 601Ps had been built.
Data (601P): *Engines* as above *Wing span* 11.18 m (36 ft 8 in) *Length* 10.61 m (34 ft 9¾ in) *Max T-O weight* 2,721 kg (6,000 lb) *Cruising speed* 476 km/h (296 mph) *Range* 2,305 km (1,432 miles) *Accommodation* six seats

Pitcairn PAA-1 Autogiro (USA) Two-seat open-cockpit autogiro of 1931 intended for private use and training. Powered by a 93 kW (125 hp) Kinner B-5 engine.

Piper PA-38-112 Tomahawk.

Piper PA-38-112 Tomahawk (USA) Side-by-side two-seat trainer/utility aircraft introduced in 1978. Power is provided by an 83.5 kW (112 hp) Lycoming O-235-L2C engine. 1,109 had been built by the end of 1978.
Data: *Engine* as above *Wing span* 10.36 m (34 ft 0 in) *Length* 7.04 m (23 ft 1¼ in) *Max T-O weight* 757 kg (1,670 lb) *Max level speed* 202 km/h (126 mph) *Range* 867 km (539 miles)

Piper PA-39 Twin Comanche (USA) In 1970 Piper introduced two new versions of the Twin Comanche as the PA-39TC and the Turbo TC C/R with two 119 kW (160 hp) Lycoming IO-320-B1A and IO-320-C1A engines respectively. 145 had been built by 1974.

Piper PA-44-180 Seminole.

Piper PA-60-290 Aerostar 600A.

Pitts S-2S Special.

Pitcairn Mailwing, Super Mailwing and Sport Mailwing (USA) The Mailwing and Super Mailwing were single-seat mailplanes produced in several versions during the latter 1920s and early 1930s for operation over the US air mail routes. Power was provided by a 164 kW (220 hp) Wright Whirlwind engine. The Sport Mailwing was a passenger or sporting version of the series.

Pitcairn PA-18 Autogiro (USA) Two-seat open-cockpit autogiro intended for private use and training. Power was provided by a 119 kW (160 hp) Kinner R-5 engine.

Pitcairn PA-19 Autogiro (USA) Four-seat cabin autogiro powered by a 313 kW (420 hp) Wright R-975E-2 Whirlwind radial engine.

Pitcairn PA-34 Autogiro (USA) Two-seat observation direct-control autogiro powered by a 313 kW (420 hp) Wright R-975E-2 Whirlwind radial engine.

Pitcairn PCA-2 Autogiro (USA) Three-seat open-cockpit autogiro powered by a Wright R-975 Whirlwind radial engine.

Pitts S-1 Special (USA) Single-seat sporting and aerobatic biplane originally designed by Mr Curtis Pitts in 1943–44 and first flown in September 1944. Currently available as the S-1A for amateur construction (plans available); S-1E with wings of symmetrical aerofoil section, for amateur construction; and S-1S factory-built production aircraft, also available in kit form. Pitts have been used with success in national and international aerobatic competitions.

Pitts S-2A Special (USA) Two-seat version powered by a 149 kW (200 hp) Lycoming IO-360-A1A engine. Flown by the Rothman Tobacco Company and the Carling Black Label aerobatic teams.

Polikarpov I-15 in Finnish markings.

Pitts Model S-2S (USA) Single-seat version of the S-2A with a modified forward fuselage to permit the installation of a 194 kW (260 hp) Lycoming AEIO-540-D4A5 engine. Production began in 1978.

Polikarpov I-1 (USSR) First flown in August 1923, the I-1 was a single-seat cantilever low-wing monoplane fighter powered by a 298 kW (400 hp) M-5 engine and armed with two forward-firing 7.62 mm machine-guns. It became the first fighter of Soviet design to go into service.

Polikarpov I-3 (USSR) Trouble with the I-1 monoplane led Polikarpov to design a new fighter as a biplane, and in 1927 the I-3 appeared. Powered by a 447 kW (600 hp) M-17 engine, it entered production and service, later being supplemented but not replaced on production lines by the superior I-5. Several hundred I-3s were built.

Data: *Engine* as above *Wing span* 11.1 m (36 ft 5 in) *Length* 8.1 m (26 ft 6 in) *Max level speed* 300 km/h (186.5 mph) *Armament* two forward-firing 7.62 mm machine-guns

Pitts S-2A Special.

Polikarpov

**Polikarpov I-153 with
underwing booster
rockets.**

Polikarpov I-5 (USSR) The first prototype of
this diminutive single-seat unequal-span biplane
flew on 29 April 1930. Power was provided by an
imported Gnome-Rhône Jupiter VII radial
engine with individual helmet-type fairings over
each cylinder head. The second prototype was
named *Klim Voroshilov* after the Soviet Defence
Minister. It had a Jupiter VI radial and was
intended for low-level operations. The third and
final prototype had a Soviet M-15 radial engine
with a ring cowling. In the summer of 1930 seven
evaluation aircraft were built, powered by the
358 kW (480 hp) M-22 radial – in fact a Russian
version of the Jupiter VI. Tests were successful
and series production was undertaken. A total of
803 was built and the type formed the main
equipment of Soviet fighter units until 1936.

Standard armament of the I-5 was two synchronised 7.62 mm PV-1 machine-guns and up to
40 kg (88 lb) of bombs could be carried on
underwing racks. The circular-section fuselage
had a metal tubular framework with metal sheet
covering forward and fabric aft. The wooden
wings were fabric covered. The axle-type undercarriage could be fitted with wheel spats.

A number of I-5s were still in use at the time of
the German invasion of the Soviet Union in June
1941, when a few were pressed into service by
Black Sea naval airmen for ground attack. Interestingly, I-5s had previously been used in Soviet
Zveno 'parasite' experiments, being launched in
the air from the TB-3 mother ship.
Data (M-22 engine): *Engine* as above *Wing span*
10.2 m (33 ft 5½ in) *Length* 6.78 m (22 ft 3 in)
Max T-O weight 1,355 kg (2,987 lb) *Max level speed*
278 km/h (173 mph) *Range* 725 km (450 miles)

Polikarpov I-15 *bis*.

Polikarpov I-15 fighter series (USSR)
Designed by Nikolai Polikarpov in 1933, the
TsKB-3 was a compact unequal-span single-seat
fighter biplane with its upper wing gulled into the
top of the fuselage, immediately in front of the
open pilot's cockpit. The prototype was flown in
October 1933 powered by a 469.5 kW (630 hp)
Wright Cyclone engine. Plans were made to
power production machines by the Soviet
521.6 kW (700 hp) M-25 radial, but before it
became available 59 I-15s were completed with
imported Cyclones and 392 with the lower-
powered M-22 radial. Two hundred and twenty-
three M-25-powered machines followed. The I-15
fuselage was of steel-tube construction, fabric-
covered. The wings were braced either side by
single profiled I-form struts. The fixed landing

gear had single cantilever-strut main units and
was provided with wheel spats.

The Soviet government sent large numbers of
I-15s to the Republican government of Spain for
use in the 1936 Civil War. Licence production was
also undertaken in Spain and at least 100
machines were delivered before the war ended
early in 1939. A few I-15s remained in Nationalist
service during World War II. Armament comprised four 7.62 mm machine-guns and four 25 kg
bombs could also be carried. In combat the I-15
proved superior to the Heinkel He 51 and a
redoubtable antagonist to the Fiat CR.32. It was
named 'Chato' by the Republicans.

Main complaint against the I-15 was poor pilot
visibility. The I-15*bis* (or I-152) was therefore
evolved with a conventional strut-braced upper
wing centre-section. Power was provided by a
559 kW (750 hp) M-25V radial with a long-chord
cowling. Increased weight led to a slight drop in
maximum speed of 3 km/h (2 mph), down to
364 km/h (226 mph). Most of the 2,408 I-15*bis*
built had the PV-1s replaced by more rapid-firing
ShKAS machine-guns, and there was provision
for six RS-82 rockets and a 150 kg (331 lb) bomb
load. The few I-15*bis* fighters sent to Spain arrived
too late to enter combat. The type was used
against the Japanese at Khalkin Gol and
Nomonhan in 1939 and was also supplied to the
Chinese Nationalists. In the Soviet Union it
served during the first two years' fighting against
the invading Germans, having been relegated
largely to ground-attack duties.

Under the mistaken impression that future
wars would still require biplane fighters, the
Soviet Command initiated design of the I-153 (or
I-15*ter*) in October 1937. It went into production
in the autumn of 1938. Reverting to the upper
gull-wing of the I-15, the new fighter had a much
stronger structure and was fitted with a fully
retractable undercarriage. Known as the Chaika
(Gull), the I-153 remained in production until the
end of 1940: 3,457 being completed. The original
M-25V engine was replaced by the more powerful
745.2 kW (1,000 hp) M-62 radial and armament
was four 7.62 mm ShKAS machine-guns plus six
RS-82 rockets and up to 100 kg (220 lb) of bombs.
The first I-153s delivered fought against the
Japanese on the Manchukuo border in 1939. The
type also saw large-scale service in the early years
of World War II against Germany (latterly with
ground-attack regiments), having been used also
against Finland during the 'Winter War'.
Data (I-153): *Engine* as above *Wing span* 10.0 m
(32 ft 9¾ in) *Length* 6.18 m (20 ft 3 in) *Max T-O
weight* 2,110 kg (4,652 lb) *Max level speed* 444 km/h
(276 mph)

North American B-25 Mitchell.

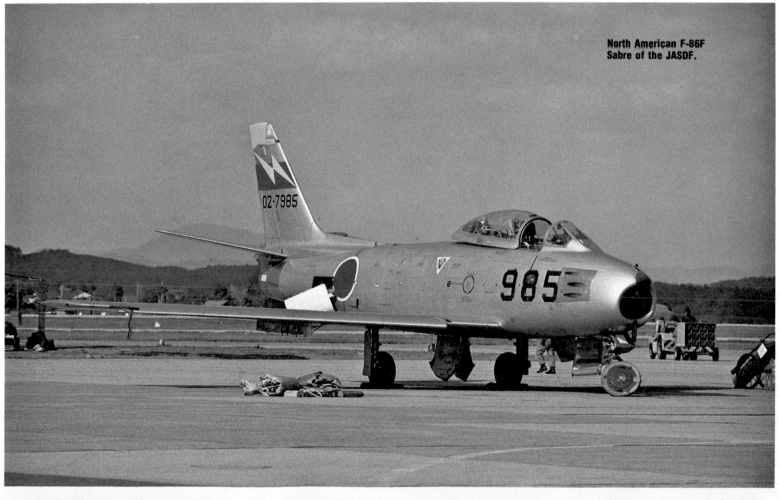

North American F-86F Sabre of the JASDF.

North American P-51D Mustangs (three in foreground) of the British-based 8th Air Force.

North American X-15.

North American RA-5C
Vigilante.

Northrop F-5E Tiger IIs.

Panavia Tornado IDS
(interdictor-strike)
version.

Percival Prentice T.1.

**Pilatus PC-6/B2-H2
Turbo-Porter.**

Pilatus PC-7
Turbo-Trainers.

Polikarpov I-16s.

Polikarpov I-16 (USSR) The Polikarpov TsKB-12 single-seat fighter prototype flew for the first time on 31 December 1933. A small series of 30 Type 1 machines powered by the same Soviet-built M-22 radial engine of 358 kW (480 hp) followed, five of them taking part in the 1935 May Day fly-past over Red Square, Moscow. They were the first cantilever low-wing single-seat fighters with retractable landing gears to go into service anywhere in the world.

The I-16 was characterised by its stubby, sharply tapering fuselage of monocoque construction, skinned with plywood. The curved, tapering wing trailing edge and horizontal tailplane leading edge were both profiled into the fuselage so that they almost met. The wing itself had metal sheet covering the leading edge and centre-section, while remaining surfaces were fabric covered. The wide-track inward-retracting main landing gear legs were manually operated.

The second prototype was designated TsKB-12*bis* and powered by an imported Wright Cyclone radial engine. A small series was built as the Type 4. However, large-scale production of the fighter began with the 521.6 kW (700 hp) M-25-powered Type 5 in 1935. Armament comprised two 7.62 mm machine-guns and an enclosed cockpit was fitted for the first time. Maximum speed was 454 km/h (282 mph).

The rather tricky flight characteristics of the I-16 led to the development of the two-seat UTI-4 advanced trainer which was built in parallel with the fighter. The four-gun M-25A-powered I-16 Type 6 was followed by the Type 10, built in greater quantity than any other version. It had an open cockpit with a fixed windscreen and four 7.62 mm ShKAS machine-guns – two wing-mounted and two synchronised in the upper fuselage decking. Power was provided by the M-25V engine delivering 559 kW (750 hp). In 1938 two further versions were built: the twin 20 mm cannon-armed I-16P; and the I-16 Type 17 which had its armament increased by a ventrally mounted 12.7 mm UBS machine-gun and introduced a tailwheel in place of the previously standard tailskid. From the period of the Nomonhan fighting against the Japanese, I-16s were fitted with launchers for six RS-82 rockets.

The final production versions of the I-16 were the Type 18 with the 686 kW (920 hp) M-62 engine, and the Type 24 with either the M-62 or an M-63 delivering 820 kW (1,100 hp). The Type 24 had a redesigned wing and provision for external fuel tanks. Production was phased out during 1940, but the I-16 was returned to production briefly during the hectic days of 1941. The eventual production total was 7,005, excluding 1,639 UTI-4 trainers.

Meanwhile in the autumn of 1936 Polikarpov I-16 Type 5 fighters had been delivered to the Spanish government at the beginning of the Civil War. These were followed by the Type 6 and the Type 10 fighters – the latter being known as the 'Super Rata' to the opposing Nationalists. All I-16s were dubbed 'Mosca' (fly) by the Republicans. The total number delivered was 278, supplemented by a small number completed in Span-ish factories. After the Nationalist victory a further 30 Type 10 aircraft were built in Spain. I-16s were also supplied to the Chinese Nationalists from 1937 and fought with Russian air regiments against the Japanese at Nomonhan in 1939, as previously noted. They were also widely employed during the 'Winter War' against Finland. When the Germans launched Operation Barbarossa against the Soviet Union in June 1941, the I-16 was still the most numerous Soviet fighter aircraft. While often outclassed, the I-16 was able to give a good account of itself in the hands of skilled pilots. The type became famous in 1941 for the so-called 'taran attack', when Soviet fighter pilots deliberately rammed German fighters and bombers, frequently destroying the enemy and their own aircraft in the process.

Data (I-16 Type 24): *Engine* as above *Wing span* 9.0 m (29 ft 6 in) *Length* 6.1 m (20 ft 1 in) *Max T-O weight* 1,912 kg (4,215 lb) *Max level speed* 500 km/h (311 mph) *Range* 400 km (249 miles)

Polikarpov I-17 (USSR) The TsKB-15 single-seat fighter prototype was a diminutive low-wing monoplane of slim configuration, powered by an imported 626 kW (840 hp) Hispano-Suiza 12Y in-line engine. With an inward-retracting undercarriage, it flew in September 1934 and was followed by the TsKB-19 with the M-100 (Soviet version of the Hispano engine). Armament comprised a 20 mm cannon and four 7.62 mm machine-guns. Production of a small number as the I-17-2 was reported, but it is not known if the type was used by first-line units. A third prototype (the TsKB-33) had reduced armament in an attempt to cut down weight and increase performance. The projected use of this version as a parasite fighter to be launched from a multi-engined 'mother ship' was subsequently abandoned.

Polikarpov R-5 (USSR) An unequal-span two-seat biplane constructed largely of wood with fabric covering, the R-5 reconnaissance light

Polikarpov R-5.

bomber flew in prototype form in 1928. Pilot and observer/gunner were seated close together in tandem open cockpits – the pilot beneath a cut-out in the upper wing trailing edge. The BMW VIb in-line engine of the prototype was replaced by the 507 kW (680 hp) Soviet-built M-17B in production aircraft. The R-5 could operate on skis or twin-floats (the latter designated R-5a or MR-5), as well as on the more normal axle-type fixed undercarriage. Standard armament was a fixed 7.62 mm PV-1 machine-gun and a DA-1 weapon of the same calibre operated by the observer. Up to 250 kg (551 lb) of bombs could be carried on underwing racks.

Many variants of the R-5 were used in the Soviet Union. These included the single-seat R-5T torpedo bomber; the heavily armed R-5Sh ground-attack aircraft; and the SSS of 1934 with 533 kW (715 hp) M-17F engine, spatted landing gear and new ShKAS machine-guns. Civil versions were the P-5 and P-5a, the latter with cabin accommodation for four passengers, and an enclosed pilot's cockpit.

Some 7,000 of all versions of the R-5 were built. Military operations included the Spanish Civil War (31 R-5s serving with the Republicans), the campaigns in 1938–39 against the Japanese in the Far East, the 'Winter War' against Finland, and the fighting against Germany from 1941. At the time of the German invasion most R-5s had been relegated to training and liaison duties, but several hundred returned to first-line duties to equip light night-bombing 'nuisance raid' units alongside the ubiquitous Polikarpov U-2.

Data: *Engine* as above *Wing span* 15.5 m (50 ft 10¼ in) *Length* 10.56 m (34 ft 10¼ in) *Max T-O weight* 3,247 kg (7,158 lb) *Max level speed* 228 km/h (141.5 mph) *Range* 1,100 km (684 miles)

Captured Polikarpov Po-2.

Polikarpov R-Z.

Polikarpov R-Z (USSR) The robust and reliable R-Z was a single-bay unequal-span light bomber biplane developed from the R-5. Production totalled some 1,000 machines, built from 1936 to 1938. It differed externally from the R-5 in having a fin and rudder assembly of new design; the ventral radiator for its 611 kW (820 hp) M-34R in-line engine relocated between the new landing-gear legs; and pilot and observer/gunner protected by a raised transparent canopy. Armament comprised a fixed synchronised 7.62 mm PV-1 machine-gun and a ShKAS weapon of the same calibre on a heavy ring mounting operated by the observer. Maximum bomb load was 400 kg (882 lb).

R-Z biplanes were sent to Spain in February 1937, giving a good account of themselves with the Republican forces. Known as 'Natasha', the type carried out many devastating attacks in formation and at low level on enemy troop concentrations and targets, such as railway junctions. Great use was made on the outward journey of defensive crossfire from the ShKAS machine-guns, but the formations split up after the attack and each pilot made his own way back to base by adopting hedge-hopping tactics. Casualties were remarkably light. The R-Z also took part in Far Eastern operations against the Japanese and in the early stages of the German invasion in 1941, but with negligible effect.

Data: *Engine* as above *Wing span* 15.5 m (50 ft 10¼ in) *Length* 9.7 m (31 ft 10 in) *Max T-O weight* 3,500 kg (7,716 lb) *Max level speed* 290 km/h (180.5 mph) *Range* 1,000 km (621 miles)

Polikarpov Po-2 (U-2) (USSR) By the time the last Po-2 two-seat single-bay light biplane left the production line in 1954, some 40,000 examples of the type had been built over 25 years. This remarkable little aircraft started as a prototype in 1928. Construction was intended to be very simple with interchangeable upper and lower wing sections. Unfortunately the new aircraft did not fly well and shortly afterwards a radically altered machine was evolved. Powered by a 74.5 kW (100 hp) M-11 engine (later boosted to give 108 kW; 145 hp), the U-2 originally went into service on a large scale as a primary trainer for military and civil use; although many other versions were evolved. These included agricultural aircraft for crop spraying; air ambulances; passenger versions with enclosed cabins behind the open pilot's cockpit; and floatplanes.

The Soviet Union's entry into World War II gave a new lease of life to the little Polikarpov biplane. The U-2VS military series was evolved, including the U-2NAK for night artillery observation; the GN with loudspeaker for night propaganda missions; and the famous LNB version which operated in the light night-bomber 'nuisance-raider' role, armed with up to 250 kg (551 lb) of bombs. Many military Po-2s (as they were redesignated after Polikarpov's death in 1944) were armed with a single 7.62 mm ShKAS machine-gun on a ring mounting over the rear cockpit. A favourite Soviet nickname for the Po-2 was 'Kukuruznik' (corn cutter).

The Po-2 remained in widespread use for a variety of civil tasks in the Soviet Union and Eastern Europe for a decade after World War II, surviving to receive the NATO reporting name *Mule*.

Data: *Engine* as above *Wing span* 11.4 m (37 ft 4¾ in) *Length* 8.1 m (26 ft 7 in) *Max T-O weight* 1,016 kg (2,240 lb) *Max level speed* 170 km/h (105.5 mph) *Range* 430 km (267 miles)

Pomilio PC, PD and PE (Italy) Two-seat high-performance armed reconnaissance biplanes operated by the Italian air force from 1917. The first version to go into service was the PC, powered by a 194 kW (260 hp) Fiat A-12 engine and armed with one forward-firing and one rear-mounted Revelli machine-guns. Unfortunately this proved unstable in flight and so production quickly changed to the modified PD which accounted for most of the 545 PC/PDs built in 1917.

The major production version of the series was the PE powered by a 223.6 kW (300 hp) Fiat A-12*bis* engine and which eventually equipped 18 Squadriglie (30 Squadriglie equipped with all versions); production of the PD and PE in 1918 totalling 1,075 aircraft. Armament for the PE was one forward-firing machine-gun and one rear-mounted Lewis gun. The final version was the PY, only seven of which were built in 1918.

The Pomilio brothers used the basic PD/PE layout for a 298 kW (400 hp) Liberty-powered light bomber designed for the US Army as the BVL-12, six of which were built after the Armistice. The brothers also designed the FVL-8 single-seat biplane fighter for the US Army, six of which were built.

Data (PE): *Engine* as above *Wing span* 11.8 m (38 ft 8 in) *Length* 8.94 m (29 ft 4 in) *Max T-O weight* 1,537 kg (3,389 lb) *Max level speed* 194 km/h (120.5 mph) *Endurance* 3 h 30 min

Port Baby (UK) Flying-boat of World War I, powered by three Rolls-Royce Eagle engines. Eleven were operated by the RNAS.

Porterfield monoplane series (USA) The Porterfield company was incorporated in August 1934 and development of a two-seat high-wing monoplane continued until March 1935, when it was placed in production. In the first year of production more than 100 aircraft were sold, supplied with 30 kW (40 hp), 37.25 kW (50 hp), 48.4 kW (65 hp) and 56 kW (75 hp) Continental and 67 kW (90 hp) Warner Scarab engines.

Porterfield Zephyr (USA) Two-seat open-cockpit parasol-wing monoplane powered by a Continental A-40-4 engine.

Potez IX (France) Following on from the Potez VII single-engined transport and the curious Potez VIII two-seat biplane of post-war design

(with engine mounted vertically), the Potez IX of 1921 was produced. It resembled the VII except for having a deeper fuselage with a cabin for four passengers, behind which was the open pilot's cockpit. Power was provided by a 275.7 kW (370 hp) Lorraine-Dietrich 12Da engine. Thirty aircraft flew on routes to London, Warsaw and Budapest, finally being withdrawn in 1928.

Potez XV and XVIII (France) Displayed at the 1921 Paris Salon Aéronautique, the Potez XV was a two-seat reconnaissance biplane which entered production in 1923 (more than 450 built). Power was provided by a 298 kW (400 hp) Lorraine-Dietrich 12Db, with twin Lamblin radiators located between the landing-gear legs. Armament comprised a fixed forward-firing 7.92 mm Vickers machine-gun and single or twin Lewis guns on a Scarff-type mounting. About 300 Potez XVs went to French observation regiments, while others were supplied to Denmark, Romania, Spain and Poland. The latter country operated both reconnaissance (A2) and bomber (B2) versions: 110 aircraft being delivered from France and a further 135 built under licence. Bulgaria purchased 30 examples of a variant designated Potez XVIII.

An experimental variant of the Potez XV, the XV S, was used to test the new wings and landing gear for the Potez 25 and was also flown as a twin-float seaplane.

Data (Potez XV): *Engine* as above *Wing span* 12.68 m (41 ft 7¼ in) *Length* 8.7 m (28 ft 6½ in) *Max T-O weight* 1,950 kg (4,299 lb) *Max level speed* 202 km/h (125.5 mph) *Armament* (bomber version) guns as above, plus two 50 kg bombs carried on a special rack under the fuselage

Potez 25 (France) The prototype Potez 25 general-purpose and reconnaissance biplane was built in 1925 at the new Meaulte factory and was a development of the Potez XV and the experimental Potez 24. Production eventually totalled about

Polikarpov Po-2 air ambulance with underwing panniers.

The unsuccessful but impressive twelve-passenger Potez XXII of 1922, powered by three Gnome-Rhône-built Bristol Jupiter engines.

Potez 25.

4,000 aircraft in 87 variants, the last remaining in service in Indo-China until 1945.

The French Aéronautique Militaire utilised four versions which included the A2 observation aircraft (Lorraine or Salmson engine); ET2 advanced trainer (Salmson); Type 25/5 A2 observation or Cn2 night fighter (Renault); and the famous Potez 25TOE Colonial version (Lorraine), 1,948 of which were delivered to French forces and 322 were exported to 17 countries. The French Navy also flew 12 Potez 25/35s (Lorraine) for target towing. Poland, Portugal and Yugoslavia licence-built nearly 400 Potez 25s between them.

Many notable 'showing the flag' and record flights were made by Potez 25s, the best-remembered being the famous 'Croisière Noire' by 30 veteran Potez 25TOEs between November 1933 and January 1934, led by Vuillemin (late C-in-C Armée de l'Air) and covering 23,000 km (14,300 miles), mostly over French Africa.

A small number of two-seat Potez 25 A2s were also produced for civil use, mainly for Aéropostale.

Data (Potez 25TOE): *Engine* one 335.3 kW (450 hp) Lorraine-Dietrich 12Eb *Wing span* 14.14 m (46 ft 4¾ in) *Length* 9.1 m (29 ft 10½ in) *Max T-O weight* 2,238 kg (4,934 lb) *Max level speed* 208 km/h (129 mph) *Armament* fixed forward-firing Vickers and two rear-mounted Lewis machine-guns, plus up to 200 kg (441 lb) of bombs

Potez 27 (France) Despite its designation, the Potez 27 represented a half-way stage between the Potez XV and Potez 25. It featured the engine, fuselage, landing gear and cabane struts of the former, married to the wings of the latter. The prototype flew in 1924. Twenty were exported to Poland, where the PWS company licence-built a further 155, and thirty went to Romania, where they were used for reconnaissance and light bombing (up to 200 kg; 441 lb of bombs) duties.

Potez 29 (France) The Potez 29 transport aircraft of 1927 resulted from a marriage of the wings, tail unit and landing gear of the Potez 25 with a new fuselage. An enclosed cabin was provided for the two pilots immediately in front of the main cabin for five–six passengers. Civil orders totalled 28, including 15 Potez 29-4s each with a 357.7 kW (480 hp) Gnome-Rhône Jupiter 9 radial engine. Potez 29s flew with the French Aéropostale and CIDNA airlines and with Aeroput of Yugoslavia.

From 1929 came a series of orders for the Potez 29-2 ambulance-liaison version for the French Army. Production eventually totalled 120 aircraft, each powered by a 335.3 kW (450 hp) Lorraine-Dietrich 12Eb engine. These remained in Armée de l'Air service right through the 1930s and during World War II, carrying out casualty-evacuation duties mainly during the fighting in French overseas territories.

Data (Potez 29-2): *Engine* as above *Wing span* 14.5 m (47 ft 7 in) *Length* 10.68 m (35 ft 0½ in) *Max T-O weight* 2,650 kg (5,842 lb) *Max level speed* 219 km/h (136 mph)

Potez 32 (France) The Potez 32 was a strut-braced high-wing monoplane with enclosed accommodation for a crew of two and up to five passengers. Some 50 were built which flew air mail services from 1928 onwards with CIDNA, Air Orient and Aéropostale. Exports included seven to Canada. Power was provided by either a 171.4 kW (230 hp) Salmson 9Ab or a 283 kW (380 hp) Gnome-Rhône Jupiter 9Aa engine.

Potez 33 (France) At least 54 Potez 33s were built, mostly for French service (in Madagascar and elsewhere), although Belgium purchased 12 and others went to Brazil and Portugal. A development of the Potez 32, it was a general-purpose aircraft, with duties including liaison and crew training. Externally it differed from its predecessor in having an open dorsal-gunner's cockpit and a divided landing gear.

Potez 36 (France) A two-seat strut-braced high-wing monoplane of 1929 with folding wings which had slots in the leading edges. Nearly 300 were built in many variants, the most prolific being the Potez 36/13 (71 kW; 95 hp Salmson 7Ac) and Potez 36/14 (71 kW; 95 hp Renault 4 Pb). The type made a powerful bid to capture the potential market for a safe and comfortable pleasure aircraft.

Potez 39 (France) The Potez 39 was an all-metal parasol-wing monoplane with tandem open cockpits. The prototype, built to an official French requirement for an observation aircraft, flew for the first time in January 1930. The Armée de l'Air ordered initially 100 aircraft in May 1932. Total production amounted to 244, including some Potez 391s with 387.5 kW (520 hp) Lorraine-Dietrich 12 engines, 12 of which were purchased by Peru (plus a Potez 391b twin-float seaplane). A number of Potez 39s were still in French service in September 1939, mainly for training duties.

Data (Potez 390): *Engine* one 432 kW (580 hp) Hispano-Suiza 12Hb *Wing span* 16.0 m (52 ft 6 in) *Length* 9.98 m (32 ft 9 in) *Max T-O weight* 2,280 kg (5,017 lb) *Max level speed* 230 km/h (143 mph) *Armament* one forward-firing machine-gun and two rear-mounted Lewis guns, plus up to 120 kg (265 lb) of bombs

Potez 43 (France) Two–three-seat high-wing cabin tourer developed from the Potez 36 and powered by an 89.4 kW (120 hp) Renault 4 Pdi engine. One hundred and sixty-seven examples were built for civil use and 33 as Potez 438s for military liaison duties between 1932 and 1934.

Potez 53 (France) Low-wing racing monoplane powered by a 223.6 kW (300 hp) Potez 9Bb radial engine. Two built, one flown by Georges Detré winning the 1933 Coupe Deutsch by covering

Potez 39.

F-ALRL

2,000 km (1,242.72 miles) at an average speed of 322.8 km/h (200.58 mph).

Potez 54 (France) Built as a private venture by Henry Potez, the prototype flew for the first time on 14 November 1933 as a multi-role military aircraft. It was a high-wing strut-braced monoplane with a retractable landing gear. The pilot's cabin was enclosed. Armament comprised 7.5 mm Darne machine-guns in manually operated nose, dorsal and ventral turrets (the last retractable), plus up to 550 kg (1,212 lb) of bombs carried internally or 900 kg (1,984 lb) externally. Power was provided by two 514 kW (690 hp) Hispano-Suiza 12Xirs/Xjrs (Potez 540) or two 536.5 kW (720 hp) Lorraine Petrel 12 Hdrs/Hers (Potez 542) engines. A total of 259 of both versions was built for the Armée de l'Air, serving mainly with reconnaissance Groupes. However by World War II the Potez 54 had been relegated to training or transport duties.

A prototype Potez 541, powered by a Gnome-Rhône engine, was followed by ten similar Potez 543s for Romania in 1936.

Data (Potez 540): *Engines* as above *Wing span* 22.1 m (72 ft 6 in) *Length* 16.2 m (53 ft 1 in) *Max T-O weight* 5,908 kg (13,025 lb) *Max level speed* 310 km/h (192.5 mph) *Range* 1,250 km (777 miles)

Potez 56 (France) The Potez 56 was an attractive low-wing cabin monoplane with a retractable landing gear and powered by two 138 kW (185 hp) Potez 9Ab radial engines. The prototype flew for the first time on 18 June 1934. This aircraft, plus 20 production Potez 56-1s, were operated as commercial airliners by Sté Potez Aero Service over the French Mediterranean coast from 1935; Régie Air Afrique over North Africa; and by SARTA (later LARES) in Romania. Six aircraft were also acquired by the Chilean airline LAN. Accommodation was provided in each for a pilot and six passengers, plus air mail.

The first military variant was the naval Potez 56E of January 1936, intended for carrier operations. It was followed by three military P.566 T3 general-purpose aircraft, each powered by two 179 kW (240 hp) Potez 9Eo radial engines and featuring a dorsal gun turret and a ventral observation gondola. During 1937–38 the French Navy took delivery of 22 Potez 567s, intended for gunnery target towing. The final version was the Potez 568 pilot trainer for the Armée de l'Air, in which the instructor sat behind the pupil; 26 being built up to August 1940.

Potez 58 (France) Essentially an improved version of the Potez 43 produced as a three-seat tourer and powered by a 97 kW (130 hp) Potez 6B radial engine. A total of 203 was completed between 1934 and 1936, 99 as militarised Potez 585s for liaison or ambulance duties.

Potez 60 (France) Two-seat open-cockpit parasol-wing light tourer and trainer of 1935, powered by a 44.7 kW (60 hp) Potez 3B engine. A total of 155 was built for club use under the auspices of the French government-sponsored Popular Aviation Movement.

Potez 62 (France) Sixteen-passenger strut-braced high-wing monoplane airliner, first flown

Potez 540.

in prototype form on 28 January 1935. Twelve Potez 62-0s and 13 Potez 63-1s were built for Air France, powered by two 648.3 kW (870 hp) Gnome-Rhône 14K and 536.5 kW (720 hp) Hispano-Suiza 12Xrs engines respectively; nine of the 62-0s subsequently being re-engined with 670.7 kW (900 hp) Gnome-Rhône 14Ns and the remaining three brought up to 62-1 standard. These operated the Paris–Marseilles–Rome and to the Far East services, and in 1936 began flying the South American Buenos Aires–Santiago route over the Andes.

Data (Potez 62-0): *Engines* as above *Wing span* 22.45 m (73 ft 7¾ in) *Length* 17.32 m (56 ft 10 in) *Max T-O weight* 7,500 kg (16,535 lb) *Max level speed* 325 km/h (202 mph) *Range* 1,000 km (621 miles)

Potez 56.

Potez 63 (France) The Potez 63 was built originally to a French Air Ministry programme calling for a 'Multiplace légère de Défense', literally a light multi-seat defensive aircraft. In practice the specification called for an aircraft to perform the three roles of fighter control (three-seat C3); daylight interception (two-seat C2); and night-fighter (two-seat Cn2). The first prototype flew on 25 April 1936. It was a pleasant-looking all-metal stressed-skin cantilever monoplane with a retractable landing gear. Ten further prototypes were tested before production orders were placed in 1937 for 80 Potez 630s (two 432 kW; 580 hp Hispano-Suiza 14 radials) and 80 Potez 631s (Gnome-Rhône 14 Mars radials). The Potez 633 B2 was a light bomber version with a partially glazed nose, 40 of which were ordered by Romania and others by Greece. In the event only 21 of the Romanian aircraft were delivered, the rest retained by France. The Potez 637 A3 was a three-seat reconnaissance version with a ventral gondola for the observer, 60 of which were built. The final production version was the Potez 63-11 with an extensively redesigned fully glazed nose and a new short crew canopy. A total of 702 production aircraft was built.

Potez

Potez 63-11.

Potez 630/631s served with day- and night-fighter Groupes and with 'Sections de Commandement' attached to single-seat fighter units from the outbreak of World War II. Armament comprised two forward-firing and one rear-mounted 7.7 mm machine-guns. Potez 637s equipped five reconnaissance Groupes and during the battle for France suffered heavy losses. Potez 63-11s were delivered from November 1939 and served with 40 GAO (observation Groupes) and 13 reconnaissance Groupes by May 1940.
Data (Potez 63-11): *Engines* as above *Wing span* 16.0 m (52 ft 6 in) *Length* 10.93 m (35 ft 10½ in) *Max T-O weight* 4,530 kg (9,987 lb) *Max level speed* 425 km/h (264 mph) *Armament* normally one forward-firing and one rear-mounted 7.5 mm MAC guns, but increased for ground attack by adding ventral packs with two additional forward-firing and two rearward-firing guns
Potez 65 (France) This was a military transport development of the Potez 62. Fifty were built, the first making its maiden flight on 2 June 1937. The fuselage was specially adapted for the carriage of freight with floor trap-door access for items such as aero-engines, which could be winched aboard. As alternatives, the Potez 65 could airlift 14 fully equipped troops or accommodate six stretcher cases and four seated patients as an ambulance. In an emergency a reasonable bomb load could be carried. Five Potez 65s were exported to Romania; the remainder served with the Armée de l'Air, originally with GIA I/601 and I/602 (France's only pre-war paratroop units) but later on general transport duties.

Power was provided by two 536.5 kW (720 hp) Hispano-Suiza 12X liquid-cooled engines.
Potez 841 and 842 (France) Four-engined light transports, the first prototype flying in April 1961. Each was designed to accommodate 24 passen-

gers and differed from each other in having Pratt & Whitney PT6A-20 and Turboméca Astazou XII turboprops respectively.
Potez SEA IV (France) The Société d'Etudes Aéronautiques was formed in 1916 by Henry Potez and Marcel Bloch (famous nowadays as Marcel Dassault). Following the experimental SEA I, the SEA IV appeared. It was a robust two-bay equal-span two-seat reconnaissance bomber powered by a 275.7 kW (370 hp) Lorraine-Dietrich 12Da liquid-cooled engine. Production started in November 1918 but was cancelled in 1919 after 115 had been completed. A number were subsequently issued to French observation units.

Potez 842 prototype.

Potez SEA VII (France) The SEA VII was an adaptation of the military two-seat SEA IV for passenger-carrying. It retained the same 275.7 kW (370 hp) Lorraine-Dietrich 12Da engine and two-bay biplane configuration. The fuselage behind the pilot's cockpit was, however, modified by having a square cabin structure fitted to provide enclosed accommodation for two passengers, who reached it by means of a ladder fixed to the left of the fuselage. Twenty-five SEA VIIs were operated by Cie Franco-Roumaine on routes to Eastern Europe during the early 1920s.

Potez 841.

Pottier P.50 Bouvreuil (France) Single-seat racing monoplane, plans for which are available to amateur constructors.

Pottier P.70S (France) Single-seat sporting monoplane, plans for which are available to amateur constructors.

Pottier P.80S (France) Small single-seat sporting monoplane, plans for which are available to amateur constructors.

Pottier P.100S and P.110S (France) Small high-wing monoplanes accommodating two and three persons respectively.

Pottier P.170S (France) Tandem two-seat version of the P.70S, plans for which are available to amateur constructors.

Pottier P.180S (France) Side-by-side two-seat version of the P.80S, plans for which are available to amateur constructors.

Practavia Sprite (UK) The Sprite is a two-seat all-metal aerobatic aircraft suitable for amateur construction from plans or kits.

Praga BH-39 (Czechoslovakia) Two-seat primary-training biplane produced as the BH-39NZ of 1931 (89.4 kW; 120 hp Walter NZ engine), BH-39G of 1936 (112 kW; 150 hp Walter Gemma) and BH-39AG of 1937 (112 kW; 150 hp Armstrong Siddeley Genet Major).

Praga BH-41 (Czechoslovakia) Two-seat advanced training biplane of 1931 powered by a 223.6 kW (300 hp) Skoda-built Hispano-Suiza 8Fb engine.

Praga E-114 Air Baby (Czechoslovakia) Two-seat cabin monoplane produced in E-114B (1934) and E-114D (1936) versions powered by 31.3 kW (42 hp) Praga B and 46.2 kW (62 hp) Praga D engines respectively.

Praga E-114D.

PS-40 and PS-41 (USSR) Special transport versions of the Tupolev SB-2 and SB-2*bis* twin-engined light bombers respectively, both used by Aeroflot. There was also a PS-41*bis*.

PS-42 (USSR) Believed to have been a 70-passenger version of the TB-7 four-engined heavy bomber of 1936 which was developed into the production Petlyakov Pe-8.

PS-89 (USSR) Twin M-17-engined 12-passenger cantilever low-wing monoplane airliner of 1935, a few of which were produced for Aeroflot.

Procaer F15E Picchio.

PWS 10 (Poland) The prototype of this single-seat braced parasol-wing monoplane fighter flew for the first time in May 1930. It was powered by a 335.3 kW (450 hp) Skoda-built Lorraine 12Eb engine. Wing structure was of wood, with plywood covering up to the rear spar, the whole fabric covered. The fuselage was of welded steel-tube construction, with metal panelling to the rear of the cockpit, the remainder fabric covered. Armament comprised twin forward-firing machine-guns. Only 65 production aircraft were built, serving until replaced by PZL P.7s between 1932 and 1933. Maximum level speed was 258 km/h (160 mph).

PWS 12 and PWS 14 (Poland) The PWS 12 two-seat advanced-training biplane appeared in

Praga E-241 (Czechoslovakia) Two-seat advanced training biplane of 1936 powered by a 268 kW (360 hp) Walter Pollux II engine.

Procaer F15 Picchio (Italy) Four-seat light cabin monoplane, the latest production version of which is the F15E powered by a 224 kW (300 hp) Continental IO-520-F engine.

Procaer/General Avia F15F (Italy) Derivative of the F15E designed by General Avia. A pre-production series was to be undertaken by Procaer.

Procter Petrel (UK) Two-seat light monoplane based on the Kittiwake I single-seat lightplane but with increased wing area. It has been optimised for glider towing.

Practavia Sprite.

PWS 10.

PZL P-6 at the National Air Races at Cleveland in 1931.

PZL P-7a.

Second prototype PZL P-1.

1929. It was easily convertible into a single-seater for aerobatic training. Power was provided by a 164 kW (220 hp) Skoda-built Wright J-5B radial engine. Production aircraft had fuselages constructed of welded steel tubes and were sometimes referred to as PWS 14s.

PWS 16 (Poland) Two-seat trainer developed from the PWS 12.

PWS 18 (Poland) Licence-built Avro Tutor two-seat trainer.

PWS 20T (Poland) Eight-passenger high-wing transport aircraft of 1929 powered by a Lorraine 12Eb engine. The single example built was operated by LOT. Maximum level speed was 200 km/h (124 mph).

PWS 24T (Poland) Basically a smaller four-passenger version of the PWS 20 powered initially by a Wright J-5 engine. About ten were built, most eventually having a 313 kW (420 hp) Pratt & Whitney Wasp Junior engine fitted.

PWS 26 (Poland) A further development of the PWS 12/16 series powered by the same J-5 engine. Two hundred and forty were built for training and liaison duties, a number being used as 'nuisance' raiders during the German invasion. Armament comprised a 7.7 mm machine-gun.

PWS 54T (Poland) Three–four-passenger high-wing transport aircraft of 1932 powered by a J-5 engine. Operated for a brief period by LOT.

PWS RWD-8 (Poland) Two-seat 82 kW (110 hp) Walter Junior- or Skoda-powered parasol-wing monoplane trainer. Four hundred and forty were built by PWS for the Polish Air Force (see **RWD**).

PZL P-1 (Poland) Progenitor of an important family of Polish single-seat fighters, the P-1 of 1929 introduced the shoulder-mounted gull-wing monoplane configuration designed by Zygmunt Pulawski – known internationally as the 'Pulawski wing'. The landing gear of the P-1 was also a 'first': its independent main legs having oleo-pneumatic shock-absorbers located within the profile of the all-metal fuselage. The smooth contours of the aircraft owed much to the Hispano-Suiza in-line engine, but Poland was standardising its military designs on licence-built Bristol radial engines and the two P-1 prototypes were abandoned in favour of the P-7.

PZL P-5 (Poland) Two-seat light biplane powered normally by the 71 kW (95 hp) de Havilland Gipsy engine. Maximum speed was 165 km/h (102 mph).

PZL P-7 (Poland) During 1930–31 two P-6 and two P-7 fighter prototypes were built and tested. All were powered by the Bristol Jupiter radial engine, but the P-7s were fitted with superchargers for high-altitude operations. The P-6/I was flown at the American National Air Races in Cleveland in 1931 and achieved considerable publicity. The Polish authorities, however, preferred the high-altitude P-7 and between 1931 and 1933 149 series aircraft were built at the PZL Warsaw factory, featuring simple engine ring cowlings and faired headrests. Armed with two fixed synchronised 7.7 mm Vickers E machine-guns, the P-7a formed the entire equipment of Poland's fighter squadrons by the autumn of 1933, making the Polish Air Force the first in the world with only all-metal monoplane fighters in first-line service. On 28 October of that year P-7a fighters made a mass goodwill flight to Romania.

Retaining the P-1's remarkable 'Pulawski

PZL P-7as.

PZL P-11c.

wing' and landing-gear design but with a new fuselage of circular section and modified tailplane, the 361.4 kW (485 hp) Jupiter VIIF-powered P-7a gave outstanding service – still equipping one fighter squadron in September 1939. A few P-7s escaped to Romania when Poland collapsed.

Data (P-7a): *Engine* as above *Wing span* 10.3 m (33 ft 9½ in) *Length* 7.16 m (23 ft 6 in) *Max T-O weight* 1,355 kg (2,976 lb) *Max level speed* 317 km/h (197 mph) *Range* 560 km (348 miles)

PZL P-11 (Poland) In 1930 the P-7 fighter was developed to take the more powerful Bristol Mercury engine, but further development had to be taken over by Wsiewolod Jakimiuk after Pulawski's death in an air crash. The P-11/I first prototype flew in the summer of 1931, although still with a Jupiter radial. The P.11/II (which followed at the end of the year) was Mercury-powered. It achieved renown at aviation meetings in Warsaw and Zurich during 1932. The P-11/III was the production prototype and competed in the American National Air Races in Cleveland during August 1932. The first series aircraft were 49 P-11a fighters for Romania with 391 kW (525 hp) Gnome-Rhône Mistral engines, followed by 30 P-11as with 385.3 kW (517 hp) Mercury IV.S2 engines, ordered for the Polish Air Force. In construction and appearance these aircraft resembled the P-7, the main external difference being a larger tail fin.

Principal production version of the aircraft was, however, the P-11c powered by a 417.3 kW (560 hp) Mercury V engine in early examples and a 480.7 kW (645 hp) Mercury VI later. One hundred and seventy-five examples were delivered during 1935–36, replacing the P-7 as the standard Polish fighter. Like its predecessors, the P-11c was of all-metal construction with aluminium-alloy sheet covering, but wing and fuselage were modified and a new vertical tailplane incorporated. Only about 40 aircraft had a four-gun armament, the rest relying on two 7.7 mm machine-guns.

Between 1936 and 1938 the Romanian IAR factory built 70 P-11f fighters, similar to the P-11c but powered by a Romanian-built 443.4 kW (595 hp) Gnome-Rhône 9K Mistral radial. The P-11c and P-11f were manoeuvrable, compact and sturdy, but by the late 1930s virtually obsolete. Lack of a suitable new fighter led to the

PZL P-12 amphibian in which Pulawski was killed.

conversion of a standard P-11c to become the prototype P-11g (Kobuz), tested in August 1939. This version was put into production, but no deliveries were made before the Polish collapse. It closely resembled the later and refined P-24. Therefore, the P-11c faced overwhelming odds in September 1939, flying with 12 Polish squadrons and claiming 126 German aircraft. Surviving P-11s flew to Romania, which subsequently used them alongside P-11fs against the Soviet Union in 1941.

Data (P-11c with Mercury VI engine): *Engine* as above *Wing span* 10.72 m (35 ft 2 in) *Length* 7.55 m (24 ft 9¼ in) *Max T-O weight* 1,630 kg (3,593 lb) *Max level speed* 390 km/h (242.5 mph) *Range* 700 km (435 miles)

PZL P-19 (Poland) Three-seat light cabin monoplane powered by an 89.4 kW (120 hp) de Havilland Gipsy III engine.

PZL P-23 and P-43 (Poland) Four prototypes of the P-23 were tested during 1934–35. A three-seat all-metal cantilever low-wing monoplane with a fixed, spatted landing gear, it was intended as a reconnaissance bomber which would operate tactically in co-operation with Polish ground forces. Forty P-23A aircraft were delivered late in 1936, to be followed by 210 P-23B machines. Named 'Karaś' (Carp), the B version equipped 11 Polish squadrons in September 1939, by which time Stanislaw Prauss' design was approaching obsolescence. Power was provided by a 507 kW (680 hp) Pegasus VIII radial engine. Pilot and observer were housed under a glazed canopy, while a bomb-aiming gondola also accommodated the ventral gun position. Armament com-

PZL P-11s.

PZL P-23A Karas A.

PZL P-24F.

PZL P-43A for Bulgaria.

PZL P-24C.

PZL P-37 Loś.

prised three 7.7 mm machine-guns and up to 700 kg (1,543 lb) of bombs.

The P-43 was an export development for Bulgaria. An order for 12 P-43As was followed by one for 42 P-43Bs. The P-43B had a 730 kW (980 hp) Gnome-Rhône 14N engine fitted and an additional forward-firing machine-gun. Maximum speed was 365 km/h (227 mph). Nine undelivered P-43Bs were requisitioned by the Polish government in September 1939.

Data (P-23B): *Engine* as above *Wing span* 13.95 m (45 ft 9 in) *Length* 9.68 m (31 ft 9¼ in) *Max T-O weight* 3,526 kg (7,773 lb) *Max level speed* 319 km/h (198 mph) *Range* 1,250 km (777 miles)

PZL P-24 (Poland) Final gull-wing monoplane fighter to stem from the P-1, the refined P-24 was first tested in May 1933. The second of two prototypes captured the world speed record for radial-engined fighters in June 1934, attaining 414 km/h (257.25 mph). Produced entirely for export, the P-24 was powered by a Gnome-Rhône 14K radial delivering in excess of 671 kW (900 hp). Among a number of refinements introduced on the P-24 were a fully enclosed pilot's cockpit and streamlined wheel spats. Most powerful of various armament combinations was two 20 mm cannon plus two 7.7 mm machine-guns. Polish production continued right up to September 1939.

Of 60 P-24As bought by Turkey during 1936–37, 26 had four-machine-gun armament. Subsequently about 100 P-24Cs were built in Turkey. Fourteen P-24Bs were delivered to Bulgaria and 36 P-24Fs and P-24Gs to Greece. Romania imported six 'pattern' P-24Es in 1936; the IAR factory then licence-building 50 more. Greek P-24s engaged the invading Germans and Italians in 1940–41, while Romanian P-24s operated during the early fighting on the Russian front.

Data (P-24F): *Engine* as above *Wing span* 10.68 m (35 ft 0½ in) *Length* 7.6 m (24 ft 11¼ in) *Max T-O weight* 2,000 kg (4,409 lb) *Max level speed* 430 km/h (267 mph) *Range* 700 km (435 miles)

PZL P-37 (Poland) When the first P-37 prototype made its maiden flight in June 1936 it represented one of the most advanced bomber designs in the world at that time. A cantilever low-wing all-metal monoplane, it had beautiful lines because of its oval-section semi-monocoque fuselage. The first prototype and initial 10 production aircraft had angular single-fin-and-rudder tail assemblies. The remaining prototypes and the other 80 or so series machines completed by September 1939 had redesigned tailplanes with twin fins and rudders. The landing gear was especially designed for load-bearing, each main unit having a twin-wheel assembly.

Named 'Loś' (Elk), the first 30 production aircraft constituted the A series and were soon relegated to advanced training duties. Remaining machines were known as the Los B and were powered by two 684 kW (918 hp) Pegasus XX radial engines. Defensive armament comprised three 7.7 mm machine-guns on flexible mountings in the nose and in dorsal and ventral positions. Maximum offensive load (carried in internal bays) was 2,580 kg (5,688 lb).

The P-37 was popular with its crews but was not employed effectively by the Polish Air Force command. In September 1939 many were lost in attacking moving troops and armour without effective escort. More than 30 P-37s reached Romania in September 1939 and were used by that country during the early months of action against the Soviet Union.

Data (P-37B): *Engines* as above *Wing span* 17.93 m (58 ft 10 in) *Length* 12.92 m (42 ft 4½ in) *Max T-O weight* 8,900 kg (19,621 lb) *Max level speed* 445 km/h (277 mph) *Range* 1,500 km (933 miles)

PZL 101A Gawron (Poland) Development of the Yak-12, first flown in April 1958. Models appeared for agricultural duties, ambulance and utility work: 330 being built in Poland for domestic use and export. The standard power plant was a 194 kW (260 hp) Ivchenko AI-14R radial.

PZL 102 Kos (Poland) The original prototype PZL 102 two-seat semi-aerobatic light monoplane flew in May 1958. Production aircraft followed in 1959. The final production version was the PZL 102B powered by a 71 kW (95 hp) Continental C-90-12F engine.

PZL 104 Wilga 35 (Poland) The Wilga is a light general-purpose aircraft intended for a wide variety of general aviation and flying club duties. The prototype flew for the first time in April 1962. The current versions are the Wilga 35A (Aeroclub), Wilga 35P (passenger/liaison), Wilga 35R (agricultural) and Wilga 35S (ambulance) versions. The 35A can tow a single glider of up to 650 kg (1,433 lb) weight or two or three smaller gliders.
Data (Wilga 35A): *Engine* one 194 kW (260 hp) Ivchenko AI-14RA supercharged radial *Wing span* 11.12 m (36 ft 5¾ in) *Length* 8.1 m (26 ft 6¾ in) *Max T-O weight* 1,300 kg (2,866 lb) *Max level speed* 201 km/h (125 mph) *Range* 680 km (422 miles) *Accommodation* passenger version carries four persons

PZL 106A Kruk (Poland) Single-seat agricultural aircraft powered by a 447 kW (600 hp) PZL-3S radial engine. Production began in 1976 and 58 had been built by the autumn of 1978.

PZL 110 Koliber (Poland) Licence-built Socata Rallye two–four-seat light aircraft.

PZL-MD-12F (Poland) Four-engined photographic-survey aircraft, first flown in 1962 and intended to replace the survey version of the Li-2.

PZL-Mielec (Antonov) An-2 (Poland) see **Antonov**

PZL-Mielec M-15 Belphegor (Poland) Three-seat agricultural aircraft, first flown in 1973. Power is provided by a 14.7 kN (3,306 lb st) Ivchenko AI-25 turbofan engine.

PZL-Mielec M-18 Dromader (Poland) Single-seat agricultural aircraft, first flown in 1976. A firefighting version was also flown in 1978. Power is provided by a 746 kW (1,000 hp) PZL Kalisz ASz-621R supercharged radial engine.

PZL-Mielec M-20 Mewa (Poland) Polish assembled and manufactured Piper Seneca II twin-engined business aircraft for distribution in Eastern Europe.

PZL 101A Gawron.

PZL 104 Wilga 35.

PZL 106A Kruk two-seat training version, with instructor's seat in place of hopper.

PZL-Mielec TS-11 Iskra (Poland) Tandem two-seat primary and basic trainer, armament trainer, light ground attack and single-seat combat trainer and reconnaissance aircraft. First flown in 1960 and powered in its latest Iskra-BisD form by one 9.81 kN (2,205 lb st) SO-3 turbojet engine. Operated by India, Indonesia and Poland.

PZL 106A Kruk.

PZL 110 Koliber.

PZL-MD-12F.

PZL-Swidnik

PZL-Mielec M-15 Belphegor.

PZL-Mielec M-18 Dromader.

PZL-Mielec M-20 Mewa.

Quickie Aircraft Corporation Quickie.

PZL-Swidnik (Mil) Mi-2 cropduster.

PZL-Swidnik (Mil) Mi-2 (Poland) Known to NATO as *Hoplite*, the Mi-2 helicopter was designed by Mil. Development continued in the USSR until the prototype had completed its initial State trials programme of flying. Then, in accordance with an agreement signed in 1964, further development, production and marketing were assigned exclusively to the Polish aircraft industry.

Production began in 1965 and more than 2,800 have been built in 24 different versions for civil and military use; the majority of these have been exported, including more than 2,000 to the USSR. Data: *Engines* two 298 or 335 kW (400 or 450 shp) Polish-built Isotov GTD-350P turboshafts *Main rotor diameter* 14.5 m (47 ft 6¾ in) *Length of fuselage* 11.94 m (39 ft 2 in) *Max T-O weight* 3,700 kg (8,157 lb) *Max level speed* 210 km/h (130 mph)

Range 580 km (360 miles) *Accommodation* eight passengers or up to 700 kg (1,543 lb) of internal freight

PZL-Swidnik Kania (Poland) Modified version of the Mi-2 powered by two Allison 250-C20B turboshafts.

Quickie Aircraft Corporation Quickie (USA) Single-seat light sporting aircraft of canard configuration, kits for the construction of which are available to amateur builders.

R23, R24, R25 and R26 (UK) The R23 airship was built by Vickers mainly for training and experimental (mooring mast, etc) duties. It was 163 m (535 ft) long, had a volume of 26,674 m³ (942,000 cu ft) and was originally powered by four 186.3 kW (250 hp) Wolseley engines, later changed for four similarly rated Rolls-Royce engines. It flew for a total of 321 hours 30 minutes. R24, R25 and R26 were identical, except that the latter had three Rolls-Royce and one 149 kW (200 hp) Maybach engines. Like R23, R24 and R25 were launched in 1917, whereas R26 was launched in 1918.

R31 (UK) Built by Shorts and launched in 1918, the R31 spent only 9 hours in the air and was scrapped in 1919 because of dangerous rotting of the wooden framework.

R32 (UK) R32 was the sister ship to the R31 but completed about 260 flying hours, originally as a passenger airship and later as a training airship with the US Navy. It was 187 m (614 ft) long and powered by five Rolls-Royce engines.

R33 (UK) Built by Armstrong Whitworth, the R33 was 196 m (643 ft) long and powered by five 186.5 kW (250 hp) Sunbeam engines. Launched in 1919, it had a stormy career: being deleted, recommissioned, damaged and finally deleted for reasons of economy in 1927, having flown for about 800 hours.

R34 (UK) The R34 was almost identical to the R33. After about 500 hours of flying it broke up in a ground-landing accident in 1921 (see **Chronology** 9–13 July 1919).

R36 (UK) Built by Vickers and launched in 1921. Made seven flights lasting about 80 hours, but was damaged in a landing accident on 21 June 1921 and finally broken up in 1927.

R38 (UK) Built by Shorts, the R38 was launched in 1921 but crashed into the Humber in the same year (see **Chronology** 24 August 1921). It was 212 m (695 ft) long and powered by six 261 kW (350 hp) Cossack engines.

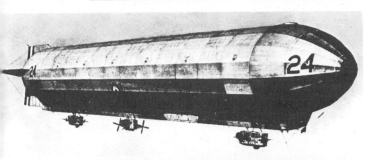

R100 (UK) The R100 was built by the Airship Guarantee Company (a subsidiary of Vickers) and launched in 1929. It was 216 m (709 ft) long and had a total volume of 146,000 m³ (5,156,000 cu ft). Power was provided by six 521.6 kW (700 hp) Rolls-Royce engines. It made a total of nine flights and was finally sold for scrap in 1931 following the R101 disaster (see **Chronology** 29 July and 13–16 August 1930).

R101 (UK) The R101 was built at the Air Ministry Establishment at Cardington and was 220 m (722 ft) long. Power was provided by five 432.2 kW (580 hp) Beardmore engines. It made a total of 12 flights, lasting 127 hours 11 minutes (see **Chronology** 4–5 October 1930).

Rand Robinson KR-1 (USA) Single-seat lightweight sporting monoplane, plans for which are available to amateur constructors (about 6,000 sets sold by February 1979).

Rand Robinson KR-2 (USA) Slightly larger two-seat version of the KR-1, plans and kits for which are available to amateur constructors (about 4,500 sets of plans and 2,800 kits sold by February 1979)

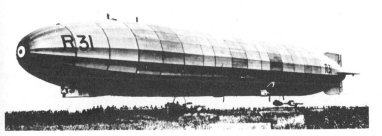

Rearwin Cloudster (USA) Two–three-seat light cabin monoplane powered by an 89.4 kW (120 hp) Ken Royce engine.

Rearwin Junior (USA) Two-seat light high-wing monoplane of 1931 powered by a 37.25 kW (50 hp) Aeromarine or 41 kW (55 hp) Jacobs engine.

Rearwin Skyranger (USA) Two-seat light cabin monoplane powered by a 56 kW (75 hp) Continental A-75 engine.

Rearwin Speedster (USA) Two-seat light cabin monoplane powered by a 93 kW (125 hp) Menasco C-4 or similar engine up to 108 kW (145 hp).

Rearwin Sportster (USA) Two-seat light cabin monoplane powered by a Ken Royce 5E, Ken Royce 5G or Warner Scarab Junior engine of 52–67 kW (70–90 hp).

Rearwin Model 8135T (USA) Two-seat tandem trainer derived from the Cloudster and designed specially for instrument training in co-operation with Pan American Airways.

Rand Robinson KR-2.

Reggiane Re 2000 Falco I, Re 2001 Falco II and Re 2005 Sagittario (Italy) Appearing in 1938, the Re 2000 was a single-seat fighter powered by a 745.2 kW (1,000 hp) Piaggio P.XI RC 40 radial engine. It had a maximum speed of 541 km/h (336 mph). A small number were acquired by the Italian Navy and others were exported to Sweden and Hungary (also licence-built).

In 1941 and 1943 respectively the Re 2001 and Re 2005 appeared, powered by 857 kW (1,150 hp) Daimler-Benz DB 601A (Re 2001) and 1,099 kW (1,475 hp) DB 605A (Re 2005) engines. They represented major redesigns, although some of the Re 2000's lines were still apparent. Maximum speed and manoeuvrability were improved and the Regia Aeronautica received 252 and 48 prior to Italy's surrender to the Allies. A small number of Re 2001s and Re 2005s thereafter served with the Fascist Republican Air Force.

R24.

Constructing the R100 rigid airship at the Vickers works.

Rand Robinson KR-2.

Reggiane Re 2000 Falco Is.

R31.

Reims FTB 337.

Reggiane Re 2001 Falco II.

Reggiane Re 2005 Sagittario.

Reggiane Re 2002 Ariete fighter-bomber (foreground), of which no more than fifty were flown operationally by the Regia Aeronautica from 1942. Powered by an 876 kW (1,175 hp) Piaggio P.XIX RC 45 radial and armed with four machine-guns and 650 kg (1,433 lb) of bombs, it had a maximum speed of 530 km/h (329 mph).

Renard R.31.

Replica Plans SE-5A.

Data (Re 2001): *Engine* as above *Wing span* 11.0 m (36 ft 1 in) *Length* 8.36 m (27 ft 5 in) *Max T-O weight* 3,267 kg (7,202 lb) *Max level speed* 545 km/h (339 mph) *Range* 1,040 km (646 miles) *Armament* two 12.7 mm and two 7.7 mm machine-guns, plus optionally one 250 kg bomb

Reims/Cessna series (France/USA) Reims Aviation of France manufactures under licence Cessna designs for sale in Europe (see **Cessna**). One such aircraft is the Skymaster, from which Reims has developed the FTB 337, powered by two 168 kW (225 hp) Continental TSIO-360-D turbocharged engines and suitable for navigation and IFR training, counter-insurgency missions, maritime or overland patrol, and sea and land rescue (four underwing attachments for stores).

Renard R.17 (Belgium) Four-seat cabin monoplane powered by an 89.4 kW (120 hp) or 119 kW (160 hp) Renard radial engine.

Renard R.30 (Belgium) Six-passenger colonial cabin monoplane powered by three 89.4 kW (120 hp) Renard radial engines.

Renard R.31 (Belgium) Two-seat open-cockpit high-wing reconnaissance monoplane of 1932 powered by a 358 kW (480 hp) Rolls-Royce Kestrel IIS engine. Entered service with the Belgian Air Force. Built by Renard between 1935 and 1936 and under licence by SABCO.

Replica Plans SE-5A (Canada) Single-seat sporting biplane designed as an 85% scale rep-

resentation of the SE-5a fighter of World War I. Plans are available to amateur constructors.

R.E.P. Type N (France) Shoulder-wing monoplane of pre-World War I design powered by a 59.6 kW (80 hp) Gnome or Le Rhône rotary engine. Used by two French escadrilles for reconnaissance duties up to 1915; Escadrille R.E.P. 15 assigned to the 5th Army at the outbreak of the war (see **[Robert] Esnault-Pelterie R.E.P. types**).

R.E.P. Parasol (France) Two-seat parasol-wing monoplane of pre-World War I design powered by a 59.6 kW (80 hp) Gnome rotary engine. Twelve flown as observation aircraft by the RNAS before and during the early part of the war.

Republic F-84 Thunderjet (USA) The Thunderjet was developed under the joint supervision of the Republic company and the USAAF Air Materiel Command as a jet-powered single-seat fighter to replace piston-engined fighters. Like all early American jets, the Thunderjet had straight wings and flew for the first time in prototype form on 28 February 1946. The second prototype was flown over the measured course at Muroc in September 1946, but the highest speed obtained was 983.3 km/h (611 mph): this represented an American speed record, although falling short of the world record.

The 13 YF-84As were powered by 17.8 kN (4,000 lb st) Allison J35-A-15 turbojet engines and differed from the prototypes in brake, armament and other minor details. All were subsequently converted to F-84B standard, which was the first production model. Armament comprised six 0.50 in machine-guns, while provision was made from the 86th aircraft for rockets on retractable mounts. Delivery of the F-84B began in 1947. The B was followed by the similar C.

Data (F-84G): *Engine* as above *Wing span* 11.1 m (36 ft 4¾ in) *Length* 11.62 m (38 ft 1¼ in) *Max T-O weight* 10,670 kg (23,525 lb) *Max level speed* 1,001 km/h (622 mph) *Combat radius* 1,609 km (1,000 miles)

Republic F-84F Thunderstreak (USA) This aircraft was originally intended to be a swept-wing version of the F-84E Thunderjet powered by an Allison J35-A-29 engine. A prototype using an F-84E fuselage and an A-25 engine was built and flown in six months – its first flight being made on 3 June 1950. The impending delivery of the high-powered 32 kN (7,200 lb st) Sapphire engine (for which Curtiss-Wright had acquired a licence) resulted in the decision to re-engine the F-84F – the re-engined prototype flying on 14 February 1951. As a result of successful trials, the J-65-W-1 or -3 Sapphire-engined F-84F entered production and more than 2,711 were eventually built by July 1957, half for NATO countries. The first F-84F was delivered on 3 December 1952 and the type entered service in 1954. Maximum level speed was 1,058 km/h (658 mph).

Republic F-84E Thunderjets.

The 4,457th and last Republic F-84 Thunderjet.

The F-84D was a development of the B with thicker metal skins and ailerons; hinged gun deck; winterised fuel system; changes to permit use of gasoline instead of kerosene; and substitution of mechanical linkage for hydraulic compression of shock-strut travel to shorten the landing gear for retraction.

Use of a 22.24 kN (5,000 lb st), Allison J35-A-17 turbojet engine introduced the F-84E. This also had a longer fuselage to give more room in the cockpit; wingtip tanks fitted with fins to permit full manoeuvrability with tanks fitted; and structural modifications to increase the permissible *G* loads. In addition to the fixed armament, it could carry 32 × 5 in rockets; two 11.5 in and 16 × 5 in rockets; two 1,000 lb bombs and 18 × 5 in rockets or other stores. The F-84E was also the first version supplied under MDAP to other NATO countries.

Progressive development of the F-84E produced the F-84G fitted with in-flight refuelling. It was the first USAF fighter bomber announced as being equipped to carry the atomic bomb. Power was provided by a 24.9 kN (5,600 lb st) Allison J35-A-29 engine. Using in-flight refuelling, a group of F-84Gs taking part in 'Operation Longstop' in August 1953 flew 7,218 km (4,485 miles) from Georgia to Lakenheath in England: the longest non-stop flight then achieved by jet fighters. The G was the final 'straight wing' variant, production of all versions totalling 4,457.

Republic RF-84F Thunderflash (USA) The Thunderflash was a tactical-reconnaissance version of the F-84F. Unlike the Thunderstreak which had a nose air-intake, this aircraft had wing-root intakes to enable it to carry cameras, radar and electronic equipment in the nose. It went out of production in December 1956 after 715 had been built. It served with the USAF, US Air National Guard and the air forces of Belgium, France, Italy, Greece, Norway, Turkey and the Netherlands.

Republic F-105 Thunderchief (USA) The F-105 was developed to meet the USAF requirements for a supersonic single-seat fighter bomber able to deliver nuclear weapons – as well as heavier loads of conventional bombs and rockets – at very high speeds over long ranges. Design work began in 1951 and the first prototype flew on 22 October 1955.

Republic RF-84F Thunderflash.

Republic F-84F Thunderstreaks.

Republic F-105D Thunderchief fighter-bombers.

Early version of the Republic P-47D Thunderbolt has its guns synchronised.

Republic P-47M Thunderbolt with triple rocket tubes under each wing.

Republic YP-43 Lancer.

Seventy-five F-105Bs and three JF-105Bs were produced with one 111 kN (25,000 lb st, with afterburning) Pratt & Whitney J75-P-3 or -5 turbojet engine each. Following these were the F-105D all-weather fighter bomber (more than 600 built); F-105F two-seat dual-purpose trainer/tactical fighter (143 built); and F-105G two-seat all-weather 'hunter killer' – a 'Wild Weasel' ground-defence suppression conversion of the F-105F which was used in Vietnam against anti-aircraft missile sites. The F-105D/F/G versions remain operational with the USAF and Reserve.

Data (F-105D): *Engine* one 117.9 kN (26,500 lb st) Pratt & Whitney J75-P-19W turbojet *Wing span* 10.65 m (34 ft 11 in) *Length* 20.43 m (67 ft 0¼ in) *Max T-O weight* 23,968 kg (52,840 lb) *Max level speed* 2,230 km/h (1,385 mph) *Range* 3,330 km (2,070 miles) *Armament* one General Electric M-61 Vulcan automatic multi-barrel 20 mm gun in port side of nose. Loads are: (1) 2,460 litre (650 US gal) centreline tank, 1,703 litre (450 US gal) tank on one inner wing pylon, nuclear store on other inner pylon; (2) 450 gal tanks on centreline and inner wing pylons, nuclear weapon in bomb bay; (3) 650 gal centreline tank, two 3,000 lb bombs on inner wing pylons; (4) 650 gal centreline tank, two 450 gal tanks on inner wing pylons, four Sidewinder missiles on outer wing pylons; (5) three rocket packs on centreline, two on each inner wing pylon and one on each outer pylon; (6) nine BLU-1/B firebombs or nine MLU-10/B mines in similar arrangement to rocket packs, or 16 leaflet bombs, 750 lb bombs, or MC-1 toxic bombs. Typical armament for the F-105G would comprise four Shrike missiles or two AGM-78B Standard ARMs. Adaptation of the F-105 to carry the latest missiles carried out during early 1970s

Republic P-43 Lancer (USA) The Lancer was a single-seat interceptor fighter that first appeared in service evaluation YP-43 form in 1940. With a Pratt & Whitney R-1830 Twin Wasp radial engine and bulky fuselage, it was clearly a product of the Republic Aviation Corporation. Production for the USAAF (also supplied to the RAAF with reconnaissance equipment fitted) and China totalled 272 aircraft in three versions.

Data (P-43): *Engine* one 894 kW (1,200 hp) Pratt & Whitney R-1830-35 Twin Wasp *Wing span* 10.97 m (36 ft 0 in) *Length* 8.68 m (28 ft 5¾ in) *Max T-O weight* 3,245–3,600 kg (7,155–7,936 lb) *Max level speed* 565 km/h (351 mph) *Range* 1,287 km (800 miles) *Armament* two 0.50 in and two 0.30 in machine-guns, plus six 20 lb bombs

Republic P-47 Thunderbolt (USA) Largest and heaviest single-engined fighter of World War II, the P-47 was redesigned with a larger engine in 1940 to take account of the aerial fighting in Europe and to carry increased armament and fuel capacity. The aircraft was designed around the turbocharged Pratt & Whitney R-2800 Double Wasp: the air inlet passing under the engine but inside the cowl, through pipes to the exhaust-driven turbocharger under the rear fuselage, the compressed air then being ducted back above the wing to the engine. To absorb the power – which in late models reached 2,086.5 kW (2,800 hp) with water injection – a four-bladed propeller of 3.7 m (12 ft 2 in) diameter was needed. This meant a long landing gear, hinged well-outboard in the elliptical wing. It was not easy to accommodate the heavy armament even further out on the wing; the four 0.50 in guns in each wing having ammunition boxes stretching almost to the tips.

The prototype flew on 6 May 1941 and after extensive development the first production P-47B was delivered in March 1942 to the 56th Fighter Group. This Group reached the 8th Air Force in England in January 1943. Its size caused the P-47 to be criticised and at first it was thought that the only thing it could do well was dive out of the fray. It was called 'The Juggernaut', shortened to 'The Jug' – a name which stuck. Gradually its immense firepower and ability to survive damage forced reassessment. No fewer than 15,660 were built, serving on all fronts as long-range escorts and, especially, as ground-strafing fighter bombers.

The P-47C introduced a longer fuselage; the D a later sub-type of R-2800 engine; the D-25 a 'teardrop' (bubble) canopy; and the D-30 a dorsal fin. No fewer than 12,602 were D series, all equipped to carry the eight heavy guns plus three to five external stores, such as bombs or drop-tanks to a total weight of 1,134 kg (2,500 lb). Final batches and the P-47M and N had further improvements, the M being a stripped model to catch flying bombs, and the N an ultra-long-range escort for the Pacific theatre with a new long-span wing, internal fuel capacity of 4,337 litres (954 US gal) and extra radio. The N also introduced zero-length rocket launchers, rockets having been carried on earlier models in triple tubes of 114 mm (4.5 in) calibre.

When the bubble-hood P-47D-25 and -30 became dominant, the older models were called 'razorbacks' because of their narrow curving top line. Large numbers of D models served with the Soviet Union and the RAF, chiefly on the Burmese Front. There were many experimental models, one of which set a speed record for piston-engined aircraft at 811 km/h (504 mph). *Data (P-47D): Engine* one 1,889 kW (2,535 hp) Pratt & Whitney R-2800-59 Double Wasp radial *Wing span* 12.4 m (40 ft 9¼ in) *Length* 11.03 m (36 ft 1¼ in) *Max T-O weight* 8,800 kg (19,400 lb) *Max level speed* 690 km/h (428 mph) *Range* 950 km (590 miles) *Armament* eight 0.50 in machine-guns, plus two 1,000 lb and a 500 lb bomb or ten 5 in rockets

Republic RC-3 Seabee (USA) Four-seat light pusher-engined amphibious flying-boat, the prototype of which appeared in November 1944.

RFB Fantrainer 400 (Germany) Tandem two-seat basic- and IFR-training aircraft designed as a replacement for the Piaggio P.149D primary trainer used by the Luftwaffe. First flown on 27

One of the two P-47D Thunderbolts converted to TP-47G two-seat fighter trainer standard.

Republic RC-3 Seabee.

RFB Fantrainer 400.

October 1977. Power is provided by a 313 kW (420 hp) Allison 250-C20B turboshaft engine in the Fantrainer 400 configuration. An uprated version has been offered to the USAF as a T-37 replacement, powered by a 448 kW (600 shp) Allison 250 or Avco Lycoming LTS 101 turboshaft.

Rikugun Ki 79 (Japan) Advanced trainer of World War II powered by a 335.3 kW (450 hp) Hitachi Ha 13A engine.

Robin DR 400/100 2 + 2 (France) Two–four-seat light monoplane powered by a 74.5 kW (100 hp) Lycoming O-235-H2C engine.

Robin DR 400/120 Petit Prince (France) Three–four-seat light training and touring monoplane powered by an 88 kW (118 hp) Lycoming O-235-L2A engine.

Robin DR 400/140B Major (France) Four-seat light monoplane powered by a 119 kW (160 hp) Lycoming O-320-D engine. Deliveries began in 1979.

Republic P-47N Thunderbolts.

Robin DR 400/140B Major.

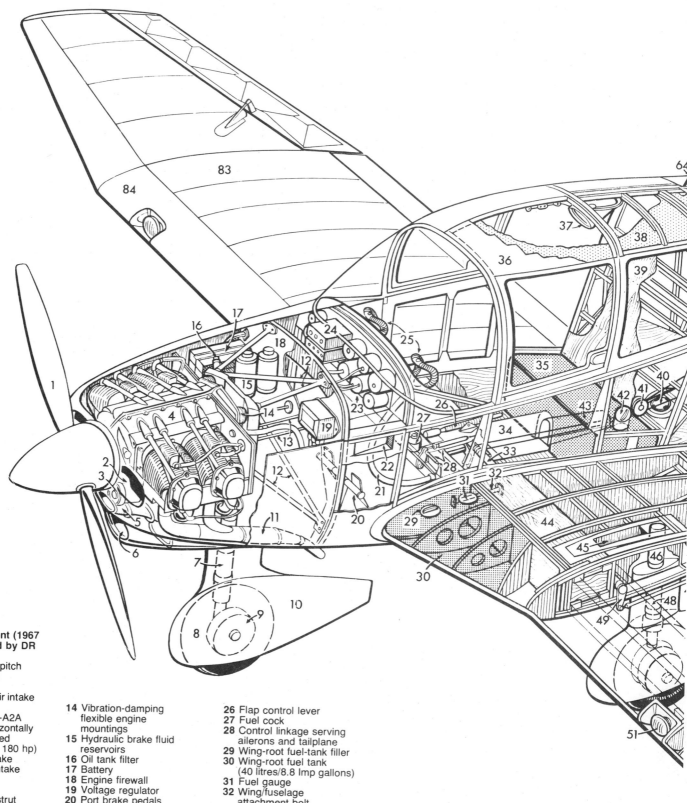

Robin DR 253 Regent (1967 Regent, superseded by DR 400/180)

1 Two-blade fixed-pitch Sensenich metal propeller
2 Engine-cooling air intake
3 Generator
4 Lycoming O-360-A2A four-cylinder horizontally opposed air-cooled engine (134 kW; 180 hp)
5 Oil-cooler air intake
6 Carburettor air intake
7 Oleo-pneumatic nosewheel shock-absorber strut (offset to starboard)
8 Steerable nosewheel
9 Manu-hydraulic brake drum
10 Nosewheel fairing spat
11 Exhaust silencer manifold
12 Engine-bearing struts
13 Nosewheel steering rods

14 Vibration-damping flexible engine mountings
15 Hydraulic brake fluid reservoirs
16 Oil tank filter
17 Battery
18 Engine firewall
19 Voltage regulator
20 Port brake pedals
21 Curved control columns
22 Cabin air-conditioning intake
23 Instrument panel
24 Radio navigation and communication equipment
25 Handgrips of dual controls

26 Flap control lever
27 Fuel cock
28 Control linkage serving ailerons and tailplane
29 Wing-root fuel-tank filler
30 Wing-root fuel tank (40 litres/8.8 Imp gallons)
31 Fuel gauge
32 Wing/fuselage attachment bolt
33 Aileron control-cable conduit
34 Central tunnel for control cables
35 Fuselage fuel tank (110 litres/24 Imp gallons)
36 Forward-hinged cabin access doors (port and starboard)

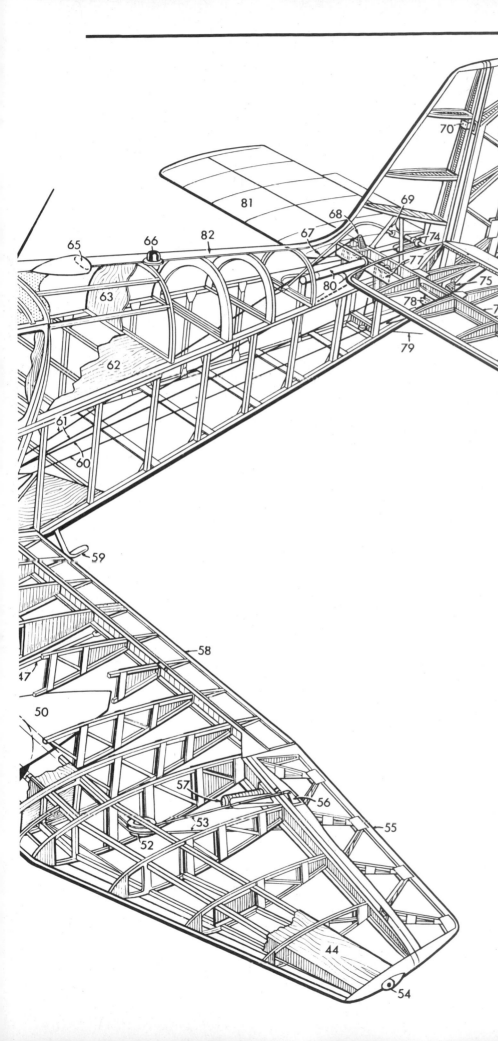

37 Cabin loudspeaker
38 Cabin inner roof lining
39 Cabin rear bulkhead
40 Radio compass
41 Tail control-cable pulleys
42 Fuselage fuel filler
43 Cable passage through fuel tank
44 Ply-covered box spar
45 Reinforced box for undercarriage anchorage
46 Undercarriage attachment shaft
47 Flap control rod
48 Mainwheel shock-absorbing strut
49 Flap-rod linkage to torsion tube
50 Mainwheel fairing spat
51 Landing lamp
52 Aileron cable pulley
53 Aileron cables
54 Navigation lamp
55 Aileron on outer (16° dihedral) wing section
56 Upper aileron control bracket
57 Internal aileron mass balance
58 Aluminium alloy wing flap
59 Cabin access step
60 Rudder control cables
61 Tailplane control cables

62 Baggage compartment floor
63 Baggage compartment rear bulkhead
64 VHF aerial
65 Cabin air outlet
66 Anti-collision revolving beacon
67 Tailplane tab control
68 Tailplane incidence control brackets (upper and lower)
69 Fin bracing struts
70 Upper rudder hinge
71 Rudder
72 Position light
73 Tailplane trim tab
74 Tailplane tab control fork
75 Rudder control bracket
76 Single spar of one-piece variable-incidence tailplane
77 Tailplane axis bearers
78 Lower rudder hinge
79 VOR antenna
80 Tailplane mass balance
81 Fabric-covered all-wooden tail unit
82 Plywood-covered all-wooden fuselage
83 Fabric-covered all-wooden wing and aileron
84 Plywood-covered leading edge

Robin

Rockwell Alpine Commander.

Robin DR 400/160 Chevalier (France) Four-seat light monoplane powered by a 119 kW (160 hp) Lycoming O-320-D engine.

Robin DR 400/180 Régent (France) Four–five-seat member of the wooden DR 400 series powered by a 134 kW (180 hp) Lycoming O-360-A engine.

Robin DR 400/180 Régent.

Robin R 2112.

Robin DR 400/180R Remorqueur (France) Member of the DR 400 range designed for use as a glider-towing aircraft, although it can be flown as a normal four-seat tourer. Powered by a 134 kW (180 hp) Lycoming O-360-A engine.

Rockwell Gran Turismo Commander.

Robin HR 100/250TR President (France) Four–five-seat all-metal monoplane powered by a 186 kW (250 hp) Lycoming IO-540-C4B5 engine.

Robin R 1180 Aiglon (France) All-metal four-seat light monoplane powered by a 134 kW (180 hp) Lycoming O-360-A3AD engine.

Robin R 2000 series (France) Two-seat aerobatic light monoplanes derived from the Robin HR 200 which they superseded. Produced as the R 2100A (80.5 kW; 108 hp Lycoming O-235-H engine); R 2112 (82 kW; 110 hp Lycoming); R 2160 Acrobin (119 kW; 160 hp Lycoming O-320-D); and R 2160A Rafale (119 kW; 160 hp Lycoming AEIO-320).

Rockwell Commander 700.

Robinson Model R22 (USA) Two-seat lightweight helicopter powered by a 112 kW (150 hp) Lycoming O-320-A2B engine. First flown on 28 August 1975. Orders for 524 received by the beginning of 1979. Max level speed 180 km/h (112 mph).

Rockwell Model 111 and Model 112/Alpine Commander (USA) The Alpine Commander is a four-seat cabin monoplane powered by a 156.6 kW (210 hp) Lycoming TO-360-C1A6D turbocharged engine. It is the current version of the Model 112, the first prototype of which flew on 17 December 1970. Deliveries of production aircraft began in 1972. The Model 111 was similar to the Model 112 but had a non-retractable landing gear.

Data (Alpine Commander): *Engine* as above *Wing span* 10.85 m (35 ft 7¼ in) *Length* 7.63 m (25 ft 0½ in) *Max T-O weight* 1,338 kg (2,950 lb) *Max level speed* 315 km/h (196 mph) *Range* 1,106 km (687 miles)

Rockwell Model 114/Gran Turismo Commander (USA) Known as the Model 114 when introduced in 1976, the Gran Turismo Commander is basically similar to the Alpine Commander but powered by a 194 kW (260 hp) Lycoming IO-540-T4B5D engine.

Rockwell Commander 685 (USA) Pressurised seven–nine-seat business transport evolved from the Turbo Commander 690 but powered by two 325 kW (435 hp) Continental GTSIO-520-F engines. Maximum cruising speed is 412 km/h (256 mph).

Rockwell Commander 700 (USA/Japan) Six–eight-seat light transport developed and being produced in collaboration with Fuji in Japan. Design began in Japan (under designation

Robinson Model R22.

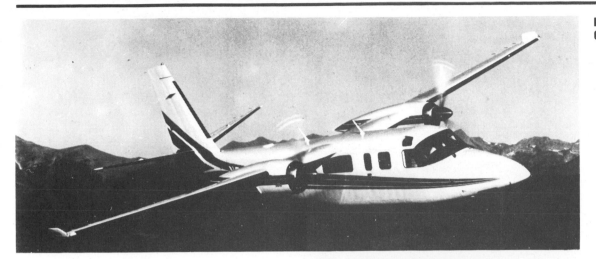

Rockwell Jetprop Commander 980.

FA-300) in 1971. The first prototype flew on 13 November 1975 and the first production aircraft was delivered in August 1978.

Data: *Engines* two turbocharged 253 kW (340 hp) Lycoming TIO-540-R2ADs *Wing span* 12.94 m (42 ft 5½ in) *Length* 12.03 m (39 ft 5¾ in) *Max T-O weight* 3,151 kg (6,947 lb) *Cruising speed* 393 km/h (244 mph) *Range* 2,226 km (1,384 miles)

Rockwell Commander 710 (USA/Japan) First flown in 1976, this is a pressurised aircraft developed jointly by Rockwell and Fuji, powered by two 335.3 kW (450 hp) engines.

Rockwell Hawk Commander (USA) Eight–nine-seat pressurised transport aircraft with an airframe based on the Shrike Commander but with reduced wing span and powered by two 451 kW (605 ehp) AiResearch TPE 331-43BL turboprops. Deliveries began in 1966.

Rockwell Lark Commander (USA) Four-seat high-wing all-metal business/sport/trainer powered by a 134 kW (180 hp) Lycoming O-360-A2F engine. Deliveries began in 1968.

Rockwell Jetprop Commander 840 and 980 (USA) Replacements for the Turbo Commander 690B, the prototypes of which were shown in 1979. Seating will be for 7, 8 or up to 11 persons and power will be provided by two Garrett-AiResearch TPE331-5 and TPE331-10 turboprop engines respectively.

Rockwell Quail Commander and Sparrow Commander (USA) see **AAMSA**

Rockwell Snipe Commander (USA) Version of the Ag Commander single-seat agricultural aircraft which subsequently became known as the Snipe Commander, powered by a 335.3 kW (450 hp) Pratt & Whitney IR985 engine.

Rockwell Turbo Commander 690B.

Rockwell Shrike Commander Esquire and Courser Commander (USA) The Esquire was produced as a six-seat de luxe version of the Shrike Commander. Power was provided by two 216 kW (290 hp) Lycoming IO-540-E1B5 engines. The Courser Commander was the name applied to the former Grand Commander before production ended.

Rockwell Shrike Commander 500S (USA) Four-seat light business/utility transport powered by two 216 kW (290 hp) Lycoming IO-540-E1B5 engines. Maximum cruising speed is 346 km/h (215 mph). In production.

Rockwell Turbo Commander 690B (USA) Pressurised transport aircraft powered by two 522 kW (700 shp) Garrett-AiResearch TPE 331-5-251K turboprop engines. It is the last of the Turbo Commander series which began in 1964, re-emerged in 1971 with the Model 681B, and subsequently included the Model 690 and Model 690A (more than 150 built). The Model 690B was available in two versions in 1979 (now superseded by the Jetprop Commanders), the seven-seat Executive I and II.

Data (Model 690B): *Engines* as above *Wing span* 14.23 m (46 ft 8 in) *Length* 13.52 m (44 ft 4¼ in) *Max T-O weight* 4,683 kg (10,325 lb) *Max cruising speed* 526 km/h (327 mph) *Range* 2,718 km (1,689 miles)

Rockwell Sabreliner series (USA) The prototype Sabreliner flew for the first time on 16 September 1958 and had been designed and built to the USAF 'UTX' requirement for a combat-readiness trainer and utility aircraft. In January 1955 the USAF ordered the first of 143 T-39A pilot-proficiency/administrative-support aircraft; followed by six radar-trainer versions as T-39Bs.

Rockwell Shrike Commander 500S.

Rockwell

Rockwell Sabreliner 60.

Rockwell Sabreliner 75A.

Rockwell International B-1.

In 1961 the US Navy ordered 42 radar interception officer trainers, designated T-39D; subsequently also acquiring seven CT-39E (commercial Sabreliner 40) rapid-response airlift aircraft for high-priority passengers, ferry pilots and freight, and a number of CT-39G staff transports (based on the commercial Sabreliner 60). The only other military version proper is the T-39F, a conversion of the T-39A for the USAF to train 'Wild Weasel' ECM operators for F-105G Thunderchiefs. Argentina also operates the Sabreliner 75A as a military aircraft.

Commercial versions of the Sabreliner which are no longer available have included: the Series 40, the basic version for a crew of two and nine passengers and powered by two 14.68 kN (3,300 lb st) Pratt & Whitney JT12A-8 turbojets (earlier Sabres could be brought up to Series 40 standard); Series 40A with the wing of the Series 75 and the fuselage, landing gear and engines of the Series 40; Series 60 for a crew of two and ten passengers and lengthened from 13.34 m (43 ft 9 in) to 14.73 m (48 ft 4 in); Series 70 for a crew of two and 8–12 passengers; and Series 75A with increased tailplane span, new landing gear, antiskid system, improved galley, seating and toilet, new air-conditioning system, and 19.26 kN (4,315 lb st) General Electric CF700-2D-2 turbofan engines.

The current version is the Series 65, accommodating a crew of two and eight–ten passengers and powered by two 16.46 kN (3,700 lb st) Garrett-AiResearch TFE731-3-1D turbofan engines. Deliveries of the Series 65 began in July 1979. The Series 85 is a new version currently under development. It is to have true intercontinental range, a supercritical wing, advanced-technology turbofan engines and a cabin 7.62 m (25 ft 0 in) long.

Rockwell Sabreliner 65.

Data (Sabreliner 65): *Engines* as above *Wing span* 15.37 m (50 ft 5⅛ in) *Length* 14.3 m (46 ft 11 in) *Max T-O weight* 10,886 kg (24,000 lb) *Max operating speed* Mach 0.85 *Range* 4,818–5,393 km (2,994–3,351 miles)

Rockwell Thrush Commander-600 and -800 (USA) Single-seat agricultural aircraft powered by 448 kW (600 hp) Pratt & Whitney R-1340 Wasp and 596.5 kW (800 hp) Wright R-1300-1B Cyclone radial engines respectively.

Rockwell International B-1 (USA) The B-1 was designed as a new low-altitude penetration bomber to replace the Boeing B-52s of USAF Strategic Air Command by 1980. It was to be the third and most flexible component of the US Triad defence system, comprising also land-based and submarine-launched ballistic missiles.

The B-1 prototypes were assembled in USAF facilities known as Plant 42 at Palmdale, California. The first aircraft flew on 23 December 1974. The fourth B-1 had its maiden flight on 14 February 1979 and is the only example fitted with the complete B-1 offensive and defensive weapons systems. The first and second prototypes have been retired in order to utilise limited funding in tests of the most advanced aircraft; this resulted from the June 1977 announcement by President Carter that production of the B-1 would be cancelled and priority given instead to the cruise missile development programme. Authority was given for the test and development programme to continue in order to provide a technical base in the event of the alternative systems running into difficulty

In 1978 B-1 derivative designs were included in continuing Department of Defense studies to evaluate various types of aircraft as cruise missile carriers.

Data: *Engines* four 133.4 kN (30,000 lb st, with afterburning) General Electric YF101-GE-100 turbofans *Wing span* (spread) 41.67 m (136 ft

8½ in), (swept) 23.84 m (78 ft 2½ in) *Length* (incl nose probe) 45.78 m (150 ft 2½ in) *Design max T-O weight* 179,170 kg (395,000 lb) *Max level speed* (approx) Mach 2.2 *Max range* (without refuelling) intercontinental

Rockwell International OV-10 Bronco (USA)
The Bronco is a two-seat multi-purpose counter-insurgency aircraft which flew for the first time in 1965. The initial production version was the OV-10A, first flown in August 1967. It was delivered to the US Marine Corps for light armed reconnaissance, helicopter escort and forward air control duties (18 loaned to the US Navy), and to the USAF for use in the forward air control role and for limited quick-response ground support (pending the arrival of tactical fighters).

The OV-10A was followed by the OV-10B, six supplied to the Federal German government for target towing; OV-10B(Z), structurally similar to the B but with provision for a 13.12 kN (2,950 lb st) General Electric J85-GE-4 turbojet engine to be mounted above the wing to increase performance for target towing (12 delivered to the Federal German government); OV-10C, 32 delivered to the Royal Thai Air Force; OV-10D Night Observation System (NOS) version, converted from the OV-10A with a 20 mm gun turret under the rear fuselage, forward-looking infra-red sensor under the lengthened nose, laser target designator within the FLIR turret, uprated engines (775.5 kW; 1,040 shp), and wing pylons capable of carrying rocket pods, flare pods, free-fall stores and drop-tanks; OV-10E, similar to the OV-10A for the Venezuelan Air Force (16); and OV-10F, similar to the OV-10A for Indonesia (16).
Data (OV-10A): *Engines* two 533 kW (715 ehp) Garrett-AiResearch T76-G-416/417 turboprops *Wing span* 12.19 m (40 ft 0 in) *Length* 12.67 m (41 ft 7 in) *Overload T-O weight* 6,552 kg (14,444 lb) *Max level speed* 452 km/h (281 mph) *Combat radius* 367 km (228 miles) *Armament* four 272 kg (600 lb) weapon attachment points under wings and one 544 kg (1,200 lb) under fuselage. Two 7.62 mm M-60C machine-guns carried in each sponson. Provision for one AIM-9D Sidewinder air-to-air missile under each wing. Max weapon load 1,633 kg (3,600 lb)

Rockwell International T-2 Buckeye (USA)
The first T2J-1 prototype Buckeye jet trainer, built for the US Navy, flew on 31 January 1958. Five versions were produced subsequently, beginning with the T-2A, 217 of which were built (no longer in service). The T-2B (97 built) is similar to the A but powered by two 13.34 kN (3,000 lb st) Pratt & Whitney J60-P-6 turbojet engines. The T-2C entered production in 1968 and is generally similar to the B, but has 13.12 kN (2,950 lb st) General Electric J85-GE-4 turbojet engines (231 ordered by Naval Air Training Command).

The final two versions built were the T-2D and T-2E, both of which are generally similar to the C. The former differs in avionics and by the deletion of carrier landing capability (24 delivered to the Venezuelan Air Force). The T-2F has new avionics and an accessory kit to permit utilisation in an attack role, providing six wing store stations with a combined capacity of 1,588 kg (3,500 lb) – 40 delivered to the Hellenic Air Force Training Command as advanced and tactical jet trainers.
Data (T-2C): *Engines* as above *Wing span* 11.62 m (38 ft 1½ in) *Length* 11.67 m (38 ft 3½ in) *Max T-O weight* 5,983 kg (13,191 lb) *Max level speed* 852 km/h (530 mph) *Max range* 1,722 km (1,070 miles)

Rockwell International

Rockwell International XFV-12A (USA) Single-seat all-weather V/STOL fighter/attack prototype powered by one modified 133.4 kN (30,000 lb st) Pratt & Whitney F401-PW-400 afterburning turbofan engine.

Rogozarski IK-3 (Yugoslavia) Twelve production IK-3 fighters delivered to the Yugoslav Air Force in mid-1940, each powered by a 685.5 kW (920 hp) licence-built Hispano-Suiza 12 engine. Maximum level speed 526 km/h (327 mph).

Rohrbach Rocco and Rostra (Germany) The Rocco of 1927 was a ten-passenger flying-boat powered by two 484.4 kW (650 hp) Rolls-Royce Condor III engines mounted above the monoplane wings. Deutsche Luft-Hansa operated the only example built. The Rostra was basically similar in layout to the Rocco but powered by two 391 kW (525 hp) Gnome-Rhône-built Jupiter VI engines. Unlike the Rocco, its wings were pure cantilever and the stabilising floats were slightly further apart. It was designed as a freight-carrying or postal flying-boat.

Rollason Turbulent.

Rollason Condor.

Rohrbach Roland (Germany) Designed by Dr Ing Adolf Rohrbach, the Roland was a triple-engined airliner of 1926 accommodating ten passengers in a large cabin. Between 1927 and 1929 Deutsche Luft-Hansa received nine Rolands (171.4 kW; 230 hp BMW IV or 238.5 kW; 320 hp BMW Va engines) with enclosed accommodation for the pilots and high-mounted wings.

Rohrbach Romar (Germany) The Romar was basically a larger three-engined version of the Rocco, accommodating 12 passengers in two cabins in the standard version and 16 passengers in the Romar II. Power was provided by 536.5 kW (720 hp) BMW VI engines mounted as pushers. Four Romar/Romar IIs were built: three used by Deutsche Luft-Hansa on its Baltic services and one delivered to the French Navy.

Rollason (Druine) Turbulent and Condor (UK) Licence-built Druine Turbulent (single-

seat) and Condor (two-seat), the former powered by a 33.5 kW (45 hp) 1,500 cc Ardem Mk IV (modified Volkswagen motorcar engine) or 41 kW (55 hp) Ardem Mk V engine.

Rolladen-Schneider LS3 and LS4 (Germany) The LS3 and LS3a are single-seat FAI 15-metre Class sailplanes. The LS3-17 is an extended-span (17-metre) version. The LS4 is a new Standard Class sailplane, first flown in 1979.

Romano R.82 (France) Designed as an aerobatic trainer, the R.82 flew for the first time in prototype form in March 1936. Eventually 150 were built for the Armée de l'Air and 30 for the Aéronavale, powered by 208.6 kW (280 hp) Salmson 9Aba radial engines.

Romeo Ro.1 and Ro.1*bis* (Italy) Licence-built versions of the Fokker C.VD and C.VE with 335.3 kW (450 hp) and 410 kW (550 hp) Bristol Jupiter engines respectively.

Romeo Ro.5 (Italy) Two-seat light high-wing monoplane of the late 1920s powered by a 63.3 kW (85 hp) Fiat A.50 engine or a similarly rated Walter engine in the Ro.5*bis*. A number were purchased by the Italian Air Force (see also **Meridionali**).

RotorWay Scorpion (USA) Basically the production version of the earlier Javelin prototype, which first flew in 1965. The Scorpion is a single-seat light helicopter, plans and kits of components for which were available to amateur constructors.

RotorWay Scorpion Too (USA) Developed from the earlier Scorpion, the Scorpion Too is a two-seat light helicopter. RotorWay offers a package deal which includes components to build the helicopter, the 99 kW (133 hp) RotorWay RW 133 engine (or a turbocharged version) and a complete flight and maintenance training programme.

RotorWay Scorpion Too.

Royal Aircraft Factory B.E.2 (UK) The B.E. designation at first indicated 'Blériot Experimental', Louis Blériot being credited with having originated the tractor-engined aeroplane. With the appearance of aircraft from the Royal Aircraft Establishment it was taken to mean 'British Experimental'.

The original B.E. was designed by and built under the supervision of Geoffrey de Havilland, later Capt de Havilland of the RFC and chief designer for the Air raft Manufacturing Company. A later type of the same general design was the B.E.2, a tandem two-seat biplane with incredibly stable flying characteristics which, in several versions, was employed throughout World War I as a reconnaissance aircraft.

The first version to enter service with the RFC was the B.E.2a, built in very small numbers and the first aircraft to reach France at the outbreak of World War I. Flying alongside a Blériot monoplane, a B.E.2a made the first RFC reconnaissance over German lines on 19 August 1914. The first version built in reasonable numbers was the B.E.2b (which introduced ailerons) followed by the mass-produced B.E.2c which superseded earlier versions from April 1915. Power was provided by a 67 kW (90 hp) RAF 1a engine and wing dihedral was introduced. It was also the first armed version, carrying a machine-gun in the forward cockpit. This gun arrangement greatly restricted the observer's field of fire, which was reversed on the B.E.2d but reintroduced on the final and most numerous version, the B.E.2e.

Royal Aircraft Factory B.E.2e, with machine-gun in forward cockpit.

winter of 1915–16 and again during 'Bloody April' in 1917. In total more than 3,200 B.E.2s were built.

Data (B.E.2c): *Engine* as above *Wing span* 11.28 m (37 ft 0 in) *Length* 8.31 m (27 ft 3 in) *Max T-O weight* 971.5 kg (2,142 lb) *Max level speed* 116 km/h (72 mph) *Endurance* 3 h

Royal Aircraft Factory B.E.8 (UK) Follow-up to the B.E.2 powered by a 59.6 kW (80 hp) Gnome rotary engine. Small numbers served as reconnaissance and then training aircraft with the RFC.

Royal Aircraft Factory B.E.12a.

Royal Aircraft Factory B.E.12 (UK) Built as an interim fighter for 1916, the B.E.12 was basically a more powerful single-seat version of the B.E.2, armed initially with one machine-gun on the upper wing and later two guns in a similar arrangement or one synchronised gun. In combat on the Western Front the early versions proved of little worth and were soon employed more successfully as light bombers. Even with a 149 kW (200 hp) Hispano-Suiza engine, the final B.E.12b was not up to the necessary standard and was transferred for home defence or occasionally anti-submarine duties. Maximum level speed of the 112 kW (150 hp) RAF 4a-powered B.E.12a was 159 km/h (99 mph).

Original Royal Aircraft Factory B.E.2.

Royal Aircraft Factory B.E.2a.

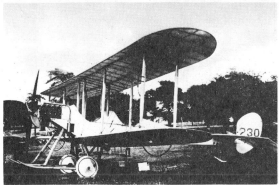

Royal Aircraft Factory F.E.2b.

With the B.E.2d/e in service, the B.E.2c (and earlier versions) was flown as a training aircraft, and a number were employed successfully at home in attacking airships and used on other fronts. Throughout its career the B.E.2 performed very useful work but was over-stable and slow. With the deployment of fighter aircraft, it proved a sitting duck and was the main victim during the so-called 'Fokker Scourge' which lasted the

Royal Aircraft Factory

Royal Aircraft Factory F.E.8.

Royal Aircraft Factory R.E.8s.

Royal Aircraft Factory R.E.7.

Royal Aircraft Factory F.E.2 (UK) The F.E. designation originally indicated 'Farman Experimental', Henry Farman being credited with having originated the pusher type. It was later taken to mean 'Fighter Experimental' and originally applied to a service aircraft in the form of the F.E.2.

Following a handful of F.E.2as, the F.E.2b was built as a two-seat fighting biplane powered by an 89.4 kW (120 hp) or 119 kW (160 hp) Beardmore pusher engine. Production of this version totalled 1,939 aircraft. The observer was accommodated in the lower forward cockpit and armed with forward-firing and rearward-firing Lewis guns. To operate the latter he had to stand up in the cockpit – undoubtedly a difficult firing position with the aircraft in combat. With the D.H.2, the F.E.2b helped subdue the Fokker Eindecker and also performed useful reconnaissance and bombing duties. It formed the initial equipment of No 100 Squadron, the RFC's first squadron created specifically for night bombing. Interestingly No 100's first raid was made on 5 April 1917 on Douai airfield, home of Manfred von Richthofen's élite squadron.

The only other version to enter RFC service was the F.E.2d, powered by a 186.3 kW (250 hp) Rolls-Royce Eagle I engine and with increased fire-power. Just over 250 were built, entering service in the latter half of 1916. By mid-1917 the fighter's main role had changed to home defence, being used to intercept Zeppelin airships and Gotha heavy bombers.
Data (F.E.2b): *Engine* as above *Wing span* 14.55 m (47 ft 9 in) *Length* 9.83 m (32 ft 3 in) *Max T-O weight* 1,377.5 kg (3,037 lb) *Max level speed* 146 km/h (91 mph) *Range* 400 km (248 miles)
Royal Aircraft Factory F.E.8 (UK) Single-seat biplane fighter of 1916 powered by a 74.5 kW (100 hp) Gnome Monosoupape rotary engine.

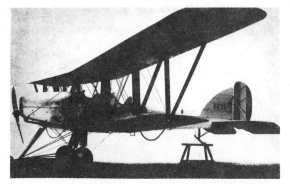

More than 180 served with the RFC but were obsolete. Maximum level speed was 151 km/h (94 mph).
Royal Aircraft Factory R.E. 5 (UK) The R.E. designation indicated 'Reconnaissance Experimental' and the R.E.5, only 24 of which were built for the RFC, was operated successfully as a reconnaissance and light-bombing biplane during the early stages of World War I. Power was provided by an 89.4 kW (120 hp) engine, giving a maximum speed of 125 km/h (78 mph).
Royal Aircraft Factory R.E.7 (UK) Used mainly by the RFC during 1916, the R.E.7 was a two-seat (later occasionally three-seat) bombing biplane powered by a 112 kW (150 hp) RAF 4a engine. Two hundred and fifty were completed. Maximum level speed was 137 km/h (85 mph).
Royal Aircraft Factory R.E.8 (UK) Known as the 'Harry Tate', the R.E.8 looked a little like a scaled-up B.E.2. During the course of the latter half of World War I no less than 4,077 were built for the RFC/RAF and a few for Belgium. R.E.8s for British service standardised on the 112 kW (150 hp) RAF 4a engine. During a brief spell on the Western Front in late 1916 several were lost through accidents, resulting in their temporary withdrawal. However from early 1917 the aircraft settled to a steady career as a reconnaissance aircraft and light bomber on the Western Front and in Palestine and Italy, remaining active until the Armistice.
Data: *Engine* as above *Wing span* 12.98 m (42 ft 7 in) *Length* 8.5 m (27 ft 10½ in) *Max T-O weight* 1,215 kg (2,678 lb) *Max level speed* 164 km/h (102 mph) *Endurance* 4 h 15 min *Armament* one forward-firing Vickers and one/two rear-mounted Lewis machine-guns, plus 118 kg (260 lb) of bombs

Royal Aircraft Factory S.E.5 and S.E.5a (UK) The S.E. designation indicated 'Scouting Experimental' and was first applied to an operational aircraft as the S.E.2a, which flew with the RFC in the early months of World War I.

The S.E.5 first appeared in 1916 and was the Royal Aircraft Factory's long-awaited single-seat tractor-engined fighter proper. Unlike most Allied fighters of the period, it was powered by an in-line engine which made it a much easier aircraft for an inexperienced pilot to fly. Early production aircraft (with 112 kW; 150 hp Hispano-Suiza engines) became operational in the first half of 1917, joined soon after by the more powerful S.E.5a. They quickly made an impression over the Western Front in the skilled hands of pilots like Albert Ball (the RFC's first great ace of the

war), James McCudden and top ace Edward Mannock (73 victories). The movable Lewis gun mounted on the upper wing proved a most useful weapon for 'blasting' enemy aircraft from below. Various engines were fitted to the S.E.5a. Production of both fighters totalled more than 5,200 by the Armistice.

Data (S.E.5a): *Engine* one 149 kW (200 hp) Wolseley Viper or 149–179 kW (200–240 hp) Hispano-Suiza *Wing span* 8.11 m (26 ft 7½ in) *Length* 6.38 m (20 ft 11 in) *Max T-O weight* 902 kg (1,988 lb) *Max level speed* 222 km/h (138 mph) *Range* 547 km (340 miles) *Armament* one Vickers and one Lewis machine-guns

Rumpler 6B (Germany) Single-seat twin-float fighter biplane of 1916, powered by a 119 kW (160 hp) Mercedes D.III engine. About ninety built, each armed with one Spandau machine-gun.

Rumpler B.I (Germany) Two-seat unarmed reconnaissance aircraft powered by a 74.5 kW (100 hp) Mercedes D.I engine. One hundred and ninety-eight were built, serving on Western and Eastern Fronts for the first year or so of World War I.

Rumpler C.I (Germany) Armed and more powerful version of the B.I, entering service in 1915.

The C.I and C.Ia reconnaissance and light-bombing versions were powered by 119 kW (160 hp) Mercedes D.III and 134 kW (180 hp) Argus As.III engines respectively; while a later training variant standardised on the 112 kW (150 hp) Benz Bz.III. Armament comprised initially one rear-mounted Parabellum machine-gun, supplemented eventually by a forward-firing Spandau. Several hundred C.I-series aircraft were built. Maximum level speed of the C.I was 150 km/h (93 mph).

After the war a number of C.Is were converted for commercial passenger carrying. According to the 1920 *Jane's* the C.I was the first biplane to be provided with a radiator below the trailing edge of the upper wing, in the propeller slipstream.

Rumpler C.III to C.VII (Germany) The 164 kW (220 hp) Benz Bz.IV-engined C.III appeared in 1917 as a two-seat reconnaissance biplane developed from the earlier C.I but with many revisions improving both appearance and performance. It was not a success and was superseded by the much improved and acclaimed C.IV, which had a 194 kW (260 hp) Mercedes

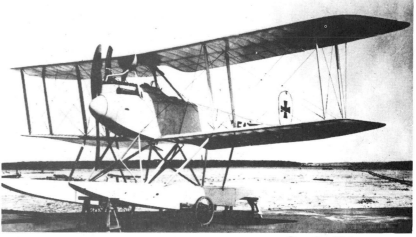

Rumpler 6B-1.

D.IV engine and re-contoured wings. It was the first Rumpler to be fitted with an inverted-camber tailplane. Used on the Western Front and elsewhere, the C.IV was only bettered by the 179 kW (240 hp) Maybach Mb.IV-engined C.VII. One sub-variant of the C.VII (known as the *Rubild*) used a high-compression engine for high-altitude photographic-reconnaissance duties. The C.VII was the main German long-distance reconnaissance aircraft at the end of the war. Meanwhile the C.V had also entered service with a D.IV engine. After the war the C.IV was operated as a commercial passenger type.

Data (C.IV): *Engine* as above *Wing span* 12.65 m (41 ft 6 in) *Length* 8.4 m (27 ft 7 in) *Max T-O weight* 1,530 kg (3,373 lb) *Max level speed* 170 km/h (105.5 mph) *Endurance* 3 h 30 min *Armament* one forward-firing Spandau and one rear-mounted Parabellum machine-gun, plus up to 100 kg (220 lb) of bombs

Rumpler C.VIII (Germany) Two-seat training biplane of 1917 powered by a 134 kW (180 hp) Argus As.III engine.

Rumpler D.I (Germany) Single-seat fighter powered by a 134 kW (180 hp) Mercedes D.IIIa

Royal Aircraft Factory S.E.5as.

Wing-mounted Lewis gun on a Royal Aircraft Factory S.E.5a.

Rumpler-built Taube.

Rutan VariEze.

RWD-5 bis.

Rutan Defiant.

engine: the outcome of seven preceding different experimental aircraft devoted to weight and resistance saving. A small number of production aircraft were built in 1918 but did not become operational (a full description appears in the 1920 *Jane's*).

Rumpler G types (Germany) It is a curious fact that no example of the Rumpler G type twin-engined bomber was captured or traced during World War I, in spite of its engagement on active service on all fronts. The G.I appeared in 1915 and was probably the major production version, 58 being completed. It was a large three-seat biplane powered by two 112 kW (150 hp) Benz Bz.III or later 119 kW (160 hp) Mercedes D.III engines mounted as pushers. In March 1915 a Benz-powered example made several high-altitude demonstration flights with 12–16 passengers, reaching 2,400 m (7,875 ft) in 55 minutes with 12 people.

The G.I was followed into service by the 164 kW (220 hp) Benz Bz.IV-powered G.II and 194 kW (260 hp) Mercedes D.IVa-powered G.III, some of which remained operational into 1918. Maximum level speed of the G.I was 146 km/h (91 mph).

Rutan VariViggen.

Rutan Defiant (USA) Four-seat twin 119 kW (160 hp) Lycoming O-320-engined light aircraft of 'push and pull' configuration, with rear-mounted swept cantilever wings (with 'winglet' surfaces) and a canard foreplane. First flown in June 1978.

Rutan VariViggen (USA) Two-seat (or 2 + 2) light aircraft with cropped delta wings, plans for which are available to amateur constructors (900 sets sold by early 1979).

Rutan VariEze (USA) Two-seat high-performance sporting aircraft of tail-first configuration, plans for which are available to amateur constructors (about 2,000 sets sold by early 1979).

RWD types (Poland) RWD aeroplanes were originally produced by the Aeronautical Section of the Technical High School at Warsaw, the letters RWD standing for the initials of the designers Rogalski, Wigura and Drzewiecki. Among the first aircraft built was the RWD-5 (78.25 kW; 105 hp Cirrus-Hermes engine) which became famous for its flight across the South Atlantic from Dakar to Natal.

In 1933 the Doswiadczalne Warsztaty Lotnicze was formed to take over the assets and liabilities of the Aeronautical Section and to continue the construction of RWD aircraft. Then followed the RWD-8 two-seat training monoplane (82 kW; 110 hp Walter Junior or Skoda engine), the licence for which was acquired by the Polish government and was built in quantity at the government factory and also under licence in Estonia and Yugoslavia; the RWD-9, which was specially designed for, and won, the 1934 Challenge de Tourisme International; the RWD-10 single-seat aerobatic trainer; RWD-13 three-seat cabin monoplane, which was successful at the 1937 Zurich meeting; the RWD-14 (see **LWS**); RWD-15 four-seat cabin monoplane; and subsequent open-cockpit and cabin monoplanes for training and touring, including the two-seat RWD-19, RWD-21 and RWD-23.

Ryan B.1 Brougham (USA) The B.1 Brougham was a five-seat cabin monoplane which was basically a commercial version of Lindbergh's *Spirit of St Louis* (although actually designed as a cabin version of the M-1). It was powered by a 168 kW

Ryan B.1 Brougham.

(225 hp) Wright J-5 Whirlwind radial engine. In 1928 production rate was 20 a month and the 150 B-1 Broughams produced were sold to customers in the USA and exported. The price in 1928 was $12,200.

Data: *Engine* as above *Wing span* 12.8 m (42 ft 0 in) *Length* 8.46 m (27 ft 9 in) *Max T-O weight* 1,497 kg (3,300 lb) *Max level speed* 203 km/h (126 mph)

Ryan B.3, B.5 and B.7 Brougham (USA) The B.3 of 1928 was basically an enlarged six-seat version of the B.1, nine of which were constructed. The B.5 (61 built) and B.7 (8 built) were similar to the B.3 except for power plants and slight changes to the fuselage lengths and tail surface areas. They were produced in 1929 prior to the introduction of the Foursome. Power was provided by a 223.6 kW (300 hp) Wright J-6 and a 313 kW (420 hp) Pratt & Whitney Wasp engine respectively.

Ryan C.1 Foursome (USA) The Foursome was a smaller version of the Brougham with seating for four on deeply upholstered car-type seats and an improved control system. Power was provided by a 179 kW (240 hp) Wright J-6 engine. Three were constructed.

Ryan Cloudster (USA) Modification of the Douglas Cloudster accommodating ten passengers in a large cabin.

Ryan FR-1 Fireball (USA) The Ryan Model 28 Fireball single-seat fighter was the first aircraft to be put into production with a combined power plant of a conventional piston engine driving a propeller and a turbojet engine (in the rear fuselage). Design work began in 1943 and production was proceeding at the time of the Japanese capitulation. On 6 November 1945 a Fireball (with its piston engine unserviceable) made a successful landing on the deck of the aircraft carrier USS *Wake Island* off San Diego, using only its turbojet engine: this was claimed to be the first occasion on which a pure-jet landing was made on a carrier.

The prototype XFR-1 was powered by a 1,006 kW (1,350 hp) Wright R-1820-72W piston engine and a 7.12 kN (1,600 lb st) General Electric I-16 (J-31) turbojet, first flying on 25 June 1944. The production version was the FR-1 which was similarly powered. Only 66 were built – the remaining 634 FR-1s on order being cancelled at the end of World War II. These served with the US Navy until the end of 1947, finally on board USS *Badoeng Strait*.

Data: *Engines* as above *Wing span* 12.19 m (40 ft 0 in) *Length* 9.86 m (32 ft 4 in) *Max T-O weight* 5,285 kg (11,650 lb) *Max level speed* 684 km/h (425 mph) *Normal range* 1,658–2,607 km (1,030–1,620 miles) *Armament* four 0.50 in Browning machine-guns, plus up to 454 kg (1,000 lb) of bombs or rocket projectiles

Ryan Navion (USA) The Navion was designed by North American Aviation. Two versions were subsequently produced by Ryan: one as the Navion A with a 153 kW (205 hp) Continental E-185-3 or -9 engine; the other as the Navion B or Super 260 with a 194 kW (260 hp) Lycoming GO-435-C2 engine. Total production was 1,238 aircraft.

The Navion was also used as a liaison and

Ryan B.5 Brougham.

Ryan FR-1 Fireball.

Ryan Navion.

observation aircraft by the US Army and Air National Guard. These aircraft carried the designation L-17B (163 built) and were powered by the E-185-3 engine (the L-17A having been built earlier by North American Aviation). The L-17C was a modification of the L-17A by Ryan (35 produced). L-17s were operated during the Korean War.

Data (Super 260): *Engine* as above *Wing span* 10.19 m (33 ft 5 in) *Length* 8.38 m (27 ft 6 in) *Max T-O weight* 1,293 kg (2,850 lb) *Max level speed* 280 km/h (174 mph)

Ryan S-T, ST and PT series (USA) In 1927 Mr T. Claude Ryan severed his connections with the original Ryan Company but continued to operate the Ryan School of Aeronautics which he had established in 1922. In 1933 he saw an opportunity to re-enter the manufacturing field and developed the S-T (Sport-Trainer) tandem two-seat open-cockpit monoplane, five of which were built.

Ryan STM.

Ryan PT-20.

Ryan PT-22-type seaplane for the Dutch Navy.

From the S-T Ryan developed the 92 kW (125 hp) Menasco C-4-engined STA (71 built); 112 kW (150 hp) STA Special (11 built); and STM. The latter was produced as the single-seat STM lightweight fighter or advanced trainer powered by the same Menasco C-4S engine as the STA Special (small numbers exported to Bolivia, Ecuador, Guatemala, Honduras, Mexico and Nicaragua), two-seat STM-2 and STM-S2 (108 built as landplanes and seaplanes for the Netherlands East Indies), and STM-2E/P (50 built for China).

Meanwhile the Ryan Company had been one of the three firms selected by the US government for the mass production of military training aircraft under a type standardisation programme: it was the first to manufacture in quantity an all-metal low-wing primary trainer for the US forces. Following the XPT-16 prototype for the USAAF (first flown on 3 February 1939), Ryan built 15 service evaluation YPT-16s; 40 PT-20s (most of which had their Menasco L-365-1 engine replaced by a similarly rated Kinner, becoming P-20As); 100 PT-21s and 100 NR-1s for the USAAF and US Navy respectively (98.4 kW; 132 hp Kinner R-440-3 engines and similar to the experimental ST-3 prototypes); and 1,048 PT-22 Recruits (119 kW; 160 hp Kinner R-540-1 engines) including 25 for the Dutch Navy.

Ryan M-1.

The PT-22 was also based on the ST-3 and remained in production until 1942, when the Ryan Company produced the ST-4 (PT-25). This was a new two-seater built almost entirely of plastic-bonded wood as a result of a request to convert the PT-22 all-metal trainer to non-strategic materials in order to release essential metals for more urgent purposes. The PT-25 type failed to enter production.

Data (PT-22): *Engine* as above *Wing span* 9.17 m (30 ft 1 in) *Length* 6.83 m (22 ft 5 in) *Max T-O weight* 844 kg (1,860 lb) *Max level speed* 211 km/h (131 mph) *Range* 566 km (352 miles)

Ryan M-1 (USA) The first M-1 high-wing monoplane flew on 14 February 1926. A total of 16 was built, the most successful being the nine 149 kW (200 hp) Wright J-4B Whirlwind-powered mailplanes, each accommodating a pilot and mail or two passengers (a full description appears in the 1927 *Jane's*). Whirlwind-powered M-1s were used by Pacific Air Transport on the Seattle–Los Angeles mail route and by Colorado Airways on the Cheyenne–Pueblo mail route. Maximum level speed was 209 km/h (130 mph).

Ryan M-2 (USA) Approximately 21 M-2s were built and were similar in most respects to the early M-1s, being two-seaters powered by Wright-built Hispano-Suiza or other engines in the 112–149 kW (150–200 hp) range.

Ryan NYP (USA) Only one NYP was built: this was the aircraft used by Lindbergh on his solo transatlantic flight. First flown on 28 April 1927, it was a special improved version of the M-1 powered by a 176.6 kW (237 hp) Wright J-5C Whirlwind radial engine. Accommodation was provided for a pilot only – a large-capacity auxiliary fuel tank occupying the forward fuselage and completely obscuring direct forward vision. In a flying time of 33 hours 39 minutes, Lindbergh completed his transatlantic flight between New York and Paris, winning the $25,000 prize offered by the hotelier Raymond Orteig and the admiration of the world (see **Chronology** 20–21 May 1927; a full description of the NYP appears in the 1927 *Jane's*).

Ryan S-C (USA) Three-seat cabin monoplane powered by a 108 kW (145 hp) Warner Super Scarab engine. Ten production aircraft were built from 1938.

Ryan Standard (USA) Modification of Curtiss biplanes, produced as four-passenger commercial aircraft, each powered by a 112 kW (150 hp) Hispano-Suiza engine. Nine completed in 1922.

Ryan VZ-3RY Vertiplane (USA) V/STOL research aircraft, first flown on 7 February 1958.

Ryan X-13 Vertijet (USA) Rolls-Royce Avon turbojet-powered VTOL research aircraft designed to take off in a vertical attitude from a special mobile ground servicing trailer. First flown on 10 December 1955.

Ryan XF2R-1 (USA) Experimental fighter used to gain experience with the XT31-GE-2 (TG-100) engine. First flown in November 1946.

Ryan XV-5A/B (USA) 'Fan-in-wing' VTOL research aircraft, first flown on 25 May 1964.

Saab 17 (Sweden) The Saab 17 was the first aircraft to be designed and built by Saab. It was

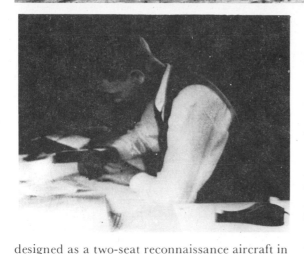

and faster Saab 18B powered by Swedish-built DB 605B engines; with a speed of 570 km/h (354 mph) at the time of its appearance, it was one of the world's fastest twin-engined all-metal bombers.

A third version (designated T 18B) with the DB 605B engines – but with increased armament – was also produced in quantity before production ceased in 1948. Several Heavy Attack Wings of the Swedish Air Force were equipped with Saab 18Bs and T 18Bs. Subsequently the Saab 18A was converted for reconnaissance duties only. All were withdrawn by 1956.
Data (T 18B): *Engines* two 1,099 kW (1,475 hp) Swedish-built Daimler-Benz DB 605Bs *Wing span* 17.0 m (55 ft 9½ in) *Length* 13.2 m (43 ft 5 in) *Max T-O weight* 8,800 kg (19,400 lb) *Max level speed* 575 km/h (357 mph) *Max range* 2,600 km (1,616 miles) *Armament* two 13.2 mm and one 7.9 mm machine-guns, plus 1,500 kg (3,306 lb) of bombs, rocket projectiles or a torpedo. The T 18B was subsequently fitted with a 57 mm Bofors cannon

designed as a two-seat reconnaissance aircraft in 1938 but in the following year was redesigned as a dive-bomber. The first prototype flew on 23 May 1940 and production for the Swedish Air Force started soon afterwards. Large numbers were built as dive-bombers, bombers and reconnaissance aircraft with different engines. The type remained in service into the 1950s although out of first-line use. In 1947 16 Saab 17A light bombers were supplied to the Royal Ethiopian Air Force.
Data: *Engine* one 793.6 kW (1,065 hp) Swedish-built Pratt & Whitney R-1830-S1C3G radial, (17B) Bristol Mercury 24, (17C) Piaggio P.XI*bis Wing span* 13.75 m (45 ft 1 in) *Length* 10.0 m (32 ft 10 in) *Max T-O weight* 3,790 kg (8,356 lb) *Max level speed* 435 km/h (270 mph)
Saab 18 (Sweden) The original version of the Saab 18 attack bomber first appeared in 1942, powered by two Swedish-built R-1830 Twin Wasp engines. It was followed in 1944 by the new

Saab 21A (Sweden) Single-seat fighter and attack aircraft, first revealed in 1945. It was the only pusher-engined fighter in the world to reach the production stage during World War II. The last of 299 was delivered in 1948.
Data: *Engine* one 1,099 kW (1,475 hp) SFA licence-built DB 605B mounted as a pusher in the aft central nacelle *Wing span* 11.6 m (38 ft 1 in) *Length* 10.45 m (34 ft 3 in) *Max T-O weight* 4,150 kg (9,149 lb) *Max level speed* 640 km/h (398 mph) *Armament* one 20 mm cannon and two 13.2 mm machine-guns in the nose and two 13.2 mm wing guns. Provision for an eight-gun pack and rockets in A 21A attack model
Saab 21R (Sweden) First flown on 10 March 1947, the Saab 21R was the first jet fighter to be designed and built in Sweden. Production aircraft built for the Swedish Air Force (based on the Saab

Saab

Saab 17s.

S 18A reconnaissance version of the Saab 18.

B 18B version of the Saab 18.

Saab 21A.

Saab 21Rs.

21A-type airframe) were powered by de Havilland Goblin turbojet engines. Maximum level speed was 800 km/h (497 mph).

Saab 29 (Sweden) The Saab 29 was the first swept-wing jet fighter to be put into large-scale production in Western Europe. The first of three prototypes was test-flown on 1 September 1948, powered by a de Havilland Ghost turbojet engine; a series prototype was flown in July 1950. All production aircraft were fitted with 22.24 kN (5,000 lb st) Ghost engines built under licence in Sweden; the Saab 29F was fitted with an afterburner.

The first production version was the J 29A, followed in 1953 by the J 29B with increased internal fuel tankage; A 29 attack aircraft; S 29C photographic-reconnaissance version; J 29D and E experimental aircraft; and the J 29F interceptor fighter, the fifth and last production version.

Data: (J 29B): *Engine* as above *Wing span* 11.0 m (36 ft 1 in) *Length* 10.13 m (33 ft 2½ in) *Normal T-O weight* 6,060 kg (13,360 lb) *Max level speed*

1,060 km/h (659 mph) *Max range* 2,700 km (1,678 miles) *Armament* four 20 mm cannon, plus rockets

Saab 32 Lansen (Sweden) First flown as a prototype on 3 November 1952, the Lansen jet-powered aircraft was designed to the requirements of the Swedish Air Force. The first production version was the A 32A, an all-weather attack aircraft powered by a 44.1 kN (9,920 lb st) Swedish-built Rolls-Royce Avon 100-series turbojet engine. The J 32B was produced as the all-weather fighter and night-fighter version with a 67.6 kN (15,200 lb st, with afterburning) Avon 200-series turbojet, while the S 32C was produced for photographic-reconnaissance duties. The A 32A and S 32C remain in service.

Data (A 32A): *Engine* as above *Wing span* 13.0 m (42 ft 7¾ in) *Length* 14.65 m (48 ft 0¾ in) *Max T-O weight* 13,000 kg (28,660 lb) *Max level speed* 1,125 km/h (700 mph) *Max range* 3,220 km (2,000 miles) *Armament* four 20 mm Hispano cannon, plus two RB04 air-to-surface missiles, 24 rockets or up to 1,000 kg (2,205 lb) of bombs

Saab 35 Draken (Sweden) The Saab 35 Draken single-seat fighter was designed mainly to intercept bombers in the transonic speed range. It is, however, able to carry substantial weapon loads for attack duties or cameras for photographic reconnaissance.

The Draken is of the 'double delta' configuration (developed exclusively in Sweden) which provides large space for fuel, armament and equipment, in combination with low structure weight, low drag and a high air-intake efficiency. The first of three prototypes of the Saab 35 made its maiden flight on 25 October 1955. During 1956 the aircraft was ordered into quantity production and the first production Saab 35A (J 35A) flew on 15 February 1958. Several versions of the Draken have been built and are listed below:

J 35A Initial production version with Svenska Flygmotor RM6B (Rolls-Royce Avon 200 series) turbojet and Swedish-developed afterburner, giving approximately 64 kN (14,400 lb st) with afterburner. It entered service with the

Piper PA-17 Vagabond.

Republic F-105
Thunderchiefs.

Rockwell Alpine
Commander (foreground),
Turbo Commander 690B
(centre) and Shrike
Commander 500S.

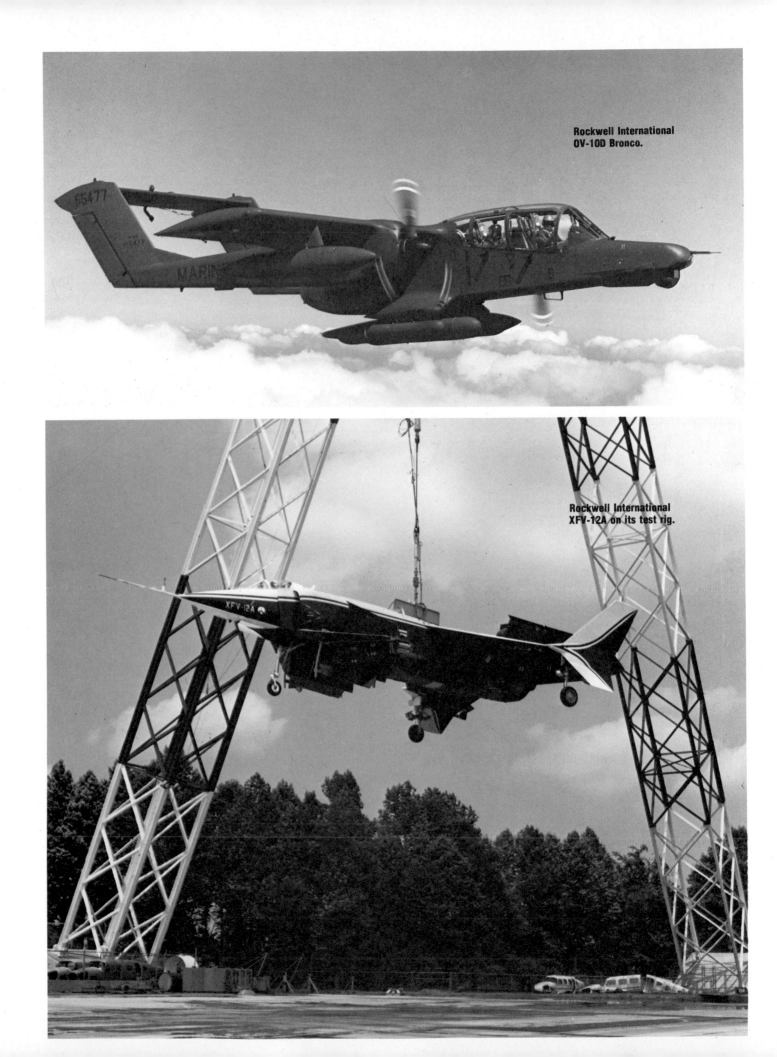

Rockwell International
OV-10D Bronco.

Rockwell International
XFV-12A on its test rig.

RotorWay Scorpion Toos.

Saab 32 Lansens.

Saab SF 37 Viggen.

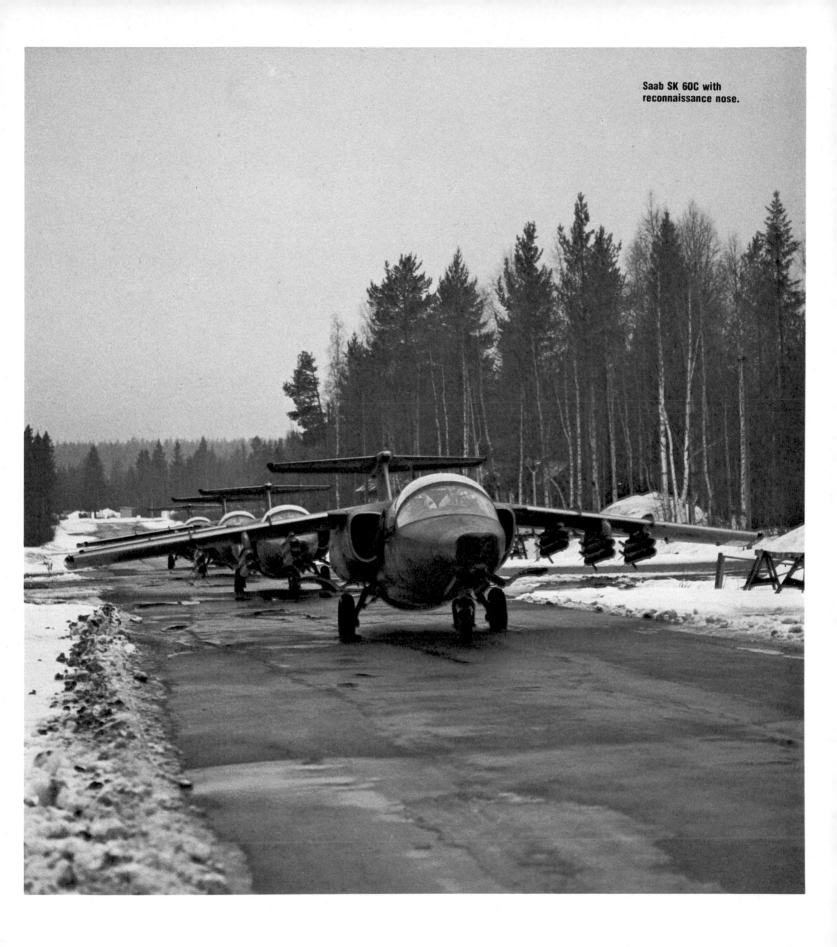

Saab SK 60C with reconnaissance nose.

Saab Safari.

Saab A 32As.

Saab 210, built and flown to evaluate the double-delta configuration.

Swedish Air Force early in 1960. An aerodynamically improved and lengthened rear fuselage, with dual tail wheel unit to facilitate aerodynamic braking during landing, was introduced on this version during 1960. Some were converted to SK 35Cs; most of the others were converted to J 35B standard. No longer operational.

J 35B Development of J 35A with Saab S7 collision-course fire-control system and electronic equipment designed especially for integration with Sweden's semi-automatic air-defence control system. The J 35B first flew on 29 November 1959. No longer operational.

SK 35C Two-seat dual-control trainer version of J 35A with different front fuselage. Same weapons capability as tactical versions. The first SK 35C flew on 30 December 1959.

J 35D Development of J 35B with more powerful Flygmotor RM6C (Rolls-Royce RB 146 Series 300 Avon) turbojet engine. Increased fuel capacity. First flew on 27 December 1960. No longer operational.

S 35E Reconnaissance version based on J 35D with a total of seven cameras for use at all heights. First S 35E flew on 27 June 1963. It has been in service since late 1965.

J 35F Development of J 35D with normal armament of two Saab-produced Rb 27 Falcon HM-55 (radar-guided) and two Rb 28 Falcon HM-58 (infra-red) air-to-air missiles. Infra-red target seeker in fairing under nose. One 30 mm Aden M/55 cannon in starboard wing. Ordered in greater numbers than any other version and built in large numbers as the final Swedish Air Force version.

Saab 35X Export version (35XD for Denmark, 35S for Finland) for tactical strike and reconnaissance. Increased internal fuel and external

Saab S 35E Draken.

weapons load (maximum 4,500 kg; 9,920 lb). Danish Air Force designations F-35 (fighter), RF-35 (reconnaissance) and TF-35 (trainer).

Data (Saab 35S Draken): *Engine* one 78.5 kN (17,650 lb st, with afterburning) Volvo Flygmotor RM6C (Rolls-Royce Avon 300 series) turbojet *Wing span* 9.4 m (30 ft 10 in) *Length* 15.35 m (50 ft 4 in) *Max overload weight* 16,000 kg (35,275 lb) *Max level speed* 2,124 km/h (1,320 mph) *Radius of action* 1,003 km (623 miles) *Armament* nine attachment points (each 454 kg; 1,000 lb) for external stores: three under each wing and three under fuselage. Stores can consist of air-to-air missiles and pods of unguided air-to-air rockets (19 ×7.5 cm), 12 × 13.5 cm Bofors air-to-ground rockets, nine 1,000 lb or 14 × 500 lb bombs, or fuel tanks. Two or four RB24 (Sidewinder) air-to-air missiles can be carried under wings and fuselage. Two 30 mm Aden cannon (one in each wing) can be replaced by extra internal fuel tanks. With two 1,275 litre (280 Imp gal) and two 500 litre (100 Imp gal) drop-tanks, two 1,000 lb or four 500 lb bombs can be carried.

Saab 37 Viggen (Sweden) The Saab 37 Viggen multi-mission combat aircraft can be readily adapted to fulfil the four primary roles of attack,

Saab J 29Fs.

Saab

Saab AJ 37 Viggen.

Saab 90 Scandia.

Saab 91B Safir.

Saab 105Ö delivered to Austria.

interception, reconnaissance and training. The aircraft has an advanced aerodynamic configuration, using a foreplane fitted with flaps in combination with a main delta wing to confer STOL characteristics.

The first of seven prototypes flew on 8 February 1967 and by April 1969 all six single-seat prototypes were flying. The seventh Viggen was the prototype for the two-seat SK 37 operational trainer.

The AJ 37 is the single-seat all-weather attack version with secondary interceptor capability. It was the initial production version. The JA 37 is the single-seat interceptor, with Volvo Flygmotor RM8B engine, of improved performance and with secondary capability for attack missions. An initial batch of 30 JA 37s was ordered in September 1974, out of a planned total procurement of 149 to re-equip eight or more Draken fighter squadrons of the Swedish Air Force in 1978–85. Two further batches (60 and 59) were ordered in May 1978. First flight by a production JA 37 was made on 4 November 1977. Deliveries began in 1979.

The SF 37 and SH 37 are single-seat all-weather armed photographic-reconnaissance and single-seat maritime-reconnaissance versions of the Viggen respectively: the former produced as a replacement for the S 35E Draken and the latter as a replacement for the S 32C version of the Lansen. The SK 37 is the tandem two-seat dual-control trainer. Proposed versions of the Viggen are the Saab 37X export version – essentially similar to the JA 37 – and the A 20 attack version.

Initially 175 aircraft of the AJ 37, SF/SH 37 and SK 37 versions were ordered for the Swedish Air Force; in December 1973 it was announced that five or more aircraft (AJ 37s) were to be built within the same overall budget cost. More than 200 Viggens had been delivered of the 329 on order by mid-1979.

Data (AJ 37): *Engine* one 115.7 kN (26,015 lb st, with afterburning) Volvo Flygmotor RM8A turbofan *Wing span* 10.6 m (34 ft 9¼ in) *Length* 16.3 m (53 ft 5¾ in) *Max T-O weight* 15,000–20,500 kg (33,070–45,195 lb) *Max level speed* above Mach 2 *Tactical radius* over 1,000 km (620 miles) *Armament* primary armament is the Swedish RB04E air-to-surface homing missile for use against naval targets; or the Saab RB05A air-to-surface missile for use against ground, naval and certain airborne targets. To these can be added pods of Bofors 135 mm air-to-surface rockets, up to 16 bombs, or 30 mm Aden gun pods. The AJ 37 version can be adapted to perform interception missions armed with RB24 (Sidewinder) or RB28 (Falcon) air-to-air missiles. Armament of the JA 37 is an underbelly pack containing one 30 mm Oerlikon KCA long-range cannon, plus medium- and short-range homing air-to-air missiles

Saab 90 Scandia (Sweden) The Scandia twin-engined airliner was originally conceived in 1944 and made its first flight on 16 November 1946. SAS and VASP took delivery of production aircraft for services in Europe and Brazil respectively. Power was provided by two 1,341 kW (1,800 hp) Pratt & Whitney R-2180-E1 Twin Wasp radial engines and accommodation was for 24–32 passengers.

Saab 91 Safir (Sweden) Four-seat cabin monoplane, first flown on 20 November 1945. About 320 Safirs were sold to customers in 20 countries, including some equipped as executive transports and others used by air forces and for airline pilot training. The Saab 91B was powered by a 141.5 kW (190 hp) Lycoming O-435-A engine, but the final production version (the Saab 91D) had a 134 kW (180 hp) Lycoming O-350-A1A engine fitted.

Saab 105 (Sweden) The Saab 105 twin-jet multi-purpose military aircraft was designed originally for training and ground-attack duties, with reconnaissance, target flying and liaison as secondary roles. It normally seats two pilots side-by-side on ejection seats; four-seats can be fitted in place of the ejection seats. The first prototype flew on 29 June 1963.

Seven versions were built, of which the SK 60A, B and C (150 built) went to the Swedish Air Force. The Saab 105Ö was the export version delivered to Austria.

Data (SK 60A): *Engines* two 7.29 kN (1,640 lb st) Turboméca Aubisque turbofans *Wing span* 9.5 m (31 ft 2 in) *Length* 10.5 m (34 ft 5 in) *Max T-O weight* 4,500 kg (9,920 lb) *Max level speed* 770 km/h (478 mph) *Range* 1,780 km (1,106 miles) *Armament* six underwing attachment points for up to 700 kg (1,543 lb) of weapons, including two 30 mm gun pods, 12 × 13.5 cm rockets or two RB05 air-to-surface missiles.

Saab Safari TS (Sweden) The prototype Safari two–three-seat light monoplane flew for the first time on 11 July 1969. The initial production version, with a 149 kW (200 hp) Lycoming IO-360-A1B6 engine, was superseded by the current Safari TS in 1978, powered by a 157 kW (210 hp) Continental turbocharged engine.

Saab Supporter (Sweden) First flown in 1972, the Supporter is basically a Safari with the ability to carry weapons on six underwing hardpoints for military training, ground air control, reconnaissance, artillery observation, liaison and target-towing duties.

SABCA S.2 (Belgium) Four-passenger high-wing commercial transport of 1926, a single example of which was operated by Sabena.

SABCA S.40 E (Belgium). Two-seat light training monoplane powered by a 104.3 kW (140 hp) Renault 4 Pei engine. Adopted by the Belgian Air Force.

Saab Supporters in Pakistani Air Force markings.

Sablatnig P.I.

Sablatnig N.I and P.I (Germany) Wartime Sablatnig floatplanes were also built under licence by LVG and LFG and their success led (towards the end of the war) to the building of N-class two-seat night-bombing landplanes powered by Argus, Benz and Maybach engines. It is possible that a small number of N.I.s were delivered for operational use, but this cannot be substantiated. A modification of the N.I design was produced after the war as the four-seat P.I, a very small number of which were operated commercially by Danish Air Express and Lloyd-Luftverkehr Sablatnig.

Sablatnig P.III (Germany) The P.III was a purpose-built parasol-wing commercial aircraft accommodating six passengers. Small numbers were operated by Lloyd-Luftverkehr Sablatnig, Deutsche Luft-Hansa, Danish Air Express, Aeronaut (of Estonia) and the Swiss Air Force.

Sablatnig SF floatplanes (Germany) Josef Sablatnig designed his first aircraft for the German Navy as the SF-1, a two-seat reconnaissance floatplane powered by a 119 kW (160 hp) Mercedes engine. Maximum speed was 125 km/h (77.5 mph) and it could climb to 1,000 m in about ten minutes. This effort resulted in the formation of the Sablatnig aircraft firm in October 1915. Although the SF-1 remained a prototype only, 26 similarly powered SF-2s, 91 112 kW (150 hp) Benz Bz.III-powered SF-5s and 33 Benz Bz.III-powered SF-8s followed, being used as reconnaissance aircraft and trainers from 1916 until the end of the war.

Saiman 200, 202 and 204 (Italy) Two-seat training biplane (149 kW; 200 hp Alfa 115-I engine), two-seat cabin monoplane (89.4 kW; 120 hp Alfa 110) and four-seat cabin monoplane (134 kW; 180 hp Alfa 115) respectively, a number of which were produced for civil use and others delivered to the Regia Aeronautica.

Saab Safari.

Salmson

Salmson 2A.2.

Full-scale representation of the Salyut 3/4 type of space station.

Santos-Dumont 14*bis*.

Cosmonauts at the central control panel of Salyut 4.

Salmson 2A.2 (France) The Salmson 2A.2 was a two-seat reconnaissance aircraft, first flown in April 1917. Armament comprised one forward-firing 0.303 in Vickers machine-gun and two rear-mounted Lewis guns. Power was provided by a 194 kW (160 hp) Salmson-built Canton-Unné radial engine which gave a maximum speed equal to that of most contemporary single-seat fighters. Strong construction (with an all-moving tail unit) and good manoeuvrability enabled the aircraft to be flown as a two-seat fighter or light bomber when required – the pilot's excellent forward view from his cockpit under the leading edge of the upper wing helping in this respect.

A total of about 3,200 2A.2s was built. Most went to French escadrilles, although 705 were delivered to the AEF as observation aircraft. After the war the type was licence-built in Japan, while ex-military examples were used as makeshift commercial airliners, often with enclosed accommodation for two passengers.
Data: *Engine* as above *Wing span* 11.8 m (38 ft 8¾ in) *Length* 8.5 m (27 ft 10½ in) *Max T-O weight* 1,340 kg (2,954 lb) *Max level speed* 185 km/h (115 mph) *Endurance* 3 h

Salmson-Moineau SM-1 (France) Unsuccessful and ugly reconnaissance biplane of 1916 powered by a Salmson-built Canton-Unné radial engine driving two tractor propellers. A very small number became operational for a brief period.

Salmson Cri-Cri (France) Two-seat parasol-wing training monoplane of 1936 produced in large numbers for the 'Aviation Populaire' movement. Power was provided by a 44.7 kW (60 hp) Salmson 9Adr radial engine.

Salyut (USSR) Salyut spacecraft serves as orbital scientific stations for the crews of Soyuz manned spacecraft. Basically the station is a stepped cylinder about 13.0 m (42 ft 8 in) long, from 2.13 m (7 ft) to 4.0 m (13 ft) in diameter, with a weight of 18½ tons (See **Chronology** for launch dates, etc).

SAML S.1 and S.2 (Italy) The SAML S.1 was basically an improved Aviatik B.I powered by a 194 kW (260 hp) Fiat A.12 engine. Maximum level speed was 151 km/h (94 mph). From the S.1 was developed the shorter-span S.2 powered by the same A.12 or a 223.6 kW (300 hp) A.12*bis* engine, the latter giving a maximum speed of 162 km/h (100.5 mph). Armament for the S.1 comprised a single rear-mounted Revelli machine-gun; the S.2 having also a forward-firing Revelli gun. A total of 660 S.1s and S.2s was operated by 16 squadriglie da Ricognizione from 1917, stationed in Italy, Macedonia, Albania and elsewhere. Although basically reconnaissance types, the aircraft also undertook observation and light bombing duties, as a bomber carrying a 40 kg (88 lb) warload.
Data (S.1): *Engine* as above *Wing span* 13.8 m (45 ft 3½ in) *Length* 8.5 m (27 ft 11 in) *Max T-O weight* 1,420 kg (3,130 lb) *Max level speed* 151 km/h (94 mph) *Range* 500 km (311 miles)

Santos-Dumont 14bis (France/Brazil) The 14*bis* (see **Chronology** 12 November 1906) was a tail-first biplane with a wing span of 11.2 m (36 ft 9 in). Length was 9.7 m (31 ft 10 in). Power was eventually provided by a 37.25 kW (50 hp) Antoinette engine, giving a maximum speed of 40 km/h (25 mph). It first 'hopped' on 13 September 1906 for a distance of about 7.0 m (23 ft). On 23 October 1906 it covered a distance of about 60 m (197 ft) and so won the 3,000-franc Archdeacon Prize for the first observed flight in Europe of more than 25 metres.

Santos-Dumont Demoiselle (France/Brazil) The Demoiselle appeared in several forms from

1907 and was a single-seat high-wing monoplane powered by a small tractor engine mounted in the wing leading edge. It is best remembered as the world's first low-cost 'homebuilt' aircraft for the light-in-weight enthusiast.

Saro Cloud (UK) The Cloud amphibious flying-boat was produced in two forms: as a civil eight-seater and as a military trainer. In the latter role the RAF received 16 from 1933. The large cabin provided accommodation for eight pupils; six pupils and wireless and electrical equipment, navigation instruments and signalling apparatus; or four pupils and the above equipment for navigational training. Alternatively, the Cloud could be used for flying training, to simulate the conditions to be met with a larger service type of flying-boat. Power was provided by two 253.4 kW (340 hp) Armstrong Siddeley Double Mongoose engines. Other less successful flying-boats and amphibians built by Saro included the six-seat three-engined Windhover with an auxiliary upper wing.

Saro Cutty Sark (UK) Saro or Saunders-Roe produced the Cutty Sark four-seat cabin flying-boat (or amphibian) as its first new design after formation in 1928. It was adopted for flying-boat and navigational training by Air Service Training Ltd (two 112 kW; 150 hp Armstrong Siddeley Genet Major engines) and was exported as a coastal-reconnaissance aircraft (de Havilland Gipsy Major engines).

Saro Lerwick (UK) The Lerwick was a general-purpose monoplane flying-boat powered by two 1,025 kW (1,375 hp) Bristol Hercules II or IV engines. A normal crew of six was carried. It entered service with RAF Coastal Command in 1939 and just 21 were built.

Saro London (UK) The London was an open-sea reconnaissance biplane flying-boat, powered in its Mk I form by two Bristol Pegasus III engines and in Mk II form by two 715.4 kW (960 hp) Bristol Pegasus X engines. Thirty-one went into service with RAF Coastal Command from 1937.

Saunders-Roe SR.A/1 (UK) Post-war products of this company are better known as Saunders-Roe types rather than Saro. The SR.A/1 was an experimental single-seat fighter flying-boat that first flew on 16 July 1947. It was the world's first turbojet-powered flying-boat and the first flying-boat to exceed 805 km/h (500 mph) in level flight.

Saunders-Roe SR.53 (UK) Experimental mixed-power interceptor, first flown on 16 May 1957.

Saunders-Roe Duchess (UK) Projected jet-propelled medium-range 92-passenger flying-boat, considered for commercial operation by Tasman Empire Airways.

Saunders-Roe Princess (UK) Long-range 220-passenger flying-boat, first flown on 20 August 1952. Power was provided by ten Bristol Proteus 600 Series turboprop engines, four in coupled pairs and two as single units. Expected to be ordered by BOAC, it remained a prototype only.

Saunders-Roe

Saunders-Roe SR.A/1.

Saunders-Roe SR.53.

Saunders-Roe Princess.

Commercial version of the Savoia S.13.

Saunders-Roe Skeeter.

Saunders-Roe Skeeter (UK) The Skeeter two-seat light helicopter was originally designed and built by the Cierva Autogiro Company before it was taken over by Saunders-Roe in 1951. Production Skeeters were operated by the British Army as the AOP.10 and 12, the RAF as the T.11 trainer, and by the Army and Navy of the German Federal Republic as the Mk 50 and Mk 51 respectively. Power was provided by the 149 kW (200 hp) or 160 kW (215 hp) de Havilland Gipsy Major engine.

Saunders ST-27.

Saunders ST-27 (Canada) Turboprop re-manufacture of the Hawker Siddeley Heron Series 2 as a third-level and commuter airliner powered by two 559 kW (750 shp) PT6A-34 turboprop engines.

Savoia S.12 and S.13 (Italy) See **Schneider Trophy contestants**

Savoia S.16 (Italy) Five-seat biplane flying-boat of 1919 powered by a single Fiat A.12*bis* or Lorraine engine. Several were operated commercially.

Savoia-Marchetti S.55 (Italy) An epoch-making design in every sense, the S.55 prototype flew in 1925. In an era still committed to the biplane flying-boat, it had a revolutionary formula: a cantilever shoulder-wing monoplane with twin hulls and delicate booms supporting a twin-fin triple-rudder tail assembly. Side-by-side pilots' cockpits were located in the leading edge of the wing centre-section. Twin tandem engines were carried on struts over the wing. Originally these were 298 kW (400 hp) Lorraines, but power was gradually increased to 559 kW (750 hp) Assos on the 1933 S.55X.

Total production exceeded 200. The type formed the main equipment of Italy's maritime-bombing squadriglie for many years, 13 remaining on charge (but in reserve) in 1939. The S.55C and S.55P civil passenger versions operated Mediterranean routes for a decade.

The S.55 achieved great fame through spectacular long-distance flights: Lieut-Col the Marchese de Pinedo flew the *Santa Maria* from Sardinia to Buenos Aires and then through South America and the USA in 1927; later Brazilian, American and Russian crews achieved world headlines. The S.55 will be chiefly remembered, however, for the remarkable mass formation flights led by the famous Italo Balbo. The first began in December 1930 when specially modified S.55As covered 10,400 km (6,460 miles) between Italy and Brazil. The second flight (three years later) was even more impressive: 24 S.55X machines overflew the Alps and continued in stages via Iceland, Greenland and Labrador to Chicago for the 1933 Century of Progress Exposition. The international press coined the phrase 'Aerial Armada' to describe the flights.

Data (S.55X): *Engines* as above *Wing span* 24.36 m (78 ft 11 in) *Length* 16.31 m (54 ft 2 in) *Max T-O weight* 7,700 kg (16,975 lb) *Max level speed* 236 km/h (146.5 mph) *Range* 3,500 km (2,174 miles) *Armament* four gunners' posts in the bow and stern of each hull and an offensive load of a torpedo or up to 1,000 kg (2,205 lb) of bombs carried under the wing centre-section

Savoia-Marchetti S.59 (Italy) This biplane flying-boat was produced in two forms: the standard S.59 with a 298 kW (400 hp) Lorraine-Dietrich engine and the S.59*bis* with a 372.6 kW

(500 hp) Isotta-Fraschini Asso 500Ri engine.
Examples of both versions went into commercial
and military service during the 1920s.

Savoia-Marchetti S.62 (Italy) Operated mainly
as military flying-boats with the Regia
Aeronautica, although commercial examples
were produced, the initial S.62 and later S.62*bis*
were powered by 372.6 kW (500 hp) and 559 kW
(750 hp) Isotta-Fraschini Asso engines respectively. As a three-seat reconnaissance aircraft, it
was armed with Lewis machine-guns in the nose
cockpit and two more in a midships cockpit. The
S.62*bis* had the open midships position replaced
by a twin-gun turret.

Savoia-Marchetti S.64 (Italy) Developed
specifically for attempts at world duration and
distance records. Power was provided by a
372.6 kW (500 hp) Fiat A.22T engine. During
May and June 1928 the S.64 set up three new
world records, culminating with a distance of
8,188.8 km (5,088.275 miles) covered in a closed
circuit.

Savoia-Marchetti S.59.

Savoia-Marchetti
S.62*bis*.

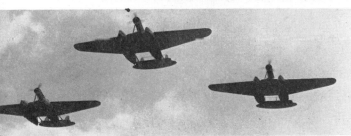

bought 20 production aircraft with defensive dorsal turret and ventral step machine-gun posts, but
nothing was heard of them in action against the
Japanese.

Savoia-Marchetti S.73 (Italy) The S.73P was a
long-range commercial transport powered by
three 521.6 kW (700 hp) Piaggio Stella IXRC or
other engines of similar output. Accommodation
provided for 18 passengers. Deliveries to commercial operators began in 1935; many were
impressed by the Regia Aeronautica as troop
transports during World War II, although a
specific military version was produced as the
S.73M.

Savoia S.16*ter*.

Savoia-Marchetti S.74 (Italy) Twenty/twenty-
seven-passenger commercial transport of 1934
powered by four 521.6 kW (700 hp) Piaggio Stella
XR engines. A small number went into service.

Savoia-Marchetti S.M.75 Marsupiale (Italy) A
twenty-four-seat passenger transport powered by
three 559 kW (750 hp) Alfa-Romeo 126RC.34
radial engines. The S.M.75 prototype flew in
November 1937. Production for military and civil
use continued until 1943, 90 machines being delivered to the Italian authorities and five exported
to Hungary. The latter were finally converted for
military use with dorsal and ventral gun turrets. A
number of Italian S.M.75s were also militarised.

Savoia-Marchetti S.55s.

Savoia-Marchetti S.66 (Italy) First appearing in
1931, the S.66 prototype was a larger development of the S.55 accommodating 14 passengers
and powered by three A.22R engines. Production
aircraft were fitted with 521.6 kW (700 hp) Fiat
A.24R engines, raising accommodation to 18.
S.66s entered commercial service and at least one
was taken on charge by the Regia Aeronautica.

Savoia-Marchetti S.71 (Italy) Eight-passenger
commercial monoplane of 1930 powered by three
179 kW (240 hp) Walter Castor, 253.4 kW
(340 hp) Walter Pollux II, or 276 kW (370 hp)
Piaggio Stella VII engines. Several were produced. Maximum level speed with the Stella
engines was 270 km/h (168 mph).

Savoia-Marchetti S.72 (Italy) The S.72 prototype bomber/transport flew in 1932. Powered
by three 410 kW (550 hp) Pegasus II radials, it
followed the popular high-wing, fixed landing-
gear formula of the time. An altitude record with
5,000 kg (11,023 lb) payload was established in
June 1934. The Nanking Chinese government

Savoia-Marchetti S.66.

Savoia-Marchetti S.73.

Savoia-Marchetti

Savoia-Marchetti S.M.75 Marsupiale.

Savoia-Marchetti S.M.82 Canguro.

Savoia-Marchetti S.M.79-II.

Savoia-Marchetti S.M.79 Sparviero (Italy) By far the most important Italian bomber of World War II, this tough three-engined aircraft established a reputation that contrasted with most Italian weapons of the day, and it was flown with courage and skill. The prototype appeared in late 1934 and subsequently had a varied career, setting records and winning races with various engines and painted in civil or military markings. The basic design continued the company's tradition of mixed construction with steel tubes, light alloy, wood and fabric (this being the only way to produce in quantity with available skills and tools); but compared with other designs, it had a much more highly loaded wing which demanded long airstrips.

The S.M.79-I was powered by three 559 kW (750 hp) Alfa-Romeo 126 RC.34 radials. It carried a 12.7 mm Breda-SAFAT gun firing ahead from the roof of the cockpit in a humpback that enabled bullets to clear the nose propeller; a second firing to the rear from the hump; a third aimed down and to the rear from the gondola under the rear fuselage; and, often, a 7.7 mm firing from each beam window, this needing a crew of at least five. The bombardier occupied the gondola, with his legs projecting down in two retractable tubes during the bombing run. Up to 1,000 kg (2,205 lb) of bombs were carried in an internal bay; alternatively two 450 mm (17.7 in) torpedoes could be hung externally.

The 79-I established an excellent reputation in combat with the Aviación Legionaria in Spain in 1936–39; while other units called Aerosiluranti (aerial torpedoes) pioneered use of these large fast bombers in the anti-shipping role. In October 1939 the Regia Aeronautica began to receive the 79-II with 745.2 kW (1,000 hp) Piaggio P.XI RC.40 engines (one batch had the Fiat A.80 of similar power), and this was the dominant version in action subsequently. About 1,200 served with the Regia Aeronautica, including a handful of the III sub-type with forward-firing 20 mm cannon and no ventral gondola. Post-war a few of various versions survived as utility transports until 1952.

About 100 were exported to Brazil, Iraq and Romania – all of the twin-engined S.M.79B variety. Romania built the 79JR under licence with two 894 kW (1,200 hp) Junkers Jumo 211Da liquid-cooled engines. These were used in numbers on the Eastern Front; initially as bombers with visual aiming position in the nose and subsequently mainly as utility transports.
Data (S.M.79-II): *Engines* as above *Wing span* 21.2 m (69 ft 6½ in) *Length* 16.2 m (53 ft 1¾ in) *Max T-O weight* 11,300 kg (24,192 lb) *Max level speed* 434 km/h (270 mph) *Range* 2,000 km (1,243 miles)

Savoia-Marchetti S.M.81 (Italy) Designed in parallel with the S.73 passenger aircraft, the S.M.81 was a robust cantilever low-wing monoplane with three radial engines and a divided, spatted landing gear. The first flight of the prototype took place on 8 February 1935 and initial production deliveries were made just two months later. S.M.81s were sent directly to support the Italian campaign in Ethiopia. In all 534 S.M.81s were built in a number of versions, employing five different types of engine. Known as the 'Pipistrello' (Bat), the S.M.81 served in Spain and in the campaign in East Africa in 1941. Subsequently it was relegated to night operations, training and transport duties.

Armament normally comprised retractable twin-gun dorsal and ventral turrets and single 7.7 mm Lewis guns firing through hatches either side of the rear fuselage. A semi-retractable bomb-aimer's gondola was located under the nose. Maximum bomb load was 2,000 kg (4,409 lb).
Data: *Engines* three 432.2 kW (580 hp) Alfa Romeo 125 radials *Wing span* 24.0 m (78 ft 9 in) *Length* 17.8 m (58 ft 6 in) *Max T-O weight* 9,300 kg (20,503 lb) *Max level speed* 340 km/h (211 mph) *Range* 2,000 km (1,243 miles)

Savoia-Marchetti S.M.82 Canguro (Italy) The S.M.82 of 1938 was a development of the S.M.75, from which it differed by having a deeper fuselage, greater loaded weight, redesigned fin and rudder, and the addition of a hydraulically operated retractable gun turret on top of the fuselage to the rear of the pilot's cockpit. Initially powered by three 633.4 kW (850 hp) Alfa Romeo 128 engines, it could accommodate up to 40 fully armed troops or be used as a long-range heavy bomber. It was widely used by the Regia Aeronautica and some were operated by the Luftwaffe from 1943.

Savoia-Marchetti S.M.83 (Italy) First flying in 1938, the S.M.83 was a ten-passenger commercial transport powered initially by three 559 kW (750 hp) Alfa Romeo 126 RC.34 radial engines. Production totalled 23 aircraft.

Savoia-Marchetti S.M.84 (Italy) The S.M.84 of 1941 was basically a new version of the S.M.79 fitted with twin fins and rudders, a dorsal turret and incorporating other minor changes. Production aircraft went into service with the Regia Aeronautica.

Savoia-Marchetti S.M.85 (Italy) Single-seat twin-engined dive bomber and ground-attack monoplane. Power was provided by two 372.6 kW (500 hp) Piaggio P.VII RC.35 engines. A small number served with the Regia Aeronautica.

Savoia-Marchetti S.M.95 (Italy) Four-engined 30–38-passenger transport. First flown in 1943, but most were produced post-war for civil and military service. One was operated by the RAF for VIP transport duties.

Savoia-Marchetti S.M.102 (Italy) Twin-engined short-range transport of 1949 accommodating eight passengers. Small number built.

Savoia-Pomilio S.P. series (Italy) Originating in 1916, the S.P. series of reconnaissance, artillery observation and bombing biplanes were operated widely by Italian squadrons. More than 850 were built as S.P.2s (194 kW; 260 hp Fiat A.12); S.P.3s (223.6 kW; 300 hp Fiat A.12*bis*); and S.P.4s (two 112 kW; 150 hp Isotta-Fraschini V.4Bs). The final 29 S.P.4s were built as late as 1918.

Data (S.P.2): *Engine* as above *Wing span* 16.74 m (54 ft 11 in) *Length* 10.77 m (35 ft 4 in) *Max T-O weight* 1,700 kg (3,748 lb) *Max level speed* 120 km/h (74.5 mph) *Range* 450 km (280 miles)

SCAN 20 (France) The SCAN 20 was designed and built in secret in 1941 and flight tests were made immediately following liberation. It was a single 179 kW (240 hp) Salmson 8-powered training flying-boat, 23 of which were delivered to the French Navy during the early 1950s.

SCAN 30 (France) Licence-built Grumman Widgeon.

Scenic/AJI Turbo Star 402 (USA) Scenic Air Lines acquired from AJI in early 1977 all engineering and manufacturing rights for the turboprop conversions of the Cessna Models 402 and 414.

Schavrov Sch-2 (USSR) Two-seat open-cockpit amphibian of early 1930, a number of which were operated as passenger/mail-carrying, ambulance and patrol aircraft. Power was provided by a 74.5 kW (100 hp) M-11 engine mounted on the leading edge of the upper wing.

Scheibe Bergfalke-IV, SF-25C and C-S Falke '76, SF-25E Super-Falke, SF-28A Tandem-Falke, and SF-H34 (Germany) Tandem two-seat training and competition sailplane; side-by-side two-seat motor glider (C-S Falke '76 is the current model); side-by-side two-seat increased-wing-span development of the SF-25C-S motor glider; tandem two-seat motor glider; and tandem two-seat training and sporting sailplane respectively.

Schempp-Hirth Nimbus 2, HS-7 Mini-Nimbus and Janus (Germany) Single-seat Open Class sailplane; single-seat 15-metre Contest Class sailplane; and tandem two-seat high-performance training sailplane respectively.

Scheutzow Bee (USA) Light utility helicopter powered by a 134 kW (180 hp) Lycoming IVO-360-A1A engine.

Schleicher ASK 13, ASW 19 B, ASW 20, ASW 20L and ASK 21 (Germany) Tandem two-seat training and high-performance sailplane; single-seat Standard Class sailplane; single-seat 15-metre Contest Class sailplane; 16.5 m (54 ft

Savoia-Marchetti S.M.83.

Savoia-Marchetti S.M.95.

SCAN 20.

Schavrov Sch-2.

Savoia-Marchetti S.M.85.

Schempp-Hirth Nimbus II.

1½ in) wing-span version of the ASW 20; and tandem two-seat competition and training sailplane respectively.

Schneider Trophy contestants Few people, other than aviation enthusiasts, historians or those connected with aviation in a civil or service capacity, have any real appreciation of the significance of the Schneider Trophy contests. Dismissed so often as 'early aeroplane races', it is perhaps unfortunate that there is not a better and wider appreciation of the significant influence exerted by these contests upon the development of high-powered, compact engines and, to a lesser extent, the improvement of streamlined airframe structures.

Sopwith Tabloid, winner of the second Schneider Trophy contest, here seen with a wheeled landing gear.

Savoia S.12.

At the time when Frenchman Jacques Schneider announced (on 5 December 1912) his intention to sponsor an international competition to be contested by seaplanes, aviation was still largely a 'fun' thing linked with motor and balloon races. However Schneider believed – as did other forward-thinking men – that the aeroplane could be developed to provide a fast, safe means of communication over continental or intercontinental ranges. Like many he thought that aircraft which could operate from and to water surfaces would be ideal for such a role. This was based on one fact and one mistaken belief: that seven-tenths of the Earth's surface is covered with water, thus providing natural areas fit for the operation of suitable aircraft; that in the event of a forced- or crash-landing, water would prove more yielding than land!

To set the scene in a context of aviation achievement: by the end of 1911 the world air

Supermarine Sea Lion II.

speed record stood at 133.14 km/h (82.73 mph), distance record at 722.92 km (449.2 miles) and altitude record at 3,910 m (12,828 ft). The world's first aircraft to operate from water (a floatplane glider designed jointly by Gabriel Voisin and Ernest Archdeacon) had flown on 8 June 1905. Almost five years later (on 28 March 1910), Henri Fabre had flown the world's first successful powered seaplane a distance of about 450 m (1,476 ft)–first flight of an aircraft of his own design. First flight from water in America was recorded by Glenn Curtiss on 26 January 1911; and in Britain by Cmdr Oliver Schwann – very briefly – on 18 November 1911.

It is not surprising, therefore, that when the world's first hydro-aeroplane meeting was held at Monaco (at the end of March 1912), the performance of these aircraft was somewhat limited and their structure hardly suited for such a role. All were landplanes with floats attached: that of Maurice Farman had its floats secured between each pair of bicycle wheels which comprised its main landing gear, with another float at the tail. Performance of these aircraft in their original landplane form was hardly startling: with the addition of heavy drag-inducing floats – well-braced to maintain structural integrity – speed diminished to well below normal.

A major problem of aviation's early days was to obtain an engine of adequate power. Assuming that one had an engine/airframe combination which could be flown, even the slightest increase in load made it non-viable; but in the 'stick and string' era there was little chance of making significant aerodynamic improvement to the airframe. The constant cry was for more power.

One design team, the French Seguin brothers, had started in 1907 to develop a more powerful and more reliable engine. At that time liquid-cooled engines derived from the motorcar industry and were big and heavy. The specially designed radial engines for aircraft use were air-cooled and lighter in weight; but their low power and the slow forward speed of the aircraft meant that cooling was marginal.

The rotary engine developed by the Seguin brothers had propeller, cylinders and crankcase rotating as one. The crankshaft – with related connecting rods and pistons attached – was stationary and fixed indirectly to the airframe. The cylinders milling in the airstream were adequately cooled, and the flywheel inertia of this rotating mass ensured smooth running, even at

small throttle openings. Because the cooling was effective, comparatively high power outputs became possible and the Gnome engine, as it was called, had a power/weight ratio almost twice as good as the rest of the world's aero-engines. It was the Gnome-powered Henri Farman biplane (piloted by M. Fischer) that was declared winner at the Monaco meeting.

The first Schneider Trophy contest – scheduled as one item in the full programme of the 1913 Monaco Hydro-Aeroplane Meeting – could hardly be regard as a major international event. Six French and one American pilot were involved, the latter flying a French Nicuport monoplane; but this number was reduced to four after the preliminary open-water trials had taken their toll. The race was flown on 16 April 1913 over a 28-lap course totalling 280 km (173.98 miles). It was won by Maurice Prévost, flying a Deperdussin monoplane powered by a 119 kW (160 hp) Gnome engine, at a speed of 73.63 km/h (45.75 mph). Clearly the penalty imposed by the heavy floats had a major effect on speed: the wheeled Deperdussin monoplane which won the Gordon-Bennett contest held in America in September 1912 had averaged 169.8 km/h (105.5 mph).

A French win meant that the venue for the next contest and its organisation were the responsibility of the Aéro-Club de France: once again Monaco was chosen. This second contest was to prove the most truly international of the entire series, with entries from Britain, France, Germany, Switzerland and the USA. Flown on 20 April 1914, seven starters flew the same course as the previous year and C. Howard Pixton of Britain recorded an average speed of 139.66 km/h (86.78 mph), almost double the average of the previous contest.

Britain's winning entry evolved from the new Sopwith Aviation Company, established by Tommy (later Sir Thomas) Sopwith at Kingston upon Thames, Surrey in 1913. One of the company's earliest products was a two-seat biplane known as the Tabloid, intended from the outset to compete in air races. Seizing the opportunity to gain valuable publicity for the new company, a floatplane version of the Tabloid was provided with a new 74.5 kW (100 hp) power plant, known as the Gnome Monosoupape (single valve) engine, which dispensed with inlet valves and was, consequently, lighter in weight.

The intervention of World War I meant that it was not until 1919 that the British Royal Aero Club was able to stage the next contest at

Gloster III.

Bournemouth, Hampshire (now Dorset). It proved inconclusive, with Britain, France and Italy competing under conditions of sea fog. Only Sgt Guido Janello (piloting a Savoia S.13 flying-boat) completed the course and, despite spirited protests, was disqualified on the grounds that he had not flown accurate laps. As an appreciation of his efforts, however, it was ruled that Italy should stage the next contest.

This meant that Venice was host in 1920. But with immediate post-war financial stringencies, America, Britain and France could not afford to compete and Germany was excluded by the terms of the Versailles Treaty. Only Italy fielded a team and Lt Luigi Bologna flew his Savoia S.12 biplane flying-boat over the course to record an Italian victory. Thus the Aéro-Club d'Italia became responsible for the next contest, to be held at Venice a second time. Once again, only the Italians competed, the French entry being damaged during trials. Two Macchi M.7s and an M.19 were flown; but the only one to complete the course was the M.7 piloted by Giovanni de Brigantl at an average speed of 189.74 km/h (117.90 mph).

Italy now needed only one more win to secure the Schneider Trophy for all time. When the 370.5 km (230.22 mile) course at Naples was flown on 12 August 1922, one British and three Italian aircraft had been prepared to compete. One of the most exciting contests of the entire series, with all four aircraft completing the course, it was won narrowly by Henry Biard flying the British Supermarine Sea Lion II at an average speed of 234.48 km/h (145.7 mph).

Supermarine's entry was made possible by the generosity of Napiers, Shell and Wakefield, as well as the Steam Navigation Company who transported aircraft and team to Naples: illustrating the steeply rising cost of participation. The Sea Lion II was a conversion of the company's Sea King II amphibian flying-boat, lightened and refined by the skill of R. J. Mitchell and powered by a 335.5 kW (450 hp) Napier Lion engine.

Supermarine Sea Lion II winning the 1922 Schneider Trophy contest.

Macchi M.39.

Schneider Trophy contestants

Curtiss R3C-3, a re-engined R3C-2, stalled and capsized during practice for the 1926 Schneider Trophy contest.

Supermarine S.5.

Two Supermarine S.6Bs flank the S.6.

Savoia-Marchetti S.65, entered in the 1929 Schneider Trophy contest.

The 1923 contest held at Cowes, Isle of Wight on 28 September, brought together Britain, France and the USA. It was the latter that took first and second place with Curtiss CR-3 racing biplanes powered by 346.8 kW (465 hp) Curtiss D-12 engines. The winner's speed of 285.6 km/h (177.38 mph) completely outclassed the British Sea Lion III, which averaged 252.94 km/h (157.17 mph). This was the same aircraft which had won the contest in 1922, still further 'cleaned up' by Mitchell and provided with a 410 kW (550 hp) Lion engine. Even then Supermarine could not have afforded to field an entry; the Sea Lion had been loaned by the Air Ministry which had acquired it after the 1922 contest. America's success was due largely to the Curtiss D-12 engine in combination with a Curtiss-Reed propeller:

details of this engine are given in the entry for the Fairey Fox.

There was no contest in 1924 – due to be held at Baltimore, Maryland – because only America was ready to participate. Sportingly the US National Aeronautic Association ruled 'no contest', giving overseas competitors twelve months in which to prepare. In fact this was little enough, for the moment in time had come when specialised aircraft and engines were necessary to attain speeds of 322 km/h (200 mph) or more. Thus, in 1925, America won easily with a developed version of the CR-3 (designated R3C-2) powered by a 447 kW (600 hp) Curtiss V-1400 and flown by Lieut J. H. 'Jimmy' Doolittle at an average of 374.28 km/h (232.57 mph).

Britain had entered the almost revolutionary Supermarine S.4, a cantilever all-wood monoplane seaplane designed by R. J. Mitchell and powered by a 521.6 kW (700 hp) Napier Lion engine. This crashed during trials and the equally new Gloster III biplane seaplane could do no better than gain second place at an average of 320.53 km/h (199.17 mph).

The 1926 contest at Hampton Roads, Virginia was won by Italy – virtually on the orders of Benito Mussolini who had ensured the provision of new aircraft and engines for propaganda purposes. This enabled Mario Castoldi of the Macchi company to create the M.39 which (via the M.52, M.52R and M.67) resulted in the world-beating M.72. This was flown by Francesco Agello in late 1934 to set up a world record of 709.20 km/h (440.68 mph). All of these Macchi aircraft were powered by Fiat engines of progressively increasing output, ranging from 657–2,310 kW (882–3,100 hp). By 1934, however, the Schneider Trophy had already passed permanently into British possession, following wins with the Supermarine S.5 at Venice in 1927, flown by Flt

Lieut S. N. Webster at 453.29 km/h (281.66 mph); the Supermarine S.6 at Calshot in 1929, piloted by Fl Off H. R. Waghorn at 528.88 km/h (328.63 mph); and finally in 1931, again at Calshot, when the Supermarine S.6B flown by Flt Lieut J. N. Boothman completed the course uncontested at 547.305 km/h (340.08 mph).

Success for Britain resulted from the genius of R. J. Mitchell who developed the S.5 from the cantilever-wing S.4. Principal changes involved lowering the wing; adopting wire bracing between wing, floats and fuselage; reducing the cross-sectional area of floats and fuselage; and installing a 671 kW (900 hp) Napier Lion VIIA with surface radiators. This output, however, represented the Lion at full development and the S.6 for 1929 was powered by the specially developed Rolls-Royce R engine of 1,416 kW (1,900 hp). The S.6 itself was virtually an enlarged S.5 of all-metal construction with floats which included fuel tanks and surface radiators for engine coolant. External oil coolers passed down each side of the fuselage, being linked in the fin to complete a return circuit. The Trophy-winning S.6B was little changed from the S.6, being lengthened slightly by virtue of longer floats needed to cater for the more powerful 1,752.4 kW (2,350 hp) Rolls-Royce R engine and by having increased cooling surfaces for both engine lubricating oil and coolant.

Britain's final participation was made possible only by the gift of £100,000 from Lady Houston, for at that time the government was not prepared to put up such a sum of money. By then the founder of the contest was no more, for Jacques Schneider had died on 1 May 1928. The contests, then, had done little towards directly achieving his dream of long-range international transport. They were, however, to make possible the development of high-powered reliable engines and bring a far wider understanding of how to build rugged and aerodynamically efficient structures. In so doing nations acquired the knowledge to design and construct a completely new generation of aircraft.

Scottish Aviation Pioneer (UK) The Pioneer began life as a three-seat light military communications aircraft built to Specification A.4/45 and powered by a 179 kW (240 hp) de Havilland Gipsy Queen 34 engine. The original military requirement failed to materialise and so the basic design was developed into a civil light transport aircraft as the (Prestwick) Pioneer.

On 5 May 1950 the first prototype of the 387.5 kW (520 hp) Leonides-powered Pioneer II flew. It was selected for service as a five-seat communications and casualty-evacuation (one stretcher and an attendant) aircraft for the RAF and production CC.1s were flown from mid-1953. By March 1960 a total of 53 Pioneer IIs had been delivered, most to the RAF but five to the Royal Ceylonese Air Force and others to Iran and Malaya.

Scottish Aviation Twin Pioneer (UK) The Twin Pioneer was a twin-engined light general-purpose aircraft suitable for civil and military use. The prototype first flew on 25 June 1955, followed by the first production aircraft on 28 April 1956.

Scottish Aviation Twin Pioneer Series 3s for Malaya.

By the spring of 1964 a total of 91 Twin Pioneers had been built for service with 15 operators in 20 countries, including 32 CC.1s and 7 CC.2s for the RAF. The final production version was the Series 3 which could be equipped for a wide variety of duties in addition to normal passenger and freight transport roles. These included photographic survey, geophysical survey, executive transport and air ambulance (six stretchers and five sitting casualties/attendants) versions.

The general-purpose military Twin Pioneer was operated by the RAF in troop (13), paratroop (11) and freight transport, casualty evacuation, photographic survey, supply-dropping and light bombing roles.

Data (Series 3): *Engines* two 477 kW (640 hp) Alvis Leonides 531 radials *Wing span* 23.33 m (76 ft 6 in) *Length* 13.8 m (45 ft 3 in) *Max T-O weight* 6,620 kg (14,600 lb) *Max cruising speed* 256 km/h (159 mph) *Range* 338–1,180 km (210–733 miles) *Armament* (as could be carried by the RAF CC.I) two Browning or one Bren gun fired through doorway, plus up to 907 kg (2,000 lb) of high-explosive or anti-personnel bombs carried under sponsons

Scottish Aviation Bulldog and Jetstream (UK) See **BAe**

SECAN Type S.U.C. 10 Courlis (France) Four-seat cabin monoplane of 1946 with a pusher-mounted 149 kW (200 hp) Mathis engine and the tail carried by twin booms. A series of 30 was built.

SECAT RG-60 (France) Single-seat open-cockpit light biplane powered by a 30 kW (40 hp) Train engine.

SECAT RG-75 (France) Two-seat cabin monoplane powered by a 52 kW (70 hp) Régnier 4-D.2 engine.

SECAT S-5 (France) Development of the S-4 Mouette two-seat high-wing monoplane of 1938 powered by a 52 kW (70 hp) Régnier 4-D.2 engine.

Scottish Aviation Pioneer CC.1.

SEPECAT Jaguar International.

SEPECAT Jaguar GR.1.

SEPECAT Jaguar (UK/France) The Jaguar (evolved from the Breguet Br 121 project) was designed by Breguet and BAe to meet a common requirement of the French and British air forces laid down in early 1965. This called for a dual-role aircraft to be used as an advanced and operational trainer and a tactical support aircraft of light weight and high performance, to enter French service in 1972 and with the RAF in 1973. The Jaguar M French naval version was abandoned in 1973. Five versions of the Jaguar have been built:

Jaguar A French single-seat tactical support version, the first prototype of which was flown on 23 March 1969. Total of 160 ordered. By 1 March 1979 117 Jaguar As had been delivered. The first operational Armée de l'Air Jaguar unit (Esc. 1/7 'Provence') was formed at St Dizier in eastern France on 19 June 1973.

Jaguar B (RAF designation Jaguar T.2) British two-seat operational training version, the prototype of which was first flown on 30 August 1971. Total of 37 ordered, all of which had been delivered by end of 1976.

Jaguar E French two-seat advanced training version, the first prototype of which was flown on 8 September 1968. Total of 40 ordered, all of which have been delivered.

Jaguar S (RAF designation Jaguar GR.1) British single-seat tactical support version, basically similar to A but with an advanced inertial navigation and weapon-aiming system (NAVWASS) controlled by a digital computer. The first prototype was flown on 12 October 1969. Total of 165 ordered, all of which have been delivered. The first production GR.1 flew on 11 October 1972 and this version now equips eight RAF front-line squadrons. RAF Jaguars are to be refitted with uprated Adour engines, designated Mk 104 and equivalent to the Mk 804 which powers the Jaguar International.

Jaguar International Export version, first flown on 19 August 1976. Differs little from the original single-seat Jaguar except in having more powerful Adour turbofan engines (initially the RT. 172-26 Adour Mk 804, rated at 38.25 kN; 8,600 lb st with afterburning).

Other customer options now on offer include over-wing pylons compatible with Magic or similar dogfight missiles; a multi-purpose radar such as the Thomson-CSF Agave, with which flight trials were completed in March 1977; anti-shipping weapons such as Harpoon, Exocet and Kormoran; and night sensors such as low-light-level TV. Initial orders placed by the Sultan of Oman's Air Force (12) and Ecuadorean Air Force (12). Deliveries to Ecuador began in January 1977 and were completed by October that year. Deliveries to SOAF began on 7 March 1977 and were completed in the spring of 1978.

The Jaguar International is also being offered in a maritime strike version, similarly powered by Adour 'Dash 26' (current standard) or 'Dash 58' (optional) turbofan engines. Main differences from the standard Jaguar International are the fitting of a Thomson-CSF Agave multi-purpose nose radar and ability to carry up to four anti-shipping missiles such as Harpoon, Exocet or Kormoran on the underwing and underfuselage hardpoints. The capacity to carry Magic air-to-air missiles on the overwing pylons is retained.

Data (RAF Jaguar): *Engines* two 38.25 kN (8,600 lb st, with afterburning) Turboméca Adour Mk 104 turbofans *Wing span* 8.69 m (28 ft 6 in) *Length* 16.83 m (55 ft 2½ in) *Max T-O weight* 15,500 kg (34,000 lb) *Max level speed* 1,593 km/h (990 mph) *Tactical attack radius* (with external fuel) 1,315 km (818 miles) *Armament* (Jaguar A and S) two 30 mm cannon (DEFA 553 in Jaguar A, Aden in Jaguar S) in lower fuselage aft of cockpit. One stores attachment point on fuselage centreline and two under each wing. Centreline and inboard wing points can each carry up to 1,000 kg (2,000 lb) of weapons, and the outboard underwing points up to 500 kg (1,000 lb) each. Maximum external stores load 4,535 kg (10,000 lb). Jaguar As in service can carry the AN 52 tactical nuclear weapon. Typical alternative loads include one Martel AS.37 anti-radar missile and two 1,200 litre (264 Imp gallon) drop-tanks; eight 1,000 lb bombs; various combinations of free-fall and retarded bombs, BL755 or Belouga cluster bombs, Magic missiles and air-to-surface rockets, including the 68 mm SNEB rocket

Sequoia Model 300 Sequoia (USA) Side-by-side two-seat utility and aerobatic monoplane, plans and kits for which are available to amateur constructors.

Sequoia Model 301 (USA) Tandem two-seat version of the Model 300.

Sequoia Model 302 Kodiak (USA) Four-seat development of the Model 300, the prototype of which was scheduled to fly in late 1979.

Seversky BT-8 (USA) Two-seat basic training monoplane powered by a 335.3 kW (450 hp) Pratt & Whitney R-985-11 Wasp Junior radial engine. Thirty delivered to the USAAC.

SEPECAT Jaguar E.

Seversky P-35 (USA) First flown in prototype form in 1935, the P-35 was a single-seat fighter monoplane with a retractable landing gear (which retracted backwards into fairings under the centre-section). Armament comprised one 0.50 in and one 0.30 in machine-guns mounted in the top cowling. In 1938 76 P-35s were delivered to the USAAC, each powered by a 708 kW (950 hp) Pratt & Whitney R-1830-9 Twin-Wasp radial engine.

An export version of the P-35s was also produced as the EP-1 powered by a 782.5 kW (1,050 hp) R-1830-45 Twin-Wasp engine and armed with two 0.30 in Colt MG-40 and two 0.50 in Colt MG-53 machine-guns, plus provision for five 17 lb fragmentation bombs if required. One hundred and twenty EP-1s were ordered by Sweden, which received 60 (Swedish designation S9). The remaining aircraft ordered passed into US service as P-35As: two-thirds of which were lost during the Japanese attack on the Philippines in December 1941.

Data (P-35): *Engine* as above *Wing span* 10.97 m (36 ft 0 in) *Length* 7.72 m (24 ft 4 in) *Max T-O weight* 2,855 kg (6,295 lb) *Max level speed* 454 km/h (282 mph) *Range* 1,931 km (1,200 miles) *Armament* one 0.30 in Colt MG-40 and one 0.50 in Colt MG-53 machine-guns, plus fragmentation bombs

Seversky 2PA (USA) Basically a two-seat version of the EP-1 powered by a 745.2 kW (1,000 hp) Wright R-1820 Cyclone radial engine. It was designed to accommodate several different types of outer wing sections to provide fuel tankage for exceptionally long range. Armament included a rear-mounted 0.30 in Colt MG-40 machine-gun and up to 420 kg (924 lb) of bombs. Twenty were exported to Japan and two to the USSR. Some fifty out of a total of fifty-two ordered by Sweden were impressed for the US Army as AT-12 trainers.

Seversky SEV-3 (USA) The SEV-3 was a three-seat twin-float amphibious monoplane, first flown in June 1933. Power was provided by a 313 kW (420 hp) Wright R-975-E2 Whirlwind radial engine in the SEV-3XAR version. It was the first

Seversky SEV-3M-WW, three of which were bought by Colombia.

Shchetinin M-5.

product of the Seversky company and set two world speed records for amphibians in 1933 and 1935, the latter (by the higher-powered SEV-3M-WW) at 370.814 km/h (230.413 mph) remained unbeaten in 1978.

Shcherbakov ShchE-2 (USSR) Twin M-11D-engined troop, freight or ambulance monoplane. Entered service during World War II and was adopted subsequently for use over short ranges by Aeroflot.

Shchetinin M-5 (Russia) Armed two–three-seat training and reconnaissance flying-boat powered by a 74.5 kW (100 hp) Gnome Monosoupape engine mounted in pusher configuration. The Imperial Russian Navy received approximately 300 from 1915.

Shchetinin M-9 (Russia) Larger development of the M-5 powered by a 112 kW (150 hp) Salmson-built Canton-Unné or 164 kW (220 hp) Renault engine mounted in pusher configuration. Up to 65 kg (143.3 lb) of bombs could be carried. Approximately 500 M-9s were built (delivered from 1916), serving in the Baltic and Black Sea areas. M-9s also fought in the 'White and Red' conflicts of 1919.

Shchetinin M-11 (Russia) Fighter aircraft of 1916.

Shchetinin M-15 and M-20 (Russia) Further developments of the M-5/M-9 series, the former powered by a 104.3 kW (140 hp) Hispano-Suiza engine. Armed with the usual flexibly mounted Lewis gun

Seversky P-35.

Seversky EP-1.

Shchetinin M-9.

Shenandoah

Shenandoah.

Shin Meiwa US-1.

Short Folder.

Shenandoah (USA) Shenandoah was a government-built Zeppelin-type rigid airship for the US Navy, designated ZR1. It was launched in 1921 and was 207.4 m (680 ft 6 in) long, powered by six 266 kW (357 hp) Packard engines. It made its first flight on 4 September 1923 and served until 3 September 1925, when it broke in two during a squall over Caldwell, Ohio. The forward half of the airship rose to 3,050 m (10,000 ft) but was brought to rest on the ground by the crew. Twenty-nine of the 43 crew survived the incident.

Shin Meiwa PS-1 and US-1 (Japan) In January 1966 Shin Meiwa was awarded a contract to develop a new anti-submarine flying-boat for the JMSDF. Company designated SS-2, the flying-boat was also adapted for amphibious operation as the SS-2A. In the ASW configuration the SS-2 received the JMSDF designation PS-1, while as a search and rescue aircraft it was designated US-1.

The first PS-1 prototype flew on 5 October 1967. By March 1979 Shin Meiwa had delivered two prototypes and 22 production PS-1s to the JMSDF (one more has been ordered), serving with the 31st Air Group for ASW duties.

The first US-1 flew on 16 October 1974. It was delivered to the JMSDF on 5 March 1975, followed by three more for search and rescue duties. A further three had been funded by early 1979.

In co-operation with the JMSDF and the National Fire Agency, Shin Meiwa converted the first PS-1 prototype into a water-bombing testbed; it could deliver a total of 185 tonnes (182.1 tons) of water, picked up 70 km (43.5 miles) from base, to a site 10 km (6 miles) away, in 3 hours 36 minutes. The proposed production version could deliver 315 tonnes (310 tons) to a site the same distance from its base before needing to refuel.

Data (PS-1): *Engines* four 2,282 kW (3,060 ehp) Ishikawajima-built General Electric T64-IHI-10 turboprops *Wing span* 33.15 m (108 ft 9 in) *Length* 33.46 m (109 ft 9¼ in) *Max T-O weight* 43,000 kg (94,800 lb) *Max level speed* 547 km/h (340 mph) *Range* 2,168 km (1,347 miles) *Armament and operational equipment* weapons bay on upper deck (aft of tactical compartment) in which is stored AQA-3 Jezebel passive long-range acoustic search equipment with 20 sonobuoys and launchers, Julie active acoustic echo ranging with 12 explosive charges, four 330 lb anti-submarine bombs, and smoke bombs. External armament includes underwing pod between each pair of engine nacelles, each containing two homing torpedoes, and a launcher beneath each wingtip for three 5 in air-to-surface rockets

Short 74 (UK) Two-seat carrier-borne floatplane powered by a 74.5 kW (100 hp) Gnome rotary engine. Eighteen were operated by the RNAS at the beginning of World War I.

Short 166 (UK) Developed from the Short 'Folder' (so named because of its folding wings, using the Patent Folding Wing device of 1913) via the Short 135. The Short 166 was a torpedo-bombing floatplane powered by a 149 kW (200 hp) Salmson engine. Twenty-six were built for the RNAS.

Short 184 (UK) The Short 184 was the first seaplane to be employed successfully in a naval engagement, and an official letter written to Messrs Short Bros with regard to the work performed by a Short 184 in spotting enemy ships during the Battle of Jutland in May 1916 stated: '... the flight made by Flight Lieut Rutland, with Assistant Paymaster Trewin, as observer, which Sir David Beatty praises so highly, was carried out on a 225 hp Short Seaplane.' A Short 184 had previously become the first aeroplane to sink a ship with a torpedo (see **Chronology** 12 August 1915).

First entering service with the RNAS in early 1915, the Short 184 had a long and highly successful career and remained fully active until the Armistice – more than 900 being completed. Its initial power plant of a 167.7 kW (225 hp) Sunbeam gave rise to the often quoted incorrect designation Short 225; several different engines were fitted during the production run. A number of Short 184s were taken on charge post-war by other countries.

Data: *Engine* as above *Wing span* 19.36 m (63 ft 6 in) *Length* 12.38 m (40 ft 7½ in) *Max T-O weight*

Short 74.

2,522 kg (5,560 lb) *Max level speed* 141.5 km/h (88 mph) *Endurance* 2 h 45 mins *Armament* one rear-mounted Lewis gun, plus a 14 in torpedo or bombs

Short 320 (UK) The 320 was the ultimate torpedo-carrying seaplane to come from the Short stable during World War I, representing a combination of the best features of the earlier types combined with a more powerful 238.7 kW (320 hp) Sunbeam engine. Main armament comprised an 18 in torpedo. The RNAS received 110 examples. Increased size and weight kept performance below that of the Short 184 and it therefore failed to equal the reputation of the earlier aircraft.

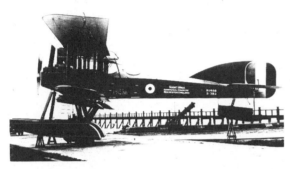

Short 827 and 830 (UK) These were two-seat floatplanes of typical Short styling powered by 112 kW (150 hp) Sunbeam and 149 kW (200 hp) Salmson or 104.3 kW (140 hp) Canton-Unné engines respectively. They were flown by the RNAS as reconnaissance and bombing aircraft from 1914. Some 120 were eventually built.

Short T.5 (UK) Large two-seat trainer of 1911 powered by a 52 kW (70 hp) Gnome rotary engine. Maximum level speed 93 km/h (58 mph). Still in service as a naval type at the outbreak of war.

Short Bomber (UK) Basically a landplane version of the Short 184 powered normally by a 186.3 kW (250 hp) Rolls-Royce Eagle III engine and featuring a four-wheel main landing gear. Eighty-two production aircraft were built for the RNAS out of 110 ordered, some of which were later transferred to the RFC and one was presented to the French government. Maximum level speed was 124 km/h (77 mph).

Short Calcutta and Rangoon (UK) Short's connection with sea-going aeroplanes started in 1911. Success with the S.27 (see **Chronology** May 1912) and torpedo bombers of World War I gave the company the experience and confidence to concentrate its post-war effort on the development of all-metal flying-boats, achieving remarkable results.

The Calcutta was designed primarily for long-distance Empire sea routes and Imperial Airways had five for the Mediterranean section of the England–India air route and on the Nile section of the England–Africa route. Power was provided by three 391.2 kW (525 hp) Bristol Jupiter XIF radial engines and accommodation was for 15 passengers.

From the Calcutta Short developed the Rangoon as a long-range reconnaissance type for the RAF. Six were produced and went into service in 1931. These were basically similar to the Calcutta, except that the pilots were accommodated in an enclosed cockpit, in the nose was an open cockpit with Scarff gun-ring and aft of the biplane wings were staggered cockpits for two gunners. Maximum level speed of the Rangoon was 185 km/h (115 mph).

Short Belfast (UK) The Belfast was a four-engined heavy transport for the RAF, the first of which flew on 5 January 1964. It was specifically designed for the carriage of heavy freight, including the largest types of guns, vehicles, guided missiles and other loads and had 'beaver-tail' rear loading doors capable of permitting the unhindered passage of any load that the fuselage could contain. As a troop transport it could carry 200 men, and was often used to carry helicopters overseas. Ten were built for the RAF, first entering service with No 53 Squadron in January 1966 as the Belfast C.1. No longer operated by the RAF. Data: *Engines* four 4,270 kW (5,730 ehp) Rolls-Royce Tyne RTy.12 turboprops *Wing span* 48.42 m (158 ft 9½ in) *Length* 41.69 m (136 ft 5 in) *Max T-O weight* 104,300 kg (230,000 lb) *Max cruising speed* 566 km/h (352 mph) *Range* 8,530 km (5,300 miles)

Short Calcutta.

Short 320.

Short Belfast.

Short 830.

Short Bomber.

Short

Short Empire Flying Boat *Canopus* being rolled out.

Short S.30 Empire Flying Boat *Cabot*.

Short Empire Flying-Boat (UK) In 1935 the British government took the bold decision to carry all mail within the Empire at the ordinary surface rate (in Britain then equal to 0.625 p). Combined with.increasing passenger traffic, this called for a sudden expansion of Imperial Airways and the equally bold decision was taken to buy 28 of a totally new flying-boat 'off the drawing board' from Short Brothers. Flying-boats were then favoured because they could be more heavily loaded than landplanes, the latter being constricted by the small and rough fields available. The prototype S.23 made its very successful maiden flight on 4 July 1936. It was named *Canopus* and all sister-ships had names beginning with C, the boats also being known as the C class.

Short G-class *Golden Hind*.

Short Kent.

Features included light-alloy stressed-skin construction; a cantilever high wing with electric Gouge flaps; four 685.6 kW (920 hp) Bristol Pegasus Xc radial engines driving DH Hamilton two-position propellers; and a streamlined nose incorporating an enclosed flight deck for captain, first officer, navigator and flight clerk. A steward's pantry was amidships and in the normal configuration seats were arranged in front and rear cabins for 24 passengers. On long hauls sleeping accommodation was provided for 16, with a promenade lounge. On some routes experience showed that the mail capacity had to be raised from 1.5 to 2 tonnes, reducing the passenger seats to 17.

Promenade cabin of a Short Empire Flying Boat.

All 28 were delivered, plus three for Qantas (Australia). Two were long-range boats with increased weight and transatlantic range. Eleven S.30s (eight for Imperial and three for Tasman Empire Airways) had 663 kW (890 hp) Perseus XIIc sleeve-valve engines and greater range – the first four also being equipped for flight refuelling to greater weight. The final two boats were S.33s with increased weight and Pegasus engines.

During World War II most of these great aircraft served on long routes all over the world. Four were impressed for RAF use with radar (two being destroyed in Norway in May 1940) and most were re-engined with the same 752.6 kW (1,010 hp) Pegasus 22 engines as the Sunderlands (the derived military version). Their achievements were amazing: one made 442 crossings of the Tasman Sea, two evacuated 469 troops from Crete and one was flown out of a small river in the Belgian Congo in 1940. Others maintained schedules on the North Atlantic, between Britain and Africa, the dangerous Mediterranean route from Gibraltar to Malta and Cairo, and the Horseshoe route between Australia, India and South Africa. Most were retired in 1947.

Data (S.23 LR): *Engines* as above *Wing span* 34.75 m (114 ft 0 in) *Length* 26.84 m (88 ft 0 in) *Max T-O weight* 19,732 kg (43,500 lb), (flight-refuelling and S.33) 24,041 kg (53,000 lb) *Max level speed* 311 km/h (200 mph) *Range* 1,245 km (760 miles)

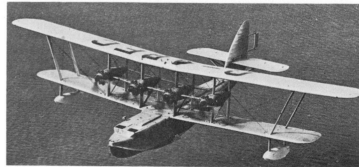

Short G class (UK) The G class flying-boat was a development of the Empire 'boat and designed for service with Imperial Airways over the North Atlantic. Three were completed as mail carriers as it was not intended to carry passengers until experience had been gained in operation of a regular service across the Atlantic. They were, however, taken over by the authorities and converted into military flying-boats. One (formerly named *Golden Fleece*) was lost while on patrol in the Bay of Biscay. The other two were returned to BOAC in 1941 and modified back for civil use. Power was provided by four Bristol Hercules IV engines.

Short Kent (UK) The Kent was a 15-passenger flying-boat designed to the requirements of Imperial Airways. Fitted with four 413.6 kW (555 hp) Bristol Jupiter XF.BM engines, the general design followed closely upon the Calcutta which the Kent replaced. Three were built, the first flying on 24 February 1931, named *Scipio*.

Short Sandringham 2.

Short Sandringham (UK) The Sandringham was a four-engined civil flying-boat, the basic airframe of which did not differ from that of the Sunderland. The modifications were confined to secondary structural changes and to the complete re-arrangement of the interior.

The Sandringham 1 was powered by 745.2 kW (1,000 hp) Bristol Pegasus 38 engines and accommodated 24 passengers by day or 16 by night. It was supplied to BOAC. The Sandringham 2 went to the Aviacion del Litoral Fluvial Argentina and was powered by 894 kW (1,200 hp) Pratt & Whitney R-1830-92 Twin Wasp engines and accommodated 28 passengers on the lower deck and 17 on the upper. The similar 21-passenger Sandringham 3 also went to Argentina. The 30-passenger R-1830-90D Twin Wasp-powered Sandringham 4 was supplied to Tasman Empire Airways, while the 22/16-passenger (day/night) Sandringham 5 (similar to 4) was BOAC's second version. Norwegian Air Lines received the 37-passenger Sandringham 6 (similar to 3), while the final Sandringham 6 version (similar to 4) was supplied to BOAC.
Data (Mk 1): *Engines* as above *Wing span* 34.39 m (112 ft 9½ in) *Length* 26.28 m (86 ft 3 in) *Max T-O weight* 24,401 kg (56,000 lb) *Max level speed* 346 km/h (215 mph) *Range* 2,575 km (1,600 miles)

Shorts SC.7 Skyvan (UK) Design of the Skyvan light civil or military STOL utility transport was started as a private venture in 1959. The prototype flew for the first time on 17 January 1963. This was designated Series 1 and then 1A (Continental then Astazou II engines). It was followed by the 16 Series 2 initial production aircraft with Astazou XII turboprop engines. The current ver-

sions are the civil Series 3 and 3A and the military Series 3M. Production of the de luxe Skyliner all-passenger version of the Series 3/3A has ended. Total orders for the Series 3/3A/3M and Skyliner had reached 127 by mid-1979.
Data: *Engines* two 533 kW (715 shp) Garrett-AiResearch TPE 331-201 turboprops *Wing span* 19.79 m (64 ft 11 in) *Length* 12.6 m (41 ft 4 in) *Max T-O weight* 6,577 kg (14,500 lb) *Max cruising speed* 327 km/h (203 mph) *Range* 1,115 km (694 miles) *Accommodation* (Srs 3) 19 passengers,

Short Scion-Senior.

Shorts 330.

or 12 stretcher patients and attendants; or 2,085 kg (4,600 lb) of freight, vehicles or agricultural equipment; (Srs 3M) 22 troops, 16 paratroops, etc

Short Scion and Scion-Senior (UK) The Scion was a twin-engined light five-passenger transport aircraft powered by two 67 kW (90 hp) Pobjoy engines. The prototype flew for the first time on 18 August 1933. The Scion-Senior was basically a larger four-engined version, accommodating nine passengers.

Short Scylla (UK) Flown in 1934, Short produced two landplane derivatives of the Kent flying-boat for Imperial Airways, powered by four Perseus or Pegasus engines at different times. Accommodation was for 36 passengers.

Shorts 330 (UK) Twin-turboprop transport aircraft, first flown as a prototype on 22 August 1974. By mid-1979 orders for 43 had been placed and 27 had been delivered. Power is provided by two 862 kW (1,156 shp) Pratt & Whitney Aircraft of Canada PT6A-45A turboprop engines and accommodation is normally for 30 passengers.

Short Seaford (UK) Further development of the Sunderland series, eight of which were completed

Short SC.1 VTOL research aircraft of 1957, powered by five Rolls-Royce RB.108 turbojet engines (four mounted vertically and one horizontally).

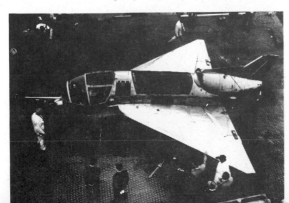

Short

Short Seamew.

Short Singapore III.

Short Stirling IIIs.

Short Solent.

Short Sturgeon TT.2 target-towing aircraft.

for the RAF, delivered in 1946 (see **Sunderland**).
Short Sealand (UK) The Sealand twin-engined light commercial amphibian flying-boat was first flown on 22 January 1948. Power was provided by 253.4 kW (340 hp) de Havilland Gipsy Queen 70-4 engines and accommodation was for five to eight passengers. Only a small number were produced, including three for the Indian Navy.
Short Seamew (UK) Designed as a light anti-submarine aircraft and first flown in 1953.
Short Singapore III (UK) The Singapore III reconnaissance and coastal patrol flying-boat was basically the production version of the earlier Singapore II, itself developed from the twin Buzzard-engined Singapore I of 1926. Thirty-seven Singapore IIIs were delivered to the RAF, entering service in the spring of 1935. The last few aircraft were withdrawn in late 1941, when they were transferred to the Royal New Zealand Air Force. Power was provided by four 417.3 kW (560 hp) Rolls-Royce Kestrel IIMS and IIIMS engines mounted in tandem pairs between the biplane wings.

Short Solent (UK) The Solent was the civil version of the Seaford flying-boat, 18 of which were operated by BOAC as 30-passenger Solent 2s (12) and 34-passenger Solent 3s (6) before the company abandoned the use of flying-boats in 1950. Power for these was provided by Bristol Hercules 637 engines. Four Solent 4s were operated by Tasman Empire Airways with Hercules 733 engines and accommodation for 42 day passengers.
Short Stirling (UK) The Stirling's design was

based on Air Ministry Specification B.12/36. It was the first of the large four-engined bombers to go into service with the RAF. The original layout of the bomber was tried out by the construction of a half-scale model fitted with four 97 kW (130 hp) Pobjoy engines. Flying trials with this proved the feasibility of the design, which included several novel and previously untried features.

The prototype Stirling (with four Bristol Hercules II engines) flew for the first time on 14 May 1939. This aircraft crashed on landing after its maiden flight, but a second prototype was completed and was flying in the autumn of 1939. Deliveries of production aircraft to the RAF began in August 1940, the early aircraft being built by the parent company. An organisation system of dispersal was soon put into operation, whereby the main components were built in more than 20 different factories.

The first production version for the RAF was the Stirling I powered by four 1,185 kW (1,590 hp) Bristol Hercules XI radial engines and without a dorsal turret fitted. Mk Is were first used in action on the night of 10–11 February 1941. The Stirling II, only a few of which were completed, was a conversion of the Mk I with Wright R-2600-A5B Cyclone engines. The Mk III had four 1,229.5 kW (1,650 hp) Bristol Hercules XVI engines and featured a mid-upper turret. From 1943, when the Stirling was no longer a suitable bomber, many were fitted for glider towing (Horsa glider).

Unlike the Mk III, the Stirling IV was produced from new as a long-range troop transport and glider tug, the nose and upper turrets being removed and replaced by fairings, although the four-gun tail turret was retained. Up to 24 paratroops or 34 airborne troops could be carried. The final version of the Stirling was the Mk V, an unarmed military transport and freighter with a redesigned nose. Total production of the Stirling –

the Mk III of which was the major variant – was about 2,380.

Data (Mk III): *Engines* as above *Wing span* 30.2 m (99 ft 1 in) *Length* 26.59 m (87 ft 3 in) *Max T-O weight* 31,751 kg (70,000 lb) *Max level speed* 435 km/h (270 mph) *Range* 950–3,235 km (590–2,010 miles) *Armament* eight 0.303 in Browning machine-guns, two in nose and mid-upper turrets and four in tail turret, plus up to 6,350 kg (14,000 lb) of bombs

Short Sturgeon (UK) Originally designed as a twin-engined naval reconnaissance bomber for operation from the *Ark Royal* and *Hermes*-class aircraft carriers. With the end of the war, the need for such an aircraft receded and so a new specification was drawn up to convert the Sturgeon into a high-performance carrier-based target tug, suitable for towing targets for ground-to-air firing practice, photographic marking of ground-to-air firing, target towing for air-to-air practice by night and day, 'throw-off' target practice and radar calibration. The FAA received a small number during the early 1950s.

Short Sunderland (UK) The Sunderland maritime-patrol and reconnaissance flying-boat was designed to meet the requirements of Air Ministry Specification R.2/33 and was virtually a military version of the Empire 'boat. The prototype flew for the first time in October 1937, just over a year after the first Empire began its trials. By the outbreak of war there were three squadrons of RAF Coastal Command operational with it and others in the process of re-equipping or forming. The Sunderland was notable for being the first flying-boat to be equipped with power-operated gun turrets.

The first production version was the Sunderland I powered by Bristol Pegasus 22 engines and armed with eight 0.303 in machine-guns: two in a Fraser-Nash nose turret, four in a Fraser-Nash tail turret, and two on hand-operated mountings in the upper part of the hull aft of the wing trailing edge.

The Sunderland II had Pegasus XVIII engines, but was otherwise similar to the Mk I, although late models were fitted with a two-gun dorsal turret in place of the manually operated guns. The Mk III used the same power plant as the Mk II, but had a modified hull with a streamlined front step and a dorsal turret as standard. The final military version was the Sunderland V, the IV having become the Seaford. Power for the Mk V was provided by 894 kW (1,200 hp) Pratt & Whitney R-1830-90B Twin Wasp engines. Armament comprised four fixed 0.303 in

SIA 7B.

machine-guns in the nose, two similar beam guns and four in the tail turret.

In 1943 a number of Sunderlands were de-militarised, equipped to carry 20 passengers and turned over to BOAC.

Data (Mk III): *Engines* as above *Wing span* 43.39 m (112 ft 9½ in) *Length* 26.01 m (85 ft 4 in) *Max T-O weight* 26,308 kg (58,000 lb) *Max level speed* 338 km/h (210 mph) *Range* 2,865–4,667 km (1,780–2,900 miles) *Armament* machine-guns as above, plus 907 kg (2,000 lb) of bombs

Showa L2D2 (Japan) Japanese version of the Douglas DC-3 transport, known to the Allies during world War II as *Tabby*. A total of 450 built, 70 by Nakajima.

SIA 5 (Italy) Derivative of the Farman M.F.11 for the Italian Army Air Service, powered by a 74.5 kW (100 hp) Fiat A.10 or similar engine.

SIA 7 (Italy) The SIA 7B1 and 7B2 were two-seat reconnaissance and light bombing biplanes of 1917 and 1918 respectively, differing mainly in that the 7B1 was powered by a 186.3 kW (250 hp) Fiat A.12 engine, while the 7B2 had a strengthened structure and a 223.6 kW (300 hp) Fiat A.12*bis* engine. The Italian Army Air Service received more than 500 7B1s and 72 7B2s. The AEF also received 19 7B2s, but these were used as trainers.

Data (7B2): *Engine* as above *Wing span* 13.32 m (43 ft 8½ in) *Length* 9.06 m (29 ft 8¾ in) *Max T-O weight* 1,100 kg (2,425 lb) *Max level speed* 200 km/h (124 mph) *Armament* one forward-firing and one rear-mounted Revelli machine-guns, plus bombs

SIA 9 (Italy) In February 1918 the SIA 9B appeared as a larger, heavier and much more powerful development of the SIA 7B2. Power was provided by a massive 521.6 kW (700 hp) Fiat A.14 engine, but the increased weight of the aircraft meant that only a slight increase in maximum speed was realised. The 9B was not ordered by the Italian Army but instead by the Italian

Short Sunderland V.

SIAI-Marchetti S.205.

SIAI

SIAI-Marchetti SA.202 Bravo.

Navy, which received only 62 of 500 ordered by the end of the war. Meanwhile Fiat, of which SIA was only the aircraft manufacturing branch during the war, dropped the name SIA and produced a version of the 9B2 as the R.2. However R.2s saw very little action during the final weeks of the war, the 129 built remaining in service in reduced numbers until 1925.

Data (9B): *Engine* as above *Wing span* 15.5 m (50 ft 10¼ in) *Length* 9.7 m (31 ft 10 in) *Max T-O weight* 1,900 kg (4,189 lb) *Max level speed* 205 km/h (127 mph) *Range* 600 km (373 miles)

SIAI S.8 (Italy) The S.8 was a reconnaissance and anti-submarine two-seat biplane flying-boat of 1917, powered by a 126.7 kW (170 hp) Isotta-Fraschini I.F. V-4B or 89.4 kW (120 hp) Colombo F-150 engine mounted in pusher configuration. A total of 172 was produced for the Italian Navy.

Data: *Engine* as above *Wing span* 12.77 m (41 ft 10¾ in) *Length* 9.75 m (32 ft 0 in) *Max T-O weight* 1,425 kg (3,142 lb) *Max level speed* 142 km/h (88.25 mph) *Armament* two Revelli machine-guns flexibly mounted in the bow cockpit

SIAI S.12 and S.13 (Italy) Biplane flying-boats, better known as Savoia types and used for the Schneider Trophy races (see **Schneider Trophy contestants**).

SIAI S.16 to S.64 (Italy) See **Savoia** and **Savoia-Marchetti**

SIAI-Marchetti SF.260Ms.

In 1968 the S.208 version became available, produced basically as a five-seat, more powerful version of the S.205, with some 60% of its structural components in common. By February 1973 approximately 80 S.208s had been delivered to customers in Europe and Africa, including 44 S.208Ms to the Italian Air Force for liaison and training duties. A version for general duties, including agricultural and ambulance work, was developed as the S.208AG.

The current versions are the S.205/20R four-seater with a 149 kW (200 hp) Lycoming IO-360-A1B6D (selected as a second-level trainer by the Italian Aero Club, to which delivery of 140 S.205ACs began in 1977); and S.208A five-seater with a 194 kW (260 hp) Lycoming O-540-E4A5 engine (available also in cargo, ambulance or agricultural versions).

Data (S.205/20R): *Engine* as above *Wing span* 10.86 m (35 ft 7½ in) *Length* 8.0 m (26 ft 3 in) *Max T-O weight* 1,300 kg (2,866 lb) *Max level speed* 221 km/h (137 mph) *Range* 1,258 km (782 miles)

SIAI-Marchetti S.210 (Italy) Six-seat twin-engined version of the S.205 powered by two 149 kW (200 hp) Lycoming TIO-360-As.

SIAI-Marchetti S.211 (Italy) Lightweight low-cost basic trainer and light-attack aircraft powered by a 9.8 kN (2,200 lb st) Pratt & Whitney Aircraft of Canada JT15D-1 turbofan engine. The first flight is expected in 1981.

SIAI-Marchetti/FFA SA.202 Bravo (Italy/Switzerland) Two-seat light training aircraft (see **FFA AS.202 Bravo**).

SIAI-Marchetti SF.260 (Italy) The prototype for the SF.260 series, known as the F.250, flew for the first time on 15 July 1964. The version developed initially for civil production was manufactured at first under licence from Aviamilano by SIAI-Marchetti and is designated SF.260. Subsequently SIAI-Marchetti became the official holder of the type certificate and of all manufacturing rights of the SF.260. It has continued to develop the civil version, the current version being the SF.260C three-seater powered by the same type of engine as used in the current military versions (approximately 30–40 civil SF.260s, including SF.260As and SF.260Bs, had been built by the spring of 1978).

SIAI-Marchetti S.208M.

SIAI-Marchetti S.210.

SIAI-Marchetti S.205 and S.208 (Italy) Design of the S.205 four-seat all-metal light monoplane was started in March 1964 and by April of the following year three examples had been completed. Each had a 134 kW (180 hp) Lycoming engine fitted, but a wide range of versions subsequently became available with different engines and equipment.

Three military versions of the SF.260 are available as the SF.260M two–three-seat trainer (operated by 13 air forces); SF.260W Warrior trainer/tactical-support version of the SF.260M (operated by five air forces and the Dubai Police Air Wing); and the SF.260SW Sea Warrior for surveillance, search and rescue, and supply missions (no orders announced by mid-1979).

By mid-1979 more than 600 civil and military SF.260s of all models had been completed, most of which were for export.

Data (SF.260M): *Engine* one 194 kW (260 hp) Lycoming O-540-E4A5 *Wing span* 8.35 m (27 ft 4¾ in) *Length* 7.1 m (23 ft 3½ in) *Max T-O weight* 1,200 kg (2,645 lb) *Max level speed* 340 km/h (211 mph) *Range* 1,650 km (1,025 miles) *Armament* (SF.260W Warrior) two or four underwing hardpoints able to carry external stores on NATO standard pylons up to a maximum of 300 kg (661 lb) when flown as a single-seater. Loads can include one or two SIAI gun pods, each with one 7.62 mm FN machine-gun, rockets, general purpose or fragmentation bombs, two throwers for 74 mm explosive cartridges, one cartridge thrower and a photo-reconnaissance pod, or auxiliary fuel tanks

SIAI-Marchetti SM.95 (Italy) Four-engined commercial airliner accommodating 30 or 38 passengers.

SIAI-Marchetti SM.102 (Italy) Twin-engined light transport aircraft accommodating eight passengers.

SIAI-Marchetti SM.1019E (Italy) Two-seat STOL light monoplane powered by a 298 kW (400 shp) Allison 250-B17 turboprop engine. Suitable for observation, light ground attack or utility duties. The prototype first flew on 24 May 1969. Eighty SM.1019EIs were ordered for the ALE (Italian Army Light Aviation), deliveries beginning in the summer of 1978. Optional armament or equipment on two underwing hardpoints includes 2.75 in rocket launchers, gun

Siemens-Schuckert D.IV.

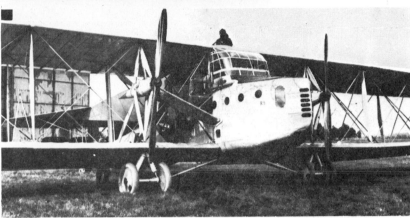

Siemens-Schuckert R.V.

pods, missiles, bombs, auxiliary fuel tanks or a reconnaissance pod. Maximum level speed is 296 km/h (184 mph).

Siebel Si.204 (France) Twin-engined eight-passenger transport aircraft (Si.204A) and military instrument trainer (Si.204D), production of which began in 1942 at the SNCAC factory at Bourges for French and Luftwaffe service (see **SNCAC NC 701/702 Martinet**).

Siemens-Schuckert D.I (Germany) The D.I single-seat fighter biplane entered service in 1917 and was basically a copy of the French Nieuport. Its 82 kW (110 hp) Siemens-Halske Sh.I engine gave a maximum speed of only 155 km/h (96.5 mph), resulting in most of the aircraft ordered being cancelled, while those delivered were operated mainly on the Eastern Front.

Siemens-Schuckert D.III and D.IV (Germany) The D.III represented a complete break from the D.I type and was a more modern aircraft. Powered by a 119 kW (160 hp) Sh.III engine, covered by a neat cowl, it had a rounded-section fuselage made of three-ply wood, shaped to offer minimum head resistance. Ailerons were fitted to upper and lower wings and a new tail unit of unusual shape was fitted. Production D.IIIs, about 50 of which were ordered with this engine and 30 with the 119 kW (160 hp) Sh.IIIa, entered service in January 1918.

At the same time as the D.III was being delivered, the new D.IV was being tested at the official fighter competitions. Although basically similar to the earlier type, it had slightly reduced-span wings. Power plant was the Sh.IIIa, although the 1920 *Jane's* states a 149 kW (200 hp) Siemens engine. Rate of climb exceeded that required and, with good manoeuvrability and sufficient speed, the D.IV was ordered into production. It is thought that some 50 or so D.IVs

SIAI-Marchetti SM.1019E.

Siemens-Schuckert D.I.

Siemens-Schuckert

Sikorsky CH-53E.

had become operational by the Armistice, although production had far exceeded this.

Data (D.IV): *Engine* as above *Wing span* 8.35 m (27 ft 4¾ in) *Length* 5.7 m (18 ft 8¼ in) *Max T-O weight* 735 kg (1,620.5 lb) *Max level speed* 190 km/h (118.5 mph) *Endurance* 2 h *Armament* two forward-firing Spandau machine-guns

Siemens-Schuckert E.I and E.III (Germany) Basically similar to other German single-seat monoplane fighters of 1915–16, the E.I and E.III were powered by 82 kW (110 hp) Siemens-Halske Sh.I and 74.5 kW (100 hp) Oberursel U.I rotary engines respectively. Only a very small number were built, each armed with one forward-firing Spandau machine-gun. Maximum speed was 135 km/h (84 mph).

Siemens-Schuckert R.I to R.VII (Germany) Siemens-Schuckert was the second firm in Germany to take up the construction of giant bombing aircraft, following close upon the Zeppelin enterprise. The first two giant models were begun in 1914. The first, designed by Forsman in December 1914 and built in early 1915, was virtually a copy of the Sikorsky biplane and had four Mercedes engines mounted on the lower wings. This proved underpowered and development ended.

The contemporary giant, designed by Steffen, had three centrally mounted engines inside the fuselage, which drove through an automatic disengaging clutch to a main gear in case one engine stopped. From the main gear, universally jointed transmission shafts led to reduction gears for two large propellers mounted at the first set of interplane struts. The first example (the R.I) was powered by 112 kW (150 hp) Benz Bz.III engines. Seven aircraft in total were built with various engine installations, the most common being 164 kW (220 hp) Benz Bz.IVs. The four Bz.IV-powered R types were operated as heavy bombers on the Eastern Front and the other three became trainers. Maximum speed achieved was 130 km/h (81 mph).

Sikorsky CH-53E (USA) The Sikorsky S-65 was chosen in 1973 for development with a three-engined power plant to provide the US Navy and Marine Corps with a heavy-duty multi-purpose helicopter. Other changes to increase performance included installation of a new seven-blade main rotor of increased diameter and blades of titanium construction, and an uprated transmission of 9,798 kW (13,140 shp) capacity to cater for future developments.

The first prototype YCH-53E made a flight on 1 March 1974, during which low-altitude hovering and limited manoeuvres were carried out. It was lost subsequently in an accident on the ground, but the programme was resumed on 24 January 1975 with the second YCH-53E. This aircraft has flown at an AUW of 33,793 kg (74,500 lb), the highest gross weight achieved by any helicopter outside the USSR.

In February 1978 Sikorsky was awarded a contract to initiate full-scale production, with initial approval for six aircraft. Later the same year the US Navy exercised an option for an additional 14 CH-53Es. The US Navy plans to use the CH-53E for vertical on-board delivery operations; to support mobile construction battalions; and for the removal of battle-damaged aircraft from carrier decks. In amphibious operations it would be able to airlift 93% of a US Marine division's combat items and would be able to retrieve 98% of the Marine Corps' tactical aircraft without disassembly.

The CH-53E is also the largest helicopter capable of full operation from the Navy's existing and planned ships, requiring only 10% more deck space than the twin-turbine H-53. It offers double the lift of the latter aircraft with an increase of only 50% in engine power. It is anticipated that CH-53Es will begin to join the US fleet in late 1980.

Data: *Engines* three 2,756 kW (3,696 shp) General Electric T64-GE-415 turboshafts *Main rotor diameter* 24.08 m (79 ft 0 in) *Length of fuselage* 22.48 m (73 ft 9 in) *Max T-O weight* 33,339 kg (73,500 lb) *Max level speed* 315 km/h (196 mph) *Range* 2,075 km (1,290 miles) *Accommodation* up to 55 troops

Sikorsky R-4 (USA) The R-4 was the first helicopter in the world to be put into series production and the first military helicopter to be operated in sizeable numbers. The experimental prototype (the XR-4) flew for the first time on 13 January 1942 and was a two-seat development of the earlier VS-300. It was delivered by air from Stratford, Connecticut to Wright Field, Dayton, Ohio by easy stages and under various weather conditions without any trouble. On the basis of

Sikorsky R-4.

the successful trials which followed, a limited production order for three YR-4As was placed for the USAAF, followed by orders for 27 YR-27Bs and eventually 100 R-4Bs. These were used for training and service trials, one being sent to Burma and another to Alaska. A few were also allocated to the US Navy and US Coast Guard, although nearly half those built were supplied to Britain as Hoverfly Is.

In May 1943 tests in America were conducted by the War Shipping Administration and Coast Guard to prove the feasibility of operating the helicopter from the platform of a ship, using a tanker in Long Island Sound. However the R-4s were normally used for training, experimental-observation and rescue duties.

Data (R-4B): *Engine* one 138 kW (185 hp) Warner R-550-1 or R-550-3 Super Scarab *Main rotor diameter* 11.58 m (38 ft 0 in) *Length* 14.68 m (48 ft 2 in) *Max T-O weight* 1,152 kg (2,540 lb) *Max level speed* 121 km/h (75 mph) *Range* 210 km (130 miles)

Sikorsky R-5 (USA) see **Sikorsky S-51**

Sikorsky S-16.

Sikorsky S-38.

Sikorsky R-6A (USA) The R-6A was a direct development of the R-4 and, despite its later designation, was not as advanced as the R-5. The prototype, retaining the basic shape of the R-4 but in refined form, was flown for the first time on 15 October 1943. Eventually more than 220 helicopters were produced for the USAAF for observation duties (and training). A small number of these were transferred to the US Navy and to the RAF and FAA as Hoverfly IIs. Power was provided by a 182.5 kW (245 hp) Franklin O-405-9 engine, giving a maximum speed of 161 km/h (100 mph). Construction of the fuselage was interesting. The framework was all-metal but the cabin itself was constructed of aluminium, moulded plastic-impregnated glass-fibre cloth and Plexiglas windows. The engine compartment and rotor pylon were covered by a cowling made of paper-based moulded plastic. The rear fuselage carrying the tail rotor was a light metal monocoque.

Sikorsky S-16 (Russia) Armed two-seat reconnaissance biplane of 1915 powered by a 59.6 kW (80 hp) Gnome rotary engine.

Sikorsky S-20 (Russia) Single-seat scout of 1917 powered by an 82 kW (110 hp) Le Rhône rotary engine.

Sikorsky S-36 (USA) Eight-seat amphibious flying-boat powered by two 149 kW (200 hp)

Wright Whirlwind engines. It entered service with Pan American Airways in 1928.

Sikorsky S-38 (USA) The S-38 was a nine-seat commercial amphibian powered by two 313 kW (420 hp) Pratt & Whitney Wasp radial engines. A sesquiplane wing arrangement was employed and the tail unit was carried on two outriggers running aft from the main wing and braced to the heel of the hull by two struts. It was a successful design and many were built for airline use (including Pan American Airways, entering service in October 1938), private use and for the US Navy/USAAC. The type also set several world records for speed and altitude with specific loads.

Data: *Engines* as above *Wing span* 21.84 m (71 ft 8 in) *Length* 12.27 m (40 ft 3 in) *Max T-O weight* 4,753 kg (10,478 lb) *Max level speed* 200 km/h (125 mph)

Sikorsky S-39 (USA) A smaller single-engined development of the S-38 powered by a Pratt & Whitney Wasp Junior engine and accommodating five persons.

Sikorsky S-40 (USA) When built the Sikorsky S-40 was the largest amphibian in the world. Powered by four 428.5 kW (575 hp) Pratt & Whitney Hornet engines, it had accommodation for 28 passengers and the added luxury of a smoking room with three chairs. It entered service with Pan American Airways on 19 November 1931.

Sikorsky R-6A.

Sikorsky S-40.

Sikorsky

Sikorsky S-41.

Sikorsky S-42.

Sikorsky VS-44A Excalibur.

Sikorsky S-43.

Sikorsky S-41 (USA) Fifteen-passenger development of the S-38 powered by three 428.5 kW (575 hp) Pratt & Whitney Hornet engines. Also used in small numbers by the US Navy.

Sikorsky S-42 (USA) First flown on 29 March 1934, the S-42 was a large 36-passenger commercial flying-boat powered by four 559 kW (750 hp) Pratt & Whitney Hornet engines. It differed from earlier Sikorsky flying-boats in having a two-step hull with a long stern which supported the tail unit directly. Full use was made of a hydraulically controlled wing flap which extended across the straight portion of the wing. Within a brief period of time the S-42 had established ten altitude-with-load world records.

Ten S-42s were delivered to Pan American Airways, the last three as S-42Bs with increased wing span (from 34.8 m; 114 ft 2 in) and loaded weight and incorporating refinements in fairing and hull design. The original S-42 was used in survey flights across the Pacific in 1935 by Pan American Airways. In 1937 an S-42B surveyed the route from San Francisco to New Zealand, via Honolulu; a similar aircraft was used on the inaugural and scheduled mail and passenger service between New York and Bermuda, the latter shared with Imperial Airways and begun on 16 June 1937. At about the same time the final S-42B delivered to PAA (named *Clipper III*) made three

survey flights across the Atlantic by way of Newfoundland and Foynes.

Data (S-42B): *Engines* as above *Wing span* 36.0 m (118 ft 2 in) *Length* 20.73 m (68 ft 0 in) *Max T-O weight* 19,050 kg (42,000 lb) *Max level speed* 302 km/h (188 mph) *Range* 1,930 km (1,200 miles)

Sikorsky S-43 (USA) Eleven–fifteen-passenger commercial amphibian powered by two 559 kW (750 hp) Pratt & Whitney Hornet engines and known as the *Baby Clipper* as a smaller version of the S-42. Production aircraft went into service with Pan American Airways and a number of other airlines for operations in Norway, West Africa, Russia, China, Hawaiian and Philippine islands and South America. The US Navy/Marine Corps and USAAC also used the type as a general-purpose aircraft.

Data: *Engines* as above *Wing span* 26.21 m (86 ft 0 in) *Length* 15.6 m (51 ft 2 in) *Max T-O weight* 8,845 kg (9,500 lb) *Max level speed* 306 km/h (190 mph) *Range* 1,247 km (775 miles)

Sikorsky VS-44A Excalibur (USA) The VS-44A was a commercial version of the experimental XPBS-1 patrol-bomber flying-boat, which had been built for the US Navy and flown in 1937. Accommodating 40 passengers over short ranges or 16 with sleeping bunks, it was developed for American Export Airlines for use on its transatlantic service, which was inaugurated in 1942. Power was provided by four 894 kW (1,200 hp) Pratt & Whitney Twin Wasp engines. The last commercial use of the VS-44A came in the early 1960s, when Avalon Air Transport operated an ex-AEA aircraft.

Sikorsky S-51 and R-5 (USA) With the success of the R-4, Sikorsky developed two new and more refined helicopters for military use. One was the R-6A (see entry) and the other the R-5 (later becoming H-5). The R-5 had a completely new cabin area accommodating two persons in tandem and power was provided by a 335.3 kW

Sikorsky S-43.

(450 hp) Pratt & Whitney R-985-AN-5 engine. The first XR-5 experimental prototype flew on 18 August 1943. Eventually the USAF received 50 R-5As, some later being converted into three-seaters.

From the R-5 Sikorsky developed the four-seat commercial S-51, which was the first Sikorsky helicopter to be licensed by the CAA for commercial operation. This went into production in 1946 and examples were produced until 1951, more than 300 being built (probably including those delivered to the US Navy and RCAF). The S-51 was also the first helicopter to be series-built by Westland Aircraft in Britain after a manufacturing licence had been granted. The Westland-built

helicopter was known as the Dragonfly and the first flew in 1948. Dragonflies were supplied to the RAF and FAA and to commercial operators (see **Chronology** 1 Oct 1947, 1 June 1948, 20 Feb 1949 and 1 June 1950).
Data: *Engine* as above *Main rotor diameter* 14.63 m (48 ft 0 in) *Length* 17.39 m (57 ft 0½ in) *Max T-O weight* 2,495 kg (5,500 lb) *Max level speed* 165 km/h (103 mph)
Sikorsky S-52 (USA) As a new side-by-side two-seat light helicopter, the S-52 was developed for civil use and as a military liaison type. It was the first US helicopter to be fitted with all-metal rotor blades and flew for the first time in February 1947. In 1948 it established three international helicopter records for speed and height. Subsequent modification produced the S-52-2 as a

three–four-seater, fitted with a more powerful 182.5 kW (245 hp) Franklin engine. This version was ordered for the US Navy and Coast Guard.
Sikorsky S-55 (USA) The S-55 was a 12-seat utility helicopter suitable for passenger, air mail or cargo transport and for air rescue and military service. The most important feature of the design was the location of the power plant in the nose of the fuselage and so mounted that the drive shaft sloped up to the base of the rotor pylon, clear of the main cabin situated below the main rotor. This left a totally clear and spacious cabin for passengers or cargo. The prototype flew for the first time on 7 November 1949.

Apart from being adopted by the USAF, US Army, US Navy, US Marine Corps and US Coast Guard (eventually as the H-19 Chickasaw), it was sold in large numbers to commercial operators and was exported in military and civil versions. In addition it was licence-built in the UK by Westland Aircraft as the Whirlwind for military and civil use (the Series 3 with a 783 kW; 1,050 shp Bristol Siddeley Gnome H.1000 turboshaft engine fitted) and elsewhere. On 1 September 1953 Sabena began the first international helicopter service in the world using S-55s.
Data (H-19 Chickasaw, with Wright engine): *Engine* one 596 kW (800 hp) Wright R-1300-3 *Main rotor diameter* 16.15 m (53 ft 0 in) *Length of fuselage* 12.88 m (42 ft 3 in) *Max T-O weight* 3,583 kg (7,900 lb) *Max level speed* 180 km/h (112 mph) *Range* 580 km (360 miles) *Accommodation* crew of two and up to ten fully armed troops, six stretchers in ambulance role, or freight

Sikorsky S-51.

Sikorsky H-5H, operated by the USAF from 1959.

Sikorsky S-52-2, flown by the US Navy and Coast Guard as the HO5S-1.

Prototype two-seat Sikorsky S-52.

Loading a stretcher into a USMC Sikorsky HO5S-1 during the Korean War.

Sikorsky

Sikorsky

US Marine Corps Sikorsky HRS-1 (S-55) carries supplies to a hilltop position during the Korean War.

Westland-built turbine-powered development of the S-55, flown by the RAF as the Whirlwind HAR.10 search and rescue aircraft.

Sikorsky S-56, flown by the US Army as the H-37 Mojave.

Two Sikorsky S-58s operated by Sabena.

Sikorsky S-56 (USA) The S-56 was a twin-engined single-rotor transport helicopter of comparable size to a DC-3 airliner. First flown in prototype form on 18 December 1953, it was subsequently produced for the US Marines as the HR2S-1 (later CH-37C) assault transport and for the US Army as the H-37A and B (later CH-37A and B) cargo and troop transport. A total of 154 S-56s was built up to May 1960. Power was provided by two Pratt & Whitney R-2800 engines.

Sikorsky S-58 (USA) The first prototype of this helicopter flew on 8 March 1954 and the first production aircraft on 20 September 1954. In addition to the many versions that entered service with the US Navy (as the H-34 Seabat), US Army (as the H-34 Choctaw) and the USMC (as the H-34 Seahorse), three commercial versions were produced as the S-58B and D passenger freighters, similar to the military H-34s, and the S-58C scheduled passenger-carrying version with two entrance doors on the starboard side of the cabin. The first commercial deliveries were made (S-58C) in 1956–57. A very large number of S-58s

were also exported for civil and military use, bringing the total number of helicopters built by Sikorsky by the end of production in January 1970 to 1,821 – mostly for military operation.

In addition Westland Aircraft of the UK produced a turbine-engined version as the Wessex, initially for the Royal Navy as an anti-submarine helicopter but subsequently also for the RAF and for export. Wessex HAS.1s first entered service with the Royal Navy in July 1961. Sikorsky also developed a turbine-powered S-58 as the S-58T, with the aim of producing kits to convert piston-engined helicopters into the new version.

Data (CH-34A Choctaw): *Engine* one 1,137 kW (1,525 hp) Wright R-1820-84B/D radial *Main rotor diameter* 17.07 m (56 ft 0 in) *Length of fuselage* 14.25 m (46 ft 9 in) *Max normal T-O weight* 5,900 kg (13,000 lb) *Max level speed* 196 km/h (122 mph) *Range* 400 km (247 miles) *Accommodation* crew of two and 16–18 passengers, eight stretchers or freight

Data (Wessex Mk 60): *Engine* one 1,156 kW (1,550 shp) Rolls-Royce Bristol Gnome Mk 110 or Gnome Mk 111 turboshaft *Main rotor diameter* as above *Length of fuselage* 14.74 m (48 ft 4½ in) *Max T-O weight* 6,169 kg (13,600 lb) *Max level speed* 214 km/h (133 mph) *Range* 538 km (334 miles) *Accommodation* crew of two and ten passengers at airline standard; eight stretchers, two sitting casualties and a medical attendant; 15 survivors in a rescue role; or freight

Sikorsky S-61A and S-61B (USA) The first version of the S-61 ordered into production was the SH-3A (formerly HSS-2) Sea King amphibious anti-submarine helicopter. The original US Navy contract for this aircraft was received on 23 September 1957; the prototype flew for the first time

on 11 March 1959 and deliveries to the Fleet began in September 1961. The S-61 series now includes a number of military and commercial variants, which are listed below:

SH-3A Sea King Initial anti-submarine version for the US Navy powered by 932 kW (1,250 shp) General Electric T58-GE-8B turboshaft engines. A total of 255 was produced by Sikorsky. Also standard equipment in the Japan Maritime Self-Defence Force.

CH-124 Designation of 41 aircraft (similar to SH-3A) ordered for the Canadian Armed Forces.

S-61A Amphibious transport, generally similar to the US Navy's SH-3A. Accommodates 26 troops, 15 stretchers, cargo, or 12 passengers in VIP configuration. Rolls-Royce Gnome H.1200 turboshafts available as alternative to standard General Electric T58 engines. Nine delivered to Royal Danish Air Force with additional fuel tankage for long-range air-sea rescue duties. One S-61A delivered to Construction Helicopters.

S-61A-4 Nuri Thirty-eight aircraft for the Royal Malaysian Air Force, each with 31 seats, rescue hoists and auxiliary fuel tanks as standard equipment. These aircraft are used for troop transport, cargo carrying and rescue.

HH-3A Variant of SH-3A for search and rescue duties with the US Navy.

SH-3D Sea King Standard anti-submarine helicopter of the US Navy with T58-GE-10 engines and more fuel than SH-3A. First SH-3D (delivered in June 1966) was one of ten for the Spanish Navy, which later ordered 12 more. Four were delivered to the Brazilian Navy and 72 to the US Navy. SH-3Ds are also manufactured under licence by Agusta in Italy.

S-61D-4 Four for Argentine Navy, similar to SH-3D.

VH-3D Eleven delivered to replace VH-3As of USAF Executive Flight Detachment.

SH-3G US Navy conversion of 105 SH-3As into utility helicopters, by removing anti-submarine warfare equipment. Six equipped with Minigun pods for search and rescue missions in combat conditions.

SH-3H Multi-purpose version of the SH-3G. Contracts from the US Navy call for conversion of 163 existing aircraft to increase fleet helicopter capability against submarines and low-flying missiles. General Electric T58-GE-10 engines are fitted.

Data (SH-3D): *Engines* two 1,044 kW (1,400 shp) General Electric T58-GE-10 turboshafts *Main rotor diameter* 18.9 m (62 ft 0 in) *Length of fuselage* 16.69 m (54 ft 9 in) *Normal T-O weight* 8,449 kg (18,626 lb) *Max level speed* 267 km/h (166 mph) *Range* 1,005 km (625 miles) *Armament* provision for 381 kg (840 lb) of weapons, including homing torpedoes

Sikorsky S-61L and S-61N (USA) Although basically similar to the S-61A and B, the S-61L and N commercial transports incorporate a number of changes, including a longer fuselage. The S-61L is the non-amphibious configuration with a modified landing gear, rotor head and

The Westland Wessex HAS.1 evolved from the S-58.

Sikorsky S-58T.

stabiliser. Accommodation is for up to 30 passengers. First flight of the prototype S-61L was made on 6 December 1960. Production has been completed.

The S-61N is similar to the S-61L, but with a sealed hull for amphibious operation and stabilising floats as on the SH-3. Accommodation is provided for 26–28 passengers. The prototype was first flown on 7 August 1962. It is now available also in Mark II form with General Electric CT58-140-1 or -2 turboshaft engines (earlier aircraft have 1,007 kW; 1,350 shp engines), enabling it to carry 22 passengers on an 86°F (30°C) day, compared with the former 10. This version is in production.

The Payloader is a stripped-down version of the S-61N, weighing nearly 907 kg (2,000 lb) less than the standard version but capable of lifting a payload of more than 4,990 kg (11,000 lb). It is intended for logging, general construction, power-line installation and similar operations. Sponsons are replaced by a fixed main-wheel landing gear.

On 6 October 1964 the S-61L and S-61N became the first transport helicopters to receive FAA approval for IFR operations. A total of 116 commercial S-61s had been delivered by 8 June 1979.

Data (S-61N Mk II): *Engines* two 1,118 kW (1,500 shp) General Electric CT58-140-1/2

Sikorsky S-61N.

Sikorsky

Sikorsky HH-3F Pelican.

Sikorsky HH-52A.

First two Sikorsky CH-53D/Gs built for Germany.

Sikorsky S-64E Skycrane.

turboshafts *Main rotor diameter* 18.9 m (62 ft 0 in) *Length overall* 22.2 m (72 ft 10 in) *Max T-O weight* 9,980 kg (22,000 lb) *Max cruising speed* 241 km/h (150 mph) *Range* (standard tanks) 453 km (282 miles)

Sikorsky S-61R (USA) Although based on the SH-3A, this amphibious transport helicopter introduced many important design changes. They include provision of a hydraulically operated rear ramp for straight-in loading of wheeled vehicles; a 907 kg (2,000 lb) capacity winch for internal cargo handling; retractable tricycle-type landing gear; pressurised rotor blades for quick and easy inspection; gas-turbine auxiliary power supply for independent field operations; self-lubricating main and tail rotors; and built-in equipment for the removal and replacement of all major components in remote areas.

The first S-61R flew on 17 June 1963, followed by the first CH-3C a few weeks later. Deliveries have been made to USAF Aerospace Defense Command, Air Training Command, Tactical Air Command, Strategic Air Command and Aerospace Rescue and Recovery Service. Production by Sikorsky has ended, but S-61R variants continue to be available from Agusta of Italy. There have been four Sikorsky-built versions, as listed below:

CH-3C Two 969.5 kW (1,300 shp) T58-GE-1 turboshaft engines. After a total of 41 had been built for the USAF, production was switched to the CH-3E. All aircraft delivered as CH-3Cs were modified to CH-3E standard.

CH-3E Designation applicable since 1966, following introduction of uprated engines (1,118 kW; 1,500 shp T58-GE-5s). A total of 42 was built as new aircraft to this standard.

HH-3E For USAF Aerospace Rescue and Recovery Service. Additional equipment comprises armour, self-sealing fuel tanks, retractable flight-refuelling probe, defensive armament and rescue hoist. Two 1,118 kW (1,500 shp) T58-GE-5 turboshafts. A total of 50 HH-3Es was converted from CH-3Es and are known as Jolly Green Giants.

HH-3F Similar to HH-3E for US Coast Guard, which has given them the name Pelican. It has advanced electronic equipment for search and rescue duties. No armour plate, armament or self-sealing tanks. Deliveries began in 1968 and a total of 40 was built.

Data (CH-3E): *Engines* two 1,118 kW (1,500 shp) General Electric T58-GE-5 turboshafts *Main rotor diameter* 18.9 m (62 ft 0 in) *Length of fuselage* 17.45 m (57 ft 3 in) *Max T-O weight* 10,000 kg (22,050 lb) *Max level speed* 261 km/h (162 mph) *Range* 748 km (465 miles) *Accommodation* normally 25 fully equipped troops; alternatively 30 troops, 15 stretchers, or 2,270 kg (5,000 lb) of cargo

Sikorsky S-62 (USA) The prototype S-62 flew for the first time on 14 May 1958 using the transmission and rotor system of the S-55 and was the first amphibious helicopter produced by Sikorsky. The S-62A initial production version has accommodation for ten passengers. Twenty-five were also built under licence in Japan by Mitsubishi. The S-62B is similar to the S-62A but has the S-58 main rotor system reduced in diameter to that of the earlier model. The last commercial model produced was the S-62C, which is similar to the HH-52A. About 50 commercial S-62s were built. The HH-52A is a search and rescue helicopter for the US Coast Guard. Deliveries began in 1963 and 99 were produced. Sikorsky also delivered S-62s to the Indian Air Force and the Thailand Police Force.

Data (HH-52A): *Engine* one 932 kW (1,250 shp) General Electric T58-GE-8B turboshaft derated to 544.5 kW (730 shp) *Main rotor diameter* 16.16 m (53 ft 0 in) *Length of fuselage* 13.58 m (44 ft 6½ in) *Max T-O weight* 3,674 kg (8,100 lb) *Max level speed* 175 km/h (109 mph) *Range* 764 km (474 miles)

Sikorsky

Accommodation crew of two and 12 passengers; alternative cargo layout

Sikorsky S-64 Skycrane (USA) First flown on 9 May 1962, the Skycrane is a heavy flying-crane helicopter. It was designed initially for military transport duties. Equipped with interchangeable pods, it is suitable for use as a troop transport and for mine-laying, cargo and missile transport, anti-submarine or field hospital operations. Attachment points are provided on the fuselage and landing gear to facilitate securing of bulky loads. Pickup of loads is made easier by the pilot's ability to shorten or extend the landing gear hydraulically.

The US Army placed an initial order for six in 1963, delivery taking place in the winter of 1964–65. These are designated CH-54A Tarhe. Two commercial Skycranes of Tarhe type were delivered to the Rowan Drilling Company in 1969. The S-64E is the civil version proper, while the CH-54B Tarhe was a second US Army version with increased payload capacity, bringing the total number of CH-54A/Bs ordered to 80. A commercial counterpart of the CH-54B was developed as the S-64F.

Data (CH-54A/S-64E): *Engines* two Pratt & Whitney JFTD12-4A (military T73-P-1) turboshafts, each 2,903 kW (1,000 shp) max continuous rating *Main rotor diameter* 21.95 m (72 ft 0 in) *Length of fuselage* 21.41 m (70 ft 3 in) *Max T-O weight* 19,050 kg (42,000 lb) *Max level speed* 203 km/h (126 mph) *Range* 370 km (230 miles) *Accommodation* detachable military pod can carry 45 combat-equipped troops, 24 stretchers, cargo or other equipment. Alternative use of helicopter as a flying crane with a platform or slung load

Sikorsky S-65A (USA) First flown on 14 October 1964, the S-65A is a twin-turbine heavy assault transport helicopter. It is currently in service with the US Navy (as the CH-53A Sea Stallion), USAF (HH-53B/C) and US Marine Corps (CH-53D) and with Israel, Austrian Air Force (as the S-65-Oe for rescue duties in the Alps) and the German armed forces. Eight USAF HH-53Cs are being modified for night search and rescue operations under the Pave Low 3 programme.

Data (CH-53D): *Engines* two 2,927 kW (3,925 shp) General Electric T64-GE-413 turboshafts *Main rotor diameter* 22.02 m (72 ft 3 in) *Length of fuselage* 20.47 m (67 ft 2 in) *Max T-O weight* 19,050 kg (42,000 lb) *Max level speed* 315 km/h (196 mph) *Range* 413 km (257 miles) *Accommodation* crew of three and 55 troops, 24 stretchers or internal or external freight

Sikorsky S-65 (MCM) (USA) In 1970 the US Navy announced plans to establish helicopter mine countermeasures (MCM) squadrons. The first unit, Helicopter Mine-Countermeasures Squadron 12 (HM-12), borrowed 15 CH-53As from the US Marine Corps, pending production of specially equipped helicopters.

In February 1972 Sikorsky announced that the US Navy had ordered 30 helicopters under the designation RH-53D. The first RH-53D flew on 27 October 1972 and first deliveries were made to HM-12 in September 1973. The RH-53D is designed to tow existing and future equipment evolved to sweep mechanical, acoustic and magnetic mines. Power is provided by two General Electric T64-GE-413A/415 turboshafts. Provision is made for two 0.50 in machine-guns to detonate surfaced mines.

Sikorsky S-69.

Sikorsky S-69 (USA) Two-seat research helicopter built to test the Advancing Blade Concept (ABC) rotor system. Power is provided by a 1,360 kW (1,825 shp) Pratt & Whitney Aircraft of Canada PT6T-3 Turbo Twin Pac and two 13.35 kN (3,000 lb st) Pratt & Whitney J60-P-3A turbojets mounted in pods on the sides of the fuselage.

Sikorsky S-70 Black Hawk (USA) In August 1972 the US Army selected Sikorsky and Boeing Vertol as competitors to build three prototypes each of their submissions for the Utility Tactical Transport Aircraft System (UTTAS) requirement. Sikorsky's first YUH-60A flew on 17 October 1974. Fly-off evaluation against Boeing Vertol's YUH-61A prototypes began in early 1976. In December 1976 Sikorsky's design was declared the winner.

Designed to carry 11 fully equipped troops plus a crew of three, the UH-60A has a large cabin which enables it to be used without modification for medical evacuation, reconnaissance, command and control purposes or troop resupply. For external-lift missions its cargo hook has a capacity of up to 3,630 kg (8,000 lb). One helicopter can be accommodated in a C-130, two in a C-141 and six in a C-5A.

The UH-60A (now named Black Hawk) is

Sikorsky

Sikorsky S-72.

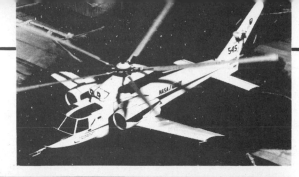

Sikorsky S-76 Spirit,

Sikorsky Le Grand.

Sikorsky VS-300 in early form, with Igor Sikorsky at the controls.

intended to serve as the US Army's primary combat-assault helicopter. The Army plans to procure a total of 1,107 by the mid-eighties. The first flight of a production aircraft was made in October 1978 and Black Hawks were delivered for pilot training to the US Army Aviation Center, Fort Rucker, Alabama, in April 1979. The first delivery of production aircraft to an operational unit was made on 19 June 1979.

Two special variants of the Black Hawk were reported in 1979 as the EH-60A ECM variant and EH-60B for SOTAS (Stand-Off Target Acquisition System) missions. The first EH-60B prototype was scheduled to fly in late 1980. Army plans envisage eventual production of more than 100 SOTAS helicopters.

Data: *Engines* two 1,151 kW (1,543 shp) General Electric T700-GE-700 advanced-technology turboshafts *Main rotor diameter* 16.36 m (53 ft 8 in) *Length of fuselage* 15.26 m (50 ft 0¾ in) *Mission T-O weight* 7,474 kg (16,478 lb) *Max level speed* 296 km/h (184 mph) *Range* 600 km (373 miles) *Armament* provision for one or two M-60 side-firing machine-guns

Sikorsky S-70L Seahawk (USA) Sikorsky's S-70L (designated SH-60B Seahawk by the US Navy) won the Navy's LAMPS (Light Airborne Multi-Purpose System) Mk III competition in 1977. It is based on the Black Hawk and is intended for anti-submarine (ASW) and anti-ship surveillance and targeting (ASST) missions. It will be deployed on board *Spruance*-class ASW destroyers, Aegis-equipped guided-missile des-

troyers and guided-missile frigates. The US Navy has indicated a requirement for 204 helicopters. The first prototype was rolled out in August 1979.

Sikorsky S-72 (USA) The S-72 is a research helicopter, specially designed to carry out research on a wide range of advanced rotor systems. The optional wings and fuselage-mounted turbofan engines permit flight testing of rotors that would otherwise be too small to sustain the helicopter in the air.

Sikorsky S-76 Spirit (USA) The Spirit is a new twin-turbine general-purpose all-weather commercial helicopter, of which 265 had been ordered by September 1979. Initial deliveries began in February 1979.

Data: *Engines* two 485 kW (650 shp) Allison 250-C30 turboshafts *Main rotor diameter* 13.41 m (44 ft 0 in) *Length overall* 16.0 m (52 ft 6 in) *Max T-O weight* 4,536 kg (10,000 lb) *Max cruising speed* 286 km/h (178 mph) *Range* (with 12 passengers) 748 km (465 miles) *Accommodation* crew of two and up to 12 passengers; other layouts are available

Sikorsky VS-300 (USA) Igor Sikorsky's early attempts to construct a helicopter in 1909–10 had been unsuccessful, but on 14 September 1939 the new VS-300 achieved its first tethered flight, followed by a free flight on 13 May 1940 (see **Chronology**). Powered initially by a 56 kW (75 hp) Lycoming and later by a 74.5 kW (100 hp) Franklin engine, it had full cyclic-pitch control. The VS-300 went through various changes during development, in its final form showing sufficient promise to warrant construction of the new two-seat XR-4.

Data: *Engine* as above *Main rotor diameter* 9.14 m (30 ft 0 in) *Length* 8.48 m (27 ft 10 in) *Max T-O weight* 585 kg (1,290 lb) *Cruising speed* 64–80 km/h (40–50 mph) *Range* 80–120 km (50–75 miles) *Accommodation* pilot only

Sikorsky Le Grand and Ilya Mourometz (Russia) Officially named *Russian Knight* but more usually known as *Le Grand*, Sikorsky's 74.5 kW (100 hp) Argus-engined passenger-carrying biplane was the first four-engined aeroplane in the world and the first with a fully enclosed passenger cabin (accommodating four passengers, with a sofa, table and wash room). It flew for the first time on 13 May 1913 for ten minutes (with Sikorsky himself as pilot), subsequently completing 53 flights without major problems. One flight carrying eight passengers (on 2 August 1913) lasted 1 hour 54 minutes. Its career ended when it

SEPECAT Jaguar GR.1s.

Shin Meiwa PS-1
water-bomber.

Sikorsky R-4B.

Sikorsky S-51.

Sikorsky HH-3F Pelican.

Sikorsky S-76 Spirit.

Spad VII.

Stinson SR-9C Reliant.

**Supermarine Spitfire
F.21s and a single F.22
(centre).**

**Supermarine Swift in use
as a missile testbed.**

was destroyed on the ground by an engine falling from a passing aeroplane.

From *Le Grand* Sikorsky developed the *Ilya Mourometz*, the first four-engined bomber built and the first to enter operational service. The prototype was flown in January 1914 and in the following month established a world height-with-load record by achieving an altitude of 2,000 m (6,560 ft) with 16 persons on board. Subsequent aircraft differed slightly. The Type B was powered by two 149 kW (200 hp) and two 100.6 kW (135 hp) Salmson-built Canton-Unné engines. Between 70 and 80 heavy bombers of all versions were eventually built, serving successfully during World War I.

Data (*Le Grand*): *Engines* as above *Wing span* 28.0 m (91 ft 11 in), (*Ilya Mourometz* Type B) 31.0 m (101 ft 6 in) *Length* 20.0 m (65 ft 8 in) *Max T-O weight* (approx) 4,080 kg (9,000 lb) *Cruising speed* (approx) 88 km/h (55 mph) *Max level speed* (*Ilya Mourometz* Type B) 96 km/h (60 mph)

Silvercraft SH-4A.

Silvercraft SH-200.

Silvercraft SH-4 (Italy) First flown in March 1965, the SH-4 is a three-seat light general-purpose helicopter powered by a 175 kW (235 hp) Franklin 6A-350-D1B engine (derated to 127 kW; 170 hp). The standard version is suitable for pilot training, utility, survey, police, ambulance, military liaison and observation duties. An agricultural version was also produced as the SH-4A. The SH-4/4A is no longer in production. A replacement for the SH-4 was built as the SH-200, first flown in April 1977.

Sindlinger HH-1 Hawker Hurricane (USA) Single-seat sporting aircraft designed as a ⅝-scale representation of a Hawker Hurricane IIC. Plans and certain components are available to amateur constructors.

SIPA S.10 (France) French version of the Arado Ar 396, built as the company's first post-war product. Twenty-eight produced.

SIPA S.11, S.111, S.12 and S.121 (France) The S.11 (50 built for the French Air Force) and S.111 (S.11s converted to S.111 standard) were modified versions of the S.10 two-seat advanced trainer, fitted with Renault 125 engines (440 kW; 590 hp SNECMA S-12-SO2-3H, French-built Argus As 411). The S.12 was similar to the S.11 but was constructed entirely of metal; 52 S.12s were built for the French Air Force together with 58 S.121 lightweight derivatives. For use in Algeria, a number of S.111s and S.121s were modified to carry rockets and bombs for ground attack under the designations S.111A and S.121A.

SIPA S.901 (France) Two-seat light training monoplane which won a 1948 contest to produce an aircraft to be built for use in the schools of the Service de l'Aviation Légère et Sportive.

SITAR Gardan GY 100 Bagheera, Gardan GY 90 Mowgli and GY 110 Sher Khan (France) The Bagheera was built as a three–four-seat light monoplane powered by a 112 kW (150 hp) Lycoming O-320-E engine. Production began in 1968. A smaller and simplified version of the Bagheera was designed as the two-seat Mowgli, intended primarily for amateur construction using kits or plans. The Sher Khan was a projected enlarged four-seat version of the Bagheera with a retractable landing gear (see **Socata GY 80**).

Skylab 1 (USA) Skylab 1 was launched on 14 May 1973 from Cape Kennedy by a Saturn V into a near perfect orbit of 463 km (271 miles). Initial

1914 *Ilya Mourometz*.

Sindlinger HH-1 Hawker Hurricane.

SIPA 111.

SIPA 901s.

Skylab programme official emblem.

The crew of Skylab 2 leave the spacecraft after their 28-day mission on board Skylab 1.

Skyote Aeromarine Skyote.

Close-up view of Skylab 1 showing where the micrometeoroid shield should have been and where a parasol solar shield was later deployed. The damaged and partially deployed solar panel can be seen.

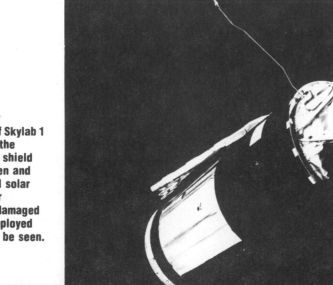

astronauts could either deploy or fasten into position. In addition cutting tools with extended handles, 3 m (10 ft) rods and poles, were made for pushing or pulling the partially deployed main solar array. These steps were performed successfully by the crew of Skylab 2 (comprising a modified Apollo Command Module and Service Module), which was launched on 25 May.

The S-IVB Orbital Workshop or Skylab 1 itself was devised to explore further and extend man's usefulness in space. It was basically a modified S-IVB stage of a Saturn V launch vehicle, with its 283 m³ (10,000 cu ft) hydrogen tank equipped as living and working areas for three astronauts. Floor-to-ceiling partitions divided the living and working area into an experimental section, wardroom, sleep compartments and waste compartment. Three openings were cut into the sides of the S-IVB stage: one provided a 46 cm (18 in) wide observation window, and two were for airlocks through which experiments could be put in space (see **Chronology**).

lift-off was successful, but after 63 seconds, as the vehicle reached maximum aerodynamic pressure, one section of the micrometeoroid shield deployed prematurely. It was torn off completely by the air pressure and caused one of the main solar arrays to break off also.

A more serious situation developed on the day following the launch when temperature measurements indicated that the Orbital Workshop was being overheated by the Sun. This was due to the loss of the micrometeoroid shield, which had a special thermal paint pattern to limit absorption of solar energy. Rapid steps were taken by NASA officials on the ground to devise repair plans that would overcome the heating problems. Schemes were devised for a variety of 'sunshades' which

Skyote Aeromarine Skyote (USA) Single-seat aerobatic biplane, plans and wing kits for which are available to amateur constructors.

(Vickers) Slingsby Vega and T.61E Venture (UK) Single-seat 15-metre Contest Class sailplane and a special licence-built version of the Scheibe SF-25B Falke motor glider respectively. Forty T.61Es have been ordered by the Ministry of Defence for the Air Training Corps.

Smith DSA-1 Miniplane (USA) Single-seat sporting biplane, plans for which are available to amateur constructors.

Smyth Model S Sidewinder (USA) Two-seat sporting monoplane, plans and kits of parts for which are available to amateur constructors.

SNCAC NC 701 and NC 702 Martinet (France) For early development of these aircraft see **Siebel Si 204**. Post-war SNCAC put the aircraft back into production as the NC 701 (Si 204D) and NC 702 (Si 204A) powered by Renault 12S engines (440 kW; 590 hp SNECMA S-12-SO2-3Hs, French-built Argus As 411s). About 300 or so were built. The NC 702 version accommodated a crew of two and eight passengers (four on each side of a central aisle), with a toilet and luggage compartment aft. As a freighter, the interior equipment was removed and the cabin divided into four compartments. Among the many operators of the Martinet were Air France and ČSA of Czechoslovakia.

Data (NC 702): *Engines* as above *Wing span* 21.83 m (71 ft 7¼ in) *Length* 12.81 m (42 ft 0½ in) *Max T-O weight* 5,600 kg (12,346 lb) *Cruising speed* 325 km/h (202 mph) *Max range* (auxiliary fuel tanks) 2,000 km (1,243 miles) *Normal range* 810–1,400 km (503–870 miles)

SNCAC NC 840 Chardoneret (France) Four-seat cabin monoplane of the late 1940s.

SNCAC NC 853, NC 854, NC 856 and NC 860 (France) The NC 853 was a two-seat light monoplane powered by a 56 kW (75 hp) Minie 4DC-32 engine. From it were developed the 48.4 kW (65 hp) Continental A65-powered NC 854 and the four-seat NC 856 (78.25 kW; 105 hp Walter). A twin-engined development of the NC 856 was the NC 860. The company ceased trading in 1949.

SNCAC NC 900 (France) French-built version of the Focke-Wulf 190A, first flown in March 1945. Forty delivered to the French Air Force and 24 to the French Navy.

SNCASE Aquilon, Mistral and Vampire (France) SNCASE aircraft are best known as Sud-Est types (see entries), although the French-built de Havilland Vampire and Venom

SNCAC NC 840 Chardoneret.

SNCASE Aquilon.

derivatives are the exception and are better known under the full SNCASE name.

SNCASE undertook the licence production of the Vampire FB.5 for the French Air Force. The first French-built Mk 5 flew on 27 January 1950. The definitive French production version (Mk 53) was powered by a Hispano-Suiza-built Rolls-Royce Nene engine. Because the aircraft was fabricated with French materials and was mainly fitted with French equipment and instruments, it was given the name Mistral. Altogether SNCASE built 430 Vampires/Mistrals.

The Aquilon was a French-built de Havilland Sea Venom, of which 109 production aircraft were produced for the Navy, including 19 Aquilon 204 trainers.

SNCASO SO.30 Bretagne and SO.95 Corse (France) See **Sud-Ouest**

SNECMA C.450-01 Coléoptère (France) Jet-powered VTOL research aircraft, first flown on 6 May 1959. Special features were its annular wing and retractable foreplanes in the fuselage nose.

Snow S-2 (USA) Single-seat agricultural monoplane, first delivered to customers in its S-2B form in 1958. Three versions of the S-2C were produced up to 1965, bringing the total number of S.2s of all versions to 260.

Socata GY 80 Horizon (France) In 1962 Sud-Aviation obtained the licence to build and market the four-seat all-metal Horizon from M. Yves Gardan (see **SITAR**). The initial 75 aircraft had either 112 kW (150 hp) or 119 kW (160 hp) Lycoming O-320 engines, but the smallest engine

Smith DSA-1 Miniplane.

Smyth Model S Sidewinder.

SNCAC NC 701.

SNCASE Vampire Mk 5s.

Socata

SNECMA C.450-01
Coléoptère.

Snow S-2.

Aircraft of the basic
Rallye series are similar
externally. This light
Rallye airframe is used
for the Galopin,
Garnement and Galérien.

Socata ST 10 Diplomate.

Socata Guerrier in ground
support configuration,
with rocket packs and
gun pods.

was dropped thereafter and a 134 kW (180 hp) O-360 was introduced. A total of 260 Horizons was produced.

Socata M 360-6 Jupiter (France) Six–seven-seat twin-engined (in nose and tail as a 'push and pull' type) executive transport.

Socata Rallye series (France) The prototype Rallye-Club first flew on 10 June 1959. The 3,000th Rallye built in France was delivered in May 1977, excluding versions built under licence in Poland by PZL-Warszawa. The seven versions currently available are the Galopin two-seater (cleared for spinning) or three–four-seater (spins prohibited) powered by an 82 kW (110 hp) Lycoming O-235-L2A engine; Garnement with a 115 kW (155 hp) Lycoming O-320-D2A; Galérien specialised glider- and banner-towing version with a 134 kW (180 hp) Lycoming O-360-A3A; Gaillard four-seater, with an O-360-A3A engine (742 built by 1979); Gabier with a 175 kW (235 hp) Lycoming O-540-B4B5 engine (103 built by 1979); Gaucho agricultural version of the Gabier; and Guerrier military two–three-seater with an O-540-B4B5 engine and four underwing stores pylons for armed and support missions.

Data (Gaillard): *Engine* as above *Wing span* 9.74 m (31 ft 11 in) *Length* 7.24 m (23 ft 9 in) *Max T-O weight* 1,050 kg (2,315 lb) *Max level speed* 240 km/h (150 mph) *Range* 1,110 km (690 miles)

Socata Rallye Tampico and Tobago (France) New series of all-metal light aircraft introduced to the 1979 Rallye range as the four-seat TB 9 Tampico (119 kW; 160 hp Lycoming O-320-D2A) and four–five-seat TB 10 Tobago (134 kW; 180 hp Lycoming O-360-A1AD).

Socata ST 10 Diplomate (France) Initially known as the Provence, the Diplomate is a four-seat light monoplane powered by a 149 kW (200 hp) Lycoming IO-360-C1B engine. Fifty-six had been delivered by 1974, including 12 to Varig as pilot trainers.

Socata (Aérospatiale) TB 30 Epsilon (France) Two-seat primary flying trainer powered by a 224 kW (300 hp) Lycoming AEIO-540-L1A5D engine. Two prototypes were built for the French Air Force in 1979.

Soko G2-A Galeb (Yugoslavia) The first prototype Galeb two-seat armed jet trainer flew in May 1961. Production began in 1963 for the Yugoslav Air Force and has continued to fulfil repeat Yugoslav and export orders. The first overseas customer was the Zambian Air Force, in early 1971.

There are two current versions of the Galeb: the G2-A standard Yugoslav Air Force version and the G-2A-E export version with updated equipment (entered production in 1975).

Data: *Engine* one 11.12 kN (2,500 lb st) Rolls-Royce Viper 11 Mk 22-6 turbojet *Wing span* 10.47 m (34 ft 4½ in) *Length* 10.34 m (33 ft 11 in) *Max T-O weight* (strike version) 4,300 kg (9,480 lb) *Max level speed* 812 km/h (505 mph) *Range* 1,240 km (770 miles) *Armament* all production aircraft have two 0.50 in machine-guns in nose, plus underwing pylons for two 50 kg or 100 kg bombs and four 57 mm rockets or two 127 mm rockets, or clusters of small bombs and expendable bomblet containers of up to 150 kg (330.5 lb) weight (300 kg; 661 lb total)

Soko G2-A Galebs.

Soko J-1/RJ-1 Jastreb (Yugoslavia) The basic J-1 Jastreb is a single-seat light attack version of the Galeb, developed and produced for service with the Yugoslav Air Force. Currently in production and service are four versions: the J-1 standard attack version for the Yugoslav Air Force; J-1-E export version with updated equipment; RJ-1 tactical reconnaissance version for the Yugoslav Air Force; and the RJ-1-E export reconnaissance version. In addition there is also a training version, designated TJ-1 (see entry).
Data: *Engine* one 13.32 kN (3,000 lb st) Rolls-Royce Viper 531 turbojet, plus provision for two 4.44 kN (1,000 lb thrust) JATO rockets under fuselage *Wing span* over tip-tanks 11.68 m (38 ft 4 in) *Length* 10.88 m (35 ft 8½ in) *Max T-O weight* 5,100 kg (11,243 lb) *Max level speed* 820 km/h (510 mph) *Range* 1,520 km (945 miles) *Armament* three 0.50 in Colt-Browning machine-guns in nose. Total of eight underwing weapon attachments for bombs, napalm tanks or rockets

Soko P-2 Kraguj (Yugoslavia) Single-seat light-weight close-support aircraft powered by a 253.4 kW (340 hp) Lycoming GSO-480-B1A6 engine. Small number were operated by the Yugoslav Air Force, each armed with one 7.7 mm machine-gun in each wing and with six underwing attachments for bombs, napalm tanks or rockets.

Soko TJ-1 Jastreb Trainer (Yugoslavia) Two-seat operational conversion and pilot proficiency training version of the Jastreb, designed for maximum commonality with the J-1 and retaining full operational capability of the ground-attack version. Deliveries to the Yugoslav Air Force and for export began in 1975.

Soko/CIAR Orao/IAR-93 (Yugoslavia/Romania) This twin-jet ground-attack fighter is under development to meet the joint requirement of the air forces of Romania and Yugoslavia. In the latter country it is known as the Orao (Eagle); its Romanian designation is IAR-93. The aircraft was originally known as the Jurom.

It is believed that the first prototype flew in August 1974. On 15 April 1975 it was demonstrated publicly during the Victory Day parade held at a military airfield near Belgrade. Two further prototypes have reportedly been built, followed by nine pre-production aircraft.

It is anticipated that 200 or more of these aircraft may be built eventually for the two air forces, including a proportion of two-seat operational trainers. The initial production batch is reported to be around 40, including two-seaters.
Data (estimated): *Engines* two 17.8 kN (4,000 lb st, without afterburning) Rolls-Royce Viper Mk 632-41 turbojets *Wing span* 7.56 m (24 ft 9¾ in) *Length* 12.9 m (42 ft 4 in) *Max T-O weight* 10,300 kg (22,700 lb) *Max level speed* 1,226 km/h (762 mph) *Combat radius* 650 km (404 miles) *Armament* two 30 mm cannon, plus up to 3,000 kg (6,615 lb) of external stores

Soko P-2 Kraguj.

Sokol M.1D/E (Czechoslovakia) Three-seat landplane and seaplane respectively (see **Let Mraz M.1 Sokol**).

Solar MS-2 (USA) Eight-passenger sesquiplane airliner of 1931 powered by a 313 kW (420 hp) Pratt & Whitney radial engine.

Sopwith 1½-Strutter (UK) The Sopwith '1½-Strutter' was so called (unofficially) because of its wing strut arrangement. It had one pair only of the conventional vertical parallel struts joining the wings and a second pair of short struts running from the fuselage to a point on the upper wing where the usual second pair of vertical struts would normally be located. First flown as a prototype in late 1915, it was a two-seater powered by an 82 kW (110 hp) Clerget rotary engine. Production aircraft with this engine or a Le Rhône or 97 kW (130 hp) Clerget entered service with the RFC and RNAS from the spring of 1916, having the first synchronised Vickers machine-gun and the first rear-mounted Scarff ring for a Lewis gun fitted as standard to a British aircraft.

With the arrival of improved single-seat fighters in German service, the 1½-Strutter gradually fell into obsolescence as a fighter. The majority of the 5,700 or so aircraft built were of French manufacture and these did not enter service until a year after the first British examples. From the beginning the 1½-Strutter had undertaken light bombing duties and it was in this role (and reconnaissance) that it was mainly

Two-seat version of the Soko/CIAR Orao/IAR-93 (foreground) with single-seater.

Sopwith 1½-Strutter.

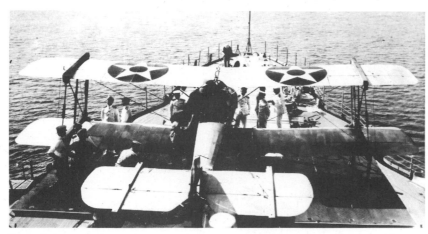

Rare photograph of a Sopwith 1½-Strutter on board a US Navy vessel in 1920.

Sopwith 807.

Sopwith B.1 single-seat bomber of 1917, powered by a 149 kW (200 hp) Hispano-Suiza engine. Although flown on several operational missions on the Western Front, it was not adopted by the RNAS and remained a prototype.

Sopwith 2F.1 Camels. The fuselage of this version was constructed in two sections for easy stowage on board naval vessels.

Sopwith 860.

employed thereafter, the RNAS also using specially adapted single-seaters. Extended life was also assured by deployment on less demanding fronts, but from early 1918 it was used mainly as a trainer. Several other countries also flew the type, the AEF alone receiving more than 500 French-built aircraft.

In 1915 a 1½-Strutter set a new British height record when Sopwith's test pilot flew one to 5,600 m (18,393 ft).

Data: *Engine* as above *Wing span* 10.21 m (33 ft 6 in) *Length* 7.69 m (25 ft 3 in) *Max T-O weight* 1,120 kg (2,250 lb) *Max level speed* 158–171 km/h (98.5–106 mph) *Endurance* 3¾–4½ h *Armament* as above; some aircraft had non-standard armament, notably two Lewis guns firing upwards. Specialised single-seat bomber version had internal bomb bay in place of rear cockpit

Sopwith 807 (UK) Gnome Monosoupape-powered two-seat seaplane of 1914, operated in very small numbers by the RNAS.

Sopwith 860 (UK) Torpedo-carrying seaplane powered by a 168 kW (225 hp) Sunbeam engine. Small number used by the RNAS.

Sopwith Camel (UK) The Camel is remembered as the most successful British single-seat fighter of World War I and is credited with 1,294 'kills'. It ranked with the German Fokker D.VII but did not achieve the extended post-war service of the German type. It also had its vices, the most obvious of which was the high torque produced by the large rotary engine, giving it a vicious right pull. This was acceptable to experienced pilots, who found it a positive advantage for rapid manoeuvring during dogfights, but it caused the demise of many pilots during their conversion period (the S.E.5 had an in-line engine and so was preferred by many pilots).

Camels entered service with the RFC and RNAS in mid-1917 and remained in first-line use until the Armistice. A total of 5,490 was built, serving also with Belgian and AEF squadrons and with other air forces. It was a Camel that shot down the German ace Rittmeister Manfred von Richthofen (the 'Red Baron') at the hands of Captain Roy Brown of No 209 Squadron, RAF, over Sailly-le-Sec on 21 April 1918 (see **Chronology** 1 and 11 Aug 1918).

Data (F.I): *Engine* one 97 kW (130 hp) Clerget rotary (or other engines from an 82 kW; 110 hp Le Rhône to a 112 kW; 150 hp Bentley B.R.1) *Wing span* 8.53 m (28 ft 0 in) *Length* 5.72 m (18 ft 9 in) *Max T-O weight* 659 kg (1,453 lb) *Max level speed* 185 km/h (115 mph) *Endurance* 2 h 30 min *Armament* two forward-firing Vickers machine-guns

Sopwith Cuckoo (UK) The prototype Cuckoo torpedo-bomber flew in June 1917 and was powered by a Hispano-Suiza engine. Production aircraft first appeared with 149 kW (200 hp) Sunbeam Arabs as T.1 Cuckoos and entered service in the latter half of 1918, first going to sea on board HMS *Argus* in October. In the first batch of Cuckoos built by Blackburn were three with Wolseley Viper engines; these became Mk IIs together with others built immediately after the war. Armament of the Cuckoo was an 18 in torpedo. Maximum level speed was 166 km/h (103 mph).

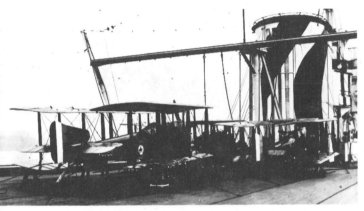

combat and helped to establish its reputation as a 'pilot's aircraft'. With the arrival of the S.E.5 and Camel, the Pup was downgraded and many performed home-defence duties. Some were occasionally armed with Le Prieur rockets for anti-Zeppelin patrols.

Sopwith 5F.1 Dolphin.

One of the best remembered exploits of the Pup was its use in determining the feasibility of landing conventionally wheeled aircraft on board aircraft carriers. On 2 August 1917 a Pup, flown by Squadron Cdr E. H. Dunning, landed on the deck of HMS *Furious*, so recording the first landing of an aeroplane on a moving ship. Grab straps attached to the aircraft enabled deck crew to pull it to rest. Unfortunately, when another landing was attempted on 7 August, the Pup stalled and went over the side of the carrier into the sea and Dunning was killed. Nevertheless the results were sufficiently encouraging for the experiments to continue and the Royal Navy became the first service in the world with an effective carrier force. A total of 1,770 Pups was built (see **Chronology** 2 and 7 Aug 1917 and 21 Aug 1917).

Sopwith T.1 Cuckoos on board HMS *Furious*.

Data: *Engine* one 59.6 kW (00 hp) Le Rhône rotary or 74.5 kW (100 hp) Gnome Mono-

Sopwith Dolphin (UK) The Dolphin was designed as a single-seat Hispano-Suiza-engined fighter, but was better suited as a ground-attack aircraft. The prototype flew for the first time in May 1917. Production aircraft, of which several hundred were delivered to the RFC/RAF from early 1918, were powered by the 149 kW (200 hp) Hispano-Suiza engine of the prototype or a more powerful 223.6 kW (300 hp) version. Maximum level speed varied over 188–211 km/h (117–131 mph) according to engine. Armament comprised two fixed Vickers guns and two wing-mounted Lewis guns. It was particularly active in the ground-attack role during the German spring offensive.

Sopwith Dragon.

Sopwith Dragon (UK) Single-seat fighter of 1919 developed from the Snipe. Power was provided by a 268 kW (360 hp) ABC Dragonfly radial engine. Production aircraft were built but failed to become operational.

Sopwith Pup (UK) The Pup or Scout Tractor was Sopwith's follow-up fighter to the 1½-Strutter and got its name as a smaller single-seat version. It entered service with the RNAS and RFC in the latter half of 1916, just as the Strutter was getting out of its depth in the face of the German Halberstadt and early Albatros fighters on the Western Front.

Sopwith Pup.

Although underpowered, the Pup was a remarkably fine aircraft with good maximum speed and climb and excellent manoeuvrability – especially when the torque of the engine was exploited for fast turns. The battles of Ypres, Messines and Cambrai kept the Pup locked in

Sopwith

Sopwith Pup being lifted onto the deck of HMS *Furious*.

soupape *Wing span* 8.08 m (26 ft 6 in) *Length* 5.89 m (19 ft 3¾ in) *Max T-O weight* 556 kg (1,225 lb) *Max level speed* 179 km/h (111 mph) *Endurance* 3h *Armament* one Vickers or Lewis machine-gun

Sopwith Salamander (UK) Ground-attack version of the Snipe, of which a very small number became operational during World War I.

Sopwith Baby.

Sopwith TF.2 Salamander.

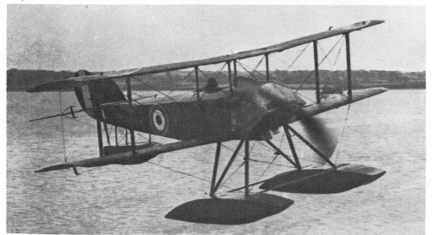

Sopwith Schneider.

Sopwith Schneider and Baby (UK) The Schneider for the RNAS was a direct development of the seaplane with which Pixton had won the 1914 Schneider Trophy. Power was provided by a 74.5 kW (100 hp) Gnome Monosoupape engine. It became a standard type on board ships of the Royal Navy and was active in the Mediterranean and elsewhere, performing fighter and anti-submarine duties (carrying bombs), but was most useful as a reconnaissance aircraft.

The Baby, or Sopwith Fighting Seaplane to

Sopwith 7F.1 Snipe.

give it its company name, entered service with the RNAS in early 1916 and was basically a more powerful version of the Schneider, using as standard a Clerget engine of 82 or 97 kW (110 or 130 hp). As with the Schneider, armament comprised a single Lewis machine-gun plus bombs for certain duties. Babies remained active right up to the Armistice.

Data (Baby with a 97 kW; 130 hp engine): *Engine* as above *Wing span* 7.82 m (25 ft 8 in) *Length* 7.01 m (23 ft 0 in) *Max T-O weight* 778 kg (1,715 lb) *Max level speed* 158 km/h (98 mph) *Endurance* 2 h

Sopwith Snipe (UK) The Sopwith Snipe was the RAF's standard single-seat fighter of the post-World War I period until replaced by the Gloster Grebe and Armstrong Whitworth Siskin in 1923. A squadron comprised the fighter element of the force which took over responsibility of policing in Iraq from October 1922, in the famous 'air control' operations. However it had first appeared in early 1918 and by the Armistice was in service with several squadrons (see **Chronology** 27 Oct 1918).

Data: *Engine* one 171.4 kW (230 hp) Bentley B.R.2, except the prototype, which had a 112 kW (150 hp) B.R.1 *Wing span* 9.14 m (30 ft 0 in) *Length* 6.02 m (19 ft 9½ in) *Max T-O weight* 916 kg (2,020 lb) *Max level speed* 195 km/h (121 mph) *Endurance* 3 h *Armament* two forward-firing Vickers machine-guns, plus four 25 lb bombs

Sopwith Spinning Jenny (UK) Two-seat biplane of 1914, used in very small numbers by the RNAS on anti-airship duties.

Sopwith Tabloid (UK) The original Tabloid appeared in 1913 as a civil two-seater but in the following year was selected for military service as a single-seat scout. It therefore became the first single-seat scout anywhere to go into production for military use. From February 1915 a number of

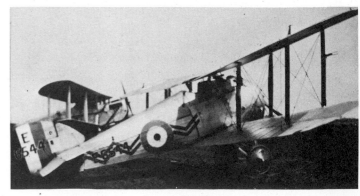

Tabloids were fitted with Lewis machine-guns. The type is best remembered as the light bomber which made the first successful British bombing raid on Germany. It is worth quoting from a letter sent to the Admiralty on 28 December 1914 that appeared in the 1918 *Jane's*: 'With reference to the recent attack on the German Airsheds at Cologne and Düsseldorf, carried out by Squadron Commander Spenser D. A. Grey and Flight Lieutenant R. L. G. Marix, you may be interested to learn that the machines used were your "Sopwith Tabloid aeroplanes" . . . It is reported from Berlin that a new Zeppelin fitted with the latest silent motors, which had just been moved into the shed at Düsseldorf and a Machinery Hall alongside the Airship Shed, were destroyed by Flight Lieutenant Marix. The roof of the Airship Shed has fallen in.' In fact the airship destroyed by Marix was Z.IX.

The Tabloid was powered by a 74.5 kW (100 hp) Gnome Monosoupape engine, giving a maximum speed of 148 km/h (92 mph).

Sorrell SNS-7 Hiperbipe.

Sopwith Tabloid.

Sopwith Triplanes.

Sopwith Triplane (UK) Said to have been the progenitor of the Fokker Dr.I triplane – and therefore various other less successful German triplanes – the Triplane single-seat fighter was nicknamed 'Tripehound'. First flown in prototype form on 28 May 1916, it had been evolved as a faster-climbing derivative of the Pup, with even better manoeuvrability and improved vision for the pilot. Wing span remained the same as for the Pup, but each wing was of much narrower chord and had an aileron fitted.

Initial production Triplanes, with 82 kW (110 hp) Clerget rotary engines, had been ordered for the RFC. In the event they were delivered to the RNAS, as were later examples with 97 kW (130 hp) Clerget engines fitted. The top exponent of the Triplane was Raymond Collishaw, who commanded 'B' Flight of No 10 (Naval) Squadron from April 1917 – a unit which received some of the first Triplanes. Known as the 'Black Flight' because of the colour of its Triplanes and the names given to individual aircraft (*Black Maria*, *Black Sheep*, etc), it was composed exclusively of Canadian pilots, who accounted for 87 kills between May and July. Collishaw managed to average more than one kill every two days throughout June. He ended the war as the highest-scoring RNAS pilot, with 60 victories.

The whole triplane era of World War I only lasted a little more than a year, higher-powered Camels replacing RNAS Triplanes and the Fokker Dr.I's career coming to an abrupt end with the death of Richthofen in April 1918.

The exact number of Triplanes that became operational with the RNAS is not clear. What is known is that the first prototype was followed by three more fitted with Clerget and Hispano-Suiza engines of 112 kW (150 hp) and 149 kW (200 hp). A further 148 aircraft were built, of which five were presented to France, another three were loaned and probably returned, and one went to Russia.

Data: *Engine* as above *Wing span* 8.08 m (26 ft 6 in) *Length* 5.74 m (18 ft 10 in) *Max T-O weight* 699 kg (1,541 lb) *Max level speed* 182 km/h (113 mph) *Endurance* 2 h 45 min *Armament* one or two forward-firing Vickers machine-guns

Sorrell SNS-7 Hiperbipe (USA) Two-seat aerobatic biplane, plans and certain components for which are available to amateur constructors.

Launch of Soyuz 15.

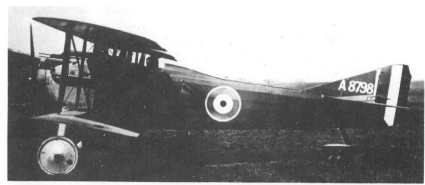

British-built Spad VII.

Spad XIII.

Spad XIV.

Spad XII.

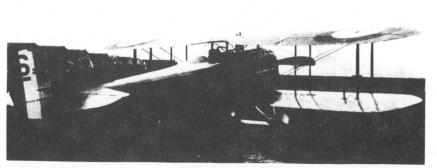

America; the AEF received nearly 190 for combat and training duties. In addition to French production, 200 were built in Britain by the Air Navigation Company and Mann, Egerton.
Data: *Engine* as above *Wing span* 7.8 m (25 ft 7¼ in) *Length* 6.1 m (20 ft 3½ in) *Max T-O weight* 705 kg (1,554 lb) *Max level speed* 192 km/h (119 mph) *Endurance* 2 h 15 min *Armament* one forward-firing Vickers machine-gun

Spad XI (France) Armed two-seat reconnaissance biplane powered by a 175 kW (235 hp) Hispano-Suiza engine. It entered service from 1917 with French, Belgian and eventually AEF squadrons, but was not a success. Some were employed occasionally as light bombers.

Spad XII (France) Basically a Spad VII with a 149 kW (200 hp) Hispano-Suiza 8 Bc engine which incorporated a 37 mm cannon. Several hundred were built but it was not successful.

Soyuz spacecraft (USSR) Developed for the Russian Earth-orbital space station programme, Soyuz spacecraft each comprise three basic sections or modules: a laboratory-cum-rest compartment (orbit module); a descent compartment (landing module); and a propulsion and instrument section (service module). The orbital module is mounted on the extreme nose of the craft and communicates with the landing module via a hermetically sealed hatch. It can accommodate up to four cosmonauts (see **Chronology** from 23 April 1967).

Space Shuttle (USA) See **NASA**

Spacelab (Germany) Under development by a ten-nation consortium led by VFW-Fokker/ERNO, Spacelab is the largest European space project initiated in the last decade and will be the only manned payload for the American Space Shuttle. A typical payload will comprise a large module and two pallets with an overall length of 13.8 m (45 ft 3 in).

The first launch of the Space Shuttle and a Spacelab is scheduled for 1981. Four payload specialists will work in two shifts for periods of 7 to 30 days. Spacelab will remain in the cargo bay of the Orbiter during the mission and will be brought back to Earth with the Orbiter. The payload specialists will be able to work under normal atmospheric conditions in the pressurised module. For work on the pallet section pressure suits will be necessary.

Spad VII (France) The Spad VII was a robust single-seat fighter of distinctive appearance. Most of the 6,000 or so built were powered by the 130.4 kW (175 hp) Hispano-Suiza 8 Ac engine, although the first production aircraft had the smaller 112 kW (150 hp) H-S 8 Aa fitted.

The fighter entered service in September 1916 but initial deliveries were slow. Eventually it equipped squadrons of 11 countries, including France, Britain, Belgium, Italy, Russia and

Spad XIII (France) Although more than 8,470 Spad XIIIs were built up to the Armistice, production was still increasing and twice this number were on order from French and American manufacturers. In the event no American-built Spads were delivered for operation, the 893 flown by the AEF all originating in France.

The Spad XIII was a better armed and more powerful derivative of the VII, also incorporating refinements to improve manoeuvrability. It was one of the fastest fighters of the war and was inevitably the mount of many famous pilots, including Capitaine Georges Guynemer and Captain 'Eddie' Rickenbacker. French squadrons received XIIIs from May 1917, in many cases in place of VIIs; several Italian and Belgian squadrons were also equipped. Post-war the fighter served with all four air forces mentioned, plus three other countries, well into the 1920s.
Data: *Engine* one 175 kW (235 hp) Hispano-Suiza 8 Be, initial production aircraft had 149 kW (200 hp) H-S 8 B *Wing span* 8.2 m (26 ft 11 in) *Length* 6.2 m (20 ft 4 in) *Max T-O weight* 820 kg (1,808 lb) *Max level speed* 218–222 km/h

(135–138 mph) *Endurance* 2 h *Armament* two forward-firing Vickers machine-guns

Spad XIV (France) Single-seat seaplane fighter powered by a 149 kW (200 hp) Hispano-Suiza 8 Bc engine. Forty served with the French Navy in 1918.

Spad A.2 (France) The A.2 was a two-seat fighter biplane with the 82 kW (110 hp) Le Rhône engine and propeller inset into the forward fuselage. Armament comprised a Lewis gun on a flexible mounting in the nose. About 100 were built in 1915–16 for French and Russian service but these were quickly replaced by more conventional aircraft.

Spad A.4 (France) Similar to the A.2 but with a 59.6 kW (80 hp) Le Rhône engine. Ten or twelve were delivered to Russia.

Sparmann S-1 (Sweden) Light single-seat monoplane, designed for primary and advanced military and civil training. Power was provided by a 97 kW (130 hp) de Havilland Gipsy Major engine. A number were delivered to the Swedish Air Force in about 1936.

Spartan Cruiser (UK) Spartan Aircraft Limited produced up to 1935 a three-engined six–ten-seat commercial monoplane known as the Cruiser, developed from the Saro-Percival Mailplane of 1931. Powered in its Mk III version by 97 kW (130 hp) de Havilland Gipsy Major engines. Cruisers were used on internal air routes in the UK and were also in service in Yugoslavia, Czechoslovakia, Egypt and India.

Spartan C-2 to C-5, Executive and Zeus (USA) Prior to 1934 Spartan produced the C-3 three-seat biplane (see **NP-1** entry) and a number of four- and five-seat cabin monoplanes in various forms under the type designations C-4 and C-5. These were followed in early 1934 by a light two-seat side-by-side sporting and training monoplane, the C2-60 powered by a 44.7 kW (60 hp) Jacobs L-3 engine. The company also delivered to the Mexican government six C2-175 trainers with 130.4 kW (175 hp) engines.

Spartan C-3.

The best remembered product of the company is the Executive: a four–five-seat cabin monoplane powered by a 298 kW (400 hp) Pratt & Whitney R-985 Wasp Junior engine and featuring a retractable landing gear. Executives were produced for the civil market, but in 1942 16 were pressed into military service as UC-71 staff transports. From the Executive, Spartan also developed the two-seat military Zeus, small numbers of which were exported to Mexico and China.

Spartan NP-1 (USA) In 1940 Spartan produced its first military design, the NS-1 primary training biplane for the US Navy. It was based on the earlier C-3 which had been produced by the Mid-Continent Aircraft Company. Power was provided by a 167.7 kW (225 hp) Lycoming R-680-8 engine. Altogether 201 were built, designated NP-1s by the US Navy.

Spencer Amphibian Air Car Model S-12-D and -E (USA) Four-seat amphibians, plans for which are available to amateur constructors.

Spezio DAL-1 Tuholer (USA) Two-seat open-cockpit sporting monoplane, plans for which are available to amateur constructors

SPCA VII Type 40T (France) This was a five-passenger (plus a crew of two) high-wing monoplane airliner of 1930 powered by three 100.6 kW (135 hp) Salmson 9Nc engines. Two were used on the Tananarive–Broken Hill air service, connecting Madagascar with the Imperial Airways African route at the latter place (in what was then Northern Rhodesia).

Spad A.4 in Russian service.

Spartan Zeus prototype.

Arrow two-seat light biplane, built by Spartan Aircraft Limited in the UK. Powered by a 78 kW (105 hp) Cirrus Hermes II engine.

Spencer Amphibian Air Car.

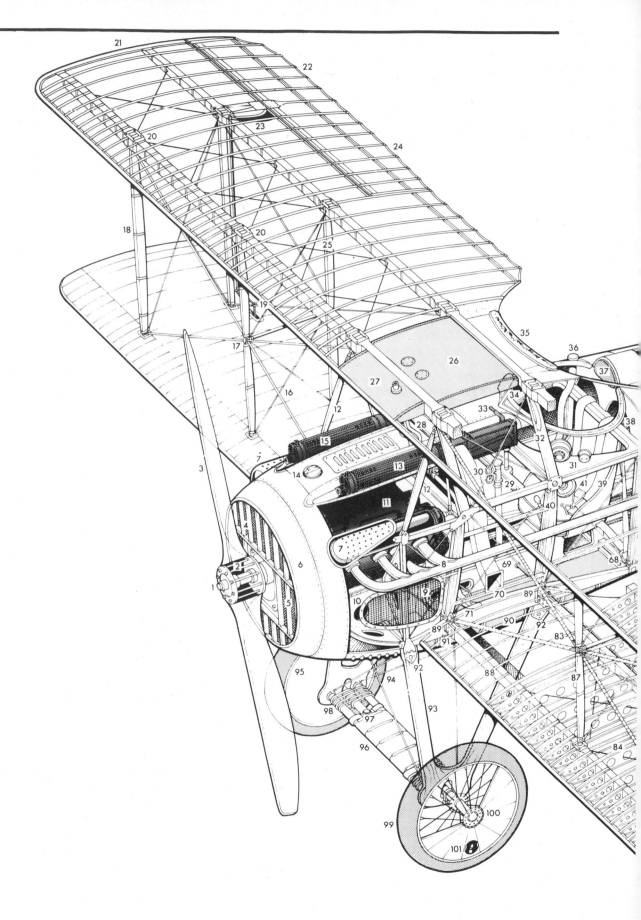

Spad XIII
1 Propeller hub
2 Propeller fixing bolts
3 Narrow-chord wooden propeller
4 Radiator shutters (open)
5 Water radiator
6 Radiator nose fairings
7 Engine blister fairings
8 Exhaust pipe
9 Ventilation air intake
10 Engine mounting structure
11 Hispano-Suiza 8 Be engine
12 Centre-section front bracing strut
13 Port 0.303 in Vickers machine-gun (staggered aft)
14 Radiator filler cap
15 Starboard 0.303 in Vickers machine-gun (staggered forward)
16 Bracing wires
17 Bracing-wire support strut
18 Interplane strut
19 Aileron operating linkage
20 Spar joints
21 Leading-edge carry-round
22 Starboard aileron
23 Aileron horn
24 Steel-wire trailing edge
25 Wing internal wire bracing
26 Service petrol tank
27 Radiator header tank
28 Ammunition boxes between guns
29 Control column
30 Gun triggers
31 Instrument shelf
32 Centre-section strut
33 Gun cocking lever
34 Split windscreen
35 Padded trailing-edge section
36 Petrol tank filler
37 Pilot's headrest
38 Padded cockpit coaming
39 Pilot's seat
40 Throttle control
41 Seat harness
42 Plywood decking
43 Headrest fairing
44 Dorsal structure
45 Dorsal stringers
46 Upper longeron
47 Rudder and elevator control cables

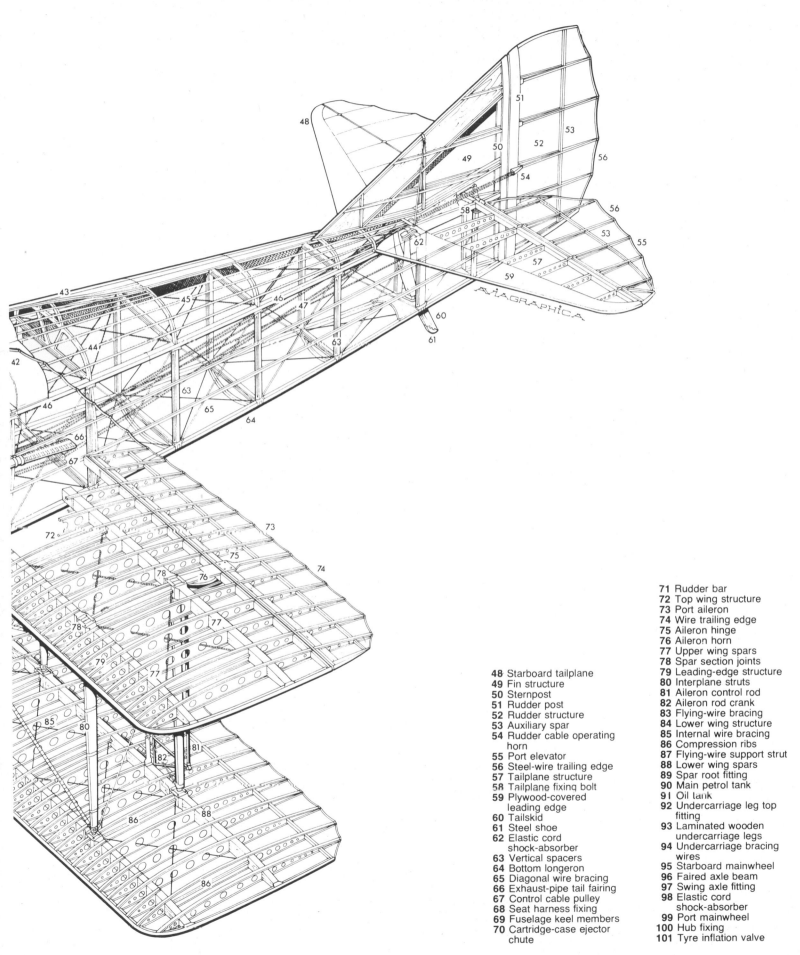

48 Starboard tailplane
49 Fin structure
50 Sternpost
51 Rudder post
52 Rudder structure
53 Auxiliary spar
54 Rudder cable operating horn
55 Port elevator
56 Steel-wire trailing edge
57 Tailplane structure
58 Tailplane fixing bolt
59 Plywood-covered leading edge
60 Tailskid
61 Steel shoe
62 Elastic cord shock-absorber
63 Vertical spacers
64 Bottom longeron
65 Diagonal wire bracing
66 Exhaust-pipe tail fairing
67 Control cable pulley
68 Seat harness fixing
69 Fuselage keel members
70 Cartridge-case ejector chute

71 Rudder bar
72 Top wing structure
73 Port aileron
74 Wire trailing edge
75 Aileron hinge
76 Aileron horn
77 Upper wing spars
78 Spar section joints
79 Leading-edge structure
80 Interplane struts
81 Aileron control rod
82 Aileron rod crank
83 Flying-wire bracing
84 Lower wing structure
85 Internal wire bracing
86 Compression ribs
87 Flying-wire support strut
88 Lower wing spars
89 Spar root fitting
90 Main petrol tank
91 Oil tank
92 Undercarriage leg top fitting
93 Laminated wooden undercarriage legs
94 Undercarriage bracing wires
95 Starboard mainwheel
96 Faired axle beam
97 Swing axle fitting
98 Elastic cord shock-absorber
99 Port mainwheel
100 Hub fixing
101 Tyre inflation valve

Sperry M-1 Messenger.

Sport Aircraft Mini Coupe.

Sportavia Avion-Planeur RF4D (farthest aircraft) and RF5.

Sportavia Avion-Planeur RF-7.

SPCA 81.Col.2 and 90.Col.3 (France) Single-engined four-seat cabin monoplane and three-engined passenger/ambulance/freight-carrying monoplane respectively, reportedly used in French Morocco.

SPCA Météore 63 (France) Three-engined five-passenger biplane flying-boat of 1926, three of which were operated by Air Union.

Sperry M-1 Messenger (USA) The Messenger of 1921 was designed by the Engineering Division of the US Army Air Service and was a single-seat light communications biplane powered by a 44.7 kW (60 hp) Lawrence L-4 engine. A total of 42 was built, a few of which were modified into experimental radio-controlled flying 'torpedoes'. The Sperry company ceased trading soon after production ended, following the death of Lawrence Sperry in a flying accident in a Messenger.

Spitfire Mks I and II (USA) The Mk I is a three-seat light helicopter powered by a 313 kW (420 hp) Allison 250-C20B turboshaft engine. The Mk II is a four-seat light helicopter.

Sport Aircraft Mini Coupé (USA) Single-seat lightweight sporting monoplane, plans for which are available to amateur constructors.

Sportavia RF5B Sperber (Germany) Tandem two-seat motor glider powered by a 50.7 kW (68 hp) Limbach SL 1700 E Comet engine. Improved high-performance version of the Avion-Planeur RF5.

Sportavia SFS 31 Milan (Germany) Essentially a combination of the Avion-Planeur RF4D fuselage and tail unit with the wings of the Scheibe SF-27K sailplane, producing a single-seat light monoplane powered by a 29 kW (39 hp) Rectimo 4 AR 1200 engine.

Sportavia Avion-Planeur RF4 (Germany) Single-seat motor glider combining the characteristics of a small sporting aeroplane and a training sailplane. Powered by a 30 kW (40 hp) converted Volkswagen 1,200 cc motorcar engine. Sportavia took over production of the Avion-Planeur series (designed by Fournier) from Alpavia in 1966.

Sportavia SFS 31 Milan.

Sportavia Avion-Planeur RF5 (Germany) Two-seat motor glider powered by a 50.7 kW (68 hp) Limbach SL 1700 E Comet engine.

Sportavia Avion-Planeur RF7 (Germany) Basically a shorter-span version of the RF4 with increased tailplane span and the power plant of the RF5.

Sportavia RD 180 Sportsman (Germany) Four-seat lightweight sporting monoplane powered by a 134 kW (180 hp) Lycoming O-360-A3A engine. Entered production in 1976 as the RF6C, but the designation was changed to the present style in 1978.

Spratt Model 107 (USA) Two-seat lightweight flying-boat with pivoted controllable parasol wings. Plans are available to amateur constructors.

Stal-2 and -3 (USSR) The Stal-2 of 1932 was a five-seat braced high-wing cabin monoplane powered by a 223.6 kW (300 hp) M-26 engine. Maximum speed was 210 km/h (130 mph). The Stal-3 was an enlarged six-seat version of the Stal-2 powered by a 357.7 kW (480 hp) M-22 engine. Both versions were operated by Aeroflot.

Stampe et Renard (Belgium) This company produced a modernised version of the Stampe et Vertongen S.V.4 as the S.V.4D, intended primarily as an ab initio training aircraft to replace machines in the class of the Tiger Moth and original S.V.4B/C, but also suitable for glider-towing. Power was provided by a 123 kW (165 hp) Rolls-Royce Continental IO-360-A engine.

Stampe et Vertongen S.V.4 and earlier types (Belgium) This company was established in 1922 and specialised in the construction of school and advanced training aircraft, the early types of which were known by the initials RSV (Renard-Stampe-Vertongen). Early products included the RSV 22-180 two-seat advanced training biplane; RSV 28-180 Type III two-seat advanced trainer biplane, specially equipped to teach blind flying; Stampe et Vertongen 26-Lynx two-seat training biplane; 32-G-II two-seat light biplane; and Type III two-seat aerobatic and long-distance touring biplane.

The S.V.4 two-seat training or touring biplane entered production in 1933. Powered by a 97 kW (130 hp) de Havilland Gipsy Major engine, it was supplied as a military trainer to the Belgian government as the S.V.4B. It was also produced under licence in France by SNCAN as the S.V.4C (1,000 built) with the 104.3 kW (140 hp) Renault 4Pei engine fitted. Large numbers of S.V.4s remain flying today with clubs. Maximum level speed is 180 km/h (112 mph).

Stampe et Vertongen S.V.5 (Belgium) Two-seat military training and general-purpose biplane powered by a 253.4 kW (340 hp) Armstrong Siddeley Serval/Cheetah radial engine. A number of S.V.5s were supplied to the Latvian government.

Standard E-1 (USA) Designed in 1917 as a single-seat biplane fighter but ordered by the Army Air Service as an advanced trainer. Delivery of 33 74.5 kW (100 hp) Gnome-powered and 135 59.6 kW (80 hp) Le Rhône-powered E-1s/M-Defences began just before the end of the war.

Standard H-3 and H-4 (USA) In 1916 Sloan Aircraft produced a biplane suitable for reconnaissance and training duties. Twelve were delivered to the Army, powered by 93 kW (125 hp) Hall-Scott A-5 engines. These later became known as Standard H-3s when the company was taken over. Three similar aircraft were delivered to the US Navy as H-4-H twin-float trainers in 1917.

Standard J series (USA) Tandem two-seat biplane trainers developed from the H series. The initial version was the SJ powered by a 74.5 kW (100 hp) Hall-Scott A-7A engine. It proved somewhat underpowered and so the JR Pursuit and J-1 were introduced, powered by 130.4 kW (175 hp) Hall-Scott A-5A engines, giving a maximum speed of 153 km/h (95 mph). The 1918 *Jane's* said this about the JR Pursuit version: 'As may be seen from the firm's own figures for performance, the machine cannot be used for war purposes. . . . Nevertheless, in the advanced stages of training, after a pupil has left the slow preliminary types, and before putting him onto war aeroplanes, the machine should find a distinct field of usefulness.'

Sportavia RS 180 Sportsman.

Spratt Model 105, landplane counterpart of the Model 107.

Stampe et Vertongen S.V.4B.

Standard E-1.

Starck

Standard J-1.

Standard Mailplane.

Starck AS-37 (France) Two-seat light aircraft employing the narrow-gap, sharply staggered biplane wing configuration. Plans are available to amateur constructors.

State Aircraft Factories current types (China) Longest established of the Chinese national aircraft factories is the works at Shenyang. This had its origin in the Mukden plant of the Manshu Aeroplane Manufacturing Company, one of several aircraft and aero-engine manufacturing facilities established in Manchuria by the Japanese invaders in 1938. Although it was thought that the advanced version of the F-6 (see below) was built at Shenyang, it now appears to be designated A-5 (not F-6*bis*) and built at Nanchang. The F-9B engine is reportedly designated WP-6.

The Shenyang F-6 and Nanchang A-5 are MiG-19 fighters, the latter in a highly developed form (see **Mikoyan MiG-19**). The F-7 is a copy of the MiG-21, while the designations F-8, F-9 and F-12 refer to Chinese-designed fighters powered respectively by single and twin Tumansky R-11

Starck AS-37.

Stearman PT-13.

turbojet engines (F-8 and F-9) and a new fighter currently under development and possibly using technology gleaned from the MiG-23. The Harbin B-5 is a Chinese-produced version of the Ilyushin Il-28 three-seat tactical bomber, while the Sian B-6 is a Chinese-built Tupolev Tu-16 bomber. The Harbin H-5 is the Chinese-built Mil Mi-4 helicopter. Shenyang BT-5 and BT-6 are versions of the Yakovlev Yak-18 basic trainers, while the designation Shenyang C-10 (Y-10) refers to a jet airliner, the prototype of which was nearing completion in 1979. Finally the Harbin C-5 (Y-5) is a Chinese-built Antonov An-2 general-purpose biplane, and the Harbin C-11 (Y-11) is a new Chinese twin-engined utility aircraft designed as a modern replacement for the C-5 (Y-5).

Stearman NS, N2S and PT-series Kaydet (USA) Having produced the Cloudboy trainer and various other aircraft including the three-seat open-cockpit C-3R and 4E commercial biplanes, Stearman built a new tandem two-seat primary trainer. About 10,000 were eventually produced for the US Navy and US Army Air Corps/Force and for export from 1934 as Kaydets.

Under the designation NS-1, the US Navy ordered 41 Stearman Model 73 trainers in 1934, powered by 168 kW (225 hp) Wright R-790-8 engines (J-5s). In the following year the company received contracts for the construction of 46 aeroplanes: 26 for the USAAC (Model 75s) and 20 for the US Navy (Model 73s) as PT-13s and NS-1s respectively. Power for the PT-13s was provided by 164 kW (220 hp) Lycoming R-680-5 engines. In the following year deliveries and orders included four Model 73s and three Model 76 advanced trainers (313 kW; 420 hp Pratt & Whitney Wasp Junior engines) to the Philippine Constabulary; 92 PT-13As (164 kW; 220 hp Lycoming R-680-7 engines) to the USAAC; 30 Model 76s to the Brazilian Army Air Service; and six Model 76s to the Argentine Navy.

From 1939 Stearman (now a division of Boeing, see entry) produced the PT-13B for the USAAC and similar N2S-2 for the US Navy, powered by 209 kW (280 hp) Lycoming R-680-11 and R-680-8 engines respectively. The final PT-13 derivative was the Army's PT-13D of 1942, powered by the R-680-17 engine. The USAAC's PT-17 and PT-18 were similar except for being powered by 164 kW (220 hp) Continental R-670-5 and 168 kW (225 hp) Jacobs R-755-7 engines respectively, both based on the Model 75. The Navy ordered the 164 kW (220 hp) Continental R-670-14-engined N2S-1 as a naval version of the PT-17, which in fact preceded the N2S-2 mentioned above. The final Navy versions of the Stearman were the N2S-3, N2S-4 and N2S-5, basically similar to the N2S-1 but with Continental R-670-4, R-670-5 and R-680-17 engines respectively.

The final PT designation was applied to the PT-27, ordered by the USAAF on behalf of the RCAF. The Stearman designation A75L3 applied to PT-13-type trainers supplied to Venezuela, while the designation A75N1 was carried by Stearmans for Peru. Export versions were also

delivered to the British and Chinese governments.
Data (N2S-5): *Engine* as above *Wing span* 9.8 m
(32 ft 2 in) *Length* 7.63 m (25 ft 0¼ in) *Max T-O
weight* 1,232 kg (2,717 lb) *Max level speed* 200 km/h
(124 mph) *Endurance* 4 h 45 min

Stearman Cloudboy (USA) Two-seat trainer
powered by a Wright R-975-E, Pratt & Whitney
Wasp Junior, Kinner C-5 or Lycoming R-670
engine. Developed version became the Kaydet.

Steen Skybolt (USA) Two-seat aerobatic biplane, plans (more than 2,000 sold) and
fuselage/wing kits for which are available to
amateur constructors.

Stewart JD₂FF Foo
Fighter.

and lengthened O-49As (later L-1As) from 1940,
plus a number of L-1B/C ambulance aircraft. A
further seven Vigilants, followed by 55 Vigilant Is
and 41 IAs, were assigned to the RAF under
Lease–Lend. Delivery of only 20 can be confirmed,
although the number received must have been
higher.

Stinson L-5 Sentinel (USA) The Sentinel was
developed from the Voyager for liaison and communications duties, powered by a 141.6 kW
(190 hp) Lycoming O-435-1 engine. Three versions were produced for the USAAF: the L-5 and
L-5A standard two-seat short-range aircraft, the
latter being identical to the L-5 except for having
a 24 volt electrical system; and the L-5B or Sentinel II. The L-5B was an adaptation of the L-5 to
carry one stretcher or light cargo up to a maximum of 91 kg (200 lb). The fuselage aft of the rear
wing spar was deepened and retained the rectangular cross-section to the fin. A large door aft of
the observer's door opened downwards to permit
the loading of a stretcher. In service all L-5s had
their wheel fairings removed. During World War
II more than 3,000 Sentinels were delivered.
Many were also operated by the RAF in Burma,
supplied under Lease–Lend.
Data: *Engine* as above *Wing span* 10.36 m (34 ft
0 in) *Length* 7.35 m (24 ft 1¼ in) *Max T-O weight*
979 kg (2,158 lb) *Max level speed* 208 km/h
(129 mph)

Stinson Airliner (USA) The Airliner was produced as the eight-passenger Model A (three
194 kW; 260 hp Lycoming R-680-5 engines) and
the slightly smaller six-passenger Model B (two
R-680-5 engines). One operator of the Model A
was American Airlines.

Stinson SM-1F Detroiter and Junior (USA)
The SM-1F Detroiter (unrelated to the Detroiter
biplane of 1926) was a six-seat commercial cabin

Stearman N2S-5.

Steen Skybolt.

Stephens Akro.

Stewart JD₁HW1.7
Headwind.

Stephens Akro (USA) Single-seat sporting
monoplane, plans for which are available to
amateur constructors.

Stewart JD₂FF Foo Fighter (USA) Single-seat
lightweight sporting biplane, plans for which are
available to amateur constructors.

Stewart JD₁HW1.7 Headwind (USA) Single-
seat light monoplane, plans for which are available to amateur constructors.

Stinson O-49/L-1 Vigilant (USA) The Vigilant
was a two-seat braced high-wing liaison and
observation/spotter aircraft powered by a
223.6 kW (300 hp) Lycoming R-680-9 engine.
The USAAF received 324 as O-49s (later L-1s)

Stinson L-5 Sentinel.

Stinson SR Reliant.

monoplane powered by a 223.6 kW (300 hp) Wright J-6 Whirlwind radial engine. Between 28 August and 14 September 1927 a Detroiter named *Pride of Detroit* was flown from Newfoundland to Tokyo, including a direct flight across the Atlantic. The same aircraft won the 1927 National Air Tour. In the following year two Detroiters finished ahead of every other single-engined aeroplane in the Reliability Air Tour. Detroiters also set up new world duration and endurance records in 1928–29.

However the type is best remembered as the first American aeroplane to incorporate in its design an entirely enclosed cabin, engine starter, brakes on the wheels, a sound-proof cabin and cabin heat for winter flying. It was eventually succeeded by the Reliant.

The Junior of 1928 was basically a smaller four-seat version of the Detroiter monoplane, designed for a Wright J-5 or J-6 Whirlwind engine but normally powered by a 156.5 kW (210 hp) Lycoming engine.

Stolp SA-300 Starduster Too.

Stinson SM-6B Wasp (USA) Eight-seat cabin monoplane of the latter 1920s powered by a 317 kW (425 hp) Pratt & Whitney Wasp engine.

Stinson Detroiter (USA) The original Detroiter of 1926 was a four-seat cabin biplane powered by a 149 kW (200 hp) Wright Whirlwind engine. A number were operated by North-West Airways

Stinson Voyager 150.

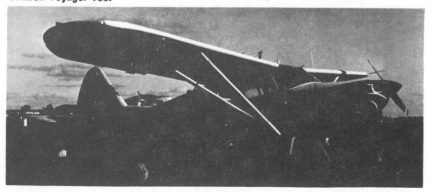

and Florida Airways on the Chicago–Minneapolis and Atlanta–Miami air mail routes respectively.

Stinson SR Reliant (USA) The Reliant was originally produced as a four–five-seat commercial monoplane and was used widely in the US by sportsmen and business executives. Although commercial production ceased on America's entry into World War II, the Reliant was built during 1942–43 in a modified and more powerful form for assignment to the British government as the AT-19 three-seat navigation and communications aircraft for use by the Royal Navy (500 under Lease–Lend). In addition, civil Reliants were impressed into military service during the war by the US Navy, USAAF and RAF, the first having previously received two (in 1935) as light transports, one of which went to the US Coast Guard.

Data (AT-19): *Engine* one 216 kW (290 hp) Lycoming R-680-13 *Wing span* 12.8 m (41 ft 10½ in) *Length* 8.95 m (29 ft 4¼ in) *Max T-O weight* 1,814 kg (4,000 lb) *Max level speed* 227 km/h (141 mph)

Stinson Voyager (USA) Production of the original three-seat Stinson 105 Voyager was discontinued by the Stinson Division of Consolidated Vultee when America entered the war. However preparations were made during 1944–45 to resume production with the new Model 125 Voyager as soon as the war ended, and the prototype was test-flown in December 1944 with a 93 kW (125 hp) Lycoming engine. The standard postwar Voyager was fitted instead with a 112 kW (150 hp) Franklin 6A4-150-B3 engine as the Model 108 Voyager 150.

Stolp SA-300 Starduster Too (USA) Two-seat sporting biplane, plans for which are available to amateur constructors.

Stolp SA-500 Starlet (USA) Single-seat swept parasol-wing monoplane, plans for which are available to amateur constructors.

Stolp SA-700 Acroduster 1 (USA) Single-seat fully aerobatic biplane, plans for which are available to amateur constructors.

Stolp SA-750 Acroduster Too (USA) Two-seat aerobatic biplane, plans for which are available to amateur constructors.

Stolp SA-900 V-Star (USA) Basically a low-cost low-horsepower biplane version of the SA-500 Starlet.

Stout 2-AT/Pullman and AT-4 (USA) The 2-AT or Pullman was a six-passenger (plus two crew or pilot and one passenger) high-wing airliner of 1924, normally powered by a single 298 kW (400 hp) Liberty engine (317 kW; 425 hp Pratt & Whitney Wasp tested experimentally). It was used by Ford Air Transport Services and Florida Airways, by the former from 1926 on its Detroit–Chicago and Detroit–Cleveland air mail services.

From the Pullman was developed the AT-4, an 11-passenger airliner powered by three 149 kW (200 hp) Wright Whirlwind engines. However in 1925 Mr Henry Ford of motor car fame bought the company. As a division of the Ford Motor Company Stout produced the 223.6 kW (300 hp) Wright J-6 Whirlwind-engined 4-AT-E and subsequent Trimotor airliners, better known as Ford types (see **Ford**).

Sud-Aviation SE 3200 and SA 3210 Frelon (France) Sud-Aviation was formed on 1 March 1957 from the Ouest-Aviation (Sud-Ouest) and Sud-Est Aviation companies. One of its first major projects was the Frelon, a large helicopter of conventional layout powered by three Turboméca Turmo III turboshaft engines. The first SE 3200 prototype flew on 10 June 1959. The planned production version was the SA 3210 powered by three 931.5 kW (1,250 shp) Turmo IIIC engines. The Frelon was developed into the larger Super Frelon (see **Aérospatiale**).

Sud-Aviation SE 5000 Baroudeur (France) Among the large number of experimental military aircraft produced in France during the 1950s was the Baroudeur, an experimental tactical-support fighter designed to operate independently of airfields with long runways. Powered by a turbojet engine, it had retractable skids for take-off and landing or could take off from a rocket-powered trolley. It was first flown on 1 August 1953.

Sud-Aviation SO 1221 Djinn (France) The Djinn was a two-seat light helicopter powered by a Turboméca Palouste IV turbo-air generator

which drove the two-bladed rotor by compressed air. The prototype flew for the first time on 16 December 1953. Of the total of 178 Djinns produced, 47 served as agricultural aircraft in ten countries and 100 went to the French Army.

Sud-Aviation SO 4050 Vautour (France) The Vautour was a swept-wing combat aircraft designed and built for tactical support, bombing and all-weather fighting. It was in service until recently with the air forces of France (II-Bs and II-Ns) and Israel (25 II-As). The first prototype flew on 16 October 1952 and exceeded Mach 1 in a shallow dive during its early trials.

Three production versions were produced for the French Air Force: the Vautour II-A single-seat tactical fighter bomber, first flown on 30 April 1956 (30 built); Vautour II-B two-seat bomber, first flown on 31 July 1957 (40 built); and Vautour II-N two-seat all-weather fighter, first flown on 10 October 1956 (70 built).

Data (Vautour II-N): *Engines* two 34.34 kN (7,720 lb st) SNECMA Atar 101E-3 turbojets *Wing span* 15.09 m (49 ft 6½ in) *Length* 15.57 m (51 ft 1 in) *Max T-O weight* 20,700 kg (45,635 lb)

Sud-Aviation

Sud-Aviation Vautour II-Bs and Vautour II-N (second from right).

Sud-Aviation Vautour II-B.

Sud-Aviation Fennec.

Sud-Est SE 161 Languedoc.

Sud-Est SE 2010 Armagnac.

Max level speed 1,100 km/h (686 mph) *Range* 4,000 km (2,485 miles) *Armament* four 30 mm DEFA cannon, plus 232 rockets in two packs in fuselage and underwing attachments for four Matra R 511 air-to-air missiles

Sud-Aviation Fennec (France) Sud-Aviation modified a total of 135 ex-USAF North American T-28A basic trainers into general-purpose military aircraft for service with the French Air Force, making them suitable for reconnaissance, convoy protection, light close support and other duties. Most of these subsequently passed to the air forces or navies of Argentina, Morocco and Tunisia.

Sud-Est SE 161 Languedoc (France) The SE 161 was originally designed as the SO (Bloch) 161 four-engined airliner. The prototype flew at Bordeaux in 1939 but did not complete its tests until January 1942. Although ordered in series by the Vichy government from SNCASE in December 1941, no aircraft other than the prototype (which was confiscated by the Germans) was delivered during the war. However it was put into production after the liberation of France to the order of the provisional government, the first post-war production SE 161 flying on 17 September 1945.

By the end of 1950 72 Languedocs (out of an eventual total of 100) had been delivered to Air France and the French Air Force and Navy. Various Languedoc airframes were also used for experimental purposes, including as carrier aircraft for the Leduc ramjet aircraft (see entry). Data: *Engines* four 782.5 kW (1,050 hp) Pratt & Whitney R-1830-92 Twin Wasps *Wing span* 29.38 m (96 ft 5 in) *Length* 24.25 m (79 ft 7 in) *Max T-O weight* 20,577 kg (45,364 lb) *Max level speed* 440 km/h (273 mph) *Range* 3,200 km (1,988 miles) *Accommodation* main cabin accommodated as standard 33 passengers in 11 rows of 3; alternative arrangements for 12 or 24 passengers or freight

Sud-Est SE 200 (France) Originally designed to a French Air Ministry specification of 1936 for a transatlantic flying-boat, this large six-engined long-range commercial aircraft was designed by Lioré et Olivier as the H-49. Construction of four prototypes was started: two were completed and seized by the Germans but were destroyed by RAF bombing raids; the remaining two were completed after the war. Accommodation was provided for 80 passengers by day and 40 by night.

Sud-Est SE 2010 Armagnac (France) The prototype of this four-engined airliner flew for the first time on 2 April 1949. Four of the first six airliners laid down were delivered to TAI, but these proved uneconomical and were quickly taken out of service. However in 1953 SAGETA was formed, eventually operating seven Armagnacs between Toulouse and Saigon (not direct). Power was provided by 2,608 kW (3,500 hp) Pratt & Whitney R-4360 B13 Wasp Major engines and accommodation was provided for 84, 107 or 160 passengers.

Sud-Ouest SO 30P Bretagne (France) The SO 30P Bretagne was the production version of an aircraft the original design of which began during World War II. As a transport for 30, 37 or 43 passengers or freight, the SO 30P was fitted with three types of power plant. Most had two 1,341 kW (1,800 hp) Pratt & Whitney R-2800-B43s (occasionally supplemented by two Turboméca Pallas auxiliary turbojets), although at least one had 1,788.5 kW (2,400 hp) R-2800-CA18s and others were experimentally fitted with Hispano-Suiza-built Rolls-Royce Nene and SNECMA Atar 101 turbojet engines. A total of 45 Bretagnes were built, serving with sev-

eral airlines (including Air France and Air Algérie) as well as the French Air Force and Navy – the latter as a result of termination of certain airline contracts or because of the end of hostilities in Indo-China.

Sud-Ouest SO 93, 94 and 95 Corse II (France) Twin 440 kW (590 hp) Renault 12S-engined 8-seat, 10-seat and 13-seat postal light commercial aircraft respectively of post-war construction. During the war the SO 90 prototype had made a dramatic and secret first flight to Algiers (North Africa) under the noses of the members of the Italo-German Armistice Commission carrying nine passengers. It is believed that 60 production SO 95 Corse IIs were built from 1947 for the French Navy, plus a handful for commercial service with overseas airline operators.

Sud-Ouest SO 175 (France) The original Bloch 175 had gone into production just before the German occupation of France as a three-seat reconnaissance bomber (see **Bloch 175**). After the war the French Navy needed a replacement torpedo-bomber and ordered a new version of the Bloch 175 to fulfil this task. In addition to the Bloch 175Ts, Sud-Ouest built a number of SO 175T derivatives powered by two Gnome-Rhône N 48/N 49 radial engines and armed with three cannon and rockets. Maximum speed of the SO 175T was 510 km/h (317 mph).

Sukhoi Su-2 (USSR) Two-seat attack monoplane powered by an 820 kW (1,100 hp) M-88 radial engine. Used in limited numbers between 1940 and 1942.

Sukhoi Su-6 (USSR) Two-seat ground-attack monoplane powered by a 1,490.4 kW (2,000 hp)

or 1,639.4 kW (2,200 hp) radial engine. Small number delivered during 1942–43.

Sukhoi Su-7B (USSR) The Su-7B single-seat ground-attack fighter (NATO reporting name *Fitter-A*) was first seen in prototype form during the 1956 Soviet Aviation Day Display and appeared in formations of up to 21 aircraft in the 1961 Tushino display. It subsequently became the standard tactical fighter bomber of the Soviet Air Force, with which about 400 continue in service. Others have been supplied to Afghanistan, Algeria, Cuba, Czechoslovakia, Egypt, Hungary, India, Iraq, North Korea, Peru, Poland, Romania, Syria and Vietnam.

Early production models had the pitot boom mounted centrally above the air intake, but it is offset to starboard on current versions. Another change was made in the brake-chute installation. Early aircraft had a single ribbon-type parachute attached under the rear fuselage; later Su-7Bs have twin brake-chutes in a housing at the base of the rudder. The size of the blast panels on the sides of the front fuselage by the wing-root guns was also increased, implying that the cannon now fitted have a higher muzzle velocity or rate of fire.

Among further changes that led to use of the revised designation Su-7BM (for Modifikatsirovanny: modified) was the introduction of a low-pressure nosewheel tyre, requiring blistered doors to enclose it when retracted.

A variant of the Su-7 seen first at Domodedovo in 1967 is the two-seat Su-7U, with the second cockpit in tandem aft of the standard cockpit and with a slightly raised canopy. A prominent dorsal spine extends from the rear of the aft canopy to the base of the tail fin. The two-seater is a standard operational trainer and has the NATO reporting name *Moujik*.

Data (Su-7BM): *Engine* one 98.1 kN (22,046 lb st,

Sud-Ouest SO 30P Bretagne, with underwing Palas auxiliary turbojets.

Sukhoi Su-7BM.

Sud-Ouest SO 95 Corse II.

Sukhoi Su-2.

Sukhoi Su-9s.

Sukhoi

Sukhoi Su-17 *Fitter-C*.

Artist's impression of the Sukhoi Su-24.

with afterburning) Lyulka AL-7F-1 turbojet *Wing span* 8.93 m (29 ft 3½ in) *Length* 17.37 m (57 ft 0 in) *Max T-O weight* 13,500 kg (29,750 lb) *Max level speed* Mach 1.6 *Range* 1,450 km (900 miles) *Armament* two 30 mm NR-30 guns in wing-root leading edges. Four underwing attachments for rocket pods or bombs (usually two 750 kg and two 500 kg). When underbelly fuel tanks are fitted, max external weapon load is 1,000 kg (2,205 lb)

Sukhoi Su-9 and Su-11 (USSR) First seen at Tushino during the 1956 Aviation Day display, the prototype of these single-seat all-weather fighters (allocated the NATO reporting name *Fishpot-A*) had a small conical radome above its engine air intake. This was replaced by a centre-body air intake on the production version, which entered standard service with the Soviet Air Force in two forms as follows:

Su-9 (*Fishpot-B*) Initial version, operational since 1959 and still in service. Powered by an 88.25 kN (19,840 lb st) Lyulka AL-7F afterburning turbojet. Examples included in the Tushino display of 1961 carried four of the Soviet Air Force's then-standard radar-homing air-to-air missiles (NATO reporting name *Alkali*) on underwing attachments, plus two under-fuselage fuel tanks side-by-side. No fixed armament.

Su-11 (*Fishpot-C*) First seen publicly in 1967, the Su-11 is a much-improved development of the Su-9 with a Lyulka AL-7F-1 turbojet (98.1 kN; 22,046 lb st, with afterburning) and a standard armament of two underwing missiles (NATO *Anab*), one with a radar homing head and one with an infra-red homing head. It also has a lengthened nose of less tapered form than that of the Su-9.

In 1977 the Su-9 and Su-11 equipped some 25% of the Soviet home-defence interceptor force. There is also a tandem two-seat training version known to NATO as *Maiden*.
Data (Su-11, estimated): Engine as above *Wing span* 8.43 m (27 ft 8 in) *Length* 17.0 m (56 ft 0 in) *Max T-O weight* 13,600 kg (30,000 lb) *Max level speed* Mach 1.8

Sukhoi Su-15 (USSR) Known to NATO as *Flagon*, ten examples of the Su-15 single-seat twin-jet delta-wing fighter participated in the flying display at Domodedovo in July 1967. It was developed to meet a Soviet Air Force requirement for a Mach 2.5 interceptor to replace the Su-11 and is in service with the Soviet Air Force in several forms:

Flagon-A has simple delta wings and a conical radome and is powered by turbojets reported to be Tumansky R-11F2-300s, each rated at 60.8 kN (13,668 lb st) with afterburning.

Flagon-B was an experimental STOL version with three lift-jet engines mounted vertically in the centre-fuselage.

Flagon-C is the two-seat training version of *Flagon-D*, probably with combat capability.

Flagon-D is generally similar to *Flagon-A*, but with longer-span wings of compound sweep, produced by reducing the sweepback at the tips via a very narrow unswept section. It was the first major production version.

Flagon-E has new turbojet engines reported to be Tumansky R-13F-300s, each rated at 64.73 kN (14,550 lb st), and uprated avionics. This has been the major production version since the second half of 1973.

Flagon-F is the latest version, generally similar to *Flagon-E*.

About 1,000 Su-15s were believed to form the backbone of the 2,600 interceptors based in the Soviet Union in 1979.
Data (estimated): Engines as above *Wing span* 10.53 m (34 ft 6 in) *Length* 20.5 m (68 ft 0 in) *Max T-O weight* 16,000 kg (35,275 lb) *Max level speed*

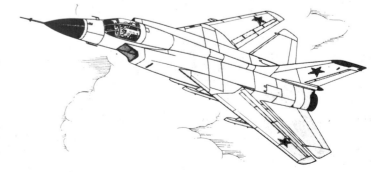

Mach 2.3–2.5 *Combat radius* 725 km (450 miles) *Armament* single pylon for external store under each wing. Normal armament comprises one radar-homing and one infra-red-homing air-to-air missile (NATO *Anab*). Side-by-side pylons under centre-fuselage for further weapons or external fuel tanks

Sukhoi Su-17 (USSR) The Su-17 is a single-seat variable-geometry tactical fighter which first entered service in the early 1970s. Power is provided by an uprated Lyulka AL-21F-3 turbojet engine (109 kN; 24,500 lb st, with afterburning). Two versions have been identified and these are known to NATO as *Fitter-C* and *-D*. The former is the original version, of which it was announced in the USA in 1972 that at least one or two squadrons were operational with the Soviet Air Force, while *Fitter-D* has a small undernose radome and a laser marked-target seeker in its centrebody.

Both *Fitter-C* and *-D* have also been assigned to Soviet Naval Aviation units in the Baltic Sea, where they could be employed in limited anti-shipping strike roles or to support amphibious operations.

Data (estimated): *Engine* as above *Wing span* (spread) 14.0 m (45 ft 11¼ in), (swept) 10.6 m (34 ft 9½ in) *Length* 18.75 m (61 ft 6¼ in) *Max T-O weight* 17,700 kg (39,020 lb) *Max level speed* Mach 2.17 *Combat radius* 630 km (391 miles) *Armament* including the wing-fence stores attachments, eight weapon pylons can be fitted under the wings and fuselage for up to 5,000 kg (11,023 lb) of bombs, rocket pods and guided missiles. Two 30 mm NR-30 wing-root guns

Sukhoi Su-20 and Su-22 (USSR) The Su-20 is an export version of *Fitter-C* and is currently operational with seven air forces, including the Polish Air Force, which has about ten squadrons. The Su-22 is a variant of the Su-20 with a lower equipment standard. Delivery of 36 Su-22s to Peru began in 1977.

Sukhoi Su-24 (USSR) Known to NATO as *Fencer*, the Su-24 is a two-seat variable-geometry fighter-bomber powered by two unidentified afterburning turbojet engines (possibly Lyulka AL-21Fs, each rated at 111.2 kN; 25,000 lb st). It entered squadron service in December 1974 and by the spring of 1979 at least 250 were serving in first-line squadrons in the European theatre.

Data (estimated): *Engines* as above *Wing span* (spread) 17.15 m (56 ft 3 in), (swept) 9.53 m (31 ft 3 in) *Max T-O weight* 30,850 kg (68,000 lb) *Max level speed* above Mach 2 *Combat radius* 322 km (200 miles)

Superior Satellite (USA) Two-seat light cabin monoplane derived from the Culver Model V and powered by a 67 kW (90 hp) Continental C90 engine. The first production Satellite flew on 20 December 1957.

Supermarine S.4, S.5, S.6 and S.6B (UK) See **Schneider Trophy contestants**

Supermarine Attacker (UK) The Attacker was designed to Specification E.10/44, drawn up in 1944 to provide without delay a fighter which would use the Rolls-Royce Nene engine. To simplify production the wings and tailwheel landing gear of the Spiteful were incorporated.

The first prototype flew on 27 July 1946 and had been designed to RAF requirements. The second and third prototypes were built as naval aircraft. Successful carrier trials took place in October 1947 on HMS *Illustrious* and the Attacker was subsequently ordered for the Royal Navy and the Royal Pakistan Air Force.

The FAA received three versions: the F.1 interceptor fighter and the FB.1 fighter-bomber, both with 22.7 kN (5,100 lb st) Rolls-Royce Nene 3 turbojet engines, and the FB.2 with a Nene 102 engine. The RPAF received 36 F.1-type Attackers without folding wings and other naval equipment. The FAA Attacker first entered service in August 1951.

Data (FB.2): *Engine* as above *Wing span* 11.25 m (36 ft 11 in) *Length* 11.43 m (37 ft 6 in) *Max normal T-O weight* 5,579 kg (12,300 lb) *Max level speed* 950 km/h (590 mph) *Max range* 1,915 km (1,190 miles) *Armament* four 20 mm British Hispano Mk 5 cannon, plus two 1,000 lb bombs or 12 × 60 lb rocket projectiles

Supermarine Scapa (UK) All-metal reconnaissance flying-boat developed from the Southampton and powered by two 391 kW (525 hp) Rolls-Royce Kestrel IIIS radial engines mounted in nacelles applied directly to the undersurface of the upper wing centre-section. Fourteen were built for the RAF, entering service in 1935.

Supermarine Sea Otter.

Supermarine Scimitar (UK) Known originally as the Supermarine N.113, the Scimitar F.1 was a large single-seat, twin-engined naval carrier-borne interceptor fighter and strike aircraft for the Royal Navy. The prototype flew for the first time on 20 January 1956 and deck-landing trials were successfully completed on HMS *Ark Royal* in July 1957. The first of 76 production aircraft flew on 11 January 1957 and the first operational squadron (No 803) was formed in the summer of 1958 and embarked on HMS *Victorious* in the following September.

Data: *Engines* two 50 kN (11,250 lb st) Rolls-Royce Avon Mk 202 turbojets *Wing span* 11.33 m (37 ft 2 in) *Length* 16.87 m (55 ft 4 in) *Max T-O weight* (approx) 18,144 kg (40,000 lb) *Max level speed* 1,143 km/h (710 mph) *Armament* originally armed with four 30 mm Aden guns, and had provision for 96 unguided air-to-air rockets. Alternative armaments later added included Sidewinder air-to-air missiles. In the strike role it could carry a tactical nuclear bomb or four large bombs, etc

Supermarine Seafire Mk 47 on board HMS *Triumph*.

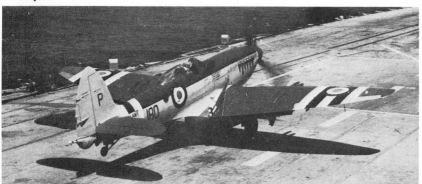

Supermarine Seafire (UK) The Seafire was a naval version of the Spitfire specially adapted for operation from aircraft carriers. It had folding wings and was provided with catapult, deck-arrester gear and other specialised equipment. Many versions were built with Merlin and Griffon engines, first entering service with No 807 Squadron in mid-1942 and going to sea on board HMS *Furious*. The last were finally withdrawn from first-line duties in 1952.

Supermarine Seagull III (UK) This amphibious biplane was designed for fleet spotting and reconnaissance duties and first appeared in 1921. Six were built for the FAA, operating from HMS *Eagle*. Power was provided by a 335.3 kW (450 hp) Napier Lion V engine.

Supermarine Southampton Mk I.

Supermarine Seagull III.

Supermarine 381 Seagull (UK) Not to be confused with the Seagull III, this Seagull was built to Specification S.14/44 to replace the Walrus and Sea Otter. It successfully completed deck-landing trials in 1949 but failed to win orders from the Royal Navy.

Supermarine Sea Lion (UK) See **Schneider Trophy contestants**

Supermarine Sea Otter (UK) The Sea Otter amphibious biplane was designed to replace the Walrus on reconnaissance and general duties, including air-sea rescue. It was produced before World War II and went into service with the RAF and FAA during the war. A total of 290 was built. After the war a number were modified for civil use with the normal military equipment removed. Power was provided by one 637 kW (855 hp) Bristol Mercury 30 radial, giving a maximum level speed of 241 km/h (150 mph).

Supermarine Southampton (UK) First appearing in 1925, the Southampton was a wooden or metal-hulled (Mk I and Mk II respectively) biplane flying-boat powered by two 335.3 kW (450 hp) Napier Lion V engines. The RAF received 68 and these were used by naval co-operation squadrons, mainly for reconnaissance duties. Maximum level speed was 174 km/h (108 mph).

Supermarine Spiteful and Seafang (UK) The Spiteful was designed to meet Specification F.1/43 and was a direct descendant of the Spitfire. It featured new wings with straight-tapered leading and trailing edges and squared tips, a larger tail unit and other refinements. Production was cancelled at the end of the war after only 17 had been built from an order for 373. The naval version of the Spiteful was the Seafang, which was also cancelled.

Supermarine Spitfire (UK) The first Supermarine aeroplane to have the name Spitfire suggested for it was the experimental single-seat fighter designed to Specification F.7/30. It was produced in 1934 and was a cantilever low-wing

soundness of the basic design was proved in six years of war, throughout which the Spitfire, in its many progressively developed forms, remained a first-line fighter.

Apart from its fighter and fighter-bomber duties, the Spitfire was also used during the war for photographic-reconnaissance duties, the first such mission by an unarmed Spitfire being undertaken on 18 November 1939.

Supermarine Spitfire VC at a Sicilian airfield in 1943.

monoplane with inverted gull wings and a fixed landing gear. Power was provided by a 447 kW (600 hp) Rolls-Royce Goshawk engine. From the type – which did not proceed beyond the prototype stage – was evolved as a private venture a new prototype to which the name Spitfire seemed more appropriate and around which Specification F.37/34 was written. Into this aircraft R. J. Mitchell incorporated the results of experience gained in the design of the high-speed Schneider Trophy racing seaplanes.

The first production version of the Spitfire was the Mk I powered by a 767.5 kW (1,030 hp) Rolls-Royce Merlin II or III engine, initially driving a two-blade wooden propeller but subsequently a three-blade duralumin type. Armament varied from eight 0.303 in machine-guns to two 20 mm cannon and four guns. First deliveries went to No 19 and No 66 Squadrons, RAF, in mid-1938. The Spitfire II and III had Merlin XII and XX engines respectively, while the Spitfire PR.III was the first special photographic-reconnaissance version.

Although the Spitfire Mk XII was the first to have the Rolls-Royce Griffon engine fitted – in the form of a 1,293 kW (1,735 hp) Griffon III or IV – a single Mk IV had flown with a Griffon IIB in 1941, later being redesignated Spitfire XX. The Mk XII entered service in early 1943. The Spitfire V that went into service in 1941 was the first mark to be fitted with tropical equipment, to carry drop-tanks (VB and VC) and to serve in large numbers outside the British Isles.

By 1941 high-flying German Focke-Wulf 190s were proving too good for the Spitfire V (which in 1943 had its wings clipped for service as a low-altitude fighter) and so the Spitfire VIII was evolved to counter it, initially fitted with a Merlin 61 engine. But before this version entered service in 1943, the Spitfire IX had become operational; this mark was eventually produced in standard fighter (F.IX), low-altitude fighter (LF.IX), and high-altitude (HF.IX) forms.

The Spitfire XVI was powered by a Packard-built Merlin 266 engine, the equivalent of the British-built Merlin 66. The final versions of the fighter were the Mks 22 and strengthened 24, fitted with Merlin 61, Griffon 85 or other engines, bringing the total number of Spitfires built to well over 20,000. The last missions performed by RAF Spitfires took place in Malaya in 1954.

The prototype F.37/34, fitted with one of the first Rolls-Royce Merlin engines, flew for the first time on 5 March 1936. With a fixed-pitch wooden propeller it had a maximum speed of 550 km/h (342 mph), which classed it at the time as the fastest military aeroplane in the world. The

Supermarine Spitfire prototype on view to the public in 1936 alongside a Walrus, the prototype Wellesley and prototype Wellington.

Supermarine Spitfire VCs under construction.

Supermarine

Supermarine Spitfires seek out the enemy.

Data (Mk XIV): *Engine* one 1,527.7 kW (2,050 hp) Rolls-Royce Griffon 65 *Wing span* 11.23 m (36 ft 10 in) *Length* 9.96 m (32 ft 8 in) *Max T-O weight* 3,851 kg (8,490 lb) *Max level speed* 721 km/h (448 mph) *Range* 1,368 km (850 miles) *Armament* two 20 mm cannon and four 0.303 in machine-guns, plus bombs

The following table first appeared in the 1946–47 *Jane's*. Although not totally accurate, it gives a good indication of the differences between the Spitfire Mks I to XVI.

Supermarine Stranraer (UK) The Stranraer was an all-metal long-range reconnaissance and bombing flying-boat powered in its production form by two 652 kW (875 hp) Bristol Pegasus X radial engines mounted in monocoque nacelles immediately below the upper wing centre-section. Seventeen were ordered for the RAF on 29 August 1935, followed by six more the following year. These entered service in 1936. The Canadian Vickers company also produced the Stranraer for the Department of National Defence, about half

Mark	Power plant	Function	Weight loaded (lb)	Max. Speed (mph) at operational height	Normal range (miles)	Ceiling (ft)	Remarks
SPITFIRE IA	Merlin II or III	Fighter	5,332	367	—	—	
SPITFIRE IB	Merlin III	Fighter	5,784	—	—	—	
SPITFIRE IIA	Merlin XII	Fighter	6,317	—	—	—	
SPITFIRE IIB	Merlin XII	Fighter	6,527	—	—	—	
SPITFIRE PR. IV	Merlin 45 or 46	Photo-Reconnaissance	7,178	372	1,460	38,000	Unarmed
SPITFIRE VA	Merlin 45 or 46	Fighter	6,417	45=369 46=365	VB {45=480 46=460} VC {45=470 46=450}	45=37,000 46=38,000	First to be fitted with fuselage drop-tank or bomb
SPITFIRE VB	Merlin 45 or 46	Fighter	6,622				
SPITFIRE VC	Merlin 45 or 46	Fighter	6,785				
SPITFIRE F. VI	Merlin 47	Fighter	6,797	364	475	40,000	
SPITFIRE F. VII	Merlin 61 or 64	Fighter	7,875	408	660	43,000	
SPITFIRE HF. VII	Merlin 71	High-alt. Fighter	7,875	416	660	44,000	
SPITFIRE PR. VII	Merlin 45 or 46	Photo-Reconnaissance	6,585	369	710	37,000	8 × 0.303 in m.g.
SPITFIRE F. VIII	Merlin 61, 63 or 63A	Fighter and Fighter-Bomber	7,767	408	660	43,000	
SPITFIRE LF. VIII	Merlin 66	Low-alt. Fighter	7,767	404	660	41,500	
SPITFIRE HF. VIII	Merlin 70	High-alt. Fighter	7,767	416	660	44,000	
SPITFIRE F. IX	Merlin 61 or 63	Fighter	7,300	over 400	434	40,000	
SPITFIRE LF. IX	Merlin 66	Low-alt. Fighter	7,300	404	434	42,500	
SPITFIRE HF. IX	Merlin 70	High-alt. Fighter	7,300	416	434	45,000	
SPITFIRE PR. X	Merlin 64 or 77	Photo-Reconnaissance	8,159	416	1,370	43,000	Unarmed
SPITFIRE PR. XI	Merlin 61, 63, 63A or 70	Photo-Reconnaissance	7,872	422	over 1,200	44,000	Unarmed
SPITFIRE F. XII	Griffon III or IV	Fighter and Fighter-Bomber	7,280	393	329	40,000	
SPITFIRE PR. XIII	Merlin 32	Photo-Reconnaissance	6,364	348	500	38,000	4 × 0.303 in m.g.
SPITFIRE F. XIV	Griffon 65	F., F.B. or F. Recce	8,490	over 450	{F.XIV=460 FR.XIV=620}	over 40,000	
SPITFIRE F. XVI	Merlin 266	Low-alt. Fighter or Fighter-Bomber	7,300	over 400	434	40,000	

Supermarine Stranraers.

Supermarine Swift FR.5s.

the ten ordered being completed in 1938. Maximum level speed was 266 km/h (165 mph). Armament comprised machine-guns in bow (also a bombing station), midship and extreme tail positions, plus bombs. A torpedo or spare engine could be transported in the lower centre-section.

Supermarine Swift (UK) The Swift was a single-seat swept-wing fighter powered by a Rolls-Royce Avon axial-flow turbojet engine. On 10 July 1952 the prototype established an international point-to-point record between London and Brussels, covering 320 km (200 miles) in 18 minutes 3.3. seconds, representing a speed of 1,071.7 km/h (665.9 mph). On 25 September 1953 a Swift F.4 raised the world speed record to 1,184 km/h (735.7 mph) over a 3 km course.

The RAF received a total of about 60 Swift F.1s, F.2s and F.3s, with an Avon RA.7 turbojet engine and two 30 mm Aden cannon; four Aden cannon and a new wing planform with compound leading-edge taper; and with an Avon RA.7R engine with afterburner and changes to the rear fuselage respectively. These versions were not used operationally. The Swift F.4 had an all-moving tail of increased area. Only the FR.5 was used for any length of time and was a fighter-reconnaissance aircraft with a longer nose to accommodate a camera. Deliveries began in 1956. Sixty were flown by the RAF; one further aircraft ordered crashed on delivery and several others were not completed.

Data (FR.5): *Engine* one 42 kN (9,450 lb st, with afterburning) Rolls-Royce Avon 114 turbojet *Wing span* 9.86 m (32 ft 4 in) *Length* 12.88 m (42 ft 3 in) *Max T-O weight* 9,707 kg (21,400 lb) *Max level speed* 1,102 km/h (685 mph) *Range* 773 km (480 miles)

Supermarine Walrus (UK) The Walrus amphibious biplane originally appeared in 1933 under the name Seagull V and was supplied to the Australian government under that name. In 1935 it was adopted by the Admiralty as a standard ABR (amphibian-boat-reconnaissance) type for employment on all ships equipped with catapults. It was subsequently renamed Walrus. Apart from service on ships of the Royal Navy, the aircraft was used for training, communications and air-sea rescue duties at home and abroad by the RAF. A total of 740 was built in two versions: the Mk I with a metal hull and the Mk II (built by Saunders-Roe) with a wooden hull. These were extensively used throughout World War II.

Data (Walrus II): *Engine* one 577.5 kW (775 hp) Bristol Pegasus VI radial *Wing span* 13.97 m (45 ft

Supermarine Walrus I.

10 in) *Length* 11.45 m (37 ft 7 in) *Max T-O weight* 3,259 kg (7,200 lb) *Max level speed* 217 km/h (135 mph) *Cruising range* 966 km (600 miles) *Armament* two or three Vickers K guns, plus bombs

Swallow types (USA) The Swallow Aeroplane Manufacturing Company (later Swallow Aircraft Company) was the successor to the E. M. Laird Company and its early aircraft were refined Laird designs. Swallow's first product was the Commercial Three-Seater (a refined Laird Swallow) built around the 67 kW (90 hp) Curtiss OX-5 engine. This type proved very popular in the Middle West for passenger-carrying and was the subject of continuous improvement. In about 1926 Swallow produced a number of mail planes based on the successful New Swallow aircraft for the Elko (Nevada)–Pasco (Washington) air mail service of Varney Air Lines.

In 1927 the company produced the four-seat Super Swallow, followed by the three-seat Swallow Commercial TP trainer, two-seat Swallow Coupé light cabin monoplane of the 1930s (93 kW; 125 hp Menasco C-4 engine), and the Swallow LT-65 two-seat low-wing monoplane of 1940.

Swearingen Merlin IIIB.

Swearingen Merlin IVA.

Tachikawa Army Ki-9.

Swales SD-3-15T (UK) Single-seat sailplane currently in production.

Swearingen Merlin IIA and IIB (USA) The Merlin IIA was first flown in prototype form on 13 April 1965 and production aircraft were delivered from August 1966. It was produced as an eight-seat executive aircraft with a new pressurised fuselage mated to modified Beechcraft Queen Air wings and a Twin Bonanza landing gear. Power was provided by two 410 kW (550 shp) Pratt & Whitney Aircraft of Canada PT6A-20 turbo-props. Thirty-three were built, followed by production of the Merlin IIB, powered by 495.5 kW (665 shp) Garrett AiResearch TPE 331-1-151G turboprop engines. Eighty-seven IIBs had been delivered by February 1972. Maximum cruising speed of the IIB is 475 km/h (295 mph).

Swearingen Merlin III (USA) The Merlin III differs from the Merlin IIB by having a new tail unit; slightly longer fuselage; and the wings, landing gear and engines of the Metro. The current Merlin IIIB is an 8–11-seat all-weather pressurised executive transport powered by two 671 kW (900 shp) Garrett-AiResearch TPE 331-10U-501G turboprop engines. It differs from the earlier Merlin IIIs by having additional windows; major system and flight deck improvements; and a wide selection of new interiors. A total of 92 IIIs and IIIAs had been delivered by 1 January 1979, when production ended. Customers included the Belgian Air Force and Argentine Army and Air Force. The first production IIIB was delivered in December 1978.

Data (IIIB): *Engines* as above *Wing span* 14.1 m (46 ft 3 in) *Length* 12.85 m (42 ft 2 in) *Max T-O weight* 5,670 kg (12,500 lb) *Max cruising speed* 571 km/h (355 mph) *Range* 4,567 km (2,838 miles)

Swearingen Merlin IVA (USA) Corporate version of the Metro II commuter airliner, differing principally in its internal configuration, which provides accommodation for 12–15 passengers, with a private toilet and 4.05 m³ (143 cu ft) of baggage volume. Initial deliveries of the earlier Merlin IV were made in 1970. A total of 50 Merlin

Swearingen Metro II.

IV/IVAs had been delivered by the beginning of 1979. Power for the Merlin IVA is provided by two 701 kW (940 shp) Garrett-AiResearch TPE 331-3UW-303G turboprops.

Swearingen Model SA-226TC Metro II (USA) The Metro II is a 19–20-passenger all-weather pressurised, air-conditioned airliner. It differs from the earlier Metro by the introduction of larger windows and major systems and flight deck improvements. A total of 86 Metro/Metro IIs had been delivered by the beginning of 1979.

Swearingen Merlin Maritime Surveillance Aircraft (USA) This is a new multi-mission aircraft developed from the Metro II, configured specifically for maritime surveillance. A crew of seven and all the avionics/surveillance equipment necessary for a maritime mission are carried, but it is designed also for quick conversion for passenger, cargo or other roles.

SZD sailplanes (Poland) Six sailplanes and a motor glider are currently built by SZD: the SZD-30C Pirat single-seat Standard Class; SZD-41A Jantar Standard single-seat Standard Class; SZD-42-1 Jantar 2 single-seat high-performance Open Class; SZD-42-2 Jantar 2B single-seat Open Class; SZD-48 Jantar Standard 2 single-seat Standard Class; SZD-50-2 Puchacz tandem two-seat high-performance training sailplane; and the SZD-45A Ogar side-by-side two-seat school and training motor glider.

Tachikawa Army Ki-9 (Japan) Intended to take different power plants – the 261 kW (350 hp) Ha-13a radial for the basic training role and a 112 kW (150 hp) engine for primary training – the Ki-9 was tested during 1935. Centre of gravity problems soon resulted in the scrapping of the lower-powered prototype, but two 261 kW (350 hp) prototypes showed promise and were developed into the production Type 95-1 intermediate trainer.

An unequal-span, single-bay two-seat biplane with a fixed divided undercarriage, the Ki-9 soon became the standard Army basic trainer. The Model A was followed by the Model B (Ki-9Kai), which had a simplified and strengthened landing gear, a shorter fuselage and reduced take-off weight. A total of 2,615 series aircraft was built, serving at all the major Japanese Army flying schools. Captured aircraft were used by a number of Far Eastern air arms post-World War II, and a number of Ki-9s had been used on Kamikaze missions in the summer of 1945.

Data (Ki-9): *Engine* as above *Wing span* 10.32 m (33 ft 10¼ in) *Length* 7.53 m (24 ft 8½ in) *Max T-O weight* 1,425 kg (3,142 lb) *Max level speed* 240 km/h (149 mph)

Tachikawa Army Ki-17 (Japan) Two prototype Ki-17 two-seat biplanes flew in the summer of 1935 and were followed by 558 production aircraft which went into service at army flying schools as the Type 95-3 Primary Trainer. Known as *Cedar* by the Allies, the Ki-17 was an equal-span single-bay biplane of remarkably light structure. Power was provided by a 112 kW (150 hp) Hitachi Ha-12 uncowled radial engine.

Tachikawa Army Ki-36 and Ki-55 (Japan) A two-seat, all-metal low-wing monoplane with a fixed, spatted cantilever undercarriage, the Ki-36 was designed by Ryokichi Endo for the army co-operation role. Following tests with two prototypes – the first of which flew on 20 April 1938 – the type went into service in 1939 as the Army Type 98 Direct Co-operation aircraft. Good visibility was provided by the deep crew canopy, the rear of which was flush with the fuselage decking. The pilot's view downwards was guaranteed by the swept-back wing leading edge and the observer was provided with glazed floor panels.

Armed with two 7.7 mm Type 89 machine-guns and up to 150 kg (331 lb) of bombs, the Ki-36 demonstrated excellent short-field characteristics and served in China and then in the Pacific up to 1943. It received the Allied code name *Ida*. Power was provided by a single 380 kW (510 hp) Hitachi Ha-13a radial engine.

The Ki-55 Army Type 99 Advanced Trainer version went into production in 1939. Many Ki-36s ended their careers as trainers and some of both versions were expended in 1945 Kamikaze attacks. A total of 2,721 Ki-36s and Ki-55s was built up to January 1944.

Data (Ki-36): *Engine* as above *Wing span* 11.8 m (38 ft 8½ in) *Length* 8.0 m (26 ft 3 in) *Max T-O weight* 1,660 kg (3,660 lb) *Max level speed* 348 km/h (216 mph)

Tachikawa Army Ki-54 (Japan) Intended originally as a crew trainer, the Ki-54 was a neat low-wing all-metal monoplane with two 335.3 kW (450 hp) Ha-13a radial engines and a retractable landing gear. The Type 1 Advanced

Tachikawa Army Ki-36s.

Trainer (Ki-54a) entered service in 1941 to train pilots for twin-engined flying. It was followed by the Type 1 Operations Trainer (Ki-54b) with equipment for training bomber crews and four gunners' positions – including two dorsal manually operated turrets. In 1943 the eight-passenger Type 1 Transport went into production. Final version was the Type 1 Patrol Bomber (Ki-54d), built in small numbers for anti-submarine work and carrying eight 60 kg depth charges. Total production of all versions was 1,368. The Allies allocated the code name *Hickory* to the Ki-54.

Tainan Mita 111 (Japan) Tandem two-seat training and sporting sailplane.

Taylor J.T.1 Monoplane.

Taylor J.T.1 Monoplane (UK) Single-seat fully aerobatic ultra-light monoplane, plans for which are available to amateur constructors.

Taylor J.T.2 Titch (UK) Single-seat light monoplane, plans for which are available to amateur constructors.

Taylor Bird (USA) Two-seat ultra-light monoplane designed by Mr C. Gilbert Taylor; plans, materials and component parts are available to amateur constructors.

Taylor Chummy (USA) The Taylor Brothers Aircraft Corporation was incorporated in 1929. It marketed the Chummy two-seat high-wing monoplane powered by a 67 kW (90 hp) Kinner K-5 or Brownback Tiger engine.

Tachikawa Army Ki-17.

Tachikawa Army Ki-74 long-range bomber, powered by two Mitsubishi Ha-104 engines. Internal bomb load was 1,000 kg (2,205 lb).

Incomplete Taylor Bird.

Taylor J-2 Cub.

Taylorcraft Model F-19 Sportsman 100.

In addition to new aircraft, the USAAF impressed civil Model BF-65, BFT-65, BC-12, BI-12, BF-12, BF-50 (with Franklin, Continental and Lycoming engines) and Model DC-65, DL-65 and DF-65 aircraft (similar engines) as L-2F, L-2G, L-2H, L-2J, L-2K, L-2L and L-2C, L-2D and L-2E types respectively.

Data (L-2A): *Engine* as above *Wing span* 10.8 m (35 ft 5 in) *Length* 6.93 m (22 ft 9 in) *Max T-O weight* 590 kg (1,300 lb) *Max level speed* 145 km/h (90 mph)

Taylorcraft TG-6 (USA) Three-seat training glider evolved from the Tandem Trainer.

Taylorcraft Model BC-12D (USA) Post-war production began with the BC-12D, which was basically similar to the pre-war B-12 but incorporated improvements found in the military L-2 Grasshopper series. In the first six months of 1946 2,800 were delivered – the maximum daily output reaching 50 – but shortage of engines held up final assembly. However in late 1946 the Taylorcraft Aviation Corporation got into financial difficulties and the assets of the firm were put up at public auction in March 1947. The assets were acquired by C. G. Taylor, once again giving him control of the company he began. The new company was named Taylorcraft Incorporated.

Taylor Cub (USA) In 1931 the President and Treasurer of the former Taylor Brothers Aircraft Corporation headed the newly incorporated Taylor Aircraft Company, which marketed the Cub two-seat high-wing monoplane. The President was C. Gilbert Taylor and the Secretary and Treasurer W. T. Piper. During 1935 the Taylor company produced 211 Cubs and in the following year 550 New Cubs. However in 1937 William T. Piper formed the Piper Aircraft Corporation from the Taylor Aircraft Company with the Cub as his first model – having purchased all rights in the aircraft. Meanwhile C. G. Taylor had formed the Taylorcraft Aviation Company, which became the Taylor-Young Airplane Company in 1937 and finally the Taylorcraft Aviation Corporation in 1940.

Taylorcraft Auster series (USA) See **Auster**

Taylorcraft Model A, B and D (USA) The Model A was the first product of Taylorcraft/ Taylor-Young; it was a two-seat high-wing cabin monoplane first offered with a 30 kW (40 hp) Continental engine. More than 100 Model As were built by the company in the first six months of operations. It was followed by the basically similar Models B and D, offered with several engine choices, and the D Tandem Trainer with tandem seating in a narrower fuselage.

Taylorcraft L-2 Grasshopper (USA) The L-2 was a special version of the Tandem Trainer; a large number (more than 1,800) were supplied to the USAAF for observation and light liaison duties, designated L-2, L-2A, L-2B and L-2M. Power for each version was provided by a 48.4 kW (65 hp) Continental O-170-3 engine. To provide increased vision for the pilot and observer, the fabric formerly covering the cabin roof and the rear deck of the fuselage to a point about midway to the tail was replaced by transparent 'Vinylite' panels. For the same reasons, the root ends of the wings were cut away at the trailing edge.

Taylorcraft types of 1947 to 1958 (USA) Aircraft produced by Taylorcraft Inc were the two-seat Ace (Continental A65); four-seat Model 15 Tourist (Continental A65); two-seat Traveler (Continental A65); two-seat De Luxe 65 and De Luxe 85 (Continental A65 and C85); two-seat Traveler (later version, with a Continental A65); two-seat Sportsman (Continental C85); four-seat Tourist (Continental C145-2); two-seat Model 19 Sportsman (Continental C85-12F), two-seat Special De Luxe (lower-powered and low-cost version of the Sportsman, with a Continental A65 engine); four-seat Model 20 Ranch Wagon (167.7 kW; 225 hp Continental O-470-J); Model 20AG Topper (agricultural version of the Ranch Wagon); Seabird (floatplane version of the Ranch Wagon); and four-seat Model 20 Zephyr 400 (Continental O-470-J).

Taylorcraft Model F-19 Sportsman 100 (USA) The Taylorcraft Aviation Corporation was re-formed in 1968, primarily to provide production support for earlier aircraft. In 1973 construction of the pre-production Model F-19 Sportsman 100 began and by early 1979 more than 120 had been completed. This aircraft, based on the Taylorcraft Model B of pre-World War II origin, is a two-seat trainer/sporting aircraft powered by a 74.5 kW (100 hp) Continental O-200-A engine.

Ted Smith Aerostar 600/601/601P (USA)
First flown in prototype form in October 1967, the Aerostar is a six-seat light transport aircraft. It was produced until recently in three forms: the Model 600A (two 216 kW; 290 hp Lycoming IO-540-K1F5 engines, European models designated 600AE); Model 601B (increased wing span and powered by two 216 kW; 290 hp Lycoming IO-540-S1A5 turbocharged engines, European models designated 601BE); and Model 601P (as for 601B, but with higher-flow-rate turbochargers to supply bleed air for cabin pressurisation, European models designated 601PE). Maximum level speed of the Model 601B is 486 km/h (302 mph).

TEDDE Turner T-40A, Super T-40A and T-40C (USA) Two-seat sporting monoplanes, plans for which are available to amateur constructors.

Tellier T.3, T.4, T.5 and T.C.6 (France)
Developed from the T.2 prototype of 1916, the T.3 was a two-seat open-cockpit biplane flying-boat powered by a 149 kW (200 hp) Hispano-Suiza 8 Ba engine. Production began in the first half of 1917 and a total of 96 was eventually produced by several manufacturers; 60 were operated by the French Navy for anti-submarine and convoy-escort duties in the Mediterranean and Atlantic; 34 by US Navy units based in France; and two by the RNAS for gun trials at Grain.

In addition to the standard T.3s, the French Navy received a more heavily armed version of the T.3 designated T.C.6, carrying a 47 mm cannon (55 built). Post-war developments included the 261 kW (350 hp) Sunbeam-engined T.4 and the twin 223.6 kW (300 hp) Hispano-Suiza-engined T.5, known as Nieuport-Telliers after Nieuport had taken over Tellier flying-boat interests.
Data (T.3): *Engine* as above *Wing span* 15.6 m (51 ft 2¼ in) *Length* 11.84 m (38 ft 10 in) *Max T-O weight* 1,750 kg (3,858 lb) *Max level speed* 145 km/h (90 mph) *Armament* one machine-gun in the bow, plus light bombs

Temco Model 51 Pinto (USA) The Temco Model 51 was the first primary jet trainer accepted by one of the US military services. The prototype first flew on 26 March 1956 and was sent shortly afterwards to the US Navy base at Patuxent River, Maryland, for evaluation with the Beech Model 73 Jet Mentor. As a result of these trials the Navy ordered 14 Model 51s (designated TT-1) for use by its Air Training Command at Pensacola, Florida, to 'determine the feasibility of beginning a student pilot's flight training in jet-propelled aircraft.' This evaluation programme began in January 1959. Power for the TT-1 was provided by one 4.1 kN (920 lb st) Continental J69-T-9 turbojet engine.

Tervamaki ATE-3 and JT-5 (Finland) Single-seat light autogyros. Plans for the JT-5 are available to amateur constructors.

Thaden T-4 (USA) The T-4 was a five-seat braced high-wing cabin monoplane of the latter 1920s powered by a 223.6 kW (300 hp) Wright Whirlwind engine. The company was taken over by the Pittsburgh Metal Airplane Company in 1929.

Ted Smith Aerostar 600A.

THK-2 to -16 (Turkey) See **MKEK**

Thomas T-2 (USA) Two-seat reconnaissance biplane of 1915, 24 of which were delivered to the RNAS.

Thomas-Morse MB-3 (USA) The Thomas-Morse MB-3 represented one of the first attempts to produce a modern combat aircraft of indigenous design for service with the American forces fighting in World War I. However the prototype did not fly until 21 February 1919. Overall performance was such that a total of 250 MB-3/3As was ordered for the USAAS as replacements for Spad and other single-seat fighters of European origin. Eventually MB-3s were relegated to training duties; a few also flew with the Marine Corps.

A refined version of the MB-3 was subsequently produced as the MB-6, which was estimated to have a maximum speed of 298 km/h (185 mph), but this failed to enter production.
Data (MB-3A): *Engine* one 223.6 kW (300 hp) Wright H-3 *Wing span* 7.92 m (26 ft 0 in) *Length* 6.1 m (20 ft 0 in) *Max T-O weight* 1,152 kg (2,540 lb) *Max level speed* 227 km/h (141 mph) *Endurance* 2 h 15 min *Armament* two forward-firing machine-guns

Thomas-Morse MB-3A, built by Boeing.

Thomas-Morse O-19 (USA) From 1928 Thomas-Morse produced 180 two-seat all-metal armed observation biplanes for the USAAC under the designation O-19 and powered by the 335.3 kW (450 hp) Pratt & Whitney R-1340 Wasp engine. In the following year the company was taken over by the Consolidated Aircraft Corporation.

Thomas-Morse S-4 and S-5 (USA) The S-4 was a single-seat advanced trainer of which about 600 were built, most going to the USAAS but a few also to the US Navy from 1917. The S-4B initial production version and a number of S-4Cs were powered by 74.5 kW (100 hp) Gnome rotary engines, but the vast majority of aircraft produced were 59.6 kW (80 hp) Le Rhône-powered S-4Cs. The designation S-5 was applied to a handful of S-4Bs fitted with float landing gears and operated by the US Navy.

Thorp T-18 Tigers.

Thulin Type K.

Transall C-160F.

Thomas-Morse SH-4 (USA) More powerful floatplane version of the Thomas T-2, 14 of which were delivered to the US Navy as reconnaissance and training aircraft.

Thorp T-18 Tiger (USA) Two-seat high-performance sporting monoplane, plans for which are available to amateur constructors.

Thulin Type A and Type K (Sweden) Phil Dr Enoch Thulin started the Thulin Aeroplane Manufacturing Company in 1915. These works developed into one of the biggest industrial concerns in Sweden, constructing aeroplanes and aero engines during World War I and other products immediately after. However Dr Thulin was killed in a flying accident in 1919 while performing an exhibition flight.

The first aeroplane to be produced was the Type A, based on the Blériot monoplane. Twenty-five were built, including two for the Swedish Army. A number of other types followed, including the slow and underpowered Type K single-seat monoplane fighter, of which most of the 18 built went to Holland after the war.

Timm N2T-1 Tutor (USA) Timm Aircraft Corporation developed a system of plastic construction based on its patented Aeromold process (plastic-bonded plywood), and its first product using this method was a two-seat open-cockpit primary training monoplane of 1940. The US Navy ordered 262 aircraft under the designation N2T-1.

Transall C-160 (France/Germany) The C-160, first flown on 25 February 1963, was developed to meet the specific requirements of the Federal German and French governments for a military transport aircraft capable of carrying troops, casualties, freight, supplies and vehicles, and of operating from semi-prepared surfaces.

Initial production of the C-160A (6 pre-production aircraft), C-160D (90 for Germany), C-160F (60 for France), C-160T (20 for Turkey) and C-160Z (9 for South Africa) was shared among the three participating companies of Aérospatiale, MBB and VFW-Fokker and ended in 1972. In 1977 the French government gave its approval to the launching of a new production series, primarily to satisfy a requirement of the French Air Force for 25–30 additional aircraft. The main improvements in this new batch are updated electronics equipment, increased max T-O weight, and extended range resulting from a reinforced wing with an optional additional fuel tank in its centre-section.

Data (French Air Force/export versions): *Engines* two 4,549 kW (6,100 ehp) Rolls-Royce Tyne RTy.20 Mk 22 turboprops *Wing span* 40.0 m (131 ft 3 in) *Length* 32.4 m (106 ft 3½ in) *Max T-O weight* 51,000 kg (112,435 lb) *Max level speed* 513 km/h (319 mph) *Range* (with 16,000 kg; 35,275 lb payload) 1,852 km (1,151 miles) *Accommodation* As above to a maximum payload of 17,000 kg (37,478 lb)

Transavia PL-12 Airtruk (Australia) The three-seat prototype Airtruk agricultural (PL-12) and multi-purpose (PL-12-U) sesquiplane flew for the first time on 22 April 1965. Delivery of production Airtruks began in December 1966 and 100 had been built by January 1979 for customers in Australia, Europe, Asia and Africa (see also **Bennett**).

Travel Air types (USA) In 1924, in association with Clyde Cessna and Lloyd Stearman, Walter Beech formed the Travel Air Manufacturing Company, and developed a range of commercial and training aeroplanes that were most popular in the US. When Travel Air was absorbed by the Curtiss-Wright group in 1929, Beech was elected Vice-President of the Curtiss-Wright Corporation. In 1930 on the merging of the Travel Air interests with the Curtiss-Robertson Airplane Manufacturing Company (to form the Curtiss-Wright Airplane Company), Beech resigned and formed the Beech Aircraft Company (see **Beechcraft**).

The first Travel Air product was a three-seat biplane of 1925 powered initially by a 67 kW (90 hp) Curtiss OX-5 engine. The name 'Special' was used in the 1926 *Jane's* for a version with a

Tupolev *Bear-D*.

Tupolev Tu-134.

**Replica of the Vickers
F.B.5 Gunbus.**

Vought A-7A Corsair IIs.

Vultee BT-13.

Waco VKS-7.

Westland Lysander.

Westland Sea King HAR.3.

**Westland Wessex HAS.1,
a development of the
Sikorsky S-58.**

Yakovlev Yak-23.

119 kW (160 hp) Curtiss C-6A engine. Subsequently the biplane was developed into several designated versions beginning with the Type 2000 (OX-5 engine) and continuing with the Type 3000 (112–134 kW; 150–180 hp Hispano-Suiza); Type 4000 (164 kW; 220 hp Wright J-5 Whirlwind); Type 8000 (100.6 kW; 135 hp Fairchild-Caminez); and Type 9000 (93 kW; 125 hp Siemens-Halske).

The Travel Air 5000 was a five-seat commercial monoplane powered by a Wright J-5 engine. It featured an enclosed pilot's cockpit situated in front of the passenger cabin in line with the front spar of the wing. It was built to the requirements of the Department of Commerce and several were operated by National Air Transport. A special version (known as the Woolaroc) was adapted for long-distance flying and used by Col 'Art' Goebel and Lieut W. S. Davis, USN, on their flight across the Pacific from Oakland, California, to Hawaii, for which they were awarded the Dole Prize.

The Travel Air 6000 was a Wright J-5-C Whirlwind-powered six-seat commercial cabin monoplane, subsequently developed into the 223.6 kW (300 hp) Wright J-6 Whirlwind-powered Type 6000B with a redesigned pilot's cockpit. The Travel Air Mystery was a single-seat sporting and racing open-cockpit braced low-

wing monoplane which at its first appearance at the 1929 National Air Races won the Free-For-All Speed Contest.

With the taking over of Travel Air by Curtiss-Wright (as noted above), developments of the biplane and Type 5000 appeared as the Curtiss-Wright 12 two-seater and Curtiss-Wright 10 respectively. In addition to these Curtiss-Wright marketed several products of basically Travel Air origin.

Trident TR-1 Trigull (Canada) Six-seat light amphibian powered by a 223.6 kW (300 hp) Lycoming IO-540-M1A5D engine. Production deliveries began in mid-1980.

Tri Turbo Tri Turbo-3 (USA) Conversion of the Douglas DC-3 to utilise three turboprop engines.

Tupolev ANT-9.

Tupolev ANT-9 (USSR) The ANT-9, designed by A. N. Tupolev, was a high-wing nine-passenger all-metal transport aircraft covered with a corrugated skin. It first flew in 1929 and was powered by three radial engines (Gnome-Rhône Titans or Wright Whirlwinds) and as the ANT-9-M-17 with two water-cooled M-17 engines. Examples were operated by Aeroflot and Deruluft on wheel and ski landing gears.

Tupolev ANT 11 (USSR) The ANT 14 was a 40.4 m (132 ft 6 in) wing span all-metal high-wing monoplane powered by five 357.7 kW (480 hp) Gnome-Rhône Jupiter engines. It first flew in 1931, named *Pravda*, and was used for propaganda.

Tupolev ANT-20 and 20*bis* (USSR) The ANT-20 *Maxim Gorki* was a very large all-metal monoplane with a 63.0 m (206 ft 8¼ in) wing span and powered by six wing-mounted 671 kW (900 hp) AM-34R water-cooled engines and a further two installed as a tandem pair above the centre section. It first flew on 19 May 1934 and was used for propaganda. It was lost in a collision

Transavia PL-12 Airtruk.

Travel Air biplane of 1929.

Tupolev ANT-20 *Maxim Gorki*.

Tupolev R-6.

on 18 May 1935. Developed from it was the six-engined ANT-20*bis* (PS-124), a 60–64-passenger aircraft which first saw service in 1940 on the Moscow–Mineralnye Vody route. About 16 ANT-20*bis* were subsequently used as troop and cargo transports.

Tupolev ANT-35 (PS-35) (USSR) Modern-looking all-metal cantilever low-wing airliner of 1935 accommodating ten passengers. Powered by two 633.4 kW (850 hp) M-85 (Gnome-Rhône 14N-type) radial engines driving three-bladed propellers. Retractable tailwheel-type landing gear fitted. Small number operated by Aeroflot.

Tupolev ANT-44 (USSR) Four-engined flying-boat operated in limited numbers during World War II.

Tupolev I-4.

Civil-registered ANT-3 flown to several European cities in 1926.

Tupolev I-4 (ANT-5) (USSR) As late as 1927 the Red Air Force was still heavily dependent on aircraft of non-Soviet design. At that time it had well over 300 aircraft originating from the Junkers and Fokker companies alone. In a major effort to catch up with foreign technology, several indigenous new designs were initiated, one of which was the ANT-5. With A. N. Tupolev acting as supervisor and P. Sukhoi as chief designer, the aircraft appeared as a single-seat sesquiplane fighter of all-metal construction, corrugated skinning being employed. Power was provided by a 343 kW (460 hp) M-22 engine. Production began in 1928 and by 1932 more than 240 had been built. Production eventually totalled 370 aircraft.
Data: *Engine* as above *Wing span* 11.4 m (37 ft 4 in) *Length* 7.3 m (23 ft 10½ in) *Max T-O weight* 1,365 kg (3,009 lb) *Max level speed* 257 km/h (160 mph) *Armament* two forward-firing machine-guns

Tupolev MDR-4.

Tupolev R-3 (ANT-3) (USSR) Best remembered as the first Soviet-designed two-seat military aircraft and first all-metal aircraft to achieve series production, the ANT-3 was a reconnaissance aircraft of 1925. Between 1927 and 1929 one hundred and nine were built; most had a

335.3 kW (450 hp) M-5 engine fitted, although other power plants were used. Armament comprised two forward-firing Vickers and two rear-mounted Lewis machine-guns, plus 200 kg (441 lb) of bombs as required. Maximum level speed was 205 km/h (128 mph).

Tupolev R-6 (ANT-7) (USSR) Basically a scaled-down TB-1 bomber, the ANT-3 first appeared in 1929. The 400 or so aircraft built were produced in two major and two lesser forms. The initial form was as the R-6 long-range reconnaissance aircraft, followed by the KR-6 escort fighter. Both appear to have been powered by two 533 kW (715 hp) M-17F engines mounted in the leading edges of the cantilever low monoplane wings and armed with five 7.62 mm DA-2 machine-guns in twin-gun nose and midship cockpits and a retractable ventral turret. Up to 500 kg (1,102 lb) of bombs could also be carried. In addition a seaplane version was built for the Navy as the KR-6P or MR-6 torpedo bomber, while passenger transport versions appeared under the P-6 designation.
Data: *Engines* as above *Wing span* 23.2 m (76 ft 1¼ in) *Length* 15.06 m (49 ft 4¾ in) *Max T-O weight* 6,470 kg (14,264 lb) *Max level speed* 230 km/h (143 mph) *Range* 800 km (497 miles)

Tupolev MDR-2 (ANT-8) (USSR) All-metal cantilever monoplane armed reconnaissance flying-boat of 1931; it closely resembled the Rohrbach Rocco except that the twin 484 kW (650 hp) M-17 engines were mounted as pushers. Maximum level speed was 217 km/h (135 mph).

Tupolev MDR-4 (ANT-27) (USSR) Further development of the MDR-1 and similar MDR-2 production reconnaissance flying-boat, but larger and powered by three 708 kW (950 hp) supercharged M-34R engines mounted in tractor configuration. Fifteen were built and entered service in 1936. The MDR-5 reverted to twin M-17 engines.

Tupolev RD-DB-1 (ANT-25) (USSR) The ANT-25 was a low-wing monoplane with a retractable landing gear and powered by a 708 kW (950 hp) M-34 engine. It had been

designed in 1932 on the lines of the Dewoitine 'Trait d'Union' monoplane which met its end in the forests of Siberia. It was completed in 1933 and was later prepared for a flight from Moscow to San Francisco, across the North Pole, but an oil leak prevented the aircraft from proceeding on its ambitious journey. In 1936 it was used in an attempt to beat the world distance record in a closed circuit and succeeded in remaining airborne for 56 hours 20 minutes. In July 1936 the ANT-25 flew non-stop from Moscow to Nikolayevsk-on-Amur, a distance of 8,400 km (5,220 miles) across the Arctic wastes.

From the ANT-25 a military version was developed as the RD-DB-1 bomber. This was not very successful and only a small number were produced. Maximum speed of the ANT-25 was 240 km/h (149 mph), that of the RD-DB-1 was 210 km/h (131 mph).

Tupolev SB-1 (ANT-39) and SB-2 (ANT-40) (USSR) Developed in parallel with the 559 kW (750 hp) M-25-engined prototype SB-1, the prototype SB-2 was also an all-metal cantilever low-wing medium bomber. The SB-1 (ANT-39) entered limited production with 618 kW (830 hp) M-34 engines and was flown with the Republicans during the Spanish Civil War, remaining operational at least to the end of the 1930s. Maximum speed of the SB-1 was 350 km/h (217 mph).

The much more important SB-2 (ANT-40) entered production in early 1936 and was produced eventually in three forms. The original M-100 engines gave way to 641 kW (860 hp) M-100As and later still to 715 kW (960 hp) M-103s. With the last-named engine the type was designated SB-2*bis*.

Total production of the SB-2 and variants is normally put at more than 6,600. The majority of the 210 supplied to Spain during the Civil War were lost. In the Winter War against Finland an SB-2 was the first Finnish kill, shot down by a Fokker D.XXI. Nevertheless it was a good aircraft and remained operational throughout World War II, also being produced as the PS-41 transport. A variant of the SB-2 was also produced in Czechoslovakia as the B-71.

Data (SB-2*bis*): *Engines* as above *Wing span* 20.33 m (66 ft 8½ in) *Length* 12.27 m (40 ft 3 in) *Max T-O weight* 6,500 kg (14,330 lb) *Max level speed* 450 km/h (280 mph) *Range* (full load) 1,500 km (932 miles) *Armament* four 7.62 mm machine-guns, plus 600 kg (1,323 lb) of bombs

Tupolev TB-1 (ANT-4) (USSR) The TB-1 was a large twin-engined cantilever low-wing monoplane bomber of all-metal construction. Open

cockpits were provided for the crew of six. The prototype, first flown on 26 November 1925, was named *Stranya Sovietov* (land of the Soviets) and in 1929 made an epic flight in stages from Moscow to New York. Production bombers, fitted with 507 kW (680 hp) M-17 engines in the wing leading edges, were produced between 1929 and 1932 (216 built, which may have included the TB-1P floatplanes for the Navy). At this time the Soviet heavy bomber force was the most powerful in the world. By the mid-1930s TB-1s were being withdrawn from first-line service, but with modification some lasted another decade as G-1 transports.

Data: *Engines* as above *Wing span* 28.7 m (94 ft 2 in) *Length* 18.0 m (59 ft 0½ in) *Max T-O weight* 6,810 kg (15,013 lb) *Max level speed* 207 km/h (128 mph) *Range* 1,000 km (621 miles) *Armament* six 7.62 mm machine-guns, plus 1,000 kg (2,205 lb) of bombs

Tupolev TB-3 (ANT-6) (USSR) Developed from the twin-engined TB-1, the TB-3 was a four-engined and much larger heavy bomber. Eight hundred and eighteen were built between 1931 and 1938. The design was under constant revision during the production run and as new versions appeared so even more impressive height-with-load records were set up. In October 1936 Nioukhtinov, flying a modernised version of the ANT-6 with a smooth skin covering, reached an altitude of 7,032 m (23,071 ft) while carrying a 10,000 kg (22,046 lb) load. On the same day he reached 2,000 m (6,560 ft) with a much heavier load. These were but two of many record flights.

The prototype ANT-6 first flew in December 1930 powered by Curtiss Conqueror engines. Production aircraft appeared for service in early

Tupolev TB-1 during the Zveno experiments (see TB-3).

Tupolev ANT-25 flown from Moscow to the United States via the North Pole on 17 June 1937.

Tupolev TB-3.

Tupolev

Tupolev Tu-2.

1932, initially fitted with 507 kW (680 hp) M-17Fs. Defensive armament comprised a staggering ten 7.62 mm machine-guns. The crew of ten still occupied open cockpits. Improved performance was achieved by the successive use of 619 kW (830 hp) M-34, M-34R, M-34RN and subsequently M-34RNF engines and making many refinements to the airframe, including replacement of the corrugated-metal skin with a smooth skin from 1935. Late production aircraft also featured manually operated nose and dorsal gun turrets and the crew was reduced to six.

TB-3s took an active part in the fighting against the Japanese during the late 1930s and were again used during the 'Winter War' with Finland. The bomber's last combat missions were performed in 1941 although by then it was normally employed only as the converted G-2 30-troop/paratroop transport.

Tupolev Tu-12.

TB-3s carried on the Zveno parasite experiments begun by the TB-1, carrying two Polikarpov I-5 fighters above the wings and two I-16s beneath for air launching.

Data (late model): Engines as above Wing span 41.8 m (137 ft 3 in) Length 25.2 m (82 ft 8 in) Max T-O weight 18,700–18,875 kg (41,225–41,612 lb) Max level speed 288 km/h (179 mph) Normal range 960 km (597 miles) Armament eight 7.62 mm DA-2 machine-guns, plus up to 3,000 kg (6,614 lb) of bombs

Tupolev Tu-14.

Tupolev Tu-2 and Tu-6 (USSR) During World War II Tupolev produced only one major new design, the Tu-2 three–four-seat attack bomber, for which he was awarded a Stalin Prize in 1943. Production began in 1942 as a replacement for the Pe-2 and ended in 1948. The production rate was too low to enable it to completely supersede the earlier type. Nevertheless its improved perfor-

Tupolev SB-2.

mance made it one of the best Soviet aircraft of the war. Post-war it was supplied to China and Poland and was again in action during the Korean War. The reporting name *Bat* was applied to the aircraft by NATO. The Tu-6 was a high-altitude reconnaissance version of the Tu-2. Data: *Engines* two 1,378.6 kW (1,850 hp) ASh-82FNV radials *Wing span* 18.85 m (61 ft 10½ in) *Length* 13.8 m (45 ft 3½ in) *Max T-O weight* 12,800 kg (28,220 lb) *Max level speed* 550 km/h (342 mph) *Range* 1,400–2,500 km (870–1,553 miles) *Armament* two 20 mm or 23 mm cannon (one in each wing root), three rearward-firing 12.7 mm Beresin machine-guns in dorsal, ventral and aft of pilot positions, plus 2,270 kg (5,000 lb) of bombs

Tupolev Tu-4 (USSR) Tupolev was responsible for the analysis and redesign for Russian production of the Boeing B-29 Superfortress, three specimens of which had made forced landings near Vladivostok in 1944. A very large number were built, powered by 1,490.5 kW (2,000 hp) ASh-73TK radial engines. The Tu-4 received the NATO reporting name *Bull*.

Tupolev Tu-12 (USSR) The initial Soviet-built jet-powered bomber, first seen during the 1947 Aviation Day flypast. Only a very small number were built and these were probably not used by an operational squadron.

Tupolev Tu-14 (USSR) This twin-jet attack bomber was closely related to the Tu-12 and was allocated the NATO reporting name *Bosun*. Power was provided by two 26.5 kW (5,955 lb st) VK-1 turbojet engines and it is believed to have served with the Soviet Naval Air Force for shore-based attack duties. Armament comprised two 23 mm cannon in the nose and twin guns in the tail. Two torpedoes or bombs were carried in the fuselage bomb bay. Only a small number were built. Maximum level speed was estimated at 900 km/h (559 mph) and range at 2,900 km (1,802 miles).

Tupolev Tu-16 (USSR) Known to NATO as *Badger*, the Tu-16 made its first major public appearance in 1954. About half of the 2,000 built remain operational. Some 300 are deployed with medium-range squadrons of the Soviet strategic

nuclear force, supported by a few Tu-16 in-flight refuelling tankers and more than 100 reconnaissance and ECM variants. Naval units have nearly 300 Tu-16s carrying air-to-surface missiles, 90 tankers and 70 reconnaissance and ECM models. Versions of the Tu-16 are listed below, except for *Badger-B*, which is no longer in service:

Badger-A First Soviet long-range strategic jet bomber, carrying a crew of seven. Defensive armament of seven 23 mm cannon. Nine supplied to Iraq. More than 80 operational with Chinese Air Force, mostly built in China.

Badger-C Anti-shipping version. A large air-to-surface winged missile (NATO reporting name *Kipper*) is carried under fuselage.

Badger-D Maritime/electronic reconnaissance version. Nose is similar to that of *Badger-C*. Enlarged undernose radome; three blister fairings in tandem under centre-fuselage.

Badger-E Similar to *Badger-A* but with cameras in bomb bay.

Badger-F Basically similar to *Badger-E* but with electronic intelligence pod on a pylon under each wing.

Badger-G Similar to *Badger-A* but with underwing pylons for two rocket-powered missiles (NATO reporting name *Kelt*). One photographed in December 1977 carried a new missile (NATO *Kingfish*) on port underwing pylon. Some *G*s were included in the 25 Tu-16s supplied to Egypt.

Badger-H Stand-off or escort ECM aircraft with primary function of chaff dispensing.

Badger-J Specialised ECM jamming aircraft.

Badger-K Electronic reconnaissance variant.

Data (estimated): *Engines* two 93.2 kN (20,950 lb st) Mikulin AM-3M turbojets *Wing span* 32.93 m (108 ft 0½ in) *Length* 34.8 m (114 ft 2 in) *Normal T-O weight* (approx) 68,000 kg (150,000 lb) *Max level speed* 945 km/h (587 mph) *Range* (max bombs) 4,800 km (3,000 miles) *Armament* forward dorsal and rear ventral barbettes each containing two 23 mm cannon. Two further cannon in tail position controlled by an automatic gun-ranging radar set. Seventh (fixed) cannon in nose of versions without nose radar. Up to 9,000 kg (19,800 lb) of bombs. Naval versions can carry air-to-surface stand-off missiles

Tupolev Tu-22 (USSR) Known to NATO as *Blinder*, the Tu-22 was first shown publicly in the 1961 Aviation Day flypast over Moscow. This bomber and maritime-patrol aircraft was the first operational Soviet supersonic bomber. A total of 22 Tu-22s took part in the 1967 display at Domodedovo, most carrying *Kitchen* missiles.

Tupolev Tu-16 *Badger-F.*

About 250 Tu-22s were built in four versions, listed below:

Blinder-A Basic reconnaissance bomber with fuselage weapon bay for free-fall bombs. *Blinder-A* entered only limited service, its max range of 2,250 km (1,400 miles) being inadequate for the originally intended strategic role.

Blinder-B Generally similar to *Blinder-A* but equipped to carry air-to-surface nuclear missile (*Kitchen*) recessed in weapon bay. About 125 *Blinder-A*s and *Blinder-B*s are believed to remain operational with the Soviet bomber force, plus about 24 serving with the Libyan Air Force.

Blinder-C Maritime-reconnaissance version. Modifications to nosecone, dielectric panels, etc suggest possible electronic intelligence role or equipment for electronic countermeasures (ECM) duties. About 60 delivered for operation primarily over sea approaches to the Soviet Union, from bases in the Southern Ukraine and Estonia.

Blinder-D Training version. Cockpit for instructor in raised position aft of standard flight deck, with stepped-up canopy.

A missile-armed long-range interceptor version of *Blinder* has been reported in service, as a possible replacement for the Tu-28P.

Data (*Blinder-A* and *-B*, estimated): *Engines* two 120.1 kN (27,000 lb st, with afterburning) turbojets *Wing span* 27.7 m (90 ft 10½ in) *Length* 40.53 m (132 ft 11½ in) *Max T-O weight* 83,900 kg (185,000 lb) *Max level speed* Mach 1.4 *Max range* 2,250 km (1,400 miles) *Armament* weapons bay in centre-fuselage; single 23 mm NS-23 gun in radar-directed tail turret

Tupolev Tu-26 (Tu-22M) (USSR) Official US sources first acknowledged the existence of a Soviet variable-geometry medium bomber in the autumn of 1969. Such an aircraft was not unexpected, as the Tu-22 (NATO *Blinder*) was clearly incapable of performing a long-range strategic-bombing role in the 'seventies.

Tupolev Tu-22 *Blinder-A.*

Tupolev Tu-26
Backfire-B.

Tupolev Tu-142 *Bear-D.*

Tupolev Tu-28P/Tu-128
Fiddler.

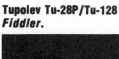

A prototype of the new bomber is said to have been observed in July 1970. At least two prototypes were built initially; up to 12 pre-production models followed, for development testing, weapons trials and evaluation, by the beginning of 1973. Their official designation was reported to be Tu-26 but the designation Tu-22M has also been mentioned; the NATO reporting name allocated to the aircraft is *Backfire*. There are two known versions of *Backfire*:

Backfire-A Initial version, with large landing-gear fairing pods on the wing trailing edges. There is evidence to suggest that the large size of these fairings, with the wheels stowed beneath the wing, caused excessive drag. Redesign almost eliminated the fairings from subsequent aircraft, requiring a revised main landing gear, retracting into the fuselage. Therefore it is believed that *A* only equips one squadron.

Backfire-B Developed version with landing-gear fairing pods eliminated except for shallow fairings under the wings and no longer protruding beyond the trailing edge. Increased wing span. More than 125 *Backfire-B*s are in service, with production continuing at a rate of about 30 per year. Many of them have been allocated to medium-range bomber squadrons of the Soviet Strategic Nuclear Forces, but at least 50 are deployed in a maritime role by Soviet Naval Aviation.

Data (estimated): *Engines* two turbofans, probably in the 196.1 kN (44,090 lb st) class with afterburning *Wing span* (spread) 34.45 m (113 ft 0 in), (swept) 26.21 m (86 ft 0 in) *Length* 40.23 m (132 ft 0 in) *Max T-O weight* 122,500 kg (270,000 lb) *Max level speed* Mach 2 *Max unrefuelled combat range* 8,050 km (5,000 miles) *Armament* air-to-surface missile (*Kitchen*) and/or other stores. Twin 23 mm guns in radar-directed tail mounting

Tupolev Tu-28P/Tu-128 (USSR) Largest fighter ever put into squadron service, this super-sonic twin-jet interceptor was seen for the first time at Tushino in 1961. It is thought to have the service designation Tu-28P (US Department of Defense has used Tu-128); its NATO reporting name is *Fiddler*. It carries a crew of two in tandem. Armament comprises two *Ash* missiles under each wing.

Data (estimated): *Engines* two turbojets in the 120.1 kN (27,000 lb st) range *Wing span* 20.0 m (65 ft 0 in) *Length* 26.0 m (85 ft 0 in) *Max T-O weight* 45,000 kg (100,000 lb) *Max level speed* Mach 1.75 *Range* (max fuel) 4,989 km (3,100 miles)

Tupolev Tu-70 (USSR) Seventy-two-passenger airliner developed from the Tu-4. Did not enter service.

Tupolev Tu-95 and Tu-142 (USSR) This huge Tupolev bomber flew for the first time in the late summer of 1954. It was first seen at Tushino in July 1955 and subsequently became standard equipment in the Soviet Air Force. It is often referred to as the Tu-20, but its correct Soviet designation is Tu-95 in its air force versions and Tu-142 in its naval versions.

As well as maintaining its important strategic attack role as the Soviet counterpart of the USAF's B-52 Stratofortress, the Tu-95 is in major service with the Soviet Naval Air Force for maritime reconnaissance and to provide targeting data to the launch control and guidance stations responsible for both air-to-surface and surface-to-surface anti-shipping missiles. The six versions identified are listed below by their NATO reporting names and all remain operational.

Bear-A Basic strategic bomber with chin radar and defensive armament comprising three pairs of 23 mm cannon in remotely controlled dorsal and ventral barbettes and manned tail

Tupolev Tu-104s.

gun turret. Internal stowage for two nuclear or a variety of conventional free-fall weapons. Total of about 100 *Bear-A*s and *Bear-B*s remain operational with the Soviet bomber force.

Bear-B First seen in the 1961 Aviation Day flypast with additional radar equipment in wide undernose radome and carrying a large air-to-surface missile (NATO reporting name *Kangaroo*). Some *Bear*s of Dalnaya Aviatsiya now carry *Kitchen* air-to-surface missiles. *Bear-B* is used also for maritime patrol with flight-refuelling nose probe and, sometimes, a stream-lined blister fairing on the starboard side of the rear fuselage. Defensive armament retained.

Bear-C Maritime patrol version. Generally similar to *Bear-B* but with streamlined blister fairing on both sides of rear fuselage. Refuelling probe standard.

Bear-D It is now known that *Bear-D* has an extremely important function in support of operations involving surface-to-surface and air-to-surface missiles. It provides data on the location and nature of potential targets to mis-sile launch crews on board ships and aircraft which are themselves too distant from the target to ensure precise missile aiming and guidance. About 45 serve with Soviet Naval Air Fleet.

Bear-E Maritime-reconnaissance version basi-cally similar in configuration to *Bear-A* but with a refuelling probe above its glazed nose and the rear fuselage blister fairings of *Bear-C*.

Bear-F First identified in 1973, this is a much-refined anti-submarine version. About 15 of this version were operational in early 1979.

Data (*Bear-F* estimated): *Engines* four 11,033 kW (14,795 ehp) Kuznetsov NK-12MV turboprops *Wing span* 51.1 m (167 ft 8 in) *Length* 49.5 m (162 ft 5 in) *Max T-O weight* 188,000 kg (414,470 lb) *Over-target speed* 805 km/h (500 mph) *Range* 12,550 km (7,800 miles)

Tupolev Tu-104 (USSR) Designed in 1953 as part of a major programme to modernise Aeroflot's fleet; construction began in 1954 and the prototype flew on 17 June 1955. This rapid progress was achieved by adapting the wing, tail unit, undercarriage, engine installation and nose of the Tu-16 bomber and designing only a larger main fuselage.

The low-mounted wing was a two-spar struc-ture with anhedral and 35° sweepback at quarter chord. The two 66.2 kN (14,881 lb st) Mikulin RD-3 or AM-3 axial-flow turbojets were mounted on the fuselage and buried in the wing roots. The aircraft had neither thrust reversers nor noise suppressors but had tail-mounted braking parachutes.

The Tu-104 was the second type of jet transport to enter service and has remained in continuous service longer than any other. Equipped to carry 50 passengers, it entered service on 15 September 1956, on Aeroflot's Moscow–Omsk–Irkutsk route. Probably only 20 Tu-104s were produced, including Tu-104G trainers; the initial main pro-duction aircraft being the 70-passenger Tu-104A with the same dimensions but powered by 85.3 kN (19,180 lb st) AM-3M turbojets. The Tu-104A entered service in 1957 and was the only one to achieve export orders – six for CSA in Czechoslovakia.

The third version to enter service, with Aeroflot on the Moscow–Leningrad route on 15 April 1959, was the 100-passenger Tu-104B with 95.1 kN (21,384 lb st) RD-3M-500 engines and 1.21 m (3 ft 11½ in) longer fuselage. In April 1960 a Tu-104E achieved 959.23 km/h (596 mph) but nothing is known of this version.

On 15 April 1965 Aeroflot began using 85-seat Tu-104Ds, later with 100 seats; these were almost certainly modified Tu-104As. The 115-passenger Tu-104B was introduced in 1967.

About 200–250 Tu-104s were built; many remain in service and a few have seen military service, including cosmonaut training.

Data (Tu-104A): *Engines* as above *Wing span* 34.54 m (113 ft 4 in) *Length* 38.85 m (127 ft 5½ in) *Max T-O weight* 76,000 kg (167,551 lb) *Cruising speed* 750–800 km/h (466–497 mph) *Range* 2,650 km (1,647 miles)

Tupolev Tu-114 Rossiya.

Tupolev

Tupolev Tu-110 (USSR) First shown at Vnukovo Airport, Moscow, in July 1957, the Tu-110 was a four-jet version of the Tu-104. It did not go into production.

Tupolev Tu-114 Rossiya (USSR) Largest and heaviest commercial airliner in the world when it appeared in 1957, the Tu-114 was completed to coincide with the 40th anniversary of the Russian Revolution. It was a civil counterpart to the Tu-95 *Bear* bomber. The standard version accommodated 120–220 passengers (about 20 were in service), while at least one Tu-114D was built with a slimmer fuselage to carry a small number of passengers, mail and urgent freight over very long distances. Power was provided by four 11,033 kW (14,795 ehp) Kuznetsov NK-12MV turboprop engines. Maximum cruising speed was 910 km/h (565 mph).

Tupolev Tu-126 *Moss.*

Tupolev Tu-124 (USSR) Although similar to the Tu-104 in general configuration, the Tu-124 is 25% smaller and was the first Soviet transport aircraft with turbofan engines. The prototype flew for the first time in June 1960 and as the Tu-124 had accommodation for 44 passengers. This was developed into the Tu-124V standard version for 56 passengers, Tu-124K for 36 passengers and Tu-124K2 de luxe version for 22 passengers.

The Tu-124 was designed to replace the piston-engined Il-14 on Aeroflot's short/medium routes and entered service on 2 October 1962.
Data (Tu-124V): *Engines* two 53 kN (11,905 lb st) Soloviev D-20P turbofans *Wing span* 25.55 m (83 ft 9½ in) *Length* 30.58 m (100 ft 4 in) *Max T-O weight* 38,000 kg (83,775 lb) *Max cruising speed* 870 km/h (540 mph) *Range* 1,220 km (760 miles)

Tupolev Tu-126 (USSR) Known to NATO as *Moss*, the Tu-126 has been produced for the AWACS (airborne warning and control system) role and at least 10 or 12 are operational with the Soviet air defence forces. Based on the Tu-114 four-turboprop transport, it carries above its fuselage a large rotating 'saucer' type early warn-

ing radar. It can be used to direct advanced interceptors onto incoming strike aircraft or to assist strike aircraft to elude enemy interceptors picked up by its radar.

Tupolev Tu-134 (USSR) Known originally as the Tu-124A, this aircraft is a rear-engined twin-turbofan development of the Tu-124. The initial version accommodates 64–72 passengers and is powered by Soloviev D-30 engines. The Tu-134A has a lengthened fuselage to accommodate 76–80 passengers. More than 200 Tu-134s and Tu-134As are believed in service with Aeroflot and both versions have been exported.
Data (Tu-134A): *Engines* two 66.7 kN (14,990 lb st) Soloviev D-30 Srs II turbofans *Wing span* 29.01 m (95 ft 2 in) *Length* 37.05 m (121 ft 6½ in) *Max T-O weight* 47,000 kg (103,600 lb) *Max cruising speed* 885 km/h (550 mph) *Range* 1,890–3,020 km (1,174–1,876 miles)

Tupolev Tu-144 (USSR) The Tu-144 is a 140-passenger supersonic airliner which was first flown in prototype form on 31 December 1968. On 5 June 1969 it exceeded Mach 1 for the first time and on 26 May 1970 became the first commercial transport to exceed Mach 2. Regular supersonic flights by Aeroflot began on 26 December 1975, between Moscow's Domodedovo Airport and Alma-Ata, capital of Kazakhstan, carrying freight and mail. Scheduled passenger flights began on 1 November 1977. However this service was terminated after 102 flights had been made following an accident to one of the Tu-144s on a non-commercial flight. There was no further news of route flying by aircraft until the Tu-144D, with new engines, made a proving flight from Moscow to Khabarovsk in June 1979. Thirteen Tu-144s were built, including prototypes.
Data (Tu-144): *Engines* four 196.1 kN (44,090 lb st) Kuznetsov NK-144 turbofans *Wing span* 28.8 m (94 ft 6 in) *Length* 65.7 m (215 ft 6½ in) *Max T-O weight* 180,000 kg (396,830 lb) *Max cruising speed* Mach 2.35 *Max range* 6,500 km (4,030 miles)

Tupolev Tu-144.

Tupolev Tu-154 (USSR) The three-engined Tu-154 was intended to replace the Tu-104, Il-18 and An-10 on medium/ long stage lengths of up to 6,000 km (3,725 miles). The first prototypes flew on 4 October 1968 and mail and cargo flights with the seventh aircraft began in May 1971. Initial passenger-carrying services were flown for a few days in the early summer of 1971 and regular services began on 9 February 1972 over the 1,300 km (800 miles) route between Moscow and Mineralnye Vody, in the North Caucasus. International services began with a proving flight between Moscow and Prague on 1 August 1972.

A developed version of the airliner is the Tu-154A, which made its first scheduled flight in 1973. This version superseded the Tu-154 in production. Whereas the earlier version has 93.2 kN (20,950 lb st) Kuznetsov NK-8-2 engines and accommodation for 128–167 passengers, this has 103 kN (23,150 lb st) NK-8-2U engines and increased maximum take-off and landing weights. In 1977 production switched to the further improved Tu-154B (since refined to the Tu-154B-2) fitted with Thomson-CSF/SFIM automatic flight control and navigation equipment. Max take-off and zero-fuel weights have been increased. Up to 180 passengers can be carried. Production of all models exceeded 250 by mid-1979, of which more than 200 serve with Aeroflot.
Data (Tu-154B): *Engines* as above *Wing span* 37.55 m (123 ft 2½ in) *Length* 47.9 m (157 ft 1¾ in) *Max T-O weight* 96,000 kg (211,650 lb) *Normal cruising speed* (Tu-154A) 900 km/h (560 mph) *Range* 2,750–4,000 km (1,708–2,485 miles)

UTVA-66s.

mann. Power was provided by a 59.6 kW (80 hp) engine. The designation U.6 was applied to a new open-cockpit two-seater which was followed by the single-seat parasol-wing U.7 Kolibri powered by a 500 cc Douglas or 1,000 cc ABC Scorpion engine. It proved one of the most successful German lightplanes of the period.

The U.8 was a light commercial passenger-carrying (three) monoplane of 1924 developed from the U.5. Power was provided by 74.5 kW (100 hp) Siemens & Halske Sh 12 or Bristol Lucifer engine. Only a handful were produced for commercial use, two going to Deutsche Luft-Hansa, later operated by Aero Lloyd. The U.8b was a version with leading- and trailing-edge flaps and slots (co-invented by Dr Ing Lachmann). The U.10 was an improved two-seat school and training aircraft of 1924, while the U.10a was the seaplane version. Perhaps the most interesting aircraft produced by the company was the U.11 Kondor, an extremely modern-looking commercial transport aircraft of 1925 accommodating a crew of three and eight passengers and powered by four 74.5 kW (100 hp) Sh 12 engines mounted under the wings. The sole example built was sold to Deutsche Luft-Hansa.

The company ceased to exist in 1926 and was

Tupolev Tu-154B.

Udet U.1 to U.12 (Germany) Udet-Flugzeugbau was formed in the early 1920s by the World War I fighter ace Ernst Udet and others. It initially worked on developing the U.1 prototype single-seat lightplane powered by a 22.4 kW (30 hp) engine. From it was developed the U.2 two-seater powered by a 41 kW (55 hp) Siemens engine. The first U.2 flew from Munich to Hamburg in 5 hours 5 minutes in 1923 en route to the Gothenburg Aero Show, where it was exhibited. The U.2 became the first product of the company to enter production, seven being built.

The U.3 was a more powerful two-seater, while the U.4 was a similar single-seater. Also in 1923 the company built the U.5, a three-seat parasol-wing cabin monoplane designed by Herr Herr-

succeeded by Bayerische Flugzeugwerke (which became Messerschmitt). The final product was the U.12 Flam Flamingo, a two-seat open-cockpit primary trainer (see **BFW**).

Ufag C.I (Austria-Hungary) Ungarische Flugzeugwerke was formed during World War I by Baron von Skoda. The C.I was a two-seat reconnaissance and observation biplane powered by a 171.4 kW (230 hp) Hiero engine. Fairly large numbers were built for service in 1918, later production models changing from an 'all-moving' vertical tail surface to a conventional fin and rudder layout and introducing an extra forward-firing machine-gun to the earlier single forward-firing and rear-mounted guns. Maximum level speed was 190 km/h (118 mph).

Umbaugh

UTVA-75.

Umbaugh-18A (USA) Two-seat light autogyro, the first production examples of which were scheduled for delivery in mid-1962.

UTVA-56 and -60 (Yugoslavia) The UTVA-56 was a four-seat cabin monoplane powered by a 194 kW (260 hp) Lycoming GO-435-C2B2 engine. It was first flown on 22 April 1959. Subsequently UTVA began the work of modifying the design for series production at the beginning of 1960. In particular, the engine was replaced by a 201 kW (270 hp) GO-480. Five production versions were eventually made: the U-60-AT1 basic four-seat utility; U-60-AT2 trainer; U-60-AG agricultural; U-60-M ambulance; and U-60H floatplane.

UTVA-65 Privrednik and Super Privrednik-350 (Yugoslavia) Single-seat agricultural monoplanes, the Super Privrednik being a high-powered version with a 261 kW (350 hp) Lycoming IGO-540-A1C engine.

UTVA-66 (Yugoslavia) Four-seat general utility and ambulance aircraft, first flown in about 1967. Numbers were supplied to the Yugoslav Air Force with provision for carrying a machine-gun pack under each wing. Power is provided by a 201 kW (270 hp) Lycoming GSA-480-B1J6 engine, giving a maximum level speed of 230 km/h (143 mph).

UTVA-75 (Yugoslavia) Two-seat light monoplane suitable for training, glider-towing and utility duties. The prototype first flew on 20 May 1976 and the type is currently in production.
Data: *Engine* one 134 kW (180 hp) Lycoming IO-360-B1F *Wing span* 9.73 m (31 ft 11 in) *Length* 7.11 m (23 ft 4 in) *Max T-O weight* 960 kg (2,116 lb) *Max level speed* 220 km/h (136 mph) *Range* (with drop-tanks) 2,000 km (1,242 miles) *Armament* military examples have standard fittings for light weapon loads underwing

Valmet L-70 Miltrainer (Finland) Two-seat training or two–four-seat touring lightplane powered by a 149 kW (200 hp) Lycoming AEIO-360-A1B6 engine. The prototype first flew on 1 July 1975. Thirty L-70s were ordered as Vinkas by the Finnish Air Force, delivery of which began in 1979.

Valmet VH-II and VH-III Vihuri (Finland) Two-seat advanced training monoplanes powered by 611 kW (820 hp) Bristol Mercury radial engines. The prototype first flew on 6 February 1951 as the VH-I. The first production aircraft for the Finnish Air Force were produced as VH-II Vihuris from 1953. A second slightly modified series of the Vihuri was produced for the Air Force as the VH-III; all delivered by the latter half of 1956.

Vans RV-3 (USA) Single-seat sporting monoplane, plans for which are available to amateur constructors.

Varga Model 215OA Kachina (USA) Two-seat lightweight sporting/training monoplane powered by a 112 kW (150 hp) Lycoming O-320-A2C engine.

Vertol (USA) See also **Boeing Vertol** and **Piasecki**

Vertol Model 42A (Canada) Tandem-rotor helicopter produced exclusively in Canada. Power was provided by a Wright R-1820-103 engine. Accommodation was provided for 19 passengers, 1,280 kg (2,820 lb) of internal cargo or a 2,268 kg (5,000 lb) slung load.

Vertol Model 44 (USA) The Model 44 was an improved version of the Piasecki H-21 and was available as the Model 44A utility passenger/cargo transport with fabric seats and no sound-proofing (19 civilian or 20 military passengers, 12 stretchers and two attendants or 2½ tons of externally slung freight); Model 44B 14–15-seat commercial passenger transport (also operated as a military type); and Model 44C executive transport version with a custom-designed interior. Power was provided by a 1,062 kW (1,425 hp)

Vertol Model 44B.

VFW-Fokker 614.

Wright Cyclone engine. Sales included Model 44Bs to the French government, Swedish Navy, RCAF and New York Airways. The Swedish and New York Airways helicopters had water-tight lower fuselages and rubberised floats to permit emergency alighting on and take-off from water. The RCAF helicopters were operated by Spartan Air Services for supply duties along the Mid-Canada early-warning radar chain. Maximum level speed was 204 km/h (127 mph).

VFW-Fokker VAK 191B (Germany) Experimental STOL tactical-reconnaissance fighter, first flown on 10 September 1971.

VFW-Fokker 614 (Germany) Short-haul transport accommodating 40–44 passengers as standard and powered by two 32.4 kN (7,280 lb st) Rolls-Royce M45H Mk 501 turbofans. The first prototype flew on 1 August 1968, and 16 had been built by early 1977, including three for the Luftwaffe.

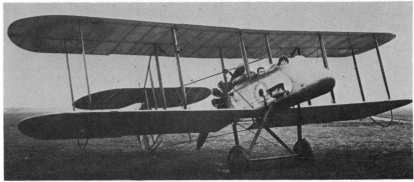

Vickers F.B.9.

Vickers F.B.5 and F.B.9 (UK) The Vickers F.B.5 (Fighting Biplane No 5), more affectionately known as the 'Gunbus', was designed specifically as a fighter aircraft long before the development of interrupter gear, the invention which would later allow guns to be fired through the propeller disc. A central nacelle structure mounted above the lower wing provided accommodation for a gunner/observer forward, with the pilot in a separate cockpit aft of the gunner. The engine was mounted at the rear of the nacelle, driving a pusher propeller. Thus the machine-gun was placed at the front of the aircraft, firing forward and providing the gunner with an excellent view and field of fire. The tail unit was carried on lightweight open-frame wire-braced structures; landing gear was of tailskid type.

Early F.B.5s were armed with a belt-fed Maxim or Vickers machine-gun, but these were difficult to train quickly on their ball-and-spigot mounting and the ammunition belts limited the amount of movement and field of fire. An improvement came with the lighter, drum-fed Lewis machine-gun, which proved to be a far more effective weapon when these aircraft were introduced on the Western Front in early 1915. They were used by the RFC for escort, artillery ranging, photography and reconnaissance, and the RNAS also had a small number for similar duties.

The F.B.9 was an improved version in which efforts had been made to reduce drag as much as possible. It entered service in June 1916, some taking part in the Battle of the Somme. Most of the 95 that were built, however, were used as trainers in Britain.

Data (F.B.5): *Engine* one 74.5 kW (100 hp) Gnome Monosoupape rotary *Wing span* 11.13 m (36 ft 6 in) *Length* 8.28 m (27 ft 2 in) *Max T-O weight* 930 kg (2,050 lb) *Max level speed* 113 km/h (70 mph) *Range* 402 km (250 miles) *Armament* one 0.303 in Lewis machine-gun

Vickers F.B.12 (UK) Single-seat fighter of 1916, a small number of which were built with one of several different engines fitted as a pusher – including the 74.5 kW (100 hp) Gnome Monosoupape.

Vickers F.B.14 (UK) Tractor-engined biplane of 1916 best suited for reconnaissance duties. Engines ranged on the small number of production aircraft from an 89.4 kW (120 hp) Beardmore to a 186.3 kW (250 hp) Rolls-Royce Eagle.

Vickers F.B.19 (UK) Designed as a single-seat fighter biplane and first flown in 1916. Only a small number were built as 74.5 kW (100 hp) Gnome Monosoupape-powered Mk Is and 82 kW (110 hp) Clerget or Le Rhône-powered Mk IIs. These served mainly as home-defence fighters, although a few were sent abroad. Armament comprised one Vickers machine-gun.

Vickers Valentia (UK) The Valentia was a development of the earlier Victoria troop-carrier, differing by having two 484.4 kW (650 hp) Bristol Pegasus II.L3 or II.M3 engines (the latter for use in India) and an improved landing gear. Accommodation was for a crew of two and 22 troops; lockers were used for equipment and rifle-racks and stretcher supports were provided. Bomb racks could also be fitted if required. Twenty-eight were built as new and 54 Victorias were brought up to this standard.

Vickers Valetta (UK) The Valetta was a military transport aircraft, the prototype of which flew for the first time on 30 June 1947. The C.1 was the

Vickers F.B.5 Gunbus.

Vickers F.B.12 (left) and F.B.14.

Vickers F.B.19.

standard RAF version for use by Airborne Forces; could be used in various roles, such as troop-carrying, freighting, paratroop-carrying, supply-dropping and as an ambulance. The C.2 was a special VIP version for 9 to 15 passengers. The T.3 was designed specifically for use as a navigational flying classroom. A number of T.3s were later converted into T.4s with radar fitted in an extended nose. Production totalled 260 aircraft. Power was provided by two 1,472 kW (1,975 hp) Bristol Hercules 230 radial engines.

Vickers Valentia.

Vickers Valetta C.1.

Vickers Valiant B.1.

Vickers Valiant (UK) As World War II came to an end, the strategic bombers which had served Britain so well throughout the war had become dated as a result of wartime developments. The immature turbine engine promised power that would enable new-generation aircraft to operate at greater heights and higher speeds; because of such enhanced performance they would require no defensive armament. Airborne electronics had been designed to locate enemy aircraft, moving ever faster in three-dimensional space, or to pinpoint one's position in the sky for navigational purposes or accurate bombing attack by day or night. And the atomic bombs which had spurred the end of war in the Pacific meant that a single aircraft could launch a devastating attack on any potential enemy.

Such thinking led to the development of the RAF's V-bomber force, comprising the Avro Vulcan, Handley Page Victor and Vickers Valiant – the latter being the first to enter squadron service. Designed to Air Ministry specification B.9/48, it was a cantilever shoulder-wing monoplane of all-metal stressed-skin construction. The wing had compound sweepback on the leading edge, somewhat similar to that of the Handley Page Victor, air-brakes, double-slotted flaps and powered ailerons. The fuselage was a circular-section semi-monocoque structure, incorporating a pressurised cell to contain the crew of five, and a large bomb bay which later proved capable of accommodating a Blue Steel stand-off weapon. The tail unit was conventional, but the tailplane was mounted almost half-way up the fin to keep it clear of the efflux from the four turbojet engines, buried in the inner wing adjacent to the fuselage. Landing gear was of retractable tricycle type. Despite being an advanced concept, the Valiant

was largely conventional in construction. One unusual feature was the extensive use of electrical power for the actuation of practically all movable units, even powered controls. The only exception was a minor hydraulic system for brakes and powered steering, but even this had its pumps driven by electric motors.

Two prototypes were ordered initially, one to be powered by four Rolls-Royce RA.3 Avon turbojets and the other by four Armstrong Siddeley Sapphires. The first prototype made its maiden flight on 18 May 1951, but was lost in an accident on 12 January 1952. The second prototype flew first on 11 April 1952, but was powered by RA.7 turbojets instead of the Sapphires as planned originally.

Named Valiant, B.1s began to enter service in January 1955, the first of the V-bombers to serve with the RAF. They were followed by B(PR).1 long-range strategic reconnaissance; B(PR)K.1 multi-purpose bomber, photo-reconnaissance, tanker; and BK.1 bomber/tanker aircraft. Production totalled 111 examples, including one B.2 pathfinder prototype. Used extensively in service, Valiants dropped the first British hydrogen and atomic bombs and during operations in the Suez campaign operated with high-explosive bombs.

Intended for fast high-altitude strategic bombing (a role frustrated by the evolution of potent surface-to-air missiles), the Valiant – in company with other V-bombers – was switched to low-level operations. There seems little doubt that the stresses imposed by such a role accelerated the wing-spar metal fatigue first reported in late 1964, and which led to the scrapping of all Valiants in January 1965.

Data (BK.1): *Engines* four 44.5 kN (10,000 lb st) Rolls-Royce Avon RA.28 turbojets *Wing span* 34.85 m (114 ft 4 in) *Length* 32.99 m (108 ft 3 in) *Max T-O weight* 63,503 kg (140,000 lb) *Max level speed* 912 km/h (567 mph) *Range* (with external tanks) 7,242 km (4,500 miles) *Armament* up to 4,536 kg (10,000 lb) of bombs

Vickers Valparaiso (UK) Two-seat fighter and reconnaissance biplane of 1924. A few were supplied to Chile and Portugal, the latter building 13 more under licence and operating them for a decade. Portuguese aircraft were powered by 335.3 kW (450 hp) Napier Lion, 313 kW (420 hp) Bristol Jupiter and 268 kW (360 hp) Rolls-Royce Eagle IX engines.

quently production ended after the original orders had been completed: 20 for BEA and 23 for Trans-Canada Airlines.

On 10 October 1969 the first of nine freighter conversions of the Vanguard, called Merchantman, was flown for BEA. Several remain in service with British Airways.

Data (Type 953 for BEA): *Engines* four 3,715 kW

Vickers Vanguard 953.

Vickers Vanguard (UK) The very considerable success of the Vickers Viscount (see entry) in airline service was due to the smoothness, economy and reliability of its turbine engines. In one enormous leap it had raised cruising speed almost 100% by comparison with the piston-engined Vickers Viking; it carried two or three times as many passengers (according to type) and offered increased range. In early 1953, not long after the Viscount entered service with British European Airways (BEA), discussions began to initiate the design of a successor. Both BEA and Trans-Canada Airlines were interested in a generally similar aircraft; compromise in design to satisfy the views of these two operators resulted in the low-wing configuration and 'double-bubble' fuselage to provide a large underfloor cargo hold beneath the main cabin.

The power plant considered originally for inclusion in the design was the Rolls-Royce Dart. But Rolls-Royce intimated that development of a new engine, the RB.109, was then well under way and it (later known as the Tyne) was chosen to power this new transport. Construction was entirely conventional except for the wing, which introduced integrally machined skins of light alloy to provide spanwise stiffening at low cost, and three shear webs instead of the single spar in the Viscount wing. When tied together by closely spaced ribs it produced a rigid box structure and outboard of the centre-section it was sealed to form integral fuel tanks.

First flight of the prototype Vanguard, as the new aircraft had been named, was made on 20 January 1959. But because of the normal development programme of a new civil airliner – coupled with delays caused by problems with the new power plant – it was not until 1 February 1961 and 1 March 1961 that these aircraft began regular service with Trans-Canada Airlines and BEA respectively. By then this and other second-generation turboprop-powered airliners had been deposed by the development and introduction into service of economical turbojet-powered airliners such as the Boeing Model 707. Conse-

(4,985 ehp) Rolls-Royce Tyne Mk 506 *Wing span* 35.97 m (118 ft 0 in) *Length* 37.45 m (122 ft 10½ in) *Max T-O weight* 63,957 kg (141,000 lb) *Max level speed* 684 km/h (425 mph) *Range* 3,331 km (2,070 miles)

Vickers Varsity (UK) The Varsity general-purpose aircrew trainer retained the general characteristics of the Valetta C.1, but had a tricycle landing gear and a slightly longer fuselage. For bomb-aiming training, a bomb bay and bomb-aiming station were provided in the form of a pannier fitting against the fuselage underbelly. The prototype first flew in July 1949 and Varsity T.1s went into service with the RAF in 1951. A total of 163 was built.

Vickers Vernon (UK) The Vernon was the first military transport aircraft to be designed and built as such and was a derivative of the Commercial Vimy. Fifty-five were produced for the RAF for service in Iraq. Each was powered by two 268.3 kW (360 hp) Rolls-Royce Eagle VIII or 335.3 kW (450 hp) Napier Lion engines and accommodated 12 troops.

Vickers Victoria (UK) The Victoria 22-troop transport was built between the Vernon and Valentia. Production for the RAF totalled 94 aircraft. Entering service in 1926, it was powered by two 425 kW (570 hp) Napier Lion engines. A commercial counterpart, the Vanguard, was less successful.

Vickers Victoria.

Vickers

The Victoria is best remembered for its role during the Kabul airlift, when people and baggage were transported out of Kabul during tribal disturbances (see **Chronology** 23 Dec 1928–25 Feb 1929). Maximum level speed was 177 km/h (100 mph).

Vickers Viking (UK) Five-seat amphibious biplane of 1919 powered by a 279.5 kW (375 hp) Rolls-Royce Eagle engine mounted as a pusher. A small number were produced for civil and overseas military service.

Vickers Viking (UK) This Viking was a twin-engined 24–27-seat transport and was the first completely new post-World War II airliner to fly in the world. British European Airways operated a fleet of 49 on its European network and total production was 163. BEA aircraft were, in fact, modified to allow them to carry up to 34 or 38 tourist-class passengers when required. Four also flew with the Queen's Flight.

Data (Viking 1B): *Engines* two 1,259 kW (1,690 hp) Bristol Hercules 634 radials *Wing span* 27.2 m (89 ft 3 in) *Length* 19.86 m (65 ft 2 in) *Max T-O weight* 15,422 kg (34,000 lb) *Cruising speed* 423 km/h (263 mph)

Vickers Vildebeest (UK) The all-metal Vildebeest was adopted by the RAF as a standard torpedo-carrying and bombing biplane and went into service in Mk I form in 1933. Powered by a 462 kW (620 hp) Bristol Pegasus IM3 engine, it was of unusual shape, with the pilot occupying an open cockpit below the leading edge of the upper wing and the observer aft of the wings in a shallower and lower section of the fuselage. A prone bombing position was provided below the pilot's seat. Armament comprised one fixed Vickers gun firing through the propeller and one Lewis gun on a Scarff ring over the back cockpit. The crutch for the 18 in torpedo or bomb rack was under the fuselage between the two legs of the landing gear.

The Mk I was followed into service by the Mks II to IV, powered by 484.4 kW (650 hp) Pegasus IIM3 and 603.6 kW (810 hp) Bristol Perseus

VIII engines. Total production for the RAF was just over 200, about half of which were still operational at the outbreak of World War II. In addition the Vildebeest was adopted by the Spanish Ministry of Marine as a standard torpedo-carrying seaplane and a batch of about 27 were ordered from the Spanish CASA firm, which had acquired a manufacturing licence. These were powered by 443.4 kW (595 hp) Hispano-Suiza 12Nbr engines. Subsequently the RNZAF also acquired more than 30 Vildebeests.

Data (Mk IV): *Engine* as above *Wing span* 14.94 m (49 ft 0 in) *Length* 11.48 m (37 ft 8 in) *Max T-O weight* 3,856 kg (8,500 lb) *Max level speed* 251 km/h (156 mph), (Mk I) 227 km/h (141 mph), (Spanish aircraft) 220 km/h (137 mph) *Range* 1,006 km (625 miles)

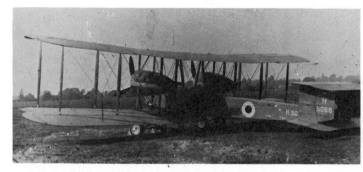

Vickers Vimy (UK) Design of the Vickers F.B.27 was initiated in 1917 to meet the requirement to provide bomber aircraft able to attack strategic targets in Germany from bases in Britain. Such aircraft as the de Havilland D.H.10 Amiens and Handley Page V/1500 were also built. The de Havilland and Vickers designs were of similar size, but the Handley Page V/1500 was almost twice as large.

The F.B.27 was a three-bay biplane of then-conventional construction, with a biplane tail unit which had twin fins and rudders. The wing centre-section – almost one-third span – had the fuselage at its centre with large struts supporting the upper wing. At the outer ends of this centre-section the engines were mounted midway between the upper and lower wings. Two twin-wheel main landing-gear units were mounted beneath the lower wing, one directly below each engine. Outboard of this centre-section the wings had dihedral.

The largest aircraft then built by Vickers, it posed many construction problems; but despite this the first prototype flew on 30 November 1917 – little more than four months after the design had been started. This aircraft was powered by two 149 kW (200 hp) Hispano-Suiza engines (subsequently re-engined with 194 kW; 260 hp Salmsons). Three further prototypes followed, powered respectively with 194 kW (260 hp) Sunbeam Maoris, 223.6 kW (300 hp) Fiat A-12s and

268.3 kW (360 hp) Rolls-Royce Eagle VIIIs. It was the latter installation which was selected for production aircraft.

With the introduction of official aircraft names in 1918, the F.B.27 became the Vimy. But only a single example had been placed on an operational footing before the Armistice, which meant that none were used operationally in World War I. However a total of 99 was built for service with the RAF post-war, remaining in first-line service until replaced by Virginias in 1924–25. The veteran bomber was then revived as an advanced instructional aircraft for training pilots in multi-engined flying. For this purpose Jupiter VI or Jaguar engines were fitted.

The Vimy is remembered especially in aviation history for the post-war long-distance flights which pointed the way to the air lanes that would link the world. First was the flight by Capt John Alcock and Lt Arthur Whitten-Brown across the North Atlantic, from St John's, Newfoundland, to Clifden, Eire, during 14–15 June 1919 in a time of 16 hours 27 minutes. Next was the England–Australia flight of the brothers Capt Ross and Lt Keith Smith, together with Sgts Bennett and Shiers. Taking off from Hounslow (not far from today's Heathrow Airport) on 12 November 1919, they landed safely at Darwin on 10 December 1919 in an elapsed flying time of 135 hours 55 minutes. Last of the trio of great Vimy flights was an attempt by Lt-Col Pierre van Ryneveld and Sqn Ldr Christopher J. Q. Brand of the South African Air Force to link London and Cape Town. On 4 February 1920 they took off from Brooklands, unfortunately making a crash landing between Cairo and Khartoum. Loaned a second Vimy by an RAF unit in Egypt, they continued to Bulawayo, Southern Rhodesia, where they failed to get airborne because of 'hot and high' conditions. They finally completed their flight to Cape Town in a third borrowed aircraft (a de Havilland D.H.9), arriving at their destination on 20 March 1920. They, like Alcock and Brown and the Ross brothers, were awarded knighthoods for their achievement.

In addition to the Vimy bomber, a small number of commercial and ambulance aircraft were built, known simply as Commercial Vimys. Data (Vimy Mk II): *Engines* two 268.3 kW (360 hp) Rolls-Royce Eagle VIIIs *Wing span* 20.73 m (68 ft 0 in) *Length* 13.27 m (43 ft 6½ in) *Max T-O weight* 5,670 kg (12,500 lb) *Max level speed* 166 km/h (103 mph) *Range* 1,770 km

Vickers Vincent.

(1,100 miles) *Armament* two Lewis machine-guns, plus up to 1,123 kg (2,475 lb) of bombs

Vickers Vincent (UK) The Vincent was a three-seat general-purpose version of the Vildebeest, designed essentially for tropical service in the Middle East and therefore carrying comprehensive equipment. Fitted with a 484.4 kW (650 hp) Bristol Pegasus IIM3 engine, it (like the Vildebeest) had sufficient fuel as standard for a 1,006 km (625 mile) flight while cruising at 195 km/h (121 mph); this range could be increased to 2,012 km (1,250 miles) by the use of an auxiliary fuel tank attached in the position normally occupied by the torpedo. A number of Vildebeests were converted into Vincents and, with new production aircraft, the RAF operated just under 200 from 1934. The last were withdrawn in 1941.

Data: *Engine* as above *Wing span* and *Length* as for Vildebeest *Max T-O weight* (normal) 3,674 kg (8,100 lb) *Max level speed* 229 km/h (142 mph) *Range* as above *Armament* machine-guns as for Vildebeest, plus up to 454 kg (1,000 lb) of bombs. Equipment included automatic reconnaissance cameras

Vickers Virginia (UK) Designed to meet the requirements of Air Ministry Specification 1/21, the Vickers Virginia proved to be the backbone of the RAF's heavy night bomber force in the inter-war years. In fulfilling such a role from 1924 to 1937, this rugged and reliable aircraft made a considerable contribution to the development of the ideas and the experience of men who were the founder members of Bomber Command in World War II.

Two aircraft were ordered initially, designated Virginia I and Virginia II. The former was the first to fly (on 24 November 1922), powered by

Vickers Commercial Vimy.

Vickers Virginia bombers.

two 335.3 kW (450 hp) Napier Lion engines. It was basically an enlarged version of the Vickers Vimy (see entry), but had its Napier Lion engines mounted on the lower wings and enclosed in rectangular nacelles. Construction was mainly of wood and fabric with a fairly extensive amount of wire bracing. The second Virginia differed by having close-fitting engine cowlings; a Lamblin cooling radiator mounted between the landing-gear legs; a lengthened nose to provide more room for the bomb-aimer and, for the same reason, a slight decrease in intended bomb load; and a variable-incidence tailplane which could be adjusted in flight. Initially both the Virginias were unstable in flight, leading to modifications which included dihedral on both wings instead of on the lower wing only, introduction of larger rudders, an additional fin, and resiting of the engines further forward.

The first production contract was for two Virginia Mk III aircraft, generally similar to the Virginia II but provided with dual controls and changes in armament. Like the earlier prototypes, these were subsequently modified to later standards. Four additional aircraft were ordered in 1923. Power plant comprised two 349 kW (468 hp) Napier Lion Series II engines. Again, these aircraft were later updated, being fitted with metal wings, and ended their lives as Mk Xs. The two Virginia Mk IVs which followed differed in electrical equipment and bomb load. First major production version (22 built) was the Mk V, which had a third rudder, first test-flown on a Mk IV aircraft; otherwise these aircraft were generally similar to the Mk III. They were modified subsequently to later marks. Interestingly, Vimys were still being delivered at this time.

The Virginia Mk VI (25 built) was the first production version to include dihedral on both upper and lower wings as standard; design of the wing-folding mechanism was improved. It was followed by 11 Mk VIIs, which introduced still further changes to improve stability – including introduction of Frise ailerons and sweepback on both wings. These represented such an improvement in flight characteristics that many earlier aircraft were modified subsequently to this Mk VII standard.

To provide adequate defence for these large and comparatively slow bombers there had been a number of experiments to locate gunners in 'fighting tops' – nacelles attached to the trailing edge of the upper wing. Apart from the aerodynamic problems, the gunners suffered from the cold and it was decided to introduce instead a gunner's position at the tail-end of the fuselage. This involved not only modification of the rear fuselage but increased tailplane span and a lengthened nose to maintain good stability. These aircraft (eight built) became designated Mk IX and some earlier aircraft were converted subsequently to this standard. Final version was the Mk X, which introduced a metal structure with fabric covering (50 built). A large number of earlier aircraft were converted to include the more powerful engines, hydraulic wheel brakes, landing lights, and auto pilot which distinguished this, the last of the series.

First entering service in 1924, Virginias remained in first-line deployment until 1937 and for four more years several remained in use, especially for parachute training.

Data (Mk X): *Engines* two 432.2 kW (580 hp) Napier Lion VBs *Wing span* 26.72 m (87 ft 8 in) *Length* 18.97 m (62 ft 3 in) *Max T-O weight* 7,983 kg (17,600 lb) *Max level speed* 174 km/h (108 mph) *Range* 1,585 km (985 miles) *Armament* one Lewis gun forward, twin Lewis guns in tail position, plus up to 1,361 kg (3,000 lb) of bombs.

Vickers Viscount (UK) During World War II the US had gained a considerable start in the design and development of long-range transport aircraft. To Britain the Viscount represented the belief and hope that its lead in the new turbine engine allied to the industry's enthusiasm would erode some of America's advantage in post-war civil aviation.

That this hope failed to materialise was due to a number of factors and space does not allow for their discussion here. Suffice it to say that production exceeded 440 aircraft and orders from Capital Airlines of Washington for 60 aircraft represented a major triumph for the British aircraft industry.

The origin of the Viscount can be traced back to the war-time Brabazon Committee, which was charged with the task of steering Britain's aircraft industry in the right direction in the immediate post-war years. One of its recommendations was the development of a turboprop-powered short/

medium-range airliner (identified originally as the Brabazon IIB), and in April 1945 Vickers were instructed to proceed with its design and development, then identified by the company as the VC2 project.

This was the first of the company's designs to be brought to fruition under the leadership of George (later Sir George) Edwards, following the death of Rex Pierson. The project undoubtedly benefited from the fact that Edwards was facing his first major design/production challenge, one which he met with tremendous practical ability and enthusiasm. As finalised, a circular-section pressurised fuselage was chosen with low-set monoplane wings, a Vickers-style tail unit, retractable tricycle-type landing gear and four of Rolls-Royce's new Dart turboprops.

Despite the efforts of Edwards, his design team and Vickers' engineers, interest in the project waned when BEA had doubts about the aircraft's economics in the autumn of 1947. Enthusiasm was at a low ebb when the Viscount 630 prototype flew for the first time on 16 July 1948. Its smooth performance and superb handling qualities left no doubt that the company had produced an exceptional aeroplane, and with BEA's co-operation a higher gross weight/increased capacity specification for 43 passengers was drawn up. A prototype of this new version was ordered by the Ministry of Supply in February 1949. By the time this flew for the first time on 28 August 1950, BEA had already bolstered Vickers' enthusiasm by ordering 20 (later 26) Viscount 701s on 3 August.

It was the beginning of a success story: the world's first turbine-powered aircraft to operate a revenue passenger service, and the first to demonstrate the smooth reliability of turbine power plants to a new generation of passengers who would soon be travelling across the face of the earth for both business and pleasure.
Data (Type 810): *Engines* four 1,483 kW (1,990 ehp) Rolls-Royce Dart R.Da.7/1 Mk 525 turboprops *Wing span* 28.56 m (93 ft 8½ in) *Length* 26.11 m (85 ft 8 in) *Max T-O weight* 32,885 kg (72,500 lb) *Max cruising speed* 575 km/h (357 mph) *Range* (with max payload) 2,554 km (1,587 miles) *Accommodation* five crew and 57–65 passengers
Vickers Vixen (UK) Similar to the Valparaiso. Small number were supplied to Chile from 1925.
Vickers Wellesley (UK) The Wellesley evolved from Vickers' design for a general-purpose day and night bomber and coastal-defence torpedo-carrier biplane to satisfy Air Ministry Specification G.4/31, the company having decided to develop and build a monoplane aircraft to meet the same specification. When evaluated there was little doubt that the monoplane was superior, with the result that the Air Ministry contract for the biplane was cancelled, being replaced on 10 September 1935 by one for 96 examples of the monoplane under a rewritten G.22/35 specification.

Named the Wellesley, it was the first RAF aircraft to utilise the geodetic form of construction devised by Barnes (later Sir Barnes) Wallis; offering a lightweight structure of great strength, it was adopted later for the Wellington (see entry).

Vickers Viscount 802.

The other highly unusual feature was the provision of a pannier beneath each wing to serve as a bomb container. The low-set monoplane wing was also of geodetic construction, the main landing gear was hydraulically retractable, and power plant comprised a single Bristol Pegasus radial piston engine.

Wellesley Mk Is entered RAF service in April 1937 but by the outbreak of World War II most of them had been transferred to the Middle East, where they remained operational into 1941. The type is remembered especially in service with the RAF's Long Range Development Flight, which was established at RAF Upper Heyford, Oxon, in January 1938. Equipment comprised six Wellesleys modified by the installation of Pegasus Mk XXII engines installed in NACA long-chord cowlings, and driving constant-speed propellers; plus other changes which included strengthened landing gear, increased fuel capacity and the introduction of an autopilot. Between 5 and 7 November 1938, two of a flight of three of these aircraft (led by Sqn Ldr R. Kellett) succeeded in establishing a new world long-distance record, covering non-stop the 11,526 km (7,162 miles) between Ismailia, Egypt, and Darwin, Australia, in just over 48 hours.
Data (Wellesley I): *Engine* one 689.3 kW (925 hp) Bristol Pegasus XX radial *Wing span* 22.73 m (74 ft 7 in) *Length* 11.96 m (39 ft 3 in) *Max T-O weight* 5,035 kg (11,100 lb) *Max level speed* 367 km/h (228 mph) *Cruising speed* 303 km/h (188 mph) *Range* 4,168 km (2,590 miles) *Armament* two Vickers 0.303 in machine-guns, plus up to 907 kg (2,000 lb) of bombs

Vickers Wellesley Is.

Vickers

Vickers Wellington IA.

Vickers Wellington with a
degaussing ring.

Vickers Wellington (UK) The Wellington, which served Bomber Command so well in the early years of World War II, is remembered by the RAF and the people of Britain as the 'Wimpey' – a nickname derived from an American cartoon character possessing the proud name J. Wellington Wimpey. It was designed to meet an Air Ministry requirement for a long-range medium bomber under Specification B.9/32 and evolved as a mid-wing monoplane with a fuselage of oval cross-section. Both of these major structures were of the geodetic construction which Barnes Wallis had introduced in the Wellesley.

But experience with the latter and development of the geodetic concept made it possible for the individual components (which were built up into the 'basket-weave' structure) to be smaller and lighter in weight without any loss of structural integrity by comparison with the Wellesley. Wings, fuselage and tail unit were fabric-covered; power plant comprised two wing-mounted engines; and the tailwheel-type landing-gear units were hydraulically retractable.

'Heavy' defensive armament – comprising five machine-guns in nose and tail turrets and a ventral dustbin – would, it was believed, enable a flight of these aircraft to put up such a curtain of fire that fighter escort would be superfluous. Those who held such beliefs (as for the Boeing B-17 Fortress developed in America) were to discover their error very quickly.

The prototype Wellington made its first flight on 15 June 1936, but it was not until October 1938 that production aircraft began to enter RAF service. Less than one year later (on 4 September 1939) Wellingtons were in action against targets in Germany. Early deployment on daylight raids showed that these and other British bomber aircraft were extremely vulnerable to fighter attack. Following the loss of ten Wellingtons from a force of 24 despatched on an armed reconnaissance of Wilhelmshaven on 18 December 1939, the type was withdrawn from daylight operations. As a night bomber, however, the Wellington proved an invaluable weapon during the early years of Bomber Command's offensive against Germany.

Wellington production was to total 11,461 aircraft and embraced many versions. These included Mk I bombers (782 kW; 1,050 hp Bristol

Pegasus XVIIIs) and the DWI with degaussing ring to trigger magnetic mines. Differing engines distinguished the 853.25 kW (1,145 hp) Rolls-Royce Merlin X-powered Mk II; 1,021.5 kW (1,370 hp) Bristol Hercules XI Mk III; and Pratt & Whitney Twin Wasp Mk IV. The Wellington Mk V was a high-altitude aircraft with pressurised cabin, no nose turret and increased wing span, followed by the high-altitude Mk VI with 1,192.3 kW (1,600 hp) Rolls-Royce Merlin 60 or 62 R6SM engines. Mk VII was designated an experimental model and Mk VIII was the first of many reconnaissance versions. Mk IX aircraft were Mk Is modified as troop carriers. The Mk X with Hercules VI or XVI engines was the last bomber. Wellingtons Mk XI, XII and XIII were ASV radar-equipped aircraft for Coastal Command. The Mk XIV with Hercules XVII engines was the final reconnaissance version. In addition to these specific versions there were many variants, and Wellingtons were also used for training and transport.

Data (Mk X): *Engines* two 1,182 kW (1,585 hp) Hercules VI radials *Wing span* 26.26 m (86 ft 2 in) *Length* 19.68 m (64 ft 7 in) *Max T-O weight* 13,380–14,288 kg (29,500–31,500 lb) *Max level speed* 410 km/h (255 mph) *Cruising speed* 290 km/h (180 mph) *Range* (with 680 kg; 1,500 lb bomb load) 3,034 km (1,885 miles) *Armament* two machine-guns in nose turret, four in tail turret, two in beam positions; plus up to 1,814 kg (4,000 lb) of bombs.

Vickers Warwick (UK) The Warwick was a slightly enlarged version of the Wellington and employed the same geodetic form of construction. It was designed originally to Specification B.1/35 to replace the Wellington. But because the generation of four-engined bombers was also being produced at the same time, it was subsequently adapted for reconnaissance duties with Coastal Command and first went into service in 1943. Other models were built for transport and air-sea rescue duties. The final version, the GR.V, entered service in 1945 and carried bombs, mines or depth-charges. About 840 production Warwicks were built.

Data (GR.V): *Engines* two 1,878 kW (2,520 hp) Bristol Centaurus VII radials *Wing span* 29.5 m (96 ft 8½ in) *Length* 21.5 m (70 ft 6 in) *Max T-O weight* 20,411 kg (45,000 lb) *Max level speed* 467 km/h (290 mph) *Armament* nose and mid-upper turrets of earlier versions removed and replaced by one 0.50 in gun in the nose and two in beam positions. Four-gun tail turret. Up to 907 kg (2,000 lb) of weapons as listed above

Vickers Vancouver (Canada) The Vancouver was a biplane flying-boat fitted with two Wright J-6 Whirlwind engines mounted as tractors. The prototype had been designed and built to the order and specification of the Department of National Defence to meet the urgent need for a type suitable for forest-fire protection duties; the transportation of bulky and general freight; and training. Following trials with the Vancouver I prototype, five production Mk IIs were ordered immediately. Subsequently Canadian Vickers designed the Mk IIA military derivative for

Vickers Warwick ASR.1 air-sea rescue aircraft.

coastal-patrol duties, fitting it with three gun positions and bomb racks under the lower wings. Four of the Mk IIs were brought up to this standard for the RCAF.

Vickers Vedette (Canada) The Canadian Vickers company produced small numbers of the Vedette three-seat flying-boat during the latter 1920s and early 1930s for use on transport, forest-fire detection and photographic-survey work. During 1929 alone 22 were built, the majority being delivered to the various branches of the Department of National Defence and the Ontario Provincial government, although six were purchased by Chile. The Mk VI was powered by a single pusher-mounted 223.6 kW (300 hp) Wright J-6 Whirlwind engine giving a maximum speed of 176 km/h (110 mph).

Victa Airtourer (Australia) Two-seat fully aerobatic light monoplane powered by a 74.5 kW (100 hp) Rolls-Royce Continental O-200-A (AT-100 version) or 85.7 kW (115 hp) Lycoming O-235-C1B (AT-115 version) engine. A total of 172 Airtourers had been completed when production ended in 1966.

Victa Airtrainer CT/4 (Australia) See **Aerospace Airtrainer**

VL Myrsky II (Finland) The Myrsky II was a single-seat fighter of 1942 powered by a 793.6 kW (1,065 hp) Swedish-built Pratt & Whitney SC3G Twin Wasp engine. Forty-seven were built. Maximum level speed 530 km/h (329 mph).

VL Pyry II (Finland) Advanced fighter-trainer powered by a 313 kW (420 hp) Wright R-975-E3 Whirlwind radial engine. Forty were built in 1941. Max level speed 330 km/h (205 mph).

Voisin biplane flown by Louis Paulhan.

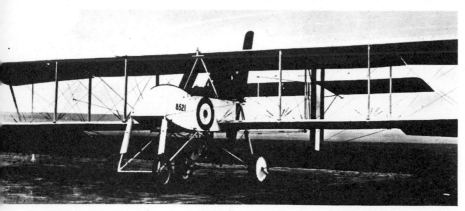

Voisin Type V flown by the RFC.

Voisin Type X.

Voisin Type VIII flown by the AEF.

Voisin biplane (France) In March 1907 the brothers Gabriel and Charles Voisin produced their first classic biplane at their factory in Billancourt. It was a box-kite-type biplane with a forward elevator, rudder in the biplane tail and powered by a 15 kW (20 hp) Buchet pusher-mounted engine. Produced for Henry Kapferer, this aeroplane never flew, but subsequent examples built for such famous aviators as Léon Delagrange, Moore-Brabazon, Paulhan and Henry Farman thereafter achieved considerable success. Farman remained airborne for more than one minute on 9 November and so was second only to the Wright brothers. During 1908–09 this aircraft was modified and subsequently made several important flights (see **Chronology** 13 Jan 1908). It is believed that about 20 of these biplanes had been built by 1909.
Data: *Engine* as above *Wing span* 10.2 m (33 ft 6 in) *Max T-O weight* 520 kg (1,146 lb)

Voisin Types I to X (France) The 1917 *Jane's* says about the Voisin combat types: 'These machines, now generally fitted with Salmson engines, have done an immense amount of work in the war, being capable of carrying big weights, either of bombs or machine-gun and ammunition. Towards the end of 1915 the need for higher speeds and climbs put this type somewhat out of date. Various improved types have been introduced during 1916–17, with higher powers.'

When this entry was written by C. G. Grey there was no way he could have known that the Voisin 'Chicken Coop' would last the war out, despite possessing a maximum speed more readily associated with the first unarmed scouting types of 1915. Indeed the Types I and II – with 52 kW (70 hp) Gnome and 59.6 kW (80 hp) Le Rhône engines respectively – were in service with two French escadrilles (V14 and V21 attached to

the Fourth Army) at the outbreak of World War I. Only some of the early Voisins were armed; one such aircraft was the Voisin Type III (89.4 kW; 120 hp Salmson-built Canton-Unné 9M engine) flown by Sergent Joseph Franz and Caporal Quénault of Escadrille VB 24, who were responsible for shooting down an Aviatik two-seater over Reims on 5 October 1914 with the forward-mounted Hotchkiss machine-gun, recording the first ever air combat kill.

The Voisin Types IV, V and VI were also Salmson-Canton-Unné-powered but, unlike earlier models, some carried up to 60 kg (132 lb) of bombs in specially developed racks, which released the observer from having to throw them manually out of the aircraft. Another favourite weapon of the period was the fléchette, a steel dart capable of passing right through the body of a ground soldier and so much feared. Fléchettes contained in racks of 250 were first dropped from aircraft of No 3 Squadron, RFC, in the autumn of 1914. Between 1915 and 1917 Voisins were also flown by the RFC and RNAS.

By 1916 the 105 km/h (65 mph) maximum speed of the Type V and 120 km/h (74 mph) of the Type VI left them extremely vulnerable, yet the frail look of the Voisin masked a robust structure. In an attempt to increase speed and so prolong the Voisin's career, the Type VIII was powered by a 164 kW (220 hp) Peugeot 8Aa engine, giving a maximum speed of 135 km/h (84 mph) and allowing an increase in bomb load. A number were also fitted with two machine-guns or a 37 mm cannon. More than 1,000 Type VIIIs were built, followed by 223.6 kW (300 hp) Renault Re 12 Fe-engined Type Xs – the last version to enter service and operated mainly as a night-reconnaissance bomber until the Armistice.

Excluding the ten Type VIII/Xs used by the AEF as trainers, approximately 210 Voisins were still operational at the time of the Armistice, forming the equipment of nine night-bomber and five reconnaissance/observation escadrilles.
Data (Type X): *Engine* as above *Wing span* 17.9 m (58 ft 10 in) *Length* 10.35 m (33 ft 11½ in) *Max T-O weight* 2,200 kg (4,850 lb) *Max level speed* 135 km/h (84 mph) *Range* 500 km (311 miles) *Armament* one Hotchkiss machine-gun, plus up to 300 kg (661 lb) of bombs

Voisin-Farman I (France) See **Farman**
Volmer VJ-22 Sportsman (USA) Two-seat light amphibian, plans for which are available to amateur constructors.

Voskhod spacecraft (USSR) Voskhod is believed to have been a modified Vostok with a launch weight of about 5,683 kg (12,529 lb). It was fitted with small solid-propellant braking rockets to lower the impact speed when landing by parachute from a mission. A crew of two was carried. It was from Voskhod 2 that Alexei Leonov performed the first extra-vehicular activity (see **Chronology** 18 Mar 1965).

Vostok spacecraft (USSR) The Vostok was the first spacecraft to take a man into orbit (see **Chronology** 12 Apr 1961). The capsule was a near-spherical re-entry module covered in ablative material and designed for automatic and ground control, although manual controls could be used in an emergency. Unlike American spacecraft, pressurisation was for an atmosphere equivalent to that on Earth. The service module contained batteries, the attitude control system and tanks of UDMH and nitric acid for the restartable retro-rockets. A crew of one was carried. Launch weight was about 4,713 kg (10,390 lb).

Vought A-7 Corsair II (USA) On 11 February 1964 the US Navy named the former LTV Aerospace Corporation winner of a design competition for a single-seat carrier-based light attack aircraft. The requirement was for a subsonic aircraft able to carry a greater load of non-nuclear weapons than the A-4E Skyhawk. To keep the costs down and speed up delivery it had been stipulated by the Navy that the new aircraft should be based on an existing design; the LTV design study was based therefore on the F-8 Crusader. The first prototype flew on 27 September 1965.

The initial production attack version for the US Navy was the A-7A powered by a non-afterburning 50.5 kN (11,350 lb st) Pratt & Whitney TF30-P-6 turbofan engine. Delivery of 199 to the Navy was completed in 1968. From it was developed the A-7B powered by a 54.3 kN (12,200 lb st) TF30-P-8 (196 delivered). The designation A-7C was applied to the first 67 TF-30-engined A-7Es to eliminate confusion with subsequent Allison-powered A-7Es. Recently 65 A-7Bs and A-7Cs have been modified into TA-7C tandem two-seat trainers.

The A-7D was a tactical fighter version of the Corsair II for the USAF, with a non-afterburning Allison TF41-A-1 (Spey) turbofan of 64.5 kN (14,500 lb st). Production of 459 was completed in 1976. The A-7E was another navy version equipped as a light attack/close support/interdiction aircraft and powered by a 59.6 kN (13,400 lb st) TF30-P-408 non-afterburning turbofan engine.

As a prototype of a two-seat version of the A-7 envisaged as an advanced trainer, or as a new operational configuration for tactical duties such as electronic countermeasures, Vought has produced a single YA-7E. The final production versions of the Corsair II are the A-7H, a land-based A-7E of which 60 were delivered to the Hellenic Air Force; TA-7H two-seat trainer for the Hellenic Air Force (five delivered); and the A-7K, a two-seat version of the A-7D which will enter service in 1981 with the US Air National Guard.

Vought A-7A Corsair II.

Deliveries of all versions totalled 1,488 by the beginning of 1979.

Data (A-7E): *Engine* as above *Wing span* 11.8 m (38 ft 9 in) *Length* 14.06 m (46 ft 1½ in) *Max T-O weight* 19,050 kg (42,000 lb) *Max level speed* 1,112 km/h (691 mph) *Ferry range* (internal fuel) 3,671 km (2,281 miles) *Armament* one forward-firing M-61A-1 20 mm Vulcan multi-barrel cannon; two stations under fuselage and six under wings for more than 6,805 kg (15,000 lb) of external stores including air-to-air missiles, air-to-surface missiles, bombs, rockets, gun pods and drop-tanks

Vought F-8 Crusader (USA) The prototype Crusader single-seat carrier-based fighter flew for the first time on 25 March 1955. The first production F-8A flew on 20 September of the same year and this version began reaching US Navy operational squadrons in March 1957. It was produced as a day fighter powered initially by a 71.2 kN (16,000 lb st) Pratt & Whitney J57-P-12 turbojet and on later aircraft a 72 kN (16,200 lb st) P-4A engine. A photo-reconnaissance version was also produced as the RF-8A. All examples of the F-8A are now operated as TF-8A trainers.

Several other versions of the Crusader were produced. The F-8B had a J57-P-4A engine and improved radar; the F-8C a 75.2 kN (16,900 lb st) J57-P-16 engine; the F-8D with limited all-weather capability and an 80 kN (18,000 lb st) J57-P-20 engine; the F-8E with improved all-weather capability and an enlarged nose radome;

Vought F-8D Crusaders.

Vought

Vought O2U-4 Corsairs.

the F-8E (FN) export version of the F-8E for the French Navy (provision for Matra R.530 missiles in addition to Sidewinders) with blown flaps; the RF-8G (modernised RF-8A with updated equipment); and the F-8H/J/K/L modernised versions of the F-8D/E/C/B respectively, with updated equipment and attack capability. The F-8H also serves with the air force of the Philippines.

Data (F-8E): *Engine* as above *Wing span* 10.87 m (35 ft 8 in) *Length* 16.61 m (54 ft 6 in) *Max T-O weight* 15,420 kg (34,000 lb) *Max level speed* 2,127 km/h (1,322 mph) *Combat radius* 965 km (600 miles) *Armament* four 20 mm Colt cannon in nose. Four Sidewinder missiles. Late production F-8Es have two underwing pylons for weapons including two 1,000 lb or 2,000 lb bombs, four 500 lb bombs, 12 × 250 lb bombs or 24 Zuni rockets. Eight more Zunis can replace the Sidewinders

Vought FU-1 (USA) Single-seat fighter version of the UO-1 powered by a 164 kW (220 hp) Wright engine. Twenty built for the US Navy.

Vought O2U Corsair (USA) Two-seat armed observation biplane powered by a 335.3 kW (450 hp) Pratt & Whitney R-1340 engine. Nearly 290 built for the US Navy from 1926.

Vought O3U and SU series (USA) Continuing its highly successful Corsair biplane range, Vought produced in 1930 the new O3U-1 for the US Navy. This led to several new O3U observation and SU scouting types being produced, powered by Pratt & Whitney Wasp or Hornet radial engines in the 410–447 kW (550–600 hp) range. All remained two-seaters, armed with one forward-firing 0.30 in and two rear-mounted machine-guns. Altogether nearly 330 were built, two-thirds as O3Us.

Vought OS2U Kingfisher (USA) The XOS2U-1 prototype of this two-seat observation/scout monoplane was delivered to the US Navy in 1938 and the first production

OS2U-1s went into service in 1940. Two further and generally similar series, the OS2U-2 and -3, followed – the latter also going into production at the Naval Aircraft Factory as the OS2N-1. The British Kingfisher I was a counterpart of the OS2U-3. Total production amounted to about 1,925 aircraft.

Data (OS2U-3 floatplane): *Engine* one 335.3 kW (450 hp) Pratt & Whitney R-985-AN-2 Wasp Junior radial *Wing span* 10.96 m (35 ft 10^{11}/$_{16}$ in) *Length* 10.25 m (33 ft 7^3/$_{16}$ in) *Max T-O weight* 2,722 kg (6,000 lb) *Max level speed* 275 km/h (171 mph) *Range* 1,460 km (908 miles) *Armament* one forward-firing and one rear-mounted 0.30 in machine-gun, plus two 100 lb or eight 30 lb bombs

Vought SBU (USA) First appearing in 1933, the SBU was a two-seat scout-bomber biplane fitted with a 521.6 kW (700 hp) Pratt & Whitney R-1535 Twin Wasp radial engine and new NACA 'flapped' cowling. Eighty-four were initially ordered for the US Navy as SBU-1s, followed by 40 SBU-2s. These served for several years from 1935, but all were out of service before America's entry into World War II. Maximum level speed was 330 km/h (205 mph).

Vought SB2U Vindicator (USA) The SB2U was this company's first low-wing monoplane and, like the earlier SBU, was a scout/bomber. Night-flying and deck-landing arrester gear were provided. Power for the initial production version was a Pratt & Whitney R-1535-96 radial engine. The generally similar SB2U-2 version was followed by the SB2U-3, which also formed the basis for the V-156 export model; some of these were delivered to France and the remainder of the order to Britain as the Chesapeake. Unfortunately the Vindicator was not as successful as Vought's earlier biplanes and was soon relegated to a training role.

Data (SB2U-3): *Engine* one 559 kW (750 hp) Pratt & Whitney R-1535-02 Wasp radial *Wing span* 12.8 m (42 ft 0 in) *Length* 10.45 m (34 ft 3^3/$_4$ in) *Max T-O weight* 4,723 kg (9,420 lb) *Max level speed* 391 km/h (243 mph) *Range* 1,126 km (700 miles) *Armament* one forward-firing 0.30 in and one rear-mounted machine-gun, plus two 500 lb or four 110 lb bombs

Vought UO-1 (USA) Two-seat biplane of 1922 powered in its final form by a 149 kW (200 hp) Wright J-3 radial engine. More than 140 were delivered to the US Navy with wheel or float landing gears, becoming standard observation aircraft and remaining operational for many years.

Vought VE-7 (USA) The VE-7 was designed in 1917 and first flew in the following year as a two-seat biplane trainer powered by a 112 kW (150 hp) Hispano-Suiza engine. A wheel or float landing gear could be fitted. The US Navy received 129 VE-7s, a number of which had been modified into single-seat fighters armed with one forward-firing Vickers gun.

Vought VE-9 (USA) The VE-9 was basically a VE-7 with a 134 kW (180 hp) Hispano-Suiza engine. A small number were built for the US Navy.

Vought OS2U-1s.

VSO 10 (Czechoslovakia) Single-seat high-performance sailplane, deliveries of which began in 1979.

Vultee A-31 and A-35 Vengeance (USA) The Vultee Model 72 two-seat dive bomber was designed to a British specification by Vultee and was put into production by both Vultee and Northrop. When the US entered the war, the Vengeance was given the USAAF designation A-31.

Vengeance I deliveries to Britain began in 1942 and these, like later Vengeance IIs and IIIs, were powered by the 1,192.3 kW (1,600 hp) Wright R-2600-19 Cyclone radial engine. British armament and equipment consisted of four 0.303 in machine-guns in the wings and two on a flexible mounting in the rear cockpit. Eventually the USAAF ordered the Vengeance II as the A-31A but in the event received only a few for non-operational use. The RAAF also received some early Vengeance Is.

The A-35 version of the Vengeance was powered by a 1,267 kW (1,700 hp) Wright R-2600-13 engine and was ordered by the USAAF. The first 100 delivered retained the earlier 0.303 in guns. With four 0.50 in guns fitted they became A-35As. The A-35B was the first fully American version fitted with US equipment and six 0.50 in wing guns as standard. Eight hundred and thirty one were built: 562 were supplied to Britain as Vengeance IVs, a small number were delivered to the Brazilian government, and the rest went into USAAF service.

The Vengeance was used operationally only by the RAF and the Royal Indian Air Force in the India-Burma theatre. The USAAF A-35s were mainly used as high-speed target tugs. Production of the Vengeance ceased in the autumn of 1944 after 1,528 had been built.

Data (A-35B): *Engine* as above *Wing span* 14.64 m (48 ft 0 in) *Length* 12.12 m (39 ft 9 in) *Max T O weight* 6,123 kg (13,500 lb) *Max level speed* 449 km/h (279 mph) *Normal range* 966 km (600 miles) *Armament* machine-guns as above, plus normally two 500 lb bombs. As an overload could carry extra 250 lb bombs

Vultee BT-13 and BT-15 Valiant (USA) The original contract for the BT-13 two-seat basic trainer was awarded in September 1939. Production ceased in the summer of 1944 after 11,537 Valiants had been delivered to the USAAF as BT-13s/BT-15s and the US Navy as SNVs. There

Vultee A-35 Vengeance.

were also several variants of the design: the BT-13 and SNV types using the 335.3 kW (450 hp) Pratt & Whitney R-985-AN-1 or -3 as the basic power plant, and the BT-15 with the Wright R-975-11.

Vultee V-1A (USA) Eight-passenger commercial monoplane powered by one Wright R-1820-G2 Cyclone radial engine.

Vultee V-11 and V-12 (USA) These were two–three-seat attack bombers developed from the V-1A commercial transport for export only. Power for the V-11 was provided by a 577.5 kW (775 hp) Wright SR-1820-F52/53 radial engine. One hundred on order by early 1938 were delivered to China, Turkey, Brazil and the USSR.

From the V-11 Vultee developed the V-12 powered by a 670.7 kW (900 hp) Wright GR-1820-G105A engine. China purchased 26 and followed up by ordering 52 examples of a version with a new power plant. The USAAF also received a variant as the YA-19, but this was not successful.

Vultee YA-19.

Vultee V-48/P-66 Vanguard (USA) Developed as a single-seat fighter for export, powered by an 894.2 kW (1,200 hp) Pratt & Whitney R-1830-53C4-G engine. Most production aircraft, given the USAAF designation P-66, found their way to China from 1940.

Waco early types (USA) The Waco Aircraft Corporation was formed in 1929 from the Advance Aircraft Company, itself formed in 1923 from the previous Weaver Aircraft Company that first traded under the name WACO.

In 1923 Advance produced the Waco 6, a three-seat commercial open-cockpit biplane powered by a 67 kW (90 hp) Curtiss OX-5 engine. The company grew rapidly and by the end of 1926 356 Waco aircraft were in use, 200 of which were built in 1926 alone. The six-passenger Civil Transport Aircraft powered by a 149 kW (200 hp) Hall-Scott Model L-6 was subsequently followed by the Waco 9 and 10, both similar to the Waco 6 although the 10 could be fitted with engines ranging from a Curtiss OX-5 to a 167.7 kW (225 hp) Wright Whirlwind. By 1929 Advance was the largest producer of commercial

Vought VE-7H floatplane.

Waco

aircraft in the US, with production said to have been greater than that of all other US aircraft manufacturers combined. It had 40 distributors and 150 dealers in the US, as well as representation in Canada, China, Australia, Mexico and South America. By 1934 25 countries were covered.

For the 1930s Waco aircraft were given letter designations. The Model A was a two-seat convertible open- or enclosed-cockpit biplane; Model C a four–five-seat cabin biplane; Model D a two-seat high-performance open or enclosed commercial or armed military biplane; Model E a five-seat cabin monoplane; Model F a three-seat open-cockpit commercial biplane; Model N a four-seat cabin biplane with a tricycle landing gear; and Model S a four–five-seat cabin biplane. All were available with a wide range of engines.

In an attempt to win USAAC orders for a new primary trainer, Waco produced the F-T based on the commercial biplanes but with tandem seating for two in open cockpits. However like its rival the St Louis PT-15, only one prototype and 13 service test examples were purchased (designated PT-14s).

Waco CG-3A.

Waco CG-3A (USA) Designed as a transport glider accommodating nine fully armed troops (two acting as pilot and co-pilot). One hundred were built and delivered to the USAAF by Commonwealth Aircraft and were later used for training glider pilots.

Waco CG-4A (USA) The CG-4A was the only American-built troop-carrying glider to be used by the Allied forces in the airborne invasion of Sicily and France. Apart from a batch of 13 gliders delivered to the US Navy, the 13,900+ CG-4As built went to the USAAF. They were produced by Waco and 15 other companies from 1942.

Accommodation was provided for two pilots and 13 fully armed troops, cargo or ordnance. Typical loads consisted of one ¼-ton Jeep with its crew of four and extra equipment; or one standard 75 mm howitzer and carriage with the gun crew of three, ammunition and supplies. The normal entrance for troops was through doors at the aft end of the compartment. The nose of the fuselage was hinged to fold upwards to give direct entry into the main hold for loading the truck, howitzer or other heavy equipment.
Data: *Wing span* 25.5 m (83 ft 8 in) *Length* 14.73 m (48 ft 3¾ in) *Max permissible overloaded weight* 4,082 kg (9,000 lb) *Normal T-O weight* 3,402 kg (7,500 lb) *Normal towed speed* 161 km/h (100 mph)

Waco CG-13A (USA) The CG-13A was a large glider capable of carrying a maximum of 42 airborne troops and their equipment or the equivalent weight in military vehicles or ordnance. The first prototype was delivered to the USAAF in March 1942 and, as a result of extensive trials, a small production order was placed with the Northwestern Aeronautical Corporation for service evaluation aircraft, the first of which was towed off the ground on 2 December 1943. Production was undertaken by Northwestern and the Ford Motor Company, but only 132 production CG-13As were built.

Waco CG-15A (USA) The CG-15A was a development of the CG-4A with reduced wing span, a strongly reinforced nose, improved landing-gear shock absorbers and the addition of flaps to counteract the effect of the shortened span. With these changes the maximum permissible towing speed was increased to 290 km/h (180 mph), permitting the glider to be towed by fighters. Only 427 were built, most as 15-seaters but some accommodating 16 men or 1,814 kg (4,000 lb) of equipment.

Waco UC-72 (USA) The Model VKS-7F (of the Model S series) four-seat cabin biplane was specially evolved to meet the requirements for a cross-country navigational trainer for the civilian training programme early in 1942. All production of this type of aircraft ceased after it. However 44 Models C, E, N and S which were in use at the outbreak of war were acquired by the USAAF from private owners and commercial operators and given UC-72 designations ranging from UC-72 and UC-72A to UC-72O.

Waco J2W and XJW (USA) These military designations applied to three Waco Model C cabin biplanes and two three-seat open-cockpit biplanes purchased by the US Coast Guard and US Navy respectively in the mid-1930s. The Navy aircraft were fitted with 'skyhooks' for parasite experiments with USS *Macon*.

Wag-Aero CUBy (USA) Modern version of the Piper Cub. Four versions are offered in kit form (or plans only) for construction by amateur builders.

Wag-Aero Wag-A-Bond (USA) Two aircraft are offered which can be constructed by amateur enthusiasts: one as a replica of the Piper PA-15 Vagabond, known as the Classic, and the other as the Traveler, a modified and updated version of the Vagabond.

War Aircraft series (USA) Plans are available to amateur constructors of a series of ½-scale World War II combat aircraft replicas, including the Focke-Wulf Fw 190, Chance Vought F4U Corsair and Republic P-47 Thunderbolt. Other types are at the prototype stage.

Wassmer WA 4/21 (France) Four–five-seat cabin monoplane powered by a 186.3 kW (250 hp) Lycoming IO-540 engine. The prototype first flew in March 1967 and production aircraft followed.

Wassmer WA-40A Super 4 Sancy (France) Four–five-seat cabin monoplane powered by a 134 kW (180 hp) Lycoming O-360-A1A engine. The prototype first flew in June 1959 and production aircraft were offered in three versions, differing in equipment only. A total of 180 was built.

Wassmer WA-41 Baladou (France) Version of the WA-40A Super 4 with a non-retractable landing gear. Power was provided by a 134 kW (180 hp) O-360-A2A engine.

Wassmer WA-51 Pacific and WA-52 Europa (France) Four-seat cabin monoplanes powered by a 112 kW (150 hp) Lycoming O-320-E2A and 119 kW (160 hp) O-320 engine respectively. The airframes are built up of large components moulded in thin layers of glassfibre, reinforced for strength (see below).

Wassmer WA-54 Atlantic (France) The Atlantic is generally similar to the WA-52 Europa but powered by a 134 kW (180 hp) Lycoming O-360-A engine. The prototype first flew in February 1973 and production began in June of the same year. By January 1977, a total of 190 Pacifics, Europas and Atlantics had been built. Production of all three models has ended.

Wassmer WA-80 Piranha (France) Two-seat light training and general-purpose monoplane powered by a 74.5 kW (100 hp) Rolls-Royce Continental O-200-A engine. By January 1977 orders for 20 had been received and ten had been built. It is no longer in production.

Watanabe Navy E9W1 (Japan) During the early 1930s a number of countries experimented with submarine-borne seaplanes which could be rapidly dismantled and carried in a sealed hangar on the submarine's deck. The Japanese carried the idea further and built ten single-seat twin-float biplanes under the designation Navy Type 91 Reconnaissance Seaplane (E6Y1) between 1930 and 1934. At least 32 later Watanabe E9W1s went into service with a number of fleet submarines in 1936 under the designation Navy Type 96 Small Reconnaissance Seaplane. Power for each was provided by a 223.6 kW (300 hp) radial engine.

Watanabe Navy K9W/Kokusai Army Ki-86 (Japan) Following the purchase of 22 Bücker Jungmann trainers during 1939, 339 more were built by Watanabe (later Kyushu) under licence. They were designated Navy Type 2 Primary Trainer Momiji. Later the Japanese Army instructed the Nippon Kokusai company to build the type. A total of 1,037 was completed between 1943 and 1945 as Army Type 4 Primary Trainers.

Watanabe Navy K10W1 (Japan) Based on an imported example of the North American NA-57 (BT-9), production of a considerably modified version was undertaken from 1941 as the Type 2 Intermediate Trainer. A total of 176 was built.

Watson GW-1 Windwagon (USA) Single-seat light monoplane, plans for which are available to amateur constructors.

Wassmer WA-41 Baladou.

Weatherley Model 201C (USA) Single-seat agricultural aircraft powered by a 335.6 kW (450 hp) Pratt & Whitney R-985 radial engine. The Model C is the latest version of the Model 201 series (more than 100 built by April 1979), developed from the earlier Model WM-62C, itself a conversion of the Fairchild M-62 airframe.

Weedhopper JC-2-1 Weedhopper (USA) Single-seat light open monoplane, kits of parts for which are available to amateur constructors.

Weiss W.M. 10 (Hungary) Having produced a number of Fokker F.VIIIs under licence for use on domestic air routes, Weiss produced its first aeroplane of original design in 1931 as the W.M.10. This was a two-seat light biplane suitable for primary training or sport flying. Power was provided by an 89.4 kW (120 hp) W.M. Sports II engine.

Weiss W.M.13 (Hungary) The W.M.13 was similar to the W.M.10 but powered by an 89.4–97 kW (120–130 hp) W.M. Sport III engine.

Wendt WH-1 Traveler (USA) Two-seat sporting monoplane, plans for which are available to amateur constructors.

Werkspoor Jumbo (Netherlands) Single example of a large commercial transport biplane powered by a Gnome-Rhône-built Jupiter VI engine. Operated from 1931 by KLM.

Western PGK-1 Hirondelle (Canada) Two-seat light monoplane, plans and wood kits, pre-formed engine cowlings, windscreens and fuel tanks for which are available to amateur constructors.

Westland Belvedere (UK) See **Bristol Type 192**

Watson GW-1 Windwagon.

Westland

Westland Commando VIP transport in Egyptian service.

Westland Commando (USA) First flown on 12 September 1973, the Commando is a tactical helicopter based on the Sea King. It is intended to operate with maximum efficiency in the primary roles of tactical troop transport, logistic support and cargo transport, and casualty evacuation. Up to 28 troops can be carried.

Westland Dragonfly (UK) See **Sikorsky S-51**

Westland Lynx (UK) The Lynx is one of three types of aircraft covered by the Anglo-French helicopter agreement confirmed on 2 April 1968. Westland has design leadership in the Lynx, which is a medium-sized helicopter intended to fulfil general-purpose, naval and civil transport roles. It is the first British aircraft to be designed entirely on a metric basis.

The first of 13 Lynx prototypes flew on 21 March 1971. On 20 and 22 June 1972 respectively the fifth Lynx (XX153) piloted by Roy Moxam set up Class E1e international speed records of 173.61 knots (321.74 km/h; 199.92 mph) over a 15–25 km straight course and 171.868 knots (318.504 km/h; 197.909 mph) over a 100 km closed circuit.

A Lynx Intensive Flying Trials Unit was formed in September 1976 at RNAS Yeovilton, Somerset, as a joint Royal Navy/Royal Netherlands Navy operational evaluation unit. Deck handling tests on board HMS *Birmingham* off Portland were completed in February 1977. Several versions of the Lynx have been produced and are listed below:

Lynx AH.1 General-purpose and utility version for the British Army. Capable of operation on tactical troop transport, logistic support, armed escort of troop-carrying helicopters, anti-tank strike, search and rescue, casualty evacuation, reconnaissance and command post

Westland Lynx AH.1.

duties. Total of 100 ordered by early 1978. First production aircraft flown on 11 February 1977.

Lynx HAS.2 Version for Royal Navy for advanced shipborne anti-submarine and other duties. Ferranti Seaspray search and tracking radar in modified nose. Capable of operation on anti-submarine classification and strike, air-to-surface vessel search and strike, search and rescue, reconnaissance, troop transport, fire support, communication and fleet liaison, and vertical replenishment duties. Total of 60 ordered by mid-1978. First production aircraft flown on 10 February 1976.

Lynx (French Navy) Navy version generally similar to British HAS.2 but with more advanced target-detection equipment. Total of 26 ordered by early 1978; 19 delivered by early 1979.

In addition to orders from the British and French armed forces, 24 naval Lynx have been ordered by the Royal Netherlands Navy, of which 18 are at the increased AUW of 4,763 kg (10,500 lb). The first batch of six (Dutch naval designation UH-14A) have been delivered and are being used for search and rescue, communications and training duties. The other 18 will be used in the ASW role: ten (designation SH-14B) will be equipped with Alcatel dunking sonar and eight (designation SH-14C) with MAD.

Nine naval Lynx are on order for the Brazilian Navy, two for the Argentinian Navy and three for Qatar. The Royal Danish Navy and Royal Norwegian Air Force have ordered seven and six respectively and the Federal German Navy 12. An initial batch of 50 Lynx will also be built in Egypt. By mid-1979 the total number of Lynx ordered was 299.

Data (general-purpose model): *Engines* two 559 kW (750 shp) Rolls-Royce BS.360-07-26 Gem turboshafts *Main rotor diameter* 12.8 m (42 ft 0 in) *Length of fuselage* 12.06 m (39 ft 7 in) *Max T-O weight* 4,763 kg (10,500 lb) *Max continuous cruising speed* 282 km/h (175 mph) *Max endurance* 3 h 26 min *Accommodation* crew of two and ten troops or paratroops, cargo etc *Armament* for armed escort, anti-tank or air-to-surface strike missions, can be equipped with one 20 mm AME 621 or similar cannon or a pintle-mounted 7.62 mm GEC Minigun inside cabin; or a Minigun beneath cabin, in Emerson Minitat installation. External pylon can be fitted on each side of cabin for a variety of stores, including two Minigun or other self-contained gun pods; two pods of 18 or two of seven 68 mm or 2.75 in rockets; or up to six Aérospatiale AS.11, or eight Aérospatiale/MBB Hot or Hughes TOW, or similar air-to-surface missiles. An additional six or eight missiles can be carried in cabin for rearming in forward areas. For ASW role (naval) armament includes two Mk 44 or Mk 46 homing torpedoes, one each on an external pylon on each side of fuselage, and six marine markers; or two Mk 11 depth charges. For anti-surface ship role armament includes BAe CL834 Sea Skua semi-active homing missiles for attacking light surface craft; alternatively four AS.12 or similar wire-guided missiles

Westland Lysander (UK) First flown as a prototype on 15 June 1936, the Lysander or 'Lizzie' was a two-seat army co-operation monoplane powered in its Mk I form by a 663.2 kW Bristol Mercury XII radial engine. This version entered RAF service at the end of 1938. The Mk II version was powered by a 674.4 kW (905 hp) Bristol Perseus XII engine and, in company with the Mk I, was active with the British Expeditionary Force in France from September 1939. They were also widely used in North Africa until replaced by Curtiss Tomahawks. Many were thereafter used as target tugs and for air-sea rescue.

Examples of the later Mk III version powered by 648.3 kW (870 hp) Bristol Mercury 30 engines were similarly employed, although a number found their way into the Special Air Service and made use of their STOL performance to drop and pick up agents in enemy-occupied Europe. Production of the Lysander, including those built in Canada, totalled nearly 1,600.

Data (Mk I): *Engine* as above *Wing span* 15.24 m (50 ft 0 in) *Length* 9.3 m (30 ft 6 in) *Max T-O weight* 2,685 kg (5,920 lb) *Max level speed* 369 km/h (229 mph) *Range* 966 km (600 miles) *Armament* two forward-firing 0.303 in machine-guns, one in each wheel fairing, and one rear-mounted gun. Up to six light bombs carried on special stub wings fitted to the landing-gear legs

Westland Sea King (UK) The Sea King was developed originally by Westland to meet the Royal Navy's requirement for an advanced anti-submarine helicopter with prolonged endurance. It can also undertake secondary roles, such as search and rescue, tactical troop transport, casualty evacuation, cargo carrying and long-range self-ferry.

The Sea King development programme stemmed from a licence agreement for the S-61 helicopter concluded originally with Sikorsky in 1959. This permitted Westland to utilise the basic airframe and rotor system of the Sikorsky SH-3D. Considerable changes were made in the power plant and in specialised equipment to meet British requirements. Several versions of the Sea King have been produced and are listed below:

Westland Sea King HAS.2.

Sea King HAS. 1 ASW version for the Royal Navy, ordered in 1967. First production HAS. 1 was flown for the first time on 7 May 1969. Total of 56 built, delivery of which was completed in May 1972.

Sea King HAS. 2 Uprated version for ASW and SAR duties with the Royal Navy. Twenty-one ordered, the first of which flew on 18 June 1976.

Sea King HAR. 3 Uprated version for SAR duties with the RAF. Sixteen ordered. First HAR.3 flew on 6 September 1977 and deliveries began in August 1978.

Sea King HC.4 Utility version of the Commando Mk 2 for the Royal Navy

Sea King Mk 41 Search and rescue version for the Federal German Navy. First example was flown on 6 March 1972. Twenty-two ordered, of which production and delivery were completed in 1974.

Sea King Mk 42 ASW version for the Indian Navy. Delivery was completed in 1974. A follow-on order was announced in June 1977 for three uprated aircraft, designated Mk 42A, with hauldown capability for small-ship operation.

Sea King Mk 43 SAR version for Norwegian Air Force. Ten ordered initially, all of which were delivered in 1972. A follow-on order was placed in June 1977 for additional aircraft to uprated standard.

Sea King Mk 45 ASW version for the Pakistan Navy. Six ordered, delivery of which was completed during 1975.

Sea King Mk 47 ASW version. Six ordered by Saudi Arabia on behalf of Egyptian Navy.

Sea King Mk 48 SAR version for Belgian Air Force. Five ordered, including one aircraft with VIP interior capability. Delivery completed in November 1976.

Sea King Mk 50 Developed from the Mk 1 for the Royal Australian Navy, which ordered ten. First flight 30 June 1974. Production included offset manufacture in Australia to 30% of the contract value. Deliveries began in the autumn

Westland Lysander I.

Westland

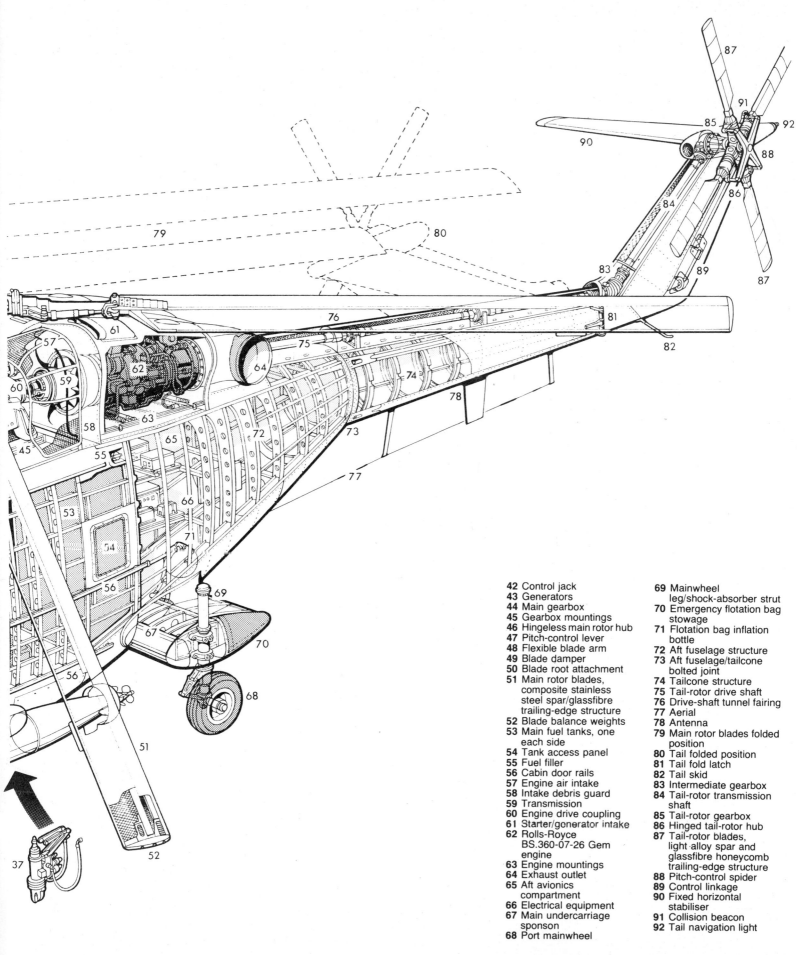

42 Control jack
43 Generators
44 Main gearbox
45 Gearbox mountings
46 Hingeless main rotor hub
47 Pitch-control lever
48 Flexible blade arm
49 Blade damper
50 Blade root attachment
51 Main rotor blades, composite stainless steel spar/glassfibre trailing-edge structure
52 Blade balance weights
53 Main fuel tanks, one each side
54 Tank access panel
55 Fuel filler
56 Cabin door rails
57 Engine air intake
58 Intake debris guard
59 Transmission
60 Engine drive coupling
61 Starter/generator intake
62 Rolls-Royce BS.360-07-26 Gem engine
63 Engine mountings
64 Exhaust outlet
65 Aft avionics compartment
66 Electrical equipment
67 Main undercarriage sponson
68 Port mainwheel

69 Mainwheel leg/shock-absorber strut
70 Emergency flotation bag stowage
71 Flotation bag inflation bottle
72 Aft fuselage structure
73 Aft fuselage/tailcone bolted joint
74 Tailcone structure
75 Tail-rotor drive shaft
76 Drive-shaft tunnel fairing
77 Aerial
78 Antenna
79 Main rotor blades folded position
80 Tail folded position
81 Tail fold latch
82 Tail skid
83 Intermediate gearbox
84 Tail-rotor transmission shaft
85 Tail-rotor gearbox
86 Hinged tail-rotor hub
87 Tail-rotor blades, light alloy spar and glassfibre honeycomb trailing-edge structure
88 Pitch-control spider
89 Control linkage
90 Fixed horizontal stabiliser
91 Collision beacon
92 Tail navigation light

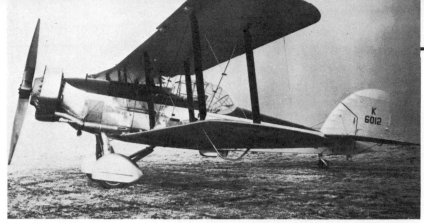

Westland Wallace II.

Westland Wapiti HAs.

Westland Wasp HAS.1.

of 1974. The Mk 50 was the first fully uprated version of the Sea King to fly. It is capable of operation in the roles of anti-submarine search and strike, vertical replenishment, tactical troop lift, search and rescue, casualty evacuation, and self-ferry.

A total of 233 Sea King and Commando aircraft had been ordered by mid-1979.

Data (current versions): *Engines* two 1,238 kW (1,660 shp) Rolls-Royce Gnome H.1400-1 turboshafts *Main rotor diameter* 18.9 m (62 ft 0 in) *Length of fuselage* 17.01 m (55 ft 9¾ in) *Max T-O weight* 9,525 kg (21,000 lb) *Cruising speed* 208 km/h (129 mph) *Range* 1,230 km (764 miles) *Accommodation* (non-ASW models) up to 22 troops, 9 stretchers and two medical attendants; or 2,720 kg (6,000 lb) of internal or 2,948 kg (6,500 lb) of external cargo *Armament* (ASW) up to four Mk 46 homing torpedoes or four Mk 11 depth charges or one Clevite simulator. For secondary role a mounting is provided on the aft frame of the starboard door for a general-purpose machine-gun

Westland Wallace (UK) The Wallace was designed as a two-seat general-purpose biplane capable of day bombing, reconnaissance, photography, army co-operation and night-flying duties. It could also be employed, in certain cases, as a two-seat fighter.

Later achieving fame for its epic flight over Mount Everest (see **Chronology** 3 Apr 1933), the Wallace first appeared in prototype form in 1931 as a development of the Wapiti. The main change was the replacement of the Wapiti's Jupiter engine with a Bristol Pegasus, although alterations to the airframe included a new landing gear. Eventually 64 Wapitis were modified to Wallace standard, powered by the 424.8 kW (570 hp) Pegasus IIM3 engine. These entered service with the RAF from 1933. One aircraft was used as a tanker.

With the Wallace I in service, Westland produced a Wallace II in 1935 powered by a 507 kW (680 hp) Pegasus IV engine. A novel feature was the use of a sliding canopy over the front cockpit and a 'lobster' hood over the rear cockpit, providing the crew with greater comfort and thereby increasing efficiency. The lowered waistline of the forward cockpit improved view. The rear hood was formed of transparent segments that could be locked together to enclose the gunner or folded back to give him a free field of fire for the gun. Production of this version totalled 107, which included three converted Wapitis.

Data (Mk II): *Engine* as above *Wing span* 14.15 m (46 ft 5 in) *Length* 10.41 m (34 ft 2 in) *Max T-O*

weight 2,608 kg (5,750 lb) *Max level speed* 254 km/h (158 mph) *Max range* up to 1,802 km (1,120 miles) *Armament* one forward-firing Vickers machine-gun and one rear-mounted Lewis gun, plus 263–515 kg (580–1,130 lb) of bombs

Westland Wapiti (UK) The Wapiti was a two-seat general-purpose biplane incorporating in its design several de Havilland D.H.9A component parts as requested by the Air Ministry. The prototype first flew in March 1927 and the initial order for 25 production Mk Is included one specially modified aircraft with a more luxurious rear cockpit for the Prince of Wales to fly in.

Mk Is were powered by 313 kW (420 hp) Bristol Jupiter VI engines, but subsequent Mk IIs and Mk IIAs had 343 kW (460 hp) Jupiter VI and 391.2 kW (525 hp) Jupiter VIIIF or similar engines respectively. Small numbers of lengthened Wapiti Vs and unarmed Mk VI trainers brought total production for the RAF to 501; while the type was also adopted by Australia, South Africa (also built under licence), Canada, India and China.

Data (IIA): *Engine* as above *Wing span* 14.15 m (46 ft 5 in) *Length* 9.91 m (32 ft 6 in) *Max T-O weight* 2,449 kg (5,400 lb) *Max level speed* 225 km/h (140 mph) *Range* 579 km (360 miles) *Armament* one forward-firing Vickers machine-gun and one rear-mounted Lewis gun, plus up to 227 kg (500 lb) of bombs

Westland Wasp and Scout (UK) The Wasp light helicopter originated as the Saunders-Roe P.531 and first flew on 20 July 1958. As the production Westland Wasp, it flew on 28 October 1962 and deliveries to the Royal Navy began the

following year; approximately 80 were ordered as HAS.1s. Operated as an anti-submarine helicopter from Royal Navy frigates, it is now being replaced by the Lynx. Wasps remain operational in four other countries.

The Scout is the British Army's equivalent of the Wasp and is flown as a two–five-seat general-purpose helicopter. One hundred and fifty were delivered as AH.1s. Other users are the Australian Navy and Ugandan Police Air Wing.

Data (Scout): *Engine* one derated 511 kW (685 shp) Rolls-Royce Bristol Nimbus 101 or 102 turboshaft *Main rotor diameter* 9.83 m (32 ft 3 in) *Length of fuselage* 9.24 m (30 ft 4 in) *Max T-O weight* 2,045 kg (5,300 lb) *Max level speed* 211 km/h (131 mph) *Range* 510 km (315 miles) *Accommodation* crew of two and, optionally, three passengers, freight or a stretcher

Westland Welkin (UK) Single-seat high-altitude twin-engined fighter, put into production in 1945 but did not enter squadron service.

Westland Widgeon (UK) The Widgeon was a developed version of the Dragonfly (licence-built Sikorsky S-51) with an entirely redesigned forward fuselage to seat five. Power was provided by an Alvis Leonides 521/2 radial engine. The prototype flew for the first time on 23 August 1955 and production models, mostly conversions of Dragonflies, were used in many parts of the world.

Data: *Engine* as above *Main rotor diameter* 14.99 m (49 ft 2 in) *Length of fuselage* 12.44 m (40 ft 10 in) *Max T-O weight* 2,676 kg (5,900 lb) *Max level speed* 177 km/h (110 mph) *Max range* 483 km (300 miles)

Westland Wyvern (UK) The Wyvern was a single-seat naval strike aircraft which first flew as a prototype on 12 December 1946. The small number of pre-production Wyverns were designated TF.1s and were powered by Rolls-Royce Eagle 22 piston engines. The later TF.2 was the first to introduce the specified turboprop engine, in the form of the Armstrong Siddeley Python fitted with two Rotol four-bladed co-axial contra-rotating propellers. The first TF.2 flew on 22 March 1949 and began aircraft carrier trials on board HMS *Illustrious* on 21 June 1950.

Following the T.3 two-seat dual-control trainer version, first flown on 11 February 1950, the S.4 appeared. This was the major production version, incorporating airframe refinements. S.4s entered service with the RN in 1953 and subsequently went to sea on board HMS *Albion* and *Eagle*. It was withdrawn from service in 1958. One hundred and ten TF.2s and S.4s were built.

Data (S.4): *Engine* one 2,735 kW (3,670 shp) plus

Westland Whirlwind I, powered by two 660 kW (885 hp) Rolls-Royce Peregrine I engines. Of 200 ordered for the RAF, only 112 were delivered, first becoming operational as long-range fighters and fighter-bombers in late 1940. Maximum speed was 579 km/h (360 mph).

Westland Wyvern carrying 16 rockets and a torpedo.

5.25 kN (1,180 lb st) Armstrong-Siddeley Python 3 turboprop *Wing span* 13.42 m (44 ft 0 in) *Length* 12.88 m (42 ft 3 in) *Max T-O weight* 11,113 kg (24,500 lb) *Max level speed* 616 km/h (383 mph) *Range* more than 1,448 km (900 miles) *Armament* four 20 mm cannon; external stores included three 1,000 lb bombs, 16 × 60 lb rockets or a 20 in torpedo

White WW-1 Der Jäger D.IX (USA) Single-seat sporting biplane. Plans, kits of materials and difficult to construct parts in finished form are available to amateur builders.

White and Thompson No 3 (UK) Two-seat anti-submarine flying-boat powered by an 89.4 kW (120 hp) Beardmore engine. Eight were delivered to the RNAS in 1915: six to Dover, Fort George and Dundee and then a further two, one with dual controls.

White and Thompson Bognor Bloater (UK) Two-seat coastal patrol biplane with a wooden monocoque fuselage and powered by a 52 kW (70 hp) Renault engine. Twelve were ordered for the RNAS but only ten delivered in 1915, the final two being used for spares and not assembled.

Wibault 7 (France) This single-seat fighter was a great advance over most of its fabric-covered contemporaries. A parasol-wing monoplane, it had a special thick-section metal wing covered by dural strips reinforced at each rib junction by 'pressed fold' skin joints, the whole process being a Wibault patent. The first prototype flew in 1924 with a metal fuselage covered in dural panels. The second prototype was followed by six evaluation machines. These featured corrugated dural sheeting over the fuselage and tailplane, a wide-track landing gear which incorporated oleo-pneumatic shock-absorbers, and modified wing and tailplane

Westland Widgeon.

Vickers-built Wibault 72.

profiles. A further prototype was used as a demonstrator in Spain. Production Wibault 72s had strengthened wing bracing, and it is believed that 60 were delivered to the French Aéronautique Militaire.

A new prototype, the Wibault 73, powered by a liquid-cooled Lorraine 12 Fb engine in place of the 358 kW (480 hp) Gnome-Rhône Jupiter 9 Ad uncowled radial of the Wibault 72, attracted the attention of the Polish Government. It eventually ordered 25 licence-built examples of the original Wibault 72 type and three Wright-powered Wibault 7s from the PZL company. Seven Wibault 73s did, however, go to Paraguay, three of which were still in service 1932 and were used during the Gran Chaco conflict with neighbouring Bolivia.

In Britain 26 Wibault 72s were licence-built by Vickers as Models 121s. One was retained by the RAF for evaluation and the rest were sold to Chile. The French Navy ordered 18 Wibault 74s for Escadrille 7C1 flying from the carrier *Béarn*, and 18 examples of the Wibault 75 photographic-reconnaissance version. The Wibault 74 differed from the Wibault 72 only in having a strengthened rear fuselage and a carrier arrester hook.

The Wibault fighter was rugged as well as manoeuvrable, as proved when an aircraft of the 32nd Aviation Regiment suffered severe wing damage in a mid-air collision during manoeuvres over Dijon on 27 May 1932. Incredibly the pilot was able to make a safe emergency landing. Armament of all versions of the Wibault 7 was twin Vickers 7.92 mm machine-guns.

Data (Wibault 72): *Engine* as above *Wing span* 10.95 m (35 ft 11 in) *Length* 7.55 m (24 ft 9¼ in) *Max T-O weight* 1,520 kg (3,351 lb) *Max level speed* 222 km/h (138 mph)

Wölfert airship with a Daimler engine.

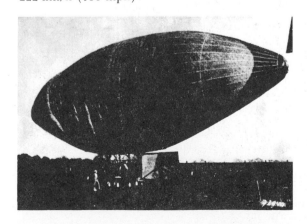

Wibault-Penhoët 280T–283T (France) In 1931 the original Wibault Company merged with the Chantiers de Saint-Nazaire Penhoët to form Wibault-Penhoët. The company's 280 series of three-engined cantilever low-wing airliners were a familiar sight at Croydon and other international airports in the 1930s. The French government bought the two prototypes. Subsequently six production Wibault-Penhoët 282Ts were introduced on the Air Union London–Paris service in 1933. Each had an enclosed cabin for the two crew members and a main cabin for ten passengers. The prototypes originally had fixed divided-type landing gears with exposed struts, but they were later brought up to Wibault-Penhoët 282 standard with trousered units. Ten 1934 Wibault-Penhoët 283Ts closely resembled the earlier batch, but had improved range.

From 1934 to 1938 all the Wibault-Penhoëts were operated by Air France on its routes to London and Berlin. A number of Wibault-Penhoët 282s and 283s, still in flying condition in September 1939, were taken over by the Armée de l'Air for military transport duties. Subsequent Wibault-Penhoët designs included the 360 T5 five-seat cabin monoplane.

Data (Wibault-Penhoët 283T): *Engines* three 261 kW (350 hp) Gnome-Rhône Titan Major 7Kd radials *Wing span* 22.61 m (74 ft 2¼ in) *Length* 17.0 m (55 ft 9 in) *Max T-O weight* 6,350 kg (13,999 lb) *Max level speed* 251 km/h (156 mph) *Range* 1,000 km (621 miles)

Wicko Monoplane and Warferry (UK) Foster, Wikner Aircraft Company was formed in 1936 to manufacture the Wicko two-seat braced high-wing monoplane powered by a 97 kW (130 hp) de Havilland Gipsy Major engine. A modified version with accommodation for a third person was known as the Warferry. The 1941 *Jane's* states that the RAF used the Monoplane as a communications type. Three civil Warferrys were impressed by the RAF during World War II.

Wideröes C.5 Polar (Norway) Six-seat general utility monoplane of 1948 powered by a 335.3 kW (450 hp) Pratt & Whitney R-985 Wasp Junior radial engine. The Polar took part in the Norwegian-British-Swedish expedition to the Antarctic in 1950–51.

Wight 840 (UK) Two-seat twin-float anti-submarine biplane powered by a 168 kW (225 hp) Sunbeam engine. Main armament was a 14 in torpedo. A total of 88 was ordered from Wight, Beardmore, Dalmuir and Portholme Aerodrome, of which up to 19 may not have been delivered and 20 were delivered as spares. In service with the RNAS from 1915 to 1917.

Wight Baby seaplane (UK) Three examples of the Baby seaplane were delivered to the RNAS. In addition Wight built a single example of a Gnome-powered aircraft, designation unknown.

Wight Pusher Seaplane (UK) Of pre-World War I design, the Pusher Seaplane was a large two–three-seat reconnaissance seaplane powered by a 149 kW (200 hp) Salmson-built Canton-Unné engine. Eleven were acquired by the RNAS. At least one was sent to the Dardanelles on board HMS *Ark Royal* in 1915.

Wight Seaplane (UK) The two-seat Wight Seaplane, sometimes referred to as the 'Converted' Seaplane, was a naval development of an earlier landplane bomber. Power was provided by one 238.5 kW (320 hp) Rolls-Royce Eagle VI, 197.5 kW (265 hp) Sunbeam Maori or 179 kW (240 hp) Renault engine. Fifty were ordered for the RNAS (plus a further batch of 30 that was cancelled), of which ten were completed as landplanes and five were not delivered.

Willows Airship No 1 (UK) The first of the Willows Airships was launched in 1905 and was a great success, being easily steerable with its swivelling propeller. Power was provided by a 5.2 kW (7 hp) Peugeot engine, giving a maximum speed of 19.3 km/h (12 mph). Length was about 22.59 m (74 ft 0 in).

Windecker AC-7 Eagle 1 (USA) Four-seat cabin monoplane powered by a 212.4 kW (285 hp) Continental IO-520-C engine.

Wing Derringer (USA) Two-seat light aircraft powered by a 119 kW (160 hp) Lycoming IO-320-B1C engine.

Wittman Tailwind Models W-8 and W-10 (USA) Two-seat cabin monoplanes, plans and prefabricated components for which are available to amateur constructors.

Wölfert NR airship (Germany) The Wölfert airship, launched in 1886, was 28.0 m (91 ft 10 in) long and originally driven by three hand-operated propellers. In 1888 it was fitted with a 1.5 kW (2 hp) Daimler engine.

Wölfert NR airship Deutschland (Germany) Following experiments with an earlier airship, launched in 1879 and driven by hand-operated propellers, Wölfert launched the NR in 1886. Power was provided by a tiny Daimler benzine engine. Wölfert then experimented with a benzine vaporiser which set fire to the airship. Both Wölfert and his passenger Knabe were killed in the resulting explosion, becoming the first people to die in an airship accident.

Wren 460 (USA) Four-seat STOL light monoplane based on the Cessna 182. A small number were produced from 1965.

Wright Flyer and early gliders (USA) At 10.35 am on Thursday 17 December 1903 at Kill Devil Hills, Kitty Hawk, North Carolina, Orville Wright piloted the Flyer biplane on a flight which lasted just 12 seconds and covered about 36.5 m (120 ft), so recording the world's first powered, sustained and controllable flight of a man-carrying aeroplane. The 9 kW (12 hp) engine and airframe were of Orville and Wilbur Wright's design and manufacture. On 23 June 1905 the first flight took place of the Flyer III powered by an 11–15.6 kW (15–21 hp) Wright engine. This was the first practical version of the Flyer, being fully controllable.

The origins of the Flyer can be traced back to the 1.52 m (5 ft) span biplane kite which they flew in August 1899. Convinced that the biplane configuration was the most satisfactory, they designed and built Glider No 1 (5.18 m; 17 ft 0 in span) and flew it in 1900 as a kite and glider. In the following year Glider No 2 was completed with a wing span of 6.71 m (22 ft 0 in). No 2

Wright Glider No 1 being flown as a kite.

Wright Flyer takes off for the first time.

featured anhedral on the wings, while for control a hip cradle was installed which enabled the pilot to warp the wings by swinging his body. Up to this point the Wrights had used some technical data pooled by other aviators, but the results were considered so poor that they decided to make further investigations of their own.

Having tested many aerofoil sections in a wind tunnel and on a bicycle (not the first wind tunnel, see **Chronology** 1871), the brothers built Glider No 3 in August and September 1902. This had a much greater wing span of 9.78 m (32 ft 1 in). With No 3 the brothers made nearly 1,000 gliding flights. During the course of the experiments, the twin fixed fins were replaced by a single movable rudder, operated by the old hip-cradle method. So successful was the modified No 3 that it was decided the time had come to construct a powered version, which became the Flyer.
Data (Flyer): *Engine* as above *Wing span* 12.29 m (40 ft 4 in) *Length* 6.43 m (21 ft 1 in) *Max T-O weight* 340.2 kg (750 lb) *Approximate max level speed* 48 km/h (30 mph)

Wright Model A (USA) The Model A or 'standard' biplane was similar to the original Flyer but had seats for a pilot and passenger. One was bought by the US Army (see **Chronology** 17 Sep 1908 and 2 Aug 1909). During 1908 and 1909 Wilbur Wright, Comte Charles de Lambert,

Wright Model A.

Walter H. Brookins and Ralph Johnston established world speed, height and distance records in 'A's. Data: *Engine* one 22.4 kW (30 hp) Wright *Wing span* 12.5 m (41 ft 0 in) *Length* 8.84 m (29 ft 0 in) *Max T-O weight* 544 kg (1,200 lb) *Max level speed* 64 km/h (40 mph)

Wright Models B to R (USA) The Model B of 1910 was basically a 22.4–26 kW (30–35 hp) version of the Model A, but with a wheel and skid landing gear and rear-mounted instead of forward-mounted elevators. The US Army received two for use as pilot trainers. The Model C was a further improvement featuring for the first time proper dual controls. The Army purchased seven with 37.25 kW (50 hp) engines, while the US Navy purchased a 44.7 kW (60 hp) version as the C-H (hydro) with three-step floats. The Model D was similar to the C but was a single-seater, two of which went to the Army.

Out of alphabetical sequence was the Model R or Roadster of 1910 powered by a 22.4–26 kW (30–35 hp) engine. From the Roadster was developed the famous Baby Wright, a single-seat racing version.

Yakovlev Yak-1.

Wright Model K.

Among the other civil and military Wright aircraft of the period were the Model Ex, a special smaller single-seat duplicate of the B for exhibition work; and the Model F, basically an attempt to produce a new and more modern military aircraft by fitting the usual wings and pusher propellers to a conventional fuselage and tail unit. The Model H-S was a shorter-span and less powerful version. Also rejected, but by the Navy, was the Model G Aeroboat, a 44.7 kW (60 hp) Wright-engined flying-boat.

The final aircraft produced by the Wright Aeronautical Company were the Models K and L. The K was a conventional twin-float seaplane, only the twin propellers (tractor) chain-driven from a single engine giving its origin away. The Navy purchased a single example. The Model L was a 52 kW (70 hp) single-seat scouting biplane of 1915.

WSK Mielec TS-8 Bies (Poland) Two-seat fully aerobatic trainer, first flown on 23 July 1955 and equipped for night and all-weather flying. The third prototype was shown in public at the Poznan Fair in July 1956. On 28 December 1956 a Bies set a new international height record for aircraft in the FAI Class C.1c, by attaining an altitude of 7,084 m (23,242 ft). Production aircraft were delivered to the Polish Air Force.
Data: *Engine* one 238.5 kW (320 hp) Narkiewicz WN-3 radial *Wing span* 10.5 m (34 ft 5½ in)

Length 8.5 m (27 ft 11 in) *Max T-O weight* (as instrument trainer) 1,600 kg (3,525 lb) *Max level speed* 312 km/h (194 mph) *Range* 800 km (497 miles)

WSK-PZL Swidnik SM-1 (Poland) See **Mil Mi-1**

Yakovlev Yak-1/-3/-7/-9 (USSR) Alexander Yakovlev was to become world-famous for the family of fighter aircraft which sprang from his Yak-1. Their qualities were such that they must rank alongside their contemporaries in this category of combat aircraft, namely the American P-51 Mustang, the British Supermarine Spitfire, Germany's Messerschmitt Bf 109 and Japan's Mitsubishi A6M Zero-Sen.

In 1938 details were circulated of an official requirement for a new single-seat fighter and several aircraft were evolved to meet this specification. None were more impressive on first sight than Yakovlev's I-26 and early flight tests were to confirm the old engineer's adage that 'if it looks right it is right'. Construction of small numbers of pre-production aircraft began before official testing was completed in 1939, with the result that a small contingent was seen for the first time in 1940 participating in the May Day fly-past over Moscow. By the end of 1940 several units had received allocations for evaluation and familiarisation, but before production was well established the German invasion of Russia had begun.

Before Russia's entry into World War II, the principal factory at Fili, near Moscow, was said to be capable of producing from 300 to 350 twin-engined bombers a year. Similarly, the plant at Gorki was said to be able to turn out five single-seat fighters a day. Other factories were however seriously short of skilled labour and only partly in operation. With the start of hostilities and to guard against their production factories being destroyed or captured by the enemy, plans were made and implemented for all important projects to be transferred to new facilities in east Russia, and high on the priorities of this move was the new fighter, by then identified as the Yak-1. Almost unbelievably the first examples began to appear within six weeks of the move and by the end of the year several hundred had been delivered to the Red Air Force.

Of mixed construction, the Yak-1 was of cantilever low-wing monoplane configuration. Wings were all-wood with fabric covering, but the Frise-type ailerons had fabric-covered light alloy frames, and the trailing-edge flaps were all-metal. The fuselage was a welded steel-tube structure with light alloy skins forward and fabric covering aft, and the tail unit a mixed wood and steel-tube structure. Landing gear was of the retractable tailwheel type, with the main units retracting inward into the undersurface of the wing centre-section. An 820 kW (1,100 hp) Klimov M-105 in-line engine was used to power the prototype and early production aircraft; this was a developed version of the Hispano-Suiza 12Ycrs. Further development of this engine resulted in the M-105PF introduced later and which, with two-speed supercharger, provided 925 kW (1,240 hp) for take-off.

Armament was to vary considerably, the initial production version carrying an engine-mounted 20 mm cannon and two 7.62 mm fuselage-mounted machine-guns; later variants had machine-guns of 12.7 mm calibre and underwing hardpoints that could accommodate launch rails for rocket projectiles, or bomb racks.

Inevitably the constant request was for more effective combat aircraft, with greater speed, manoeuvrability and payload. This led first to the Yak-1M. The major problem, of course, was that no time could be spared for significant changes on the production line, since output was paramount. This meant that Yakovlev and his team were limited to reductions in weight and drag to achieve their goal. Thus the Yak-1M represented but an interim step in the desired direction, with reduced wing span and area, limitations in the armament and modifications to the cooling systems. And to enhance the pilot's view for combat, the rear fuselage was cut down and an all-round clear-view canopy introduced.

When tested in 1942 this was to demonstrate considerably improved performance – especially in terms of manoeuvrability – and was to become regarded as a most formidable close-combat fighter. Further refinements were made at a later date, confined largely to aerodynamic improvements. But with the introduction of the Klimov M-105PF-2 offering slightly more power, plus a new three-bladed constant-speed propeller, the resulting aircraft became redesignated Yak-3. When this entered service in July 1943, it was found that at altitudes below about 5,000 m (16,400 ft) it was superior to both the Focke-Wulf Fw 190A and the Messerschmitt Bf 109G. Evaluation was to show that at its optimum altitude it was faster than early versions of the Spitfire. Final variant of this Yak-3 development was the -3U with a 1,230 kW (1,650 hp) Klimov M-107A engine, all-metal airframe and armament of one 37 mm and two 20 mm cannon; this entered service just too late to be used operationally during World War II.

A two-seat trainer conversion of the Yak-1 (designated initially UTI-26) led to it entering production in late 1941 under the designation Yak-7V. In addition to the two-seat configuration, this also had the improvements which had produced the Yak-1M. Its performance was so good that when it was decided to evolve a night-fighter version of the Yak-1, the -7V was selected as its basis. This was a single-seat aircraft, differing from the trainer version in having improved equipment and advanced radio, and this duly entered production as the Yak-7A. A day-fighter

version was evolved shortly afterwards, under the designation Yak-7B, which differed only by equipment changes. This latter version was to be built extensively after successful introduction into service in 1942, but was later relegated to second-line duties when the definitive Yak-9 began to reach the VVS in quantities.

Developed directly from the Yak-7, the Yak-9 was to prove so successful that more than 17,000 of this version alone were built. It originated during 1942 when a longer-range variant of the Yak-7 was proposed. This was required to offset the major shortcomings of the Yak-1/-7Bs then in wide-scale service, namely their very limited range.

To achieve an improvement in range, the wooden wing of the Yak-1 was redesigned with lightweight metal spars replacing the original wooden units, thus providing for the introduction of larger-capacity fuel cells within the wings. Other changes included the installation of a 969 kW (1,300 hp) M-105PF-1 engine; small modifications to the structure; some variations in equipment; and armament comprising a 20 mm cannon and one or two 12.7 mm machine-guns. The resulting Yak-9 was ready in time to be introduced into the Battle of Stalingrad and certainly made its presence felt.

Not surprisingly, the capability of this version was to lead to many variants, including the Yak-9B fighter-bomber, which had a small fuselage bomb bay; the Yak-9D long-range fighter, which had a 1,014 kW (1,360 hp) M-105PF-3 engine and increased fuel capacity; Yak-9DD long-range escort fighter with provision to carry fuel drop-tanks; the Yak-9PVO night interceptor; and Yak-9R, a reconnaissance version of the -9B. Variations in anti-armour weapons accounted for the Yak-9DK (45 mm cannon); Yak-9T-37 (37 mm cannon and one 12.7 mm machine-gun); and the basically similar Yak-9T-45, which substituted a 45 mm cannon for the 37 mm weapon. Post-war development led to the all-metal Yak-9U with 1,230 kW (1,650 hp) M-107A and revised armament; a fighter-interceptor version known as the -9P; and -9UF reconnaissance and Yak-9U dual-control trainers.

Production of this remarkable family of fighters was to exceed 37,000, and many, especially Yak-9Ps, were to remain in service with Russia's satellite nations for some years after the end of World War II.

Data (Yak-1, early production): *Engine* one 820 kW (1,100 hp) Klimov M-105P. *Wing span* 10.0 m (32 ft 9¾ in) *Length* 8.48 m (27 ft 9¾ in) *Max T-O weight* 2,820 kg (6,217 lb) *Max level speed* 536–580 km/h (333–360 mph) *Range* 850 km (528 miles) *Armament* one 20 mm engine-mounted cannon, two 7.62 mm machine-guns, up to 200 kg (440 lb) of bombs, or six 25 kg (56 lb) rocket-impelled fragmentation bombs carried on special guide-rail-type racks, three under each wing.
Data (Yak-9D): *Engine* one 1,014 kW (1,360 hp) Klimov M-105PF-3 *Wing span* 10.0 m (32 ft 9¾ in) *Length* 8.55 m (28 ft 0½ in) *Max T-O weight* 3,200 kg (7,055 lb) *Max level speed* 592 km/h (368 mph) *Range* 1,040–1,410 km (646–

Yakovlev

Yakovlev Yak-12.

876 miles) *Armament* one 20 mm engine-mounted cannon and one 12.7 mm machine-gun

Yakovlev Yak-2 and Yak-4 (USSR) In 1939 the new BB-22 bomber flew with two M-103 engines. It was put into production as the Yak-2, but with the arrival of the improved Yak-4 was converted for secondary duties. The Yak-4 was a direct development of the Yak-2, powered by 820 kW (1,100 hp) M-105 engines. It was really a high-speed dive-bomber, attack and reconnaissance aircraft rather than a straight bomber and the 1941 *Jane's* quoted designation P-2 for it under the 'Shtormovik' class. However in service it was not entirely successful and production was cut short, the type being used mainly as a reconnaissance aircraft. Maximum level speed was 540 km/h (335.5 mph).

Yakovlev Yak-4.

Yakovlev Yak-7.

Yakovlev Yak-6 (USSR) The Yak-6 was actually known in the early 1930s as the AIR 6 and was a two–three-seat smaller version of the five-seat AIR 5. Power was provided by a 74.5 kW (100 hp) M-11 engine, giving a maximum speed of 170 km/h (106 mph). It is believed that the Yak-6 was operated commercially as an air taxi.

Yakovlev Yak-17UTI.

Yakovlev Yak-11 (USSR) Known to NATO as *Moose*, the Yak-11 was a two-seat intermediate trainer and became a standard type with the Soviet forces and those of a large number of other countries. Production was also undertaken in Czechoslovakia as the C-11. Power was provided by a 545 kW (730 hp) ASh-21 engine.

Yakovlev Yak-12 (USSR) The Yak-12 was a single 179 kW (240 hp) AI-14R-engined high-wing light general-purpose aircraft built in several versions from the late 1940s. It was known to NATO as *Creek*.

Yakovlev Yak-18.

Yakovlev Yak-14 (USSR) Four-seat liaison and training monoplane of similar type to the Yak-12 but powered by a 108 kW (145 hp) M-11M engine.

Yakovlev Yak-15 (USSR) The first Soviet jet fighter, the Yak-15 was developed from an experimental Yak-3 fitted with a turbojet engine. Power for the Yak-15 was provided by an 8.8 kN (1,980 lb st) RD-10 (Junkers Jumo 004B). The prototype flew for the first time on 24 April 1946 and production aircraft followed. Olga Yam-schikova, an employee of the company, is said to have flown the fighter and was therefore probably the first woman to fly a turbojet-powered fighter. Wing span was 9.2 m (30 ft 2¼ in) and maximum speed up to 810 km/h (503 mph).

Yakovlev Yak-16 (USSR) Ten-passenger transport aircraft powered by two 559 kW (750 hp) ASh-21 radial engines.

Yakovlev Yak-17 (USSR) This was basically an improved and more powerful version of the Yak-15 fitted with a 9.8 kN (2,200 lb st) RD-10A turbojet engine. Armament remained two 23 mm NS-23 cannon in the nose. It was known to NATO as *Feather*. A two-seat training version was also built as the Yak-17UTI (*Magnet*).

Yakovlev Yak-18 (USSR) Normally a single or two-seat training and aerobatic aircraft powered by a 223.6 kW (300 hp) Ivchenko AI-14RF radial engine. It has been built in several versions since the prototype flew in 1946 (see **Yak-52**). The current Yak-18T is an extensively redesigned four-seater powered by a 269 kW (360 hp) Vedeneev M-14P radial engine.

Yakovlev Yak-23 (USSR) Known to NATO as *Flora*, the Yak-23 was a further improvement of the Yak-15/17 series, this time of all-metal construction and powered by a 15.7 kN (3,530 lb st) RD-500 turbojet engine. It was not produced in very great numbers but served with the Soviet Air Force and with Bulgaria, Czechoslovakia and Poland. Maximum level speed was 885 km/h (550 mph).

Yakovlev Yak-25.

Yakovlev Yak-24 (USSR) The Yak-24, known to NATO as *Horse*, was a tandem-rotor helicopter first flown in prototype form in 1955. It was first seen in public at Tushino in 1955. It entered service with the Soviet Air Force and was produced for commercial operation with Aeroflot, the Yak-24A being the basic 30-passenger version. Power was provided by two 1,267 kW (1,700 hp) ASh-82V engines, giving a maximum speed of 210 km/h (130 mph).

Yakovlev Yak-18T.

Yakovlev Yak-23 in Polish markings.

Yakovlev Yak-25, Yak-26 and Yak-27 (USSR) The original version of this twin-jet all-weather fighter entered service with the Soviet Air Force in 1955. Early production aircraft, known to NATO as *Flashlight-A*, were subsequently re-engined with two Klimov RD-9 turbojets as the Yak-25F. The Yak-25R (*Flashlight-B*) was produced as the multi-purpose tactical version. The Yak-26 *Mangrove* and *Flashlight-C* and Yak-27 *Flashlight-D*

were training, improved all-weather interceptor and tactical reconnaissance versions respectively. Data (*Flashlight-C*, estimated): *Engines* two 39.23 kN (8,820 lb st) Klimov RD-9 turbojets *Wing span* 11.75 m (38 ft 6 in) *Length* 18.9 m (62 ft 0 in) *Normal T-O weight* 11,350 kg (25,000 lb) *Max level speed* 1,009 km/h (627 mph)

Yakovlev Yak-28 (USSR) First seen in numbers at the 1961 Soviet Day flypast, the Yak-28 was developed as a supersonic multi-purpose aircraft. It is known to NATO by the reporting names *Brewer* and *Firebar*, depending on the role. Several versions have been reported, as follows:

Brewer-A to -C (**Yak-28**) Two-seat tactical-attack versions. Single cockpit for pilot with blister canopy, and glazed nose for navigator/bomb aimer. Corresponding to Yak-26 (*Mangrove*) and produced to replace the Il-28 in the Soviet Air Force. Guns semi-submerged in each side of the fuselage on some aircraft; on starboard side only on others. Internal bomb bay between underfuselage radome and the rear main landing-gear unit. Now used only in places of secondary importance.
Brewer-D Reconnaissance version with cameras in bomb bay.
Brewer-E First Soviet operational ECM escort aircraft, deployed in 1970. Underfuselage radome deleted. Active ECM unit built into bomb bay, from which it projects in form of a semi-cylindrical pack. Attachment under each outer wing, outboard of external fuel tank, for a rocket pod.
Firebar Tandem two-seat all-weather fighter derivative of Yak-28, corresponding to Yak-27. Nose radome. Internal weapons bay deleted. *Anab* air-to-air missile under each wing instead of guns. Identified as Yak-28P (Perekhvatchik: interceptor) at 1967 Domodedovo display, the suffix 'P' indicating that the design had been adapted for the fighter role.
Maestro (**Yak-28U**) Trainer version of *Firebar*.

Yakovlev Yak-24s.

Yakovlev Yak-28 **Brewer-C.**

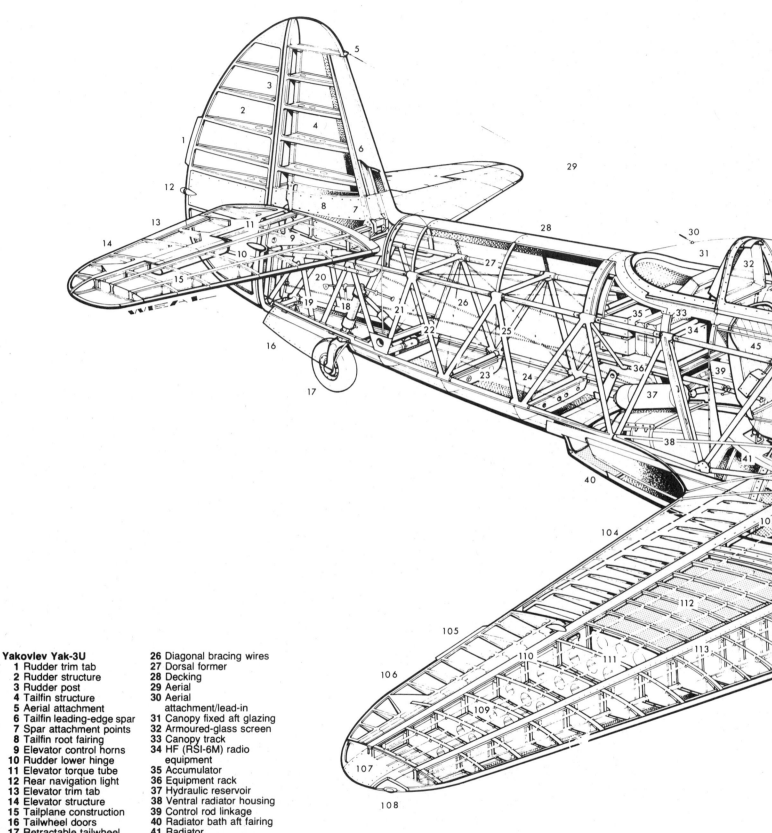

Yakovlev Yak-3U
1 Rudder trim tab
2 Rudder structure
3 Rudder post
4 Tailfin structure
5 Aerial attachment
6 Tailfin leading-edge spar
7 Spar attachment points
8 Tailfin root fairing
9 Elevator control horns
10 Rudder lower hinge
11 Elevator torque tube
12 Rear navigation light
13 Elevator trim tab
14 Elevator structure
15 Tailplane construction
16 Tailwheel doors
17 Retractable tailwheel
18 Tailwheel oleo
19 Tailwheel well
20 Wheel-impact door-closure struts
21 Tailwheel retraction jack
22 Lifting tube
23 Tubular-steel fuselage framework
24 Ventral former
25 Elevator control cables
26 Diagonal bracing wires
27 Dorsal former
28 Decking
29 Aerial
30 Aerial attachment/lead-in
31 Canopy fixed aft glazing
32 Armoured-glass screen
33 Canopy track
34 HF (RSI-6M) radio equipment
35 Accumulator
36 Equipment rack
37 Hydraulic reservoir
38 Ventral radiator housing
39 Control rod linkage
40 Radiator bath aft fairing
41 Radiator
42 Seat support frame
43 Pilot's seat pan
44 Trim-tab control console (port)
45 Padded (armoured) seat back
46 Switchbox
47 Aft-sliding cockpit canopy
48 Reflector sight

49 One-piece moulded armoured-glass windscreen
50 Instrument panel coaming
51 Control column
52 Instrument panel starboard console
53 Control linkage
54 Rudder pedal bar
55 Bulkhead
56 Frame
57 Gun support tray
58 Bracket
59 Shpital'ny-Vladimirov B-20 (MP-20) 20 mm cannon (port and starboard)

60 Port flap
61 Guide rollers
62 Aileron push-rod control linkage
63 Aileron trim tab
64 Port aileron
65 Port wing tip
66 Port navigation light
67 Pitot tube
68 Forward spar
69 Port outboard fuel tank
70 Fuel filler cap
71 Supercharger intake scoop
72 Intake ducting
73 Gun cocking mechanism fairings

74 Supercharger housing
75 Cowling frame
76 Engine bearer/firewall attachment
77 Oil tank
78 Ammunition boxes
79 Cowling aft frame
80 Exhaust stubs
81 Blast tubes
82 Gun muzzle troughs
83 Filler cap
84 Coolant header tank
85 Propeller pitch mechanism
86 VISh-107 variable-pitch metal propeller
87 Propeller spinner

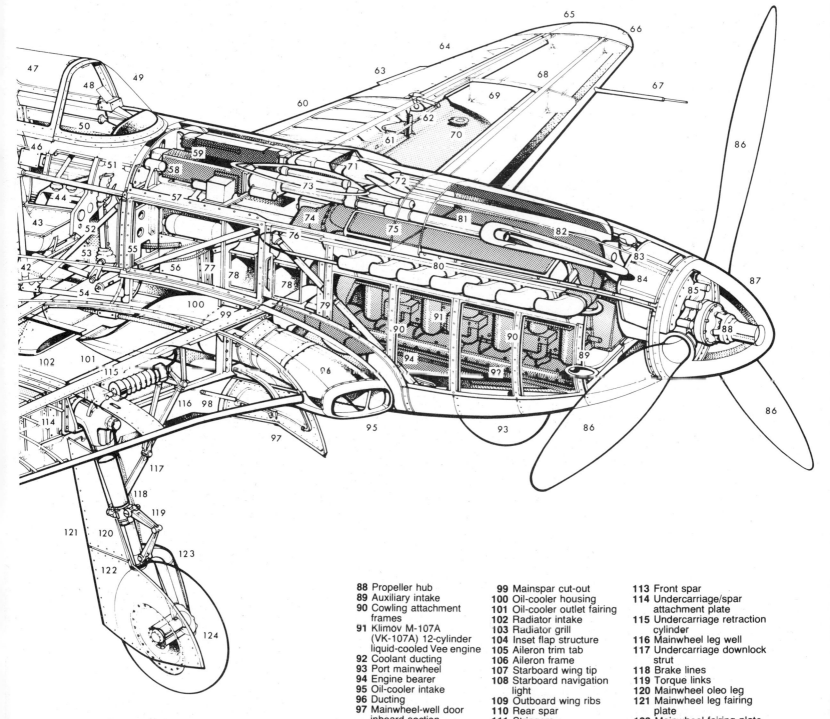

88 Propeller hub
89 Auxiliary intake
90 Cowling attachment frames
91 Klimov M-107A (VK-107A) 12-cylinder liquid-cooled Vee engine
92 Coolant ducting
93 Port mainwheel
94 Engine bearer
95 Oil-cooler intake
96 Ducting
97 Mainwheel-well door inboard section
98 Wheel-impact door-closure struts

99 Mainspar cut-out
100 Oil-cooler housing
101 Oil-cooler outlet fairing
102 Radiator intake
103 Radiator grill
104 Inset flap structure
105 Aileron trim tab
106 Aileron frame
107 Starboard wing tip
108 Starboard navigation light
109 Outboard wing ribs
110 Rear spar
111 Stringers
112 Starboard outboard fuel tank

113 Front spar
114 Undercarriage/spar attachment plate
115 Undercarriage retraction cylinder
116 Mainwheel leg well
117 Undercarriage downlock strut
118 Brake lines
119 Torque links
120 Mainwheel oleo leg
121 Mainwheel leg fairing plate
122 Mainwheel fairing plate
123 Axle fork
124 Starboard mainwheel

Yakovlev

Yakovlev Yak-36
Forger-A.

Normal cockpit layout replaced by two individual single-seat cockpits in tandem, each with its own canopy. Front canopy sideways-hinged to starboard; rear canopy rearward-sliding.

More than 300 Yak-28P *Firebar*s continue to form a significant component of the Soviet home-defence interceptor force. *Brewer*s are being relegated from front-line attack to support roles, with the emphasis on ECM, reconnaissance and operational training.

Data (Yak-28P, estimated): *Engines* two afterburning turbojets, rated at 58.35 kN (13,120 lb st) each *Wing span* 12.95 m (42 ft 6 in) *Length* 21.65 m (71 ft 0½ in) *Max T-O weight* 15,875 kg (35,000 lb) *Max level speed* Mach 1.1 *Range* 1,930–2,575 km (1,200–1,600 miles) *Armament* two *Anab* air-to-air missiles

Yakovlev Yak-36 (USSR) Known to NATO as *Forger*, this is the VTOL combat aircraft deployed by the Soviet Navy on the *Kiev* and *Minsk*, the first two of its 40,000 ton carrier/cruisers to put to sea. Two versions have been observed on the ships: the *Forger-A* basic single-seat combat aircraft, and *Forger-B* two-seat training version. Estimates put the thrust of *Forger-A*'s primary power plant (possibly based on the Lyulka AL-21) at around 78.0 kN (17,500 lb st), and the thrust of each Koliesov lift-jet engine, installed in the fuselage immediately aft of the cockpit to provide vertical thrust, at 25.0 kN (5,600 lb st).

Data (*Forger-A*, estimated): *Engines* as above *Wing span* 7.0 m (23 ft 0 in) *Length* 15.0 m (49 ft 3 in) *Max T-O weight* 10,000 kg (22,050 lb) *Max level speed* Mach 1.3

Yakovlev Yak-40 (USSR) The Yak-40 is a three-turbofan short-haul transport aircraft. The prototype flew for the first time on 21 October 1966 and production was initiated in 1967. It made its first passenger flight in Aeroflot service on 30 September 1968. By the summer of 1976 more than 800 had been built, most for service with Aeroflot, some as air ambulances. Others serve with the Soviet forces. Considerable numbers have also been exported to eight countries. Data: *Engines* three 14.7 kN (3,300 lb st) Ivchenko AI-25 turbofans *Wing span* 25.0 m (82 ft 0¼ in) *Length* 20.36 m (66 ft 9½ in) *Max T-O weight* 16,000 kg (35,275 lb) *Max level speed* 600 km/h (373 mph) *Max range* 2,000 km (1,240 miles) *Accommodation* 27–32 passengers

Yakovlev Yak-42 (USSR) On the basis of experience with the Yak-40, the Yakovlev design bureau has developed for Aeroflot this larger civil airliner with a similar three-engined layout. The first of three prototypes flew on 7 March 1975, furnished as a 100-passenger local-service version. The second had accommodation for 120 passengers.

Data (performance estimated): *Engines* three 63.2 kN (14,200 lb st) D-36 high-bypass-ratio turbofans *Wing span* 34.2 m (112 ft 2½ in) *Length* 36.38 m (119 ft 4¼ in) *Max T-O weight* 52,000 kg (114,640 lb) *Normal cruising speed* 820 km/h (510 mph) *Range* 1,000 km (620 miles)

Yakovlev Yak-50 (USSR) Sporting aircraft, which won the 1976 world aerobatic championships. Power is provided by a 268 kW (360 hp) Vedeneev (Ivchenko) M-14P radial engine, giving a maximum speed of 320 km/h (199 mph).

Yakovlev Yak-52 (USSR) Announced in 1978, this is a tandem two-seat variant of the Yak-50 and is expected to replace the Yak-18 as the standard ab initio trainer for Soviet pilots. Maximum level speed is 285 km/h (177 mph).

Yeoman YA1 Cropmaster (Australia) Single/two-seat agricultural monoplane, the prototype of which first flew on 15 January 1960. Production versions followed.

Yermolaev Yer-2 and Yer-4 (USSR) Several hundred Yer-2 twin-engined medium bombers were built in Russia during World War II, armed with three machine-guns or four machine-guns and two cannon in nose, dorsal and ventral positions, plus up to 5,000 kg (11,000 lb) of bombs. The Yer-4 was a subsequent development of the Yer-2.

Yokosuka Navy B3Y1 (Japan) The three-seat

Yakovlev Yak-42.

B3Y1 (Navy Type 92 Carrier-Borne Torpedo Bomber) was the production version of the Type 13KAI – an improved Mitsubishi B1M designed at the Yokosuka Naval Air Arsenal. Power was provided by a 559 kW (750 hp) Type 91 engine and armament comprised one 7.7 mm forward-firing and one 7.7 mm rear-mounted machine-guns and an 800 kg torpedo or bombs.

A total of 130 was built from 1933 at the Aichi works. In service these proved a disappointment and were not well suited to carrier operations. During the Sino-Japanese conflict that began again on 7 July 1937 B3Y1s flew from the aircraft carrier *Hosho* against mainland targets, supported by others operated from land bases.

Data: *Engine* as above *Wing span* 13.5 m (44 ft 4 in) *Length* 9.5 m (31 ft 2 in) *Max T-O weight* 3,200 kg (7,055 lb) *Max level speed* 220 km/h (136 mph)

Yokosuka Navy B4Y1 (Japan) The B4Y1 (Navy Type 96) was a 626 kW (840 hp) Nakajima Hikari-engined torpedo bomber, 200 of which went into service from 1936 on board Japanese aircraft carriers. Armament comprised one rear-mounted 7.7 mm machine-gun and an 800 kg torpedo or bombs.

Data: *Engine* as above *Wing span* 15.0 m (49 ft 3 in) *Length* 10.15 m (33 ft 3¼ in) *Max T-O weight* 3,600 kg (7,936 lb) *Max level speed* 278 km/h (173 mph) *Range* 1,575 km (979 miles)

Yokosuka D4Y Suisei (Japan) Known to the Allies as *Judy*, the D4Y was designed by the Yokosuka Naval Air Arsenal (Depot) as No 13 Experimental Carrier-borne Bomber and was accepted for production in 1942 as the Type 2 Reconnaissance Aircraft, Model 11. In mid-1943 it was reconverted to a carrier-based dive-bomber as the Model 12 Suisei (Comet), adapted for catapult launching. The Model 11 versions were powered by the 879.3 kW (1,180 hp) Aichi Atsuta 21 engine, the Japanese version of the German Daimler-Benz DB 601A, while the Model 12 had the 1,043.3 kW (1,400 hp) Atsuta 32 engine; the two versions of the aircraft were designated D4Y1 and D4Y2 respectively.

A radial-engined version was also produced as the D4Y3 or Model 33, fitted with a 1,162.5 kW (1,560 hp) Mitsubishi Kinsei 62. In other respects it was identical to the Model 12. Benefiting from the increase in power the D4Y3 was faster than the D4Y1 and – according to the 1945–46 *Jane's* – faster than the D4Y2, with a

Yokosuka MXY 7 Ohka.

maximum speed of 624 km/h (388 mph) at 5,640 m (18,500 ft). However it is normally accepted that the D4Y2 was the fastest with a speed of 580 km/h (360 mph), although this is open to doubt. D4Y3s were normally operated from land bases and all types ended their careers on suicide attacks against Allied shipping. Production of all versions amounted to 2,319 aircraft.

Data (D4Y2): *Engine* as above *Wing span* 11.5 m (37 ft 8¾ in) *Length* 10.2 m (33 ft 7 in) *Max T-O weight* 3,910 kg (8,620 lb) *Max level speed* 580 km/h (360 mph) *Max range* 2,110 km (1,310 miles) *Armament* two forward-firing 7.7 mm and one rear-mounted 7.92 mm machine-guns, plus one 500 kg or 250 kg bomb and other light bombs

Yokosuka E14Y1 (Japan) Known to the Allies as *Glen*, the E14Y1 was a small two-seat reconnaissance seaplane for use from submarines. Power was provided by a 268 kW (360 hp) engine and armament comprised just one rear-mounted 7.7 mm machine-gun.

Yokosuka K1Y, K2Y, K4Y and K5Y (Japan) Biplane trainers, all used at one time or another during World War II.

Yokosuka MXY-7 Ohka (Japan) Known to the Allies as *Baka* (the Japanese word for idiot or fool), the Ohka suicide aircraft was seemingly inspired by the German flying bomb used in Europe.

The Ohka consisted of a cylindrical fuselage 6.0 m (19 ft 10 in) long, mid-cantilever wings of 5.0 m (16 ft 5 in) span and a twin-ruddered tail unit. The nose of the fuselage carried a warhead of some 1,200 kg (2,645 lb) of trinitro-aminol and was provided with a nose fuse and four base fuses. Behind the warhead was the pilot's cockpit with blister canopy and simple controls. The propulsion unit of the Model 11 major production version (755 built) consisted of three Type 4 Mk 1 Model 20 rocket tubes, giving a combined thrust of 7.85 kN (1,765 lb st) – the rockets being ignited electrically by the pilot.

The aircraft was carried normally under the

Yokosuka D4Y1 Suisei.

Yokosuka P1Y1 Ginka.

Yokosuka

Zenair Zénith-CH 200.

belly of a *Betty* bomber and was launched at an altitude of about 8,240 m (27,000 ft) and at a speed of 280–320 km/h (175–200 mph), some 88 km (55 miles) from the target. The first 83 km (52 miles) to the target were covered at a gliding speed of 368 km/h (230 mph) and at a gliding angle of about 5°. The rockets were then ignited, increasing the level speed to 860 km/h (535 mph). In the final dive to the target the maximum speed of 990 km/h (615 mph) was reached. Although the pilot was provided with some light armour for protection from behind, he had no means of getting out of the projectile once it was secured to the shackles of the carrier aircraft before take-off.

Ohka attacks began on 21 March 1945, when 16 were sent to attack a US Navy task force off Kyushu. However the Ohka-carrying bombers and Zero escort fighters were intercepted by Grumman Hellcats and all bombers, Ohkas (jettisoned by the bombers) and many of the Zero fighters were destroyed. The first successful attack by an Ohka is believed to have been made on 1 April 1945, when three were launched at US Navy ships near Okinawa, damaging the battleship USS *West Virginia* and cargo vessels. However on 12 April the US Navy destroyer USS *Mannert L. Abele* was sunk – the first successful attack.

Yokosuka P1Y1 Ginka (Japan) Known to the Allies as *Frances*, this aircraft was designed by Yokosuka but built by Nakajima. The basic 1940 design was for a land-based bomber (crew of three), but it was later adapted for night-fighting duties as the P1Y1-S, while others were used as torpedo bombers and reconnaissance aircraft.

The P1Y1 was powered by two 1,356 kW (1,820 hp) Nakajima Homare 11 radial engines.

Zeppelin LZ1.

Armament comprised two 20 mm Japanese-built Oerlikon (Type 99) cannon or a cannon and a 13.2 mm machine-gun, one in a section of the symmetrical transparent nose and one on a flexible mounting in the rear cockpit; plus an 880 kg torpedo, two 500 kg or 250 kg bombs, or small anti-personnel bombs. Later and improved versions of the aircraft were appearing as P1Y2 types when the war ended. Production of the P1Y1 versions totalled 1,002 from 1943.

Data (P1Y1): *Engines* as above *Wing span* 20.0 m (65 ft 7½ in) *Length* 15.0 m (49 ft 2½ in) *Max T-O weight* 10,500 kg (23,149 lb) *Max level speed* 570 km/h (354 mph) *Normal range* about 2,000 km (1,243 miles)

Zenair Zénith-CH 200 (Canada) Two-seat all-metal light monoplane, plans for which are available to amateur constructors.

Zenair CH 50 Mini Z (Canada) Single-seat light monoplane, first flown in 1979.

Zenair Tri-Z-CH 300 (Canada) Three-seat 'stretched' version of the CH 200, plans for which are available to amateur constructors.

Zenair Z-CH 100 (Canada) Single-seat light monoplane, plans for which are available to amateur constructors.

Zeppelin LZ1 (Germany) In May 1894 Count Ferdinand von Zeppelin headed the newly formed Joint Stock Company for Promotion of Airship Flight and work began soon after on Luftschiff Zeppelin 1. What became the first rigid airship was constructed in a floating shed on Lake Constance (see **Chronology** 2 July 1900). The LZ1 made only three flights, its main problems being lack of speed and control, and was broken up in 1901. Construction of the LZ2 did not begin until 1905. LZ1 had, however, set Germany (and in particular Count von Zeppelin) ahead of the world in the design and construction of the large dirigible. Between 1910 and 1914 five Zeppelin airships operated by Delag carried 35,000 passengers safely between cities in Germany (the first passenger services by air in the world), and the exploits of military Zeppelin raiders during World War I are legend.

Data (LZ1): *Engines* two 11 kW (14.75 hp) Daimlers *Length* 128.0 m (420 ft 0 in) *Max level speed* 28 km/h (17.3 mph) *Volume* 11,300 m³ (399,000 cu ft)

Zeppelin airships (Germany) Individual airships can be found under their names (for exam-

906

leaving Hirth no choice but to make a forced landing in a mountainous wooded valley. The resulting crash left the aircraft an almost total wreck, but without injury to the crew. It was subsequently rebuilt. Soon after it was sent to the Eastern Front, where it carried out numerous flights with the German Navy, to which it belonged, but was later returned for further testing. It was while under test that it again crashed, killing two persons, including Klein.

From the first prototype were evolved the V.G.O. II and III (R.II and R.III) powered by five Maybach and six 119 kW (160 hp) Mercedes

Zeppelin Staaken R.VI.

ple *Graf Zeppelin* and *Hindenburg*). The fate of the wartime Zeppelin airships can be found in the **Chronology**.

Zeppelin LZ CII (Germany) Two-seat long-range Maybach Mb IV-engined reconnaissance aircraft, 19 of which were operated by the Swiss Air Force from 1920 until 1928.

Zeppelin (Lindau) D.I (Germany) Interesting cantilever biplane fighter of 1918 powered by a 119 kW (160 hp) BMW IIIa engine. It was the brainchild of Dr Claude Dornier, but remained a prototype.

Zeppelin Staaken R series (Germany) Thirty-two R-type heavy bombers were built during World War I, a few of which were shot down. Others were finally employed as seaplanes for seaside and weekend flights from Berlin to the Baltic and North Sea after the Armistice.

In the first month of the war Count von Zeppelin asked for two types of giant aeroplane, entrusting to Dipl Eng Dornier the design of the huge metal naval aircraft and to Prof Baumann (with Hellmuth Hirth and Klein) the design of a machine of 1 ton carrying capacity capable of a 700 km return flight. The flying-boat became the Zeppelin (Lindau) Rs I, which led to the construction of three monoplane derivatives. Drawings for the landplane bomber were begun in September 1914 and were finished by December. From January 1915 progress in the construction of the prototype was slowed down only by the delay in the arrival of the three 179 kW (240 hp) Maybach engines.

The first flight of the V.G.O. I prototype was made on 11 April 1915 at the hired Gotha works. As engine trouble was experienced, the giant aircraft was flown in May to Friedrichshafen. It took until the autumn to sort out the problems and on the return flight to Gotha the aircraft ran into a snowstorm. One engine and then another stopped,

D.III engines respectively. The R.II crashed before delivery to the Army but the R.III was used on the Eastern Front. According to the 1920 *Jane's* this had a service ceiling of 3,000 m (9,850 ft). Next came the single R.IV powered by four 164 kW (220 hp) Benz Bz.IV and two 119 kW (160 hp) Mercedes D.IIIs, and the single R.V of 1916 powered by five Mb.IVs and with a service ceiling of 4,000 m (13,125 ft).

The R.VI was the only version to enter quantity production (18 built). Powered by four 194 kW (260 hp) Mercedes D.IVa or Mb.IV engines, these were built by Zeppelin, Albatros, Aviatik and Schütte-Lanz from 1916 until 1918. Meanwhile the single R.VII was built in 1917, followed by three R.XIVs with five Mb.IVs each and a service ceiling of 4,500 m (14,760 ft), the R.XIVa and three R.XVs with five Mb.IVs each. The final aircraft of the series was the R.XVI powered by two 164 kW (220 hp) Benz Bz.IV and two 410 kW (550 hp) Benz Bz.VI engines. Four or five seaplanes of similar type to the R bombers were also built.

Data (R.VI): *Engines* as above *Wing span* 42.2 m (138 ft 5½ in) *Length* 22.2 m (72 ft 6 in) *Max T-O weight* 11,500 kg (25,353 lb) *Max level speed*

Zlin 42.

Zlin Z 50 L.

Zlin 726 Universal.

130 km/h (81 mph) *Armament* four Parabellum machine-guns, plus bombs

Zlin 22 (Czechoslovakia) Two–three-seat training and touring monoplane of 1946 powered by a 56 kW (75 hp) Praga D engine.

Zlin 26 Trener (Czechoslovakia) Two-seat trainer, aerobatic trainer and sporting monoplane of 1948 powered by a 78.25 kW (105 hp) Walter Minor 4-III engine (163 built).

Zlin 42 (Czechoslovakia) Two-seat light training and touring monoplane. The prototype first flew on 17 October 1967. Production of the initial version began in 1971; powered by a 134 kW (180 hp) M 137 A engine. The current production version is the Zlin 42M, production of which began in 1974. Power is provided by a 134 kW (180 hp) Avia M 137 AZ engine.

Zlin 43 (Czechoslovakia) Two–four-seat training and touring monoplane of 1968 powered by a 157 kW (210 hp) Avia M 337 A engine.

Zlin Z 50 L (Czechoslovakia) Fully aerobatic single-seat monoplane powered by a 194 kW (260 hp) Lycoming AEIO-540-D4B5 engine. The prototype first flew on 18 July 1975. Eighteen production aircraft had been built by 1979, all of which have been flown in World Aerobatic Championships with considerable success.

Zlin 126 Trener, 226, 326 and 526 (Czechoslovakia) The Zlin 126 Trener of 1953 was a development of the earlier Zlin 26 powered by a similar engine. Wing span was slightly increased and length decreased. A total of 166 was built. The Zlin 226 of 1955–56 was a further development of the Zlin 26/126 series with a more powerful 119 kW (160 hp) Walter Minor 6-III engine and increased length. Three versions were produced (364 built): the Z 226A single-seat aerobatic trainer; Z 226B version fitted for glider-towing; and the Z 226T standard trainer. The Zlin 326 of 1957 and Z 526 of 1966 were named Trener-Masters and were produced with wings of increased span (436 and 291 built respectively).

Zlin 726 Universal (Czechoslovakia) Latest version of the Zlin 26 Trener series powered by a 134 kW (180 hp) Avia M 137 AZ engine in the standard version and a 157 kW (210 hp) Avia M 337 AK in the Z 726 K version. Accommodation is provided for two in tandem.

JANE'S
Encyclopedia of Aviation

Supplement

New Aircraft A–Z
1980–89

Compiled and edited by Michael J. H. Taylor

Note: An asterisk after the heading/country indicates additional material to an existing entry. In these cases, refer to the main A–Z in addition to the supplement information.

Aeritalia G222 (Italy)* In addition to the standard G222 transport, G222RM flight calibration, G222SAA firefighting, G222T VIP transport with Rolls-Royce Tyne engines, and G222VS and GE electronic warfare versions have been built.

Aeritalia G222

Nigerian Aermacchi MB-339A

Aérospatiale AS 332L Super Puma

Aermacchi MB-339 (Italy)* In addition to the MB-339A training and light ground attack version, Aermacchi has developed the MB-339PAN version to equip the Frecce Tricolori Italian Air Force aerobatic team, MB-339B advanced trainer with improved attack capability and using a 19.57 kN (4,400 lb st) Viper Mk 680-43 turbojet, MB-339C improved trainer/attack version of the 'B' with a digital nav/attack system and other avionics changes, and the single-seat MB-339K attack aircraft (with training capability) using the Mk 680 engine and armed with two fixed 30 mm DEFA cannon plus 1,935 kg (4,265 lb) of other weapons/stores. The 'K' was first flown on 30 May 1980.

Aero L-39 Albatros (Czechoslovakia)* Current versions of the Albatros are the L-39C basic and advanced jet trainer, L-39 Z0 trainer with four weapon stations (total 1,150 kg; 2,535 lb load) and an underfuselage 23 mm cannon, L-39 ZA with similar cannon and weapon stations but the load increased to 1,290 kg (2,844 lb), and the latest L-39 MS trainer with an uprated engine and improved avionics and equipment.

Aero Mercantil Gavilan (Colombia) This is a newly flown eight-seat all-metal high-wing lightplane, powered by a 261 kW (350 hp) Textron Lycoming TIO-540-W2A piston engine.

Aérospatiale AS 332 Super Puma/Super Puma Mk II (France)* The AS 332 Super Puma, first flown in prototype form on 13 September 1978, has since that time been the subject of continuing production and development with almost 300 ordered by 31 countries; some 75 per cent of this

total had been delivered by early 1988. Current production versions, now powered by two uprated Turbomeca Makila IA1 turboshafts each with a maximum continuous rating of 1,184 kW (1,588 shp), are as follows: AS 332B1, standard fuselage military version with reinforced floor and seating two crew and 21 troops; naval AS 332F1, suitable for ASW, anti-ship and SAR roles, equipped with folding tail rotor pylon and ship landing assist gear; civil AS 332L1 introducing increased fuel and cabin lengthened by 0.76 m (2 ft 6 in) to seat two crew and up to 24 passengers; and military AS 332M1 with the fuel and cabin revisions of the AS 332L to seat two crew and up to 25 troops. A Super Puma Mk II, of which a development aircraft was flown on 6 February 1987, will introduce uprated main transmission and a new main rotor for better operating performance without revision of the Makila IA1 powerplant. When the Super Puma Mk II enters service in the early 1990s it is the intended carrier of the Orchidée high-performance radar, able to detect and pinpoint enemy troops and vehicles at ranges up to 150 km (93 miles).

Aérospatiale Epsilon (France) Tandem two-seat military primary and basic trainer, first flown on 22 December 1979. Deliveries to the French Air Force began in 1983 in unarmed form. Armed version for export has four underwing stations for 300 kg (661 lb) of weapons when flown by a single pilot. Togo received the first armed examples in 1986–7. One 224 kW (300 hp) Textron Lycoming AEIO-540-L1B5D piston engine.

Aérospatiale SA 365F Dauphin 2 (France) Details of earlier versions of the Dauphin 2 can be found in the main text, the designation SA 365F

being given first to 24 aircraft ordered by Saudi Arabia in October 1980; SA 365F variants have been ordered subsequently by the Chilean Navy (4), French Navy (3) for the carrier plane-guard role, and by Ireland (5) for fishery surveillance and SAR duties. Saudi Arabia's Dauphin 2s will comprise four with Omera ORB 32 radar for the SAR role, and 20 anti-ship helicopters suitable for operation from both shore bases and frigates, each carrying Crouzet MAD gear, Thomson-CSF Agrion 15 radar on a roll-stabilized mounting, and Aérospatiale AS.15TT all-weather missiles. Power for the SA 365F is provided by two 522 kW (700 shp) Turbomeca Arriel IM turboshafts, and an SA 365N1 type 11-blade 'fenestron' is introduced to improve hovering performance.

Aérospatiale SA 365M Panther (France) The prototype of this military multi-mission development of the Dauphin 2 was first flown on 29 February 1984. Based on the standard SA 365N1 airframe, the primary changes include more composite materials and armoured crew seats to maximize survivability in combat zones, the introduction of Turbomeca TM333-1M turboshafts with a continuous rating of 560 kW (751 shp), and the provision of equipment to permit the use of armament and to allow for night operations. Roles can include aerial command post, anti-air (fixed- or rotary-wing aircraft), anti-tank, armed or unarmed reconnaissance, casualty evacuation, close support, electronic warfare, freight transport, high-speed assault transport, target designation and SAR.

Aérospatiale SA 365N1 Dauphin 2 (France)* Current production version of the civil Dauphin 2, the SA 365N1 is powered by two improved Turbomeca Arriel turboshaft engines, each with a maximum continuous rating of 437 kW (586 shp), and introduces the larger eleven-blade 'fenestron' tail rotor. Providing standard accommodation for a pilot and co-pilot/passenger forward and eight seats to the rear, optional layouts include a pilot and 13 passengers, four/six-seat VIP configuration, and two aeromedical versions.

Aérospatiale SA 366 Dauphin 2 (France) To meet US Coast Guard needs for an SRR (Short Range Recovery) helicopter, Aérospatiale submitted a proposal based on the Dauphin 2 and, in early 1979, was awarded a contract. Identified as the SA 366G, and with the Coast Guard designation HH-65A Dolphin, current orders total 99; the first was delivered on 19 November 1984 and more than half the total have been accepted. Basically similar to the SA 365N, the SA 366G differs primarily in its powerplant (two 507 kW [680 shp] Textron Lycoming LTS101-750A-1 turboshafts) and with advanced communications and all-weather navigation and search equipment of US manufacture. Following an 18-month evaluation of two ex-USCG trials aircraft, the Israel Defence Force has contracted for 20 (to HH-65A standard) for ASW, fire control and SAR duties.

Aerotec A-135 Tangará (Brazil) Developed from the prototype A-132, this aircraft is a tandem two-seat dual-control primary trainer, exhibited as a mock-up in 1986. Power is provided by a 149 kW (200 hp) Textron Lycoming AEIO-360-A1B6 piston engine. Not in production in 1988.

Agusta A 109 (Italy)* Helicopters delivered since September 1981 have been to the A 109 Mk II standard, featuring higher transmission rating, tail rotor changes, redesigned tailboom, improved avionics and other changes. In 1985 a version with a wide-body was also made available, providing more cabin space. Other versions of the Mk II can perform such military roles as attack, anti-ship, electronic warfare, scouting, command and control, patrol, and RPV launch. The military A 109K uses two 538 kW (722 shp)

Prototype Aérospatiale Epsilon

Aérospatiale SA 365M Panther

Aérospatiale HH-65A Dolphin

Agusta A109 MK4

Agusta A 129 Mangusta

Turbomeca Arriel 1K engines to improve 'hot and high' performance, while the Italian Air Force has taken delivery of A 109 EOA's with 335.5 kW (450 shp) Allison 250-C20R/1s for observation and support roles.

Agusta A 129 Mangusta (Italy)* This helicopter, intended for service with the Italian Army in light anti-tank, attack and advanced scout roles, underwent several design changes between receipt of development approval in early 1978 and attainment of its current layout during 1980. The first 'proper' flight by the first of five prototypes was recorded on 15 September 1983, but it was not until mid-1986 that manufacture began of the first 15 of 60, although the army has indicated its requirement for an additional 30 aircraft plus reserves, and there is also Netherlands interest in a batch of 20 for that Army. The A 129 is typical of military attack helicopters; its main rotor and rotor head have ballistic tolerance to 12.7 mm ammunition, plus considerable tolerance against 23 mm hits; the landing gear is designed to withstand heavy landings at descent rates in excess of 10 m (33 ft)/s; and it has separate tandem cockpits for pilot (rear) and co-pilot/gunner. Stub wings mid mounted on the fuselage have four underwing attachments for a maximum 1,200 kg (2,645 lb) stores load, including missiles, gun pods and rocket launchers.
Data: *Engines* two Rolls-Royce Gem 2 Mk 1004D turboshafts each with max continuous rating of 615 kW (825 shp) *Main rotor diameter* 11.90 m (39 ft 0.5 in) *Length* (incl rotors) 14.29 m (46 ft 10.5

in) *Max T-O weight* 4,100 kg (9,039 lb) *Dash speed* 315 km/h (196 mph) *Max endurance* 3 hrs

AIDC AT-3 (Taiwan) The prototype of this tandem two-seat trainer and light attack aircraft flew for the first time on 16 September 1980 and production aircraft have been joining the air force since 1984. A single-seat attack and maritime strike version is also now in production as the Lui-Meng, able to carry a 2,720 kg (6,000 lb) weapon load that can include air-to-air missiles. The fuselage weapons bay can also be used to house machine-gun packs. Powered by two 15.57 kN (3,500 lb st) Garrett TFE731-2-2L turbofan engines, the AT-3 can attain 904 km/h (562 mph).

AIDC IDF (Taiwan) In late 1988 Taiwan put on public display its first indigenously developed fighter, which was expected to make its maiden flight in 1989. Intended eventually to replace the air force's Starfighters and F-5s, its development has been assisted by several American companies. It is a lightweight single-seater of conventional layout, powered by two afterburning Garrett TFE731 turbofan engines. The radar is believed to be a General Electric AN/APG-67, as developed for the Northrop F-20 Tigershark, and air-to-air armament comprises Tien Chien missiles.

Air Tractor series (USA) Agricultural aircraft available from Air Tractor are the AT-301 Air Tractor with a 447 kW (600 hp) Pratty & Whitney R-1340 radial engine and a 1,211 litre (320 US gallon) chemical hopper or a 1,325 litre (350 US gallon) hopper (AT-301B), AT-400 Turbo Air Tractor with a 507 kW (680 shp) Pratt & Whitney Canada PT6A-15AG/-27/-28 turboprop engine and 1,514 litre (400 US gallon) hopper, AT-401 Air Tractor that is similar to the AT-301 but with a larger hopper and greater wing span, AT-501 with a 447 kW (600 hp) R-1340-S3H1G radial engine and 1,900 litre (502 US gallon) hopper, AT-502 with a 507 kW (680 shp) PT6A turboprop engine and 1,900 litre hopper, and the AT-503 anti-narcotics sprayer, agricultural and firefighting aircraft with an 820 kW (1,100 shp) PT6A-45R turboprop engine and a 1,900 litre hopper.

Airbus A300-600 (France/West Germany/Spain/UK)* Since 1984 has been the current production A300, following the earlier B2 and B4 series (mentioned in the main text and built to a total of 248). There are three versions, first being the basic A300-600 which offers a moderate increase in passenger/freight capacity and is available with 249 kN (56,000 lb st) Pratt & Whitney PW4156 or 262.4 kN (59,000 lb st) General Electric CF6-80C2A1 turbofans. The extended range A300–600R (formerly -600ER) is offered with 273.6 kN (61,500 lb st) CF6-80C2A5 or 258 kN (58,000 lb st) PW4158 engines. Third is the A300-600 Convertible which can have the same optional powerplants, but for its passenger or mixed passenger/cargo role introduces a large forward upper deck cargo door, reinforced cabin floor and other special equipment.

Airbus A310 (France/West Germany/Spain/

UK)* Basically a shorter-fuselage version of the A300, the A310 is certificated for a maximum 280 passengers but is normally configured to seat from 210 to 250. New advanced technology wings of smaller span and area were introduced, together with smaller horizontal tail surfaces, plus standard pylons able to mount all optional General Electric and Pratt & Whitney engines. First A310s into revenue service, on 12 and 21 April 1983, were those delivered respectively to Lufthansa and Swissair. Firm orders for A310s were approaching the 200 mark in 1989, with the following versions available: A310-200 which is the basic passenger model, complemented by the A310-200C Convertible and A310-200F Freighter. Extended-range version is the A310-300, first flown on 8 July 1985, which has its standard extra fuel carried in the tailplane; it can have an optional tank installed in the cargo hold to provide a maximum range with 218 passengers of 9,175 km (5,700 miles). The A300 has as standard the drag-reducing delta-shaped wing-tip fences developed by BAe.

Airbus A320 (France/West Germany/Spain/UK) This member of the Airbus family, a short/medium-range single-aisle twin turbofan commercial transport, was the first airliner other than Concorde to use fly by wire control for normal operations. Other features include an advanced wing with drag-reducing delta-shaped wingtip fences; a centralized maintenance system; composite materials for major sections of the main structure; and side-stick controls on the flight deck (replacing control columns). Standard accommodation is for a flight crew of two, four cabin attendants and a maximum of 179 passengers in a high density layout. Following a production go-ahead, on 2 March 1984, the first was flown initially on 22 February 1987. Production began with the A320-100, replaced by the current A320-200 in Autumn 1988; convertible and all-freight versions are under consideration. Optional powerplant, of two International Aero Engines 111.2 kN (25,000 lb st) V2500-A1 turbofans, was scheduled for introduction after certification in 1989.

Data: *Engines* two 104.5–111.2 kN (23,500–25,000 lb st) CFM International CFM56-5-A1 turbofans *Wing span* 33.91 m (111 ft 3 in) *Length* 37.57 m (123 ft 3 in) *Max T-O weight* 73,500 kg (162,040 lb) *Max range* (150 passengers) 5,318 km (3,305 miles)

Airbus A330 (France/West Germany/Spain/UK) A twin-engined medium/long-range version of the Airbus 340 (which see), to which it is basically similar except for having twin- rather than four-engined powerplant. When the A330 first enters airline service, currently scheduled for September 1993, it will be powered by two 291.4 kN (65,500 lb st) General Electric CF6-80C2 turbofans to offer an estimated operating speed of Mach 0.82. Optional engines to become available at a later date will include developments of the Pratt & Whitney PW4000 and Rolls-Royce RB211-524L series, using a common pylon and mount. In a typical two-class configuration, with 328 passengers and baggage, the estimated range for the A330 is 9,000 km (5,585 miles)

Airbus A340 (France/West Germany/Spain/UK) Announced simultaneously with the A330 which, because of the similarity of the two aircraft, is effectively one unit of a combined programme. It is planned that the A340 will be the first to fly, in April 1991, with the programme being launched by a four-engined A340-300 which is the basic long-range version seating 375 passengers as standard, or 440 in an optional high-density layout. Both the A340 and A330 will benefit from a degree of commonality with earlier members of the family and, in particular, will incorporate the new technological features developed for the A320, except for the drag-reducing wingtip fences. Instead both A340 and A330 have a wing of new design which has at the tips what are usually known as winglets, but which Airbus names as wingtip devices. Three versions of the A340 have been announced to date, comprising the initial A340-300, an A340-300 Combi which will have great flexibility of payload, and a longer-range A340-200. Airbus already has orders and options for more than 100 A340-300s, and the type is scheduled to enter airline service in May 1992.

Data: *Engines* four 138.8 kN (31,200 lb st) CFM International CFM56-5C-2 turbofans *Wing span* 58.65 m (192 ft 5 in) *Length* 63.65 m (208 ft 10 in) *Max T-O weight* 251,000 kg (553,360 lb) *Typical speed* Mach 0.82 *Range* (estimated) with 295 passengers and baggage 12,325 km (7,655 miles)

Airtech CN-235 (Indonesia/Spain) The name Airtech was adopted for the joint company formed by Construcciones Aeronauticas SA (CASA) of Spain and Industri Pesawat Terbang Nusantara (IPTN) of Indonesia to design and manufacture a twin-turboprop transport. Known as the Airtech CN-235, and optimised for short-haul operations, the first Series 10 production aircraft was flown initially on 19 August 1986. Production deliveries began in December 1986 and February 1987, from IPTN and CASA respectively. A cantilever high-wing monoplane of typical transport configuration, the CN-235 is suitable for both civil and military use (the latter designated CN-235 M) and total orders, now close on 120 aircraft, are in equal proportions. Powerplant for the Series 10 comprises two General Electric CT7-7A turboprops, but the current Series 100 differs by using CT7-9C engines in composite nacelles.

Data: *Engines* two General Electric CT7-9C turboprops with a T-O rating of 1,305 kW (1,750 shp) *Wing span* 25.81 m (84 ft 8 in) *Length* 21.35 m (70 ft 0.75 in) *Max T-O weight* 15,100 kg (33,290 lb) *Max cruising speed* 452 km/h (280 mph) *Range* (CN-235 M with max payload) 1,240 km (770 miles)

Airtech Canada DC-3/2000 (Canada) Re-engined Douglas DC-3, first flown in March 1987 with Polish 745.7 kW (1,000 hp) PZL Kalisz ASz-62IR radials. Future 'production' conversion likely to use 895 kW (1,200 hp) engines.

Airtech Canada DHC-2/PZL-3S Beaver (Canada) Re-engined de Havilland Canada DHC-2 Beaver, using Polish 447.4 kW (600 hp) PZL-3S radial power plant.

Airtech Canada DHC/1000 Otter (Canada) Re-engined de-Havilland Canada DHC-3 Otter, using Polish 745.7 kW (1,000 hp) PZL Kalisz ASz-62IR radial power plant. Max level speed 232 km/h (144 mph).

AMX International AMX (Brazil/Italy) An Italian Air Force specification for a small tactical fighter-bomber led to project definition by the indigenous companies Aeritalia and Aermacchi SpA. These have since been joined by EMBRAER of Brazil, forming AMX International to develop and produce the single-seat AMX, with current requirements of 187 for the IAF and 79 for the Brazilian Air Force. A tandem two-seat combat trainer/special missions version is under development, with respective requirements of 37 and 14, and the first of three prototypes was scheduled to fly in the summer of 1989. The first of five Italian single-seat AMX prototypes was flown initially on 15 May 1984, and the first of two Brazilian prototypes on 16 October 1985. Deliveries of production aircraft have started, and it is estimated that current

requirements will be met by 1994. Computer regulated powered controls (with manual reversion) ensure optimum low altitude/high speed performance, adequate avionics enabling this to be carried out by day or night and in poor visibility. The possibility of roles such as battlefield interdiction, close air support, offensive counter-air and reconnaissance has given emphasis to good take-off and landing performance, ensuring operational capability from a variety of bases. Production aircraft for the two air forces differ in avionics and weapons delivery systems, and Brazilian Air Force AMXs have twin 30 mm cannon instead of the multi-barrel 20 mm cannon of IAF aircraft.

Data: *Engines* one 49.1 kN (11,030 lb st) Rolls-Royce Spey Mk 807 non-afterburning turbofan *Wing span* 8.874 m (29 ft 1.5 in) *Length* 13.575 m (44 ft 6.5 in) *Max T-O weight* 12,500 kg (27,558 lb) *Max cruising speed* Mach 0.86 *Radius of action* 370–520 km (230–323 miles)

Antonov An-72 (USSR)* The first of two prototypes of this twin-turbofan light STOL transport made the type's initial flight on 22 December 1977. These prototypes were subsequently allocated the NATO reporting name *Coaler-A*, but the production version of the An-72, identified as *Coaler-C*, has been optimized for freighting to supersede the Antonov An-26. By comparison with the prototypes, *Coaler-C* has its wing span increased by 6.06 m (19 ft 10.5 in) and overall length by 1.50 m (4 ft 11 in). It is powered by high-set engines which exhaust over the upper surface of the wing and its large slotted flaps to increase lift, has multi-wheel landing gear with low-pressure tyres for operation from unprepared airfields or surfaces covered with ice or snow, and a rear loading ramp/door to allow vehicles to be driven directly into the hold. To ease the pilot's workload equipment includes a Doppler based automatic navigation system, linked to an onboard computer and which can be pre-programmed before flight.

Data: *Engines* two 63.74 kN (14,330 lb st) Lotarev D-36 turbofans with thrust reversers as standard *Wing span* 31.89 m (104 ft 7.5 in) *Length* 28.07 m (92 ft 1.25 in) *Max T-O weight* 34,500 kg (76,060 lb) *Max level speed* 705 km/h (438 mph) *Range* (with max payload) 4,200 km (2,610 miles)

Antonov An-74 (USSR) The An-74, which is identified by NATO as *Coaler-B*, is basically identical to the An-72 *Coaler-C*, except for revised landing gear, the introduction of a de-icing system, and by having a larger radome. Intended primarily for operation in Arctic and Antarctic regions, it is equipped for such a role by having provisions for the installation of wheel/ski landing gear, carries an increased flight crew (four instead of the An-72's two), and has more comprehensive and advanced navigation aids, including an inertial navigation system. It is regarded as an all-weather aircraft, the de-icing system covering wing and tail unit leading edges, and the engine inlets. It has been stated that its tasks in the Polar regions would include airdropping various supplies to Antarctic expeditions, help establish scientific stations on Arctic ice floes, and the surveillance and recording of icefield movements. In addition to *Coaler-B*, an AEW&C (Airborne Early Warning and Control) variant has been seen and is probably in an early stage of production. This, which has been given the NATO reporting name *Madcap*, has a modified, sweptforward fin and rudder, above which is mounted a typical AEW&C rotodome.

Antonov An-124 (USSR) Antonov's giant long-range heavy-lift freight transport is perhaps better known by the name *Ruslan* given to the second prototype; this appeared at the Paris Air Show in 1985 to give the public at large its first view of this remarkable aircraft. Allocated the very appropriate NATO reporting name of *Condor* (nature's largest bird), the first prototype flew initially on 26 December 1982. It is the world's second largest transport aircraft. In overall configuration it is similar to the Lockheed C-5 Galaxy, and features meriting mention include its 24-wheel landing gear that permits operation from unprepared fields, compressed snow and other terrain; upward hinged visor nose and rear fuselage ramp/door for simplified loading/unloading; fly by wire control system; and the use of 5,500 kg (12,125 lb) of composite materials in the aircraft's structure which give a weight saving in excess of 2,000 kg (4,410 lb). Included among records set by the An-124 is a payload of 171,219 kg (377,473 lb) lifted to a height of 10,750 m (35,269 ft) on 26 July 1985.

Data: *Engines* four 229.5 kN (51,590 lb st) Lotarev D-18T turbofans *Wing span* 73.30 m (240 ft 5.75 in) *Length* 69.10 m (226 ft 8.5 in) *Max T-O weight* 405,000 kg (892,872 lb) *Max cruising speed* 865 km/h (537 mph) *Max range* (with max payload) 4,500 km (2,795 miles)

Antonov An-225 Mriya (USSR) This, the world's largest aircraft, is a six-engined and enlarged development of the An-124. Carrying all six 229.5 kN (51,590 lb st) Lotarev D-18T turbofans under its wings, it weighs about 600 tonnes. A prototype was first displayed in November 1988, and this made its maiden flight from Kiev on 21 December that year.

Data: *Wing span* 88.4 m (290 ft) *Length* 84 m (275 ft 7 in) *Max T-O weight* 600,000 kg (1,322,770 lb) *Cruising speed* (estimated) 850 km/h (530 mph) *Range* (estimated) 4,500 km (2,795 miles)

Arocet AT-9 (USA) Side-by-side two-seat training aircraft, based on the Stoddard–Hamilton Aircraft Glasair III. Powered by one 313 kW (420 shp) Allison 250-B17D turboprop engine. Can carry weapons on two underwing stations.

Atlas Cheetah (South Africa) Taking note of Israel's upgrading of Dassault–Breguet Mirage III/5 airframes, Atlas Aircraft Corporation has

carried out very similar work in order to update the single- and two-seat Mirage IIIs operated by the SAAF. The initial example of the resulting aircraft, named as the Cheetah, was first seen publicly on 16 July 1986, and early conversions were reported to be in operational service some 12 months later. In this extensive refurbishing programme it is claimed that some 50 per cent of the airframe is reconstructed and flight systems improved, but the major changes include an extended and drooped fuselage nose and the adoption of non-movable canards, strakes on the nose, and 'dog-tooth' wing leading edges. The resulting Cheetah thus appears very similar to the IAI Kfir, causing speculation that Atlas may have gained some guidance from IAI, and it is assumed that the resulting Cheetah shares similar performance benefits to those gained by the Kfir. It is believed that more advanced avionics have been introduced, including multi-mode radar, Doppler or terrain following radar, and an infra-red seeker.

Australian Autogyro Skyhook (Australia) Single-seat light autogyro, designed by Ted Minty. Offered in three standards, with either

Volkswagen, Porsche or Rotax engine. Mk II and III models have enclosed accommodation. Maximum speed 161 km/h (100 mph).

Aviolight P.86 Mosquito (Italy) First flown on 27 April 1986, this is a two-seat high-wing light-plane powered by a 56 kW (75 hp) Limbach L 2000 piston engine.

Avions de Transport Régional ATR 42 (France/Italy) ATR was formed in February 1982 by Aérospatiale and Aeritalia to jointly develop and produce a twin-turboprop regional transport aircraft. The new company moved ahead quickly, with the first of two development aircraft being flown on 16 August 1984 and the first production delivery made on 2 December 1985. Current production is centred on the ATR 42-300 which accommodates a crew of two and 42 to 50 passengers. Variants under consideration are the ATR 42 F commercial freighter, ATR 42 L civil freighter/ATM 42 L military freighter, and SAR 42 search and rescue/maritime surveillance aircraft.

Data: *Engines* two Pratt & Whitney Canada PW120 turboprops, each flat rated at 1,342 kW (1,800 shp) *Wing span* 24.57 m (80 ft 7.5 in) *Length* 22.67 m (74 ft 4.5 in) *Max T-O weight* 16,700 kg (36,817 lb) *Max cruising speed* 495 km/h (307 mph) *Max range* with 46 passengers 1,946 km (1,209 miles)

Aeritalia L'ATR 42

BAe 146 CC.Mk 2

Avions de Transport Régional ATR 42

Avions de Transport Régional ATR 72 (France/Italy) The decision to develop a 'stretched' version of the ATR 42 was announced by the company in mid-1985, with work on two development aircraft beginning shortly afterwards. The designation ATR 42 referred to that aircraft's minimum 42-passenger capacity, and it seems likely that the 'stretched' ATR 72 was designated with the same idea in mind. However, accommodation of this version is currently stated to be 64 to 74 passengers according to layout. Generally similar to its predecessor, the ATR 72 has wings of increased span (27.05 m/88 ft 9 in) and area, a lengthened (27.166 m/89 ft 1.5 in) fuselage, revised landing gear and is powered by two 1,790 kW (2,400 shp) Pratt & Whitney Canada PW124/2 turboprops. Orders and options already total more than 50 aircraft, and initial production deliveries were scheduled for August 1989.

Avtek Model 400A (USA) Composites built 6/9-seat business aircraft, powered by two 507 kW (680 shp) Pratt & Whitney Canada PT6A-3L/R turboprop engines. First flown on 17 September 1984, after which it underwent important redesign. Production deliveries are expected to start in 1990.

Ayres Thrush series (USA) Having bought the rights to the Rockwell International Thrush Commander-600 and 800 agricultural aircraft in 1977, Ayres currently offers the Thrush S2R-600 with a 447 kW (600 hp) Pratt & Whitney R-1340 Wasp radial engine and a 1,514 litre (400 US gallon) hopper, Turbo-Thrush S2R in various forms with 373–559 kW (500–750 shp) Pratt & Whitney Canada PT6A turboprop engines, and the Bull Thrush S2R-R1820/510 with an 895 kW (1,200 hp) Wright R-1820 Cyclone radial engine and a 1,930 litre (510 US gallon) hopper. The Turbo-Thrush S2R-T65/400 NEDS is the designation of an anti-narcotics version of the Turbo-Thrush with a 1,026 kW (1,376 shp) PT6A-65AG turboprop engine and purchased by the US State Department, while the Turbo Sea Thrush is a water-bomber version of the Turbo-Thrush by Terr-Mar Aviation.

BAe 146 (UK)* The first 82–93 passenger Series 100 flew for the first time on 3 September 1981. Dan-Air became the first operator, starting scheduled services on 27 May 1983. Subsequent versions have been the lengthened 82–112 passenger Series 200, lengthened 100-passenger Series 300, 146-QT Quiet Trader freighter based on the Series 200 (a future Series 300 freighter may become the Series 350), Statesman executive versions of the Series 100 and 200, 146M/MSL/STA military freighters, 146M milit-

ary flight-refuelling tanker version, and the 146 CC.Mk 2 version of the Series 100 for the RAF's Royal Flight.

Data (Series 200): *Engines* four 31.00 kN (6,970 lb st) Textron Lycoming ALF 502R-5 turbofans *Wing span* 26.34 m (86 ft 5 in) *Length* 28.60 m (93 ft 10 in) *Max T-O weight* 42,185 kg (93,000 lb) *Economical cruising speed* 709 km/h (440 mph) *Range* 2,180 km (1,355 miles) with full passenger load

BAe ATP (UK) British Aerospace has developed the ATP regional transport as a successor to the BAe Super 748. This retains the cabin cross-section of the Super 748, but has a lengthened fuselage to accommodate from 60 to 72 passengers according to layout. First flown in prototype form on 6 August 1986, certification was gained in March 1988, with British Midland Airways operating the first revenue service on 9 May 1988. In addition to the civil transport, several military variants have been proposed.

Data: *Engines* two 1,978 kW (2,653 shp) Pratt & Whitney Canada PW126 (JAR) turboprops *Wing span* 30.63 m (100 ft 6 in) *Length* 26.00 m (85 ft 4 in) *Max T-O weight* 22,930 kg (50,550 lb) *Cruising speed* 496 km/h (308 mph) *Range with max payload* 1,065 km (662 miles)

BAe EAP (UK) Derived from ACA (Agile Combat Aircraft) research and development, British Aerospace built an experimental aircraft programme (EAP) technology demonstrator aircraft. First flown on 8 August 1986, experience with EAP and related development work is contributing to the Eurofighter EFA programme. In configuration it is a single-seat aircraft with a delta wing and active foreplanes, incorporates a quadruplex digital fly by wire control system, and is powered by two Turbo-Union RB199-34R Mk 104D turbofans each rated in the 75.5 kN (17,000 lb) class with afterburning. With a max T-O weight of 14,515 kg (32,000 lb), the EAP has demonstrated a max speed in excess of Mach 2.0.

BAe Hawk 200 Series (UK) A single-seat multi-role combat aircraft developed from the Hawk two-seat trainer (which see in main text), its structure differs primarily in redesign of the forward fuselage for a single-seat cockpit and by introduction of a taller fin, and thus retaining

BAe 146 QT

BAe EAP

BAe ATP

some 80 per cent airframe commonality with the original Hawk. Power is provided by a 26.0 kN (5,845 lb st) Rolls-Royce Turbomeca Adour Mk 871 turbofan. The original Hawk 200 demonstrator flew initially on 19 May 1986 and the first pre-production aircraft on 24 April 1987. Armament for the multi-role capability includes one or two internally mounted 25 mm Aden guns, and up to 3,084 kg (6,800 lb) of varied stores on four

BAe Hawk 200

BAe EAP

BAe

BAe Jetstream 31s

Beechcraft 1900 Exec-Liner

Beechcraft Model 400 Beechjet

Beechcraft Model 2000 Starship 1

underwing pylons. An initial order for Hawk 200s (60) has been received from Saudi Arabia.

BAe Jetstream 31 and Super 31 (UK)* The Jetstream 31 is the current version of the Jetstream commuter and executive transport, first flown on 28 March 1980. Two 701 kW (940 shp) Garrett TPE331-10UG turboprop engines. Commuter layout provides for up to 19 passengers, and executive layout for 8–10. Other possible seating arrangements include a quick change interior for 18 commuter or 12 executive passengers. A Royal navy training version is the Jetstream T. Mk 3. The Super 31, launched in 1987, has two 760 kW (1,020 shp) TPE331-12 engines.

BAe Sea Harrier (UK)* Used with success during the 1982 Falklands War, when 28 Royal Navy Sea Harriers flew 2,376 missions and claimed 22 Argentine aircraft in air-to-air combat without loss (although four were lost during the campaign to ground fire and on-route accidents), the Sea Harrier FRS.Mk 1 continues to offer V/STOL fighter, reconnaissance and strike capability while operating from the three Royal Navy *Invincible* class aircraft carriers. Standard air-to-air armament since the Falklands has been four Sidewinders, while strike weapons can include two Sea Eagle or Harpoon anti-ship missiles or 2,270–3,630 kg (5,000–8,000 lb) of other weapons. 30 mm Aden guns can replace the underfuselage strakes. Between 1991 and 1994 all Royal Navy aircraft will be redelivered in upgraded FRS.Mk 2 form, having Ferranti Blue Vixen radar replacing the original Blue Fox, provision for AMRAAM air-to-air missiles, greater wing span and other changes.

The Indian Navy also operates Sea Harriers, as FRS.Mk 51s (plus trainers) and with Magic missiles replacing Sidewinders, operating from the carriers *Vikrant* and *Viraat*.

Data: *Engine* one 95.6 kN (21,500 lb st) Rolls-Royce Pegasus Mk 104 vectored thrust turbofan *Wing span* 7.70 m (25 ft 3 in) *Length* 14.50 m (47 ft 7 in) *Max T-O weight* 11,884 kg (26,200 lb) *Max level speed* over 1,185 km/h (736 mph) *Radius of action* 463–750 km (288–460 miles)

Beechcraft 1300 Commuter (USA) Beech has developed from the Super King Air B200 (which see in main text) a twin-engined regional airliner seating up to 13 passengers which is suitable for

operation over long routes. Launch customer for this new commuter aircraft is Mesa Airlines of Farmington, New Mexico.

Beechcraft 1900 Exec-Liner and 1900C Airliner (USA) Twelve-to-eighteen passenger executive (Exec-Liner) and 19-passenger commuter or freight-carrying airliner, first flown on 3 September 1982 and powered by two 820 kW (1,100 shp) Pratt & Whitney Canada PT6A-65B turboprop engines. Military examples of the Airliner have been purchased, including C-12J transports for the USAF's Air National Guard and by the Egyptian Air Force for electronic surveillance duties.

Beechcraft Model 400 Beechjet (USA) In late 1985 Beech acquired from Mitsubishi the latter company's Diamond II business jet programme. Now marketed as the Model 400 Beechjet, this twin turbofan-powered aircraft (Pratt & Whitney Canada JT15-D5s of 12.9 kN/2,900 lb st) has standard accommodation for two flight crew and eight passengers.

Beechcraft Model 2000 Starship 1 (USA) The prototypes of Beech's new Starship 1 eight/

eleven-seat business aircraft must currently be numbered among the more unusual aircraft seen in American skies. Starship 1 is unusual because of its canard configuration, a conventional fuselage mounting low-set variable geometry foreplanes in the nose, and at the rear a swept wing with wingtip stabilisers that each incorporate a rudder. Power is provided by wing-mounted turboprops driving pusher propellers. However unconventional, Beech has more than 50 Starships on order, the first production aircraft scheduled for delivery in mid-1989.

Beechcraft Super King Air 300 (USA) 783 kW (1,050 shp) Pratt & Whitney Canada PT6A-60A turboprop-powered version of the Super King Air, first flown in 1981. Max T-O weight is increased to 6,350 kg (14,000 lb).

Bell Model 209/AH-1 HueyCobra/SuperCobra (USA)* The US Army designations for the AH-1S models of the HueyCobra known as Upgun, Modernised and Production are AH-1E, F and P respectively. The AH-1W SuperCobra is a new version of AH-1 for the USMC, powered by two 1,260 kW (1,690 shp) General Electric T700-GE-401 turboshaft engines. Forty-four newly built helicopters had joined the USMC by 1988, and AH-1Ts are to be upgraded to this standard. A night targeting system is being developed for the SuperCobra. In addition to the US Army's and USMC's HueyCobras, SeaCobras and SuperCobras, users of the HueyCobra are Israel, Japan, Jordan, South Korea, Pakistan and Thailand.

Bell Model 406/OH-58D/AH-58D Warrior and Model 406 CS (USA) In September 1981 the US Army selected Bell's Model 406 proposal as winner of its Army Helicopter Improvement Program (AHIP). This aimed to modify some 578 current OH-58A Kiowa helicopters (see Bell Kiowa in main text) to OH-58D scout configuration by the introduction of a mast mounted sight and a cockpit control and display subsystem. The programme started in 1985 and almost 100 have been completed, this total including 15 of an armed version designated AH-58D Warrior. The designation Model 400 CS (Combat Scout) applies to a lighter and less sophisticated variant of the OH-58D which has been developed by Bell.

Bell Model 412 and Agusta Griffon (Canada/Italy) This derivative of the US Bell Model 212 is produced in Canada by a division of Textron Canada Ltd. It features two 843 kW (1,130 shp) continuous rating turboshaft engines within the Pratt & Whitney Canada PT6T-3B-1 Turbo Twin Pac power plant, driving a four-blade advanced technology rotor. The Model 412SP (special performance) has greater take-off weight and more fuel, while an armed military version with an 0.50-in machine gun in an undernose turret and able to carry also 38 rockets on the fuselage sides is known as the Military 412SP. IPTN of Indonesia and Agusta of Italy are also producing Model 412SPs under agreements, while Agusta has also developed its own multi-role military version as the Griffon, able to offer a much wider range of weapons that encompass TOW anti-armour and Sea Skua anti-ship missiles.

Data (Model 412SP): *Engines* as above *Main rotor diameter* 14.02 m (46 ft 0 in) *Length overall* 17.07 m (56 ft 0 in) *Max T-O weight* 5,397 kg (11,900 lb) *Max cruising speed* 230 km/h (143 mph) *Range* 656–695 km (408–432 miles)

Bell Model 206B JetRanger, 206L-3 LongRanger and Model 212 (Canada)* All these US helicopters are now produced at the Bell facility in Canada (see Model 412 entry).

Bell-Boeing V-22 Osprey (USA) First flown on 19 March 1989, the Osprey is likely to become the world's first operational tilt-rotor aircraft. The USAF requires the CV-22A 12-troop/cargo transport version, the US Navy the HV-22A for search and rescue, logistics support and special warfare, while the USMC's planned MV-22A will be the main version for amphibious assault. At each end of the 14.02 m (46 ft 0 in) span wings is an engine nacelle housing a 4,586 kW (6,150 shp) Allison T406-AD-400 turboshaft engine. These drive 11.58 m (38 ft 0 in) rotors which are tilted upward to perform as rotors when the aircraft flies as a helicopter, and are tilted forwards to act as large propellers for high speed horizontal flight. Estimated maximum speed is 556 km/h (345 mph).

Boeing B-52 Stratofortress A total of 167 B-52Gs and 96 B-52Hs remained in USAF service in 1988, operated by 12 Wings of the Eighth and Fifteenth Air Forces, Strategic Air Command. Ninety-eight B-52Gs and all Hs are now assigned to carry the AGM-86 air-launched cruise missile in addition or instead of SRAMS and/or other weapons, with a full complement comprising 12 ALCMs under the wings and 8 on a rotary launcher in the weapon bay. The remaining B-52Gs undertake non-strategic roles, including 30 equipped to carry Harpoon anti-ship missiles for maritime support. Gradually more B-52s will be assigned non-nuclear roles.

Boeing E-6A Tacamo (USA) Required to provide an airborne link between US National Command Authorities and the US Navy's nuclear submarine fleet, which is the current role of the Lockheed EC-130Q Tacamo (TAke Charge And Move Out), the E-6A Tacamo shares virtually a common airframe with the Boeing E-3 Sentry AWACS aircraft (which see in main text). The US Navy has a requirement for 16 E-6As, which

Pakistan Army AH-1S HueyCobra

Boeing

Boeing Model 737-300

Boeing Model 747-400

Boeing Model 767

differ primarily from the E-3 by the avionics equipment installed for the Tacamo role.

Boeing EC-18B ARIA (USA) USAF designation of four ex-airline Boeing Model 707-323Cs converted to perform Advanced Range Instrumentation Aircraft roles, each housing a large radar antenna in the modified nose to support missile tests and space programmes.

Boeing Model 737-300/400/500 (USA) These new versions of the Model 737 (which see in main text) have variations in fuselage length and power plant affecting accommodation and range. The -300 (length 33.40 m/109 ft 7 in) seats from 128 to 149 passengers, the -400 (length 36.45 m/119 ft 7 in) from 146 to 170 passengers, and the -500 (length 31.0 m/101 ft 9 in) from 108 to 132 passengers.

Boeing Model 747-300/400 (USA) These are new versions of the Model 747 (which see in main text). The -300 introduces an extended (by 7.11 m/23 ft 4 in to the rear) upper deck to increase upper deck accommodation from 32 to a maximum of 69. The -400 is an advanced long-range version which adopts the extended upper deck of the -300. It introduces an extension of 1.83 m (6 ft 0 in) at each wingtip plus outward-canted winglets, weight-saving wing structure, a two-crew flight deck and optional engines in the 258.0 kN (58,000 lb) class to give increased range and better fuel economy.

Boeing Model 757 (USA)* First flown on 19 February 1982, the Model 757 short/medium-range airliner is offered in 757-200 178–239 passenger form, 757-200PF package freighter form accommodating fifteen 2.24 × 3.18 m (7 ft 4 in × 10 ft 5 in) pallets, and 757-200M Combi form for a mix of cargo and passengers. Eastern Air Lines opened Model 757 commercial services on 1 January 1983.
Data: *Engines* two 166.4 kN (37,400 lb st) Rolls-Royce 535C, 178.4 kN (40,100 lb st) Rolls-Royce 535E4, Pratt & Whitney PW2037, or 185.5 kN (41,700 lb st) Pratt & Whitney PW2040 turbofans *Wing span* 38.05 m (124 ft 10 in) *Length* 47.32 m (155 ft 3 in) *Max T-O weight* 113,395 kg (250,000 lb) *Cruising speed* Mach 0.8 *Range* typically 7,200 km (4,474 miles)

Boeing Model 767 (USA)* First flown on 26 September 1981, this medium-range airliner is offered in 767-200 216–290 passenger, the heavier 767-200ER extended range, lengthened 767-300 269-passenger, and 767-300ER extended-range versions. United Air Lines opened commercial services on 8 September 1982.
Data (767-200): *Engines* two General Electric CF6, Pratt & Whitney JT9D or PW4050/4052, or Rolls-Royce RB211 turbofan engines, in the 213.5–269.6 kN (48,000–60,600 lb st) class *Wing span* 47.57 m (156 ft 1 in) *Length* 48.51 m (159 ft 2 in) *Max T-O weight* 136,078–142,880 kg (300,000–315,000 lb) *Cruising speed* Mach 0.8 *Range* 7,135 km (4,433 miles); other versions can attain up to 11,230 km (6,978 miles)

Brooklands Optica Scout Mk II (UK) Formerly the Edgley Optica, this slow speed observation aircraft first flew on 14 December 1979. Features include a 194 kW (260 hp) Textron Lycoming IO-540-V4A5D piston engine driving a ducted pusher fan and accommodation for three in the helicopter-style 'bubble' cabin pod. Loiter speed at 40% engine power is 130 km/h (81 mph).

CAC J-7, F-7M Airguard, CAC/Grumman Super-7 and CAIGC JJ-7 (China) J-7 is the Chinese designation for locally-built versions of the Mikoyan MiG-21. Exported models are known in the west as F-7s. F-7M Airguard appeared in 1984 as an upgraded version of the J-7/F-7, fitted with some western avionics that include improved ranging radar and communications radio, a head-up display and weapon aiming computer, IFF and so on. Four underwing weapon stations (instead of two). Airguards are included in the inventory of the Chinese forces and are among many hundreds of exported F-7s. A tandem two-seat training version of the J-7 first flew in 1985 as the JJ-7, produced by GAIGC at Guizhou. The Super-7 represents as much reworked derivative of the J-7, under development by CAC and Grumman of the USA. It introduces a 'solid' nose to house the newly fitted Westinghouse APG-66 radar; the General Electric F404/RM12, Turbo-Union RB199 or similar engine (when selected) will receive air from fuselage side intakes; fixed armament will be a two-barrel 23 mm cannon; the longer (15.04 m; 49 ft 4 in) fuselage will feature a dorsal spine housing extra fuel; the pilot will have a more modern canopy and modern avionics; and the increased-area wings (7.92 m; 26 ft span) will feature leading-edge slats and more weapon stations.

CAMC Z-8 (China) First flown on 11 December 1985, this is a heavy transport helicopter based on the French Aérospatiale Super Frelon. Power is provided by three Wozhou-6 turboshaft engines. Ten Z-8s comprise the initial production batch. Take-off weight is 13,000 kg (28,660 lb).

Canadair Challenger 600, 601 and CL-601RJ (Canada)* CL-600 executive, commuter and cargo transport is now known as the Challenger 600, first flown on 8 November 1978 and powered by two 33.36 kN (7,500 lb st) Textron Lycoming ALF 502L-2 or -3 turbofan engines. Challenger 601 is similar, using 40.66 kN (9,140 lb st) General Electric CF34-1A or 3A turbofans and featuring winglets. 601 was first flown on 17 September 1982. Up to 19 passengers or 2,365 kg (5,215 lb) of freight. Examples of both versions are also in military service. Canadair CL-601RJ is the projected 'stretched' version of the 601, able to accommodate up to 48 passengers and using CF34-3A engines. Not yet built.

Data (601): *Engines* as above *Wing span* 19.61 m (64 ft 4 in) *Length* 20.85 m (68 ft 5 in) *Max T-O weight* 19,550 kg (43,100 lb) *Max cruising speed* 851 km/h (529 mph) *Range* 6,370 km (3,959 miles)

Canadair CL-215T (Canada)* Turboprop version of the CL-215, powered by two 1,775 kW (2,380 shp) Pratt & Whitney Canada PW123AF engines. Cruising speed 385 km/h (240 mph). CL-215s can be retrofitted to this standard.

Caproni Vizzola C22J Ventura (Italy) This is a very light side-by-side two-seat basic jet trainer and sporting aircraft, powered by two 1.28 kN (288 lb st) Microturbo TRS 18-1 turbojets. Constructed of aluminium alloy and glassfibre. Max take-off weight is 1,255 kg (2,767 lb) and max cruising speed is 482 km/h (299 mph). Two underwing stations can be provided for 250 kg (551 lb) of weapons.

CASA C-101 Aviojet (Spain)* The Aviojet, currently in service with the air forces of Chile, Honduras, Jordan and Spain, has been developed into four basic versions: C-101EB initial production trainer for Spanish use from 1980, with a 15.57 kN (3,500 lb st) Garrett TFE731-2-2J turbofan engine; C-101BB export version with armament and a 16.46 kN (3,700 lb st) TFE731-3-1J engine; C-101CC light attack model with a 19.13 kN (4,300 lb st) TFE731-5-1J turbofan engine and 2,250 kg (4,960 lb) of weapons in addition to an optional 30 mm DEFA cannon pack (used by Chile as the ENAER A-36 Halcon and by Jordan); and the C-101DD trainer with additional avionics that include a head-up display and weapon aiming computer.

Data (C-101CC): *Engine* as above *Wing span* as noted previously *Max T-O weight* 6,300 kg (13,889 lb) *Max level speed* 769 km/h (478 mph) *Radius of action* typically 519 km (322 miles)

Cessna Model 208 Caravan I (USA) First flown on 9 December 1982, the Caravan I is a 10/14-seat utility monoplane, with alternative loads including 1,360 kg (3,000 lb) of cargo. A longer version is the Model 208B, able to carry a 1,587 kg (3,500 lb) cargo load in the cabin and in an underfuselage cargo pod. Cargo versions in Federal Express use are known as Cargomasters and Super Cargomasters. Power is provided by one 447 kW (600 shp) Pratt & Whitney Canada PT6A-114 turboprop engine.

Cessna Model 425 Conquest I (USA) Twin-turboprop business aircraft, developed from the Golden Eagle. Previously named Corsair. A total of 232 were delivered before production was suspended.

Cessna Model 441 Conquest II (USA)* Production of this latest version was suspended at the end of 1987 after delivery of 360 aircraft.

Cessna Model 550 Citation II (USA) First flown on 31 January 1977, this 8/12-seat executive jet is powered by two 11.12 kN (2,500 lb st) Pratt & Whitney Canada JT15D-4 turbofan engines.

Cessna Model S550 Citation S/II (USA) Heavier development of the Citation II, with larger supercritical wings, other airframe changes, and has seating for eight to ten persons. Two JT15D-

CAC F-7M Airguard

Canadair Challenger 601

4B turbofans for improved high-altitude performance. Fifteen taken into US Navy service as T-47A radar trainers.

Cessna Model 560 Citation V (USA) Developed from the Citation S/II, with two 12.89 kN (2,900 lb st) JT15D-5A turbofans and a lengthened fuselage to give improved accommodation for the eight passengers.

Cessna Model 650 Citation III (USA) First flown on 30 May 1979, this 8/11-seat executive jet is powered by two 16.24 kN (3,650 lb st) Garrett TFE731-3B-100S turbofan engines and offers long range.

Chadwick C-122S (USA) Pilot-only ultralight helicopter, powered by a 47 kW (63 hp) Rotax 503 piston engine. Other versions are under development for police, agricultural, two-seat training and RPV uses.

Christen A-1 Husky (USA) Two-seat high-wing monoplane, first flown in 1986 and powered by a 134 kW (180 hp) Textron Lycoming O-360-C1G piston engine.

Claudius Dornier Seastar (West Germany) Fourteen-seat amphibian of mainly composite material construction, with the two 373 kW (500 shp) Pratt & Whitney Canada PT6A-112 turboprop engines carried in tandem (one tractor and one pusher) above the strut-mounted wing. First flown on 24 April 1987 in current CD2 form.

CMC Leopard (UK) Unusually configured four-seat business aircraft, built mainly of glassfibre. Power is provided by two 1.42 kN (319 lb st) Noel Penny Turbines NPT 301-3 turbojet engines on the prototype.

Colani Cormoran CCE-208 (West Germany) New and unusual 4 or 5-seat light aircraft of composite material construction. Extremely streamline fuselage, with flush glazing. One 164 kW (220 hp) Porsche PFM N03 or 183 kW (245 hp) turbocharged PFM T03 piston engine mounted in the fuselage, driving a three-blade pusher propeller carried aft of the high-mounted tailplane via a driveshaft.

Conair Firecat and Turbo Firecat (Canada) Firecat is a modification of ex-military Grumman Trackers, now used for firefighting. 3,296 litre (870 US gallon) tank for fire retardant in the fuselage. A re-engined turboprop version is the Turbo Firecat, using two 761 kW (1,020 shp) Pratt & Whitney Canada PT6A-67AF engines and also able to carry 173 litres (46 US gallons) of foam concentrate.

Conair F27 Firefighter (Canada) Modification of the Fokker F27 Friendship for firefighting duties, carrying 6,364 litres (1,681 US gallons) of retardant. Retains passenger carrying capability or can be fitted with other specialised equipment. The first conversion was certificated in 1986.

Dassault-Breguet IV-P (France) Designation of 19 Mirage IV-As, modified to carry the ASMP air-to-surface nuclear missile. Thomson-CSF Arcana pulse-Doppler radar and other avionics updates. Redelivered between 1983 and 1988, equipping two operational squadrons and an operational conversion unit. One lost by 1988.

Dassault-Breguet Mirage 50M (France) Designation of existing Mirage IIIs, 5s and 50s modified for improved capability and performance, featuring foreplanes and other changes.

Dassault-Breguet Gardian 2 (France) Maritime reconnaissance version of the Mystère-Falcon 200, suitable for anti-shipping, electronic warfare, over-the-horizon targeting and mid-course guidance, and target-towing duties. Equipment choices include Thomson-CSF Varan surveillance radar. Chilian Navy became the initial customer.

Dassault-Breguet Gardian 50 (France) Maritime surveillance and environmental protection version of the Mystère-Falcon 50, with Thomson-CSF Varan radar and much else.

Dassault-Breguet Mystère-Falcon 100 (France) This heavier 4–8-passenger executive jet superseded the Mystère-Falcon 10. Two 14.4 kN (3,230 lb st) Garrett TFE731-2 turbofan engines.

Dassault-Breguet Mystère-Falcon 200 (France) Developed from the Mystère-Falcon 20 and first flown on 30 April 1980. Up to 12 passengers, or it can be specially equipped for such tasks as cargo-carrying, air ambulance, photography, electronic warfare, calibration, training and target towing. Two 23.13 kN (5,200 lb st) Garrett ATF 3-6A-4C turbofan engines.

Dassault-Breguet Mystère-Falcon 900 (France) The company's intention to develop a three-turbofan intercontinental executive transport was announced in Spring 1983. Little time was lost in construction of the first prototype, flown initially on 21 September 1984, and to speed certification it was followed by a development aircraft flown first on 30 August 1985. Some days later this second M-F 900 made a non-stop flight of 7,973 km (4,954 miles) from Paris to Little Rock, Arkansas for a US demonstration tour. Of similar configuration to, but larger than the Mystère-Falcon 50, the M-F 900 is powered by three 20 kN (4,500 lb st) Garrett TFE731-5AR-1C turbofans, can accommodate a crew of two and up to 19 passengers, and has a maximum range of 6,968 km (4,329 miles) with 15 passengers. About 40 are in service and Japan has ordered two for long-range maritime patrol.

Dassault-Breguet Atlantique 2 (or ATL2) (France)* This aircraft, known previously as the ANG (Atlantic Nouvelle Génération), is a derivation of the original Breguet 1150 Atlantic (which see in main text), now known generally as the Atlantic 1. With a French government requirement for an Atlantic 1 replacement, work began in January 1979 to build two ATL2 prototypes by modification of two Atlantic 1 airframes, the first of them flying initially on 8 May 1981. Satisfactory testing led to a production decision on 24 May 1984, with plans to build 42 for the French Navy. The primary difference between the two versions is the adoption of advanced constructional techniques that will ensure that the Atlantique 2 has a service life of 30 years. Intended, like its predecessor, as a maritime patrol aircraft, the ATL2 is suitable also for transport, search and rescue, EEZ patrol and minelaying.

Data: *Engines* two 4,549 kW (6,100 ehp) Rolls-Royce Tyne RTy.20 Mk 21 turboprops *Wing span* 37.42 m (122 ft 9.25 in) *Length* 31.62 m (103 ft 9 in) *Max T-O weight* 46,200 kg (101,850 lb) *Max speed* 648 km/h (402 mph)

Dassault-Breguet Mirage 2000 (France)* The Mirage 2000 is destined to become the French Air Force's main warplane. Prototype development led to the first production single-seat Mirage 2000C being flown on 20 November 1982 and the first Mirage 2000B two-seat trainer on 7 October 1983. Production deliveries of Mirage 2000Cs began in 1983, resulting in Escadron de Chasse 1/2 'Cigognes' being the first combat unit to become operational, on 2 July 1984. Prior to that, on 3 February 1983, the first of two prototypes of the Mirage 2000N was flown; this version is a two-seater intended for low-altitude penetration of enemy airspace while carrying the ASMP nuclear ASM. In addition to nuclear-armed Mirage 2000Ns, the French Air Force is procuring 10 Mirage 2000N1 aircraft for conventional attack roles, and has identified an eventual requirement for between 300 and 400 Mirage 2000s of all versions. The capability of the Mirage 2000 has ensured export interest, customers to date including Abu Dhabi (22 2000EAD, 8 2000RAD and 6 2000DAD), Egypt

(16 2000EM and 4 2000BM), Greece (36 2000EGM and 4 2000BGM), India (45 2000H and 4 2000TH), and Peru (initially 24 2000P and 2 2000DP, but since reduced to a total of 12 aircraft). Dassault-Breguet private venture update programmes, identified as 2000-3 and 2000-5, will introduce respectively multifunction cockpit displays, and Thomson-CSF RDY radar and a new central processing unit.

Data (2000C): *Engine* one 95.1 kN (21,385 lb st) with afterburning SNECMA M53-P2 turbofan *Wing span* 9.13 m (29 ft 11.5 in) *Length* 14.36 m (47 ft 1.25 in) *Max T-O weight* 17,000 kg (37,480 lb) *Max level speed* Mach 2.2+ *Armament* two 30 mm DEFA 554 guns; five underfuselage and four underwing attachments with a maximum capacity of 6,300 kg (13,890 lb); typical interceptor weapons comprise two Matra Super 530D or 530F missiles (inboard) and two Matra 550 Magic or Magic 2 missiles (outboard)

Dassault-Breguet Rafale (France) Identified first as ACX, the name Rafale A was given to the experimental prototype intended to lead to later production Rafales for the French Air Force and Navy. The production Rafale is expected to be able to meet all air threats, carry 6 to 10 advanced air-to-air missiles or, alternatively, deliver a warload of at least 3,500 kg (7,715 lb) on targets up to 650 km (400 miles) distant. The need for a thrust-to-weight ratio considerably in excess of one has dictated a structure comprised extensively of advanced alloys and composite materials, and the conflicting requirements of low speed/high lift adequate for STOL operations, combined with exceptional manoeuvrability, high angle-of-attack flight in combat and maximum speed capability, have led to a compound-sweep delta wing configuration allied to a large movable foreplane. Other features include a zero-zero ejection seat inclined at 30 40°, hands on throttle and stick controls, and a digital fly by wire control system. Rafale A was first flown on 4 July 1986. Planned production versions are the military Rafale D and naval Rafale M.

Data (Rafale A): *Engines* two General Electric F404-GE-400 augmented turbofans in 71.2 kN (16,000 lb st) class *Wing span* 11.2 m (36 ft 9 in) *Length* 15.8 m (51 ft 10 in) *Combat weight* 14,000 kg (30,865 lb) *Max level speed* (estimated) Mach 2

Dassault-Breguet/Dornier Alpha Jet (France/West Germany)* Well over 500 Alpha Jets have been delivered to the air forces of France, West Germany, Belgium, Cameroun, Egypt, Ivory Coast, Morocco, Nigeria, Qatar and Togo. Cur-

First prototype Dassault-Breguet Atlantique 2

Dassault-Breguet Rafale A

Dätwyler

Dornier 228

rent versions do not carry letter designations as previously used, with the exceptions of the MS1 trainer and MS2 close support versions assembled in Egypt for the indigenous air force, but are known by names or roles. Therefore, the currently available models are the advanced trainer/light attack; close support; alternative close support (equipped with inertial platform, laser rangefinder, head-up display and more), Alpha Jet 2 upgraded attack aircraft with the new nav/attack system of the 'alternative' version, more powerful 14.12 kN (3,175 lb st) SNECMA/Turbomeca Larzac 04-C20 turbofan engines and other features that include the ability to carry air-to-air missiles; Alpha Jet 3 trainer with modern controls and displays that include cathode-ray tube raster head-up display combined with collminated display, multi-function displays, TV monitor and much else; and Lancier, a day and night attack development of the Alpha Jet 2 for an expanded range of missions and carrying radar, forward-looking infra-red system, and other equipment.

Dätwyler MD-3 Swiss Trainer (Switzerland) Two versions of this side-by-side two-seat primary trainer are to be made available, the MD-3-115 using an 82 kW (110 hp) Textron Lycoming O-235-N2A piston engine and the MD-3-160 with a 119 kW (160 hp) O-320-D2A engine. The prototype first flew on 12 August 1983.

de Havilland Canada DHC-8 Dash 8/8M/Series 300 and 400 (Canada) Expanding its product line with a twin turboprop quiet short-range transport, the company flew the first Dash 8 prototype on 20 June 1983. The initial Series 100 can have Pratt & Whitney Canada PW120A 1,491 kW/2,000 shp (Model 102) or PW121 1,603 kW/2,150 shp (Model 103) engines and is available in Commuter (local service) or Corporate (extended range) versions. The basic commuter accommodates a flight crew of two, cabin attendant and 36 passengers, with 40-passenger, mixed passenger/cargo or corporate layouts optional. The first Dash 8 Series 100 was delivered on 23 October 1984 and more than 150 were ordered by Spring 1988. The military potential of the DHC-8 is vested in the Dash 8M, with two CAF CC-142 passenger/cargo transports operating, four CT-142 navigation trainers due to enter service, and two USAF E-9A flying data links in use off Florida's Gulf Coast. Initial deliveries of the Dash 8 Series 300 – a 'stretched' (by 3.43 m/11 ft 3 in) transport with 1,775 kW (2,380 shp) PW123 engines and seating for 50 to 56 passengers – were scheduled for early 1989.

A 64/70-seat Dash 8 Series 400 with an additional 3.05 m (10 ft) of 'stretch' and more powerful engines could be in service in the early 1990s if there is sufficient interest.

Dornier 128-6 (West Germany) No longer in production, this was first flown on 4 March 1980 as the production turboprop development of the STOL Do 28 Skyservant. Two crew plus up to 10 passengers, five stretchers, 1,273 kg (2,806 lb) of cargo, or maritime patrol equipment (in 128-6MPA form, using undernose MEL Marec radar – used by Cameroun). Two 298 kW (400 shp) Pratt & Whitney Canada PT6A-110 turboprop engines.

Dornier 228 (West Germany) First flown on 28 March 1981, this transport is available in various versions and with two fuselage lengths to allow accommodation for 15 or 19 passengers (21 or 25 troops in military form). Other versions include three models with differing equipment for maritime patrol and another for signal intelligence (sigint). 228–203F freighter version can carry a 2,300 kg (5,070 lb) cargo load.

Data (228–201): *Engines* two 579 kW (776 shp) Garrett TPE331-5-252D turboprops *Wing span* 16.97 m (55 ft 8 in) *Length* 16.56 m (54 ft 4 in) *Max T-O weight* 5,980 kg (13,183 lb) *Max cruising speed* 428 km/h (266 mph) *Range* 305 km (189 miles) allowing for substantial reserves; 228–101 has range of 1,740 km (1,080 miles) with full passenger load

Egrett-1 (West Germany/USA) First flown on 24 June 1987, this is a single-seat high-altitude surveillance and relay aircraft developed by E-Systems, Garrett Turbine Engine Company and Grob. The airframe, constructed mainly of composite materials, uses a 28.80 m (94 ft 6 in) wing, enabling a 10–12 hour endurance. Power is provided by a 731 kW (980 shp) Garrett TPE331-14 turboprop engine. Special mission avionics are carried in removable ventral panniers.

EH Industries EH 101 (Italy/UK) This helicopter was developed initially by Agusta of Italy and Westland of the UK, through a new joint company established in 1980, as a replacement for the ASW Sea King helicopter. The first prototype made its maiden flight on 9 October 1987, and production naval aircraft will be delivered during the early 1990s. Before this, however, in about 1991, examples of the 30-passenger commercial version will be delivered to customers. A third variant is the military EH 101, accommodating 35 troops. This uses similar 1,230 kW

(1,649 shp) General Electric CT7-6 turboshaft engines to the commercial model. The Royal Air Force requires military examples. The naval version has also been selected by Canada.

Slightly smaller than the Sea King, the EH 101 is capable of shore- and ship-based operations and its disposable load is greater. This translates into four torpedoes or other weapons, or up to a 4,309 kg (9,500 lb) payload. Mission equipment for the naval ASW role includes Ferranti Blue Kestrel (specified for the Royal Navy version) or similar search radar, dipping sonar, sonobuoys and associated processing system, and ESM. The naval version is also capable of being equipped for anti-ship surveillance and tracking, and anti-ship strike, over-the-horizon targeting, search and rescue, and amphibious assault.
Data (naval): *Engines* three 1,071 kW (1,437 shp) General Electric T700-GE-401A turboshafts *Rotor diameter* 18.59 m (61 ft 0 in) *Length overall* 22.81 m (74 ft 10 in) *Max T-O weight* 13,530 kg (29,829 lb) *Cruising speed* 296 km/h (184 mph) *Range* 926 km (576 miles) in commercial form with full passenger load

EMBRAER EMB-120 Brasilia (Brazil)* Mentioned briefly in the original A–Z as the Araguaia, the Brasilia became the developed production model of the EMB-120, first flying as a prototype on 27 July 1983 and delivered to customers from June 1985. Basically a pressurised 30 passenger commercial transport, with optional mixed configuration (24 or 26 passengers plus 900 kg; 1,984 lb of freight) or executive layout, it has also gone into military service with the Brazilian Air Force.
Data: *Engines* two 1,342 kW (1,800 shp) Pratt & Whitney Canada PW118 turboprops *Wing span* 19.78 m (64 ft 10¾ in) *Length* 20.0 m (65 ft 7½ in) *Max T-O weight* 11,500 kg (25,350 lb) *Max cruising speed* 552 km/h (343 mph) *Range* 1,750 km (1,087 miles) with max passenger load
EMBRAER EMB-312 Tucano (Brazil) Designed as a basic trainer for the Brazilian Air Force, the first EMB-312 prototype was flown on 16 August 1980. Production deliveries (118) began on 29 September 1983 with completion in September 1986; designated T-27 by the FAB, this air arm retains an option on a further 50. In 1988

EMBRAER EMB-312 Tucanos serving with Paraquay

EMBRAER had delivered more than 350 from a total of almost 600 orders and options, firm orders including the air forces of Argentina (30), Egypt/Iraq (120), Honduras (12), Paraquay (6), Peru (20) and Venezuela (3). The basic EMBRAER version has instructor and student in tandem on ejection seats, is powered by a 559 kW (750 shp) Pratt & Whitney Canada PT6A-25C turboprop engine, and carries an underwing weapon load of 1,000 kg (2,205 lb). A version of the EMB-312 (built by Short Brothers in the UK) was selected for an RAF requirement (130); it differs by introducing structural strengthening, a ventral airbrake, new cockpit layout, British equipment and an 820 kW (1,100 shp) Garrett TPE331-12B turboprop, giving a maximum level speed of 507 km/h (315 mph). The first delivery of a Shorts-built production Tucano T.Mk1 to the RAF was made in June 1988.
ENAER A-36 and T-36 Halcón (Chile) Chilean-built versions of the Spanish CASA C-101 Aviojet, used by the Chilean Air Force as T-36 jet trainers and A-36 light attack aircraft. ENAER is also working on a naval anti-ship strike version carrying Sea Eagle missiles, designated A-36M. A-36 has a 19.13 kN (4,300 lb st) Garrett TFE731-5 turbofan engine and the T-36 a 16.46 kN (3,700 lb st) Garrett TFE731-3 turbofan engine.
ENAER T-35 Pillán (Chile) Formed in 1984 from the former IndAer, Empresa Nacional de Aeronáutica de Chile is building for the Chilean Air Force a tandem two-seater for aerobatic, basic, intermediate and instrument flying training. Its design, finalized by Piper in the USA, is based on that company's Cherokee series and uses many components of the PA-28 and PA-32. Powered by a 224 kW (300 hp) Textron Lycoming IO-540-K1K5 engine, versions include the Chilean Air Force T-35A primary trainer (60 ordered) and T-35B instrument trainer (20), Spanish Air Force T-35C primary trainer (40, local designation E.26 Tamiz), and Panamanian Air Force T-35D primary trainer (4 + 6 options). ENAER has flown with the standard engine a single-seat T-35S prototype, to be powered by a 313 kW (420 shp) Allison 250-B17 in production form, and with a variant of this latter engine the T-35T turboprop trainer known as the Aucán; this last programme has been suspended.

EH Industries E4 101

Fokker 50

Enstrom F-28 and 280 (USA)* Current models of these three-seat helicopters are the F-28F Falcon, F-28F-P Sentinel police version and Model 280FX improved version of the previous Shark. One 168 kW (225 hp) Textron Lycoming HIO-360-F1AD piston engine.

Extra 230 and 300 (West Germany) Single- and two-seat aerobatic monoplanes, the former powered by a 149 kW (200 hp) Textron Lycoming AEIO-360-A1E piston engine and first flown on 14 July 1983.

Fairchild Model SA227-AC Metro III and Expediter I (USA) The 19/20-passenger Metro III commuter airliner was developed from the Metro II and has increased payload and take-off weights. Power is provided by two 746 kW (1,000 shp) Garrett TPE331-11U-612G turboprop engines. Military examples have gone into Swedish and USAF Air National Guard (C-26A) service. A freighter version is named Expediter I.

Prototype FAMA IA 63 Pampa

FAMA IA 63 Pampa (Argentina) Known formerly as Fábrica Militar de Aviones, and since late 1987 as Fábrica Argentina de Materiales Aeroespaciales, FAMA has designed and developed the IA 63 Pampa for the military pilot training needs of the Fuerza Aérea Argentina (FAA). The first of three prototypes was flown initially on 6 October 1984 and deliveries of production aircraft began in early 1988. FAA planned procurement is for 64 aircraft, with a possibility of an additional 40 for combat proficiency training. A basic and advanced jet trainer seating instructor (rear) and student in tandem on ejection seats, the IA 63 is powered by a single 15.6 kN (3,500 lb st) Garrett TFE731-2-2N turbofan giving a maximum speed of 755 km/h (469 mph). A weapon load of 1,160 kg (2,557 lb) on five underwing and fuselage stations gives full scope for military training and light attack.

Fokker 50 (Netherlands) Developed from the F27 Friendship (see Fokker-VFW F.27 in main text) and benefitting from continued use of a proven airframe, the Fokker 50 incorporates a number of differences. These include introduction of composite materials into the structure, use of advanced avionics, improved engines, and removal of the cargo door. The cabin accommodates 46–58 passengers, who also benefit by the addition of more windows. Power is now provided by new technology engines, namely two 1,864 kW (2,500 shp) Pratt & Whitney Canada PW125B turboprops. The first new production Fokker 50 was flown initially on 13 February

1987, with first deliveries to airlines being made shortly afterwards. Maritime and surveillance versions are available and include the unarmed patrol Maritime Mk 2; armed surveillance, ASW and ASV Maritime Enforcer Mk 2; border surveillance/standoff reconnaissance Sentinel Mk 2; and AEW King Bird Mk 2.

Fokker 100 (Netherlands) Like the Fokker 50, the Fokker 100 is also derived from an earlier aircraft, in this case the F.28 Mk 4000 (which see in the main text under Fokker-VFW F.28), but is a more comprehensive development than that of the Fokker 50. The wings have been redesigned and extended (span now 28.08 m/92 ft 1.5 in), the fuselage lengthened (by 5.92 m/19 ft 5 in) and having a new flight deck with CRT displays and new cabin interior with standard accommodation for 107 instead of 85 passengers. Considerably more powerful (61.6 kN/13,850 lb st) Rolls-Royce Tay Mk 620-15 turbofans were installed initially, but Tay Mk 650-15s developing 67.2 kN (15,100 lb st) were to be available as options from early 1989. New and improved systems have been introduced, together with the advanced avionics now available for commercial aircraft. With the optional power plant and at a max T-O weight of 44,450 kg (98,000 lb), the Fokker 100 has a range of 2,844 km (1,767 miles) with 107 passengers.

Fokker 100

Ganzavia GAK-22 Dino (Hungary) First flown in 1988, this is a side-by-side two-seat biplane, with a fully enclosed cockpit and negative-staggered cantilever wings. Power is provided by an 86 kW (115 hp) Textron Lycoming O-235-H2C piston engine.

General Avia F.20 TP Condor (Italy) This four-seat aircraft, powered by two 298 kW (400 shp) Allison 250-B17B turboprop engines, was developed from the F.20 Pegaso and is intended for a range of military uses. It can be fitted with four underwing stations for auxiliary fuel tanks and/or light weapons including those suited to anti-armour and attack.

General Dynamics F-16 Fighting Falcon (USA)* Delivery of the F-16A to the USAF took place between 1979 and 1985, starting with the 388th Tactical Fighter Wing. This version is now also flown by the US Air National Guard and US Air Force Reserve, Belgium, Denmark, Egypt, Indonesia, Israel, Malaysia, the Netherlands, Norway, Pakistan, Singapore, Thailand and Venezuela. F-16B is the two-seat operational training version, delivered to the same air forces. Subsequent versions have been the F-16ADF air defence fighter for the US Air National Guard to replace F-4s and F-106s; F-16C and D improved and current single- and two-seat multi-role versions with day and night capability for fighter, beyond visual range intercept and attack roles, featuring an advanced cockpit, Westinghouse AN/APG-68 radar and the ability to carry AMRAAM, AGM-65D Maverick and other advanced weapons; F-16N and TF-16N single- and two-seat adversary training fighters for the US Navy; F-16 Recce reconnaissance aircraft; and the SX-3 proposed future variant for the JASDF for service from about 1997. Cs and Ds are offered with either a 122.8 kN (27,600 lb st) with afterburning General Electric F110-GE-100 turbofan engine or a 104.3 kN (23,450 lb st) with afterburning Pratt & Whitney F100-PW-220 engine. Max weapon load is 5,443 kg (12,000 lb). Users of the F-16C/D are the USAF since 1984, Bahrain, Egypt, Greece, Israel, South Korea and Turkey.

General Dynamics F-111G (USA) This new F-111 model represents the conversion of existing FB-111A strategic bombers into dual-role aircraft for future basing in Europe. Expected to be deployed from 1990, they will be operated by Tactical Air Command.

Grob G 115, G 116 and GF 200 (West Germany) First flown in 1985, the G 115 is a two-seat light monoplane powered by an 86 kW (115 hp) Textron Lycoming O-235-H2C piston engine. The G 116, first flown in 1988, is a four-seat development with a 134 kW (180 hp) O-360 engine. The entirely different four-seat GF 200 again uses composite materials for its airframe but is of more unusual design, with the Porsche engine driving a pusher propeller carried at the tail beneath the high-mounted tailplane. The prototype GF 200 is expected to fly in 1989.

Grumman F-14 Tomcat (USA)* F-14As delivered to the US Navy between 1984 and April 1987, when production ended, have similarly rated TF30-P-414A turbofan engines. F-14As received by the US Navy totalled 545 full production and 12 research and development aircraft. As an interim measure before the F-14D becomes available from 1990, the US Navy has been receiving F-14A(Plus)s, basically similar to the F-14A but using 102.75 kN (23,100 lb st) F110-GE-400 turbofan engines. Delivery of thirty-eight F-14A(Plus)s began in 1988, and 32 F-14As are being upgraded to this standard. The

Egyptian General Dynamics F-16Cs

Grumman X-29A Forward Swept Wing Demonstrator

F-14D uses this same F110 power plant but also incorporates major changes to the avionics (digital) and adopts the new Hughes AN/APG-71 radar. Weapon options will include AMRAAM. Delivery of some 127 new F-14Ds will start in early 1990, and perhaps 400 earlier aircraft will eventually be brought up to this standard. F110-GE-400-engined Tomcats have important performance gains.

Grumman S-2T Turbo Tracker (USA) Under a US Navy foreign military sales programme, Grumman was contracted to develop and produce a turboprop engine conversion for existing Tracker ASW aircraft, with updates also to the Tracker's mission avionics. Taiwan's entire fleet of 32 Trackers are the first to be upgraded. Two 1,227 kW (1,645 shp) Garrett TPE331-1-5AW turboprop engines.

Grumman X-29A Forward Swept Wing Demonstrator (USA) Allocated the USAF designation X-29A, this aircraft (with the unusual configuration of all-moving canard foreplanes mounted ahead of rear-mounted forward swept wings) is intended to evaluate the potential of such a design which offers the promise of a new generation of lightweight and efficient tactical fighters. The first of two demonstrator X-29s was flown initially on 14 December 1984 and had completed 200 test flights by 8 June 1988, during which it had demonstrated a maximum speed of Mach 1.46.

Grumman (General Dynamics) EF-111A Raven (USA)* In January 1987 Grumman received a

USAF contract to upgrade the avionics of the EF-111As. The package includes improved cockpit control-display functions and navigation/terrain following radars, and installation of two new digital computers, a global positioning system, and a ring laser gyro inertial navigation system. Production modernization kits were scheduled for delivery during 1990.

Gulfstream Aerospace Gulfstream IV and SRA-4 (USA) Gulfstream IV is a 14/19-passenger executive jet, powered by two 61.6 kN (13,850 lb st) Rolls-Royce Tay Mk 611-8 turbofan engines. Developed from the Gulfstream III, it first flew on 19 September 1985. Three are also used by the US Navy as EC-20Fs, having replaced ERA-3 Skywarriors in the ECM training role. The SRA-4 is a special missions version, offered for a variety of tasks including maritime patrol, reconnaissance, surveillance, anti-submarine warfare, anti-ship, evacuation and so on.

Gulfstream Aerospace Gulfstream IV

Gyroflug SC 01 Speed Canard (West Germany) This tandem two-seat sporting aircraft is constructed of glassfibre and carbonfibre, and has the unusual configuration of rear-mounted sweptback wings with winglets and a straight foreplane. The SC 01B is powered by an 86.5 kW (116 hp) Textron Lycoming O-235-P2A engine and the SC 01B-160 uses a 119 kW (160 hp) O-320-D1A engine. The prototype first flew on 2 December 1980.

HAL HPT-32 (India)* Following the initial flight of the first HPT-32 prototype, on 6 January 1977, development continued for the next four years with the third prototype, flown on 31 July 1981, being representative of the production version for the Indian Air Force. Suitable for a wide variety of training and support tasks, the HPT-32 was designed as a two-seat (side by side) fully aerobatic piston engined basic trainer. Deliveries to the IAF (40) and Indian Navy (8) were completed by 31 March 1987, but production of an additional 40 aircraft has continued in anticipation of further orders. In current form the HPT-32 is powered by a 194 kW (260 hp) Textron Lycoming AEIO-540-D4B5 piston engine, which gives this useful little aircraft a maximum cruising speed of 213 km/h (132 mph).

HAMC Y-12

HAL Light Combat Aircraft (India) After the Indian Air Force identified a requirement for an air superiority and light close support aircraft for service in the 1990s, the Indian government announced that an LCA (Light Combat Aircraft) was to be developed. The original feasibility study, covering a single-seat aircraft incorporat-

ing composite construction and powered by a turbofan engine, specifies such advanced features as fly by wire flight controls, ring laser gyro system, multi-function radar, digital databus and engine controls, and a central weapons management system. In order to speed project definition, Dassault-Breguet in France has been requested to provide technological assistance. An indigenous afterburning engine has been put under development for the LCA, but with a first flight anticipated in the early 1990s General Electric F404-F2J3 turbofans have been ordered to power the six prototypes.

HAMC SH-5 (China) The design, development and construction in China of a large turboprop powered amphibian flying-boat was unknown in the West until 1980, when two were seen under construction by officials of the US aircraft industry. The prototype flew initially on 3 April 1976, and it is believed that, following the construction of two more prototypes, production began in 1984. The type entered PLA Navy service on 3 September 1986, and several are now in use. The Harbin Aircraft Manufacturing Corporation (HAMC) SH-5 (known in the West as the PS-5) appears to incorporate design features similar to those of the Shin Meiwa PS-1 and the Beriev Be-12. Powered by four 2,349 kW (3,150 ehp) Harbin WJ-5A-1 engines, the SH-5 has a wing span of 36.00 m (118 ft 1.25 in) and maximum take-off weight of 45,000 kg (99,208 lb). It is intended to carry out various differing tasks, including anti-submarine and anti-surface-vessel warfare, freighting, minelaying, patrol, surveillance, and search and rescue. It was reported recently that the Chinese are seeking to upgrade the ASW and avionics capability of the SH-5.

HAMC Y-11 (China)* Mentioned briefly under *State Aircraft Factories* in the original A–Z, the Y-11 is a nine- or ten-seat or 870 kg (1,918 lb) of cargo general purpose transport. It first flew in about 1975. Other main roles include agricultural, forestry and survey, for the former having a 900 litre (198 Imp gallon) chemical hopper. Two 213 kW (285 hp) Quzhou Huosai-'a radial engines.

HAMC Y-12 (China) Larger development of the Y-11 type, accommodating up to 17 passengers, 1,700 kg (3,748 lb) of cargo or 1,200 litres (264 Imp gallons) of chemicals (in agricultural form). Powered by two 507 kW (680 shp) Pratt & Whitney Canada PT6A-27 turboprop engines.

Hawk GafHawk 125 (USA) One 875 kW (1,173 shp) Pratt & Whitney Canada PT6A-65B/R turboprop-engined freighter, featuring a nearly square-section cabin with a rear-loading cargo door. First flown on 19 August 1982.

Hoffman H-40 (West Germany) The H-40 is a side-by-side two-seat light aircraft, constructed of glassfibre and carbonfibre and with an impressive 10.84 m (35 ft 6¾ in) wing span. Power is provided by a 71 kW (95 hp) Limbach L 2400 DB1 piston engine.

IAC TA16 Seafire (USA) Four-seat amphibious flying-boat, representing the ready-assembled production derivative of the Thurston TA16 Trojan. One 186 kW (250 hp) Textron Lycoming O-540-A4D5 piston engine.

IAI 1125 Astra (Israel) Two crew and six passenger business aircraft, first flown on 19 March 1984. Deliveries began in 1986. Two 16.23 kN (3,650 lb st) Garrett TFE731-3A-200G turbofan engines.

IAI Kfir (Israel)* Total Kfir production was 212 aircraft. The latest models are the single-seat Kfir-C7 and two-seat operational training TC7, representing upgrade of earlier C2/TC2 models. C7 is powered by one 83.41 kN (18,750 lb st) with afterburning General Electric J79-J1E turbojet engine, and has upgraded avionics, HOTAS (hands on throttle and stick) controls, and nine weapon stations for a 6,085 kg (13,415 lb) load. Colombia received C7/TC7s. The US Navy and US Marine Corps also received modified Kfir C1s as temporary 'aggressor' training aircraft, designated F-21As. However, the former have already been superseded by F-16N/TF-16Ns. Chile may purchase Kfirs with SNECMA engines to replace F-5s.

IAI Lavi (Israel) The Lavi multi-role combat aircraft was designed for the Israeli Air Force by Israel Aircraft Industries. A single-seater optimized for close air support and interdiction, with secondary air defence capability, the IAF had planned on procurement of at least 300, including 60 examples of the two-seat trainer model. Seeking to give the air force a fast and highly manoeuvrable aircraft, one that combined also

good combat radius and weapon load, a 'swept delta' wing (designed by Grumman in the USA) was selected, complemented by all-moving foreplanes of similar planform. Power plant is a single Pratt & Whitney PW1120 turbojet, rated at 91.7 kN (20,620 lb st) with afterburning, which is aspirated via a ventral single-shock inlet based on that of the General Dynamics F-16. Advanced avionics were chosen for the Lavi, and armament comprised an internally mounted 30 mm cannon plus four underwing and seven underfuselage stores attachments for a variety of bombs, missiles and rockets. The realisation of this new and sophisticated aircraft proved too great for the IAF's budget, and although B-1 and B-2 prototypes had flown (in 1986 and 1987 respectively) the Israeli government terminated the programme on 30 August 1987.

IAI Nammer (Israel) Israel Aircraft Industries has proposed the Nammer upgrade of the Mirage III/5. Its General Electric/Flygmotor F404/RM12 turbofan engine, rated at 80.7 kN (18,140 lb st) with afterburning, would provide a maximum high altitude speed of Mach 2.2 and an external stores load of up to 6,260 kg (13,800 lb).

ICA IAR-28MA (Romania) Two-seat light aircraft, developed from the IS-28M2. One 60 kW (80 hp) Limbach L2000 EOI piston engine. Taken into service by the Romanian Air Force from 1984.

ICA IAR-317 Airfox (Romania) The ICA at Brasov modified the airframe of an IAR-316B Alouette III to provide a light ground attack, military liaison and training helicopter for the Romanian armed forces, the prototype being flown in April 1984. The resulting IAR-317 differs primarily by introducing a slim tandem cockpit with an elevated rear seat and by the provision of attachments for external weapons. Though exhibited at the 1985 Paris Air Show, the current status of this programme is uncertain.

IAv Craiova IAR-99 Soim (Romania) Comparatively little is known of the design and development of this new Romanian advanced jet trainer/light attack aircraft. First flown in prototype form during December 1985, it is a cantilever low-wing monoplane with retractable tricycle landing gear and has accommodation for a crew of two in tandem, the rear seat being elevated. There are four underwing stations for stores/weapons, and power is provided by one 17.8 kN (4,000 lb st) Rolls-Royce Viper Mk 632-41 turbojet which is mounted in the aft fuselage.

Data: *Engine* see above *Wing span* 10.16 m (33 ft 4 in) *Length* 11.009 m (36 ft 1.5 in) *Max T-O weight*

US Marine Corps IAI F-21A Kfir

ICA IAR-28MA

IAI Lavi

5,641 kg (12,436 lb) *Max level speed* 850 km/h (528 mph)

ICA IAR-825TP Triumf (Romania) To provide the Romanian Air Force with an economical and modern military trainer, ICA at Brasov initiated design of the IAR-825TP turboprop-powered aircraft, the prototype being flown for the first time on 12 June 1982. A cantilever low-wing monoplane of conventional all-metal construction, it provides accommodation for an instructor and pupil seated in tandem in a single cockpit enclosed by a one-piece side-opening canopy. The prototype was flown on the power of one 507 kW (680 shp) Pratt & Whitney Canada PT6A-15AG turboprop, but production aircraft, of which the current status is uncertain, will have a more powerful version of this engine.

Data: *Engine* one 559 kW (750 shp) Pratt & Whitney Canada PT6A-25C *Wing span* 10.00 m (32 ft 9.75 in) *Length* 8.99 m (29 ft 6 in) *Max T-O weight* 2,300 kg (5,070 lb) *Max level speed* (PT6A-15AG) 470 km/h (292 mph) *Endurance* 2.5 hrs

Prototype ICA IAR-825TP Triumf

IL PZL I-22 Iryd (Poland) Modern tandem two-seat advanced jet trainer and light close air support/reconnaissance aircraft, first flown as a prototype on 3 March 1985. Not yet in service in 1988. Two 10.79 kN (2,425 lb st) PZL Rzeszów SO-3W22 turbojet engines. 1,200 kg (2,646 lb) weapon load on four underwing stations, plus a two-barrel 23 mm cannon in an underfuselage pack.

Ilyushin Il-76 (USSR)* The Il-76, first flown in prototype form on 25 March 1971, has since given distinguished service in a number of variants which have seen use for both civil and military roles. In addition to the cargo variants of the Il-76 which have the NATO reporting name *Candid*, there are specialized versions for AEW&C (Airborne Early Warning & Control) and flight refuelling which have the respective NATO reporting names of *Mainstay* and *Midas*. The former, like the Boeing E-3 Sentry, carries a large rotodome strut-mounted above the rear fuselage; other equipment for this role includes comprehensive ECM, a state of the art IFF system, and a flight refuelling probe mounted in the nose, forward of the flight deck. More than 12 examples of *Mainstay* are reported to be in service and production is expected to continue at a rate of about five per year. The *Midas* flight refuelling tanker is configured for three-point probe and drogue type refuelling operations, equipped with a refuelling pod beneath each wing and a hose-reel unit in the rear fuselage. *Midas* entered service during 1987 in support of both tactical and strategic combat aircraft, replacing in this role the Myasishchev M-4 *Bison*.

Ilyushin Il-86 (USSR)* Ilyushin's Il-86 wide-body passenger transport, which has the NATO reporting name *Camber*, began scheduled operations with Aeroflot on 26 December 1980; the type's first international service, between Moscow and East Berlin, began on 3 July 1981. Over half of a planned production total of 100 are already in service, during which they have not met all performance expectations. To overcome this the prototype of a new version, to be powered by 157 kN (35,300 lb st) Soloviev PS-90A (D-90) high bypass ratio turbofans, is scheduled to make its maiden flight in 1990. Since the Il-86 entered service the maximum T-O weight has been increased to 208,000 kg (458,560 lb), and the maximum range with a 40,000 kg (88,185 lb) payload is quoted by the manufacturer as 3,600 km (2,235 miles). However, some operators have indicated that such payload range cannot be achieved and that, with the payload quoted above, the maximum range is nearer to 2,500 km (1,550 miles).

Ilyushin Il-96-300 (USSR) Inadequate range of the Ilyushin Il-86 would appear to have given concern, and to address this shortcoming work has been going on for some time on a longer-range aircraft to supplant it. This now has the designation Il-96-300. While similar in appearance to the Il-86, it is a new type with an increased wing span (57.66 m/189 ft 2 in), utilising a wing of supercritical section which incorporates winglets at the wingtips. Other performance improvement will come from the use of advanced structural materials, the adoption of state of the art technology, and the introduction of more powerful Soloviev PS-90A (D-90A) turbofans each rated at about 157 kN (35,300 lb st). It is anticipated that the first production examples of the Il-96-300 will enter airline service in the early 1990s. It has also been reported that a twin-engined version of the Il-96 is under development, to be powered by Lotarev D-18 turbofans each developing between 275 and 314 kN (61,750 and 70,500 lb st).

Ilyushin Il-114 (USSR) Ilyushin's Il-114 twin-turboprop short-range passenger and freight transport is intended to accommodate a flight crew of two, a cabin attendant and up to 60 passengers. Access to the cabin is via an airstair type door in the forward port side of the fuselage. A cantilever low-wing monoplane of conventional appearance, it has retractable tricycle landing gear with twin wheels on each unit, and is to be powered by two wing mounted 1,864 kW (2,500 shp) Isotov TV7-117 turboprop engines. A prototype was scheduled to fly during early 1989, with the type entering airline service in the early 1990s.

Data: *Engines* see above *Wing span* 30.00 m (98 ft 5.25 in) *Length* 25.46 m (83 ft 6.5 in) *Max T-O weight* 20,250 kg (44,640 lb) *Max cruising speed* (estimated) 500 km/h (310 mph)

IRGC Fajr (Iran) This side-by-side two-seat composites light monoplane is the first aircraft to come from Iran. The first flight was announced in February 1988. Duties could include training and liaison.

Island Aircraft ARV-1 Super2 (UK) Side-by-side two-seat lightplane, powered by a 57.4 kW (77 hp) Hewland Engineering AE 75 piston engine. First flown on 11 March 1985. Deliveries began in 1986 in kit and ready assembled forms.

Jaffe SA-32T Turbo Trainer (USA) Designed by Swearingen as a two-seat military trainer, based on the SX-300 sportplane. Powered by a 313 kW (420 shp) Allison 250-B17D turboprop engine.

Kamov *Hokum* (USSR) Reports that the Kamov bureau had a new combat helicopter at the flight test stage were confirmed during 1984, this new aircraft being allocated the NATO reporting name *Hokum*, by which name the aircraft is currently identified. Details of its configuration are based upon an artist's impression and, consequently, are not necessarily accurate, but in overall configuration it retains Kamov's typical three-blade coaxial contra-rotating rotor system and tail unit. The streamlined fuselage (more like that of a conventional fighter aircraft) has an elevated rear seat for the two-man crew seated in tandem, retractable landing gear, and stub wings beneath the side-mounted engines on which can be mounted a variety of weapons. *Hokum* is believed to be intended primarily for an air-to-air role and, if put in production, would give the Soviet Air Force a helicopter which has no counterpart in the West.

Kamov Ka-27 (USSR) Fairly typical of Kamov helicopters, the Ka-27 has two three-blade coaxial contra-rotating rotors and a tail unit comprising a fixed incidence tailplane mounting elevators and endplate fins with rudders. Landing gear is of quadricycle configuration, and power is provided by two 1,660 kW (2,225 shp) Isotov TV3-117V turboshafts which are mounted side by side above the cabin. Three versions of the military Ka-27 have been reported, that with the NATO reporting name *Helix-A* being the basic ASW version which has been in operational use since 1982. More than 60 are in Soviet Naval Aviation service, and eight have been requested by India. *Helix-B* is a ship-borne version for the amphibious assault role; it can be used to carry infantry, launch smart weapons, or designate targets. *Helix-D* fulfils a

SAR and plane guard role aboard Soviet carriers. It can be identified by an external fuel tank on each side of the cabin and by the winch.

Kamov Ka-28 (USSR) This company designation is allocated to an export version of the Kamov Ka-27 ASW helicopter, to which it appears to be identical and consequently has the same NATO reporting name of *Helix-A*. The first example was seen during 1988, the aircraft in question being in Yugoslav service and included in an air show lineup in that country. Power is provided by two Isotov TV3-117BK, each developing 1,618 kW (2,170 shp), which is slightly less than the output of the TV3-117V turboshafts that power versions of *Helix* in Soviet service.

Kamov Ka-32

Kamov Ka-32 (USSR) Kamov's Ka-32, which was first displayed publicly in 1981, is a civil version of the Ka-27 and consequently was allocated the NATO reporting name *Helix-C*. It is available in two variants, the Ka-32T being the basic flying crane/transport version with seats for three aircrew on a large air-conditioned flight deck, and accommodation for up to 16 passengers or cargo in a cabin which is heated and ventilated. The second version is the maritime Ka-32S which is intended for such roles as ice patrol, transporting to and from ships, offshore support and SAR. In order that the Ka-32S can fulfil such maritime roles in adverse weather conditions it has a more comprehensive avionics suite than the Ka-32T, this including undernose radar.

Kamov Ka-27

Data: *Engines* as for Ka-27 *Rotor diameter* (each) 15.90 m (52 ft 2 in) *Max T-O weight* 12,600 kg (27,775 lb) *Max level speed* 250 km/h (155 mph)

Kamov Ka-126 (USSR) Kamov's Ka-126, which has the NATO reporting name *Hoodlum-B*, is a turboshaft conversion of the piston-engined Ka-26 *Hoodlum-A* (which see in main text). A prototype with a turboshaft engine installed was flown by Kamov during 1986 and ICA Brasov in Romania is now responsible for 'production' conversions, this involving the installation of a single 537 kW (720 shp) Glushenkov TVD-100 turboshaft above the cabin. This power plant gives the Ka-126 a significant increase in endurance, payload and range capability, and it is anticipated that many of the Ka-26s in service will undergo conversion.

Learjet 55c

Kawasaki T-4 (Japan) To meet the requirement of the Japan Air Self-Defence Force for a new intermediate trainer, the Japan Defence Agency named Kawasaki as prime contractor to produce a new aircraft, with Fuji and Mitsubishi each to have a 30 per cent share in the production programme. Based on a Kawasaki design, the T-4 is a cantilever mid-wing monoplane of basic all-metal construction, with only moderate use of composite materials. Carried on retractable tricycle landing gear, it seats the instructor and pupil (forward) in a tandem cockpit which is pressurized and air-conditioned. Power is provided by two 16.32 kN (3,670 lb st) Ishikawajimas-Harima F3-IHI-30 turbofans, giving a maximum level speed of Mach 0.9. The T-4 has no built in armament, but can carry practice bombs or missiles. The first of four prototypes was flown initially on 29 July 1985, the first production T-4 on 28 June 1988, and the first 12 production aircraft (from a requirement for about 200) were expected to be in service by early 1989.

King's Model 44 Angel (USA) Eight-seat or three-seat and cargo utility monoplane, powered by two 224 kW (300 hp) Textron Lycoming IO-540-M piston engines driving pusher propellers. Developed for missionary work and first flown in early 1984. Production could start in 1989.

Lake LA-250 Renegade, Turbo Renegade and Seawolf (USA) Renegade is a 186 kW (250 hp) Textron Lycoming IO-540-C4B5-engined and six-seat development of the Lake LA4-200 Amphibian. A turbocharged version is named Turbo Renegade. A military version of Renegade is the Seawolf, capable of maritime patrol, photographic reconnaissance, search and rescue, fishery protection, strike and other duties with the appropriate avionics and equipment installed.

Learjet 31 (USA) Basically a long wing span (with winglets) version of the Learjet 35A/36A, first flown on 11 May 1987. Deliveries began in 1988.

Learjet 55C (USA) Four/eight-passenger executive jet, powered by two 16.46 kN (3,700 lb st) Garrett TFE731-3A-2B turbofan engines. Extended range (55C/ER) and long-range (55C/LR) versions are also available.

Let L-610 (Czechoslovakia) Forty passenger short-haul commuter airliner, first flown in 1988. Two 1,358 kW (1,822 shp) Motorlet M 602 turboprop engines. Range 870–2,405 km (540–1,495 miles).

Lockheed C-5B Galaxy (USA) First flown on 10 September 1985, the C-5B is a new production version of this heavy logistics transport. Fifty have been delivered since 1986, incorporating as standard all the improvements retrofitted to C-5As. Dimensions remain the same. Power is provided by four 191.2 kN (43,000 lb st) General Electric TF39-GE-1C turbofan engines. Max T-O weight 379,655 kg (837,000 lb). Max level speed 919 km/h (571 mph). Range 5,525–10,410 km (3,434–6,469 miles). Payload 118,388 kg (261,000 lb).

Lockheed P-3 Sentinel

Lockheed S-3B and ES-3A Viking (USA) The new S-3B designation will apply to perhaps an eventual total of 160 S-3A Vikings after modification to this later standard under a weapons system improvement programme. New production S-3Bs could follow. Improvements have been made to the radar processing system, acoustic processing system and electronic support measures, while other changes include a new sonobuoy telemetry receiver system and carriage of Harpoon anti-ship missiles. In another programme, 16 S-3As were to be modified into ES-3A electronic reconnaissance aircraft, replacing EA-3B Skywarriors.

Lockheed P-3 Sentinel (USA) Airborne early warning and control version of the P-3 Orion, using a Grumman E-2C Hawkeye type radar installation for military operated models. The US Customs Service has received the first aircraft, equipped with the General Electric AN/APS-125 radar system, for use in anti-narcotics operations.

Lockheed F-117A (USA) First flown in June 1981, this is a highly classified stealth reconnaissance attack aircraft, of which some 56 are operated by the USAF's 4450th Tactical Group at Nellis Air Force Base, stationed at Tonapha Test Range in Nevada. Three have been lost in accidents. Possibly powered by two 48 kN (10,800 lb st) non-afterburning General Electric F404-GE-400 turbofan engines, features include a radar absorbant airframe shaped as an arrow head and skinned with many flat panels, twin canted tailfins to help mask the above-fuselage engine nozzles, an internal weapons bay, and a flush cockpit for the single crew member. As it cannot use radar because of its stealth mission, navigation is by the global positioning system. Dimensions have not been released. Estimated weapon load and max take-off weight are 1,814 kg (4,000 lb) and 20,400 kg (45,000 lb) respectively.

seven passengers (standard) or ten passengers (high density). There are individual production lines in Germany and Japan, the former having produced the lion's share to date (some 150 aircraft) with Japan building about 10 per cent of

Lockheed F-117A

MBB BO 108

Lockheed TR-1 and ER-2 (USA) Sharing the same basic airframe as the Lockheed U-2R (which see in main text), there are three versions of the TR-1. These comprise the single-seat tactical reconnaissance TR-1A, and a two-seat trainer version designated TR-1B. The ER-2, which is generally similar to the TR-1A, is equipped specially for use by NASA as an Earth resources research aircraft.

Maule M-7 and MX-7 Star Craft (USA) Turboprop versions of the Super Rocket and Star Rocket, using the 313 kW (420 shp) Allison 250-B17C power plant.

Maule MX-7 Star Rocket and Super Rocket (USA) The Star Rocket is a STOL four-seat light aircraft, powered by either a 134 kW (180 hp) Textron Lycoming O-360-C1F or 175 kW (235 hp) O-540 piston engine. The M-6 Super Rocket was developed from the earlier M-5-235C version, featuring revised wings. Engine choices as for the MX-7-235 version of the Star Rocket. The M-7-235 Super Rocket is a five-seater, with similar engine choices but featuring increased wing span and weights.

MBB/Kawasaki BK 117 and BK 117M (West Germany/Japan) Joint development of the BK 117 multi-purpose helicopter by MBB and Kawasaki was agreed on 25 February 1977, the first (Kawasaki-built) production aircraft flown initially on 24 December 1981. Deliveries of the first production BK 117 A-1s began in early 1983, later followed by the BK 117 A-3 with enlarged tail rotor and increase in maximum T-O weight, and BK-117 A-4 with improved tail rotor head and increased transmission limit on T-O power. Current production version, the BK 117 B-1, has as powerplant two new Textron Lycoming LTS 101-750B-1 engines giving improved performance. Optional accommodation caters for a pilot and six passengers (executive),

this figure. MBB in Germany has developed without the collaboration of Kawasaki a multi-role military version of the BK 117 which is designated BK 117M. It differs primarily by having high-skid landing gear to allow the mounting of an underfuselage gun turret, and outrigger pylons for a wide range of weapons.

MBB BO 108 (West Germany) This new helicopter has the configuration of a scaled-down BK 117 and is being used to evaluate new helicopter technologies. Its two 335.5 kW (450 shp) Allison 250-C20R-3 turboshaft engines drive a four-blade bearingless main rotor with elastomeric damping. Much of the airframe is constructed of composite materials. The first BO 108 flew in 1988.

McDonnell Douglas AH-64A Apache (USA)* Originally developed by Hughes, delivery of production Apaches to the US Army began in January 1984, allowing the 3rd Squadron of the 6th Cavalry Regiment to achieve initial operational capability by July 1986. A total of 357 Apaches had been received by mid-1988, when production continued to US Army active and National Guard units. Ongoing development includes programmes to provide air-to-air missile armament and to evaluate a future ship-based version.

McDonnell Douglas AH-64A Apache

McDonnell Douglas

Artist's impression of the McDonnell Douglas F-15S/MTD

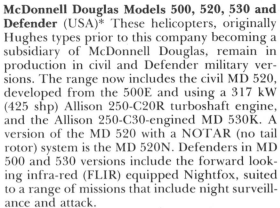

McDonnell Douglas Model 530F Lister

McDonnell Douglas 530MG Defender

McDonnell Douglas Models 500, 520, 530 and Defender (USA)* These helicopters, originally Hughes types prior to this company becoming a subsidiary of McDonnell Douglas, remain in production in civil and Defender military versions. The range now includes the civil MD 520, developed from the 500E and using a 317 kW (425 shp) Allison 250-C20R turboshaft engine, and the Allison 250-C30-engined MD 530K. A version of the MD 520 with a NOTAR (no tail rotor) system is the MD 520N. Defenders in MD 500 and 530 versions include the forward looking infra-red (FLIR) equipped Nightfox, suited to a range of missions that include night surveillance and attack.

US Navy McDonnell Douglas F/A-18A Hornets

McDonnell Douglas F-15 Eagle (USA)* The USAF had received 850 Eagles by early 1988, equipping active and Air National Guard units. Export users include Israel (F-15A, B and C) and Saudi Arabia (F-15C and D). The JASDF is also receiving 187 F-15Js and DJs, 173 of which are being built by Mitsubishi in Japan. Two 104.3 kN (23,450 lb st) with afterburning Pratt & Whitney F100-PW-220 turbofan engines have been the standard power plant for production Eagles since 1985. The USAF has also been receiving since 1988 examples of the two-seat attack and air superiority dual-role F-15E, with a 10,670 kg (23,500 lb) weapon load, for day/night, adverse weather high-weapon load attack missions, long-range interdiction and air superiority. Avionics include Hughes AN/APG-70 radar, FLIR, Martin Marietta LANTIRN navigation/targeting pods, a Lear Siegler Astronautics flight control system for coupled automatic terrain following, and a Honeywell ring laser gyro inertial navigation system for highly accurate navigation. Either F110 or Pratt & Whitney F100 engines can be installed. The USAF expects to receive 392 F-15Es. An advanced STOL/manoeuvring technology demonstrator Eagle (the F-15S/MTD) has also been flown, intended to lead to a version that can cope with the short take-off and landing runs associated with war-damaged runways. It will also have improved manoeuvring capability. The programme is investigating two-dimensional engine thrust vectoring/reversing nozzles, an integrated flight and engine system, a rough and soft field STOL undercarriage, and advanced pilot and aircraft interfaces. A modified F-15B has initiated this research programme.

McDonnell Douglas F/A-18 Hornet (USA)* A total of 410 single-seat F/A-18A and two-seat operational training F/A-18B Hornets joined the US Navy/Marine Corps between 1980 and 1987, when production switched to the F/A-18C and D versions with changes to the avionics, and provision for AMRAAM and imaging IR Maverick missiles. The first F/A-18C was delivered in September 1987. Cs and Ds delivered from October 1989 have the ability to perform all-weather night attack missions. The Canadian Armed Forces received CF-18As and Bs from October 1982, the Royal Australian Air Force received AF-18As and ATF-18As from early 1985, and the Spanish Air Force received EF-18As and Bs from 1986. The US Navy/Marine Corps will eventually receive a total of 1,168 Hornets. The maximum weapon load and take-off weights in fighter and attack configurations are, respectively, 7,710 kg (17,000 lb), 16,650 kg (36,710 lb) and 22,328 kg (49,224 lb) for the F/A-18C model.

McDonnell Douglas KC-10A Extender (USA) First flown on 12 July 1980, this is a military in-flight refuelling and cargo-carrying derivative

of the DC-10 airliner. Sixty have joined the USAF, each powered by three 233.53 kN (52,500 lb st) General Electric CF6-50C2 turbofan engines and accommodating 68,610 litres (18,125 US gallons) of fuel in seven lower fuselage compartment cells in addition to its own standard fuel capacity. Maximum cargo capacity is 76,843 kg (169,409 lb).

McDonnell Douglas MD-11 (USA) Derived from the DC-10, this new medium/long-range airliner has a longer fuselage accommodating up to 323 passengers, winglets, cambered aerofoil tailplane, an all-digital two-man flight deck and other advanced features. Power will be provided by three 266.9 kN (60,000 lb st) Pratt & Whitney PW4360, 289–311 kN (65,000–70,000 lb st) Rolls-Royce RB211-524L or 273.6 kN (61,500 lb st) General Electric CF6-80C2D1F turbofan engines. Maximum range will be 12,990 km (8,070 miles) for the basic version. Other versions will be the 277-passenger MD-11ER short-fuselage extended-range model, MD-11 Combi mixed passenger and cargo model, MD-11F freighter, and the MD-11 Super Stretch accommodating 370 passengers in a longer fuselage. The first MD-11 flew in 1989, allowing the start of commercial services in 1990.

McDonnell Douglas MD-80 Series (USA) Current designation of DC-9 Super 80 series aircraft. 172-passenger MD-81 has Pratt & Whitney JT8D-209 turbofan engines, MD-82 has -217 engines, longer-range MD-83 has -219 engines, 109–139 passenger short fuselage MD-87 has -217C engines, 142-passenger MD-88 has -219 engines and an electronic flight instruments cockpit display system, while the Executive Jet has executive and corporate versions of the MD-83 and MD-87. The highest weight versions are the MD-83 and MD-88, at 72,575 kg (160,000 lb) max take-off weights (optional weight for the MD-88), while the MD-82 has the greatest payload weight, of 19,709 kg (43,450 lb).

McDonnell Douglas/BAe Harrier II (USA/UK)*
Collaboration by McDonnell Douglas and BAe on development of the AV-8A Harrier has led to the Harrier, II which has the designations AV-8B and TAV-8B (USMC) and Harrier GR.Mk 5 (RAF). By comparison with the earlier AV-8A/Harrier GR.Mk 3, the new Harrier II incorporates many structural changes to augment lift, enhance manoeuvrability and air combat capability, improve weapon load, and cater for higher operating weights; engine air intakes have been redesigned to allow greater thrust; and on-board equipment has been improved progressively to give better operational capability and allow the pilot to manage the aircraft more effectively. Among airframe changes are the new larger composite-built supercritical wings, with leading edge root extensions. Major production version is the AV-8B for the USMC, which has a requirement for 295; the first pilot production aircraft was flown on 29 August 1983, and by early 1989 six operational and one training squadron had been formed. The prototype of a night attack version was flown on 26 June 1987 and this variant has entered production. The designation EAV-8B applies to 12 export single-seaters for the Spanish Navy, all of them delivered, and the TAV-8B is a two-seat operational trainer version of which the USMC requires 28. The RAF's initial production order covered 60 Harrier GR.Mk 5s, and a follow-on contract for 34 was announced during 1988. However, under a programme known as Nightbird, a two-seat night attack version of the Harrier has been developed by BAe, this having the unofficial designation Harrier GR.Mk 7. It is planned that the last 34 on order will be completed to this Mk.7 configuration and, ultimately, aircraft from the original contract will be retrofitted to this standard.

Data (AV-8B): *Engine* one 95.42 kN (21,450 lb st) Rolls-Royce F402-RR-406A (Pegasus 11) vectored thrust turbofan *Wing span* 9.25 m (30 ft 4 in) *Length* 14.12 m (46 ft 4 in) *Max T-O weight* 14,061 kg (31,000 lb) *Max speed* Mach 0.91

McDonnell Douglas/BAe T-45A Goshawk (USA/UK) The BAe Hawk (see main text) was selected by the US Navy on 18 November 1981 as an undergraduate jet pilot trainer to replace the T-2C Buckeye and TA-4J Skyhawk. For US Navy requirements the T-45A differs from the standard Hawk by being modified for carrier operations. Scheduled to enter service in late 1990, current Navy plans cover the procurement of 300 production aircraft.

Melex T45 Turbine Dromader (USA) Turboprop conversion of the Polish M-18 Dromader agricultural aircraft, using a Pratt & Whitney Canada PT6A-45AG engine derated to 735 kW (986 shp). A firefighting water-bomber version is being developed.

Microjet 200 B (France) Lightweight side-by-

McDonnell Douglas KC-10A Extender

USMC McDonnell Douglas/BAe AV-8B Harrier II

Mikoyan MiG-31

side two-seat jet trainer, with a max take-off weight of just 1,300 kg (2,865 lb). Some use of composite materials in the airframe. Powered by two 1.45 kN (326 lb st) Microturbo TRS 18-1 turbojet engines, exhausting through jetpipes in the rear of the fuselage sides. First flown on 19 May 1983 in pre-production form.

Mikoyan MiG-29 (USSR) Soviet development of an air superiority fighter in the class of the American F-16 and Hornet was detected by satellite in the late 1970s. When production was confirmed the NATO reporting name *Fulcrum* was allocated. The MiG-29 has been in operational service since 1985 and with this aircraft the Soviet Union has matched (and in some respects surpassed) any fighter of the West. This achievement extends beyond performance upgrading, for the introduction of an infra-red search/track sensor and pulse Doppler lookdown/shootdown radar provides new capability for Soviet aircraft in terms of day/night all-weather operation and freedom from the restrictions of ground control interception. Other technologies include the use of a helmet aiming sight and very advanced missiles. In configuration the MiG-29 is a cantilever low-wing monoplane with twin tailfins/rudders and all-moving horizontal tail surfaces, retractable tricycle landing gear and powerplant of two afterburning turbofans. It is built in two versions, *Fulcrum-A* being the operational single-

Mikoyan Mig 29A Falcrum

seater which has been identified in four variants exhibiting minor changes, probably indicating different stages of development resulting from squadron service. *Fulcrum-B* identifies the combat trainer, which seats the pupil forward of the normal cockpit. More than 450 MiG-29s are believed to be operational with Soviet air forces, and the type has been delivered to East Germany, India, North Korea, Syria and Yugoslavia.
Data: *Engines* two Tumansky R-33D turbofans, each 81.4 kN (18,300 lb st) with afterburning *Wing span* 11.36 m (37 ft 3.25 in) *Length* 17.32 m (56 ft 10 in) *Max T-O weight* 18,000 kg (39,700 lb) *Max level speed* Mach 2.3 *Armament* One 30 mm cannon plus 6 AA-10 (*Alamo-A*) and AA-11 (*Archer*) AAMs or attack weapons

Mikoyan MiG-31 (USSR) Rumours that the Mikoyan bureau was developing an improved version of the MiG-25 *Foxbat* (which see in main text) began circulating in the 1970s, but it was not until 1982 that NATO allocated the reporting name *Foxhound* to an aircraft then being dubbed Super Foxbat by the Western press. A first provisional three-view drawing of this air-

craft appeared in 1983, but it was not until the Autumn of 1985 that it was possible to confirm this as being fairly accurate. Clearly developed from the MiG-25, with generally similar wings, it introduced such features as wingroot leading-edge extensions, enlarged engine air inlets, and tandem seating for a two-man crew. It remained to be discovered that *Foxhound* had Tumansky turbojet engines developing 137.3 kN (30,865 lb) afterburning thrust and gained new combat capability by introduction of active countermeasures dispensers, an infra-red search/track sensor, and a pulse Doppler radar with lookdown/shootdown and multiple target engagement capability. It is now known that the type entered service with Soviet air defence regiments in early 1983, and it is believed that some 160 are now operational.
Data (estimated): *Wing span* 14.00 m (45 ft 11.25 in) *Max T-O weight* 41,150 kg (90,725 lb) *Max level speed* Mach 2.4 *Armament* Eight AA-8 (*Aphid*) and AA-9 (*Amos*) AAMs

Mil Mi-17 (USSR) First seen publicly at the Paris Air Show in 1981, the Mil Mi-17 (NATO reporting name *Hip-H*) is basically an updated version of the Mil Mi-8 (*Hip*) (which see in the main text). The Mi-17 retains basically the same airframe as the Mi-8, except that the tail rotor is to the port (rather than starboard) side of the vertical stabiliser. Primary change is the installation of more powerful Isotov TV3-117MT turboshafts, each with a T-O rating of 1,417 kW (1,900 shp) which give an expanded performance envelope by comparison with the Mi-8, including an increase of 1,000 kg (2,205 lb) in max T-O weight.

Mil Mi-24 and Mi-25 (USSR)* In addition to the *Hind-A, B, C* (training) and *D* versions of this helicopter detailed in the original A–Z, the *Hind-E* has been identified as a version of the 'D' but carrying 12 AT-6 *Spiral* anti-armour missiles and the ability to launch AA-8 *Aphid* air-to-air missiles, *Hind-F* has a 30 mm gun on the fuselage side and no nose gun position, and *Hind-G* appears to be used for radiation sampling and was evident during the Chernobyl nuclear power station disaster. Mi-25 is the designation of *Hinds* exported to Angola, India, Peru and perhaps elsewhere, with some changes in equipment.
Data (*Hind-D*): *Engines* two 1,640 kW (2,200 shp) Isotov TV3-117 turboshafts *Rotor diameter* 17.0 m (55 ft 9 in) *Length overall* 21.5 m (70 ft 6 in) *Take-off weight* 11,000 kg (24,251 lb) *Max level speed* 310 km/h (192 mph) *Range* 750 km (465 miles) *Armament* 1,500 kg (3,300 lb) load

Mil Mi-26 *Halo* (USSR)* First flown in prototype form on 14 December 1977, the Mil Mi-26 heavy

lift helicopter is (apart from the Mil Mi-12 of which only a prototype was built) the heaviest rotary-wing aircraft yet flown, and the first to operate successfully with an eight-blade main rotor. Its large fuselage, which incorporates clamshell rear loading doors and ramp, accommodates a flight crew of five, plus a four-seat passenger compartment aft of the flight deck. The main hold can cater for a maximum cargo load of 20,000 kg (44,090 lb) or, alternatively, can seat about 85 combat equipped troops. *Halo* first entered squadron service in early 1983 and more than 50 are now operational.

Mil Mi-28 (USSR) Existence of the Mil Mi-28 combat helicopter (to which NATO has allocated the reporting name *Havoc*) has been known since 1984, but some doubt seems to exist as to whether it has yet emerged from the prototype development stage. In configuration it has a five-blade main and three-blade tail rotor, a fuselage incorporating tandem cockpits (that at the rear elevated for the pilot) with integral armour surrounding them, non-retractable tail-wheel type landing gear, and with power provided by two unidentified turboshaft engines. Stub wings have underwing hardpoints for anti-armour and air-to-air missiles and rockets, and armament includes a heavy calibre gun in an undernose turret.
Data (estimated): *Main rotor diameter* 17.00 m (55 ft 9 in) *Max T-O weight* 8,000 kg (17,635 lb) *Max level speed* 300 km/h (186 mph)

Mil Mi-34 (USSR) Intended primarily for pilot training and/or competition flying at international level, Mil's Mi-34 (NATO reporting name *Hermit*) is a two/four-seat lightweight helicopter that would clearly be suitable also for other general purpose roles. Of conventional pod and boom configuration on skid landing gear, the Mi-34 has four-blade main and two-blade tail rotors, and is powered by a 242 kW (325 hp) Vedeneyev M-14-26 radial piston engine mounted within the fuselage. The first flight of a prototype was made during 1986 but no production decision had been made in early 1989.

Mooney 205 (USA) This is a more aerodynamic development of the Mooney 201, first appearing in 1986.

Mooney 252TSE (USA) This four-seat monoplane appeared in 1985 as a Turbo Mooney 231 replacement, powered by a 156.5 kW (210 hp) Continental TSIO-360-MB-1 turbocharged engine.

Mooney PFM (USA) Similar to the Mooney 252TSE but with a lengthened fuselage and using a 162 kW (217 hp) Porsche PFM 3200-N03 piston engine. First flown in May 1987.

Mudry CAP 230 (France) Developed from the CAP 21 as a single-seat aerobatic monoplane with a 224 kW (300 hp) Textron Lycoming AEIO-540-L1 piston engine. First flown on 8 October 1985.

NAC Fieldmaster (UK) Two-seat agricultural monoplane, first flown on 17 December 1981. Also suited to firefighting. The chemical hopper forms part of the fuselage. Current standard engine is a 559 kW (750 shp) Pratt & Whitney Canada PT6A-34AG turboprop engine. Deliveries began in 1987.

NAC Firecracker (UK) Tandem two-seat trainer, powered by a 533 kW (715 ehp) Pratt & Whitney Canada PT6A-25A turboprop engine. First flew on 1 September 1983. Military examples can opt for the 559 kW (750 shp) -25D engine if more power is required, and weapons can be carried on four underwing stations.

NAC Freelance (UK) Four-seat utility light-plane, powered by a 134 kW (180 hp) Textron Lycoming O-360-A4M piston engine. First flown on 29 September 1984. Also suitable for agricultural, ambulance, photography, towing and other roles.

NAMC CJ-6 and Haiyan (China) The CJ-6 is a Chinese tandem two-seat basic trainer, first flown in 1958. Power is provided by a 213 kW (285 hp) Zhuzhou Huosai-6A radial engine. Based on the Soviet Yak-18A design/Chinese CJ-5, which it superseded. The Haiyan is a civil modification of the CJ-6, developed for agricultural, forestry and patrol duties. One 257 kW (345 hp) engine of similar type.

NAMC L-8 Karakorum 8 (China) To be flown around 1990, this is a tandem two-seat jet trainer and light attack aircraft of typical modern design. Power is provided by a 15.57 kN (3,500 lb st) Garrett TFE731-2A turbofan engine.

NAMC Q-5/A-5 (China) Known to NATO as *Fantan*, the Q-5 single-seat close air support and attack aircraft was developed in China and based on the J-6 (MiG-19). It uses similar wings but with new flaps and no spoilers, and the fuselage has a 'solid' nose and is longer. Initial examples used the longer fuselage to house an internal weapons bay, but more recently this bay has been used to carry a huge increase in the internal fuel load.

The prototype Q-5 made its maiden flight on 5

Pakistani NAMC A-5C Fantans

June 1965. It continues to be built and developed, the current Mk III version going to the Air Force to keep the number in use at about 500, while the People's Navy uses a further 100 or thereabouts as interceptors. The current export model is the A-5C, perhaps 140 being operated by Pakistan, while the earlier A-5B is used by North Korea (some 40). Although none of these carry attack radar in the nose, current development of the A-5K/A-5M versions introduce this. The prototype A-5K Kong Yun flew for the first time in late 1988 and carries French Thomson-CSF radar, a head-up display, an inertial navigation system, laser rangefinder and more. Two prototype A-5Ms with Italian avionic systems and other changes have also flown, the first on 30 August 1988. However, one was lost in an accident that October.

Data (Mk III): *Engines* two 31.87 kN (7,165 lb st) with afterburning Shenyang Wopen 6 turbojets *Wing span* 9.70 m (31 ft 10 in) *Length* 16.26 m (53 ft 4 in) *Max T-O weight* 12,000 kg (26,455 lb) *Max level speed* 1,210 km/h (752 mph) *Range* 2,000 km (1,242 miles) with auxiliary fuel tanks *Armament* two fixed 23 mm cannon plus up to 2,000 kg (4,409 lb) of attack and/or air-to-air weapons on ten stations

Nash Petral (UK) Two-seat lightplane, first flown on 8 November 1980 and powered by a 134 kW (180 hp) Textron Lycoming O-360-A3A piston engine.

with a 'zig-zag' trailing-edge. Flap-elevons along the trailing-edge and a system of vectored thrust using the engine exhaust over the flaps provide control. There are no vertical tail surfaces. The aircraft's configuration, plus the special composite materials used for airframe construction and other features, are designed to offer very low radar, infra-red and acoustic signatures for an enemy to detect. The eventual total force is expected to be 132, with all but 12 having a nuclear strategic role. Operational deployment will not begin until well into the next decade, with Whiteman Air Force Base in Missouri as the first B-2A station.

Data (provisional): *Engines* four General Electric F118-GE-100 non-afterburning turbofans *Wing span* 52.43 m (172 ft 0 in) *Length* 21.03 m (69 ft 0 in) *Max T-O weight* about 136,077 kg (300,000 lb) *Max level speed* high subsonic *Range* 8,050–12,000 km (5,000–7,500 miles) *Armament* probably 16 cruise missiles or nuclear bombs in the nuclear strategic bomber role

OMAC Laser 300 (USA) Seven/ten-seat business aircraft, with rear-mounted sweptback wings (with tipfins) and foreplanes. Power is provided by a 559 kW (750 shp) Pratt & Whitney Canada PT6A-135A turboprop engine mounted in the rear of the fuselage and driving a pusher propeller. First flown on 11 December 1981. Delivery of production aircraft is expected to begin in 1989.

Panavia Tornado (UK/West Germany/Italy)* The first Tornado IDSs for the RAF (as Tornado GR.Mk 1s) were delivered to No IX Squadron at RAF Honington in January 1982. The RAF has since received its 228, of which those based in West Germany now have the capability to carry tactical nuclear weapons. In late 1988, No 2 Squadron became the first RAF unit to fly the Tornado in reconnaissance form. The RAF has nine IDS squadrons, seven based in West Germany. The West German Luftwaffe and Marineflieger has received 211 and 111 IDSs

Northrop B-2A

Northrop B-2A (USA) Rolled out for public viewing on 22 November 1988, a prototype of this new stealth bomber confirmed speculation that it was indeed a flying-wing. The wing has about a 35° angle of leading-edge sweepback,

respectively, and the former is in the process of receiving 35 examples of an ECR variant (electronic combat and reconnaissance). The Italian Air Force received the first of its 100 IDSs (some for air superiority role) in August 1982. In

addition, the IDS was ordered by Jordan, Malaysia and Saudi Arabia, but in 1989 Jordan postponed its eight.

The Tornado ADV entered RAF service from 9 October 1985 in F.Mk 2 form, with Turbo-Union RB199-34R Mk 103 turbofans. From the 19th aircraft (of 165 ordered) they have been in F.Mk 3 form, with Mk 104 turbofans and other changes. F.Mk 2s are being modified to later standard in most respects except for those relating to the power plant, thereafter being designated F.Mk 2A. Oman and Saudi Arabia became customers also for the ADV.

Panavia is also teaming with Rockwell International in order to submit a version of the IDS for the competition to find a future replacement for the F-4G Phantom II Wild Weasel.

Data (IDS): *Engines* two 71.2 kN (16,000 lb st) with afterburning Turbo-Union RB199-34R Mk 101 turbofans *Wing span* as previously detailed *Length* 16.72 m (54 ft 10¼ in) *Max T-O weight* about 27,215 kg (60,000 lb) *Max level speed* Mach 2.2 *Radius of action* 1,390 km (863 miles) *Armament* external weapon load is about 9,000 kg (19,840 lb), including Kormoran, ALARM, HARM, Aspide, and Sidewinder missiles, MW-1 munitions dispenser, and so on. Some have tactical nuclear capability.

Partenavia AP 68TP-300 Spartacus (Italy) Out of production since 1988, this is an 8/9-seat transport derived from the P.68. Total number delivered to customers was 11.

Partenavia AP 68TP-600 Viator (Italy) Basically a 10-seat general-purpose transport but currently used also for photogrammetric and other roles, developed from the Spartacus and featuring a longer fuselage and a retractable undercarriage. Two 244.5 kW (328 shp) Allison 250-B17C turboprop engines. First flown on 29 March 1985.

Piaggio P.180 Avanti (Italy) First flown on 23 September 1986, this is a highly unusual 5 to 9-passenger executive transport. Of metal and composites construction, it features rear-mounted straight wings carrying two 634 kW (850 shp) Pratt & Whitney Canada PT6A-66 turboprop engines mounted in pusher configuration and a foreplane. Production deliveries will probably begin in 1990–91.

Pilatus PC-7 Turbo-Trainer (Switzerland)* This two-seat aircraft is suitable as standard for basic, aerobatic and transition training and, with the necessary equipment installed, for instrument and tactical training. It is currently available with optional Martin-Baker lightweight Mk CH 15A ejection seats. Since the first production PC-7 was flown on 18 August 1978, a total of close on 400 have been sold and most of them delivered. Military customers include the air forces of Abu Dhabi (24), Angola (18), Austria (16), Bolivia (36), Burma (17), Guatemala (12), Iran (35), Iraq (52), Malaysia (44), Mexico (75), Switzerland (40) and the Chilean Navy (10).

Data: *Engine* one 485 kW (650 shp) Pratt & Whitney Canada PT6A-25A turboprop *Wing span* 10.40 m (34 ft 1 in) *Length* 9.78 m (32 ft 1 in) *Max T-O weight* 2,700 kg (5,952 lb) *Max cruising speed* 412 km/h (256 mph) *Max endurance* 4 hrs 22 min

Panavia Tornado F.Mk 2

Pilatus PC-7

Pilatus PC-9 (Switzerland) This single/two-seat advanced trainer, is similar in appearance to the PC-7 Turbo-Trainer but actually shares little of the same structure. Built basically of light alloy, glassfibre-reinforced plastics are introduced for a number of fairings, and easily noted external differences include the 'stepped' tandem cockpit with ejection seats as standard, a ventral airbrake and mainwheel doors. Power plant is a more powerful version of the P&WC PT6A turboprop than that of the PC-7. Following the first flights of two pre-production aircraft in May and July of 1984, and the receipt of Aerobatic category

Pilatus PC-9 operated by Burma

certification on 19 September 1985, initial production deliveries began. Customers include the Tamdaw Lay (Burma) Burma Air Force (4), Royal Saudi Air Force (30), approximately 25 for undisclosed customers and, most importantly, 67 for the Royal Australian Air Force which designates them PC-9/A; of these 48 are being built in Australia by Hawker de Havilland and ASTA. The first four aircraft were handed over to the RAAF in December 1987.

Data: *Engine* one Pratt & Whitney Canada PT6A-62 turboprop flat rated at 708 kW (950 shp) *Wing span* 10.124 m (33 ft 2.5 in) *Length* 10.175 m (33 ft 4.75 in) *Max T-O weight* 3,200 kg (7,055 lb) *Max level speed* 556 km/h (345 mph) *Max range* 1,642 km (1,020 miles)

Piper PA-42-1000 Cheyenne 400 (USA) Eight-seat business aircraft, delivered to customers from July 1984. Two 1,226.5 kW (1,645 shp) Garrett TPE331-14A/B turboprop engines.

Piper PA-46-310P Malibu (USA) Six-seat pressurised light monoplane, powered by a 231 kW (310 hp) Continental TSIO-520-BE piston engine. Customer deliveries started in late 1983.

Piper PA-34-220T Seneca III (USA) Improved version of the six-seat Seneca, with two 164 kW (220 hp) Continental TSIO/LTSIO-360-KB turbocharged piston engines. Also produced under an agreement in Poland as the PZL Mielec M-20 Mewa, with similarly rated PZL-F engines.

Promavia Jet Squalus F1300 NGT (Belgium) This new jet trainer has been developed to take a trainee pilot through all levels of training until transferred for aspects of the advanced course. The first prototype made its maiden flight on 30 April 1987. Instructor and trainee on side-by-side ejection seats. Engine exhausts under fuselage, aft of wings. Four underwing stations for up to 600 kg (1,322 lb) of weapons or equipment, including 12.7 mm or 20 mm guns, or rocket launchers.

Data: *Engine* currently one 5.916 kN (1,330 lb st) Garrett TFE76 turbofan *Wing span* 9.04 m (29 ft 8 in) *Length* 9.36 m (30 ft 8½ in) *Max T-O weight* 2,400 kg (5,290 lb) *Max level speed* 584 km/h (363 mph) *Ferry range* 1,850 km (1,149 miles)

RFB Fantrainer 400 and 600 (West Germany)*
Details of the Fantrainer 400 can be found in the main text, the first German-built production aircraft to fly (on 12 August 1984) being a Fantrainer 600 which differs primarily by having an Allison 250-C30 turbofan. The Royal Thai Air Force ordered 31 Fantrainer 400s and 16 Fantrainer 600s in August 1982. Only two were fully built in Germany, delivered in 1984. The others are being assembled from components in Thailand. The Luftwaffe has also evaluated the Fantrainer, as a possible replacement for the Piaggio P.149D.

Data: *Engine* one 485 kW (650 shp) Allison 250-C30 turbofan *Wing span* 9.74 m (31 ft 11.5 in) *Length* 9.48 m (31 ft 1.25 in) *Max T-O weight* 2,000 kg (4,409 lb) *Max speed* 463 km/h (288 mph)

Piper Seneca III built in Poland as the M-20 Mewa

Prototype RFB Fantrainer 400

Robin ATL (France) Two- or four-seat lightweight monoplane, suited to private and club use and available in several versions with differing engines. Airframe constructed of wood, composite materials and fabric. Powered by one 48 kW (65 hp) JPX 4T 60A piston engine in two-seat Club form, when the max take-off weight is 580 kg (1,278 lb). First flown 17 June 1983.

Robin DR 400/100 Cadet (France) Two-seat development of the DR 400/120 Dauphin (known prior to 1979 as the Petit Prince*), with the maximum take-off weight reduced to 800 kg (1,764 lb). Similar Textron Lycoming engine.

Robin R 3000 (France) Series of low-wing monoplane light aircraft, the R 3000/140 having a maximum take-off weight of 1,050 kg (2,315 lb) and a max level speed of 250 km/h (155 mph) on the power of a 119 kW (160 hp) Textron Lycoming O-320-D2A piston engine. First flown 8 December 1980.

Rockwell International B-1B (USA) Developed from the cancelled B-1, the first of 100 production B-1B strategic bombers made its maiden flight on 18 October 1984 and all have been delivered. Three have since been lost. The 96th Bomb Wing at Dyess Air Force Base in Texas was the first to achieve initial operational capability, in September 1986.

The four-crew B-1B differs from the B-1 in making better use of stealth or 'low observable' technology, with a radar signature one-hundredth that of the B-52. It has been strengthened, has a more adaptable bomb-bay arrangement, and uses fixed engine air intakes and less

Rockwell International B-1B

sophisticated engine nacelles/overwing fairings, which reflect its considerably lower speed and its main role as a low-altitude subsonic bomber (but capable of supersonic speed). To assist it to elude enemy detection and attack, on board systems include radar location and warning, electronic jamming, infra-red countermeasures, chaff and flares. The defensive electronic countermeasures suite centres on the Eaton AN/ALQ-161 system.
Data: *Engines* four 136.9 kN (30,780 lb st) with afterburning General Electric F101-GE-102 turbofans *Wing span* (spread) 41.67 m (136 ft 8½ in), (swept) 23.84 m (78 ft 2½ in) *Length* 44.81 m (147 ft 0 in) *Max T-O weight* 216,363 kg (477,000 lb) *Max level speed* about Mach 1.25 *Range* 12,000 km (7,455 miles) without in-flight refuelling *Armament* twenty AGM-86B ALCMs on 6 under-fuselage stations and on bomb-bay rotary launcher. Alternatively, 24 SRAM short-range missiles, or 12–24 nuclear or eighty-four 500 lb conventional bombs/mines in the three bays.

Saab 35 Draken (Sweden)* Some fifty Swedish Air Force J 35F fighters have been modified to J 35J standard for continued service until replaced by Gripens in the 1990s. Each has two extra underwing stations, and modifications have been made to the radar, weapon systems, IFF and infra-red target seeker, plus other changes. All were redelivered between 1987–89. These operate with three squadrons of F10 Wing. Austria has also received (in 1987–88) 24 upgraded J 35Ds, now redesignated 35OEs.

Saab 340A and B (Sweden) Originally developed by Saab and Fairchild as the SF 340, the American company relinquished its share in this transport aircraft in 1985 but continued as a sub-contractor until 1987. The first prototype made its maiden flight on 25 January 1983 and the first production 340A to be delivered to a customer began scheduled services with the Swiss operator Crossair in June 1984. By mid-1988 orders had been received for 137 340As. Accommodation is for up to 35 passengers. A version with 1,394 kW (1,870 shp) General Electric CT7-9B engines for improved 'hot and high' performance should be available from 1989 as the 340B. This version

also has a larger tailplane, a 12,927 kg (28,500 lb) max take-off weight, and extended range.
Data (340A): *Engines* two 1,294 kW (1,735 shp) General Electric CT7-5A2 turboprops *Wing span* 21.44 m (70 ft 4 in) *Length* 19.72 m (64 ft 8½ in) *Max T-O weight* 12,700 kg (28,000 lb) *Max cruising speed* 504 km/h (313 mph) *Range* 1,167 km (725 miles)

Saab JAS 39 Gripen (Sweden) With the requirement for a new multi-role combat aircraft to replace attack, recce and lastly interceptor versions of the Viggen, as well as all J 35 Drakens (see entries in main text) remaining in Swedish Air Force service, Saab-Scania, Volvo Flygmotor, Ericsson Radio Systems and FFV Aerotech combined their talents to propose a design. In June 1981 this group submitted its proposals to the Swedish Defense Materiel Administration and, following evaluation of the details against combat aircraft of other nations, the programme was approved on 6 May 1982. This covered development and then construction of 140 production Gripens, for delivery between 1992 and the end of the century. The first of five prototypes was rolled out on 26 April 1987, and this first flew on 9 December 1988. Gripen has delta wings and all-moving foreplanes, and one of the most significant concepts of the design is the use of carbonfibre-reinforced plastics for some 30 per cent of the fail-safe airframe structure with resultant weight savings of up to 25 per cent. Power plant comprises a single General Electric F404J afterburning turbofan which, developed

Prototype Saab JAS 39 Gripen

and produced as the RM12 in collaboration with Volvo Flygmotor, has an initial thrust rating of 80.5 kN (18,100 lb st) with afterburning. Advanced features include a triple-redundant digital fly by wire flight control system, programmable head-down CRT displays in the cockpit, and state of the art avionics. Armament will include an internally-mounted 27 mm Mauser BK27 automatic cannon and there are six underwing hardpoints for a wide variety of weapons.
Data: *Wing span* 8.00 m (26 ft 3 in) *Length* 14.10 m (46 ft 3 in) *T-O weight* about 8,000 kg (17,635 lb)

SAC J-8 II (China) Known to NATO as *Finback*, this indigenously designed air superiority fighter from the Shenyang aircraft company was taken into operational service in 1988, having been under development since the 1960s. Initial operational J-8 IIs do not have the benefit of western avionics being supplied under the US Peace Pearl programme for subsequent aircraft, for which Grumman is responsible. The latter, initially for fifty aircraft, will include (for each) a Westinghouse APG-66 fire control radar, head-up display, computers and a databus, and an inertial navigation system. *Finback* has delta wings plus a full tail unit with an all-moving tailplane. Construction is of metal.

Data: *Engines* two 65.9 kN (14,815 lb st) with afterburning Liyang Wopen 13A II turbojets *Wing span* 9.34 m (30 ft 8 in) *Length* 21.59 m (70 ft 10 in) *Max T-O weight* 17,800 kg (39,240 lb) *Max level speed* Mach 2.2 *Range* 2,200 km (1,365 miles) *Armament* one 23 mm cannon plus PL-2B and PL-7 air-to-air missiles, bombs, rockets, etc on seven stations

Sadler A-22 (USA) Single-seat lightweight ground attack development of the Vampire ultralight aircraft, with a 224 kW (300 hp) Chevrolet piston engine. Four underwing stations for 454 kg (1,000 lb) of weapons; provision for two 7.62 mm guns in the wings. Max take-off weight is 907 kg (2,000 lb) and the max level speed is 362 km/h (225 mph).

Schweizer Model 330 Sky Knight (USA) Developed from the Model 300C, this 3/4-seat helicopter is powered by an Allison 225-C10A turboshaft engine that is derated to 149 kW (200 shp). Cockpit instrumentation incorporates two CRT displays. The prototype first flew on 14 June 1988.

Shorts 330-UTT (UK) Military transport version of the 330, with a 3,630 kg (8,000 lb) payload. Accommodation for cargo, 33 troops, 30 para-

troopers or 15 stretchers plus four other persons. Royal Thai Army received the first examples in 1984–85.

Shorts Sherpa (UK) Freighter, based on the 330-200. Features a wide cargo door/ramp in the rear of the fuselage. Maximum load is 3,175 kg (7,000 lb). First flown on 23 December 1982. Deliveries include 18 designated C-23As for the USAF, used to transport spares between European military bases.

Shorts 360 (UK) First flown on 1 June 1981, this is a 36–39 passenger commuter transport. Power is provided by two 1,062 kW (1,424 shp) Pratt & Whitney Canada PT6A-67R turboprop engines. The current production model is the 360-300. The 360-300F is a freighter version, with a 4,536 kg (10,000 lb) load capacity.

SIAI-Marchetti S.211 (Italy)* First flown on 10 April 1981, this modern tandem two-seat jet trainer and light attack aircraft is in service with Haiti, Singapore and Uganda.

Data: *Engine* one 11.12 kN (2,500 lb st) Pratt & Whitney Canada JT15D-4D turbofan *Wing span* 8.43 m (27 ft 8 in) *Length* 9.31 m (30 ft 6½ in)

Max T-O weight 3,150 kg (6,944 lb) *Max cruising speed* 667 km/h (414 mph) *Range* 1,668 km (1,036 miles) *Armament* 660 kg (1,455 lb) of weapons on four underwing stations

SIAI-Marchetti SF.260 TP (Italy) Turboprop development of the SF.260, powered by a 261 kW (350 shp) Allison 250-B17D engine. Max level speed 422 km/h (262 mph).

Sikorsky H-60 Black Hawk (USA)* By early 1988 the US Army had received more than 900 of its expected 2,251 UH-60A Black Hawk assault transport helicopters. In addition, the US Marine Corps has received 9 VH-60A VIP helicopters, and the US Army will receive from 1990 the first of 22 initial long-range MH-60K special mission helicopters with Texas Instruments AN/APQ-168 terrain following radar, forward-looking infra-red, uprated power plant, and armament that may include Stinger air-to-air missiles.

Sikorsky H-76 Eagle (USA) Military version of the S-76B, first flown in 1985. Wide equipment and weapon choice includes a mast or roof mounted sight, head-up display, laser range-finder, and anti-armour, anti-ship and/or air-to-air missiles or other weapons.

Sikorsky H-76N (USA) Basically a new naval version of the S-76B, with the engine choices of the S-76 Mk II/S-76B. Suited to anti-submarine and anti-ship warfare, attack, search and rescue, over-the-horizon targeting and other roles. Mission avionics and equipment can include (de-pending on role) MEL Super Searcher or Ferranti Seaspray 3 radar, dipping sonar, forward-looking infra-red, and electronic counter-measures.

Sikorsky MH-53E Sea Dragon (USA) Mine countermeasures version of the CH-53E Super Stallion, delivered to the US Navy from June 1986. Japan is receiving similar S-80Ms. The designation S-80E applies to exported Super Stallions.

Sikorsky S-70C (USA) Commercial derivative of the H-60, powered by two 1,212 kW (1,625 shp) General Electric CT7-2C or 1,285 kW (1,723 shp) CT7-2D turboshaft engines. Twelve-to-nineteen passengers or 3,630 kg (8,000 lb) of slung cargo, or special cabin interiors for other tasks such as survey or evacuation.

Sikorsky S-76 Mk II (USA) General purpose helicopter for civil or military uses, superseding the S-76 from 1982. Higher rated power plant, comprising two 485 kW (650 shp) Allison 250-C30S turboshaft engines, and other improvements (kits available to bring earlier S-76s up to this standard). Max take-off weight is 4,672 kg (10,300 lb). A heavier version that is particularly useful for 'hot and high' operations is the S-76B, with two 716 kW (960 shp) Pratt & Whitney PT6B-36 turboshaft engines. This has a slung payload and max take-off weight of 1,497 kg (3,300 lb) and 5,170 kg (11,400 lb) respectively.

Sikorsky SH-60B Seahawk, SH-60F Ocean Hawk and HH-60 (USA)* The first prototype SH-60B (derived from the Black Hawk) made its maiden flight on 12 December 1979. Deploy-

Slingsby T67M Firefly trainers in Hong Kong

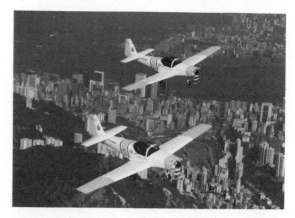

Soko G-4 Super Galeb

ment of production Seahawks by the US Navy began in 1984, for anti-submarine and anti-ship surveillance and targeting roles as LAMPS Mk III helicopters. Eventually, Seahawks will be carried on board 95 frigates, guided missile cruisers and destroyers. Mission equipment includes Texas Instruments AN/APS-124 search radar, MAD, sonobuoy launcher and receivers, magnetic tape memory system, acoustic processor and ESM. Weapons can be two torpedoes or Penguin anti-ship missiles. It has also been selected by the JMSDF as the SH-60J and by the Royal Australian Navy as the S-70B-2. The SH-60F Ocean Hawk recently entered US Navy service to protect the inner zone of a carrier battle group from enemy submarines, replacing Sea Kings. This derivative version has dipping sonar, a third weapon station and other changes. Models of the naval H-60 for combat search and rescue and special warfare are designated HH-60H by the US Navy, while the US Coast Guard has HH-60Js for medium-range recovery missions.

Data (SH-60B Seahawk): *Engines* two 1,260 kW (1,690 shp) General Electric T700-GE-401 turboshafts, superseded by two 1,417 kW (1,900 shp) T700-GE-401Cs in helicopters built since 1988 *Main rotor diameter* 16.36 m (53 ft 8 in) *Length overall* 12.47 m (40 ft 11 in) *Max T-O weight* 9,925 kg (21,884 lb) *Max level speed* 234 km/h (145 mph)

Skytrader ST1700 Conestoga and MD Evader (USA) Developed from the Dominion Skytrader, the Conestoga is a STOL commuter or cargo transport, powered by two turboprop engines. The cabin provides for various arrangements, including 18 passengers or cargo. The Evader is a military derivative, suited to carrying up to 26 troops, cargo, or casualties. Provision is made for four underwing stations, with weapon choices including gun pods, while two fuselage stations offer a Sidewinder self-defence capability. Neither version was in production in 1988.

Skytrader Scout-STOL (USA) Multi-role aircraft, of similar type to the Evader but smaller and much lighter. Can carry 16 passengers/troops or cargo, or it can perform such tasks as patrol, surveillance, photographic, fishery protection and gunship among others. Two 373 kW (500 shp) Teledyne Continental TP-500 turboprop engines. Deliveries began in 1989, for patrol and fishery protection.

Skytrader 1400 Commuterliner and Scout-A (USA) New 19-passenger and paratroop STOL transports respectively, based on the Scout-STOL but with 533 kW (715 shp) Garrett TPE331-5 turboprop engines and a lengthened fuselage. Delivery of Commuterliners was expected to start in late 1989.

Slingsby T67 and T67M Firefly (UK) Developed versions of the Fournier RF6B, intended for civil two-seat training, aerobatic and sport flying (T67) and military (or civil) training (T67M Firefly). T67B uses an 86.5 kW (116 hp) Textron Lycoming O-235-N2A piston engine, T-67C, D and T67M Firefly 160 a 119 kW (160 hp) O-320

engine and the T67M200 Firefly a 149 kW (200 hp) AEIO-360-A1E engine.

Socata Trinidad (France) Four- or five-seat light aircraft, similar to the Tobago but with a retractable undercarriage and higher-powered engine. TB 20 version uses a 186 kW (250 hp) Textron Lycoming IO-540-C4D5D piston engine. TB 21 Trinidad TC version has a turbocharged TIO-540-AB1AD engine. First flown on 14 November 1980.

Soko G-4 Super Galeb (Yugoslavia) Tandem two-seat basic jet trainer and light attack aircraft, powered by one 17.8 kN (4,000 lb st) Rolls-Royce Viper Mk 632 turbojet engine. First flown on 17 July 1978. Operated by the Yugoslav Air Force. Ventral pod for a 23 mm twin-barrel cannon. Four underwing stations for other weapons. Total weapon load is 1,950 kg (4,300 lb).

Soko J-22 Orao/CNIAR IAR-93 (Yugoslavia/Romania)* First flown on 31 October 1974, these similar close air support, attack and reconnaissance aircraft have entered operational service in four versions. Yugoslavia has received single- and two-seat training versions of the Orao 1, each powered by two 17.79 kN (4,000 lb st) Turbomecanica/Orao/Rolls-Royce Viper 632-41R non-afterburning turbojet engines. It has also received single-seat Orao 2s, using two 22.24 kN (5,000 lb st) with afterburning Viper 633-41 turbojet engines and with the payload increased from 1,500 kg (3,305 lb) to 2,800 kg (6,173 lb). Romania's equivalents are the IAR-93A and B, although the latter is built in single- and two-seat forms.

Data (Orao 2): *Engines* as above *Wing span* 9.62 m (31 ft 6¾ in) *Length* 14.90 m (48 ft 10½ in) *Max T-O weight* 11,250 kg (24,802 lb) *Max level speed* 1,160 km/h (720 mph) *Radius of action* 260–530 km (161–329 miles)

Sukhoi Su-25 (USSR) Designed and developed to provide the Soviet forces with a single-seat attack aircraft comparable to the USAF's A-10A Thunderbolt II, the Su-25 was first identified by satellite while at the Ramenskoye flight test centre, accounting for the provisional US designation Ram-J. Not until 1982 was the NATO reporting name *Frogfoot* allocated, this being when the type was first deployed to Afghanistan before gaining full operational capability in 1984. In the Afghan theatre much effort was devoted to evolving methods of ensuring optimum co-ordination between *Frogfoot* and Mil Mi-24 helicopter gunships. A cantilever shoulder-wing monoplane of all-metal construction, the fuselage of the Su-25 incorporates armour protection around the cockpit (which has a bullet-proof windscreen) and is carried on retractable tricycle landing gear. Power is provided by two 41.5 kN (9,340 lb st) Tumansky R-13-300 turbojets. *Aphid* or *Atoll* AAMs, a chaff/flare dispenser, *Odd Rods* IFF and Sirena 3 radar warning system cater for self-defence, while for offensive use there is a twin-barrel 30 mm gun and an estimated 4,500 kg (9,920 lb) of weapons including anti-personnel, chemical cluster and incendiary bombs and rockets on eight underwing pylons. About 210 Su-25s are believed to be operational with Soviet forces, one squadron with the Czechoslovak Air Force, and a number have reportedly gone to Iraq.
Data: *Engines* see above *Wing span* 14.30 m (46 ft 11 in) *Length* 15.40 m (50 ft 6.75 in) *Max T-O weight* 19,200 kg (42,330 lb) *Max level speed* Mach 0.8
Sukhoi Su-26 (USSR) Single-seat aerobatic monoplane, first flown in June 1984. Construction includes considerable use of glassfibre. Modified Su-26s for the 1986 World Aerobatic Championships were designated Su-26M. One 268 kW (360 hp) Vedeneyev M-14P radial engine.
Sukhoi Su-27 (USSR) Generally similar in configuration to the Mikoyan MiG-29, implying that it and the MiG may stem from similar research, Sukhoi's new all-weather fighter is however considerably bigger and has more powerful engines; this is highlighted by the fact that its max T-O

weight is 50 per cent greater than that of the MiG-29. Prototypes of the Su-27 began flight testing during 1977, and these have the NATO reporting name *Flanker-A*. Production aircraft, identified from the prototypes by having square wingtips carrying rails for air-to-air missiles, an extended tailcone, and relocated tail fins, are known as *Flanker-B*. A third variant for carrier-based operations has been reported but no details have so far become available. Although photographed by a Norwegian Air Force Orion during 1986, and thus gaining excellent detail of the aircraft's external appearance, no confirmation of the Su-27's dimensions, weights and performance have been published to date. However, illustration of its capability has been given by the P-42, a specially prepared aircraft used to set a number of international records, which was flown to an altitude of 12,000 m in 55.542 seconds, namely a height of almost 12 km (7.5 miles) in less than a minute. Such performance, combined with a pulse Doppler radar giving lookdown/shootdown capability, makes *Flanker-B* a formidable adversary.
Data (estimated): *Engines* two Tumansky R-32 turbofans, each rated at 133.25 kN (29,995 lb st) with afterburning *Wing span* 14.70 m (48 ft 2.75 in) *Length* 21.60 m (70 ft 10.5 in) *Max T-O weight* 27,200 kg (60,000 lb) *Max level speed* Mach 2.0
Summit Sentry O2-337 (USA) Multi-role light-plane, based on the Cessna T337. Four underwing stations for weapons or other stores. In service with Haiti, Honduras, Nicaragua, Senegal and Thailand (navy).
Super Rotor AC-4 Andorinha and M-1 Montalvá (Brazil) Single- and two-seat autogyros, first flown in 1972 and 1985 respectively. Available ready assembled and in kit form. AC-4 uses 63 kW (85 hp) and M-1 uses 72 kW (97 hp) converted Volkswagen 1,600 cc engine.
Swearingen SA-30 Fanjet (USA) Six-seat executive jet, powered by two 8.01 kN (1,800 lb st) Williams International FJ44 turbofan engines. First flight is expected in 1989.
TBM Corporation TBM 700 (Finland/France/USA) Valmet of Finland, Socata of France and Mooney of the USA have teamed to develop this 6/8-seat pressurised business aircraft. The first

Summit Sentry O2-337s in Haiti

prototype flew on 14 July 1988. Power is provided by a 522 kW (700 shp) Pratt & Whitney Canada PT6A-40/1 turboprop engine.

Teledyne Ryan Model 410 (USA) Single-seat or RPV very long endurance surveillance/reconnaissance light aircraft, powered by a 119 kW (160 hp) Textron Lycoming TIO-320-C1B turbocharged piston engine driving a pusher propeller. First flown as a prototype on 27 May 1988.

Trago Mills SAH-1 (UK) Side-by-side two-seat aerobatic lightplane, powered by an 88 kW (118 hp) Textron Lycoming O-235-L2A piston engine. First flown on 23 August 1983. Now marketed by Orca Aircraft Ltd.

Tupolev Blackjack (USSR) The Tupolev bureau, with its comprehensive experience of building large military aircraft, was the clear candidate to design and develop a new strategic bomber for the Soviet Air Force. The West had known for some time that such an aircraft was under construction, with a total of 11 completed by early 1988, these being given the NATO reporting name Blackjack. Then, on 2 August 1988, the US Defense Secretary was given an opportunity to examine one of these aircraft at the Kubinka air base, near Moscow, following which the first photograph of the Soviet's new bomber became available in the West. Considerably larger than Tupolev's Tu-26 Backfire medium bomber, it shares with the earlier aircraft such features as low mounted variable geometry wings, and vertical tail surfaces with a large dorsal fin. It differs by having four instead of two engines, these being installed in a manner reminiscent of that adopted for Tupolev's Tu-144 SST which is no longer in service, but no details are available of the power plants used. For the strategic bombing role Blackjack will carry a mix of ALCMs, bombs and short-range missiles, but the AS-15 Kent ALCM and supersonic AS-X-19 missile will be primary weapons. Production of at least 100 Blackjack bombers is anticipated.

Data (estimated): *Wing span* (spread) 55.70 m (182 ft 9 in), (swept) 33.75 m (110 ft 0 in) *Length* 54.00 m (177 ft 0 in) *Max T-O weight* 250,000 kg (551,150 lb) *Max level speed* Mach 2.0 *Radius of action (unrefuelled)* 7,300 km (4,535 miles) *Armament* 16,330 kg (36,000 lb) load

Tupolev Tu-26 (USSR)* In addition to the *Backfire-A*, *Backfire-B* has an increased wing span and other airframe changes and *Backfire-C* is an advanced version with wedge air intakes, one twin-barrel cannon and other modifications. About 320 *Backfire Bs and Cs* are in use, undertaking bomber and maritime roles.

Data (*Backfire-B*): *Engines* two 196 kN (44,090 lb st) Kuznetsov NK-144 turbofans *Wing span* (spread) 34.3 m (112 ft 6 in), (swept) 23.4 m (76 ft 9 in) *Length* 39.6 m (129 ft 11 in) *Max T-O weight* 130,000 kg (286,600 lb) *Max level speed* Mach 2 *Radius of action* 4,000 km (2,485 miles) without in-flight refuelling *Armament* 12,000 kg (26,455 lb) load

Tupolev Tu-95 and Tu-142 (USSR)* In addition

to the versions of *Bear* detailed in the original A–Z, *Bear-G* is similar to the 'C' and 'D' versions but carries two AS-4 *Kitchen* missiles and electronic intelligence avionics, *Bear-H* is a newly built bomber with a Tu-142 'F' style fuselage but of the Tu-95 shorter length and carries AS-15 *Kent* air-launched cruise missiles, and *Bear-J* is used to provide a communications link between command authorities and the Soviet Navy's nuclear ballistic missile submarines.

Tupolev Bear-H

Tupolev Tu-154C (USSR)* First detailed in 1982, the Tupolev Tu-154C is a freight carrying conversion of the Tu-154 airliner (primarily Tu-154B). It provides a clear cargo volume of 72 m^3 (2,542 cu ft) in the main cabin, and has a freight door in the port side of the cabin and cargo handling mat/tracks. Nominal range of this version with 20,000 kg (44,100 lb) of cargo is 2,900 km (1,800 miles).

Tupolev Tu-155 (USSR) A Tupolev Tu-154 which has had its centre turbofan removed and replaced by a Kuznetsov NK-88 engine is being used under the designation Tu-155 as a testbed for cryogenic fuels. On 15 April 1988 this aircraft made its first flight using liquid hydrogen, and it is planned to test the NK-88 with liquified natural gas.

Tupolev Tu-204 (USSR) To replace the Tu-154 currently in service, Tupolev is developing a new medium-range transport in the 170–214 passenger class under the designation Tu-204. To be powered by four 157 kN (35,300 lb st) Soloviev PS-90A (D-90A) turbofans, this will incorporate wings of supercritical section with wingtip winglets, a fly by wire control system, beneficial use of composite materials, advanced CRT displays, and a triplex automatic approach and landing system. Production is expected to begin in the early 1990s with 80–90 being built for Aeroflot; it is planned that the Tu-204 will be operated also by CSA of Czechoslovakia.

Data (estimated): *Engines* see above *Wing span* 42.00 m (137 ft 9.5 in) *Length* 45.00 m (147 ft 7.75 in) *Max T-O weight* 93,500 kg (206,130 lb) *Max level speed* 900 km/h (559 mph)

UTVA-75A11 (Yugoslavia) Single-seat agricultural monoplane, powered by a 224 kW (300 hp) Texton Lycoming IO-540-L1A5D piston engine. First flown in 1988. Max load is 780 kg (1,720 lb).

UTVA-75A21 (Yugoslavia) Side-by-side two-seat lightplane, powered by a 134 kW (180 hp) Textron Lycoming IO-360-B1F piston engine. First flown on 19 May 1976. Used by flying clubs and the Yugoslav Air Force.

UTVA-75A41 (Yugoslavia) Four-seat lightplane, developed from the UTVA-75A21. Suited to utility, glider-towing and training duties. First flown in 1986.

UTVA Lasta (Yugoslavia) Tandem two-seat primary trainer and light attack aircraft, powered by a 224 kW (300 hp) Textron Lycoming AEIO-540-Z1B5D piston engine. First flown in 1985 and used by the Yugoslav Air Force. Weapon load on two underwing stations is 400 kg (882 lb).

Valentin Taifun 11 S (West Germany) Valentin, known also for its gliders, first flew in 1988 the prototype of this four-seat composites light aircraft. Power in provided by an 86 kW (115 hp) Textron Lycoming O-235-H2C piston engine. The wing span is an impressive 11.6 m (38 ft 1 in).

Valmet L-90 TP Redigo (Finland) Larger and more powerful development of the company's L-70 Miltrainer, for similar uses. First flown on 1 July 1986. Powered by a 313 kW (420 shp) Allison 250-B17F turboprop engine.

Venga TF-10 (Canada) New tandem two-seat lightweight jet trainer, also suitable for attack carrying (pilot only) 845 kg (1,863 lb) of weapons on five external stations. Conventional layout, with twin outward-canted tailfins, but with a modular airframe constructed of glassfibre and PVC foam. Prototype, powered by one 13.01 kN (2,925 lb st) General Electric J85-GE-5 turbojet, was expected to make its first flight in late 1988. Estimated max level speed is 899 km/h (558 mph).

Verilite Model 100 Sunbird (USA) Side-by-side two-seat light monoplane, powered by a 52 kW (70 hp) Emdair CF-092B piston engine. First flown on 5 October 1987.

Westland Super Lynx (UK)* New all-weather, day and night version of the naval Lynx, currently under development. Two 835 kW (1,120 shp) Gem 42-1 turboshaft engines, driving advanced technology rotors. Extended range and load, with weapons including Sting Ray torpedoes and Sea Skua and Penguin anti-ship missiles. 360° radar and dipping sonar.

WSK-PZL Mielec M-21 Dromader Mini (Poland) Smaller development of the M-18 Dromader agricultural aircraft, powered by a 447 kW (600 hp) PZL-3SR radial engine and having a 900–1,200 kg (1,984–2,645 lb) payload. First flown on 18 June 1982.

WSK-PZL Mielec M-24 Dromader Super (Poland) First flown on 14 July 1987, this is a new large agricultural aircraft, powered by a 746 kW (1,000 hp) PZL Kalisz ASz-62IR radial engine and having a hopper capable of accommodating 2,700 litres (594 Imp gallons) of liquid or 1,800 kg (3,968 lb) of dry chemicals. Airframe is slightly larger than that of the M-18 Dromader.

WSK-PZL Mielec M-26 Iskierka (Poland) Tandem two-seat military and civil trainer, powered by a 153 kW (205 hp) PZL-F6A-350CA piston engine in M-26 00 form and a 224 kW (300 hp) Textron Lycoming AEIO-540-L1B5D engine in M-26 01 form. The initial prototype first flew on 15 July 1986.

WSK-PZL Swidnik W-3 Sokól (Poland) Expected to supersede the Mi-2 as the company's main production helicopter in the 1990s, this helicopter accommodates a crew of two plus 12 passengers or four stretchers and an attendant or 2,100 kg (4,630 lb) of cargo. Power is provided by two 662 kW (888 shp) PZL-10W turboshaft engines. The first prototype flew initially on 16 November 1979.

WSK-PZL Warszawa-Okecie PZL-105 (Poland) Designed to supersede the Wilga, this six-seat general-purpose strut-braced high-wing monoplane first flew in 1989. Power is provided by a 209 kW (280 hp) PZL AI-14RD/RDP radial engine.

WSK-PZL Warszawa-Okecie PZL-106BT Turbo-Kruk (Poland) 544 kW (730 shp) Walter M 601 D turboprop-powered version of the Kruk, with some airframe changes and a 1,300 kg (2,866 lb) chemical load.

WSK-PZL Warszawa-Okecie PZL-126 Mrówka (Poland) Very small and streamlined single-seat agricultural, ecological and general-purpose low-wing monoplane, with wingtip spraypods for low-volume liquid chemical distribution and underfuselage reel spreader. One 44.7 kW (60 hp) PZL-F 2A-120-C1 piston engine. First flown in 1988.

WSK-PZL Warszawa-Okecie PZL-130 Orlik/Turbo Orlik (Poland) Under development as a civil/military trainer, design of the PZL-130 Orlik began in 1981. The first of three prototypes was flown initially on 12 October 1984. Certification in Utility and Aerobatic categories was gained in early 1988 and construction of pre-production aircraft has been initiated. The PZL-130 is a cantilever low-wing monoplane of all-metal construction, carried on retractable tricycle landing gear and with two-seat tandem accommodation for instructor (rear) and pupil in a heated and

Prototype WSK-PZL Warszawa-Okecie PZL-130 Orlik

ventilated enclosed cockpit. Power is provided by a 246 kW (330 hp) Vedeneyev M-14Pm radial aircooled engine, giving a maximum level speed of 340 km/h (211 mph). A single example of the Turbo Orlik was built by conversion (in Canada) of the third PZL-130 prototype to take a 410 kW (550 shp) Pratt & Whitney Canada PT6A-25A turboprop engine. During its certification programme this aircraft was lost in a fatal accident, and a second prototype is under conversion to complete the programme.

Data (PZL-130): *Engine* see above *Wing span* 8.00 m (26 ft 3 in) *Length* 8.45 m (27 ft 8.75 in) *Max T-O weight* 1,600 kg (3,527 lb) *Max range* 1,416 km (880 miles)

XAC Y-7 (China) The Xian aircraft company developed an improved version of the Soviet Antonov An-24 *Coke* as the Y-7, which began passenger operations with CAAC in 1986. Further modification has produced the current Y7-100, which features winglets, a three crew flight deck, a restyled cabin for 52 passengers, better navigation and communications equipment, de-icing for the flight deck windows and other updates. Much of the equipment and restyling work was contracted to western suppliers.

Yakovlev Yak-41 (USSR) Claimed designation of a new V/STOL combat aircraft being developed to supersede the Yak-38.

Yakovlev Yak-42M (USSR) Lengthened version of the Yak-42, accommodating up to 168 passengers. Three 73.6 kN (16,550 lb st) Lotarev D-436 turbofan engines. Entered service in about 1987.

Yakovlev Yak-53 (USSR) Single-seat aerobatic trainer, powered by a 268 kW (360 hp) Vedeneyev M-14P radial engine.

Yakovlev Yak-55 (USSR) Single-seat aerobatic aircraft, first used at the 1982 World Championships. Same engine as the Yak-53.

Zlin Z 37T Agro Turbo (Czechoslovakia) Turboprop version of the Z-37A Cmelák agricultural aircraft, powered by a 365 kW (490 shp) Motorlet Walter M 601 Z engine. Two-seat training version is designated Z 37T-2. Deliveries began in 1985.

Zlin Z 50 L and M (Czechoslovakia) Single-seat aerobatic monoplanes, powered by a 224 kW (300 hp) Textron Lycoming AEIO-540-L1B5D and 134 kW (180 hp) Avia M 137 AZ piston engine respectively. First flown in 1981 and 1988 respectively. Similar wing spans but lighter 'M' has longer fuselage.

Zlin 142 (Czechoslovakia) Side-by-side two-seat training, aerobatic, glider-towing and touring lightplane, first flown on 29 December 1978. One 156.6 kW (210 hp) Avia M 337 AK piston engine.

INDEX TO AIRCRAFT A-Z

As the Aircraft A-Z has been set out in alphabetical order it has not been necessary to index aircraft under manufacturers' names. Therefore the index normally lists alphabetically only the model designation and/or name, followed by manufacturer's names and page number.

The same applies to aircraft mentioned in the text but without bold headings. In the case of aircraft with number designations only these are to be found under their respective company names.

Index

Index